Computing Today

Computing Today

Timothy J. O'Leary
Arizona State University

Linda I. O'Leary

McGraw Hill Technology Education

Boston Burr Ridge, IL Dubuque, IA Madison, WI New York San Francisco St. Louis
Bangkok Bogotá Caracas Kuala Lumpur Lisbon London Madrid Mexico City
Milan Montreal New Delhi Santiago Seoul Singapore Sydney Taipei Toronto

McGraw-Hill Technology Education

COMPUTING TODAY

Published by McGraw-Hill/Irwin, a business unit of The McGraw-Hill Companies, Inc. 1221 Avenue of the Americas, New York, NY, 10020. Copyright © 2004 by The McGraw-Hill Companies, Inc. All rights reserved. No part of this publication may be reproduced or distributed in any form or by any means, or stored in a database or retrieval system, without the prior written consent of The McGraw-Hill Companies, Inc., including, but not limited to, in any network or other electronic storage or transmission, or broadcast for distance learning. Some ancillaries, including electronic and print components, may not be available to customers outside the United States.

This book is printed on acid-free paper.

domestic 1 2 3 4 5 6 7 8 9 0 QPD/QPD 0 9 8 7 6 5 4 3
international 1 2 3 4 5 6 7 8 9 0 QPD/QPD 0 9 8 7 6 5 4 3

ISBN 0-07-256598 5

Publisher: *Brandon Nordin*
Editor-in-chief: *Robert Woodbury, Jr.*
Senior sponsoring editor: *Donald J. Hull*
Freelance developmental editor: *Jane Ducham*
Developmental editor: *Jennie Yates*
Marketing manager: *Andrew Bernier*
Senior producer, Media technology: *Greg Bates*
Lead project manager: *Pat Frederickson*
Manager, new book production: *Heather Burbridge*
Coordinator freelance design: *Artemio Ortiz Jr.*
Photo research coordinator: *Jeremy Chesherack*
Photo researcher: *Teri Stratford*
Supplement producer: *Matthew Perry*
Senior digital content specialist: *Brian Nacik*
Cover design: *Joanne Schopler*
Interior design: *Artemio Ortiz, Jr.*
Typeface: *10/12 New Aster*
Compositor: *GAC/Indianapolis*
Printer: *Quebecor World Dubuque Inc.*

Library of Congress Control Number: 2003114505

INTERNATIONAL EDITION ISBN 0-07-119998-5
Copyright © 2004. Exclusive rights by The McGraw-Hill Companies, Inc. for manufacture and export. This book cannot be re-exported from the country in which it is sold by McGraw-Hill. The International Edition is not available in North America.

www.mhhe.com

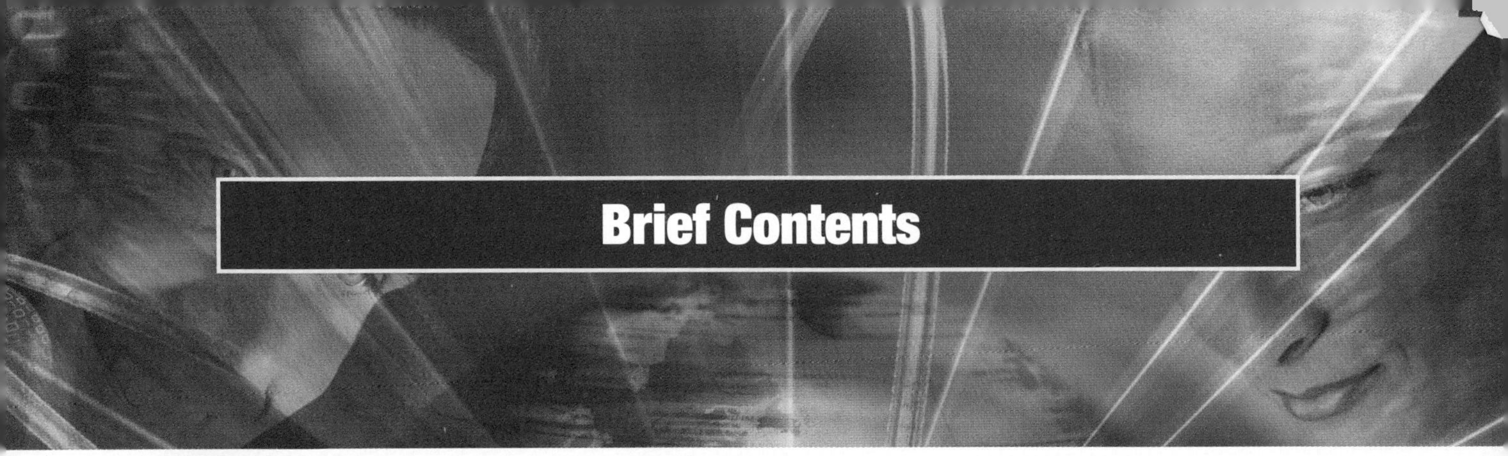

Brief Contents

Contents

Preface

INTRODUCTION

The 20th century not only brought us the dawn of the Information Age, but continued to bring us rapid changes in information technology. There is no indication that this rapid rate of change will be slowing—it may even be increasing. As we begin the 21st century, computer literacy will undoubtedly become prerequisite in whatever career a student chooses. The goal of *Computing Today* is to provide students with the basis for understanding the concepts necessary for success in the Information Age. *Computing Today* also endeavors to instill in students an appreciation for the effect of information technology on people and our environment and to give students a basis for building the necessary skill set to succeed in this new, 21st century.

ABOUT THE AUTHORS

Tim and Linda O'Leary live in the American Southwest and spend much of their time engaging instructors and students in conversation about learning. In fact, they have been talking about learning for over 25 years. Something in those early conversations convinced them to write a book, to bring their interest in the learning process to the printed page. Today, they are as concerned as ever about learning, about technology, and about the challenges of presenting material in new ways, both in terms of content and the method of delivery.

A powerful and creative team, Tim combines his years of classroom teaching experience with Linda's background as a consultant and corporate trainer. Tim has taught courses at Stark Technical College in Canton, Ohio, and at Rochester Institute of Technology in upstate New York, and is currently a professor at Arizona State University in Tempe, Arizona. Tim and Linda have talked to and taught students from 8 to 80, all of them with a desire to learn something about computers and the applications that make their lives easier, more interesting, and more productive.

Each new edition of an O'Leary text, supplement, or learning aid has benefited from these students and their instructors who daily stand in front of them (or over their shoulders). *Computing Today* is no exception.

A WORD FROM THE AUTHORS

Times are changing, technology is changing, and this text is changing, too. Do you think the students of today are different from yesterday? Mine are and I'll wager that yours are as well. On the positive side, I am amazed how much effort students put toward things that interest them and things they are convinced are relevant to them. Their effort directed at learning application programs and exploring the Web seems at times limitless. On the other hand, it is difficult to engage them in other equally important topics such as personal privacy and technological advances.

I've changed the way I teach, and this book reflects that. I no longer lecture my students about how important certain concepts like microprocessors, input devices, and utility programs are. Rather, I begin by engaging their interest by presenting practical tips related to the key concepts, by demonstrating interesting applications that are relevant to their lives, and by focusing on outputs rather than processes. Then, I discuss the concepts and processes.

Motivation and relevance are the keys. This text has several features specifically designed to engage students and to demonstrate the relevance of technology in their lives. These elements are combined with a thorough coverage of the concepts and sound pedagogical devices.

SELECTED FEATURES OF THIS BOOK

- **Visual Chapter Openers** Each chapter begins with a two-page Visual Chapter Opener with large graphics and brief text. The graphics present the structure and organization of the chapter. The text relates the graphics to topics that are covered in the chapter and discusses their importance. The objective of the visual chapter openers is to engage students and provide relevancy and motivation.
- **On the Web Explorations** Within many of the chapters, two or more On the Web Explorations are presented as marginal elements. These explorations encourage students to connect to carefully selected Web sites that provide additional information on key topics. The objective of the Web Explorations is to encourage students to expand their knowledge by using Web resources.

> **On the Web Explorations**
>
> **Dragon Soft is a leader in developing continuous-speech systems. To learn more about the company, visit our Web site at http://www.mhhe.com/oleary/CT05 and select On the Web Explorations from Tim's Toolbox.**

- **Tips** Within many of the chapters, Tips are provided that offer advice on a variety of chapter-related issues such as how to efficiently locate information on the Web, how to speed up computer operations, and how to protect against computer viruses. One objective of the Tips is to provide students with assistance on common technology-related problems or issues. The other objective is to motivate students by showing the relevance of concepts presented in the chapter to their everyday lives.

> **TIPS** Have you ever bought anything online? If not, it's likely that in the future you will join the millions that have. Here are a few suggestions on how to shop online:
>
> 1. **Consult product review sites.** To get evaluations or opinions on products, visit one of the many review sites on the Web such as www.consumersearch.com and www.epinions.com.
> 2. **Use a shopping bot.** Once you have selected a specific product, enlist a shopping bot or automated shopping assistants to compare prices. Two well-known shopping bots are located at www.mysimon.com and www.shopping.yahoo.com.
> 3. **Consult vendor review sites.** Of course, price is not everything. Before placing an order with a vendor, check their reputation by visiting vendor review sites such as www.gomez.com and www.bizrate.com.
> 4. **Select payment option.** Once you have selected the product and the vendor, the final step is to order and pay. Security of your credit card number is critical. Consider payment options available from www.private.buy.com and www.americanexpress.com/privatepayments.

- **Concept Checks** Every chapter contains strategically placed Concept Check boxes. Each box contains questions related to the material just presented. The objective of these Concept Checks is to provide students the opportunity to test their retention of key chapter concepts.

> **Concept Check**
>
> ✔ What is an information system?
>
> ✔ What is required of a competent end user?

- **Making IT Work for You** Based on student surveys, 11 special interest topics have been identified. These topics include downloading music from the Internet, creating personal Web sites, and using the Internet to place free long-distance telephone calls. Each of these 11 special interest topics is presented in a two-page Making IT Work for You section within the relevant chapter. The objective is to engage students by presenting high-interest topics and to motivate them to learn about related concepts in the chapter.

- **Making IT Work Video Series** Based on student interest and chapter content, several Making IT Work for You special interest topics have been selected for special attention. Seven short videos bring these selected topics to life. These videos are available on CD for classroom viewing and on the Web for direct student viewing. One objective of this feature is to motivate students by animating and extending the printed two-page Making IT Work for You presentation in the textbook. The other objective is to provide instructors with a presentation tool for classroom demonstrations that are integrated and further supported by the textbook.
- **Using IT at DVD Direct** Many students find information systems concepts to be very challenging. A series of four cases focused on DVD Direct, a factious Web-based movie rental company have been created. The cases appear at the end of Chapters 12, 13, 14, and 15. They have been written to allow instructors to skip all or some of the cases without losing continuity. The objective of the cases is to engage students in an interesting current application of technology and to demonstrate the relevance and importance of information systems, databases, systems analysis and design, and programming.

USING IT AT DVD DIRECT—A CASE STUDY

- **Careers in IT** Each chapter includes a job description for a different career in IT. These descriptions include job titles, responsibilities, educational requirements, and salary ranges, providing students with real-world examples within the IT field.

- **A Look to the Future** Each chapter concludes with a brief discussion of a specific recent technological advance related to material presented in the chapter. The objective of this feature is to remind students that technology is always changing and to reinforce the importance of staying informed of recent changes.

- **Visual Chapter Summaries** Each chapter ends with a multipage visual chapter summary. Like the chapter openers, the summaries use graphics to present the structure of the chapter and text to provide specifics. Using a columnar arrangement, major concepts are represented by graphics followed by detailed text summaries. The objective of the visual chapter summaries is to provide a detailed summary of key concepts and terms in an engaging and meaningful way.

- **Using Technology** Every chapter has Web-related end-of-chapter exercises that direct students to explore current popular uses of technology. In most cases, the first question requires the student to view one of the Making IT Work for You Web-delivered demonstrations and to respond to a series of related questions. Other questions require Web research. One objective of the Using Technology feature is to provide support for instructors who would prefer their students to view the Making IT Work for You videos on the Web rather than in class. The other objective is to provide a powerful tool to engage and motivate students by providing assignments related to technology that directly relates to them.

- **Expanding Your Knowledge** Every chapter has Web-related end-of-chapter exercises directing students to enhance their depth of knowledge on specific technologies introduced in the chapter. In most cases, one question requires the students to use either their free SimNet Concepts CD-ROM or their Computing Today CD and to respond to a series of related questions. Other questions require Web research into carefully selected topics. One objective of the Expanding Your Knowledge feature is to provide support for instructors who want their students to effectively use the free Interactive CD-ROM. The other objective is to support instructors who want their students to obtain greater in-depth understanding of key technologies.

- **Building Your Portfolio** Every chapter has Web-related end-of-chapter exercises directing students to prepare and to write a one- or two-page paper on critical technology-related issues. Some questions require students to summarize and analyze select emerging technologies addressed in the chapter. Other questions focus on a critical chapter-related privacy, security, and/or ethical issue. Students are required to consider, evaluate, and formulate a position. One objective of the Building Your Portfolio feature is to support instructors who want their students to develop critical thinking and writing skills. Another objective is to provide support for instructors who want their students to create written document(s) recording their technology knowledge. A third objective is to provide support for instructors who want their students to recognize, understand, and analyze key privacy, security, and ethical issues relating to technology.

- **Engaging Students** Having all these features is one thing. Making the students aware of them is another. Like in almost all textbooks, Chapter 1 of this textbook provides an overview and framework for the following chapters. Unlike other textbooks, our Chapter 1 also provides a discussion and overview of each of the above engaging features. One objective of this approach is to support instructors who want to focus their students' attention on any one or on a combination of features. The other objective is to motivate students by highlighting features that are visually interesting and relevant to their lives.

- **Tim's Toolbox** Throughout the pages of the text you will see references to Tim's Toolbox. This is a set of resources for students on the student CD-ROM and on the text's Web site, www.mhhe.com/oleary/CT05. The features inside Tim's Toolbox have been determined by the features on the pages of the text. Tim's Toolbox organizes these features on the CD and the Web site for easy access and reference. Features found in Tim's Toolbox include *Tips, On the Web Explorations, Making IT Work for You, Careers in IT,* practice tests, and more.

Instructor's Guide

RESOURCES FOR INSTRUCTORS

We understand that in today's teaching environment offering a textbook alone is not sufficient to meet the needs of the many different instructors who use our books. To teach effectively, instructors must have a full complement of supplemental resources to assist them in every facet of teaching from preparing for class, to presenting lectures, to assessing students' comprehension. *Computing Today* offers a complete, fully integrated supplements package, as described below.

Instructor's Resource Kit

The Instructor's Resource Kit contains an updated CD-ROM containing the Instructor's Manual in both MS Word and PDF formats, PowerPoint slides, and Brownstone's Diploma test generation software with accompanying test item files for each chapter. The distinctive features of each component of the Instructor's Resource Kit are described below.

- **Instructor's Manual** The Instructor's Manual contains a schedule showing how much time is required to cover the material in the chapter; a list of the chapter competencies; tips for covering difficult material; and answers to the Concept Checks. Also included are references to corresponding topics on the Interactive Companion CD-ROM, answers to all the exercises in the Chapter Review section, and answers to the On the Web Exercises. The manual also includes a helpful introduction that explains the features, benefits, and suggested uses of the IM and an index of concepts and corresponding competencies.
- **PowerPoint Presentation** The PowerPoint presentation is designed to provide instructors with a comprehensive resource for use during lecture. It includes a review of key terms and definitions, figures from the text, along with several new illustrations, anticipated student questions with answers, and additional resources that can be accessed in Internet-enabled classrooms. Also included with the presentation are comprehensive speaker's notes.
- **Testbank** The *Computing Today* edition testbank contains over 3,000 questions categorized by level of learning (definition, concept, and application). This is the same learning scheme that is introduced in the text to provide a valuable testing and reinforcement tool. The test questions are identified by text page number to assist you in planning your exams, and rationales for each answer are also included. Additional test questions, which can be used as pretests and posttests in class, can be found on the Online Learning Center, accessible through our Information Technology Supersite (www.mhhe.com/it).

Tech TV—New Video Series from McGraw-Hill Technology Education

McGraw-Hill Technology Education is pleased to announce a new relationship with Tech TV. Through this partnership, we are able to offer instructors and students new video content directly related to computing that enhances the classroom or lab experience with technology programming from business and society. Video selections from Tech TV programs such as "Cybercrime," "The Screen Savers" and "TechLive" are sometimes edgy and always informative. Use of these videos will help students understand how computing interacts with and contributes to business and society—and will also offer an advance look at emerging technology and devices. These new videos have been developed with the guidance of Professor Donald L. Amoroso of San Diego State

University. Professor Amoroso is an active teacher of large sections and has selected video segments from Tech TV that he knows will work in the classroom. He has prepared written guidance on how to best use these videos to facilitate learning. This new series gives instructors and students more power for teaching and learning in the computing classroom!

Making IT Work Video Series

Available on CD or the Web site, these videos provide cutting-edge context to help students learn the concepts presented in the text. This series of brief video presentations features the author and corresponds to specific Making IT Work for You topics from the text, making it a flexible tool for in-class and Web-delivered demonstrations while engaging students by presenting high-interest topics directly related to the concepts presented in the text. The series includes videos on:

- CD-R Drivers and Music from the Internet
- Creating a Personal Web Site
- Creating an Active Desktop
- Instant Messaging
- Locating Jobs Online
- Using TV Tuner Cards and Video Clips
- Virus Protection

SimNet CD

SimNet is a new interactive computer-based program for student learning and assessment on 77 key computer concepts. SimNet includes a learning or tutorial presentation of each of these 77 concepts, and includes exam questions (both practice questions and assessment questions) for each one.

Computing Today CD

The Computing Today CD contains animations of key concepts, videos relating to select Making IT Work for You applications, and in-depth coverage of select topics. Computing Today CD icons are located in the margins throughout the book to alert students that expanded coverage of the material in the text can be found on their Computing Today CD.

Digital Solutions to Help You Manage Your Course

PageOut—PageOut is our Course Web Site Development Center that offers a syllabus page, URL, McGraw-Hill Online Learning Center content, online exercises and quizzes, gradebook, discussion board, and an area for student Web pages. For more information, visit the PageOut Web site (www.pageout.net).

Online Learning Centers—The Online Learning Center that accompanies *Computing Today* is accessible through our Information Technology Supersite (www.mhhe.com/it). This site provides additional learning and instructional tools developed using the same three-level approach found in the text and supplements. This offers a consistent method for students to enhance their comprehension of the concepts presented in the text.

Online Courses Available—OLCs are your perfect solutions for Internet-based content. Simply put, these Centers are "digital cartridges" that contain a book's pedagogy and supplements. As students read the book, they can go online and take self-grading quizzes or work through interactive exercises. These also provide students appropriate access to lecture materials and other key supplements.

Blackboard.com

WebCT (a product of Universal Learning Technology)

O'Leary Series Applications Lab Manuals

The O'Leary Series computer applications lab manuals for Microsoft Office are available separately, or packaged with *Computing Today*. The O'Leary Series offers a step-by-step approach to developing computer applications skills and is available in both brief and introductory levels. The introductory level manuals are MOUS Certified and prepare students for the Microsoft Office User Certification Exam.

Skills Assessment

SimNet XPert (Simulated Network Assessment Product) provides a way for you to test students' software skills in a simulated environment. SimNet is available for Microsoft Office 97, Microsoft Office 2000, and Microsoft Office XP. SimNet provides flexibility for you in your course by offering:

- Pretesting options
- Posttesting options
- Course placement testing
- Diagnostic capabilities to reinforce skills
- Proficiency testing to measure skills
- Web or LAN delivery of tests
- Computer-based training tutorials (new for Office XP)
- MOUS preparation exams
- Learning verification reports
- Spanish version

For more information on skills assessment software, please contact your local sales representative, or visit us at www.mhhe.com/it.

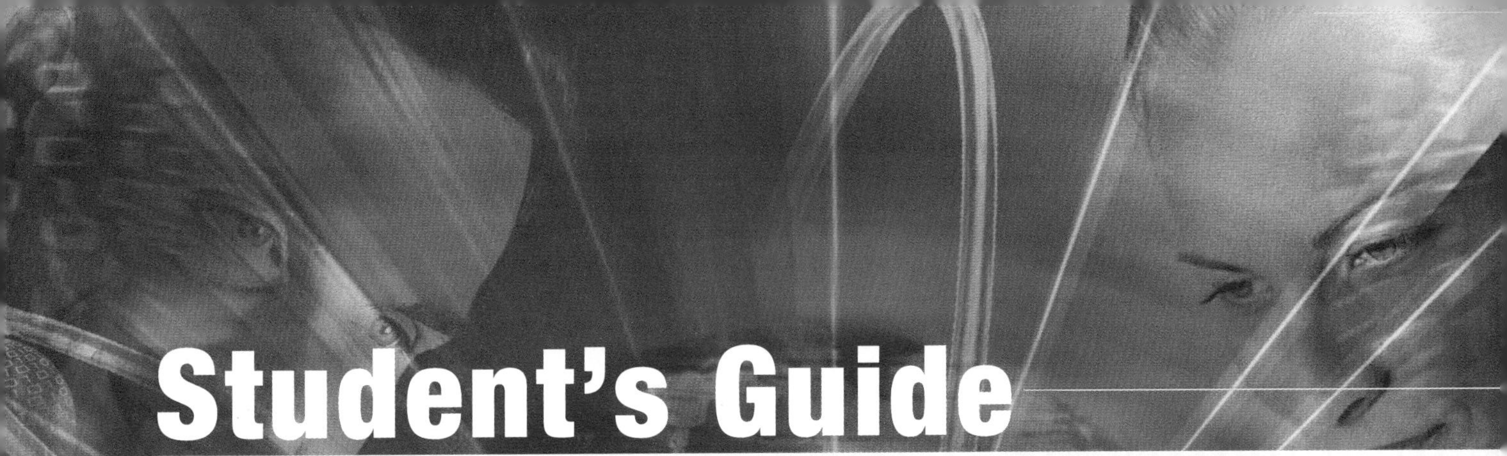

Student's Guide

STUDENT'S GUIDE TO THE O'LEARY LEARNING SYSTEM

Recently, at the end of the semester, some of my students stopped by my office to say they enjoyed the class and that they "learned something that they could actually use." High praise indeed for a professor! Actually, I had mixed feelings. Of course, it felt good to learn that my students had enjoyed the course. However, it hurt a bit that they were surprised that they learned something useful.

Here's my promise to you:

In the following pages you will find things that you can actually use now as well as that provide a foundation for understanding future technological advances.

As you read the text, notice the "Tips" scattered throughout the book. These tips offer suggestions on a variety of topics from the basics of cleaning a monitor to how to make your computer run faster and smoother. Also, notice the "Making IT Work for You" sections that demonstrate some specific computer applications you might find interesting. For example, one demonstrates how to capture and use television video clips for electronic presentations and another shows how to capture, save, and play music from the Internet.

Many learning aids are built into the text to ensure your success with the material and to make the process of learning rewarding. In the pages that follow, we call your attention to the key features in the text. We also show you supplemental materials, such as the student Online Learning Center, that you should take advantage of to ensure your success in this course.

What makes Computing Today such a powerful tool?

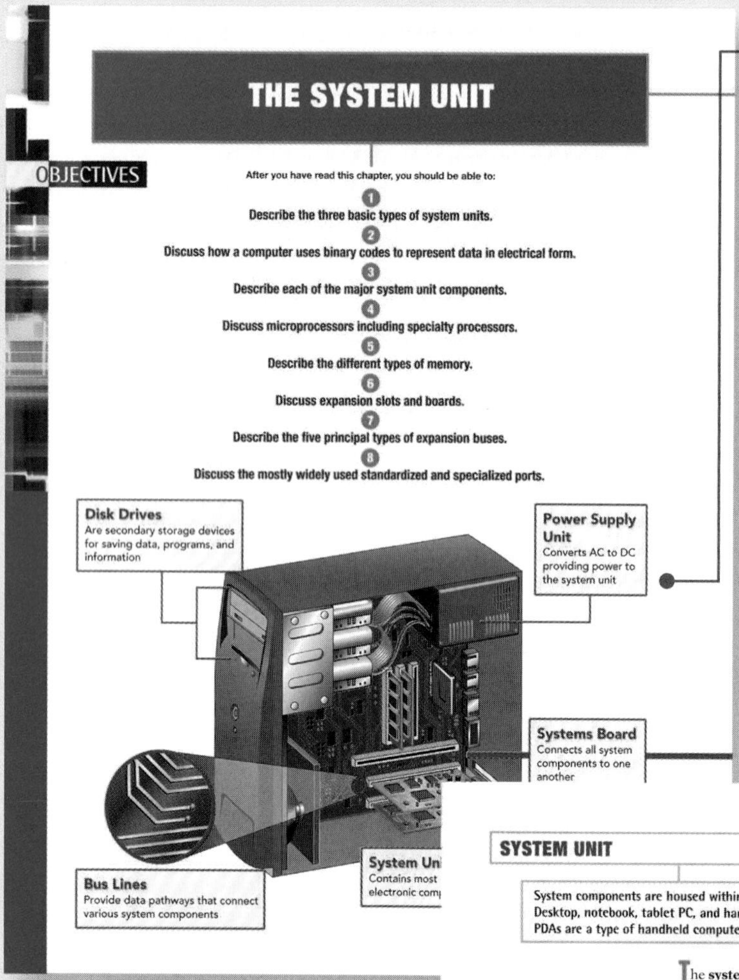
THE SYSTEM UNIT

OBJECTIVES

After you have read this chapter, you should be able to:

1. Describe the three basic types of system units.
2. Discuss how a computer uses binary codes to represent data in electrical form.
3. Describe each of the major system unit components.
4. Discuss microprocessors including specialty processors.
5. Describe the different types of memory.
6. Discuss expansion slots and boards.
7. Describe the five principal types of expansion buses.
8. Discuss the mostly widely used standardized and specialized ports.

Disk Drives Are secondary storage devices for saving data, programs, and information

Power Supply Unit Converts AC to DC providing power to the system unit

Systems Board Connects all system components to one another

System Un Contains most electronic com

Bus Lines Provide data pathways that connect various system components

Visual Chapter Openers

Each chapter begins with a two-page opening spread that provides the Chapter Competencies and a brief introduction to the chapter. Graphics present the structure and organization of the chapter visually, while text discusses the topics that will be covered and their importance.

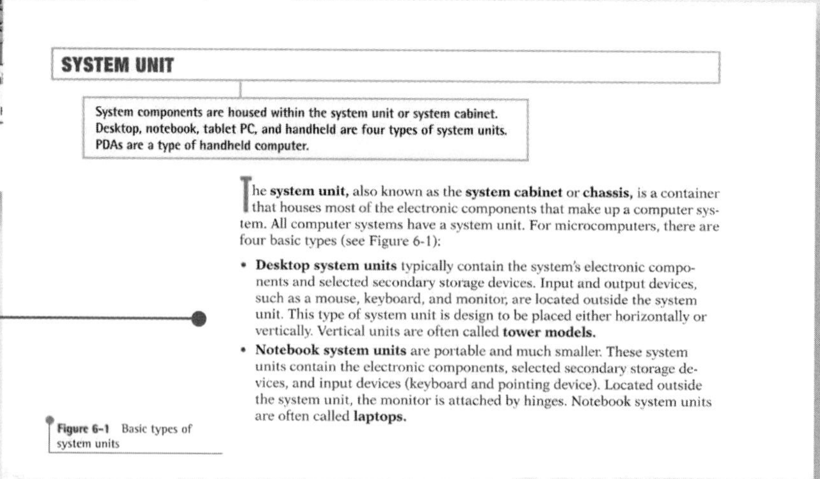
SYSTEM UNIT

System components are housed within the system unit or system cabinet. Desktop, notebook, tablet PC, and handheld are four types of system units. PDAs are a type of handheld computer.

The **system unit,** also known as the **system cabinet** or **chassis,** is a container that houses most of the electronic components that make up a computer system. All computer systems have a system unit. For microcomputers, there are four basic types (see Figure 6-1):

- **Desktop system units** typically contain the system's electronic components and selected secondary storage devices. Input and output devices, such as a mouse, keyboard, and monitor, are located outside the system unit. This type of system unit is design to be placed either horizontally or vertically. Vertical units are often called **tower models.**
- **Notebook system units** are portable and much smaller. These system units contain the electronic components, selected secondary storage devices, and input devices (keyboard and pointing device). Located outside the system unit, the monitor is attached by hinges. Notebook system units are often called **laptops.**

Figure 6-1 Basic types of system units

Key Terms

Throughout the text, the most important terms are presented in bold type and are defined within the text. You will also find a list of key terms at the end of each chapter and in the glossary at the end of the book.

How does Computing Today use the Web and provide practical real world tips?

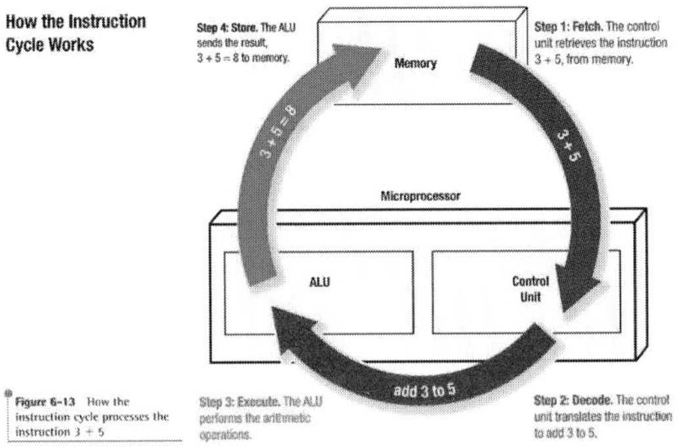
How the Instruction Cycle Works

Step 4: Store. The ALU sends the result, 3 + 5 = 8 to memory.
Step 1: Fetch. The control unit retrieves the instruction 3 + 5, from memory.
Memory
3+5=8
3+5
Microprocessor
ALU
Control Unit
add 3 to 5
Step 3: Execute. The ALU performs the arithmetic operations.
Step 2: Decode. The control unit translates the instruction to add 3 to 5.

Figure 6-13 How the instruction cycle processes the instruction 3 + 5

Unit	Speed
Microsecond	Millionth of a second
Nanosecond	Billionth of a second
Picosecond	Trillionth of a second

Figure 6-14 Processing speeds

There are two types of microprocessor chips.

- **CISC chips:** The most common type of microprocessor is the **complex instruction set computer (CISC) chip.** This design was popularized by Intel and is the basis for their line of microprocessors. It is the most widely used chip design with thousands of programs written specifically for it. Intel's Pentium microprocessors are CISC chips. While Intel is the leading manufacturer of microprocessors, other manufacturers produce microprocessors using a nearly identical design. These chips, referred to as **Intel-compatible** processors, are able to process programs originally written specifically for Intel chips. For example, AMD Corporation produces Intel-compatible chips known as Athlon and Hammer.
- **RISC chips: Reduced instruction set computer (RISC) chips** use fewer instructions. This design is simpler and less costly than CISC chips. The PowerPC is a RISC chip produced by Motorola. SPARC is a RISC chip produced by Sun. These chips are used in many of today's most powerful microcomputers known as **workstations.**

On the Web Explorations

Motorola is a leader in RISC research and development. To learn more about the company, visit our Web site at http://www.mhhe.com/oleary/CT05 and select On the Web Explorations from Tim's Toolbox.

See Figure 6-15 for a table of popular microprocessors.

SPECIALTY PROCESSORS

In addition to microprocessor chips, a variety of more specialized processing chips have been developed. One of the most common is coprocessors. **Coprocessors** are specialty chips designed to improve specific computing opera-

Tips

Tips appear within nearly every chapter and are provided to offer advice on a variety of chapter-related issues, such as how to efficiently locate information on the Web, how to speed up computer operations, and how to protect against computer viruses. Tips assist you with common technology-related problems or issues, and motivate you by showing the relevance of concepts presented in the chapter to everyday life.

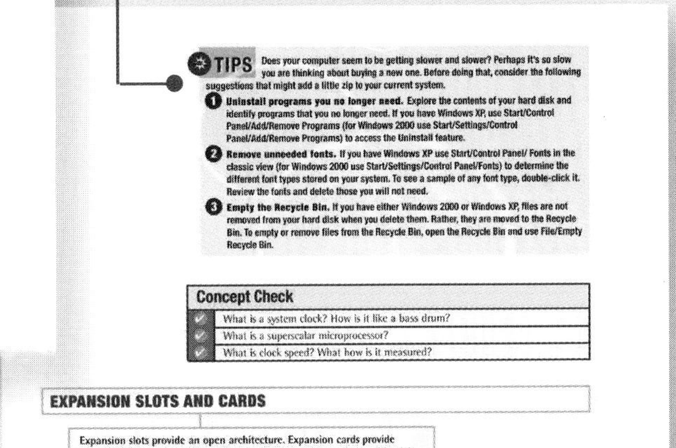
TIPS Does your computer seem to be getting slower and slower? Perhaps it's so slow you are thinking about buying a new one. Before doing that, consider the following suggestions that might add a little zip to your current system.

1. **Uninstall programs you no longer need.** Explore the contents of your hard disk and identify programs that you no longer need. If you have Windows XP, use Start/Control Panel/Add/Remove Programs (for Windows 2000 use Start/Settings/Control Panel/Add/Remove Programs) to access the Uninstall feature.
2. **Remove unneeded fonts.** If you have Windows XP use Start/Control Panel/ Fonts in the classic view (for Windows 2000 use Start/Settings/Control Panel/Fonts) to determine the different font types stored on your system. To see a sample of any font type, double-click it. Review the fonts and delete those you will not need.
3. **Empty the Recycle Bin.** If you have either Windows 2000 or Windows XP, files are not removed from your hard disk when you delete them. Rather, they are moved to the Recycle Bin. To empty or remove files from the Recycle Bin, open the Recycle Bin and use File/Empty Recycle Bin.

Concept Check

- What is a system clock? How is it like a bass drum?
- What is a superscalar microprocessor?
- What is clock speed? What how is it measured?

EXPANSION SLOTS AND CARDS

Expansion slots provide an open architecture. Expansion cards provide connections for video, sound, network, TV tuner cards, and more. PC cards are for notebook and handheld computers.

Computers are known for having different kinds of "architectures." Machines that have **closed architecture** are manufactured in such a way that users cannot easily add new devices. Most microcomputers have **open architecture.** They allow users to expand their systems by providing **slots** on the system board. Users can insert optional devices known as **expansion cards** into these slots. (See Figure 6-24.)

Expansion cards are also called **plug-in boards, controller cards, adapter cards,** and **interface cards.** They plug into slots located on the system board. Ports on the cards allow cables to be connected from the expansion cards to devices outside the system unit. (See Figure 6-25.) There are a wide range of different types of expansion cards. Some of the most commonly used expansion cards are:

- **Video cards:** Also known as **graphics cards,** these cards connect the system board to the computer's monitor. The cards convert the internal electronic signals to video signals so they can be displayed on the monitor.
- **Sound cards:** These cards accept audio input from a microphone and convert it into a form that can be processed by the computer. Also, these cards convert internal electronic signals to audio signals so they can be heard from external speakers.

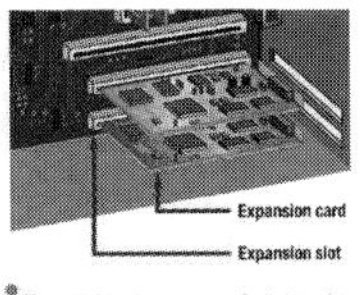

Expansion card
Expansion slot

Figure 6-24 Expansion cards fit into slots on the system board

On the Web Explorations

Two or more On the Web Explorations appear within nearly every chapter and are presented as marginal elements. These explorations ask you to connect to carefully selected Web sites that provide additional information on key topics, encouraging you to expand your knowledge by using Web resources.

Computing Today Web site

Throughout the text, the Computing Today Web site at http://www.mhhe.com/oleary/CT05 is referenced. The text directs you to this Web site for additional material, Web links, and exercises to boost interest and enhance your comprehension of the material.

How does Computing Today get you involved in current technologies?

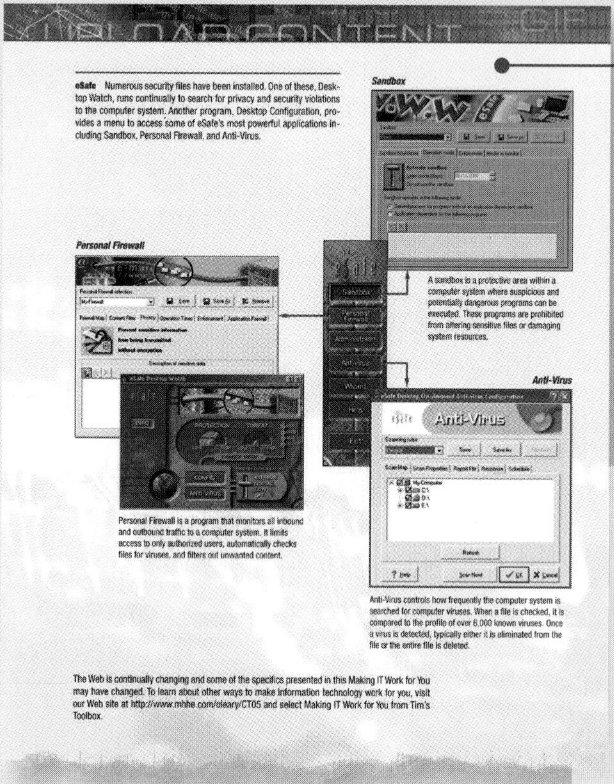

eSafe Numerous security files have been installed. One of these, Desktop Watch, runs continually to search for privacy and security violations to the computer system. Another program, Desktop Configuration, provides a menu to access some of eSafe's most powerful applications including Sandbox, Personal Firewall, and Anti-Virus.

Sandbox

A sandbox is a protective area within a computer system where suspicious and potentially dangerous programs can be executed. These programs are prohibited from altering sensitive files or damaging system resources.

Personal Firewall

Personal Firewall is a program that monitors all inbound and outbound traffic to a computer system. It limits access to only authorized users, automatically checks files for viruses, and filters out unwanted content.

Anti-Virus

Anti-Virus controls how frequently the computer system is searched for computer viruses. When a file is checked, it is compared to the profile of over 6,000 known viruses. Once a virus is detected, typically either it is eliminated from the file or the entire file is deleted.

The Web is continually changing and some of the specifics presented in this Making IT Work for You may have changed. To learn about other ways to make information technology work for you, visit our Web site at http://www.mhhe.com/oleary/CT05 and select Making IT Work for You from Tim's Toolbox.

Making IT Work for You

Special interest topics are presented in a two-page Making IT Work for You section within the chapter relating to that topic. These topics include protecting against computer viruses, downloading music from the Internet, and using the Internet to place free long-distance telephone calls.

Making IT Work Video Series

Seven of the Making IT Work for You features have been expanded into video presentations available on the Web and from the Computing Today CD. These videos expand and animate the material in the book.

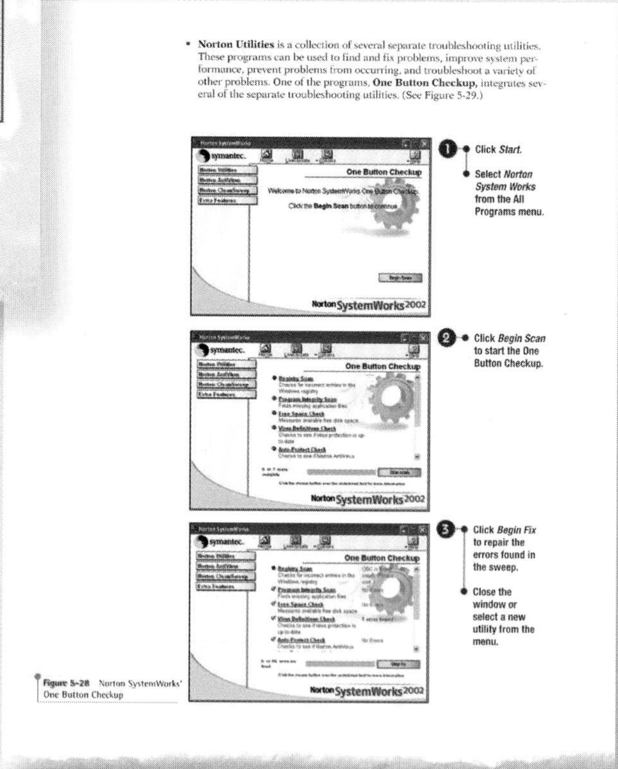

- **Norton Utilities** is a collection of several separate troubleshooting utilities. These programs can be used to find and fix problems, improve system performance, prevent problems from occurring, and troubleshoot a variety of other problems. One of the programs, **One Button Checkup,** integrates several of the separate troubleshooting utilities. (See Figure 5-29.)

1. Click *Start*.
   Select *Norton System Works* from the All Programs menu.
2. Click *Begin Scan* to start the One Button Checkup.
3. Click *Begin Fix* to repair the errors found in the sweep.
   Close the window or select a new utility from the menu.

Figure 5-28 Norton SystemWorks' One Button Checkup

How does Computing Today teach you about careers and the future in information technology?

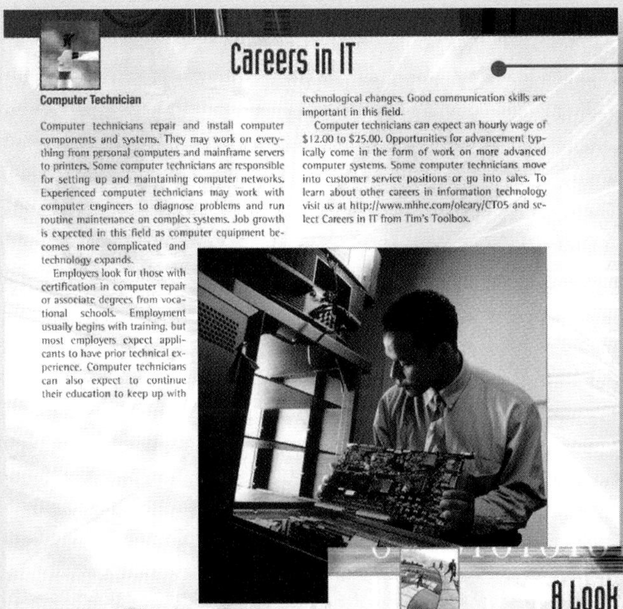

Careers in IT

Computer Technician

Computer technicians repair and install computer components and systems. They may work on everything from personal computers and mainframe servers to printers. Some computer technicians are responsible for setting up and maintaining computer networks. Experienced computer technicians may work with computer engineers to diagnose problems and run routine maintenance on complex systems. Job growth is expected in this field as computer equipment becomes more complicated and technology expands.

Employers look for those with certification in computer repair or associate degrees from vocational schools. Employment usually begins with training, but most employers expect applicants to have prior technical experience. Computer technicians can also expect to continue their education to keep up with technological changes. Good communication skills are important in this field.

Computer technicians can expect an hourly wage of $12.00 to $25.00. Opportunities for advancement typically come in the form of work on more advanced computer systems. Some computer technicians move into customer service positions or go into sales. To learn about other careers in information technology visit us at http://www.mhhe.com/oleary/CT05 and select Careers in IT from Tim's Toolbox.

Careers in IT

Some of the fastest growing career opportunities are in information technology. Every chapter includes a job description for a different career in IT. These descriptions include job titles, responsibilities, educational requirements, and salary ranges. Among the careers covered are webmaster, software engineer, and database administrator. You will learn how the material they are studying relates directly to a potential career path.

A Look to the Future

Xybernaut Corporation Makes Wearable Computers a Reality

Wouldn't it be nice if you could conveniently access the Internet wirelessly at any time during the day? What if you could send and receive e-mail from your waist-mounted computer? What if you could maintain your personal schedule book, making new appointments with others on the fly? What if you could play interactive games, and surf the Web from anywhere?

Of course you can do all this and more using wireless technology and PDAs. Many people currently use this technology when they are away from their home or office. What if these users could accomplish these tasks with an even smaller, more portable and less intrusive system? Will people be wearing computers rather than carrying them? What if your computer featured a head-mounted display?

Xybernaut Corporation is currently marketing a personal wearable computer called POMA®. The device is described as a personal multimedia appliance. It is composed of a processor that runs Windows CE, a wireless pointing device, and a head-mounted display. The display allows you to see the equivalent of a desktop monitor via a small screen that is worn in front of one eye. This screen is only one inch square and weighs a mere 3 ounces. The device includes an MP3 player that plays songs and displays videos, and abridged versions of Windows Office programs.

Devices made by Xybernaut® are currently evaluated for use in airports by security personal. These devices are currently being used by the U.S. Department of Defense for military applications and by the Toronto Blue Jays to end long lines at ticket windows. When coupled with face recognition technology Xybernaut's Mobile Assistant® V allows security personnel the advantage of portability and instant communication with the command center. Police and security officers may someday use this technology to check IDs and verify your identity. Experts say that wearable computers will be used by surgeons in operating rooms to "view" their patients.

Will we be wearing computers soon? Some of us already are. And some experts predict the majority of us will employ a wearable computer before the end of the decade. Many computer manufacturers are currently working on wearable computers, and there is even a wearable computer fashion show that showcases the latest designs. Many people are already "wearing" their computers, and making use of this mobile technology to read e-mail while waiting in lines or even studying their notes for the next exam. What do you think? Will Americans someday grab their keys and their computers before they leave the house? Will your computer one day be housed in your jacket?

A Look to the Future

Each chapter concludes with a brief discussion of a recent technological advance related to chapter material, reinforcing the importance of staying informed.

How does Computing Today reinforce key concepts

Visual Chapter Summaries

These summaries appear in at least two pages at the end of each chapter. Using a columnar arrangement, major concepts are presented by graphics followed by detailed text summaries, providing a summary of key concepts and terms in an engaging and meaningful way.

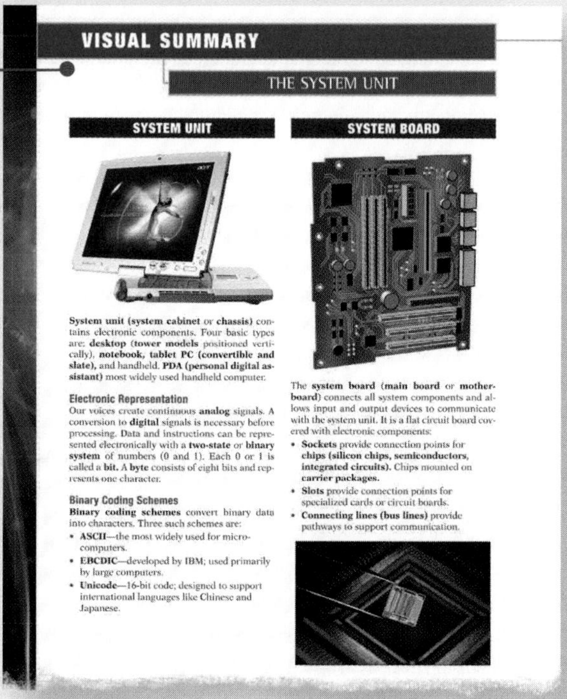

VISUAL SUMMARY

THE SYSTEM UNIT

SYSTEM UNIT

System unit (system cabinet or **chassis)** contains electronic components. Four basic types are: **desktop (tower models** positioned vertically), **notebook, tablet PC (convertible and slate),** and handheld. **PDA (personal digital assistant)** most widely used handheld computer.

Electronic Representation

Our voices create continuous **analog** signals. A conversion to **digital** signals is necessary before processing. Data and instructions can be represented electronically with a **two-state** or **binary system** of numbers (0 and 1). Each 0 or 1 is called a **bit.** A **byte** consists of eight bits and represents one character.

Binary Coding Schemes

Binary coding schemes convert binary data into characters. Three such schemes are:

- **ASCII**—the most widely used for microcomputers.
- **EBCDIC**—developed by IBM; used primarily by large computers.
- **Unicode**—16-bit code; designed to support international languages like Chinese and Japanese.

SYSTEM BOARD

The **system board (main board** or **motherboard)** connects all system components and allows input and output devices to communicate with the system unit. It is a flat circuit board covered with electronic components:

- **Sockets** provide connection points for **chips (silicon chips, semiconductors, integrated circuits).** Chips mounted on **carrier packages.**
- **Slots** provide connection points for specialized cards or circuit boards.
- **Connecting lines (bus lines)** provide pathways to support communication.

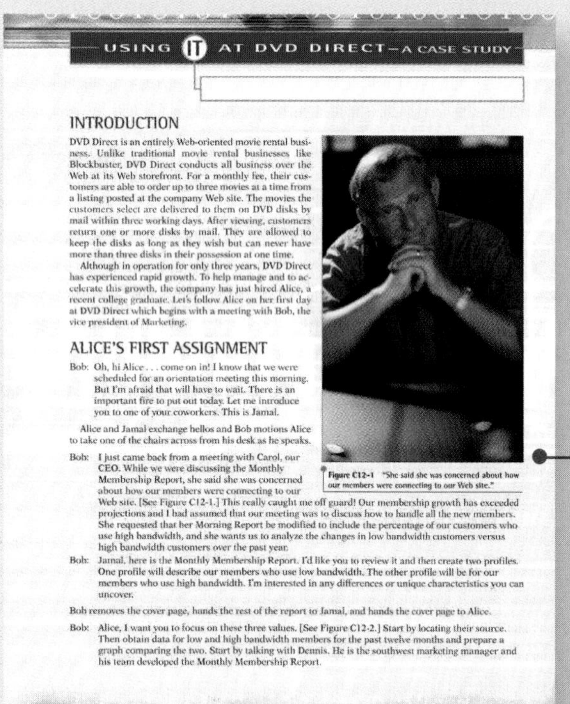

USING IT AT DVD DIRECT—A CASE STUDY

INTRODUCTION

DVD Direct is an entirely Web-oriented movie rental business. Unlike traditional movie rental businesses like Blockbuster, DVD Direct conducts all business over the Web at its Web storefront. For a monthly fee, their customers are able to order up to three movies at a time from a listing posted at the company Web site. The movies the customers select are delivered to them on DVD disks by mail within three working days. After viewing, customers return one or more disks by mail. They are allowed to keep the disks as long as they wish but can never have more than three disks in their possession at one time.

Although in operation for only three years, DVD Direct has experienced rapid growth. To help manage and to accelerate this growth, the company has just hired Alice, a recent college graduate. Let's follow Alice on her first day at DVD Direct which begins with a meeting with Bob, the vice president of Marketing.

ALICE'S FIRST ASSIGNMENT

Bob: Oh, hi Alice . . . come on in! I know that we were scheduled for an orientation meeting this morning. But I'm afraid that will have to wait. There is an important fire to put out today. Let me introduce you to one of your coworkers. This is Jamal.

Alice and Jamal exchange hellos and Bob motions Alice to take one of the chairs across from his desk as he speaks.

Bob: I just came back from a meeting with Carol, our CEO. While we were discussing the Monthly Membership Report, she said she was concerned about how our members were connecting to our Web site. [See Figure C12-1.] This really caught me off guard! Our membership growth has exceeded projections and I had assumed that our meeting was to discuss how to handle all the new members. She requested that her Morning Report be modified to include the percentage of our customers who use high bandwidth, and she wants us to analyze the changes in low bandwidth customers versus high bandwidth customers over the past year.

Bob: Jamal, here is the Monthly Membership Report. I'd like you to review it and then create two profiles. One profile will describe our members who use low bandwidth. The other profile will be for our members who use high bandwidth. I'm interested in any differences or unique characteristics you can uncover.

Bob removes the cover page, hands the rest of the report to Jamal, and hands the cover page to Alice.

Bob: Alice, I want you to focus on these three values. [See Figure C12-2.] Start by locating their source. Then obtain data for low and high bandwidth members for the past twelve months and prepare a graph comparing the two. Start by talking with Dennis. He is the southwest marketing manager and his team developed the Monthly Membership Report.

Figure C12-1 "She said she was concerned about how our members were connecting to our Web site."

Using IT at DVD Direct—A Case Study

Beginning in Chapter 12 and continuing through Chapter 15, Using IT at DVD-Direct—A Case Study is an up-close look at what you might expect to find on the job in the real world. You will follow Alice, a recent college graduate hired as a marketing analyst, as she navigates her way through Accounting, Marketing, Production, Human Resources and Research, gathering and processing data to help manage and accelerate the growth of the three year-old company. This case study is supported with end of chapter exercises and the Computing Today CD.

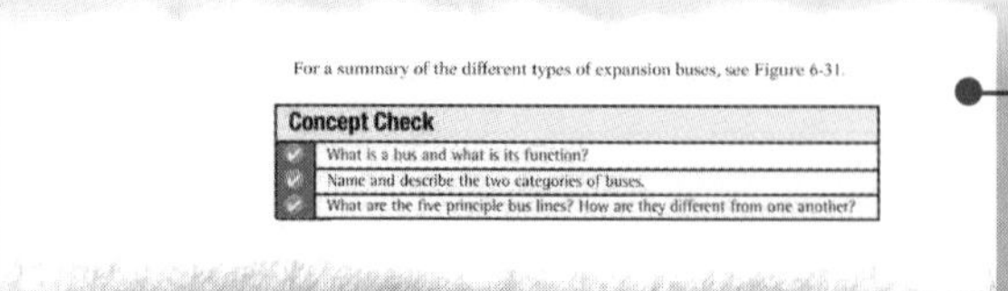

For a summary of the different types of expansion buses, see Figure 6-31.

Concept Check
What is a bus and what is its function?
Name and describe the two categories of buses.
What are the five principle bus lines? How are they different from one another?

Concept Check

Located at points throughout each chapter, the Concept Check cues you to note which topics have been covered and to self-test your understanding of the material

How does Computing Today help you to evaluate your knowledge of the material in each chapter?

Chapter Review

Following the Visual Summary, the chapter Review includes material designed to review and reinforce chapter content. It includes a **Key Terms List** that reiterates the terms presented in the chapter, a **Crossword Puzzle** to challenge your understanding of the chapter material, **Multiple Choice** questions to help test your recall of information presented in the chapter. **Matching** exercises to test your recall of terminology presented in the chapter, and **Open-Ended** questions or statements to help review your understanding of the key concepts presented in the chapter.

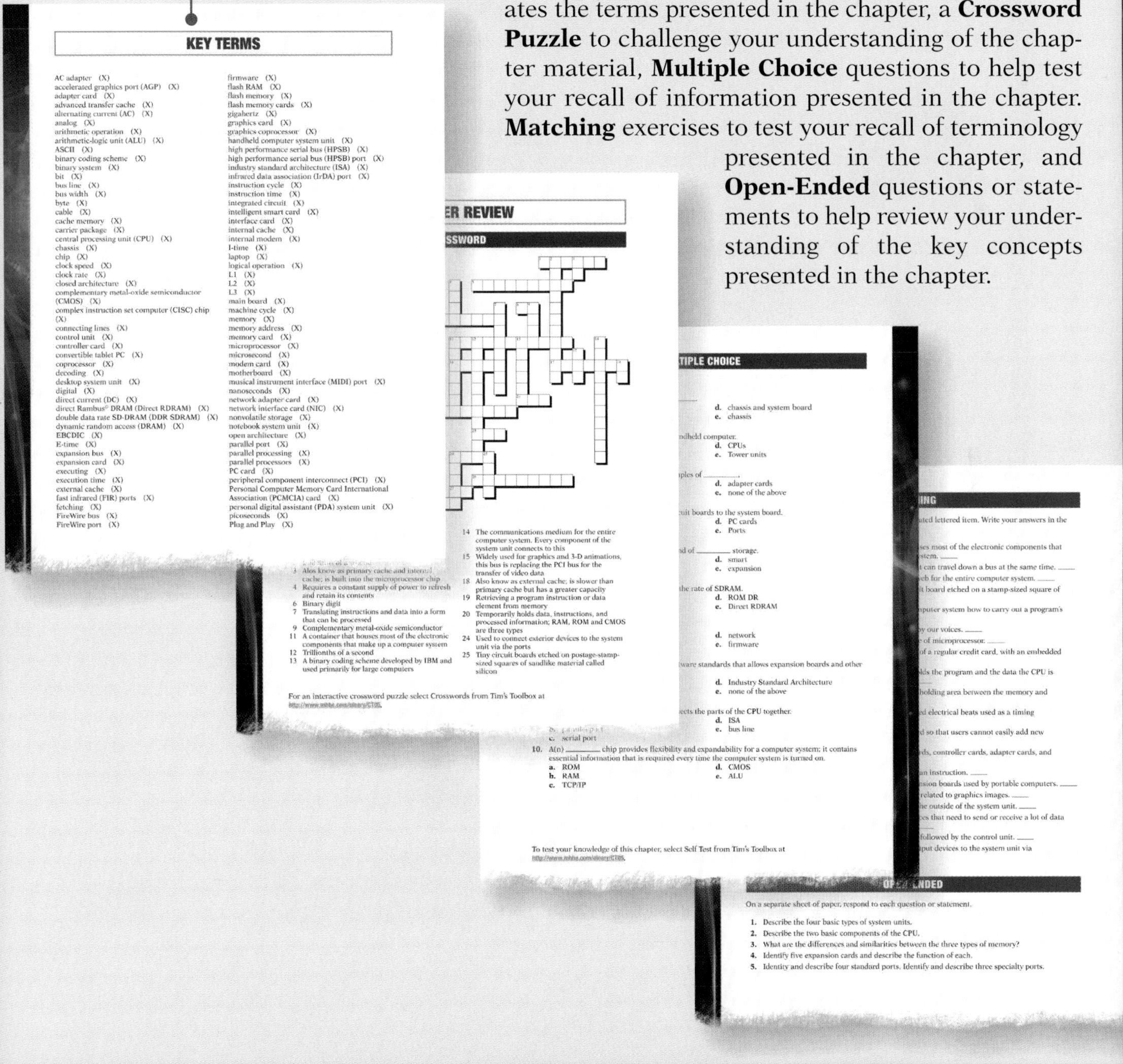
KEY TERMS
ER REVIEW
SSWORD
TIPLE CHOICE
On a separate sheet of paper, respond to each question or statement.
1. Describe the four basic types of system units.
2. Describe the two basic components of the CPU.
3. What are the differences and similarities between the three types of memory?
4. Identify five expansion cards and describe the function of each.
5. Identify and describe four standard ports. Identify and describe three specialty ports.

How does Computing Today encourage you to develop and utilize critical thinking skills?

Using Technology

In each chapter, Using Technology presents four questions designed to help you gain a better understanding of how technology is being used today. One question typically relates the chapter's Making IT Work for You topics. Additional questions focus on interesting applications of technology that relate directly to you. Topics include: Online Auctions, Online Personal Information Managers, Desktop and Notebook Computers.

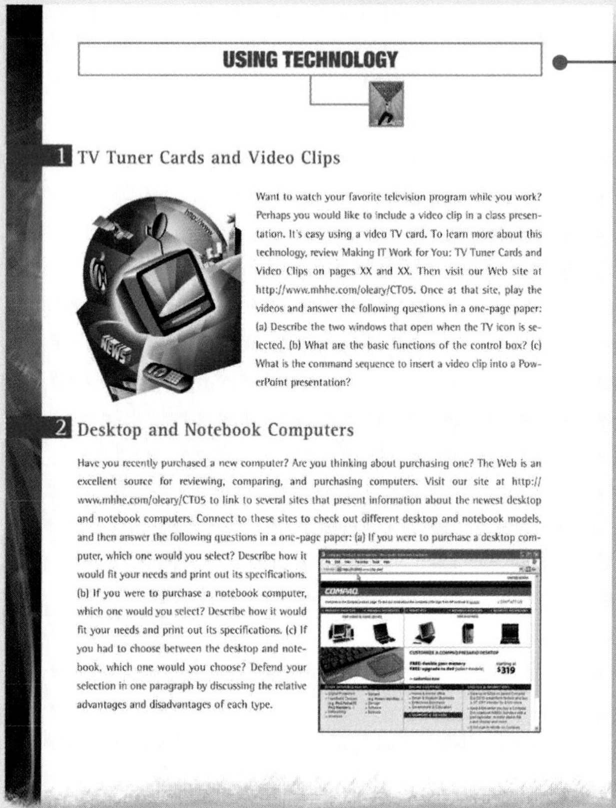

USING TECHNOLOGY

1 TV Tuner Cards and Video Clips

Want to watch your favorite television program while you work? Perhaps you would like to include a video clip in a class presentation. It's easy using a video TV card. To learn more about this technology, review Making IT Work for You: TV Tuner Cards and Video Clips on pages XX and XX. Then visit our Web site at http://www.mhhe.com/oleary/CT05. Once at that site, play the videos and answer the following questions in a one-page paper: (a) Describe the two windows that open when the TV icon is selected. (b) What are the basic functions of the control box? (c) What is the command sequence to insert a video clip into a PowerPoint presentation?

2 Desktop and Notebook Computers

Have you recently purchased a new computer? Are you thinking about purchasing one? The Web is an excellent source for reviewing, comparing, and purchasing computers. Visit our site at http://www.mhhe.com/oleary/CT05 to link to several sites that present information about the newest desktop and notebook computers. Connect to these sites to check out different desktop and notebook models, and then answer the following questions in a one-page paper: (a) If you were to purchase a desktop computer, which one would you select? Describe how it would fit your needs and print out its specifications. (b) If you were to purchase a notebook computer, which one would you select? Describe how it would fit your needs and print out its specifications. (c) If you had to choose between the desktop and notebook, which one would you choose? Defend your selection in one paragraph by discussing the relative advantages and disadvantages of each type.

Expanding Your Knowledge

In each chapter, Expanding Your Knowledge presents four questions that help you gain a deeper understanding of select topics. Typically, one question relates to a topic contained on your Computing today CD, such as How Instant Messaging Works, How Streaming Media Works, and How Virus Protection Works. Additional questions in Expanding Your Knowledge typically relate to a tutorial on your SimNet CD, including tutorials about The Internet, Web, and Electronic Commerce.

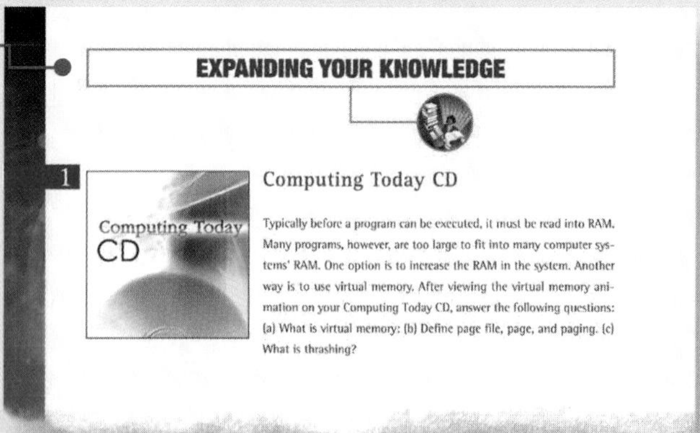

EXPANDING YOUR KNOWLEDGE

1 Computing Today CD

Typically before a program can be executed, it must be read into RAM. Many programs, however, are too large to fit into many computer systems' RAM. One option is to increase the RAM in the system. Another way is to use virtual memory. After viewing the virtual memory animation on your Computing Today CD, answer the following questions: (a) What is virtual memory: (b) Define page file, page, and paging. (c) What is thrashing?

How does Computing Today help you create a portfolio that demonstrates your knowledge of technology?

BUILDING YOUR PORTFOLIO

1 Microprocessors

The microprocessor is the "brains" of the system unit. It has two basic components: control unit and arithmetic-logic unit. Microprocessors approximately double their speed every year and a half. New technologies make for faster chips and faster PCs. Research the latest microprocessors from industry leaders Intel, AMD, and Cyrix. Then write a one-page paper titled "Current Microprocessors" that addresses the following points: (a) Describe the chips you located. (b) How does each of these chips differ from their last generation? What improvements have been made? (c) Describe any special features that these chips offer and explain each.

BUILDING YOUR PORTFOLIO

Processor Serial Numbers **3**

When the Intel Pentium III microprocessor was released, each unit originally contained a unique Processor Serial Number, or PSN. This PSN could be used by online e-commerce sites to identify and to track individuals by the computer they used. This tracking would be similar to keeping track of car owners by their license plate numbers. Write a one-page paper that addresses the following items: (a) What are the benefits of a PSN for a computer user? For society? Explain your answers. (b) What privacy issues does a PSN raise for a computer user? (c) Describe how a PSN could be misused.

Building Your Portfolio

Two questions in Building Your Portfolio typically relate to key technologies. Topics include: electronic commerce, artificial intelligence, Linux, microprocessors digital input, and firewalls. Two additional questions in Building Your Portfolio typically relate to security, privacy, and ethical issues. The issues presented include: HTML source code, antitrust legislation, Processor serial numbers, CD-R and Music Files, and electronic monitoring. One objective of the Building Your Portfolio feature is to develop critical thinking and writing skills. Another objective is to create written documents recording your technology knowledge. A third objective is to recognize, understand, and analyze key privacy, security, and ethical issues relating to technology.

How do the Interactive CD-ROMs that accompany Computing Today work together with the text to enhance learning?

SimNet CD

The SimNet CD is a complete computer-based learning and assessment program for topics you will study in Computing Today. The learning component offers three modes: Teach Me (introduces topics using text, graphics, and interactivity), Show Me (animates and explains key topics), and Let Me Try (provides practice for critical skills). The assessment component consists of two separate pools of questions, one for Exams and one for Pre-Tests, so that you can see and practice questions similar to what will be on the test. CD icons are located in the margins throughout the text to alert students that tutorials on the SimNet CD relating to the text material are available to help them assimilate the concepts.

Computing Today CD

The Computing Today CD contains animations of key concepts, videos relating to select Making IT Work for You applications, and indepth coverage of select topics. Computing Today CD icons are located in the margins throughout the book to alert students that expanded coverage of the material in the text can be found on their Computing Today CD.

Computing Today

INFORMATION TECHNOLOGY, THE INTERNET, AND YOU

OBJECTIVES

After you have read this chapter, you should be able to:

1. Explain the five parts of an information system: people, procedures, software, hardware, and data.
2. Distinguish between system software and application software.
3. Discuss the four kinds of system software programs.
4. Distinguish between special-purpose and general-purpose application software.
5. Identify the four types of computers and the three types of microcomputers.
6. Describe the different types of computer hardware including the system unit, input, output, storage, and communication devices.
7. Define data and describe document, worksheet, database, and presentation files.
8. Explain computer connectivity, the wireless revolution, and the Internet.

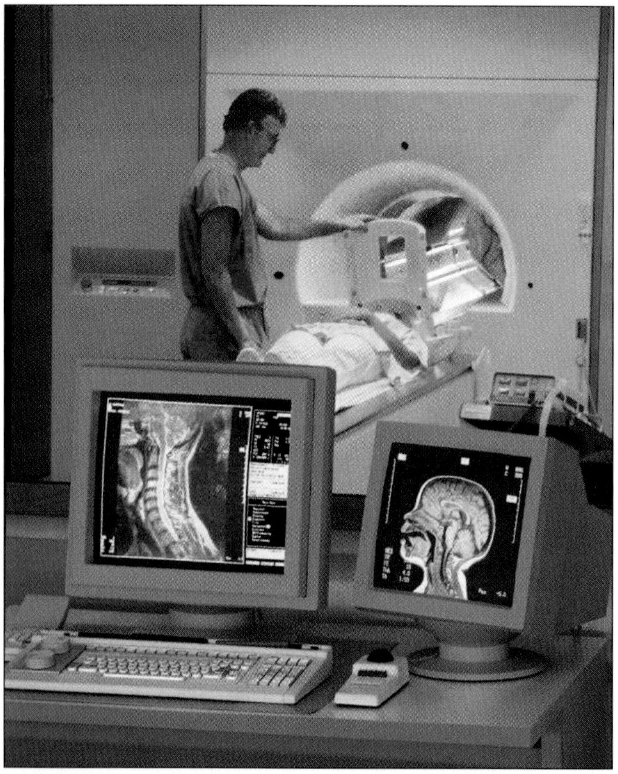

CHAPTER 1

Information Technology (IT): Just as the Internet and the Web have affected all of us, they have affected computer technology as well. Today, communication links to the Internet are a common feature of almost all computer systems. Information technology is a modern term that describes this combination of traditional computer and communication technologies.

The purpose of this book is to help you use and understand information technology. This involves two aspects: computer competency and computer knowledge. Computer competency refers to acquiring computer-related skills. These skills are indispensable tools for today. They include how to efficiently and effectively use popular application packages and the Internet. Computer knowledge is a deeper understanding of how technology works. It provides a foundation for you to understand how technology is being used today and how you might use technology in the future. For example, knowing how the Internet works provides the foundation for you to understand the potential of electronic commerce and to understand how information about you can be collected and dispensed without your consent.

In this chapter, we first present an overview of an information system: people, procedures, software, hardware, and data. It is essential to understand these basic parts and how connectivity through the Internet and the Web expands the role of information technology in our lives. In subsequent chapters, we will describe these parts of an information system in detail.

Fifteen years ago, most people had little to do with computers, at least directly. Of course, they filled out computerized forms, took computerized tests, and paid computerized bills. But the real work with computers was handled by specialists—programmers, data entry clerks, and computer operators.

Then microcomputers came along and changed everything. Today it is easy for nearly everybody to use a computer. Now:

- Microcomputers are common tools in all areas of life. Writers write, artists draw, engineers and scientists calculate—all on microcomputers. Students and businesspeople do all this, and more.
- New forms of learning have developed. People who are homebound, who work odd hours, or who travel frequently may take courses on the Web. A college course need not fit within the usual time of a quarter or a semester.
- New ways to communicate, to find people with similar interests, and to buy goods are available. All kinds of people are using electronic mail, electronic commerce, and the Internet to meet and to share ideas and products.

What about you? How are you using information technology? Many interesting and practical uses have recently surfaced to make our personal lives richer and more entertaining. These applications range from recording digital video clips to creating personalized Web sites.

To be competent and knowledgeable with IT, you need to know the five parts of an information system: people, procedures, software, hardware, and data. Additionally, you need to understand connectivity, the wireless revolution, the Internet, and the Web and to recognize the role of information technology in your personal and professional life.

INFORMATION SYSTEMS

An information system has five parts: people, procedures, software, hardware, and data. Connectivity allows computers to connect and share information, thereby greatly expanding the capability and usefulness of an information system.

When you think of a microcomputer, perhaps you think of just the equipment itself. That is, you think of the monitor or the keyboard. Yet, there is more to it than that. The way to think about a microcomputer is as part of an information system. An **information system** has five parts: *people, procedures, software, hardware,* and *data.* (See Figure 1-1.)

- **People:** It is easy to overlook people as one of the five parts of a microcomputer system. Yet this is what microcomputers are all about—making **people, end users** like you, more productive.
- **Procedures:** The rules or guidelines for people to follow when using software, hardware, and data are **procedures.** These procedures are typically documented in manuals written by computer specialists. Software and hardware manufacturers provide manuals with their products. These manuals are provided either in printed or electronic form.
- **Software:** A **program** consists of the step-by-step instructions that tell the computer how to do its work. **Software** is another name for a program or programs. The purpose of software is to convert **data** (unprocessed facts) into **information** (processed facts). For example, a payroll program would instruct the computer to take the number of hours you worked in a week

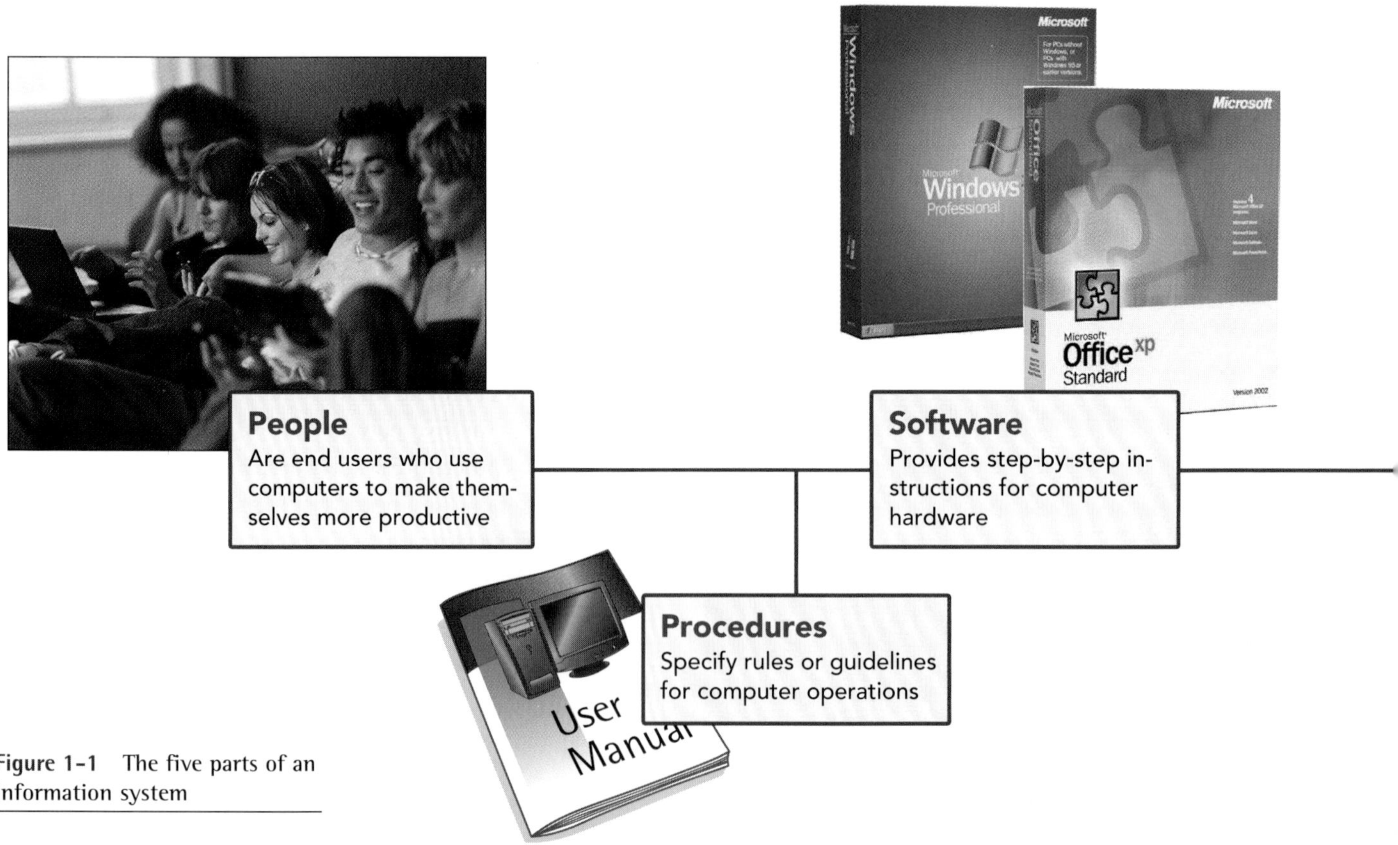
Microsoft
Windows Professional
Microsoft
Office xp Standard
People
Are end users who use computers to make themselves more productive
Software
Provides step-by-step instructions for computer hardware
Procedures
Specify rules or guidelines for computer operations
User Manual

Figure 1-1 The five parts of an information system

(data) and multiply it by your pay rate (data) to determine how much you are paid for the week (information).

- **Hardware:** The equipment that processes the data to create information is called **hardware.** It includes the keyboard, mouse, monitor, system unit, and other devices. Hardware is controlled by software.
- **Data:** The raw, unprocessed facts, including text, numbers, images, and sounds are called data. Processed, data yields information. Using the example above, the data (number of hours worked and pay rate) are processed (multiplied) to yield information (weekly pay).

Almost all of today's computer systems add an additional part to the information system. This part, called **connectivity,** allows computers to connect and to share information. These connections, including Internet connections, can be by telephone lines, by cable, or through the air. Connectivity allows users to greatly expand the capability and usefulness of their information systems.

In large computer systems, there are specialists who write procedures, develop software, and capture data. In microcomputer systems, however, end users often perform these operations. To be a competent and knowledgeable end user, you must understand the essentials of **information technology (IT),** including software, hardware, and data.

Concept Check

- ✔ What are the five parts of an information system?
- ✔ What is the difference between data and information?
- ✔ What is connectivity?

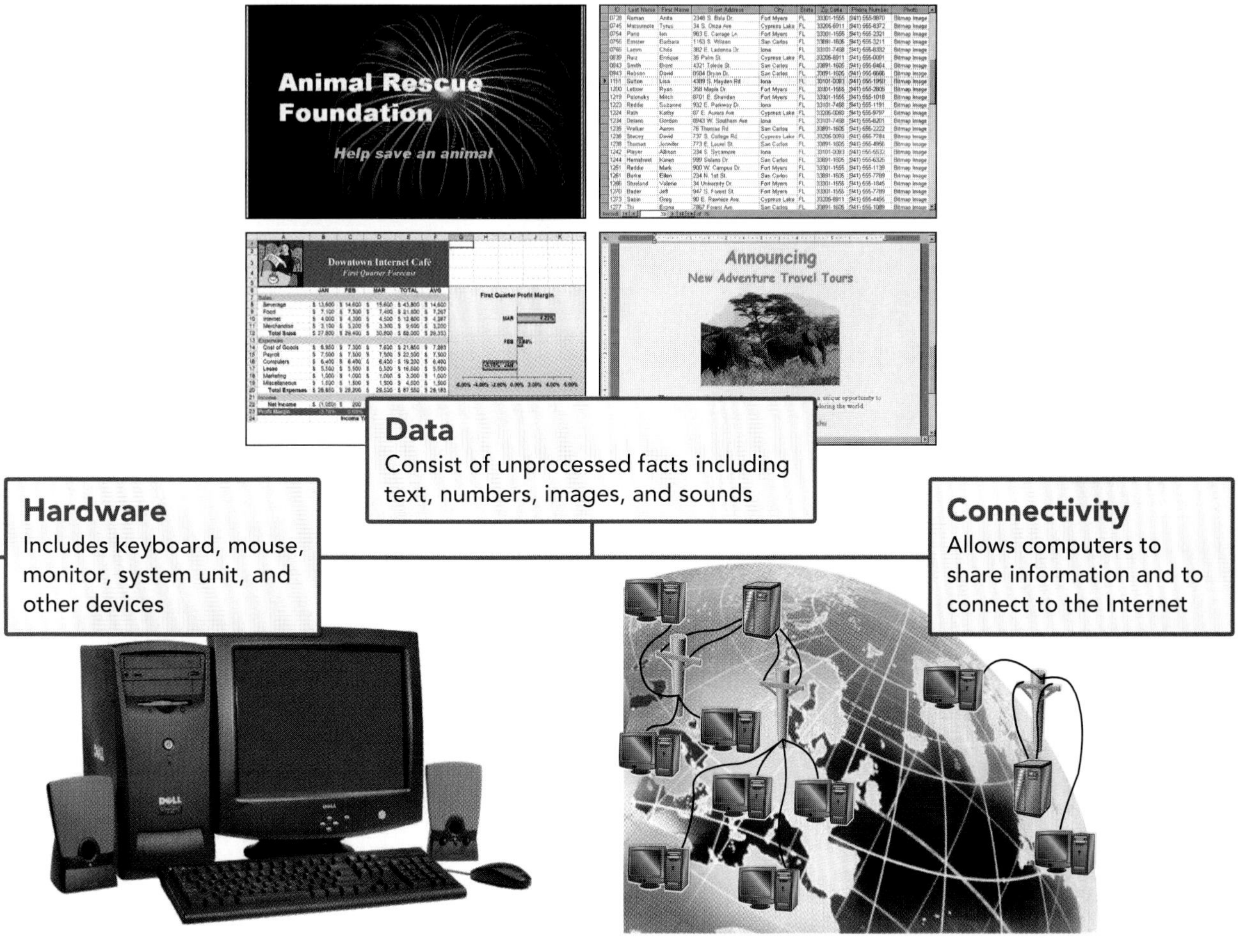

PEOPLE

People are the most important part of an information system. Features in this book include Making IT Work for You, Tips, and two interactive CDs.

Although easy to overlook, people are surely the most important part of any information system. Our lives are touched every day by computers and information systems. Many times the contact is direct and obvious, such as when we create documents using a word processing program or when we connect to the Internet. Other times, the contact is not as obvious. Consider just the four examples in Figure 1-2.

Throughout this book you will find a variety of features designed to help you become computer competent and knowledgeable. These features include Making IT Work for You, Tips, and two interactive CDs.

- **Making IT Work for You.** In the chapters that follow, you will find Making IT Work for You features that present interesting and practical IT applications. Using a step-by-step procedure, you are provided with specific instructions on how to use each application. Figure 1-3 presents a list of these applications.

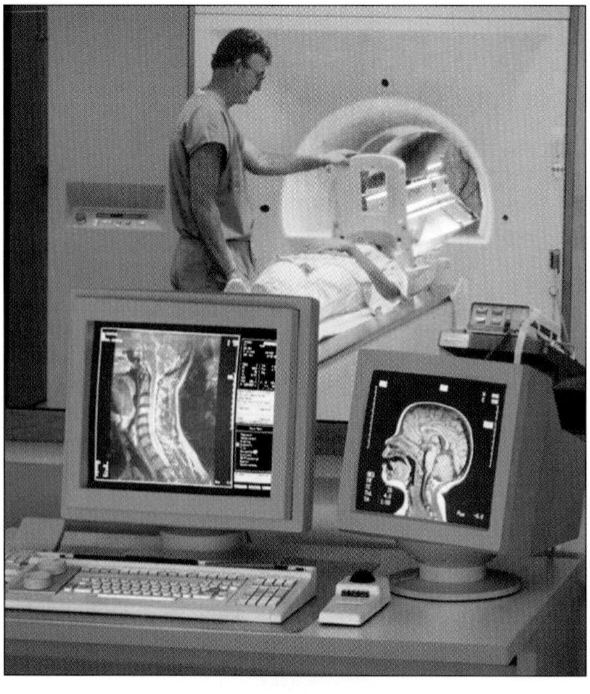

Figure 1-2 Computers in business, entertainment, education, and medicine

MAKING IT WORK FOR YOU

INFORMATION TECHNOLOGY TOPICS

Information technology touches our lives every day in a personal way. Many interesting and practical uses of IT have recently surfaced to make our lives richer and more entertaining. In the following chapters, you will find these applications presented in detail.

Instant Messaging Do you enjoy chatting with your friends? Have you ever worked on a group project and had problems getting everyone together for a meeting? Perhaps instant messaging is just what you're looking for. See page 48.

Web-based Applications Would you like access to free general-purpose applications from anywhere in the world? Would you like to be able to access to your data files from almost any computer? You can have it all with Web-based applications. See page 84.

Personal Web Site Do you have anything to share with the world? Would you like to create a personal Web without having to learn any special Web publishing programs? Would you like to put your personal Web site on the Web without having to pay for server time? Many services are available to get you started for FREE! See page 138.

Virus Protection Has your computer ever been attacked by a computer virus? If not, chances are that it will be in the near future. Fortunately, special software is available to protect you against computer viruses . . . some of the software is even free! See page 186.

TV Tuner Cards and Video Clips Want to watch your favorite television program while you work? Perhaps you would like to include a video clip from a television program or from a VHS tape in a class presentation. It's easy using a TV tuner card. See page 228.

Digital Photography Want to edit your photos on your computer? Would you like to share your photos with family and friends over the Web? Digital photography makes it easy to do. See page 264.

Internet Telephony Would you like to make long distance calls at little or no cost? You can use your computer to make long distance calls to almost any telephone in the world. All you need is the right software and an Internet connection to get started. See page 300.

Music from the Internet Did you know that you can use the Internet to locate music, download it to your computer, and create your own compact discs? All it takes is the right software, hardware, and a connection to the Internet. See page 338.

Home Networking Computer networks are not just for corporations and schools anymore. If you have more than one computer, you can use a wireless home network to share files and printers, to allow multiple users access to the Internet at the same time, and to play interactive computer games. See page 380.

Spyware Are you concerned about maintaining your privacy while you are surfing the Web? Did you know that programs known as spyware could be monitoring your every move? Fortunately, these programs are relatively easy to detect and remove. See page 418.

Job Opportunities Did you know that you can use the Internet to find a job? You can browse through job openings, post your resume, and even use special programs that will search for the job that's just right for you. See page 612.

Figure 1-3 Making IT Work for You topics

- **Tips.** We all can benefit from a few tips or suggestions. Throughout this book you will find numerous Tips ranging from the basics of keeping your computer system running smoothly to how to protect your privacy while surfing the Web. For a partial list of the Tips presented in the following chapters, see Figure 1-4. For a complete list, go to http://www.mhhe.com/oleary/CT05 and select Tips from Tim's Toolbox.
- **Interactive CDs.** This text is accompanied by two interactive CDs. One, **SimNet Concepts,** presents a series of interactive tutorials on a variety of important IT subjects. The other CD, **Computing Today,** contains animations of key concepts, videos relating to select Making IT Work for You applications, and in-depth coverage of select topics. (See Figure 1-5.)

TIPS

- **Controlling spam.** Do you get a lot of unwanted e-mail advertisements? Americans receive over 200 billion spam e-mails every year. There are some basic steps that you can take to keep your inbox spam-free. See page 46.
- **Recovering from a power failure.** Have you ever been working on a document when the power goes off? Your original document and all your recent changes are gone. Fortunately, most applications automatically save your work every few minutes to a temporary recovery or backup file. It's easy to get back under way again.
- **Improving slow computer operations.** Does your computer seem to be getting slower and slower? Consider a few suggestions that might add a little zip to your current system. See page 224.
- **Improving hard disk performance.** Does your internal hard-disk drive run a lot and seem slow? Are you having problems with lost or corrupted files? To clean up the disk and speed up access, consider defragging. See page 329.
- **Protecting your privacy.** Are you concerned about your privacy while on the Web? Consider some suggestions on protecting your identity online. See page 417.

Figure 1-4 Selected Tips

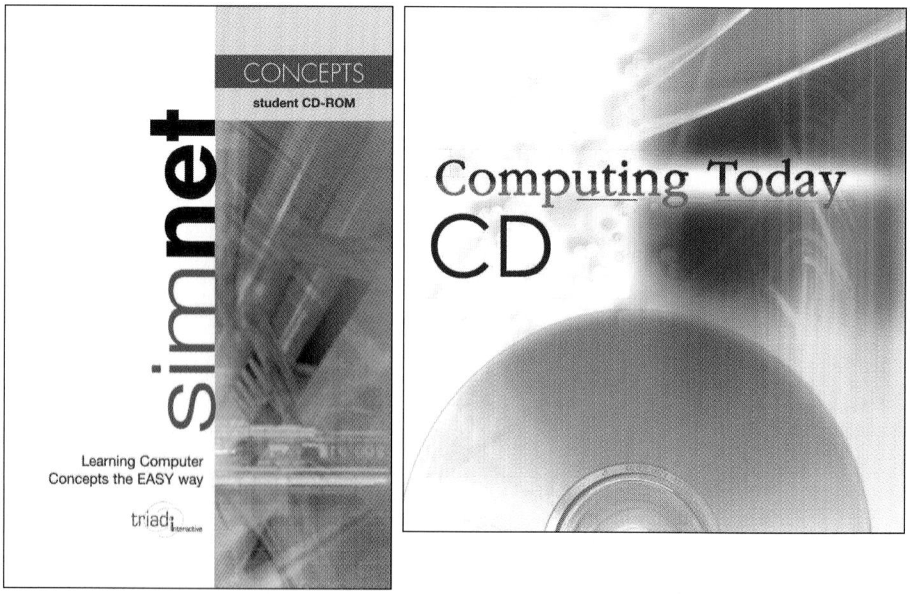

Figure 1-5 Two interactive CDs: SimNet Concepts and the Computing Today CD

SOFTWARE

There are two kinds: system software and application software. System software includes operating systems, utilities, and device drivers. Application software is categorized as general-purpose and special-purpose.

Software, as we mentioned, is another name for programs. Programs are the instructions that tell the computer how to process data into the form you want. In most cases, the words software and programs are interchangeable. There are two major kinds of software—*system software* and *application software.* You can think of application software as the kind you use. Think of system software as the kind the computer uses.

SYSTEM SOFTWARE

The user interacts primarily with application software. **System software** enables the application software to interact with the computer hardware. System software is "background" software that helps the computer manage its own internal resources.

System software is not a single program. Rather it is a collection of programs:

- **Operating systems** are programs that coordinate computer resources, provide an interface between users and the computer, and run applications. Windows XP and the Mac OS X are two of the best-known operating systems for today's microcomputer users. (See Figure 1-6.)
- **Utilities,** also known as **service programs,** perform specific tasks related to managing computer resources. For example, the Windows utility called Disk Defragmenter locates and eliminates unnecessary file fragments and rearranges files and unused disk space to optimize computer operations.
- **Device drivers** are specialized programs designed to allow particular input or output devices to communicate with the rest of the computer system.

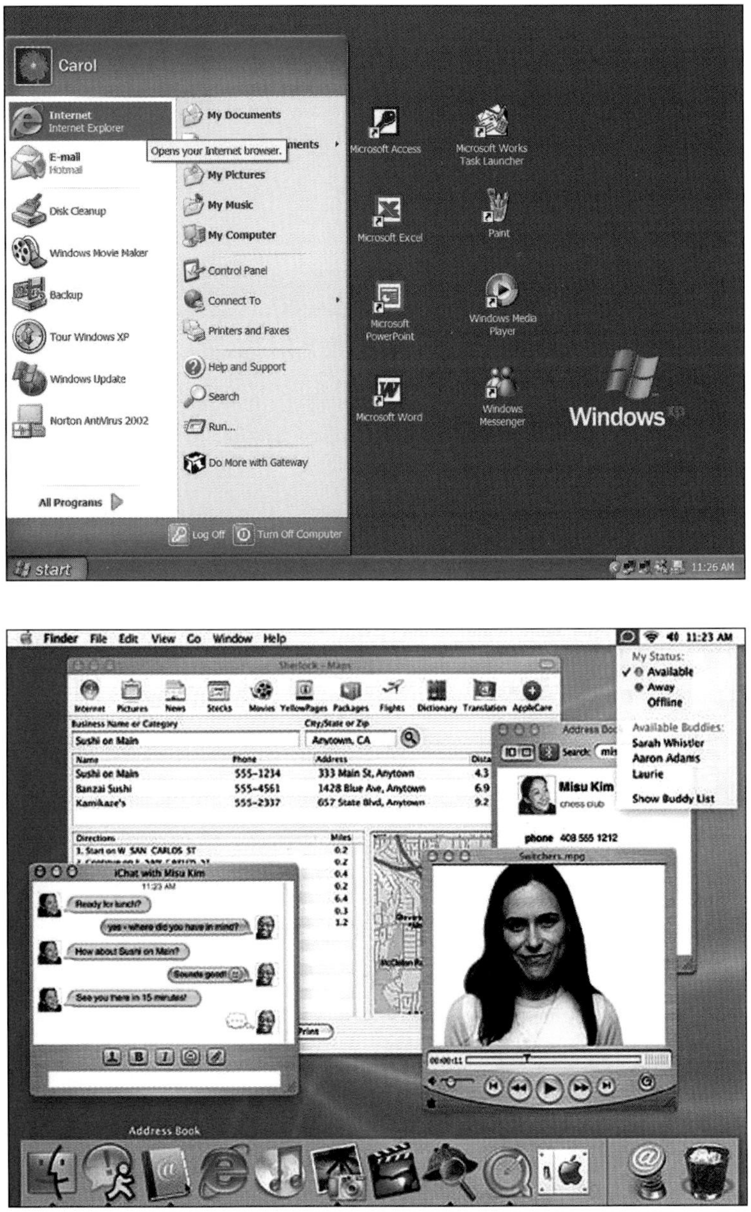

Figure 1-6 Windows and Mac operating systems

APPLICATION SOFTWARE

Application software might be described as end user software. These programs can be categorized as either *general-purpose* or *special-purpose applications.*

General-purpose applications, or **basic applications,** are widely used in nearly all career areas. They are the kinds of programs you have to know to be considered computer competent. One of these basic applications is a browser to

TIPS Have you used the Internet? If so, then you probably already know how to use a browser. For those of you who do not, here are a few tips to get you started.

1. **Start browser.** Typically, all you need to do is double-click the browser's icon on the desktop.
2. **Enter URL.** In the browser's location box, type the URL (uniform resource locator, or address) of the Internet or Web location (site) that you want to visit.
3. **Press ENTER.** On your keyboard, press the ENTER key to connect to the site.
4. **Read and explore.** Once connected to the site, read the information displayed on your monitor. Using the mouse, move the pointer on the monitor. When the pointer changes from an arrow to a hand, click the mouse button to explore other locations.
5. **Close browser.** Once you are done exploring, click on your browser's CLOSE button.

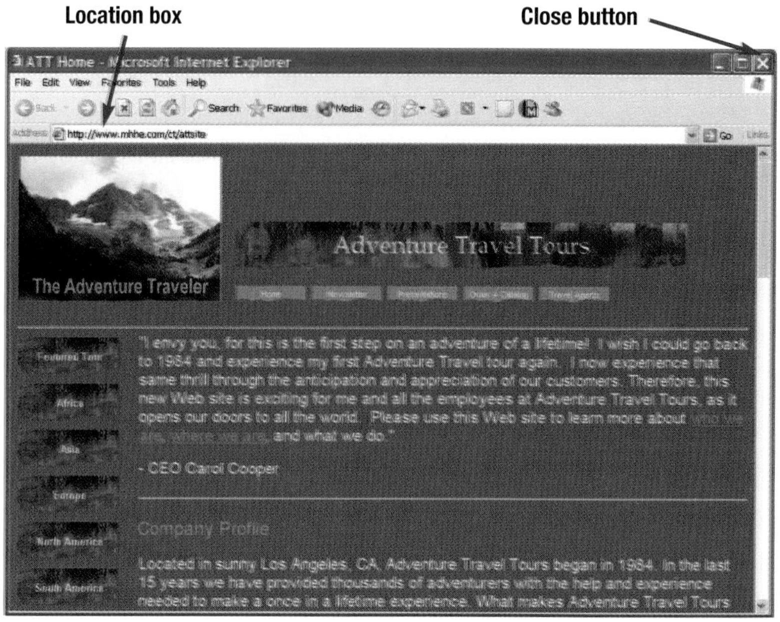

Figure 1-7 Internet Explorer browser

Figure 1-8 Basic applications

Type	Description
Browser	Connect to Web sites and display Web pages
Word processor	Prepare written documents
Spreadsheet	Analyze and summarize numerical data
Database management system	Organize and manage data and information
Presentation graphics	Communicate a message or persuade other people

Figure 1-9 Specialized applications

Type	Description
Graphics	Includes programs designed to create presentations, to analyze data, or to create and edit images
Audio and video	Capture and edit audio and video files
Multimedia	Develop interactive presentations that include audio, video, text, and/or graphical elements
Web authoring	Create and edit Web pages
Artificial intelligence	Programs that attempt to mimic or simulate human senses, thought processes, and/or actions.

navigate, explore, and find information on the Internet. (See Figure 1-7.) The two most widely used browsers are Microsoft's Internet Explorer and Netscape's Navigator. For a summary of the basic applications, see Figure 1-8.

Special-purpose applications, also known as **advanced applications,** include thousands of other programs that are more narrowly focused on specific disciplines and occupations. Some of the best known are graphics, audio and video, multimedia, Web authoring, and artificial intelligence programs. For a description of these programs, see Figure 1-9.

Concept Check

- Describe the two major kinds of software.
- Describe three types of system software programs.
- Define and compare general-purpose and special-purpose applications.

HARDWARE

Four types of computers are supercomputer, mainframe computer, minicomputer, and microcomputer. Microcomputer hardware consists of the system unit, input/output, secondary storage, and communications devices.

Computers are electronic devices that can follow instructions to accept input, process that input, and produce information. This book focuses principally on microcomputers. However, it is almost certain that you will come in contact, at least indirectly, with other types of computers.

TYPES OF COMPUTERS

There are four types of computers: supercomputers, mainframe computers, minicomputers, and microcomputers.

- **Supercomputers** are the most powerful type of computer. These machines are special high-capacity computers used by very large organizations. For example, NASA uses supercomputers to track and control space explorations.
- **Mainframe computers** occupy specially wired, air-conditioned rooms. Although not nearly as powerful as supercomputers, mainframe computers are capable of great processing speeds and data storage. (See Figure 1-10.) For example, insurance companies use mainframes to process information about millions of policyholders.

Figure 1-10 Mainframe computer

- **Minicomputers,** also known as **midrange computers,** are refrigerator-sized machines. Medium-sized companies or departments of large companies typically use them for specific purposes. For example, production departments use minicomputers to monitor certain manufacturing processes and assembly line operations.
- **Microcomputers** are the least powerful, yet the most widely used and fastest-growing, type of computer. There are four types of microcomputers: *desktop, notebook, tablet PC,* and *handheld computers.* (See Figure 1-11.) **Desktop computers** are small enough to fit on top of or alongside a desk yet are too big to carry around. **Notebook computers,** also known as **laptop computers,** are portable, weigh between 4 and 10 pounds, and fit into most briefcases. A **tablet PC** is a type of notebook computer that accepts your handwriting. This input is digitized and converted to standard text that can be further processed by programs such as a word processor. **Handheld computers** are the smallest and are designed to fit into the palm of one hand. Also known as **palm computers,** these systems typically combine pen input, writing recognition, personal organizational tools, and communications capabilities in a very small package. **Personal digital assistants (PDA)** are the most widely used handheld computer.

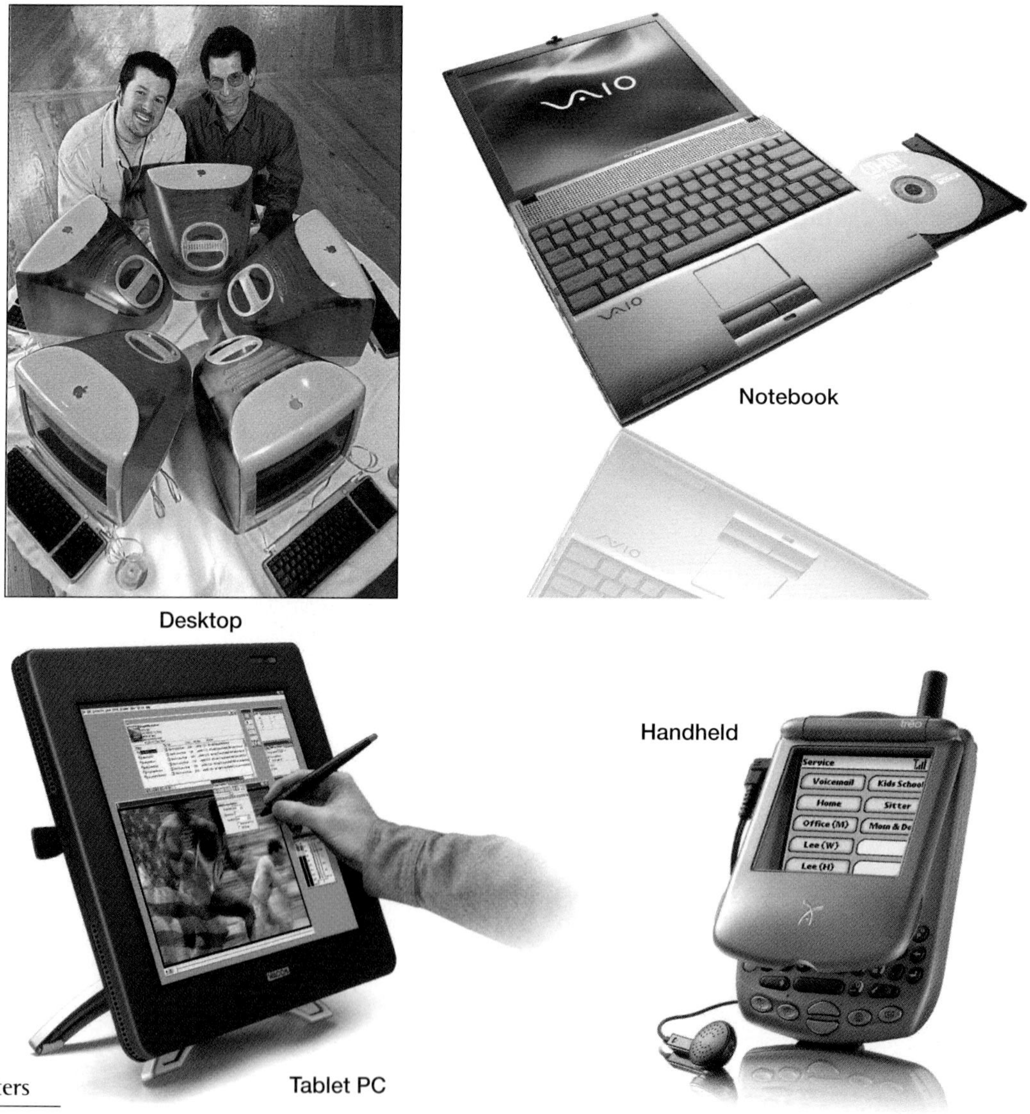

Figure 1-11 Microcomputers

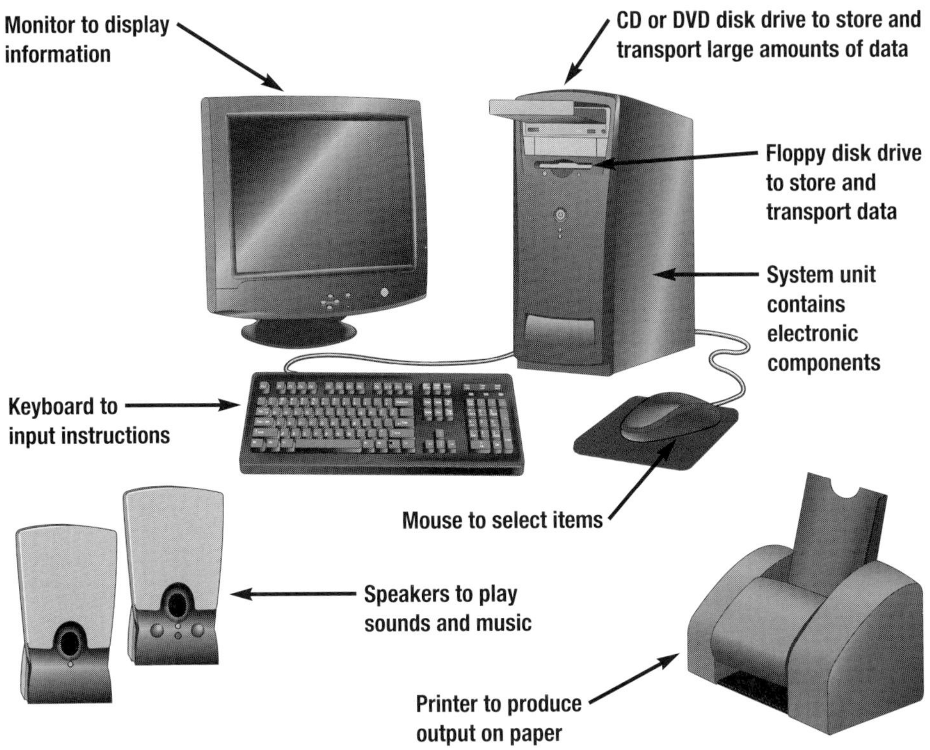
Monitor to display information
CD or DVD disk drive to store and transport large amounts of data
Floppy disk drive to store and transport data
System unit contains electronic components
Keyboard to input instructions
Mouse to select items
Speakers to play sounds and music
Printer to produce output on paper

Figure 1-12 Microcomputer system

MICROCOMPUTER HARDWARE

Hardware for a microcomputer system consists of a variety of different devices. See Figure 1-12 for a typical desktop system. This physical equipment falls into four basic categories: system unit, input/output, secondary storage, and communication. Because we discuss hardware in detail later in this book, we will present just a quick overview of the four basic categories of microcomputer hardware: system unit, input/output, secondary storage, and communication.

- **System unit:** The system unit, also known as the **system cabinet** or **chassis,** is a container that houses most of the electronic components that make up a computer system. (See Figure 1-13.) Two important components of the system unit are the *microprocessor* and *memory.*

On the Web Explorations

Intel is a leading manufacturer of microprocessors. To learn more about this company, visit our Web site at http://www.mhhe.com/oleary/CT05 and select On the Web Explorations from Tim's Toolbox.

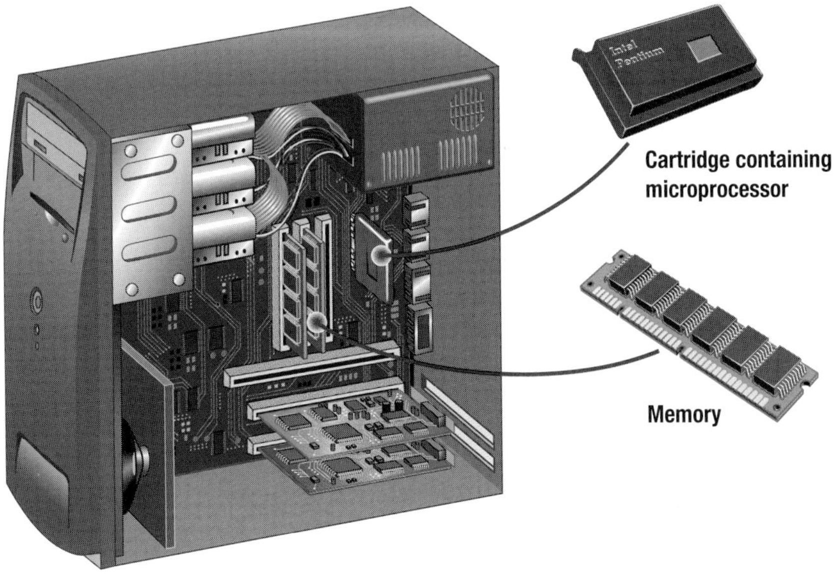
Cartridge containing microprocessor
Memory

Figure 1-13 System unit

The **microprocessor** controls and manipulates data to produce information. Many times the microprocessor is contained within a protective cartridge. **Memory,** also known as **primary storage** or **random access memory (RAM),** holds data and program instructions for processing the data. It also holds the processed information before it is output. Memory is sometimes referred to as **temporary storage** because its contents will typically be lost if the electrical power to the computer is disrupted.

- **Input/output: Input devices** translate data and programs that humans can understand into a form that the computer can process. The most common input devices are the **keyboard** and the **mouse.** (See Figure 1-14.) **Output devices** translate the processed information from the computer into a form that humans can understand. The most common output devices are **monitors** or **video display screens** (see Figure 1-15) and **printers.**
- **Secondary storage:** Unlike memory, **secondary storage devices** hold data and programs even after electrical power to the computer system has been turned off. The most important kinds of secondary media are *floppy, hard,* and *optical disks.* **Floppy disks** are widely used to store and transport data from one computer to another. (See Figure 1-16.) They are called floppy because data is stored on a very thin flexible, or floppy, plastic disk. **Hard disks** are typically used to store programs and very large data files. Using a rigid metallic platter, hard disks have a much greater capacity and are able to access information much faster than floppy disks. **Optical disks** use laser technology and have the greatest capacity. (See Figure 1-17.) The two basic types of optical disks are **compact discs (CDs)** and **digital versatile** (or **video**) **discs (DVDs).**

On the Web Explorations

Toshiba is a leader in the development of DVD. To learn more about this company, visit our Web site at

http://www.mhhe.com/oleary/CT05 and select On the Web Explorations from Tim's Toolbox.

Figure 1-14 Keyboard and mouse

Figure 1-15 Monitor

Figure 1-16 A 3½-inch floppy disk

Figure 1-17 An optical disk

- **Communication:** At one time, it was uncommon for a microcomputer system to communicate with other computer systems. Now, using **communication devices,** a microcomputer can communicate with other computer systems located as near as the next office or as far as halfway around the world using the Internet. The most widely used communication device is a **modem**, which modifies telephone communications into a form that can be processed by a computer. Modems also modify computer output into a form that can be transmitted across standard telephone lines.

Concept Check

- ✔ What are the four types of computers?
- ✔ Describe the four types of microcomputers.
- ✔ Describe the four basic categories of microcomputer hardware.

DATA

Data are unprocessed facts. Processing data creates information. Four common file types are document, worksheet, database, and presentation.

Data are raw, unprocessed facts, including text, numbers, images, and sounds. As we have mentioned earlier, processed data becomes information. When stored electronically in files, data can be used directly as input for the information system.

Four common types of files (see Figure 1-18) are:

- **Document files,** created by word processors to save documents such as memos, term papers, and letters.
- **Worksheet files,** created by electronic spreadsheets to analyze things like budgets and to predict sales.
- **Database files,** typically created by database management programs to contain highly structured and organized data. For example, an employee database file might contain all the workers' names, social security numbers, job titles, and other related pieces of information.
- **Presentation files,** created by presentation graphics programs to save presentation materials. For example, a file might contain audience handouts, speaker notes, and electronic slides.

Concept Check

- ✔ Define data.
- ✔ What is the difference between data and information?
- ✔ List four common types of files.

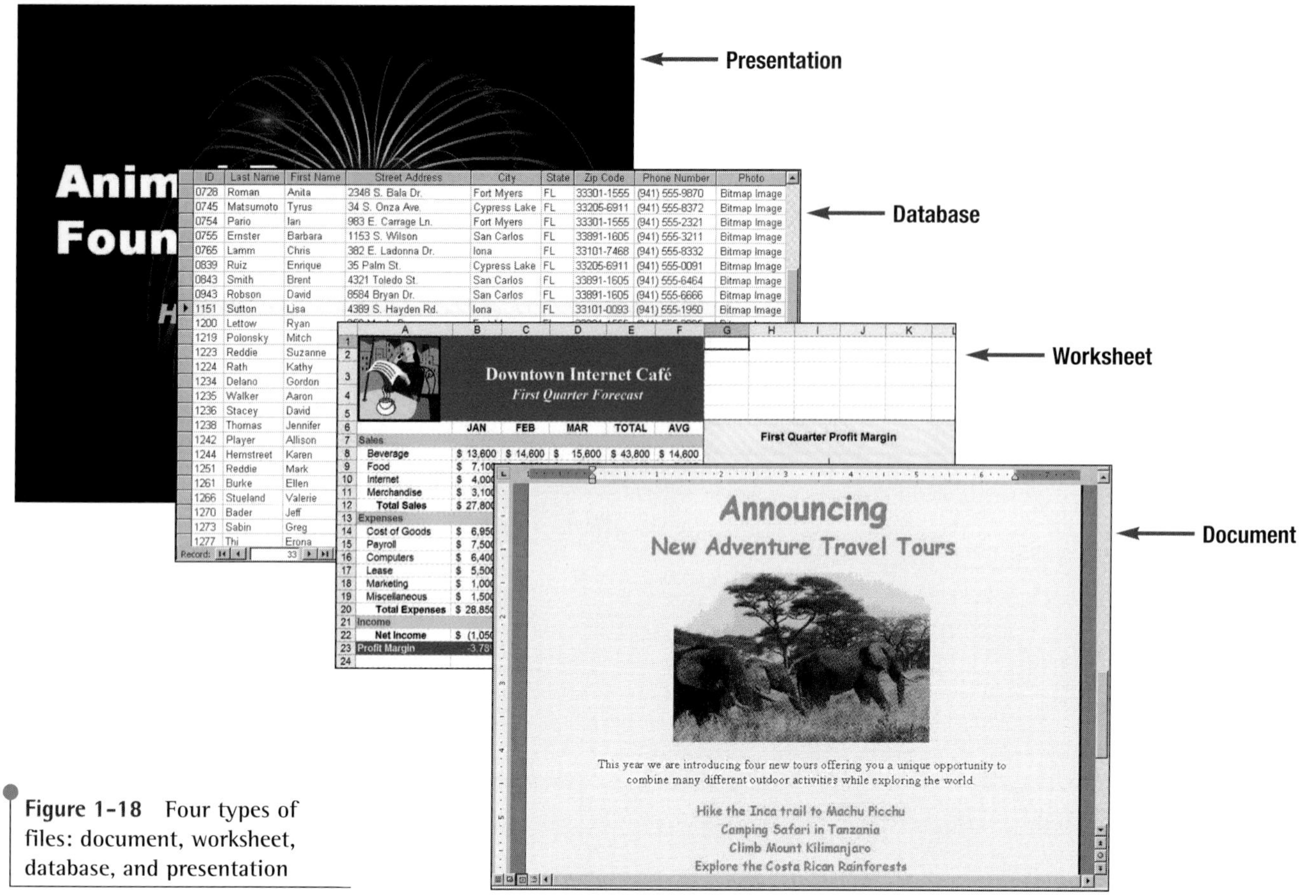

Figure 1-18 Four types of files: document, worksheet, database, and presentation

CONNECTIVITY, THE WIRELESS REVOLUTION, AND THE INTERNET

Connectivity allows sharing of information worldwide. The wireless revolution is expected to alter communications and computer systems. The Internet is the largest network in the world.

Connectivity is the capability of your microcomputer to share information with other computers. Data and information can be sent over telephone lines or cable and through the air. Thus, your microcomputer can be connected to other computers, to the Internet, and to many computerized data banks and other sources of information worldwide.

The single most dramatic change in connectivity in the past five years has been the widespread use of mobile or wireless communication devices. Once used exclusively for telephone communications, these devices are now widely used to connect people and computers located almost anywhere in the world. For just a few of these devices, see Figure 1-19. Many experts predict that these wireless applications are just the beginning of the **wireless revolution,** a revolution that is expected to dramatically affect the way we communicate and use computer technology.

Figure 1-19 Wireless communication devices

Connectivity and the wireless revolution are significant developments, for they expand the uses of the microcomputer severalfold. Central to the concept of connectivity is the **network** or **computer network.** A network is a communications system connecting two or more computers. Networks connect people as close as the next office and as far away as halfway around the world.

The largest network in the world is the **Internet.** It is like a giant highway that connects you to millions of other people and organizations located throughout the world. (See Figure 1-20.) The Internet is a huge computer network available to nearly everyone with a microcomputer and a means to connect to it. The **Web,** also known as the **World Wide Web** or **WWW,** provides a multimedia interface to the numerous resources available on the Internet.

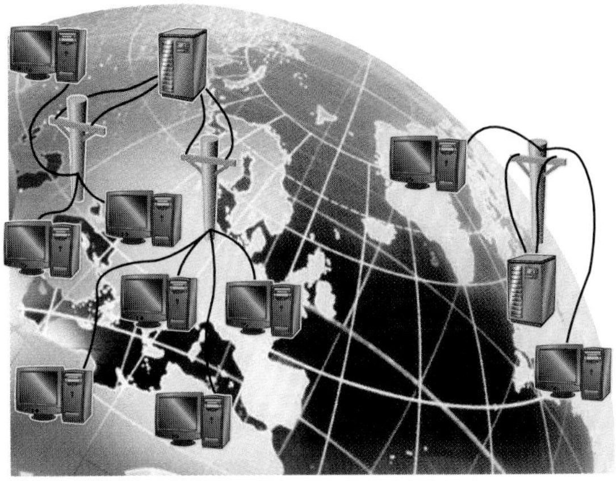

Figure 1-20 The Internet connects millions of people and computers worldwide

Concept Check

- ✓ Define connectivity and the wireless revolution.
- ✓ What is a network?
- ✓ What is the Internet?

Careers in IT

Some of the fastest growing career opportunities are in information technology. Every chapter following this chapter includes a detailed job description for a different career in IT. These descriptions, include job titles, responsibilities, educational requirements, and salary ranges. For a list of just a few of these careers, see Figure 1-21. For a complete list and full descriptions, visit our site at http://www.mhhe.com/oleary/CT05 and select Careers in IT from Tim's Toolbox.

Webmasters develop and maintain Web sites and Web resources. Webmasters also monitor and initiate steps to increase the traffic at Web sites. Salaries range from $45,000 to $70,000. See page 61 for details.

Software engineers analyze users' needs and create application software. They have a background in programming and focus on the design and development of programs. Salaries range from $50,000 to $85,000. See page 346 for details.

Database administrators use specialized database management software to determine the most efficient ways to organize and access a company's data. Additionally, they are responsible for maintaining database security and backing up the corporate databases. Salaries range from $35,000 to $75,000. See page 501 for details.

Systems analysts address specific organization needs for information. Working with end users and other computer professionals, they follow the steps in the systems life cycle which includes preliminary investigation, analysis, design, development, implementation, and maintenance. Salaries range from $35,000 to $70,000. See page 540 for details.

Computer programmers create, test, and troubleshoot programs used by computers. Most programmers work for companies that create and sell software, but programmers may also be employed in various other businesses. Salaries range from $45,000 to $75,000. See page 584 for details.

Figure 1-21 Select Careers in IT

A Look to the Future

Using and Understanding Information Technology Means Being Computer Competent and Knowledgeable

The purpose of this book is to help you use and understand information technology. We want to help you become computer competent in today's world and to provide you a foundation of knowledge so that you can understand how technology is being used today and anticipate how technology will be used in the future. This will enable you to benefit from four important information technology developments: the ever evolving Internet and Web, more powerful software, more powerful hardware, and organizational use of computers.

THE INTERNET AND THE WEB

The Internet and the Web are considered by most to be the two most important technologies for the 21st century. Understanding how to efficiently and effectively use the Internet to browse the Web, communicate with others, and locate information are indispensable computer competencies. Understanding how the Internet and the Web work provides a foundation to appreciate their positive aspects such as the enormous potential of electronic commerce. These issues are presented in Chapter 2, The Internet, the Web, and Electronic Commerce.

POWERFUL SOFTWARE

The software now available can do an extraordinary number of tasks and help you in an endless number of ways. You can create professional looking documents, analyze massive amounts of data, create dynamic multimedia Web pages, and much more. Today's employers are expecting the people they hire to be able to effectively and efficiently use a variety of different types of software. General-purpose and special-purpose applications are presented in Chapters 3 and 4. System software is presented in Chapter 5.

POWERFUL HARDWARE

Microcomputers are now much more powerful than they used to be. Indeed, the newer models have the speed and power of room-size computers of only a few years ago. New communication technologies such as wireless networks are dramatically changing the ways to connect to other computers, networks, and the Internet. However, despite the rapid change of specific equipment, their essential features remain unchanged. Thus, the competent and knowledgeable end user should focus on these features. Chapters 6 through 10 explain what you need to know about hardware: the central processing unit, input, output, secondary storage, and communication. A Buyer's Guide and an Upgrader's Guide are presented at the end of this book for those considering the purchase or upgrade of a microcomputer system.

SECURITY AND PRIVACY

What about people? Is there a downside to all these technological advances? Experts agree that we as a society must be careful about the potential of technology to negatively impact our personal privacy and security. Additionally, we need to be aware of potential physical and mental health risks associated with using technology. Finally, we need to be aware of negative effects on our environment caused by the manufacture of computer-related products. Thus, Chapter 11 explores each of these critical issues in detail.

ORGANIZATIONS

Almost all organizations rely on the quality and flexibility of their information systems to stay competitive. As a member or employee of an organization, you will undoubtedly be involved in these information systems. Therefore, you need to be knowledgeable about the different types of organizational information systems and how they are used. Accordingly, we devote Chapters 12 through 15 to detail what you need to know about information systems and how to develop, modify, and maintain these systems.

CHANGING TIMES

Are the times changing any faster now than they ever have? Most people think so. Those who were alive when radios, cars, and airplanes were being introduced certainly lived through some dramatic changes. Has technology made our own times even more dynamic? Whatever the answer, it is clear we live in a fast-paced age. The Evolution of the Computer Age section presented at the end of this book tracks the major developments since computers were first introduced.

Most people and businesses have become aware that they must adapt to changing technology or be left behind. Almost all major organizations have plans to keep track of technology and to use it in their competitive strategies. Nearly every corporation in the world has a presence on the Internet. Delivery services such as Federal Express and UPS provide customers with the ability to personally track the delivery of their packages. Retail stores such as JCPenney and Wal-Mart provide catalog support and sales. Banks such as Wells Fargo and Citibank support home banking and electronic commerce. You can even purchase tickets to music, theater, and sporting events on the Internet.

Clearly, such changes do away with some jobs—those of many bank tellers and cashiers, for example. However, they create opportunities for other people. New technology requires people who are truly capable of working with it. These are not the people who think every piece of equipment is so simple they can just turn it on and use it. Nor are they those who think each new machine is a potential disaster. In other words, new technology needs people who are not afraid to learn about it and who are able to manage it. The real issue, then, is not how to make technology better. Rather, it is how to integrate the technology with people. In Chapter 16 we discuss these issues, your future, and information technology.

After reading this book, you will be in a very favorable position compared with many other people in industry today. You will learn not only the basics of hardware, software, connectivity, the Internet, and the Web—you will also learn the most current technology. You will be able to use these tools to your advantage—to be a winner.

VISUAL SUMMARY

INFORMATION TECHNOLOGY, THE INTERNET, AND YOU

INFORMATION SYSTEMS

The way to think about a microcomputer is to realize that it is one part of an **information system.** Five parts of an information system:

1. **People** are obviously the essential part of the system! The purpose of information systems is to make people, or **end users** like you, more productive.
2. **Procedures** are rules or guidelines to follow when using software, hardware, and data. They are typically documented in manuals written by computer professionals.
3. **Software (programs)** provides step-by-step instructions to control the computer to convert data into information.
4. **Hardware** consists of the physical equipment. It is controlled by software and processes data to create information.
5. **Data** consists of unprocessed facts including text, numbers, images, and sound. **Information** is data that has been processed by the computer.

Connectivity is an additional part to today's information systems. It allows computers to connect and share information. To be **computer competent** and **knowledgeable,** end users need to understand **information technology (IT).**

PEOPLE

People are the most important part of an information system. People are touched hundreds of times daily by computers. This book contains several features to demonstrate how people just like you use computers. These features include:

- **Making IT Work for You** presents several interesting and practical applications. Topics include creating personal Web sites, using digital photography, and searching for job opportunities.
- **Tips** offer a variety of suggestions on such practical matters as how to improve slow computer performance and how to protect your privacy while on the Web.
- **Interactive CDs** included with this book are **SimNet Concepts** and **Computing Today CD.** These CDs provide tutorials, animations, videos, and in-depth coverage of select topics.

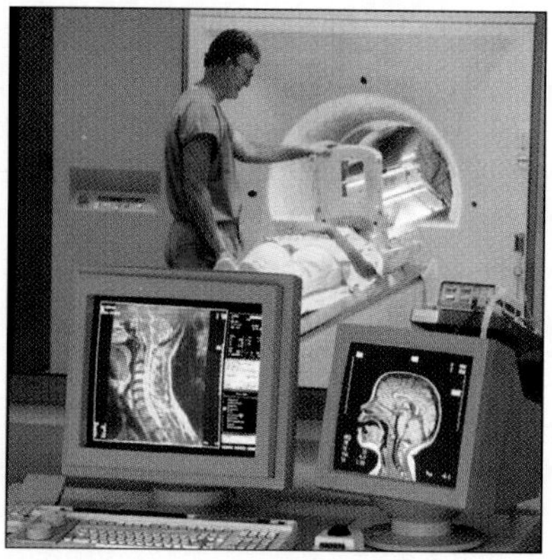

To prepare for your future as a competent and knowledgeable end user, you need to understand the basic parts of an information system: people, procedures, software, hardware, and data. Also you need to understand connectivity through the Internet and the Web and to recognize the role of technology in your professional and personal life.

SOFTWARE

Software, or **programs,** consists of system and application software.

System Software

System software enables application software to interact with computer hardware. It consists of a variety of programs including:

- **Operating systems** coordinate resources, provide an interface for users and computer hardware, and run applications. Windows XP and Mac OS X are operating systems.
- **Utilities (service programs)** perform specific tasks to manage computer resources.
- **Device drivers** are specialized programs to allow input and output devices to communicate with the rest of the computer system.

Application Software

Application software includes general and special-purpose applications. **General-purpose (basic applications)** are widely used in nearly all career areas.

Special-purpose applications (advance applications) focus on specific disciplines and occupations. These programs include **graphics, audio and video, multimedia, Web authoring,** and **artificial intelligence** programs.

HARDWARE

Hardware is the physical equipment in an information system.

Types of Computers

Supercomputer, mainframe, minicomputer (midrange), and **microcomputer** are four types of computers. Microcomputers can be **desktop, notebook (laptop), tablet PC,** or **handheld (palm). PDAs** are the most widely used handheld computer.

Microcomputer Hardware

There are four basic categories of hardware devices:

- **System unit** (**system cabinet** or **chassis**) contains the electronic circuitry, including the **microprocessor** and **memory (primary storage, random access memory, RAM, temporary storage).**
- **Input/output devices** are translators between humans and computers. **Input devices** include **keyboard** and **mouse. Output devices** include **monitors (video display screens)** and **printers.**
- **Secondary storage devices** store data and programs. Typical media include **floppy, hard,** and **optical disks** (**CD** and **DVD**).
- **Communication devices** connect the system unit to other computers and the Internet. A **modem** modifies signals for processing and communication.

DATA

Data describe and are the raw facts about something. Common file types include:

- **Document files** created by word processors.

- **Worksheet files** created by spreadsheet programs.

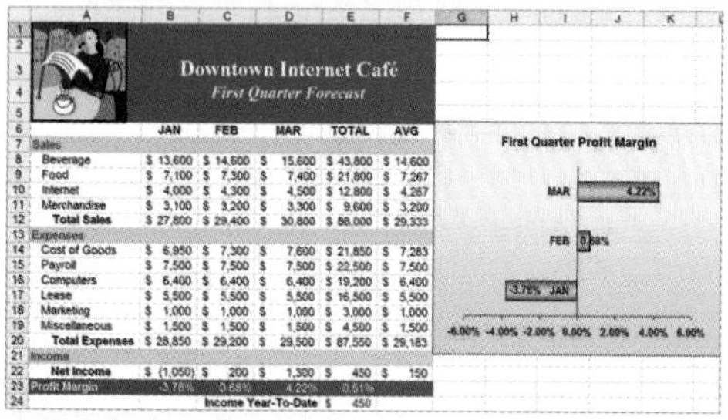

- **Database files** created by database management programs.

- **Presentation files** created by presentation graphics programs.

CONNECTIVITY AND THE INTERNET

Connectivity

Connectivity is a concept describing the ability of end users to tap into resources well beyond their desktops. **Computer networks (networks)** are connected computers that share data and resources.

The Wireless Revolution

The **wireless revolution** is the widespread and increasing use of mobile (wireless) communication devices.

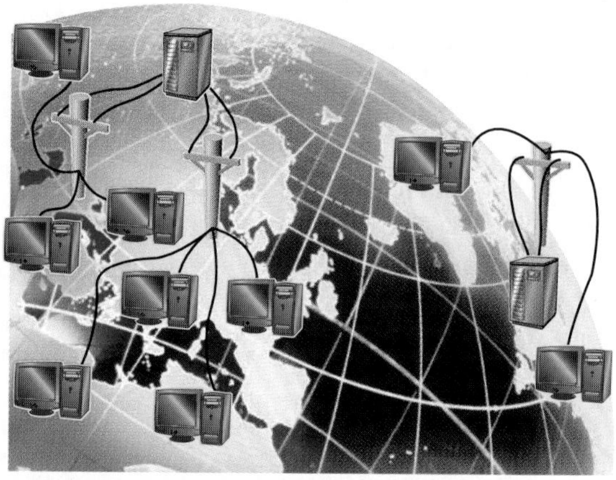

Internet

The **Internet** is the world's largest computer network. The **Web,** also known as the **World Wide Web (WWW),** provides a multimedia interface to resources available on the Internet.

KEY TERMS

advanced application (10)
application software (9)
basic application (9)
chassis (13)
communication device (15)
compact disc (CD) (14)
computer competency (3)
computer knowledge (3)
computer network (17)
Computing Today CD (8)
connectivity (5)
data (5)
database file (15)
device driver (9)
desktop computer (12)
digital versatile disc (DVD) (14)
digital video disc (DVD) (14)
document file (15)
end user (4)
floppy disk (14)
general-purpose application (9)
handheld computer (12)
hard disk (14)
hardware (5)
information (4)
information system (4)
information technology (IT) (5)
input device (14)
Internet (17)
keyboard (14)
laptop computer (12)
mainframe computer (11)
memory (14)
microcomputer (12)
microprocessor (14)
midrange computer (12)
minicomputer (12)
modem (15)
monitor (14)
mouse (14)
network (17)
notebook computer (12)
operating system (9)
optical disk (14)
output device (14)
palm computer (12)
people (4)
personal digital assistant (PDA) (12)
presentation file (15)
primary storage (14)
printer (14)
procedures (4)
program (4)
random access memory (RAM) (14)
secondary storage device (14)
service program (9)
software (4)
special-purpose application (10)
supercomputer (11)
SimNet Concepts (8)
system cabinet (13)
system software (9)
system unit (13)
tablet PC (12)
temporary storage (14)
utility (9)
video display screen (14)
Web (17)
wireless revolution (16)
worksheet file (15)
World Wide Web (WWW) (17)

To test your knowledge of these key terms with animated flash cards, select Flash Cards from Tim's Toolbox at http://www.mhhe.com/oleary/CT05.

CHAPTER REVIEW

CROSSWORD

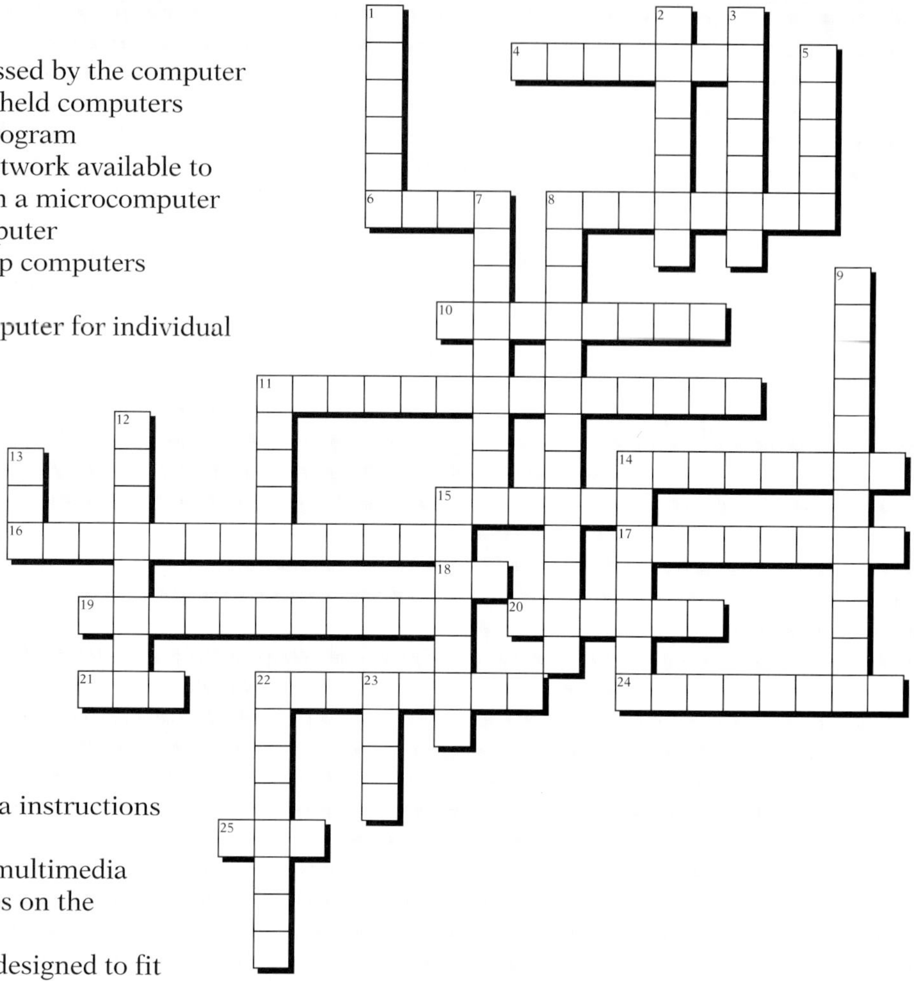

ACROSS

4 Displays data processed by the computer
6 Also known as handheld computers
8 Another word for program
10 A huge computer network available to nearly everyone with a microcomputer
11 CPU of a microcomputer
14 Also known as laptop computers
15 End users
16 Small, low-cost computer for individual users
17 Is a type of notebook computer that accepts handwritten input
18 Computer systems large or micro that provide understanding to the end user
19 Data that has been processed by a computer system
20 Holding area for data instructions and information
21 A service providing multimedia interface to resources on the Internet
22 Computers that are designed to fit into the palm
24 Input device
25 Internet service using hypertext

DOWN

1 Computer that is portable and fits into most briefcases
2 Also known as a service program, manages computer resources
3 Instructions for the computer to follow in order to process data
5 Device that rolls and directs the cursor
7 Can process several million program instructions per second
8 Fastest calculating device
9 Desk-sized computer between micro and mainframe
11 Short for modulator-demodulator
12 Also known as minicomputer
13 Volatile temporary storage
14 Arrangement in which various communications channels are connected
15 Device that produces printed-paper output
22 The equipment that processes the data to create information
23 Raw unprocessed facts

Interactive crossword puzzles are available by selecting Crosswords from Tim's Toolbox at http://www.mhhe.com/oleary/CT05.

MULTIPLE CHOICE

Circle the letter or fill in the correct answer.

1. Computer ________ refers to acquiring computer related skills.
   - **a.** competency
   - **b.** aware
   - **c.** connectivity
   - **d.** networked
   - **e.** active
2. The ________ consist(s) of the equipment: keyboard, mouse, monitor, system unit, and other devices.
   - **a.** people
   - **b.** procedures
   - **c.** hardware
   - **d.** system unit
   - **e.** information
3. The ________ is one of the system software programs.
   - **a.** word processor
   - **b.** database management system
   - **c.** operating system
   - **d.** application software
   - **e.** information system
4. Browsers, word processors, and spreadsheets are ________ applications.
   - **a.** special-purpose
   - **b.** general-purpose
   - **c.** advanced
   - **d.** artificial intelligence
   - **e.** multimedia
5. A ________ computer is another name for a notebook computer.
   - **a.** PDA
   - **b.** laptop
   - **c.** midrange
   - **d.** DVD
   - **e.** handheld
6. ________ is sometimes referred to as temporary storage.
   - **a.** PDA
   - **b.** CD
   - **c.** RAM
   - **d.** DVD
   - **e.** Secondary storage
7. The type of disk that uses laser technology:
   - **a.** concentric
   - **b.** layered
   - **c.** hard
   - **d.** floppy
   - **e.** optical
8. A ________ file might contain audience handouts, speaker notes, and electronic slides.
   - **a.** document
   - **b.** database
   - **c.** worksheet
   - **d.** presentation
   - **e.** floppy disk
9. The term ________ refers to the widespread use of mobile communication devices.
   - **a.** IT
   - **b.** wireless revolution
   - **c.** PDA
   - **d.** RAM
   - **e.** WWW
10. The largest network in the world is called the ________.
    - **a.** Internet
    - **b.** WWW
    - **c.** World Wide Web
    - **d.** Web
    - **e.** all of the above

To test your knowledge of this chapter, select Self Test from Tim's Toolbox at http://www.mhhe.com/oleary/CT05.

MATCHING

Match each numbered item with the most closely related lettered item. Write your answers in the spaces provided.

- **a.** application software
- **b.** computer network
- **c.** connectivity
- **d.** database files
- **e.** document file
- **f.** hard disks
- **g.** information
- **h.** input device
- **i.** mainframe computer
- **j.** microcomputers
- **k.** optical disks
- **l.** output device
- **m.** primary storage
- **n.** procedures
- **o.** program
- **p.** secondary storage device
- **q.** supercomputers
- **r.** system software
- **s.** system unit
- **t.** the Internet

1. Guidelines for people to follow when using software, hardware, and data. _____
2. Consists of the step-by-step instructions that tell the computer how to do its work. _____
3. Although not the most powerful, this type of computer is capable of great processing speeds and data storage. _____
4. The capability of a microcomputer to share information with other computers. _____
5. Software that enables the application software to interact with the computer hardware. _____
6. End user software. _____
7. The most powerful type of computer. _____
8. Data that has been processed through the computer. _____
9. Translates processed information from the computer into a form that humans can understand. _____
10. Container that houses most of the electronic components that make up a computer system. _____
11. The least powerful and most widely used type of computer. _____
12. Translates data and programs that humans can understand into a form that the computer can process. _____
13. Created by database management programs. _____
14. Holds data and programs even after electrical power to the system has been turned off. _____
15. Typically used to store programs and very large data files. _____
16. Use laser technology and have the greatest capacity of all secondary storage. _____
17. Created by word processors to save documents. _____
18. Holds data and program instructions for processing data. _____
19. Communications system connecting two or more computers. _____
20. The largest network in the world. _____

OPEN-ENDED

On a separate sheet of paper, respond to each question or statement.

1. Explain the five parts of an information system. What part do people play in this system?
2. What is system software? What kinds of programs are included in system software? What is the difference between system software and application software? What are the most common basic applications?
3. Define and compare general-purpose and special-purpose application software. Describe some different types of general-purpose applications. Describe some types of special-purpose applications.
4. Describe the different types of computers. What is the most common type? What are the types of microcomputers?
5. What is connectivity? How are the wireless revolution and connectivity related? What is a computer network? What are the Internet and the Web?

USING TECHNOLOGY

Making a habit of keeping current with technology trends is a key to your success with information technology. In each of this book's chapters, the Using Technology feature will present four questions designed to help you gain a better understanding of how technology is being used today.

The first question in Using Technology typically relates to one of the Making IT Work for You topics. Some of these topics are listed below. Select the two that you find the most interesting and then describe why they are of interest to you and how you might use (or, are using) those applications.

- **Instant Messaging** Do you enjoy chatting with your friends? Have you ever worked on a group project and had problems getting everyone together for a meeting? Perhaps instant messaging is just what you're looking for. See page 72.

- **TV Tuner Cards and Video Clips** Want to watch your favorite television program while you work? Perhaps you would like to include a video clip from a television program or from a VHS tape in a class presentation. It's easy using a TV tuner card. See page 228.
- **Digital Photography** Want to edit your photos on your computer? Would you like to share your photos with family and friends over the Web? Digital photography makes it easy to do. See page 280.
- **Home Networking** Computer networks are not just for corporations and schools anymore. If you have more than one computer, you can use a wireless home network to share files and printers, to allow multiple users access to the Internet at the same time, and to play interactive computer games. See page 400.
- **Job Opportunities** Did you know that you can use the Internet to find a job? You can browse through job openings, post your resume, and even use special programs that will search for the job that's just right for you. See page 624.

USING TECHNOLOGY

2 In each of the following chapters, questions in Using Technology focus on interesting applications of technology that relate directly to you. Some of those applications are listed below. Select the two that you find the most interesting and then describe why they are of interest to you and how you might use (or, are using) those applications.

- Online Auctions Have you ever participated in an online auction? You can purchase or sell all types of goods from baseball cards to used and new automobiles. What are some of the pros and cons? How can you protect yourself as a buyer and as a seller? See page 73.
- Online Personal Information Manager Do you have a PDA? Many people do and they have become very dependent on them to record personal schedules, addresses, telephone numbers, e-mail addresses, and much more. What if the PDA gets lost? One way to protect yourself is to back up the information onto another computer. Or, you could use an online personal information manager. See page 481.
- Utility Suites Are you concerned about keeping your computer tuned up and safe from computer viruses? Most of us are and all of us should be. One way to keep your system operating smoothly and safely is to use a utility suite. McAfee and Symantec are producers of two well-known utility suites. See page 202.

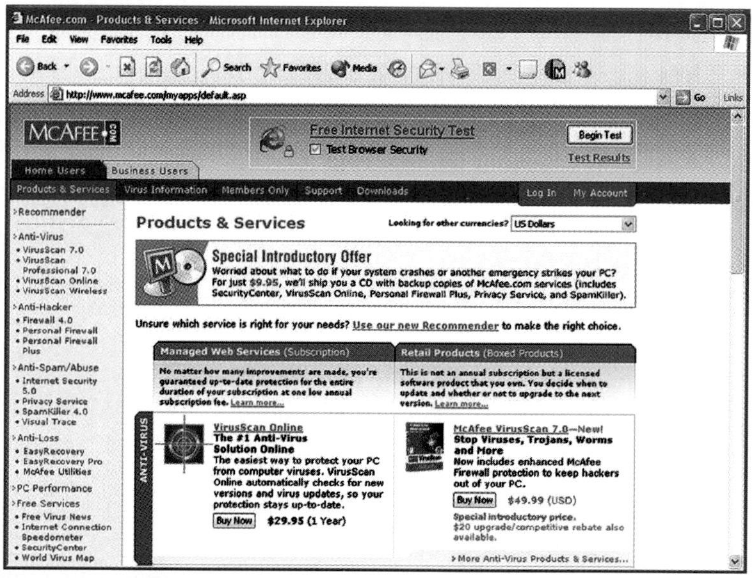

- Desktop and Notebook Computers Are you thinking about buying a new computer? Would you prefer a desktop or notebook? Perhaps you are considering a tablet PC or a handheld computer. The Web is an excellent resource for reviewing, comparing, and purchasing computers. See page 246.
- TiVo Would you like to avoid the hassles and limitations of your video tape recorder? TiVo is a device that automatically will record television programs digitally. It allows you to pause a live television broadcast, view slow motion, and much more. See page 356.
- Anonymous Web Browsing Have you ever wanted to send an e-mail message to someone without them knowing where it came from? Did you know that your activities on the Web can be traced? The Anonymizer can change all that and more. See page 444.

EXPANDING YOUR KNOWLEDGE

A deeper knowledge of select topics can greatly enhance your understanding of information technology. In each of the following chapters, the Expanding Your Knowledge feature presents four questions designed to help you gain a deeper understanding of select topics.

Typically, one question in Expanding Your Knowledge relates to a topic contained on your **Computing Today CD.** Some of those topics are listed below. Select the two that you find the most interesting and then describe why they are of interest to you and why they are important.

- How Instant Messaging Works One of the fastest growing applications on the Internet is instant messaging. This extension to e-mail provides a way for friends and colleagues to communicate and share information from almost anywhere in the world. See page 74.
- How Web-based Applications Work Some predict that many organizations will be using Web-based applications in the near future. These organizations will not be required to own, install, upgrade, or store applications. Additionally, applications and application files can be accessed from almost anywhere in the world. See page 122.
- How Web Site Development Works Developing or publishing a Web site is a common activity for organizations of all types and for people from all walks of life. The process of creating a Web site consists of five steps: planning, analyzing and designing, creating, going online, and maintaining. See page 160.
- How Computer Viruses Work Computer viruses are destructive and dangerous programs that can migrate through networks and operating systems. They often attach themselves to other programs, e-mail messages, and databases. It is essential to protect your computer systems from computer viruses. See page 204.
- How Digital Photography Works While traditional cameras capture images on film, digital cameras capture images, and convert them into a digital form. These images can be viewed immediately and saved to a disk or into the cameras memory. See page 282.
- How Internet Telephones Work Internet telephones offer a low cost alternative to making long distance calls. Using the Internet telephone (or other appropriate audio input and output devices), the Internet, a special service provider, a sound card, and special software you can place long distance calls to almost anywhere in the world. See page 316.
- How Wireless Networks Work Wireless home networks are becoming very popular. These LANs are easy to set up and use. They allow different computers to share resources including a common Internet connection and printer. See page 402.

EXPANDING YOUR KNOWLEDGE

2

In each of the following chapters, one question in Expanding Your Knowledge typically relates to a tutorial on your **SimNet** CD. Some of those tutorials are listed below. Select the two that you find the most interesting and then describe why they are of interest to you and why they are important.

- The Internet, Web, and Electronic Commerce Internet service providers, Web browsers, Web pages, HTML, e-mail, electronic commerce, and more are presented in this tutorial. See page 75.
- Applications Software This tutorial presents browsers, word processors, spreadsheets, database administrators, presentation graphics, and more. See page 123.
- System Software This tutorial describes the Windows operating systems and commonly used Windows utilities. Other operating systems are presented including Mac OS. See page 205.
- The System Unit This tutorial describes components within the system unit including the motherboard, CPU, memory, expansion boards, and expansion cards. See page 248.
- Input and Output This tutorial describes keyboards, mice, digital cameras, monitors, printers, plotters and more. See page 283.
- Secondary Storage Removable and nonremovable disks are presented in this tutorial. Also, CDs are compared to DVDs. See page 359.
- Connectivity, the Wireless Revolution, and Communications This tutorial presents connectivity concepts, Web sites specifically designed for wireless handheld devices, and different network configurations. See page 403.
- Privacy and Security A variety of ergonomic, privacy, and security issues are presented. The most significant security risks for end users are discussed. See page 446.

BUILDING YOUR PORTFOLIO

A portfolio typically consists of printed material that documents an individual's skills and knowledge. The process of creating a portfolio helps individuals to recognize and to organize their accomplishments. A well-designed and complete portfolio can be an essential tool for landing that perfect job. In the following chapters, the Building Your Portfolio feature presents four questions designed to help you create a portfolio to document your computer competency and knowledge.

Two questions in Building Your Portfolio typically relate to key technologies. Some of these technologies are listed below. Select the two that you find the most interesting and then describe why they are of interest to you and why a prospective employer would be impressed with this knowledge.

- Electronic Commerce Electronic commerce is one of the most exciting Web applications. Different types include businesses to consumer (B2C), consumer to consumer (C2C), and business to business (B2B). Each of these has significant economic potential for nearly all organizations. See page 76.
- Artificial Intelligence A technology that promises widespread implications is artificial intelligence. This technology attempts to simulate human senses, thought processes, and actions. Many software manufacturing companies are producing programs with built-in artificial intelligence. See page 162.
- Linux Linux is a powerful operating system used by many computer professionals today. Some experts project that it will replace Windows as the most widely used operating system for powerful microcomputers and servers on the Web. See page 206.

- Microprocessors One of the most important components of any microcomputer systems is the microprocessor. For the past several years, microprocessor speeds have doubled every year and a half. Many manufacturers including Intel, AMD, and Cyrix expect this trend to continue. See page 250.
- Digital Input Before any type of data or information can be processed by a computer, it must be in digital form. The capability of input devices to convert handwriting, sketches, and images into a digital form has greatly expanded computer capabilities. See page 284.

BUILDING YOUR PORTFOLIO

2 In each of the following chapters, two questions in Building Your Portfolio typically relate to security, privacy, and ethical issues. Some of these issues are listed below. Select the two that you find the most interesting and then describe why they are of interest to you and why they are important issues.

- **HTML Source Code** A common way to create interesting and dynamic Web pages is to examine how professionals create their sites. Once connected to most Web sites, you can display the HTML source code used to create that site. Additionally, you can make a copy of the code and save it on your computer system. Some argue that this is unethical and illegal. Others argue that this is an acceptable way to create personal and professional sites. See page 163.
- **Antitrust** Microsoft Corporation has been involved with extensive antitrust legal battles over the past few years. The issue has been that Microsoft's Windows operating system has been tailored to use Microsoft application software. The suite claims that this provides Microsoft an unfair advantage over other companies that produce competing application software. While many support this view, others contend that all corporations use whatever they can to improve their competitive positions. See page 207.
- **Processor Serial Numbers** When the Intel Pentium III microprocessor was released, each unit originally contained a unique Processor Serial Number, or PSN. This PSN could be used by online e-commerce sites to identify and track individuals by the computer they used. This tracking would be similar to keeping track of car owners by their license plate numbers. Intel anticipated that the PSN would help electronic commerce and add security to Internet sales. Others argued that the tracking capabilities were an invasion of personal privacy. Soon after introduction, the PSNs were discontinued. See page 251.
- **CD-R and Music Files** For the past few years, one of the most popular Web activities has been to share or download music from the Web to create custom CDs. Even though recent legal rulings support the illegality of reproducing music that has been copyrighted, sharing music continues to be a widely practiced Web activity. While some suggest that stronger enforcement is needed, others suggest that enforcement is impossible and not needed. See page 361.
- **Electronic Monitoring** Surveillance of individuals is greater today than ever before. For example, the FBI has proposed the widespread use of a technology known as Carnivore to help them track terrorists. This technology supports widespread monitoring of individual Internet activity and e-mail. Privacy advocates claim that this would be an unnecessary and unneeded invasion of personal privacy. See page 405.

NOTES

THE INTERNET, THE WEB, AND ELECTRONIC COMMERCE

OBJECTIVES

After you have read this chapter, you should be able to:

1. Discuss the origins of the Internet and Web.
2. Describe how to access the Web using providers and browsers.
3. Discuss Web sites including common types of Web pages and multimedia content.
4. Discuss Internet communications including e-mail, instant messaging, and discussion groups.
5. Describe search tools including search engines, metasearch engines, specialized search engines, and research on the Web.
6. Discuss electronic commerce including B2B, B2C, C2C, and security.
7. Describe Web utilities: Telnet, FTP, plug-ins, and filters.

Browsers
Connect to Web sites and display Web pages
Welcome to E! Online - Microsoft Internet Explorer
http://www.eonline.com/
WindowsMedia.com : Music
Web Sites
Include all types of multimedia

CHAPTER 2

Want to communicate with a friend across town, in another state, or even in another country? Perhaps you would like to send a drawing, a photo, or just a letter. Looking for travel or entertainment information? Perhaps you're researching a term paper or exploring different career paths. Where do you start? For these and other information-related activities, try the Internet and the Web.

The Internet is often referred to as the Information Superhighway. In a sense, it is like a highway that connects you to millions of other people and organizations. Unlike typical highways that move people and things from one location to another, however, the Internet moves your ideas and information. Rather than moving through geographic space, you move through cyberspace—the space of electronic movement of ideas and information. The Web provides an easy-to-use, exciting, multimedia interface to connect to the Internet and to access the resources available in cyberspace. It has become an everyday tool for all of us to use. For example, you can create personal Web sites to share information with others, use instant messaging to chat with friends, and collaborate on group projects.

Competent and knowledgeable end users need to be aware of the resources available on the Internet and the Web. Additionally, they need to know how to access these resources, to effectively communicate electronically, to efficiently locate information, to understand electronic commerce, to use Web utilities, and to be knowledgeable about extranets, intranets, and security issues.

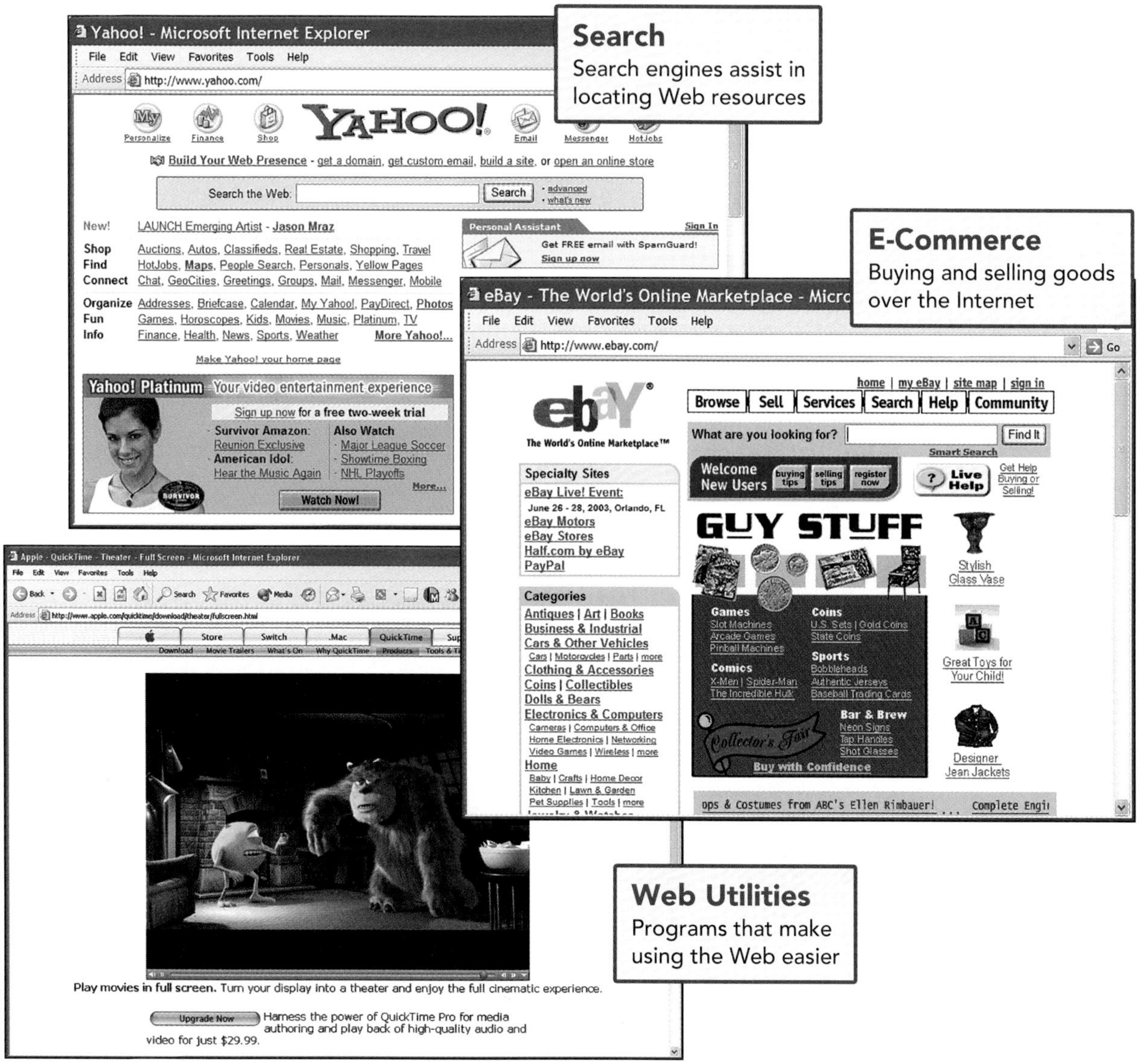
Search
Search engines assist in locating Web resources
E-Commerce
Buying and selling goods over the Internet
Web Utilities
Programs that make using the Web easier

THE INTERNET AND THE WEB

The Internet launched by ARPANET is a worldwide network. The Web introduced at CERN is a multimedia interface. Internet uses include communication, shopping, searching, entertainment, and education.

On the Web Explorations

Many individuals and institutions played a part in the development of the Internet and the Web. To learn more about the history of the Internet and Web visit our site at

http://www.mhhe.com/oleary/CT05

and select On the Web Explorations from Tim's Toolbox.

The **Internet,** or **Net,** was launched in 1969 when the United States funded a project that developed a national computer network called **Advanced Research Project Agency Network (ARPANET).** The Internet is a large network that connects smaller networks all over the globe together. The **Web,** also known as **WWW** and the **World Wide Web,** was introduced in 1992 at the **Center for European Nuclear Research (CERN)** in Switzerland. Prior to the Web, the Internet was all text—no graphics, animations, sound, or video. The Web made it possible to include these elements. It provided a multimedia interface to resources available on the Internet. From these early research beginnings, the Internet and the Web have evolved into one of the most powerful tools of the 21st century.

It is easy to get the Internet and the Web confused, but they are not the same thing. The Internet is the actual physical network. It is made up of wires, cables, and satellites. Being connected to this network is often described as being **online.** The Internet connects over 65 million computers and resources throughout the world. The Web is a multimedia interface to resources available on the Internet. Every day over a billion users from every country in the world use the Internet and the Web. (See Figure 2-1.) What are they doing? The most common uses are the following:

- **Communicating** is by far the most popular Internet activity. You can exchange e-mail with your family and friends almost anywhere in the world. You can join and listen to discussions and debates on a wide variety of special-interest topics. You can chat live with others. You can even create your own personal Web page for friends and family to visit.
- **Shopping** is one of the fastest-growing Internet applications. You can visit individual stores or a **cybermall** which provides access to a variety of different stores. You can window shop, look for the latest fashions, search for bargains, and make purchases. (See Figure 2-2.) You can purchase goods using checks, credit cards, or electronic cash.

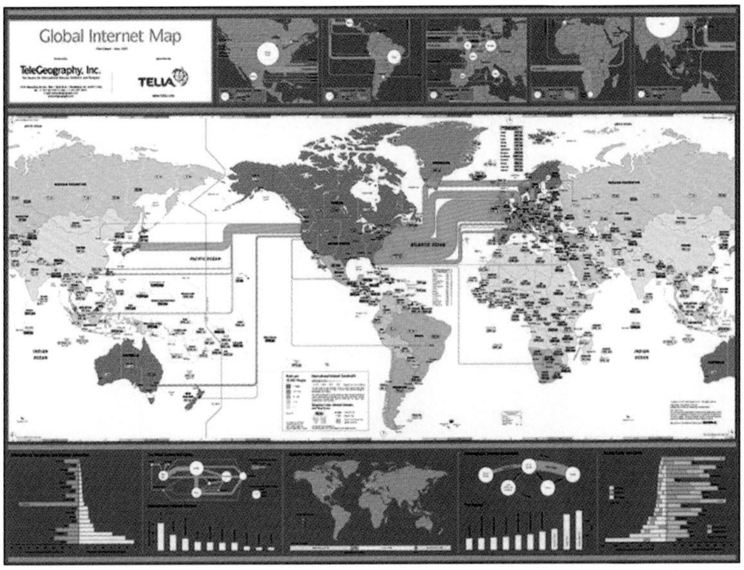

Figure 2-1 A TeleGeography, Inc. (TGI) map depicts global Internet connections

Figure 2-2 Shopping over the Internet is one of the Web's fastest growing activities

- **Searching** for information has never been more convenient. You can access some of the world's largest libraries directly from your home computer. You can visit **virtual libraries,** search through their stacks, read selected items, and even check out books. You will also find the latest local, national, and international news. Many newspapers maintain an online presence and include interactive and multimedia presentations related to current news stories.
- **Entertainment** options are nearly endless. You can find music, movies, magazines, and computer games. You will find live concerts, movie previews, book clubs, and interactive live games. (See Figure 2-3.)

Figure 2-3 Entertainment site

- **Education** or **e-learning** is another rapidly emerging Web application. You can take classes on almost any subject. There are courses just for fun and there are courses for high school, college, and graduate school credit. Some cost nothing to take and others cost a lot.

The first step to using the Internet and Web is to get connected, or to gain access to the Internet.

Concept Check

- ✓ Describe how the Internet and the Web started.
- ✓ What is the difference between the Internet and the Web?
- ✓ List and describe five of the most common uses of the Internet and the Web.

ACCESS

Providers give us access to the Internet. National, regional, and wireless are three types of ISPs. Browsers provide access to Web resources.

The Internet and the telephone system are similar—you can connect a computer to the Internet much like you connect a phone to the telephone system. Once you are on the Internet, your computer becomes an extension of what seems like a giant computer—a computer that branches all over the world. When provided with a connection to the Internet, you can use a browser program to the Web.

PROVIDERS

The most common way to access the Internet is through a **provider** or **host computer.** The providers are already connected to the Internet and provide a path or connection for individuals to access the Internet. Your college or university most likely provides you with free access to the Internet either through their local area networks or through a dial-up or telephone connection. There are also some companies that offer free Internet access.

Commercial Internet service providers (**ISPs**) include national, regional, and wireless service providers.

- **National service providers** like America Online (AOL) are the most widely used. They provide access through standard telephone connections. Users can access the Internet from almost anywhere within the country for a standard fee without incurring long-distance telephone charges. (See Figure 2-4.)
- **Regional service providers** also use telephone lines. Their service area, however, is smaller, typically consisting of several states. If users access the Internet from outside the regional area, they incur long-distance connection charges in addition to the service's standard fees.
- **Wireless service providers** do not use telephone lines. They provide Internet connections for computers with wireless modems and a wide array of wireless devices.

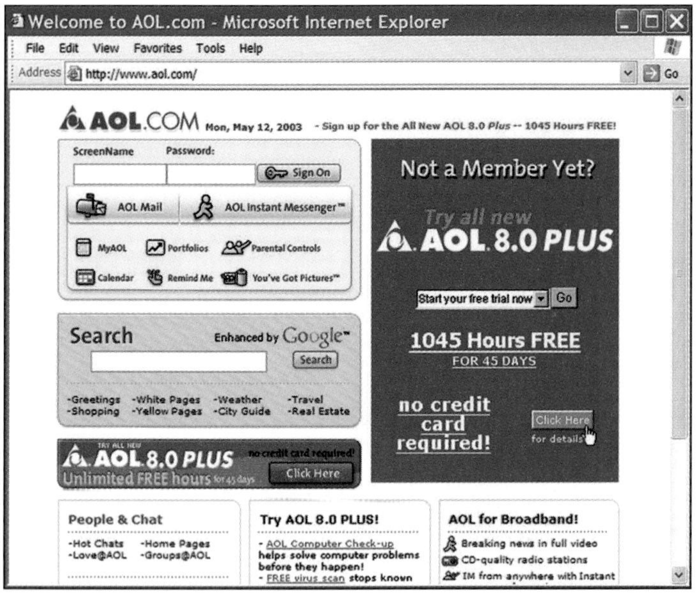

Figure 2-4 America Online ISP

As we will discuss in Chapter 10, users connect to ISPs using one of a variety of connection technologies including **dial-up, DSL, cable,** and **wireless modems.** This creates a **client/server network.** The user's computer is the **client** that requests services from the provider's computer or **server.** To learn more about service providers, visit some of the sites presented in Figure 2-5.

BROWSERS

Browsers are programs that provide access to Web resources. This software connects you to remote computers, opens and transfers files, displays text and images, and provides in one tool an uncomplicated interface to the Internet and Web documents. Browsers allow you to explore, or to **surf,** the Web by easily moving from one Web site to another. Two well-known browsers are Netscape Navigator and Microsoft Internet Explorer. (See Figure 2-6.)

For browsers to connect to resources, the **location** or **address** of the resources must be specified. These addresses are called **uniform resource**

Figure 2-5 Internet service providers

Provider	Type	Site
America Online (AOL)	National	www.aol.com
AT&T WorldNet	National	www.att.net
BellSouth	Regional	www.bellsouth.net
Qwest Internet Service	Regional	www.qwest.net
OmniSky	Wireless	www.omnisky.com
SprintPCS	Wireless	www.sprintpcs.com
Free Internet	Free	www.freeinternet.com
NetZero	Free	www.netzero.com

Figure 2-6 Internet Explorer

Figure 2-7 Two basic parts of a URL

locators (URLs). All URLs have at least two basic parts. (See Figure 2-7.) The first part presents the protocol used to connect to the resource. As we will discuss in Chapter 10, **protocols** are rules for exchanging data between computers. The protocol *http://* is the most widely used Web protocol. The second part presents the **domain name** or the name of the server where the resource is located. In Figure 2-7 the server is identified as www.mtv.com. (Many URLs have additional parts specifying directory paths, file names, and pointers.) The last part of the domain name following the dot (.) is the **domain code.** It identifies the type of organization. For example, *.com* indicates a commercial site. The URL *http:// www.mtv.com* connects your computer to a computer that provides information about MTV.

Figure 2-8 MTV Web site

Once the browser has connected to the Web site, a document file is sent back to your computer. This document contains **Hypertext Markup Language (HTML)** commands. The browser interprets the HTML commands and displays the document as a **Web page.** For example, when your browser first connects to the Internet it opens up to a Web page specified in the browser settings. This page presents information about the site along with references and **hyperlinks** or **links** that connect to other documents containing related information —text files, graphic images, audio, and video clips. (See Figure 2-8.)

These documents may be located on a nearby computer system or on one halfway around the world. The computer that stores and shares these documents is called a **Web server.** The references appear as underlined and colored text and/or images on the Web page. To access the referenced material, all you do is click on the highlighted text or image. A link is automatically made to the computer containing the material, and the referenced material appears on your display screen.

Web pages can also contain links to special programs, called **applets** that are typically written in a programming language called **Java.** (Java and other programming languages will be presented in Chapter 15.) These programs can be quickly downloaded and run by most browsers. Java applets are widely used to add interest and activity to a Web site by presenting animation, displaying graphics, providing interactive games, and much more.

To learn more about browsers, consult your Computing Today CD or visit Tim's Toolbox at http://www.mhhe.com/oleary/CT05.

On the Web Explorations

Popup ads often appear while you surf the Web. They can be a real annoyance. There are many programs available to eliminate these ads. To learn more about getting rid of popup ads visit our Web site at http://www.mhhe.com/oleary/CT05 and select On the Web Explorations from Tim's Toolbox.

Computing Today CD

Concept Check

- What is the function of an ISP? Describe three types of ISPs.
- What is the function of a browser?
- What are URLs, HTML, Web pages, hyperlinks, applets, and Java?

WEB SITES

A Web site is a group of related pages. Portals and directories, news and information, exploration and education, business, advocacy, and personal are types of Web pages. Media players are programs that play audio and video files.

A **Web site** is a group of related Web pages and/or other resources located on a Web server. Typically, the first page of a Web site is referred to as its **home page.** (See Figure 2-9.) For example, a Web site may have a home page that includes links to other resources and pages. Some Web sites are extremely complex, with many different pages and information. To help you navigate on these complicated sites, a diagram called a **site map** or **site index** may be provided. (See Figure 2-10.)

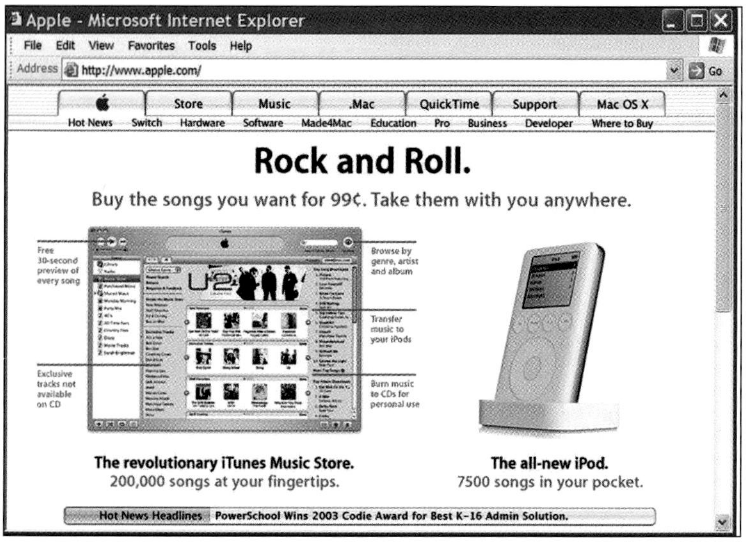

Figure 2-9 Apple home page

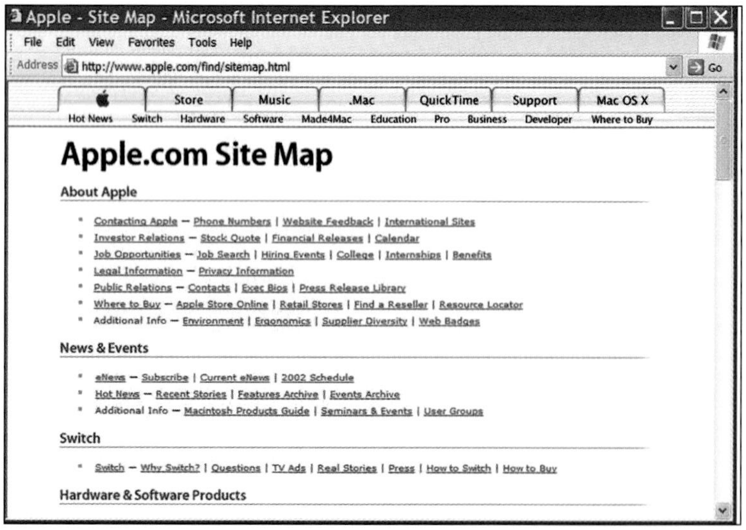

Figure 2-10 Site map for the Apple Web site

WEB PAGES

There are millions of Web pages published on the Web. Each may serve a different purpose or audience, but most of them share some common features. Many web sites have a **FAQ (Frequently Asked Questions)** page that provides answers to commonly asked questions. For example, a software company might provide a FAQ page to answer questions about how to use their products. Many Web pages have a separate scrollable window called a **frame.** These frames may provide a table of contents for the site with links to various areas of the site. (See Figure 2-11.)

There are many different types of Web pages on the Internet. Some of the most common include portals and directories, news and information, exploration and education, business, advocacy, and personal.

- **Portals and Directories:** With all of the information available on the Internet and Web it can be difficult to locate exactly what you are looking for. Portals and directories are designed to ease navigation and organize resources. **Portals,** also known as **Web portals,** offer a variety of services including searching, e-mail, sports updates, financial data, news, shopping, and links to other selected Web sites. Portals are designed to encourage you to visit them each time you are on the Web, to act as your home base, and to use as a gateway to their resources. There are two basic types of portals. **Horizontal portals** are designed to appeal to a wide audience. They offer general-interest services and

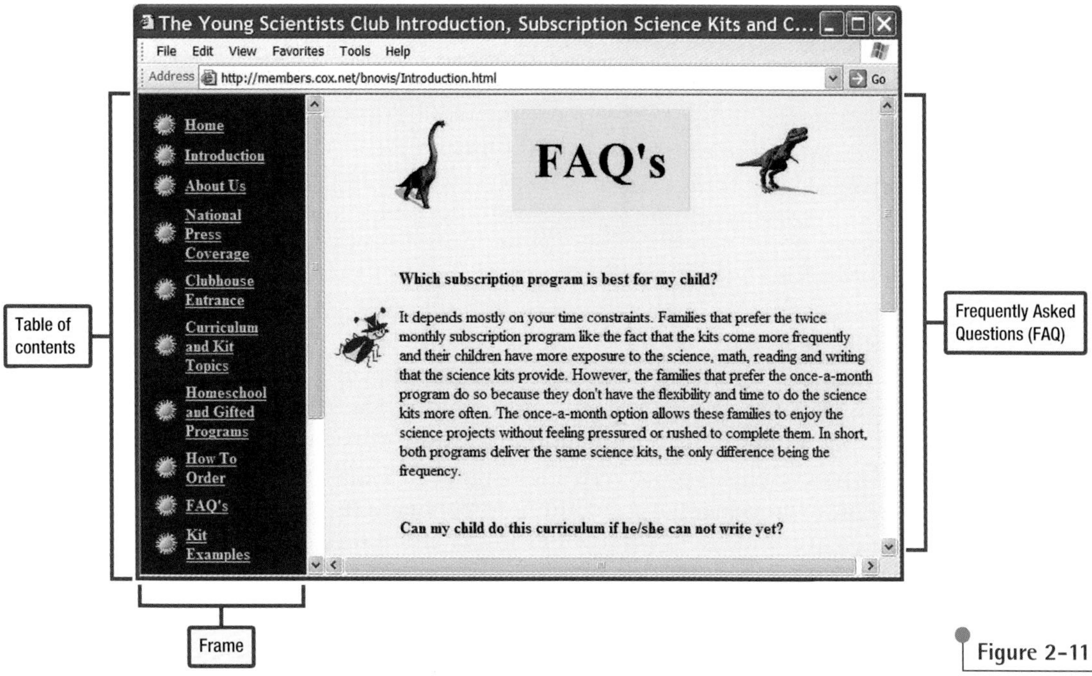

Figure 2-11 FAQ and Frames

Type	Site
Horizontal	www.yahoo.com
Horizontal portal	www.aol.com
Vertical for sports	www.cbs.sportsline.com
Vertical for news	www.usatoday.com
Vertical for computers	www.zdnet.com

Figure 2-12 Popular Web portals

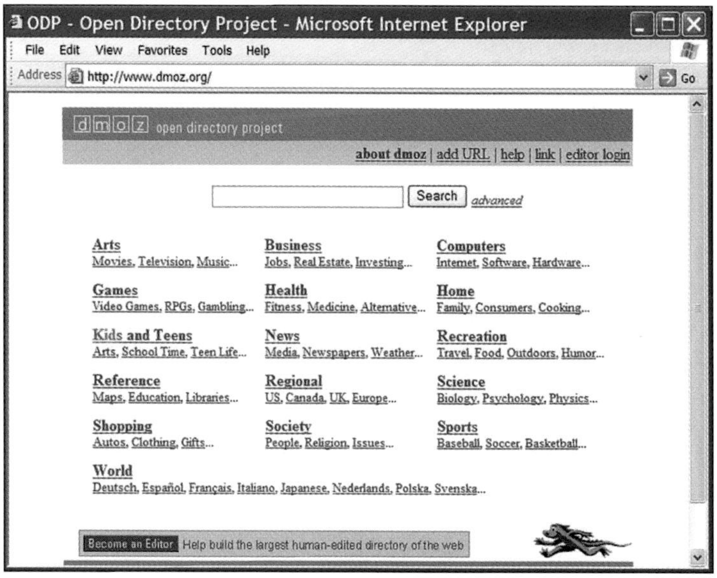

Figure 2-13 The Open Directory Project organizes Web pages by categories

links. **Vertical portals** present more focused content appealing to special-interest groups. (See Figure 2-12.) While Web portals offer access to services, **directories** provide access to content organized into categories such as the arts, business, and computers. Some common directories are The Open Directory Project and Google Directory. (See Figure 2-13.)

- **News and Information:** Many newspaper and television news programs have Web sites that provide information on breaking news. For example, CNN presents current news content and archives on the Web. To learn more about news sites visit some of the sites presented in Figure 2-14. These sites frequently include multimedia presentations related breaking news and provide expanded coverage. The content at these sites is usually linked to resources found elsewhere on the Web. The U.S. government, many universities, and even private groups maintain Web sites that are designed to inform. For example, the NASA site offers a history of space flight.

Organization	Site
ABC News	www.abcnews.com
CNN	www.cnn.com
New York Times	www.nytimes.com
Newsweek	www.newsweek.com
Washington Post	www.washingtonpost.com

Figure 2-14 News sites

Company	Site	Cost of Course
Dell	www.educateu.com	$30 to $1,300
Digital Think	www.digitalthink.com	$99 to $1,000
EduPoint.com	www.edupoint.com	$10 to $1,000
Learn2.com	www.learn2.com	$20 to $100

Figure 2-15 E-learning sites

- **Exploration and Education:** Many of the resources traditionally found in libraries are now available on the Web. For example, some prestigious libraries have put access to rare and unusual documents on their Web sites. Several major universities and many companies support e-learning by offering courses or degree programs over the Internet. To learn more about e-learning visit some of the sites presented in Figure 2-15.
- **Business:** Most large corporations, and many small businesses, maintain a Web site to advertise their products or services. A presence on the Web is considered by many businesses an essential contact with their customers. Most business Web sites offer information about their products or services, contact information, and an outline of their company on their site.
- **Advocacy:** This type of Web site usually supports a cause, or makes a statement on an issue, with the intent to persuade its readers. For example, an environmental site may offer information on a variety of ecological issues with the intention of persuading readers to carpool, contact their representatives in government, or donate money to further a cause. (See Figure 2-16.)

Figure 2-16 Greenpeace maintains an advocacy Web site

- **Personal:** People all over the world maintain Web sites that describe the places where they live, the things they like to do, and the other people in their lives. Some personal sites act as a resume and others are used to keep friends and family updated with family photos. One new type of personal page is a **blog,** or **Weblog.** This type of page is easily updatable and is commonly used as a diary of events. While some blogs are used for business or advocacy capacities, the over-whelming majority of blogs are personal sites that share feelings and experiences in a public forum. There are even directories dedicated to locating specific blogs by topic or type. (See Figure 2-17.) For a summary of the different types of Web pages, see Figure 2-18.

Directory	Address
Bloghop	www.bloghop.com
Eaton Web Portal	portal.eatonweb.com
Weblogs	www.weblogs.com

Figure 2-17 Blog directories and engines

Type	Description
Portals and directories	Offer navigational and organizational services
News and information	Provide news and expanded information
Exploration and education	Support online libraries and e-learning
Business	Advertises products and services
Advocacy	Promotes cause; intended to influence
Personal	Shares personal feelings and experiences

Figure 2-18 Types of Web Pages

MULTIMEDIA

You have probably visited Web sites that played music and videos. Web sites that include these elements are using multiple kinds of media, or **multimedia** (photos, music, video, text, etc.) to enhance your experience. Multimedia is a common feature on the Web.

To listen to audio or play video files on your computer, typically you use a **media player.** These players are programs that support a variety of multimedia-related activities including:

- Playing audio and video files, as well as CDs and DVDs.
- Listening to radio stations.
- Locating digital media files on the Internet.

One of the best known media players is Microsoft's Windows Media Player. This program is included with most versions of Windows XP. It can also be obtained directly from Microsoft at www.microsoft.com. To see how Windows Media Player helps you locate and play video from the Internet, see Figure 2-19.

Another common use of Windows Media Player is to listen to **Internet Radio** or radio broadcasts over the Internet. The process of broadcasting audio or video over the Internet is known as **Webcasting.** Typically, Webcasting involves streaming media. **Streaming media,** also known as **streaming audio** and **streaming video,** is a technique for delivering audio and video files over a network without downloading an entire file before it plays. After playing, the files are not stored on to your computer. To learn more about streaming media see your Computing Today CD or visit Tim's Toolbox at http://www.mhhe.com/oleary/CT05.

Computing Today CD

1 Click ***Start.***

Select ***Windows Media Player*** from the ***Start Menu*** or the ***All Programs*** menu.

Media Player

2 Select a video clip from the ***Media Guide.***

Click on the bandwidth link below the graphic if necessary.

Select bandwidth

Figure 2-19 Using Windows Media Player to locate and play video from the Internet

continued

3 Click the ***View Full Screen*** **button.**

Watch the video clip.

Figure 2-19 concluded

Concept Check

✔ What is a Web site? What is a homepage? What is a site map?
✔ Describe six common types of Web pages.
✔ What is a media player? What are streaming audio and streaming video?

COMMUNICATION

E-mail is the transmission of electronic messages and the most popular Internet activity. Instant messaging extends e-mail to direct, live communication. Discussion groups include mailing lists, newsgroups, and chat groups.

As previously mentioned, communication is the most popular Internet activity, and its impact cannot be overestimated. At a personal level, friends and family can stay in contact with one another even when separated by thousands of miles. At a business level, electronic communication has become a standard and many times preferred way to stay in touch with suppliers, employees, and customers. The three most popular types of Internet communication are e-mail, instant messaging, and discussion groups.

E-MAIL

E-mail or **electronic mail** is the transmission of electronic messages over the Internet. At one time, e-mail consisted only of basic text messages. Now e-mail routinely includes graphics, photos, and many different types of file attachments. People all over the world send e-mail to each other. You can e-mail your family, your co-workers, and even your Senator. All you need to send and receive e-mail is an e-mail account, access to the Internet, and an e-mail program. Two of the most widely used e-mail programs are Microsoft's Outlook Express and Netscape's Mail.

A typical e-mail message has three basic elements: header, message, and signature. (See Figure 2-20.) The **header** appears first and typically includes the following information:

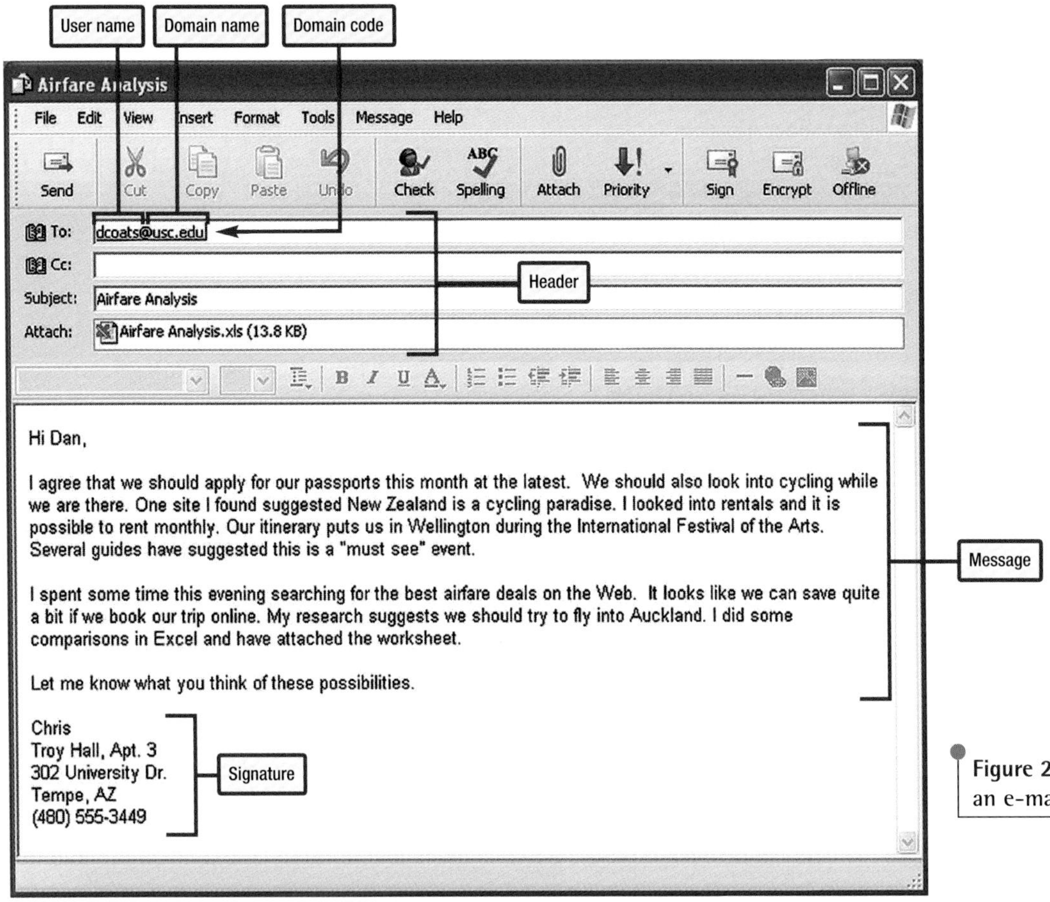

Figure 2-20 Basic elements of an e-mail message

Figure 2-21 Two parts of an e-mail address

- **Addresses:** Addresses of the persons sending, receiving, and, optionally, anyone else who is to receive copies. E-mail addresses have two basic parts. (See Figure 2-21.) The first part is the user's name and the second part is the domain name, which includes the domain code. In our example e-mail, *dcoats* is Dan's username. The server providing e-mail service for Dan is *usc.edu*. The domain code indicates that the provider is an educational institution.
- **Subject:** A one-line description, used to present the topic of the message. Subject lines typically are displayed when a person checks his or her mailbox.
- **Attachments:** Many e-mail programs allow you to attach files such as documents and worksheets. If a message has an attachment, the file name appears on the attachment line.

The letter or **message** comes next. It is typically short and to the point. Finally, the **signature line** provides additional information about the sender. Typically, this information includes the sender's name, address, and telephone number.

On the Web Explorations

Almost all ISPs and online service providers offer e-mail service to their customers. But you can get this service for free from Hotmail, Juno Online Services, USA Net Inc., and Yahoo!. To learn more about these free services, visit our site at: http://www.mhhe.com/oleary/CT05 and select On the Web Explorations from Tim's Toolbox.

TIPS Are you tired of sorting through an inbox full of spam? Americans receive over 200 billion spam e-mails every year. Here are a few simple tips to help ensure that your inbox is spam-free:

1. **Choose a complex address.** sally_smith@hotmail.com is much more likely to get spam than 4it3scoq2@hotmail.com. Consider using a more complicated, and less personal, user name.
2. **Keep a low profile.** Many spammers collect e-mail addresses from personal Web sites, chat rooms, and message boards. Use caution when handing out your address and be sure to read the privacy policy of a site before you hand over your address.
3. **Don't ever respond to spam.** Once you respond to spam, either in interest or to opt out of a list, you have confirmed the address is valid. Valid addresses are worth more to spammers, who then sell the address to others.
4. **Use a filter.** Most e-mail programs have a filter option that screens incoming e-mail based on a set of preferences you choose. You can set up your inbox to accept only mail from certain addresses, or block mail from others.
5. **Consider a software solution.** There are plenty of programs available to help protect your inbox. For example, MailWasher provides an effective and free program available at www.mailwasher.com.

E-mail can be a valuable asset in your personal and professional life. However, like many other valuable technologies, there are drawbacks too. Americans receive billions of unwanted and unsolicited e-mails every year. This unwelcome mail is called **spam.** While spam is indeed a distraction and nuisance, it can also be dangerous. For example, **computer viruses** or destructive programs are often attached to unsolicited e-mail. Computer viruses and ways to protect against them will be discussed in Chapter 5.

INSTANT MESSAGING

Instant messaging (IM) is an extension of e-mail that allows two or more people to communicate via direct, live communication. To use instant messaging, you specify a list of **friends** (also known as **buddies** or **contacts**) and register with an instant messaging server. Whenever you connect to the Internet, special software informs your messaging server that you are online. In response, the server will notify you if any of your contacts are online. At the same time, it notifies your contacts that you are online. You can then send messages directly back and forth to one another. Many new instant messaging programs also include videoconferencing features, file sharing, and remote assistance. To see how Instant Messaging works, see Figure 2-22. Also consult your Computing Today CD or visit us at http://www.mhhe.com/oleary/CT05 and select Animations from Tim's Toolbox.

Computing Today CD

The most widely used instant messaging services are AOL's Instant Messenger, Microsoft's Messenger, and Yahoo! Messenger. One limitation, however, is that many instant messaging services do not support communication with other services. For example, at the time of this writing, a user registered with AOL cannot use AOL's Instant Messenger software to communicate with a user registered with Yahoo! Messenger. Recently, however, some software companies have started providing **universal instant messenger** programs that overcome this limitation. For example, Imici Messenger, Odigo, and Trillian provide instant messaging services that do support communication with other services.

Instant messaging has had a significant impact on how we communicate. It has impacted personal communications as well as business communications. Many business people use instant messaging to collaborate with nearby, and far away, co-workers to quickly resolve critical business issues.

See Making IT Work for You: Instant Messaging on page 48.

Concept Check

Define e-mail. What are the three basic elements of a typical e-mail message?
What is SPAM?
Define instant messaging? What is a universal instant messenger?

How Instant Messaging Works

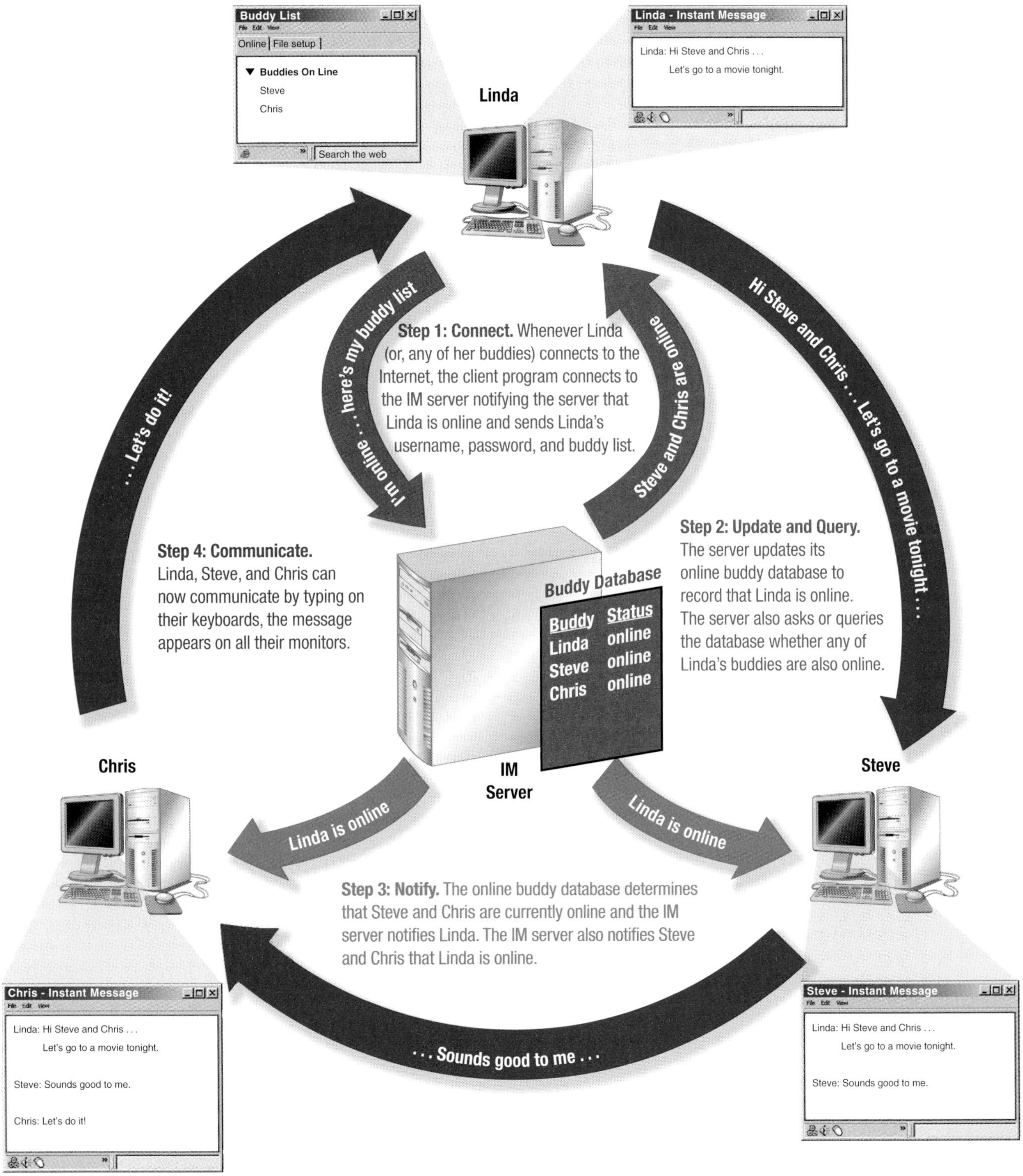
Buddy List
File Edit View
Online | File setup
▼ Buddies On Line
Steve
Chris
Search the web
Linda - Instant Message
File Edit View
Linda: Hi Steve and Chris . . .
Let's go to a movie tonight.
Linda
I'm online . . . here's my buddy list
Steve and Chris are online
Hi Steve and Chris . . . Let's go to a movie tonight . . .
. . . Let's do it!
Step 1: Connect. Whenever Linda (or, any of her buddies) connects to the Internet, the client program connects to the IM server notifying the server that Linda is online and sends Linda's username, password, and buddy list.
Step 2: Update and Query. The server updates its online buddy database to record that Linda is online. The server also asks or queries the database whether any of Linda's buddies are also online.
Step 4: Communicate. Linda, Steve, and Chris can now communicate by typing on their keyboards, the message appears on all their monitors.
Buddy Database
Buddy Status
Linda online
Steve online
Chris online
IM Server
Chris
Steve
Linda is online
Linda is online
Step 3: Notify. The online buddy database determines that Steve and Chris are currently online and the IM server notifies Linda. The IM server also notifies Steve and Chris that Linda is online.
. . . Sounds good to me . . .
Chris - Instant Message
File Edit View
Linda: Hi Steve and Chris . . .
Let's go to a movie tonight.
Steve: Sounds good to me.
Chris: Let's do it!
Steve - Instant Message
File Edit View
Linda: Hi Steve and Chris . . .
Let's go to a movie tonight.
Steve: Sounds good to me.

Figure 2-22 How Instant Messaging Works

MAKING IT WORK FOR YOU

INSTANT MESSAGING

Do you enjoy chatting with your friends? Are you working on a project and need to collaborate with others in your group? Perhaps instant messaging is just what you're looking for. It's easy and free with an Internet Connection and the right software.

Messages and File Transfer After installing free instant messaging software, you can exchange messages and files with friends. For example, you could use Windows Messenger as follows:

1

- **Add Contacts by clicking *Add a Contact* and following the on-screen instructions.**
- **Double-click the Contact name of a friend that appears in the *Online* section.**
- **Enter your message into the window that appears.**
- **Click the *Send* button.**

Your message appears on your friend's screen instantly. Your friend can then continue the conversation by following the same steps above.

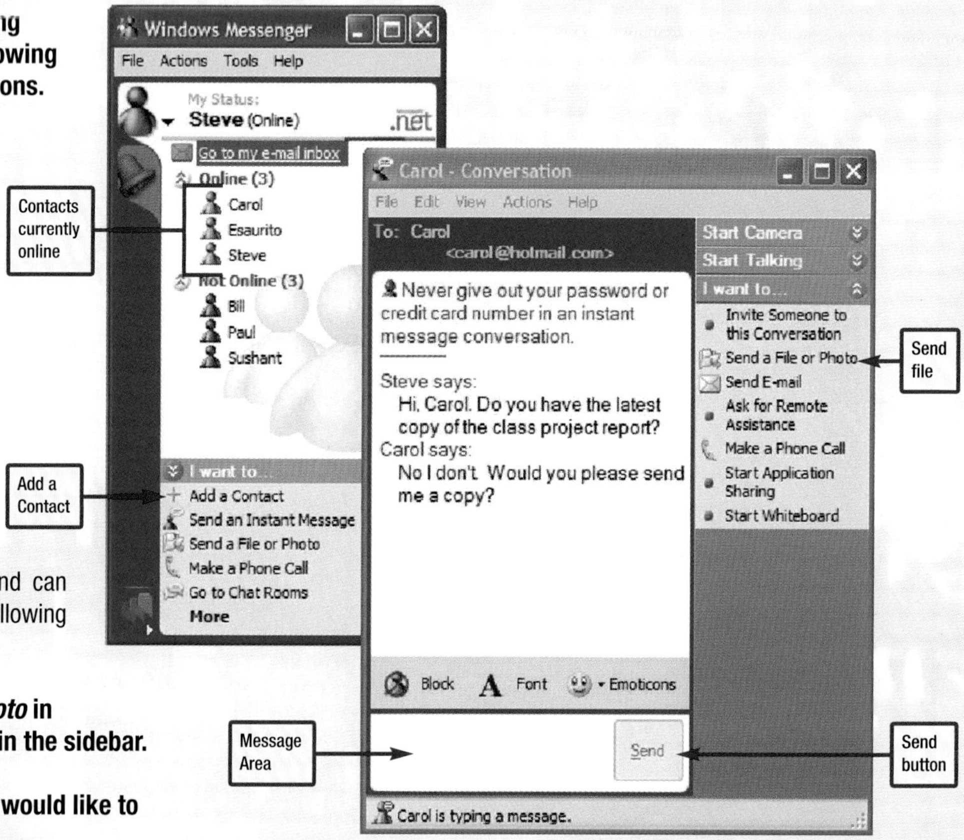

2

- **Click *Send a File or Photo* in the *I want to . . .* menu in the sidebar.**
- **Browse for the file you would like to share, and click *Open*.**
- **Your friend will be given an option to accept the transfer. Once the friend accepts, the file is transferred to him or her.**

You can continue your conversation without interruption while the file is being transferred.

Video Conferencing In addition to typing text messages, some instant messaging software allows you to have voice or video conversations over the Internet so you can see and hear the person you are collaborating with. To do this, both users must have a microphone and speakers, as well as Web cameras for video conferencing. You could hold a video conference using Windows Messenger by following these steps:

1. **Start a conversation with a Contact as shown in the Messages and File Transfer section.**
   - **Click *Start Camera* in the sidebar.**
   - **Your friend will be given the option to accept the video conference. Once he or she accepts, the video conference begins.**
   - **As you speak, adjust the Speakers and Microphone sliders to comfortable levels.**

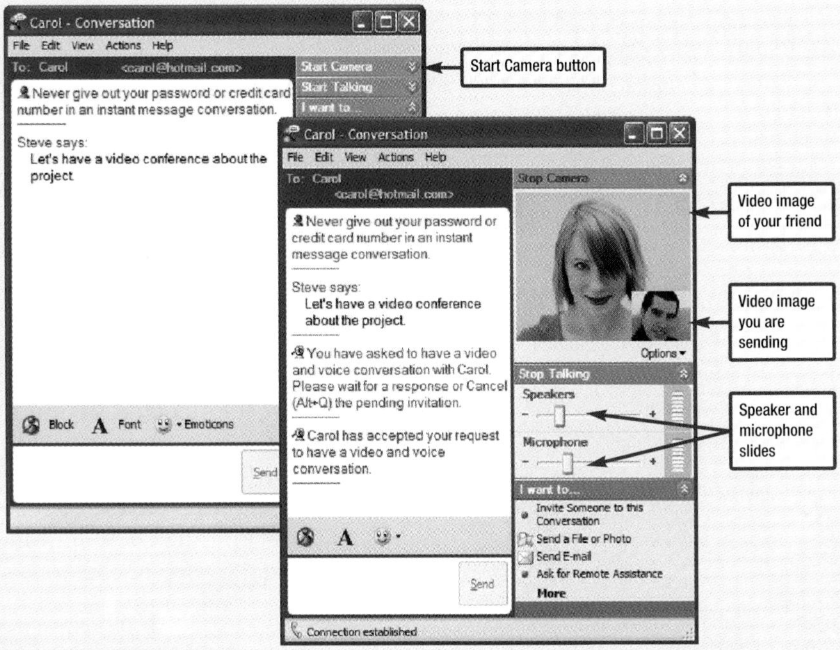

Placing an Internet Phone Call Placing an Internet phone call is one other way to keep in touch using instant messaging software. An Internet phone call allows you to call a regular telephone from your computer using the Internet. To use this feature, you must sign up with an Internet Phone service provider. For example, you could make an Internet phone call using Windows Messenger by following these steps:

1. **Click *Make a Phone Call* in the *I want to . . .* menu.**

If you have not yet signed up for an Internet Phone account, you will be given the opportunity at this point.

2. **In the Phone window that appears, type the phone number you wish to dial.**
   - **Click the *Dial* button.**
   - **During the phone conversation, adjust the Speakers and Microphone sliders to comfortable levels.**
   - **Click the *Hang Up* button to end the call.**

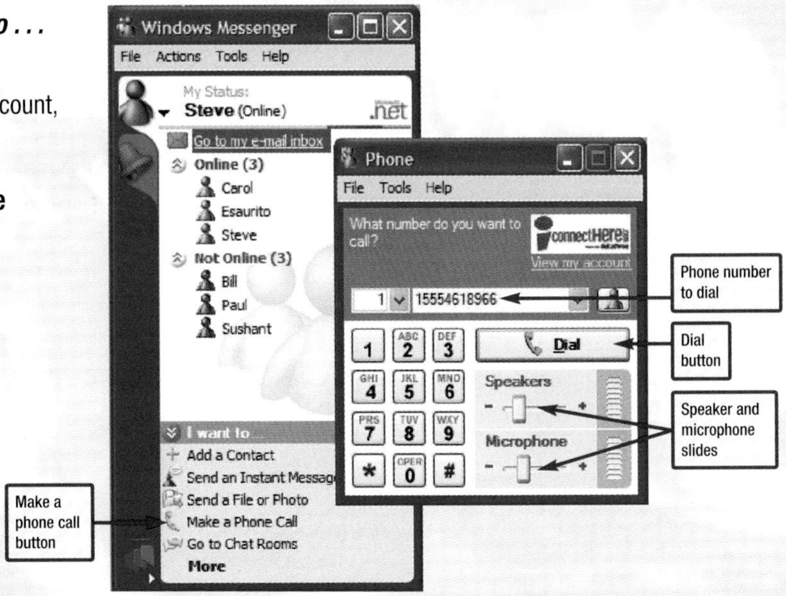

The Web is continually changing and some of the specifics presented in this Making IT Work for You may have changed. Visit our Web site at http://www.mhhe.com/oleary/CT05 and select Making IT Work For You from Tim's Toolbox to learn about other ways to make technology work for you.

DISCUSSION GROUPS

You can also use e-mail to communicate in **discussion groups** with people you do not know but with whom you wish to share ideas and interests. You can participate in forums and debates that range from general topics like current events and movies to specialized forums like computer troubleshooting and Hollywood animations. Discussion groups include mailing lists, newsgroups, and chat groups.

Description	Subscription Address
Music and bands	dbird@netinfo.com.au
Movies	moviereview@cuenet.com
Jokes	jokeaday.com
Travel	tourbus@listserv.aol.com

Figure 2-23 Popular mailing lists

- **Mailing lists** allow members of a mailing list to communicate by sending messages to a **list address.** Each message is then copied and sent via e-mail to every member of the mailing list. To participate in a mailing list, you must first subscribe by sending an e-mail request to the mailing list **subscription address.** (See Figure 2-23.) Once you are a member of a list, you can expect to receive e-mail from others on the list. You may find the number of messages to be overwhelming. If you want to cancel a mailing list, send an e-mail request to "unsubscribe" to the subscription address.
- **Newsgroups,** unlike mailing lists, use a special network of computers called the **UseNet.** Each of these computers maintains the newsgroup listing. There are over 10,000 different newsgroups organized into major topic areas that are further subdivided into subtopics. (See Figure 2-24.) Contributions to a particular newsgroup are sent to one of the computers on the UseNet. This computer saves the messages on its system and periodically shares all its recent messages with the other computers on the UseNet. Unlike mailing lists, a copy of each message is not sent to each member of a list. Rather, interested individuals check contributions to a particular newsgroup, reading only those of interest. There are thousands of newsgroups covering a wide variety of topic areas. (See Figure 2-25.)
- **Chat groups,** like IM, allow direct live communication, or communication. Unlike IM, chat groups are typically comprised of individuals who have never met face-to-face. To participate, you join a chat group, select a **channel** or topic, and communicate live with others by typing words on your computer. Other members of your channel immediately see those words on their computers and can respond in the same manner. One popular chat service is called **Internet Relay Chat (IRC).** This software is available free from several locations on the Internet. Using the chat-client software, you log on to the server, select a channel or topic in which you are interested, and begin chatting. To participate, you need access to a server or computer that supports IRC. This is done using special chat-client software.

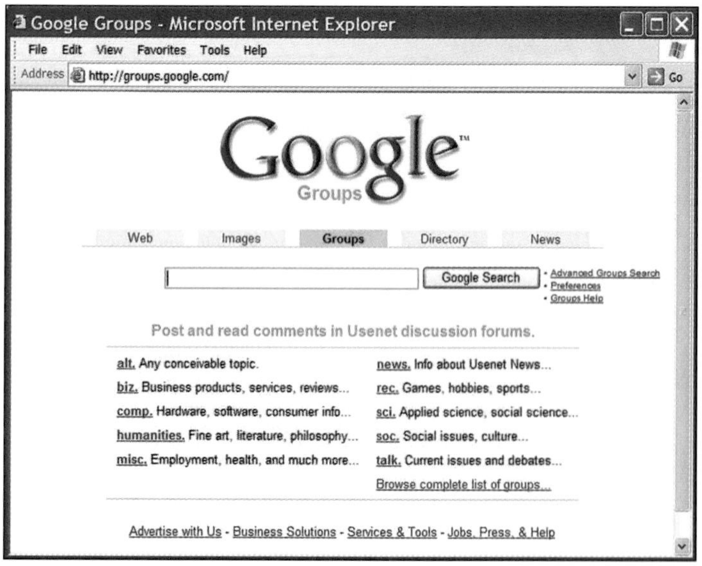

Figure 2-24 Google Groups connects you to UseNet

Before you submit a contribution to a discussion group, it is recommended that you observe or read the communications from others. This is called **lurking.** By lurking, you can learn about the culture of a discussion group. For example, you can observe the level and style of the discussions. You may decide that a particular discussion group is not what you were looking for—in which case, unsubscribe. If the discussions are appropriate and you wish to participate, try to fit into the prevailing culture. Remember that your contributions will likely be read by hundreds of people.

For a list of commonly used discussion group terms, see Figure 2-26.

Description	Newsgroups
Aerobics fitness	misc.fitness.aerobic
Cinema	rec.arts.movies
Mountain biking	rec.bicycles.off-road
Music	rec.music.hip-hop
Clip art	alt.binaries.clip-art

Figure 2-25 Popular newsgroups

Term	Description
Flaming	Insulting, putting down, or attacking
Lurking	Reading news but not joining in to contribute
RFD	Request for discussion
Saint	Someone who aids new users by answering questions
Thread	A sequence of ongoing messages on the same subject
Wizard	Someone who has comprehensive knowledge about a subject

Figure 2-26 Common discussion group terms

Concept Check

- ✔ What is a discussion group? Discuss mailing lists, newsgroups, and chat groups.
- ✔ Compare and contrast mailing lists and newsgroups.
- ✔ What is a chat group? What are channels?

SEARCH TOOLS

Search services locate information. Metasearch engines submit search requests to several search engines simultaneously. Specialized search engines focus on subject-specific Web sites. Basic activities for conducting research on the Web are locating information, evaluating the information, and citing references.

The Web can be an incredible resource providing information on nearly any topic imaginable. Are you planning a trip? Writing an economics paper? Looking for a movie review? Trying to locate a long-lost friend? Information sources related to these questions, and much, much more are available on the Web.

With over 2 billion pages and more being added daily, the Web is a massive collection of interrelated pages. With so much available information, locating the precise information you need can be difficult. Fortunately, a number of organizations called **search services** or **search providers** operate Web sites that can help you locate the information you need. They maintain huge databases relating to information provided on the Web and the Internet. The information stored at these databases includes addresses, content descriptions or classifications, and keywords appearing on Web pages and other Internet informational resources. Special programs called **agents, spiders,** or **bots** continually look for new information and update the search services' databases. Additionally, search services provide special programs called search engines that you can use to locate specific information on the Web.

SEARCH ENGINES

Search engines are specialized programs that assist you in locating information on the Web and the Internet. To find information, you go to a

TIPS

Are you going to use a search tool to locate some information? Here are a few tips that might help.

1. **Start with the right approach.** For general information, use a direct search. For specific information, use a key word search.
2. **Be as precise as possible.** Use specific key words that relate directly to the topic.
3. **Use multiple words.** Use quotation marks to identify key words.
4. **Use Boolean operators.** Typically, these include words such as "and," "not," "or."
5. **Check your spelling.** Misspelling is one of the most common problems.
6. **Keep moving.** Look only at the first page of search results. If necessary, try another search using different key words.

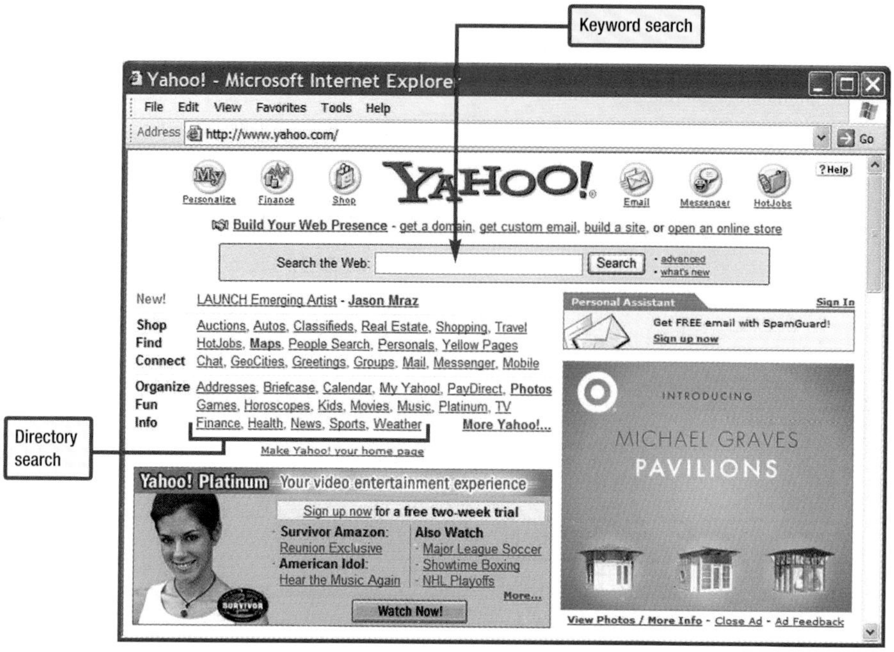

Figure 2-27 Yahoo's search engine provides keyword and directory search

search service's Web site and use their search engine. For example, see Figure 2-27 for Yahoo's search engine. This search engine, like most others, provides two different search approaches.

- **Keyword search:** In a **keyword search,** you enter a keyword or phrase reflecting the information you want. The search engine compares your entry against its database and returns a list of **hits,** or sites that contain the keywords. Each hit includes a hyperlink to the referenced Web page (or other resource) along with a brief discussion of the information contained at that location. Many searches result in a large number of hits. For example, if you were to enter the keyword *travel,* you would get thousands of hits. Search engines order the hits according to those sites that most likely contain the information requested and present the list to you in that order, usually in groups of 10.
- **Directory search:** Most search engines also provide a directory or list of categories or topics such as Finance, Health, and News. In a **directory search,** also known as an **index search,** you select a category or topic that fits the information that you want. Another list of subtopics related to the topic you selected appears. You select the subtopic that best relates to your topic and another subtopic list appears. You continue to narrow your search in this manner until a list of Web sites appears. This list corresponds to the hit list previously discussed.

As a rule, if you are searching for general information, use the directory search approach. For example, to find general information about music, use a directory search beginning with the category Entertainment and then select the subtopic Music. If you are searching for specific information, use the keyword approach. For example, if you were looking for a specific music file, you would use a keyword search using the album title and/or the artist's name.

A recent study by the NEC Research Institute found that any one search engine includes only a fraction of the informational sources on the Web. Therefore, it is highly recommended that you use more than one search engine when researching important topics. See Figure 2-28 for a list of some of the most widely used search engines. Or, you could use a special type of search engine called a metasearch engine.

Figure 2-28 Search engines

Search Service	Site
Alta Vista	www.altavista.com
Excite	www.excite.com
Google	www.google.com
NorthernLight	www.northernlight.com
Teoma	www.teoma.com
Yahoo!	www.yahoo.com

Metasearch Service	Site
Dogpile	www.dogpile.com
Ixquick	www.ixquick.com
Mamma	www.mamma.com
MetaCrawler	www.metacrawler.com
ProFusion	www.profusion.com
Search	www.search.com
Vivisimo	www.vivisimo.com

Figure 2-29 Metasearch sites

Figure 2-30 MetaCrawler search site

METASEARCH ENGINES

One way to research a topic is to visit the Web sites for several individual search engines. At each site, you would enter the search instructions, wait for the hits to appear, review the list, and visit selected sites. This process can be quite time-consuming and duplicate responses from different search engines are inevitable. Metasearch engines offer an alternative.

Metasearch engines are programs that automatically submit your search request to several search engines simultaneously. The metasearch engine receives the results, eliminates duplicates, orders the hits, and then provides the edited list to you. See Figure 2-29 for a list of several metasearch engines available on the Web. One of the best known is MetaCrawler, see Figure 2-30.

Topic	Site
Environment	www.eco-web.com
Fashion	www.infomat.com
History	www.historynet.com
Law	www.llrx.com/guide
Medicine	www.medsite.com

Figure 2-31 Select specialized search engines

SPECIALIZED SEARCH ENGINES

Specialized search engines focus on subject-specific Web sites. Specialized sites can potentially save you time by narrowing your search. For a list of just a few selected specialized search engines, see Figure 2-31. For example, let's say you are researching a paper about the fashion industry. You could begin with a general search engine like Yahoo! Or, you could go to a search engine that specializes specifically in fashion such as infomat.com. (See Figure 2-32.)

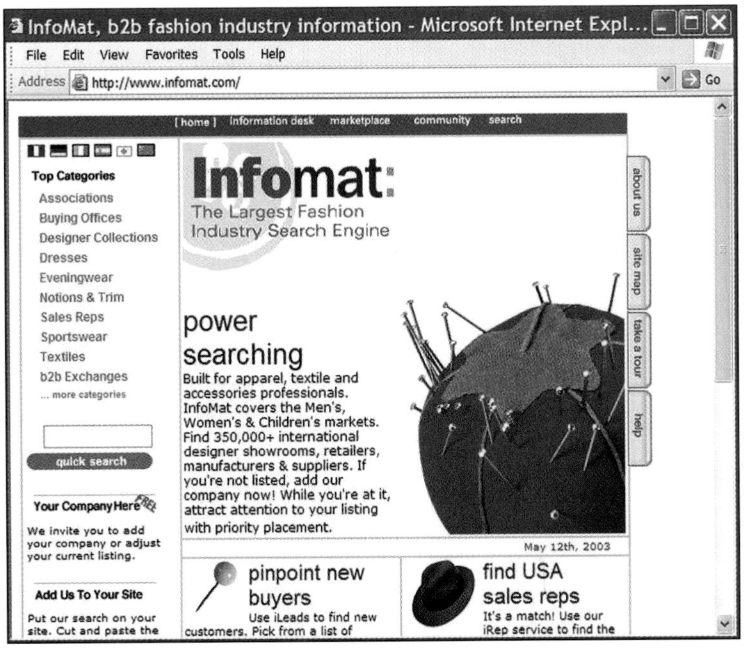

Figure 2-32 Fashion specialized search engine

RESEARCH ON THE WEB

Whether you are conducting ground-breaking research or writing a paper for one of your classes, the Web is an invaluable research tool. There are three basic activities to conducting research on the Web: locating information, evaluating the information, and citing references.

- **Locating information.** With all the information available on the Web, it is challenging to find just the information you are looking for. Discussion groups are an often overlooked resource that can provide direct access to experts. (For an extensive list of discussion group sites,

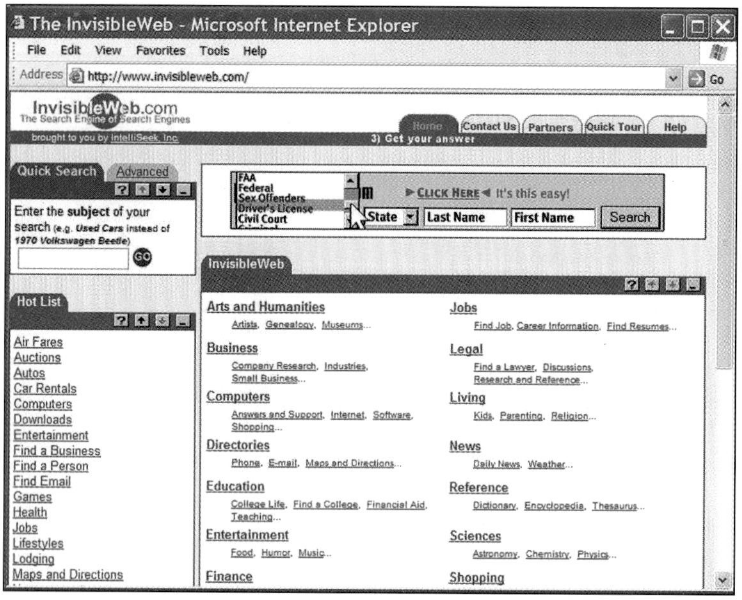

Figure 2-33 Locating specialized Web databases

connect to www.liszt.com.) In addition to using the search, metasearch, and specialized search engines listed in Figures 2-29, 2-30, and 2-31, specialized Web databases may contain untapped information resources. (For assistance in locating a database(s) relevant to a particular research topic, connect to www.invisibleweb.net.) (See Figure 2-33.)

- **Evaluating information.** Locating information is not enough. Because nearly anyone can publish information on the Web, not everything you find is equally reliable or useful. You need to carefully consider the quality of information you have located. One way is to consider a few commonsense questions. For example, who put the information there and what is the source of the information? If the site is maintained by a university, college, or government agency, the information is likely more reliable than information from a site published by an unknown individual. What is the purpose of the site? Is it designed to sell products, influence your opinion on a particular topic, or dispense information? Considering these questions and using common sense will help you evaluate the quality and reliability of information obtained from the Web.
- **Cite resources** Plagiarism is the illegal copying of someone else's words or ideas. You can use someone's words or ideas without committing plagiarism by simply acknowledging or citing the source. There are several standards to cite electronic resources. The Modern Language Association (MLA) standard is one of the most widely used for research papers. Using this standard, if the author of the information is known, the citation format is:

author name. day month year <source>

For example, the citation shown in Figure 2-34 acknowledges information created by Dan Coats (author) that was obtained on January 15, 2006, from the www.auto.com Web site (<source>). If the author's name is unknown, then the title of the Web page would replace the author's name.

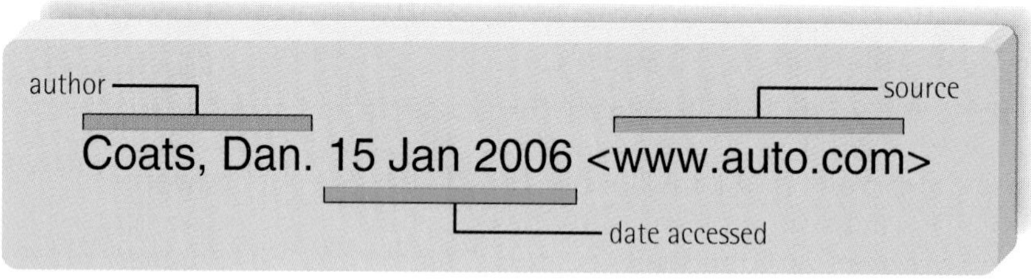

Figure 2-34 MLA citation

Concept Check

- What is the difference between a search engine and a metasearch engine?
- What is a specialized search engine? When would a specialized search engine be useful?
- Discuss the three basic activities to conducting research on the Web.

E-commerce is buying and selling over the Internet. B2C, C2C, and B2B are types of e-commerce. E-banking, e-trading, and e-tailing are B2C applications. Web auctions are C2C. Greatest challenge to e-commerce development: Security.

Electronic commerce, also known as **e-commerce,** is the buying and selling of goods over the Internet. Have you ever bought anything over the Internet? If you have not, there is a very good chance that you will within the next year or two. Shopping on the Internet is growing rapidly and there seems to be no end in sight. (See Figure 2-35.)

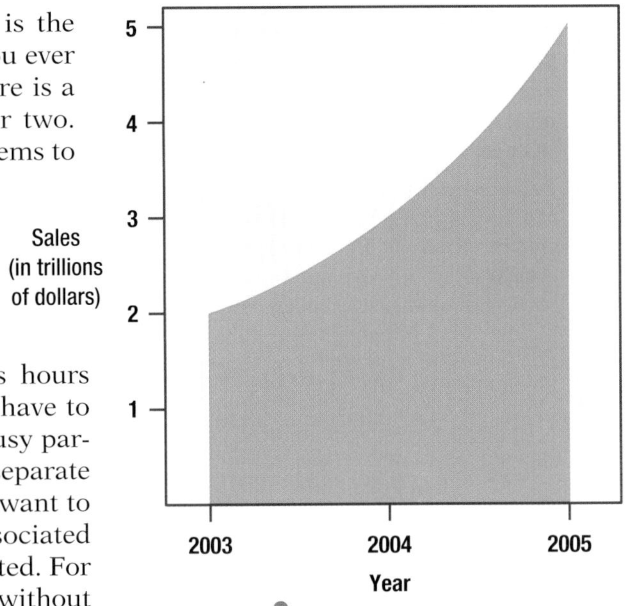

Figure 2-35 Growth in e-commerce

The underlying reason for the rapid growth in e-commerce is that it provides incentives for both buyers and sellers. From the buyer's perspective, goods and services can be purchased at any time of day or night. Traditional commerce, also known as **bricks and mortar** business, is typically limited to standard business hours when the seller is open. Additionally, buyers no longer have to physically travel to the seller's location. For example, busy parents with small children do not need to coordinate their separate schedules or to arrange for a baby sitter whenever they want to visit the mall. From the seller's perspective, the costs associated with owning and operating a retail outlet can be eliminated. For example, a music store can operate entirely on the Web without an actual physical store and without a large sales staff. (See Figure 2-36.) Another advantage is reduced inventory. Traditional stores maintain an inventory of goods in their stores and periodically replenish this inventory from warehouses. With e-commerce, there is no in-store inventory and products are shipped directly from warehouses.

While there are numerous advantages to e-commerce, there are disadvantages as well. Some of these disadvantages include the inability to provide immediate delivery of goods, the inability to "try on" prospective purchases, and questions relating to the security of online payments. Although these issues are being addressed, very few observers suggest that e-commerce will replace bricks and mortar businesses entirely. It is clear that both will coexist and that e-commerce will continue to grow.

Just like any other type of commerce, electronic commerce involves two parties: businesses and consumers. There are three basic types of electronic commerce:

Figure 2-36 Music e-commerce site

- **Business-to-consumer (B2C)** involves the sale of a product or service to the general public or end users. Oftentimes this arrangement eliminates the middleman by allowing manufacturers to sell directly to customers. Other times, existing retail stores use B2C e-commerce to create a presence on the Web as another way to reach customers.

TIPS Have you ever bought anything online? If not, it's likely that in the future you will join the millions that have. Here are a few suggestions on how to shop online:

1. **Consult product review sites.** To get evaluations or opinions on products, visit one of the many review sites on the Web such as www.consumersearch.com and www.epinions.com.
2. **Use a shopping bot.** Once you have selected a specific product, enlist a shopping bot or automated shopping assistants to compare prices. Two well-known shopping bots are located at www.mysimon.com and www.shopping.yahoo.com.
3. **Consult vendor review sites.** Of course, price is not everything. Before placing an order with a vendor, check their reputation by visiting vendor review sites such as www.gomez.com and www.bizrate.com.
4. **Select payment option.** Once you have selected the product and the vendor, the final step is to order and pay. Security of your credit card number is critical. Consider payment options available from www.private.buy.com and www.americanexpress.com/privatepayments.

- **Consumer-to-consumer (C2C)** involves individuals selling to individuals. This often takes the form of an electronic version of the classified ads or an auction. Goods are described and interested buyers contact sellers to negotiate prices. Unlike traditional sales via classified ads and auctions, buyers and sellers typically never meet face-to-face.
- **Business-to-business (B2B)** involves the sale of a product or service from one business to another. This is typically a manufacturer–supplier relationship. For example, a furniture manufacturer requires raw materials such as wood, paint, and varnish. In B2B e-commerce, manufacturers electronically place orders with suppliers and many times payment is made electronically. The most popular B2B e-commerce is for automobile parts, electronics including computers, and health care.

BUSINESS-TO-CONSUMER E-COMMERCE

The fastest growing type of e-commerce is business-to-consumer. It is used by large corporations, small corporations and start-up businesses. Whether large or small, nearly every existing corporation in the United States provides some type of B2C support as another means to connect to customers. Because extensive investments are not required to create traditional retail outlets and to maintain large marketing and sales staffs, e-commerce allows start-up companies to compete with larger established firms.

The three most widely used B2C applications are for online banking, financial trading, and shopping.

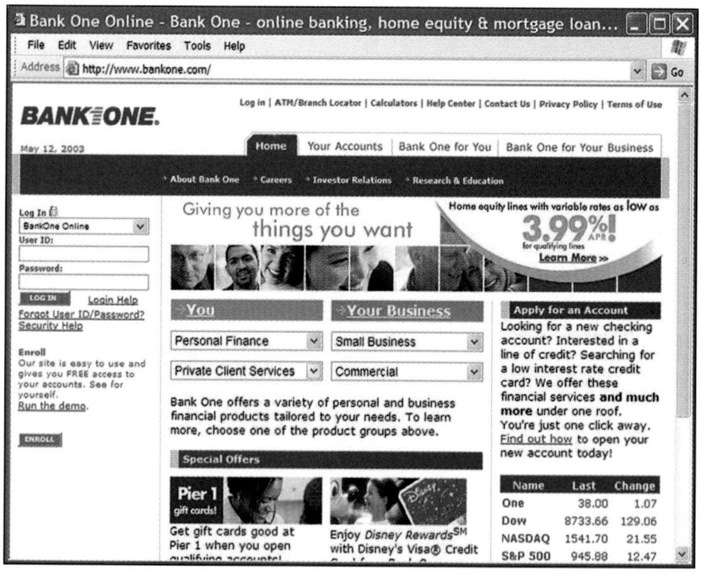

Figure 2-37 Online banking

- **Online banking,** also known as **e-banking,** is becoming a standard feature of banking institutions. Customers are able to go online with a standard browser to perform many banking operations. These online operations include accessing account information, balancing check books, transferring funds, paying bills, and applying for loans. Using these electronic services is considered safer than using an ATM. (See Figure 2-37.)
- **Online stock trading,** also known as **e-trading,** allows investors to research, buy, and sell stocks and bonds over the Internet. While e-trading is more convenient than using a traditional full-service broker, the greatest advantage is cost. Typical charges for stock trading with a full-service broker are 10 times greater than online stock trading. Of course, a full-service broker provides advice based on his or her research. However, e-trading sites typically provide research on individual stocks that many e-traders use to make their trading decisions. (See Figure 2-38.)
- **Online shopping,** also known as **e-retailing** or **e-tailing,** includes the buying and selling of a wide range of consumer goods over the Internet. There are thousands of e-commerce applications in this area. Some areas have been more successful than others. The greatest e-retailing successes have

been in the book, travel, music, and health industries. (See Figure 2-39.)

Web storefronts are virtual stores for B2C electronic commerce. Shoppers visit the stores on the Web to inspect merchandise and make purchases. A new type of program called **Web storefront creation packages** or **commerce servers** has recently evolved to help businesses create virtual stores. These programs create Web sites that allow visitors to register, browse, place products into virtual shopping carts, and purchase goods and services. And they do even more behind the scenes. They calculate taxes and shipping costs, handle a variety of payment options, update and replenish inventory, and ensure reliable and safe communications. Additionally, the storefront sites collect data about visitors and generate reports to evaluate the site's profitability. (See Figure 2-40.)

Using commerce servers, a start-up company can become operational with a Web storefront in just a few weeks for as little as $2,000 and monthly server costs of $100.

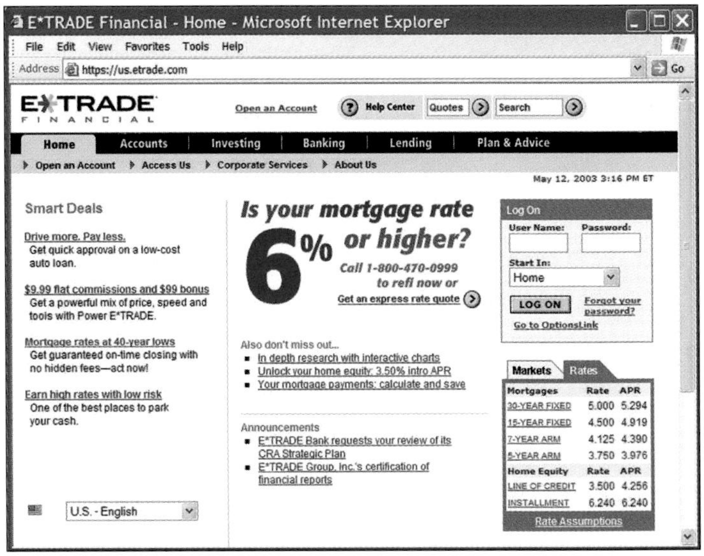

Figure 2-38 Online trading

Figure 2-39 Online shopping

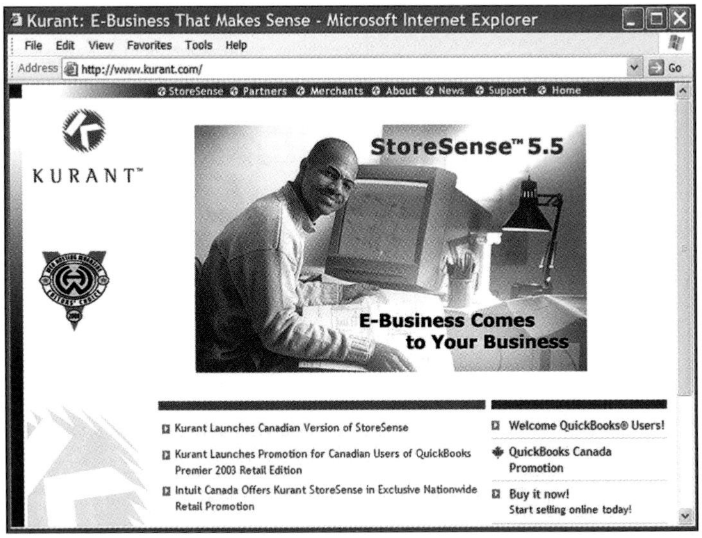

Figure 2-40 Web storefront creation package site

CONSUMER-TO-CONSUMER E-COMMERCE

A recent trend in C2C e-commerce is the growing popularity of Web auctions. **Web auctions** are similar to traditional auctions except that buyers and sellers seldom, if ever, meet face-to-face. Sellers post descriptions of products at a Web site and buyers submit bids electronically. Like traditional auctions, sometimes the bidding becomes highly competitive and enthusiastic. There are two basic types of Web auction sites:

- **Auction house sites** sell a wide range of merchandise directly to bidders. The auction house owner presents merchandise that is typically from a company's surplus stock. These sites operate like a traditional auction, and bargain prices are not uncommon. Auction house sites are generally considered safe places to shop.
- **Person-to-person auction sites** operate more like flea markets. The owner of the site provides a forum for numerous buyers and sellers to gather. While the owners of these sites typically facilitate the bidding process, they are not involved in completing transactions or in verifying the authenticity of the goods sold. (See Figure 2-41.) As with purchases at a flea market, buyers and sellers need to be cautious.

For a list of the most popular Web auction sites, see Figure 2-42.

Figure 2-41 Person-to-person Web auction site

Organization	Site
Amazon	www.auctions.amazon.com
eBay	www.ebay.com
Priceline.com	www.priceline.com
Sotheby's	www.sothebys.com
Yahoo!	www.auctions.yahoo.com

Figure 2-42 Auction sites

SECURITY

The single greatest challenge for e-commerce is the development of fast, secure, and reliable payment methods for purchased goods. The three basic payment options are check, credit card, and electronic cash.

- Checks are the most traditional and perhaps the safest. Unfortunately, check purchases require the longest time to complete. After selecting an item, the buyer sends a check through the mail. Upon receipt of the check, the seller verifies that the check is good. If it is good, then the purchased item is sent out.
- Credit card purchases are faster and more convenient than check purchases. Credit card fraud, however, is a major concern for both buyers and sellers. Criminals known as **carders** specialize in stealing, trading, and using stolen credit cards over the Internet. We will discuss this and other privacy and security issues related to the Internet in Chapter 11.
- **Electronic cash,** or **e-cash,** is the Internet's equivalent to traditional cash. It is also known as **cybercash** and **digital cash.** Buyers purchase e-cash from a third party (a bank that specializes in electronic currency) by transferring funds from their banks. (See Figure 2-43.) Buyers purchase goods using e-cash. Sellers convert the e-cash to traditional currency through the third party. Although not as convenient as credit card purchases, e-cash is more secure. For a list of e-cash providers, see Figure 2-44.

Figure 2-43 PayPal offers electronic payment

Organization	Site
ECash	www.ecash.com
EmoneyMail	www.emoneymail.com
Internet Cash	www.internetcash.com
PayPal	www.paypal.com

Figure 2-44 Electronic cash providers

Concept Check

- What is electronic commerce? Discuss the incentives for buyers and sellers to use e-commerce.
- What are the three basic types of e-commerce?
- What are the three basic payment options for electronic payment?

WEB UTILITIES

Web utilities are programs that make working with the Web and the Internet easier and safer. Telnet and FTP are Internet standards. Plug-ins operate as part of a browser. Filters block access and monitor use of selected Web sites.

Utilities are programs that make computing easier. **Web utilities** are specialized utility programs that make using the Internet and the Web easier and safer. Some of these utilities are Internet services for connecting and sharing resources over the Internet. Others are browser-related programs that either become part of your browser or are executed from your browser.

TELNET

Many computers on the Internet will allow you to connect to them and to run selected programs on them. **Telnet** is an Internet standard that allows you to connect to another computer (host) on the Internet and to log on to that computer as if you were on a terminal in the next room. There are hundreds of computers on the Internet that you can connect to. Some allow limited free access, and others charge fees for their use.

FTP

File transfer protocol (FTP) is an Internet standard for transferring files. Many computers on the Internet allow you to copy files to your computer. This is called **downloading.** You can also use FTP to copy files from your computer to another computer on the Internet. This is called **uploading.**

PLUG-INS

Plug-ins are programs that are automatically loaded and operate as a part of your browser. Many Web sites require you to have one or more plug-ins to fully experience their content. Some widely used plug-ins include:

- Acrobat Reader from Adobe—for viewing and printing a variety of standard forms and other documents saved in a special format called PDF.
- Cosmos from Silicon Graphics—for displaying three-dimensional graphics.
- Windows Media Player from Microsoft—for playing audio files, video files, and much more as discussed earlier in this chapter.
- QuickTime from Apple—for playing audio and video files. (See Figure 2-45.)

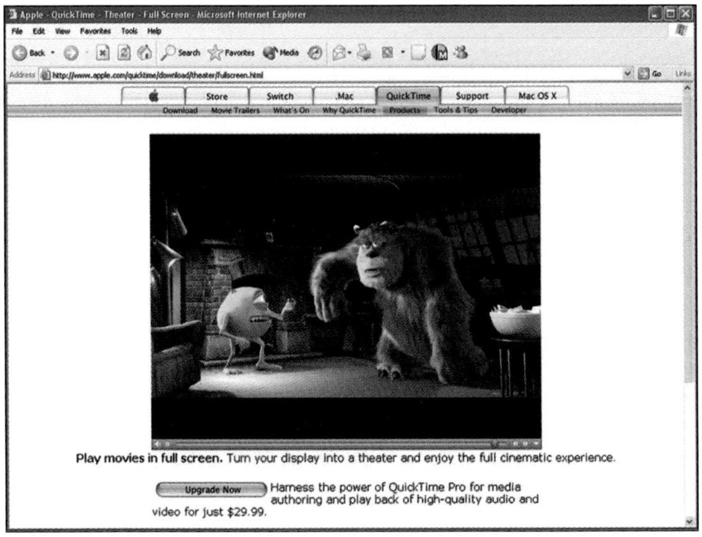

Figure 2-45 QuickTime movie at Apple.com

Plug-in	Source
Acrobat Reader	www.adobe.com
Media Player	www.microsoft.com
QuickTime	www.apple.com
RealPlayer	www.real.com
Shockwave	www.macromedia.com

Figure 2-46 Plug-in sites

- RealPlayer from RealNetworks—for playing audio and video files.
- Shockwave from Macromedia—for playing Web-based games and viewing concerts and dynamic animations.

Some of these utilities are included in many of today's browsers and operating systems. Others must be installed before they can be used by your browser. To learn more about plug-ins and how to download them, visit some of the sites listed in Figure 2-46.

FILTERS

Filters block access to selected sites. The Internet is an interesting and multifaceted arena. But one of those facets is a dark and seamy one. Parents, in particular, are concerned about children roaming unrestricted across the Internet. (See Figure 2-47.) Filter programs allow parents as well as organizations to block out selected sites and set time limits. (See Figure 2-48.) Additionally, these programs can monitor use and generate reports detailing the total time spent on the Internet and the time spent at individual Web sites, chat groups, and newsgroups. Three well-known filters are CyberPatrol, Cybersitter, and Net Nanny.

Figure 2-47 Parents play an important role in Internet supervision

Concept Check

- What are Web utilities?
- Describe Telnet and FTP.
- What are plug-ins and filters used for?

On the Web Explorations

Some privacy groups, like the Digital Freedom Network, object to the use of Web filtering programs on the grounds that they accidentally censor valuable Web content. To learn more about this issue visit our Web site at http://www.mhhe.com/oleary/CT05 and select On the Web Explorations from Tim's Toolbox.

Figure 2-48 CyberPatrol is a Web filter

TIPS

Do your children or little brother or sister use the Internet a lot? While you may want them to be able to take advantage of the educational and entertainment side of the Internet, you also want to protect them from the negative side. To help protect them from viewing inappropriate material, consider the following suggestions:

1. **Locate.** Place the computer in a common area where children can be easily supervised.
2. **Discuss.** Discuss browsing with children to explain what types of content you consider to be appropriate. Create a specific agreement and limit the amount of time your child spends on the Internet.
3. **Surf.** Spend time with your child on the Web. Visit family sites and create a shared e-mail account.
4. **Filter.** Use a filter program and/or investigate your browser's filtering capabilities. Recent versions of Internet Explorer, for example, include a Content Advisor program.
5. **Verify.** Check up on your child's Web activities. Visit their Web pages and search the Web for their screen names.

Careers in IT

Webmaster

Webmasters develop and maintain Web sites and Web resources. The job may include backup of the company Web site, updating resources, or development of new resources. Webmasters are often involved in the design and development of the Web site. Part of their job may also include monitoring and updating the interface design. Some Webmasters monitor traffic on the site and take steps to improve the publicity of the site. Webmasters may also work with marketing personnel to increase site traffic and may be involved in development of Web promotions.

Employers look for candidates with a bachelor's degree in computer science and knowledge of common programming languages and Web development software. Knowledge of HTML is considered essential. Those with experience using Web authoring software and programs like Adobe Illustrator and Macromedia Flash are often preferred. Webmasters often work in conjunction with many other departments and employees. Good communication and organizational skills are vital in this position.

Webmasters can expect to earn an annual salary of $45,000 to $70,000. This position is relatively new in many corporations and tends to have fluid responsibilities. With technological advances and increasing corporate emphasis on a Web presence, experience in this field could lead to managerial opportunities. To learn about other careers in IT, visit us at http://www.mhhe.com/oleary/CT05 and select Careers in IT from Tim's Toolbox.

A Look to the Future

Internet2 Will Be a High-Performance Network

Have you ever been unable to connect to the Internet? Have you ever waited a long time for a graphic to download? Would you like to have high-speed access to multimedia content? What if you could work in a virtual science lab? Internet2 is a project designed to develop the software and resources needed to meet these bandwidth-heavy services.

Internet2 is a collaborative project between an assembly of universities, the government, and private research groups. Over 60 private companies and 200 universities are currently working together to develop the technology and applications they believe will power the Internet in the future. Internet2 is currently 100 times faster than the Internet. Students and faculty at participating universities are currently using Internet2 to collaborate on very media-intensive files and projects. In fact, exchange of digital video is expected to become a major component of Internet2. In order to supply large and uninterrupted digital video files, Internet2 must be a high-bandwidth connect with little delay.

Faster downloads and less waiting are the ultimate goal of this group, but the main objective of their combined efforts is to provide access to new applications. For example, it is anticipated that Internet2 will provide individuals access to virtual libraries and science labs. Internet2 is also expected to enhance the distance learning experience. Current tests are allowing music students to use audio and video equipment to have music lessons with instructors in other countries. Students are using Internet2 to examine atoms with electron microscopes. Doctors are participating in video surgeries.

Internet2 is not a separate network; it is designed to use advanced networking technology and is not expected to replace the current Internet. It is a superfast connection over a fiber-optic network that is less likely to lose data or be interrupted. It is nearly 3,000 times faster than a modem connection to the Internet. Private industry is using university experiences with Internet2 to develop products for public use later. For example, Cisco Systems is currently working with universities on the next generation of network hardware.

Do you think developments like these will eventually benefit the public? What are the benefits of such collaboration between the public and private sectors? The original Internet and e-mail are the result of private and public partnership. What do you think? Will students one day attend university courses virtually? Some experts suggest the applications currently in development may make it possible.

NOTES

VISUAL SUMMARY

THE INTERNET, THE WEB, AND ELECTRONIC COMMERCE

INTERNET AND WEB

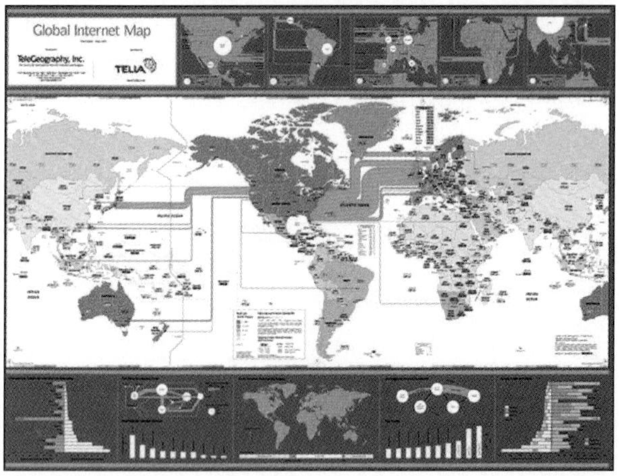

The Internet is like a highway in **cyberspace** that moves ideas and information.

Internet

Launched in 1969 with **ARPANET,** the **Internet (Net)** consists of the actual physical network made up of wires, cables, and satellites. Being connected to this network is often described as being **online.**

Web

Introduced in 1992 at **CERN,** the **Web** (**WWW** and **World Wide Web**) provides a multimedia interface to Internet resources.

Common Uses

The most common uses of the Internet and Web include:

- Communication—the most popular Internet activity.
- Shopping—**cybermalls** provide access to variety of stores.
- Searching—**virtual libraries** provide access to a variety of resources.
- Entertainment—music, movies, magazines, and computer games.
- Education—**e-learning** or taking classes in online courses.

ACCESS

Once connected to the Internet, our computer seemingly becomes an extension of a giant computer that branches all over the world.

Providers

Providers or **host computers** are connected to the Internet. **ISPs** may be **national, regional,** or **wireless.**

Connection technologies include **dial-up, DSL, cable,** and **wireless modems.** User's computer (**client**) requests services from ISP (**server**) forming **client/server network.**

Browsers

Browsers access the Web allowing you to **surf** or explore. Some related terms are:

- **URLs**—**locations** or **addresses** to Web resources; two parts are **protocol** and **domain name; domain code** identifies type of organization.
- **HTML**—commands to display **Web pages; hyperlinks (links)** are connections.
- **Web server**—computer on Internet that stores and shares documents.
- **Applets**—special programs linked to Web pages; typically written in **Java.**

To be a competent and knowledgeable end user you need to be aware of resources available on the Internet and Web, to be able to access these resources, to effectively communicate electronically, to efficiently locate information, to understand electronic commerce, and to use Web browsers and utilities.

WEB SITES

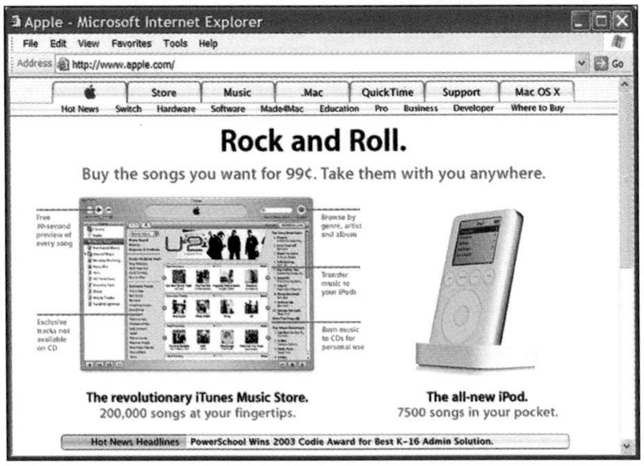

A **Web site** is a group of related Web pages. The **home page** is typically the first page at a site. A **site map** or **index** provides navigational assistance.

Web Pages

Common features include **FAQ** pages and scrollable windows called **frames.** Common types:

- **Portals and directories**—offer navigational and organizational services; **portals (Web portals)** may be **horizontal** or **vertical; directories** are organized by subject.
- **Personal**—shares personal feeling and experiences; **blogs (Web logs)** used as a diary.
- Others—including **News and Information, Exploration and Education, Business,** and **Advocacy.**

Multimedia

Multimedia is the use of multiple types of media including audio and video. Some related terms:

- **Media player**—program that accesses multimedia Web content including **Internet Radio.**
- **Webcasting**—broadcasting audio or video over the Internet; uses **streaming media (streaming audio and video)** to deliver content without downloading entire file before it plays.

COMMUNICATION

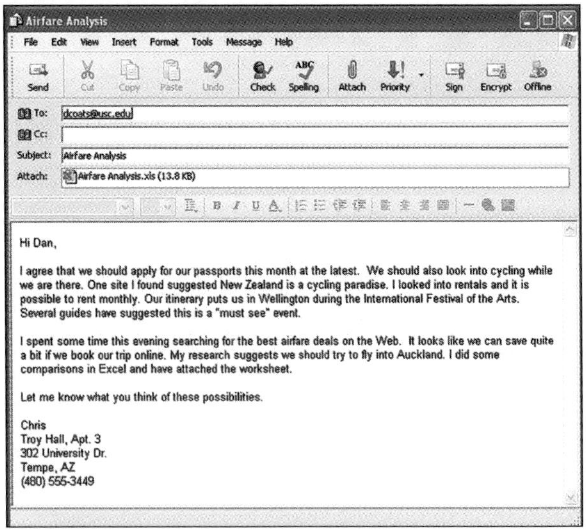

Communication includes e-mail, instant messaging, and discussion groups.

E-mail

E-mail (electronic mail) is the transmission of electronic messages. Basic elements: **header** (including **addresses, subject,** and **attachments**), **message,** and **signature line. Spam** is unwanted and unsolicited e-mail that may include a **computer virus.**

Instant Messaging

Instant messaging (IM) extends e-mail to support live communication with **friends** (**buddies** or **contacts**). **Universal instant messengers** support communication with other services.

Discussion Groups

Discussion groups use e-mail to communicate with people who may have never met face-to-face.

- Includes **mailing lists** (using **list** and **subscription addresses**), **newsgroups** (using the **UseNet**), and **chat groups** (using **channels; IRC** is a popular chat service).
- Associated terms include **flaming, lurking, RFD, saint, thread,** and **wizard.**

SEARCH TOOLS

Search services (search providers) maintain huge Web site databases to locate information. **Agents (spiders or bots)** are programs that update these databases.

Search Engines

Search engines locate information. Most provide two search approaches:

- **Keyword search**—keyword(s) entered and list of **hits** returns. Good for locating specific information.
- **Directory search (index search)**—selections made from a list of topics. Good for locating general information.

Metasearch Engines

Metasearch engines submit search requests to several search engines simultaneously. Duplicate sites eliminated, hits ordered, and composite hit list presented.

Specialized Search Engines

Specialized search engines focus on subject-specific Web sites.

Research on the Web

Basic activities are locating information, evaluating information, and citing resources.

ELECTRONIC COMMERCE

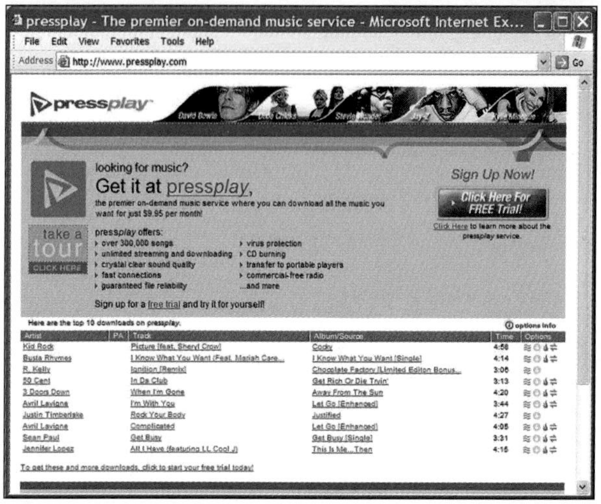

Electronic commerce, or **e-commerce,** is the buying and selling of goods over the Internet. Compared to traditional commerce (**bricks and mortar** business), e-commerce offers advantages to buyers (convenience) and sellers (cost, inventory).

Three basic types of e-commerce are:

- **Business-to-consumer (B2C)**—involves the sale of a product or service to the general public or end users.
- **Consumer-to-consumer (C2C)**—involves individuals selling to individuals.
- **Business-to-business (B2B)**—involves the sale of a product or service from one business to another.

Business-to-Consumer

B2C is fastest growing. Used by small, large, and start-up companies. Applications include:

- **Online banking (e-banking)**—customers perform banking operations online.
- **Online stock trading (e-trading)**—investors research, buy, and sell stocks and bonds; traditional trading 10 times more expensive.
- **Online shopping (e-retailing, e-tailing)**—includes wide range of consumer goods.

Web storefronts are B2C virtual stores. **Web storefront creation packages (commerce servers)** are programs for creating virtual stores.

ELECTRONIC COMMERCE

Consumer-to-Consumer

Web auctions are a growing C2C application of e-commerce. Similar to traditional auctions except that buyers and sellers rarely meet. Two basic types are:

- **Auction house sites** offer wide range of merchandise directly to bidders. Like traditional auctions.
- **Person-to-person sites** like flea market. Sites facilitate bidding process but not involved in completing transactions or verifying authenticity of goods sold.

Security

Security is greatest challenge for e-commerce development. Three basic payment options are: check, credit card, and electronic cash.

- **Check**—most traditional, perhaps safest, but requires most time.
- **Credit**—faster, more convenient than check. Criminals known as **carders** specialize in stealing, trading, and using credit cards over the Internet.
- **Electronic cash (e-cash, cybercash, digital cash)**—Internet equivalent to traditional cash. E-cash purchased and redeemed with third party or bank specializing in electronic cash.

WEB UTILITIES

Plug-in	Source
Acrobat Reader	www.adobe.com
Media Player	www.microsoft.com
QuickTime	www.apple.com
RealPlayer	www.real.com
Shockwave	www.macromedia.com

Web utilities are specialized utility programs that make using the Internet and the Web easier and safer.

Telnet

Telnet is an Internet standard that helps you connect to another computer on the Internet and use that computer as if you were a terminal in the next room.

FTP

FTP (file transfer protocol) is an Internet standard for transferring files. **Downloading** is the process of receiving a file from another computer. **Uploading** is the process of sending a file to another computer.

Plug-ins

Plug-ins are automatically loaded and operate as part of a browser. Many Web sites require specific plug-ins to fully experience their content. Some plug-ins are included in many of today's browsers; other must be installed.

Filters

Filters are used by parents and organizations to block certain sites and to monitor use of the Internet and the Web.

KEY TERMS

address (45)
Advanced Research Project Agency Network (ARPANET) (36)
agent (51)
applet (39)
attachment (45)
auction house site (57)
bot (51)
blog (42)
bricks and mortar (55)
browser (38)
buddy (46)
business-to-business (B2B) (56)
business-to-consumer (B2C) (55)
cable (38)
carder (58)
Center for European Nuclear Research (CERN) (36)
channel (50)
chat group (50)
client (38)
client-server network (38)
commerce servers (57)
computer virus (46)
contact (46)
consumer-to-consumer (C2C) (56)
cybercash (58)
cybermall (36)
dial-up (38)
digital cash (38)
directory (41)
directory search (52)
discussion group (50)
domain code (39)
domain name (39)
downloading (59)
DSL (38)
e-banking (56)
e-cash (58)
e-commerce (55)
e-learning (37)
electronic cash (58)
electronic commerce (55)
electronic mail (44)
e-mail (44)
e-retailing (e-tailing) (56)
e-trading (56)
FAQ (frequently asked questions) (40)
file transfer protocol (FTP) (59)
filter (60)
flaming (51)
frame (40)
friend (46)
header (44)
hit (52)
home page (40)
horizontal portal (40)
host computer (37)
hyperlink (39)
Hypertext Markup Language (HTML) (39)
index search (52)
instant messaging (IM) (46)
Internet (36)
Internet Radio (43)
Internet Relay Chat (IRC) (50)
Internet Service Provider (ISP) (38)
Java (39)
keyword search (52)
link (39)
list address (50)
location (38)
lurking (50)
mailing list (50)
media player (43)
message (45)
metasearch engine (53)
multimedia (43)
national service provider (38)
Net (36)
newsgroup (50)
online (36)
online banking (56)
online shopping (56)
online stock trading (56)
person-person auction site (57)
plug-in (59)
portal (40)
protocol (39)
provider (37)
regional service provider (38)
search engine (51)
search provider (51)
search service (51)
server (38)
signature line (45)
site index (40)
site map (40)
spam (46)
specialized search engine (53)
spider (51)
streaming audio (43)
streaming media (43)
streaming video (43)
subject (45)
subscription address (50)
surf (38)
Telnet (59)
uniform resource locator (URL) (38)
universal instant messenger (46)
uploading (59)
UseNet (50)
vertical portal (41)
virtual library (37)
Web (36)
Web auction (57)
Webcasting (43)
Weblog (42)
Web page (39)
Web portal (40)
Web site (40)
Web server (39)
Web storefront creation package (57)
Web storefront (57)
Web utility (59)
wireless modem (38)
wireless service provider (38)
World Wide Web (36)
WWW (36)

To test your knowledge of these key terms with animated flash cards, select Flash Cards from Tim's Toolbox at http://www.mhhe.com/oleary/CT05.

CHAPTER REVIEW

Interactive crossword puzzles are available by selecting Crosswords from Tim's Toolbox at http://www.mhhe.com/oleary/CT05.

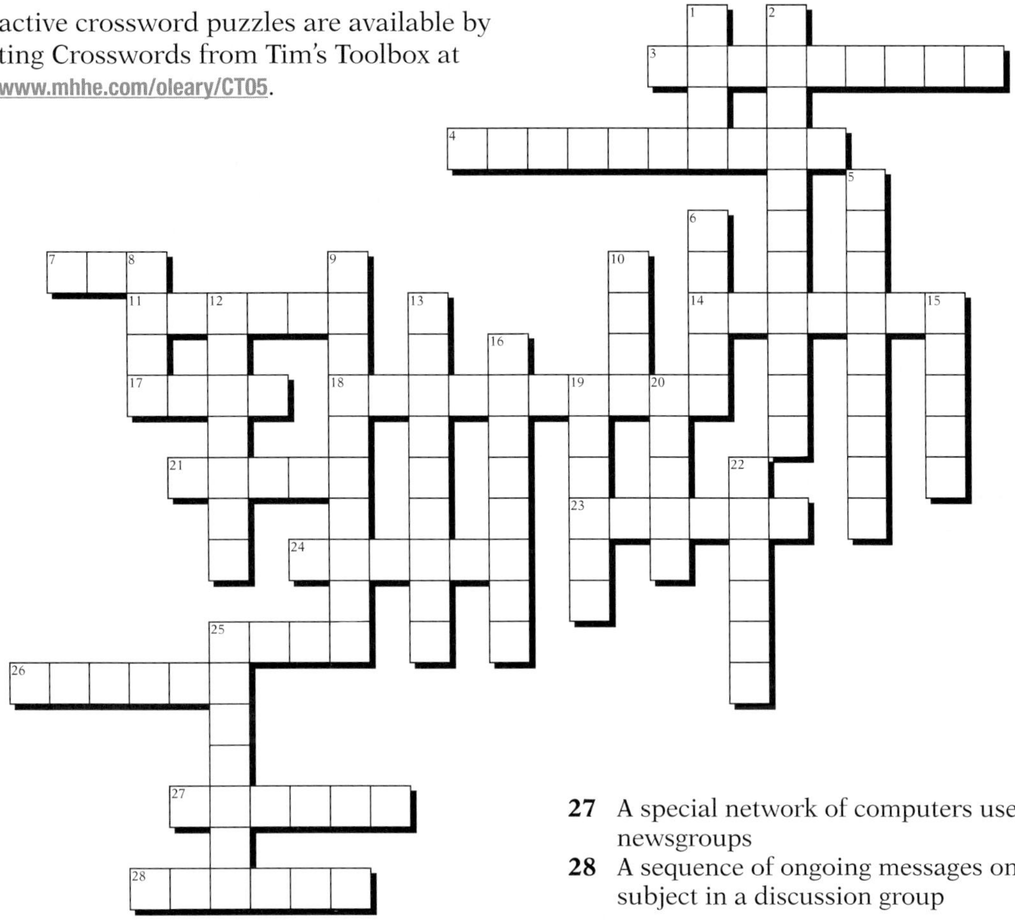

ACROSS

3 Copying files from your computer to another computer on the Internet
4 A file that is attached to an e-mail message
7 Multimedia interface to connect to the Internet
11 Being connected to the Internet
14 Another word for the location of resources on the Web; browsers look for these
17 To explore the Web
18 The space of electronic movement of ideas and information
21 Destructive programs
23 A Web utility that makes working with the Web and the Internet easier and safer
24 Someone who has comprehensive knowledge about a subject
25 This type of page is easily updatable and is commonly used as a diary of events
26 Program that continually updates search engines and databases
27 A special network of computers used by newsgroups
28 A sequence of ongoing messages on the same subject in a discussion group

DOWN

1 Unwelcome mail
2 The process of receiving a file from another computer
5 Connects to other documents containing related information—text files, graphic images, audio, and video clips
6 Scrollable windows
8 Programs that continually update search engines and databases
9 Process of broadcasting audio or video over the Internet
10 Programming language of choice used to create applets
12 Reading news but not joining in to contribute
13 Provides access to a variety of stores online
15 Someone who aids new users in an online discussion group by answering questions
16 Gives us access to the Internet
19 Along with directories, offers navigational and organizational services
20 One type of connection technology
22 The provider's computer
25 Program that provides access to Web resources

MULTIPLE CHOICE

Circle the letter or fill in the correct answer.

1. The Internet was launched in 1969 when the United States funded a project to develop a national computer network called ________.
   a. ARPANET
   b. CERN
   c. the Web
   d. WWW
   e. IRC
2. ________ use telephone lines and service an area limited to several states.
   a. Wireless service providers
   b. National service providers
   c. Local service providers
   d. Regional service providers
   e. Commercial ISPs
3. ________ present focused content to appeal to special-interest groups.
   a. Agents
   b. Horizontal portals
   c. Vertical portals
   d. Web portals
   e. UseNets
4. To participate in a chat group, select a ________ and communicate live with others.
   a. signal
   b. index
   c. engine
   d. list
   e. channel
5. ________ connect(s) to remote computers, open(s) and transfer(s) files, display(s) text and images, and provide(s) in one tool an uncomplicated interface to the Internet and Web.
   a. Bots
   b. Browsers
   c. Java
   d. Web utilities
   e. Wizards
6. In a directory or ________ search, you select a category that fits the information you want.
   a. packet
   b. keyword
   c. index
   d. specialized
   e. subject
7. In ________ commerce, individuals typically sell to other individuals without ever meeting face-to-face.
   a. C2C
   b. B2C
   c. B2B
   d. C2I
   e. I2I
8. ________ is a technique for delivering audio and video files over a network without downloading an entire file before it plays.
   a. IRC
   b. Internet radio
   c. Streaming media
   d. Simulcast
   e. UseNet
9. ________ are programs that are automatically loaded and operate as part of a browser.
   a. Plug-ins
   b. Add-ons
   c. Providers
   d. Agents
   e. Applets
10. ________ are catalogs of sites organized by subject.
    a. Directories
    b. Web logs
    c. Browsers
    d. Search engines
    e. a and d

MATCHING

Match each numbered item with the most closely related lettered item. Write your answers in the spaces provided.

- **a.** applets
- **b.** bots
- **c.** carders
- **d.** commerce server
- **e.** cyberspace
- **f.** e-cash
- **g.** e-commerce
- **h.** header
- **i.** hits
- **j.** hyperlink
- **k.** lurking
- **l.** metasearch engine
- **m.** provider
- **n.** signature line
- **o.** subscription address
- **p.** surfing
- **q.** URLs
- **r.** Web auction
- **s.** Web site
- **t.** Web storefronts

1. The space of electronic movement of ideas and information. ____
2. The most common way to access the Internet. ____
3. Addresses of Web resources. ____
4. Moving from one Web site to another. ____
5. Special programs written in Java. ____
6. A group of related Web pages. ____
7. Part of an e-mail message that includes the subject, address, and attachments. ____
8. Typically includes the sender's name, address, and telephone number. ____
9. To participate in a mailing list, you must send a request to this address. ____
10. Link that connects to other documents. ____
11. Reading and observing discussions without participating. ____
12. Special programs that look for new information and update a search service database. ____
13. The list of sites that contain the keywords of a keyword search. ____
14. Program that automatically submits a search request to several search engines simultaneously. ____
15. Buying and selling goods over the Internet. ____
16. Program for creating Web sites for virtual stores. ____
17. Virtual stores where shoppers inspect goods and make purchases. ____
18. Similar to a traditional auction, but buyers and sellers interact only on the Web. ____
19. Criminals that specialize in stealing, trading, and using stolen credit cards over the Internet. ____
20. Internet equivalent to traditional cash. ____

OPEN-ENDED

On a separate sheet of paper, respond to each question or statement.

1. Discuss the uses of the Internet. Which activities have you participated in? Which one do you think is the most popular?
2. Explain the differences between the three types of providers.
3. What are the basic elements of an e-mail message?
4. What are the types of discussion groups? Describe any groups you participate in.
5. Describe the different types of search engines. Give an example of the type of search each engine is best for.

To test your knowledge of this chapter, select Self Test from Tim's Toolbox at http://www.mhhe.com/oleary/CT05.

USING TECHNOLOGY

1 Instant Messaging

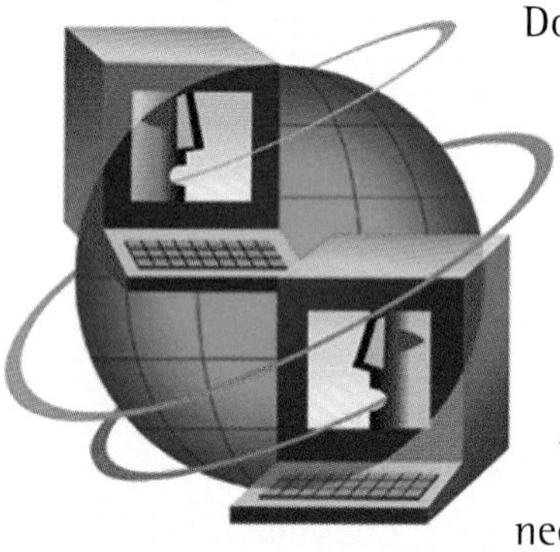

Do you enjoy chatting with your friends? Are you working on a project and need to collaborate with others in your group? Perhaps instant messaging is just what you're looking for. It's easy and free with an Internet connection and the right software. To learn more about instant messaging, review Making IT Work for You: Instant Messaging on pages 48 and 49. Then complete the following questions (a) What is Windows Messenger? What is it used for? (b) What is video conferencing? What equipment is needed to video conference? Describe a situation in which you might use video conferencing? (c) What is an Internet phone call? How is it different from a traditional telephone call? How is it similar?

2 Online Shopping

Shopping on the Internet can be fast and convenient. Connect to our Web site at http://www.mhhe.com/oleary/CT05 and select Using Technology from Tim's Toolbox to link to a popular shopping site. Once there, try shopping for one or two products, and answer the following questions: (a) What product(s) did you shop for? Could you find the product(s) at the site? If not, then search for another product(s) that you can locate at the site. (b) Describe your experience. Was the site easy to use? Did you find it easy to locate the product(s)? What are the pros and cons of shopping online versus a traditional store? Are there any products or circumstances in which you would more likely shop online? (c) Have you ever purchased anything online? If you have, describe what you bought and why you bought it online. If you have not, do you expect to in the near future? Why or why not?

Web Auctions 3

Web auctions have been a phenomenal success on the Internet. Using online auctions, individuals can list items for sale and submit bids for items listed. Connect to our Web site at http://www.mhhe.com/oleary/CT05 and select Using Technology from Tim's Toolbox to link to a popular online auction. Once there, read about how the auction works and check out a few of the items up for bid. Answer the following questions: (a) What are the advantages of using a Web auction to purchase items? What are the disadvantages? (b) What are the advantages and disadvantages to selling an item on an online auction, as opposed to a traditional method (such as a classified ad in the newspaper)? (c) What assurances are there that buyers will get what they paid for? What is the site's fraud policy? (d) Have you ever bought or sold an item at an online auction? If you have, describe what you bought and how you bought it. If you have not, do you think that you will in the near future? Why or why not?

Internet Radio 4

Internet Radio is an increasingly popular form of Webcasting. Many Web sites act as directories listing available Internet Radio "stations." Some even offer services that allow you to become an Internet DJ. Connect to our Web site at http://www.mhhe.com/oleary/CT05 and select Using Technology from Tim's Toolbox to link to a site that offers Internet Radio. Explore the site, listen to an Internet Radio station of your choice, and then answer the following questions: (a) What software is required to use Internet Radio? (b) How is Internet Radio different from traditional radio? In what ways is it better? How is it worse? (c) Have you listened to Internet Radio before? If you have, describe how often you listen to it and why you use it rather than traditional radio broadcasts. If you have not, do you think you will listen to Internet Radio again in the near future? Why or why not?

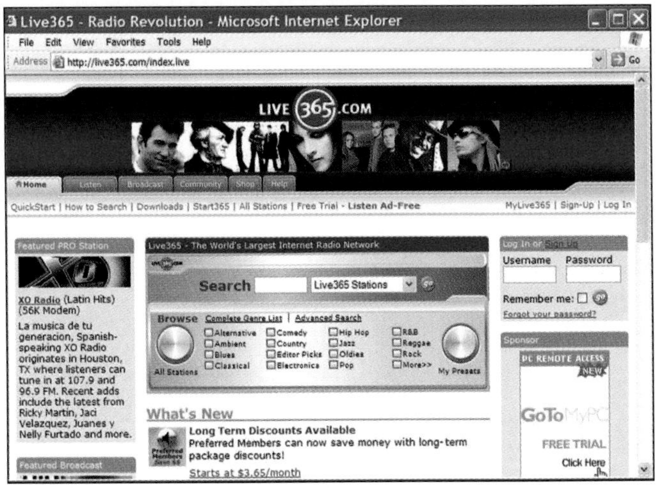

EXPANDING YOUR KNOWLEDGE

1

Computing Today CD

One of the fastest growing applications on the Internet is instant messaging. This extension to e-mail provides a way for friends and colleagues to communicate and share information from almost anywhere in the world. After viewing the instant messaging animation from your Computing Today CD or from Tim's Toolbox at http://www.mhhe.com/oleary/CT05 and studying Figure 2-22, consider the following:

As described in Step 4: Communicate, Linda, Steve, and Chris agree to meet for a movie. Then, Chris tells them that he has to leave for school and disconnects. Linda and Steve continue talking with Linda asking Steve, "Have you seen any good movies lately?"

On a single page of paper, create a drawing similar to Figure 2-22 that describes these events beginning with Step 5 when Chris says, "Bye for now—I have to leave for school."

2

Wireless Service Providers

One way for mobile users to connect to the Internet is through a wireless service provider. These providers can be found in a variety of ways including Web sites known as wireless service provider locators. Find one of these locators and use it to locate a service provider near you. Then answer the following questions: (a) Describe how the locator service works and list a few wireless providers you found. (b) What special equipment or software does a user need to connect to these providers? (c) What fees are associated with using wireless access at these locations? (d) How might expanded wireless Internet access change the way people use the Internet? Be specific in your predictions, and explain your answer.

EXPANDING YOUR KNOWLEDGE

SimNet CD 3

Complete Chapter 2: The Internet, The Web, and Electronic Commerce on your SimNet CD and then answer the following on a single page of paper.

a. Why have free ISPs not worked in the past?
b. Identify each of the numbered items on the screen below.
c. Describe the different domain codes.
d. Describe the languages other than HTML that are used to create Web pages.
e. What is the special connection that Word 2000, PowerPoint 2000, and Excel 2000 have with e-mail?

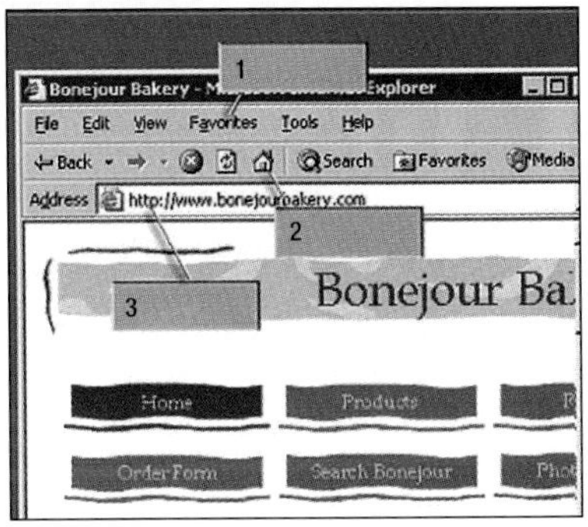

f. Discuss the different methods of communicating over the Internet.
g. What is the best way to write a search query?
h. Describe the different e-commerce business models.
i. Discuss the ways that you can increase the security of online transactions.

Domain Registration 4

Having a domain name is essential to many businesses on the Web. Individuals and businesses do not *own* domain names. Instead, names such as "yahoo.com" are *registered* with a domain name registrar for an annual fee. Conduct a Web search to locate a domain name registrar site. Review the process for registering a domain name and address the following questions: (a) List the steps involved in registering a domain name. (b) What is the cost for registering a domain name? (c) How long can a domain name be registered for? What happens if a domain name registration is not renewed after this time?

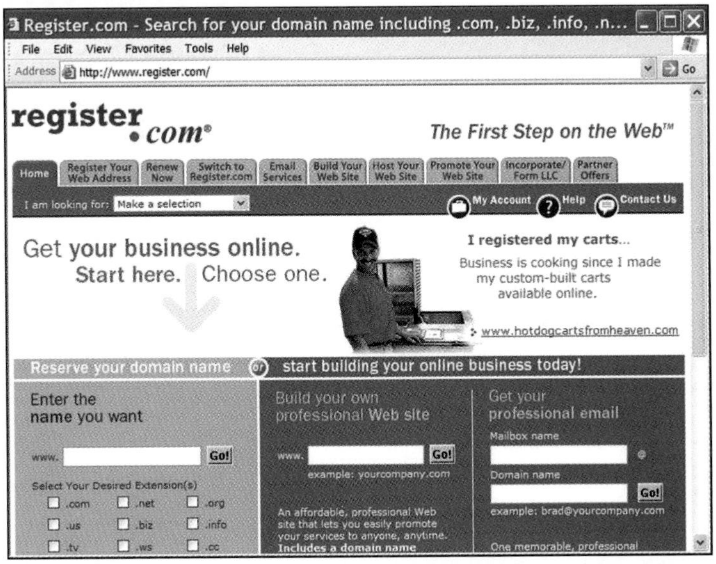

BUILDING YOUR PORTFOLIO

1 Electronic Commerce

Electronic commerce is one of the most exciting Web applications. Write a one-page paper titled "Electronic Commerce" that addresses the following in a one-page paper: (a) Define electronic commerce including B2C, C2C, and B2B. Provide examples. Compare it to traditional bricks and mortar businesses. (b) What types of businesses and consumers are most affected by electronic commerce today? What types will be affected in the future? Discuss and justify your positions. (c) What are the greatest challenges to future developments in electronic commerce? Discuss and justify your conclusions.

2 Web Portals

Web portals are the first stop for many who use the Internet. Write a one page paper titled "Web Portals" that addresses the following: (a) Define Web portals including vertical and horizontal portals, citing examples of each. (b) What features are common to Web portals? (c) Do Web portals enhance the Internet experience? Are there ways that portals limit the experience? Justify your answers.

Free Speech Online 3

Some feel that there is too much objectionable material allowed on the Internet, whereas others argue that the Internet should be completely uncensored. Consider these two viewpoints and answer the following questions in a one-page paper: (a) Should religious groups be allowed to distribute information over the Internet? What about groups that advocate hatred or oppression? (b) Is there any material you feel should not be freely available on the Web? What about child pornography? (c) If you think some regulation is required, who should determine what restrictions should be imposed? (d) The Internet is not "owned" by a particular group or country. What limitations does this impose on enforcement of restrictions?

Dot-Bombs 4

After the initial boom of e-commerce, many Internet-based businesses ran out of funding and pulled the plug. There is much speculation about why these sites, often referred to as "dot-bombs," failed to succeed in the new market the Web has created. Research two or three articles that speculate about such business collapses and address the following items in a one-page paper: (a) Summarize the reasons cited for the "dot-bombs." Do these reasons seem justified? Why or why not? (b) What types of businesses have been successful in e-commerce? What types have become "dot-bombs"? Be specific. (c) Make a prediction about the future of e-commerce. Will doing business online become more commonplace, or is it just a trend that will pass? Explain your answer.

BASIC APPLICATION SOFTWARE

OBJECTIVES

After you have read this chapter, you should be able to:

1. Discuss common features of most software applications.
2. Discuss word processors and word processing features.
3. Describe spreadsheets and spreadsheet features.
4. Discuss database management systems and database management features.
5. Describe presentation graphics and presentation graphics features.
6. Discuss integrated software and software suites.
7. Describe ways to share data between applications.

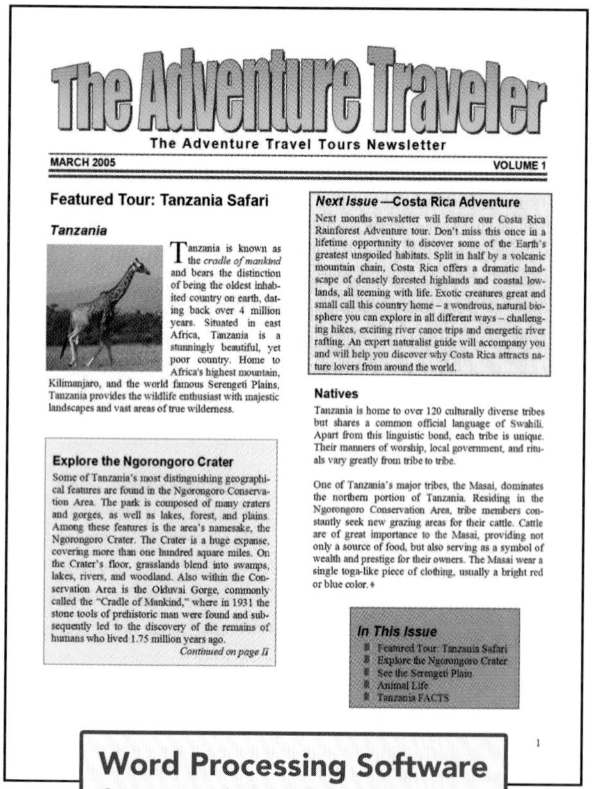

The Adventure Traveler

The Adventure Travel Tours Newsletter

MARCH 2005 VOLUME 1

Featured Tour: Tanzania Safari

Tanzania

Tanzania is known as the *cradle of mankind* and bears the distinction of being the oldest inhabited country on earth, dating back over 4 million years. Situated in east Africa, Tanzania is a stunningly beautiful, yet poor country. Home to Africa's highest mountain, Kilimanjaro, and the world famous Serengeti Plains, Tanzania provides the wildlife enthusiast with majestic landscapes and vast areas of true wilderness.

Explore the Ngorongoro Crater

Some of Tanzania's most distinguishing geographical features are found in the Ngorongoro Conservation Area. The park is composed of many craters and gorges, as well as lakes, forest, and plains. Among these features is the area's namesake, the Ngorongoro Crater. The Crater is a huge expanse, covering more than one hundred square miles. On the Crater's floor, grasslands blend into swamps, lakes, rivers, and woodland. Also within the Conservation Area is the Olduvai Gorge, commonly called the "Cradle of Mankind," where in 1931 the stone tools of prehistoric man were found and subsequently led to the discovery of the remains of humans who lived 1.75 million years ago.

Continued on page II

***Next Issue*—Costa Rica Adventure**

Next months newsletter will feature our Costa Rica Rainforest Adventure tour. Don't miss this once in a lifetime opportunity to discover some of the Earth's greatest unspoiled habitats. Split in half by a volcanic mountain chain, Costa Rica offers a dramatic landscape of densely forested highlands and coastal lowlands, all teeming with life. Exotic creatures great and small call this country home – a wondrous, natural biosphere you can explore in all different ways – challenging hikes, exciting river canoe trips and energetic river rafting. An expert naturalist guide will accompany you and will help you discover why Costa Rica attracts nature lovers from around the world.

Natives

Tanzania is home to over 120 culturally diverse tribes but shares a common official language of Swahili. Apart from this linguistic bond, each tribe is unique. Their manners of worship, local government, and rituals vary greatly from tribe to tribe.

One of Tanzania's major tribes, the Masai, dominates the northern portion of Tanzania. Residing in the Ngorongoro Conservation Area, tribe members constantly seek new grazing areas for their cattle. Cattle are of great importance to the Masai, providing not only a source of food, but also serving as a symbol of wealth and prestige for their owners. The Masai wear a single toga-like piece of clothing, usually a bright red or blue color. ♦

In This Issue

- Featured Tour: Tanzania Safari
- Explore the Ngorongoro Crater
- See the Serengeti Plain
- Animal Life
- Tanzania FACTS

1

Word Processing Software
Create text-based documents

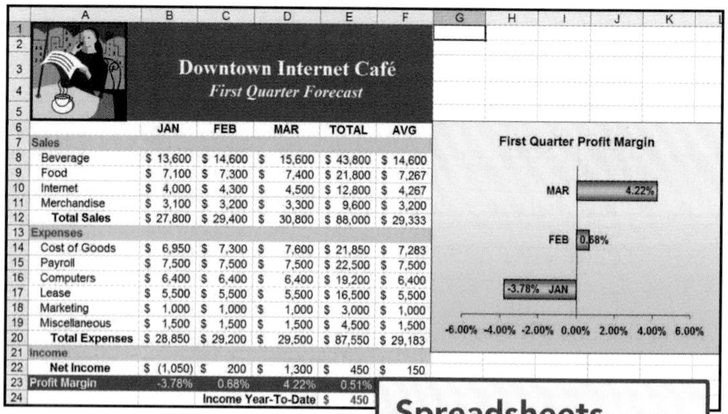

Downtown Internet Café

First Quarter Forecast

	JAN	FEB	MAR	TOTAL	AVG
Sales					
Beverage	$ 13,600	$ 14,600	$ 15,600	$ 43,800	$ 14,600
Food	$ 7,100	$ 7,300	$ 7,400	$ 21,800	$ 7,267
Internet	$ 4,000	$ 4,300	$ 4,500	$ 12,800	$ 4,267
Merchandise	$ 3,100	$ 3,200	$ 3,300	$ 9,600	$ 3,200
Total Sales	$ 27,800	$ 29,400	$ 30,800	$ 88,000	$ 29,333
Expenses					
Cost of Goods	$ 6,950	$ 7,300	$ 7,600	$ 21,850	$ 7,283
Payroll	$ 7,500	$ 7,500	$ 7,500	$ 22,500	$ 7,500
Computers	$ 6,400	$ 6,400	$ 6,400	$ 19,200	$ 6,400
Lease	$ 5,500	$ 5,500	$ 5,500	$ 16,500	$ 5,500
Marketing	$ 1,000	$ 1,000	$ 1,000	$ 3,000	$ 1,000
Miscellaneous	$ 1,500	$ 1,500	$ 1,500	$ 4,500	$ 1,500
Total Expenses	$ 28,850	$ 29,200	$ 29,500	$ 87,550	$ 29,183
Income					
Net Income	$ (1,050)	$ 200	$ 1,300	$ 450	$ 150
Profit Margin	-3.78%	0.68%	4.22%	0.51%	
		Income Year-To-Date		$ 450	

Spreadsheets
Use functions and formulas to analyze numeric data

Not long ago, trained specialists were required to perform many of the operations you can now do with a microcomputer. Secretaries used typewriters to create business correspondence. Market analysts used calculators to project sales. Graphic artists created designs by hand. Data processing clerks created electronic files to be stored on large computers. Now you can do all these tasks—and many others—with a microcomputer and the appropriate application software.

Think of the microcomputer as an electronic tool. You may not consider yourself very good at typing, calculating, organizing, presenting, or managing information. A microcomputer, however, can help you to do all these things—and much more. All it takes is the right kinds of software.

You are probably most familiar with the software available for sale in retail stores. You purchase these programs, store them on your hard disk, and run them. An emerging trend, however, is to use Web-based applications. These are programs you access from the Internet and run on your microcomputer.

Competent and knowledgeable end users need to understand the capabilities of basic application software, which includes word processors, spreadsheets, database management systems, and presentation programs. They need to know how to effectively use application programs and how to share data between applications.

APPLICATION SOFTWARE

Basic and specialized are the two categories of application software. Common interface features include icons, windows, menus, dialog boxes, help, toolbars, and buttons. ASPs provide access to Web-based applications.

As we discussed in Chapter 1, there are two kinds of software. **System software** works with end users, application software, and computer hardware to handle the majority of technical details. **Application software** can be described as end user software. It is used by end users to accomplish a variety of different tasks.

Application software in turn can be divided into two categories. One category, **basic applications,** is the focus of this chapter. These programs, also known as **general-purpose applications** and **productivity applications,** are widely used in nearly every discipline and occupation. They include word processors, spreadsheets, database management systems, and presentation graphics. The other category, **specialized applications,** also known as **special-purpose applications,** includes thousands of other programs that are more narrowly focused on specific disciplines and occupations. Some of the best known are graphics programs, audio/video editors, multimedia creation programs, Web authoring, and virtual reality programs. (A detailed discussion of these specialized applications is presented in Chapter 4.)

On the Web Explorations

Microsoft is one of the leaders in creating software applications. To learn more about the company, visit our Web site at http://www.mhhe.com/oleary/CT05 and select On the Web Explorations from Tim's Toolbox.

COMMON FEATURES

A **user interface** is the portion of the application that you work with. Most applications use a **graphical user interface (GUI)** that displays graphical elements called **icons** to represent familiar objects and a mouse. The mouse controls a **pointer** on the screen that is used to select items such as icons. Another feature is the use of windows to display information. A **window** is simply a rectangular area that can contain a document, program, or message. (Do not confuse the term *window* with the various versions of Microsoft's Windows operating systems, which are programs.) More than one window can be opened and displayed on the computer screen at one time. For example, one window might contain a graphics program, another a spreadsheet program, and yet another a word processing program. (See Figure 3-1.)

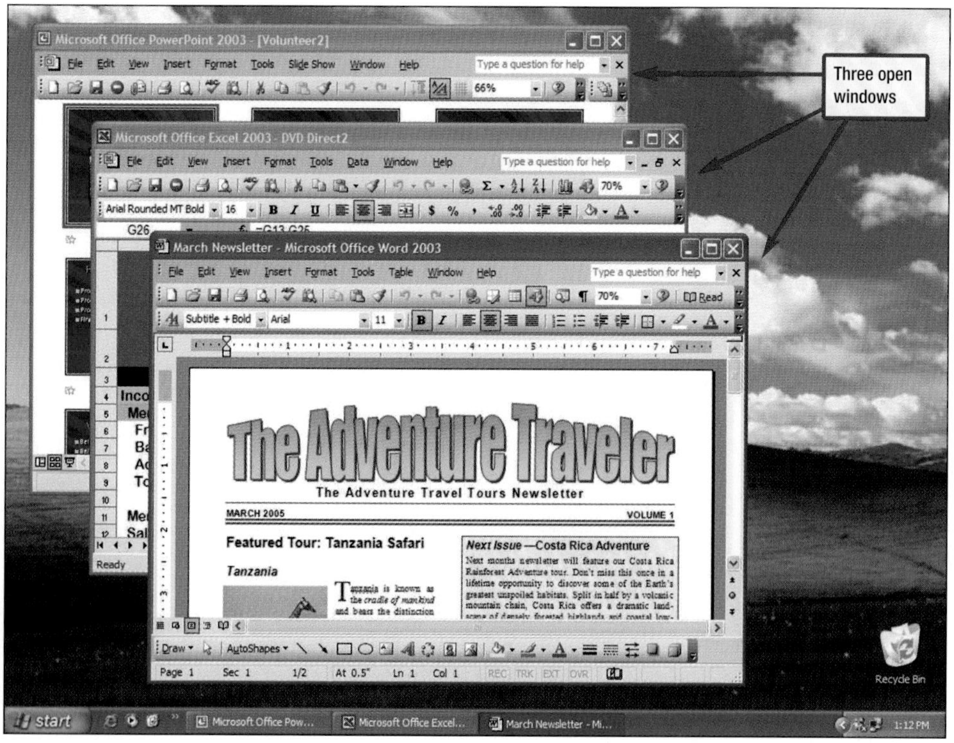

Figure 3-1 Three windows

Almost all software programs have **menus** to present commands. Typically, menus are displayed in a **menu bar** at the top of the screen. When one of the menu items is selected, a **pull-down** or **drop-down menu** appears. This is a list of options or commands associated with the selected menu. Selecting one of these options may display an additional list of menu options or a **dialog box** that provides additional information and requests user input. One of the commands on the menu bar is **Help.** This option provides access to a variety of Help features and acts as an online reference manual for the application. It is an invaluable resource for learning and using application programs.

Toolbars typically are below the menu bar. They contain small outlined areas called **buttons** that provide shortcuts for quick access to commonly used commands. For example, the **standard toolbar** contains a variety of buttons that are common to most applications including those to open, save, and print files. (See Figure 3-2.) All Microsoft Office applications have a common user interface, including similar commands and menu structures. (See Figure 3-3.)

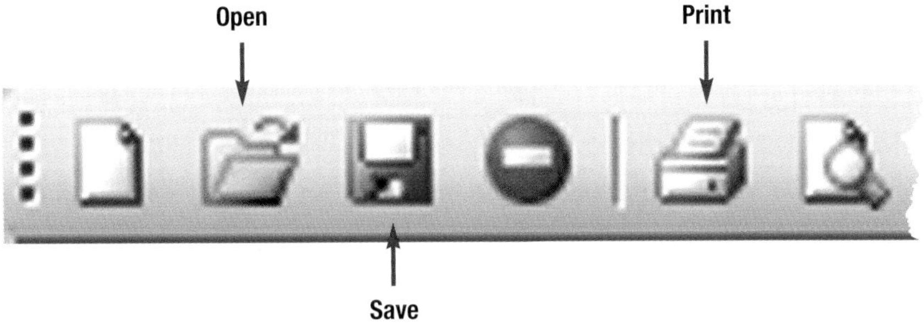

Figure 3-2 Common features on the standard toolbar

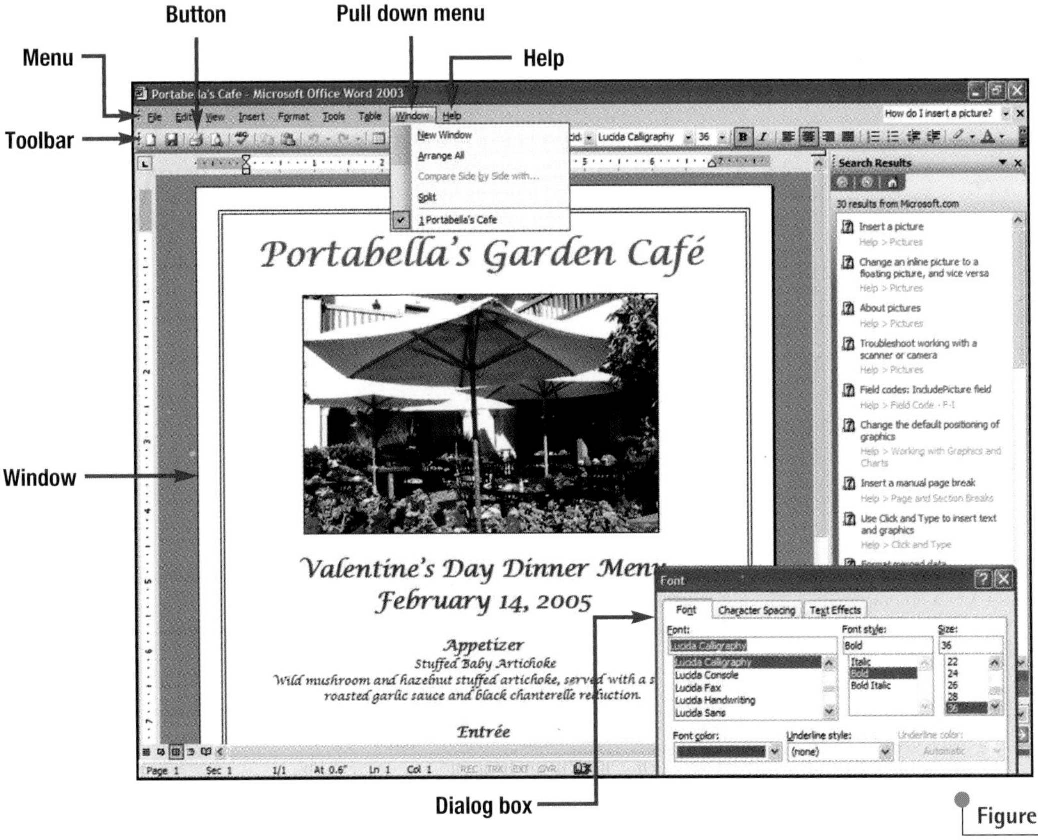

Figure 3-3 Common features

Term	Description
Clip Art	Collection of graphic illustrations including drawings, diagrams, and photographs that can be inserted into documents.
Cut, Copy, Paste	Selected items or portions of a document can be deleted (cut), copied, and inserted (paste) from one location to another.
Handwriting Recognition	Ability to accept handwritten text and drawings as input.
Spelling Checker	Identifies misspelled words and suggests alternative spellings.
Task Panes	Appear automatically to provide quick access to commands related to the current tasks being performed.
Templates	Blank forms that supply a basic structure or format for a variety of different types of documents.
Undo	Reverses (undo) the last action performed.
Voice Recognition	Ability to accept voice input for dictating text and issuing commands.
Wizards	Provide step-by-step guidance for users to perform specific tasks.

Figure 3-4 Additional common software features

The table in Figure 3-4 lists some additional common software application features.

WEB-BASED APPLICATIONS

Typically, application programs are owned by individuals or organizations and stored on their computer system's hard disks. For the application to be used, a copy of the program (or part of the program) is read into the computer system's memory. An emerging trend, however, is to free users from owning and storing applications by using Web-based applications.

Special Web sites, called **application service providers (ASPs),** allow access to their application programs. To use one of these **Web-based applications,** you would connect to the ASP, copy the application program to your computer system's memory, and then run the application. Most ASPs provide access to a wide range of application programs and charge a fee for their service. To see how Web-based applications work, see Figure 3-5. Also see Making IT Work for You: Web-based Applications on pages 84 and 85, and consult your Computing Today CD or select Animations from Tim's Toolbox at http://www.mhhe.com/oleary/CT05.

Computing Today CD

Concept Check

- What is the difference between basic and specialized applications?
- What are user interfaces, icons, and windows?
- What are menus, dialog boxes, toolbars, and buttons?
- What are Web-based applications?

How Web-based Applications Work

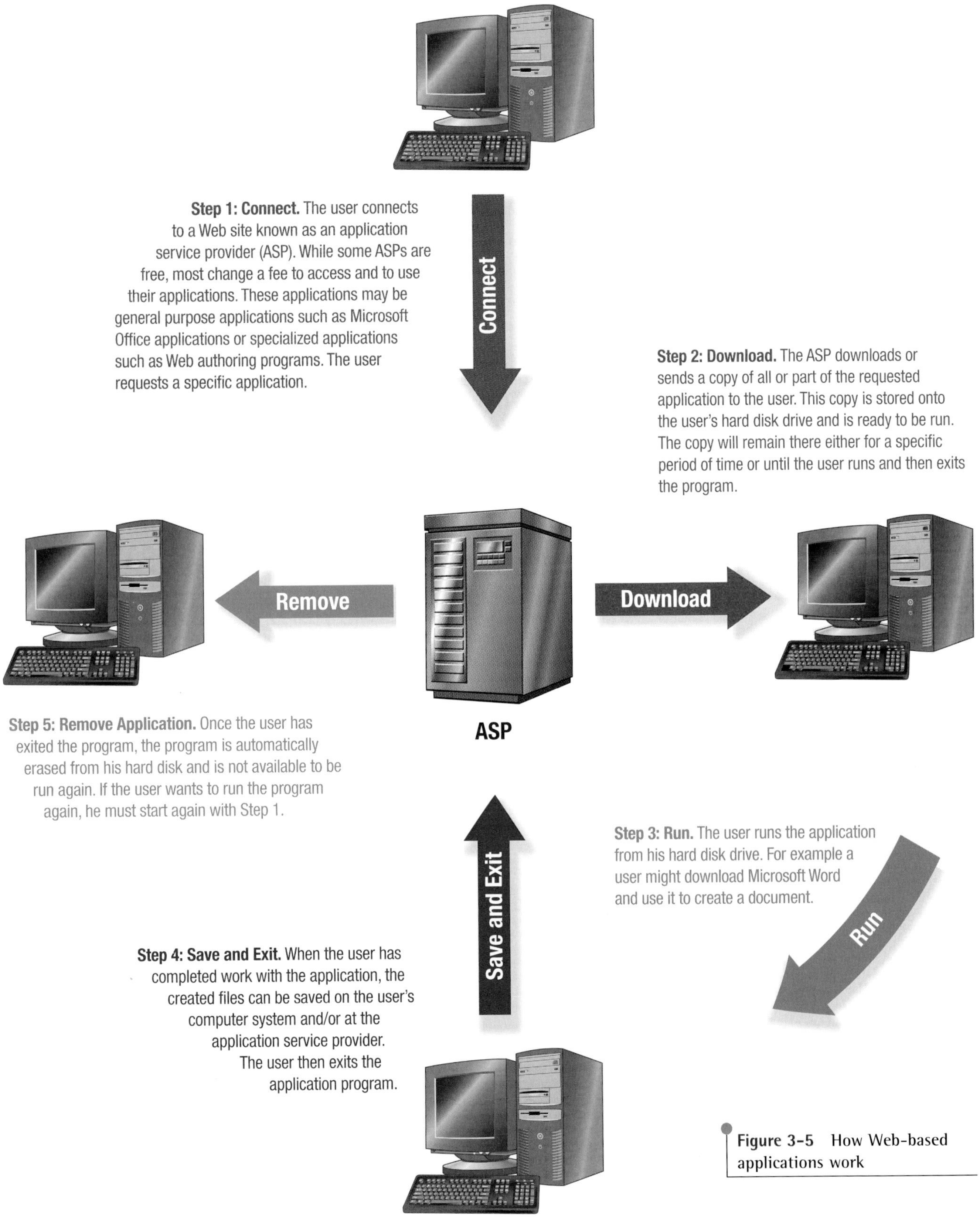
Step 1: Connect. The user connects to a Web site known as an application service provider (ASP). While some ASPs are free, most change a fee to access and to use their applications. These applications may be general purpose applications such as Microsoft Office applications or specialized applications such as Web authoring programs. The user requests a specific application.
Connect
Step 2: Download. The ASP downloads or sends a copy of all or part of the requested application to the user. This copy is stored onto the user's hard disk drive and is ready to be run. The copy will remain there either for a specific period of time or until the user runs and then exits the program.
Remove
Download
ASP
Step 5: Remove Application. Once the user has exited the program, the program is automatically erased from his hard disk and is not available to be run again. If the user wants to run the program again, he must start again with Step 1.
Step 3: Run. The user runs the application from his hard disk drive. For example a user might download Microsoft Word and use it to create a document.
Run
Save and Exit
Step 4: Save and Exit. When the user has completed work with the application, the created files can be saved on the user's computer system and/or at the application service provider. The user then exits the application program.

Figure 3-5 How Web-based applications work

WEB-BASED APPLICATIONS

Would you like access to free general-purpose applications from anywhere in the world? What about accessing your data files from any location? You can have it all with Web-based applications.

Registering Several ASP sites exist on the Web and some of them offer free services. One of the best-known sites is WebOS. Their only requirement is that you register for their service.

1
- **Connect to *www.WebOS.com.***
- **Click the *free trial* link.**
- **Follow the instructions to register for your account.**

2
- **Once you've signed up for your account, enter your Username and Password.**

The Web-based desktop appears, similar to the figure to the right.

WebOS home page

Free trial link

Web-based desktop

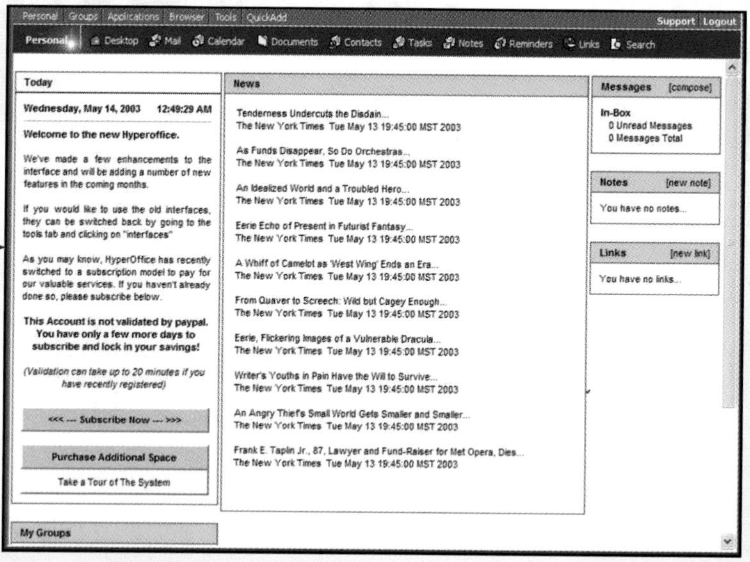

Accessing Applications Each time you connect to the WebOS site and log in, your Web-based desktop will appear. It will display numerous icons that can be used to access Web-based applications. These include notes, personal information manager, calender, and a variety of games.

Notes

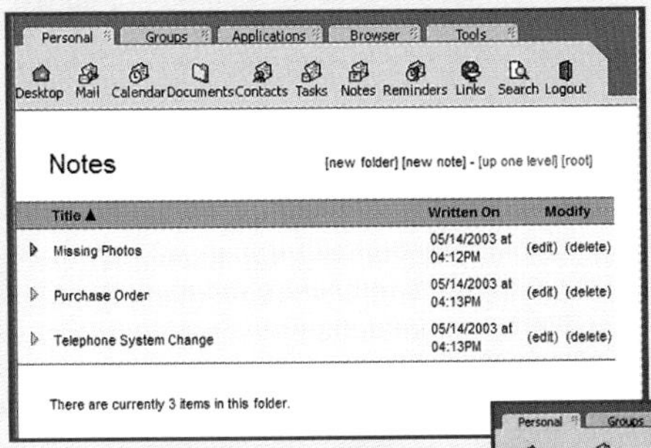

Personal Information Manager

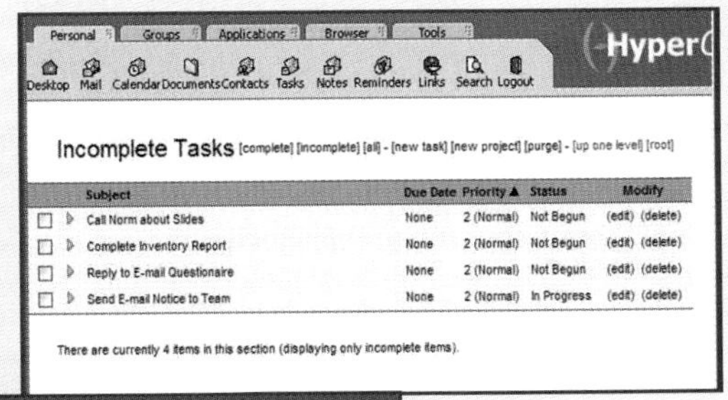

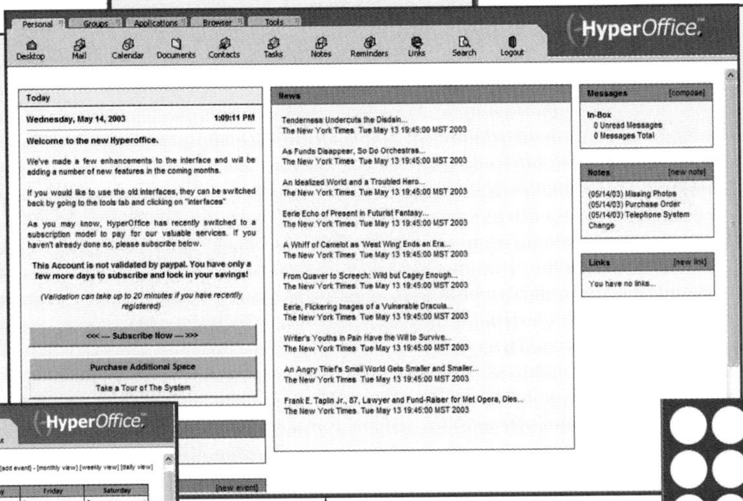

Calendar

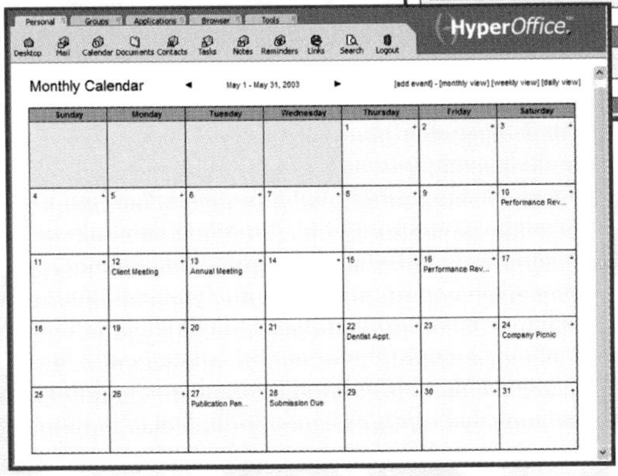

Games

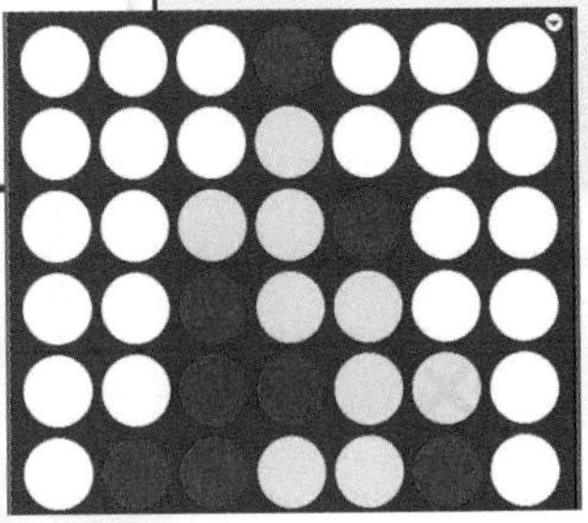

Web-Based Desktop The Web-based desktop looks and operates like the traditional Windows desktop. It contains a variety of icons that are used to load and run applications.

Some suggest that Web-based applications may replace traditional application software some time in the future. They point out that Web-based applications offer advantages beyond universal access to software and to data. One advantage is that users may no longer need to upgrade software on their hard disk when a new version becomes available. Of course, there are some potential disadvantages or challenges of Web-based applications. One challenge relates to privacy and security of personal data stored at an ASP.

The Web is continually changing and some of the specifics presented in this Making IT Work for You may have changed. To learn about other ways to make information technology work for you, visit our Web site at http://www.mhhe.com/oleary/CT05 and select Making IT Work for You from Tim's Toolbox.

WORD PROCESSORS

Word processing software creates text-based documents. Features support entering, editing, and formatting text.

Word processors create text-based **documents** and are one of the most flexible and widely used software tools. All types of people and organizations use word processors to create memos, letters, and faxes. Organizations create newsletters, manuals, and brochures to provide information to their customers. Students and researchers use word processors to create reports. Word processors can even be used to create personalized Web pages.

The three most widely used word processing programs are Microsoft Word, Corel WordPerfect, and Lotus Word Pro.

FEATURES

Word processors provide a variety of features to make entering, editing, and formatting documents easy. One of the most basic features for entering text is **word wrap.** This feature automatically moves the insertion point to the next line once the current line is full. As you type, the words "wrap around" to the next line.

There are numerous features designed to support **editing** or modifying a document. One of these is a **Thesaurus** which provides synonyms, antonyms, and related words for a selected word or phrase. You can quickly locate and replace selected words using the **find and replace** feature. **Spelling** and **grammar checkers** look for misspelled words and problems with capitalization, punctuation, and sentence structure. You can use the **AutoCorrect** feature to automatically make corrections for you. Using **AutoText,** previously specified words or phrases can be directly inserted into a document upon the user's request. Or as the user begins to enter the specified words or phrases, **AutoComplete** will complete the text and enter it into the document at the user's request.

There are numerous features designed to improve the **format** or appearance of a document. These features include:

Font	Sample
Arial	ABCabc
Impact	ABCabc
Times New Roman	ABCabc
Broadway	ABCabc

Figure 3-6 Sample fonts

- **Font** Also known as a **typeface,** a **font** is a set of characters with a specific design. Most word processors offer many different fonts including the four shown in Figure 3-6.
- **Font size** The height of a character is its **font size.** It is typically measured in **points** with each point being approximately 1/72 inch.
- **Character effects** The appearance of characters can be enhanced using such **character effects** as **bold,** ***italic,*** shadow, and colors.
- **Alignment** Text can be aligned or positioned on a line. There are four basic types of **alignment:** left, center, right, and justified.
- **Bulleted** and **numbered lists** Presenting information in bulleted or numbered lists makes the information easy to read. A sequence or list of topics can be presented as a **bulleted list.** A sequence of steps or topics can be organized as a **numbered list.**

Frequently more than one person is involved in creating a document. This is called **collaboration** and many word processors include features to support this activity. One feature is **tracking changes** in which changes to the original document are identified. For example in Figure 3-7, a draft submitted by one person has been revised by others. Their changes and comments are displayed.

The table in Figure 3-8 lists some additional word processing features commonly used to create certain types of documents.

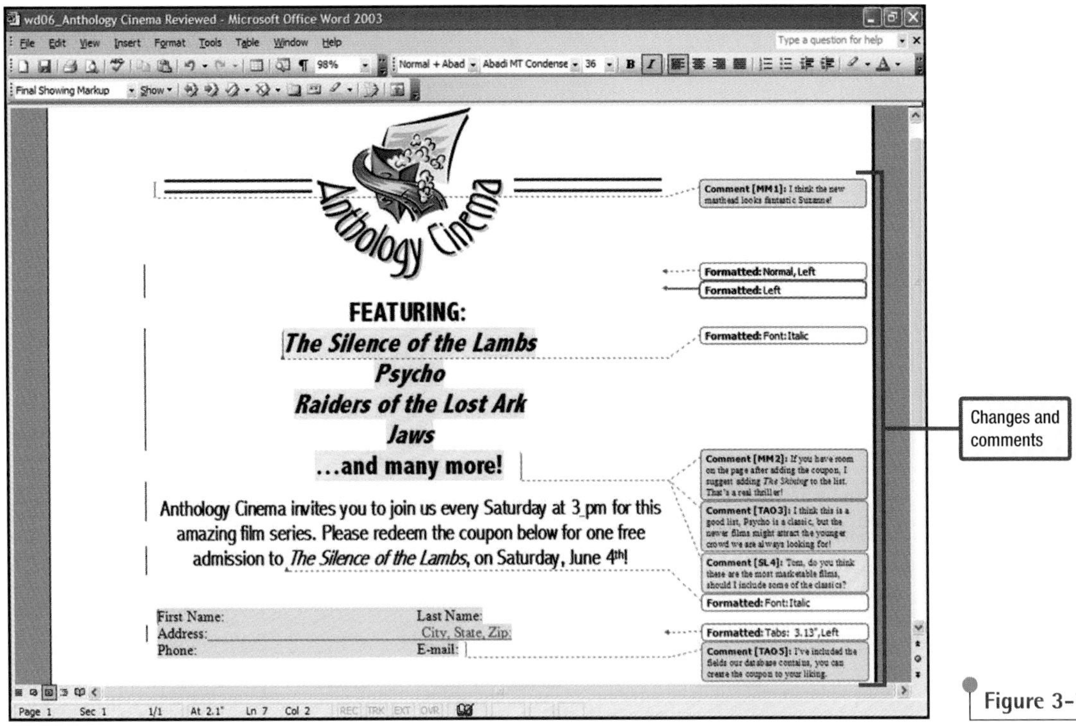

Figure 3-7 Tracking changes

Document	Features
Newsletters	WordArt to artistically modify titles, hyphenation, newsletter-style columns, and text boxes to highlight important information.
Reports	Tools to create figure captions, cross references, tables, headers, footers, footnotes, and endnotes.
Web Pages	Themes or predefined Web templates, hypertext links, and support for publishing Web pages on the Internet.

Figure 3-8 Additional word processing features

CASE

Assume that you have accepted a job as advertising coordinator for Adventure Travel Tours, a travel agency specializing in active adventure vacations. Your primary responsibilities are to create and coordinate the company's promotional materials including flyers, form letters, travel reports, newsletters, and Web pages. To see how you could use Microsoft Word, the most widely used word processing program, as the advertising coordinator for the Adventure Travel Tours, see Figures 3-9 through 3-12.

Concept Check

- ✔ What do word processors do?
- ✔ Describe editing features. Describe formatting features.
- ✔ What is collaboration? What does the tracking changes feature do?

Spelling Checker
Correcting spelling and typing errors identified by the **spelling checker** creates an error-free and professional-appearing document.

Fonts and Font Size
Using interesting **fonts** and a large **font size** in the flyer's title grabs the reader's attention.

Announcing

New Adventure Travel Trips

Attend an Adventure Travel presentation to learn about some of the earth's greatest unspoiled habitats and find out how you can experience the adventure of a lifetime. This year we are introducing four new tours and offering you a unique opportunity to combine many different outdoor activities while exploring the world.

Hike the Inca trail to Machu Picchu
Camp on safari in Tanzania
Climb Mt. Kilimanjaro
Explore the Costa Rican rain forests

Presentation dates and times are January 5 at 7 PM, February 3 at 7:30 PM, and March 8 at 7 PM. All presentations are held at convenient hotel locations. The hotels are located in downtown Los Angeles, Santa Clara and at the airport.

Call 1-800-777-0004 for presentation locations, a full color brochure, and itinerary information, costs, and trip dates.

Center Aligning
Center aligning all of the text in the flyer creates a comfortable balanced appearance.

Word Wrap
The automatic **word wrap** feature frees you to focus your attention on the content of the flyer.

Character Effects
Adding **character effects** such as bold and color makes important information stand out and makes the flyer more visually interesting.

Grammar Checker
Incomplete sentences, awkward wording, and incorrect punctuation are identified and corrections are offered by the **grammar checker**.

Figure 3-9 Flyer

CREATING A FLYER

You have been asked to create an advertising flyer for upcoming promotional presentations. After discussing the flyer's contents and basic structure with your supervisor, you start to enter the flyer's text. As you enter, the text, *words wrap* automotically at the end of each line. Also while entering the text, the *spelling checker* and *grammer checker* catch spelling and grammatical errors. Once the text has been entered, you focus your attention onto enhancing the visual aspects of the flyer. You add an interesting graphic and experiment with different character and paragraph formats including *fonts, font sizes,* colors, and *alignments.*

CREATING A REPORT

Your next assignment is to create a report on Tanzania and Peru. After conducing your research, you start writing your paper. As you enter the text for the report, you notice that the *AutoCorrect* feature automatically corrects some grammar and punctuation errors. Your report includes several figures and *tables*. You use the *captions* feature to keep track of figure and table numbers, to enter the caption text, and to position the captions. When referencing figures or tables from the text, you use the *cross reference* feature. You then carefully document your sources using *footnotes*. Finally, you prepare the report for printing by adding *header* and *footer* information.

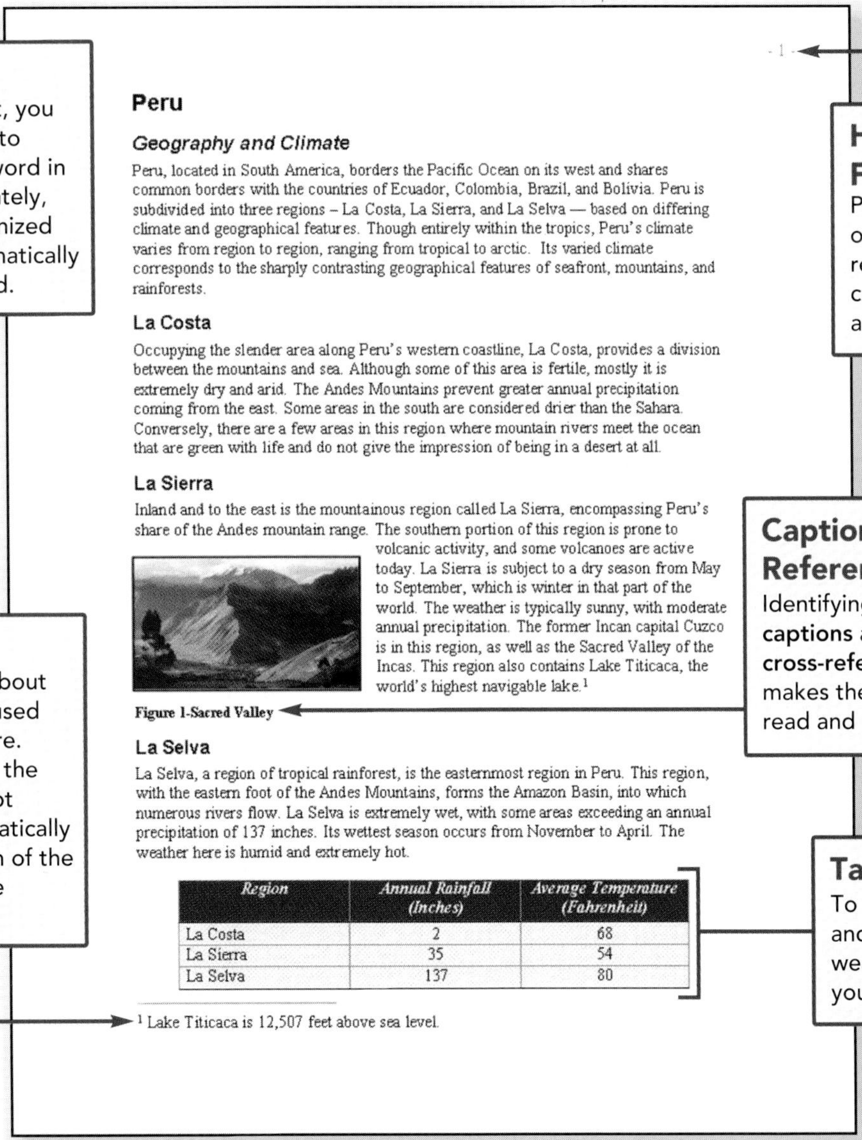
- 1 -

Peru

Geography and Climate

Peru, located in South America, borders the Pacific Ocean on its west and shares common borders with the countries of Ecuador, Colombia, Brazil, and Bolivia. Peru is subdivided into three regions – La Costa, La Sierra, and La Selva — based on differing climate and geographical features. Though entirely within the tropics, Peru's climate varies from region to region, ranging from tropical to arctic. Its varied climate corresponds to the sharply contrasting geographical features of seafront, mountains, and rainforests.

La Costa

Occupying the slender area along Peru's western coastline, La Costa, provides a division between the mountains and sea. Although some of this area is fertile, mostly it is extremely dry and arid. The Andes Mountains prevent greater annual precipitation coming from the east. Some areas in the south are considered drier than the Sahara. Conversely, there are a few areas in this region where mountain rivers meet the ocean that are green with life and do not give the impression of being in a desert at all.

La Sierra

Inland and to the east is the mountainous region called La Sierra, encompassing Peru's share of the Andes mountain range. The southern portion of this region is prone to volcanic activity, and some volcanoes are active today. La Sierra is subject to a dry season from May to September, which is winter in that part of the world. The weather is typically sunny, with moderate annual precipitation. The former Incan capital Cuzco is in this region, as well as the Sacred Valley of the Incas. This region also contains Lake Titicaca, the world's highest navigable lake.[1]

Figure 1-Sacred Valley

La Selva

La Selva, a region of tropical rainforest, is the easternmost region in Peru. This region, with the eastern foot of the Andes Mountains, forms the Amazon Basin, into which numerous rivers flow. La Selva is extremely wet, with some areas exceeding an annual precipitation of 137 inches. Its wettest season occurs from November to April. The weather here is humid and extremely hot.

Region	*Annual Rainfall (Inches)*	*Average Temperature (Fahrenheit)*
La Costa	2	68
La Sierra	35	54
La Selva	137	80

[1] Lake Titicaca is 12,507 feet above sea level.

AutoCorrect
As you entered text, you occasionally forgot to capitalize the first word in a sentence. Fortunately, **AutoCorrect** recognized the error and automatically capitalized the word.

Header or Footer
Page numbers and other document related information can be included in a **header** or **footer**.

Footnote
To include a note about Lake Titicaca, you used the **footnote** feature. This feature inserts the footnote superscript number and automatically formats the bottom of the page to contain the footnote text.

Captions and Cross References
Identifying figures with **captions** and using **cross-references** in a report makes the report easier to read and more professional.

Table
To concisely present and organize the weather information, you used a **table**.

Figure 3-10 Report

Figure 3-11 Newsletter

CREATING A NEWSLETTER

You have been asked to transform the report you created on Tanzania and Peru into a newsletter that will be sent to clients. To begin, you create a unique headline using *WordArt* at the top of the page. Using the text from the Tanzania and Peru report, you create a series of articles and format the articles so that they are displayed in *newsletter-style columns.* To improve the appearance of the text within the columns, you *hyphenate* the text within the columns. You use *text boxes* to focus the reader's attention to selective information. Finally, you use a *bulleted list* to present topics included in the newsletter.

WordArt

The newsletter's title is The Adventure Traveler. To grab the readers' attention, you use **WordArt** to stylize the title by giving it a wavy 3-D appearance.

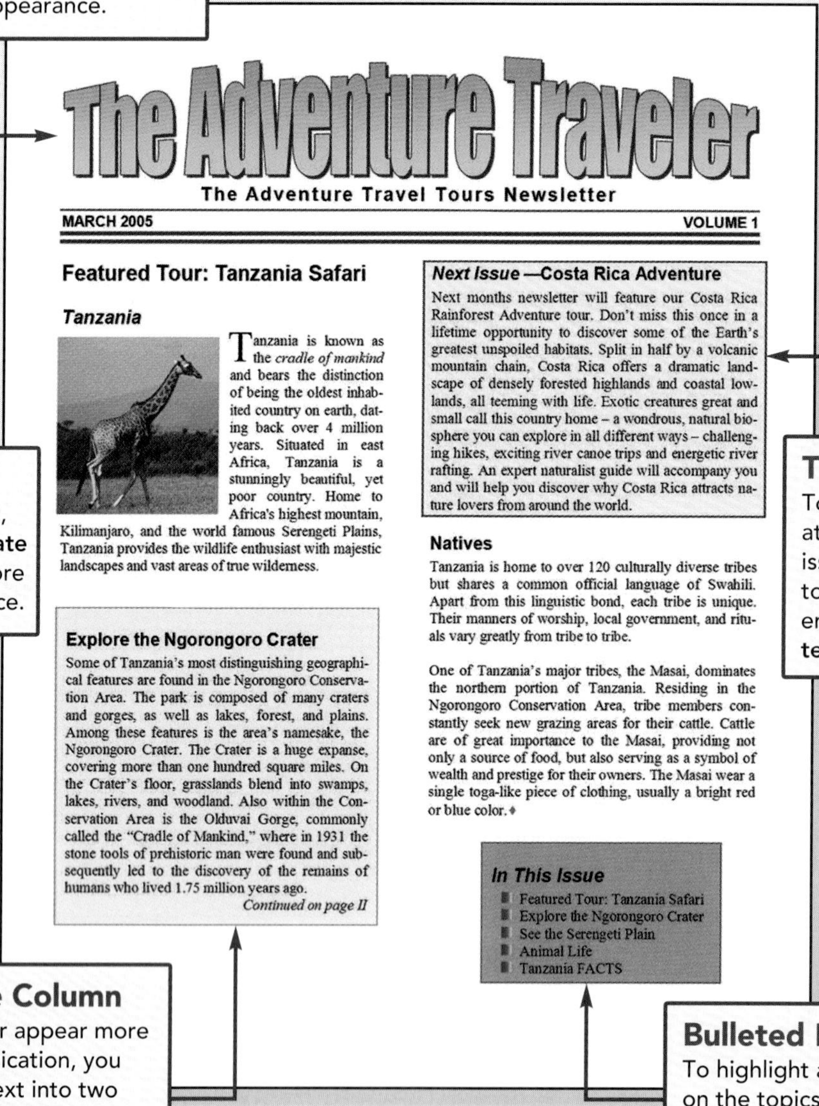

The Adventure Traveler

The Adventure Travel Tours Newsletter

MARCH 2005 VOLUME 1

Featured Tour: Tanzania Safari

Tanzania

Tanzania is known as the *cradle of mankind* and bears the distinction of being the oldest inhabited country on earth, dating back over 4 million years. Situated in east Africa, Tanzania is a stunningly beautiful, yet poor country. Home to Africa's highest mountain, Kilimanjaro, and the world famous Serengeti Plains, Tanzania provides the wildlife enthusiast with majestic landscapes and vast areas of true wilderness.

Explore the Ngorongoro Crater

Some of Tanzania's most distinguishing geographical features are found in the Ngorongoro Conservation Area. The park is composed of many craters and gorges, as well as lakes, forest, and plains. Among these features is the area's namesake, the Ngorongoro Crater. The Crater is a huge expanse, covering more than one hundred square miles. On the Crater's floor, grasslands blend into swamps, lakes, rivers, and woodland. Also within the Conservation Area is the Olduvai Gorge, commonly called the "Cradle of Mankind," where in 1931 the stone tools of prehistoric man were found and subsequently led to the discovery of the remains of humans who lived 1.75 million years ago.

Continued on page II

***Next Issue* —Costa Rica Adventure**

Next months newsletter will feature our Costa Rica Rainforest Adventure tour. Don't miss this once in a lifetime opportunity to discover some of the Earth's greatest unspoiled habitats. Split in half by a volcanic mountain chain, Costa Rica offers a dramatic landscape of densely forested highlands and coastal lowlands, all teeming with life. Exotic creatures great and small call this country home – a wondrous, natural biosphere you can explore in all different ways – challenging hikes, exciting river canoe trips and energetic river rafting. An expert naturalist guide will accompany you and will help you discover why Costa Rica attracts nature lovers from around the world.

Natives

Tanzania is home to over 120 culturally diverse tribes but shares a common official language of Swahili. Apart from this linguistic bond, each tribe is unique. Their manners of worship, local government, and rituals vary greatly from tribe to tribe.

One of Tanzania's major tribes, the Masai, dominates the northern portion of Tanzania. Residing in the Ngorongoro Conservation Area, tribe members constantly seek new grazing areas for their cattle. Cattle are of great importance to the Masai, providing not only a source of food, but also serving as a symbol of wealth and prestige for their owners. The Masai wear a single toga-like piece of clothing, usually a bright red or blue color.♦

In This Issue

- Featured Tour: Tanzania Safari
- Explore the Ngorongoro Crater
- See the Serengeti Plain
- Animal Life
- Tanzania FACTS

Hyphenate

After entering the text, you decide to **hyphenate** the text to give it a more professional appearance.

Textbox

To draw the reader's attention to the next issue's featured trip to Costa Rica, you enter the text into a **textbox**.

Newsletter-style Column

To make the newsletter appear more like a professional publication, you decide to format the text into two columns using the **Newsletter-style column** feature. This provides a professional magazine-like feel to the newsletter.

Bulleted List

To highlight and focus attention on the topics in this issue, you formatted the topics as a **bulleted list**.

CREATING A WEB PAGE

You have been asked to create a Web site to promote the upcoming trips to Machu Picchu, Tanzania, Mt. Kilimanjaro, and Costa Rica. You start by converting the recently completed advertising brochure to a *Web page*. To enhance the appearance of the page you add a *theme*. Next, you replace the image, edit the existing text, add additional documents to the site, and connect the documents to the home page using *hyperlinks*. Finally, you *publish* your Web page to make it available to the public on the Internet.

Figure 3-12 Web page

Theme
To give your Web pages a professional and well-designed appearance, you select the Expedition **theme**. This theme provides a basic layout and color scheme for the pages.

Web Page
To convert the advertising brochure file to a **Web page**, all you had to do was to save the text file as a Web Page. The file is converted to HTML code and saved as a Web page.

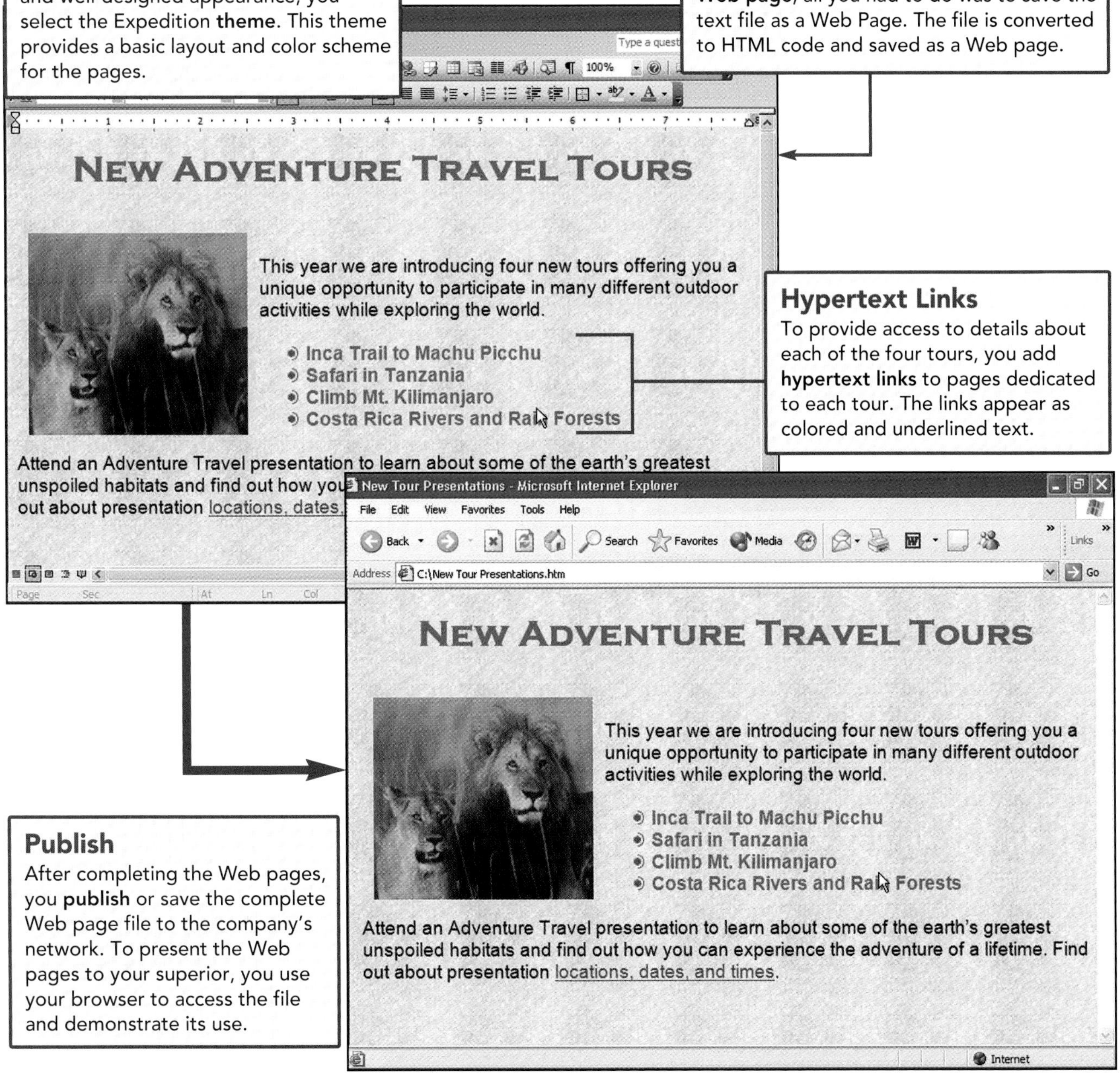

Hypertext Links
To provide access to details about each of the four tours, you add **hypertext links** to pages dedicated to each tour. The links appear as colored and underlined text.

Publish
After completing the Web pages, you **publish** or save the complete Web page file to the company's network. To present the Web pages to your superior, you use your browser to access the file and demonstrate its use.

SPREADSHEETS

Spreadsheet programs manipulate numeric data. Features include workbooks, worksheets, cells, ranges, text and numeric entries, formulas, functions, charts, recalculation, and what-if analysis.

Spreadsheet programs organize, analyze, and graph numeric data such as budgets and financial reports. Once used exclusively by accountants, spreadsheets are widely used by nearly every profession. Students and teachers record grades and calculate grade point averages. Marketing professionals analyze sales trends. Financial analysts evaluate and graph stock market trends.

The three most widely used spreadsheet programs are Microsoft Excel, Corel Quattro Pro, and Lotus 1-2-3.

FEATURES

Unlike word processors which manipulate text and create text documents, spreadsheet programs manipulate numeric data and create workbook files. **Workbook files** consist of one or more related worksheets. A **worksheet,** also known as a **spreadsheet** or **sheet,** is a rectangular grid of **rows** and **columns.** For example in Figure 3-13, the columns are identified by letters and the rows are identified by numbers. The intersection of a row and column creates a **cell.** For example the cell D8 is formed by the intersection of column D and row 8.

A cell can contain text or numeric entries. **Text entries** or **labels** provide structure to a worksheet by describing the contents of rows and columns. For example in Figure 3-13, cell B8 contains the label Food. The cell in D8 contains a number identified as the food expense.

A **numeric entry** can be a number or a formula. A **formula** is an instruction to calculate or process. For example the cell F15 contains the formula =E5−E13. This formula will calculate a value and display that value in cell F15 (Net). The value is calculated by taking the value in cell E5 (Wages) and subtracting the value in cell E13 (Total Expenses). **Functions** are prewritten formulas provided by the spreadsheet program that perform calculations such as adding a series of cells. For example, the cell E13 contains the function

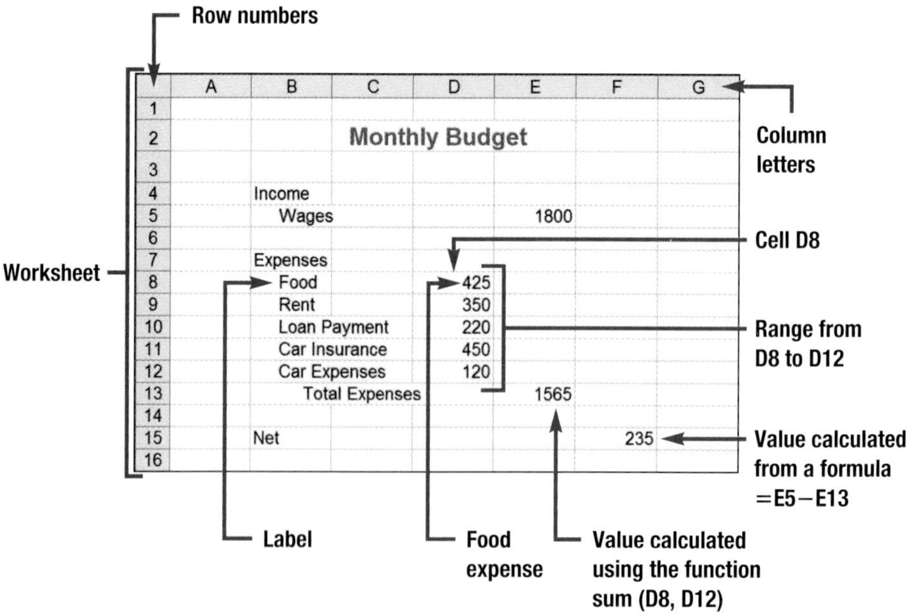

Figure 3-13 Monthly budget worksheet

SUM(D8:D12) which adds the values in the range from D8 to D12. A **range** is a series of continuous cells. In this case the range includes D8, D9, D10, D11, and D12 and displays the sum in cell E13. Spreadsheet programs typically provide a variety of different types of functions including financial, mathematical, statistical, and logical functions. Some of these functions are presented in Figure 3-14.

Analytical graphs or **charts** are visual representations of data in a worksheet. You can readily create graphs in a spreadsheet program by selecting the cells containing the data to be charted and then selecting the type of chart to display. If you change one or more numbers in your spreadsheet, all related formulas will automatically recalculate and charts will be recreated. This is called **recalculation.** The process of observing the effect of changing one or more cells is often referred to as **what-if analysis.** For example, to analyze the effect of a rent increase in the Monthly Budget worksheet in Figure 3-13, all you would need to do is replace the contents in cell D9. The entire worksheet including any charts that had been created would be automatically recalculated. There are numerous chart and analysis features. (See Figure 3-15.)

TIPS

Have you ever wanted to draw attention to a cell in a spreadsheet? AutoShapes make it easy to emphasize the contents of your worksheet. If you are using Excel 2002:

1. **Open the Drawing Toolbar.** Right click a toolbar and select the Drawing toolbar from the menu.
2. **Open the AutoShapes Menu.** Click the AutoShapes button on the Drawing toolbar to open the AutoShapes menu.
3. **Choose and Insert an AutoShape.** Select an AutoShape click on the worksheet and drag to create the shape.

Type	Function	Calculates
Financial	PMT	Size of loan payments
	PV	Present value for an investment
Mathematical	SUM	Sum of the numbers in a range of cells
	ABS	Absolute value of a number
Statistical	AVERAGE	Average or mean of the numbers in a range of cells
	MAX	Largest numbers in a range of cells
Logical	IF	Whether a condition is true; if true a specified value displayed; if not true then a different specified value displayed
	AND	Whether two conditions are true; if both true then a specified value displayed, if either one or both not true then a different specified value displayed

Figure 3-14 Selected spreadsheet functions

Category	Features	Description
Chart	Chart types	Provides variety of different types of chart including bar, column, line, and pie. Most have a 3D variation.
	Chart options	Provides various titles (chart, x-axis, y-axis), legends, and data labels
Analysis	Solver	Evaluates effect of changing the values in two or more cells
	Goal seek	Determines values required in one or more cells to achieve a goal
	Scenario	Evaluates the effect of changing different sets (scenarios) of cell values. Scenario Manager and Scenario Summary provide tools for developing, managing, and reporting scenarios.

Figure 3-15 Chart and analysis features

CASE

Assume that you have just accepted a job as manager of the Downtown Internet Café. This Café provides a variety of flavored coffees as well as Internet access. One of your responsibilities is to create a financial plan for the next year. To see how you could use Microsoft Excel, the most widely used spreadsheet program, as the manager for the Downtown Internet Café, see Figures 3-16 through 3-19.

CREATING A SALES FORECAST

Your first project is to develop a first quarter sales forecast for the Café. You begin by studying the sales at the Downtown Internet Café and talking with several managers. After obtaining sales and expense estimates, you are ready to create the first quarter forecast. You start by structuring the *worksheet* by inserting descriptive *text entries* for the row and column headings. Next, you insert *numeric entries* including *formulas* and *functions* to perform calculations. To test the accuracy of the worksheet, you change the value in some cells and compare the recalculated spreadsheet results with hand calculations.

Figure 3-16 Worksheet

Worksheets
Worksheets are used for a wide range of different applications. One of the most common is to create, analyze, and forecast budgets.

Text Entries
Text entries provide meaning to the values in the worksheet. The rows are labeled to identify the various sales and expense items. The columns are labeled to specify the months.

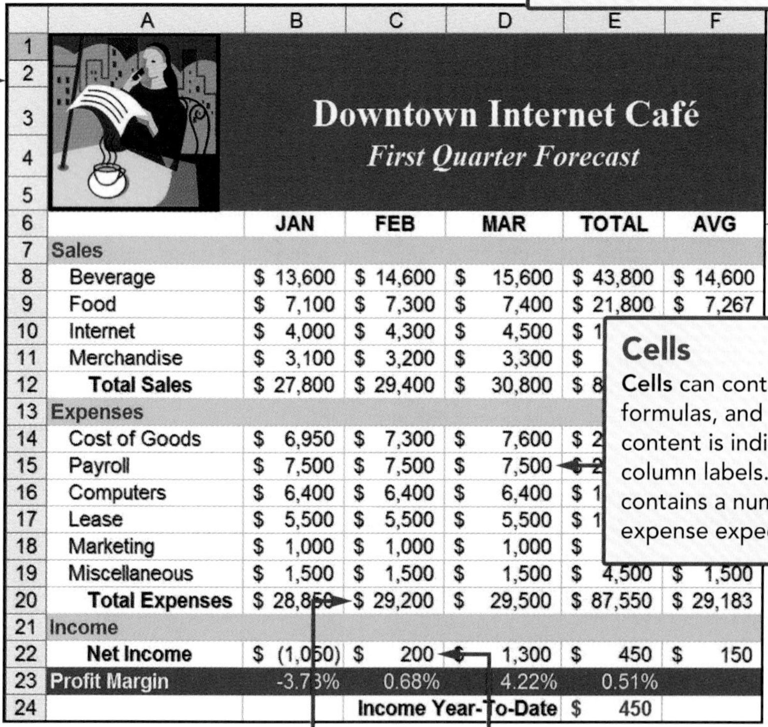

	A	B	C	D	E	F
1						
2						
3		Downtown Internet Café				
4		*First Quarter Forecast*				
5						
6		JAN	FEB	MAR	TOTAL	AVG
7	Sales					
8	Beverage	$ 13,600	$ 14,600	$ 15,600	$ 43,800	$ 14,600
9	Food	$ 7,100	$ 7,300	$ 7,400	$ 21,800	$ 7,267
10	Internet	$ 4,000	$ 4,300	$ 4,500	$ 1	
11	Merchandise	$ 3,100	$ 3,200	$ 3,300	$	
12	Total Sales	$ 27,800	$ 29,400	$ 30,800	$ 8	
13	Expenses					
14	Cost of Goods	$ 6,950	$ 7,300	$ 7,600	$ 2	
15	Payroll	$ 7,500	$ 7,500	$ 7,500	2	
16	Computers	$ 6,400	$ 6,400	$ 6,400	$ 1	
17	Lease	$ 5,500	$ 5,500	$ 5,500	$ 1	
18	Marketing	$ 1,000	$ 1,000	$ 1,000	$	
19	Miscellaneous	$ 1,500	$ 1,500	$ 1,500	$ 4,500	$ 1,500
20	Total Expenses	$ 28,850	$ 29,200	$ 29,500	$ 87,550	$ 29,183
21	Income					
22	Net Income	$ (1,050)	$ 200	$ 1,300	$ 450	$ 150
23	Profit Margin	-3.73%	0.68%	4.22%	0.51%	
24			Income Year-To-Date		$ 450	

Cells
Cells can contain labels, numbers, formulas, and functions. A cell's content is indicated by the row and column labels. For example, cell D15 contains a number or the Payroll expense expected for March.

Functions
One advantage of using **functions** rather than entering formulas is that they are easier to enter. In this case, cell C20 (Total Expenses for February) contains the function SUM(C14:C19) rather than the formula =C14+C15+C16+C17+C18+C17.

Formulas
Formulas provide a way to perform calculations in the worksheet. In this case Cell B22 (Net Income for January) contains the formula = B12 (Total Sales for January) −B20 (Total Expenses for January).

CREATING A CHART

After completing the First Quarter Forecast for the Internet Café, you decide to *chart* the sales data to better visualize the projected growth in sales. You select the 3D column *chart type* to show each month's projected sales category. Using a variety of chart options, you enter descriptive *titles* for the chart, the x-axis, and the y-axis. Then you use *data labels* to focus attention on the growing Internet sales. Finally, you insert a *legend* to define the chart's different columns.

Figure 3-17 Chart

Chart Types
To display the monthly expenses over the quarter, you consider several different **chart types** before selecting the 3D column chart. The 3D variation of the chart provides an interesting depth perception to the columns.

Titling
Clearly **titling** the chart as well as the x-axis and y-axis makes the chart easier to read and understand.

Chart
Once data is in the worksheet, it is very easy to **chart** the data. All you need to do is to select the data to chart, select the chart types, and add some descriptive text.

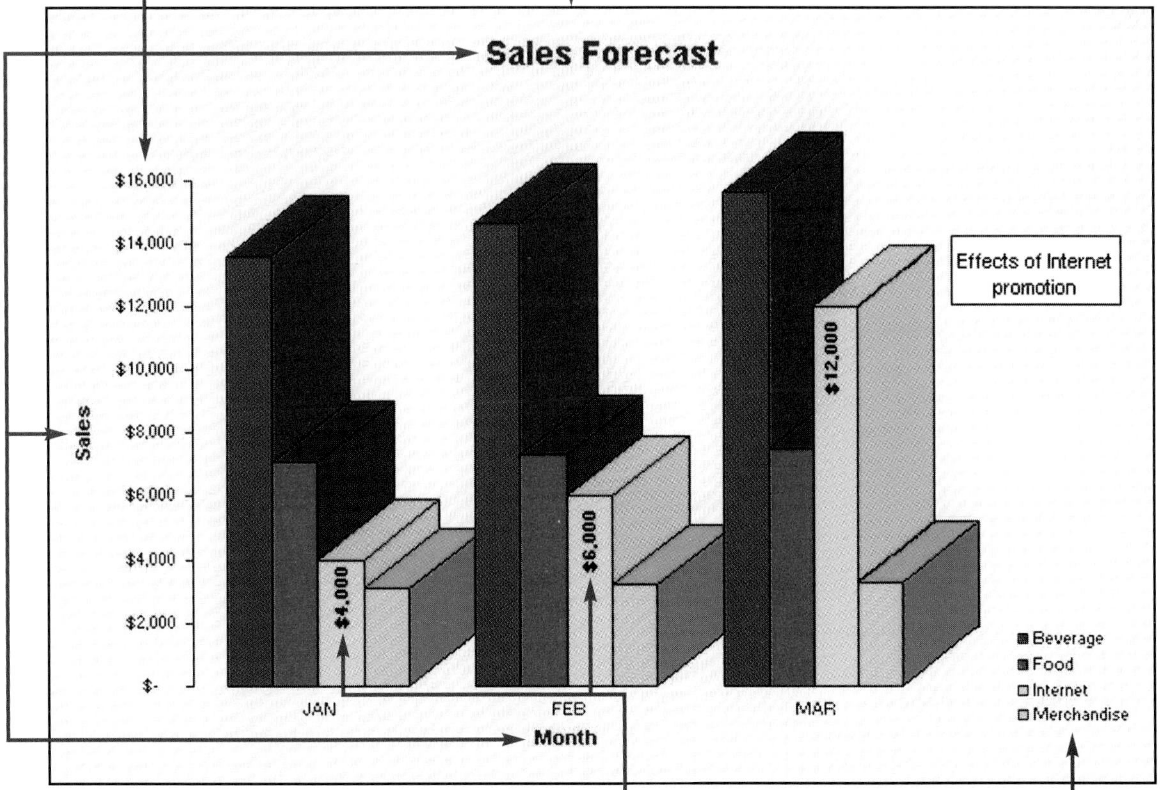

Data Labels
Data labels draw the viewer's attention to selected pieces of information in the chart.

Legend
The **legend** defines each sales expense by a color. Legends are essential to charts that depict more than one set of data.

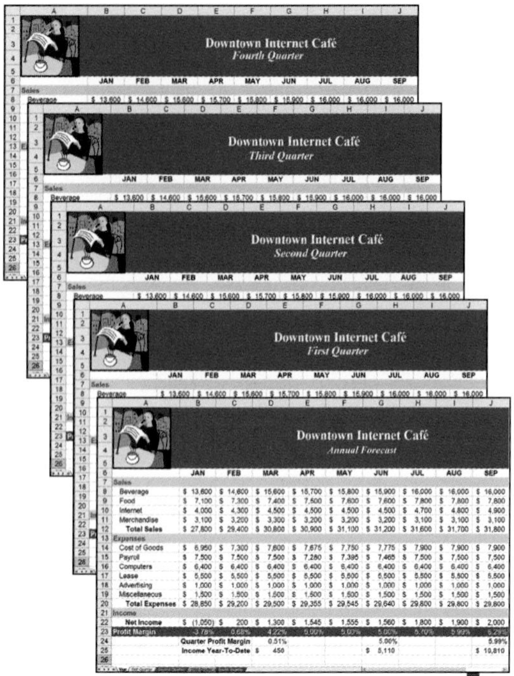

Goal Seek

A common goal in many financial workbooks is to achieve a certain level of profit. **Goal seek** allows you to set a goal and then will analyze other parts of the workbook that would need to be adjusted to meet that goal.

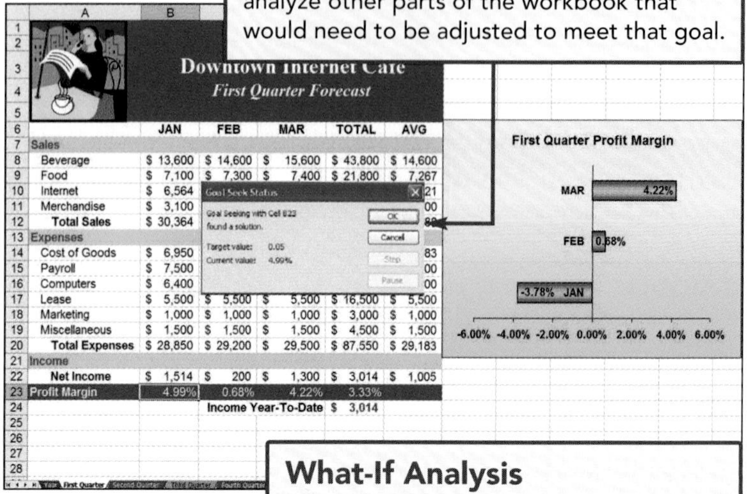

What-If Analysis

What-if analysis is a very powerful and simple tool to test the effects of different assumptions in a spreadsheet.

Workbook

The first worksheet in a **workbook** is often a summary of the following worksheets. In this case, the first workbook presents the entire year's forecast. The subsequent worksheets provide the details.

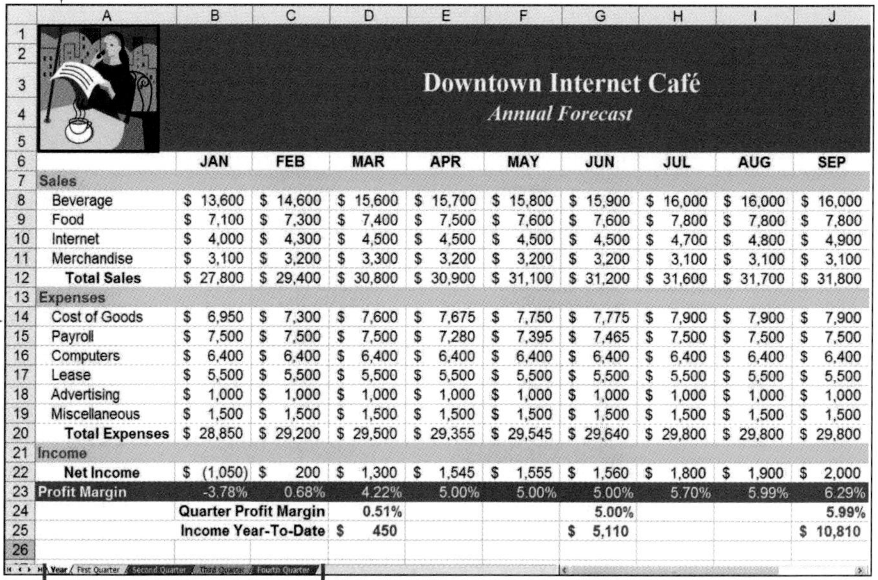

Downtown Internet Café
Annual Forecast

	JAN	FEB	MAR	APR	MAY	JUN	JUL	AUG	SEP
Sales									
Beverage	$ 13,600	$ 14,600	$ 15,600	$ 15,700	$ 15,800	$ 15,900	$ 16,000	$ 16,000	$ 16,000
Food	$ 7,100	$ 7,300	$ 7,400	$ 7,500	$ 7,600	$ 7,600	$ 7,800	$ 7,800	$ 7,800
Internet	$ 4,000	$ 4,300	$ 4,500	$ 4,500	$ 4,500	$ 4,500	$ 4,700	$ 4,800	$ 4,900
Merchandise	$ 3,100	$ 3,200	$ 3,300	$ 3,200	$ 3,200	$ 3,200	$ 3,100	$ 3,100	$ 3,100
Total Sales	$ 27,800	$ 29,400	$ 30,800	$ 30,900	$ 31,100	$ 31,200	$ 31,600	$ 31,700	$ 31,800
Expenses									
Cost of Goods	$ 6,950	$ 7,300	$ 7,600	$ 7,675	$ 7,750	$ 7,775	$ 7,900	$ 7,900	$ 7,900
Payroll	$ 7,500	$ 7,500	$ 7,500	$ 7,280	$ 7,395	$ 7,465	$ 7,500	$ 7,500	$ 7,500
Computers	$ 6,400	$ 6,400	$ 6,400	$ 6,400	$ 6,400	$ 6,400	$ 6,400	$ 6,400	$ 6,400
Lease	$ 5,500	$ 5,500	$ 5,500	$ 5,500	$ 5,500	$ 5,500	$ 5,500	$ 5,500	$ 5,500
Advertising	$ 1,000	$ 1,000	$ 1,000	$ 1,000	$ 1,000	$ 1,000	$ 1,000	$ 1,000	$ 1,000
Miscellaneous	$ 1,500	$ 1,500	$ 1,500	$ 1,500	$ 1,500	$ 1,500	$ 1,500	$ 1,500	$ 1,500
Total Expenses	$ 28,850	$ 29,200	$ 29,500	$ 29,355	$ 29,545	$ 29,640	$ 29,800	$ 29,800	$ 29,800
Income									
Net Income	$ (1,050)	$ 200	$ 1,300	$ 1,545	$ 1,555	$ 1,560	$ 1,800	$ 1,900	$ 2,000
Profit Margin	-3.78%	0.68%	4.22%	5.00%	5.00%	5.00%	5.70%	5.99%	6.29%
		Quarter Profit Margin	0.51%			5.00%			5.99%
		Income Year-To-Date	$ 450			$ 5,110			$ 10,810

Year / First Quarter / Second Quarter / Third Quarter / Fourth Quarter

Sheet Name

Each worksheet has a unique **sheet name**. To make the workbook easy to navigate, it is a good practice to always use simple yet descriptive names for each worksheet.

ANALYZING YOUR DATA

After presenting the First Quarter Forecast to the owner, you revise the format and expand the *workbook* to include worksheets for each quarter and an annual forecast summary. Each worksheet is given a descriptive *sheet name*. At the request of the owner, you perform a *what-if analysis* to test the effect of different estimates for payroll and you use *Goal Seek* to determine how much Internet Sales would have to increase to produce a profit margin of 5.00 percent for January.

Figure 3-18 Workbook

Scenario

Many times the values in a worksheet are estimates. These estimates reflect the most likely **scenario** or set of estimated values. To test the sensitivity of these estimates, a common approach is to define a worst-case set of estimates and a best-case set of estimates. A more informative forecast can be made by inserting these different scenarios into the workbook and analyzing the results.

Scenario Manager

Scenario manager is an Excel tool that helps in creating, editing, and evaluating alternative scenarios. The number of scenarios is not limited to the most likely, best case, and worst case. Any number of different scenarios can be analyzed.

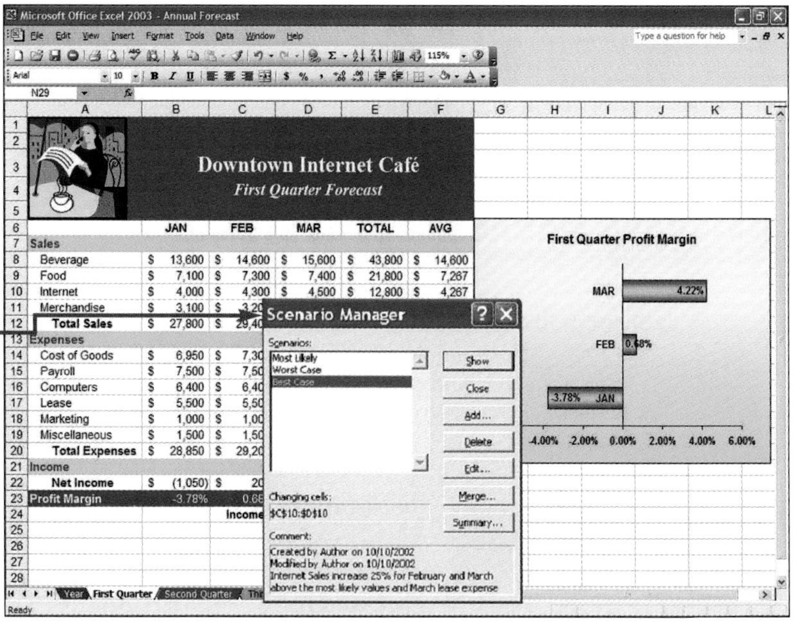

Scenario Summary

A **scenario summary** is an Excel tool that summarizes and reports the effects of the different scenarios created in the Scenario Manager. This report is created and displayed in a separate worksheet.

Scenario Summary 9/24/2004 9:28		Current Values:	Most Likely	Worst Case	Best Case
Changing Cells:					
	Internet JAN	$ 4,410	$ 4,900	$ 4,410	$ 4,410
	Internet FEB	$ 6,100	$ 4,900	$ 4,410	$ 6,100
	Internet MAR	$ 6,100	$ 4,900	$ 4,410	$ 6,100
	Lease MAR	$ 6,200	$ 6,000	$ 6,200	$ 6,200
Result Cells:					
	Profit Margin JAN	3.77%	5.25%	3.77%	3.77%
	Profit Margin FEB	8.70%	5.25%	3.77%	8.70%
	Profit Margin MAR	8.09%	5.25%	3.13%	8.09%
	Profit Margin TOTAL	6.91%	5.25%	3.56%	6.91%

Notes: Current Values column represents values of changing cells at time Scenario Summary Report was created. Changing cells for each scenario are highlighted in gray.

Profits from high Internet Sales

Figure 3-19 Scenarios

ANALYZING SCENARIOS

New information has affected the estimates for several values in the first quarter forecast. After discussing this new information and the uncertainty of forecasting the future with the owner, you revise the first quarter forecast to reflect the most likely values. Additionally, you use *scenario manager* to evaluate different *scenarios* and print a *scenario summary.* The best-case scenario is that Internet sales for February and March are 25% greater than expected. The worst-case scenario is that each month's Internet sales are 10% lower than expected and that the March lease increases from $6,000 to $6,200.

Concept Check

- What are spreadsheets used for? What is a workbook? What is a worksheet?
- Define cells, ranges, text, and numeric entries.
- Describe the following spreadsheet features: formulas, functions, charts, recalculation, and what-if analysis.

DATABASE MANAGEMENT SYSTEMS

A database is like an electronic file cabinet. DBMS structures data and provides tools. Relational databases use tables, records, fields, primary fields, joins, file sizes, and data types. Features include tools for sorting, filtering, defining criteria, querying, creating forms, and reports.

On the Web Explorations

Corel is one of the leaders in software development. To learn more about the company, visit our Web site at

http://www.mhhe.com/oleary/CT05 and select On the Web Explorations from Tim's Toolbox.

A **database** is a collection of related data. It is the electronic equivalent of a file cabinet. A **database management system (DBMS)** or **database manager** is a program that sets up, or structures, a database. It also provides tools to enter, edit, and retrieve data from the database. All kinds of individuals use databases from teachers recording grades to police officers checking criminal histories. Colleges and universities use databases to keep records on their students, instructors, and courses. Organizations of all types maintain employee databases.

Three of the most widely used database management systems designed for microcomputers are Microsoft Access, Corel Paradox, and Lotus Approach.

FEATURES

The **relational database** is the most widely used database structure. Data is organized into related **tables.** For example, an organization's personnel database might contain three tables: Employee, Location and Position, and Pay Rate. (See Figure 3-20.) The Employee table contains basic information, such as employee identification number, first name, and last name. The Location and Position table contains work location information and job title. The Pay Rate table contains employee pay rate and hours worked. All of this data could be contained in one large table; however, smaller tables make the data easier to work with and faster to process.

Each table is made up of rows called **records** and columns called **fields.** Each record contains fields of data about some specific person, place, or thing. For example, the Employee table in Figure 3-20 contains several fields including ID, Last Name, and First Name. Every record has at least one **primary key** or **primary field** that uniquely identifies the record. Social security numbers, student identification numbers, and employee identification numbers are common primary keys. Tables can be linked or **joined** by their common fields. For example in Figure 3-20, the tables are linked by the common field ID.

When a database is set up, each field is assigned a field size and data type. **Field size** is the maximum number of characters that can be entered into the field. **Data type** defines the kind of data that can be entered. To see the basic types of data, see Figure 3-21.

DBMS provides a variety of tools to create and use databases. A **sort** tool will quickly rearrange a table's records according to a selected field. For example, the Employee table could be sorted alphabetically by last name. A **filter** will locate and display records from a table that fit a set of limiting conditions or **criteria.** For example, a filter could be used to locate all employees that live in a particular city.

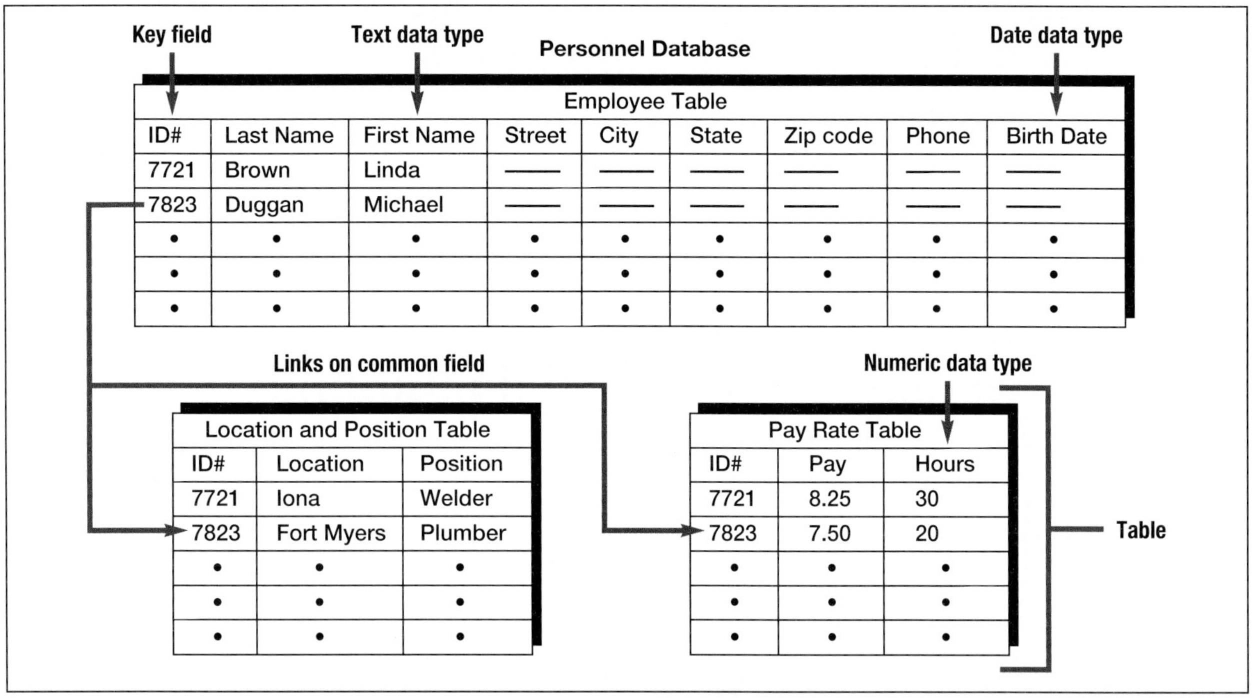

Figure 3-20 Personnel database

Data Type	Description
Text	Letters, words, and numbers that are not used in calculations. Examples include names and telephone numbers.
Numeric	Digits or numbers that can be used in calculations. Examples include number of hours worked and number of vacation days.
Currency	Similar to numeric except formatted to display decimal places and currency symbols.
Date	Month, day, and year information. Examples include the birth dates and dates hired.
Object	Photographs, video, audio, and documents created by other applications. Examples include photos of employees and employee evaluation reports created in Word.

Figure 3-21 Basic data types

The greatest power of a DBMS, however, comes from its ability to quickly find and bring together information stored in separate tables using queries, forms, and reports.

- A **query** is a question or a request for specific data contained in a database. Queries are used to view data in different ways, to analyze data, and even to change existing data. For example referring to the Personnel database shown in Figure 3-20, a query could be used to locate all employees living in a particular city and working at a specific location. This query would use data contained in Employee table and the Location and Position table.
- Database **forms** look similar to traditional printed forms. These electronic forms are displayed on the computer monitor and typically reflect the contents for one record in a table. They are primarily used to enter new records and to make changes to existing records.
- Data from tables and queries can be printed in a variety of different report formats. **Reports** can be a simple listing of an entire field in a table or a list of selected fields based on a query involving several tables. Typical database reports include sales summaries, phone lists, and mailing labels.

CASE

Assume that you have accepted a job as an employment administrator for the Lifestyle Fitness Club. One of your responsibilities is to create a database management system to replace the club's manual system for recording employee information. To see how you could use Microsoft Access, one of the most widely used relational DBMS programs, as the employment administrator for the Lifestyle Fitness Club, see Figures 3-22 and 3-23.

CREATING A DATABASE

The first step in creating the database management system is to plan. You study the existing manual system focusing on how and what data is collected and how it is used. Next, you design the basic structure or organization of the new database system to have two related *tables*, which will make entering data and using the database more efficient. Focusing on the first table, Employees, you create the table structure by specifying the *fields*, *data types*, and *primary key* field. To make the process faster and more accurate you create a form and use the form to enter the data for each employee as a *record* in the table.

Figure 3-22 Table and form

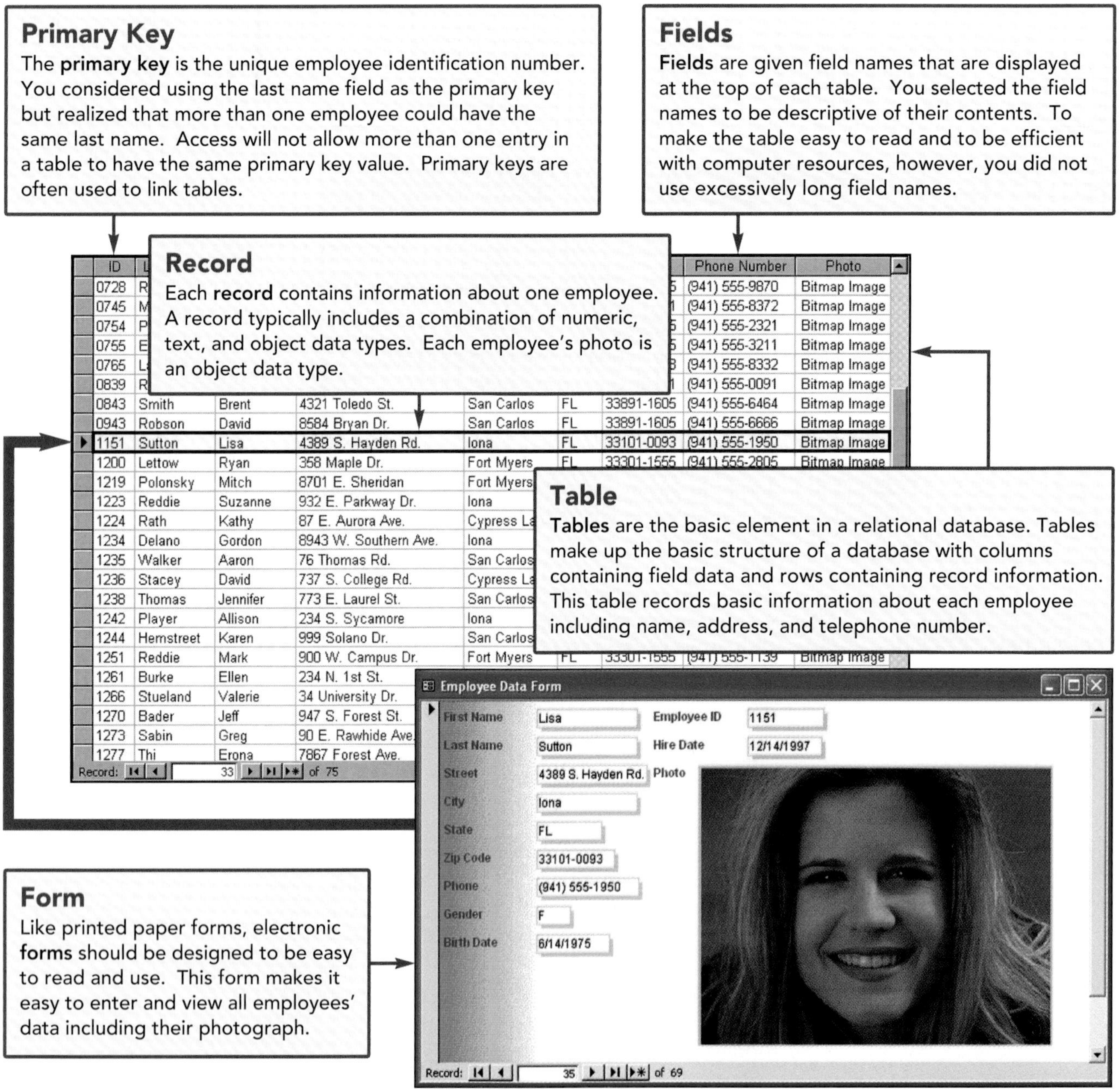

Primary Key
The primary key is the unique employee identification number. You considered using the last name field as the primary key but realized that more than one employee could have the same last name. Access will not allow more than one entry in a table to have the same primary key value. Primary keys are often used to link tables.
Fields
Fields are given field names that are displayed at the top of each table. You selected the field names to be descriptive of their contents. To make the table easy to read and to be efficient with computer resources, however, you did not use excessively long field names.
Record
Each record contains information about one employee. A record typically includes a combination of numeric, text, and object data types. Each employee's photo is an object data type.
Table
Tables are the basic element in a relational database. Tables make up the basic structure of a database with columns containing field data and rows containing record information. This table records basic information about each employee including name, address, and telephone number.
Form
Like printed paper forms, electronic forms should be designed to be easy to read and use. This form makes it easy to enter and view all employees' data including their photograph.
Employee Data Form
First Name
Lisa
Last Name
Sutton
Street
4389 S. Hayden Rd.
City
Iona
State
FL
Zip Code
33101-0093
Phone
(941) 555-1950
Gender
F
Birth Date
6/14/1975
Employee ID
1151
Hire Date
12/14/1997
Photo

Query
Your **query** requests the names, addresses, and telephone numbers of all employees living in Iona or Cypress Lake who work in Fort Myers. This query uses the Employee table and the Location and Position table.

Joined
Since the query involves two tables, they must be linked or **joined** by common fields. You chose to link the tables by the key field ID. This join is represented by the horizontal line between the two table representations.

Criteria
The query **criteria** to produce the car pool list require that both the Employees table and the Location and Position table be consulted. The Employee table is used to identify all employees living in either Iona or Cypress Lake. The Location and Position table is used to evaluate where the employees work. The criteria identify all employees who work at Fort Myers and live either in Iona or Cypress Lake.

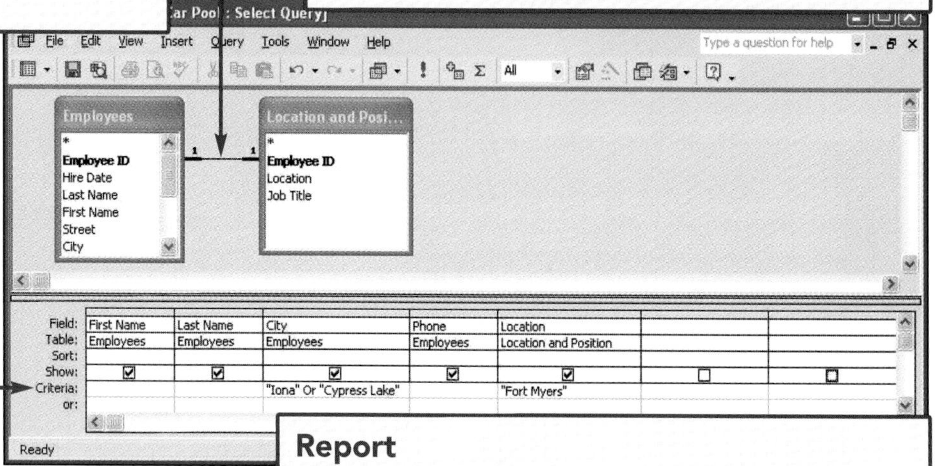

Report
From a variety of different **report** formats, you selected this format to display the names, addresses, and telephone numbers of all employees who might commute from either Cypress Lake or Iona to the Fort Myers plant.

Iona to Fort Myers Car Pool Report

Last Name	First Name	Street Address	City	Phone Number
Delucchi	Bill	950 S. Terrace Dr.	Cypress Lake	(941) 555-8195
Fromthart	Lisa	32 Redcoat Rd.	Cypress Lake	(941) 555-0110
Helfand	Eric	4801 E. Willow Dr.	Iona	(941) 555-9101
Lawrence	Nichol	433 S. Gaucho Dr.	Cypress Lake	(941) 555-7856
Lopez	Mina	4290 E. Alameda Dr.	Cypress Lake	(941) 555-5050
Nichols	Cathy	75 Brocklea Dr.	Cypress Lake	(941) 555-0001
Reddie	Suzanne	932 E. Parkway Dr.	Iona	(941) 555-1191
Schiff	Marc	235 N. Cactus Dr.	Cypress Lake	(941) 555-0010
Sutton	Lisa	4389 S. Hayden Rd.	Iona	(941) 555-1950

Sorted
To make the report easier for employees to locate their name and the names of others, you **sorted** the query results alphabetically by last name.

Figure 3-23 Query and report

CREATING A QUERY

You have continued to build the database by creating a second table containing information about each employee's work location and job title. This table is linked or *joined* with the Employee table by the common field, ID. After you completed this second table, you received a request to create car pool information for those employees who live in either Iona or Cypress Lake and work in Fort Meyers. You created a *query* using the appropriate *criteria* to create the car pool list. After *sorting* the resulting list alphabetically according to last name, you created a *report* to distribute to interested employees.

Concept Check

- What is a database? What is a DBMS? A relational database?
- What are records, fields, primary keys, joins, field sizes, and data types?
- Describe the following DBMS features: sort, filter, criteria, query, form, and report.

PRESENTATION GRAPHICS

Presentation graphics create interesting and professional presentations. Features include slides, views, and presentation styles. Other features include color schemes, slide layouts, special effects, design templates, and master slides.

Research shows that people learn better when information is presented visually. A picture is indeed worth a thousand words or numbers. **Presentation graphics** are programs that combine a variety of visual objects to create attractive, visually interesting presentations. They are excellent tools to communicate a message and to persuade people.

People in a variety of settings and situations use presentation graphics programs to make their presentations more interesting and professional. For example, marketing managers use presentation graphics to present proposed marketing strategies to their superiors. Sales people use these programs to demonstrate products and encourage customers to make purchases. Students use presentation graphics programs to create high-quality class presentations.

Three of the most widely used presentation graphics programs are Microsoft PowerPoint, Corel Presentations, and Lotus Freelance Graphics.

On the Web Explorations

Lotus is one of the leaders in developing presentation graphics. To learn more about the company, visit our Web site at

http://www.mhhe.com/oleary/CT05 and select On the Web Explorations from Tim's Toolbox.

FEATURES

An electronic presentation consists of a series of **slides.** For example, Figure 3-24 shows a PowerPoint presentation consisting of four slides. The slides are presented in the **layout view,** in which a miniature of each slide is displayed. Other views include the **normal view,** which is used to create individual slides and the **slide show view,** which is used to present the slides. The slides can be presented in a variety of ways called **presentation styles.** These styles include onscreen presentations, Web presentations, overhead slides, and 35mm slides.

Presentation programs include a variety of features to help you create effective dynamic presentations. Most include a wizard such as Microsoft's **AutoContent wizard** that steps you through the process of creating a presentation. Other features include tools to select alternative color schemes, slide layouts, special effects, design templates, and master slides.

- **Color schemes** are combinations of complementary colors to apply to a slide's background, text, and other elements.
- Each slide in a presentation can have a different **slide layout** or arrangement of items.
- **Special effects** such as animation, transitions, and builds add interest and motion to a presentation. **Animation** adds action to text and graphics and interest with prerecorded sounds. **Transitions** control how one slide moves off the screen and the next one appears. **Builds** are used to display

TIPS Planning a presentation for school or work? Here are a few tips from professionals to make it the best ever:

1. **Be prepared.** Know your audience, equipment, and presentation room.
2. **Practice and time** your presentation by giving it to a friend.
3. **Begin and end well.** Begin with a joke or story. End with a summary.
4. **Know when to move.** Move around to focus attention on you. Remain still to focus attention on your slides.
5. **Relax.** Prior to a presentation, take a short walk, stretch, or just take a few quiet moments to breathe deeply.

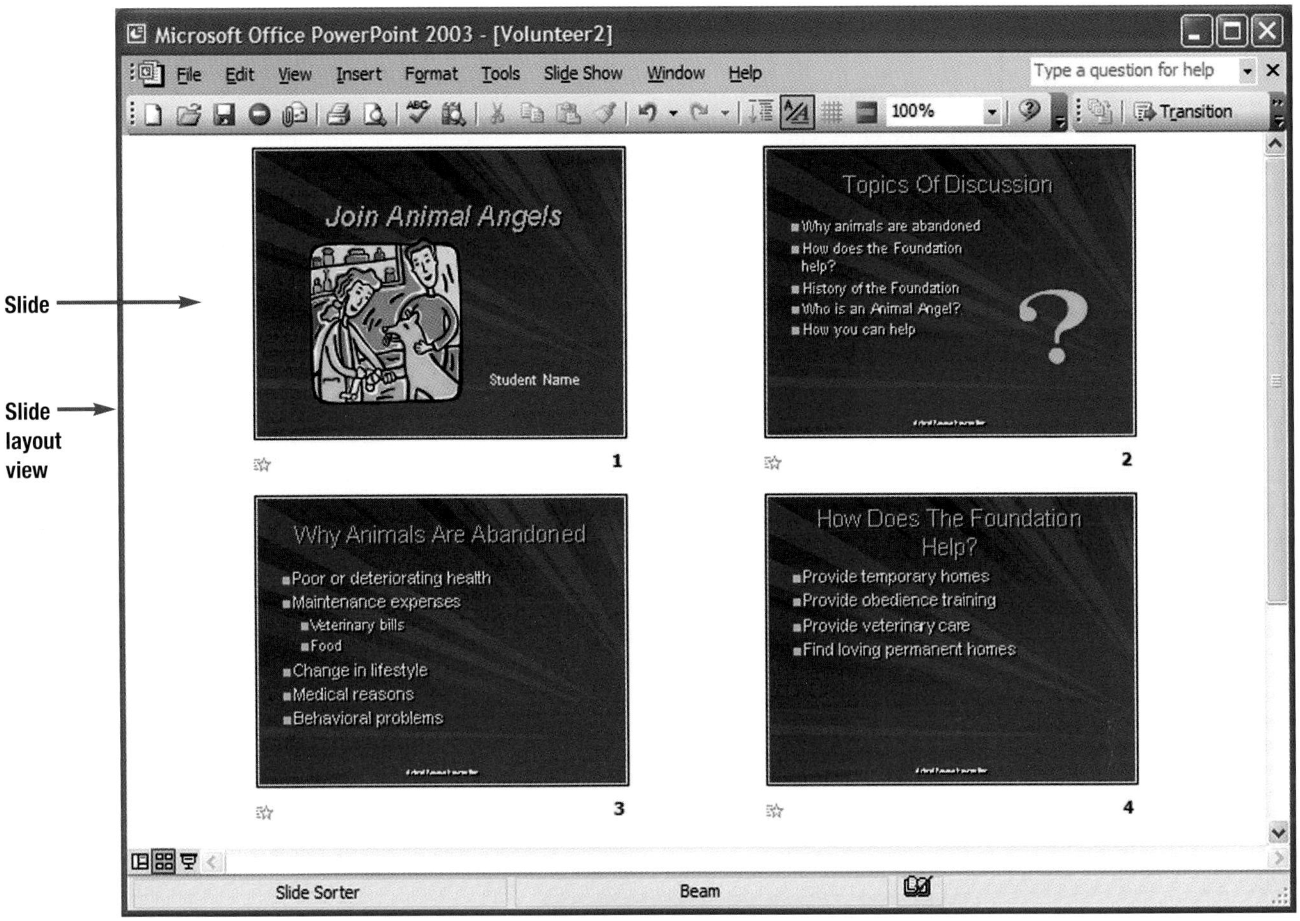
Slide
Slide layout view
Microsoft Office PowerPoint 2003 - [Volunteer2]
File Edit View Insert Format Tools Slide Show Window Help
Type a question for help
100%
Transition
Join Animal Angels
Student Name
Topics Of Discussion
Why animals are abandoned
How does the Foundation help?
History of the Foundation
Who is an Animal Angel?
How you can help
Why Animals Are Abandoned
Poor or deteriorating health
Maintenance expenses
Veterinary bills
Food
Change in lifestyle
Medical reasons
Behavioral problems
How Does The Foundation Help?
Provide temporary homes
Provide obedience training
Provide veterinary care
Find loving permanent homes
1
2
3
4
Slide Sorter
Beam

Figure 3-24 Slides

each bullet point, text, paragraph or graphic independently of the other text or objects on the slide.

- **Design templates** provide professionally selected combinations of color schemes, slide layouts, and special effects.
- The **master slide** is a special slide that does not appear in a presentation but controls all the format and placement of all slides in a presentation. The design template for a presentation can be easily changed for an entire presentation using the master slide.

CASE

Assume that you have volunteered for the Animal Rescue Foundation, a local animal rescue agency. You have been asked to create a powerful and persuasive presentation to encourage other members from your community to volunteer. To see how you could use Microsoft PowerPoint, one of the most widely used presentation graphics programs, as a volunteer for the Animal Rescue Foundation, see Figures 3-25 through 3-27.

Concept Check

- ✔ What are presentation graphics programs? What are they used for?
- ✔ What are slides, views, and presentation styles?
- ✔ What is the AutoContent Wizard? What is it used for?
- ✔ Describe the following presentation graphics features: color schemes, slide layouts, special effects, design templates, and master slides.

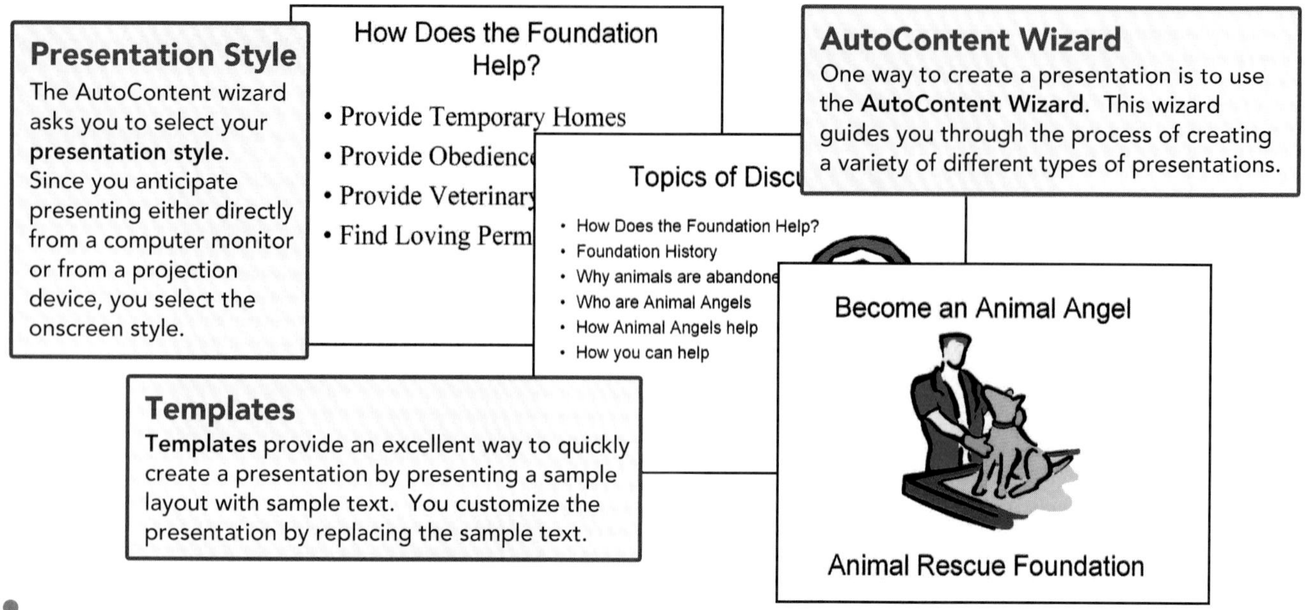
Presentation Style
The AutoContent wizard asks you to select your presentation style. Since you anticipate presenting either directly from a computer monitor or from a projection device, you select the onscreen style.
How Does the Foundation Help?
• Provide Temporary Homes
• Provide Obedienc
• Provide Veterinar
• Find Loving Perm
Topics of Disc
• How Does the Foundation Help?
• Foundation History
• Why animals are abandone
• Who are Animal Angels
• How Animal Angels help
• How you can help
AutoContent Wizard
One way to create a presentation is to use the AutoContent Wizard. This wizard guides you through the process of creating a variety of different types of presentations.
Templates
Templates provide an excellent way to quickly create a presentation by presenting a sample layout with sample text. You customize the presentation by replacing the sample text.
Become an Animal Angel
Animal Rescue Foundation

Figure 3-25 Presentation

CREATING A PRESENTATION

You start creating the presentation using the *AutoContent Wizard* and specify the *template* and *presentation style* to use. The wizard creates a sample presentation containing suggested content in each slide and uses a consistent design style throughout. After replacing the sample content with the information for your presentation, you are on your way to the director's office to show him what you have.

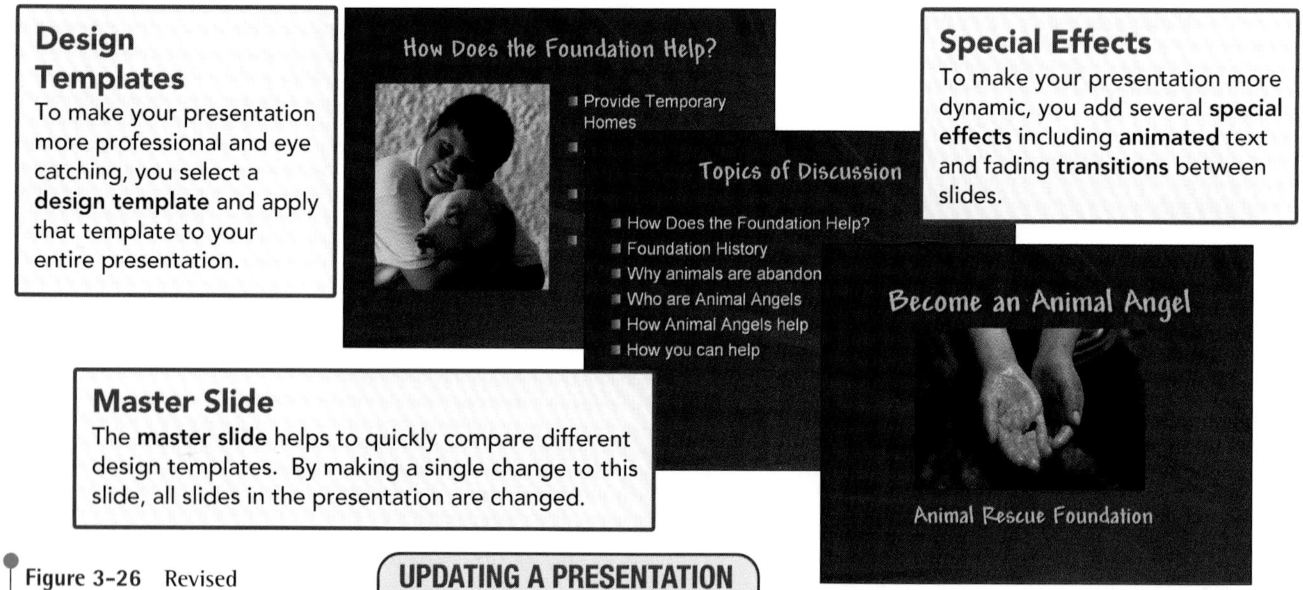
Design Templates
To make your presentation more professional and eye catching, you select a design template and apply that template to your entire presentation.
How Does the Foundation Help?
Provide Temporary Homes
Topics of Discussion
How Does the Foundation Help?
Foundation History
Why animals are abandon
Who are Animal Angels
How Animal Angels help
How you can help
Special Effects
To make your presentation more dynamic, you add several special effects including animated text and fading transitions between slides.
Become an Animal Angel
Animal Rescue Foundation
Master Slide
The master slide helps to quickly compare different design templates. By making a single change to this slide, all slides in the presentation are changed.

Figure 3-26 Revised presentation

UPDATING A PRESENTATION

After discussing the presentation with the director, you have some ideas to enhance the effectiveness of the message. First, you improve the color of selected items and add more graphics. Next, you select one of the *design templates* and make some other changes. You apply these changes to all the slides by simply adjusting the *master slide*. You add some *special effects* including *animations* and sound effects. Finally, you practice or rehearse the presentation, create speaker notes, and print out audience handouts. You're ready to give a professionally designed, dynamic presentation.

Hyperlinks
These hyperlinks provide a quick way for a viewer to jump to selected slides.

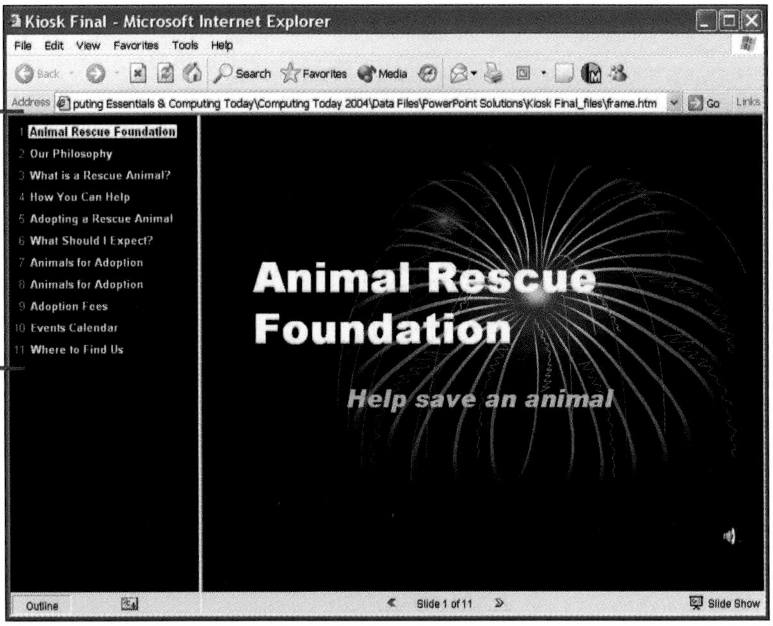
Kiosk Final - Microsoft Internet Explorer
File Edit View Favorites Tools Help
1 Animal Rescue Foundation
2 Our Philosophy
3 What is a Rescue Animal?
4 How You Can Help
5 Adopting a Rescue Animal
6 What Should I Expect?
7 Animals for Adoption
8 Animals for Adoption
9 Adoption Fees
10 Events Calendar
11 Where to Find Us
Animal Rescue Foundation
Help save an animal
Outline
Slide 1 of 11
Slide Show

HTML
By saving the presentation as a Web page, HTML commands are automatically created to display each page.

Figure 3-27 Published presentation

PUBLISHING A PRESENTATION ON THE WEB

The director is planning a presentation at a national conference. Her presentation is to describe the entire scope of the Animal Rescue Foundation. You have created this extensive presentation and present it to the director. The director is so impressed with the presentation that she has asked you to publish the presentation to the organization's Web site. You begin by adding *hyperlinks* to the first slide and then save the presentation in *HTML* format.

INTEGRATED PACKAGES

Integrated packages provide the functionality of several separate application programs within a single program. Also known as personal or home software, they provide limited capability at low cost.

An **integrated package** is a single program that provides the *functionality* of a word processor, spreadsheet, database manager, and more. The primary disadvantage of an integrated package is that the capabilities of each function (such as word processing) are not as extensive as in the individual programs (such as Microsoft Word). The primary advantages are cost and simplicity. The cost of an integrated package is much less than the cost of the individual powerful, professional grade application programs discussed thus far in this chapter. Because an integrated package is a single program, using and switching between functions is very easy and convenient.

Integrated packages are popular with many home users who are willing to sacrifice some advanced features for lower cost and simplicity. For this reason, integrated packages are sometimes classified as **personal** or **home software.** (Other personal software applications will be discussed in Chapter 4.) The most widely used integrated packages are Microsoft Works and AppleWorks. See Figure 3-28.

Figure 3-28 AppleWorks

CASE

Assume that you publish a gardening newsletter that you distribute to members of the Desert Gardening Club. Using many of the features in AppleWorks, you have prepared several articles including the feature article on planting seeds. Using the word processing function, you entered text, formatted titles and subtitles, and inserted several photographs. (See Figure 3-29.) Using the spreadsheet function, you analyzed daily rainfall for the feature article and included a chart within the article to summarize your findings. After completing the newsletter, you will use the database function and the membership database to print mailing labels.

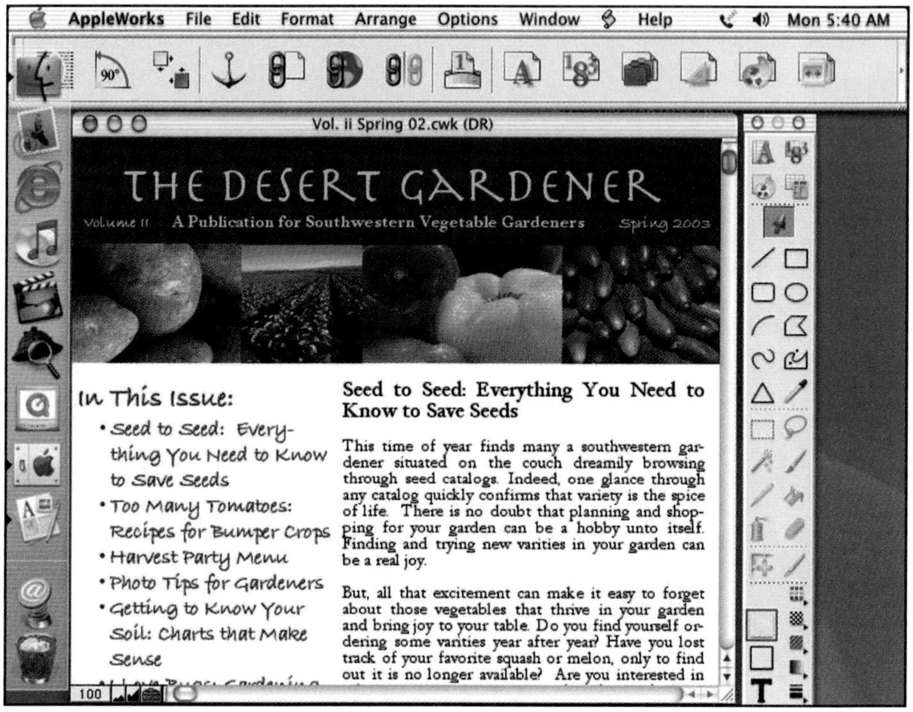

Figure 3-29 Integrated package (AppleWorks)

Concept Check
✔ What is an integrated package?
✔ Describe the advantages and disadvantages of an integrated package.
✔ Why are integrated packages classified as personal or home software?

SOFTWARE SUITES

A software suite is a group of application programs. Four types are productivity, personal, specialized, and utility.

A **software suite** is a collection of separate application programs bundled together and sold as a group. While the applications function exactly the same whether purchased in a suite or separately, it is significantly less expensive to buy a suite of applications than to buy each application separately. There are four types of suites:

- **Productivity suite** Productivity suites, also known as **business suites,** contain professional grade application programs including a word processor, spreadsheet, database manager, and more. The best known is Microsoft Office. (See Figure 3-30.) Two other well-known productivity suites are Corel WordPerfect OfficeSuite and Lotus SmartSuite.
- **Personal suite** Also known as **home suites,** these contain personal software applications or programs intended for home use. The best known is Microsoft Works Suite, which includes the Works integrated package along with Works Calendar, Streets&Trips, and more. (See Figure 3-31.)
- **Specialized suite** Specialized suites focus on specific applications. These include graphics suites, financial planning suites, and many others. (Graphics and financial planning suites will be discussed in Chapter 4.)
- **Utility suite** These suites include a variety of programs designed to make computing easier and safer. One of the best known is Norton System Works and Norton Internet Security Suite. (Utility suites will be discussed in detail in Chapter 5.)

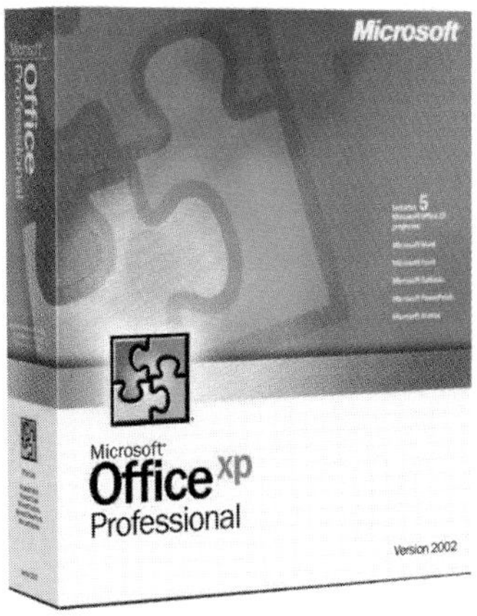

Figure 3-30 Microsoft Office XP

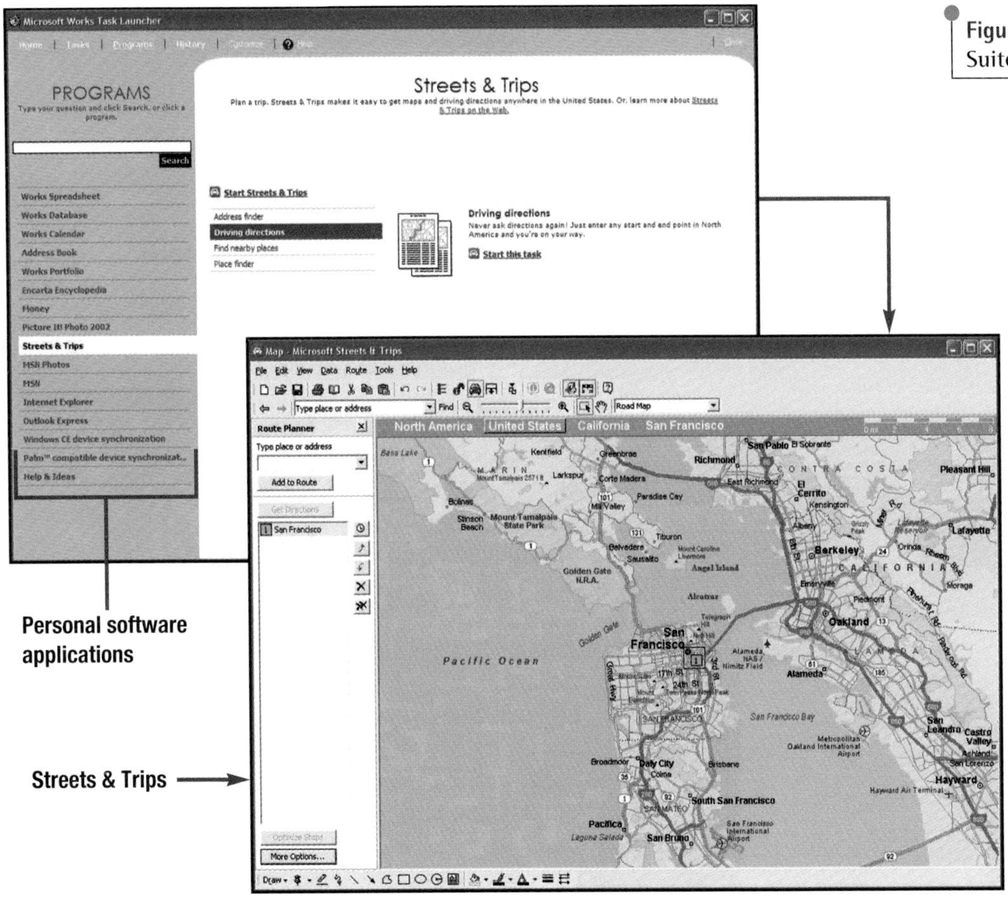

Figure 3-31 Microsoft Works Suite

Concept Check

- What is a software suite? What are the advantages to purchasing a suite?
- What are the four types of software suites?
- What is the best-known productivity suite? What is the best-known personal suite?

SHARING DATA BETWEEN APPLICATIONS

Ways to share data include copy and paste, object linking, and object embedding. Copy and paste is static. OLE is dynamic.

Many times it is convenient to share data between applications. For example, when writing a report it may be useful to include a chart from a spreadsheet or data from a database. Data created by one application can be shared with another application in a variety of different ways including copying and pasting, object linking, and object embedding.

COPY AND PASTE

The most straightforward way to share data is to copy and then paste. From the file that contains the data to be shared, you would select the item and then select the copy command. Next, go to the file where the selected data is to be inserted. Position the insertion pointer to the location where the data is to be inserted and select the paste command. The data will be inserted into this file.

This is a static copy in that any changes to one file will not affect the other file. Object linking and object embedding, however, create more dynamic relationships.

OBJECT LINKING AND EMBEDDING

Object linking and embedding (OLE) is feature that makes it easy to dynamically share and exchange data between applications. For example, you could create a text document using a word processing program that includes a chart created by a spreadsheet program and a presentation created by a graphics program. Whenever the text document is opened, the most up-to-date version of the chart would appear in the document and the presentation could be run. (See Figure 3-32.)

With **object linking,** a copy of the object from a **source file** (the file containing the object) is inserted in a **destination file** (the file receiving the object) and a *link* or connection between the two files is established. In our example, the object is a chart from a spreadsheet (source) file. If a change occurs in the spreadsheet file that affects the chart, the link between the two files will automatically update the chart in the word processing file. Object linking is useful if you want the destination document to always contain the most up-to-date data.

With **object embedding,** the object from the source file is *embedded* or added to the destination document and becomes part of the destination document. In our example, the embedded object is a presentation created by a presentation graphics program. The presentation (embedded object) can be run and edited from within the destination document. However, changes you make to the embedded object are not reflected in the original source file.

Object linking and embedding is a powerful and useful functional feature that connects separate application programs to support sharing and exchanging of data.

Destination File

A **destination file** receives objects (the Excel chart and the PowerPoint presentation) from source files.

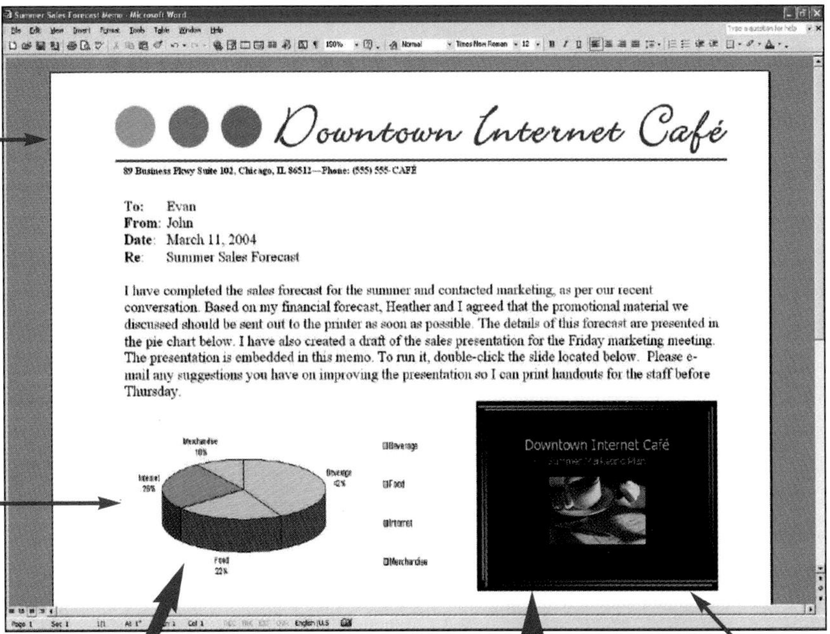

Linked Object

A **linked object** (the Excel chart) from the source file appears in the destination file. Any changes in the source file affecting the linked object are automatically made in the destination file.

Embedded Object

An **embedded object** (presentation) is part of the destination file. Double-clicking the object in the destination file causes the object to run.

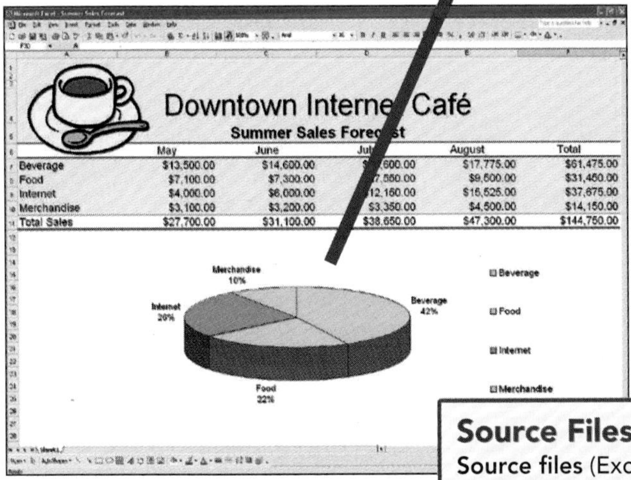

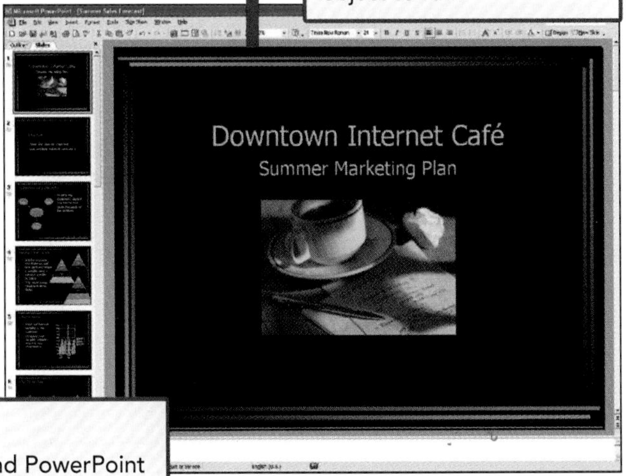

Source Files

Source files (Excel and PowerPoint files) provide objects that are either linked or embedded into a destination file.

Figure 3-32 Object linking and embedding

Concept Check

- Discuss the three ways to share data between applications.
- What are OLE, source files, and destination files?
- What is the difference between object linking and object embedding?

Careers in IT

Computer Trainer

Computer trainers instruct new users on the latest software or hardware. They are usually expected to prepare new materials for instruction and may be asked to write and maintain a course manual. A position may also include design and development of a Web site for the course. Computer trainers typically teach new users how to use the latest software and hardware. Many computer training positions are offered to those with experience with the most popular business software.

Employers look for good communication skills and teaching experience. Though a teaching degree may not be required, it may be preferred. Experience with the latest software and/or hardware is essential but this varies depending on the position. Applicants who are comfortable speaking in front of groups may be preferred. Employers often seek detail-oriented individuals with IT experience.

Computer trainers can expect to earn an annual salary of $35,000 to $50,000. However, salary is dependent on experience and may vary drastically. This position may be very autonomous. Responsibilities typically include preparation of course materials, grading coursework, and continuing education in the field. Opportunities for advancement include management of other trainers and consulting work. To learn more about other careers in information technology visit us at http://www.mhhe.com/oleary/CT05 and select Careers in IT from Tim's Toolbox.

A Look to the Future

Web-based Application Software Updates Ease Maintenance

Wouldn't it be great if you never had to buy software again? What if you could "pay as you go," only paying for those parts of a software suite you actually use? These options sound terrific to end users eager to avoid the high cost and difficulties of software maintenance. They sound even better to large and small corporations, where the costs of maintaining software and the information systems department can be huge expenditures.

Of course, that is what Web-based application service providers, ASPs, are all about. As we discussed earlier, you can use the Web to connect to an ASP and use their software. A major advantage to using an ASP is that others do all the administration work—there are no programs for you to install and configure, and you never have to worry about the hassle of upgrades.

As you've already seen, with an ASP you can access your data from any Internet-connected computer in the world. This means that if a computer is lost or damaged, no data or time has been wasted. And because any computer that can access the Internet can connect to an ASP, any platform can be used. For example, PCs and Apple computers could share data and applications in the same office. Finally using an ASP allows for a simpler and cheaper computer system, because you don't have to worry about hardware requirements or storage space.

These considerations may sound tempting to individuals who dislike installing and maintaining software, and some experts predict that eventually all software may be distributed this way. However, ASPs are currently very valuable to smaller companies with fewer dollars to spend on these labor intensive maintenance and installation tasks. ASPs allow them to customize their software in ways that would have been too expensive for them in the past.

Some experts have even suggested ASPs may become widely used by large corporations, with IT departments, who decide to outsource these projects. They predict that software may become a "service" that companies receive from an outside company. For example, a large company in the future may have a software contract with a company that agrees to supply a word processing program over the Internet. In fact, some traditional software developers are slowly moving toward Web deployment. Microsoft's .NET program is believed to be a step by the corporation toward Web services of their popular software programs.

Do you think you and other end users will use ASPs for these new services? Will we be using ASPs to create customized programs for our personal use?

VISUAL SUMMARY

BASIC APPLICATION SOFTWARE

APPLICATION SOFTWARE

There are two basic types of software. **System software** focuses on handling technical details. **Application software** focuses on completing specific tasks or applications. Two categories:

- **Basic applications** (**general-purpose applications, productivity applications**) are widely used.
- **Specialized applications** (**special-purpose applications**) are more specialized.

Common Features

Common features of most application programs include:

- **User interface**—most have **graphical user interfaces** (**GUI**) that display **icons.**
- **Windows**—rectangular areas that can contain documents, programs, and messages.
- **Menus**—present commands listed on the **menu bar;** use **pull-down** (**drop-down**) menus. **Help** menu provides access to online assistance.
- **Dialog box**—provides additional information or requests user input.
- **Toolbars**—contain **buttons** and menus; **standard toolbar** common to most applications.

Web-based Applications

Web-based applications accessed from Web sites called **application service providers** (**ASP**).

WORD PROCESSORS

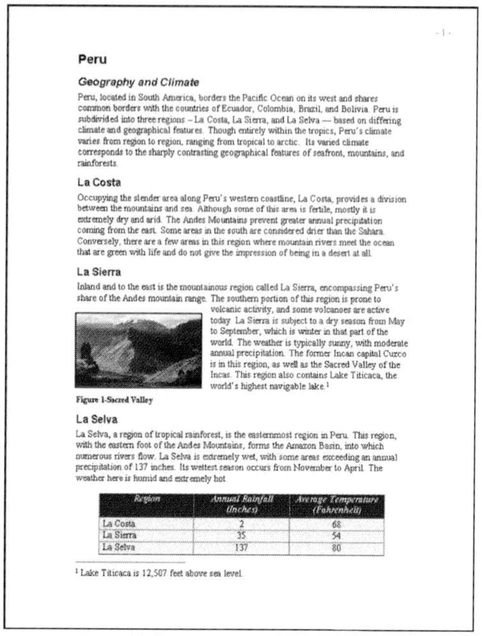

- 1 -

Peru

Geography and Climate

Peru, located in South America, borders the Pacific Ocean on its west and shares common borders with the countries of Ecuador, Colombia, Brazil, and Bolivia. Peru is subdivided into three regions – La Costa, La Sierra, and La Selva — based on differing climate and geographical features. Though entirely within the tropics, Peru's climate varies from region to region, ranging from tropical to arctic. Its varied climate corresponds to the sharply contrasting geographical features of seafront, mountains, and rainforests.

La Costa

Occupying the slender area along Peru's western coastline, La Costa, provides a division between the mountains and sea. Although some of this area is fertile, mostly it is extremely dry and arid. The Andes Mountains prevent greater annual precipitation coming from the east. Some areas in the south are considered drier than the Sahara. Conversely, there are a few areas in this region where mountain rivers meet the ocean that are green with life and do not give the impression of being in a desert at all.

La Sierra

Inland and to the east is the mountainous region called La Sierra, encompassing Peru's share of the Andes mountain range. The southern portion of this region is prone to volcanic activity, and some volcanoes are active today. La Sierra is subject to a dry season from May to September, which is winter in that part of the world. The weather is typically sunny, with moderate annual precipitation. The former Incan capital Cuzco is in this region, as well as the Sacred Valley of the Incas. This region also contains Lake Titicaca, the world's highest navigable lake.[1]

Figure 1-Sacred Valley

La Selva

La Selva, a region of tropical rainforest, is the easternmost region in Peru. This region, with the eastern foot of the Andes Mountains, forms the Amazon Basin, into which numerous rivers flow. La Selva is extremely wet, with some areas exceeding an annual precipitation of 137 inches. Its wettest season occurs from November to April. The weather here is humid and extremely hot.

Region	*Annual Rainfall (Inches)*	*Average Temperature (Fahrenheit)*
La Costa	2	68
La Sierra	35	54
La Selva	137	80

[1] Lake Titicaca is 12,507 feet above sea level.

Word processors allow you to create, edit, save, and print text-based **documents** including flyers, reports, newsletters, and Web pages.

Features

Word wrap is a basic feature that automatically moves insertion point to next line.

Editing features include:

- **Find** and **Replace** which locates (finds), removes, and inserts (replace) another word(s).
- **Spelling** and **grammar checkers** automatically locate misspelled words and grammatical problems.
- **AutoCorrect, AutoText,** and **AutoComplete** automatically correct, insert, and complete text.

Formatting features include:

- **Font (typeface, font)**—set of characters with specific design. **Font size** is measured in **points.**
- **Character effects**—include **bold,** *italic,* shadow, and colors.
- **Alignment**—positions text.
- **Bulleted** and **numbered lists**—used to present sequences of topics or steps.

To be a competent and knowledgeable end user, you need to understand the capabilities of basic application software, which includes word processors, spreadsheets, database management systems, and presentation programs. You need to know how to use these applications and how data can be shared between them.

SPREADSHEET

	A	B	C	D	E	F	G	H	I	J
1–5		Downtown Internet Café *Annual Forecast*								
6		JAN	FEB	MAR	APR	MAY	JUN	JUL	AUG	SEP
7	Sales									
8	Beverage	$ 13,600	$ 14,600	$ 15,600	$ 15,700	$ 15,800	$ 15,900	$ 16,000	$ 16,000	$ 16,000
9	Food	$ 7,100	$ 7,300	$ 7,400	$ 7,500	$ 7,600	$ 7,600	$ 7,800	$ 7,800	$ 7,800
10	Internet	$ 4,000	$ 4,300	$ 4,500	$ 4,500	$ 4,500	$ 4,500	$ 4,700	$ 4,800	$ 4,900
11	Merchandise	$ 3,100	$ 3,200	$ 3,300	$ 3,200	$ 3,200	$ 3,200	$ 3,100	$ 3,100	$ 3,100
12	Total Sales	$ 27,800	$ 29,400	$ 30,800	$ 30,900	$ 31,100	$ 31,200	$ 31,600	$ 31,700	$ 31,800
13	Expenses									
14	Cost of Goods	$ 6,950	$ 7,300	$ 7,600	$ 7,675	$ 7,750	$ 7,775	$ 7,900	$ 7,900	$ 7,900
15	Payroll	$ 7,500	$ 7,500	$ 7,500	$ 7,280	$ 7,395	$ 7,465	$ 7,500	$ 7,500	$ 7,500
16	Computers	$ 6,400	$ 6,400	$ 6,400	$ 6,400	$ 6,400	$ 6,400	$ 6,400	$ 6,400	$ 6,400
17	Lease	$ 5,500	$ 5,500	$ 5,500	$ 5,500	$ 5,500	$ 5,500	$ 5,500	$ 5,500	$ 5,500
18	Advertising	$ 1,000	$ 1,000	$ 1,000	$ 1,000	$ 1,000	$ 1,000	$ 1,000	$ 1,000	$ 1,000
19	Miscellaneous	$ 1,500	$ 1,500	$ 1,500	$ 1,500	$ 1,500	$ 1,500	$ 1,500	$ 1,500	$ 1,500
20	Total Expenses	$ 28,850	$ 29,200	$ 29,500	$ 29,355	$ 29,545	$ 29,640	$ 29,800	$ 29,800	$ 29,800
21	Income									
22	Net Income	$ (1,050)	$ 200	$ 1,300	$ 1,545	$ 1,555	$ 1,560	$ 1,800	$ 1,900	$ 2,000
23	Profit Margin	-3.78%	0.68%	4.22%	5.00%	5.00%	5.00%	5.70%	5.99%	6.29%
24		Quarter Profit Margin		0.51%			5.00%			5.99%
25		Income Year-To-Date		$ 450			$ 5,110			$ 10,810
26										

Spreadsheet programs are used to organize, analyze, and graph numeric data.

Features

Principal spreadsheet features include the following:

- **Workbook** files consist of one or more related worksheets.
- **Worksheets,** also known as **spreadsheets** or **sheets,** are rectangular grids of **rows** and **columns.** Rows are identified by numbers. Columns by letters
- **Cells** formed by intersection of a row and column; used to hold text and numeric entries.
- **Text entries** (**labels**) provide structure and **numeric entries** can be numbers or formulas.
- **Formulas** are instructions for calculations. **Functions** are prewritten formulas.
- **Range** is a series of cells.
- **Analytical graphs** (**charts**) represent data visually.
- **Recalculation** occurs whenever a value changes in one cell that affects another cell(s).
- **What-if analysis** is the process of observing the effect of changing one or more values.

DATABASE MANAGEMENT SYSTEMS

ID	Last Name	First Name	Street Address	City	State	Zip Code	Phone Number	Photo
0728	Roman	Anita	2348 S. Bala Dr.	Fort Myers	FL	33301-1555	(941) 555-9870	Bitmap Image
0745	Matsumoto	Tyrus	34 S. Onza Ave.	Cypress Lake	FL	33205-6911	(941) 555-8372	Bitmap Image
0754	Pario	Ian	983 E. Carrage Ln.	Fort Myers	FL	33301-1555	(941) 555-2321	Bitmap Image
0755	Ernster	Barbara	1153 S. Wilson	San Carlos	FL	33891-1605	(941) 555-3211	Bitmap Image
0765	Lamm	Chris	382 E. Ladonna Dr.	Iona	FL	33101-7468	(941) 555-8332	Bitmap Image
0839	Ruiz	Enrique	35 Palm St.	Cypress Lake	FL	33205-6911	(941) 555-0091	Bitmap Image
0843	Smith	Brent	4321 Toledo St.	San Carlos	FL	33891-1605	(941) 555-6464	Bitmap Image
0943	Robson	David	8584 Bryan Dr.	San Carlos	FL	33891-1605	(941) 555-6666	Bitmap Image
1151	Sutton	Lisa	4389 S. Hayden Rd.	Iona	FL	33101-0093	(941) 555-1950	Bitmap Image
1200	Lettow	Ryan	358 Maple Dr.	Fort Myers	FL	33301-1555	(941) 555-2805	Bitmap Image
1219	Polonsky	Mitch	8701 E. Sheridan	Fort Myers	FL	33301-1555	(941) 555-1018	Bitmap Image
1223	Reddie	Suzanne	932 E. Parkway Dr.	Iona	FL	33101-7468	(941) 555-1191	Bitmap Image
1224	Rath	Kathy	87 E. Aurora Ave.	Cypress Lake	FL	33205-0093	(941) 555-9797	Bitmap Image
1234	Delano	Gordon	8943 W. Southern Ave.	Iona	FL	33101-7468	(941) 555-8201	Bitmap Image
1235	Walker	Aaron	76 Thomas Rd.	San Carlos	FL	33891-1605	(941) 555-2222	Bitmap Image
1236	Stacey	David	737 S. College Rd.	Cypress Lake	FL	33205-0093	(941) 555-7784	Bitmap Image
1238	Thomas	Jennifer	773 E. Laurel St.	San Carlos	FL	33891-1605	(941) 555-4956	Bitmap Image
1242	Player	Allison	234 S. Sycamore	Iona	FL	33101-0093	(941) 555-5532	Bitmap Image
1244	Hemstreet	Karen	999 Solano Dr.	San Carlos	FL	33891-1605	(941) 555-6325	Bitmap Image
1251	Reddie	Mark	900 W. Campus Dr.	Fort Myers	FL	33301-1555	(941) 555-1139	Bitmap Image
1261	Burke	Ellen	234 N. 1st St.	San Carlos	FL	33891-1605	(941) 555-7789	Bitmap Image
1266	Stueland	Valerie	34 University Dr.	Fort Myers	FL	33301-1555	(941) 555-1845	Bitmap Image
1270	Bader	Jeff	947 S. Forest St.	Fort Myers	FL	33301-1555	(941) 555-7789	Bitmap Image
1273	Sabin	Greg	90 E. Rawhide Ave.	Cypress Lake	FL	33205-6911	(941) 555-4455	Bitmap Image
1277	Thi	Erona	7867 Forest Ave.	San Carlos	FL	33891-1605	(941) 555-1089	Bitmap Image

Record: 33 of 75

A **database** is a collection of related data. A **database management system (DBMS),** also known as a **database manager,** structures a database and provides tools for entering, editing, and retrieving data.

Features

Principal database management system features include the following:

- **Relational database** organizes data into related tables.
- **Tables** have rows (**records**) and columns (**fields**).
- **Primary key (field)** uniquely identifies each record.
- **Field size** is the maximum number of characters in a record.
- **Data type** (text, numeric, currency, date, object) defines type of data for a field.
- **Sort** is a tool to rearrange records using a particular field.
- **Filter** is a tool to locate and display records that meet a set of **criteria.**
- **Query** is a question or request for specific data contained in a database.
- **Forms** used to enter new records or edit existing records.
- **Reports** are printed output in a variety of forms.

PRESENTATION GRAPHICS

Presentation graphics combine a variety of visual objects to create attractive, visually interesting presentations. They are excellent tools to communicate a message and to persuade people.

Features

Principal presentation graphics features include the following:

- **Slides** make up a presentation.
- **Layout, normal,** and **slide show** are different presentation views.
- **Presentation styles** include onscreen, Web, overhead slides, and 35mm slides.
- **AutoContent wizard** steps users through process of creating a presentation.
- **Color schemes** provide a set of complementary colors for slides.
- **Slide layout** describes how items are arranged on a slide.
- **Special effects** include **animations, transitions,** and **builds.**
- **Design templates** provide professionally selected combinations of color schemes, slide layouts, and special effects.
- **Master slides** control the format and placement of all slides in a presentation.

INTEGRATED PACKAGES

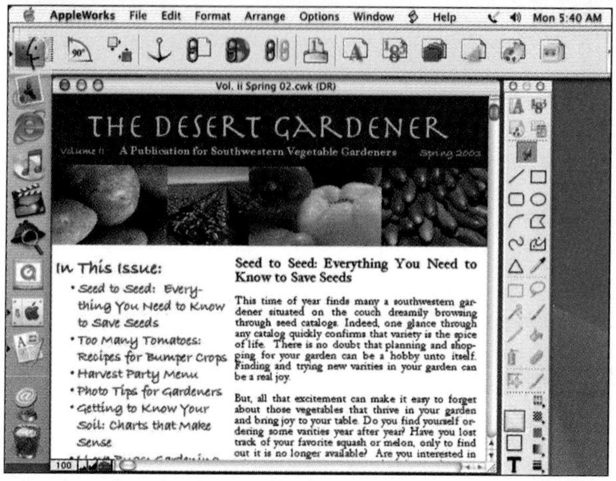

An **integrated package,** also known as **personal** or **home software,** is a single program that provides the functionality of several application packages. Some important characteristics include:

- Functions typically include word processing, spreadsheet, database manager, and more.
- Each function not as extensive or powerful as a single function application program.
- Less expensive than purchasing several individual application programs.
- Simple to use and switch between functions.
- Popular with home users who are willing to sacrifice some advanced features for cost and simplicity.

SOFTWARE SUITES

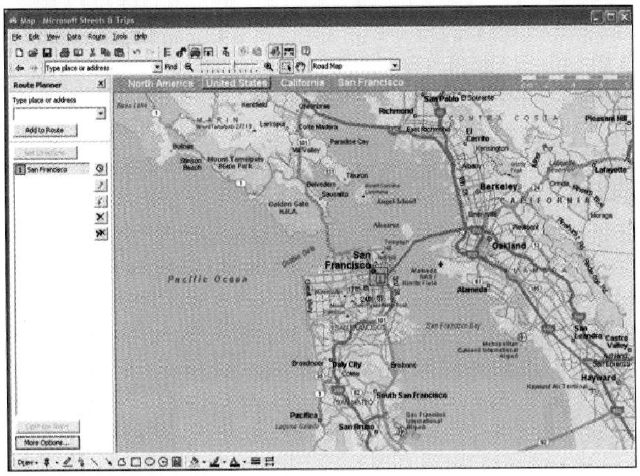

A **software suite** is a collection of individual application packages sold together. While functionally identical, application packages purchased in a suite are significantly less expensive than those purchased separately.

Four types of suites are productivity, personal, specialized, and utility:

- **Productivity** or **business suites** contain professional grade applications. Microsoft Office includes Word, Excel, Access, PowerPoint, and a collection of more specialized programs.
- **Personal** or **home suites** include a combination of personal applications. Microsoft Works includes Works Calendar, Address Book, Money, Picture IT!, Streets&Tips, and more.
- **Specialized suites** include programs for specific applications such as graphics and financial planning.
- **Utility suites** consist of programs designed to make computing easier and safer.

SHARING DATA

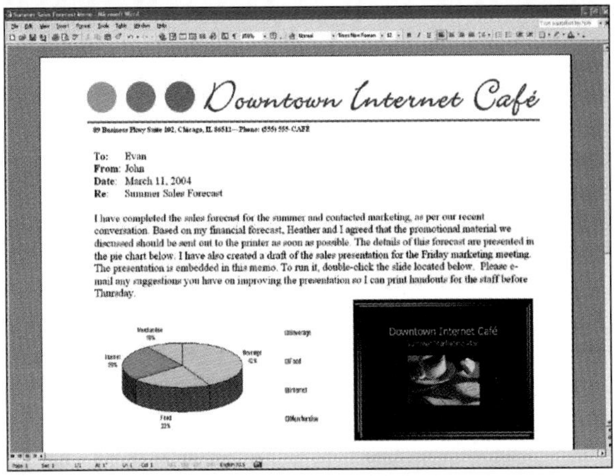

Sharing data between files created with different applications is often convenient.

Copy and Paste

Copy and paste is the most straightforward way to share between files.

- The item to be shared is simply copied from its file and then pasted into the other file.
- This creates a static copy since changes to one file will not affect the other file. Object linking and object embedding, however, create more dynamic relationships.

OLE

Object linking and embedding (OLE) is a feature to dynamically share and exchange data between files.

- With **object linking** a copy of an **object** from a **source file** is inserted into a **destination file** and a *link* between the two files is made. If a change occurs in the source file, the destination file will be updated.
- With **object embedding,** the object is embedded into the destination file and the embedded object can be run from that file. However, changes to the source file will not affect the destination file.

KEY TERMS

alignment (86)
analytical graph (93)
animation (102)
application service providers (ASPs) (82)
AutoComplete (86)
AutoContent wizard (102)
AutoCorrect (86)
AutoText (86)
basic applications (80)
build (102)
bulleted list (86)
business suite (107)
button (81)
cell (92)
character effect (86)
chart (93)
collaboration (86)
color scheme (102)
column (92)
criteria (98)
database (98)
database management system (DBMS) (98)
database manager (98)
design template (103)
destination file (108)
dialog box (81)
document (86)
drop-down menu (81)
editing (86)
filter (98)
find and replace (86)
font (86)
font size (86)
form (99)
format (86)
formula (92)
function (92)
general-purpose applications (80)
grammar checker (86)
graphical user interface (GUI) (80)
Help (81)
home software (105)
home suite (107)
icons (80)
integrated package (105)
joined (98)
label (92)
layout view (102)
master slide (103)
menu (81)
menu bar (81)
normal view (102)
numbered list (86)
numeric entry (92)
object embedding (108)
object linking (108)
object linking and embedding (OLE) (108)
personal software (105)
personal suite (107)
pointer (80)
points (86)
presentation graphic (102)
presentation style (102)
primary field (98)
primary key (98)
productivity applications (80)
productivity suite (107)
pull-down menu (81)
query (99)
range (93)
recalculation (93)
record (98)
relational database (98)
report (99)
row (92)
sheet (92)
slide (102)
slide layout (102)
slide show view (102)
software suite (106)
sort (98)
source file (108)
special effect (102)
specialized applications (80)
spelling checker (86)
spreadsheet (92)
standard toolbar (81)
system software (80)
table (98)
text entry (92)
Thesaurus (86)
toolbar (81)
tracking changes (86)
transition (102)
typeface (86)
user interface (80)
utility suite (107)
Web-based application (82)
what-if analysis (93)
window (80)
word processor (86)
word wrap (86)
workbook file (92)
worksheet (92)

To test your knowledge of these key terms with animated flash cards, select Flash Cards from Tim's Toolbox at http://www.mhhe.com/oleary/CT05.

CHAPTER REVIEW

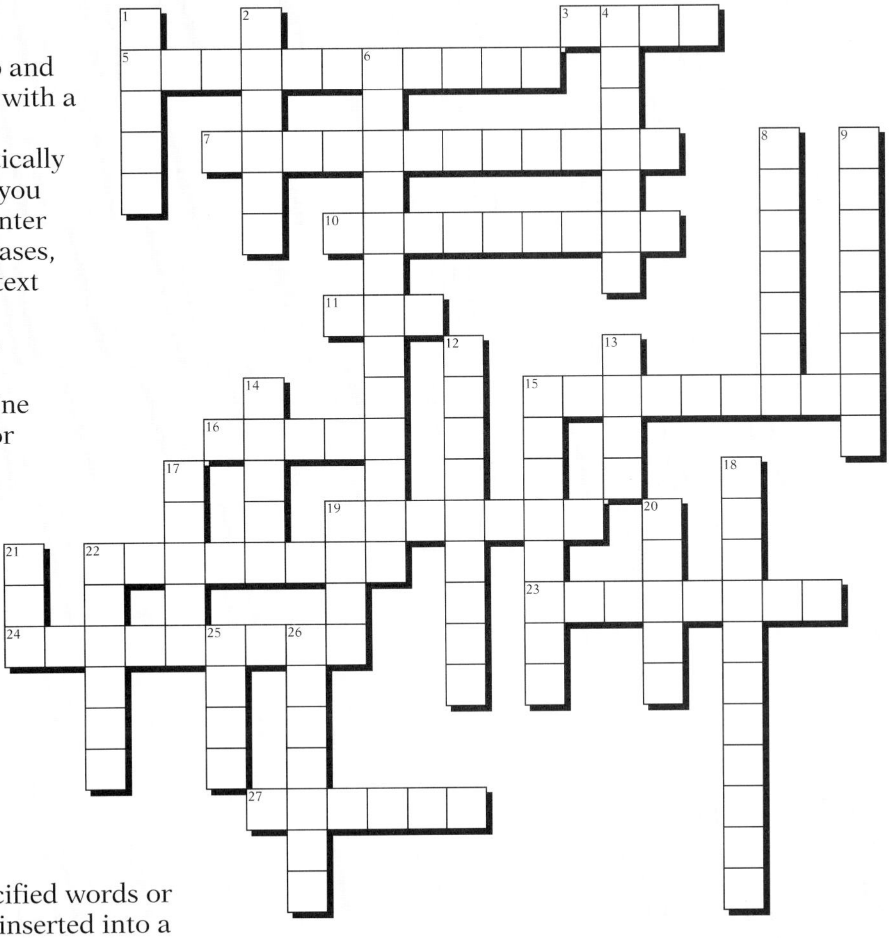

ACROSS

3 A program that sets up and provides tools to work with a database

5 A feature that automatically makes corrections for you

7 As the user begins to enter specified words or phrases, this will complete the text and enter it into the document at the user's request

10 Positioning text on a line between the margins or indents

11 Most applications use this to display graphical elements called icons

15 Provides synonyms, antonyms, and related words

16 Shorter term for worksheet or spreadsheet

19 Instructions for calculations

22 Prewritten formulas

23 Allows previously specified words or phrases to be directly inserted into a document upon the user's request

24 A rectangular grid of rows and columns

27 A rectangular area that can contain a document, program, or message

DOWN

1 A series of cells

2 Part of the grid that makes up a worksheet, identified by letters

4 Small outlined areas in a window that provide short cuts when selected

6 The result on all related formulas and charts when one or more numbers in a spreadsheet are changed

8 The mouse controls this on the screen and it is used to select items

9 A collection of related data

12 Text-based, created with word processing software

13 Intersection of a row and column

14 A way to better visualize data from a worksheet

15 These contain small outlined areas called buttons that provide short cuts to commonly used commands

17 Lists of options or commands

18 Programs that use functions and formulas to manipulate and analyze numeric data

19 A set of characters with a specific design

20 Graphical elements used to represent familiar objects

21 Part of the grid that makes up a worksheet, identified by numbers

22 A basic structure

25 Acts as an outline reference manual for the application

26 Modifying a document

For an interactive crossword puzzle select Crosswords from Tim's Toolbox at http://www.mhhe.com/oleary/CT05.

MULTIPLE CHOICE

Circle the letter or fill in the correct answer.

1. General-purpose applications are also known as ________.
   - **a.** software suites
   - **b.** advanced applications
   - **c.** basic applications
   - **d.** special-purpose applications
   - **e.** none of the above
2. Multimedia, Web authoring, graphics, and virtual reality programs are examples of ________.
   - **a.** special-purpose applications
   - **b.** general-purpose applications
   - **c.** basic applications
   - **d.** occupational applications
   - **e.** b and c
3. ________ are prewritten formulas that perform calculations automatically.
   - **a.** Functions
   - **b.** Macros
   - **c.** Templates
   - **d.** Calculators
   - **e.** none of the above
4. In a relational database, data is organized into ________.
   - **a.** fields
   - **b.** columns
   - **c.** records
   - **d.** tables
   - **e.** rows
5. Database management systems are comprised of tables that are made up of rows called ________ and columns called ________.
   - **a.** fields, records
   - **b.** records, fields
   - **c.** addresses, fields
   - **d.** ranges, sheets
   - **e.** records, ranges
6. Most presentation graphics programs provide ________ that include sample text for many different types of presentations.
   - **a.** layout files
   - **b.** templates
   - **c.** samples
   - **d.** records
   - **e.** formatting
7. The file an object is linked from is called the ________.
   - **a.** destination file
   - **b.** origin file
   - **c.** layout file
   - **d.** support file
   - **e.** source file
8. To have an object automatically updated in a destination file when a change is made to the source file, the object must be ________.
   - **a.** embedded
   - **b.** linked
   - **c.** replaced
   - **d.** resolved
   - **e.** amended
9. A(n) ________ is a single program that provides the functionality of a word processor, spreadsheet, database manager, and more.
   - **a.** general-purpose application
   - **b.** software suite
   - **c.** integrated package
   - **d.** program manager
   - **e.** none of the above
10. A ________ suite is also known as a productivity suite.
    - **a.** personal
    - **b.** utility
    - **c.** specialized
    - **d.** home
    - **e.** business

To test your knowledge of this chapter, select Self Test from Tim's Toolbox at http://www.mhhe.com/oleary/CT05.

MATCHING

Match each numbered item with the most closely related lettered item. Write your answers in the spaces provided.

a. ASP
b. cell
c. find
d. formulas
e. general-purpose applications
f. grammar checker
g. integrated package
h. OLE
i. presentation graphics
j. range
k. relational database
l. software suite
m. sort
n. spelling checker
o. template
p. toolbar
q. utility
r. what-if analysis
s. window
t. word processor

1. Word processors, spreadsheets, database management systems, and presentation graphics. ____
2. Rectangular area that can contain a document, program, or message. ____
3. A feature that contains buttons and menus to provide access to commonly used commands. ____
4. Site that provides access to Web-based applications. ____
5. Type of suite that makes computing easier and safer. ____
6. Automatically checks for problems with capitalization, punctuation, and sentence structure. ____
7. Includes the functionality of a word processor, spreadsheet, database manager, and more. ____
8. Software that creates text-based documents such as reports, letters, and memos. ____
9. Identifies incorrectly spelled words and suggests alternatives. ____
10. Tool that quickly locates any character, word, or phrase in a document. ____
11. The intersection of a row and column in a spreadsheet. ____
12. A collection of two or more cells in a spreadsheet. ____
13. Instructions for calculations. ____
14. Spreadsheet feature in which changing one or more numbers results in the automatic recalculation of all related fields. ____
15. A widely used database structure, in which data is organized into related tables. ____
16. Arranging objects numerically or alphabetically. ____
17. Programs used to communicate a message or to persuade. ____
18. Professionally designed model presentations provided in a presentation graphics program. ____
19. Individual application programs that are sold together as a group. ____
20. Powerful feature of many application programs that allows sharing of information. ____

OPEN-ENDED

On a separate sheet of paper, respond to each question or statement.

1. Explain the difference between general-purpose and special-purpose applications.
2. What is the difference between a function and a formula? How is a formula related to what-if analysis?
3. What are presentation graphics programs? How are they used?
4. Explain the difference between a linked object and an embedded object? What are the advantages of OLE?
5. What is the difference between an integrated package and a software suite? What are the advantages and disadvantages of each?

USING TECHNOLOGY

1 Web-based Applications

Would you like access to free general-purpose applications from anywhere in the world? What about accessing your data files from any location? You can have it all with Web-based applications. To learn more about Web-based applications, review Making IT Work for You: Web-based Applications on pages 84 and 85. Then complete the following questions: (a) What are Web-based applications? What are ASPs? (b) Compared to typical application programs, what are the advantages and disadvantages of Web-based applications? (c) Have you ever used a Web-based application? If you have, describe what programs you used and how you used them. If you have not, discuss why and how you might use one.

2 Presentation Graphics

For presentations, having the right software can help grab your audience's attention and improve your effectiveness as a speaker. Connect to our Web site at http://www.mhhe/com/oleary/CT05 and select Using Technology from Tim's Toolbox to link to a presentation graphics software package. Once connected, review the product's features, and answer the following questions: (a) What computer hardware and software is required to use the presentation graphics product? (b) List and describe three features that could help you organize or present your ideas. (c) What types of files can be embedded with a presentation using this software?

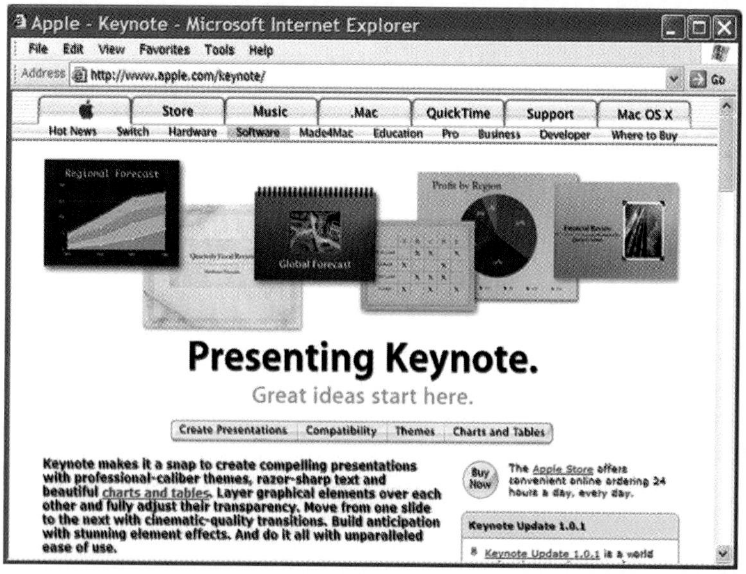

Corel Office Suite 3

Microsoft's major competitor in the office suite market is Corel. Visit our site at http://www.mhhe.com/oleary/CT05 and select Using Technology from Tim's Toolbox to connect to Corel's Web site. Review the site, and then answer the following questions: (a) What applications are provided in Corel's WordPerfect Office Suite? (b) What are the similarities and differences between the Microsoft and Corel office suites? (c) Which suite would you choose? Why?

Open Source Office Suites 4

In recent years, software projects to build open source productivity and office software have emerged. Open source means that anyone may freely download and modify the suite. Visit our Web site at http://www.mhhe.com/oleary/CT05 and select Using Technology from Tim's Toolbox to connect to one such project. Review the site, and then answer the following questions briefly: (a) What is the goal of the project? Why create an open source office suite? (b) How is this office suite different from popular commercial ones? (c) How is it similar? (d) Do you think open source office suites will be a threat to commercial ones? Justify your answer.

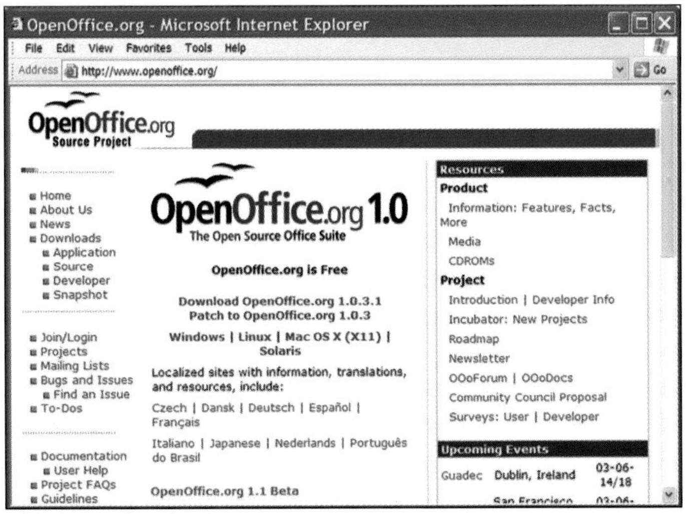

EXPANDING YOUR KNOWLEDGE

1 Computing Today CD

Some predict that many organizations will be using Web-based applications in the near future. These organizations will not be required to own, install, upgrade, or store applications. Additionally, applications and application files can be accessed from almost anywhere in the world. After viewing the "How Web-based Applications Work" animation on your Computing Today CD or from Tim's Toolbox at http://www.mhhe.com/oleary/CT05 and studying Figure 3-5 on page 83, consider the following case.

Assume that you are about to give a presentation at your company's national sales meeting. Earlier in the week you created the presentation using a Web ASP's program PRESENT and saved the presentation at the ASP's site. This presentation will be run from your notebook computer and be displayed on a projection screen large enough for everyone at the sales meeting to see. To run the program, you need access to the presentation file and the PRESENT program.

On a single page of paper, create a drawing similar to Figure 3-5 that describes how you will use the Web-based application to give the presentation.

2 Application Service Providers

Application Service Providers (ASPs) offer access to basic applications from anywhere in the world. Conduct a Web search to learn more about application service providers. Then answer the following questions: (a) List common applications provided by ASPs. (b) What are some advantages to users of ASPs beyond universal access to software and data? (c) What concerns might a user have about personal data stored at an ASP? (d) Would you use an ASP? If so, explain why. If not, explain why not.

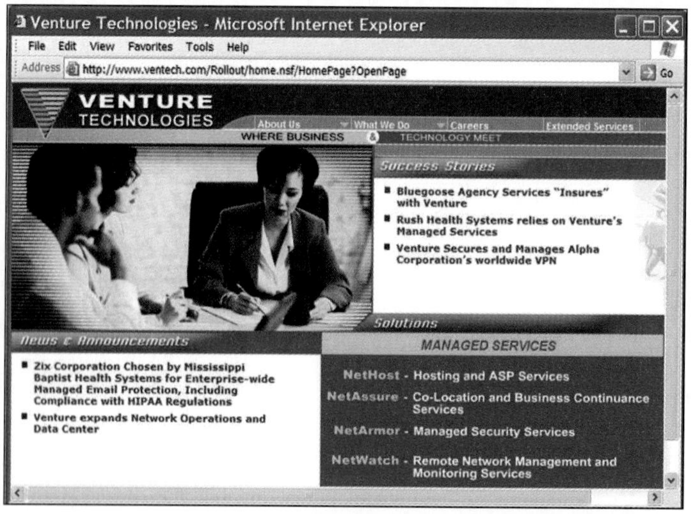

SimNet CD 3

Complete Chapter 3: Basic Application Software on your SimNet CD and then answer the following questions.

a. All of today's Web browsers are based at least in part on which original Web browser? Why are Web pages often "double-coded"?
b. Describe some of the common types of business application software.
c. Describe the basic features of a word processing application.
d. Describe the elements of a spreadsheet application.
e. Identify the two items shown below.

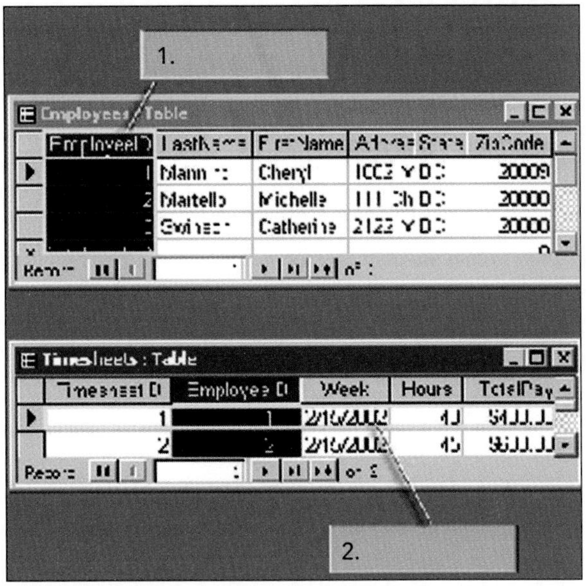

Shareware 4

One way to acquire new application software is by downloading shareware. Conduct a Web search for shareware programs. Connect to and explore a shareware site offering a program that might interest you. Then respond to the following: (a) What is shareware? Who creates it? (b) What does shareware cost to use? What about support if you have a problem using it? (c) What are the risks of using shareware? Be thorough. (d) Would you use shareware? Why or why not?

BUILDING YOUR PORTFOLIO

1 Software Suites

Software suites offer both end users and businesses some unique advantages. In a one-page paper titled "Software Suites," address the following items: (a) Define software suites. (b) Which suites are the most popular today? Why? (c) New versions of software suites are coming out all the time. As a user, how can you know when it's time to upgrade?

2 User Certification

To demonstrate competence with a particular software suite, users may become *certified* for it. This means they are officially recognized as having certain skills with the software. Choose a software suite, and research programs of certification for it. Then in a one-page paper, answer the following questions: (a) What software suite did you choose? What certification programs are available? (b) What are the requirements of certification? (c) What are the benefits of certification? Who should become certified? (d) Do you believe that software certification would be useful to you? If so, how? If not, why?

Acquiring Software 3

There are three common ways to obtain new software (use public domain software, use shareware, buy commercial software). In addition to these three ways, two others are to copy programs from a friend or purchase unauthorized copies of programs. Investigate each of these five options, and then answer the following questions in a one-page paper: (a) Define and discuss each option. Be sure to discuss both the advantages and disadvantages of each. (b) Which seems like the best method to you? Why? (c) Do you think there is anything wrong with obtaining and using unauthorized software in this manner? Identify and explore the key issues.

Software Standards 4

Most of the products you encounter every day, such as cars, electronics, and food are required by law to meet certain conditions to ensure your safety and a minimum level of quality. Software, however, can be written by anyone with few of these constraints. Fortunately, some standards of certifications do exist. Research a certification program for software vendors. Write a one-page paper to answer the following: (a) Describe the certification program you selected. What type of software is it intended for? (b) What requirements must software meet to receive certification? (c) Who performs the software tests to ensure compliance? (d) As a consumer of software, what additional certification requirements would you like to see? Explain your answer.

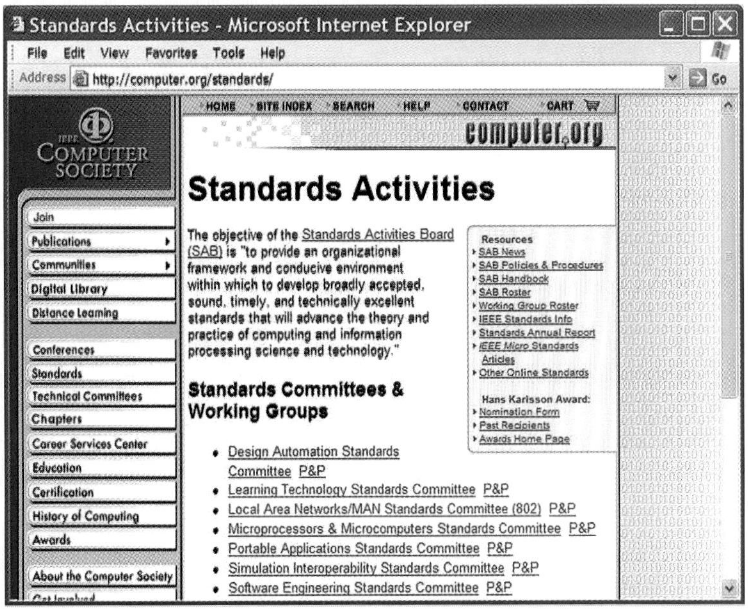

SPECIALIZED APPLICATION SOFTWARE

OBJECTIVES

After you have read this chapter, you should be able to:

1. Describe graphics software including desktop publishing, image editors, illustration programs, image galleries, and graphics suites.
2. Discuss audio and video software.
3. Describe multimedia, including story boards and multimedia authoring programs.
4. Explain Web authoring, Web site design, and Web authoring programs.
5. Discuss personal applications including PIMs, Personal Finance Managers, and Tax Preparation software.
6. Describe the impact of artificial intelligence on emerging applications.
7. Discuss virtual reality and VRML.
8. Discuss knowledge-based (expert) systems.
9. Discuss robotics, including perception systems, industrial robots, and mobile robots.

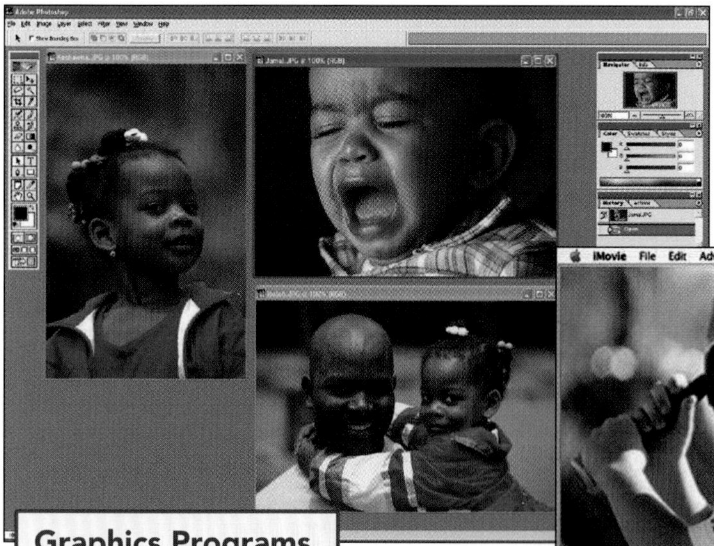

Graphics Programs
Include desktop publishing, image editors, and illustration programs

Video Editing Software
Reorganizes, adds special effects, and music to digitized video

Expect surprises—exciting and positive opportunities. The latest technological developments offer you new opportunities to extend your range of computer competency. As we show in this chapter, software that for years was available only for mainframes has recently become available for microcomputers. A whole new generation of software only recently available for microcomputers, called specialized applications, now makes it possible to perform advanced tasks at home.

The latest technological developments have created an opportunity for home users to take advantage of software previously used only in professional environments. For example, it is now possible, and quite common, for people to create their own Web sites. Home users also have access to software that helps manipulate and create graphic images. Many musicians and artists work from home to create complex and beautiful work using specialized applications.

Some of these same technological advances have allowed researchers and computer scientists to make advances in the field of artificial intelligence previously envisioned only in science fiction. Robots now provide security and assistance in homes. Virtual reality is providing opportunities in the fields of medicine and science, but also commonly appears in video games.

Competent and knowledgeable end users need to be aware of specialized applications. They need to know who uses them, what they are used for, and how they are used. These advanced applications include multimedia, Web authoring, graphics programs, audio and video editing software, and artificial intelligence, including virtual reality, knowledge-based systems, and robotics.

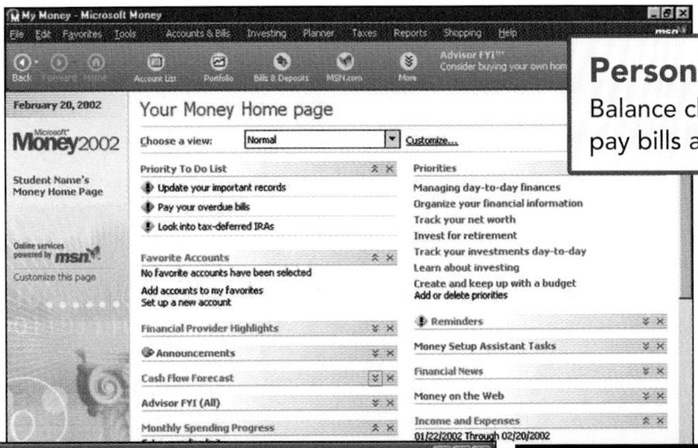

Personal Finance Managers
Balance checkbooks, track spending, pay bills and prepare taxes

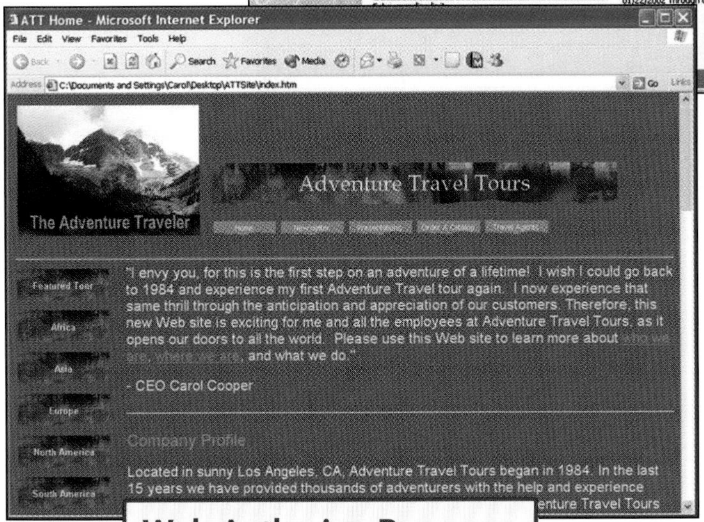

Web Authoring Programs
Create document files that display Web pages

Virtual Reality
Consists of sensory equipment to simulate alternative realities to the real world

SPECIALIZED APPLICATIONS

Specialized applications are widely used within specific professions. Applications include graphics, audio and video, multimedia, Web authoring, personal applications, and emerging applications.

In the previous chapter, we discussed basic applications including word processing, spreadsheets, and database management systems. These programs are widely used in nearly every profession. This chapter focuses on specialized applications that are widely used within specific professions. For example, graphic artists use a variety of specialized programs including image editors and illustration programs. It is important for competent and knowledgeable end users to be aware of these specialized applications and to understand how they are used. (See Figure 4-1.) Specifically, we will examine:

- Graphics programs for creating professional-looking published documents, for creating and editing images, and for locating and inserting graphics.
- Audio and video software to create, edit, and play music and videos.

Figure 4-1 Specialized applications

- Multimedia programs to create interactive presentations that integrate a variety of media including graphics, animation, sound, and video.
- Web authoring programs to create, edit, and design interesting and effective Web sites for a variety of personal and professional purposes.
- Personal applications designed to assist and provide professional assistance to individuals for organizing information, managing financial resources, and preparing tax reports.
- Emerging applications that merge artificial intelligence into a variety of different types of applications including virtual reality, knowledge-based systems, and robotics.

Of course, these are not the only types of specialized applications. They are, however, some that every knowledgeable and competent end user should be aware of.

GRAPHICS

Desktop publishers mix text and graphics. Image editors modify bitmap image files. Illustrators modify vector files. Image galleries are libraries of electronic images. Graphics suites bundle separate programs.

In Chapter 3, we discussed analytical and presentation graphics, which are widely used to analyze data and to create professional-looking presentations. Here we focus on more specialized graphics programs used by professionals in the graphic arts profession. These graphics programs include desktop publishing, image editors, and illustration programs. While desktop publishing is used to produce professional publications, image editors and illustration programs are used to modify graphic images.

DESKTOP PUBLISHING

Desktop publishing programs, or **page layout programs,** allow you to mix text and graphics to create publications of professional quality. While word processors focus on creating text and have the ability to combine text and graphics, desktop publishers focus on page design and layout and provide greater flexibility. Professional graphic artists use desktop publishing programs to create documents such as brochures, newsletters, newspapers, and textbooks.

Desktop publishing systems provide a variety of tools. (See Figure 4-2.) Four basic tools common to almost all desktop publishing programs are:

- **Selection tool** to select, move, and resize images and text.
- **Text tool** to draw text frames, insert text, and control wrapping of text.
- **Graphics tool** for creating and importing graphic elements.
- **Magnification/zoom tool** to present close-up and distance views of the document.

Popular desktop publishing programs include Adobe PageMaker, Microsoft Publisher, and QuarkXPress. While these programs provide the capability to create text and graphics, typically graphic artists import these elements from other sources including word processors, digital cameras, scanners, image editors, illustration programs, and image galleries. Word processors create text. Digital cameras and scanners provide images. Image editors and illustration

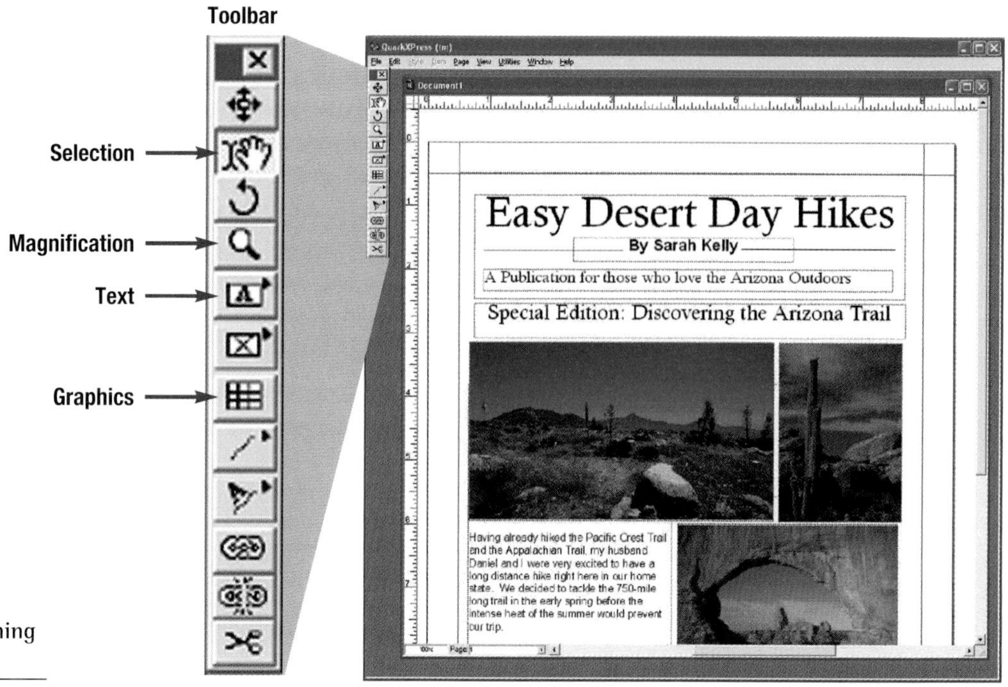

Figure 4-2 Desktop publishing tools

programs create and edit photos and other images. Image galleries provide graphics.

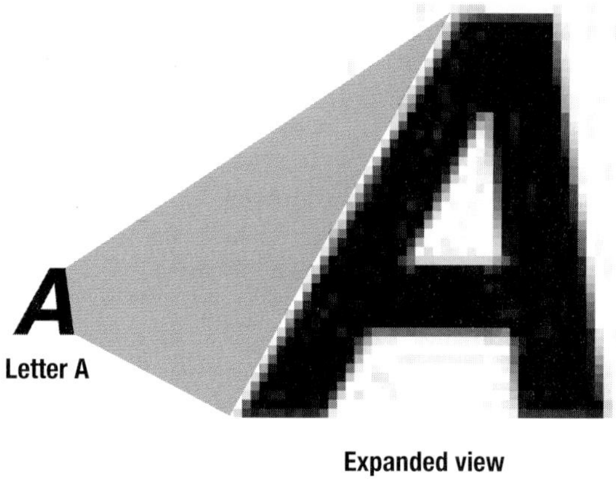

Figure 4-3 Bitmap image

IMAGE EDITORS

One of the most common types of graphic files is bitmap. **Bitmap images,** also known as **raster images,** use thousands of dots or **pixels** to represent images. Each dot has a specific location, color, and shade. For example, see Figure 4-3 for a bitmap representation for the letter A.

File names that end with .bmp, .jpg, .gif, and .tif are bitmap files. Bmp files are widely used to capture photographic and other realistic images. Jpeg and gif files are widely used for Web page images. Tiff files are used for printed documents. One limitation of bitmap images, however, is that when expanded the images can become pixilated or jagged on the edges. For example, if the letter A in Figure 4-3 were to be expanded, the borders of the letter would appear even more jagged, as indicated by the expanded view.

Image editors are programs for creating and editing bitmap images. Also known as **paint programs,** image editors provide a variety of tools including pens, brushes, and filters.

- A **pen** is used to create drawing and objects.
- A **brush** is used to fill an area or object with a color.
- **Filters** create special effects and textures for your pictures.

Popular professional image editors include Microsoft Paint, Adobe Photoshop, Corel PhotoPaint, and Paint Shop Pro. (See Figure 4-4)

On the Web Explorations

Adobe Systems Inc. is one of the leaders in the development of powerful graphics programs. To learn more about the company, visit our Web site at

http://www.mhhe.com/oleary/CT05 and select On the Web Explorations from Tim's Toolbox.

ILLUSTRATION PROGRAMS

Vector is another common type of graphic file. While bitmap images use pixels to represent images, **vector images,** also known as **vector illustrations,**

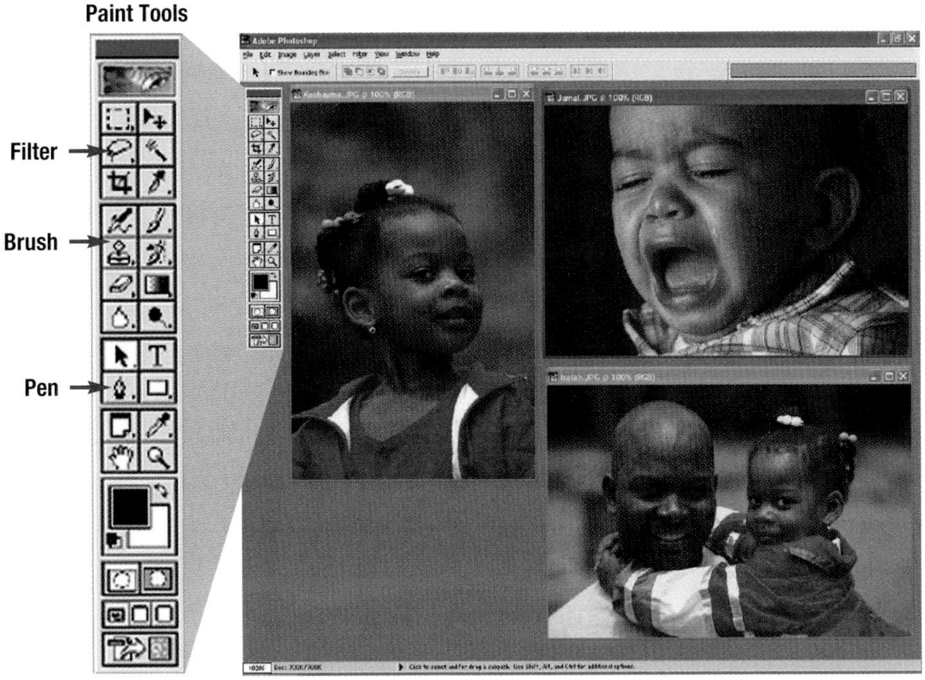
Paint Tools
Filter
Brush
Pen
Adobe Photoshop

Figure 4-4 Adobe Photoshop

Figure 4-5 Vector Image

use geometric shapes or objects. These objects are created by connecting lines and curves. Because these objects can be defined by mathematical equations, they can be rapidly and easily resized, colored, textured, and manipulated. An image is a combination of several objects. (See Figure 4-5.)

File names that end with .ai, .cdr, .drw, and .dxf are vector files. Compared to bitmap files, vector files are not good for capturing photo-realistic images. However, because the images are defined by mathematical equations, they can be expanded and resized without creating jagged edges and are widely used to create animated feature films.

Illustration programs, also known as **drawing programs,** are used to create and to edit vector images. Graphic artists use illustration programs to create line art for magazines, books, and special publications. Animators use them to create feature films. Engineers and programmers use them to create 3-D models. One exciting application is to create virtual worlds or virtual reality, as we describe later in this chapter. Popular professional illustration programs include Adobe Illustrator, CorelDraw, Macromedia FreeHand, and Micrografx Designer. (See Figure 4-6.)

IMAGE GALLERIES

Image galleries are libraries of electronic images. These images are used for a wide variety of applications from illustrating textbooks to providing visual interest to presentations. There are two basic types of electronic images in these galleries.

- **Stock photographs**—photographs on a variety of subject material from professional models to natural landscapes.
- **Clip art**—graphic illustrations representing a wide range of topics. Most applications provide access to a limited selection of free clip art. For example in Microsoft Word, you can gain access to several pieces of clip art by issuing the command Insert>Pictures>Clip Art.

There are numerous Web image galleries. (See Figure 4-7.) Some of these sites offer free images and clip art while others charge a fee.

Figure 4-6 CorelDraw

Organization	Site
ArtToday	www.arttoday.com
Borderbund	www.borderbund.com
Design Gallery Live	www.dgl.microsoft.com
GifArt	www.gifart.com
Graphics Maps	www.graphicsmap.com

Figure 4-7 Selected Web image galleries

Figure 4-8 CorelDraw

GRAPHICS SUITES

Some companies are combining or bundling their separate graphics programs in groups called **graphics suites.** The advantage of the graphics suites is that you can buy a larger variety of graphics programs at a lower cost than if purchased separately.

The most popular suite is from the Corel Corporation. The suite, called CorelDraw Graphics Suite, includes five individual Corel graphics programs plus a large library of clip art, media clips, and fonts. (See Figure 4-8.) Two other popular suites are Corel's Graphics Pack and Micrografx's ABC Graphics Suite.

For a summary of graphics programs including analytical and presentation graphics, see Figure 4-9.

Type	Purpose
Analytical graphics	Analyze and graph data
Presentation graphics	Create professional-looking presentations
Desktop publishing	Mix text and graphics to create professional-looking publications
Image editors	Create and modify bitmap images
Illustration programs	Create and edit vector images
Image gallery	Offer library of electronic images
Graphic suites	Combine separate graphics programs

Figure 4-9 Graphics

Concept Check

- What is desktop publishing?
- What is the difference between an image editor and an illustration program?
- Describe image galleries.
- What are graphics suites?

AUDIO AND VIDEO

Digital video editing software makes it easy to make digital video into professional quality home movies. Audio editing software makes it easy to record and edit music at home.

In the past, professional quality editing of home audio and video was a job for professional photo labs or studios. For example, if you wanted to assemble footage from all your Fourth of July picnics, you sent all the tapes to a lab and waited for a compilation tape. Using audio and video editing software, you can create your own compilation movies.

- **Video editing software** allows you to reorganize, add effects, and more to your digital video footage. Two commonly used video editing software programs are Apple's iMovie and Windows Movie Maker. (See Figure 4-10.) These programs are designed to allow you to assemble and edit new home videos and movies from raw digital video footage. For example, you could compose a home movie using videos of your summer vacation with captions, sound effects, and narration, and then post your video on the Web for your family and friends to view.
- **Audio editing software** allows you to create and edit audio clips. Most audio editing software also has features that allow you to add audio effects, like filters, to your tracks. For example, you can use this type of software to filter out pops or scratches in an old recording. You can even use this software to create your own MP3s. Some commonly used audio editing software programs are SonicFoundry's ACID Music and Syntrillium Software's Cool Edit. (See Figure 4-11.)

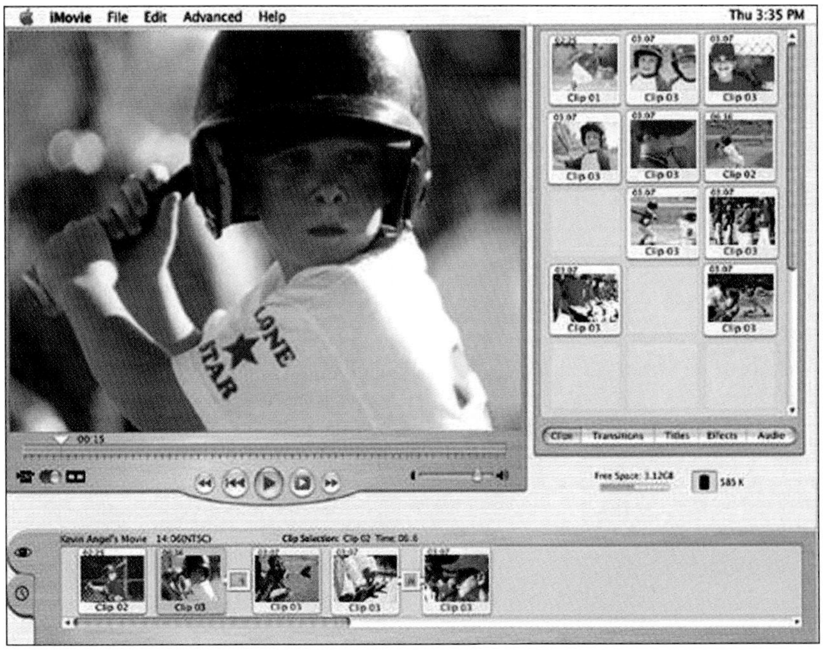

Figure 4-10 Apple iMovie

Concept Check

- What is digital video editing software?
- What is audio editing software?

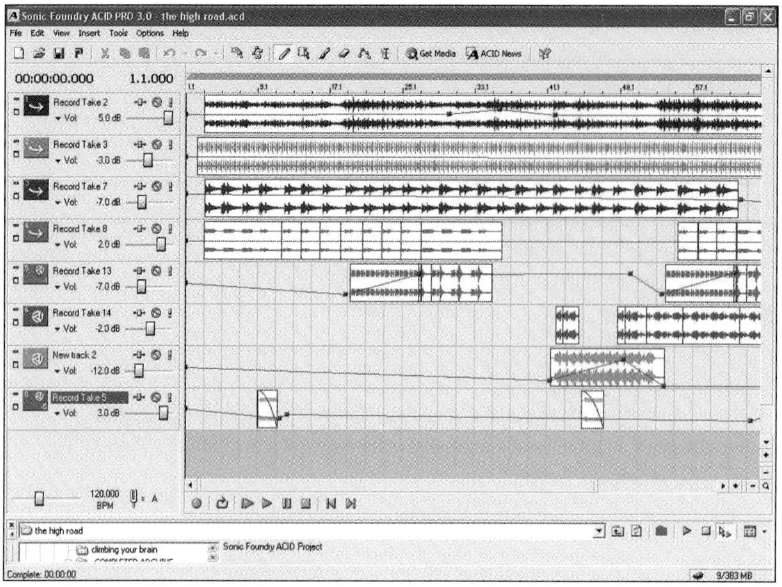

Figure 4-11 ACID Music audio software

MULTIMEDIA

Multimedia presentations can include a variety of media and should include interactivity. Pages are linked by buttons. Plan and organize, design, create, and support are steps in developing multimedia presentations. Multimedia authoring programs create presentations.

Multimedia is the integration of all sorts of media into one presentation. For example, a multimedia presentation may include video, music, voice, graphics, and text. You may have seen multimedia applied in video games, Web presentations, or even a word processing document. When word processors were first introduced, they produced simple text documents. Now, using a word processor you can create documents that not only contain text but include graphics, audio clips, animations and other types of media. Many of the basic application software programs you learned about in Chapter 3 include features that make the incorporation of multimedia in documents easy. Although these applications include multimedia features, they create documents that are generally accessed in a linear fashion and provide very limited user interaction.

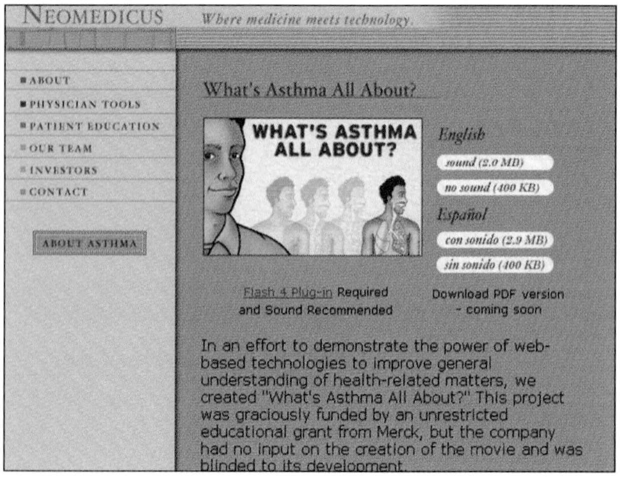

Figure 4-12 Opening page of a multimedia presentation "About Asthma"

Effective multimedia presentations incorporate user participation or interactivity. **Interactivity** allows the user to choose the information to view, to control the pace and flow of information, and to respond to items and receive feedback. When experiencing an interactive multimedia presentation, users customize the presentation to their needs. For example Figure 4-12 presents an opening page of a multimedia presentation titled "About Asthma." Users are able to select the language to be used and whether sound is included. (You can access this multimedia presentation from the Web at www.neomedicus.md.)

Once used almost exclusively for computer games, interactive multimedia is now widely used in business, education, and the home. Business uses include high-quality interactive presentations, product demonstrations, and Web page design. In education, interactive multimedia is used for in-class presentations and demonstrations, long-distance learning, and online testing over the Internet. In the home, multimedia is primarily used for entertainment.

LINKS AND BUTTONS

An interactive multimedia presentation is typically organized as a series of related pages. Each page presents information and provides **links** or connections to related information. These links can be to video, sound, graphics, and text files, and to other pages and to other resources. By clicking special areas called **buttons** on a page, you can make appropriate links and "navigate" through a presentation to locate and discover information. Typically, there are several buttons on a page. You can select one, some, or none of them. You are in control. You direct the flow and content of the presentation. (See Figure 4-13.)

Figure 4-13 Links and buttons are used to navigate the "About Asthma" multimedia presentation

DEVELOPING MULTIMEDIA PRESENTATIONS

The creation of interactive multimedia presentations follows several steps: Plan and Analyze, Design, Create, and Support. The same development process is followed, regardless of the complexity and size of the project. The steps are as follows:

- **Plan and analyze:** When planning the project you need to determine the overall objective of the project, the resources required, and the person or team of people who will work on the project. In order to specify objectives and set project requirements, analysis of the project is needed.
- **Design:** The creation of a story board is essential to the development of the project. A **story board** is a design tool used to record the intended overall logic, flow, and structure of a multimedia presentation. Figure 4-14 presents a partial overall story board. The highlighted path indicates just

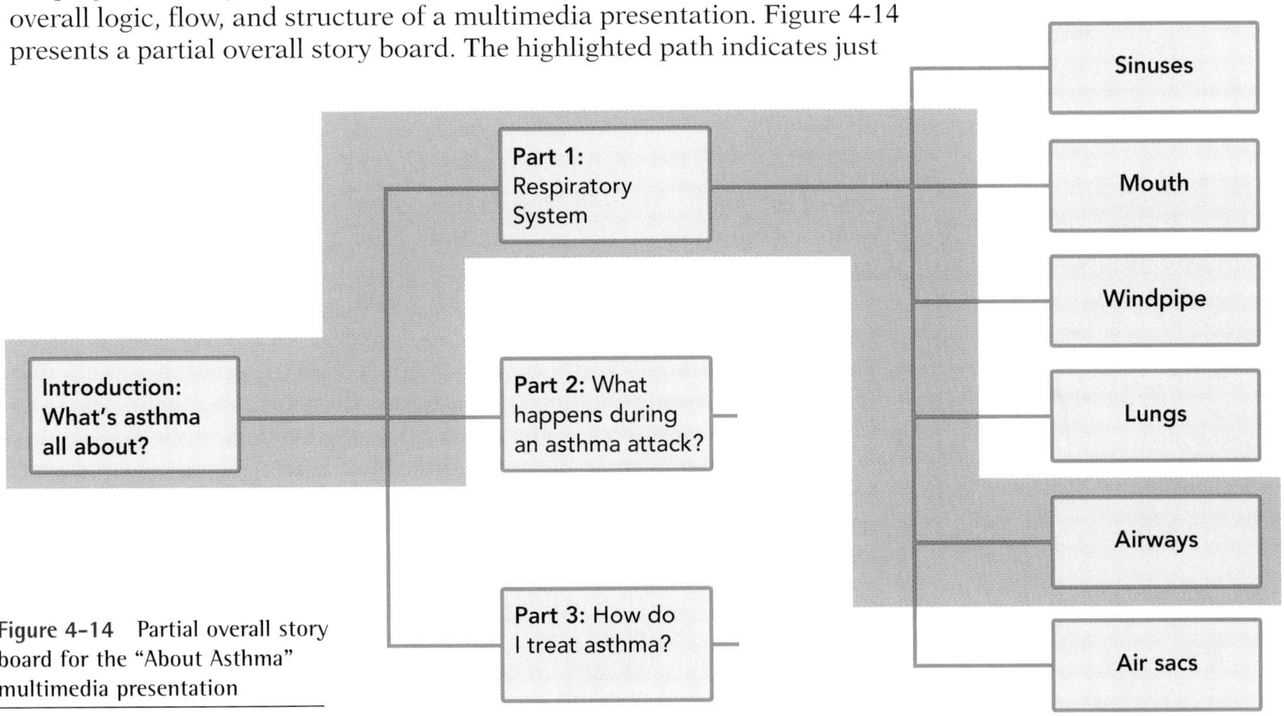

Figure 4-14 Partial overall story board for the "About Asthma" multimedia presentation

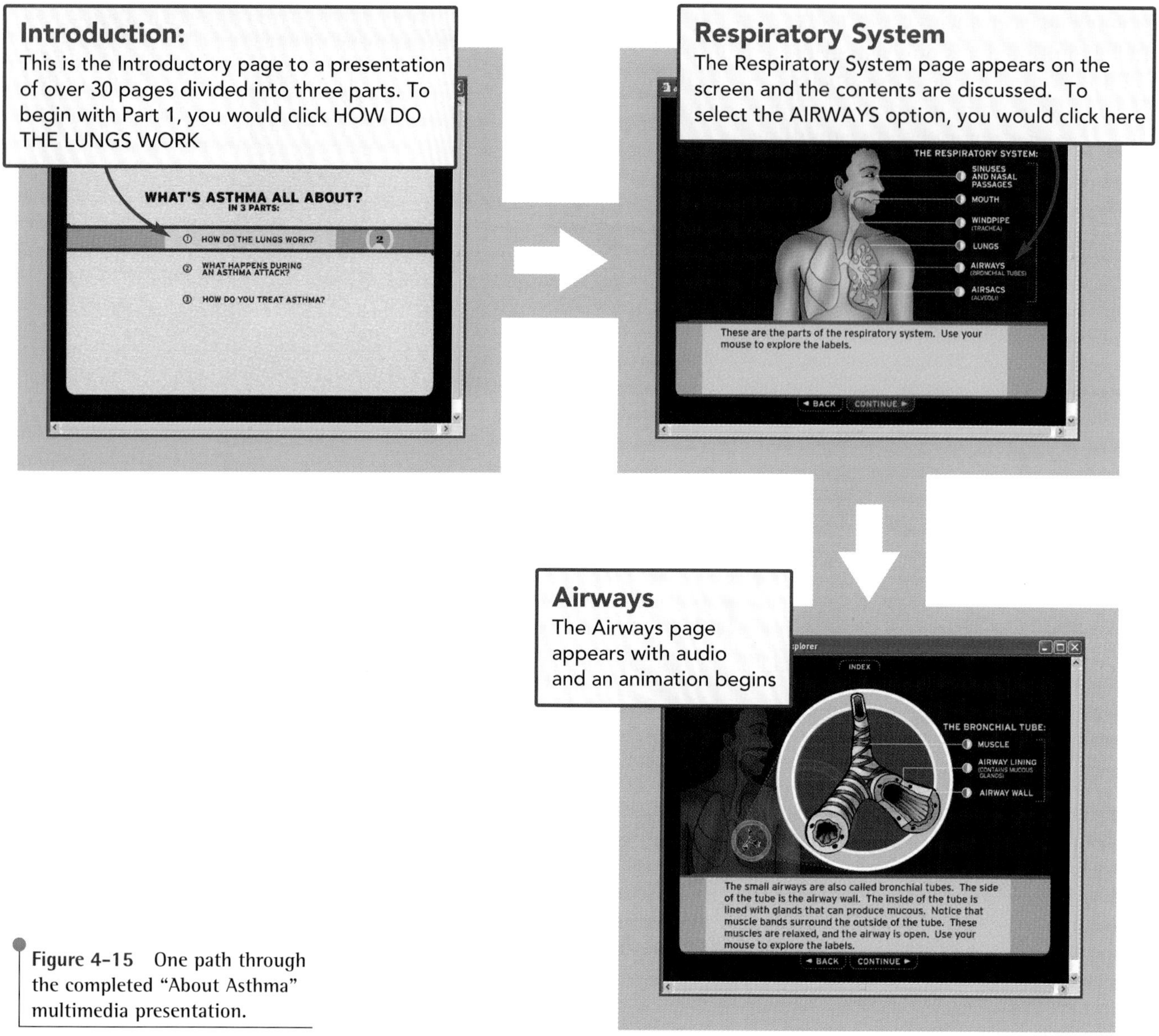
Introduction:
This is the Introductory page to a presentation of over 30 pages divided into three parts. To begin with Part 1, you would click HOW DO THE LUNGS WORK
WHAT'S ASTHMA ALL ABOUT?
IN 3 PARTS:
① HOW DO THE LUNGS WORK?
② WHAT HAPPENS DURING AN ASTHMA ATTACK?
③ HOW DO YOU TREAT ASTHMA?
Respiratory System
The Respiratory System page appears on the screen and the contents are discussed. To select the AIRWAYS option, you would click here
THE RESPIRATORY SYSTEM:
SINUSES AND NASAL PASSAGES
MOUTH
WINDPIPE (TRACHEA)
LUNGS
AIRWAYS (BRONCHIAL TUBES)
AIRSACS (ALVEOLI)
These are the parts of the respiratory system. Use your mouse to explore the labels.
◄ BACK
CONTINUE ►
Airways
The Airways page appears with audio and an animation begins
INDEX
THE BRONCHIAL TUBE:
MUSCLE
AIRWAY LINING (CONTAINS MUCOUS GLANDS)
AIRWAY WALL
The small airways are also called bronchial tubes. The side of the tube is the airway wall. The inside of the tube is lined with glands that can produce mucous. Notice that muscle bands surround the outside of the tube. These muscles are relaxed, and the airway is open. Use your mouse to explore the labels.
◄ BACK
CONTINUE ►

Figure 4-15 One path through the completed "About Asthma" multimedia presentation.

On the Web Explorations

Firstborn Multimedia is a leading developer of multimedia presentations on the Web. To learn more about this company visit our Web site at

http://www.mhhe.com/oleary/CT05

and select On the Web Explorations from Tim's Toolbox.

one of the many different paths a user could take. Each rectangle represents a single page in the presentation. Each page has a detailed story board associated with it that specifies the content, style, and design along with the links to video, audio, graphics, text, or any other media for that particular page.

- **Create:** A multimedia authoring program is used to create the interactive multimedia presentation once the different elements specified in the story boards, such as graphics, sound, and video, are available. For example, see a selection of pages from "About Asthma" in Figure 4-15. This sequence of pages matches the highlighted story board elements in Figure 4-14 and represents just one possible path through the presentation.
- **Support:** Once the multimedia presentation is complete, it is made available for use. Any errors that are identified need to be corrected. The presentation is evaluated in terms of its effectiveness to meet its goal. Future plans for revision and updating are determined, at which point the development process may begin again.

MULTIMEDIA AUTHORING PROGRAMS

Multimedia authoring programs are special programs used to create multimedia presentations. They bring together all the video, audio, graphics, and text elements into an interactive framework. Widely used authoring programs include Macromedia Director, Authorware, and Toolbook. (See Figure 4-16.)

Figure 4-16 Macromedia Director

Concept Check

- ✔ What are multimedia and interactivity?
- ✔ Describe the four steps to create an interactive multimedia presentation.
- ✔ What are multimedia authoring programs?

WEB AUTHORING

Creating Web sites is called Web authoring. Graphical maps present overall Web site design. Web authoring programs support design and HTML coding.

On the Web Explorations

Macromedia Inc. is one of the leaders in the development of multimedia authoring programs. To learn more about the company, visit our Web site at http://www.mhhe.com/oleary/CT05 and select On the Web Explorations from Tim's Toolbox.

You have probably interacted with a multimedia presentation on a Web site. There are over half a million commercial Web sites on the Internet, and hundreds more are being added every day. Corporations use the Web to reach new customers and to promote their products. (See Figure 4-17.) Individuals can even create their own personal sites on the Web. (See Making IT Work for You: Personal Web Sites on pages 138–39.) Have you ever wondered how these sites are created, or ever thought of creating your own Web site? Creating a site is called **Web authoring.** It begins with site design followed by creation of a document file that displays the Web site's content.

WEB SITE DESIGN

A Web site is an interactive multimedia form of communication. Designing a Web site begins with determining the site's overall content. The content is then broken down into a series of related pieces of information. The overall site design is commonly represented in a **graphical map.** (See Figure 4-18.)

Notice that the graphical map shown in Figure 4-18 is very similar to the story board depicted in Figure 4-14. In this case, however, each block in the map represents a Web page. Lines joining the blocks represent links to related pages of information that make up the Web site. The first page typically serves as an introduction and supplies a table of contents. The following pages present the specific pieces or blocks of information.

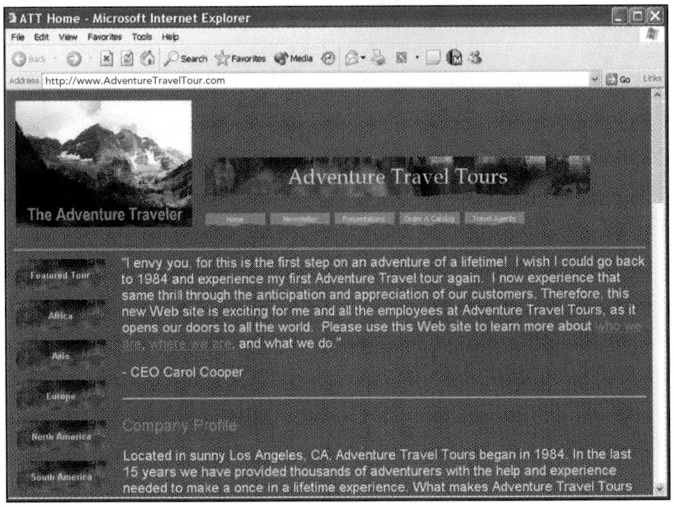

Figure 4-17 Adventure Travel Tours Web site

Multimedia elements are added to individual pages to enhance interest and interactivity. One common multimedia element found on most Web sites is moving graphics called **animations.** These anima-

PERSONAL WEB SITES

Do you have something to share with the world? Would you like a personal Web site, but don't want to deal with learning HTML? Creating your own home on the Internet is easy, and there are many services available to get you started.

How It Works A service site on the Web provides access to tools to create personal Web pages. After registering with the site, you create your Web pages using the tools provided. Once completed, the service site acts as a host for your personal Web site and others are free to visit it from anywhere in the world.

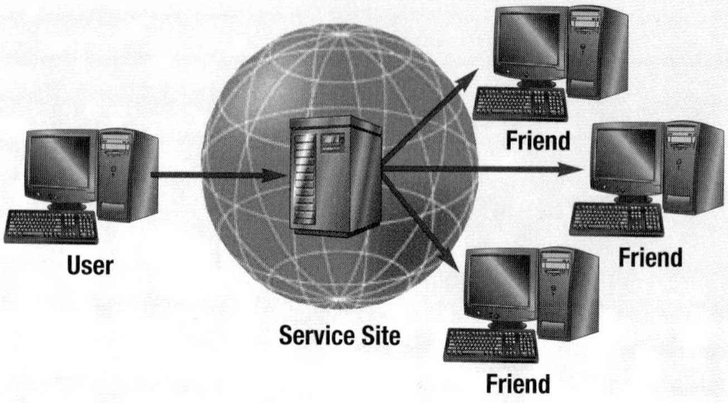

Creating a Weblog Weblogs have become a popular way to create a personal Web site. A Weblog is a Web page with dated postings, like a bulletin board. Many service sites offer Weblogs for users. For example, you could use the service site Blogger.com to start a Weblog by following these steps:

1

- **Connect to *www.blogger.com* and follow the instructions to sign up for an account.**
- **Type a name and description for your Weblog.**
- **Click *next*.**
- **Follow the on-screen instructions to choose hosting options and a URL others will visit to see your page.**

2 Select a template for your site. This design will be the colors and layout used on your Web site.

- Click *finish*.

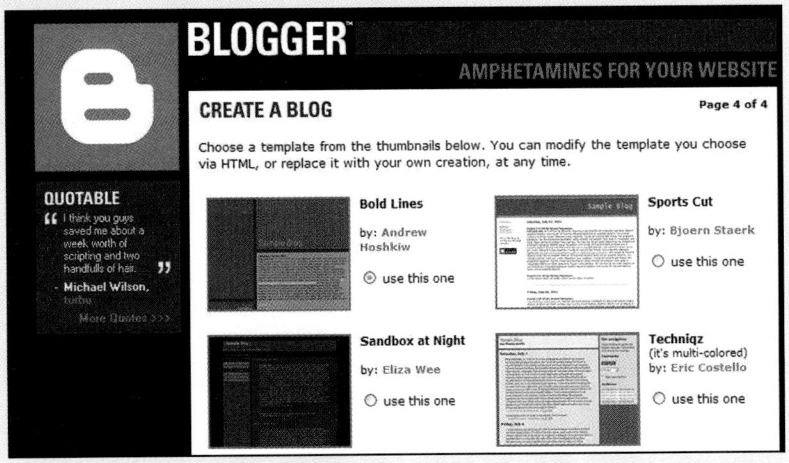

Posting to Your Weblog Once your Weblog has been created, you can add content easily by visiting a Web page and entering your information. For example, to post to a Blogger.com Weblog:

1 Connect to ***www.blogger.com*** and sign in.

- Add the text of your post to the upper pane.
- To add an image, click *Upload File* and follow the on-screen instructions.
- To add a link to another Web site, select the text for the link and click the *Hyperlink* button.

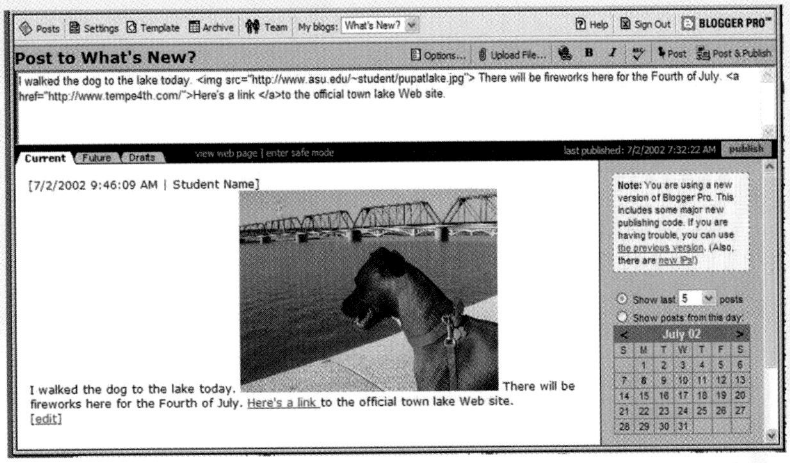

2 Click *Post* to see your new post in the lower pane.

- If you'd like to touch up your post, click [edit].
- When your post looks the way you'd like it to appear, click *publish*.
- Click *view web page* to see your page on the Internet.

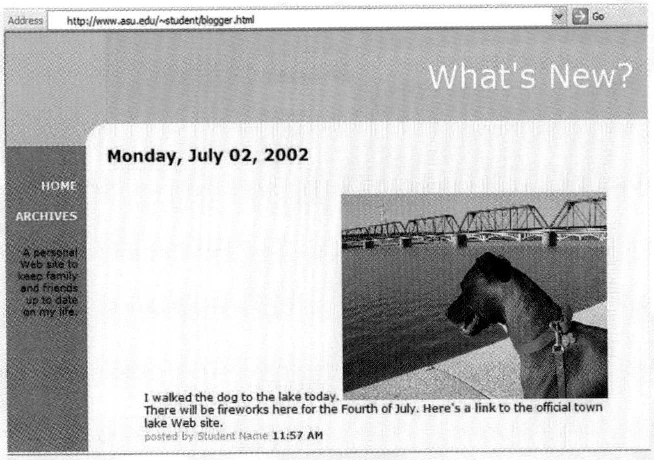

The page displayed is what others see when they visit your site.

Your Weblog is now ready for the world. To visit, all your friends and family need to do is to point their browser to the URL you specified in step 1. The Web is continually changing and some of the specifics presented in this Making IT Work for You may have changed. To learn about other ways to make technology work for you, visit our Web site at http://www.mhhe.com/oleary/CT05 and select Making IT Work for You from Tim's Toolbox.

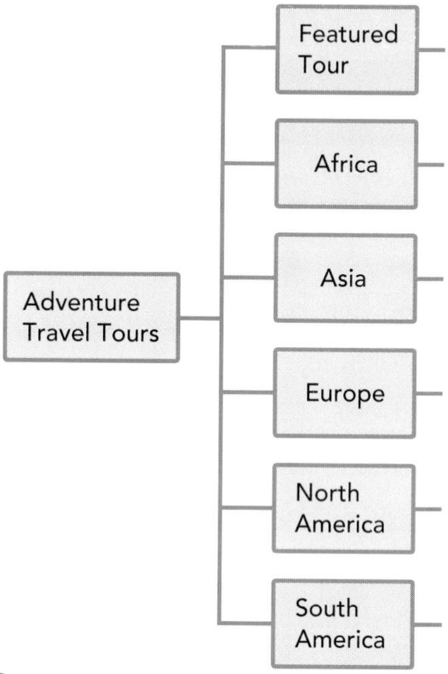

Figure 4-18 Partial graphical map for the Adventure Travel Tours Web site

TIPS Are you thinking about creating your own Web site? Perhaps you already have one and would like to spruce it up a bit? Here are a few suggestions that might help.

1. **Use a common design and theme.** Consistency in the use of colors, fonts, background designs, and navigation features gives a Web site a unified feeling and makes it easier to use.
2. **Use graphics and animations to add interest.** Graphics and animations add interest and focus the user's attention. However, they take time to download and the wait time frustrates users. Be selective and limit the size of graphics. Also reuse graphics from one page to another.
3. **Make navigating your Web site easy.** Create a simple method of navigating that allows users to get to their desired information as quickly as possible. None of your content should be more than three clicks from the home page.
4. **Design your site for a standard display.** To maximize the impact of your site for the largest number of users, design it to be viewed by a monitor with a standard 800 × 600 resolution.

tions can be simple moving text or complicated interactive features. There are many specialized programs available to aid in the creation of animation. One type of interactive animation is produced using software from Macromedia Inc. Called **Flash,** this type of animation is usually full-screen and highly dynamic and interactive. (See Figure 4-19.) Another common visual effect found on the Web is morphing. **Morphing** is a special effect in which one image seems to melt into another.

Name	Address
Bose Audio	www.bose.com
Disney	www.disney.com
FAO Schwarz	www.fao.com
Hard Rock Hotel	www.hardrockhotel.com
Sony Classical	www.sonyclassical.com

Figure 4-19 Web sites that use Flash animation

WEB AUTHORING PROGRAMS

As we mentioned in Chapter 2, Web pages are displayed using HTML documents. With knowledge of HTML and a simple text editor, you can create Web pages. Even without knowledge of HTML you can create Web pages using one of many word processing packages as demonstrated in Chapter 3.

More specialized and powerful programs, called **Web authoring programs,** are typically used to create sophisticated commercial sites. Also known as **Web page editors** and **HTML editors,** these programs provide support for Web site design and HTML coding. Widely used Web authoring programs include Macromedia Dreamweaver, NetObjects Fusion, and Microsoft FrontPage. (See Figure 4-20.) The Web site depicted in Figures 4-17 and 4-18 was created using Microsoft FrontPage. (See Figure 4-21.)

To learn more about creating your own Web site, consult your Computing Today CD or visit us on the Web at http://www.mhhe.com/oleary/ CT05 and select Expansions from Tim's Toolbox.

Figure 4-20 Microsoft FrontPage

Concept Check

- Describe Web authoring.
- What are graphical maps? What are they used for?
- What is animation? How is it used on the Web?

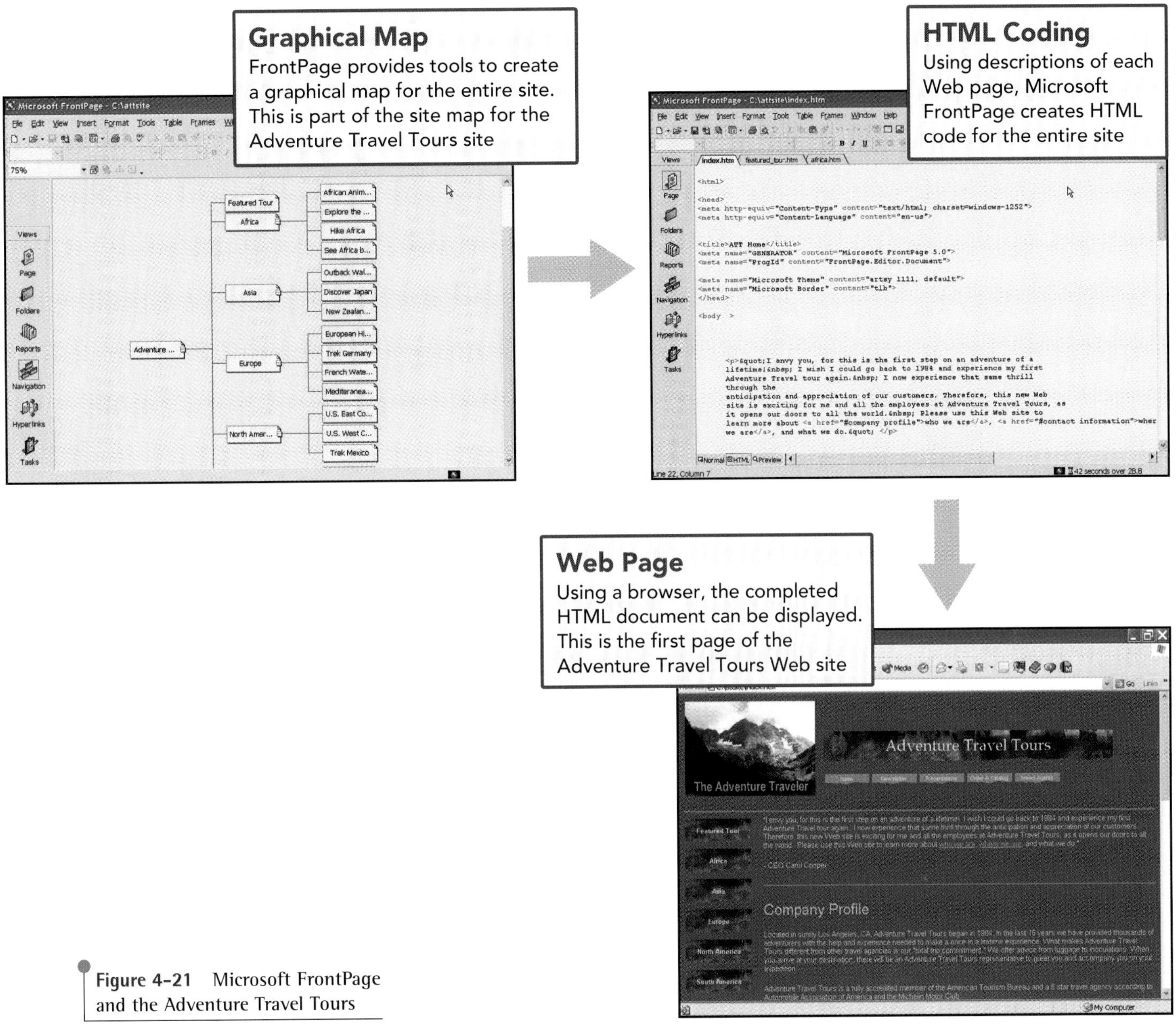
Graphical Map
FrontPage provides tools to create a graphical map for the entire site. This is part of the site map for the Adventure Travel Tours site
HTML Coding
Using descriptions of each Web page, Microsoft FrontPage creates HTML code for the entire site
Web Page
Using a browser, the completed HTML document can be displayed. This is the first page of the Adventure Travel Tours Web site
Adventure Travel Tours
The Adventure Traveler
Company Profile

Figure 4-21 Microsoft FrontPage and the Adventure Travel Tours

PERSONAL APPLICATIONS

Personal software used by individuals who sacrifice advanced features for lower cost and simplicity. Personal software includes PIMS, personal finance managers, and personal tax preparation software.

There are several ways that application programs can be categorized. One way, as discussed previously, is to distinguish between general-purpose and special-purpose programs. Another way is to distinguish between professional and personal applications. Professional applications are powerful feature-rich applications. Almost all of the applications discussed so far have been professional applications. **Personal software** or **home software,** as discussed in

Chapter 3, is intended for use by individuals who are willing to sacrifice some advanced features for lower cost and simplicity. For example, an integrated package like Microsoft Works offers the basic functionality of a software suite like Microsoft Office at a much lower cost.

There are thousands of personal applications. Many are general-purpose programs like Microsoft Works. Most, however, are special-purpose programs. Some of the most widely used personal software are personal information managers, finance managers, and tax preparation programs.

PERSONAL INFORMATION MANAGERS

Personal Information Managers (PIMs), also known as **desktop managers,** are applications that provide an easy-to-use electronic alternative to the traditional appointment calendar, address book, and notepad. Two widely used PIMs are Microsoft Outlook and Palm Desktop.

Features

Although widely used on desktop systems, PIMs are most common on handheld computers or personal digital assistants (PDAs). (See Figure 4-22.) PDAs usually communicate with your desktop computer, allowing you to back up and access your PIM data. (See Figure 4-23.) Three important features common to PIMs are:

- **Calendar:** Operates like an electronic appointment book that keeps track of events, holidays, assignments, and project schedules. Additionally, most calendars provide assistance in scheduling meetings and organizing projects.
- **Contacts:** Used to record names, addresses, and telephone , like a traditional address book. In addition, electronic address books are linked to the other parts of a PIM to save you time and energy.
- **Tasks:** A task organizer, or a to-do list, provides two basic functions. First, it records, displays, and reminds you of tasks you need to complete. Second, it works to record, display, coordinate, and communicate tasks assigned to a group.

Figure 4-22 PDAs manage personal information

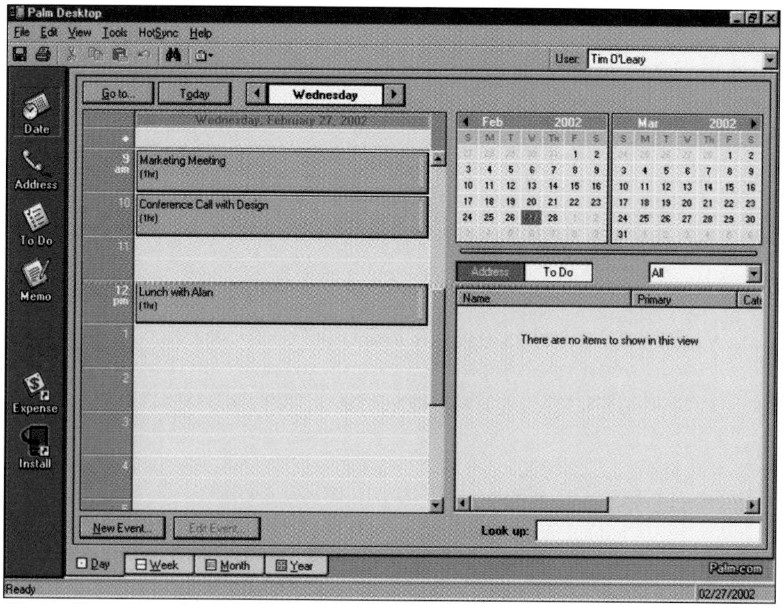

Figure 4-23 Desktop manager

Figure 4-24 Microsoft Money

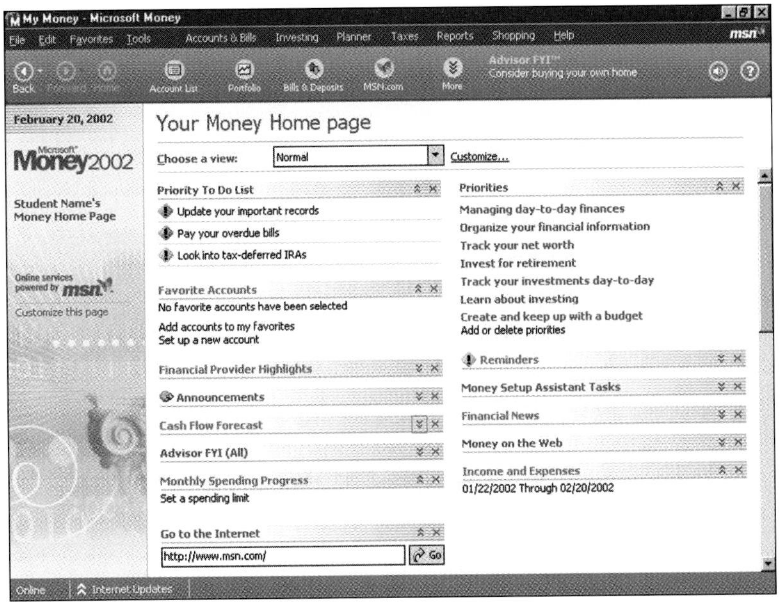

Figure 4-25 Microsoft Money

PERSONAL FINANCE MANAGERS

A **personal finance management** program helps users organize and manage their money. These programs have an easy-to-use interface and are designed to balance checkbooks, track spending, pay bills, and prepare taxes. The two most widely used personal finance management programs are Intuit's Quicken and Microsoft's Money. (See Figure 4-24.)

Features

Like PIMs, most personal finance software programs are designed to help users organize and centralize documents and assist in financial planning. These programs allow you to keep track of your checking account, credit card debt, and investment information in one place. (See Figure 4-25.)

One prominent feature offered by personal finance managers is budget planning. You can enter your financial data into the program and specify your financial goals, and the program creates a plan to help you achieve them.

Perhaps the most powerful feature of a personal finance management program is **online banking.** The program can connect to your bank account via the Internet and automatically update your check register. The program can also remind you of upcoming expenses and schedule online payments from your checking account.

These powerful and useful programs also seamlessly communicate your financial records to a tax preparation program. They can help you estimate your taxes and highlight possible deductions.

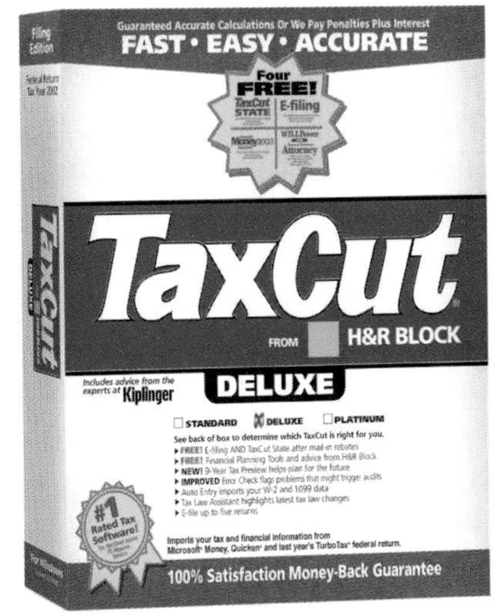

Figure 4-26 TaxCut tax preparation software

PERSONAL TAX PREPARATION

Personal tax preparation software allows you to easily input your financial records and helps you prepare and file your tax return. The program prompts you to enter your financial information and answer basic questions about your finances and then completes the forms you will need to submit to the government. Most of these programs also now offer the opportunity to electronically submit your tax return via the Internet.

The newest versions of this type of program are designed to work with personal finance managers (like Money) and include advisors designed to help you understand tax laws, anticipate deductions, and understand your investments. Two common popular tax preparation software programs are TaxCut and TurboTax. (See Figure 4-26.)

Concept Check

- Describe personal software.
- What is a Personal Information Manager? How is it used?
- What is a personal finance manager?
- What is tax preparation software designed to do? How does it relate to personal finance managers?

EMERGING APPLICATIONS

Artificial intelligence attempts to simulate human senses, thought processes, and actions. Three areas are virtual reality, knowledge-based (expert) systems, and robotics.

New and revised applications programs are appearing every day. A common thread with most of these emerging applications is the inclusion, however subtle, of artificial intelligence concepts. Clearly, artificial intelligence and its applications are one of the most exciting developments in the 21st century. You have probably seen a portrayal of a robot with the intelligence, sensibilities, and capabilities of a human in a movie or on television. Depictions of robots and computers with artificial intelligence are common. In the past such depictions were pure fiction, but computer science has made great strides in the creation of artificial intelligence and the integration of this intelligence into a wide range of applications.

The field of computer science known as **artificial intelligence (AI)** attempts to develop computer systems that can mimic or simulate human senses, thought processes, and actions. These include reasoning, learning from past actions, and using senses such as vision and touch. Artificial intelligence that corresponds to human intelligence is still a long way off. However, several tools that emulate human senses, problem solving, and information processing have been developed.

On the Web Explorations

Artificial Intelligence Enterprises is a leading developer of artificial intelligence software. To learn more about this company visit us at

http://www.mhhe.com/oleary/CT05

and select On the Web Explorations from Tim's Toolbox.

These modern applications of artificial intelligence are designed to help people and organizations become more productive. Many of these tools have practical applications for business, medicine, law, and so on. In the past, computers used calculating power to solve **structured problems,** which can be broken down into a series of well-defined steps. People—using intuition, reasoning, and memory—were better at solving **unstructured problems,** whether building a product or approving a loan. Organizations have long been able to computerize the tasks once performed by clerks. Now knowledge-intensive work and unstructured problems, such as activities performed by many managers, is being automated. Let us now consider three areas in which human talents and abilities have been enhanced with "computerized intelligence": virtual reality, knowledge-based systems, and robotics.

VIRTUAL REALITY

Suppose you could create and virtually experience any new form of reality you wished. You could see the world through the eyes of a child, a robot—or even a lobster. You could explore faraway resorts, the moon, or inside a nuclear waste dump, without leaving your chair. This simulated experience is possible with virtual reality.

Virtual reality is an artificial, or simulated, reality generated in 3-D by a computer. Virtual reality is also commonly known as **VR, artificial reality,** or

virtual environments. To navigate in a virtual space you use virtual reality hardware including headgear and gloves. The headgear has earphones and three-dimensional stereoscopic screens (one type is called Eyephones). The gloves have sensors that collect data about your hand movements (one type is called DataGlove). Coupled with software (such as a program called Body Electric), this interactive sensory equipment lets you immerse yourself in a computer-generated world. See Figure 4-27.

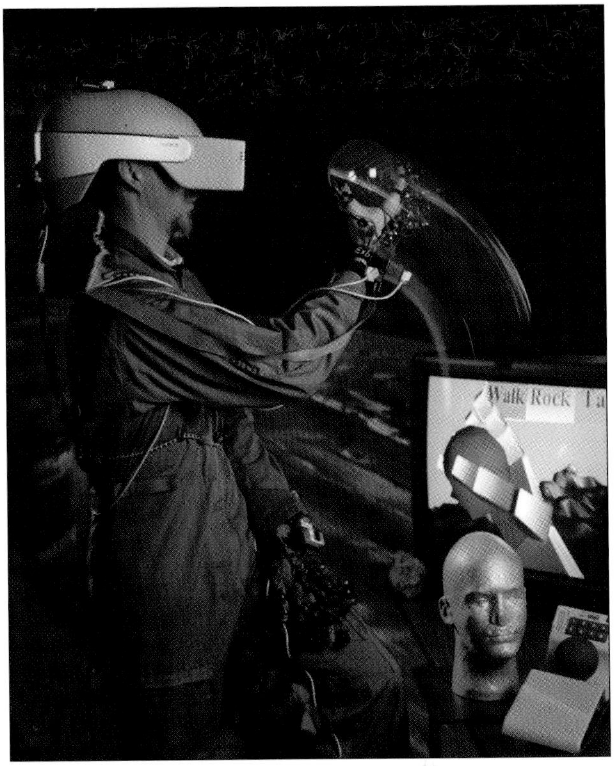

Figure 4-27 Virtual reality

Virtual reality modeling language (VRML) is used to create real-time animated 3-D scenes. Hundreds of sites exist on the Web with virtual reality applications. Users are able to experience these applications with browsers that support VRML.

Creating virtual reality programs once required very high end software costing several thousands of dollars. Recently, several lower-cost yet powerful authoring programs have been introduced. These programs utilize VRML and are widely used to create Web-based virtual reality applications. One of the best known is Cosmo Worlds from Cosmo Software.

There are any number of possible applications for virtual reality. The ultimate recreational use might be something resembling a giant virtual amusement park. More serious applications can simulate important experiences or training environments such as in aviation, surgical operations, spaceship repair, or nuclear disaster cleanup. Modern virtual reality strives to be an **immersive experience,** allowing a user to walk into a virtual reality room or view simulations on a **virtual reality wall.** (See Figure 4-28.)

Figure 4-28 Virtual reality wall

KNOWLEDGE-BASED (EXPERT) SYSTEMS

People who are expert in a particular area—certain kinds of law, medicine, accounting, engineering, and so on—are generally well paid for their specialized knowledge. Unfortunately for their clients and customers they are expensive, not always available, and hard to replace when they move on.

What if you were to somehow capture the knowledge of a human expert and make it accessible to everyone through a computer program? This is exactly what is being done with so-called knowledge-based or expert systems. **Knowledge-based systems,** also known as **expert systems,** are a type of artificial intelligence that uses a database to provide assistance to users. These systems use a database, or **knowledge base,** that contains specific facts, rules to relate these facts, and user input to formulate recommendations and decisions. The sequence of processing is determined by the interaction of the user and the knowledge base. Many expert systems use so-called **fuzzy logic,** which allows users to respond to questions in a very humanlike way. For example, if an expert system asked how your classes were going, you could respond, "great," "OK," "terrible," and so on.

Over the past decade, expert systems have been developed in areas such as medicine, geology, architecture and nature. (See Figure 4-29.) There are expert

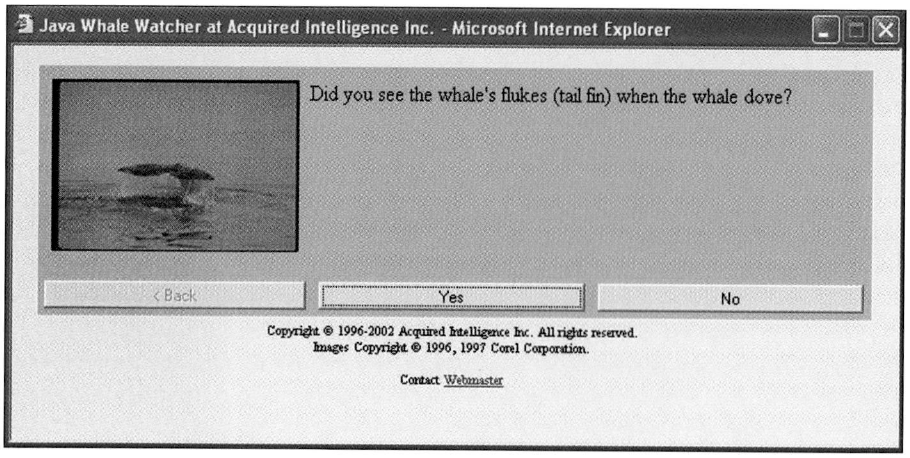
Java Whale Watcher at Acquired Intelligence Inc. - Microsoft Internet Explorer
Did you see the whale's flukes (tail fin) when the whale dove?
< Back
Yes
No
Copyright © 1996-2002 Acquired Intelligence Inc. All rights reserved.
Images Copyright © 1996, 1997 Corel Corporation.
Contact Webmaster

Figure 4-29 Whale Identification using an expert system

systems with such names as Oil Spill Advisor, Bird Species Identification, and even Midwives Assistant. A system called Grain Marketing Advisor helps farmers select the best way to market their grain.

ROBOTICS

Robotics is the field of study concerned with developing and using robots. **Robots** are computer-controlled machines that mimic the motor activities of living things. Some robots can solve unstructured problems using artificial intelligence. You may have seen household robots used for mowing the lawn or for entertainment purposes, like Sony's AIBO robotic dog. (See Figure 4-30.)

Robots are used in factories, manufacturing, home security, the military, and many other fields of human endeavor. They differ from other assembly-line machines because they can be reprogrammed to do more than one task. Robots are often used to handle dangerous, repetitive tasks. There are three types of robots:

Figure 4-30 AIBO

- **Perception systems:** Perception system robots imitate some of the human senses. For example, robots with television-camera vision systems are particularly useful. They can guide machine tools, inspect products, and secure homes.
- **Industrial robots:** Industrial robots are used to perform a variety of tasks. Examples are machines used in automobile plants to do welding, polishing, and painting. (See Figure 4-31.) Some types of robots have claws for picking up objects and handling dangerous materials.
- **Mobile robots:** Mobile robots act as transports and are widely used for a variety of different tasks. For example, the police and military use them to locate and disarm explosive devices. Mobile robots have entered the world of entertainment with their own television program called "Battlebots." You can even build your own personal robot using special robot building kits. (See Figure 4-32.)

Concept Check

- Define artificial intelligence.
- What is virtual reality?
- Describe knowledge-based systems.
- Describe three types of robots.

Figure 4-31 Industrial robot

Site	Description
battlebot.com	Offers a variety of information including links to sites offering different types of robot kits
robotkits.com	Sells beginner as well as advanced robot creation kits
robotics.org	Sells kits and offers advice for experienced builders
lynxmotion.com	Sells robotic equipment and software

Figure 4-32 Robot kits

Careers in IT

Desktop Publisher

Desktop publishers use computers to format and create publication-ready material. They may create books, magazines, newsletters, and newspapers on home computers using special application software. A large part of the job is designing page layout, importing text, and manipulating graphics. Most desktop publishers work for companies that handle commercial printing accounts. However, there are also many independent contractors.

Desktop publishing positions usually require completion of a program at a vocational school or a university. Internships and part-time work can be a valuable asset to someone pursuing this career. Employers typically look for individuals with good communication skills and artistic ability.

Desktop publishers can expect to earn an annual salary of $20,000 to $40,000. Advancement opportunities include management positions or independent contracting. To learn about other careers in information technology visit us at http://www.mhhe.com/oleary/CT05 and select Careers in IT from Tim's Toolbox.

The Future of Artificial Intelligence Is Emotional

Would you like to voice conference with your mom through robots that resemble you both and demonstrate your emotions on their rubber faces? What if you received a companion robot with a set of moral values? Would you trust a robot to trade the stocks in your portfolio? Researchers are currently at work on robots with the artificial intelligence needed to perform these tasks and more.

The Saya robot, with its artificial skin and muscles, is currently under development in Tokyo. Researchers hope that eventually it will be used as a communication device similar to a current Web cam. For example, you could connect to a robot that resembles you at your mother's house and communicate through it with her. You would see your mother through the robot's visual system. Your mother would hear your voice come from the robot and your emotions would be displayed on its face.

Other research is being conducted that will give robots a sense of values. It is hoped that these robots will be able to make decisions independently based on this set of values. Researchers in California are creating robots that act as surveillance instruments, capable of following a target without direction from a human. The robots can predict potential escape routes and pursue a subject through crowded areas.

All of these projects are designed to move beyond simple computing and into a decidedly human realm of emotional intelligence. Some experts have even suggested that human intelligence relies on emotional input for all important decision making. Thus, by definition, in order for a machine to approximate human intelligence it would have to understand and rely on emotions. If computers could read human emotion, and had emotional intelligence of their own, it could be possible for your computer to act as a stress counsellor when you stay up all night working on a project.

Computers with their own emotional intelligence could be the ultimate human companions. Computer scientists have suggested they may read your mood and play music accordingly. Or they could search through audio and video files for media you would find moving, funny, or dramatic. If computers had their own emotional sense, it is possible that they, like the humans they emulate, would require interaction for mental health.

Would you use a robot as a communication device? Do you think we should build robots with a sense of moral values? Some researchers have suggested that robots with artificial intelligence could serve as ideal supervisors and managers. What do you think? Would you like to have an "emotional" robot for a boss?

NOTES

VISUAL SUMMARY

SPECIALIZED APPLICATION SOFTWARE

GRAPHICS

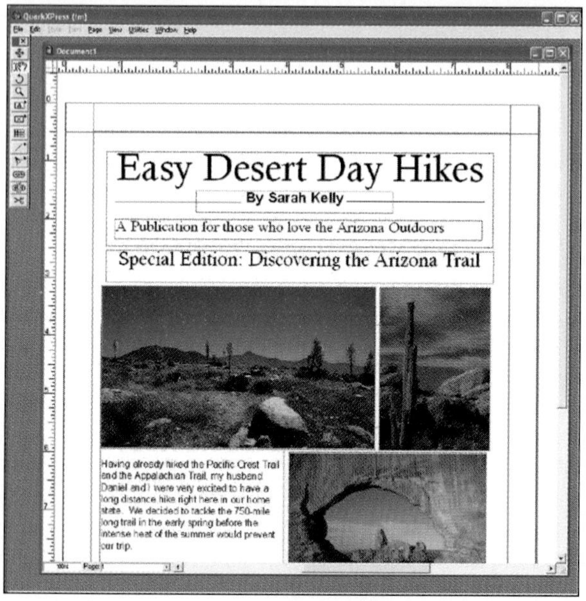

Professionals in graphic arts use specialized graphics programs. These programs include desktop publishers, image editors, illustration programs, image galleries, and graphics suites.

Desktop Publishers

Desktop publishers (**page layout programs**) mix text and graphics to create professional publications. They are widely used by graphic artists to create brochures, newsletters, newspapers, and textbooks.

Common tools include:

- **Selection** to select, move, and resize images and text.
- **Text** to draw text frames, insert text, and control wrapping of text.
- **Graphics** for creating and importing graphic elements.
- **Magnification/zoom** to present closeup and distance views of the document.

GRAPHICS

Image Editors

Image editors, also known as **paint programs,** create and modify **bitmap** (**raster**) **image** files. Images are recorded as dots or **pixels.**

Basic tools include:

- A **pen** is used to create drawing and objects.
- A **brush** is used to fill an area or object with a color.
- **Filters** create special effects and textures for your pictures.

Illustration Programs

Illustration programs, also known as **draw programs,** modify **vector images** (**vector illustrations**). In a vector file, images are recorded as a collection of objects such as lines, rectangles, and ovals.

Image Galleries

Image galleries are libraries of electronic images, widely available from the Web. Two types are **stock photographs** and **clip art.**

Graphics Suites

A **graphics suite** is a collection of individual graphics programs sold as a unit. These suites provide a variety of graphics programs at a lower cost than if purchased separately.

To be a competent and knowledgeable end user you need to be aware of specialized applications. You need to know who uses them, what they are used for, and how they are used. Specialized applications include graphics programs, audio and video editing software, multimedia, Web authoring, personal applications, and the field of artificial intelligence.

AUDIO AND VIDEO

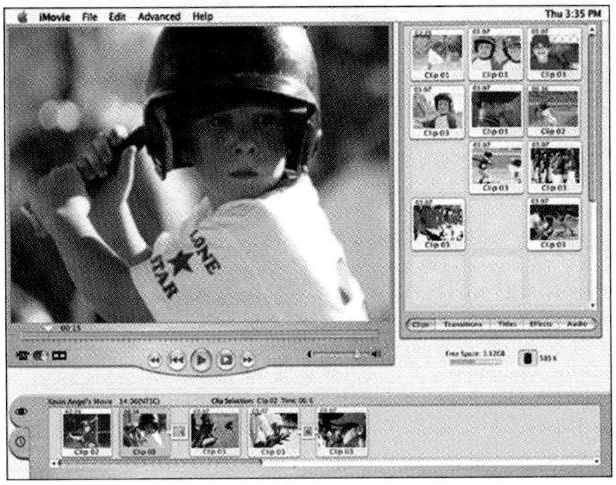

Recent advances in video and audio technology allow individuals to assemble near-professional quality video and audio footage.

Video Software

Video editing software allows you to reorganize, add effects, and more to digital video.

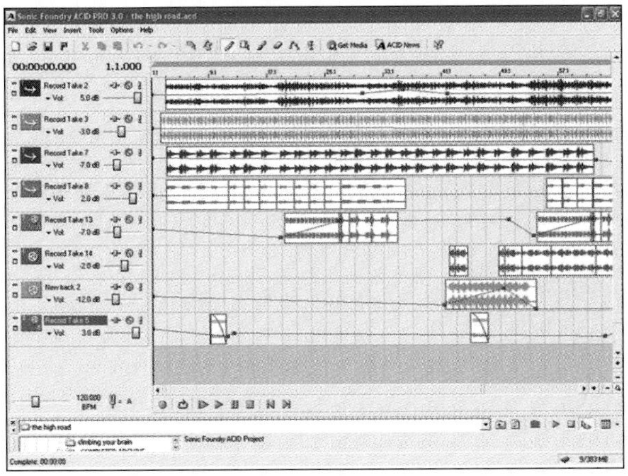

Audio Software

Audio editing software allows you to create and edit audio clips. You can add audio effects, like filters to your tracks. You can create MP3s.

MULTIMEDIA

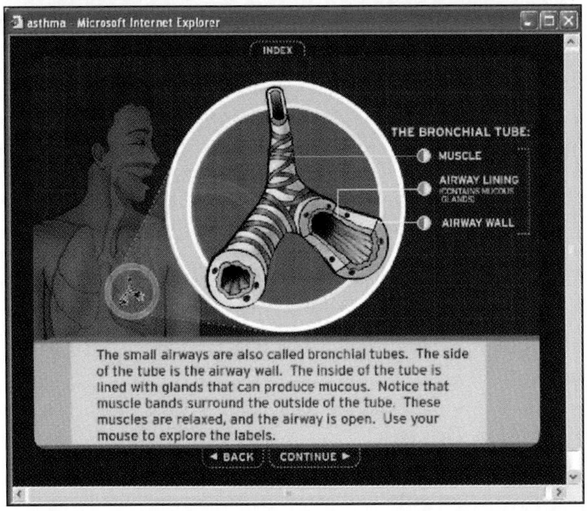

Multimedia integrates all sorts of media including video, music, voice, graphics, and text into one presentation. An essential feature is user participation or **interactivity.**

Links and Buttons

A multimedia presentation is organized as a series of related pages. Pages are **linked,** or connected, by clicking **buttons.**

Developing Multimedia Presentations

The creation of multimedia presentations involves four steps:

- **Plan and analyze**—determine objectives, resources required, and project team.
- **Design**—use **story boards** to record the intended overall logic, flow, and structure.
- **Create**—use multimedia authoring programs to create presentation and integrate various media elements.
- **Support**—identify errors, evaluate effectiveness, and revise as needed.

Multimedia Authoring Programs

Multimedia authoring programs are special programs to create multimedia presentations. They bring together video, audio, graphics, and text elements in an interactive framework.

WEB AUTHORING

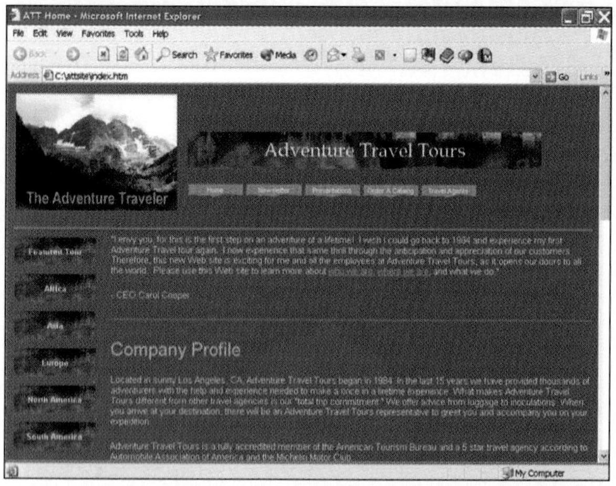

Creating Web sites is called **Web authoring.** It begins with Web site design followed by creating a document file that displays the Web site content.

Web Site Design

Web sites are an interactive multimedia form of communication.

Graphical maps use linked blocks to represent a Web site's overall content. Typically, blocks represent individual Web pages and links indicate relationships between related pages.

The first Web page usually introduces the site and supplies a table of contents. Multimedia elements are added to pages. **Animations** are moving graphics. **Flash** is a widely used type of Web animation. **Morphing** is a special effect that seems to melt one image into another.

Web Authoring Programs

Web sites can be created using a simple text editor or word processor. **Web authoring programs,** also known as **Web page editors** or **HTML editors,** are specifically designed to create Web sites. They provide support for Web site design and HTML coding.

PERSONAL APPLICATIONS

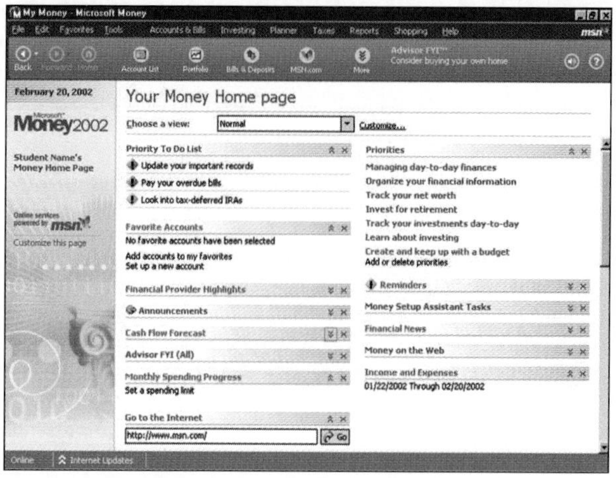

Personal software (**home software**) is used by individuals who sacrifice some advanced features for lower cost and simplicity. Three most widely used are personal information managers, personal finance managers, and tax preparation.

Personal Information Managers

Personal information managers (**PIMS** or **desktop managers**) provide electronic alternative to appointment calendar, address book, and notepad. Features include:

- **Calendar** to track events, holidays, assignments, and project schedules.
- **Contacts** to record names, addresses, and telephone numbers.
- **Tasks** to organize personal to-do items and group activities.

Personal Finance Managers

Personal finance management programs organize and manage a person's money. Features include:

- Organizes and centralizes financial documents.
- Assists in personal financial planning.
- Most include **online banking** assistance.

Personal Tax Preparation

Personal tax preparation software allows easy input of financial records and assistance in the preparation of tax return documents.

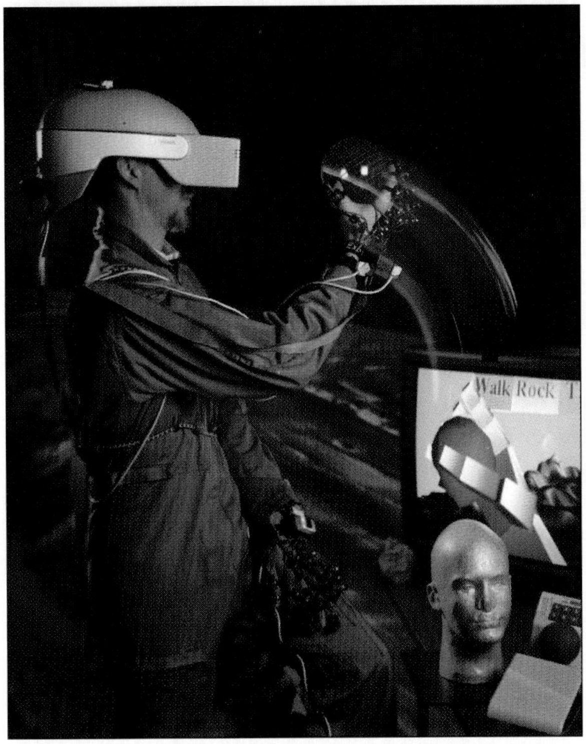

Common thread of emerging applications is the inclusion of artificial intelligence concepts.

Artificial intelligence

Artificial intelligence (**AI**) attempts to develop computer systems that mimic human senses, thought processes, and actions.

Most applications address **structured problems** which can be broken down into a series of well-defined steps. Less defined or **unstructured problems** are being addressed. Three areas are virtual reality, knowledge-based systems, and robotics.

Virtual Reality

Virtual reality (**VR, artificial reality,** or **virtual environments**) creates computer-generated simulated environments. It involves the use of interactive sensory equipment including head gear and gloves. **VRML** (**virtual reality modeling language**) is used to create or program real-time virtual reality applications.

Applications include recreational and other areas such as aviation, surgical operations, spaceship repair, and nuclear disaster cleanup. Modern applications strive for **immersive experiences** and can be viewed on **virtual reality walls.**

EMERGING APPLICATIONS

Knowlege-based Systems

Knowledge-based (**expert**) **systems** are programs that duplicate the knowledge that humans use to perform specific tasks.

Knowledge bases are databases containing facts and rules that relate facts to user input. **Fuzzy logic** allows users to respond to questions in a very humanlike way.

Some application areas include medicine, geology, architecture, and nature.

Robotics

Robotics is a field of study concerned with developing and using robots. **Robots** are computer-controlled machines that mimic the motor activities of living things. Three types of robots are:

- **Perception system**—imitate human senses. Used to guide tools, inspect products, secure homes.
- **Industrial robots**—perform a variety of tasks including welding, polishing, painting, and handling dangerous materials.
- **Mobile robots**—transport and are used in a variety of tasks. Military and police applications include locating, removing, and disarming explosive devices.

KEY TERMS

animation (137)
artificial reality (144)
artificial intelligence (AI) (144)
audio editing software (133)
bitmap image (130)
brush (130)
buttons (135)
clip art (131)
desktop managers (142)
desktop publishing program (129)
drawing program (131)
expert systems (145)
filter (130)
Flash (140)
fuzzy logic (145)
graphics tool (129)
graphical map (137)
graphics suite (132)
home software (141)
HTML editors (140)
illustration program (131)
image editors (130)
image gallery (131)
immersive experience (145)
industrial robots (146)
interactivity (134)
knowledge bases (145)
knowledge-based system (145)
links (135)
magnification/zoom tool (129)
mobile robots (146)
morphing (140)
multimedia (134)
multimedia authoring programs (137)
online banking (143)
page layout program (129)
paint programs (130)
pen (130)
perception systems (146)
personal finance management (143)
personal information managers (PIMS) (142)
personal software (141)
personal tax preparation (143)
pixels (130)
raster image (130)
robotics (146)
robots (146)
selection tool (129)
story boards (135)
stock photographs (131)
structured problem (144)
text tool (129)
unstructured problem (144)
vector (130)
vector illustration (130)
vector image (130)
video editing software (133)
virtual environments (145)
virtual reality (144)
virtual reality modeling language (VRML) (145)
virtual reality wall (145)
VR (144)
Web authoring (137)
Web authoring programs (140)
Web page editors (140)

To test your knowledge of these key terms with animated flash cards, select Flash Cards from Tim's Toolbox at http://www.mhhe.com/oleary/CT05.

CHAPTER REVIEW

CROSSWORD

ACROSS

1 Special areas on a page providing links
4 Moving graphics
8 Programming language used to create real-time animated 3-D scenes
9 Connections to related information
11 Another term for an image editor (program)
13 A type of systems robot that imitates some of the human senses
14 A type of robot that performs a variety of tasks
19 An artificial, or simulated, reality generated in 3-D by a computer
20 A most common type of graphic file
21 Also known as knowledge-based systems, a type of artificial intelligence that uses a database to provide assistance to users
23 Program used to create and to edit vector images
24 Another term for a program used to create and to edit vector images

DOWN

2 A problem that is not easily defined
3 Computer-controlled machines that mimic the motor activities of living things
5 Integrates video, music, voice, graphics, and text into interactive presentations
6 Used to fill an area or object with a color
7 A special effect in which one image seems to melt into another
10 User participation
12 Common tool used to draw text frames, insert text, and control wrapping of text
15 A problem that can be broken down into a series of well-defined steps
16 The field of study concerned with developing and using robots
17 Adds interest and focuses the user's attention. Helps create professional-looking presentations
18 Common tool used to select, move and resize images and text
22 Interactive animation, usually full-screen and highly dynamic

For an interactive crossword puzzle select Crosswords from Tim's Toolbox at http://www.mhhe.com/oleary/CT05.

MULTIPLE CHOICE

Circle the letter or fill in the correct answer.

1. A(n) ________ is typically organized as a series of related pages with links to related information.
   - **a.** graphical map
   - **b.** story board
   - **c.** multimedia presentation
   - **d.** image editor
   - **e.** virtual environment
2. ________ allows you to reorganize, add effects, and more to your digital video footage.
   - **a.** Video editing software
   - **b.** Audio editing software
   - **c.** Paint program
   - **d.** Browsers
   - **e.** Animation
3. ________ focus on page design and layout and provide greater flexibility than word processors.
   - **a.** Desktop publishers
   - **b.** Graphics editors
   - **c.** Web page editors
   - **d.** Multimedia authoring programs
   - **e.** PERT
4. ________ can be simple moving text or complicated interactive features.
   - **a.** VR
   - **b.** Graphics editors
   - **c.** Graphics suites
   - **d.** Animation
   - **e.** Vector images
5. Expert systems use ________ that contain specific facts, rules to relate these facts, and user input to formulate decisions.
   - **a.** robots
   - **b.** fuzzy logic
   - **c.** story boards
   - **d.** knowledge bases
   - **e.** interactivity
6. Many expert systems use ________, which allows users to respond to questions in a human way.
   - **a.** packets
   - **b.** fuzzy logic
   - **c.** robots
   - **d.** story boards
   - **e.** vector images
7. Police and military use ________ to locate and disarm explosive devices.
   - **a.** mobile robots
   - **b.** OSI
   - **c.** industrial robots
   - **d.** perception systems
   - **e.** fuzzy logic
8. ________ connect related pages in a multimedia presentation.
   - **a.** Robots
   - **b.** Links
   - **c.** Buttons
   - **d.** (a) and (b)
   - **e.** (b) and (c)
9. Intuition, memory, and reasoning are used to solve ________.
   - **a.** structured problems
   - **b.** unstructured problems
   - **c.** knowledge bases
   - **d.** (a) and (b)
   - **e.** none of the above
10. Draw programs are used to modify ________, while image editors are used to modify ________.
    - **a.** bitmap images, vector images
    - **b.** vector images, bitmap images
    - **c.** links, buttons
    - **d.** links, bitmap images
    - **e.** (a) and (c)

MATCHING

Match each numbered item with the most closely related lettered item. Write your answers in the spaces provided.

a. AI
b. bitmap
c. desktop publishing
d. expert system
e. Flash
f. fuzzy logic
g. graphical map
h. graphics suite
i. interactivity
j. image editor
k. multimedia
l. multimedia authoring programs
m. morphing
n. paint program
o. perception system
p. robots
q. story board
r. structured problems
s. vector image
t. Web authoring

1. Integrates all sorts of media into one presentation. ____
2. User participation in multimedia. ____
3. Graphics program for creating and editing bitmap images. ____
4. Tool for planning and structuring a multimedia presentation. ____
5. Programs used to create multimedia presentations. ____
6. Creating a Web site. ____
7. Diagram of a Web site's overall design. ____
8. Program that allows you to mix text and graphics to create publications of professional quality. ____
9. Used to create and modify bitmap files. ____
10. Group of graphics programs offered at lower cost than if purchased separately. ____
11. Special effect in which one image seems to melt into another. ____
12. Graphic file made up of thousands of pixels. ____
13. Graphics file made up of a collection of objects, such as rectangles, lines, and ovals. ____
14. Problems that can be broken down into well-defined steps. ____
15. Attempts to develop computer systems that mimic or simulate human thought processes and actions. ____
16. Provides advice to decision makers who would otherwise rely on human experts. ____
17. Animation that is usually full-screen and interactive. ____
18. Used by expert systems to allow users to respond by using qualitative terms such as great and OK. ____
19. Machines that mimic the motor activities of living things. ____
20. System that relies on sense of touch or other human senses. ____

OPEN-ENDED

On a separate sheet of paper, respond to each question or statement.

1. What are the advantages of using a desktop publishing program over a word processor?
2. Discuss the aspects of virtual reality mentioned in the chapter. What are the possibilities for this technology?
3. Discuss the different types of robotics mentioned in the chapter.
4. What are the two areas of AI? Describe each.
5. What is a paint program? How does it work?

To test your knowledge of this chapter, select Self Test from Tim's Toolbox at http://www.mhhe.com/oleary/CT05.

USING TECHNOLOGY

1 Personal Web Sites

Do you have something to share with the world? Would you like a personal Web site, but don't want to deal with learning HTML? Creating your own home on the Internet is easy, and there are many services available to get you started. To learn more about personal Web sites, review Making IT Work for You: Personal Web Sites, on pages 138 and 139. Then answer the following questions: (a) What are Weblogs? What are they used for? (b) What is Blogger.com? Describe the following features provided by Blogger.com: templates, upload file, hyperlink, post, publish, and view web page. (c) Have you ever created a Weblog or other types of personal Web site? If you have, describe how you created it and what you used it for. If you have not, discuss why and how you might use one.

2 Shockwave

Web sites aren't all just text and pictures anymore. Many are taking advantage of browser plug-ins that add new functionality and display abilities to Web browsers, as we discussed in Chapter 2. One of the most popular plug-ins is Macromedia's Shockwave. Visit our site at http://www.mhhe.com/oleary/CT05 and select Using Technology from Tim's Toolbox to link to the Macromedia site. Once connected, read about Shockwave and answer the following questions: (a) What is Shockwave? What types of content can it display? (b) How is the Shockwave plug-in obtained? (c) What types of companies are using Shockwave in their Web page designs? (d) Do you think Shockwave is a valuable Web page addition, or just a flashy distraction? Explain your answer.

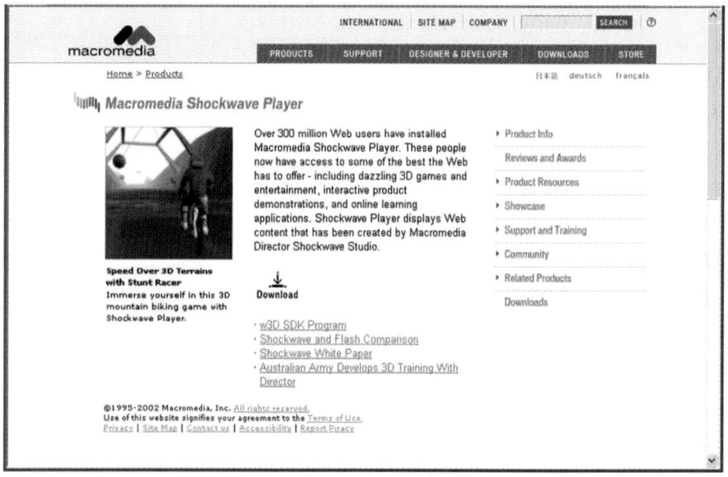

Streaming Multimedia Players 3

Streaming multimedia files come in many varieties. There are several formats for streaming audio and video files available, each with its own advantage. To play these files, a user needs software known as a *player,* which must support the type of file the user wishes to play. Visit our Web site at http://www.mhhe.com/oleary/CT05 and select Using Technology from Tim's Toolbox to link to a popular streaming multimedia player. Read about the player and then answer the following questions: (a) What types of streaming multimedia files can be played with this player? (b) How does the user receive and install the player? (c) As streaming multimedia becomes more widely available on the Internet, how might the role of player software change? Be specific.

Multimedia Web Sites 4

Many Web sites focus exclusively on providing multimedia content as product promotions. For example, you can use the Internet to see music videos or movie previews. Connect to our Web site at http://www.mhhe.com/oleary/CT05 and select Using Technology from Tim's Toolbox to link to a provider of multimedia content. Explore the site, and then briefly answer the following questions: (a) What type of content did the site provide? (b) What type of software are users required to have to use the site? (c) Did you find this site useful or entertaining? If so, describe how. If not, suggest some ways that the site could be improved.

EXPANDING YOUR KNOWLEDGE

1 Computing Today CD

Developing or publishing a Web site is a common activity for organizations of all types and for people from all walks of life. The process of creating a Web site consists of five steps: planning, analyzing and designing, creating, going online, and maintaining. After reading "Creating Your Own Web Site" from your Computing Today CD or from Tim's Toolbox at http://www.mhhe.com/oleary/CT05, consider the following case.

Assume that you are to create a Web site for an organization following the five steps discussed on your Computing Today CD and from Tim's Toolbox. You can choose any organization. It can be an athletic or a social club. It can be a professional organization or a corporation.

On a single page of paper, briefly describe the organization and discuss each step identifying specific examples or issues you might encounter during the process.

2 Streaming Multimedia

Many Web sites are now enhanced with streaming multimedia. Some sites offer streaming audio or video to augment text, such as news sites with file footage. For others, the content *is* the streaming multimedia, such as Internet radio or animation sites. Locate several Web sites that offer streaming multimedia, and pick one to review. Answer the following questions: (a) Define "streaming multimedia." (b) What type of streaming multimedia did the site offer? Who is the intended audience? (c) In what ways was the experience limited? Be specific. (d) As technology improves, streaming multimedia may become a more prominent part of the Web. Describe, in detail, two new ways in which streaming multimedia could be used in the future.

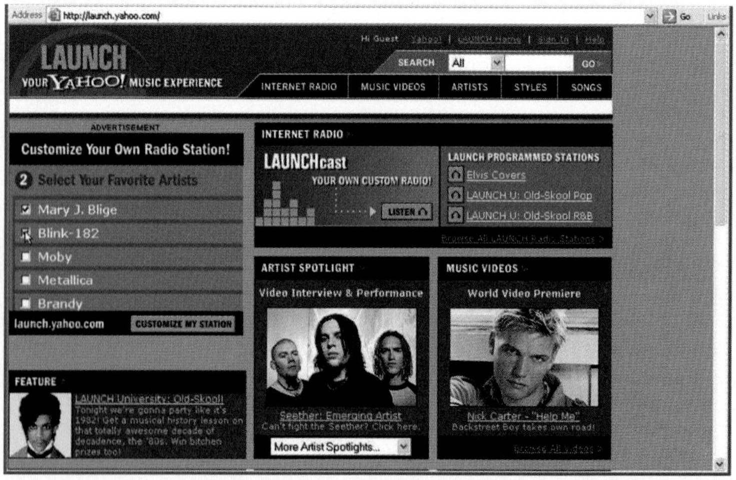

EXPANDING YOUR KNOWLEDGE

SimNet CD 3

Complete Chapter 4: Specialized Application Software on your SimNet CD and then complete the following on a single page of paper.

a. Identify each of the indicated items below.
b. Describe the Multimedia development cycle.
c. Discuss the pros and cons of using a WYSIWYG editor versus HTML code.
d. Describe the two main types of artificial intelligence.
e. Discuss some of the side effects that can occur from using virtual reality.

Robotics for the Home 4

Having a personal robot to do mundane and unpleasant tasks sounds like science fiction. However, several companies have taken development of robotics for everyday living very seriously in recent years. Visit our Web site at http://www.mhhe.com/oleary/CT05 and select Expanding Your Knowledge from Tim's Toolbox to link to some robots that could become commonplace at work, school, or home. Answer the following questions: (a) Describe the purpose of each robot project. Who and what are the robots intended for? (b) In what ways do the robots take advantage of current artificial intelligence (AI) technology? Be specific. (c) What obstacles do the designers of these robots face? How are these obstacles being addressed? Cite examples.

© Copyright 2002 Sony Corporation.
"AIBO","AIBO"logo,"LATTE" and "MACARON" are trademarks or registeredtrademarks of Sony Corporation.

BUILDING YOUR PORTFOLIO

1 Artificial Intelligence

Artificial Intelligence attempts to simulate human senses, thought processes, and actions with an eye toward productivity. Write a one-page paper titled "Artificial Intelligence" that addresses the following issues: (a) Define and describe artificial intelligence. (b) How is it currently used? How can software exhibit artificial intelligence? (c) With advancing developments in artificial intelligence, what can we expect from operating systems in the future?

2 Virtual Reality

There is a variety of applications for virtual reality technology, from entertainment to industrial. Research virtual reality on the Web, and write a one-page paper that addresses the following items: (a) Define the term "virtual reality." (b) Who is using virtual reality now? List some specific examples, and describe the technology being used. (c) Describe some existing business applications that could benefit from current or developing virtual reality technology. (c) What businesses might virtual reality *create* in the future? Hint: Describe the ways that VR could be used to do things that are not possible today. Give specific examples.

BUILDING YOUR PORTFOLIO

HTML Source Code 3

One way to learn how to create interesting and dynamic Web sites is to examine how professionals create their sites. Once connected to a Web site, you can easily display the HTML source code used to create that site. With Netscape, for example, select Document Source from the View submenu. Try this out on your own for your favorite Web site, and then answer the following questions in a one-page paper: (a) Do you see any ethical issues that relate to examining the HTML code? (b) What about copying parts of the code for your own Web site? (c) What about copying all the code? Defend your answers.

Online Expert Systems 4

Expert systems have been integrated into many Web sites for consumers. For example, health-related Web sites help patients "self-diagnose" illnesses before seeing a physician. Research Web sites that make expert systems available, and address the following items in a one-page paper: (a) Define "expert system." (b) What benefits do these expert systems offer the user? (d) Are there ways these systems could be harmful? What responsibilities do users of online expert systems have? (d) What responsibilities do providers of online expert systems have?

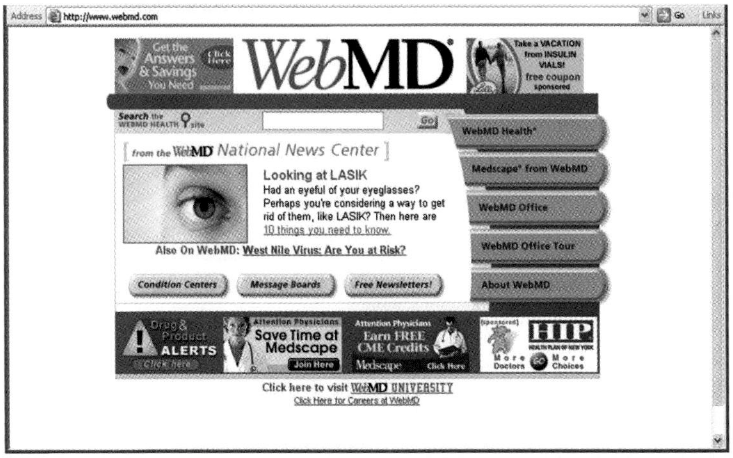

SYSTEM SOFTWARE

OBJECTIVES

After you have read this chapter, you should be able to:

1. Describe the differences between system software and application software.
2. Discuss the four types of system software.
3. Discuss the basic functions, features, and categories of operating systems.
4. Describe the Windows, Mac OS, UNIX, Linux, VSE/ESA, z/OS, Palm, and Windows CE operating systems.
5. Describe the purpose of utilities and utility suites.
6. Identify the five most essential utilities.
7. Discuss Windows utility programs.
8. Describe device drivers including printer drivers.

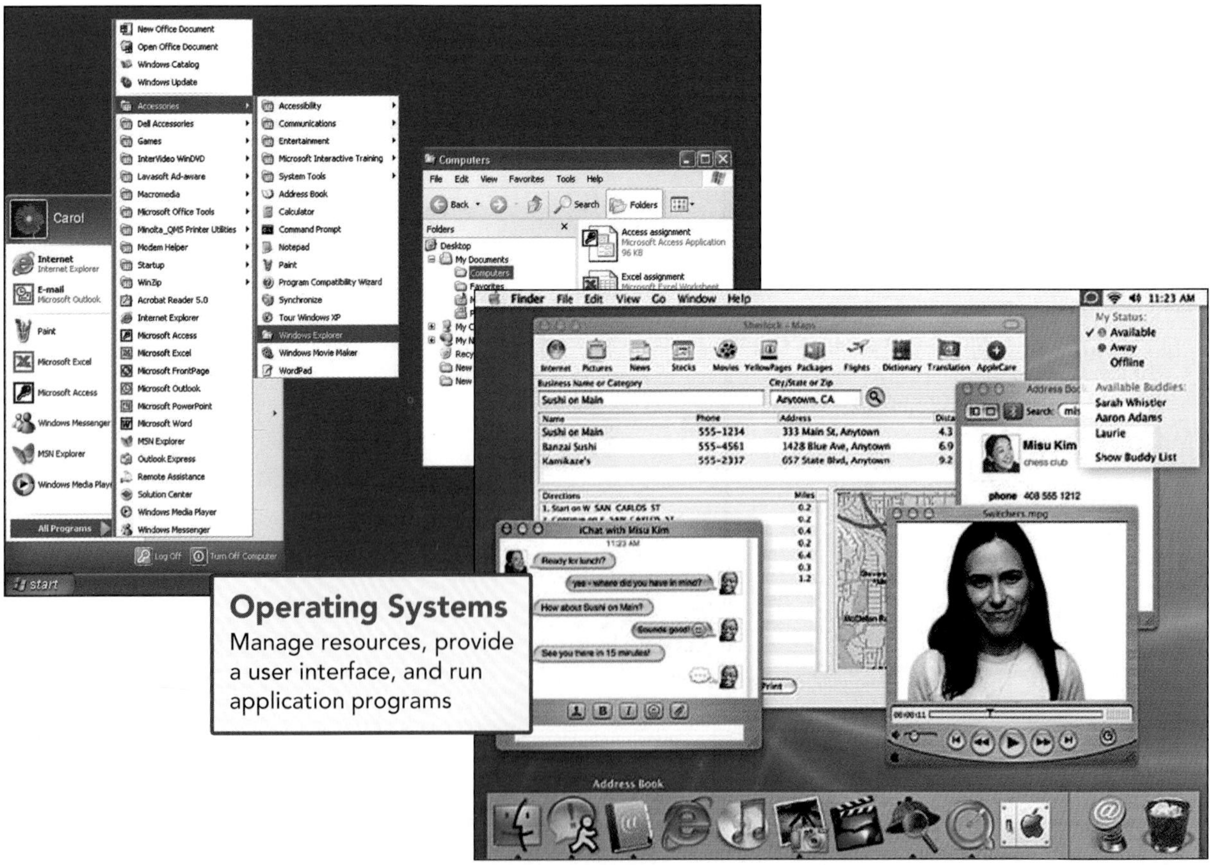

Operating Systems
Manage resources, provide a user interface, and run application programs

When most people think about computers, they think about surfing the Web, creating reports, analyzing data, storing information, making presentations, and any number of other valuable applications. We typically think about applications and application software. Most of us think about using the technology. Computers and computer applications have become a part of the fabric of our everyday lives. Most of us agree that they are great . . . as long as they are working.

We usually do not think about the more mundane and behind-the-scenes computer activities: loading and running programs, coordinating networks that share resources, organizing files, protecting our computers from viruses, performing periodic maintenance to avoid problems, and controlling hardware devices so that they can communicate with one another. These activities go on behind the scenes without our help.

That is the way it should be, and the way it is, as long as everything is working perfectly. But what if new application programs are not compatible and will not run on our current computer system? What if we get a computer virus? What if our hard disk fails? What if we buy a new digital video camera and can't store and edit the images on our computer system? What if our computer starts to run slower and slower?

These issues may seem mundane, but they are critical. This chapter covers the vital activities that go on behind the scenes. A little knowledge about these programs can go a long way to making your computing life easier. To effectively use computers, competent and knowledgeable end users need to understand the functionality of system software including operating systems, utility programs, and device drivers.

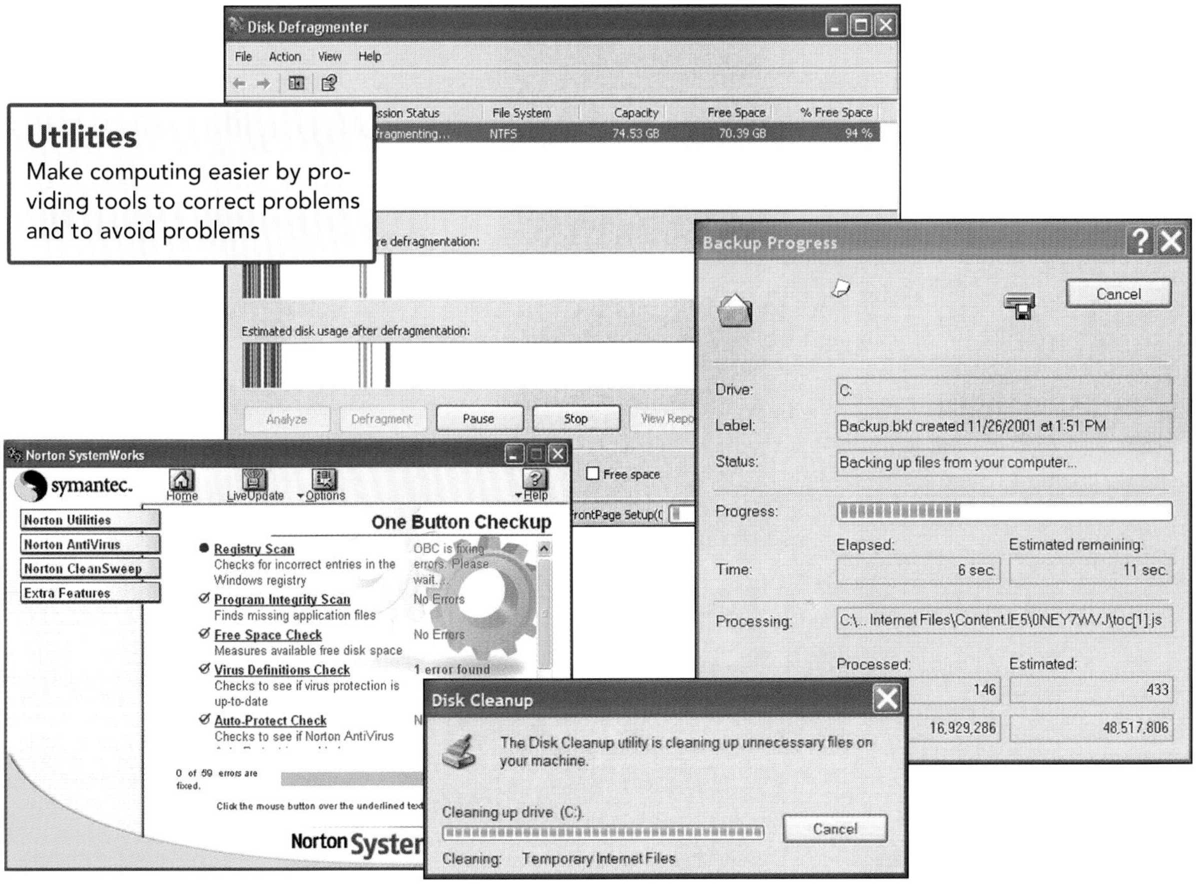

SYSTEM SOFTWARE

System software handles technical details. Operating systems, utilities, device drivers, and language translators are types of system software programs.

End users focus on applying computer technology to accomplish specific tasks. They focus on application software. For example, we use word processors to create brochures, letters, and reports. However, end users also use system software. **System software** works with end users, application software, and computer hardware to handle the majority of technical details. For example, system software controls where a word processing program is stored in memory, how commands are converted so that the system unit can process them, where a completed document or file is saved, and how the output is printed. See Figure 5-1.

System software is not a single program. Rather it is a collection or a system of programs that handle hundreds of technical details with little or no user intervention. System software consists of four types of programs:

- **Operating systems** are programs that coordinate computer resources, provide an interface between users and the computer, and run applications.
- **Utilities,** also known as **service programs,** perform specific tasks related to managing computer resources.

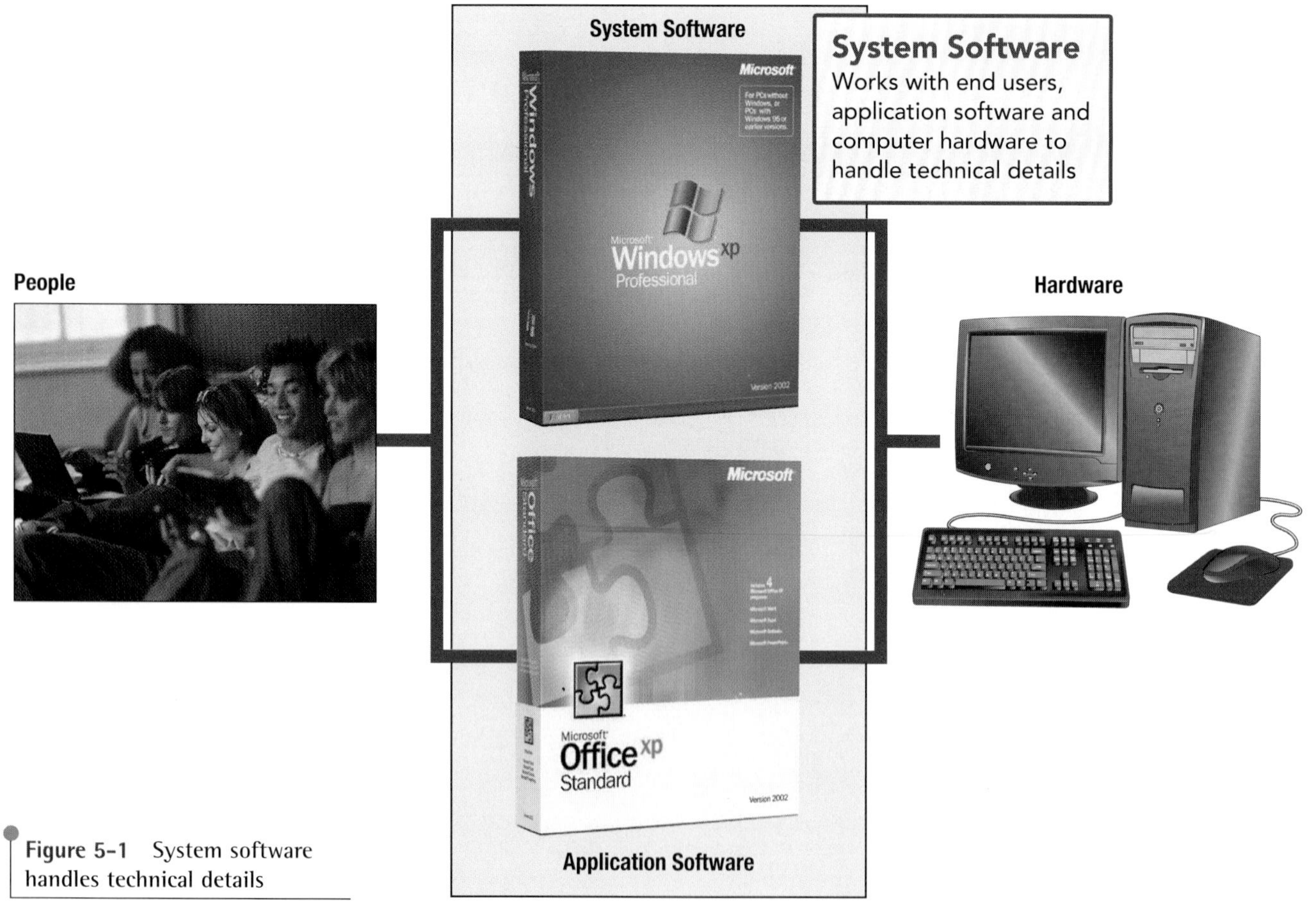

Figure 5-1 System software handles technical details

- **Device drivers** are specialized programs designed to allow particular input or output devices to communicate with the rest of the computer system.
- **Language translators** convert the programming instructions written by programmers into a language that computers understand and process.

Concept Check

- What is system software? What is it used for?
- What are the four kinds of system software programs? Briefly describe each.

OPERATING SYSTEMS

Operating systems are programs that manage resources, provide user interface, and run applications. Features include POST, desktop, files, and folders. Three categories of operating systems are embedded, network, and stand-alone. Windows, Mac OS, UNIX, Linux, VSE/ESA, z/OS, and Palm OS, are operating systems.

If you have ever used a computer to write a paper, browse the Internet, or play a game, you have already interacted with the computer's operating system. The **operating system** is a collection of programs that handle many of the technical details related to using a computer.

In many ways, an operating system is the most important type of computer program. Without it your computer would be useless. A computer without an operating system is like a racing car without a driver. No matter how powerful the racing car, it cannot operate without a driver to start it, steer it, and give it instructions. Without the driver, the racing car is just a good-looking machine. Without an operating system, a computer is just a piece of hardware.

FUNCTIONS

Every computer has an operating system and every operating system performs a variety of functions. These functions can be classified into three groups: managing computer resources, providing a user interface, and running applications. (See Figure 5-2.)

- **Resources:** These programs coordinate all the computer's resources including memory, processing, storage, and devices such as printers and monitors. They also monitor system performance, schedule jobs, provide security, and start up the computer.
- **User interface:** Users interact with application programs and computer hardware through a user interface. Many older operating systems used a **character based interface** in which users communicated with the operating system through written commands such as "Copy A: assign.doc to C:". Almost all newer operating systems use a **graphical user interface (GUI).** As we discussed in Chapter 4, a graphical user interface uses graphical elements such as icons and windows to communicate with the operating system.
- **Applications:** These programs load and run applications such as word processors and spreadsheets. Most operating systems support **multitasking,** or the ability to switch between different applications stored

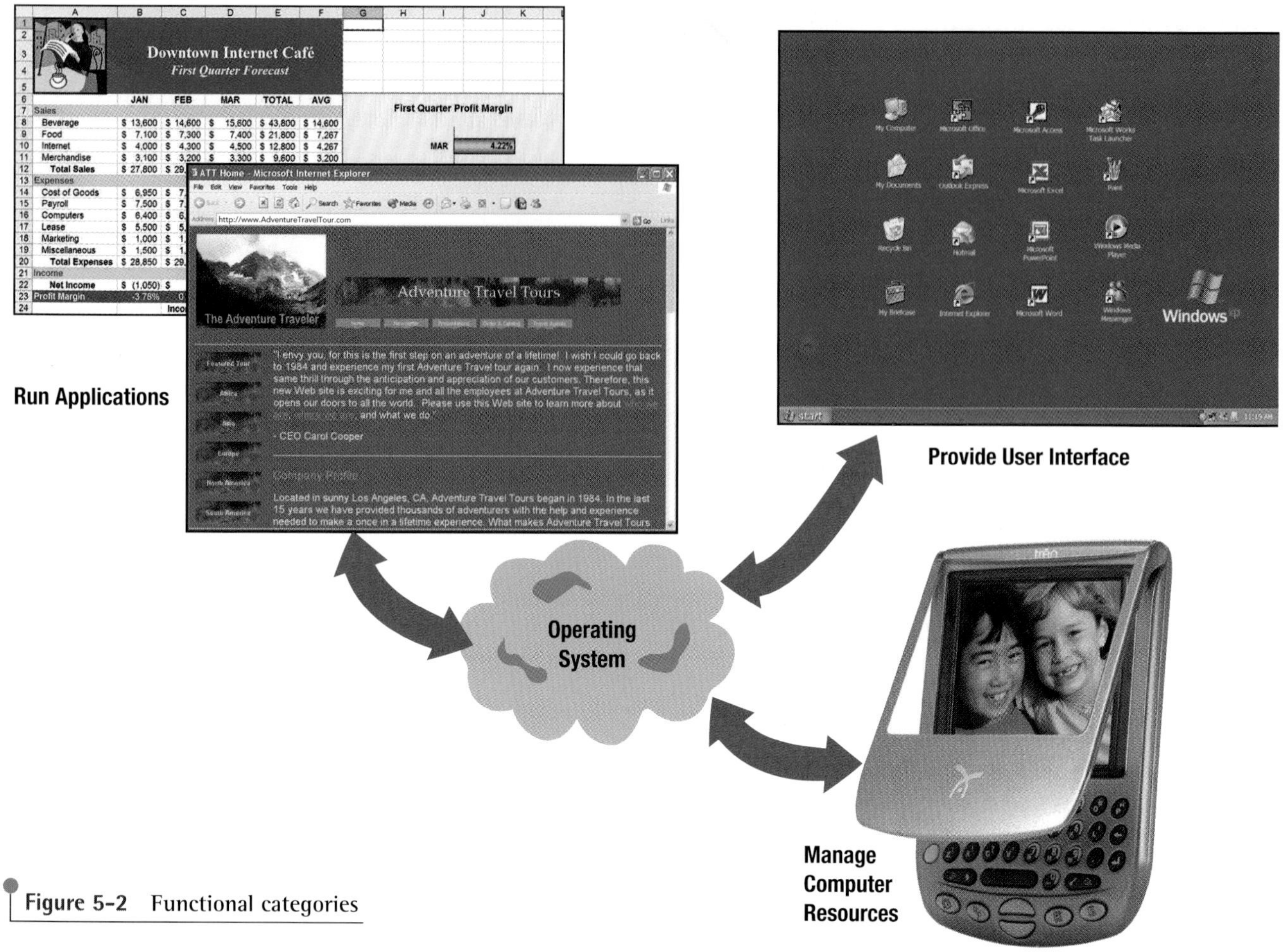

Figure 5-2 Functional categories

in memory. With multitasking, you could have Word and Excel running at the same time and switch easily between the two applications. The program that you are currently working on is described as running in the **foreground.** The other program or programs are running in the **background.**

Figure 5-3 presents some of the common functions of operating systems.

Concept Check

- What is an operating system?
- Discuss the three major groups of operating system functions.
- What is multitasking? When is a program running in the foreground? When is a program running in the background?

FEATURES

Starting or restarting a computer is called **booting** the system. There are two ways to boot a computer: a warm boot and a cold boot. A **warm boot** occurs when the computer is already on, and you restart it without turning off the power. A warm boot can be accomplished in several ways. For example, in Windows XP, a running computer can be restarted by pressing a sequence of keys. Starting a computer that has been turned off is called a **cold boot.**

Function	Description
Memory management	Controls the efficient use of computer memory by assigning data and programs to specific memory locations, monitoring to ensure validity, and deleting when no longer needed.
Process management	Supports processing functions such as multitasking.
Storage management	Keeps track of exactly where data and programs are stored on a storage medium such as a hard disk.
Device management	Uses programs called device drivers to communicate with devices such as mouse, keyboard, monitor, printer, and disk drives.
Monitor performance	Continually monitors all system resources and reports their performance.
Job scheduling	Controls the order and time in which programs and processes are run.
User interface	Provides an interface for users to communicate with the operating system.
Security	Provides password support to keep out unauthorized users.
Start-up	Starts a computer after it has been turned off or restarts a computer that is on.

Figure 5-3 Common operating system functions

In a cold boot, the computer system runs a series of programs that includes a self-testing process called **POST (power-on self test).** This test verifies that certain hardware components are operational. Next, the computer searches for the operating system programs which are typically stored on the computer's internal hard disk. Once located, select operating system files are copied into the computer's memory. Some of these files are called the **kernel** of the operating system and include programs that perform basic operations such as assigning computer resources and starting application programs. The kernel is **memory resident,** which means that it remains in memory as long as the computer is on. Finally, the operating system displays the user interface on the monitor. To learn more about booting your computer system and POST, consult your Computing Today CD or visit us on the Web at http://www.mhhe.com/oleary/CT05 and select Animations.

Computing Today CD

You typically interact with the operating system through the graphical user interface. Most provide a place, called the **desktop,** which provides access to computer resources. (See Figure 5-4.) Operating systems have several features in common with application programs including:

- **Icons**—graphic representations for a program or function.
- **Pointer**—controlled by a mouse and changes shape depending upon its current function. (See Figure 5-5.) For example, when shaped like an arrow, the pointer can be used to select items such as an icon.
- **Windows**—rectangular areas for displaying information and running programs.
- **Menus**—provide a list of options or commands.
- **Dialog boxes**—provide information or request input.
- **Help**—provides online assistance for operating system functions and procedures.

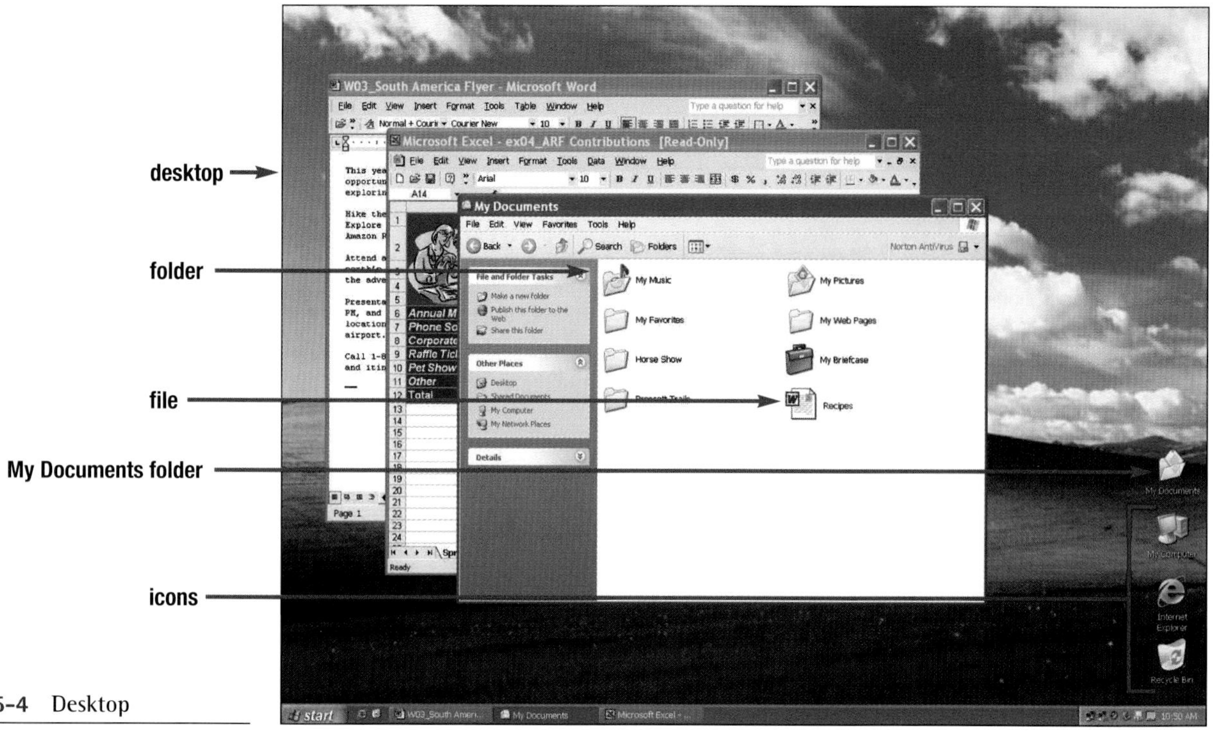

Figure 5-4 Desktop

Most operating systems store data and programs in a system of files and folders. Unlike the traditional filing cabinet, the computer files and folders are stored on a secondary storage device such as your hard disk. **Files** are used to store data and programs. Related files are stored within a **folder,** and for organization purposes, a folder can contain other folders. For example, you might organize your electronic files in the *My Documents* folder on your hard disk. This folder could contain other folders, each named to indicate their contents. One might be "Computers" and could contain all the files you have created (or will create) for this course. (See Figure 5-6.) The contents of folders can be displayed by using a file management program such as **Windows Explorer.** (See Figure 5-7.)

Concept Check

- ✓ What is the difference between a warm and a cold boot?
- ✓ What are POST, kernel, memory resident, and desktop?
- ✓ How are files and folders used? What does Windows Explorer do?

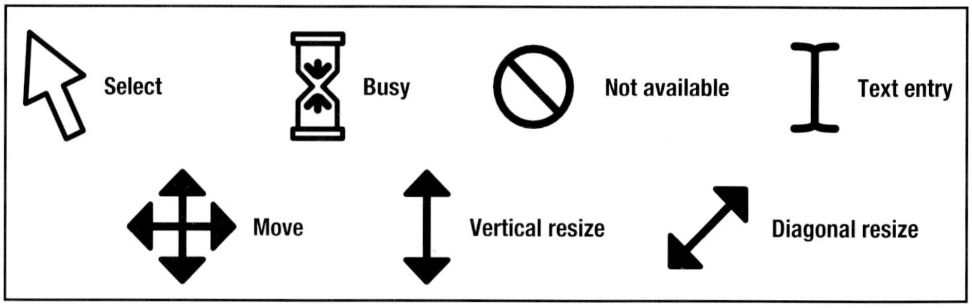

Figure 5-5 Common pointer shapes

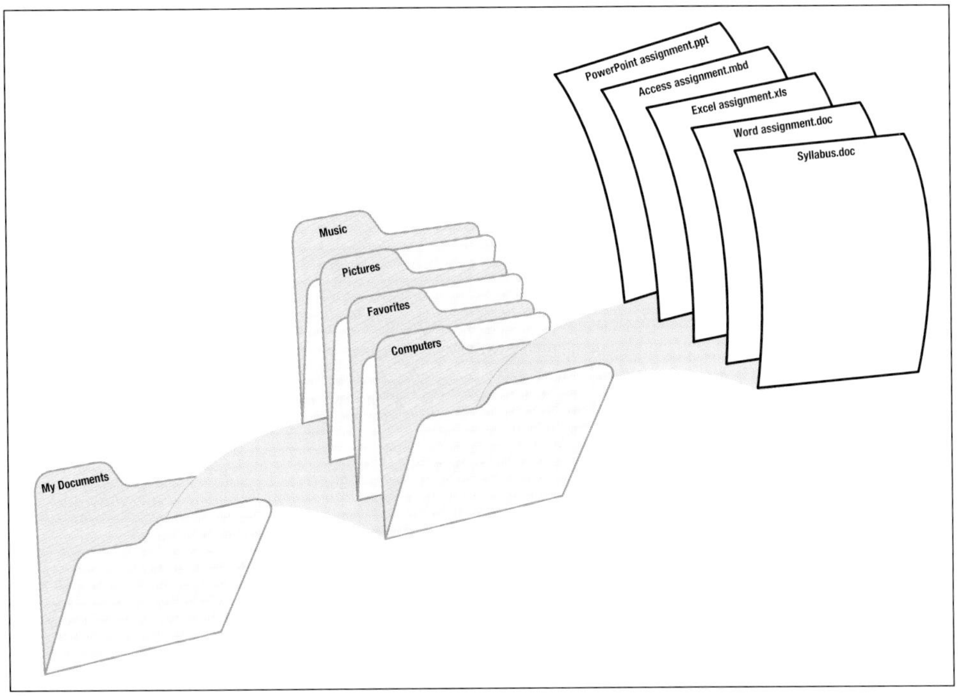

Figure 5-6 Files and folders

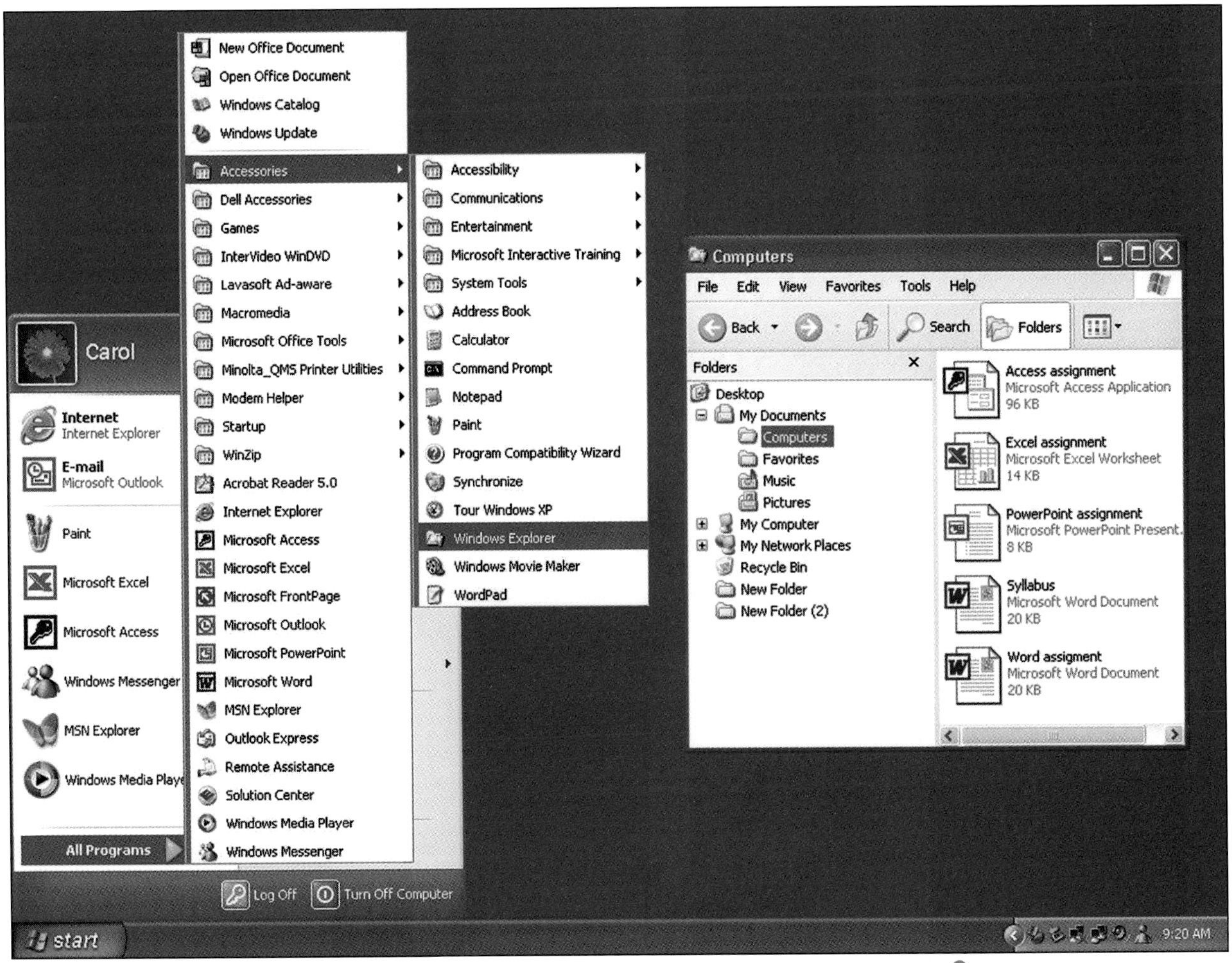

Figure 5-7 Windows Explorer

CATEGORIES

While there are hundreds of different operating systems, there are only three basic categories: embedded, network, or stand-alone.

Figure 5-8 PDAs have embedded operating systems

- **Embedded operating systems** are used for handheld computers and smaller devices like PDAs. (See Figure 5-8.) The entire operating system is stored within or embedded in the device. The operating system programs are permanently stored on ROM or read only memory chips. Popular embedded operating systems include Windows CE and Palm OS.
- **Network operating systems** (**NOS**) are used to control and coordinate computers that are networked or linked together. Many networks are small and connect only a limited number of microcomputers as depicted in Figure 5-9. Other networks like those at colleges and universities are very large and complex. These networks may include other smaller networks and typically connect a variety of different types of computers as depicted in Figure 5-10.

  Network operating systems are typically located on one of the connected computers' hard disks. Called the **network server,** this computer coordinates all communication between the other computers. Popular network operating systems include NetWare, Windows NT Server, Windows XP Server, UNIX, VSE/ESA, and z/OS.
- **Stand-alone operating systems,** also called **desktop operating systems,** control a single desktop or notebook computer. (See Figure 5-11.) These operating systems are located on the computer's hard disk. Often desktop computers and notebooks are part of a network. In these cases, the desktop operating system works with the network's NOS to share and coordinate resources. In these situations, the desktop operating system is referred to as the **client operating system.** Popular desktop operating systems include Windows, Mac OS, and some versions of UNIX. For most end users, these are the most important operating systems.

The operating system is often referred to as the **software environment** or **platform.** For example, software designed to run on Apple computers is compatible with the Mac OS environment. There are many different types of oper-

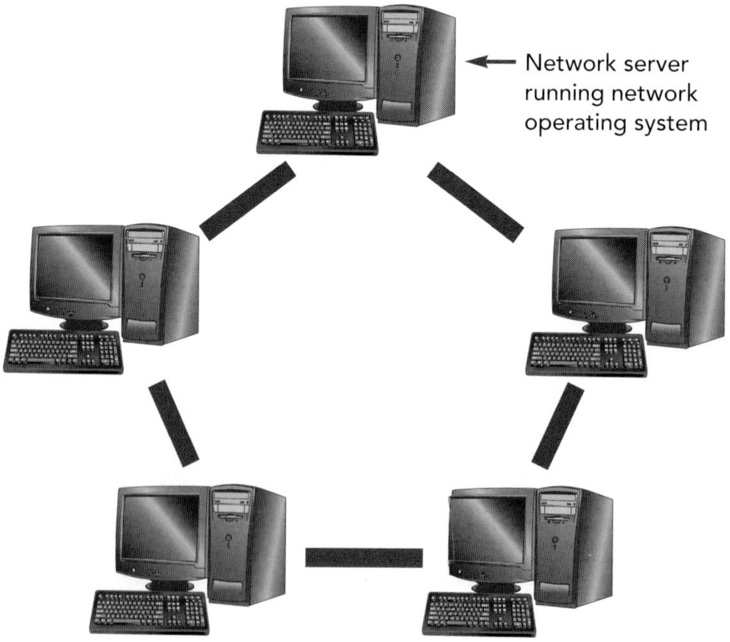

Figure 5-9 Small network

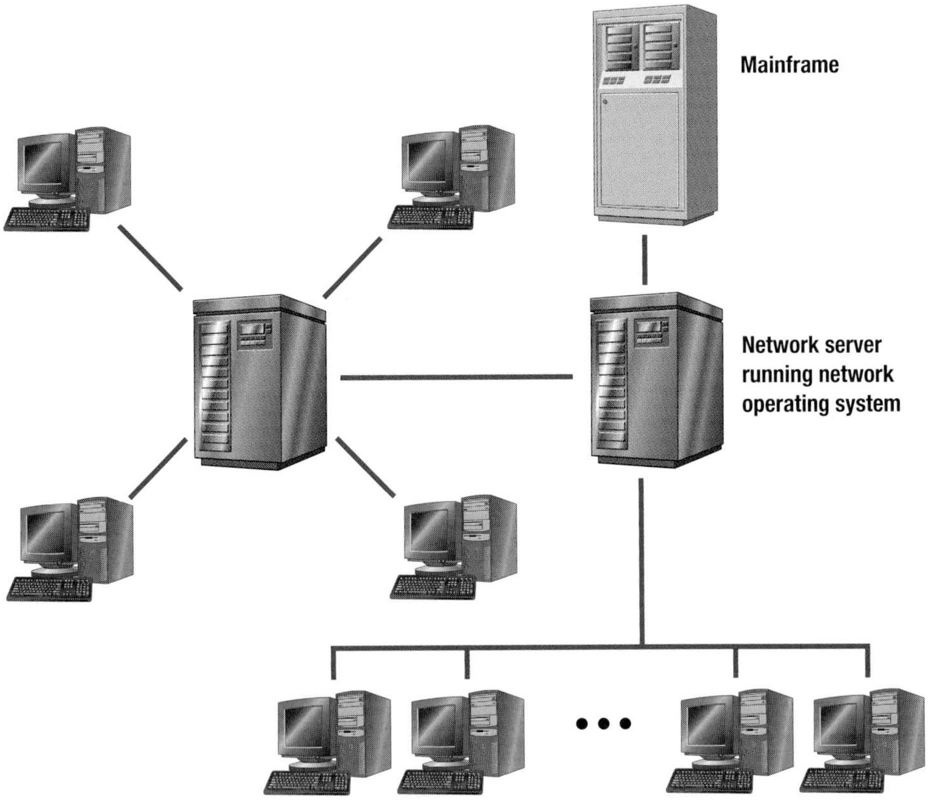

Figure 5-10 Complex network

ating systems. Windows, Mac OS, and Linux are operating systems commonly used by individuals.

Most operating systems are **proprietary operating systems,** that is, they are owned and licensed by a corporation. The Windows operating system is a proprietary operating system owned by the Microsoft Corporation. Some individuals and organizations have developed **non-proprietary operating systems** in which the operating system program or source code is provided to outside individuals. These individuals are encouraged to use, improve, and modify the programs. The objective is to produce better and more useful programs in the long run. Programs released in this way are called **open source.** For example, Linux is an open source program currently provided to software developers under an open source agreement.

Figure 5-11 Stand-alone operating systems

Concept Check

- Describe each of the three categories of operating systems.
- What is a software environment?
- What is the difference between proprietary and non-proprietary operating systems?
- What is an open source program?

WINDOWS

Microsoft's **Windows** is by far the most popular microcomputer operating system today with over 80 percent of the market. Because its market share is so large, more application programs are developed to run under Windows than any other operating system. Windows comes in a variety of different versions and is designed to run with Intel and Intel-compatible microprocessors such as the Pentium IV. For a summary of Microsoft's desktop operating systems, see Figure 5-12.

The latest release of the Windows operating system is **Windows XP.** It provides a new user interface called **Luna.** Compared to other user interfaces, Luna puts emphasis on functions over programs. For example, the new **Start menu** displays categories like E-mail and Internet, rather than individual programs such as Outlook and Internet Explorer. This menu displays a list of commands that can be used to gain access to information, change hardware settings, find information, get online help, run programs, log off a network, and shut down your computer system.

For example, you could use the Start menu to run the Internet Explorer program as shown in Figure 5-13.

Windows XP also includes **Internet Explorer,** a new **Windows Media Player,** and a new **Windows Messenger.** (To learn more about Windows Instant Messenger see Making IT Work for You: Instant Messaging on pages 48–49 in Chapter 2.) Windows XP provides support for multiple users of one microcomputer through **log on** procedures. For example, each member of a

Name	Description
DOS	Microsoft's first operating system provided a character-based interface in which commands are typed or selected from menus
Windows 95	Microsoft's first true multitasking and GUI operating system
Windows NT Workstation	Client operating system designed to work with the Windows NT Server
Windows 98	Upgrade to Windows 95
Windows 2000 Professional	Upgrade to Windows NT Workstation
Windows Millennium Edition	Also known as Windows ME, upgrade to Windows 98 specifically designed for home users
Windows XP	One of Microsoft's newest and most powerful desktop operating systems
Windows XP Tablet PC Edition	Version of Windows XP designed to support tablet pc functions such as converting handwritten input to digital form

Figure 5-12 Microsoft desktop operating systems

1 Click *Start* on the task bar to open the Start Menu.

2 Click the Internet Explorer icon to open your homepage.

Internet Explorer icon

Internet Explorer opens to the address chosen as your homepage.

homepage

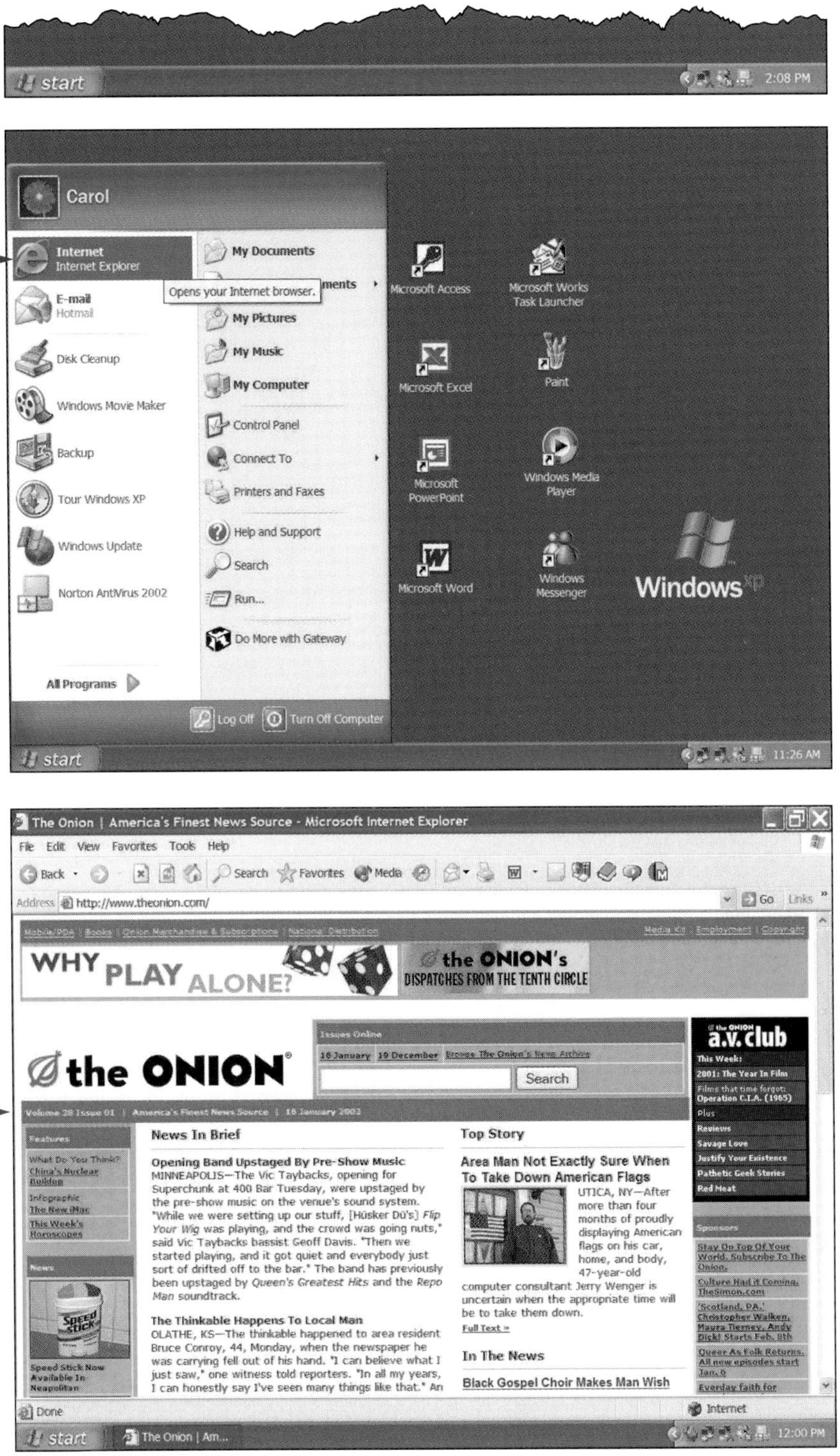

Figure 5-13 Using the Start menu with Windows XP

family could log on using separate **log on names** to access personal document files and settings. (See Figure 5-14.)

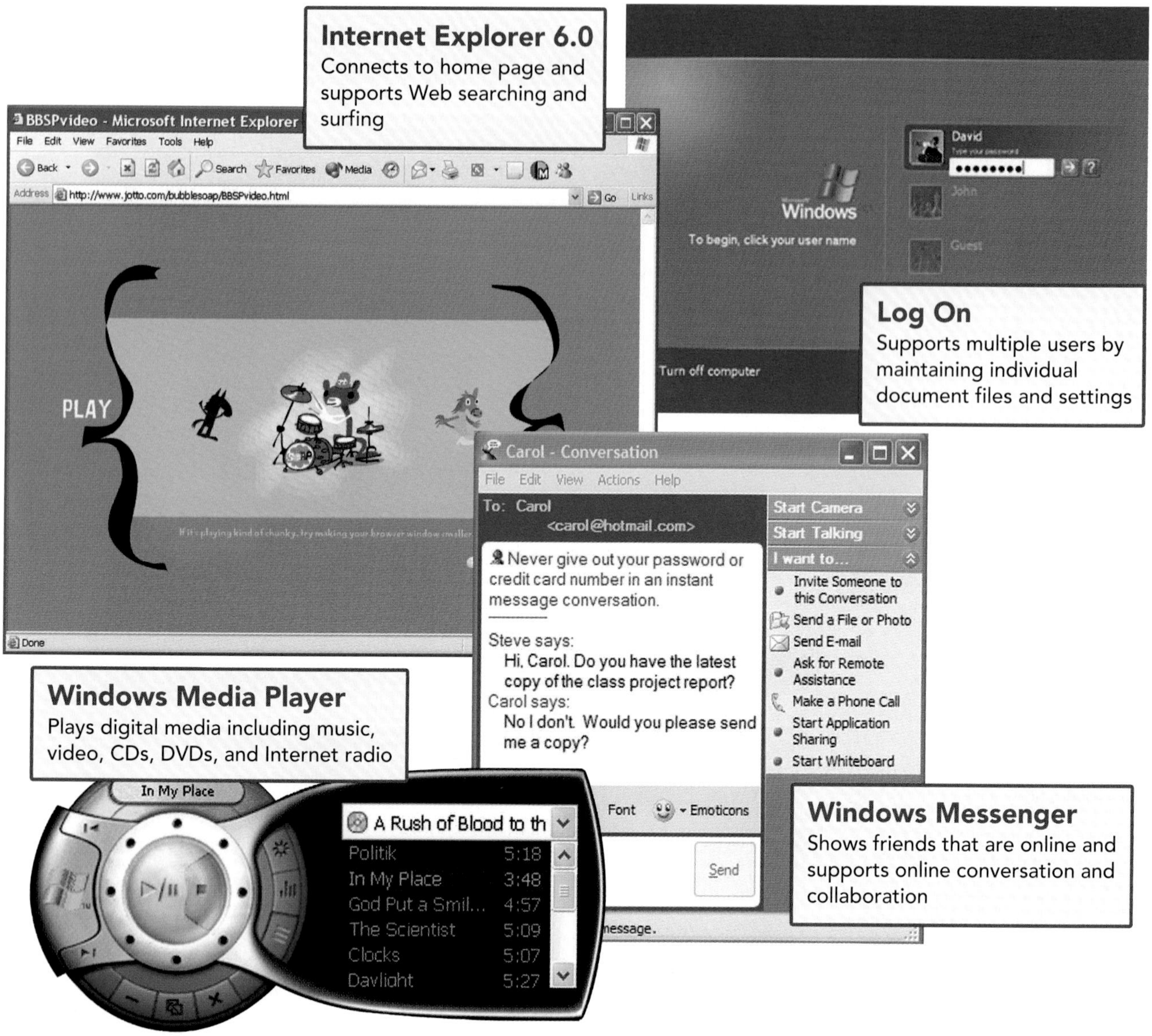

Figure 5-14 Windows Media Player, Windows Messenger, Internet Explorer, and Log On

Figure 5-15 iMac running Mac OS X

MAC OS

Macintosh introduced their first operating system and microcomputer in 1984. It provided one of the first GUIs making it easy even for novice computer users to move and delete files. Designed to run with Apple computers, **Mac OS** is not nearly as widely used as the Windows operating system. As a result, fewer application programs have been written for it. Nonetheless, Mac OS is considered to be one of the most innovative operating systems. It is a powerful, easy-to-use operating system that is popular with professional graphic designers, desktop publishers, and many home users. (See Figure 5-15.)

One of the latest versions of the Macintosh operating system, **Mac OS X,** features a new user interface called **Aqua.** It is an intuitive interface providing photo-quality icons and easy-to-use menus. The desktop features **Dock,** a tool

Figure 5-16 Mac OS X

for visually organizing files. Additionally, Mac OS X provides an updated version of its **Sherlock** search tool for locating information on the Web as well as on the user's computer system. (See Figure 5-16.)

Concept Check

- ✓ What is Windows? What is the newest version of Windows?
- ✓ What is Luna? How is it different from the classic interface?
- ✓ What is the Mac OS? What is one of the newest versions of Mac OS?
- ✓ What is Aqua? Dock? Sherlock?

UNIX AND LINUX

The **UNIX** operating system was originally designed to run on minicomputers in network environments. Now, it is also used by powerful microcomputers and by servers on the Web. There are a large number of different versions of UNIX. One receiving a great deal of attention today is **Linux.**

While Windows, the Mac OS, and many versions of UNIX are proprietary operating systems, Linux is not. It is open source software free and available from many sources, including the Web. As a graduate student at the University of Helsinki, Linus Torvalds developed Linux in 1991. He has allowed distribution of the operating system code and has encouraged others to modify and further develop the code. Linux is one of the most popular and powerful alternatives to the Windows operating system. One advantage of the Linux operating system is the flexibility of the program. For example, it provides multiple user interfaces. Two of the most widely used interfaces are **KDE** and **GNOME.** (See Figure 5-17.)

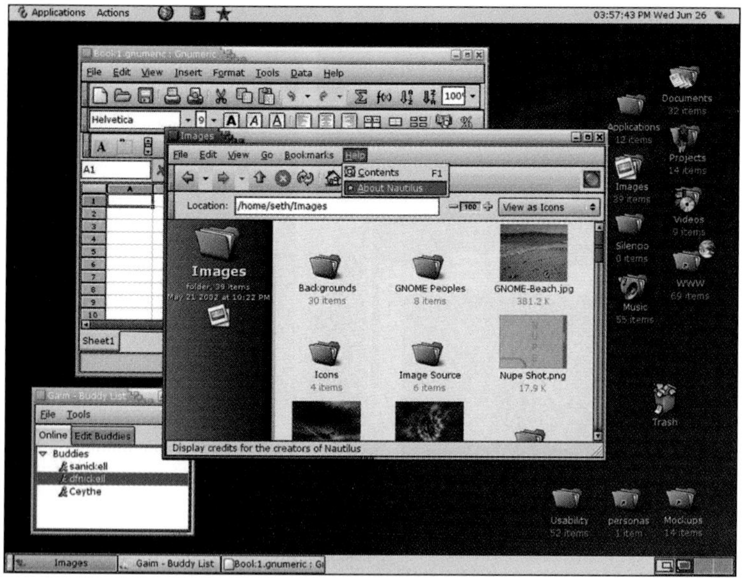

Figure 5-17 Recent version of Linux with GNOME interface

Figure 5-18 IBM zSeries 900 computer

VSE/ESA AND z/OS

Over the years, IBM has introduced numerous proprietary operating systems to support their mainframe computers. Two of the most recent are VSE/ESA and z/OS. These operating systems are designed to support IBM's newest line of powerful mainframe computers, the zSeries 800 and zSeries 900. (See Figure 5-18.) Both are capable of controlling very large and complex organizational networks. z/OSe is a version of z/OS that is specifically designed to support e-commerce and Internet communications.

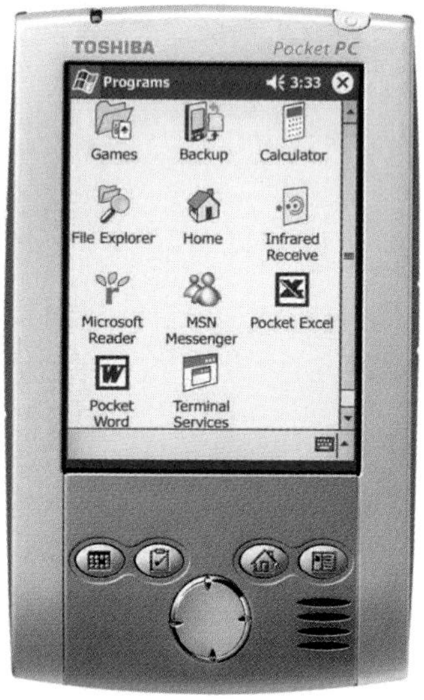

Figure 5-19 Handheld computer running Pocket PC

PALM OS AND WINDOWS CE

Palm OS is an operating system originally designed to run on PDAs manufactured by the Palm Pilot Corporation. The newest version of the Palm OS, however, runs on PDA devices designed by other companies such as Sony, Handspring, and Samsung. It has become the most widely used operating system for PDAs. Palm OS supports handwriting recognition with a system called **graffiti.** (We will discuss handwriting recognition in detail in Chapter 7.) Palm devices use a technology called **HotSync** to share and back up data with desktop and notebook computers.

Windows CE is a handheld computer operating system from Microsoft. This operating system, also known as **Pocket PC,** looks similar to the Windows XP operating system. It supports special versions of Word, Excel, and Internet Explorer. Windows CE is designed to support handheld computers from a variety of different manufacturers including Hewlett-Packard, Toshiba, and Compaq. (See Figure 5-19.)

Concept Check

- ✓ What is Linux? What are KDE and GNOME?
- ✓ What are VSE/ESA and z/OS? What are they used for?
- ✓ What is Palm OS? What is it used for? What is graffiti?
- ✓ What is Windows CE? What is it used for?

Backup, Disk Cleanup, Disk Defragmenter, and System Restore are Windows utilities. eSafe Desktop, McAfee Office, and Norton SystemWorks are utility suites.

Ideally, microcomputers continuously run without problems. However, that simply is not the case. All kinds of things can happen—internal hard disks can crash, computers can freeze up, operations can slow down, and so on. These events can make computing very frustrating. That's where utilities come in. **Utilities** are specialized programs designed to make computing easier. There are hundreds of different utility programs. The most essential are:

- **Troubleshooting** or **diagnostic** programs that recognize and correct problems, ideally before they become serious.
- **Antivirus** programs that guard your computer system against viruses or other damaging programs that can invade your computer system.
- **Uninstall** programs that allow you to safely and completely remove unneeded programs and related files from your hard disk.
- **Backup** programs that make copies of files to be used in case the originals are lost or damaged.
- **File compression** programs that reduce the size of files so they require less storage space and can be sent more efficiently over the Internet.

Most operating system programs provide some utility programs. Even more powerful utility programs can be purchased separately or in utility suites.

WINDOWS UTILITIES

The Windows operating systems are accompanied with several utility programs, including Backup, Disk Cleanup, Disk Defragmenter, and System Restore. These utilities can be accessed from the Systems Tools menu. (See Figure 5-20.)

1. Click *Start.*
2. Select *All Programs.*
   - Select *Accessories.*
   - Choose *System Tools.*

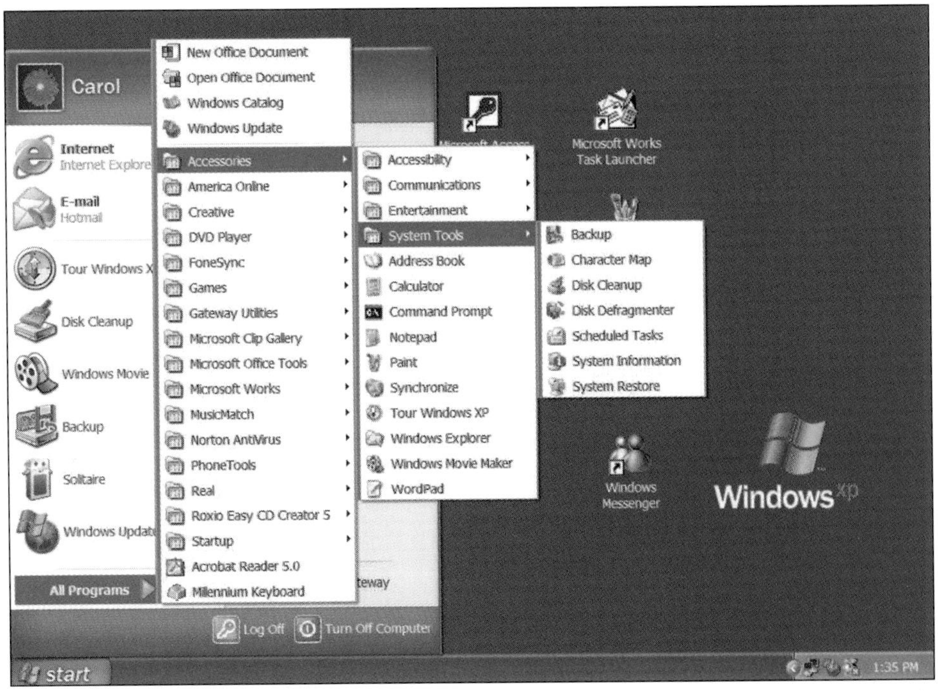

Figure 5-20 Accessing the Windows utilities

Backup is a utility program included with the many versions of Windows that makes a copy of all files or selected files that have been saved onto a disk. It helps to protect you from the effects of a disk failure. For example using the Professional edition of XP, you can select Backup from the Windows XP System Tools menu to create a backup for your hard disk as shown in Figure 5-21. (While most versions of XP include the Backup utility, the XP Home edition does not.)

1
- **Click *Start*.**
- **Select *Accessories* from the *All Programs* menu.**
- **Select *Backup* from the *System Tools* menu.**

2
- **Run the Wizard and specify your settings.**
- **Choose *Backup* and choose the files you want to include.**
- **Choose the destination for the backup.**

3
- **Finish the Wizard to back up the selected drive.**
- **Close the *Progress Window* or view the report.**

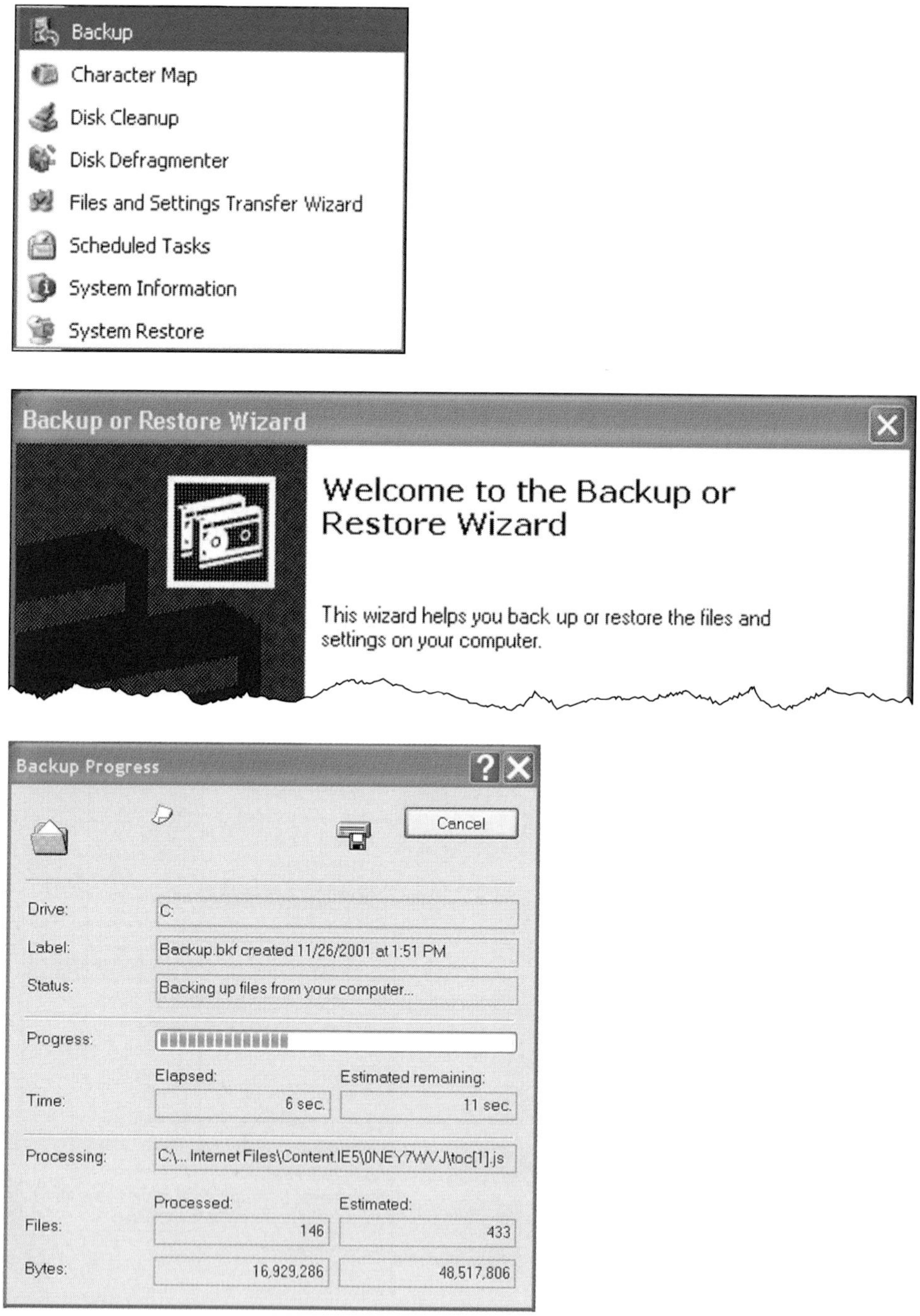

Figure 5-21 Backup utility

When you surf the Web, a variety of programs and files are saved on your hard disk. Many of these and other files are not essential. **Disk Cleanup** is a trouble-shooting utility that identifies and eliminates nonessential files. This frees up valuable disk space and improves system performance.

For example, by selecting Disk Cleanup from the Windows XP System Tools menu, you can eliminate unneeded files on your hard disk as shown in Figure 5-22.

Figure 5-22 Disk Cleanup utility

1

- **Click *Start.***
- **Select *Accessories* from the *All Programs* menu.**
- **Select *Disk Cleanup* from the *System Tools* menu.**

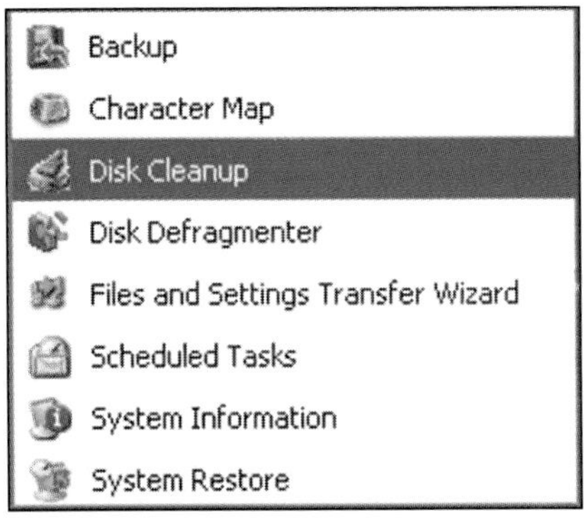

2

- **Verify the files suggested for cleanup.**
- **Click *OK.***
- **Click *Yes* to begin disk cleanup.**

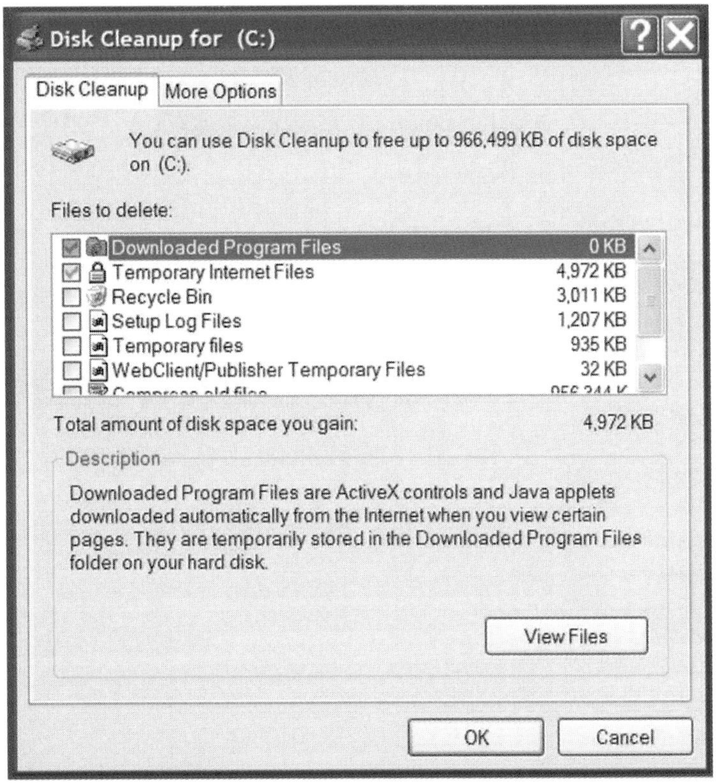

3

- **The utility cleans the selected files.**

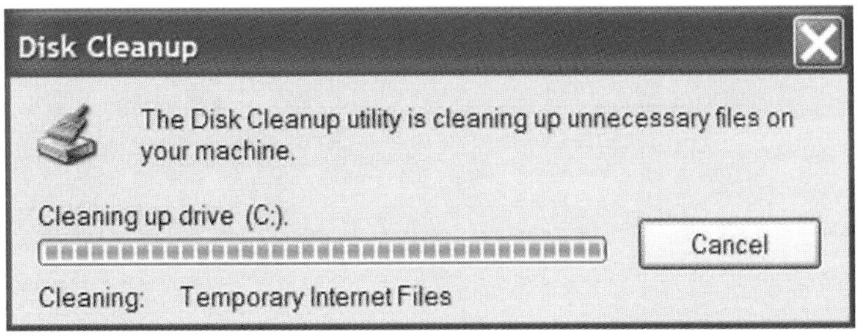

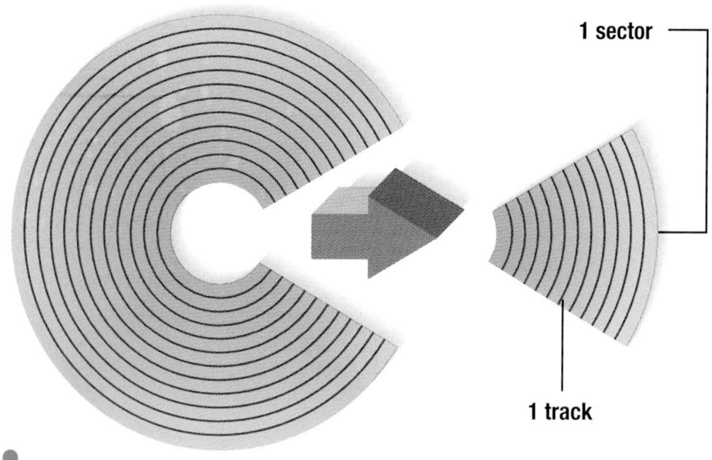

Figure 5-23 Tracks and sectors

As we will discuss in detail in Chapter 9, files are stored and organized on a disk according to tracks and sectors. A **track** is a concentric ring. Each track is divided into wedge-shaped sections called **sectors.** (See Figure 5-23.) The operating system tries to save a file on a single track across contiguous sectors. Often, however, this is not possible and the file has to be broken up, or **fragmented** into small parts and the parts stored wherever space is available. Whenever a file is retrieved, it is reconstructed from the fragments. After a period of time, a hard disk becomes highly fragmented, slowing operations.

Disk Defragmenter is a utility program that locates and eliminates unnecessary fragments and rearranges files and unused disk space to optimize operations. For example, by selecting Disk Defragmenter from the Windows XP Systems Tool menu, you can defrag your hard disk as shown in Figure 5-24.

1

- **Click *Start.***
- **Select *Accessories* from the *All Programs* menu.**
- **Select *Disk Defragmenter* from the *System Tools* menu.**

Figure 5-24 Disk Defragmenter utility

2

- **If necessary, choose the drive you want to analyze and defragment.**
- **Click the *Analyze* button to determine whether defragging is needed.**
- **View the report or, if necessary, defragment the drive.**
- **Click the *Defragment* button to begin defragging.**
- **When defragmentation is complete for the selected drive, view the report or close the window.**

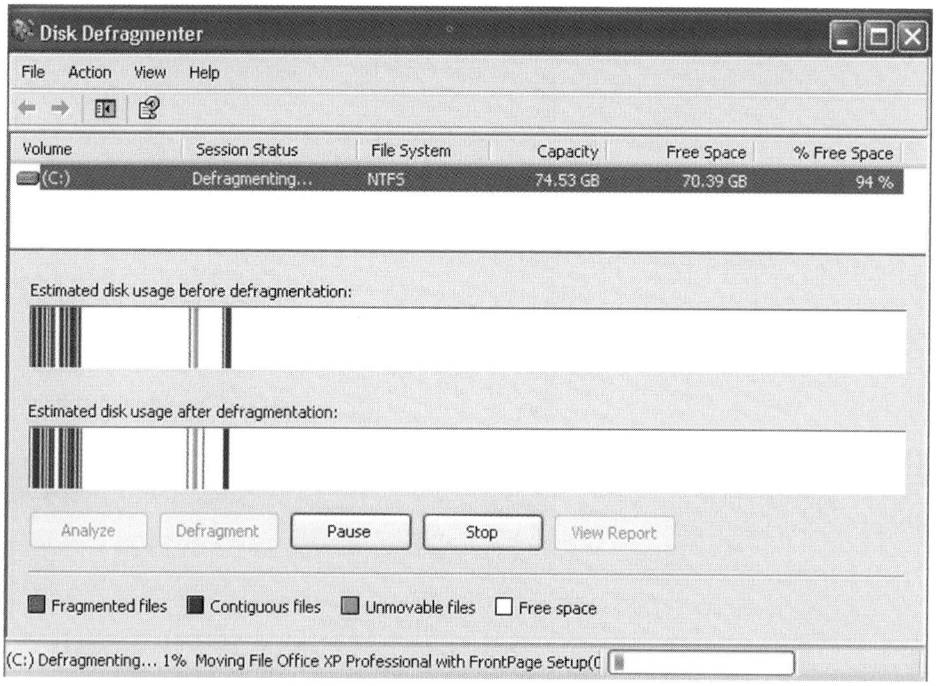

A helpful utility call **System Restore** can help undo unexpected events. For example, if you have problems installing new software or hardware, some system settings may have been incorrectly changed. Fortunately, Windows periodically saves system settings, and you can go back to these prior settings using the System Restore utility. This utility does not overwrite any documents or files you have worked on since the settings were last saved; it only eliminates potentially harmful changes. (See Figure 5-25.)

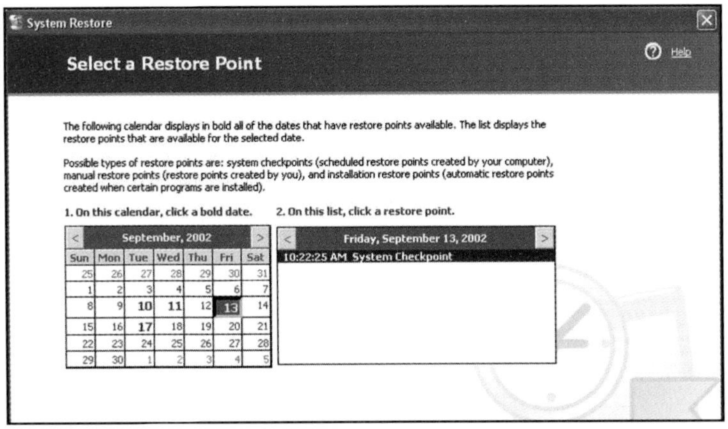

1
- Select *System Restore* from the *System Tools* menu.
- Click *Restore my computer to an earlier time.*
- Click *Next.*

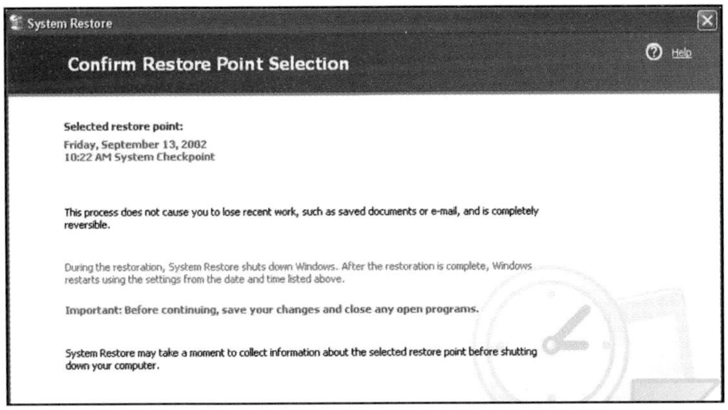

2
- Select the restore date from the calendar of options.
- Select the restore point and click *next.*

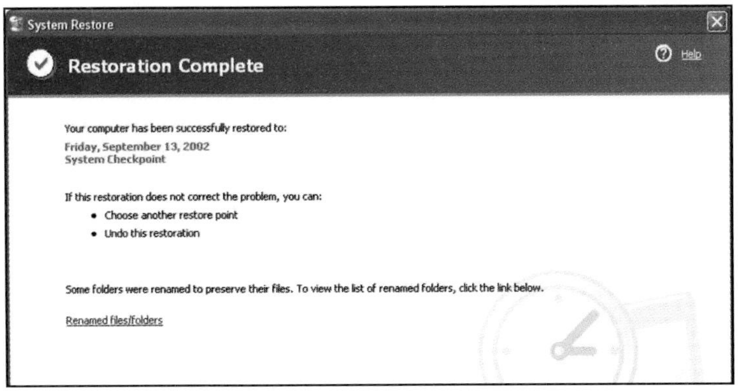

3
- Review the options presented.
- Click *Next* to restart your computer and begin the restoration
- Click *OK* to accept the changes and finish restoration.

Figure 5-25 System Restore utility

Utility	Description
Backup	Makes a copy of all or selected files
Disk Cleanup	Identifies and eliminates nonessential files
Disk Defragmenter	Eliminates unnecessary fragments and rearranges files and unused disk space to optimize operations
System Restore	Records the settings on your computer to help undo unexpected events

Figure 5-26 Windows utilities

For a summary of Windows utilities see Figure 5-26. While these and other utility programs included with Windows are effective, specialty programs offer a wider variety and higher level of support. These programs can be purchased separately or in suites.

Concept Check

- What are utilities?
- Describe each of the following utilities: Backup, Disk Cleanup, Disk Defragmenter, and System Restore.
- What are tracks, sectors, and fragments?

UTILITY SUITES

Like application software suites, **utility suites** combine several programs into one package. Buying the package is less expensive than buying the programs separately. The three well-known utility suites are eSafe Desktop, McAfee Office, and Norton SystemWorks. These suites provide a variety of utilities including programs that will protect your system from dangerous programs called **computer viruses.** You can "catch" a computer virus many ways including opening attachments to e-mail messages and downloading software from the Internet. (We will discuss computer viruses in detail in Chapter 11.)

Computing Today CD

To learn more about virus protection, consult your Computing Today CD or visit us on the Web at http://www.mhhe.com/oleary/CT05 and select Animations from Tim's Toolbox. Also see Making IT Work for You: Virus Protection on page 186–187. To see how virus protection programs work, see Figure 5-27.

Norton SystemWorks is one of the most widely used utility suites. (See Figure 5-28.) It includes the following:

- **Norton AntiVirus** is a collection of antivirus programs that can protect your system from over 21,000 different viruses, quarantine or delete existing viruses, and automatically update its virus list to check for the newest viruses.
- **Norton CleanSweep** is a collection of programs that guide you through the process of safely removing programs and files you no longer need. Additionally, they will archive, move, and make backups of programs as well as clean up your hard disk. They can also protect your existing files from damage when you install new programs.
- **Web Cleanup** is a collection of programs that check your computer system for unnecessary files including temporary files created by application programs, cache files, history files, and cookies. You can then eliminate these files with a click of a button.
- **Connection Keep Alive** prevents dial-up Internet connections from timing out by simulating online user activity during periods of inactivity.
- **GoBack Personal Edition** will retore system configurations, help to locate lost files, and repair damaged files.

On the Web Explorations

Norton is one of the leaders in developing utility software. To learn more about this company, visit our Web site at

http://www.mhhe.com/oleary/CT05

and select On the Web Explorations from Tim's Toolbox.

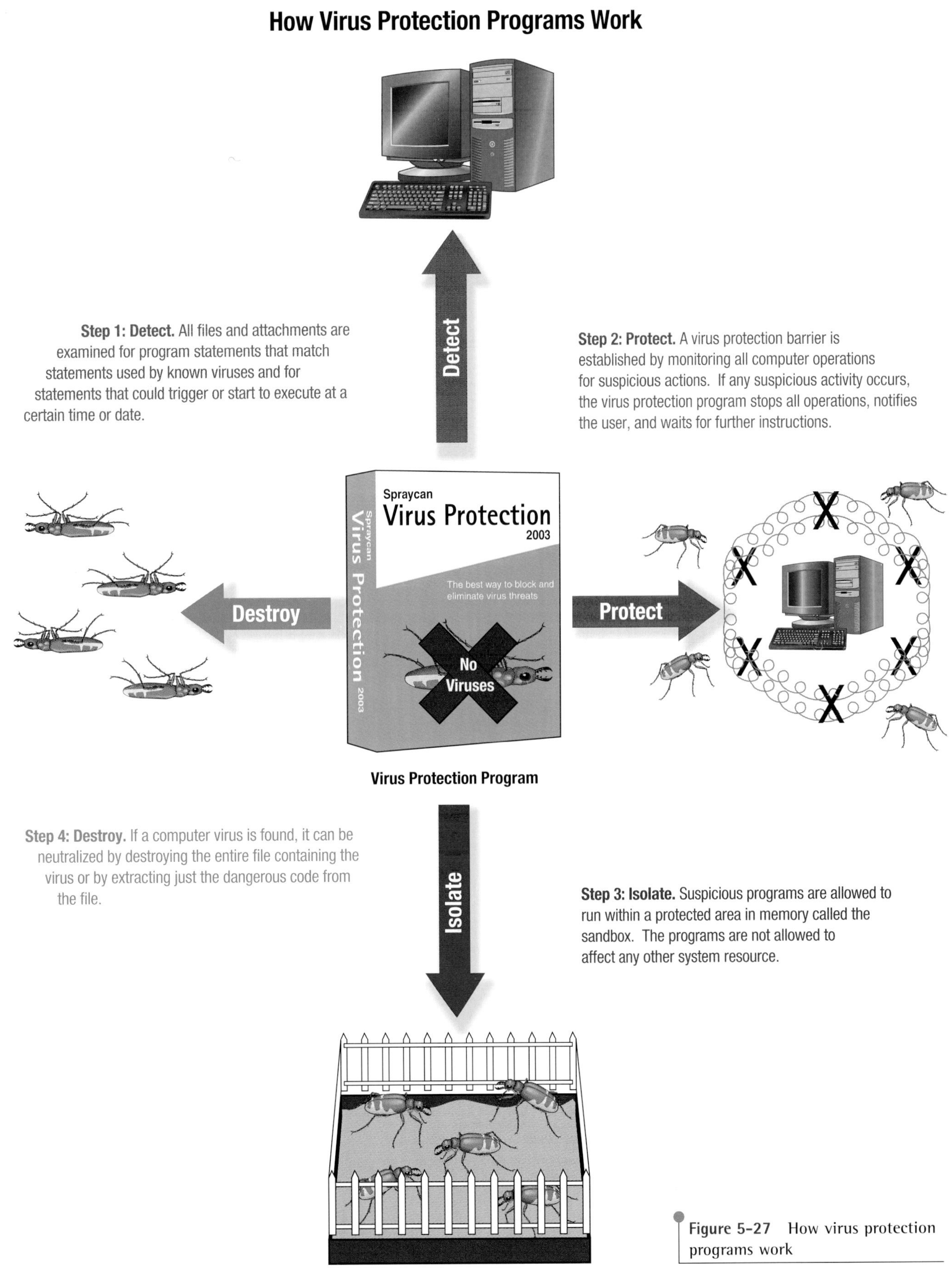
How Virus Protection Programs Work
Detect
Step 1: Detect. All files and attachments are examined for program statements that match statements used by known viruses and for statements that could trigger or start to execute at a certain time or date.
Step 2: Protect. A virus protection barrier is established by monitoring all computer operations for suspicious actions. If any suspicious activity occurs, the virus protection program stops all operations, notifies the user, and waits for further instructions.
Spraycan
Virus Protection
2003
The best way to block and eliminate virus threats
No Viruses
Destroy
Protect
Virus Protection Program
Step 4: Destroy. If a computer virus is found, it can be neutralized by destroying the entire file containing the virus or by extracting just the dangerous code from the file.
Isolate
Step 3: Isolate. Suspicious programs are allowed to run within a protected area in memory called the sandbox. The programs are not allowed to affect any other system resource.

Figure 5-27 How virus protection programs work

MAKING IT WORK FOR YOU

VIRUS PROTECTION

Worried about computer viruses? Did you know that others could be intercepting your private e-mail? It is even possible for them to gain access and control over your computer system. Fortunately, Internet security suites are available to help ensure your safety while you are on the Internet.

Getting Started The first step is to install an Internet security suite. Once installed, the software will continually work to ensure security and privacy. One such suite, eSafe, has a free evaluation version available from the Internet. To install this suite, follow the instructions below.

1
- **Connect to *www.esafedesktop.com***
- **Select *Downloads.***
- **Complete the registration form.**
- **Download the *eSafe* software.**

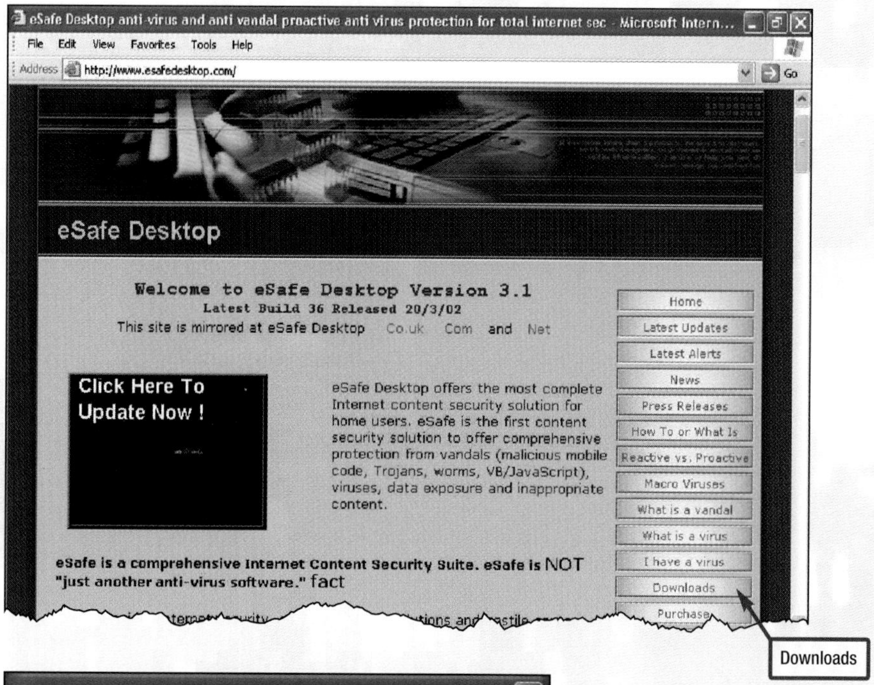

2
- **Double-click the download file.**
- **Follow the on-screen instructions to install eSafe Desktop.**

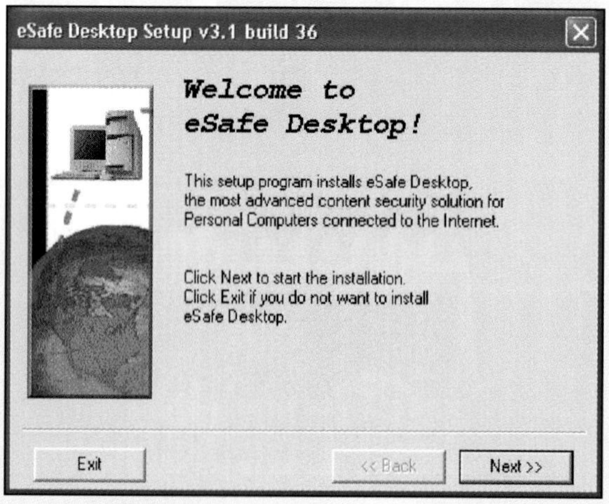

eSafe Numerous security files have been installed. One of these, Desktop Watch, runs continually to search for privacy and security violations to the computer system. Another program, Desktop Configuration, provides a menu to access some of eSafe's most powerful applications including Sandbox, Personal Firewall, and Anti-Virus.

Sandbox

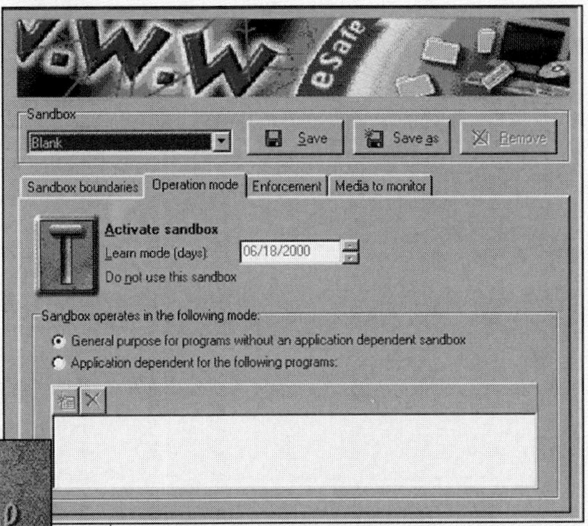

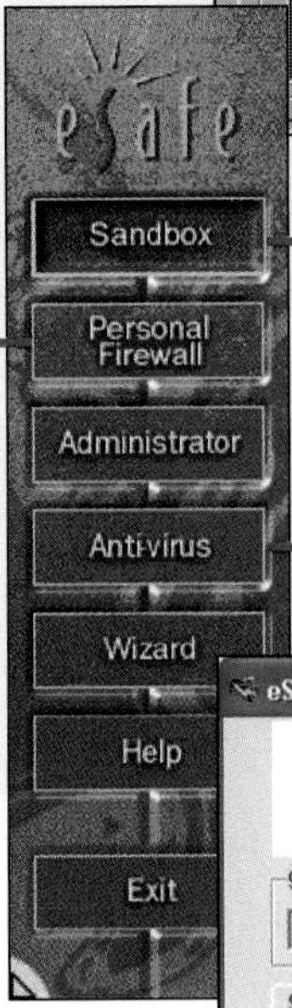

A sandbox is a protective area within a computer system where suspicious and potentially dangerous programs can be executed. These programs are prohibited from altering sensitive files or damaging system resources.

Personal Firewall

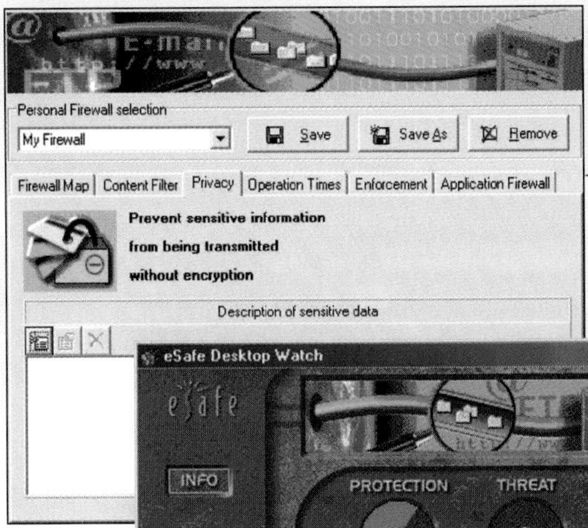

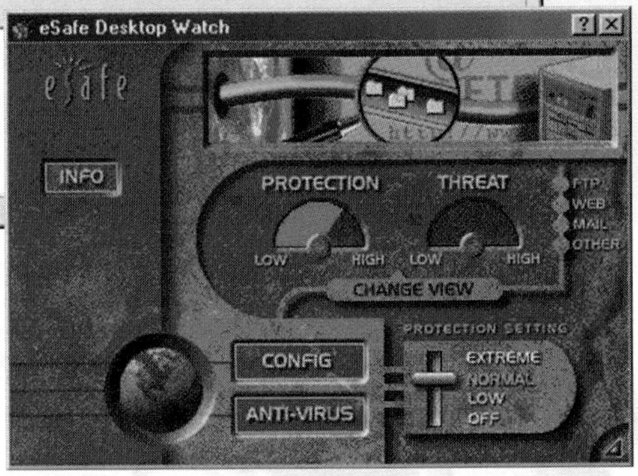

Personal Firewall is a program that monitors all inbound and outbound traffic to a computer system. It limits access to only authorized users, automatically checks files for viruses, and filters out unwanted content.

Anti-Virus

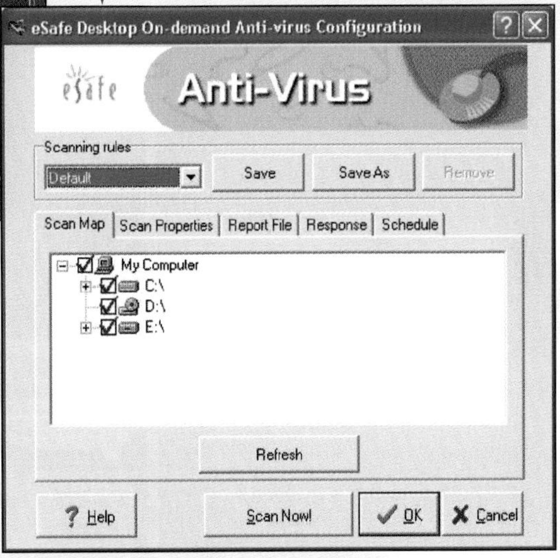

Anti-Virus controls how frequently the computer system is searched for computer viruses. When a file is checked, it is compared to the profile of over 6,000 known viruses. Once a virus is detected, typically either it is eliminated from the file or the entire file is deleted.

The Web is continually changing and some of the specifics presented in this Making IT Work for You may have changed. To learn about other ways to make information technology work for you, visit our Web site at http://www.mhhe.com/oleary/CT05 and select Making IT Work for You from Tim's Toolbox.

- **Norton Utilities** is a collection of several separate troubleshooting utilities. These programs can be used to find and fix problems, improve system performance, prevent problems from occurring, and troubleshoot a variety of other problems. One of the programs, **One Button Checkup,** integrates several of the separate troubleshooting utilities. (See Figure 5-29.)

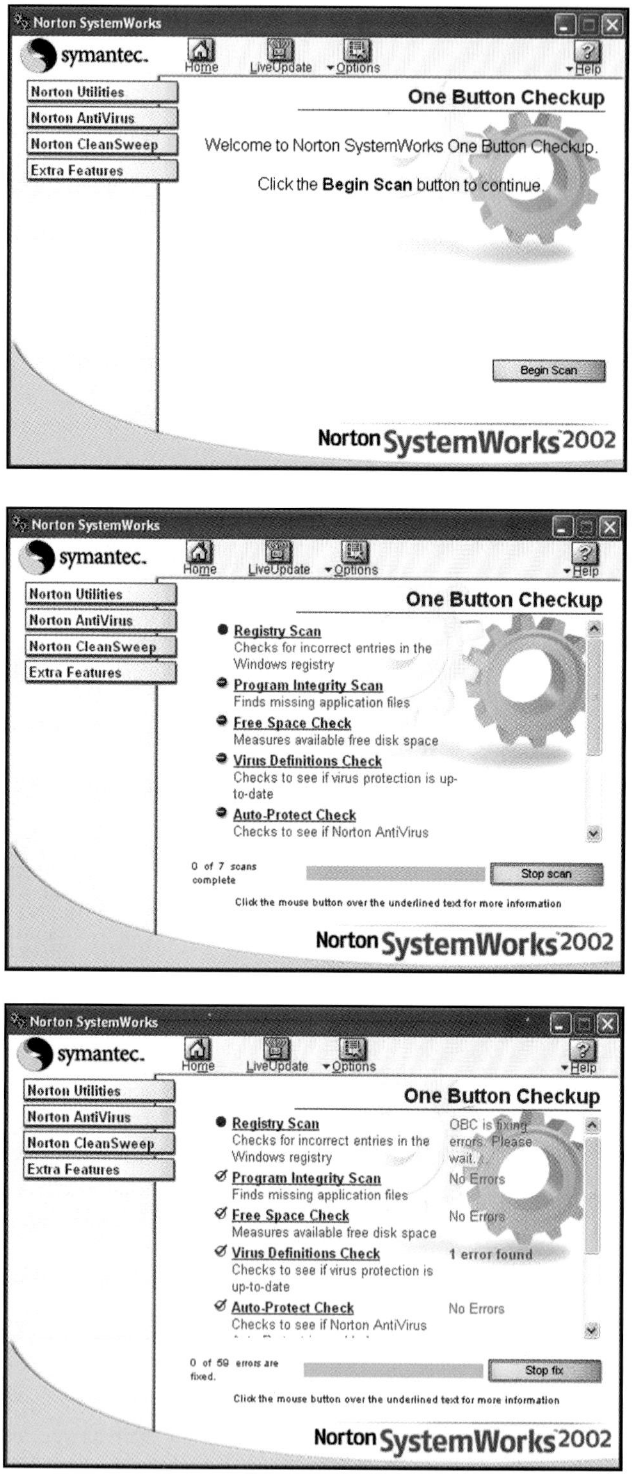

1 Click *Start.*

Select *Norton System Works* from the All Programs menu.

2 Click *Begin Scan* to start the One Button Checkup.

3 Click *Begin Fix* to repair the errors found in the sweep.

Close the window or select a new utility from the menu.

Figure 5-28 Norton SystemWorks' One Button Checkup

Concept Check

- What is the difference between a utility and a utility suite?
- What is a computer virus? How you can you protect yourself against them?

DEVICE DRIVERS

Device drivers are specialized programs that allow devices such as a mouse, keyboard, and printer to communicate with the rest of the computer system.

Every device, such as a mouse or printer that is connected to a computer system, has a special program associated with it. This program, called a **device driver** or simply a **driver,** works with the operating system to allow communication between the device and the rest of the computer system. Each time the computer system is started, the operating system loads all of the device drivers into memory.

Whenever a new device is added to a computer system, a new device driver must be installed before the device can be used. Windows supplies hundreds of different device drivers with its system software. For many devices, the appropriate drivers are automatically selected and installed when the device is first connected to the computer system. For others, the device driver must be manually installed. Fortunately, Windows provides wizards to assist in this process. For example, Windows **Add Printer Wizard** provides step-by-step guidance to select the appropriate printer driver and to install that driver. (See Figure 5-29.) If a particular device driver is not included with the Windows system software, the product's manufacturer will supply one. Many times these drivers are available directly from the manufacturer's Web site.

You probably never think about the device drivers in your computer. However, when your computer behaves unpredictably, you may find reinstalling or updating your device drivers solves your problems. Windows makes it easy to update the drivers on your computer using **Windows Update,** as shown in Figure 5-30.

To access the Add Printer Wizard

- **Select *Control Panel* from the *Start* menu.**
- **Click *Printers and faxes.***
- **Click *Add a printer.***

Figure 5-29 Add Printer Wizard

1 Access *Windows Update* in the *All Programs* list of the *Start* menu.

2 Click *Scan for Updates.*

Click *Driver Updates.*

3 Click *Add.*

Click *Review and Install Drivers.*

Click *Install Now* and *Accept* the license agreement.

Click *OK* to restart the computer.

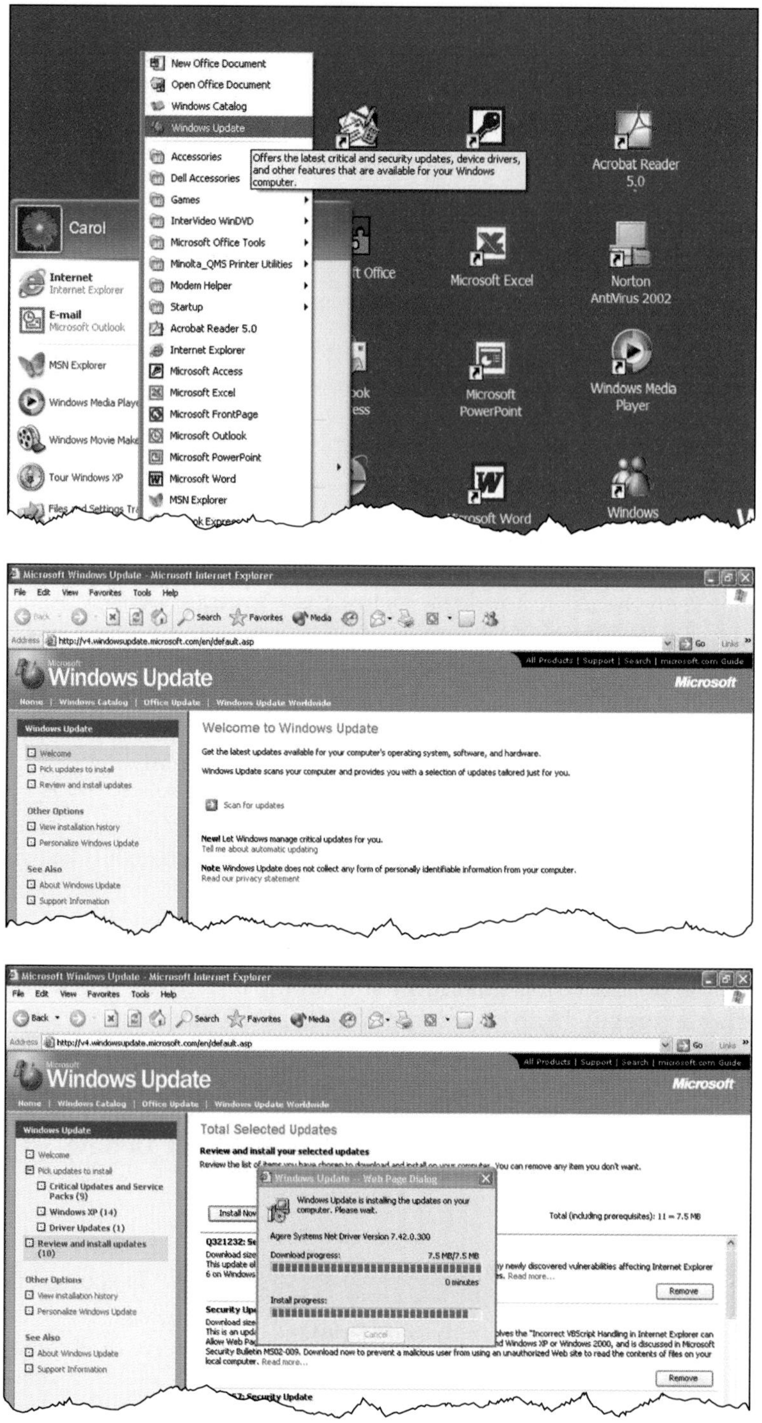

Figure 5-30 Using Windows Update

Concept Check

✓	What are device drivers?
✓	What does the Window's Add Printer Wizard do?
✓	When would you use Windows Update?

Careers in IT

Computer Support Specialist

Computer support specialists provide technical support to customers and other users. They may also be called technical support specialists or help-desk technicians. Computer support specialists manage the everyday technical problems faced by computer users. They resolve common networking problems and may use troubleshooting programs to diagnose problems. Most computer support specialists are hired to work within a company and provide technical support for other employees and divisions. However, it is increasingly common for companies to provide technical support as an outsourced service.

Employers generally look for individuals with a bachelor's degree to fill computer support specialist positions. Degrees in computer science or information systems may be preferred. However because demand for qualified applicants is so high, those with practical experience and certification from a training program increasingly fill these positions. Employers seek individuals with good analytical and communication skills. Those with good people skills and customer service experience have an advantage in this field.

Computer support specialists can expect to earn an annual salary of $25,000 to $50,000. Opportunities for advancement are very good and may involve design and implementation of new systems. Some computer support specialists become software engineers. To learn about other careers in information systems visit us at http://www.mhhe.com/oleary/CT05 and select Careers in IT from Tim's Toolbox.

A Look to the Future

IBM Builds an Aware Supercomputer

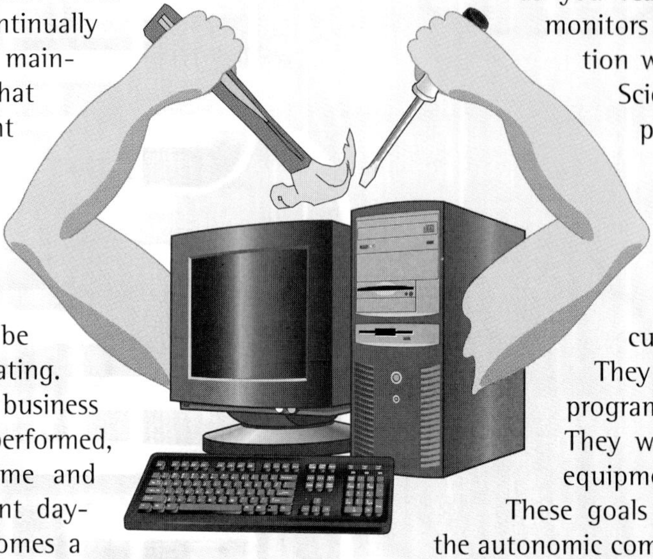

Wouldn't it be nice if computers could fix themselves? What if you never had to worry about installing or updating software? What if your computer could continually fine tune its operations to maintain peak performance? What if your computer could fight off viruses and malicious attacks from outsiders? For many people this sounds too good to be true. Maintenance and security tasks like these can be time consuming and frustrating.

Now imagine you run a business and unless these tasks are performed, you will lose valuable time and money. It is not a pleasant daydream and it quickly becomes a nightmare without properly trained systems administrators to keep servers running smoothly. Yet, many experts predict that supercomputers and business systems are not far from becoming too complex for humans to oversee. Recent news from IBM makes the dream of a self-repairing, self-updating, and self-protecting server seem ever closer.

IBM has announced plans to concentrate research efforts on developing just such a server. The project, called eLiza, hopes to free businesses from the time-consuming maintenance and complexity of business infrastructure. IBM hopes the new system will be self-regulating and virtually invisible. They believe eLiza has the potential to revolutionize the way businesses run. The foundation of the new project lies in autonomic computing.

Autonomic computing is a system that allows machines to run with little human intervention. Such computers would not have self-awareness, but rather be self-correcting. Autonomic processes in machines are modeled after autonomic processes in the human body. For example, you are not consciously breathing as you read this. Instead, your body monitors and maintains your respiration without your constant input. Scientists hope autonomic computing will behave in a similar manner and maintain self-regulating systems without intervention.

Autonomic machines would be able to sense security flaws and repair them. They would be able to sense slow programs and optimize file storage. They would be able to sense new equipment, format it, and test it. These goals are impressive and though the autonomic computer is still in development, the eLiza project at IBM is a step toward this kind of maintenance-free machine.

As technology continues to develop, many computer systems have become too complex for human maintenance. This progress makes autonomic computing more valuable now than ever. However, it is important to note that autonomic computing is not artificial intelligence, because autonomic machines do not have human cognitive abilities or intelligence. Instead, these machines have knowledge of their own systems and the capability to learn from experiences to correct errors in such systems.

Given the potential for a self-maintaining server, the possibility of a similar system designed for a microcomputer seems less like a dream and more like a reality. What do you think—will microcomputers someday care for themselves?

NOTES

VISUAL SUMMARY

SYSTEM SOFTWARE

SYSTEM SOFTWARE

System software works with end users, application programs, and computer hardware to handle many details relating to computer operations.

Not a single program but a collection or system of programs. These programs handle hundreds of technical details with little or no user intervention.

Four kinds of systems programs are operating systems, utilities, device drivers, and language translators.

- **Operating systems** coordinate resources, provide an interface between users and the computer, and run programs.
- **Utilities** (**service programs**) perform specific tasks related to managing computer resources.
- **Device drivers** allow particular input or output devices to communicate with the rest of the computer system.
- **Language translators** convert programming instructions written by programmers into a language that computers can understand and process.

OPERATING SYSTEMS

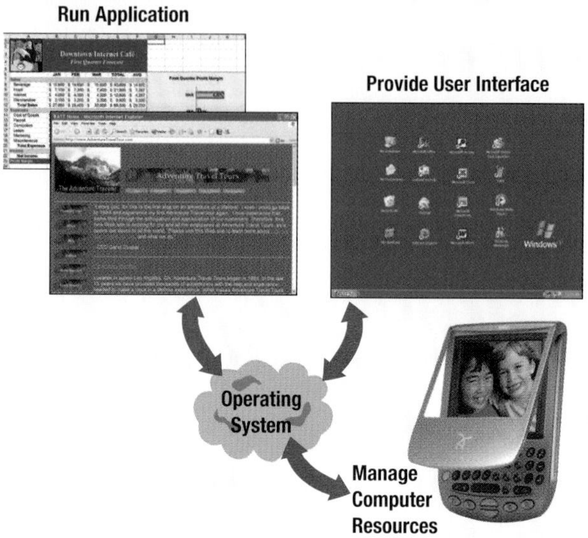

Operating systems, also known as **software environments** or **platforms,** consist of a collection of programs to handle technical details.

Functions

Operating systems perform a variety of functions. These functions can be classified into three groups:

- **Resources**—coordinate and monitor all computer resources.
- **User interface**—provides interface between users, application programs, and computer hardware. **Character based interface** uses written commands. **Graphical user interface** (**GUI**) uses graphical elements.
- **Applications**—load and run programs. **Multitasking** is ability to switch between applications stored in memory. Current program runs in **foreground.** Others run in **background.**

Features

Booting is starting or restarting a computer. **Warm boot** occurs when computer is restarted. Starting a computer after it has been turned off is a **cold boot.**

To effectively use computers, competent and knowledgeable end users need to understand the functionality of system software including operating systems, utility programs, device drivers, and language translators.

OPERATING SYSTEMS

POST (**power-on self test**) verifies that certain hardware components are operational. **Kernel** is part of the operating system that is **memory resident.** The **desktop** is the user interface provided by Windows.

Common features of application programs and operating systems include **icons, pointers, windows, menus, dialog boxes,** and **help.**

Data and programs are stored in a system of **files** and **folders. Windows Explorer** is a file management program.

Categories

There are hundreds of operating systems but only three basic categories:

- **Embedded** for handheld computers and smaller devices.
- **Network** (**NOS**) control and coordinate computers on a network. **Network server** coordinates all network communication.
- **Stand-alone** (**desktop**) for desktop and notebook computers; called **client operating systems** in networked environments.

Propriety operating systems are owned and licensed by a corporation; **non-proprietary** are free and called **open source** programs.

OPERATING SYSTEMS

Windows

Windows is the most widely used operating system. It is designed to run with Intel and Intel-compatible microprocessors. There are numerous versions with Windows XP the latest version with the following features:

- **Luna** is a new interface that emphasizes functions over programs.
- **Windows Media Player** to play digital music, video, CDs, DVDs, and Internet Radio.
- **Windows Messenger** to keep track of and communicate with online friends.
- **Log On** capability to support multiple users with individual **log on names.**

Mac OS

Apple's **Mac OS** is an innovative, powerful, easy-to-use operating system designed to run with Macintosh computers. The latest version is **Mac OS X,** which includes the following features:

- **Aqua,** an intuitive user interface providing photo-quality icons and easy-to-use menus.
- **Dock,** a tool for visually organize files.
- **Sherlock,** a tool for locating information on the Web as on the user's computer system.

OPERATING SYSTEMS

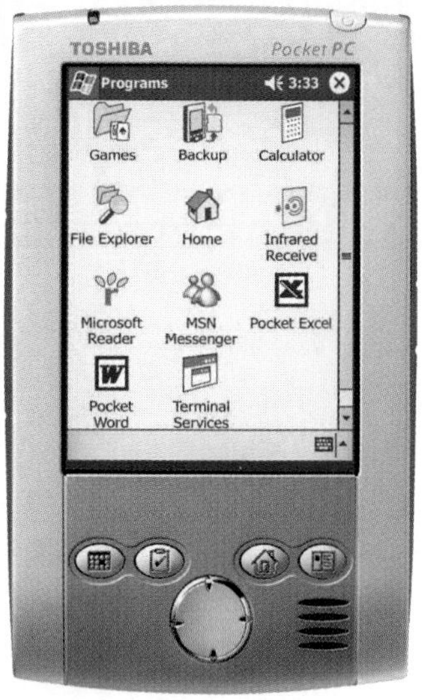

UNIX and Linux

UNIX was originally designed to run on minicomputers in network environments. Now, it is used by powerful microcomputers and servers on the Web. There are many different versions of UNIX.

One version, **Linux,** is receiving a great deal of attention today. It was originally developed by Linus Torvals in 1991. Linux is non-proprietary, free, and available from the Web. **KDE** and **GNOME** are Linux interfaces.

VSE/ESA and z/OS

VSE/ESA and **z/OS** are mainframe operating systems from IBM. z/OS is the newest with a z/OSe version designed specifically to support e-commerce and Internet communications.

Palm OS and Windows CE

Palm OS is the most widely used operating system for PDAs. Two features are:

- **Graffiti**—a handwriting recognition system included in the Palm OS.
- **HotSync**—communication support to share files and back up data with desktop and notebook computers.

Windows CE (**Pocket PC**) is a handheld operating system from Microsoft. Similar to Windows XP with support for special versions of Word, Excel, and Internet Explorer.

UTILITIES

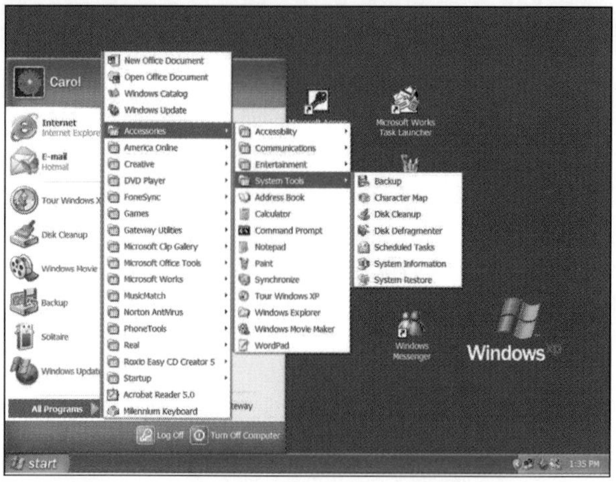

Utilities are specialized programs designed to make computing easier. The most essential utilities are:

- **Troubleshooting** (**diagnostic**) programs to recognize and correct problems.
- **Antivirus** programs to protect against computer viruses and other damaging programs.
- **Uninstall** programs to safely remove unneeded programs and related files.
- **Backup** programs to copy files in case originals are lost or damaged.
- **File compression** programs to reduce file sizes and storage requirements.

Windows Utilities

The Windows operating systems come with several utility programs accessible from the Systems Tools menu. Four such utilities are:

- **Backup**—makes a copy of individual or selected files.
- **Disk Cleanup**—identifies and eliminates unnecessary files.
- **Disk Defragmenter**—eliminates unnecessary **fragments** and rearranges files for more efficient retrieval.
- **System Restore**—records computer settings to help undo unexpected events.

UTILITIES

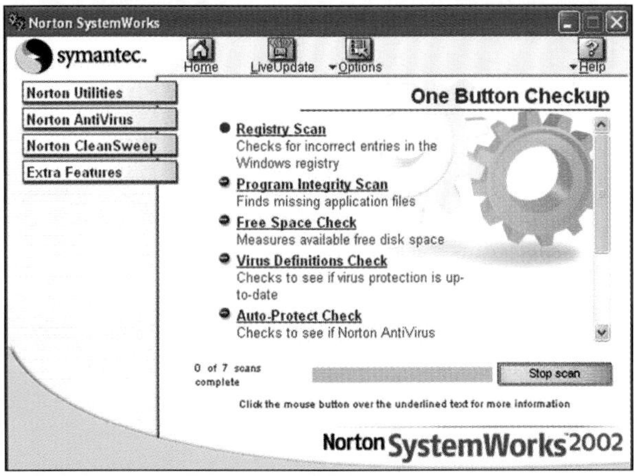

Utility Suites

Utility suites combine several programs into one package. Typically, the suite costs less than buying each program individually.

Norton SystemWorks includes several program groups:

- **Norton Utilities**—a collection of troubleshooting utilities to find problems, fix problems, improve system performance, prevent problems and more. **One Button Checkup** integrates several of these utilities.
- **Norton AntiVirus**—several antivirus programs to protect against **viruses,** quarantine or delete existing viruses, and automatically update its virus list.
- **Norton CleanSweep**—collection of programs to safely remove unneeded programs and files. Also archives, moves, backs up, and cleans hard disk as well as protects existing files from damage.
- **Web Cleanup**—collection of programs that check for unnecessary files including temporary files created by application programs, cache files, history files, and cookies. You can then eliminate these files with a click of a button.
- **Connection Keep Alive**—prevents dial-up Internet connections from timing out by simulating online user activity during periods of inactivity.
- **GoBack Personal Edition**—retores system configurations, helps locate lost files, and repairs damaged files.

DEVICE DRIVERS

Device drivers (**drivers**) are specialized programs to allow communication between hardware devices and the rest of the computer system.

While many device drivers are automatically installed, others must be installed by the user. Fortunate, Windows provides wizards such as the **Add Printer Wizard** to give step-by-step guidance.

Device drivers may need to be reinstalled or updated. **Windows Update** automates the process of updating device drivers.

KEY TERMS

antivirus (179)
application (167)
Aqua (176)
background (168)
Backup (180)
backup program (179)
booting (168)
character based interface (167)
client operating system (172)
cold boot (168)
computer virus (184)
desktop (169)
desktop operating system (172)
device driver (189)
diagnostic utility (179)
dialog box (169)
Disk Cleanup (181)
Disk Defragmenter (182)
Dock (176)
driver (189)
embedded operating systems (172)
environment (172)
file (170)
file compression utility (179)
folder (170)
foreground (168)
fragmented (182)
GNOME (177)
graffiti (178)
graphical user interface (GUI) (167)
Help (169)
HotSync (178)
icon (169)
Internet Explorer (174)
KDE (177)
kernel (169)
language translator (167)
Linux (177)
log on (174)
log on name (175)
Luna (174)
Mac OS (176)
Mac OS X (176)
memory resident (169)
menu (169)
multitasking (167)
network operating systems (NOS) (172)
network server (172)
non-proprietary operating system (173)
One Button Checkup (188)
open source (173)
operating system (166)
Palm OS (178)
platform (172)
Pocket PC (178)
pointer (169)
POST (power-on self test) (169)
proprietary operating system (173)
resource (167)
sectors (182)
service program (166)
Sherlock (177)
software environment (172)
software platform (172)
stand-alone operating system (172)
Start menu (174)
System Restore (183)
system software (166)
tracks (182)
troubleshooting utility (179)
uninstall utility (179)
UNIX (177)
user interface (167)
utility (166)
utility suite (184)
warm boot (168)
window (169)
Windows (174)
Windows Add Printer Wizard (189)
Windows CE (178)
Windows Explorer (170)
Windows Media Player (174)
Windows Messenger (174)
Windows Update (189)
Windows XP (174)

To test your knowledge of these key terms with animated flash cards, select Flash Cards from Tim's Toolbox at http://www.mhhe.com/oleary/CT05.

CHAPTER REVIEW

CROSSWORD

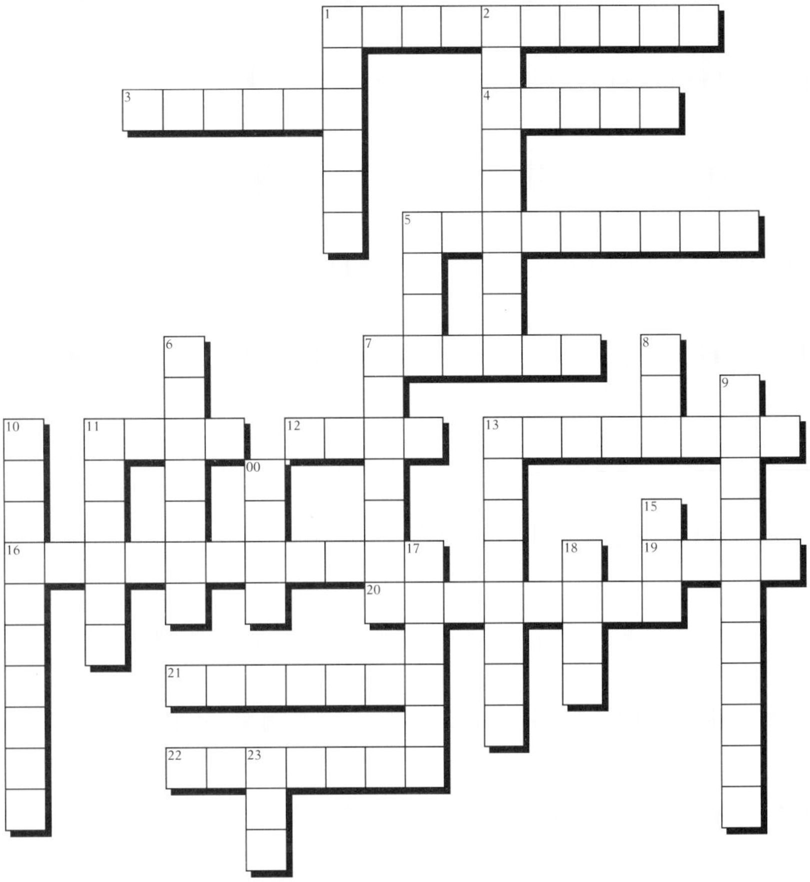

ACROSS

1 Term for when a file has to be broken up into small parts for storage
3 Operating system files that perform basic operations and are memory resident
4 One of the most popular and powerful alternatives to the Windows operating system
5 Programs that guard your computer system against damaging programs
7 A utility program that makes a copy of all files or selected files that have been saved onto a disk
11 A tool on the Mac for visually organizing files
12 Graphic representation for a program or function
13 A handheld computer operating system from Microsoft also called Windows CE
16 The operating system or platform
19 Operating system with a large number of different versions including Linux
20 Palm OS supports handwriting recognition with this system
21 Palm devices used this to share and backup data with desktop and notebook computers
22 Proprietary operating system owned by the Microsoft Corporation

DOWN

1 Related files are stored within—can also contain other folders
2 The ability to switch between different applications stored in memory
5 A new user interface featured on the latest version of the Macintosh operation system
6 Wedged-shaped sections that make up a track on a disk
7 Starting or restarting a computer
8 One of the interfaces most widely used by the Linux operation system
9 Programs such as word processing and spreadsheets
10 Window where the program being currently used is running
11 Programs that allow devices such as a mouse, keyboard and printer to communicate with the rest of the computer system
13 The operating system is often referred to as the software environment or this
14 New user interface with Windows XP that emphasizes function over programs
15 Uses graphical elements such as icons and windows to communicate with the operating system
17 Concentric rings on a disk
18 Used to store data and programs
23 Used to control and coordinate computers that are networked or linked together

For an interactive crossword puzzle select Crosswords from Tim's Toolbox at http://www.mhhe.com/oleary/CT05.

MULTIPLE CHOICE

Circle the letter or fill in the correct answer.

1. Service programs are another name for ________.
   - **a.** operating systems
   - **b.** utilities
   - **c.** device drivers
   - **d.** language translators
   - **e.** interfaces
2. In a cold boot, a self-testing series of programs called ________ begins.
   - **a.** Luna
   - **b.** POST
   - **c.** DockHotSync
   - **d.** KNE
   - **e.** Windows
3. Language translators convert human language into ________.
   - **a.** machine language
   - **b.** UNIX
   - **c.** service programs
   - **d.** operating systems
   - **e.** none of the above
4. Desktop operating systems are also called ________.
   - **a.** network operating systems
   - **b.** embedded operating systems
   - **c.** client operating systems
   - **d.** Mac operating systems
   - **e.** stand-alone operating systems
5. ________ is a program included with Windows XP that plays videos, CDs, and DVDs.
   - **a.** Log On
   - **b.** Internet Explorer 6.0
   - **c.** Windows Messenger
   - **d.** Windows Media Player
   - **e.** AUDIO
6. The ________ operating system was originally designed to run on minicomputers in network environments.
   - **a.** Windows
   - **b.** Mac OS
   - **c.** UNIX
   - **d.** Sherlock
   - **e.** Norton
7. To remove unneeded programs and related files from a hard disk you would use a ________.
   - **a.** backup program
   - **b.** trouble-shooting program
   - **c.** file compression program
   - **d.** antivirus program
   - **e.** uninstall program
8. Files that are broken into small parts and stored wherever space is available are said to be ________.
   - **a.** compressed
   - **b.** fragmented
   - **c.** lost
   - **d.** uninstalled
   - **e.** none of the above
9. ________ is a Windows program that locates and eliminates unnecessary fragments and rearranges files and unused disk space to optimize operations.
   - **a.** Disk Cleanup
   - **b.** Active Desktop
   - **c.** Sherlock
   - **d.** Disk Defragmenter
   - **e.** Resource Locator
10. Norton SystemWorks is a________.
    - **a.** Web service
    - **b.** troubleshooting program
    - **c.** utility
    - **d.** utility suite
    - **e.** none of the above

To test your knowledge of this chapter, select Self Test from Tim's Toolbox at http://www.mhhe.com/oleary/CT05.

MATCHING

Match each numbered item with the most closely related lettered item. Write your answers in the spaces provided.

- **a.** antivirus program
- **b.** backup program
- **c.** desktop operating system
- **d.** embedded operating system
- **e.** file compression program
- **f.** folders
- **g.** foreground
- **h.** icons
- **i.** Linux
- **j.** Mac OS
- **k.** multitasking
- **l.** network operating system (NOS)
- **m.** network server
- **n.** open source
- **o.** operating systems
- **p.** Palm OS
- **q.** proprietary operating system
- **r.** resources
- **s.** system software
- **t.** utilities

1. Software that deals with the complexities of computer hardware. ____
2. Programs that coordinate computer resources. ____
3. Programs that perform specific tasks related to managing computer resources. ____
4. Keyboard, mouse, printer, monitor, storage devices, and memory. ____
5. Where the active program runs. ____
6. Graphic elements that represent commonly used features. ____
7. A computer's ability to run more than one application at a time. ____
8. Operating systems completely stored within ROM memory. ____
9. Operating system used to control and coordinate computers that are linked together. ____
10. Operating system whose code is made available to outside individuals for improvements. ____
11. A computer that coordinates all communication between other computers. ____
12. An operating system located on a single stand-alone hard disk. ____
13. Operating system used by Macintosh computers. ____
14. The operating system originally designed to run on PDAs from PalmPilot. ____
15. Along with files, a component of the system that Windows stores information in. ____
16. One popular, and free, version of the UNIX operating system. ____
17. Operating system owned and operated by a company. ____
18. Program that guards your computer system against damaging and invasive programs. ____
19. Program that makes copies of files to be used if originals are lost or damaged. ____
20. Program that reduces the size of files for efficient storage. ____

OPEN-ENDED

On a separate sheet of paper, respond to each question or statement.

1. Describe system software. What are the four types of system programs?
2. Discuss operating systems. What are the basic functions of every operating system? What are the three basic operating system categories?
3. Explain the differences and similarities between Windows, Mac OS, and Linux.
4. Discuss utilities. What are they? What are the five most essential utilities? What is a utility suite?
5. Explain the role of device drivers. Discuss the Add Printer Wizard and Windows Update.

USING TECHNOLOGY

1 Virus Protection

Worried about computer viruses? Did you know that others could be intercepting your private e-mail? It is even possible for them to gain access and control over your computer systems. Fortunately, Internet security suites are available to help ensure your safety while you are on the Internet. To learn more about virus protection, review Making IT Work for You: Virus Protection on pages 186 and 187. Then answer the following questions: (a) What are viruses? What are Internet security suites? What do they do? (b) What is a personal firewall? What does it do? (c) What is a sandbox? How is it different from a personal firewall? (d) Have you ever experienced a computer virus? If you have, describe the virus, how you got it, and what you did to get rid of it. If you have not, have you taken any special precautions (discuss the precautions)? Do you think it's possible that you may have one now and not know it, or do you think that you have just been lucky?

2 McAfee Utility Suite

McAfee and Symantec are producers of some of the most widely used utility software. Visit our site at http://www.mhhe.com/oleary/CT05 and select Using Technology from Tim's Toolbox to link to their Web sites. Research their latest utility suites, and then answer the following questions: (a) What utilities are included in McAfee's suite? (b) What are the similarities and differences between McAfee's and the Symantec suite? (c) Which suite would you purchase? Why?

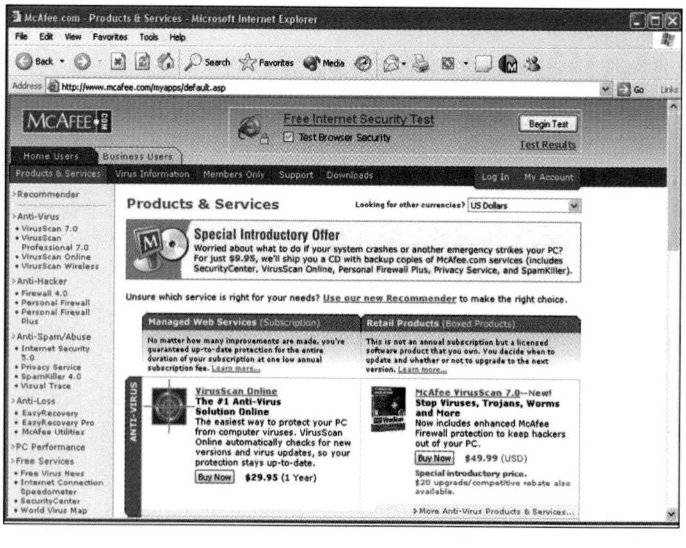

WinZip 3

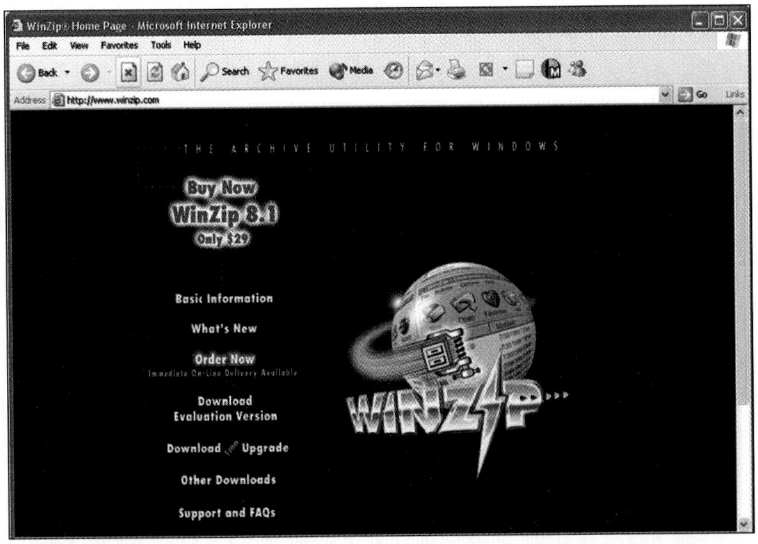

WinZip is one of the most popular file compression utilities available. Visit our Web site at http://www.mhhe.com/oleary/CT05 and select Using Technology from Tim's Toolbox to link to the WinZip Web site. Once there, read about this utility, and then answer the following: (a) What is WinZip? What does it do? (b) What is a Zip file? (c) List the most common uses for Zip files. (d) Describe in detail the procedure for creating a Zip file with WinZip.

Windows Update 4

Windows Update is a utility built into Windows that monitors and controls the process of keeping the computer up-to-date. Connect to our Web site at http://www.mhhe.com/ oleary/CT05 and select Using Technology from Tim's Toolbox to link to the Windows Update Web site. Read the information about Windows Update. Then answer the following questions: (a) How does Windows Update work? (b) How does a user know when he or she requires an update? (c) What is the process for initiating an update using Windows Update? (d) In what ways can Windows Update be automated?

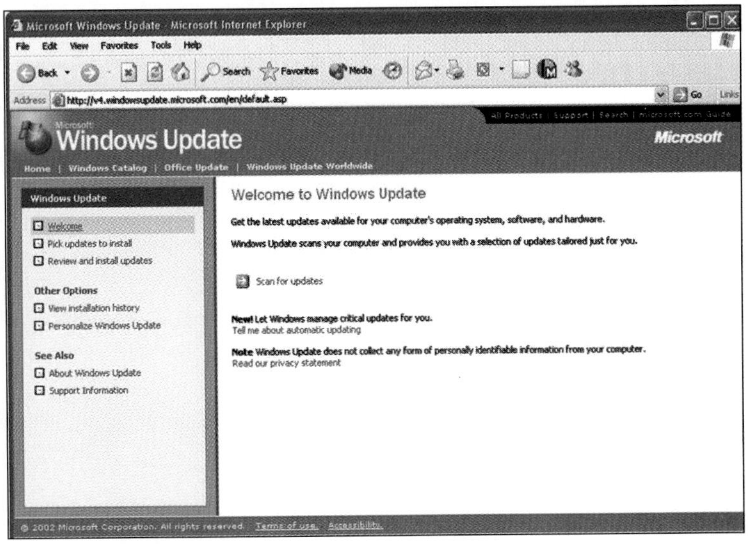

EXPANDING YOUR KNOWLEDGE

1 Computing Today CD

Computer viruses are destructive and dangerous programs that can migrate through networks and operating systems. They often attach themselves to other programs, e-mail messages, and databases. It is essential to protect your computer systems from computer viruses. After viewing the animation "How Virus Protection Programs Work" from your Computing Today CD (or from Tim's Toolbox at http://www.mhhe.com/oleary/ CT05) and studying Figure 5-27, answer the following: (a) Briefly describe the four steps taken by virus protection programs. (b) What is signature scanning? (c) What is heuristic detection and how is it different from signature scanning. (d) Do you use a virus protection program? If yes, what program(s) do you use and have they been effective? If no, do you plan to in the near future? Why or why not?

2 Mac OS X

This chapter discussed the Mac OS X operating system and its graphical user interface known as Aqua. However, this latest operating system from Apple also integrates another operating system you learned about: UNIX. Mac OS X makes use of a version of UNIX known as Darwin in a very innovative way. Visit our Web site at http://www.mhhe.com/oleary/ CT05 and select Expansions from Tim's Toolbox to link to a site that discusses Darwin. Once there, explore the site, and then answer the following questions: (a) How does Darwin relate to Mac OS X? (b) Is Darwin a proprietary or nonproprietary operating system? (c) Mac OS is a type of *desktop* operating system, but UNIX was created to be a *network* operating system. What might be some advantages to integrating the two? Are there any disadvantages? Justify your answers.

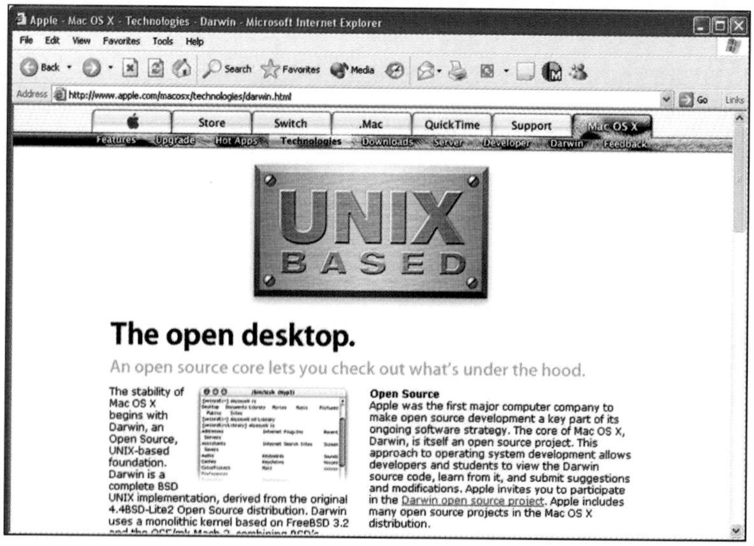

SimNet CD 3

Complete Chapter 5: System Software on your SimNet CD and then complete the following on a single page of paper.

a. Describe the difference between a GUI and command line interface.

b. Identify each of the indicated items to the right.

c. Discuss how Apple revolutionized the way we interact with computers.

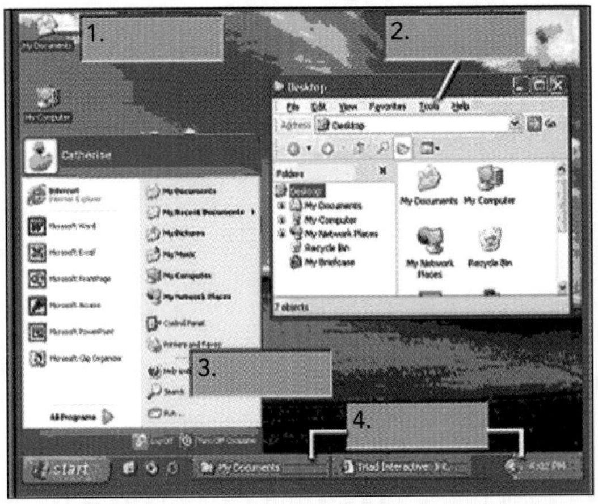

Customized Desktop 4

There are several ways to customize your computer's desktop to make it more interesting, informative, or efficient. To learn about customizations, connect to the Yahoo site at http://www.yahoo.com and look at the subject area "Computers and Internet: Desktop Customization" or search the Web using the keywords "desktop customization." Explore several options and then address the following: (a) Summarize some of the customizations you found. (b) Briefly explain how these customizations are added to a user's computer. (c) Explain how you could use these customizations to make your computing experience more enjoyable or productive.

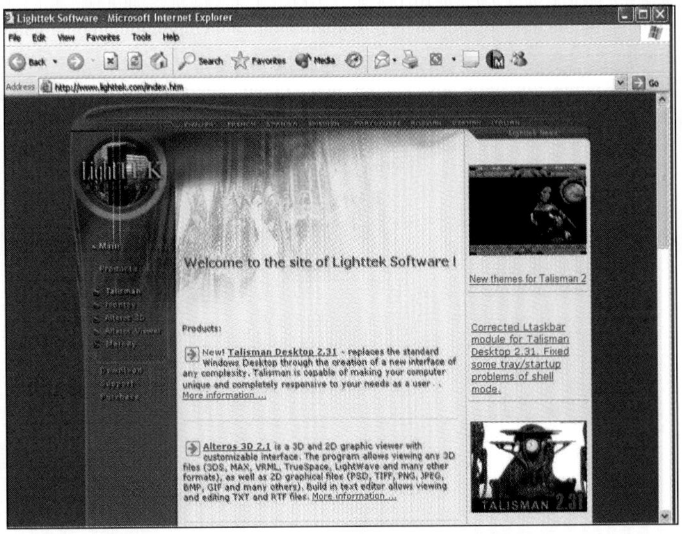

BUILDING YOUR PORTFOLIO

1 Linux

Linux is a powerful operating system used by many computer professionals. Research Linux and then write a one-page paper titled "Linux" that covers the following points: (a) What is Linux? (b) How was it developed originally? (c) How is Linux currently used? (d) How might it be used in the future? (e) Why is Linux receiving so much attention recently?

2 Operating Systems

As you've seen, operating systems are an integral part of the computing experience. Research the most common operating systems using the Internet, and write a one page paper titled "Operating Systems" that addresses the following: (a) Describe the three basic functions of an operating system. (b) What is the difference between a *proprietary* and an *open source* operating system? Give an example of each. (c) What are the most commonly used operating systems? How is each used? (d) Discuss the considerations in choosing an operating system. Which is best for you as a student? What about a large business? Justify your answers.

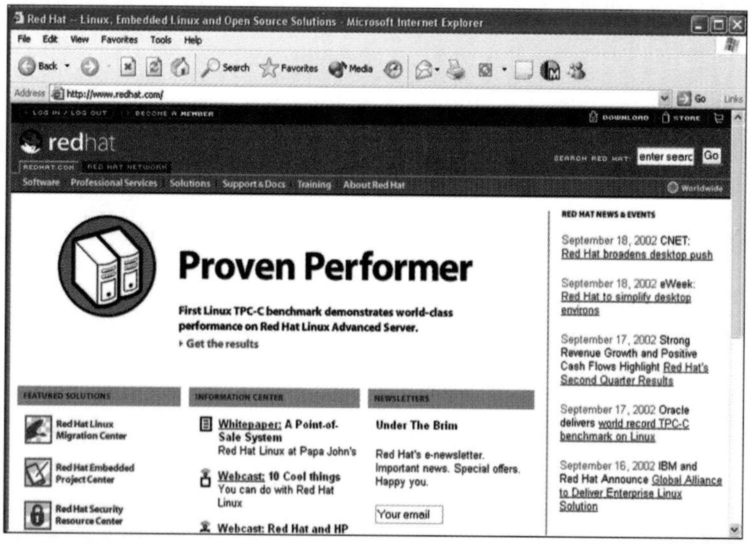

Antitrust 3

Much attention has been focused on Microsoft's legal battles over antitrust issues. It has been argued that Microsoft has an unfair marketing advantage because their Windows operating system has been tailored to use Microsoft applications. Write a one-page paper responding to the following questions: (a) Do you think Microsoft has an unfair advantage in the software market? (b) How can the outcomes of decisions on the Microsoft case affect the software available for consumers to buy? (c) What ethical obligations do you think Microsoft has to other software developers? What ethical obligations do they have to the consumer? Explain your answer.

Online Backup 4

One of the best ways to safeguard important personal or corporate data is to use an online backup service. Research three or four online backup services, and then answer the following questions in a one-page paper: (a) What are the general features of online backup services? (b) What types of emergencies do online backups help with that other backup methods do not? (c) How are backups scheduled? (d) Is this service a replacement for making backups locally? Why or why not?

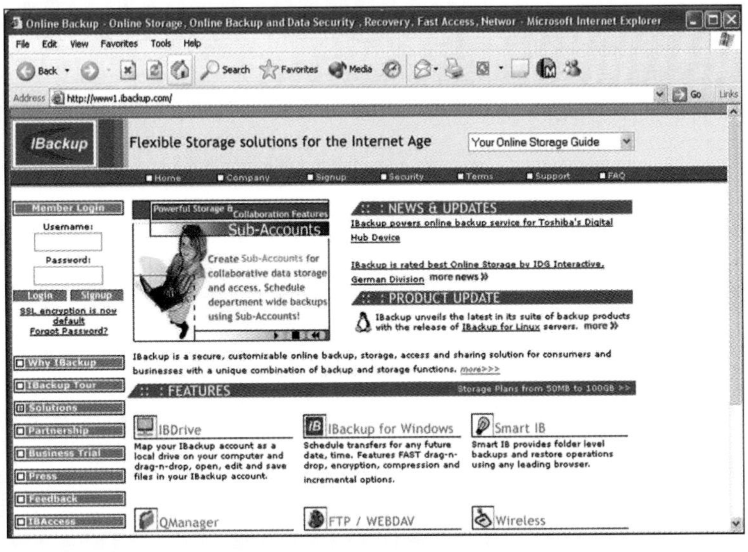

THE SYSTEM UNIT

OBJECTIVES

After you have read this chapter, you should be able to:

1. Describe the three basic types of system units.
2. Discuss how a computer uses binary codes to represent data in electrical form.
3. Describe each of the major system unit components.
4. Discuss microprocessors including specialty processors.
5. Describe the different types of memory.
6. Discuss expansion slots and boards.
7. Describe the five principal types of expansion buses.
8. Discuss the mostly widely used standardized and specialized ports.

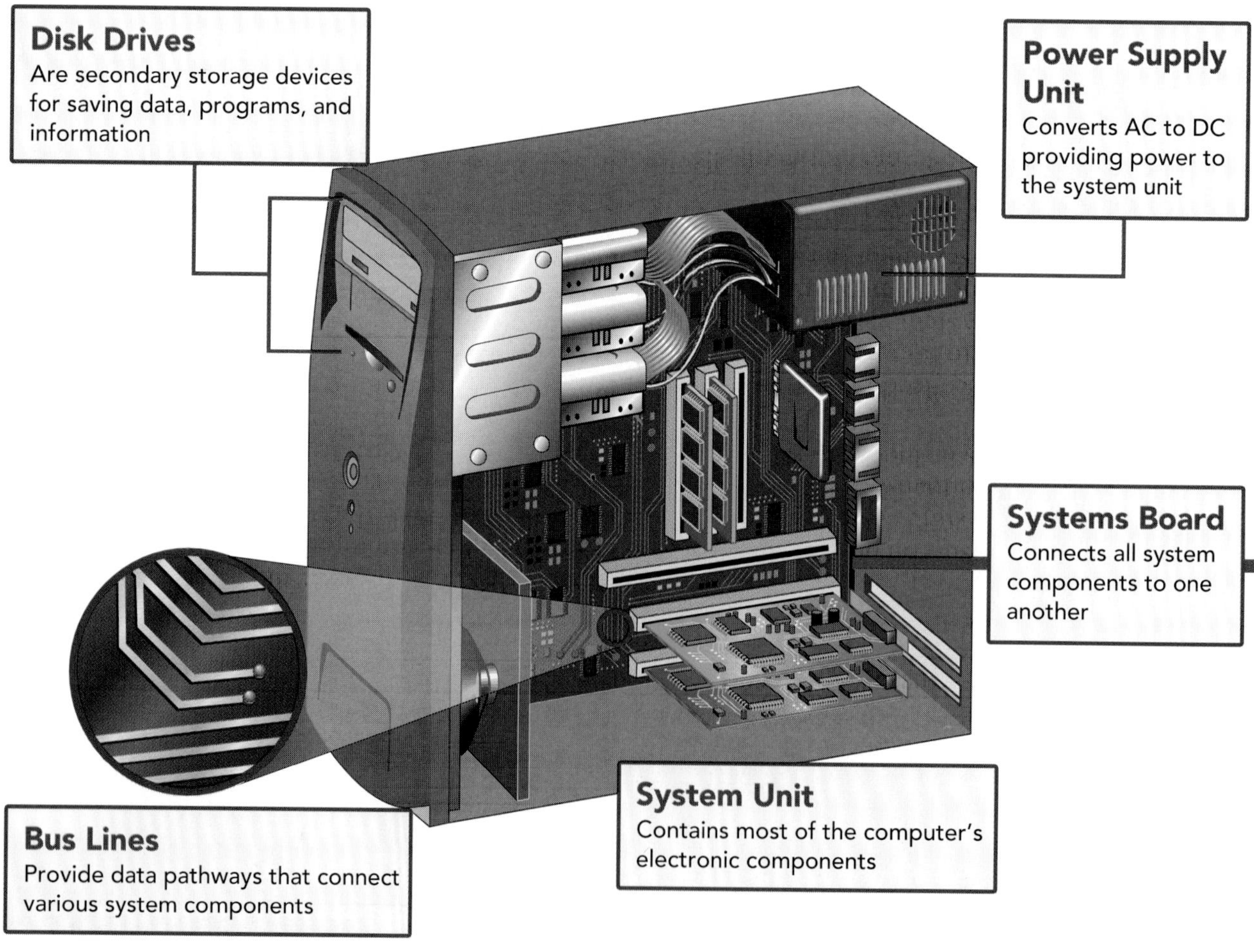
Disk Drives
Are secondary storage devices for saving data, programs, and information
Power Supply Unit
Converts AC to DC providing power to the system unit
Systems Board
Connects all system components to one another
System Unit
Contains most of the computer's electronic components
Bus Lines
Provide data pathways that connect various system components

CHAPTER 6

5 7 8 9 10 11 12 13 14 15 16

Why are some microcomputers more powerful than others? The answer lies in three words: speed, capacity, and flexibility. After reading this chapter, you will be able to judge how fast, powerful, and versatile a particular microcomputer is. As you might expect, this knowledge is valuable if you are planning to buy a new microcomputer system or to upgrade an existing system. (The Buyer's Guide and the Upgrader's Guide at the end of this book provide additional information.) It will also help you to evaluate whether or not an existing microcomputer system is powerful enough for today's new and exciting applications. For example, with the right hardware, you can use your computer to watch TV while you work and to capture video clips for class presentations.

Sometime you may get the chance to watch when a technician opens up a microcomputer. You will see that it is basically a collection of electronic circuitry. While there is no need to understand how all these components work, it is important to understand the principles. Once you do, you will then be able to determine how powerful a particular microcomputer is. This will help you judge whether it can run particular kinds of programs and can meet your needs as a user.

Competent and knowledgeable end users need to understand the functionality of the basic components in the system unit, including the system board, microprocessor, memory, system clock, expansion slots and cards, bus lines, ports, cables, and power supply units.

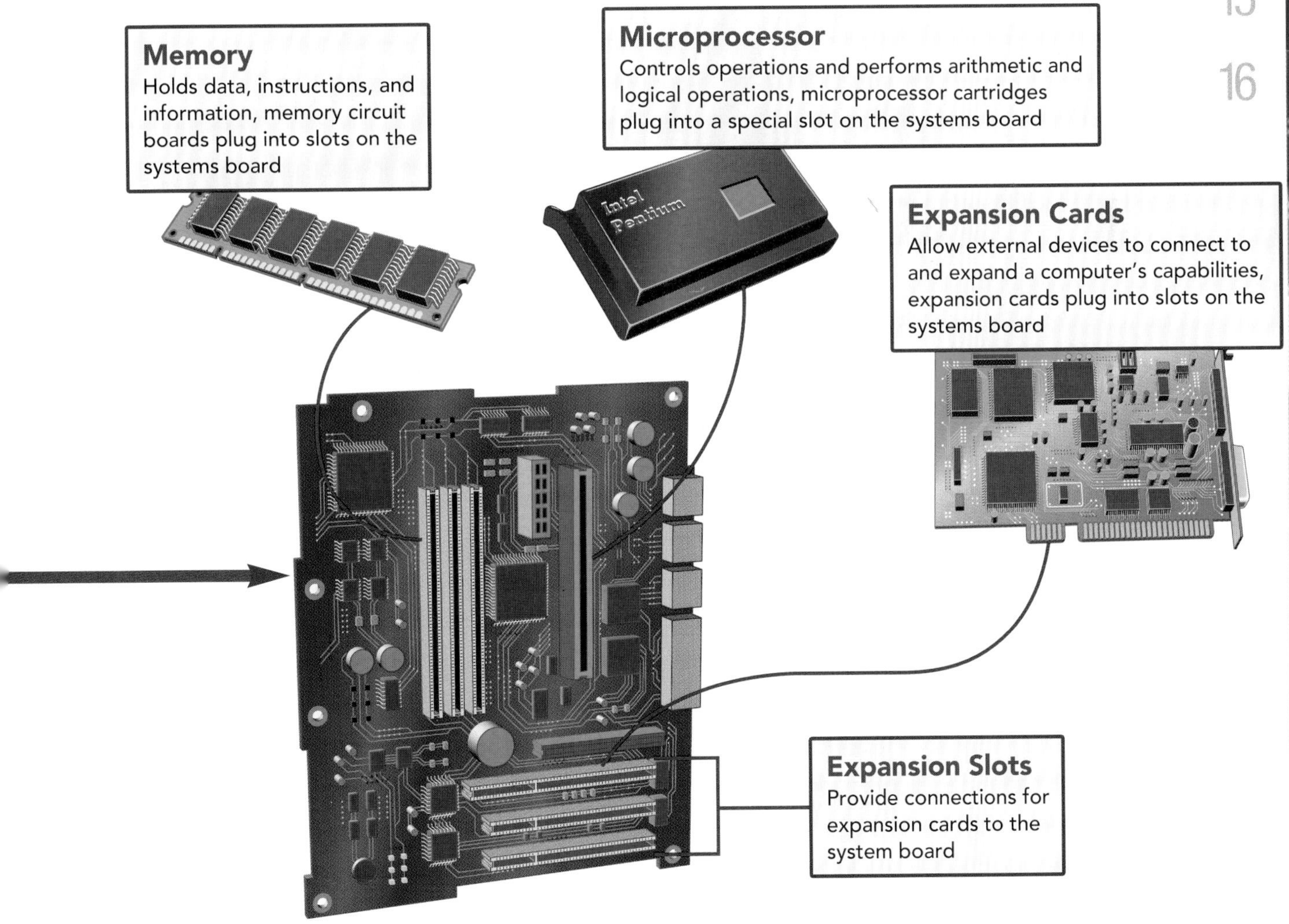
Memory
Holds data, instructions, and information, memory circuit boards plug into slots on the systems board
Microprocessor
Controls operations and performs arithmetic and logical operations, microprocessor cartridges plug into a special slot on the systems board
Intel Pentium
Expansion Cards
Allow external devices to connect to and expand a computer's capabilities, expansion cards plug into slots on the systems board
Expansion Slots
Provide connections for expansion cards to the system board

SYSTEM UNIT

System components are housed within the system unit or system cabinet. Desktop, notebook, tablet PC, and handheld are four types of system units. PDAs are a type of handheld computer.

The **system unit,** also known as the **system cabinet** or **chassis,** is a container that houses most of the electronic components that make up a computer system. All computer systems have a system unit. For microcomputers, there are four basic types (see Figure 6-1):

- **Desktop system units** typically contain the system's electronic components and selected secondary storage devices. Input and output devices, such as a mouse, keyboard, and monitor, are located outside the system unit. This type of system unit is design to be placed either horizontally or vertically. Vertical units are often called **tower models.**
- **Notebook system units** are portable and much smaller. These system units contain the electronic components, selected secondary storage devices, and input devices (keyboard and pointing device). Located outside the system unit, the monitor is attached by hinges. Notebook system units are often called **laptops.**

Figure 6-1 Basic types of system units

Desktop (tower model)

PDA

Notebook

Tablet PC

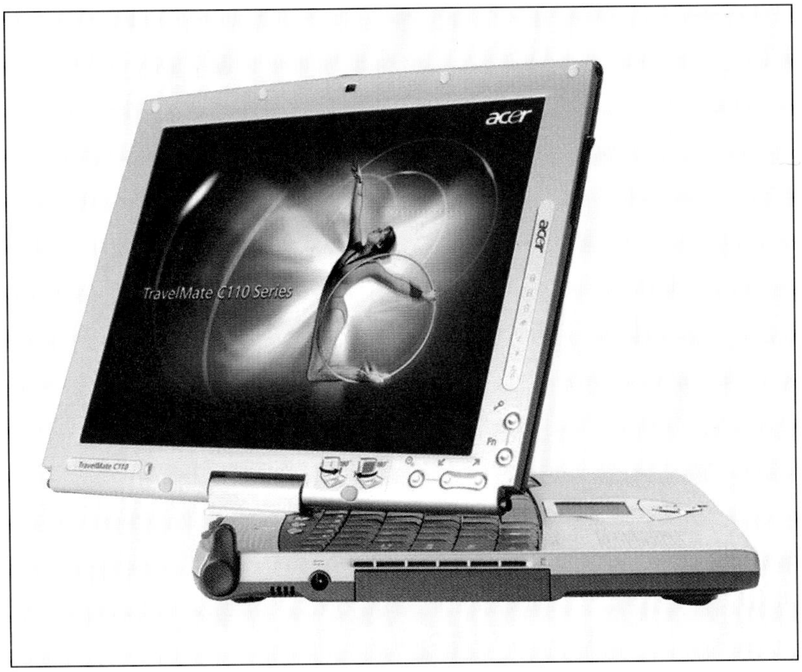

Convertible tablet PC

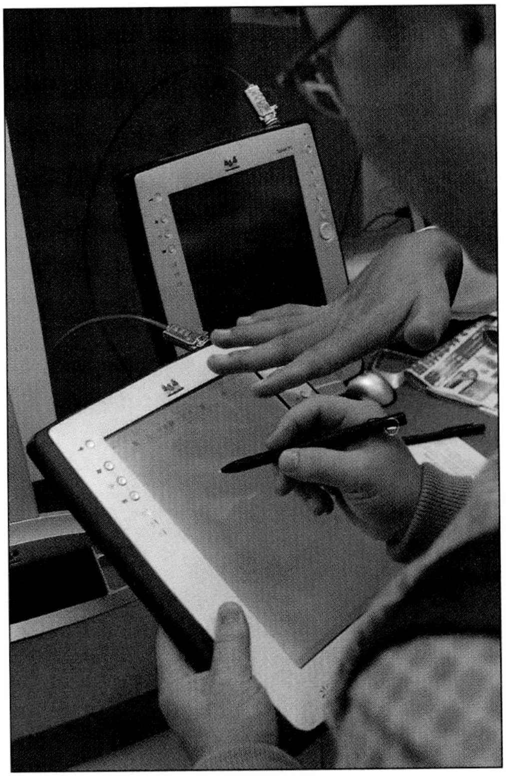

Slate tablet PC

Figure 6-2 Tablet PCs

- **Tablet PC system units** are similar to notebook system units. **Tablet PCs** are highly portable devices that support the use of a stylus or pen to input commands and data. There are two basic categories: convertible and slate. The **convertible tablet PC** is effectively a notebook computer with a monitor that swivels and folds onto its keyboard. The **slate tablet PC** is similar to a notebook computer except that its monitor is attached to the system unit and does not have a keyboard integrated into the system unit. (See Figure 6-2.)
- **Handheld computer system** units are the smallest and are designed to fit into the palm of one hand. Also known as **palm computers,** these systems contain an entire computer system including the electronic components, secondary storage, and input and output devices. **Personal digital assistants (PDA)** are the most widely used handheld computers.

While the actual size may vary, each type of system unit has the same basic system components including system board, microprocessor, and memory. Before considering these components, however, a more basic issue must be addressed. How do we as human beings communicate with and control all this electronic circuitry?

Concept Check

- ✓ What is the system unit?
- ✓ Describe the four basic types of microcomputer system units.
- ✓ What are the three basic system components that are common to all system units?

ELECTRONIC DATA AND INSTRUCTIONS

Data and instructions are represented electronically with a binary, or two-state, numbering system. ASCII, EDCDIC, and Unicode are binary coding schemes.

Have you ever wondered why it is said that we live in a *digital world?* (See Figure 6-3.) It's because computers cannot recognize information the same way you and I can. People follow instructions and process data using letters, numbers, and special characters. For example, if we wanted someone to add the numbers 3 and 5 together and record the answer, we might say "please add 3 and 5." The system unit, however, is electronic circuitry and cannot directly process such a request.

Figure 6-3 The digital world. In order for computers to process data and to efficiently share information over the Internet, it must be in a digital format.

Our voices create **analog,** or continuous signals, that vary to represent different tones, pitches, and volume. Computers, however, can only recognize **digital** electronic signals. Before any processing can occur within the system unit, a conversion must occur from what we understand to what the system unit can electronically process.

What is the most fundamental statement you can make about electricity? It is simply this: it can be either on or off. Indeed, there are many forms of technology that can make use of this **two-state** on/off, yes/no, present/absent arrangement. For instance a light switch may be on or off, or an electric circuit open or closed. A specific location on a tape or disk may have a positive charge or a negative charge. This is the reason, then, that a two-state or binary system is used to represent data and instructions.

The decimal system that we are all familiar with has 10 digits (0, 1, 2, 3, 4, 5, 6, 7, 8, 9). The **binary system,** however, consists of only two digits—0 and 1. Each 0 or 1 is called a **bit**—short for binary digit. In the system unit, the 0 can be represented by electricity being off, and the 1 by electricity being on. In order to represent numbers, letters, and special characters, bits are combined into groups of eight bits called **bytes.** Each byte typically represents one character.

BINARY CODING SCHEMES

Now let us consider an important question. How are characters represented as 0s and 1s ("off" and "on" electrical states) in the computer? The answer is in the use of **binary coding schemes.** (See Figure 6-4.) Two of the most popular binary coding schemes use eight bits or one byte. These two codes are ASCII and EBCDIC. (See Figure 6-5.) A recently developed code, unicode, uses sixteen bits.

Code	Uses
ASCII	Microcomputers
EBCDIC	Larger computers
Unicode	International languages

Figure 6-4 Binary codes

- **ASCII,** pronounced "as-key," stands for **A**merican **S**tandard **C**ode for **I**nformation **I**nterchange. This is the most widely used binary code for microcomputers. For example, the number 3 is represented in ASCII code as 0011 0011.
- **EBCDIC,** pronounced "eb-see-dick," stands for **E**xtended **B**inary **C**oded **D**ecimal **I**nterchange **C**ode. It was developed by IBM and is used primarily for large computers. For example, the number 3 is represented in EBCDIC code as 1111 0011.

Symbol	ASCII	EBCDIC	Symbol	ASCII	EBCDIC
A	0100 0001	1100 0001	X	0101 1000	1110 0111
B	0100 0010	1100 0010	Y	0101 1001	1110 1000
C	0100 0011	1100 0011	Z	0101 1010	1110 1001
D	0100 0100	1100 0100	!	0010 0001	0101 1010
E	0100 0101	1100 0101	"	0010 0010	0111 1111
F	0100 0110	1100 0110	#	0010 0011	0111 1011
G	0100 0111	1100 0111	$	0010 0100	0101 1011
H	0100 1000	1100 1000	%	0010 0101	0110 1100
I	0100 1001	1100 1001	&	0010 0110	0101 0000
J	0100 1010	1101 0001	(	0010 1000	0100 1101
K	0100 1011	1101 0010	)	0010 1001	0101 1101
L	0100 1100	1101 0011	*	0010 1010	0101 1100
M	0100 1101	1101 0100	+	0010 1011	0100 1110
N	0100 1110	1101 0101	0	0011 0000	1111 0000
O	0100 1111	1101 0110	1	0011 0001	1111 0001
P	0101 0000	1101 0111	2	0011 0010	1111 0010
Q	0101 0001	1101 1000	3	0011 0011	1111 0011
R	0101 0010	1101 1001	4	0011 0100	1111 0100
S	0101 0011	1110 0010	5	0011 0101	1111 0101
T	0101 0100	1110 0011	6	0011 0110	1111 0110
U	0101 0101	1110 0100	7	0011 0111	1111 0111
V	0101 0110	1110 0101	8	0011 1000	1111 1000
W	0101 0111	1110 0110	9	0011 1001	1111 1001

ASCII code for +

ASCII code for 3

ASCII code for 5

Figure 6.5 ASCII and EBCDIC binary coding schemes

- **Unicode** is a 16-bit code designed to support international languages like Chinese and Japanese. These languages have too many characters to be represented by the eight-bit ASCII and EBCDIC codes. Unicode was developed by Unicode, Inc., with support from Apple, IBM, and Microsoft.

When you press a key on the keyboard, a character is automatically converted into a series of electronic pulses that the system can recognize. For example, pressing the number 3 on a keyboard causes an electronic signal to be sent to the microcomputer's system unit where it is converted to the ASCII code of 0011 0011.

All instructions and data have to be converted into binary data before they can be executed. For example, the instruction to add 3 and 5 (3 + 5) requires 24 bits using the ASCII coding scheme. (See Figure 6-6.)

Coding schemes are particularly important to computer specialists to track down errors and other types of problems. But why do you suppose coding schemes are important to end users? There are several reasons. One of the most important is that data created by one computer system using one coding

How ASCII Works

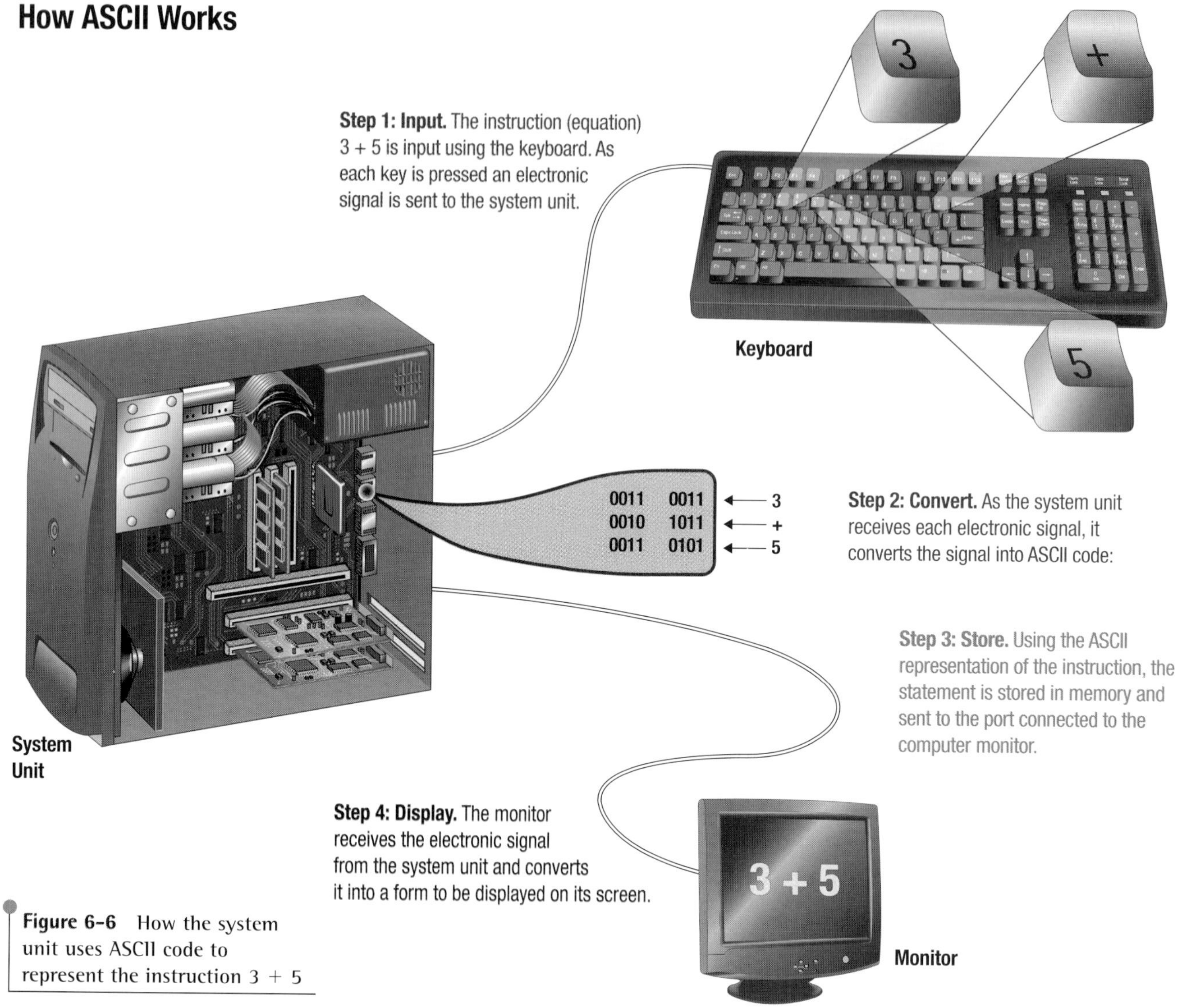

Step 1: Input. The instruction (equation) 3 + 5 is input using the keyboard. As each key is pressed an electronic signal is sent to the system unit.
3
+
5
Keyboard
0011 0011 ← 3
0010 1011 ← +
0011 0101 ← 5
Step 2: Convert. As the system unit receives each electronic signal, it converts the signal into ASCII code:
Step 3: Store. Using the ASCII representation of the instruction, the statement is stored in memory and sent to the port connected to the computer monitor.
System Unit
Step 4: Display. The monitor receives the electronic signal from the system unit and converts it into a form to be displayed on its screen.
3 + 5
Monitor

Figure 6-6 How the system unit uses ASCII code to represent the instruction 3 + 5

scheme cannot be directly accessed and used by another computer system using a different coding scheme. Generally, this is not a problem if both computers are microcomputers since both would most likely use ASCII code. And most microcomputer applications store data using this code. However, problems occur when data is shared between microcomputers and larger computers that use EBCDIC code. The data must be translated from one coding scheme to the other before processing can begin. Fortunately, special conversion programs are available to help with this translation.

Concept Check

- ✓ What are decimal and binary systems? How are they different?
- ✓ What are binary coding schemes? Name and describe three binary coding schemes.
- ✓ Describe how the system unit uses ASCII code to represent an instruction.

SYSTEM BOARD

The system board connects all system components and allows input and output devices to communicate with the system unit. Sockets, slots, and connecting lines are components of the system board.

The **system board** is also known as the **main board** or **motherboard.** The system board is the communications medium for the entire computer system. Every component of the system unit connects to the system board. It acts as a data path allowing the various components to communicate with one another. External devices such as keyboard, mouse, and monitor could not communicate with the system unit without the system board.

On a desktop computer, the system board is located at the bottom of the systems unit or along one side. (See Figure 6-7.) It is a large flat circuit board covered with a variety of different electronic components including:

- **Sockets** provide a connection point for small specialized electronic parts called chips. **Chips** consist of tiny circuit-boards etched onto squares of sandlike material called silicon. These circuit boards can be smaller than the tip of your finger. (See Figure 6-8.) A chip is also called a **silicon chip, semiconductor,** or **integrated circuit.** Chips are mounted on **carrier packages.** (See Figure 6-9.) These packages either plug directly into sockets on the system board or onto cards that are then plugged into slots on the system board. Sockets are used to connect the system board to a variety of different types of chips including microprocessor and memory chips.
- **Slots** provide a connection point for specialized cards or circuit boards. These cards provide expansion capability for a computer system. For example, a modem card plugs into a slot on the system board to provide a connection to the Internet.

On the Web Explorations

Micron Inc. is one of the largest manufacturers of system unit components. To learn more about the company, visit our Web site at http://www.mhhe.com/oleary/CT05 and select On the Web Explorations from Tim's Toolbox.

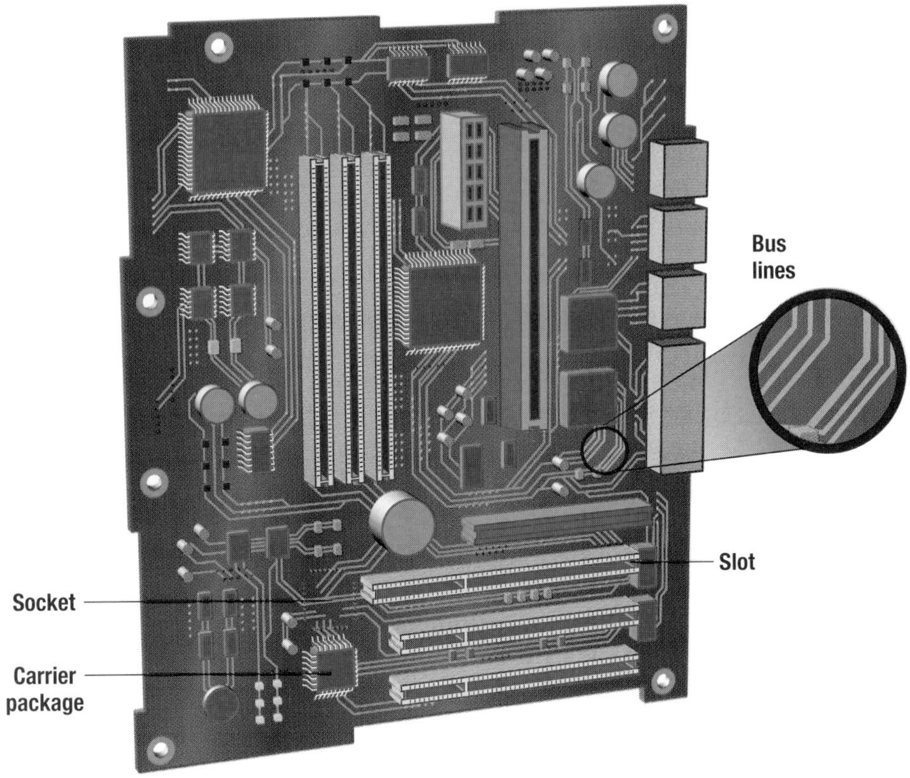

Bus
lines
Slot
Socket
Carrier
package

Figure 6-7 System board

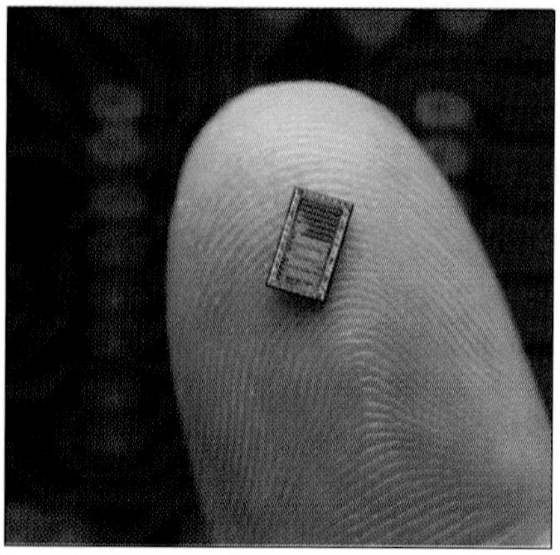

Figure 6-8 Chip

Figure 6-9 Chip being mounted onto a carrier package

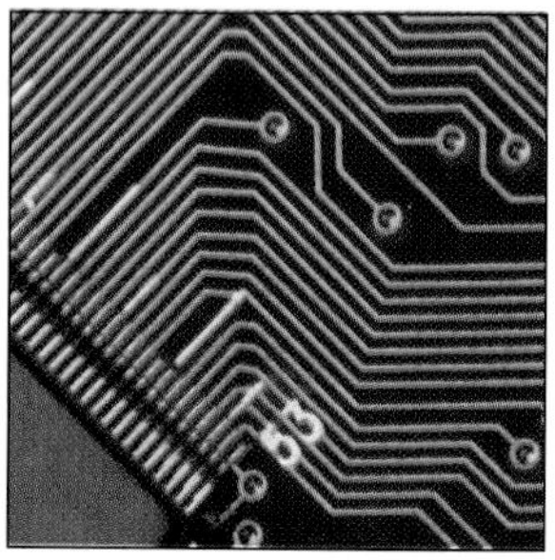

Figure 6-10 Bus Lines

- **Connecting lines** called **bus lines** provide pathways that support communication among the various electronic components that are either located on the system board or attached to the system board. (See Figure 6-10.)

Notebook and handheld system boards are smaller than desktop system boards. However, they perform the same functions as desktop system boards.

Concept Check

- ✓ What is the system board and what does it do?
- ✓ Define and describe sockets, slots, and connecting lines.
- ✓ What are chips? How are chips attached to the system board?

MICROPROCESSOR

Microprocessors have two components—control and arithmetic-logic units. Fetching, decoding, executing, and storing are instruction cycle operations. RISC and CISC are types of microprocessor chips. Coprocessors and parallel processors are specialty chips.

In a microcomputer system, the **central processing unit (CPU)** or **processor** is contained on a single chip called the **microprocessor.** The microprocessor is either mounted onto a carrier package that plugs into the system board or contained within a cartridge that plugs in to a special slot on the system board. (See Figure 6-11.) The microprocessor is the "brains" of the computer system. It has two basic components: the control unit and the arithmetic-logic unit.

- **Control unit:** The control unit tells the rest of the computer system how to carry out a program's instructions. It directs the movement of electronic signals between memory—which temporarily holds data, instructions, and processed information—and the arithmetic-logic unit. It also directs these control signals between the CPU and input and output devices.
- **Arithmetic-logic unit:** The arithmetic-logic unit, usually called the **ALU,** performs two types of operations—arithmetic and logical. **Arithmetic**

Carrier package

Cartridge

Figure 6-11 Microprocessor carrier package and cartridge

operations are, as you might expect, the fundamental math operations: addition, subtraction, multiplication, and division. **Logical operations** consist of comparisons. That is, two pieces of data are compared to see whether one is equal to (=), less than (<), or greater than (>) the other.

INSTRUCTION CYCLES

An important measurement of a computer system's power is how fast it can process a single instruction that has been stored in memory, for example, how long it takes to process an instruction such as 3 + 5. The control unit coordinates this process by following a specific series of steps called the **instruction cycle,** also known as the **machine cycle.** The instruction cycle consists of four basic operations that are repeated each time an instruction is executed. (See Figure 6-12.)

In the earlier Figure 6-6, the instruction 3 + 5 was stored in memory. To see how one instruction cycle is followed to process this instruction, see Figure 6-13.

Fetching	Retrieving a program instruction or data element from memory
Decoding	Translating instructions and data into a form that can be processed
Executing	Carrying out the commands
Storing	Saving the results in memory

Figure 6-12 Instruction Cycle Operations

The time required to *fetch* the instruction is called **instruction time,** or **I-time.** The time required to *decode* and *execute* the instruction is called **execution time** or **E-time.** The total instruction cycle time is the sum of I-time, E-time, and the time required to *store* the result. A computer's processing speed is often expressed in MIPS (millions of instruction per second). A typical microcomputer processes in excess of 300 MIPS or over 300 million instructions in a single second.

MICROPROCESSOR CHIPS

Chip capacities are often expressed in word sizes. A **word** is the number of bits (such as 16, 32, or 64) that can be accessed at one time by the CPU. The more bits in a word, the more powerful—and the faster—the computer is. As mentioned previously, eight bits group together to form a byte. A 32-bit-word computer can access 4 bytes at a time. A 64-bit-word computer can access 8 bytes at a time. Therefore, the computer designed to process 64-bit-words is faster.

Older microcomputers typically process data and instructions in millionths of a second, or **microseconds.** Newer microcomputers are much faster and process data and instructions in billionths of a second, or **nanoseconds.** Supercomputers, by contrast, operate at speeds measured in **picoseconds**—1,000 times as fast as microcomputers. (See Figure 6-14.)

How the Instruction Cycle Works

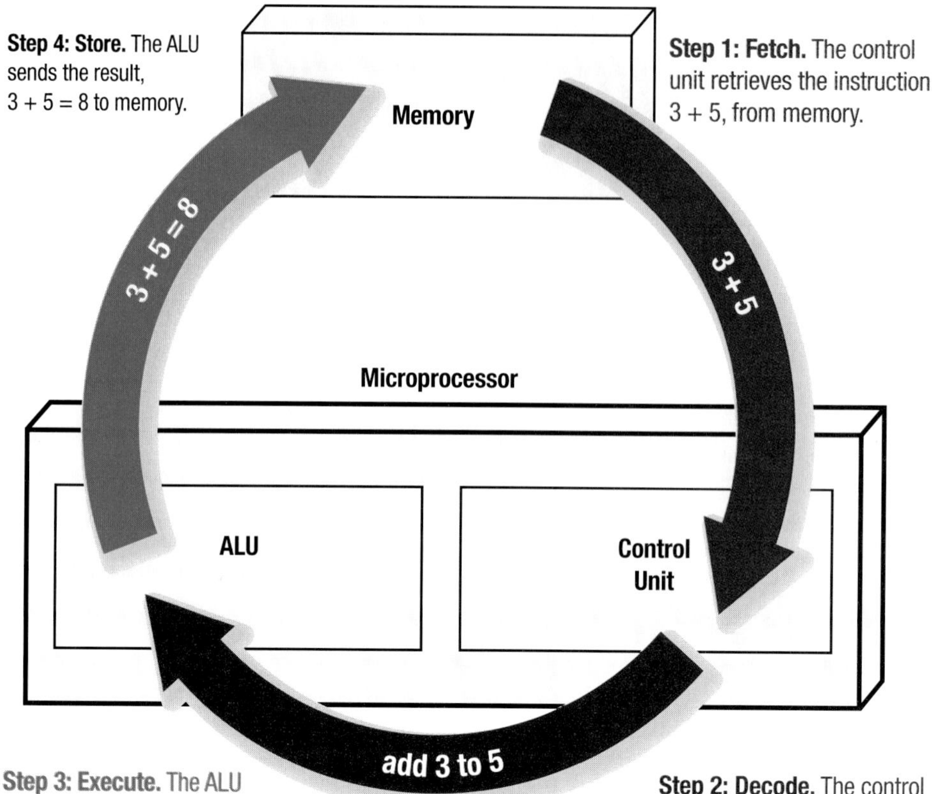
Step 4: Store. The ALU sends the result, 3 + 5 = 8 to memory.
Memory
Step 1: Fetch. The control unit retrieves the instruction 3 + 5, from memory.
3 + 5 = 8
3 + 5
Microprocessor
ALU
Control Unit
add 3 to 5
Step 3: Execute. The ALU performs the arithmetic operations.
Step 2: Decode. The control unit translates the instruction to add 3 to 5.

Figure 6-13 How the instruction cycle processes the instruction 3 + 5

Unit	Speed
Microsecond	Millionth of a second
Nanosecond	Billionth of a second
Picosecond	Trillionth of a second

Figure 6-14 Processing speeds

There are two types of microprocessor chips.

- **CISC chips:** The most common type of microprocessor is the **complex instruction set computer (CISC) chip.** This design was popularized by Intel and is the basis for their line of microprocessors. It is the most widely used chip design with thousands of programs written specifically for it. Intel's Pentium microprocessors are CISC chips. While Intel is the leading manufacturer of microprocessors, other manufacturers produce microprocessors using a nearly identical design. These chips, referred to as **Intel-compatible** processors, are able to process programs originally written specifically for Intel chips. For example, AMD Corporation produces Intel-compatible chips known as Athlon and Hammer.
- **RISC chips: Reduced instruction set computer (RISC) chips** use fewer instructions. This design is simpler and less costly than CISC chips. The PowerPC is a RISC chip produced by Motorola. SPARC is a RISC chip produced by Sun. These chips are used in many of today's most powerful microcomputers known as **workstations.**

See Figure 6-15 for a table of popular microprocessors.

On the Web Explorations

Motorola is a leader in RISC research and development. To learn more about the company, visit our Web site at

http://www.mhhe.com/oleary/CT05 and select On the Web Explorations from Tim's Toolbox.

SPECIALTY PROCESSORS

In addition to microprocessor chips, a variety of more specialized processing chips have been developed. One of the most common is coprocessors. **Coprocessors** are specialty chips designed to improve specific computing opera-

Manufacturer	Processor	Type	Typical Use
Intel	Pentium	CISC	Microcomputers
AMD	Athlon	CISC	Microcomputers
	Hammer	CISC	Workstations
Motorola	PowerPC	RISC	Apple computers
Sun	SPARC	RISC	Workstations

Figure 6-15 Popular microprocessors

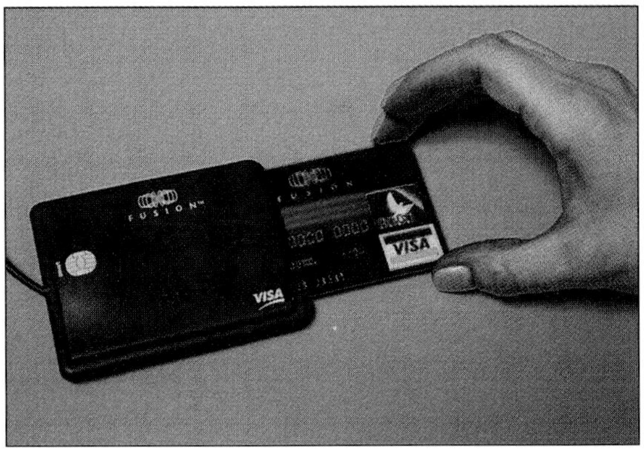

Figure 6-16 Smart Card

tions. One of the most widely used is the **graphics coprocessor.** These processors are specifically designed to handle the processing requirements related to displaying and manipulating 2-D and 3-D graphics images.

Another specialty processor is the **parallel processor.** These processors work with one or more other parallel processor chips to run or process large programs. The processors use special software that takes a large program, breaks it down into parts, and assigns the parts to separate processors. The processors then work on their respective parts simultaneously and share results as required by the program. This approach is called **parallel processing.** Although not commonly used with microcomputers, parallel processing is commonly used by supercomputers to run very large and complex programs.

Smart cards use another type of specialty processor. A **smart card** is essentially a plastic card the size of a regular credit card that has an embedded chip. While most current smart cards can store 80 times the information stored on the magnetic strip of a regular credit card, larger capacity cards are expected soon. There are two basic types of smart cards:

- **Intelligent smart cards** contain a microprocessor combined with input, output, and storage capabilities.
- **Memory cards** have only storage capabilities. (Memory cards will be discussed further in Chapter 9.)

A single smart card can replace many of the items we carry in our wallets including personal identification cards, credit cards, debit cards, and phone cards. They can be used to record personal financial and medical information. Since the information contained on the chip can be encrypted or coded and protected by a password or pin number, they offer strong security and privacy.

Visa, MasterCard, and American Express have introduced their smart cards to millions of users. (See Figure 6-16.) Many colleges and universities are distributing smart cards to their students for identification. The University of Michigan, for example, provides its students with a smart card called the Mcard that allows them to access their dorms and use their meal plans.

Concept Check

- ✔ Name and describe the two components of a microprocessor.
- ✔ What is an instruction cycle? Describe the four basic operations in an instruction cycle.
- ✔ Name and describe the two types of microprocessor chips. What does Intel-compatible mean?
- ✔ What are specialty chips? Name and discuss two types of specialty processors.

MEMORY

Memory holds data, instructions, and information. RAM, ROM, and CMOS are three types of memory chips. Dynamic, static, and flash are three types of RAM. ROM chips have built-in programs. CMOS chips provide flexibility and expandability.

Memory is a holding area for data, instructions, and information. Like microprocessors, **memory** is contained on chips connected to the system board. There are three well-known types of memory chips: random-access memory (RAM), read-only memory (ROM), and complementary metal-oxide semiconductor (CMOS).

RAM

Random-access memory (RAM) chips hold the program (sequence of instructions) and data that the CPU is presently processing. (See Figure 6-17.) RAM is called temporary or **volatile storage** because everything in most types of RAM is lost as soon as the microcomputer is turned off. It is also lost if there is a power failure or other disruption of the electric current going to the microcomputer. Secondary storage, which we shall describe in Chapter 9, does not lose its contents. It is permanent or **nonvolatile storage,** such as the data stored on diskettes. For this reason, as we mentioned earlier, it is a good idea to save your work in progress to a secondary storage device. That is, if you are working on a document or a spreadsheet, every few minutes you should save, or store, the material.

Figure 6-17 RAM chips mounted on circuit board

Before any program can be run or data used, it must be stored into RAM. Program statements and data are stored in RAM into specific locations uniquely identified by **memory addresses** or **RAM addresses.** One ASCII character or byte is typically stored at one memory address. For example, the previous Figures 6-6 and 6-13 depicted how the statement 3 + 5 is entered into memory, processed, and the result stored in memory. To see how RAM stores the instruction and result, see Figure 6-18.

As technology has advanced in recent years, the design of RAM chips has dramatically improved. There are three basic types of RAM: dynamic, static, and flash.

Dynamic RAM (DRAM) requires a constant supply of power to refresh and retain its contents. Recent advances in DRAM chips have produced three types of DRAM chips:

- **Synchronous DRAM (SDRAM)** is faster than conventional RAM chips and more expensive. SDRAM chips streamline operations by coordinating or synchronizing the movement of data and instructions between the chip and other components in the system unit.
- **Double data rate SDRAM (DDR SDRAM),** also known as **SDRAM II,** is faster, more reliable, and more expensive than SDRAM. DDR SDRAM chips are able to transfer twice (double) as much data in the same amount of times as SDRAM.
- **Direct Rambus© DRAM (Direct RDRAM)** is the fastest and most expensive.

Almost all of today's microcomputers use a combination of DRAM chips. See Figure 6-19 for a summary of the three types of DRAM.

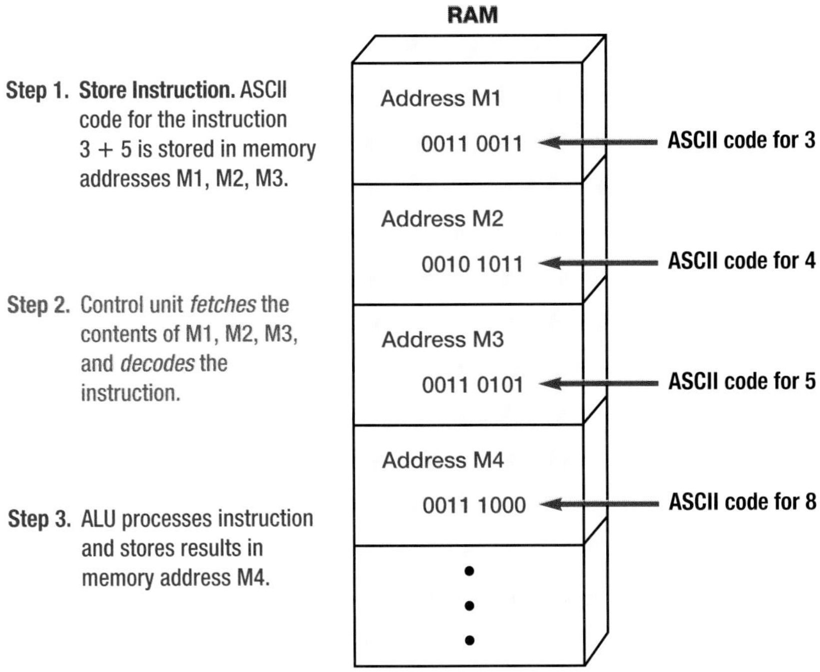
RAM
Step 1. Store Instruction. ASCII code for the instruction 3 + 5 is stored in memory addresses M1, M2, M3.
Step 2. Control unit *fetches* the contents of M1, M2, M3, and *decodes* the instruction.
Step 3. ALU processes instruction and stores results in memory address M4.
Address M1
0011 0011
ASCII code for 3
Address M2
0010 1011
ASCII code for 4
Address M3
0011 0101
ASCII code for 5
Address M4
0011 1000
ASCII code for 8

Figure 6-18 How RAM stores the instruction and result for 3 + 5

Type	Description
SDRAM	synchronizes data and instructions
DDR SDRAM	double data transfer rate
Direct RDRAM	fastest, most expensive

Figure 6-19 Types of DRAM

Static RAM (SRAM) like DRAM requires a constant supply of power. Compared to DRAM, SRAM does not require as much power, is faster, and is more reliable. SRAM is also more expensive and typically used for specialized applications. One of these applications is for **cache memory** or **RAM cache.**

Cache (pronounced "cash") memory improves processing by acting as a temporary high-speed holding area between the memory and the CPU. In a computer with a cache (not all machines have one), the computer detects which information in RAM is most frequently used. It then copies that information into the cache. When needed, the CPU can quickly access the information from the cache.

There are three different types or levels of cache:

- **Level 1 (L1),** also known as **primary cache** and **internal cache,** is built into the microprocessor chip.
- **Level 2 (L2),** also known as **external cache,** is slower than L1 but has a greater capacity. In older computers with older microprocessors, the Level 2 cache is located on a chip that is plugged into the system board. New computers with newer microprocessors have the L2 caches built into the microprocessor. This arrangement, sometimes referred to as **advanced transfer cache,** provides faster response than cache located on the system board.
- **Level 3 (L3),** the newest type of cache, works with special microprocessor L2 caches. L3 caches are not built into the microprocessor. Rather, L3 caches use SDRAM chips located on the system board.

Most of today's microcomputers have two or three types of cache. The most powerful have all three types.

Flash RAM or **flash memory** chips can retain data even if power is disrupted. This type of RAM is the most expensive and used primarily for special applications such as for digital cell telephones, digital video cameras, and portable computers.

Unit	Capacity
Megabyte (MB)	1 million bytes
Gigabyte (GB)	1 billion bytes
Terabyte (TB)	1 trillion bytes

Figure 6-20 Memory capacity

Having enough RAM is important! For example, to effectively use Excel requires 32 MB of RAM and additional RAM is needed to hold any data or other applications. Some microcomputers—particularly older ones—do not have this much memory. Additional RAM, however, can be added to these computer systems. The capacity or amount of RAM is expressed in bytes. There are three commonly used units of measurement to describe memory capacity. (See Figure 6-20.)

Even if your computer does not have enough RAM to hold a program, it might be able to run the program using **virtual memory.** Most of today's operating systems support virtual memory. With virtual memory, large programs are divided into parts and the parts stored on a secondary device, usually a hard disk. Each part is then read into RAM only when needed. In this way, computer systems are able to run very large programs. To learn more about how virtual memory works, consult your Computing Today CD or visit us on the Web at http://www.mhhe.com/oleary/CT05 and select Animations from Tim's Toolbox.

Computing Today CD

ROM

Read-only memory (ROM) chips have programs built into them at the factory. Unlike RAM chips, ROM chips are not volatile and cannot be changed by the user. "Read only" means that the CPU can read, or retrieve, data and programs written on the ROM chip. However, the computer cannot write—encode or change—the information or instructions in ROM.

ROM chips typically contain special instructions for detailed computer operations. For example, ROM instructions are needed to start a computer, give keyboard keys their special control capabilities, and put characters on the screen. ROMs are also called **firmware.**

CMOS

A **complementary metal-oxide semiconductor (CMOS)** chip provides flexibility and expandability for a computer system. It contains essential informa-

1 Double-click the time in the Quick Launch taskbar.

2 Choose *January* from the drop-down list.

Choose *2005* from the drop-down list.

Select Wednesday the 5th.

Click *Apply* to set the new system data and time on the CMOS chip.

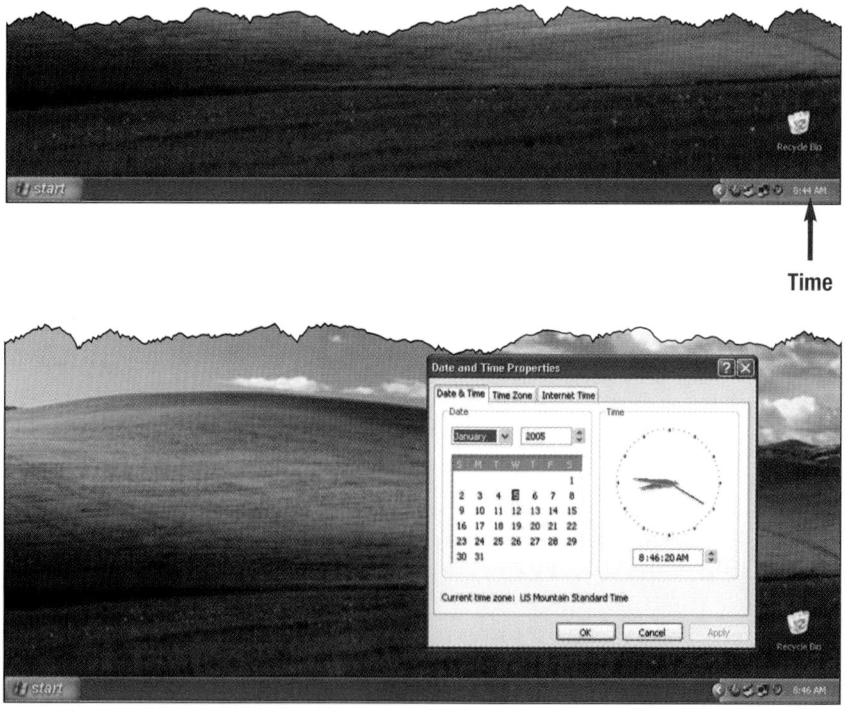

Figure 6-21 Resetting the system date and time

tion that is required every time the computer system is turned on. The chip supplies such information as the current date and time, amount of RAM, type of keyboard, mouse, monitor, and disk drives. Unlike RAM, it is powered by a battery and does not lose its contents when the power is turned off. Unlike ROM, its contents can be changed to reflect changes in the computer system such as increased RAM and new hardware devices.

One of the most common ways that users interact with a computer's CMOS chip is to reset the system date and time settings. For example, Figure 6-21 presents the steps to reset the date and time for a computer using the Windows XP operating system.

See Figure 6-22 for a summary of the three types of memory.

Type	Use
RAM	Programs and data
ROM	Fixed start-up instructions
CMOS	Flexible start-up instructions

Figure 6-22 Memory

Concept Check

- ✓ What is memory? Name and describe the three types of memory chips.
- ✓ What are the three basic types of RAM? Discuss each type.
- ✓ What is cache memory? Name and describe the three levels of cache.
- ✓ What are ROM and CMOS? What are they used for?

SYSTEM CLOCK

The system clock is like a bass drum. Superscalar microprocessors can process more than one operation per beat. Clock speed is measured in gigahertz or billions of beats per second.

The **system clock** is located on a small specialized chip that produces precisely timed electrical beats or impulses. The system clock performs a function similar to the bass drum in a marching band. Just as the bass drum determines the cadence, or how fast the band marches, the system clock emits a beat or pulse that sets the operating pace for all of the components in the system unit. Some microprocessors can only execute one operation per beat. For example, to process the instruction 3 + 5 as presented earlier in Figure 6-13 would require four beats: one beat to fetch the instruction, one beat to decode it, one beat to execute the instruction, and one beat to store the results. (See Figure 6-23.) Most newer microprocessors are **superscalar,** meaning that they are able to process more than one operation per beat of the system clock.

Unlike a bass drum which can beat faster to increase cadence, a computer's system clock has a fixed speed that cannot be varied. For that reason, a computer system's clock speed is an important measurement indicating the speed of processing or power of a computer system. The **clock speed** or **clock rate** for powerful microcomputers is measured in **gigahertz** or billions of beats per second. The faster the clock speed, the faster the computer can process information.

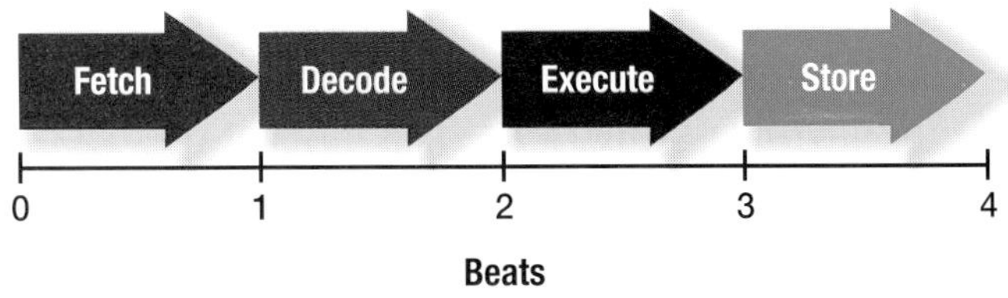

Figure 6-23 The system clock and the instruction cycle

TIPS Does your computer seem to be getting slower and slower? Perhaps it's so slow you are thinking about buying a new one. Before doing that, consider the following suggestions that might add a little zip to your current system.

1. **Uninstall programs you no longer need.** Explore the contents of your hard disk and identify programs that you no longer need. If you have Windows XP, use Start/Control Panel/Add/Remove Programs (for Windows 2000 use Start/Settings/Control Panel/Add/Remove Programs) to access the Uninstall feature.
2. **Remove unneeded fonts.** If you have Windows XP use Start/Control Panel/ Fonts in the classic view (for Windows 2000 use Start/Settings/Control Panel/Fonts) to determine the different font types stored on your system. To see a sample of any font type, double-click it. Review the fonts and delete those you will not need.
3. **Empty the Recycle Bin.** If you have either Windows 2000 or Windows XP, files are not removed from your hard disk when you delete them. Rather, they are moved to the Recycle Bin. To empty or remove files from the Recycle Bin, open the Recycle Bin and use File/Empty Recycle Bin.

Concept Check

- ✓ What is a system clock? How is it like a bass drum?
- ✓ What is a superscalar microprocessor?
- ✓ What is clock speed? What how is it measured?

EXPANSION SLOTS AND CARDS

Expansion slots provide an open architecture. Expansion cards provide connections for video, sound, network, TV tuner cards, and more. PC cards are for notebook and handheld computers.

Computers are known for having different kinds of "architectures." Machines that have **closed architecture** are manufactured in such a way that users cannot easily add new devices. Most microcomputers have **open architecture.** They allow users to expand their systems by providing **slots** on the system board. Users can insert optional devices known as **expansion cards** into these slots. (See Figure 6-24.)

Expansion cards are also called **plug-in boards, controller cards, adapter cards,** and **interface cards.** They plug into slots located on the system board. Ports on the cards allow cables to be connected from the expansion cards to devices outside the system unit. (See Figure 6-25.) There are a wide range of different types of expansion cards. Some of the most commonly used expansion cards are:

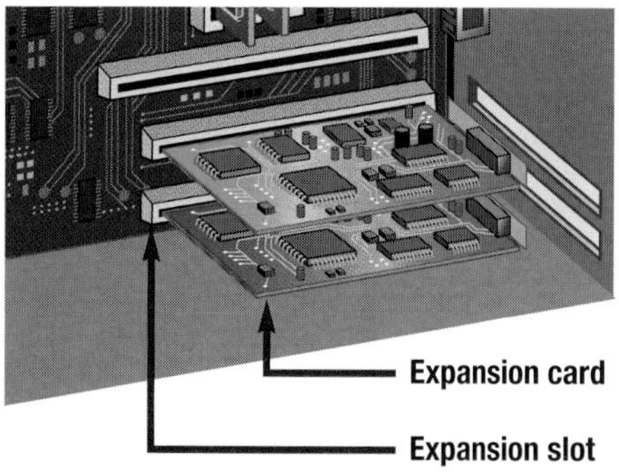

Figure 6-24 Expansion cards fit into slots on the system board

- **Video cards:** Also known as **graphics cards,** these cards connect the system board to the computer's monitor. The cards convert the internal electronic signals to video signals so they can be displayed on the monitor.
- **Sound cards:** These cards accept audio input from a microphone and convert it into a form that can be processed by the computer. Also, these cards convert internal electronic signals to audio signals so they can be heard from external speakers.

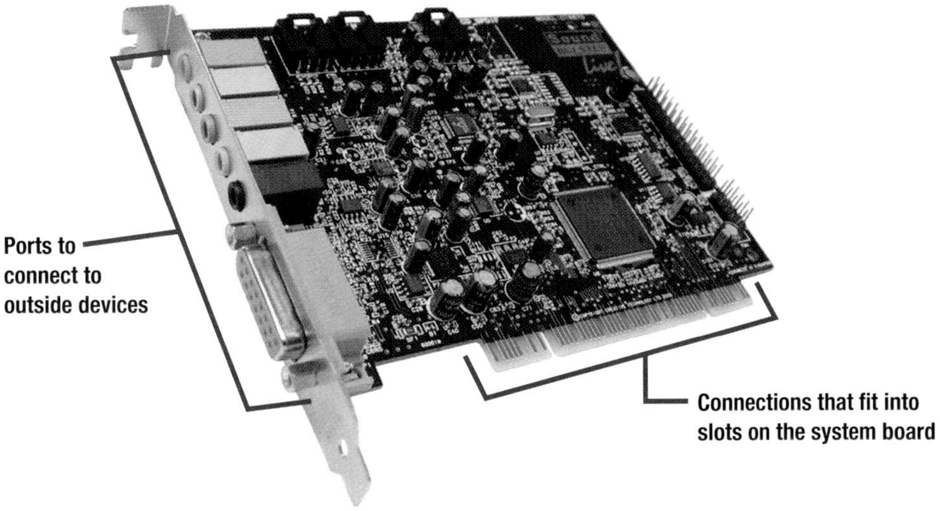

Figure 6-25 Expansion card

Figure 6-26 Modem card

- **Modem cards:** Also known as **internal modems,** these cards allow distant computers to communicate with one another by converting electronic signals from within the system unit into electronic signals that can travel over telephone lines and other types of connections. (See Figure 6-26.)
- **Network interface cards (NIC):** These cards, also known as **network adapter cards,** are used to connect a computer to one or more other computers. This forms a communication network whereby users can share data, programs, and hardware. The network adapter card typically connects the system unit to a cable that connects to the network.
- **TV tuner cards:** Now you can watch television, capture video, and surf the Internet at the same time. TV tuner cards, also known as **television boards, video recorder cards,** and **video capture cards,** contain a TV tuner and a video converter that changes the TV signal into one that can be displayed on your monitor. To see how TV tuner card works, see Figure 6-27. Also consult your Computing Today CD or visit us at http://www.mhhe.com/oleary/CT05 and select Animations from Tim's Toolbox. (To learn more about using TV tuner cards, see Making IT Work for You: TV Tuner Cards and Video Clips on pages 228 and 229.)

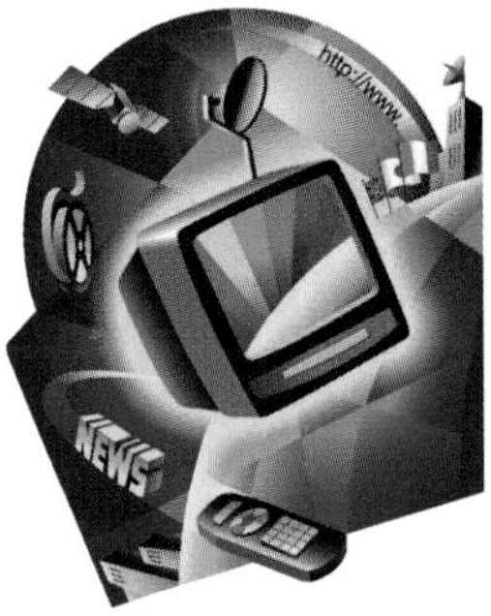

Plug and Play is a set of hardware and software standards developed by Intel, Microsoft, and others. It is an effort by hardware and software vendors to create operating systems, processing units, and expansion boards, as well as other devices that are able to configure themselves. Ideally, to install a new expansion board all you have to do is insert the board and turn on the computer. As the computer starts up, it will search for these Plug and Play devices and automatically configure the devices and the computer system. Unfortunately, not all computer systems and expansion cards have this capability. For those devices that do not, reconfiguration involves installing device drivers as discussed in chapter 5.

To meet the size constraints of notebook and handheld computers, credit card–sized expansion cards have been developed. These cards can

TIPS

Having problems or want to upgrade your system and would like professional help? Here are a few suggestions:

1. **Select a reputable computer store.** Consider local as well as national chain stores. Check them out with the Better Business Bureau.
2. **Visit the store with your computer.** Ideally, have a knowledgeable friend accompany you. Describe the problem and get a written estimate. Ask about the company's warranty.
3. **Tag your system.** If you leave the system, attach a tag with your name, address, and telephone number.
4. **Pay by credit card.** If a dispute occurs, many credit card companies will intervene on your side.

How TV Tuner Cards Work

Step 1: Input. A traditional television, VCR, or cable outlet provides video and audio input to the computer system. This input is in the form of analog signals transmitted by a cable connected to the TV tuner card.

Television

Step 2: Process. The TV tuner card is attached to the system unit via a slot on the system board. The card accepts the analog input signals and processes them into digital signals that can be further processed by the system unit.

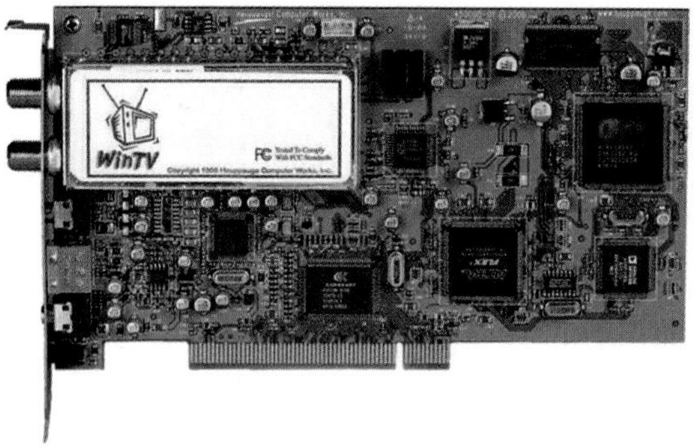

TV tuner card

Step 3: Output. After processing the signal, the audio component can be viewed on the computer system's monitor and heard on the computer system's speakers.

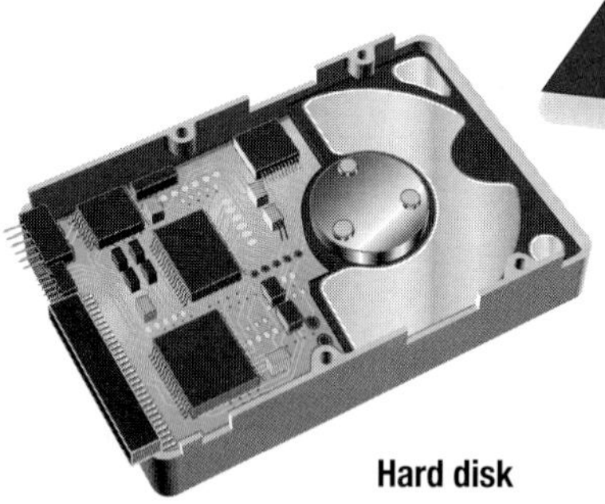

Hard disk

Step 4: Storage. The digital audio and video can be saved in files and stored on the system's hard disk or other storage device. These files can be used to replay the audio and video or to be processed later by special purpose audio and video editing software.

Monitor and Speakers

Figure 6-27 How TV tuner cards work

be easily inserted and removed. They are called **PC cards** or **Personal Computer Memory Card International Association (PCMCIA) cards.** (See Figure 6-28.)

There are three types of PC cards:

- **Type I cards** are the thinnest and are often used to expand a notebook's or handheld computer's memory. These memory expansion cards are also known as **flash memory cards.**
- **Type II cards** are thicker, typically used for communication, and include modem cards and network interface cards.
- **Type III cards** are the thickest, used to expand external storage, and include hard disk cards.

Figure 6-28 Inserting a PC card into a notebook computer

Concept Check

- What does open versus closed architecture mean?
- What are expansion slots and cards? Name five expansion cards.
- What are PC cards? Describe the three types of PC cards.

BUS LINES

Bus lines provide data pathways that connect various system components. System and expansion are two categories of buses.

A **bus line**—also known simply as a **bus**—connects the parts of the CPU to each other. Buses also link the CPU to various other components on the system board. (See Figure 6-29.) A bus is a pathway for bits representing data and instructions. The number of bits that can travel simultaneously down a bus is known as the **bus width.**

A bus is similar to a multilane highway that moves bits rather than cars from one location to another. (See Figure 6-30.) The number of traffic lanes determines the bus width. A highway (bus line) with more traffic lanes (bus width) can move traffic (data and instructions) faster. For example, a 64-bit bus is twice as fast as a 32-bit bus. Why should you even have to care about what a bus line is? The answer is that, as microprocessor chips have changed, so have bus lines. Bus design or bus architecture is an important factor relating to the speed and power for a particular computer. Additionally, many devices, such as expansion boards, will work with only one type of bus.

Figure 6-29 Bus is a pathway for bits

EXPANSION BUSES

Every computer system has two basic categories of buses. One category, called **system buses,** represented in Figure 6-30, connects the CPU to memory on the system board. The other category, called **expansion buses,** connects the CPU to slots on the system board.

Computer systems typically have a combination of different types of expansion buses. The principal types are ISA, PCI, AGP, USB, and HPSB.

- **Industry standard architecture (ISA)** was developed for the first IBM Personal Computer. Originally, it had an 8-bit bus width. Later, it was

MAKING IT WORK FOR YOU

TV TUNER CARDS AND VIDEO CLIPS

Want to watch your favorite television program while you work? Perhaps you would like to include a video clip from television and include it in a class presentation. It's easy using a TV tuner card.

Viewing You can view your favorite TV shows, even while running other applications such as Excel, by taking the steps shown here.

1
- **Click the *TV icon* on the desktop.**
- **Size and move the television window and control box window.**
- **Select the channel.**

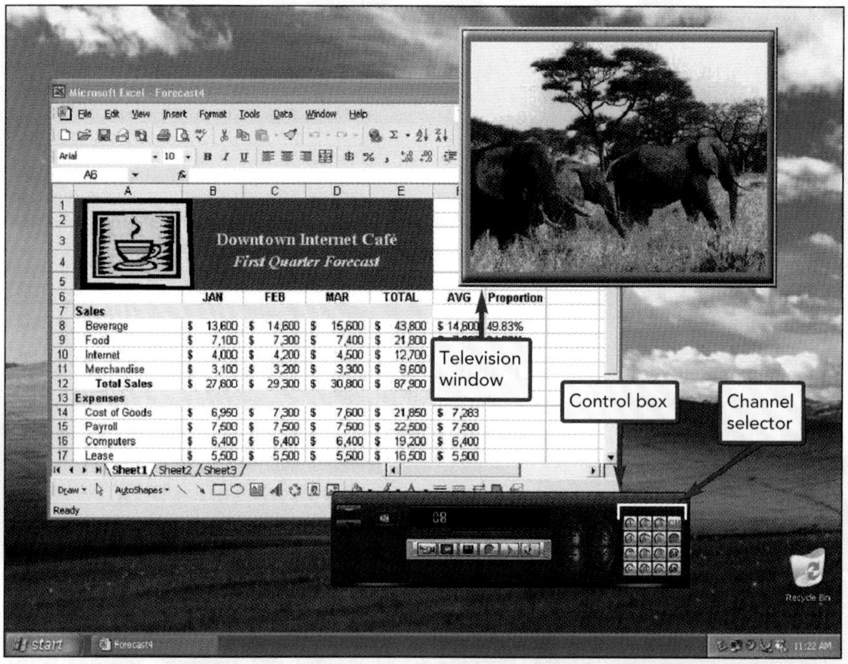

Capturing You can capture the video playing in the TV window into a digital file by taking the steps shown here.

1
- **Specify where to save the video clip on your computer by clicking the *Properties* button.**
- **Click the *Record* button to start recording.**
- **Click the *Stop* button to stop recording.**

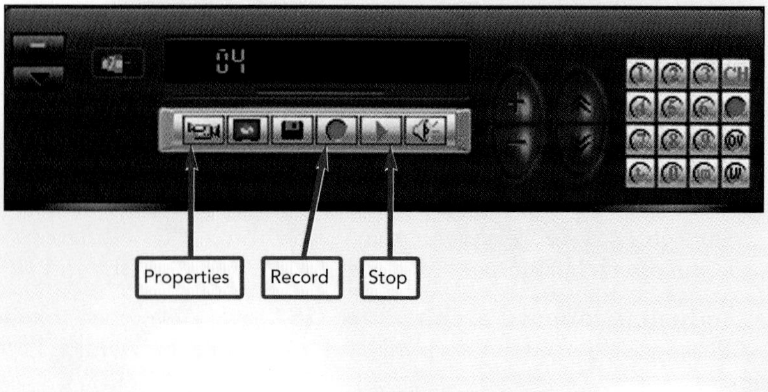

Using Once captured in a file, a video can be used in any number of ways. It can be added to a Web page, attached to an e-mail, or added to a class presentation. For example, you could include a video clip in a PowerPoint presentation by taking the steps shown here.

1 **Insert the video clip into a page in the presentation by clicking *Insert/Picture/From File.***

2 **Click on the image of the inserted video clip anytime during your presentation to play it.**

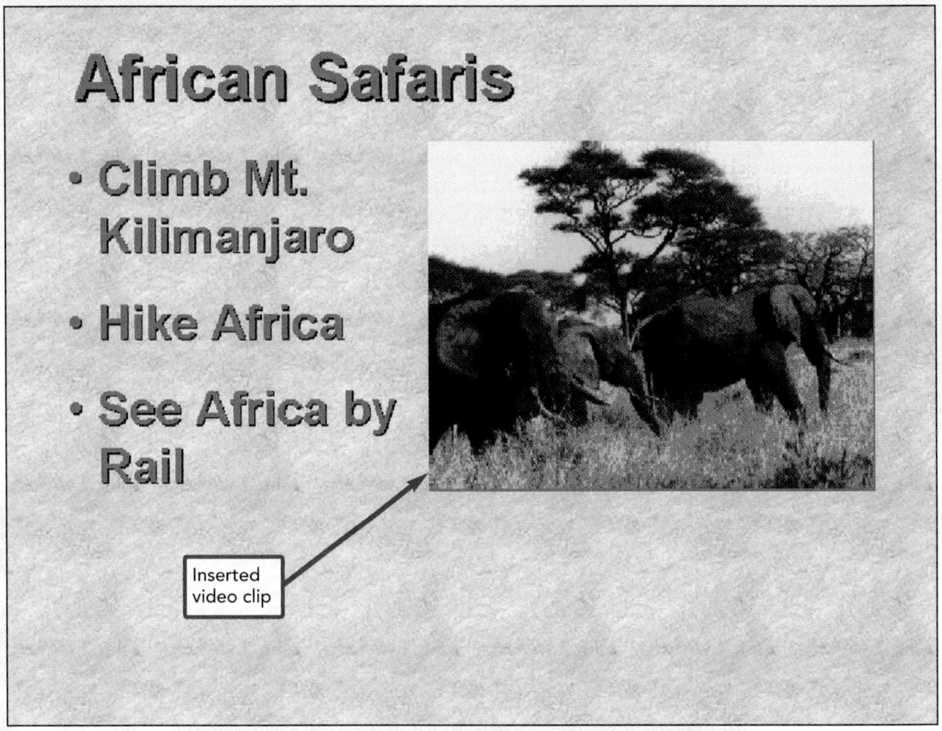

TV tuner cards are relatively inexpensive and easy to install. Some factors limiting their performance on your computer are the speed of your processor, the amount of memory, and secondary storage capacity.

TV tuner cards are continually changing and some of the specifics presented in this Making IT Work for You may have changed. To learn about other ways to make information technology work for you, visit our Web site at http://www.mhhe.com/oleary/CT05 and select Making IT Work from Tim's Toolbox.

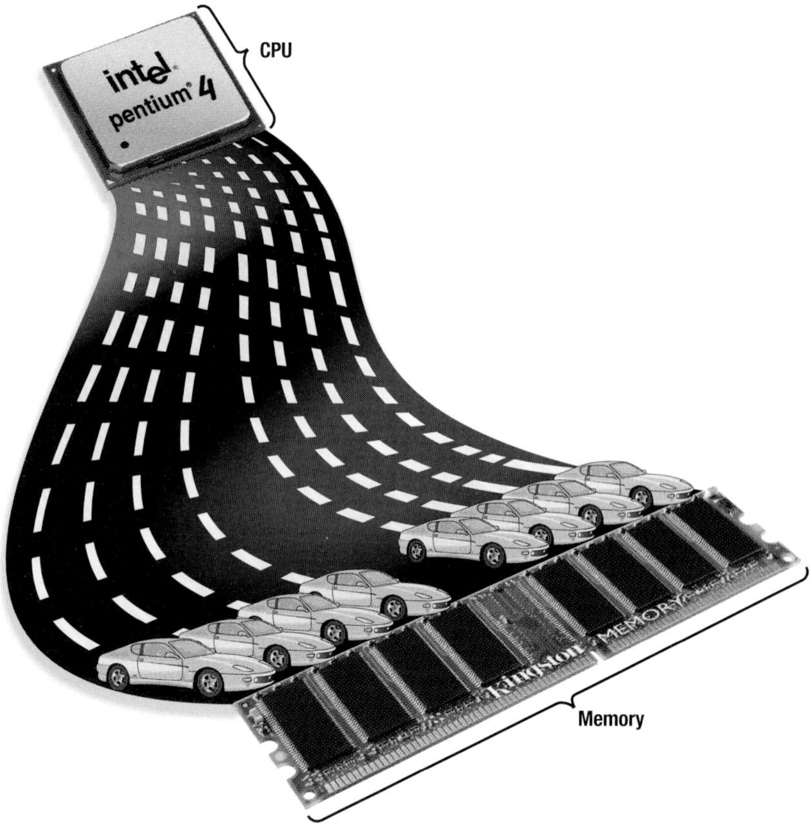

Figure 6-30 A bus is like a multilane highway

expanded to 16 bits. Although too slow for many of today's applications, the ISA bus is still widely used.

- **Peripheral component interconnect (PCI)** was originally developed to meet the video demands of graphical user interfaces. PCI is a high-speed 32-bit or 64-bit bus that is over 20 times faster than ISA buses.
- **Accelerated graphics port (AGP)** is over twice as fast as the PCI bus. While the PCI bus is used for a variety of purposes, the AGP bus is dedicated to the acceleration of graphics performance. Widely used for graphics and 3-D animations, the AGP is replacing the PCI bus for the transfer of video data.
- **Universal serial bus (USB)** combines with a PCI bus on the system board to support several external devices without using expansion cards or slots. External USB devices are connected from one to another and then on to the USB bus. The USB bus then connects to the PCI bus on the motherboard. The first universal serial bus was called USB 1.1 and is over twice as fast as the AGP bus. Recently, a new version called USB 2.0 has been introduced that is 40 times faster than USB1.1.
- **FireWire buses,** also known as **high performance serial bus (HPSB),** operate much like USB buses and perform at speeds comparable to USB 2.0. FireWire and USB 2.0 buses are used for special applications providing support for digital camcorders and video editing software.

For a summary of the different types of expansion buses, see Figure 6-31.

Concept Check

- ✔ What is a bus and what is its function?
- ✔ Name and describe the two categories of buses.
- ✔ What are the five principle bus lines? How are they different from one another?

Type	Description
ISA	Slow, being replaced by other buses
PCI	20 times faster than ISA, connects CPU, memory, and expansion slots
AGP	Twice the speed of PCI, supports accelerated graphics
USB	Uses PCI but supports many devices without using expansion cards and slots; USB 1.1 over twice as fast as AGP; USB 2.0 40 times faster than USB 2.0
FireWire	operates like USB with speeds comparable to USB 2.0

Figure 6-31 Expansion buses

PORTS

Ports are connecting sockets on the systems unit. Serial, parallel, USB, and FireWire are standard ports. MIDI, SCSI, and IrDA are specialized ports. Cables connect external devices to ports.

A **port** is a socket for external devices to connect to the system unit. (See Figure 6-32.) Some ports connect directly to the systems board while others connect to cards that are inserted into slots on the systems board. Some ports are standard features of most computer systems and others are more specialized.

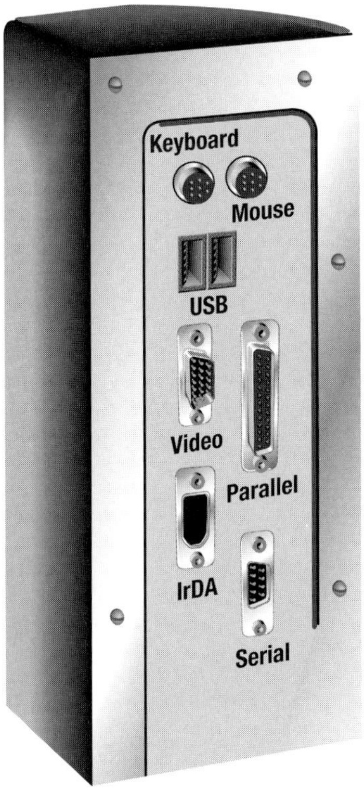

Figure 6-32 Ports

STANDARD PORTS

Many ports, like the mouse, keyboard, and video ports, are for specific devices. Others, like those listed below, can be used for a variety of different devices.

- **Serial ports** are used for a wide variety of purposes. They are often used to connect a mouse, keyboard, modem, and many other devices to the system unit. Serial ports send data one bit at a time and are very good for sending information over a long distance.
- **Parallel ports** are used to connect external devices that need to send or receive a lot of data over a short distance. These ports typically send eight bits of data simultaneously across eight parallel wires. Parallel ports are mostly used to connect printers to the system unit.
- **Universal serial bus (USB) ports** are gradually replacing serial and parallel ports. They are faster, and one USB port can be used to connect several devices to the system unit.
- **FireWire ports,** also know as **high performance serial bus (HPSB) ports,** are as fast as USB 2.0 ports and provide connections to specialized FireWire devices such as camcorders.

SPECIALIZED PORTS

In addition to standard ports, there are numerous specialty ports including MIDI, SCSI, and IrDA ports.

- **Musical instrument interface (MIDI)** ports are a special type of serial port for connecting musical instruments like an electronic keyboard to a sound card. The sound card converts the music into a series of digital instructions. These instructions can be processed immediately to reproduce the music or saved to a file for later processing. The instructions are

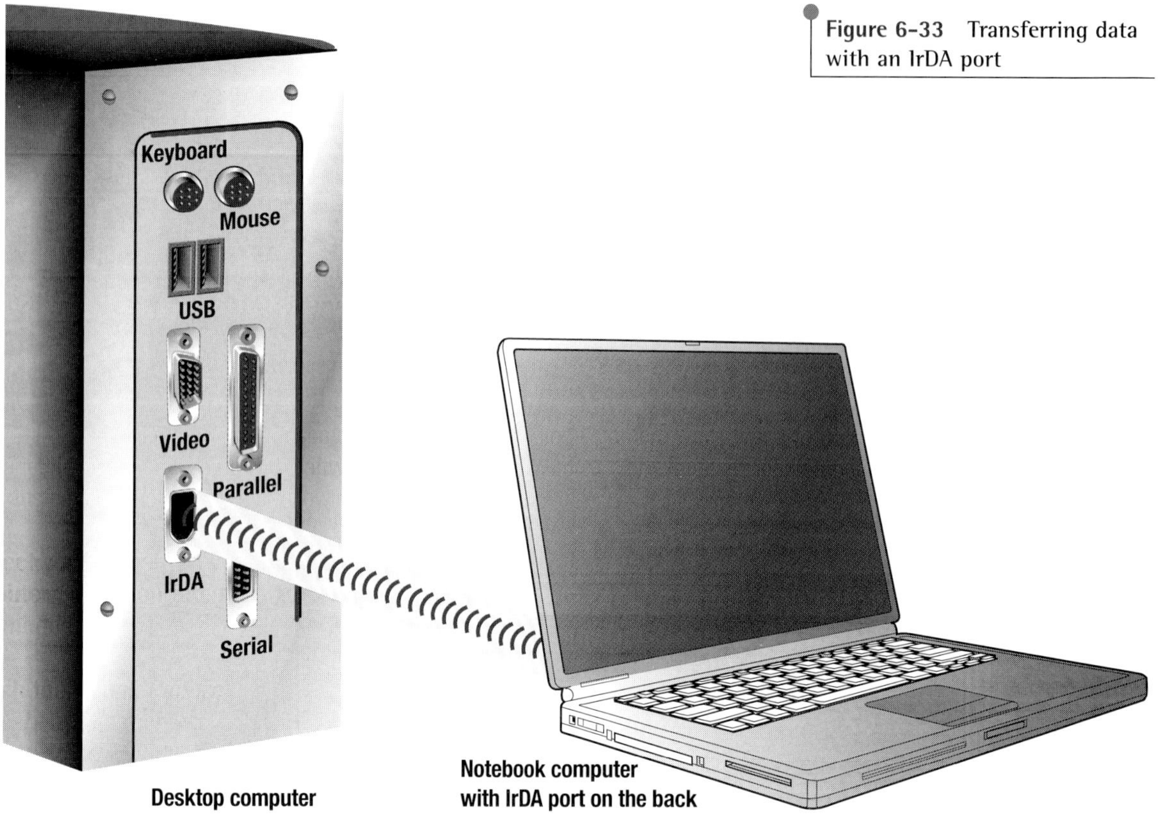

Figure 6-33 Transferring data with an IrDA port

converted to music by a **synthesizer** either located on a chip on the system board or on an external device.

- **Small computer system interface (SCSI)** ports are a special type of high speed parallel port for connecting a series of input and/or output SCSI devices to a single SCSI controller card. This arrangement allows several devices to communicate with the system unit through a single slot on the system board.
- **Infrared Data Association (IrDA)** ports are also known as **fast infrared (FIR)** ports. IrDA ports provide a wireless mechanism for transferring data between devices. Instead of cables, the IrDA ports from each device are directly aligned and infrared light waves are used to transmit data. One of the most common applications is to transfer data from either a handheld or notebook computer to a desktop computer. (See Figure 6-33.)

CABLES

Cables are used to connect exterior devices to the system unit via the ports. One end of the cable is attached to the device and the other end has a connector that is attached to a matching connector on the port. See Figure 6-34 for some of the most common types of cables.

Concept Check

- ✓ What are ports? What do they do?
- ✓ Name and describe four standard ports.
- ✓ Name and describe three specialized ports.

Cable	Port	Devices
	Mouse	Mouse
	Keyboard	Keyboard
	Serial	Mouse, modem, keyboard
	Parallel	Printer, CD-ROM drive, Zip drive
	AGP Video	Monitor
	USB	Modem, joy stick, scanner
	FireWire	Video camera

Figure 6-34 Cable connections

POWER SUPPLY

DC powers computers. Desktop computers use power supply units. Notebook and handheld computers use AC adapters and batteries.

Computers require **direct current (DC)** to power their electronic components and to represent data and instructions. DC power can be provided indirectly by converting **alternating current (AC)** from standard wall outlets or directly from batteries.

Figure 6-35 Power supply unit

- Desktop computers have a **power supply unit** located within the system unit. (See Figure 6-35.) This unit plugs into a standard wall outlet, converts AC to DC, and provides the power to drive all of the system unit components.
- Notebook computers use **AC adapters** that are typically located outside the system unit. (See Figure 6-36.) AC adapters plug into a standard wall outlet, convert AC to DC, provide power to drive the system unit components, and can recharge batteries. Notebook computers can be operated either using an AC adapter plugged into a wall outlet or using battery power. Notebook batteries typically provide sufficient power for 2–4 hours before they need to be recharged.
- Like notebook computers, handheld computers use AC adapters located outside the system unit. Unlike notebook computers, however, handheld computers typically operate only using battery power. The AC adapter is used to recharge the batteries.

Figure 6-36 AC adapter

Concept Check

- ✓ What type of power is required to operate a computer?
- ✓ List two devices that convert AC to DC.
- ✓ Discuss the power sources used by desktop, notebook, and handheld computers.

Careers in IT

Computer Technician

Computer technicians repair and install computer components and systems. They may work on everything from personal computers and mainframe servers to printers. Some computer technicians are responsible for setting up and maintaining computer networks. Experienced computer technicians may work with computer engineers to diagnose problems and run routine maintenance on complex systems. Job growth is expected in this field as computer equipment becomes more complicated and technology expands.

Employers look for those with certification in computer repair or associate degrees from vocational schools. Employment usually begins with training, but most employers expect applicants to have prior technical experience. Computer technicians can also expect to continue their education to keep up with technological changes. Good communication skills are important in this field.

Computer technicians can expect an hourly wage of $12.00 to $25.00. Opportunities for advancement typically come in the form of work on more advanced computer systems. Some computer technicians move into customer service positions or go into sales. To learn about other careers in information technology visit us at http://www.mhhe.com/oleary/CT05 and select Careers in IT from Tim's Toolbox.

A Look to the Future

Xybernaut Corporation Makes Wearable Computers a Reality

Wouldn't it be nice if you could conveniently access the Internet wirelessly at any time during the day? What if you could send and receive e-mail from your waist-mounted computer? What if you could maintain your personal schedule book, making new appointments with others on the fly? What if you could play interactive games, and surf the Web from anywhere?

Of course you can do all this and more using wireless technology and PDAs. Many people currently use this technology when they are away from their home or office. What if these users could accomplish these tasks with an even smaller, more portable and less intrusive system? Will people be wearing computers rather than carrying them? What if your computer featured a head-mounted display?

Xybernaut Corporation is currently marketing a personal wearable computer called POMA®. The device is described as a personal multimedia appliance. It is composed of a processor that runs Windows CE, a wireless pointing device, and a head-mounted display. The display allows you to see the equivalent of a desktop monitor via a small screen that is worn in front of one eye. This screen is only one inch square and weighs a mere 3 ounces. The device includes an MP3 player that plays songs and displays videos, and abridged versions of Windows Office programs.

Devices made by Xybernaut® are currently being evaluated for use in airports by security personal. These devices are currently being used by the U.S. Department of Defense for military applications and by the Toronto Blue Jays to end long lines at ticket windows. When coupled with face recognition technology Xybernaut's Mobile Assistant® V allows security personnel the advantage of portability and instant communication with the command center. Police and security officers may someday use this technology to check IDs and verify your identity. Experts say that wearable computers will be used by surgeons in operating rooms to "view" their patients.

Will we be wearing computers soon? Some of us already are. And some experts predict the majority of us will employ a wearable computer before the end of the decade. Many computer manufacturers are currently working on wearable computers, and there is even a wearable computer fashion show that showcases the latest designs. Many people are already "wearing" their computers, and making use of this mobile technology to read e-mail while waiting in lines or even studying their notes for the next exam. What do you think? Will Americans someday grab their keys and their computers before they leave the house? Will your computer one day be housed in your jacket?

VISUAL SUMMARY

THE SYSTEM UNIT

SYSTEM UNIT

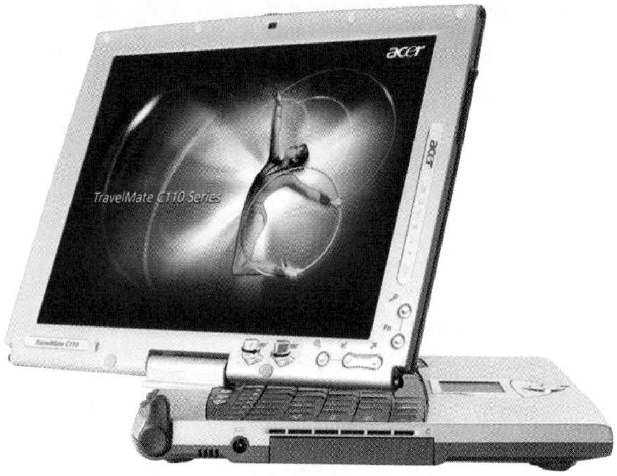

System unit (system cabinet or **chassis)** contains electronic components. Four basic types are: **desktop** (**tower models** positioned vertically), **notebook, tablet PC (convertible and slate),** and handheld. **PDA (personal digital assistant)** most widely used handheld computer.

Electronic Representation

Our voices create continuous **analog** signals. A conversion to **digital** signals is necessary before processing. Data and instructions can be represented electronically with a **two-state** or **binary system** of numbers (0 and 1). Each 0 or 1 is called a **bit.** A **byte** consists of eight bits and represents one character.

Binary Coding Schemes

Binary coding schemes convert binary data into characters. Three such schemes are:

- **ASCII**—the most widely used for microcomputers.
- **EBCDIC**—developed by IBM; used primarily by large computers.
- **Unicode**—16-bit code; designed to support international languages like Chinese and Japanese.

SYSTEM BOARD

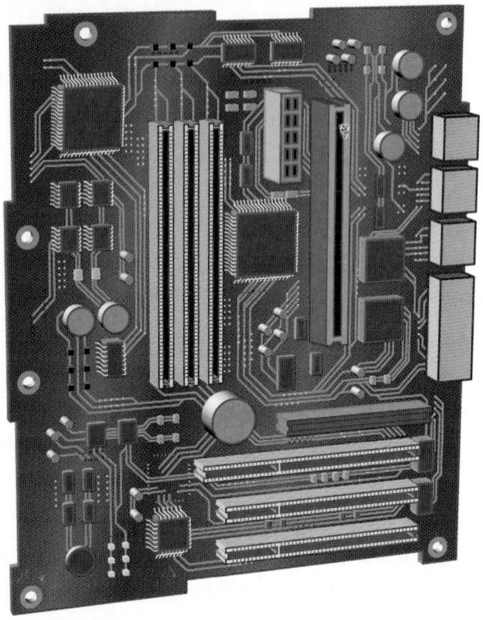

The **system board** (**main board** or **motherboard**) connects all system components and allows input and output devices to communicate with the system unit. It is a flat circuit board covered with electronic components:

- **Sockets** provide connection points for **chips (silicon chips, semiconductors, integrated circuits).** Chips mounted on **carrier packages.**
- **Slots** provide connection points for specialized cards or circuit boards.
- **Connecting lines (bus lines)** provide pathways to support communication.

To be a competent and knowledgeable end user, you need to understand how data and programs are represented electronically. Additionally, you need to understand the functionality of the basic components in the system unit: system board, microprocessor, memory, system clock, expansion slots and cards, bus lines, and ports and cables.

MICROPROCESSOR

The **microprocessor** is a single chip that contains the **central processing unit (CPU)** or **processor.** It has two basic components: **control unit** and **arithmetic-logic unit (ALU).**

Instruction Cycles

Instruction cycle (machine cycle) consists of four basic operations: **fetching, decoding, executing,** and **storing.** Time to fetch an instruction is called **instruction time (I-time).** Time to decode and execute is called **execution time (E-time).**

Microprocessor Chips

A **word** is the number of bits that can be accessed by the microprocessor at one time. Older microprocessors process data and instructions in **microseconds;** newer ones process in **nanoseconds.**

Complex instruction set computer (CISC) and **reduced instruction set computer (RISC)** chips are two different designs. RISC chips used in powerful microcomputers known as **workstations.**

Specialty Processors

Three types are: **coprocessors** such as **graphics cards** to improve specific operations; **parallel processors** to run or process large programs; and **smart card processors** such as **intelligent smart cards** and **memory cards.**

MEMORY

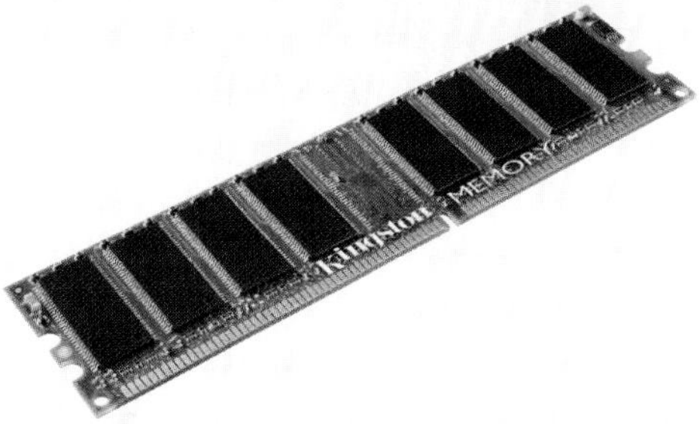

Memory holds data, instructions, and information. There are three types of **memory** chips:

RAM

RAM (random access memory) chips are **volatile storage**. Programs and data are stored in RAM **memory addresses.** Three types of RAM:

- **Dynamic RAM (DRAM)** including **SDRAM, DDR SDRAM,** and **Direct RDRAM**
- **Static RAM (SRAM)** used for **cache memory** or **RAM cache** (**L1** (**primary cache),** **L2** (**external cache**), and **L3**).
- **Flash RAM (flash memory)** does not lose its contents when power is disrupted.

Virtual memory divides large programs into parts that are read into RAM as needed.

ROM

ROM (read only memory) chips, also called **firmware,** are **nonvolatile storage** and control essential system operations.

CMOS

CMOS (complementary metal-oxide semiconductor) chips provide flexibility and expandability to computer systems.

SYSTEM CLOCK

System clock controls speed of operations. **Superscalar** microprocessors process more than one instruction per beat. **Clock speed** (**clock rate**) is measured in **gigahertz (GHz).**

EXPANSION SLOTS AND CARDS

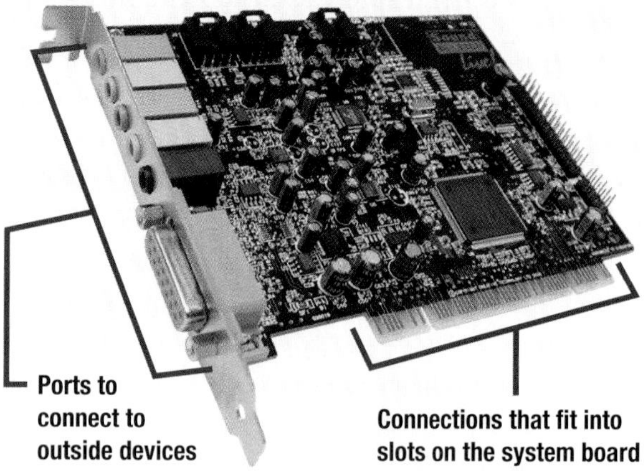
Ports to
connect to
outside devices
Connections that fit into
slots on the system board

Computers with **closed architecture** are not easily expanded. **Open architecture** computers typically have **slots** on their system boards to accept **expansion cards (plug-in boards, controller cards, adapter cards,** or **interface cards).**

Examples of **expansion cards** include:

- **Video cards**—also known as **graphics cards**, connect to monitors.
- **Sound cards**—connect to speakers.
- **Modem cards**—also known as **internal modems**, connect over a telephone line.
- **Network interface cards (NIC)**—also known as **network adapter cards**, connect to a network.
- **TV tuner cards**—contain TV tuner and video capture capabilities, also known as **television boards** and **personal video recorder cards**.
- **PC cards**—credit card–size expansion cards for portable computers, also known as **PCMCIA (Personal Computer Memory Card International Association) cards**. Three types are **Type I, II,** and **III**.

Plug and Play is a set of hardware and software standards designed to assist with the installation of expansion cards.

BUS LINES

Bus lines, also known as **buses,** provide data pathways that connect various system components. **Bus width** is the number of bits that can travel simultaneously.

Expansion Buses

System buses connect CPU and memory. **Expansion buses** connect CPU and slots. Five principal expansion buses types are:

- **ISA (Industry Standard Architecture)**—older and slower but still widely used.
- **PCI (Peripheral Component Interconnect)**—over 20 times faster than ISA; used to connect CPU, memory, and expansion boards.
- **AGP (Accelerated Graphics Port)**—over twice as fast as PCI; used to accelerate monitor graphics performance.
- **USB (Universal Serial Bus)**—combines with PCI bus to connect several external devices without inserting cards; USB 1.1 over twice as fast as AGP; USB 2.0 forty times faster than USB 1.1.
- **FireWire bus (HPSB** or **High Performance Serial Bus),** operates much like USB with speeds comparable to USB 2.0; FireWire and USB 2.0 used for special applications providing support for digital camcorders and video editing software.

PORTS

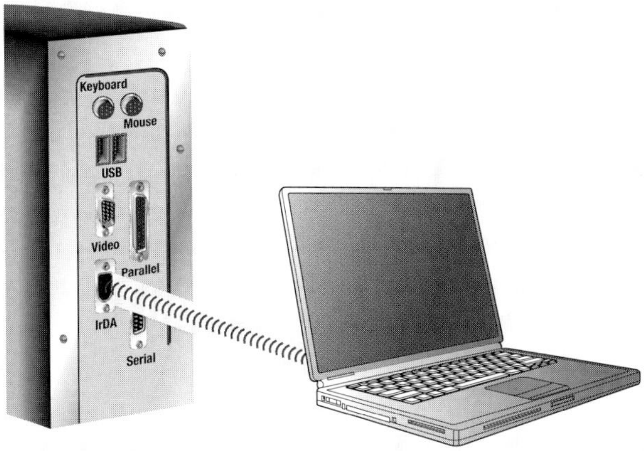

Ports are connecting sockets on the outside of the system unit. Some ports are standard while others are more specialized.

Standard Ports

Four standard ports are:

- **Serial**—send data one bit at a time.
- **Parallel**—send eight bits simultaneously.
- **USB (universal serial bus)**—faster, one port can connect several devices to system unit.
- **FireWire (HPSB or high performance serial bus)**—as fast as USB 2.0 ports; provide connections for specialized FireWire devices.

Specialized Ports

Three specialty ports are:

- **MIDI (musical instrument interface)**—special port for musical instruments such as electronic keyboards. **Synthesizers** convert MIDI instructions to music.
- **SCSI (small computer system interface)**—high speed parallel port for connecting multiple devices to a single SCSI card.
- **IrDA (Infrared Data Association)**—also known as **fast infrared (FIR) ports** provide wireless connections.

Cables

Cables are used to connect external devices to the system unit via ports.

POWER SUPPLY

Computers require **direct current (DC)** to power their components. DC power supplied is by either converting **alternating current (AC)** from standard wall outlets or directly from batteries.

- **Power supply units** convert AC to DC; they are located within desktop computer's system unit.
- **AC adapters** are used to power notebook computers and tablet PCs and to recharge their batteries.

Like notebooks and tablet PCs, handheld computers also use AC adapters to recharge their batteries; however, most handheld computers only operate using battery power and cannot operate directly from an AC adapter.

KEY TERMS

AC adapter (233)
accelerated graphics port (AGP) (230)
adapter card (224)
advanced transfer cache (221)
alternating current (AC) (233)
analog (212)
arithmetic operation (217)
arithmetic-logic unit (ALU) (216)
ASCII (212)
binary coding scheme (212)
binary system (212)
bit (212)
bus line (216)
bus width (227)
byte (212)
cable (232)
cache memory (221)
carrier package (215)
central processing unit (CPU) (216)
chassis (210)
chip (215)
clock speed (223)
clock rate (223)
closed architecture (224)
complementary metal-oxide semiconductor (CMOS) (222)
complex instruction set computer (CISC) chip (218)
connecting line (216)
control unit (216)
controller card (224)
convertible tablet PC (211)
coprocessor (218)
decoding (217)
desktop system unit (210)
digital (212)
direct current (DC) (233)
direct Rambus© DRAM (Direct RDRAM) (220)
double data rate SD-DRAM (DDR SDRAM) (220)
dynamic random access (DRAM) (220)
EBCDIC (212)
E-time (217)
expansion bus (227)
expansion card (224)
executing (217)
execution time (217)
external cache (221)
fast infrared (FIR) ports (232)
fetching (217)
FireWire bus (227)
FireWire port (231)
firmware (222)
flash RAM (221)
flash memory (221)
flash memory card (227)
gigahertz (223)
graphics card (224)
graphics coprocessor (219)
handheld computer system unit (212)
high performance serial bus (HPSB) (230)
high performance serial bus (HPSB) port (231)
industry standard architecture (ISA) (227)
infrared data association (IrDA) port (232)
instruction cycle (217)
instruction time (217)
integrated circuit (215)
Intel-compatible (218)
intelligent smart card (219)
interface card (224)
internal cache (221)
internal modem (225)
I-time (217)
laptop (210)
logical operation (217)
L1 (221)
L2 (221)
L3 (221)
main board (215)
machine cycle (217)
memory (220)
memory address (220)
memory card (219)
microprocessor (216)
microsecond (217)
modem card (225)
motherboard (215)
musical instrument interface (MIDI) port (231)
nanosecond (217)
network adapter card (225)
network interface card (NIC) (225)
nonvolatile storage (220)
notebook system unit (210)
open architecture (224)
parallel port (231)
parallel processing (219)
parallel processors (219)
PC card (227)
peripheral component interconnect (PCI) (227)
Personal Computer Memory Card International Association (PCMCIA) card (227)
personal digital assistant (PDA) system unit (211)

picosecond (217)
Plug and Play (225)
plug-in board (224)
port (231)
power supply unit (233)
primary cache (221)
processor (216)
RAM address (220)
RAM cache (221)
random-access memory (RAM) (220)
read-only memory (ROM) (222)
reduced instruction set computer (RISC) chip (218)
semiconductor (215)
serial port (231)
silicon chip (215)
slate tablet PC (211)
slot (215)
small computer system interface (SCSI) port (232)
smart card (219)
socket (215)
sound card (224)
static RAM (SRAM) (221)
storing (217)
superscalar (223)
synchronous RAM (SDRAM) (220)
synthesizer (232)
system board (215)
system bus (227)
system cabinet (210)
system clock (223)
system unit (210)
tablet PC (211)
tablet PC system unit (211)
television board (225)
tower model (210)
Type I card (227)
Type II card (227)
Type III card (227)
TV tuner card (225)
two-state system (212)
unicode (213)
universal serial bus (USB) (230)
universal serial bus (USB) port (231)
video card (224)
video capture card (225)
video recorder card (225)
volatile storage (220)
virtual memory (222)
word (217)
workstation (218)

To test your knowledge of these key terms with animated flash cards, select Flash Cards from Tim's Toolbox at http://www.mhhe.com/oleary/CT05.

CHAPTER REVIEW

CROSSWORD

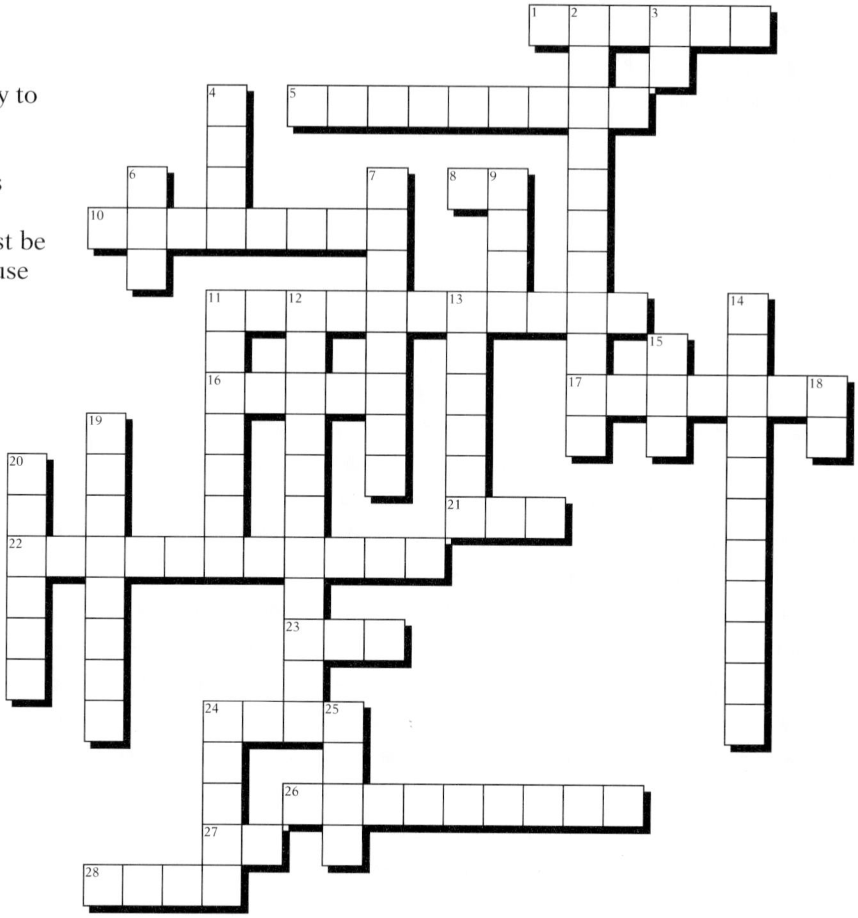

ACROSS

1 Continuous signals that vary to represent different tones, pitches, and volume
5 Carrying out the commands
8 Power from standard wall outlets or batteries that must be converted to DC power for use by computers
10 Is nonvolatile storage and controls essential system operations; also called ROM
11 Specialty chips designed to improve specific computing operations
16 The most widely used binary code for microcomputers
17 Computers can only recognize this type of electronic signal
21 Central processing unit
22 Millionths of a second
23 Network interface card
24 Complex instruction set computer chip
26 Billions of beats per second
27 Caches that use SD RAM chips located on the system board
28 Grouping of 8 bits typically representing one character

DOWN

2 Billionths of a second
3 Also know as primary cache and internal cache; is built into the microprocessor chip
4 Requires a constant supply of power to refresh and retain its contents
6 Binary digit
7 Translating instructions and data into a form that can be processed
9 Complementary metal-oxide semiconductor
11 A container that houses most of the electronic components that make up a computer system
12 Trillionths of a second
13 A binary coding scheme developed by IBM and used primarily for large computers
14 The communications medium for the entire computer system. Every component of the system unit connects to this
15 Widely used for graphics and 3-D animations, this bus is replacing the PCI bus for the transfer of video data
18 Also known as external cache; is slower than primary cache but has a greater capacity
19 Retrieving a program instruction or data element from memory
20 Temporarily holds data, instructions, and processed information; RAM, ROM, and CMOS are three types
24 Used to connect exterior devices to the system unit via the ports
25 Tiny circuit boards etched on postage-stamp-sized squares of sandlike material called silicon

For an interactive crossword puzzle select Crosswords from Tim's Toolbox at http://www.mhhe.com/oleary/CT05.

MULTIPLE CHOICE

Circle the letter or fill in the correct answer.

1. The system unit is also called the ________.
   - **a.** system cabinet
   - **b.** system board
   - **c.** system cabinet and chassis
   - **d.** chassis and system board
   - **e.** chassis
2. ________ are the most widely used handheld computer.
   - **a.** RAMs
   - **b.** Notebooks
   - **c.** PDAs
   - **d.** CPUs
   - **e.** Tower units
3. ASCII, EBCDIC, and Unicode are examples of ________.
   - **a.** two-state systems
   - **b.** integrated circuits
   - **c.** binary coding schemes
   - **d.** adapter cards
   - **e.** none of the above
4. ________ connect special cards or circuit boards to the system board.
   - **a.** Slots
   - **b.** Carrier packages
   - **c.** Unicodes
   - **d.** PC cards
   - **e.** Ports
5. Random-access memory (RAM) is a kind of ________ storage.
   - **a.** permanent
   - **b.** temporary
   - **c.** flash
   - **d.** smart
   - **e.** expansion
6. ________ chips transfer data at twice the rate of SDRAM.
   - **a.** SRAM
   - **b.** DDR RAM
   - **c.** SROM
   - **d.** ROM DR
   - **e.** Direct RDRAM
7. ROM is also known as ________.
   - **a.** semiconductor
   - **b.** slot
   - **c.** adapter
   - **d.** network
   - **e.** firmware
8. ________ is a set of hardware and software standards that allows expansion boards and other devices to install themselves.
   - **a.** Plug and Play
   - **b.** Unicode
   - **c.** System Unit
   - **d.** Industry Standard Architecture
   - **e.** none of the above
9. A(n) ________, also called a bus, connects the parts of the CPU together.
   - **a.** adapter card
   - **b.** parallel port
   - **c.** serial port
   - **d.** ISA
   - **e.** bus line
10. A(n) ________ chip provides flexibility and expandability for a computer system; it contains essential information that is required every time the computer system is turned on.
    - **a.** ROM
    - **b.** RAM
    - **c.** TCP/IP
    - **d.** CMOS
    - **e.** ALU

To test your knowledge of this chapter, select Self Test from Tim's Toolbox at http://www.mhhe.com/oleary/CT05.

MATCHING

Match each numbered item with the most closely related lettered item. Write your answers in the spaces provided.

a. analog
b. bus width
c. cables
d. cache memory
e. chip
f. CISC chip
g. closed architecture
h. control unit
i. expansion card
j. graphics coprocessor
k. instruction cycle
l. I-time
m. parallel port
n. PC card
o. port
p. RAM
q. smart card
r. system board
s. system clock
t. system unit

1. The container that houses most of the electronic components that make up a computer system. _____
2. The number of bits that can travel down a bus at the same time. _____
3. The communications web for the entire computer system. _____
4. Consists of a tiny circuit board etched on a stamp-sized square of silicon. _____
5. Tells the rest of the computer system how to carry out a program's instructions. _____
6. Type of signal created by our voices. _____
7. The most common type of microprocessor. _____
8. A plastic card, the size of a regular credit card, with an embedded chip. _____
9. Volatile storage that holds the program and the data the CPU is currently processing. _____
10. Temporary high-speed holding area between the memory and the CPU. _____
11. Produces precisely timed electrical beats used as a timing mechanism. _____
12. Machines manufactured so that users cannot easily add new devices. _____
13. Also called plug-in boards, controller cards, adapter cards, and interface cards. _____
14. Time required to fetch an instruction. _____
15. Credit card–sized expansion boards used by portable computers. _____
16. Handles computations related to graphics images. _____
17. Connecting socket on the outside of the system unit. _____
18. Connects external devices that need to send or receive a lot of data over a short distance. _____
19. Specific series of steps followed by the control unit. _____
20. Connects input and output devices to the system unit via the ports. _____

OPEN-ENDED

On a separate sheet of paper, respond to each question or statement.

1. Describe the four basic types of system units.
2. Describe the two basic components of the CPU.
3. What are the differences and similarities between the three types of memory?
4. Identify five expansion cards and describe the function of each.
5. Identify and describe four standard ports. Identify and describe three specialty ports.

NOTES

USING TECHNOLOGY

1 TV Tuner Cards and Video Clips

Want to watch your favorite television program while you work? Perhaps you would like to include a video clip in a class presentation. It's easy using a video TV card. To learn more about this technology, review Making IT Work for You: TV Tuner Cards and Video Clips on pages 228 and 229. Then visit our Web site at http://www.mhhe.com/oleary/CT05 and select Using Technology from Tim's Toolbox. Play the video and answer the following questions: (a) Describe the two windows that open when the TV icon is selected. (b) What are the basic functions of the control box? (c) What is the command sequence to insert a video clip into a PowerPoint presentation?

2 Desktop and Notebook Computers

Have you recently purchased a new computer? Are you thinking about purchasing one? The Web is an excellent source for reviewing, comparing, and purchasing computers. Visit our site at http://www.mhhe.com/oleary/CT05 and select Using Technology from Tim's Toolbox to link to several sites that present information about the newest desktop and notebook computers. Connect to these sites to check out different desktop and notebook models, and then answer the following questions: (a) If you were to purchase a desktop computer, which one would you select? Describe how it would fit your needs and print out its specifications. (b) If you were to purchase a notebook computer, which one would you select? Describe how it would fit your needs and print out its specifications. (c) If you had to choose between the desktop and notebook, which one would you choose? Defend your selection in one paragraph by discussing the relative advantages and disadvantages of each type.

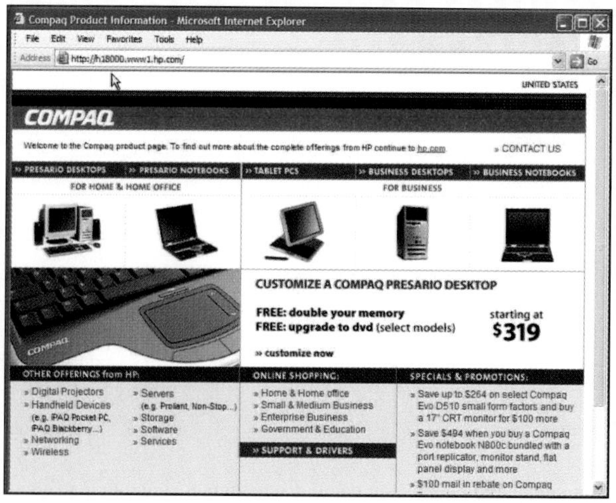

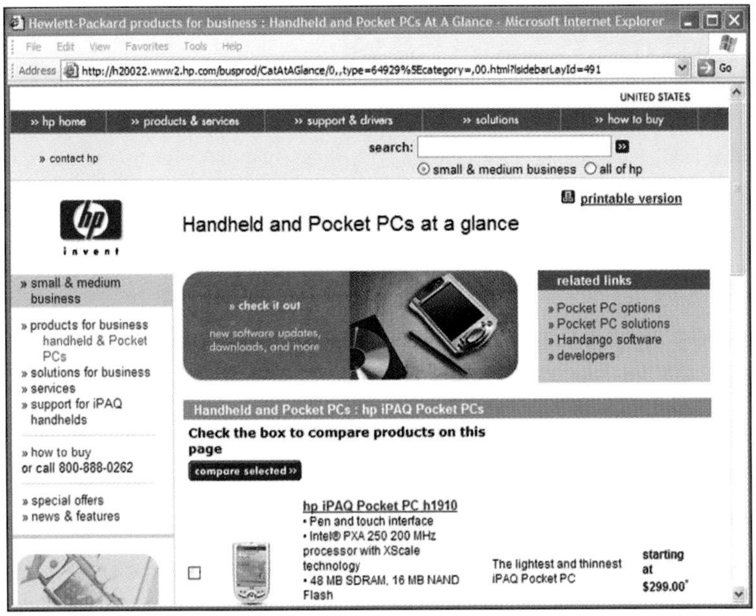

Pocket PC 3

A Pocket PC is a type of handheld computer that offers many of the same features as a desktop system, such as e-mail, Web browsing, and programs to create spreadsheets and text documents. Research Pocket PCs on the Web, and then answer the following questions: (a) What applications are available for Pocket PC that you use regularly on a desktop system? List the applications and describe how you would use them. (b) Visit the Web sites of two manufacturers of Pocket PCs. Write a product comparison by listing the following information for each: features, processor speed, memory, and price. (c) Based on your findings, if you were to purchase a Pocket PC, which would you choose? Why?

Custom System Units 4

When it is time for you to purchase your next computer, you might consider shopping online. A big advantage to choosing a computer online instead of in a store is that many computer manufacturers allow you to customize your new computer, and build it to order. Connect to the Dell Web site and use their online tools to customize and price a computer that meets your current needs. Then answer the following questions: (a) Which of the three types of system units did you configure? (b) What microprocessor did you choose? (c) How much and what type of memory option did you choose? (d) Would you purchase the computer you customized? Why or why not?

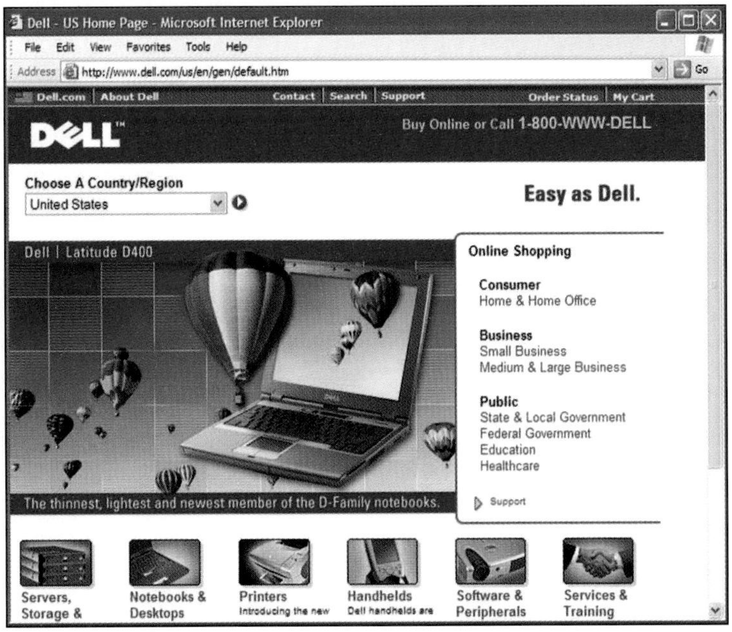

EXPANDING YOUR KNOWLEDGE

1 Computing Today CD

Typically before a program can be executed, it must be read into RAM. Many programs, however, are too large to fit into many computer systems' RAM. One option is to increase the RAM in the system. Another way is to use virtual memory. After viewing the virtual memory animation from your Computing Today CD or connecting to http://www.mhhe.com/oleary/CT05 and selecting Animations, answer the following questions: (a) What is virtual memory: (b) Define page file, page, and paging. (c) What is thrashing?

2 Expansion Cards

New or enhanced computer functionality can often be obtained with a simple hardware solution. Open architecture and Plug and Play standards make expanding microcomputer systems a much simpler task now than in the past. Expansion cards such as network adapter, modem, TV tuner and PC cards allow you to add new features easily. Select one of these categories of expansion cards and locate a specific manufacturer's card. Then answer the following: (a) Describe the specific card. (b) What are the requirements for the system unit in order to use this card? (c) How would this card add new or enhanced functionality?

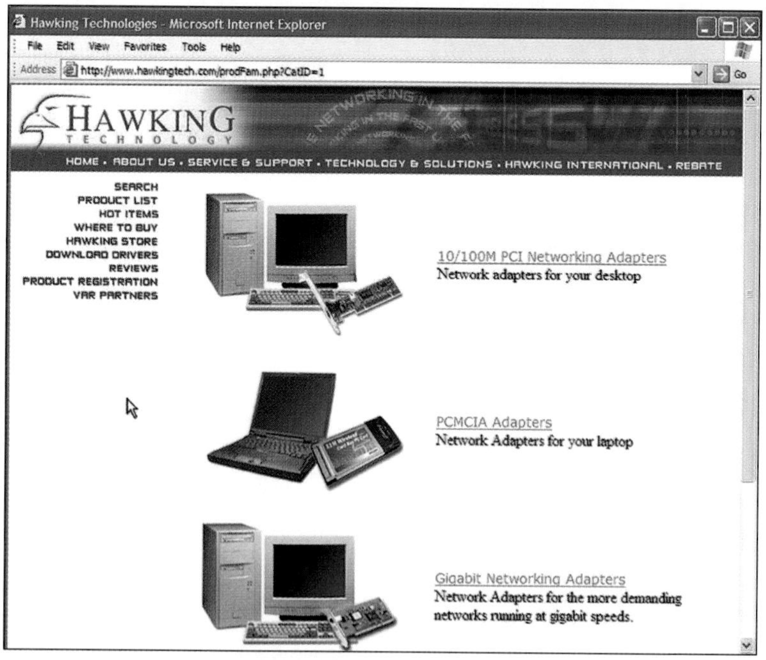

SimNet CD 3

Complete Chapter 6: The System Unit on your SimNet CD and then complete the following on a single page of paper.

a. Describe each component of the system unit.

b. Describe the most common types of buses.

c. Identify and discuss the five operations that the CPU controls.

d. What is primary difference between (1) flash memory and (2) RAM, ROM, and CMOS?

e How has clock speed changed from 1989 to 1999?

f. How are expansion cards for a desktop computer different from expansion cards for a laptop computer?

g. Describe the different types of devices that can be connected to a port.

Port Replicators 4

Port replicators allow a portable system, such as a notebook or handheld computer, to quickly connect to nonportable devices, such as printers and monitors. These nonportable devices plug in to the standard ports on the port replicator. The port replicator can be easily connected to the portable computer with a single connection. Locate a manufacturer of port replicators on the Web. Review their site, and then answer the following questions briefly: (a) Which standard ports are typically provided on a port replicator? (b) How is the replicator connected to the portable device? (c) What type of user would benefit most from a port replicator? (d) Would you use a port replicator? Why or why not?

BUILDING YOUR PORTFOLIO

1 Microprocessors

The microprocessor is the "brains" of the system unit. It has two basic components: control unit and arithmetic-logic unit. Microprocessors approximately double their speed every year and a half. New technologies make for faster chips and faster PCs. Research the latest microprocessors from industry leaders Intel, AMD, and Cyrix. Then write a one-page paper titled "Current Microprocessors" that addresses the following points: (a) Describe the chips you located. (b) How does each of these chips differ from their last generation? What improvements have been made? (c) Describe any special features that these chips offer and explain each.

2 RISC versus CISC

Both RISC and CISC architectures are widely used today, and represent two opposing philosophies of microprocessor design. Research RISC and CISC architectures on the Web or in an industry publication, and then write a one-page paper titled "RISC vs. CISC" that addresses the following topics: (a) Define RISC and CISC. (b) Describe how RISC and CISC are similar. Describe how they differ. (c) Summarize some common arguments for choosing RISC over CISC. What about for choosing CISC over RISC? (d) List some computer systems that use RISC, and some that use CISC. (e) Which architecture do you think is best? Justify your answer.

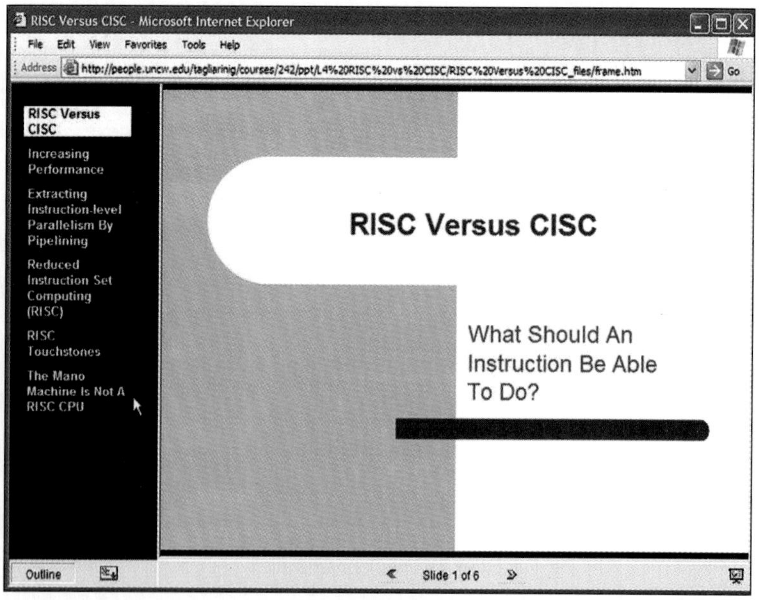

Processor Serial Numbers 3

When the Intel Pentium III microprocessor was released, each unit originally contained a unique Processor Serial Number, or PSN. This PSN could be used by online e-commerce sites to identify and to track individuals by the computer they used. This tracking would be similar to keeping track of car owners by their license plate numbers. Write a one-page paper that addresses the following items: (a) What are the benefits of a PSN for a computer user? For society? Explain your answers. (b) What privacy issues does a PSN raise for a computer user? (c) Describe how a PSN could be misused.

Smart Cards 4

There have been numerous proposals in recent years to use smart card technology for personal identification, such as driver's licenses or a national ID card. Advocates claim that this would reduce identity fraud, because the cards would contain biometric information such as a fingerprint scan. Research smart card technology on the Web, and then answer the following questions in a one-page paper: (a) What are the benefits of using smart cards for identification? List several examples. (b) What privacy concerns exist? Be specific. (c) Would you be in favor of using smart cards for personal identification? Why or why not?

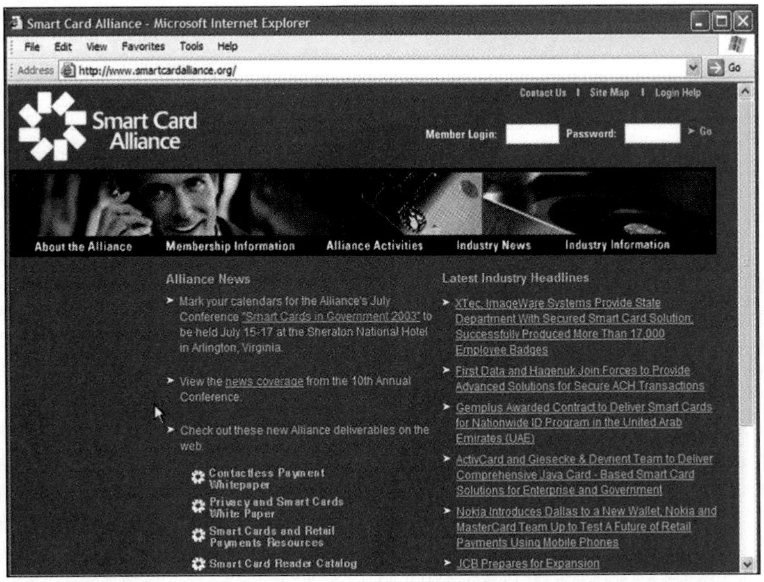

INPUT

OBJECTIVES

After you have read this chapter, you should be able to:

1. Define input.
2. Describe keyboard entry, pointing devices, and scanning devices.
3. Discuss image capturing devices.
4. Describe digitizing devices including graphics tablets and digital notebooks.
5. Discuss audio input devices for voice and music.
6. Describe assistance input devices including alternative keyboards and mice, motion capture devices, and communication aids.

Input Devices
Translate words, sounds, images, and actions that people understand into a form that the system unit can process

Touchscreen

PDA Keyboard

Digital Camera

How do you get data to the CPU? Here we describe one of the most important places where the computer interfaces with people. We input text, music, even speech, but probably never think about the relationship between what we enter and what the computer processes. People understand language, which is constructed of letters, numbers, and punctuation marks. However, computers can understand only the binary machine language of 0s and 1s. Input devices are essentially translators. Input devices translate numbers, letters, and actions that people understand into a form that computers can process.

Input devices make it possible to send words, photos, spoken words, and even music to your computer. You are already familiar with the most common input devices, like your keyboard and mouse. However, there are also many unique and specialized input devices. Some of these devices are used primarily by businesses to maintain inventory and track sales. Others are used to send music from an instrument to your computer where it can be edited, arranged, and recorded. How would you like to take digital photos, touch up your images, and share your images online? You can! All you need is a digital camera and a connection to the Internet. There are even input devices designed to make it possible for the blind to type messages in Braille.

Competent and knowledgeable end users need to know about the most commonly used input devices, including keyboards, mice, scanners, digital cameras, digitizing tablets, voice recognition devices, and MIDI. They also need to be familiar with assistive input devices like alternative keyboards and mice, motion capture devices, and communication aids.

Joystick

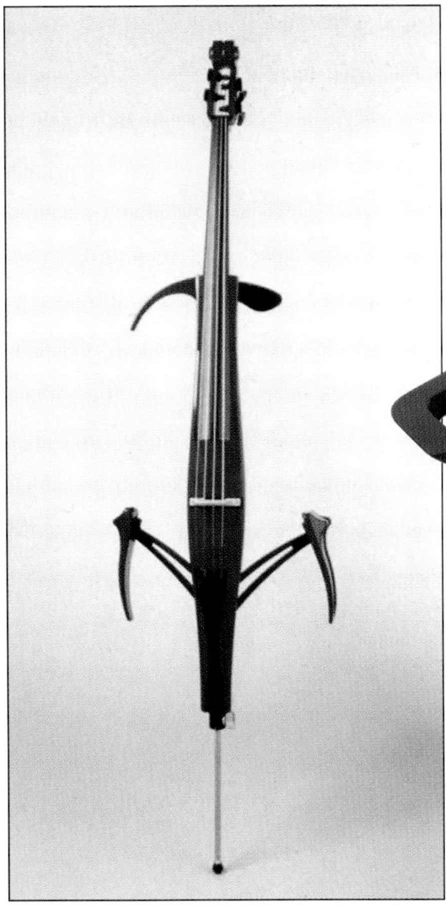

MIDI Cello

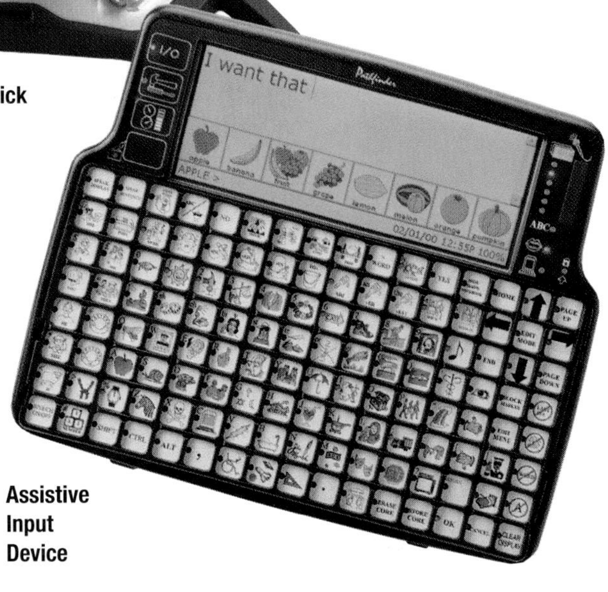

Assistive Input Device

WHAT IS INPUT?

Input consists of data and instructions. Input devices translate what people understand into a form that computers can process.

Input is any data or instructions that are used by a computer. They can come directly from you or from other sources. You provide input whenever you use system or application programs. For example, when using a word processing program, you enter data in the form of numbers and letters and issue commands such as to save and to print documents. You can also enter data and issue commands by pointing to items, using your voice, and by writing on special devices. Other sources of input include scanned or photographed images.

Input devices are hardware used to translate words, sounds, images, and actions that people understand into a form that the system unit can process. For example, when using a word processor, you typically use a keyboard to enter text and a mouse to issue commands. In addition to keyboards and mice, there are a wide variety of other input devices. (See Figure 7-1.) These include scanning, image capturing, digitizing, voice recognition, and assistive input devices.

Figure 7-1 Input devices used for fingerprint scanning, digital photography, and voice recognition.

Concept Check

- What is input?
- What are input devices?

KEYBOARD ENTRY

Keyboards translate numbers, letters, and special characters. Traditional, ergonomic, flexible, wireless, and PDA are types of keyboards. Numeric keypads, shortcuts, and toggle, combination, and programmable keys are keyboard features.

One of the most common ways to input data is by **keyboard.** As mentioned in Chapter 6, keyboards convert numbers, letters, and special characters that people understand into electrical signals. These signals are sent to, and processed by, the system unit. Most keyboards use an arrangement of keys given the name QWERTY. This name reflects the keyboard layout by taking the letters of the first six alphabetic characters found on the fourth row of keys.

Figure 7-2 Flexible keyboard

KEYBOARDS

There are a wide variety of different keyboard designs. They range from the full-sized to miniature and from rigid to flexible. The most common types are:

- **Traditional keyboards**—full-sized, rigid, rectangular keyboards that include function, navigational, and numeric keys.
- **Flexible keyboards**—fold or roll up for easy packing or storage. They are designed to provide mobile users with a full-sized keyboard with minimal storage requirements. (See Figure 7-2.)
- **Ergonomic keyboards**—similar to traditional keyboards. The keyboard arrangement, however, is not rectangular and a palm rest is provided. They are designed specifically to alleviate wrist strain associated with the repetitive movements of typing. (See Figure 7-3.)
- **Wireless keyboards**—transmit input to the system unit through the air. By eliminating connecting wires to the system unit, these keyboards provide greater flexibility and convenience.
- **PDA keyboards**—miniature keyboards for PDAs for sending e-mail, creating documents, and more. (See Figure 7-4.)

On the Web Explorations

Logitech is one of the leading ergonomic keyboard manufacturers. To learn more about the company visit our Web site at http://www.mhhe.com/oleary/CT05 and select On the Web Explorations from Tim's Toolbox.

FEATURES

A computer keyboard combines a typewriter keyboard with a **numeric keypad,** used to enter numbers and arithmetic symbols. It also has many special-purpose keys. Some keys such as the Caps Lock key are **toggle keys.** These keys turn a feature on or off. Others such as the *Ctrl* key are **combination keys,** which perform an action when held down in combination with another key. Combination keys are commonly used to perform keyboard shortcuts. **Keyboard shortcuts** allow you to use the keyboard to issue commands rather than selecting items from a menu(s). For example, Ctrl + P, is a keyboard shortcut used to print a document in Word. See Figure 7-5 for a list of commonly used keyboard shortcuts. Many keyboards also include **programmable keys,** which connect you to your favorite Web sites or perform tasks on your computer. To learn more about keyboard features see Figure 7-6.

Figure 7-3 Ergonomic keyboard

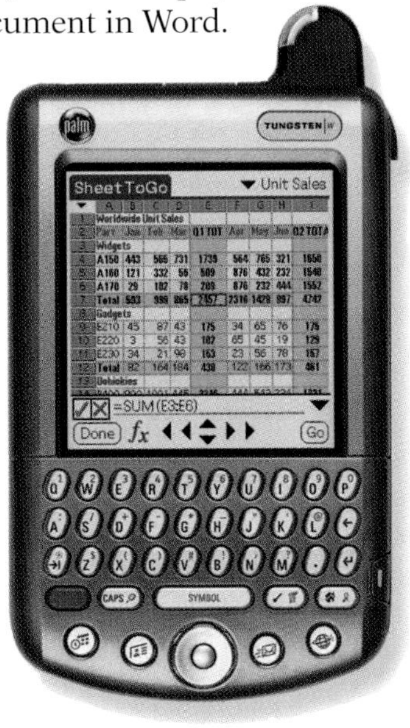

Figure 7-4 PDA with keyboard

Concept Check

- What is a QWERTY keyboard?
- What are some common keyboard features?
- Discuss the five common types of keyboard designs.

Keyboard Shortcut	Command
Ctrl + C	copy
Ctrl + F	find
Ctrl + P	print
Ctrl + S	save
Ctrl + V	paste

Figure 7-5 Common keyboard shortcuts

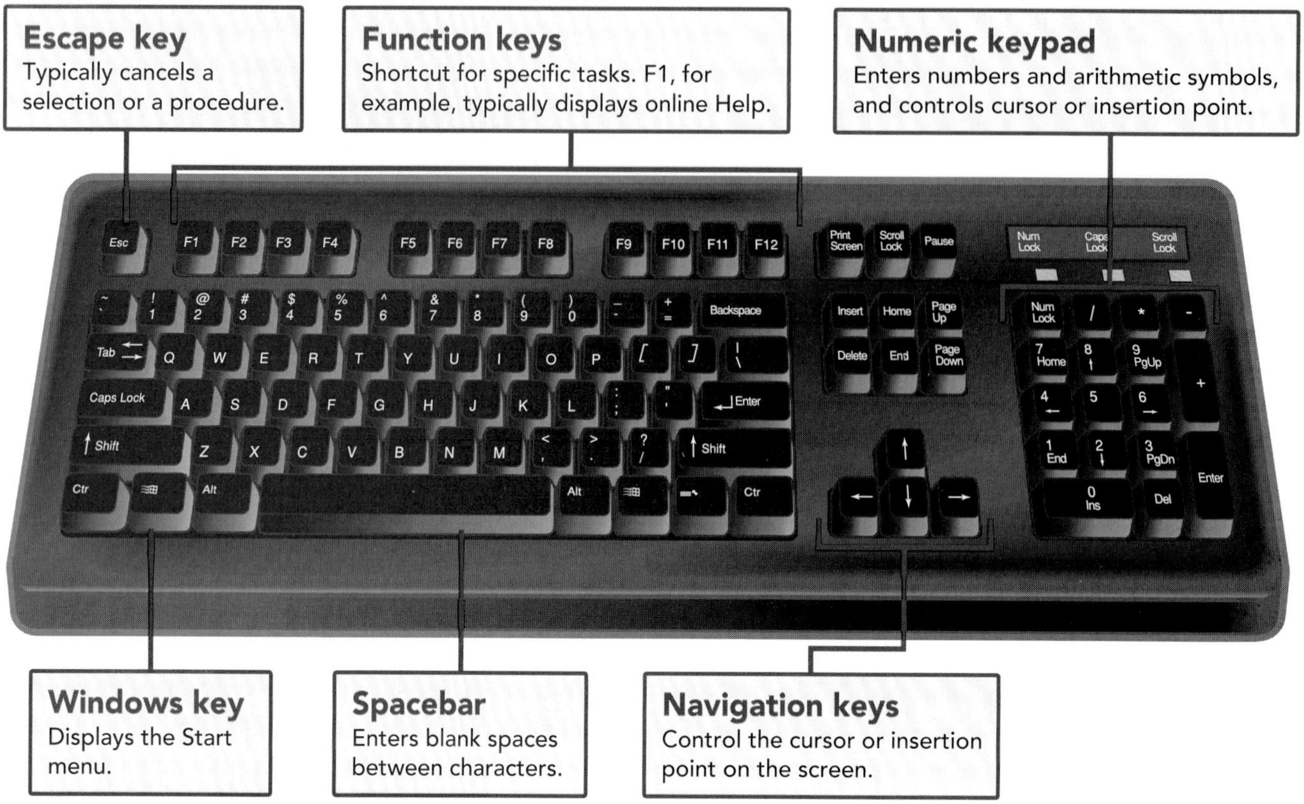
Escape key
Typically cancels a selection or a procedure.
Function keys
Shortcut for specific tasks. F1, for example, typically displays online Help.
Numeric keypad
Enters numbers and arithmetic symbols, and controls cursor or insertion point.
Windows key
Displays the Start menu.
Spacebar
Enters blank spaces between characters.
Navigation keys
Control the cursor or insertion point on the screen.

Figure 7-6 Traditional keyboard

POINTING DEVICES

A mouse controls a pointer on the monitor. Joysticks are used primarily for games. Touch screens are pressure-sensitive monitors. Light pens close circuits on special monitors. Tablet PCs and PDAs use styluses.

Pointing, of course, is one of the most natural of all human gestures. **Pointing devices** provide a comfortable interface with the system unit, by accepting pointing gestures and converting them into machine-readable input. There are a wide variety of different pointing devices including the mouse, joystick, touch screen, light pen, and stylus.

MOUSE

A **mouse** controls a pointer that is displayed on the monitor. The **mouse pointer** usually appears in the shape of an arrow. It frequently changes shape, however, depending on the application. A mouse can have one, two, or more buttons, which are used to select command options and to control the mouse pointer on the monitor. Some mice have a **wheel button** that can be rotated to scroll through information that is displayed on the monitor. Although there are several different mouse types, there are three basic designs:

- **Mechanical mouse** is generally considered the traditional type and is currently the most widely used. It has a ball on the bottom and is attached with a cord to the system unit. As you move the mouse across a smooth surface, or **mouse pad,** the roller rotates and controls the pointer on the screen. (See Figure 7-7.)

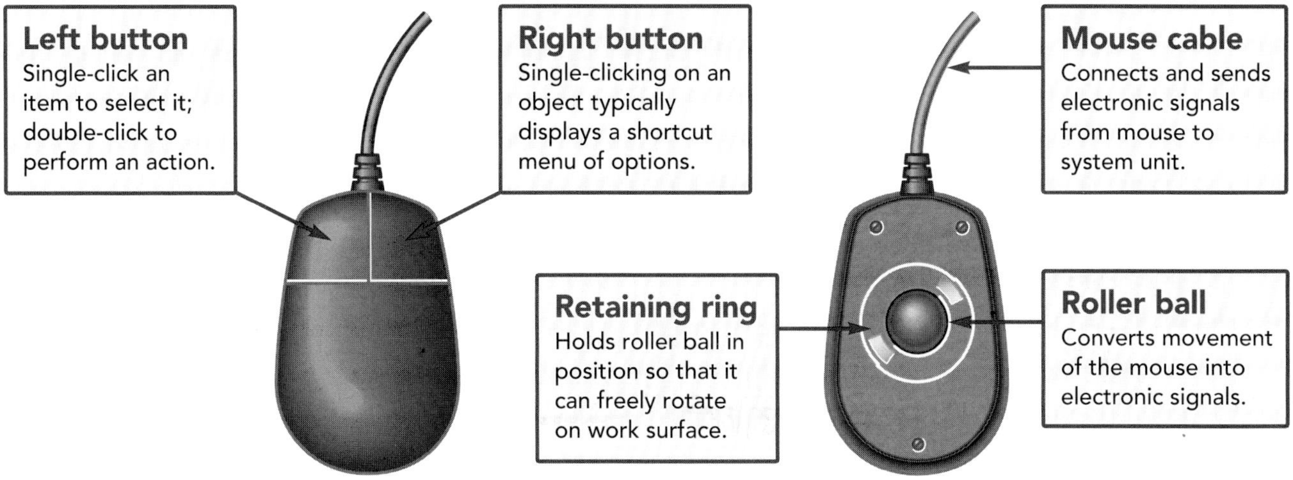
Left button
Single-click an item to select it; double-click to perform an action.
Right button
Single-clicking on an object typically displays a shortcut menu of options.
Mouse cable
Connects and sends electronic signals from mouse to system unit.
Retaining ring
Holds roller ball in position so that it can freely rotate on work surface.
Roller ball
Converts movement of the mouse into electronic signals.

Figure 7-7 Standard mouse

- **Optical mouse** has no moving parts. It emits and senses light to detect mouse movement. This newer type of mouse has some advantages compared to the mechanical mouse: it can be used on any surface, is more precise, and does not require periodic cleaning. (See Figure 7-8.)
- **Cordless** or **wireless mouse** is a battery-powered device that typically uses radio waves or infrared light waves to communicate with the system unit. These devices eliminate the mouse cord and free up desk space.

Three devices similar to a mouse are trackballs, touch surfaces, and pointing sticks. You can use the **trackball,** also known as the **roller ball, t**o control the pointer by rotating a ball with your thumb. You can use **touch surfaces,** or **touch pads,** to control the pointer by moving and tapping your finger on the surface of a pad. (See Figure 7-9.) You can use a **pointing stick,** located in the middle of the keyboard, to control the pointer by directing the stick with your finger.

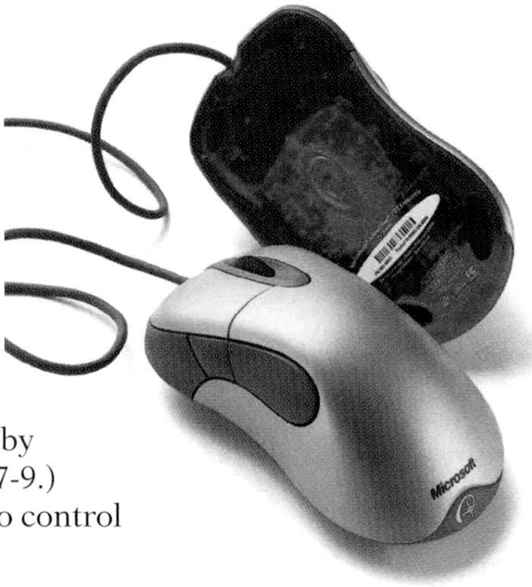

Figure 7-8 Optical mouse

Trackball

Touch Surface

Pointing Stick

Figure 7-9 Devices similar to a mouse

TIPS Are you left-handed? Do you struggle to use a mouse with your right-hand? Or would you just like to use the mouse with your left-hand to free up your right-hand? Here is a tip to easily switch the button functions on your mouse if you use Windows XP:

1. Click *Start/Control Panel* and select *Printers and Other Hardware.*
2. Choose *Mouse* from the *Control Panel Icons* list.
3. Choose the settings you would like for each of the mouse buttons from the drop-down windows.
4. Click *OK.*
5. Test your new mouse functions.

Windows XP's User Accounts make it possible to maintain these mouse settings in your profile.

JOYSTICK

A **joystick** is the most popular input device for computer games. You control game actions by varying the pressure, speed, and direction of the joystick. Additional controls such as buttons and triggers are used to specify commands or initiate specific actions. (See Figure 7-10.)

TOUCH SCREEN

A **touch screen** is a particular kind of monitor with a clear plastic outer layer. Behind this layer are crisscrossed invisible beams of infrared light. This arrangement enables someone to select actions or commands by touching the screen with a finger. Touch screens are easy to use, especially when people need information quickly. They are commonly used at restaurants, automated teller machines (ATMs), and information centers. (See Figure 7-11.)

LIGHT PEN

A **light pen** is a light-sensitive pen-like device. The light pen is placed against the monitor. This closes a photoelectric circuit and identifies the spot for entering or modifying data. For example, light pens are used to edit digital images. (See Figure 7-12.)

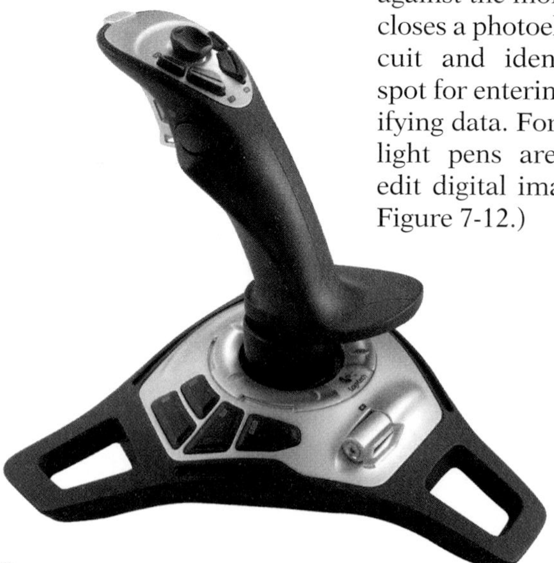

Figure 7-10 A cordless joystick used for computer games

Figure 7-11 A touch screen: a consumer application

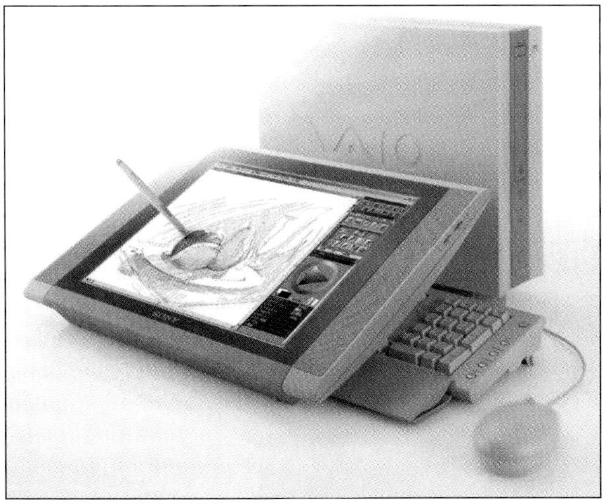

Figure 7-12 A home application of a light pen

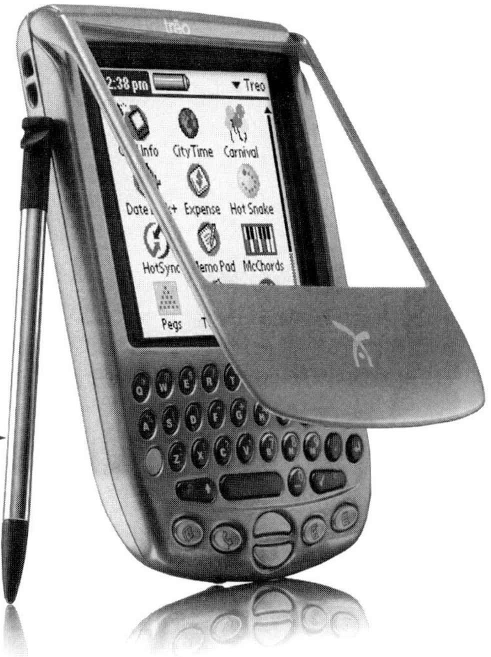

Figure 7-13 Stylus

STYLUS

A **stylus** is a pen-like device commonly used with tablet PCs and PDAs. A stylus uses pressure to draw images on a screen. A stylus interacts with the computer through handwriting recognition software. **Handwriting recognition software** translates handwritten notes into a form that the system unit can process. (See Figure 7-13.)

Concept Check

- What is a pointing device?
- Discuss five pointing devices.
- Describe the three basic mouse designs.

SCANNING DEVICES

Optical scanners copy or reproduce text and images. Bar code readers identify and price products. Character and mark recognition devices recognize special characters and marks.

Scanners move across text and images. **Scanning devices** convert scanned text and images into a form that the system unit can process. There are three types of scanning devices: optical scanners, bar code readers, and character and mark recognition devices.

OPTICAL SCANNERS

An **optical scanner,** also known simply as a **scanner,** accepts documents consisting of text and/or images and converts them to machine readable form. These devices do not recognize individual letters or images. Rather, they recognize light, dark, and colored areas that make up individual letters or images. Typically, scanned documents are saved in files that can be further processed, displayed, printed, or stored for later use. There are two basic types of scanners: flatbed and portable. (See Figure 7-14.)

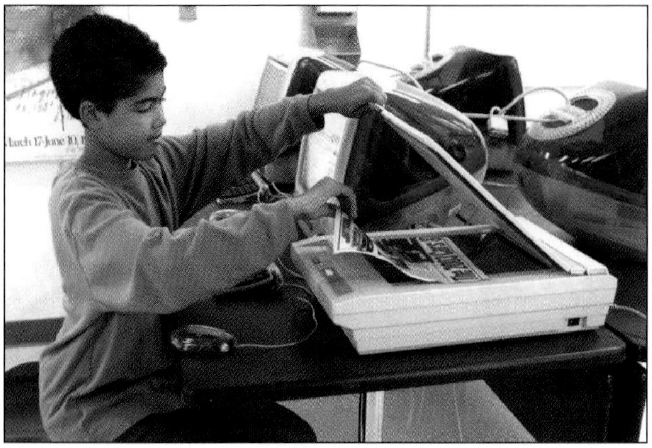

Flatbed scanner

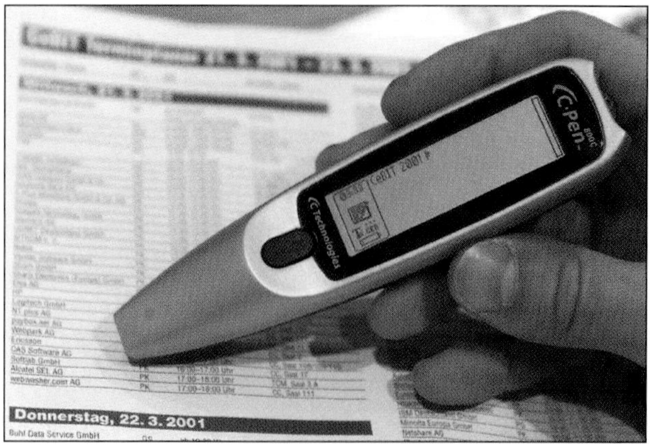

Portable scanner

Figure 7-14 Two types of scanners

- **Flatbed scanner** is much like a copy machine. The image to be scanned is placed on a glass surface and the scanner records the image from below.
- **Portable scanner** is typically a handheld device that slides across the image, making direct contact.

Optical scanners are powerful tools for a wide variety of end users including graphics and advertising professionals who scan images and combine them with text. Lawyers and students use portable scanners as a valuable research tool to record information.

BAR CODE READERS

You are probably familiar with **bar code readers** or **scanners** from grocery stores. (See Figure 7-15.) These devices are either handheld **wand readers** or **platform scanners.** They contain photoelectric cells that scan or read **bar codes,** or the vertical zebra-striped marks printed on product containers.

Figure 7-15 A bar code reader is used to record product codes

Almost all supermarkets use electronic cash registers and a bar code system called the **Universal Product Code (UPC).** At the checkout counter, electronic cash registers use a bar code reader to scan each product's UPC code. The codes are sent to the supermarket's computer, which has a description, latest price, and inventory level for each product. The computer processes this input to update the inventory level and to provide the electronic cash register with the description and price for each product. These devices are so easy to use that many supermarkets are offering customers self-checkout stations.

CHARACTER AND MARK RECOGNITION DEVICES

Character and **mark recognition devices** are scanners that are able to recognize special characters and marks. They are specialty devices that are essential tools for certain applications. Three types are:

- **Magnetic-ink character recognition (MICR)**—used by banks to automatically read those unusual numbers on the bottom of checks and deposit slips. A special-purpose machine known as a **reader/sorter** reads these numbers and provides input that allows banks to efficiently maintain customer account balances.
- **Optical-character recognition (OCR)**—uses special preprinted characters that can be read by a light source and changed into machine-readable

code. A common OCR device is the handheld wand reader discussed above. (See Figure 7-16.) These are used in department stores to read retail price tags by reflecting light on the printed characters.

- **Optical-mark recognition (OMR)** is also called **mark sensing.** An OMR device senses the presence or absence of a mark, such as a pencil mark. OMR is often used to score multiple-choice tests such as the College Board's Scholastic Aptitude Test (SAT) and the Graduate Record Examination (GRE).

Figure 7-16 A wand reader is used to record product codes

Concept Check

- How are pointing and scanning devices different?
- Describe three types of scanners.
- Describe three common character and mark recognition devices.

IMAGE CAPTURING DEVICES

Digital cameras capture still images. Digital video cameras capture motion. WebCams are specialized digital video cameras.

Optical scanners like traditional copy machines can make a copy from an original. For example, an optical scanner can make a digital copy of a photograph. **Image capturing devices,** on the other hand, create or capture original images. These devices include digital cameras and digital video cameras.

DIGITAL CAMERA

Digital cameras are similar to traditional cameras except that images are recorded digitally on a disk or in the camera's memory rather than on film, and then **downloaded,** or transferred to, your computer. (See Figure 7-17.) You can take a picture, view it immediately, and even place it on your own Web page, within minutes.

To learn more about how digital photography works see Figure 7-18. Also consult your Computing Today CD or visit us on the Web at http://www.mhhe.com/oleary/CT05 and select Animations from Tim's Toolbox. Digital photographs can be easily shared with others over the Internet. (See Making IT Work for You: Digital Photography on pages 264 and 265.)

Computing Today CD

DIGITAL VIDEO CAMERA

Unlike traditional video cameras, **digital video cameras** record motion digitally on a disk or in the camera's memory. Most have the capability to take still images as well. **WebCams (Web cameras)** are specialized digital video cameras that capture images and send them to a computer for broadcast over the Internet. WebCams have become increasing popular with individuals for video conferencing. (See Figure 7-19.)

Figure 7-17 A digital camera

How Digital Cameras Work

Step 1: Capture. Operating much like a conventional camera, a picture is taken. Unlike a conventional camera, the image is not captured on film. Rather the image is focused onto an analog electronic image capturing device such as a CCD (charge coupled device). This device captures the image on a grid of light-sensitive cells called pixels. Each pixel captures a small part of the entire image. The number of pixels indicates the clarity or resolution of the captured image.

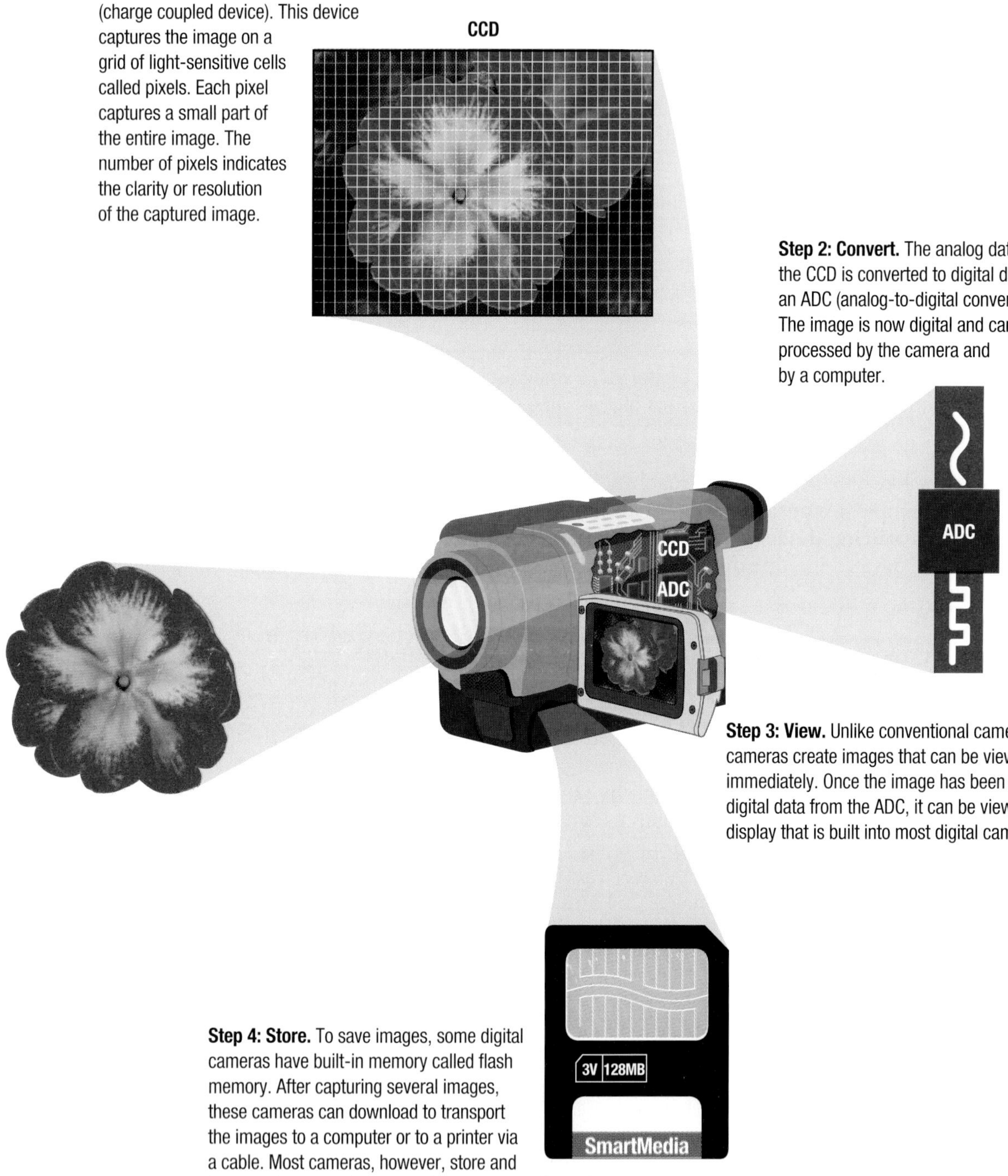

Step 2: Convert. The analog data from the CCD is converted to digital data using an ADC (analog-to-digital converter) device. The image is now digital and can be further processed by the camera and by a computer.

Step 3: View. Unlike conventional cameras, digital cameras create images that can be viewed almost immediately. Once the image has been converted to digital data from the ADC, it can be viewed using a display that is built into most digital cameras.

Step 4: Store. To save images, some digital cameras have built-in memory called flash memory. After capturing several images, these cameras can download to transport the images to a computer or to a printer via a cable. Most cameras, however, store and transport images using removable storage media such as SmartMedia cards or CompactFlash memory cards.

Figure 7-18 How digital cameras work

TIPS

Are you having trouble getting the kind of photos you want with a digital camera? Would you like to make the most of digital technology in your photos? Here are some tips to help you get started:

1. **Buttons and Knobs.** Get to know the functions of your camera before you begin. Most cameras have an automatic mode, but be sure you know how to turn on the flash, zoom the lens, and set the image resolution.
2. **Photography Basics.** Many digital cameras have an LCD screen on the back. You can use it to help frame your shots more accurately. Just be aware that using the LCD screen uses more battery power.
3. **Red-eye Reduction.** Many digital cameras have a red-eye reduction feature. When photographing people in low light, you can use this setting to eliminate glassy red-eyes in photos. Consult your owner's manual to learn more about this feature.

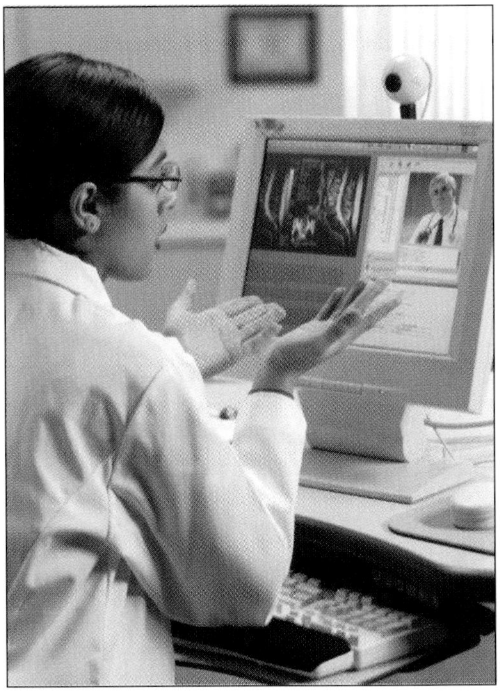

Figure 7-19 A WebCam

Concept Check

- What is the difference between scanning and image capturing?
- How are digital cameras different from traditional cameras?
- What is a WebCam?

DIGITIZING DEVICES

Graphics tablets record sketches and tracings of maps and other drawings. Digital notebooks record handwritten notes and drawings.

Digitizing devices convert a sketch or figure into a form that can be processed by a computer. Similar to slate tablet PCs, these devices have some type of flat surface and a writing device. As the user moves the writing device across the surface, the digitizing device records the movement as a series of points and sends this information to the computer. Two widely used digitizing devices are graphics tablets and digital notebooks.

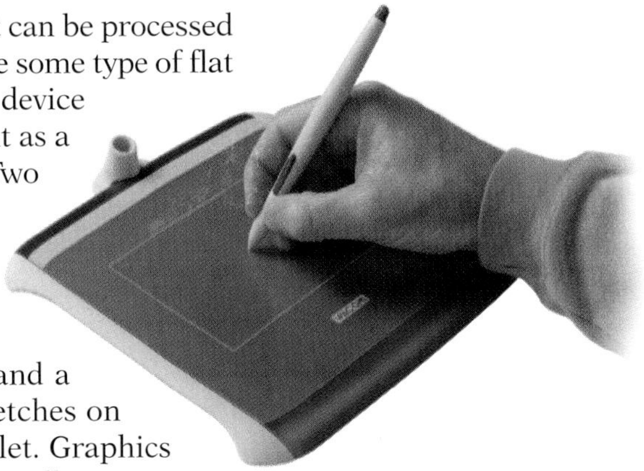

Figure 7-20 A graphics tablet

GRAPHICS TABLETS

Graphics tablets use a special graphics surface or tablet and a special stylus or pen-like device. Either the user directly sketches on the tablet or traces images that have been placed on the tablet. Graphics tablets are very specialized devices used by artists for creating illustrations, by mapmakers to record or trace maps, and by engineers to digitally save mechanical drawings. (See Figure 7-20.)

DIGITAL NOTEBOOKS

Digital notebooks are similar to tablet PCs except that they typically use regular notepads and pens. The notepad is positioned on top of an electronic pad or tablet. Using a regular pen, the user takes notes and creates drawings on the notepad. The underlying electronic pad records the movements. Students and business people frequently use these devices to record class or meeting notes. These notes can later be processed, edited, and used with a word processing program. (See Figure 7-21.)

On the Web Explorations

The Cross Pen Computing Group is a leader in developing digital notebooks. To learn more about the company, visit our Web site at http://www.mhhe.com/oleary/CT05 and select On the Web Explorations from Tim's Toolbox.

MAKING IT WORK FOR YOU

DIGITAL PHOTOGRAPHY

Digital photos are a great way to share your life with friends and family. Digital cameras are now available at very reasonable prices. With a digital camera and some special software, you can edit your photos on your computer and share them with anyone over the Internet.

Transferring Your Photos After you've taken some pictures with your digital camera, you'll want to transfer them to your computer for editing and storage. Most cameras come with software for transferring pictures. For example, using a Kodak EasyShare camera and software, you can transfer your photos with the following steps:

1

- **Connect your camera to your computer as appropriate for your model.**
- **Launch the *Kodak Picture Software* application.**
- **Click the *Get Pictures* button.**
- **Select pictures from your camera or hard drive in the dialog box that appears.**
- **Click *OK*.**

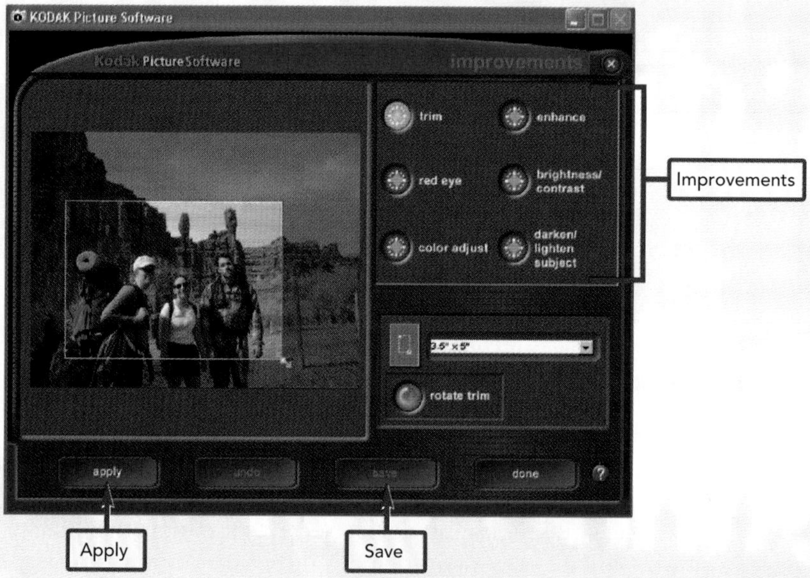

Toughing-up Your Images After you've transferred your photos to your computer, you'll want to view them. You can easily correct small imperfections such as red eye or blurriness and trim your photos to size. For example, to touch up a photo using Kodak Picture Software:

2

- **Click the *Modify* button, and then click *Improvements.***
- **Select improvements such as "color adjust" or "red eye".**
- **Click *Apply* to see an improvement.**
- **Click *Save* to save the photo with the improvement, or *Undo* to restore it.**

Sharing Your Pictures Once your photos have been touched up, you may want to share them with family and friends. One of the simplest ways to do this is by sending your photos in an e-mail message. To send a photo directly from Kodak Picture Software:

3

- **Click *Email* from the main screen.**
- **Type your e-mail address in the *from* box and addresses of friends and family in the *to* box.**
- **Type a subject in the *subject* box and a text message to accompany the photos in the *message* box.**
- **Choose images to send from the Thumbnail Viewer by clicking on them.**

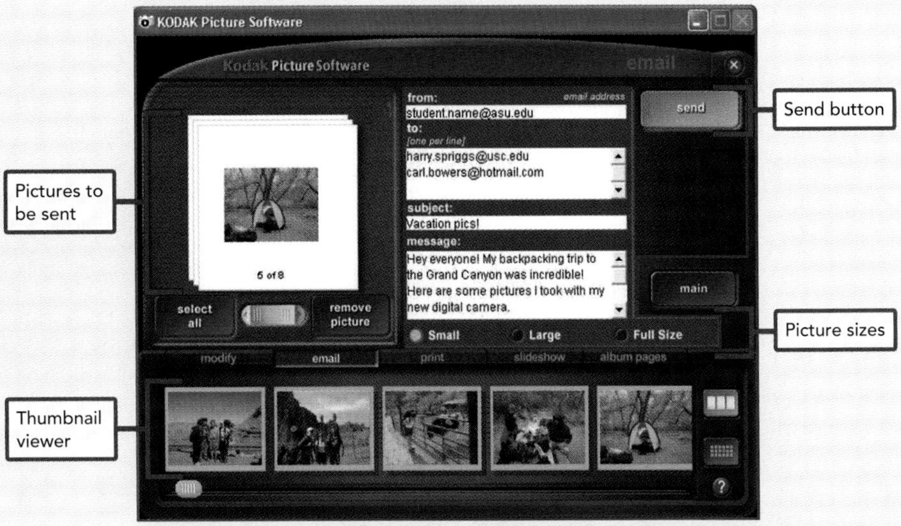

- **Select the sizing for the images to send. Note: Larger sizes are higher quality, but also make larger e-mails. Some Internet services limit e-mail sizes that can be sent or received.**
- **Click the *Send* button.**

The Web is constantly changing and some of the specifics presented in this Making IT Work for You may have changed. To learn about other ways to make information technology work for you, visit our Web site at http://www.mhhe.com/oleary/CT05 and select Making IT Work for You from Tim's Toolbox. You can also share photos on the Internet in an online album. See the Personal Web Sites Making IT Work on page 138 to find out how.

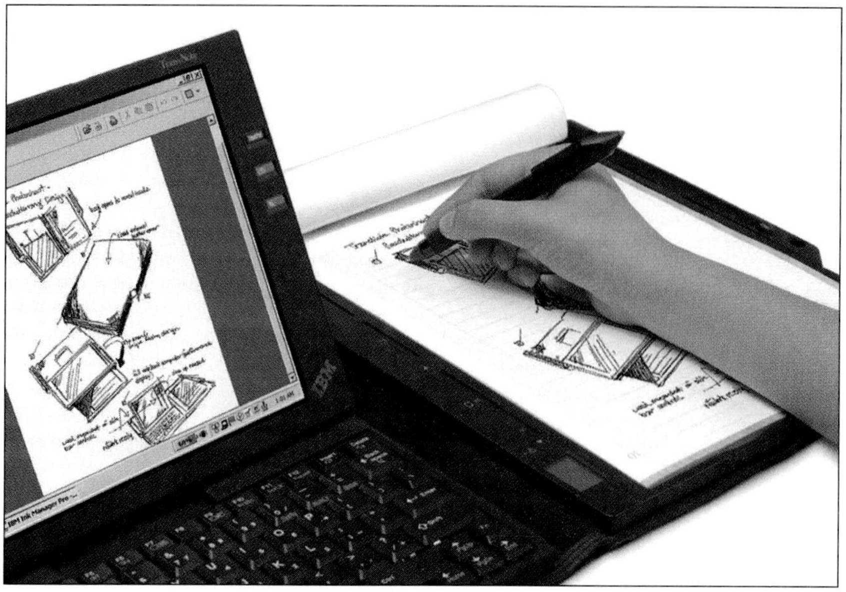

Figure 7-21 A digital notebook

Concept Check

- What are digitizing devices?
- What is a graphics tablet?
- What is a digital notebook?

AUDIO INPUT DEVICES

Audio input devices convert sounds for processing. Voice recognition systems accept voice commands to control computer operations and to create documents. MIDI is a standard for connecting musical instruments to the system unit.

Audio input devices convert sounds into a form that can be processed by the system unit. By far the most widely used audio-input device is the microphone. **Audio input** can take many forms including the human voice and music.

VOICE

Voice recognition systems use a microphone, a sound card, and special software. These systems allow users to operate computers and to create documents using voice commands. (See Figure 7-22.) Portable voice recognition systems are widely used by doctors, lawyers, and others to record dictation. (See Figure 7-23.) These devices are able to record for several hours before connecting to a computer system to edit, store, and print the dictated information. Some systems are even able to translate dictation from one language to another, such as from English to Japanese.

There are two types of voice recognition systems: discrete-speech recognition systems and continuous-speech recognition systems.

Figure 7-22 A voice recognition system: a business application

Figure 7-23 A portable voice recognition system

- **Discrete-speech recognition systems** are able to recognize individual words based on their sound. They cannot, however, distinguish between same-sound words such as *there, their,* and *they're.* This limitation requires users to review captured dictation and make corrections.
- **Continuous-speech recognition systems** are able to distinguish between same-sounding words by evaluating the context within which individual words are used. These systems are considered to be one of the key technologies for the 21st century. Two well-known systems are NaturallySpeaking from Dragon Systems and ViaVoice from IBM.

On the Web Explorations

Dragon Soft is a leader in developing continuous-speech systems. To learn more about the company, visit our Web site at http://www.mhhe.com/oleary/CT05 and select On the Web Explorations from Tim's Toolbox.

As we discussed in Chapter 3, voice recognition is a common feature with many of today's newest software applications. For example, Microsoft's Word 2003 supports voice recognition. Using Word 2003's **Language bar,** you can switch between voice command mode and dictation mode. (See Figure 7-24.)

- **Voice command mode** allows the user to select menu items, toolbars, and dialog box options. For example, to specify the use of the Times New Roman font requires the command sequence:

  Format>Font>Times New Roman>OK

  You could issue this command using a mouse or you could use a microphone and state:

  "Format font Times New Roman OK"

- **Dictation mode** allows the user to dictate text directly into a Word document. For example, consider the following sentence:

  The national economy showed rapid growth.

  You could enter this text using a keyboard or you could use a microphone and state:

  "The national economy showed rapid growth"

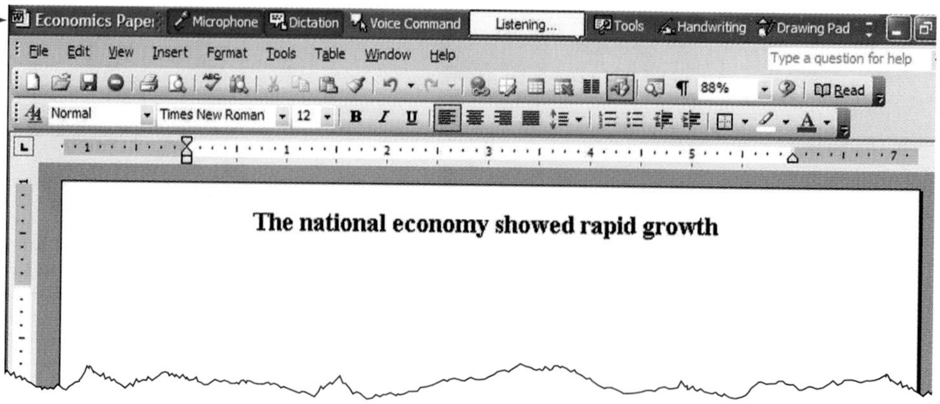

Figure 7-24 Microsoft Word 2003 voice recognition

MUSIC

Musical Interface Digital Interface or **MIDI** is a standard that allows musical instruments to connect to the system unit using MIDI ports as discussed in Chapter 6. **MIDI devices** are specialized musical instruments that provide input in the form of encoded digital signals representing musical sounds. MIDI devices can be used to create, record, and play back musical compositions. The most commonly used MIDI device is an electronic keyboard. Others include MIDI violins, guitars, and even cellos. (See Figure 7-25.)

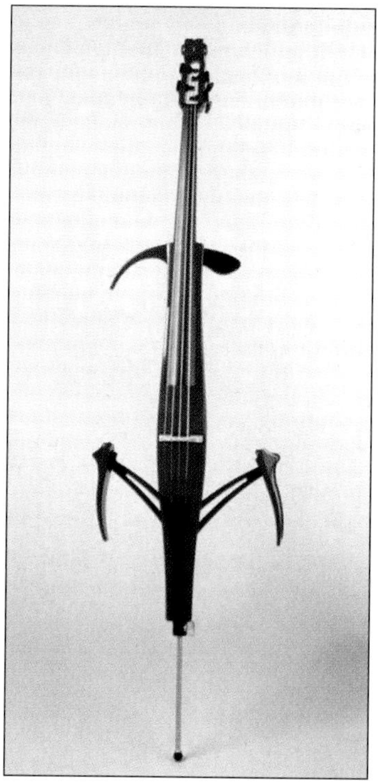

Figure 7-25 Yamaha MIDI Silent Cello

Concept Check

- Describe voice recognition systems.
- What is the difference between discrete-speech and continuous-speech recognition systems?
- What is MIDI? What are some common MIDI devices?

ASSISTIVE INPUT DEVICES

Assistive input devices allow people with disabilities to access computers and the Internet. Alternative keyboards and alternative mice allow those with limited mobility to enter input and issue commands. Motion capture devices and communication devices track movement and control computer operations.

Assistive devices, or **accessibility hardware,** allows those with visual or other physical impairments to use computers and access the Internet. Some assistive devices are specifically designed for the disabled. Other assistive devices use standard devices that have been adapted with specialized software and hardware. For example, voice recognition systems are combined with special programs that read screen content and allow input based on the user's head movements.

On the Web Explorations

Freedom Scientific is a leading developer of assistive input devices. To learn more about the company, visit our Web site at http://www.mhhe.com/oleary/CT05 and select On the Web Explorations from Tim's Toolbox.

ALTERNATIVE KEYBOARDS

Alternative keyboards are designed to allow those with limited mobility to enter data and text. There are many different types of alternative keyboards, each designed to meet the special needs of a different group. For example,

Figure 7-26 Maltron "Single-Hand" keyboard

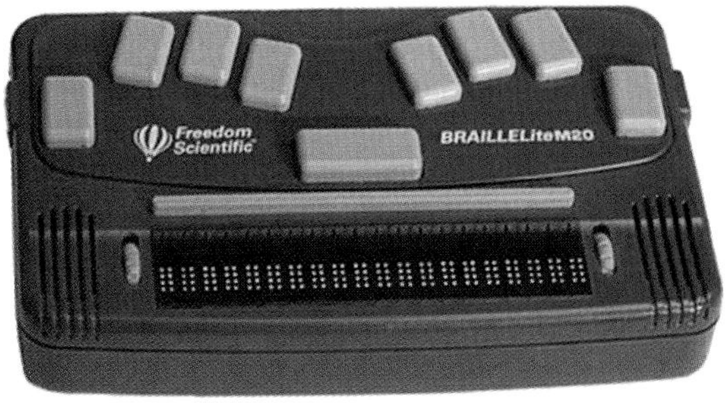

Figure 7-27 Braille Lite M20 keyboard

there are **large print keyboards** for those who have limited eyesight. There are **one-handed keyboards,** which feature a contoured arrangement of the keys for use with a single hand. (See Figure 7-26.) **Braille keyboards** use keys identified by raised dots. For example, the Braille Lite M20 keyboard uses eight braille keys. (See Figure 7-27.)

ALTERNATIVE MOUSE

Various pointing devices have been adapted or redesigned for use by the disabled. Joysticks, trackballs, touch pads, and touch screens are often modified for assistive input. However, there are also specifically designed devices. For example, some **alternative mouse** devices accept foot and/or head movements to control the mouse pointer and to select commands.

MOTION CAPTURE DEVICES

Motion capture devices are designed to follow the movements of a disabled individual and translate those movements into commands the computer can process. These input devices allow users with limited mobility to interact with a computer. One motion capture method, called **head tracking,** records head movements and uses these movements to enter data and to issue commands. A similar method tracks eye movements and eye blinks.

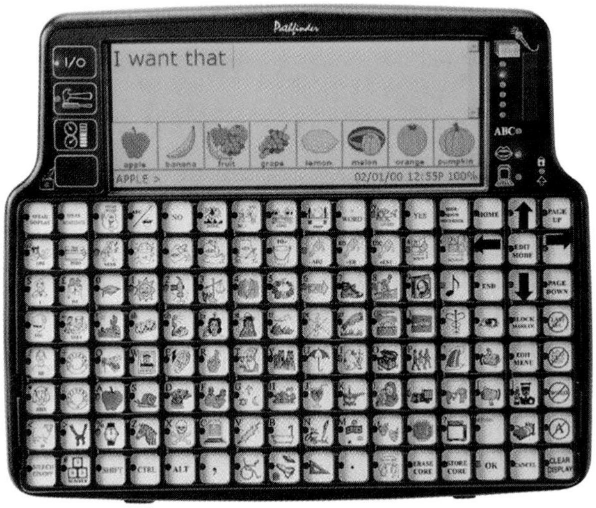

Figure 7-28 Pathfinder is a common communication device

COMMUNICATION AIDS

Communication aids use a combination of strategies to allow disabled individuals to interact with a computer and with others. Such input devices may incorporate pictures and symbols and can be programmed with spoken words and phrases. For example, the Pathfinder communication aid is a keyboard with pictures that when selected speak preprogrammed phrases. It also includes a touch screen and works with a head tracking device. (See Figure 7-28.)

Concept Check

- What is an assistive device?
- Discuss alternative keyboards and mice.
- What is a motion capture device? What are communication aids?

Careers in IT

Data Entry

Data entry workers input customer information, lists, and other types of data. Input devices are typically limited to keyboards, mice, and scanners. Because the accuracy of recorded data is so important, data entry workers are often required to verify the accuracy of data they and others have entered. Many of the tasks previously performed by data entry personnel have been automated, and the overall demand for this occupation is expected to decrease slightly. However, the demand for data entry professionals with up-to-date technical skills is expected to remain constant for the near future.

Data entry workers are expected to have a high school diploma and word processing skills. Prior experience in data entry or word processing is preferred. In order to remain marketable data entry workers must constantly update their skills and remain familiar with the latest software and hardware.

Data entry workers can expect to earn an annual salary of $20,000 to $30,000. Opportunities for advancement typically include supervisory positions, administrative positions, or transfer to other clerical positions. To learn about other careers in information technology visit us at http://www.mhhe.com/oleary/CT05 and select Careers in IT from Tim's Toolbox.

A Look to the Future

Neural Signals Inc. Creates Brain-Machine Interface

What if you could move your mouse simply by thinking about doing it? What if paralyzed people could control a wheelchair with their thoughts? These kinds of activities were previously thought to belong in the realm of science fiction. But today, researchers have already begun human trials of technology that allows humans to control machines with their thoughts. By accessing the part of the brain that controls motion and recording the electrical signals, scientists have allowed individuals without speech or motor control to "speak" using a computer cursor. What if this technology were developed enough to control prosthetic limbs? Will the human mind someday be able to directly control machines with thoughts?

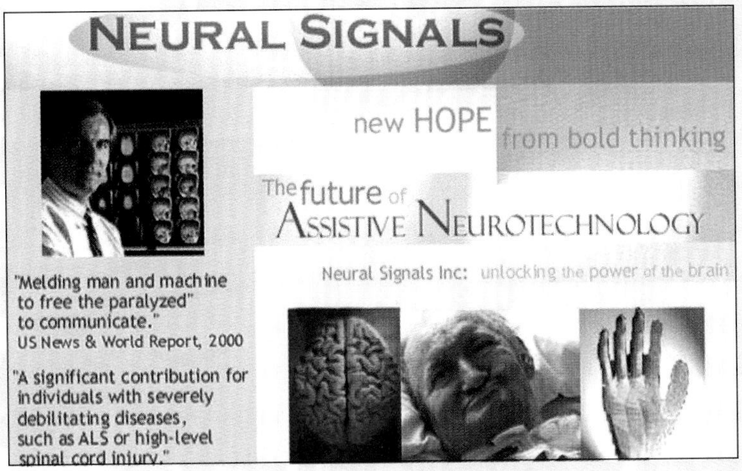

Brain-machine interface is currently pursued as a way to allow those with damaged sensory and motor functions to reconnect to the world using machines and computers. One of the most pressing groups needing this technology are those who are "locked in," incapable of communicating and physically immobile. Scientists hope that technology will allow this group to communicate and to contribute in a meaningful way. One way to accomplish this goal is to use computer technology and brain implants to bridge the gap.

Researchers at Neural Signals Inc. have begun to bridge the gap between the mind and the world using brain-machine interface. Human trials have begun using individuals with disorders that prevent them from communicating with others. At Neural Signals Inc., a patient has been able to control a mouse cursor with his thoughts. A device is implanted in the brain that encourages the growth of brain tissue and then transmits the brain signals it "hears" to a computer from an antenna. The signal interceptor implanted in the brain "reads" the signals the brain is sending and translates them into actions on a computer screen. In this way the patient is able to move a cursor using thought, or intense concentration, alone.

The ultimate goal of researchers who work with brain-machine interface is to restore mobility to the paralyzed or severely disabled. At some point researchers hope that disabled individuals could use their technology to control a motorized wheelchair or even a prosthetic limb. Additional mobility could be provided using virtual reality. Research is currently under way with the objective to create a virtual hand that will work with existing brain communication software and hardware.

What are the advantages of brain-machine interface? While this technology is currently being used to help disabled individuals, some have speculated that someday everyone will be able to control computers with their minds. The process is currently invasive and dangerous, but many suggest the benefits outweigh the risks. What do you think?

VISUAL SUMMARY

INPUT

KEYBOARD ENTRY

Input is any data or instructions that are used by a computer. **Input devices** translate words, images, and actions that people understand into a form a computer can process.

Keyboards

Keyboards are the most common way to input data. The most common types of keyboards:

- **Traditional** are full-sized, rigid, and rectangular.
- **Flexible** fold or roll up for easy packing and storage.
- **Ergonomic** are designed to alleviate wrist strain associated with repetitive movement of typing.
- **Wireless** free users from connecting wires.
- **PDA** are miniature keyboards for PDAs.

Features

Keyboard features include:

- **Numeric keypads**—used to enter numbers.
- **Toggle keys**—used to turn a feature on or off.
- **Combination keys**—perform actions when held down in combination with another key.
- **Keyboard shortcuts**—alternative to selecting items from menus.
- **Programmable keys**—connect to Web sites or perform specific tasks.

POINTING DEVICES

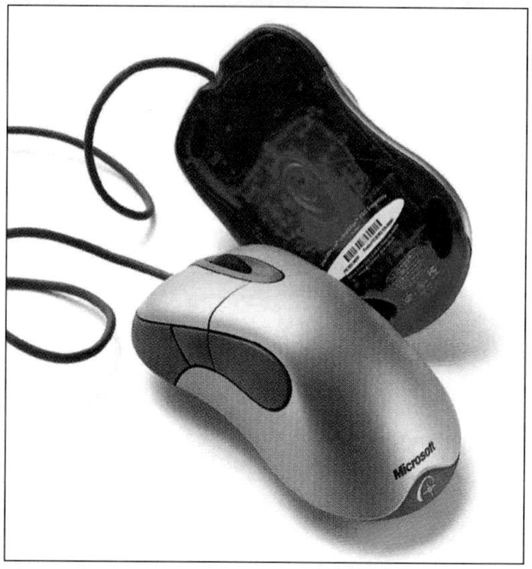

Pointing is the most natural human gesture. **Pointing devices** accept pointing gestures and convert them into machine-readable input. These devices include mice, joysticks, touch screens, light pens, and styluses.

Mouse

The most common **pointing device** is the **mouse** which controls a mouse pointer. Some have a **wheel button** to scroll information. Three basic designs are:

- **Mechanical mouse**—most widely used; has a ball at the bottom and a cord connected to the system unit; **mouse pad** provides smooth surface to roll the mouse.
- **Optical mouse**—no moving parts; uses light to detect mouse movements.
- **Cordless (wireless) mouse**—battery-powered; typically uses radio or infrared light waves.

Similar devices include:

- **Trackball (roller ball)** to control pointer by rotating a ball with thumb.
- **Touch surface (touch pad)** controls pointer by moving and tapping finger on the surface of a pad.
- **Pointing stick** controls pointer by directing the stick with a finger.

To be a competent and knowledgeable end user you need to be aware of the most commonly used input devices including keyboards, mice, scanners, digital cameras, digitizing tablets, voice recognition devices, and MIDI. You also need to be familiar with assistive input devices like alternative keyboards and mice, motion capture devices, and communication aids.

POINTING DEVICES

Joystick

Joysticks are the most popular input device for computer games. Operations controlled by varying pressure, speed, and direction of the joy-stick.

Touch Screen

Touch screens have a clear plastic layer over crisscrossed invisible beams of infrared light. Operations controlled by touching the screen with a finger.

Light Pen

Light pens are light-sensitive pen-like devices. Operations controlled by placing light pen against monitor.

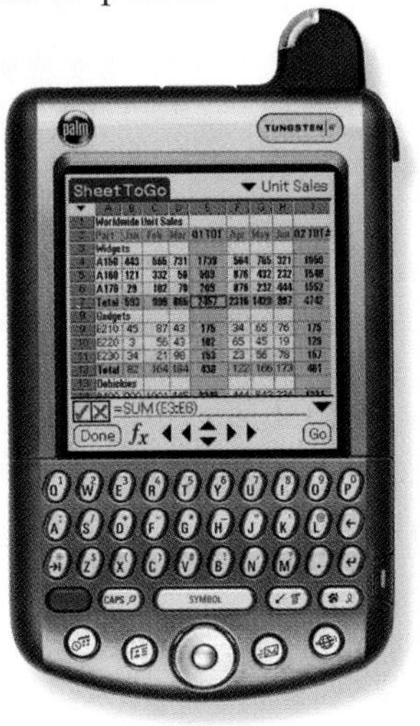

Stylus

Stylus is a pen-like device commonly used with tablet PCs and PDAs to enter notes and sketches. **Handwriting recognition software** translates handwritten notes into a form that can be processed by the system unit.

SCANNING DEVICES

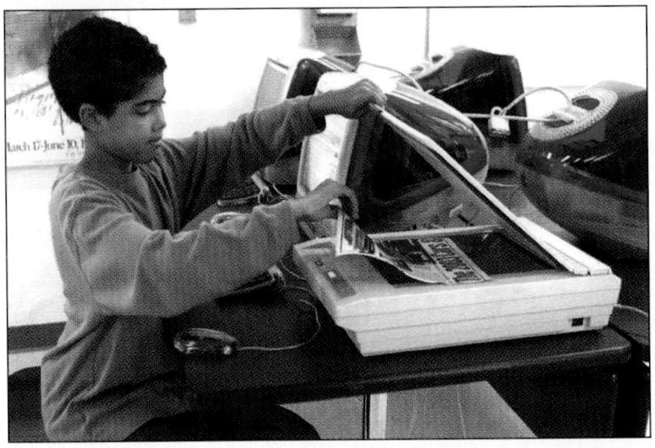

Scanners move across text and graphics. **Scanning devices** convert scanned text and images into a form that can be processed by the system unit.

Optical Scanners

Optical scanners record light, dark, and colored areas of scanned text or images. There are two types: **flatbed** and **portable.**

Bar Code Readers

Bar code readers (scanners) used with electronic cash registers in supermarkets. **Wand readers** or **platform scanners** read **UPC** codes that are used to determine product descriptions and prices and to update inventory levels.

Character and Mark Recognition Devices

Character and **mark recognition devices** can recognize special characters and marks.

- **Magnetic-ink character recognition (MICR)** used by bank's **readers/sorters** to help maintain customer account balances.
- **Optical-character recognition (OCR)** used by retail stores to provide product price information readable by customers and wand readers.
- **Optical-mark recognition (OMR, mark sensing)** used to grade multiple choice exams by recognizing items selected.

IMAGE CAPTURING DEVICES

Image capturing devices create or capture original images. These devices include digital cameras and digital video cameras.

Digital Camera

Digital cameras record images digitally on a disk. Digital images are transferred or **downloaded** to system unit for further processing and/or printing.

Digital Video Camera

Digital video cameras record motion on a disk or in the camera's memory. **WebCams (Web cameras)** are specialized digital video cameras that capture and send images over the Internet.

DIGITIZING DEVICES

Digitizing devices convert a sketch or a figure into a form that can be processed by a computer. As writing device moves across a surface, the movements are recorded as a series of points.

Graphics Tablet

Graphics tablets use a special surface and pen-like device to directly capture or trace images placed on the tablet.

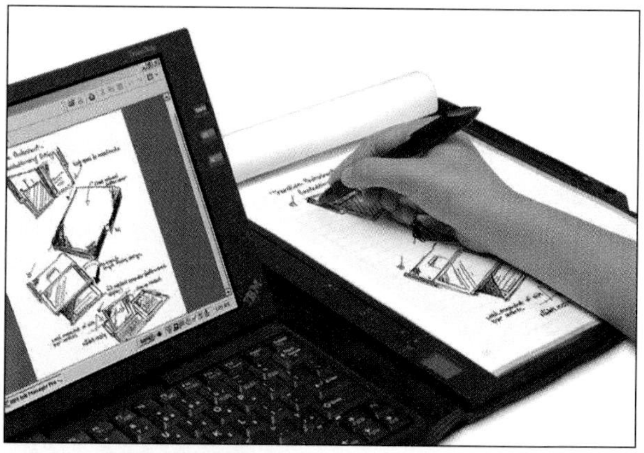

Digital Notebook

Digital notebooks use a regular notebook placed over an electronic pad. The underlying pad records the movements of the pen as the user takes notes.

AUDIO-INPUT DEVICES

Audio input can take many forms including voice and music. **Audio-input devices** convert sounds into a form that can be processed by the system unit.

Voice

Voice recognition systems are a combination of a microphone, a sound card, and special software. Two types of voice recognition systems are:

- **Discrete-speech**—recognizes only individual words.
- **Continuous-speech**—recognizes individual words and phrases in context.

Voice recognition is a common feature in much of today's software. Word 2003 has a **Language bar** to switch between two modes:

- **Voice command mode** allows users to select menu items, toolbars, and dialog box options.
- **Dictation mode** allows users to dictate text directly into documents.

Music

Musical Instrument Digital Interface (MIDI) is a standard that allows musical instruments to connect to MIDI ports in the system unit. **MIDI devices** send encoded digital signals representing musical sounds.

ASSISTIVE INPUT DEVICES

Assistive devices (accessibility hardware) allow those with visual or physical impairment to use computers and access technology. Alternative keyboards and mice, motion capture devices, and communication aids are assistive devices.

Alternative Keyboard

Alternative keyboards—designed to allow those with limited mobility to enter data and text. **Large print keyboards, Braille keyboards,** and **one-handed keyboards** are common alternatives.

Alternative Mouse

Some **alternative mice** accept foot and/or head movements to control the mouse pointer and to select commands.

Motion Capture Device

Motion capture devices are designed to follow the movements of a disabled individual and translate those movements into commands the computer can follow. **Head tracking** is a common motion capture device.

Communication Aids

Communication aids use a combination of strategies to allow disabled individuals to interact with a computer and with others.

KEY TERMS

accessibility hardware (268)
alternative keyboard (268)
alternative mouse (269)
assistive devices (268)
audio input (266)
audio input device (266)
bar code (260)
bar code reader (260)
bar code scanner (260)
Braille keyboard (269)
character recognition device (260)
combination key (255)
communication aids (269)
continuous-speech recognition system (267)
cordless mouse (257)
dictation mode (267)
digital camera (261)
digital notebook (263)
digital video camera (261)
digitizing device (263)
discrete-speech recognition system (267)
download (261)
flatbed scanner (260)
graphics tablet (263)
handwriting recognition software (259)
head tracking (269)
image capturing device (261)
input (254)
input device (254)
joystick (258)
keyboard (254)
keyboard shortcut (255)
Language bar (267)
large print keyboard (269)
light pen (258)
magnetic-ink character recognition (MICR) (260)
mark recognition device (260)
mark sensing (261)
mechanical mouse (256)
MIDI (268)
MIDI device (268)
motion capture device (269)
mouse (256)
mouse pad (256)
mouse pointer (256)
numeric keypad (255)
one-handed keyboard (269)
optical mouse (257)
optical scanner (259)
optical-character recognition (OCR) (260)
optical-mark recognition (OMR) (261)
platform scanner (260)
pointing (256)
pointing stick (257)
pointing device (256)
portable scanner (260)
programmable key (255)
reader/sorter (260)
roller ball (257)
scanner (259)
scanning device (259)
stylus (259)
toggle key (255)
touch pad (257)
touch screen (258)
touch surface (257)
trackball (257)
Universal Product Code (UPC) (260)
voice command mode (267)
voice recognition system (266)
wand reader (260)
WebCam (261)
Web camera (261)
wheel button (256)
wireless device (255)
wireless mouse (257)

To test your knowledge of these key terms with animated flash cards, select Flash Cards from Tim's Toolbox at http://www.mhhe.com/oleary/CT05.

CHAPTER REVIEW

CROSSWORD

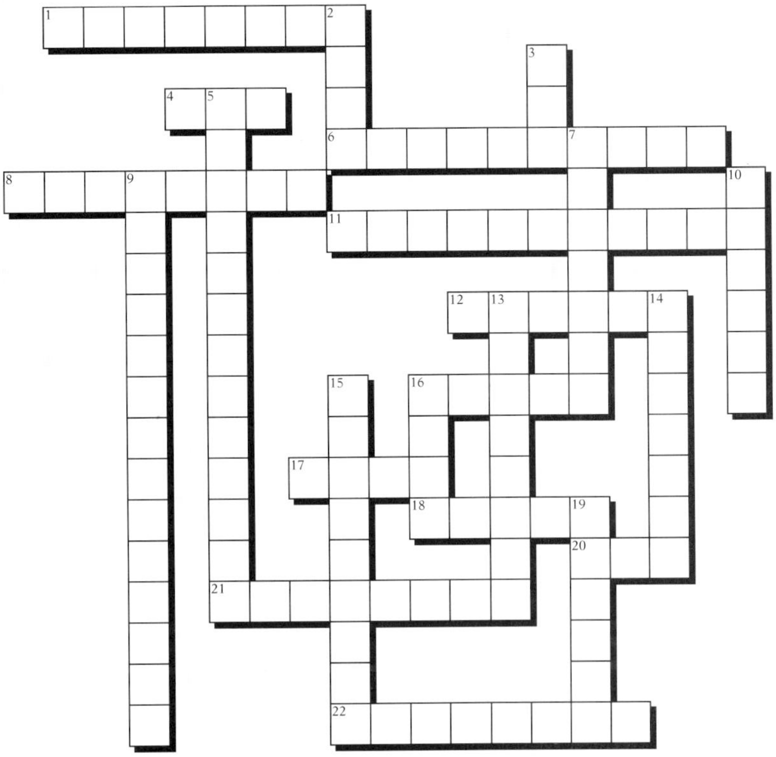

ACROSS

1 A scanner that contains photoelectric cells that scan or read bar codes
4 Universal Product Code
6 Controls the pointer by rotating a ball with your thumb
8 Input device used primarily for games
11 A mouse that accepts foot and or head movements to control the mouse pointer and to select commands
12 A pen-like device commonly used with tablet PCs and PDAs
16 Controls a pointer on the monitor
17 Another word for bar code reader
18 Putting data into the CPU. Consists of data and instructions
20 A device that senses the presence or absence of a mark
21 Translates numbers, letters and special characters
22 Closes circuits on special monitors

DOWN

2 Used by banks to read the numbers on checks and deposit slips
3 Uses preprinted characters that can be read by a light source
5 Located in the middle of the keyboard
7 A keyboard where keys are identified by raised dots
9 Converts scanned text and images into a form that the system unit can process
10 Specialized digital video camera
13 Control the pointer by moving and tapping your finger on this
14 Copies and reproduces text and images
15 Also known as the roller ball
16 A standard that allows musical instruments to connect to ports in the system unit
19 These keys turn a feature on or off

For an interactive crossword puzzle select Crosswords from Tim's Toolbox at http://www.mhhe.com/oleary/CT05.

MULTIPLE CHOICE

Circle the letter or fill in the correct answer.

1. ________ perform an operation when held down with another key.
   - **a.** Toggle keys
   - **b.** Combination keys
   - **c.** Wand readers
   - **d.** Monitors
   - **e.** Touch screens
2. ________ accept(s) pointing gestures and converts them into machine-readable input.
   - **a.** OCR
   - **b.** OMR
   - **c.** Pointing devices
   - **d.** Scanners
   - **e.** Graphics tablets
3. (A) ________ allows you to control the pointer by moving and tapping your finger on the surface of a pad.
   - **a.** touch surface
   - **b.** touch pad
   - **c.** MICR
   - **d.** mouse
   - **e.** digitizer
4. Unlike a tablet PC, a ________ uses a regular notepad and pen.
   - **a.** flatbed scanner
   - **b.** graphics tablet
   - **c.** digital camera
   - **d.** digital notebook
   - **e.** portable scanner
5. A wand reader is a type of ________ recognition device.
   - **a.** MICR
   - **b.** OCR
   - **c.** OMR
   - **d.** touch surface
   - **e.** scanner
6. ________ are specialized digital video cameras that capture images and send them to a computer for broadcast over the Internet.
   - **a.** OMR devices
   - **b.** Mark sensing devices
   - **c.** Graphics tablets
   - **d.** WebCams
   - **e.** Digital cameras
7. A(n) ________ mouse emits and senses light to detect movement.
   - **a.** mechanical
   - **b.** cordless
   - **c.** wireless
   - **d.** pointer
   - **e.** optical
8. Voice recognition systems use a microphone, a ________, and special software.
   - **a.** sound card
   - **b.** keyboard shortcut
   - **c.** toggle key
   - **d.** MIDI device
   - **e.** scanner
9. ________ is (are) a standard that allows musical instruments to connect to the system unit.
   - **a.** Instructions
   - **b.** MIDI
   - **c.** OMR
   - **d.** Input devices
   - **e.** MICR
10. Head tracking is a type of ________ device.
    - **a.** MIDI
    - **b.** OMR
    - **c.** sound capture
    - **d.** motion capture
    - **e.** touch screen

To test your knowledge of this chapter, select Self Test from Tim's Toolbox at http://www.mhhe.com/oleary/CT05.

MATCHING

Match each numbered item with the most closely related lettered item. Write your answers in the spaces provided.

a. assistive device	**1.** Type of bar code used in supermarkets. _____
b. continuous-speech recognition system	**2.** Any data or instruction used by a computer. _____
c. cordless mouse	**3.** Allows you to use the keyboard to issue commands rather than selecting items from menu(s). _____
d. digital camera	**4.** These keys turn a feature on or off. _____
e. digital notebook	**5.** Similar to a mouse, this device is located in the middle of the keyboard. _____
f. discrete-speech recognition system	**6.** Also known as a scanner, this device copies or reproduces text and images. _____
g. graphics tablet	**7.** Input devices that allow those with visual or physical impairment to use computers and access technology. _____
h. head tracking	**8.** Similar to traditional cameras except that images are recorded digitally. _____
i. keyboard shortcuts	**9.** Scanners with photoelectric cells that read bar codes. _____
j. input	**10.** Used to alleviate wrist strain that results from the repetitive movements of typing. _____
k. joystick	**11.** A standard that allows musical instruments to connect to the system unit. _____
l. ergonomic keyboard	**12.** Also known as a wireless mouse. _____
m. MIDI	**13.** Voice system that is able to distinguish between same-sounding words. _____
n. pointing stick	**14.** A pointing device widely used for computer games. _____
o. OMR device	**15.** Used by artists for creating illustrations, by mapmakers to record or trace maps, and by engineers to digitally save mechanical drawings. _____
p. optical scanner	**16.** This motion capture method records movements of disabled individuals to issue commands. _____
q. stylus	**17.** Similar to a tablet PC except that it uses a regular notepad and pen. _____
r. toggle	**18.** Device that senses the presence or absence of a mark, such as a pencil mark. _____
s. UPC	**19.** Voice system that recognizes individual words based on their sound. _____
t. wand reader	**20.** Pen-like device commonly used with tablet PCs and PDAs. _____

OPEN-ENDED

On a separate sheet of paper, respond to each question or statement.

1. Describe the most common types of keyboards.
2. Describe the different types of pointing devices.
3. Discuss the advantages and disadvantages of the three basic designs for the mouse.
4. Explain the differences between discrete-speech and continuous-speech recognition systems.
5. Describe some common assistive input devices.

USING TECHNOLOGY

1 Digital Photography

Digital photos are a great way to share your life with friends and family. Digital cameras are now available at a very reasonable cost. With a digital camera and some special software, you can edit your photos on your computer and share them with anyone over the Internet. To learn more about digital photography, review Making IT Work for You: TV Tuner Cards and Video Clips on pages 228 and 229 and answer the following questions: (a) Which button is clicked to begin the transfer of pictures from a digital camera to a computer? (b) What image touch-ups are available in the "Improvements" menu? (c) What sizing options are available for images sent as e-mail?

2 Digital Video Editing

Adobe Premiere is a popular video editing software package that can turn your computer into an editing studio. To learn more about Premiere, connect to our Web site at http://www.mhhe.com/oleary/CT05 and select Using Technology from Tim's Toolbox to link to Adobe's Web site. Once there, read about this product and then answer the following questions: (a) What features does Premiere offer? (b) How is Premiere similar to Windows Movie Maker? How is it different? (c) Who would likely use this product? (d) Describe a way that you would use video editing software. Which software would you choose? Why?

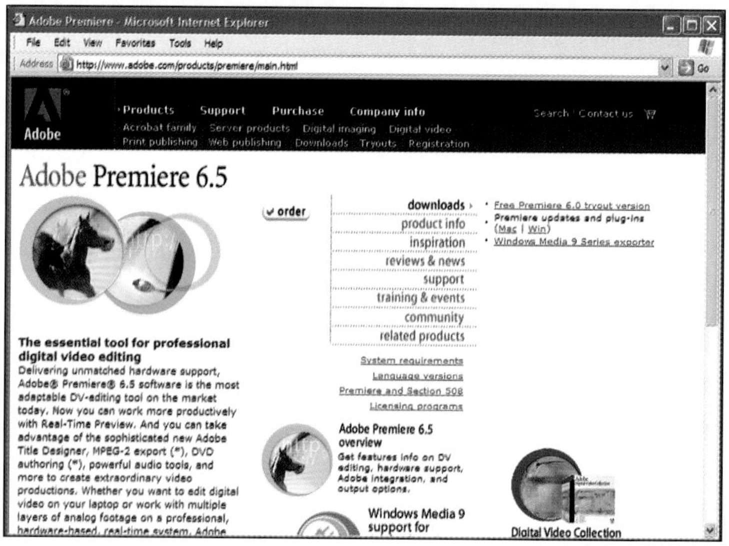

Voice Recognition 3

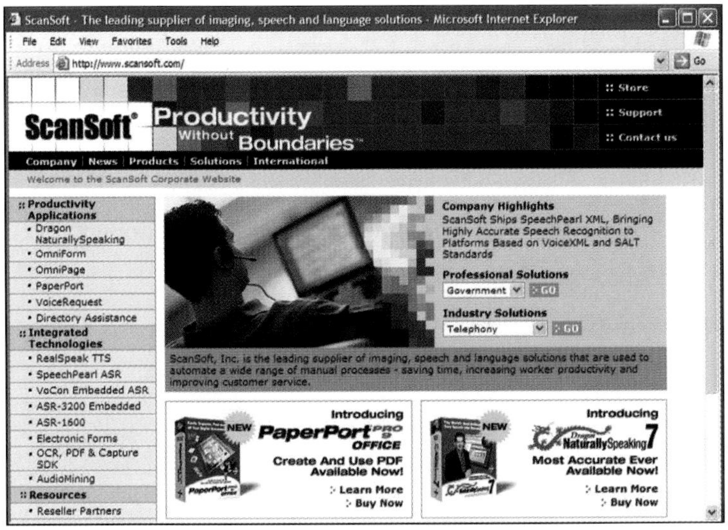

Though voice recognition technology is not yet widely used, some products do allow you to use voice recognition to control your computer or dictate a term paper. Connect to our Web site at http://www.mhhe.com/oleary/CT05 and select Using Technology from Tim's Toolbox to link to a leader in voice recognition software. Once there, read about the product's features and then answer the following questions: (a) Describe the features offered by the voice recognition software. (b) What input devices are required to use this software? (c) Do you think voice recognition software will replace keyboards and mice as primary input devices? Justify your answer.

Tablet PC 4

Tablet PCs are a hybrid between notebook computers and handhelds. Designed to be highly portable, tablet PCs offer several methods of input to accommodate different situations and user preferences. Visit our Web site at http://www.mhhe.com/oleary/CT05 and select Using Technology from Tim's Toolbox to link to a site that features tablet PCs. Review the site, and answer the following questions: (a) Describe the characteristics of a tablet PC. (b) List three different input devices that tablet PCs use. (c) For each input device you listed, describe a situation it is best suited for.

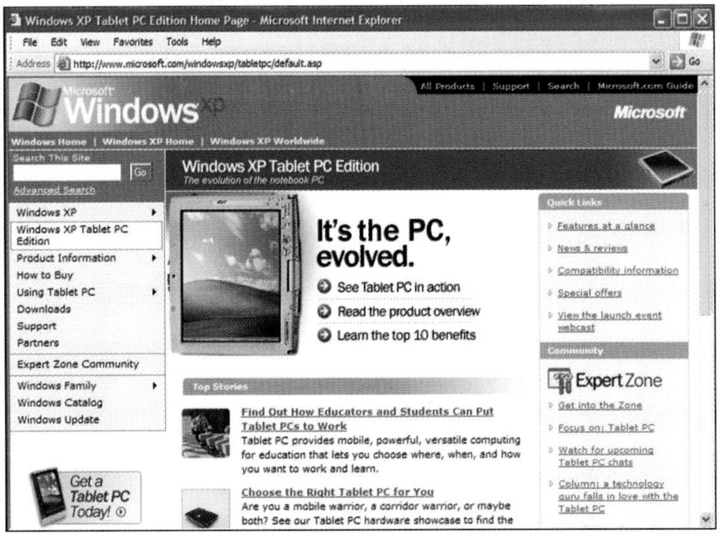

EXPANDING YOUR KNOWLEDGE

1 Computing Today CD

While traditional cameras capture images on film, digital cameras capture images, then convert them into a digital form. These images can be viewed immediately and saved to a disk or into the camera's memory. After reviewing Figure 7-18 and viewing the animation How Digital Cameras Work from your Computing Today CD or connecting to http://www.mhhe.com/oleary/CT05 and selecting Animations from Tim's Toolbox, answer the following questions:

a. What is a CCD and what is its function?
b. What is an ADC and what is its function?
c. How are images transported from a digital camera to a computer?

2 Handwriting Recognition

Handwriting recognition is a developing technology for direct input. Conduct a Web search with the key words "handwriting recognition" to learn more about this technology. Then answer the following questions: (a) What types of devices and applications use handwriting recognition now? (b) What are some applications where handwriting recognition is the best choice for input. Why is this the case? (c) What are current limitations of handwriting recognition?

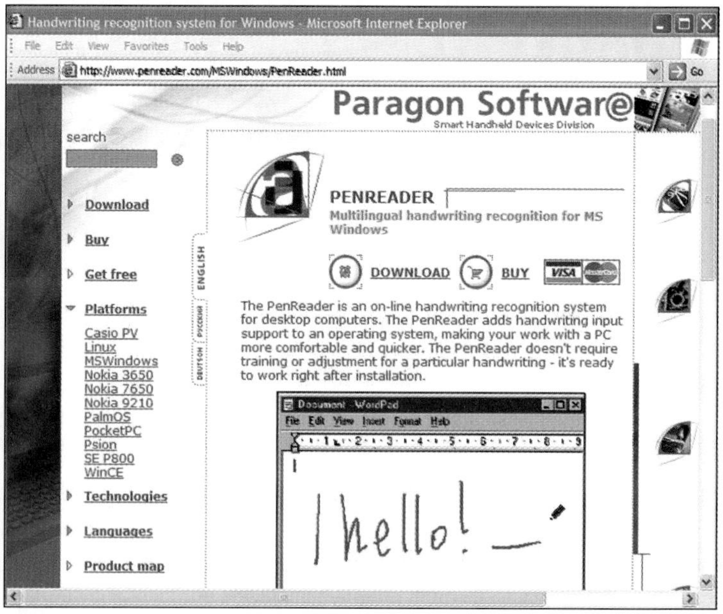

EXPANDING YOUR KNOWLEDGE

SimNet CD 3

Using your SimNet CD, complete the input sections in Chapter 7: Input and then answer the following questions on a single page.

a. Describe dataflow for input devices.
b. What are the differences between a desktop keyboard and a laptop keyboard?
c. Describe each component of a mouse.
d. Describe how a digital camera takes a picture.
e. Discuss each of the other types of input devices.

Assistive Input Devices 4

Assistive input devices help people with disabilities use computers and the Internet. Many innovative products have been developed in this field, and major research is ongoing. Connect to our Web site at http://www.mhhe.com/oleary/CT05 and select Expanding Your Knowledge from Tim's Toolbox to link to an organization that researches and creates assistive technologies. Explore the site, and answer the following questions: (a) Describe two or three assistive input devices developed by this organization. How is each one used? (b) What special software, if any, is needed to use each input device you described? (c) How are these input devices similar to standard input devices? In what ways are they specialized?

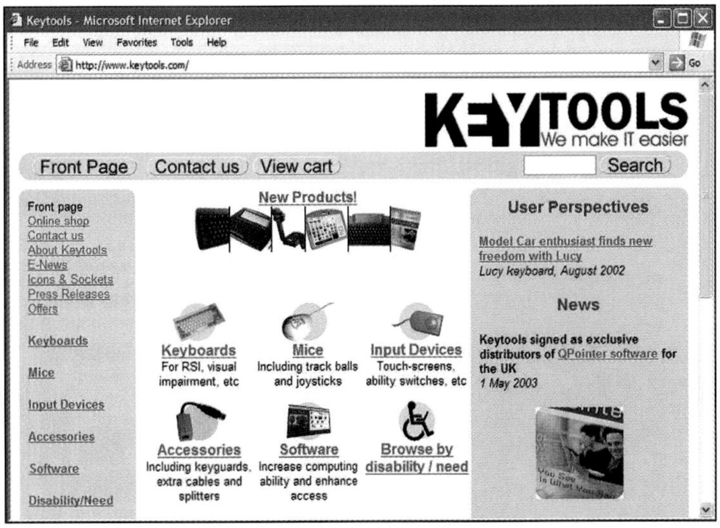

BUILDING YOUR PORTFOLIO

1 Digital Input

Digitizing devices convert sketches, figures, or images into a form that can be processed by a computer. These devices typically record the movement of a writing device as a series of points and send this information to the computer. Write a one-page paper titled "Digital Input" that answers the following questions: (a) Define digitizer, digital camera, digital video camera, and digital notebook. (b) Give examples of ways that you would use the devices above. (c) Give examples of ways that individuals in corporations use the devices above.

2 Ergonomics

Ergonomic input devices are designed to be safe and comfortable for people to use. Ergonomics is an increasingly important consideration for equipment in the workplace. Use the Web to research ergonomic input devices, and then write a one-page paper that answers the following: (a) Describe two or three ergonomic devices you researched. How does each receive input from a user? (b) How does each of these products increase comfort or prevent injury? (c) What assurances are there that ergonomic products are safer than their nonergonomic counterparts? (d) What legal issues involve ergonomics in the workplace? Cite specific examples.

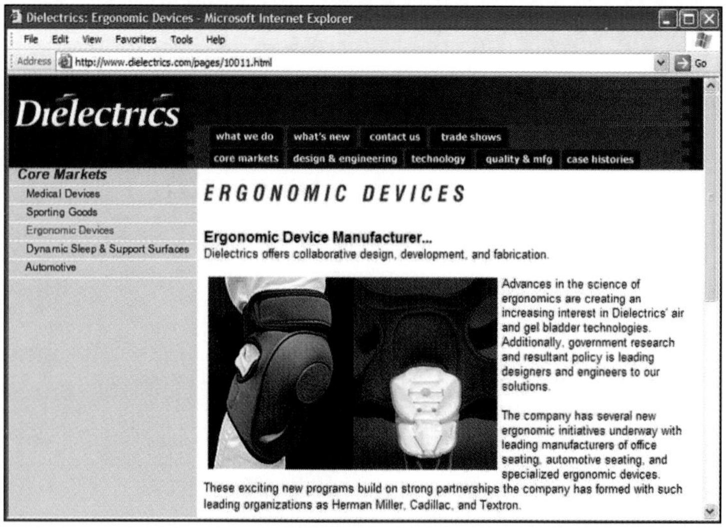

Electronic Security 3

Electronic monitoring equipment is becoming more widely used in stores, the workplace, and in public. Consider the following questions and discuss your answers. Write a one-page summary of your analysis: (a) What common applications of electronic monitoring or surveillance equipment have you noticed recently? (b) Does knowing that an electronic security device is in place make you feel more secure? (c) Have you ever felt that electronic surveillance equipment was an invasion of your privacy? (d) Consider the trade-off between security and privacy. In what cases is one more important than the other? Are these cases the same for everyone? Explain your answer.

WebCams 4

Many WebCams broadcast live views of public places, such as university campuses, football stadiums, and city centers. Anyone with a WebCam and the right software can set up a WebCam broadcast. Visit our Web site at http://www.mhhe.com/oleary/CT05 and select Building Your Portfolio from Tim's Toolbox to link to a directory of public WebCams. Once connected, browse a few WebCam broadcasts and write a one-page paper that answers the following questions: (a) What WebCam broadcasts did you view? Describe the experience. (b) How does a user list their WebCam on the directory site? (c) Do you think WebCams can be used to enhance security? Justify your answer. (d) Do you think WebCams can be a violation of personal privacy? Justify your answer.

OUTPUT

OBJECTIVES

After you have read this chapter, you should be able to:

1. **Describe output including the types of output and output devices.**
2. **Describe monitor standards and types of monitors.**
3. **Discuss printers including important features and different types of printers.**
4. **Discuss audio output devices.**
5. **Describe assistive output devices.**
6. **Discuss combination input and output devices including the most common types.**

Output Devices
Translate symbols processed by the system unit into words, sounds, images, and actions that people understand

HDTV

Flat-panel monitor

E-book

In all likelihood, you have used a computer to surf the Web, print documents, and listen to music. Have you ever wondered how information processed by the system unit is converted into a form that you can use? That is the role of output devices. While input devices convert what we understand into what the system unit can process, output devices convert what the system unit has processed into a form that we can understand. Output devices translate machine language into letters, numbers, sounds and images that people can understand.

Output devices make it possible for you to view images and text on a screen, print documents, and listen to music. You are probably familiar with the most common output devices, such as monitors, printers, and speakers. There are also many specialized output devices available to you. Combination devices include the features of input devices such as a scanner with features of output devices such as printers. These devices are called multifunctional and are increasing in popularity. Internet telephones, for example, are multifunctional devices for sending and receiving long distance telephone calls over the Internet. Some output devices are designed to assist the physically challenged. For example, some devices print documents in Braille and others read the contents of a Web page.

Competent and knowledgeable end users need to know about the most commonly used output devices, including monitors, printers, audio output devices, and assistive output devices. They need to be aware of combination input and output devices such as fax machines, multifunctional devices, Internet telephony, and terminals.

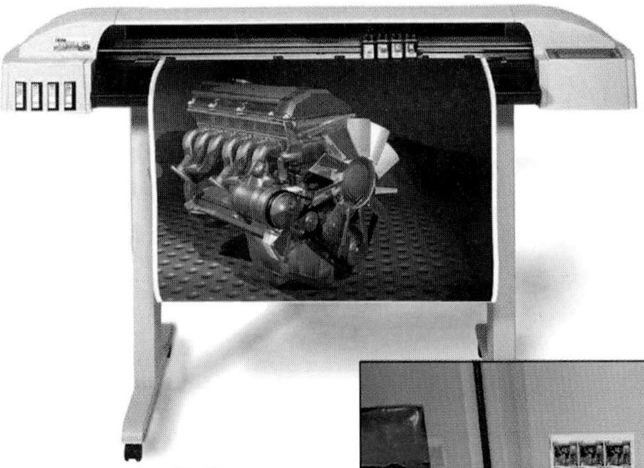
Plotter

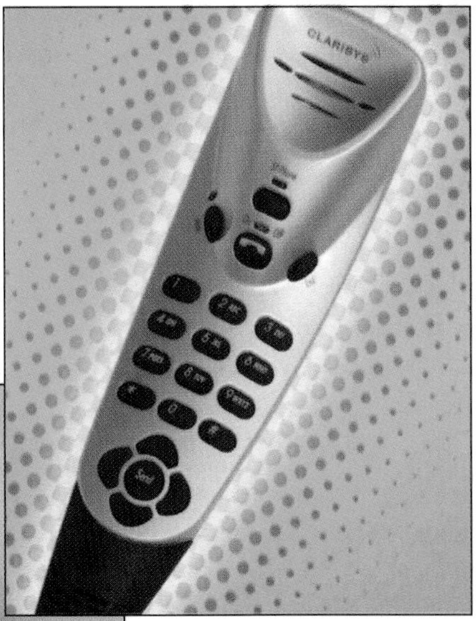
Internet telephone

Printer

WHAT IS OUTPUT?

Output is processed data or information. Text, graphics, audio, and video are types of output. Output devices translate processed information into a form for humans.

Output is processed data or information. Output typically takes the form of text, graphics, photos, audio, and/or video. For example, when you create a presentation using a presentation graphics program, you typically input text and graphics. You could also include photographs and even add voice narration. The output would be the completed presentation.

Announcing

New Adventure Travel Trips

Attend an Adventure Travel presentation to learn about some of the earth's greatest unspoiled habitats and find out how you can experience the adventure of a lifetime. This year we are introducing four new tours and offering you a unique opportunity to combine many different outdoor activities while exploring the world.

Hike the Inca trail to Machu Picchu
Camp on safari in Tanzania
Climb Mt. Kilimanjaro
Explore the Costa Rican rain forests

Presentation dates and times are January 5 at 7 PM, February 3 at 7:30 PM, and March 8 at 7 PM. All presentations are held at convenient hotel locations. The hotels are located in downtown Los Angeles, Santa Clara and at the airport.

Call 1-800-777-0004 for presentation locations, a full color brochure, and itinerary information, costs, and trip dates.

Figure 8-1 Printed document containing text and graphics

The most common types of output are text, graphics, audio, and video. (See Figure 8-1.)

- **Text**—letters, words, sentences, and paragraphs. For example, newsletters, flyers, and reports are all text documents. Text may be displayed on a monitor, printed on paper, or read as audio output.
- **Graphics**—images and pictures displayed on a monitor or printed on paper.
- **Audio**—sounds within the human hearing range, converted digital signals from the system unit into analog sounds audible to humans. Audio may be music played from speakers or voice output.
- **Video**—moving images displayed on a monitor. It is possible to play music, video, TV, and even full length movies on your computer.

Output devices are any hardware used to provide or to create output from the computer. They translate information that has been processed by the system unit into a form that humans can understand. There are a wide range of output devices. (See Figure 8-2.) The most widely used are monitors, printers, audio-output, combination, and assistive output devices.

Concept Check

- What is output?
- What are some common types of output?
- What are output devices?

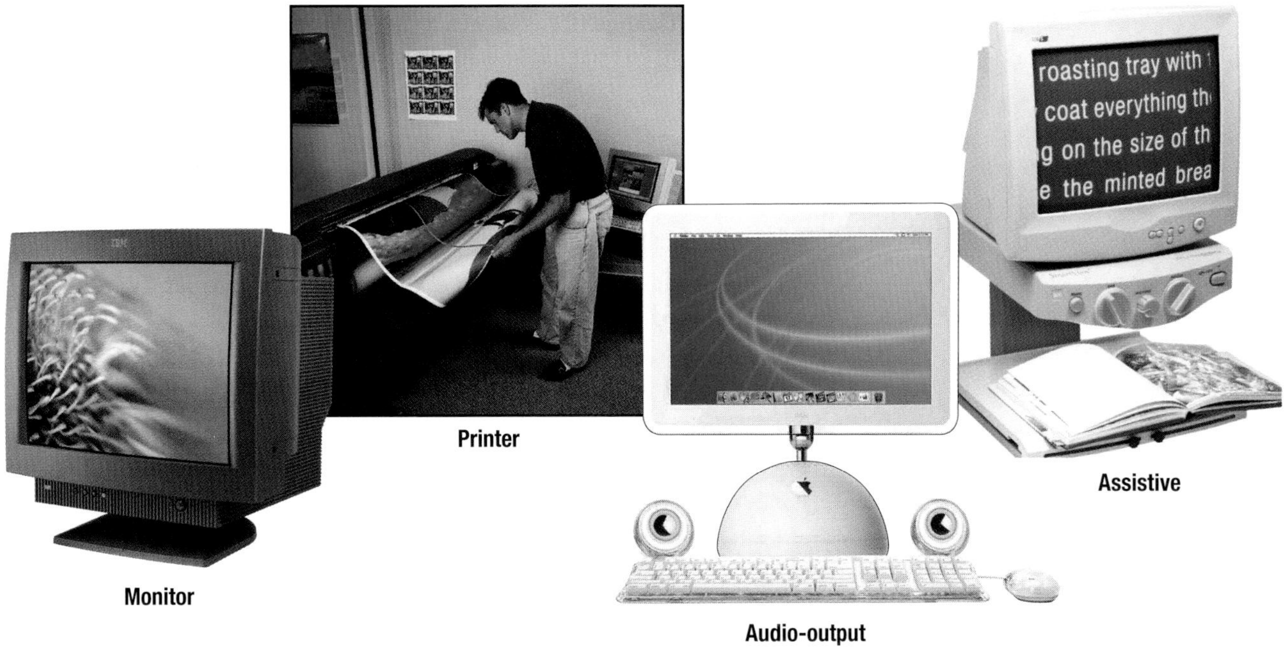
Printer
Assistive
Monitor
Audio-output

Figure 8-2 Output devices

MONITORS

Monitor features include resolution, dot pitch, refresh rate, and size. Monitor standards indicate resolution. CRT, flat-panel, and gas plasma are types of monitors. E-books, data projectors, and HDTV are specialty monitors.

The most frequently used output device is the **monitor.** Also known as **display screens** or simply as **screens,** monitors present visual images of text and graphics. The output from monitors is often referred to as **soft copy.** Monitors vary in size, shape, and cost. Almost all, however, have some basic distinguishing features.

FEATURES

The most important characteristic of a monitor is its clarity. **Clarity** refers to the quality and sharpness of the displayed images. It is a function of several monitor features including resolution, dot pitch, refresh rate, and size.

- **Resolution** is one of the most important features. Images are formed on a monitor by a series of dots or **pixels (picture elements).** (See Figure 8-3.) Resolution is expressed as a matrix of these dots or pixels. For example, many monitors today have a resolution of 1,280 pixel columns by 1,024 pixel rows for a total of 1,310,720 pixels. The higher a monitor's resolution (the more pixels) the greater the clarity of image produced.

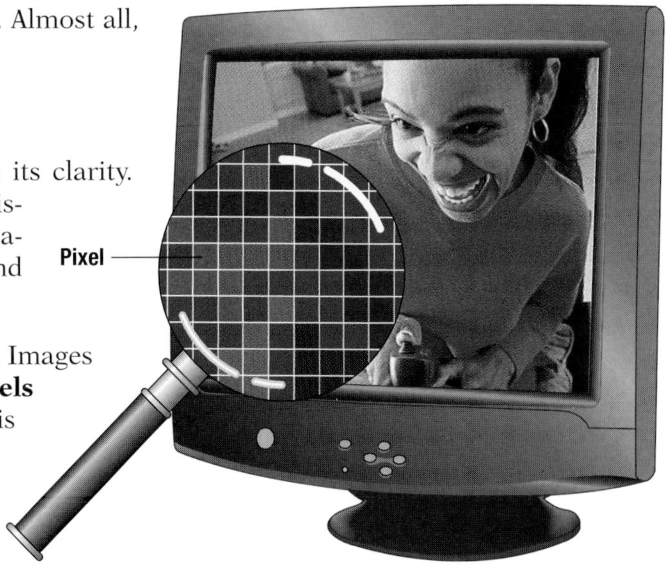
Pixel

Figure 8-3 Monitor resolution

- **Dot pitch** is the distance between each pixel. Most newer monitors have a dot pitch of .31 mm (31/100th of a millimeter) or less. The lower the dot pitch (the shorter the distance between pixels), the higher the clarity of images produced.
- **Refresh rate** indicates how often a displayed image is updated or redrawn on the monitor. Most monitors operate at a rate of 75 hertz which means that the monitor is redrawn 75 times each second. Images displayed on monitors with refresh rates lower than 75 hertz appear to flicker and can cause eye strain. The faster the refresh rate (the more frequently images are redrawn), the better the quality of images displayed.
- **Size** or **viewable size** is measured by the diagonal length of a monitor's viewing area. Common sizes are 15, 17, 19, and 21 inches. The smaller the monitor the better the quality of images displayed.

Standard	Pixels
SVGA	800 × 600
XGA	1,024 × 768
SXGA	1,280 × 1,024
UXGA	1,600 × 1,200

Figure 8-4 Resolution standards

STANDARDS

To indicate a monitor's resolution capabilities, several standards have evolved. The four most common today are SVGA, XGA, SXGA, and UXGA. (See Figure 8-4.)

- **SVGA** stands for **S**uper **V**ideo **G**raphics **A**rray. It has a minimum resolution of 800 by 600 pixels. A few years ago, SVGA was the most popular standard. Today, it is used primarily with 18-inch monitors.
- **XGA** stands for E**x**tended **G**raphics **A**rray. It has a resolution of up to 1,024 by 768 pixels. It is a popular standard today, especially with 17- and 19-inch monitors.
- **SXGA** stands for **S**uper E**x**tended **G**raphics **A**rray. This standard has a resolution of 1,280 by 1,024 pixels. It is popular with 19- and 21-inch monitors.
- **UXGA** stands for **U**ltra E**x**tended **G**raphics **A**rray. UXGA is the newest and highest standard. Although not as widely used as the XGA and SXGA monitors, its popularity is expected to increase dramatically as 21-inch monitors become more widely used. UXGA monitors are primarily used for high-end engineering design and graphic arts.

Figure 8-5 CRT monitor

CATHODE-RAY TUBE

The most common type of monitor for the office and the home is the **cathode-ray tube (CRT).** (See Figure 8-5.) These monitors are typically placed directly on the system unit or on the desktop. CRTs are similar in size and technology to televisions. Compared to other types of monitors, their primary advantages are low cost and excellent resolution. Their primary disadvantage is that they are bulky and occupy a considerable amount of space on the desktop.

Figure 8-6 A flat-panel monitor

FLAT-PANEL MONITOR

Because CRTs are too bulky to be easily transported, portable monitors known as **flat-panel monitors** or **liquid crystal display (LCD)** monitors were developed. Unlike the technology used in CRTs, the technology for portable monitors involves liquid crystals. Flat-panel monitors are much thinner and require less power to operate than CRTs. These monitors are widely used with desktop, tablet PC, and handheld computers. (See Figure 8-6.)

There are two basic types of flat-panel monitors: passive-matrix and active-matrix. **Passive-matrix** or **dual-scan monitors** create images by scanning the entire screen. This type requires very little power, but the clarity of the images is not as sharp. **Active-matrix** or **thin film transistor (TFT)** monitors do not scan down the screen; instead, each pixel is independently activated. More colors with better clarity can be displayed. Active-matrix monitors are more expensive and require more power.

> **On the Web Explorations**
>
> NEC Technologies is a leader in developing flat-panel monitors. To learn more about the company, visit our Web site at http://www.mhhe.com/oleary/CT05 and select On the Web Explorations from Tim's Toolbox.

GAS PLASMA MONITOR

Gas plasma monitors, also known as **plasma display** or **gas discharge display,** contain millions of pixels that are illuminated by charged neon gas. Originally these monitors displayed only one color, orange on black, but today gas plasma monitors display over 16 million colors. Because they are flat screens, with no distortion, plasma displays are commonly used in today's large home theater screens and HDTVs. However, these screens are more expensive to use than LCD screens because they require more power to run.

OTHER MONITORS

There are several other types of monitors. These monitors are used for more specialized applications such as reading books, making presentations, and watching television. Three of these specialized devices are e-books, data projectors, and high-definition television.

- **E-books,** also known as **e-book readers,** are handheld, book-sized devices that display text and graphics. Using content downloaded from the Web or from special cartridges, these devices are used to read newspapers, magazines, and entire books. The cost of producing and distributing e-book content is less than publishing and delivering traditional print media. Additionally, the time to create and distribute the content is much less. For these reasons and others, many experts predict that e-books will soon become as commonplace as today's traditional books. (See Figure 8-7.)
- **Data projectors** are specialized devices similar to slide projectors. These devices, however, connect to microcomputers and project computer output just as it would appear on a traditional monitor. Marketing people, educators, and students frequently use presentation graphics programs like PowerPoint to create presentations and then deliver the presentation using data projectors. Data projectors are commonly used for presentations almost anywhere from the classroom to the boardroom. (See Figure 8-8.)
- **High-definition television (HDTV)** is a recent development in the merger of microcomputers and television called **PC/TV.** HDTV delivers a much clearer and more detailed wide-screen picture than regular television. (See Figure 8-9.) Because the output is digital, users can readily freeze video sequences to create high-quality still images. The video and still images can then be digitized, edited, and stored on disk for later use. This technology is very useful to graphic artists, designers, and publishers.

For a summary of the different types of monitors, see Figure 8-10.

Figure 8-7 E-book

Figure 8-8 Data projector

Figure 8-9 HDTV

Monitor	Description
CRT	Most common type, technology like TV, low cost, excellent resolution
Flat-panel	Thin, low power requirements, liquid crystal technology, used for all types of computers, especially portables
Gas plasma	Thin, neon gas technology, no distortion, used for home theaters
E-books	Handheld specialty device for displaying electronic books
Data projectors	Specialty device for projecting computer output onto large screens
HDTV	Merges microcomputers and television technology, produces clearer and more detailed wide-screen picture than traditional television

Figure 8-10 Types of monitors

On the Web Explorations

HDTV is expected to be the standard in television broadcasting by 2006. To learn more about HDTV visit our Web site at http://www.mhhe.com/oleary/CT05 and select On the Web Explorations from Tim's Toolbox.

Concept Check

- ✔ Define these monitor features: resolution, dot pitch, refresh rate, and size.
- ✔ What are the four most common monitor standards?
- ✔ Describe CRTs, flat-panel, gas plasma, and specialty monitors.

PRINTERS

Printer features include resolution, color capability, speed, and memory. Ink-jet, laser, and thermal are common types of printers. Other types include dot-matrix, plotter, photo, and portable.

You probably use a printer with some frequency to print homework assignments, photographs, and Web pages. **Printers** translate information that has been processed by the system unit and present the information on paper. Printer output is often called **hard copy.**

FEATURES

There are many different types of printers. Almost all, however, have some basic distinguishing features including resolution, color capability, speed, and memory.

- **Resolution** for a printer is similar to monitor resolution. It is a measure of the clarity of images produced. Printer resolution, however, is measured in **dpi (dots per inch).** (See Figure 8-11.) Most printers designed for personal use average 1200 dpi. The higher the dpi, the better the quality of images produced.

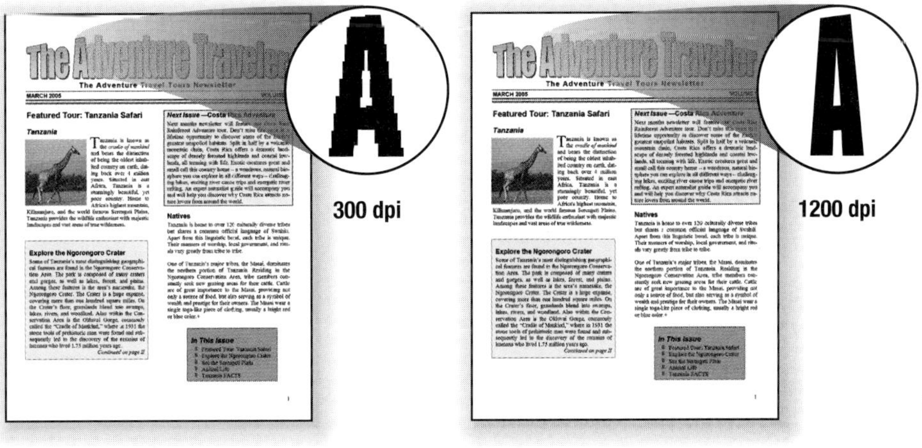

Figure 8-11 dpi comparison

- **Color capability** is provided by most printers today. Users typically have the option to print either with just black ink or with color. Because it is more expensive to print in color, most users select black ink for letters, drafts, and homework. Color is used more selectively for final reports containing graphics and for photographs.
- **Speed** is measured in the number of pages printed per minute. Typically, printers for personal use average 10 to 15 pages per minute for single color (black) output and 5 to 10 pages per minute for color output.
- **Memory** within a printer is used to store printing instructions and documents waiting to be printed. The more memory in a printer, the faster it will be able to create large documents.

TIPS

Is your ink-jet printer producing smeared pages? Are the characters looking blurry? Then it could be time to give it a cleaning. Here are a few cleaning suggestions:

1. **Disconnect.** Turn off the printer and unplug the electricity.
2. **Open.** Open the printer and locate the spray nozzles.
3. **Clean.** Wipe the nozzles with a dry, lint-free cloth or a swab moistened with distilled water.
4. **Reconnect.** When completely dry, plug in the printer and turn it on.

To prevent clogging in the future, always allow your printer to finish printing the current page and to return the print head to its resting position before removing the page or turning off the power.

INK-JET PRINTER

Ink-jet printers spray ink at high speed onto the surface of paper. This process not only produces a letter-quality image but also permits printing to be done in a variety of colors making them ideal for select special applications. (See Figure 8-12.) Ink-jet printers are the most widely used printers. They are reliable, quiet, and relatively inexpensive. The most costly aspect of ink-jet printers is replacing the ink cartridges. (See Figure 8-13) For this reason, most users specify black ink for the majority of print jobs and use the more expensive color printing for select applications. Typical ink-jet printers produce 17 to 19 pages per minute of black-only output and 13 to 15 pages of color output.

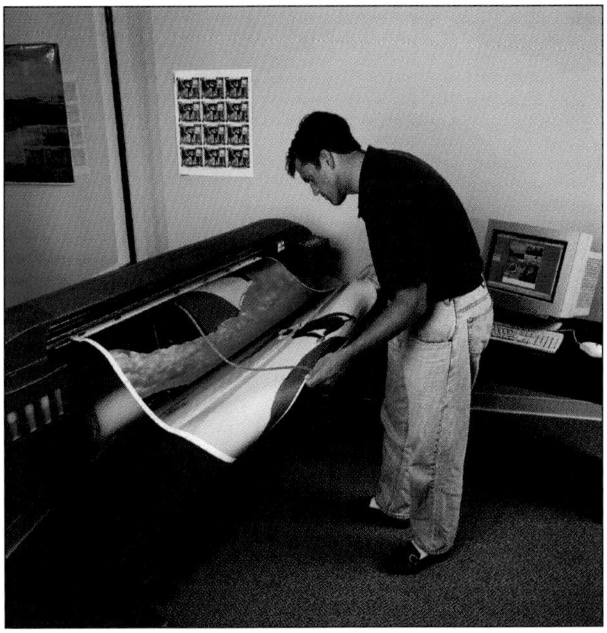

Figure 8-12 A special application ink-jet printer

LASER PRINTER

The **laser printer** uses a technology similar to that used in a photocopying machine. Laser printers use a laser light beam to produce images with excellent letter and graphics quality. More expensive than ink-jet printers, laser printers are used in applications requiring high-quality output. (See Figure 8-14.)

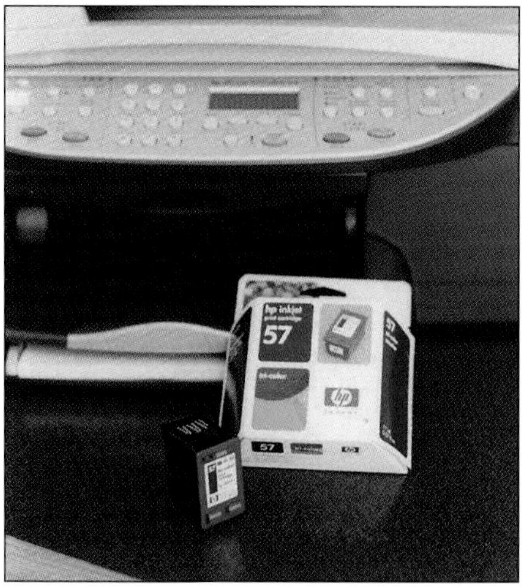

Figure 8-13 Color ink-jet cartridge

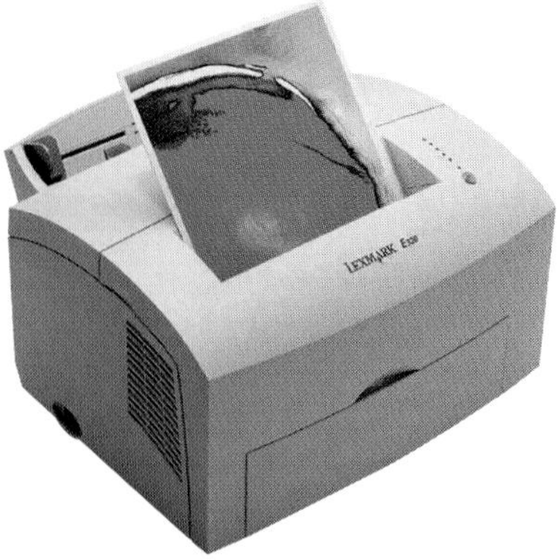

Figure 8-14 A laser printer

On the Web Explorations

Lexmark is a leading manufacturer of laser printers. To learn more about the company visit our Web site at http://www.mhhe.com/oleary/CT05 and select On the Web Explorations from Tim's Toolbox.

There are two categories of laser printers. **Personal laser printers** typically do not support color, are less expensive, and are used by many single users. They typically can print 15 to 17 pages a minute. **Shared laser printers** typically support color, are more expensive, and are used (shared) by a group of users. Shared laser printers typically print over 50 pages a minute.

THERMAL PRINTER

A thermal printer uses heat elements to produce images on heat-sensitive paper. Originally these printers were only used in scientific labs to record data. More recently, color thermal printers have been widely used to produce very high-quality color artwork and text.

Color thermal printers are not as popular because of their cost and the requirement of specially treated paper. They are a more special-use printer that produces near-photographic output. They are widely used in professional art and design work where very high-quality color is essential.

Some of the important characteristics of the three most widely used microcomputer printers are summarized in Figure 8-15.

Printer	Characteristics	Typical Use
Ink-jet	High color quality; inexpensive; sprays drops of ink on paper	Internal and external communications, advertising pieces
Laser	Very high quality; uses photocopying process	Desktop publishing, external documents
Thermal	Very high quality; uses heat elements on special paper	Art and design work

Figure 8-15 Three types of printers

TIPS Do you find extra pages in the printer when you try to print from the Web? Would you like to print your favorite articles without all the ads and hyperlinks? There are several ways to get what you want in a printout. Here are a few suggestions you can use with Internet Explorer:

1. **Preview.** To see what will be printed, choose *Print Preview* from the *File* menu. You can scroll through the pages and make sure the items you want will be printed.
2. **Choose Printer Friendly.** Many Web pages have a Printer Friendly button that removes all the ads and sidebars. Look for the button at the conclusion of most Web articles.
3. **Print Selection.** You can highlight and print only the text you would like to print. Highlight the text and graphics you would like to print and choose File/Print and check the *Selection* option under the *Page* range box.

Figure 8-16 Plotter

OTHER PRINTERS

There are several other types of printers. These printers include dot-matrix printers, chain printers, plotters, photo printers, and portable printers:

- **Dot-matrix printers** form characters and images using a series of small pins on a print head. Once a widely used microcomputer printer, they are inexpensive and reliable but quite noisy. In general, they are used for tasks where high-quality output is not required.
- **Plotters** are special-purpose printers for producing a wide range of specialized output. Using output from digitizing tables and other graphics input devices, plotters can create maps, images, and architectural and engineering drawings. They can produce high-quality, multicolor documents and also documents that are larger than most printers can handle. Plotters are widely used by graphic artists, engineers, and architects to print out designs, sketches, and drawings. (See Figure 8-16.)
- **Photo printers** are special-purpose printers designed to print photo-quality images from digital cameras. (See Figure 8-17.) Most photo printers print 3 × 5" or 4 × 6" images on glossy, photo-quality paper.
- **Portable printers** are usually small and lightweight printers designed to work with a notebook computer. Portable printers may be ink-jet or laser printers, print in black and white or color, and connect with USB or parallel port connection.

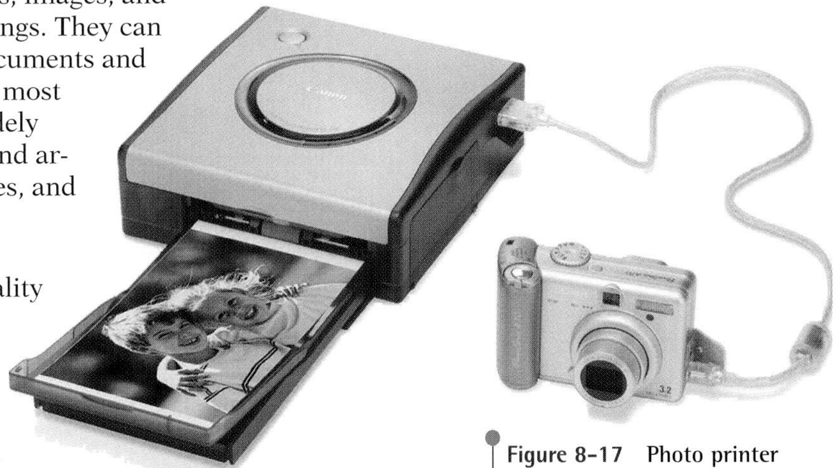

Figure 8-17 Photo printer

Concept Check

- ✓ Discuss the printer features: resolution, color capability, speed, and memory.
- ✓ What are the three printer types commonly used with microcomputers?
- ✓ Discuss dot-matrix, plotter, photo, and portable printers.

AUDIO-OUTPUT DEVICES

Audio-output devices produce sounds for people. Speakers and headphones are the most common.

Audio-output devices translate audio information from the computer into sounds that people can understand. The most widely used audio-output devices are **speakers** and **headphones.** (See Figure 8-18) These devices are connected to a sound card in the system unit. The sound card is used to capture as well as play back recorded sounds. Audio-output devices are used to play music, vocalize translations from one language to another, and communicate information from the computer system to users.

Circular speakers

Headphones

Figure 8-18 Speakers and headphones are the most widely used audio-output devices

Creating voice output is not anywhere near as difficult as recognizing and interpreting voice input. In fact, voice output is quite common. It is used with many soft-drink machines, telephones, and cars. It is used as a reinforcement tool for learning, such as to help students study a foreign language. It is also used in many supermarkets at the checkout counter to confirm purchases. One of its most powerful capabilities is to assist the physically challenged.

COMBINATION INPUT AND OUTPUT DEVICES

Fax machines send and receive images over telephone lines. Multifunction devices have input and output capabilities. Internet telephones use telephony to connect people. Dumb, intelligent, network, or Internet are types of terminals.

Many devices combine input and output devices. Sometimes this is done to save space. Other times it is done for very specialized applications. Common **combination devices** include fax machines, multifunction devices, Internet telephones, and terminals.

FAX MACHINES

A **fax machine,** also known as a **facsimile transmission machine,** is a standard tool in nearly every office. At one time, all fax machines were separate stand-alone devices for sending and receiving images over telephone lines. Now, most computer systems have that capability with the simple addition of a fax/modem board, which also operates as a modem. To send a fax, these devices scan the image of a document converting the light and dark areas into a format that can be sent electronically over standard telephone lines. To receive a fax, these devices reverse the process and print the document (or display the document on your monitor) using signals received from the telephone line.

On the Web Explorations

Hewlett-Packard is a leading manufacturer of multifunction devices. To learn more about the company, visit our Web site at http://www.mhhe.com/oleary/CT05 and select On the Web Explorations from Tim's Toolbox.

MULTIFUNCTION DEVICES

Multifunctional devices (MFD) typically combine the capabilities of a scanner, printer, fax, and copying machine. (See Figure 8-19.) These multifunctional devices offer a cost and space advantage. They cost about the same as a good printer or copy machine but require much less space than the single-function devices they replace. Their disadvantage is that the quality and functionality are not quite as good as those of the separate single-purpose devices. Even so, multifunctional devices are widely used in home and small business offices.

INTERNET TELEPHONE

Internet telephones are specialized input and output devices for receiving and sending voice communication. (See Figure 8-19). Typically, these devices connect to the system unit through an USB port and operate much like a traditional telephone.

Telephony is the transmission of telephone calls over computer networks. Also known as **Internet telephony, IP Telephony,** and **Voice-over IP (VoIP),** telephony uses the Internet rather than traditional communication lines to support voice communication. To place telephone calls using telephony requires an Internet telephone (or other appropriate input and output devices), an Internet connection, sound card, and special software. The two most popular applications are:

- Computer-to-computer communications are the least expensive and allow individuals to place long distance calls without incurring traditional long distance telephone charges. This application requires that both parties have a computer and that their computers are on and connected to the Internet when a call is placed. The required software is available from a variety of sources for free or at very low cost. MSN Explorer is one of the most widely used.
- Computer-to-traditional telephone communications allows a user to call almost any traditional telephone from their computer. Only the person making the call needs to have a computer connected to the Internet. Compared to computer-to-computer communications, however, this application requires an Internet phone service provider. The required software is typically free from the provider, however small per-minute charges are often assessed. One of the most popular Internet phone service providers is iConnectHere.

Because of its flexibility, the computer-to-traditional telephone application is the more widely used. To see how Internet telephony typically works for this type of application see Figure 8-20. Also, consult your Computing Today CD or visit us at http://www.mhhe.com/oleary/CT05 and select Animations from Tim's Toolbox. Also see Making IT Work for You: Internet Telephony on pages 300–301.

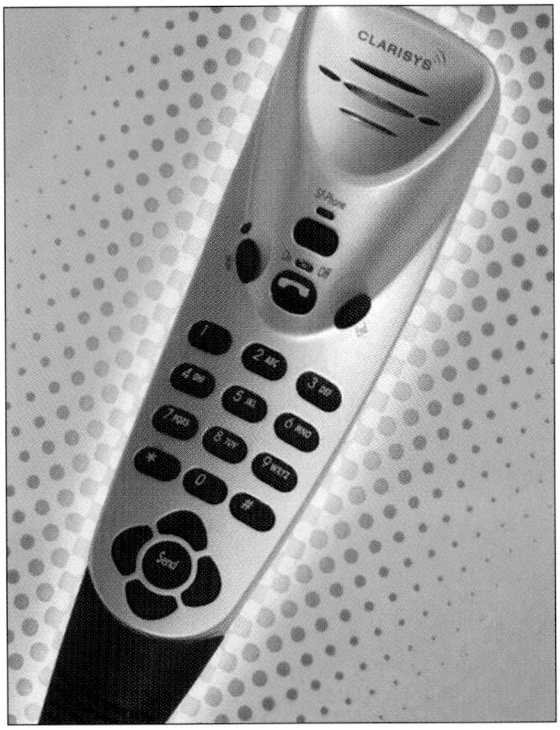

Figure 8-19 Internet telephone

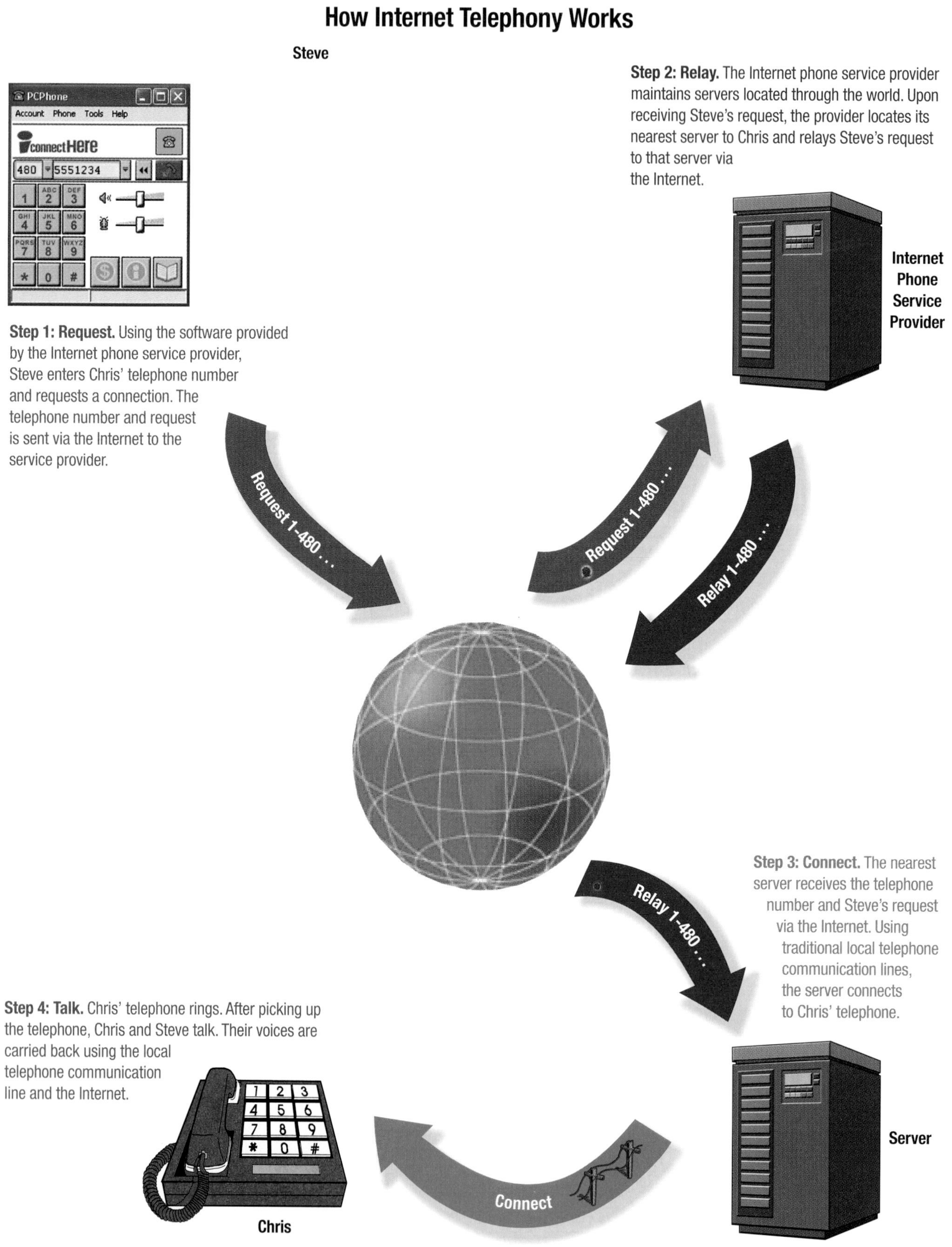
How Internet Telephony Works
Steve
PCPhone
Account Phone Tools Help
connectHere
480 5551234
Step 1: Request. Using the software provided by the Internet phone service provider, Steve enters Chris' telephone number and requests a connection. The telephone number and request is sent via the Internet to the service provider.
Request 1-480 . . .
Step 2: Relay. The Internet phone service provider maintains servers located through the world. Upon receiving Steve's request, the provider locates its nearest server to Chris and relays Steve's request to that server via the Internet.
Internet Phone Service Provider
Request 1-480 . . .
Relay 1-480 . . .
Relay 1-480 . . .
Step 3: Connect. The nearest server receives the telephone number and Steve's request via the Internet. Using traditional local telephone communication lines, the server connects to Chris' telephone.
Step 4: Talk. Chris' telephone rings. After picking up the telephone, Chris and Steve talk. Their voices are carried back using the local telephone communication line and the Internet.
Server
Connect
Chris

Figure 8-20 How Internet telephony works

Although not currently available to all locations worldwide and connection quality may vary, Internet telephone connections are rapidly gaining popularity.

TERMINALS

A **terminal** is an input and output device that connects you to a mainframe or other type of computer called a **host computer** or **server.** There are four kinds of terminals:

- A **dumb terminal** can be used to input and receive data, but it cannot process data independently. It is used only to gain access to information from a computer. Such a terminal may be used by an airline reservations clerk to access a mainframe computer for flight information. (See Figure 8-21.)

Figure 8-21 Dumb terminal

- An **intelligent terminal** includes a processing unit, memory, and secondary storage such as a magnetic disk. Essentially, an intelligent terminal is a microcomputer with communications software and a telephone hookup (modem) or other communications link. These connect the terminal to the larger computer or to the Internet. An increasingly popular type is the **Net PC,** also known as the **Net Personal Computer.** These low-cost and limited microcomputers typically have only one type of secondary storage (an internal hard disk drive), a sealed system unit, and no expansion slots.
- A **network terminal,** also known as a **thin client** or **network computer,** is a low-cost alternative to an intelligent terminal. Most network terminals do not have a hard-disk drive and must rely on a host computer or server for application and system software. These devices are becoming increasingly popular in many organizations.
- An **Internet terminal,** also known as a **Web terminal** or **Web appliance,** provides access to the Internet and typically displays Web pages on a standard television set. These special-purpose terminals offer Internet access without a microcomputer. Unlike the other types of terminals, Internet terminals are used almost exclusively in the home.

Concept Check

- ✓ What are the two most widely used audio-output devices?
- ✓ What are combination input and output devices?
- ✓ Describe the following combination devices: fax machine, MFD, Internet telephone, and terminal.

MAKING IT WORK FOR YOU

INTERNET TELEPHONY

Do you need a cheaper way to stay in touch with friends and family? Did you know you can use your computer and the Internet to make long-distance calls to regular phones? All you need is some software and an Internet connection to get started.

Creating an Account The first step is to connect to an Internet phone service provider and set up an account. You will also need to download custom software from the provider you choose. For example, follow these steps to get started with the phone service provider iConnect.Here:

1
- **Connect your browser to *www.iConnectHere.com.***
- **Click on the *Sign Up* link.**
- **Follow the on-screen instruction to select an account that meets your needs.**
- **Continue to follow the on-screen instructions to download the *PC-to-Phone* software.**

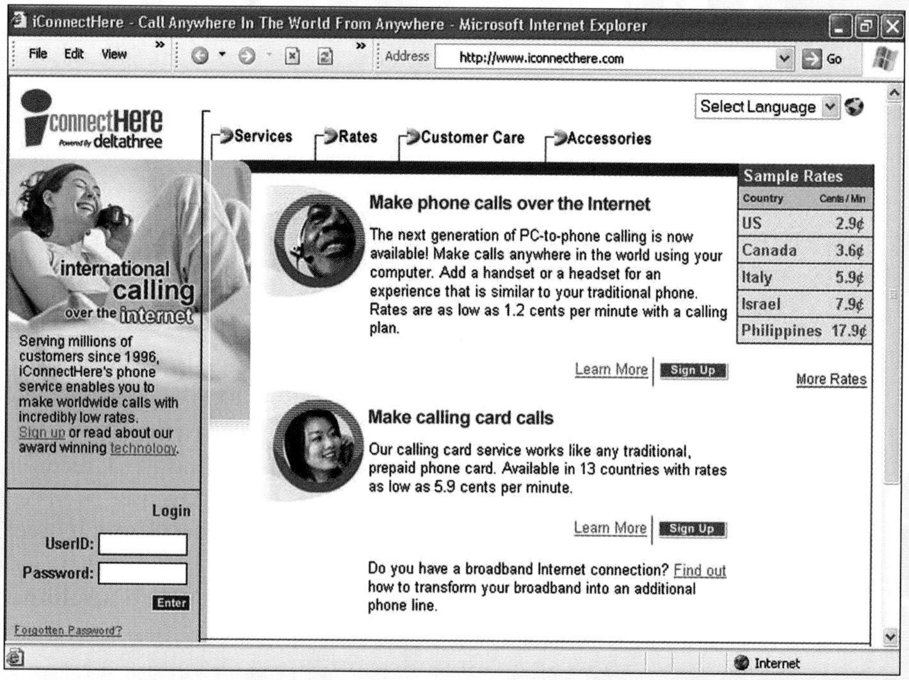

Configuring the Software When making an Internet call, you will use a regular microphone to speak and your computer's speakers or headphones to hear the conversation. Before making your first call, you will need to configure the software to work with these items as well as check your connection to the Internet. To configure the PC-to-Phone software:

2

- **If necessary, turn on your speakers or plug in your headphones and connect your microphone to your computer.**
- **Double-click the file you downloaded in the Creating an Account step to start the *Setup* wizard.**
- **Follow the wizard's instructions to select the correct input and output devices from the drop-down lists.**
- **Adjust the sliders to comfortable volume levels for your microphone input and prerecorded sample output.**
- **Use the option to test your Internet connection and take the recommended steps to resolve any detected errors.**

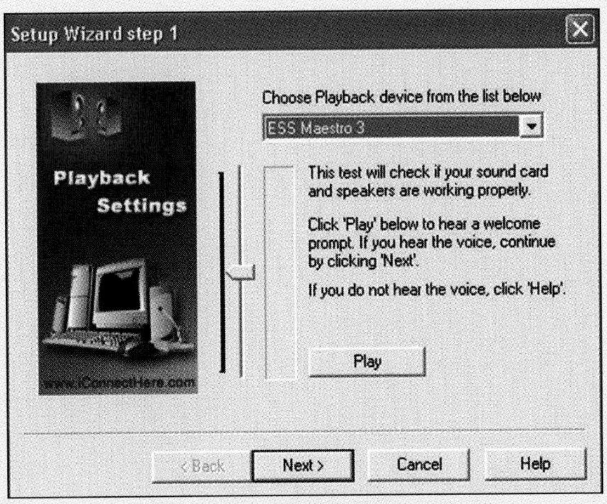

Making a Call To make an Internet call, use the specialized software like a regular phone. For example, to make a call with the PC-to-Phone software:

3

- **Start the *PC-to-Phone* software.**
- **Click the buttons on the on-screen keypad to input the phone number you wish to dial: [country code] + [area code] + [number] for example: 1 480 555 1234.**
- **Click the *Call* button to begin the call.**
- **Use the microphone and speaker sliders to make adjustments to these levels during the call.**
- **Click the *Hang Up* button to end the call.**

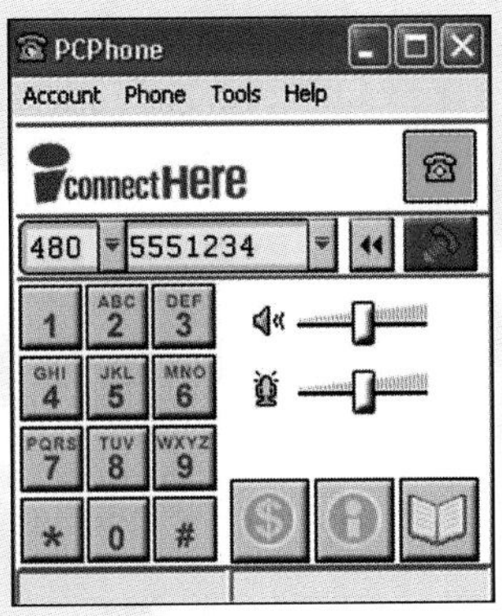

Internet telephones are continually changing and some of the specifics presented in this Making IT Work may have changed. To learn about other ways to make information technology work for you, visit our Web site at http://www.mhhe.com/oleary/CT05 and select Making IT Work for You from Tim's Toolbox.

ASSISTIVE OUTPUT DEVICES

Braille display devices use moving Braille symbols. Braille printers work like dot-matrix printers. Reading machines and screen readers are assistive output devices.

Assistive output devices make it possible for disabled individuals to print, view, or hear computer output. Some assistive devices are designed for primary use by disabled individuals. However, like assistive input devices, these tools may be modifications of commonly used output devices. (See Figure 8-22.)

BRAILLE OUTPUT DEVICES

There are several types of output devices designed to translate machine language into symbols and language the blind or visually impaired can understand. One common output device is called a Braille display. **Braille display** devices use specialized software to "read" text on a computer screen and then display the text on a type of monitor with moving Braille symbols. Braille output can also be sent to a printer. **Braille printers,** also known as **Braille embossers,** work like dot-matrix printers to output Braille on printed pages. (See Figure 8-23)

VOICE OUTPUT DEVICES

There are two basic types of voice output devices:

- **Reading machines** convert printed text to speech. These devices typically use a scanner to input printed text, a program to process or interpret the text, and speakers to provide audio output. (See Figure 8-24.)
- **Screen readers** convert text appearing on a computer monitor to speech. Screen readers use specialized programs that interpret text displayed on a monitor and speakers to vocalize the output.

Figure 8-22 Assistive output devices for the visually impaired.

Figure 8-23 Braille printer

Figure 8-24 VERA reading machine

TIPS

Does the text of your favorite Web site appear too small to read comfortably? Would you like to read the small text that appears on screen without straining your eyes? Windows XP comes with a utility designed to magnify on-screen text. Follow these steps to use this tool:

1. Click *Start/Control Panel* and select *Accessibility Options.*
2. Choose *Magnifier* from the *See Also* list.
3. Select the desired magnification level and options.
4. Minimize the Magnification Settings window.

The Magnifier follows the mouse cursor and displays the magnified text at the top of the screen. To close the Magnifier, open the Magnifier Settings window from the task bar and close the window. The Magnifier will disappear from the top of the screen.

Concept Check

- ✓ What are assistive output devices?
- ✓ Describe Braille displays and printers.
- ✓ Describe reading machines. Describe screen readers.

Careers in IT

Technical Writer

Technical writers prepare instruction manuals, technical reports, and other scientific or technical documents. Most technical writers work for computer software firms, government agencies, or research institutions. They translate technical information into easily understandable instructions or summaries. As new technology continues to develop and expand, the need for technical writers who can communicate technical expertise to others is expected to increase.

Technical writing positions typically require a college degree in communications, journalism, or English and a specialization in, or familiarity with, a technical field. However, individuals with strong writing skills sometimes transfer from jobs in the sciences to positions in technical writing.

Technical writers can expect to earn an annual salary in the range of $40,000 to $60,000. Advancement opportunities can be limited within a firm or company, but there are additional opportunities in consulting. To learn about other careers in information technology, visit us at http://www.mhhe.com/oleary/CT05 and select Careers in IT from Tim's Toolbox.

A Look to the Future

Voice Portals May Change the Way You Surf

How would you like to browse the Web by issuing voice commands? Would you like your computer to read the latest Web news to you? What if you could choose the accent and gender of your computer's voice? How would you like to call the bank and hear that same voice read your latest statement? Wouldn't it be convenient if you could use a telephone to send and receive e-mail? New speech recognition and text-to-speech advances may make it all possible.

www.wizzardsoftware.com
wizzard
Voice Fonts:
Natural Voices (TTS) Text-To-Speech Runtime Engine
Natural Voices (SDK) Software Developer's Kit
Version: Full Evaluation
Mike
Claire
Lauren
Mel
Alain
Alberto
Charles
Reiner
Anjali
Crystal
Julia
Ray
Rich
Juliette
Rosa
Audrey
Klara
Other
AT&T Natural Voices

Voice portals, sometimes called vortals, are Web sites or phone-based services that you can access and instruct with your voice. You may have used a voice portal as part of your cell phone services to access Web information. When speech recognition technology is combined with VoiceXML, you can navigate the Internet and the Web with voice commands. VoiceXML is a technology that uses tags included in Web page code to enable speech recognition software to convert the text to speech and read and decipher the content.

There are many text-to-speech programs currently available. Until recently most readers had a distinctly "computer" sounding voice. However, new developments have made readers sound much more like human voices. AT&T Natural Voices software is currently used by many businesses to answer phones and automate services. You may have "conversed" with this software when calling the local phone company to obtain your balance. Natural Voices makes it possible for companies to choose the "voice font" of the text-to-speech reader. The software provides both male and female voices with a French, Spanish, or British accent.

Speech recognition is the other component necessary for voice portals to work effectively. IBM's Voice Portal© answers a business telephone and takes voice commands to provide information and tools. This system allows users to interrupt the voice and still get the answers they need. This is seen by many as a necessary component of a successful voice portal.

Do these possibilities appeal to you? How would you like to surf the Internet with your voice? How would you like to listen to a British or French voice read the latest news from a Web page? Many people are currently making use of speech recognition software to access media. Some experts predict that voice recognition and speech-to-text software will change the way we interact with computers. Others suggest that we may someday talk to our cars and our homes using this technology. For example, you might be able to call your home and instruct it to turn on the oven to start dinner. Are you using voice recognition software now? What do you think?

NOTES

Notes

VISUAL SUMMARY

OUTPUT

OUTPUT

Announcing

New Adventure Travel Trips

Attend an Adventure Travel presentation to learn about some of the earth's greatest unspoiled habitats and find out how you can experience the adventure of a lifetime. This year we are introducing four new tours and offering you a unique opportunity to combine many different outdoor activities while exploring the world.

Hike the Inca trail to Machu Picchu
Camp on safari in Tanzania
Climb Mt. Kilimanjaro
Explore the Costa Rican rain forests

Presentation dates and times are January 5 at 7 PM, February 3 at 7:30 PM, and March 8 at 7 PM. All presentations are held at convenient hotel locations. The hotels are located in downtown Los Angeles, Santa Clara and at the airport.

Call 1-800-777-0004 for presentation locations, a full color brochure, and itinerary information, costs, and trip dates.

Output is processed data or information. The most common types of output are text, graphics, audio, and video.

- **Text**—words, sentences, and paragraphs; displayed on monitor, printed on paper, or read as audio output.
- **Graphics**—images and pictures displayed or printed on paper.
- **Audio**—sound converted from digital signals from the system unit to analog signals audible to humans.
- **Video**—moving images displayed on a monitor; includes music video, TV, and movies.

Output devices are hardware to provide or create output. Devices include monitors, printers, audio-output, combination, and assistive output.

MONITORS

Monitors (display screens, screens) present visual images of text and graphics. Monitor output is described as **soft copy.**

Features

Clarity is a function of several monitor features including resolution, dot pitch, refresh rate, and size.

- **Resolution**—expressed as matrix of **pixels (picture elements);** higher resolution gives greater clarity.
- **Dot pitch**—distance between pixels; lower dot pitch gives greater clarity.
- **Refresh rate**—number of times that screen is redrawn each second; faster refresh rate gives greater clarity.
- **Size (viewable size)**—measured by diagonal length of monitor's viewing area; larger monitors have less clarity.

Standards

Monitor resolution indicated by one of four standards.

Standard	Pixels
SVGA	800 × 600
XGA	1,024 × 768
SXGA	1,280 × 1,024
UXGA	1,600 × 1,200

To be a competent and knowledgeable end user you need to be aware of the most commonly used output devices including monitors, printers, audio output devices, and assistive output devices. Additionally, you need to know about combination input and output devices such as fax machines, multifunctional devices, Internet telephony, and terminals.

MONITORS

Cathode-Ray Tube

Cathode-ray tubes (CRTs) use technology similar to a television. Low cost with excellent resolution. However, bulky and occupy considerable space on the desktop.

Flat-Panel Monitor

Flat-Panel monitors (liquid crystal display, LCD) compared to CRTs are thinner, require less power, and used with all types of computers especially portable computers. Two types:

- **Passive-matrix (dual-scan)**—create images by scanning entire screen.
- **Active matrix (thin film transistor, TFT)**—activate individual pixels.

Gas Plasma Monitor

Gas plasma monitor (plasma display, gas discharge display) illuminates pixels with charged neon gas; thin, no distortion, more expensive than flat-panel.

Other Monitors

Three specialized types of monitors are **e-books, data projectors,** and **high-definition television (HDTV).** HDTV is merger of microcomputers and television called **PC/TV.**

PRINTERS

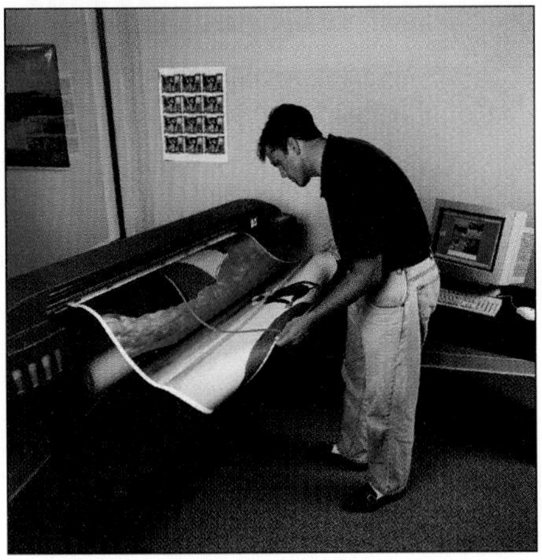

Printers translate information processed by system unit into output printed on paper. Output is described as **hard copy.**

Features

Some distinguishing features of printers include resolution, color capability, speed, and memory.

- **Resolution** for printers is similar to monitor resolution except measured in **dpi (dots per inch).** Higher dpi creates higher quality output.
- **Color capability** is available with most printers; more expensive and used selectively.
- **Speed** is measured in pages per minute.
- **Memory** within a printer used to store printing instructions and documents. Higher memory produces documents faster.

Ink-Jet Printer

Ink-jet printers spray ink to produce high quality output. These printers are inexpensive and most widely used type of printer.

Laser Printer

Laser printers use technology similar to photocopying machines. Two categories:

- **Personal laser printers** typically do not support color, are less expensive, used by single users.
- **Shared laser printers** support color, are more expensive, and shared by group of users.

PRINTERS

Thermal Printer

Thermal printers use heat elements and heat-sensitive paper. Some are used in scientific labs to record data. Recently, color thermal printers used to provide very high-quality artwork and text. These expensive printers create near-photographic output for professional art and design work.

Other Printers

- **Dot-matrix printers** form characters using small pins on a print head; inexpensive, reliable, and noisy.
- **Plotters** use output from digitizing tables and other devices to produce maps, architectural and engineering drawings.
- **Photo printers** are special-purpose printers that produce photo-quality images from digital cameras.
- **Portable printers** are small and lightweight; designed to work with notebook computers; may be ink-jet or laser, color, and typically connect to USB or parallel ports.

AUDIO-OUTPUT DEVICES

Audio-output devices translate audio information from the computer into sounds that people can understand.

- Speakers and headphones are the most widely used audio-output devices.
- These devices are connected to sound cards within the system unit; the sound card captures as well as plays back recorded sounds.
- Audio-output devices used to play music, vocalize language translations, and communicate information from the computer system.
- Creating voice output is not as difficult as recognizing and interpreting voice input. Used in soft drink machines, telephones, cars, and as a tool to reinforce learning.
- Powerful tool to assist the physically challenged.

COMBINATION DEVICES

Common combination devices include:

Fax Machines

Fax machines (facsimile transmission machines) send and receive images via standard telephone lines. Fax/modem board operates as fax and modem.

Multifunction Devices

Multifunctional devices (MFD) typically combine the capabilities of a scanner, printer, fax, and copy machine.

Internet Telephone

Internet telephones send and receive voice communication. **Telephony (Internet telephony, IP, Telephony, Voice-over IP, VoIP)** uses Internet to place very inexpensive long distance calls. It requires an Internet telephone (or other appropriate input and output device), special service provider, sound card, and software.

Terminals

Terminals connect to a **host computer** or **server.** Four kinds are **dumb** (no processing), **intelligent** (able to process, also known as **Net PC** or **Net Personal Computer**), **network** (low-cost alternative, also known as **thin client** or **network computer**), and **Internet** (access Internet without microcomputer, also known as **Web terminal** or **Web appliance**).

ASSISTIVE OUTPUT DEVICES

Assistive output devices make it possible for disabled individual to print, view, or hear computer output. Two categories are:

Braille Output Devices

There are several types of Braille devices to assist the blind or visually impaired. Two such devices are Braille displays and Braille printers.

- **Braille display**—uses specialized software to read text from a monitor and then display the text on a type of monitor with moving Braille symbols.

- **Braille printers (Braille embossers)**—work like dot-matrix printers to output Braille on printed pages.

Voice Output Devices

Reading devices convert printed text to speech. **Screen readers** convert text displayed on monitor to speech.

KEY TERMS

active-matrix monitor (290)
assistive output device (302)
audio output (288)
audio-output device (296)
Braille display (302)
Braille printer (Braille embosser) (302)
cathode ray tube monitor (CRT) (290)
clarity (289)
color capability (293)
combination device (296)
data projector (291)
display screen (289)
dot pitch (290)
dots-per-inch (dpi) (292)
dot-matrix printer (295)
dual-scan monitor (290)
dumb terminal (299)
e-book (291)
e-book reader (291)
Extended Graphics Array (XGA) (290)
facsimile (fax) machine (296)
flat-panel monitor (290)
gas plasma monitor (291)
gas discharge display (291)
graphics output (288)
hard copy (292)
headphones (296)
high-definition television (HDTV) (291)
host computer (299)
ink-jet printer (293)
intelligent terminal (299)
Internet telephone (297)
Internet telephony (297)
Internet terminal (299)
IP Telephony (297)
laser printer (293)
liquid crystal display (LCD) (290)
monitor (289)
multifunction device (MFD) (297)
network computer (299)
network terminal (299)
Net Personal Computer (Net PC) (299)
output (288)
output device (288)
passive-matrix monitor (290)
PC/TV (291)
personal laser printer (294)
photo printer (295)
pixel (289)
plasma display (291)
plotter (295)
portable printer (295)
printer (292)
reading machine (302)
refresh rate (290)
resolution (289)
screen (289)
screen reader (302)
server (299)
shared laser printer (294)
soft copy (289)
size (290)
speakers (296)
speed (293)
super extended graphics array (SXGA) (290)
super video graphics array (SVGA) (290)
telephony (297)
terminal (299)
text output (288)
thermal printer (294)
thin client (299)
thin film transistor monitor (TFT) (291)
Ultra Extended Graphics Array (UXGA) (290)
video output (288)
voice output device (302)
voice-over IP (VoIP) (297)
Web appliance (299)
Web terminal (299)

To test your knowledge of these key terms with animated flash cards, select Flash Cards from Tim's Toolbox at http://www.mhhe.com/oleary/CT05.

CHAPTER REVIEW

CROSSWORD

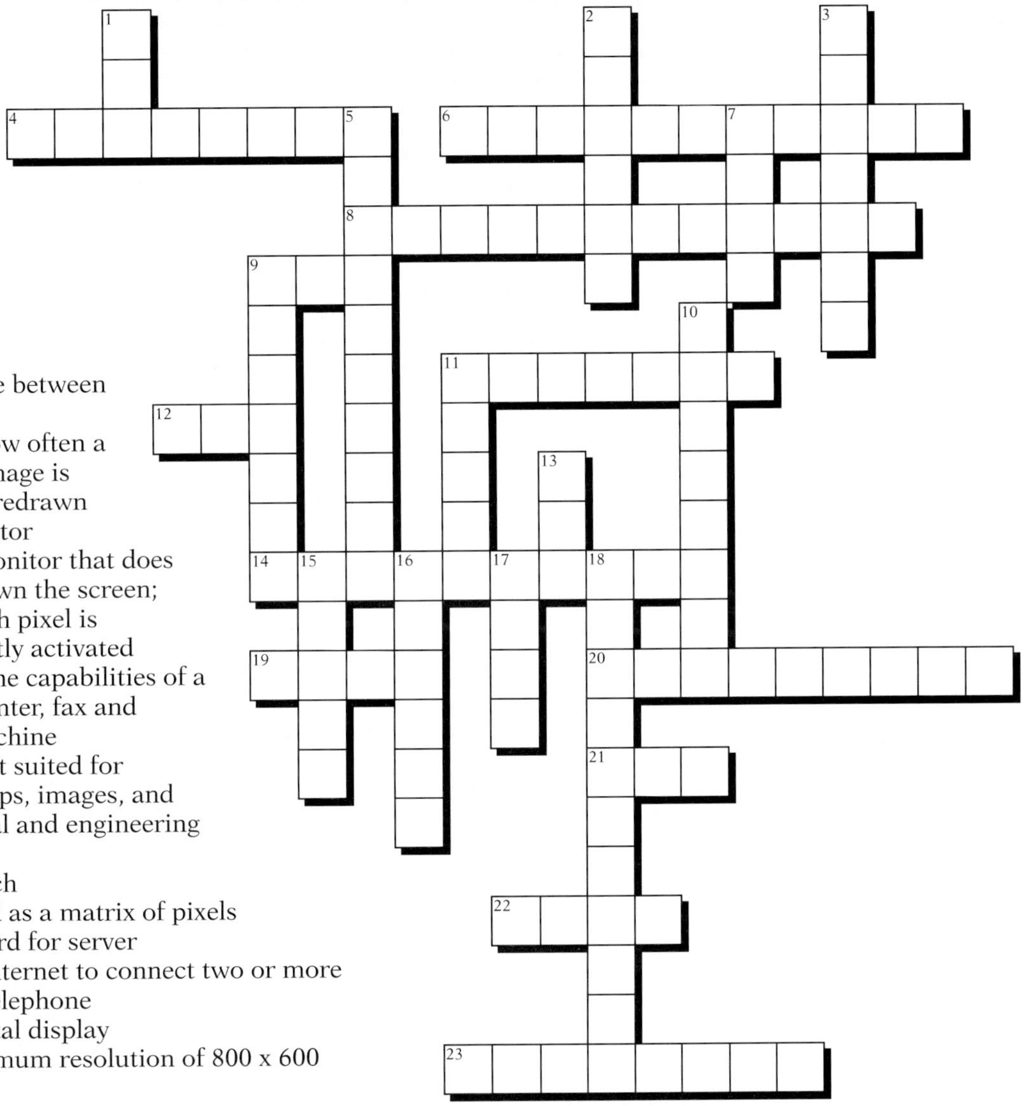

ACROSS

4 The distance between each pixel
6 Indicates how often a displayed image is updated or redrawn on the monitor
8 A type of monitor that does not scan down the screen; instead, each pixel is independently activated
9 Combines the capabilities of a scanner, printer, fax and copying machine
11 Printers best suited for creating maps, images, and architectural and engineering drawings
12 Dots-per-inch
14 Is expressed as a matrix of pixels
19 Another word for server
20 Using the internet to connect two or more people by telephone
21 Liquid crystal display
22 Has a maximum resolution of 800 x 600 pixels
23 Monitor output

DOWN

1 Cathode Ray Tube
2 Host computer
3 Refers to the quality and sharpness of the displayed images
5 One of the most widely used audio-output devices
7 Delivers a clearer and more detailed picture than regular television
9 Most frequently used output device; also known as a display screen
10 An input and output device that connects you to a mainframe
11 Picture elements
13 Thin film transistor
15 Handheld, book-sized device that displays text and graphics
16 Processed data or information
17 Ultra Extended Graphics Array
18 A terminal that includes a processing unit, memory, and secondary storage such as a magnetic disk

For an interactive crossword puzzle select Crosswords from Tim's Toolbox at http://www.mhhe.com/oleary/CT05.

MULTIPLE CHOICE

Circle the letter or fill in the correct answer.

1. A handheld, book-sized device used to read downloaded content is a(n) ________.
   - **a.** wand reader
   - **b.** e-book
   - **c.** light pen
   - **d.** graphic tablet
   - **e.** digital notebook
2. ________ are special-purpose printers that use output from digitizing tablets and other graphics input devices.
   - **a.** Fax machines
   - **b.** Portable scanners
   - **c.** Ink-jets
   - **d.** Plotters
   - **e.** Thermals
3. Speakers and headphones are the most widely used ________ devices.
   - **a.** audio-input
   - **b.** audio
   - **c.** audio-output
   - **d.** multifunctional
   - **e.** personal
4. A(n) ________ typically combines the capabilities of a scanner, printer, fax, and copying machine.
   - **a.** multifunctional device
   - **b.** output device
   - **c.** input device
   - **d.** MICR
   - **e.** dumb terminal
5. ________ uses the Internet rather than traditional communication lines to connect two or more people via telephone.
   - **a.** A multifunctional device
   - **b.** A fax machine
   - **c.** A dumb terminal
   - **d.** Telephony
   - **e.** An output device
6. A network computer is also known as a(n) ________.
   - **a.** thin client
   - **b.** intelligent terminal
   - **c.** dumb terminal
   - **d.** Net PC
   - **e.** Web terminal
7. Printers convert information output to human language or symbols and transfer it onto paper as ________.
   - **a.** soft copy
   - **b.** hard copy
   - **c.** TFT
   - **d.** dot-matrix
   - **e.** facsimile
8. ________ are typically used within organizations to serve several computers connected by a network or a mainframe computer.
   - **a.** Laser printers
   - **b.** Ink-jet printers
   - **c.** Plotters
   - **d.** Fax machines
   - **e.** Dot-matrix printers
9. ________ are less expensive and are used by many single users.
   - **a.** Personal laser printers
   - **b.** Shared laser printers
   - **c.** Ink-jet printers
   - **d.** Plotters
   - **e.** Fax machines
10. ________ use a scanner to process printed text, a program to read the text, and your speakers to output the text as voice output.
    - **a.** Braille output devices
    - **b.** Plotters
    - **c.** Reading Devices
    - **d.** Assistants
    - **e.** Magnifiers

To test your knowledge of this chapter, select Self Test from Tim's Toolbox at http://www.mhhe.com/oleary/CT05.

MATCHING

Match each numbered item with the most closely related lettered item. Write your answers in the spaces provided.

a. clarity
b. CRT
c. data projector
d. dpi
e. dumb terminal
f. fax machine
g. HDTV
h. host computer
i. ink-jet
j. Internet terminal
k. Internet telephony
l. LCD
m. output
n. passive-matrix
o. plasma display
p. plotter
q. SXGA
r. TFT
s. thermal
t. thin client

1. Processed data or information from a computer. ____
2. Specialized devices similar to slide projectors. ____
3. Indicated by resolution and measured in pixels. ____
4. Monitors that do not scan down the screen; instead each pixel is independently activated. ____
5. Super Extended Graphics Array. ____
6. Contain millions of pixels that are illuminated by charged neon gas. ____
7. Type of desktop monitor built like a television set. ____
8. The technology for portable monitors involving liquid crystals. ____
9. Uses the Internet rather than traditional communication lines to connect two or more people via telephone. ____
10. Can be used to input and receive data, but cannot process data independently. ____
11. Delivers a much clearer and more detailed wide-screen picture than regular television. ____
12. Terminal that provides Web access without a microcomputer. ____
13. These devices scan the image of a document converting the light and dark areas into a format that can be sent electronically over standard telephone lines. ____
14. Monitor that creates images by scanning the entire screen. ____
15. Measurement used to determine resolution. ____
16. Printer that sprays ink at high speed onto the surface of the paper. ____
17. Mainframe or other type of computer a terminal connects to. ____
18. Printer that uses heat elements to produce images on heat-sensitive paper. ____
19. Printer used to create maps, images, and architectural and engineering drawings. ____
20. Terminal that relies on host computer or server for software. ____

OPEN-ENDED

On a separate sheet of paper, respond to each question or statement.

1. Describe the three categories of output devices.
2. Discuss the various types of monitors and the monitor standards.
3. Describe the different types of printers.
4. What are combination input and output devices? Describe four such devices.
5. Describe the most common assistive output devices.

USING TECHNOLOGY

1 Internet Telephony

Do you need a cheaper way to stay in touch with friends and family? Did you know you can use your computer and the Internet to make long-distance calls to regular phones? All you need is some software and an Internet connection to get started. To learn more about this technology, review Making IT Work for You: Internet Telephony on pages 300 and 301. Then answer the following questions: (a) Which Internet phone service provider is featured in the examples? (b) What are the sliders used for in the Setup Wizard? (c) Which button is clicked to end a call?

2 MSN TV

MSN TV provides Internet access without the need for a traditional computer. Visit our Web site at http://www.mhhe.com/oleary/CT05 and select Using Technology from Tim's Toolbox to connect to the MSN TV home page. Once connected, read about this product and answer the following questions: (a) What is MSN TV? (b) What is required to use MSN TV? (c) What type of user might use this product? (d) Consider your own Internet and general computing needs. Is MSN TV a product for you? Why or why not?

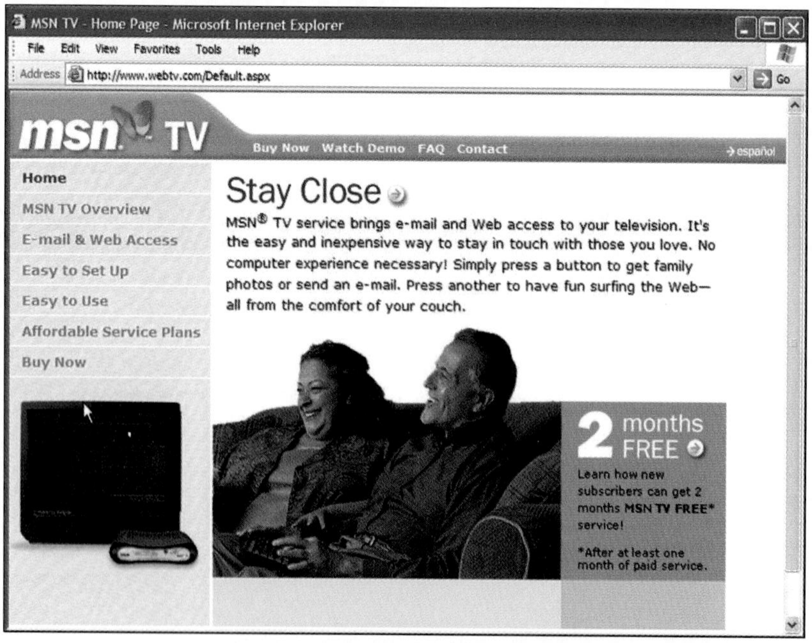

Home Automation 3

Did you know that you can control lighting, temperature, and even your television from your computer? Special hardware can be added to automate your home, and turn any electrical appliance into an output device. Visit our Web site at http://www.mhhe.com/oleary/CT05 and select Using Technology from Tim's Toolbox to link to a site that offers home automation products. Once connected, explore the site, and briefly answer the following questions: (a) How do the home automation devices communicate with a computer? (b) How are home automation devices installed? (c) What kind of users would benefit most from home automation?

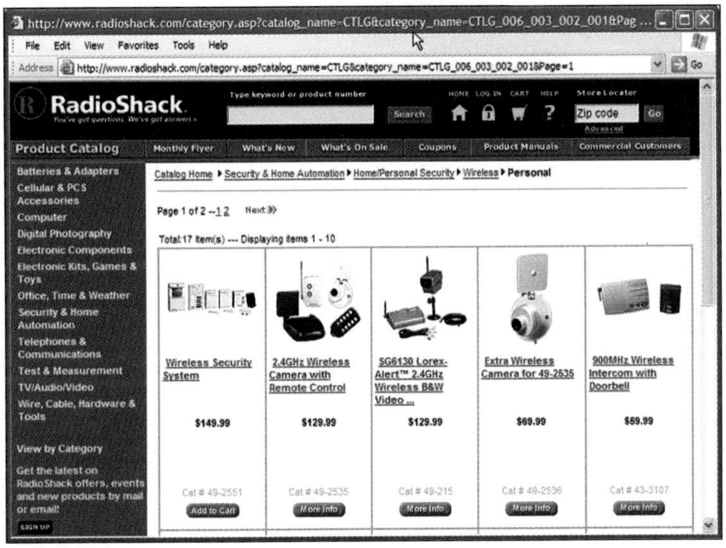

Digital Audio Receivers 4

A Digital Audio Receiver lets you use your computer to play digital music on your home stereo equipment. Connect to our Web site at http://www.mhhe.com/oleary/CT05 and select Using Technology from Tim's Toolbox to link to a manufacturer of Digital Audio Receivers. Once connected, read about the product and answer the following questions: (a) How does the Digital Audio Receiver access audio files from a computer? (b) How does the Digital Audio Receiver connect to a home stereo system? (c) In what ways does the Digital Audio Receiver differ from other audio-output devices?

EXPANDING YOUR KNOWLEDGE

1 Computing Today CD

Internet telephones offer a low cost alternative to making long distance calls. Using the Internet telephone (or other appropriate audio input and output devices), the Internet, a special service provider, a sound card, and special software, you can place long distance calls to almost anywhere in the world. After reviewing Figure 8-20 and viewing the animation How Internet Telephony Works from your Computing Today CD or from Tim's Toolbox at http://www.mhhe.com/oleary/CT05, answer the following questions: (a) What input and output devices are used? (b) What advantages and disadvantages would these devices have compared to an Internet telephone? (c) If Chris were to place a call to Steve, would she incur traditional long distance charges? Why or why not? (d) Create a drawing similar to Figure 8-20 that would represent computer-to-computer telephony. Be sure to include and number the appropriate steps.

2 E-book Readers

Although experts remain optimistic about the future of e-books, most publishing is still delivered as hard copy. One reason for this is the lack of standards for e-book output devices. Use the Web to re-search e-books, and then answer the following questions: (a) What are the most popular e-book readers available today? (b) Where can owners of e-book readers get e-books to read? (c) Can the e-book readers you located all read the same type of files? (d) What types of books are not available as e-books? (e) Do you think e-books will completely replace hard copy in the future? Justify your answer.

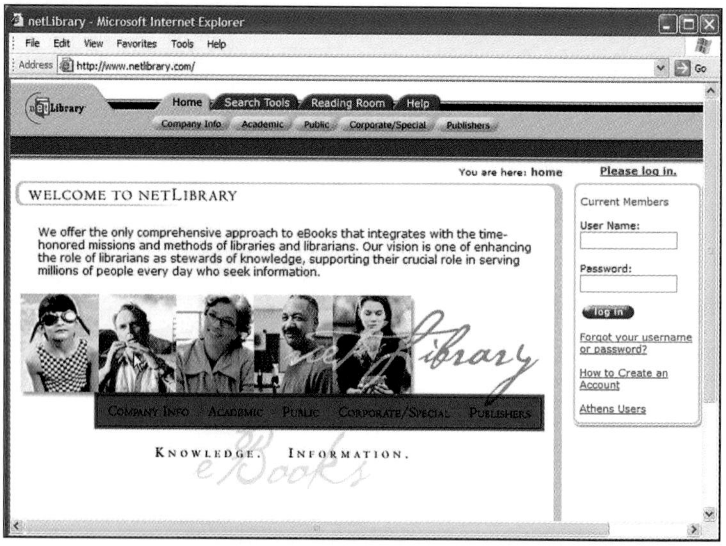

SimNet CD 3

Using your SimNet CD, complete the output sections in Chapter 8: Output and then answer the following questions in a one-page paper.

a. Label each of the components below.

b. What are some differences between a plotter and an ink-jet printer?

c. Describe the two types of monitors.

d. Describe the types of printers.

e. What type of printer is less expensive in the long run?

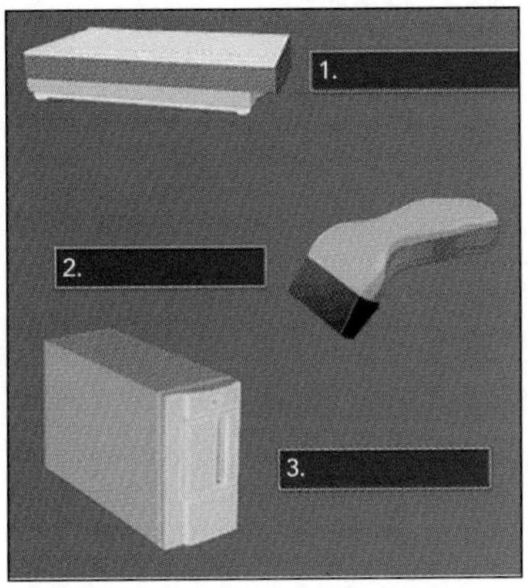

HDTV 4

The future of television seems to be High Definition Television, or HDTV. Connect to our Web site at http://www.mhhe.com/oleary/CT05 and select Expanding Your Knowledge from Tim's Toolbox to link to a site with information about HDTV. Explore the site, and answer the following questions: (a) What are the major differences between HDTV and analog (regular) television? (b) What equipment is necessary to use HDTV? (c) What screen resolutions does HDTV use? How do these compare with typical computer screen resolutions?

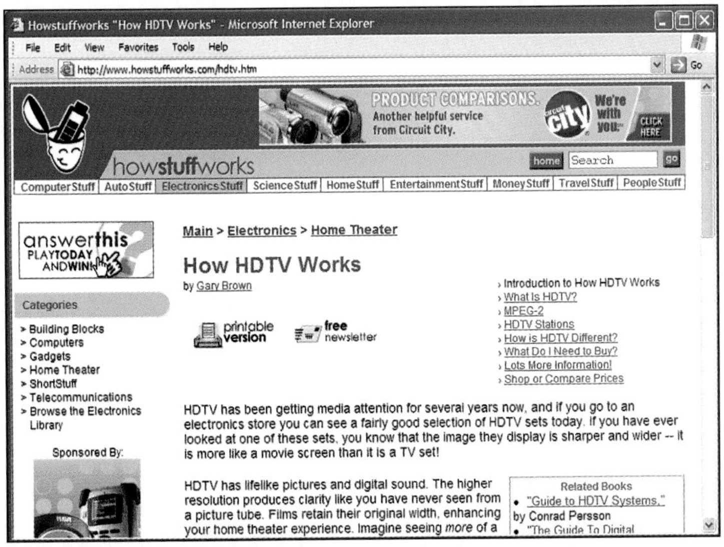

BUILDING YOUR PORTFOLIO

1 3D Printers

Special 3D printers can be used to create models of parts for fabrication. These printers can actually create 3-dimensional objects from a computer model, and many believe they will become commonplace equipment for regular users in the future. Imagine downloading and printing a spare part or product, rather than having it shipped to you! Use the Web to research 3D printers, and then answer the following questions in a one-page paper: (a) Who uses 3D printers today? (b) Describe how 3D printers work. What do 3D printers use as "ink"? (c) Can you think of any ethical or legal issues having 3D printers in the home might present? Give some examples.

2 Monitors

Monitors are perhaps the most important display device, and many options are available for monitors. Write a one-page paper titled "Monitor Options" that addresses the following topics: (a) Describe the four main standards for monitors. (b) What important characteristics are monitors compared by? (c) What are the three main types of monitors, and what kind of user is each best suited for?

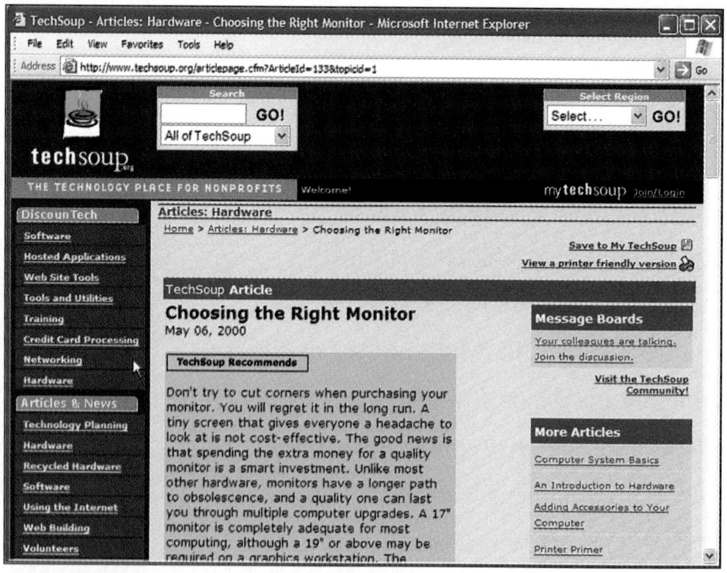

The Future of Internet Telephony 3

Internet Telephony, sometimes known as Voice Over Internet Protocol (VoIP), may well be the future of telephone service. Internet providers, cable television companies, and traditional telephone companies now offer "digital" phone service to many clients, which often uses the Internet to carry calls. Use the Web to research Internet Telephony, and write a one-page paper that addresses the following topics: (a) Define Internet Telephony. (b) How does Internet Telephony technology differ from current telephone technology? (c) What are the advantages of Internet Telephony? (d) What Internet Telephony solutions are available now? Cite specific examples.

Terminals 4

Terminals provide input and output to a host computer or server. Write a one-page paper titled "Terminal Systems" that answers the following questions: (a) What are the four kinds of terminals? Describe each. (b) What uses are each kind of terminal best suited for? (c) Why might a business choose to invest in terminals instead of individual computers? (d) As more and more productive work is done over the Internet, individual computer power becomes less important. Do you think terminals will replace computers for office tasks? Justify your answer.

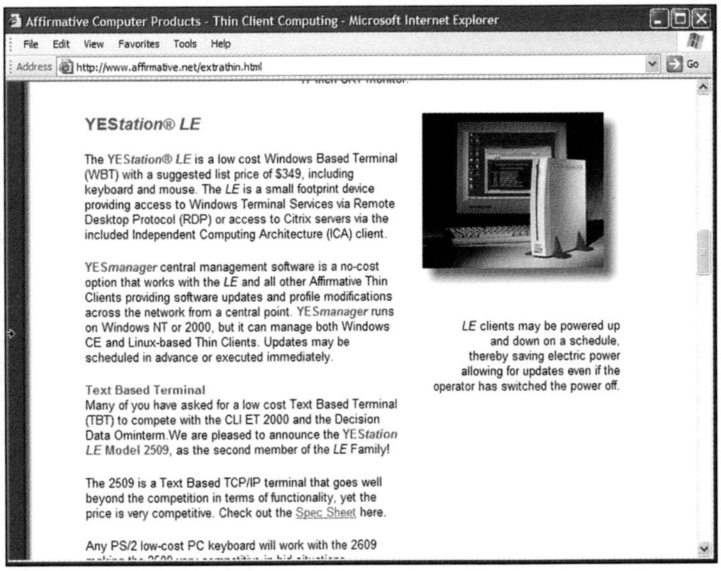

SECONDARY STORAGE

OBJECTIVES

After you have read this chapter, you should be able to:

1. Distinguish between primary and secondary storage.

2. Discuss the different types of storage media including floppy disks, hard disks, and optical disks.

2. Describe the traditional floppy disk and compare it to high capacity floppy disks.

3. Describe the following kinds of hard disks: internal hard disks, hard-disk cartridges, and hard-disk packs.

4. Describe ways to improve hard-disk operations: disk caching, redundant arrays of inexpensive disks, data compression and decompression.

5. Describe the different types of optical disks.

6. Describe other kinds of secondary storage including solid state storage, Internet drives, magnetic tape, microfilm, and microfiche.

7. Discuss secondary storage devices for portable computers.

8. Describe mass storage and enterprise storage systems.

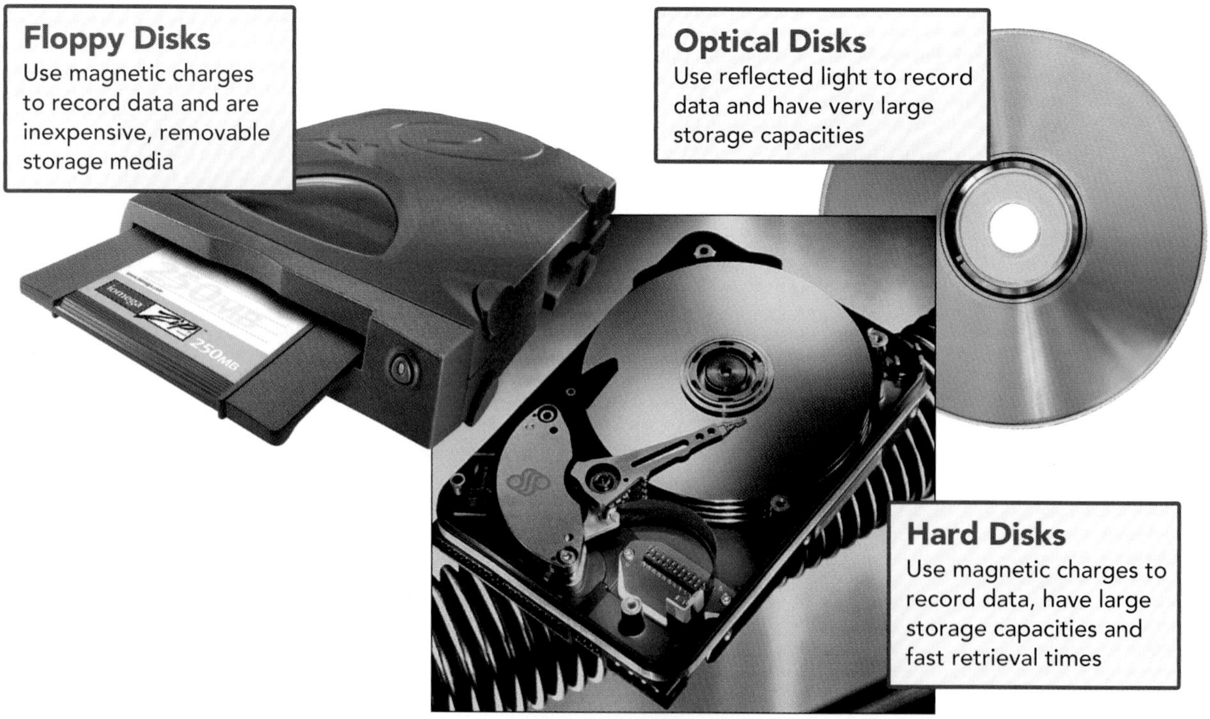

Floppy Disks
Use magnetic charges to record data and are inexpensive, removable storage media

Optical Disks
Use reflected light to record data and have very large storage capacities

Hard Disks
Use magnetic charges to record data, have large storage capacities and fast retrieval times

Secondary storage devices are used to save, to back up, and even to transport files consisting of data or programs from one location or computer to another. Not long ago, almost all files contained only numbers and letters. The demands for saving these files were easily met with low capacity floppy and hard-disk drives. For example, to save a 100-page research paper might require 400 KB of storage easily fitting onto a single floppy disk.

In the past five years, however, secondary storage devices have been required to service much greater demands. Data storage has expanded from text and numeric files to include digital music files, photographic files, video files, and much more. These new types of files require secondary storage devices that have much greater capacity. For example, a 10-minute video might require 100 MB of storage.

Today's secondary storage devices are routinely used for a variety of tasks that were impossible just a few years ago. CDs and DVDs, for example, store data that can be used over and over again. You can download music from the Internet, play it on your computer, and create custom CDs with the right hardware and software.

Secondary storage devices have always been an indispensable element in any computer system. They have similarities to output and input devices. Like output devices, secondary storage devices receive information from the system unit in the form of the machine language of 0s and 1s. Rather than translating the information, however, secondary storage devices save the information in machine language for later use. Like input devices, secondary storage devices send information to the system unit for processing. However, the information, since it is already in machine form, does not need to be translated. It is sent directly to memory (RAM), where it can be accessed and processed by the CPU.

Competent and knowledgeable end users need to be aware of the different types of secondary storage. They need to know the capabilities, limitations, and uses of floppy disks, hard disks, optical disks, and other types of secondary storage. Additionally, they need to be aware of specialty storage devices for portable computers and to be knowledgeable about how large organizations manage their extensive data resources.

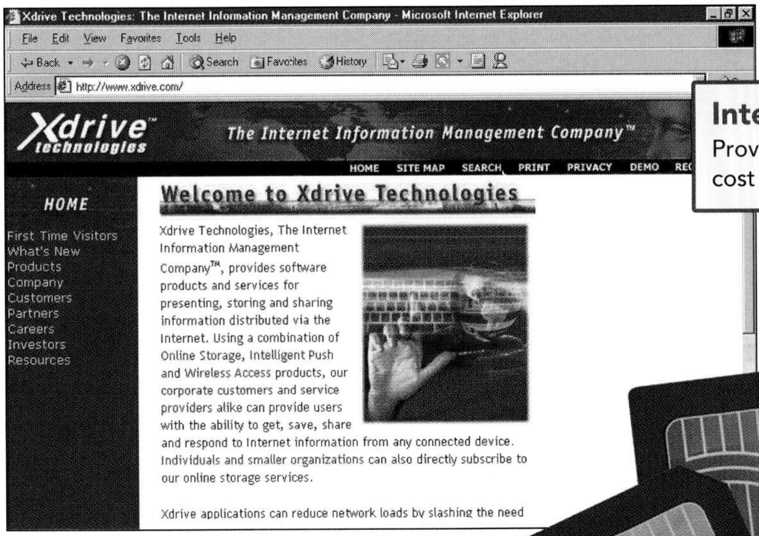

Internet Hard Drives
Provide Web-based, low-cost storage

Solid State Storage
Has no moving parts and data is stored and retrieved electronically

STORAGE

Primary storage is volatile. Secondary storage is nonvolatile. Files are written to and read from secondary storage. Important storage characteristics include media, capacity, secondary storage devices, and access speed.

An essential feature of every computer is the ability to save, or store, information. As discussed in Chapter 6, random-access memory (RAM) holds or stores data and programs that the CPU is presently processing. Before data can be processed or a program can be run, it must be in RAM. For this reason, RAM is sometimes referred to as **primary storage.**

Unfortunately, most RAM provides only temporary or **volatile storage.** That is, it loses all of its contents as soon as the computer is turned off. Its contents are also lost if there is a power failure that disrupts the electric current going into the system unit. This volatility results in a need for more permanent or **nonvolatile storage** for data and programs. We also need external storage because users need much more storage capacity than is typically available in a computer's primary or RAM memory.

Secondary storage provides permanent or nonvolatile storage. Using **secondary storage devices,** such as a floppy disk drive, data and programs can be retained after the computer has been shut off. This is accomplished by *writing* files to and *reading* files from secondary storage devices. **Writing** is the process of saving information *to* the secondary storage device. **Reading** is the process of accessing information *from* secondary storage. This chapter focuses on secondary storage devices.

Figure 9-1 Secondary storage media

Some important characteristics of secondary storage include:

- **Media** or **medium** which is the actual physical material that holds the data and programs. (See Figure 9-1.)
- **Capacity** measures how much a particular storage medium can hold.
- **Storage devices** are hardware that reads data and programs from storage media. Most also write to storage media.
- **Access speed** or **access time** measures the amount of time required by the storage device to retrieve data and programs.

Most desktop microcomputer systems have floppy, hard, and optical disk drives. Each of these has unique characteristics including access speed and cost. For a comparison of access speed and cost for various types of storage including RAM, see the Storage Pyramid represented in Figure 9-2. The base of the pyramid represents floppy disks with the slowest access speed combined with the lowest cost. The top represents RAM with the fastest access speed and highest cost.

Concept Check

- What is the difference between primary and secondary storage?
- Distinguish between writing files and reading files.
- Discuss four important characteristics of secondary storage.

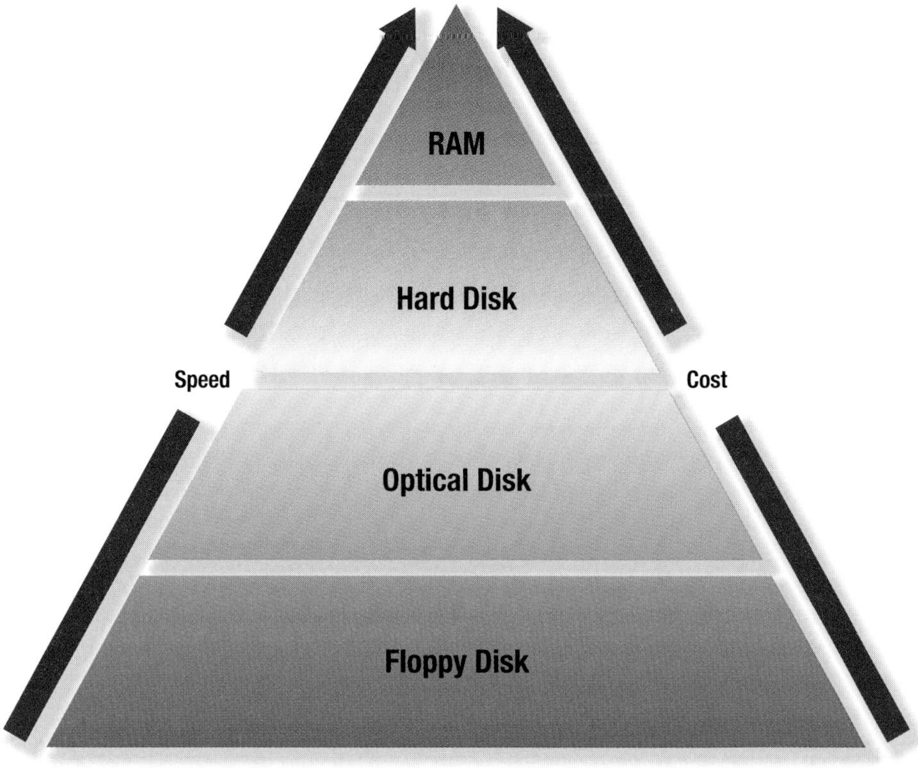

Figure 9-2 Storage pyramid

FLOPPY DISKS

Floppy disks are removable storage media. The traditional floppy disk is 1.44 MB. Data is recorded on tracks and sectors. Floppy disk drives access clusters of data. Zip, SuperDisk, and HiFD are high capacity floppy disks.

Floppy disks, often called **diskettes** or simply **disks,** are portable or removable storage media. They are typically used to store and transport word processing, spreadsheet, and other types of files. They use flat circular pieces of Mylar plastic that have been coated with a magnetic material. **Floppy disk drives (FDD)** store data and programs by altering the electromagnetic charges on the disk's surface to represent ones and zeros. Floppy disk drives retrieve data and programs by reading these charges from the magnetic disk. Characters are represented by positive (+) and negative (−) charges using the ASCII, EBCDIC, or Unicode binary codes. For example, the number 3 would require a series of 8 charges. (See Figure 9-3.)

Floppy disks are also called **flexible disks** and **floppies.** This is because the plastic disk inside the diskette cover is flexible, not rigid. There are several types of floppy disks with different capacities ranging from the traditional floppy disk to a variety of high capacity floppy disks.

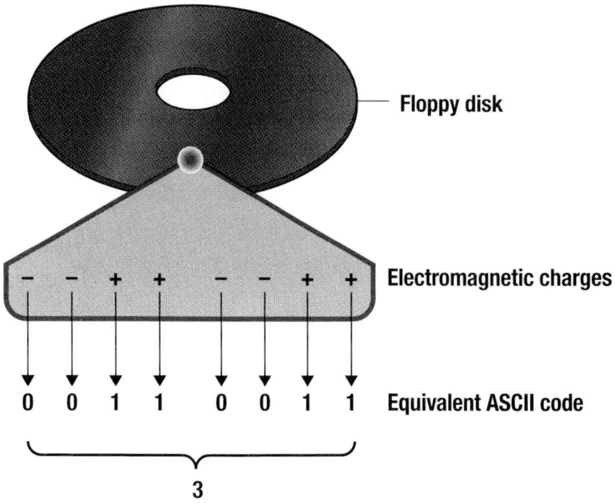

Figure 9-3 How charges on a disk surface store the number 3

TRADITIONAL FLOPPY DISK

Figure 9-4 A 1.44 MB 3½ -inch floppy disk

The traditional floppy disk is the **1.44 MB 3½-inch disk.** (See Figure 9-4.) Although introduced over 20 years ago, they are still widely used. The most common type is labelled **2HD,** which means "two-sided, high-density." Two-sided indicates that data can be stored on both sides of the disk. **Density** refers to how tightly the bits (electromagnetic charges) can be packed next to one another. These disks have a capacity of 1.44 megabytes—the equivalent of over 350 typewritten pages.

Floppy disks have a thin exterior jacket made of hard plastic to protect the flexible disk inside. (See Figure 9-5.) A **shutter** on the disk slides to the side to expose the recording surface. **Labels** provide users with an area to write or document the contents of the disk. The **write-protection notch** has a slide that opens and closes. In either position, files can be read from the floppy disk. When the notch is closed, files can be saved to the disk. If you save a file with the same name as a file already on the disk, the original file is lost. As a protection against accidentally losing important files, the write-protection notch can be set to the open position as shown in Figure 9-5. In this position, files cannot be saved to the floppy disk.

As we discussed in Chapter 5, files are stored and organized on the flexible disk according to tracks and sectors. **Tracks** are rings of concentric circles without visible grooves. Each track is divided into invisible wedge-shaped sections called **sectors.** Each track's sector can store up to 512 bytes or characters. A typical 1.44 MB 3½-inch floppy disk has 80 tracks with 18 sectors on each side. Some disks are manufactured without tracks and sectors in place. They must be adapted to the type of microcomputer and disk drive you are using. You do this using the operating system through a process called **formatting,** or **initializing.**

For most microcomputer systems, the **floppy disk drive** is mounted in the system unit and designated as the **A drive.** When a floppy disk is inserted into the drive, the disk's shutter opens and the drive's **read/write head** moves across the exposed disk's surface to either retrieve (read) information or save (write) information. The smallest amount of disk space that can be read from or written to a floppy disk is called a **cluster** or **allocation unit.**

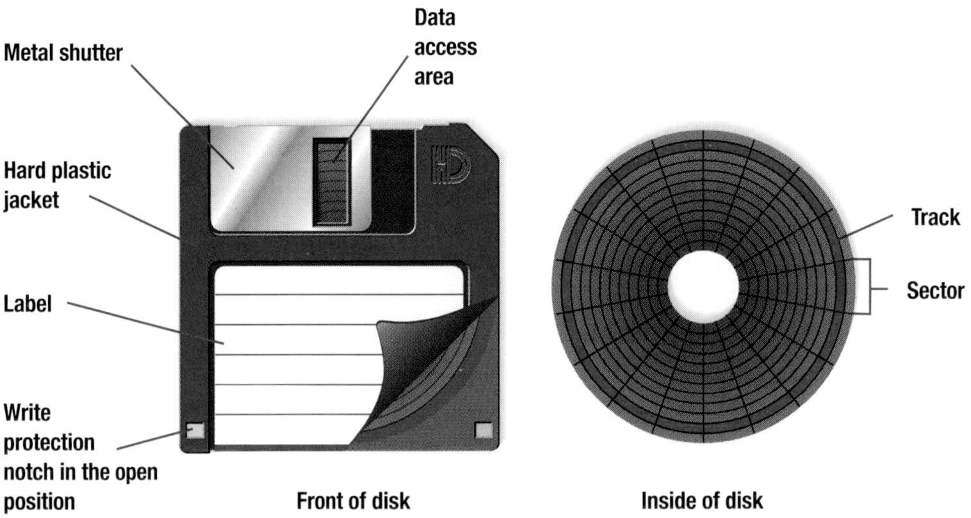

Figure 9-5 The parts of a 3½-inch floppy disk

The size of the cluster is determined by the operating system. For example, a cluster with two sectors has a capacity of 1024 bytes (512 bytes per sector multiplied by 2 sectors). When a file is stored, it will use an entire cluster even for small files. If the file is larger that the capacity of one cluster, it will use additional clusters. As discussed in Chapter 5, the operating system will attempt to store a large file in adjacent sectors and clusters. If it cannot, the file is broken up into parts or **fragments** and stored wherever possible.

To see how a floppy disk drive works, see Figure 9-6.

How a Floppy Disk Drive Works

Step 1: Insert Disk. When disk is inserted, the drive opens the shutter and positions read/write heads to just touch the data access area.

Step 2: Receive Instruction. Via cables connected to the system board, the drive receives a request to save a copy of a file located in RAM.

Step 3: Check Write Protection. The drive directs a light at the disk's write protection notch. If the light passes through (notch open) the drive refuses the request. If the light does not pass through (notch closed), the drive accepts the request.

Step 4: Check Filename. Working with the operating system, the new file name is compared to those on the disk. If a duplication occurs and data could be lost, the user is given the option to rename the new file or overwrite (lose) the existing file.

Step 5: Position Heads. The drive rotates the disk and positions the read/write heads to an open or free area on the disk's surface.

Step 6: Save File. A copy of the file is sent from RAM to the drive. The read/write heads alter the charges on the disk's surface to save the file.

Figure 9-6 How a floppy disk drive works

Figure 9-7 Zip disk and drive

HIGH CAPACITY FLOPPY DISKS

While the traditional floppy disk is very reliable and still widely used to store data, it has very limited capacity. While 1.44 MB is fine for many text and spreadsheet files, it is not sufficient to hold larger files. For example, many PowerPoint presentation files far exceed 1.44 MB. Most multimedia applications require even greater capacity. **High capacity disks,** also known as **floppy-disk cartridges,** are rapidly replacing the traditional floppy disk. Like the traditional floppy, the high capacity disks are 3½ inches in diameter. However, they are able to store more information, are thicker, and require special disk drives. The three best known high capacity disks are Zip, HiFD, and SuperDisks.

- **Zip disks** are produced by Iomega and typically have a 100 MB, 250 MB, or 750MB capacity—over 500 times as much as today's standard floppy disk. Internal Zip drives are a standard feature on many of today's system units. External Zip drives are generally connected to the system unit using parallel or USB ports. Zip disks are widely used to store multimedia, database, large text, and spreadsheet files. (See Figure 9-7.)
- **HiFD disks** from the Sony Corporation have a capacity of 200 MB or 720MB. They have one major advantage over Zip disks. HiFD drives are able to read and store data on today's 1.44 MB traditional disk as well as on their own higher capacity disks. For this reason, HiFD are popular for use with notebook computers.
- **SuperDisks** are produced by Imation and have a 120 MB or 240 MB capacity. Like HiFD drives, SuperDisk disk drives are able to use today's 1.44 MB standard disks.

Each of these will likely improve its capacity and speed in the near future. Will one of them become the next standard floppy disk? While most observers believe one will become the next standard, they are less certain which one and when this will occur. For a summary of floppy disk capacities, see Figure 9-8.

On the Web Explorations

Iomega and Imation are leaders in developing high capacity floppy disks. To learn more about the companies, visit our Web site at

http://www.mhhe.com/oleary/CT05

and select On the Web Explorations from Tim's Toolbox.

Description	Capacity
2HD	1.44 MB
Zip	100/250/750 MB
HiFD	200/720 MB
SuperDisk	120/240 MB

Figure 9-8 Typical floppy-disk capacities

TIPS Are you concerned about losing the data stored on your floppy disks? Actually, floppy disks are quite durable, and taking care of them boils down to just a few basic rules.

1. **Don't bend.** Don't bend them, flex them, or put heavy weights on them.
2. **Don't touch.** Don't touch anything visible through the protective jacket.
3. **Don't remove.** Never attempt to remove a disk when it is rotating and in use.
4. **Avoid extreme conditions.** Keep disks away from strong magnetic fields, extreme heat, and any chemicals such as alcohol and other solvents.
5. **Use storage boxes.** Store disks in a sturdy plastic storage box.

Of course the best protection is to make a backup or duplicate copy of your disk.

Concept Check

- What is the traditional floppy disk? Why is it likely to be replaced in the future?
- What are tracks, sectors, and clusters? How are they used?
- List three high capacity floppy disks.

HARD DISKS

Hard disks store files using tracks, sectors, and cylinders. Internal hard disks are fixed. Hard-disk cartridges are removable. Hard-disk packs are high capacity and removable. Disk caching, RAID, and file compression/decompression improve hard disk performance.

Like floppy disks, hard disks save files by altering the magnetic charges of the disk's surface. While a floppy disk uses a thin flexible plastic disk, a **hard disk** uses thicker, rigid metallic **platters** that are stacked one on top of another. Hard disks store and organize files using tracks, sectors, and cylinders. A **cylinder** runs through each track of a stack of platters. (See Figure 9-9.) Although not needed by floppy disks that have a single platter, cylinders are necessary to differentiate files stored on the same track and sector of different platters. When a hard disk is formatted, tracks, sectors, and cylinders are assigned.

Compared to floppy disks, hard disks are able to store and retrieve information much faster and have a greater capacity. They are, however, sensitive instruments. Their read/write heads ride on a cushion of air about 0.000001 inches thick. It is so thin that a smoke particle, fingerprint, dust, or human hair could cause what is known as a head crash. (See Figure 9-10.)

A **head crash** occurs when a read/write head makes contact with the hard disk's surface or with particles on its surface. A head crash is a disaster for a hard disk. The disk surface is scratched and some or all of the data is destroyed. At one time, head crashes were commonplace. Now, fortunately, they are rare.

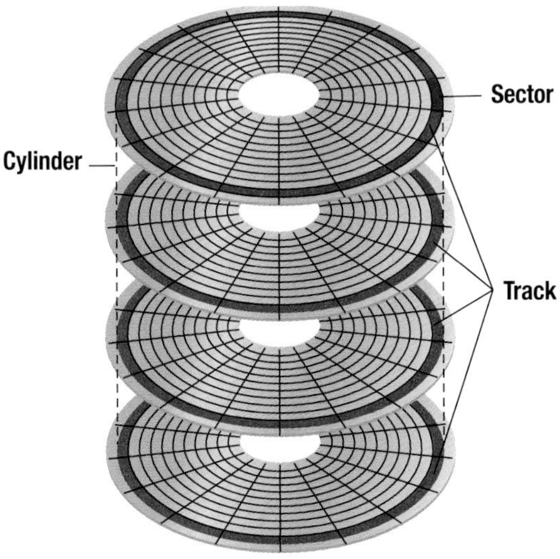

Figure 9-9 Tracks, sectors, and cylinders

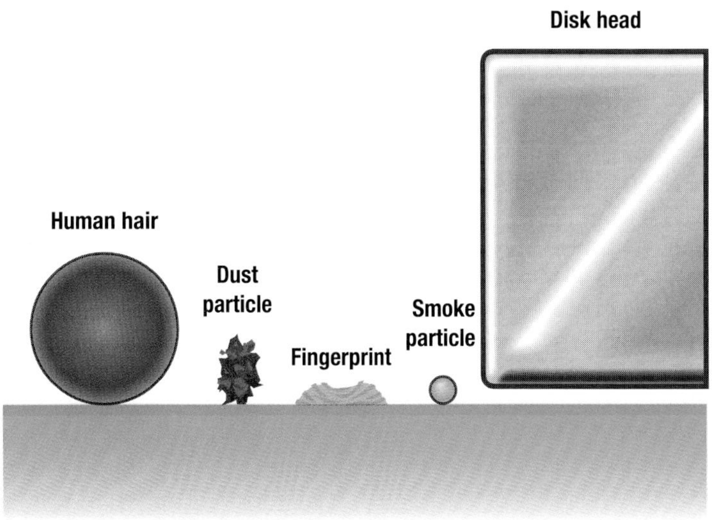

Figure 9-10 Materials that can cause a head crash

There are three types of hard disks: internal hard disk, hard-disk cartridge, and hard-disk pack.

INTERNAL HARD DISK

An **internal hard disk,** also known as a **fixed disk,** is located inside the system unit. For most microcomputer systems, the internal hard disk drive is designated as the **C drive.** It is used to store programs and large data files. For example, nearly every microcomputer uses its internal hard disk to store its operating system and major applications such as Word and Excel.

Internal hard disks have two advantages over floppy disks: capacity and access speed. A 100-gigabyte internal hard disk, for instance, can hold almost as much information as 70,000 standard floppy disks. Because hard disks rotate faster and their read/write heads are closer to the recording surface, the time required to find and retrieve information (access speed) is much faster than floppy disks. For these reasons, almost all of today's powerful applications are designed to be stored on and run from an internal hard disk. Adequate internal hard disk capacity is essential.

A typical microcomputer's internal hard disk has a motor, read/write heads, and four metallic platters sealed inside a container. The container protects against head crashes and is connected to the system board by a **hard disk controller (HDC) card.** There are two basic types of hard disk controllers:

- **Enhanced integrated drive electronics (EIDE) controller cards** can support as many as four separate hard-disk drives.
- **Small computer system interface (SCSI) controller cards** can support numerous hard drives as well as other devices. Compared to EIDE drives, SCSI disk drives are faster and more expensive.

To see how a hard disk works, see Figure 9-11.

To ensure adequate performance of your internal hard disk, you should perform routine maintenance and periodically make backup copies of all important files. For hard disk maintenance and backup procedures, refer to Chapter 5's coverage of the Windows utilities Disk Cleaner, Disk Defragmenter, Backup, and System Restore.

On the Web Explorations

Seagate is one of the leaders in developing high-capacity internal hard disks. To learn more about the company, visit our Web site at http://www.mhhe.com/oleary/CT05 and select On the Web Explorations from Tim's Toolbox.

TIPS Does your internal hard-disk drive run a lot and seem slow? Are you having problems with lost or corrupted files? The problem could be with fragmented files—files that when saved were broken into pieces (fragments) and stored in different locations on your hard disk. To clean up the disk and speed up access, consider defragging. If you are using Windows 98, 2000, or XP:

1. **Start Disk Defragmenter.** As discussed in Chapter 5, use Start/All Programs/Accessories/System Tools/Disk Defragmenter to start defragmenting your disk. Defragging rearranges the file parts so that they are stored in adjacent locations.
2. **Keep working.** You can continue running other applications while your disk is being defragmented. Unfortunately, your computer operates more slowly, and Disk Defragmenter takes longer to finish.
3. **Automate.** Use Start/All Programs/Accessories/System tools/Scheduled tasks to schedule this task to be done automatically for you in the future.

HARD-DISK CARTRIDGES

While internal hard disks provide fast access, they have a fixed amount of storage and cannot be easily removed from the system cabinet. **Hard-disk cartridges,** also known as **removable hard disks,** are as easy to remove as a cassette from a videocassette recorder. The amount of storage available to a computer system is limited only by the number of cartridges.

Hard-disk cartridges are used primarily to complement an internal hard disk. Because the cartridges are easily removed, they are particularly useful to protect or secure sensitive information. For example, personnel administrators need to have access to highly confidential employee information. When information is stored on a hard-disk cartridge, it is readily available, yet can be easily locked up when not in use. Other uses for hard-disk cartridges include

How an Internal Hard Disk Works

Step 1: Platters Rotate. All of the platters are connected to a common spindle. When the computer system is turned on, the spindle rotates the platters. For some computer systems, the platters continue to rotate as long as the system is turned on. For others, if the platters have not been used for some time, they will coast to a stop.

Step 2: Receive Instruction. Via a connection to the hard disk controller card, the internal hard disk receives a request to copy a file currently in RAM.

Step 3: Position Heads. If the platters have been coasting, they are returned to full speed. The read/write heads are mounted on a common support arm.

Step 4: Check Filename. Working with the operating system, the new filename is compared to those on the platters. If a duplication occurs and data could be lost, the user is given the option to rename the new file or overwrite (lose) the existing file.

Step 5: Save File. A copy of the file in RAM is sent to the internal drive. The correctly positioned read/write head alters the charges on the platter's surface to save the file.

Figure 9-11 How an internal hard disk works

Figure 9-12 Hard-disk cartridge and card from Iomega

Figure 9-13 PC card hard disk from Toshiba

backing up the contents of the internal hard disk and providing additional hard disk capacity.

Hard-disk cartridges for desktop computers have typical capacities of 10 to 20 GB (gigabytes). One of the most widely used hard-disk cartridges is Peerless disks from Iomega. (See Figure 9-12.) Credit card size hard-disk cartridges called **PC Card hard disks** are available for notebook computers with typical capacities up to 5 gigabytes. Two well-known PC Card hard disks are IBM's Microdrive and Toshiba's MK5002. (See Figure 9-13.)

HARD-DISK PACKS

Hard-disk packs are removable storage devices used to store massive amounts of information. (See Figure 9-14.) Their capacity far exceeds the other types of hard disks. Although you may never have seen one, it is almost certain that you have used them. Microcomputers that have access to the Internet, minicomputers, or mainframes often have access to external hard-disk packs through communication lines. Banks and credit card companies use them to record financial information.

Like internal hard disks, hard-disk packs have multiple recording platters aligned one above the other. Hard-disk packs, however, use much larger platters, use more platters, and are not enclosed in a special container. Hard-disk packs are stored in a hard plastic cover that is removed when the pack is mounted onto special drives. The drive rotates the pack and access arms move in and out between the rotating platters. Each access arm has two read/write heads. One reads the disk surface above it; the other reads the disk surface below it. All the access arms move in and out together. However, only one of the read/write heads is activated at a given moment. A disk pack with 11 disks provides 20 recording surfaces. This is because the top and bottom outside surfaces of the pack are not used. (See Figure 9-15.)

For a summary of the different types of hard disks, see Figure 9-16.

PERFORMANCE ENHANCEMENTS

Three ways to improve the performance of hard disks are disk caching, redundant arrays of inexpensive disks, and file compression/decompression.

Disk caching improves hard-disk performance by anticipating data needs. It performs a function similar to RAM caching discussed in Chapter 6. While RAM caching improves processing by acting as a temporary high-speed holding area between memory and the CPU, disk caching improves processing by acting as a temporary high-speed holding area between a secondary storage device and the CPU. Disk caching requires a combination of hardware and software. During idle processing time, frequently used data is read from the hard disk into memory (cache). When needed, the data is then accessed directly from memory. The transfer rate from memory is much faster than from hard disk. As a result, overall system performance is often increased by as much as 30 percent.

Figure 9-14 Hard-disk pack enclosed in a plastic cover

Redundant arrays of inexpensive disks (RAID) improve performance by expanding external storage, improving access speed, and providing reliable

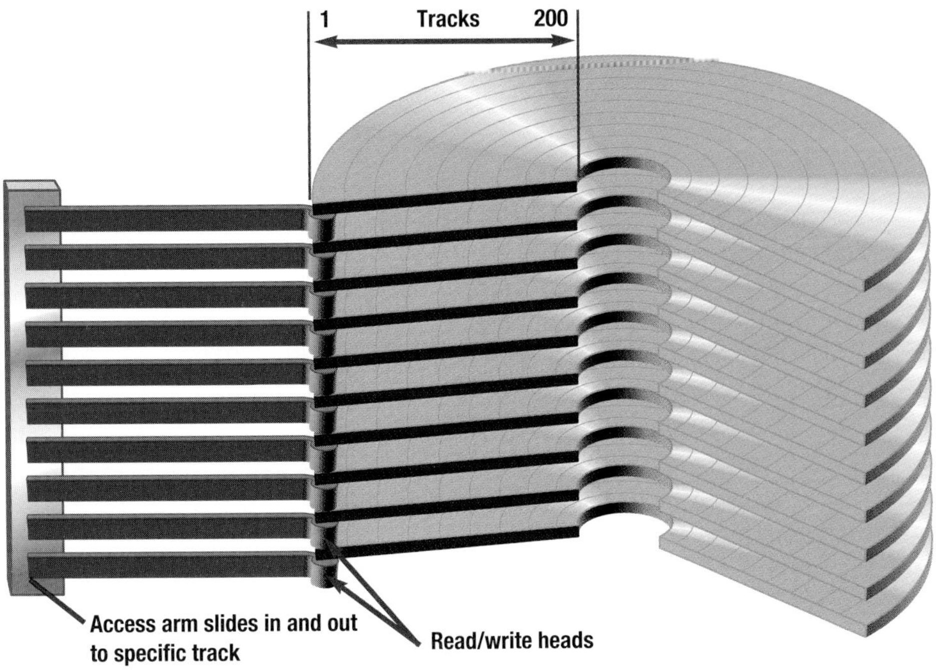
1
Tracks
200
Access arm slides in and out to specific track
Read/write heads

Figure 9-15 Hard-disk pack

storage. Several inexpensive hard-disk drives are connected to one another. These connections can be by a network or within specialized RAID devices. (See Figure 9-17.) Using special software, the connected hard-disk drives are related or grouped together and the computer system interacts with the RAID system as though it were a single large capacity hard disk drive. Files written to a RAID system are saved using more than one hard disk and are automatically duplicated. The result is expanded storage capability, fast access speed, and high reliability. For these reasons RAID is often used by Internet servers and large organizations.

Type	Description
Internal	Fast access to applications, fixed
Cartridge	Complement to internal hard disk, removable
Disk pack	Massive storage capacity, removable

Figure 9-16 Types of hard disks

File compression and **file decompression** increase storage capacity by reducing the amount of space required to store data and programs. File compression is not limited to hard-disk systems. It is frequently used to compress files on floppy disks as well. File compression also helps to speed up transmission of files from one computer system to another. Sending and receiving compressed files across the Internet is a common activity.

File compression programs scan files for ways to reduce the amount of required storage. One way is to search for repeating patterns. The repeating patterns are replaced with a token, leaving enough so that the original can be rebuilt or decompressed. These programs often shrink files to a quarter of their original size. To learn more about how file compression works, consult your Computing Today CD or visit us on the Web at http://www.mhhe.com/oleary/CT05 and select Expansions from Tim's Toolbox.

You can compress and decompress files using specialized utilities such as WinZip from Nico Mak Computing and PKZip from PKWare. Or, if these specialized utilities are not available, you can use utility programs in Windows XP. (See Figure 9-18.)

For a summary of performance enhancement techniques, see Figure 9-19.

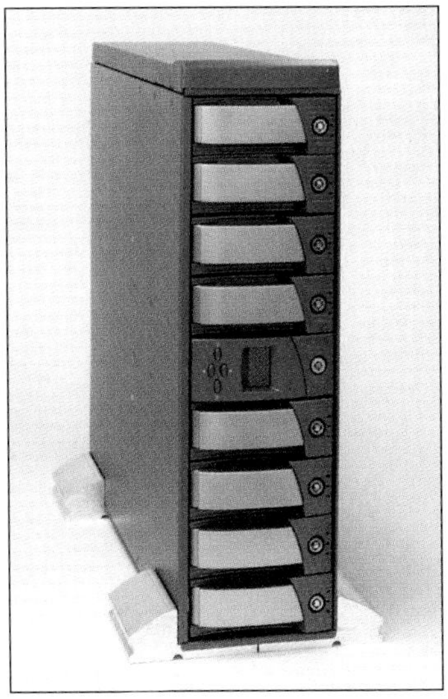

Figure 9-17 RAID storage device

Computing Today
CD

To compress a file:

1 Right click on the file to be compressed.

Choose *Compressed (zipped) Folder* from the *Send To* menu.

The compressed copy of the file is in the new zipped folder and you can delete the original uncompressed file. To see how much the original file has been compressed:

2 Right click the compressed file.

Select *Properties.*

To decompress (unzip) the file:

3 Right click the compressed file.

Select *Extract All* to access the *Compressed (zipped) Folder's Extraction Wizard.*

Follow the wizard's instructions.

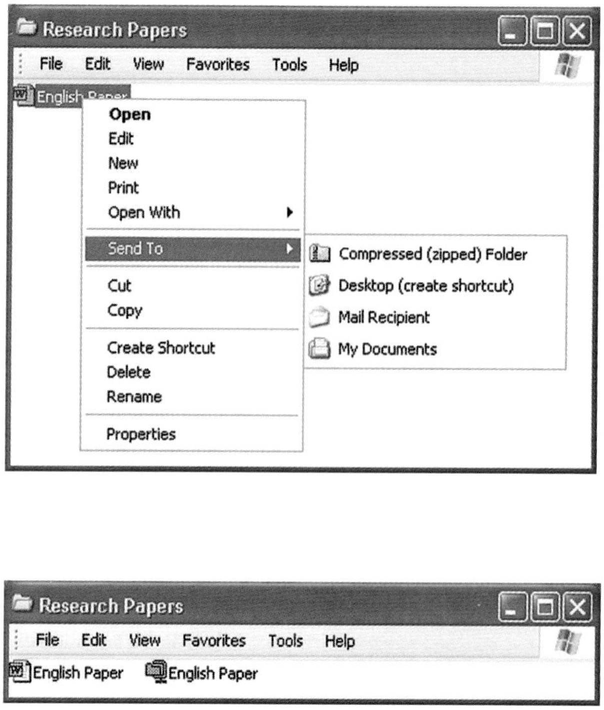

Figure 9-18 Compressing and decompressing files with Windows XP utilities

Technique	Description
Disk caching	uses cache and anticipates data needs
RAID	linked, inexpensive hard disk drives
File compression	reduces file size
File decompression	expands compressed files

Figure 9-19 Performance enhancement techniques

TIPS Are you running short of hard-disk storage space? Want to send a large file or several files at once over the Internet? You can save both space and valuable connection time by compressing the files first. Compression/decompression utility programs are available in Windows XP. If you don't have Windows XP, consider using WinZip, a popular compression program:

1. **Start.** Start the WinZip program.
2. **Create file.** Click the *New* button on the toolbar to create and name a zip file.
3. **Select.** Locate and select the file(s) you want to compress.
4. **Compress.** Click the *Add* button to compress and add the selected file(s) to the zip file.

You can now replace the selected file(s) with the much smaller zip file. To access the original files at any time, start the WinZip program, select the file(s) to decompress and click the WinZip *Extract* button.

Concept Check

- ✓ What are the major differences between floppy and hard disks? What is a head crash?
- ✓ What are the three types of hard disks? Briefly describe each.
- ✓ List and describe three ways to improve the performance of hard disks.

OPTICAL DISKS

Optical disks use laser technology to provide high capacity storage. Basic CDs include read only, write once, rewriteable, Picture CD, and Photo CD. DVDs are replacing CDs. Basic DVDs include read only, write once, and rewriteable. DataPlay disks are for digital photography and music.

Today's **optical disks** can hold over 17 gigabytes of data. (See Figure 9-20.) That is the equivalent of over several million typewritten pages or a medium-sized library all on a single disk. Optical disks are having a great impact on storage today, but we are probably only beginning to see their effects.

In optical-disk technology, a laser beam alters the surface of a plastic or metallic disk to represent data. Unlike floppy and hard disks, which use magnetic charges to represent 1s and 0s, optical disks use reflected light. The 1s and 0s are represented by flat areas called **lands** and bumpy areas called **pits** on the disk surface. The disk is read by an **optical disk drive** using a laser that projects a tiny beam of light on these areas. The amount of reflected light determines whether the area represents a 1 or a 0. To see how an optical disk drive works, see Figure 9-21.

Figure 9-20 Optical disk

Like floppy and hard disks, optical disks use tracks and sectors to organize and store files. Unlike the concentric tracks and wedge-shaped sectors used for floppy and hard disks, however, optical disks typically use a single track that spirals toward the center of the disk. This single track is divided into equally sized sectors.

Optical disks come in many different sizes including 3½, 4¾, 5¼, 8, 12, and 14 inches. The most common size is 4¾ inches. These disks are typically stored in clear protective boxes called **jewel boxes.** Data is stored on these disks in different ways or different formats. The two most common are CD and DVD.

COMPACT DISC

Compact disc, or as it is better known, **CD,** is one of the most widely used optical formats. CD drives are standard on many microcomputer systems. Typically, CD drives can store from 650 MB (megabytes) to 1 GB (gigabyte) of data on one side of a CD. One important characteristic of CD drives is their **rotational speed.** This speed is important because it determines how fast data can be transferred from the CD. For example, a 24X or 24-speed CD drive can transfer 3.6 MB per second, while a 48X drive can transfer 7.2 MB per second. The faster the drive, the faster data can be read from the CD and used by the computer system.

There are four basic types of CDs: read only, write once, rewritable, and Picture and Photo CDs:

- **Read only—CD-ROM,** which stands for **compact disc-read only memory,** is similar to a commercial music CD. *Read only* means it cannot be written on or erased by the user. Thus, you as a user have access only to the data imprinted by the publisher. CD-ROMs are used to distribute large databases and references. They are also used to distribute large software application packages.
- **Write once—CD-R,** which stands for **CD-recordable,** can be written to once. After that they can be read many times without deterioration but

TIPS

Are you concerned about damaging your optical disks? Actually, they are quite durable, and taking care of them boils down to just a few basic rules.

1. **Don't stack.** Don't stack or bend disks.
2. **Don't touch.** Don't touch the recording surfaces. Hold only by their edges.
3. **Don't remove.** Never attempt to remove a disk when it is rotating and in use.
4. **Avoid extreme conditions.** Keep disks from extreme heat and direct sunlight.
5. **Use storage boxes.** Store disks in plastic storage boxes.

Of course the best protection is to make a backup or duplicate copy of your disk.

How an Optical Disk Drive Works

Step 1: Insert disk. The disk is inserted into the drive directly or it is placed into a carrying tray that slides into the drive.

Step 2: Receive Instruction. Via a connection to the system board, the drive receives a request to read a file into RAM.

Step 3: Detector Positioned. The disk drive has a detector located beneath the disk. This detector has a laser located at its base, a prism in the middle, and a light sensing diode. The disk spins and the detector is aimed at the starting point for the file.

Step 4: Laser Projected. The laser projects a concentrated beam of light that passes directly through the prism to the underside of the disk. If the light strikes a pit, it is scattered. If the light hits a land, it is reflected directly back to the detector.

Step 5: Diode Interprets. Reflected light is redirected by the prism to a special light sensing diode. If little or no light is detected (pit), the device interprets this as a 0. If significant light is detected (land), the device interprets this as a 1.

Step 6: File read. The detector continues this to interpret the pits and lands and sends the corresponding 0's and 1's to RAM.

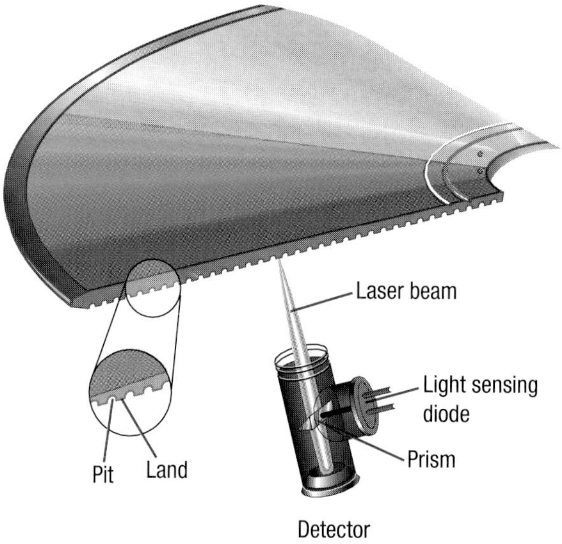
Laser beam
Light sensing diode
Prism
Pit
Land
Detector

Figure 9-21 How optical disk drives work

cannot be written on or erased. CD-R drives, also known as **CD burners,** are often used to archive data and to record music downloaded from the Internet. (See Figure 9-22.) To learn about how music is downloaded from the Internet, consult your Computing Today CD or visit us on the Web at http://www.mhhe.com/oleary/CT05 and select Animations from Tim's Toolbox. To learn more about the specifics of finding music on the Internet, creating custom CDs, and uploading to a portable player, see Making IT Work for You: Music from the Internet on pages 338 and 339.

- **Rewriteable—CD-RW** stands for **compact disc rewritable.** Also known as **erasable optical disks,** these disks are very similar to CD-Rs except that the disk surface is not permanently altered when data is recorded. Because they can be changed, CD-RWs are often used to create and edit multimedia presentations. One limitation of CD-R and CD-RW disks is that older CD-ROM drives may not be able to read them. Most newer CD-ROM drives are **multiread** or able to read both CD-R and CD-RW disks.
- **Picture CDs** and **Photo CDs** use a special format developed by Eastman Kodak to store digital images. Picture CDs are less expensive and typically used by nonprofessionals. Today, most film developers provide traditional printed pictures and digital images. The digital images are delivered by the Internet or by Picture CD. These disks are typically **single-session,** meaning that all images must be transferred at one time to the CD. Photo CDs, however, are **multisession,** meaning that new images can be added at any time.

Concept Check

- ✓ How is data represented on optical disks?
- ✓ What are CD-ROMs, CD-Rs, and CD-RWs? How are they similar? How are they different?
- ✓ What is the difference between Picture CDs and Photo CDs?

DIGITAL VERSATILE DISC

DVD stands for **digital versatile disc** or **digital video disc.** This is a newer format that is rapidly replacing CDs as the standard optical disk. DVD drives are very similar to CDs except that more data can be packed into the same amount of space. DVD discs can store 4.7 GB to 17 GB on a single DVD disk—17 times the capacity of CDs.

Many of today's more powerful microcomputer systems come with DVD drives. There are three basic types of DVDs similar to CDs: read only, write once, and rewriteable.

- **Read only—DVD-ROM** stands for **digital versatile disc-read only memory.** DVD-ROM drives are also known as **DVD players.** DVD-ROMs are having a major impact on the video market. While CD-ROMs are effective for distributing music, they can only contain just over an hour of fair-quality video. DVD-ROMs can provide over two hours of very high-quality video and sound comparable to that found in motion picture theatres. The motion picture industry is rapidly shifting video distribution from video cassettes to DVD-ROMs.
- **Write once—DVD-R** and **DVD+R** are two competing write once formats. Both stand for **DVD recordable.** Each has a slightly different way in which they format their disks. Fortunately, most new DVD players can use either format. DVD-R and DVD+R drives are typically used to create permanent archives for large amounts of data and to record videos. Currently,

How Music is Downloaded from the Internet

Step 1: Locate. There are numerous Web sites that provide access to compressed music files. Users can download these files via the Internet.

Music Web site

Step 2: Download. The compressed music files are downloaded and stored on the user's internal hard disk drive or onto a CD.

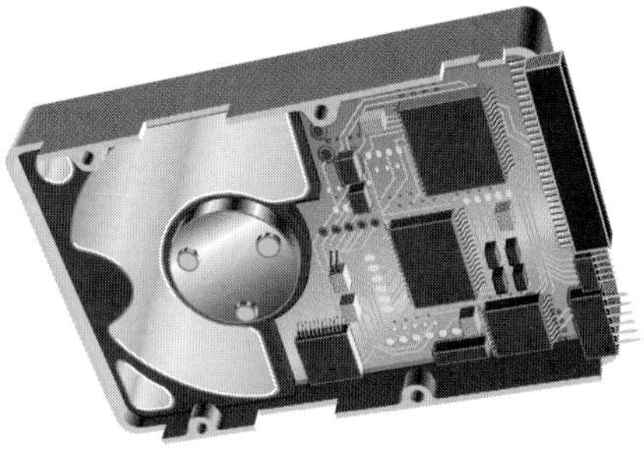

Step 3: Play. The music can be played immediately on the computer's speakers, transferred to a portable music player, or burned onto a CD-R drive.

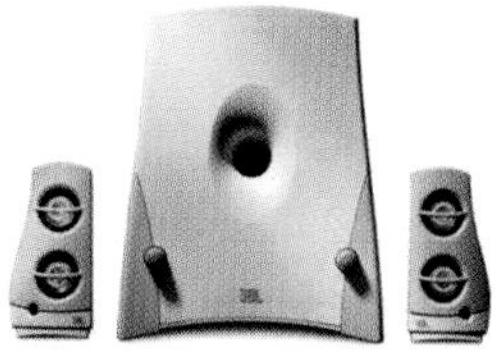

Speakers

Music player

CD

Figure 9-22 How music is downloaded from the Internet

they are not as widely used as CD-R drives because of their higher costs. This is expected to change just as soon as the costs for the write once drives become lower.

- **Rewriteable**—Unfortunately, there are several competing rewriteable formats and few DVD players can read all the standards. The three most widely used formats are **DVD-RW, DVD+RW,** and **DVD-RAM.** DVD-RW and DVD+RW stand for **DVD rewritable. DVD-RAM** stands for **DVD random-access memory.** The transition from CD rewriteable disks to DVD rewriteable disks has been slow due to the competing DVD formats. It is expected that one of these formats will soon become the standard and DVD rewriteable disks will replace CD rewriteable disks for many applications.

DATAPLAY

DataPlay is an optical write once format similar to CD-R. This format is designed for optical disks the size of a quarter with the capacity of 500 MB or enough to hold five hours of CD-quality sound. (See Figure 9-23.) Typical uses include storing and playing music files. The music industry is supporting this format, in part, because prerecorded music in the DataPlay format is more difficult to copy than with music stored on traditional CDs. Although more specialized than the other formats, DataPlay appears likely to become widely used for specialized applications, including storing digital photographs and music for portable players.

For a summary of optical disk storage capacities, see Figure 9-24.

Figure 9-23 DataPlay disks

Format	Typical Capacity	Type	Description
CD	650MB to 1 GB	CD-ROM	Read only, used to distribute databases, reference books, and software
		CD-R	Write one time only, used to archive large amounts of data
		CD-RW	Rewriteable, used to create and edit large multimedia presentations
		Picture CD	Single-session CD, used to store images
		Photo CD	Multisession CD, used to store images
DVD	17 GB to 17 GB	DVD-ROM	Read only, distribute theater-quality video and sound presentations
		DVD-R and DVD+R	Written-to one time only, used to archive very large amounts of data
		DVD-RW, DVD+RW and DVD-RAM	Rewriteable, able to create and read CD disks, used to create and edit large-scale multimedia presentations
DataPlay	500MB		Specialized format for digital photography and music.

Figure 9-24 Types of optical disks

MAKING IT WORK FOR YOU

MUSIC FROM THE INTERNET

Did you know you can use the Internet to locate and play music? You can even create your own compact disks, or transfer music to a portable player. All you need is the right software, hardware, and a connection to the Internet.

Finding Music There are many services on the Internet for finding music. The first step is to download software that connects with a music service. You can use this software to search for songs, play them, and create a *playlist* of songs you will use frequently. For example, to create a playlist with Plus Player software from MP3.com:

1

- **Connect to *http://plus.mp3.com* and download and install the PLUS Player software. Launch the software.**
- **Click *MP3.com,* then select a music category in the left pane, or click *Search* to search for a particular artist or title.**
- **Select songs from the right pane by clicking on them. Click [play] to hear a song.**
- **If necessary, click [View Playlist] to display the Playlist window.**
- **Right-click on songs you enjoy and select *Add to Playlist.***

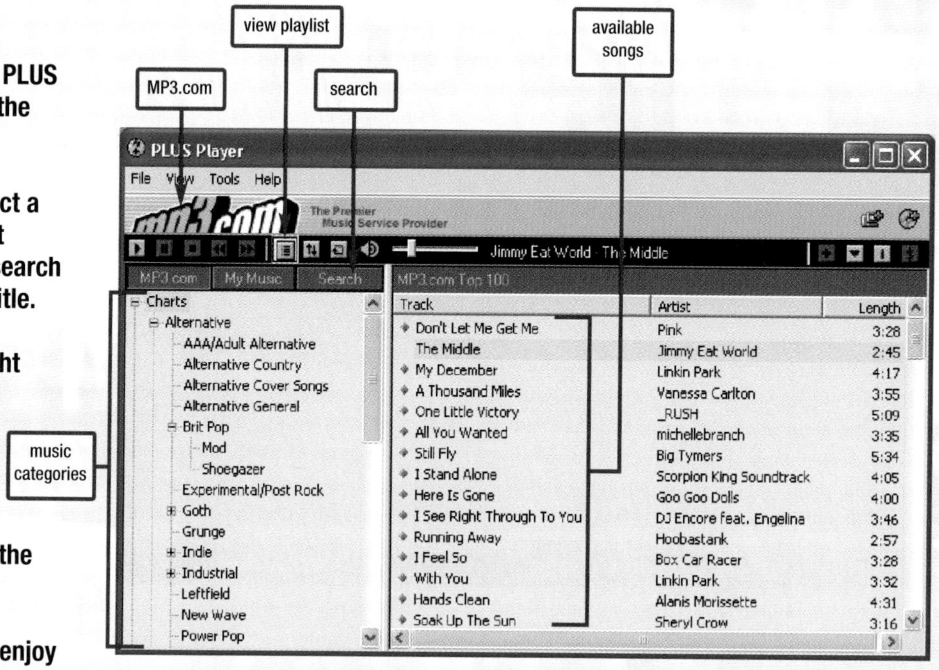

Creating A Custom CD If your computer is equipped with a CD-R or CD-RW drive, creating a custom CD is one way to take your favorite tunes from your playlists with you. To create a CD using the PLUS Play software:

1.
- **Click [Transfer 2 CD] in the Playlist window.**
- **Select a CD Type: *Data* is for CDs you will play in other computers. *Regular audio* is for regular CD players.**
- **Put the songs from your playlist in order by clicking a song title, then clicking *Move up* or *Move down.***
- **Click *Burn* to create your CD.**

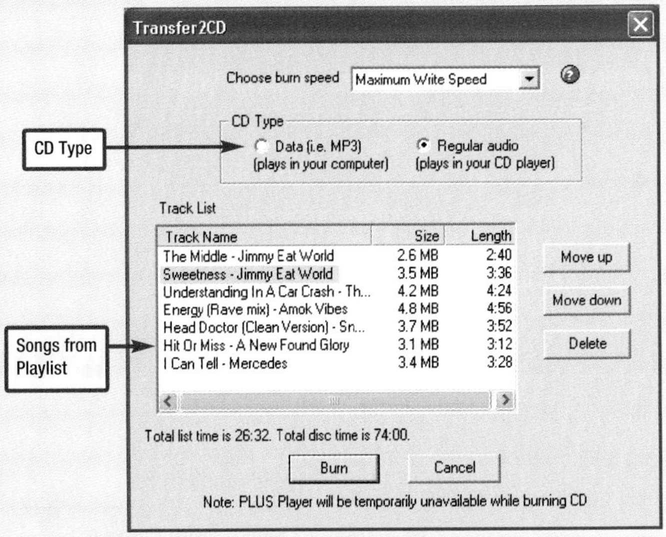

Uploading to a Portable Player Another popular way to take your songs on the go is to transfer them to a portable music player. Portable music players are lightweight digital storage devices that do not require cassettes or discs, but store music files internally. To transfer music to a portable player using the PLUS Player software:

1.
- **Click [Transfer 2 Device] in the Playlist window.**
- **Select the device that corresponds with your portable player.**
- **Click *Transfer Files.***

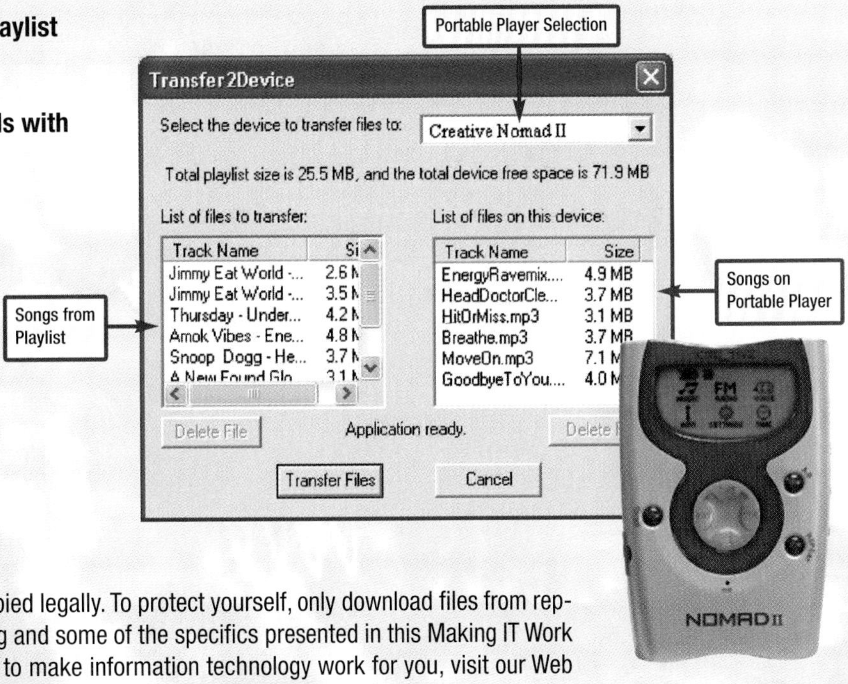

Not all music files on the Internet can be copied legally. To protect yourself, only download files from reputable sources. The Web is continually changing and some of the specifics presented in this Making IT Work may have changed. To learn about other ways to make information technology work for you, visit our Web site at http://www.mhhe.com/oleary/CT05 and select Making IT Work for You from Tim's Toolbox.

Concept Check

- Compare CD and DVD formats. Why are DVDs replacing CDs?
- What are DVD-RW, DVD+RW, and DVD-RAM?
- What are DataPlay disks used for?

OTHER TYPES OF SECONDARY STORAGE

Solid-state storage does not have moving parts. Internet drives use the Internet to store data and information. Magnetic tape provides sequential access for backup. Microfilm stores microscopic images on tape. Microfiche stores microscopic images on cards.

For the typical microcomputer user, the three basic storage options—floppy disk, hard disk, and optical disk—are complementary, not competing. Almost all microcomputers today have at least one floppy-disk drive, one hard-disk drive, and one optical drive. For many users, these secondary storage devices are further complemented with more specialized storage such as Internet hard drives, solid state storage, magnetic tape, microfilm, and microfiche.

SOLID-STATE STORAGE

Each of the secondary storage devices discussed thus far has moving parts. For example, hard disks rotate and read/write heads move in and out. Unlike these devices, **solid-state storage** devices have no moving parts. Data and information are stored and retrieved electronically directly from these devices much as they would be from conventional computer memory. While this type of storage is more expensive than the others, it is more reliable and requires less power. For these reasons, this technology is becoming widely used for specialized secondary storage.

Flash memory cards discussed in Chapter 6 are solid-state storage devices widely used in notebook computers. (See Figure 9-25.) Flash memory is also used in a variety of specialized input devices to capture and transfer data to desktop computers. For example, flash memory is used to store images captured from digital cameras and then to transfer the images to desktop and

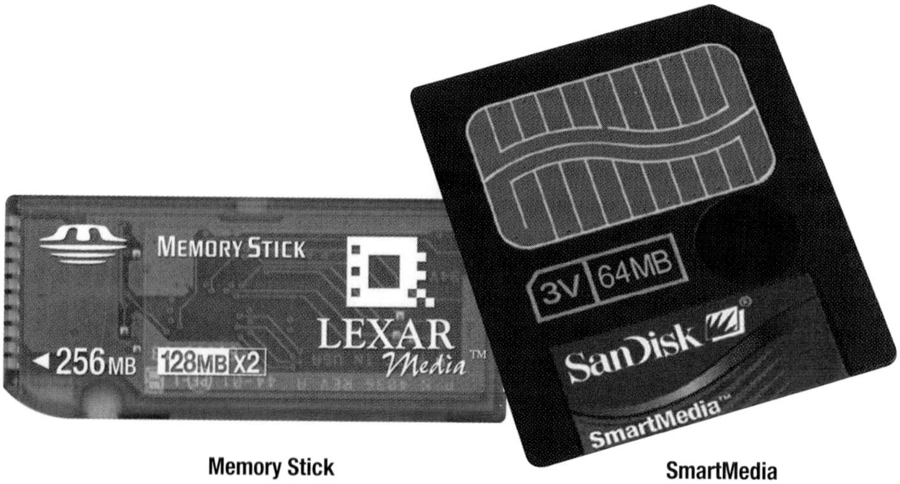

Memory Stick

SmartMedia

Figure 9-25 Flash memory cards

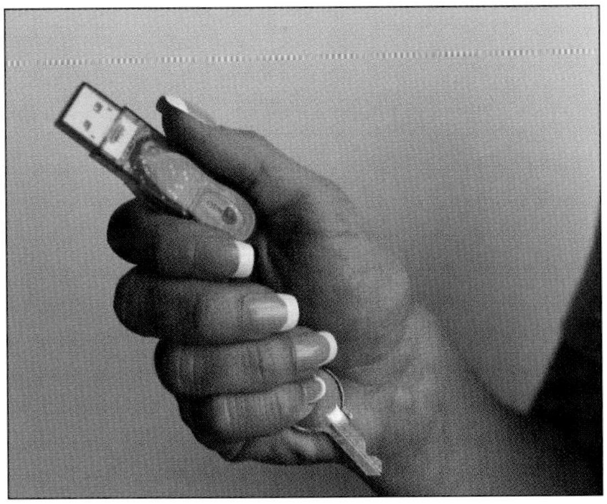

Figure 9-26 Key chain flash memory

Figure 9-27 An Internet hard drive site

other computers. Flash memory is also used to record MP3 music files and to transfer those files to computers and other devices.

Key chain hard drives have recently been introduced. These devices, also known as **key chain flash memory devices,** are so compact that they can be transported on a key ring or a necklace. (See Figure 9-28.) Key chain hard drives conveniently connect directly to a computer's USB port to transfer files and have typical capacities of 1GB. Due to their convenient size and large capacities, some predict that key chain hard-drive devices may replace the floppy disk for transporting data and information between computers and a variety of specialty devices.

INTERNET HARD DRIVES

Special service sites on the Web provide users with storage. This storage is called an **Internet hard drive,** also known as **i-drive** or **online storage.** (See Figure 9-27.)

Advantages of Internet hard drives compared to other types of secondary storage include low cost and the flexibility to access information from any location using the Internet. Because all information must travel across the Internet, however, access speed is slower. Another consideration is that users are dependent on the availability and security procedures of the service site. Because of these limitations, Internet hard drives are typically used as a specialized secondary storage device and not for storing highly personalized or sensitive information.

Typically, Internet hard drive sites focus on supplying their services either to businesses or to individuals. The business-oriented sites provide faster access and greater security for a fee. The individual-focused sites provide limited storage for much lower cost and some sites are free. (See Figure 9-28.)

Focus	Company	Location
Individual	Apple	itools.mac.com
Individual	Freedrive	www.freedrive.com
Individual	Yahoo	briefcase.yahoo.com
Business	Amerivault	amerivault.com
Business	Connected TLM	connected.com

Figure 9-28 Internet hard drive sites

MAGNETIC TAPE

To find a particular song on an audiotape, you may have to play several inches of tape. Finding a song on an audio compact disc, in contrast, can be much faster. You select the track, and the disc player moves directly to it. That, in

Figure 9-29 Magnetic tape reels

brief, represents the two different approaches to external storage. The two approaches are called **sequential access** and **direct access.**

Disks provide fast direct access. Tapes provide slower sequential access. With tape, information is stored in sequence, such as alphabetically. For example, all the grades of students at your school could be recorded on tape arranged alphabetically by their last names. To find the grades for one student, say Chris Reed, the search would begin at the start of the tape and search alphabetically past all the last names beginning with A to Q, say, before ultimately reaching Reed. This may involve searching several inches or feet, which takes time.

Like floppy and hard disks, **magnetic tape** stores data and programs by altering the electromagnetic charges on a recording surface. Although slower to access specific information, magnetic tape is an effective and commonly used tool for backing up data. At one time mainframe computers exclusively used **magnetic tape reels.** This type of tape is typically ½-inch wide and 1½ -mile long and provides massive storage capacity. (See Figure 9-29.) Now, most mainframes as well as microcomputers use **tape cartridges** or **magnetic tape streamers** to back up data. (See Figure 9-30.) The three most widely used tape cartridges are:

- **QIC (quarter-inch cartridge)** with typical capacities up to 25 GB.
- **DAT (digital audio tape)** with typical capacities up to 40 GB.
- **DLT (digital linear tape),** the most expensive with capacities up to 110 GB.

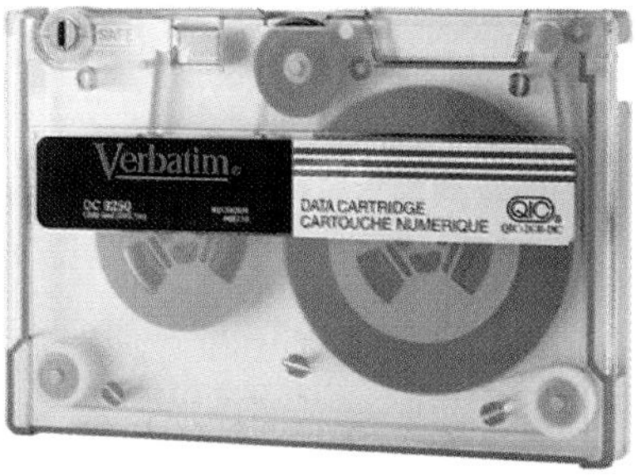

Figure 9-30 Magnetic tape cartridges

MICROFILM AND MICROFICHE

Microfilm and microfiche are best known for archiving information in libraries, large organizations, and banks. Both store very small microscopic images of documents. **Microfilm** stores the images on long rolls of film. **Microfiche** uses 4-by-6-inch cards to store the images.

The reduced images are created from original documents using a device called a **computer output microfilm (COM) recorder.** Microfilm and microfiche are widely used to provide inexpensive secondary storage for documents. They eliminate the need to archive the much larger original documents. For a summary of the other types of storage, see Figure 9-31.

Storage	Description
Internet hard drive	online storage
Solid state	no moving parts
Magnetic tape	sequential access for backup
Microfilm	microscopic images stored on tape
Microfiche	microscopic images stored on 4- by 6-inch cards

Figure 9-31 Storage devices

Concept Check

- ✓ What is solid-state storage? What is a flash memory card used for? What are key chain hard drives?
- ✓ What are Internet hard drives? What are they used for?
- ✓ What is the difference between direct and sequential access? Which type of access is provided by magnetic tape?
- ✓ What are microfilm and microfiche used for? How are they different from one another?

SECONDARY STORAGE FOR PORTABLE COMPUTERS

Notebook computers use standard types of media and specialized storage devices. Handheld computers rely on specialized media and solid-state devices. Specialty devices such as digital cameras use special secondary storage options.

Just as the popularity and use of portable computers has increased dramatically in the past few years, so has the importance of their storage devices. Although we have already discussed many of these specialized secondary storage devices, their increasingly wide-spread use warrants a review.

- Notebook computers use the standard types of media (floppy, hard, and optical disks). Compared to desktop computers, however, their disk drives are smaller and weigh less. Additionally, notebook computers use a variety of specialized storage devices including removable disk drives, PC Card hard drives, flash memory cards, and key chain hard drives. (See Figure 9-32.)
- Handheld computers have fewer secondary storage options than notebook computers. Although many handheld computers are able to read standard storage media, most rely on solid-state devices including PC Card hard disks, flash memory cards, and key chain hard drives. Wireless handheld computers use their Internet connections to access and use storage available at Internet hard drive sites.
- Specialized devices such as digital cameras and digital music players use a variety of specialized secondary storage including memory sticks, Picture CDs, Photo CDs, and DataPlay drives.

Concept Check

- ✓ Discuss secondary storage devices commonly used with notebook computers.
- ✓ What type of secondary storage is typically used by handheld computers?
- ✓ List two specialized devices and discuss some of their secondary storage options.

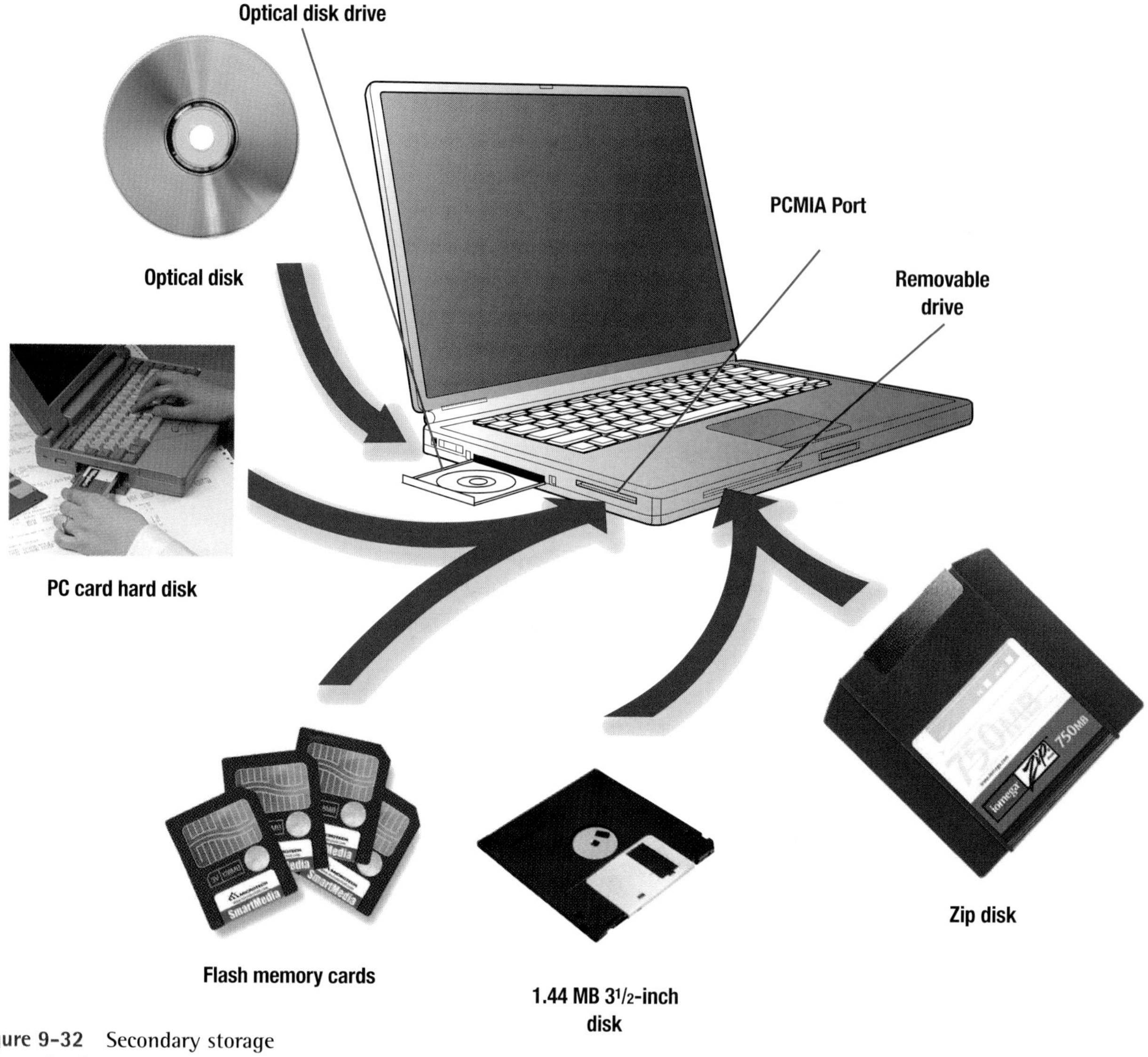
Optical disk drive
PCMIA Port
Removable drive
Optical disk
PC card hard disk
Zip disk
Flash memory cards
1.44 MB 3½-inch disk

Figure 9-32 Secondary storage for notebook computers

MASS STORAGE DEVICES

Mass storage devices are specialized high capacity secondary storage devices. Mass storage devices include file servers, RAID systems, tape libraries, optical juke boxes, and organizational Internet storage.

It is natural to think of secondary storage media and devices as they relate to us as individuals. It may not be as obvious how important these matters are to organizations. **Mass storage** refers to the tremendous amount of secondary storage required by large organizations. **Mass storage devices** are specialized high capacity secondary storage devices designed to meet organizational demands for data.

Most large organizations have established a strategy called an **enterprise storage system** to promote efficient and safe use of data across the networks

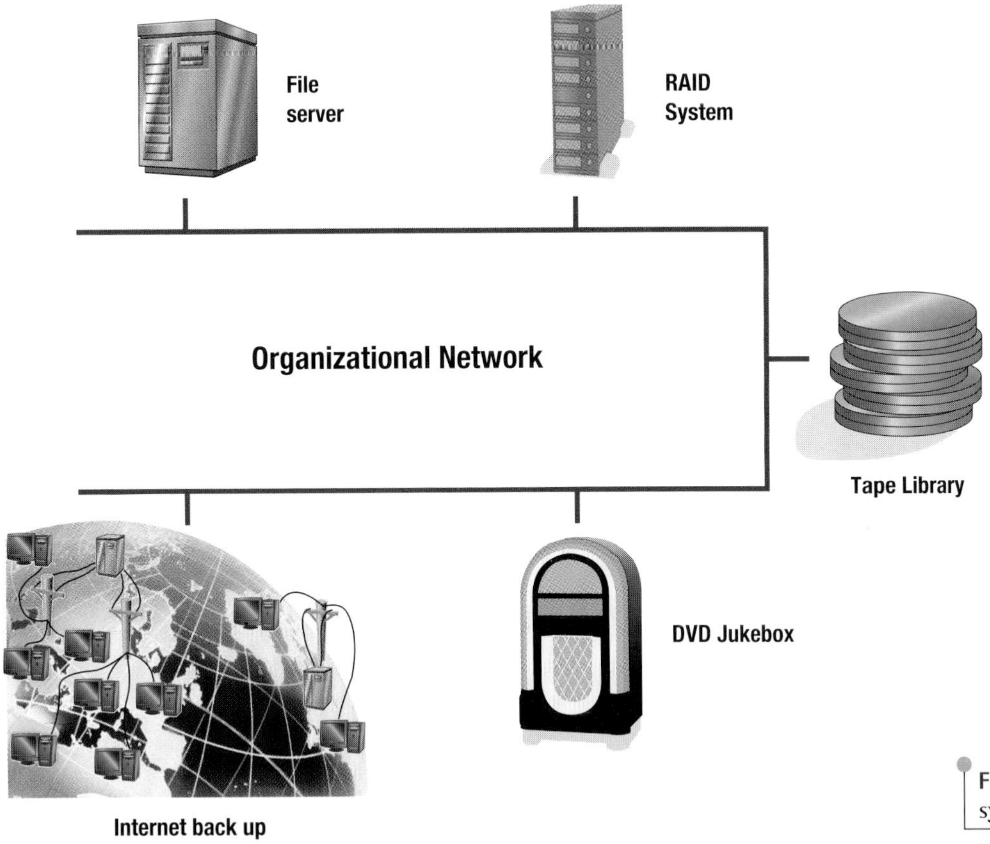
File
server
RAID
System
Organizational Network
Tape Library
DVD Jukebox
Internet back up

Figure 9-33 Enterprise storage system

within their organizations. (See Figure 9-33.) Some of the mass storage devices that support this strategy are:

- **File servers**—dedicated computers with very large storage capacity that provides users access to fast storage and retrieval of data.
- **RAID systems**—larger version of the specialized devices discussed earlier in this chapter that enhances organizational security by constantly making backup copies of files moving across the organization's networks.
- **Tape library**—device that provides automatic access to data archived on a large collection or library of tapes.
- **DVD-ROM** and **CD-ROM jukeboxes**—provide automatic access to a large collection or library of optical disks.
- **Organizational Internet storage**—high speed Internet connection to a dedicated remote organizational Internet drive site.

The availability, security, and organization of data are essential to the efficient operations of any organization. The importance of these matters is further discussed in Chapters 11 and 13.

Concept Check

- ✓ Define mass storage and mass storage devices.
- ✓ What is an enterprise storage system?
- ✓ List and describe five mass storage devices.

Careers in IT

Software Engineer

Software engineers analyze users' needs and create application software. Software engineers typically have experience in programming, but focus on the design and development of programs using the principles of mathematics and engineering. They rarely write code themselves.

A bachelor's degree in computer science and an extensive knowledge of computers and technology are required by most employers. Internships may provide students with the kinds of experience employers look for in a software engineer. Those with specific experience with networking, the Internet, and Web applications may have an advantage over other applicants. Employers typically look for software engineers with good communication and analytical skills.

Software engineers can expect to earn an annual salary in the range of $50,000 to $85,000. Advancement opportunities are usually tied to experience. Experienced software engineers may be promoted to project manager or have opportunities in systems design. To learn about other careers in information technology, visit us at http://www.mhhe.com/oleary/CT05 and select Careers in IT from Tim's Toolbox.

A Look to the Future

Blu-Ray Technology Expected to Replace DVD

Have you ever run out of space on a disk? Would you like to record 13 hours of broadcast television or movies on a single optical disk? How would you like to store hours of music on one CD? Have you ever found yourself with old disks that you can no longer access? The pace that technology is keeping sometimes makes keeping your data a challenge. Some say the transition to CDs from floppy disks is currently under way. Yet, already the manufacturers of electronics and secondary storage are looking for the new standard in storage.

Nine of the largest manufacturers of electronics, including Hitachi, Pioneer, and Sony, have recently agreed to support new optical disk technology that will allow users to record and play back much more information than currently available. This new storage medium will come encased in a disk cartridge that will protect the surface, and the data, from damage by dust and scratches. This new storage is called Blu-Ray, because the new disks use blue laser light instead of the red laser light used in traditional CD players. Blu-Ray discs may ultimately hold over 30GB on one-sided disks, and over 50GB on two-sided disks. New compression technology may make it possible to record multiple layers of data on one side of a disk. Most manufacturers hope to begin licensing new products and equipment with this latest development in the very near future.

Current DVD and CD players and recorders use red laser light. This technology can store 4.7 GB on a standard optical disk. It is not fast enough to record high quality video. Blue laser light can be focused more accurately and compactly on a disk. HDTV broadcasts and streaming audio and video can be recorded on these new disks. It is possible to store 27 GB on a standard optical disk using Blu-Ray technology.

Existing CD and DVD players and recorders will not be able to play or record on the new optical disks. It is expected that new players and recorders may incorporate both red and blue laser technology to accommodate both technologies. Manufacturers and media developers hope that cooperation on Blu-Ray will help prevent the problems of incompatibility that limited the expansion of DVD in its early development. They hope that this new larger, and easy-to-use format, will expedite the transition to these new disks.

Does this kind of increased storage capacity appeal to you? It is expected that Blu-Ray technology could eventually increase storage capacity on a dual layer disk to 50 GB. Do you think increased storage capacity will continue to be important as broadband and larger hard disks become more common?

VISUAL SUMMARY

SECONDARY STORAGE

STORAGE

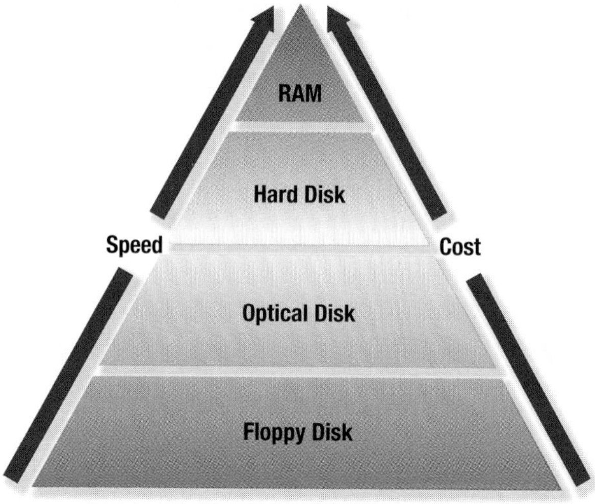

RAM is **primary storage.** Most RAM is **volatile** meaning that it loses its contents whenever power is disrupted. **Secondary storage** provides **nonvolatile** storage. Secondary storage retains data and information after the computer system is turned off.

Writing is the process of saving information to **secondary storage devices. Reading** is the process of accessing information from secondary storage devices.

Important characteristics of secondary storage include:

- **Media** or **medium**—actual physical material that retains data and programs.
- **Capacity**—how much a particular storage medium can hold.
- **Access time** or **access speed**—time required to retrieve data from a secondary storage device.

The **Storage Pyramid** shows the relationship of access speed and cost for various types of storage. Floppy disks are the slowest and least expensive. RAM is the fastest and most expensive.

FLOPPY DISKS

Floppy disks are also known as **diskettes, disks, flexible disks,** and **floppies.** Data and programs are stored by charging disk surface.

Traditional Floppy Disk

The traditional floppy disk is the **1.44 MB 3½-inch disk. 2DH** indicates **two-sided high density** disk. Disks have **shutters** that open to provide access to the recording surface, **labels** to record disk content, and **write-protection notches** to allow or prohibit writing to the disk.

Files are organized according to **tracks** (concentric circles) and **sectors** (wedge-shapes). **Formatting** or **initializing** may be required to establish tracks and sectors.

Floppy disk drives (FDD) are typically located within system unit and designated as the **A drive.** A **cluster (allocation unit)** is smallest disk space that **read/write heads** can read from or write to a floppy disk.

High Capacity Floppy Disks

Floppy-disk cartridges (high capacity disks) have greater capacity and are replacing the traditional floppy disk.

To be a competent and knowledgeable end user you need to be aware of the different types of secondary storage. You need to know their capabilities, limitations, and uses. There are four widely used storage media: floppy disk, hard disk, optical disk, and other types of secondary storage.

HARD DISKS

Compared to floppy disks, **hard disks** use rigid metallic **platters** that provide much greater capacity. Files are organized according to **tracks, sectors,** and **cylinders.**

A **head crash** occurs when hard disk makes contact with the drive's read/write heads.

Three types of hard disks are internal hard disks, hard-disk cartridges, and hard-disk packs.

Internal Hard Disk

Internal hard disks (fixed disk) are located within system unit and typically identified as the **C drive.** They typically have four platters enclosed in a protective container. Internal hard disks are connected to the system board by a **hard disk controller (HDC)** card. Two basic types are:

- **Enhanced integrated drive electronics (EIDE) controller cards** can support up to four hard disk drives.
- **Small computer system interface (SCSI) controller cards** can support numerous hard-disk drives; faster and more expensive than EIDE drives.

Hard-Disk Cartridge

Unlike internal hard disks, **hard-disk cartridges (removable hard disks)** are removable and capacity limited only by the number of cartridges. **PC Card hard disks** are for notebooks.

HARD DISKS

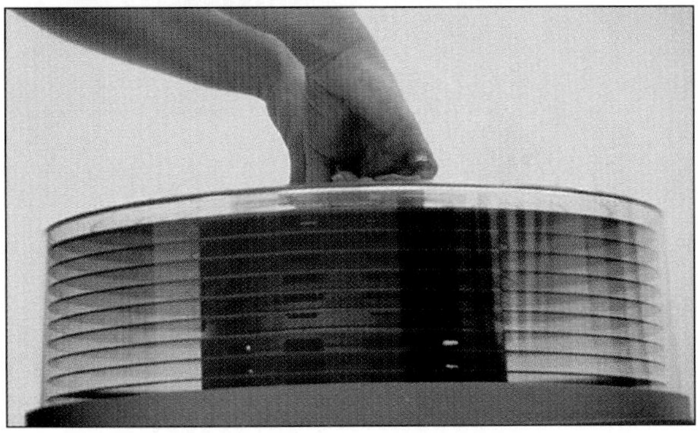

Hard-Disk Pack

Hard-disk packs are removable, have several platters and extensive capacity. A disk pack typically has 11 platters with 20 recording surfaces.

Performance Enhancements

Three ways to improve hard disk performance are disk caching, RAIDS, and file compression and file decompression.

- **Disk caching**—provides temporary high speed holding area between memory and the CPU; improves performance by anticipating data needs and reducing time to access data from secondary storage.
- **RAIDS (redundant array of inexpensive disks)**—several inexpensive hard-disk drives are connected together; improves performance by providing expanded storage, fast access, and high reliability.
- **File compression** and **decompression**—files compressed before storing and then decompressed before being used again; improves performance through efficient storage.

OPTICAL DISKS

Optical disks use laser technology. 1s and 0s are represented by **pits** and **lands. Jewel boxes** protect optical disks. **Rotational speed** of **optical disk drives** affects access speed.

Compact Discs

Compact discs (CDs) have typical capacity of 650 MB to 1 GB. Four types:

- **CD-ROM**—read only, used to distribute databases, reference, and software.
- **CD-R**—write once; CD-R drives also known as **CD burners;** used to create custom music CDs and to archive data.
- **CD-RW**—used for large multimedia presentations. **Multiread** CD-ROM drives can use CD-R and CD-RW disks.
- **Picture** and **Photo CD**—Picture CDs are **single-session.** Photo CDs are **multisession.**

Digital Versatile Discs

DVDs (digital versatile discs, digital video discs) have far greater capacity than CDs. Three types: **DVD-ROM (DVD Players** identified as **CD-R/DVD** also read CD format), **DVD-R,** and **DVD+RW (DVD+RAM** a competing standard).

DataPlay

DataPlay is a specialized format used for music and digital photography.

OTHER TYPES

The three basic storage options (floppy, hard, and optical) are complementary and not competitive. Many users complement with more specialized devices such as solid-state storage, Internet hard drives, magnetic tape, microfilm, and microfiche.

- **Solid-state storage**—no moving parts. **Flash memory cards** are solid-state storage devices. **Key chain hard drives (key chain flash memory devices)** provide very compact storage.
- **Internet hard drives (i-drive, online storage)**—Web-based, low-cost storage. Accessible from any Internet connection, these drives are often slow and security is an issue.
- **Magnetic tape—sequential access** (disks provide **direct access**) used primarily for backing up data. **Magnetic tape reels** were widely used with mainframes. Now **tape cartridges (magnetic tape streamers)** most widely used for mainframes and microcomputers. **QIC, DAT,** and **DLT** are types of tape cartridges.
- **Microfilm** and **microfiche**—microscopic images of documents stored on film (microfilm) or on cards (microfiche). Images produced by **COM (computer output on microfilm)** recorders.

PORTABLE STORAGE

Portable computer use has increased dramatically. Correspondingly, their secondary storage devices have become more and more important.

- Notebook computers use standard media as well as specialized devices including removable disk drives, PC Card hard drives, and Flash memory cards.
- Handheld computers have fewer storage options. Many can read standard media; however, the majority rely on including PC Card hard drives and flash memory cards. Wireless devices often use Internet hard drives.
- Specialized devices include digital cameras and digital music players. These devices use a variety of specialized secondary storage devices including memory sticks, Picture CDs, Photo CDs, and DataPlay disks.

MASS STORAGE

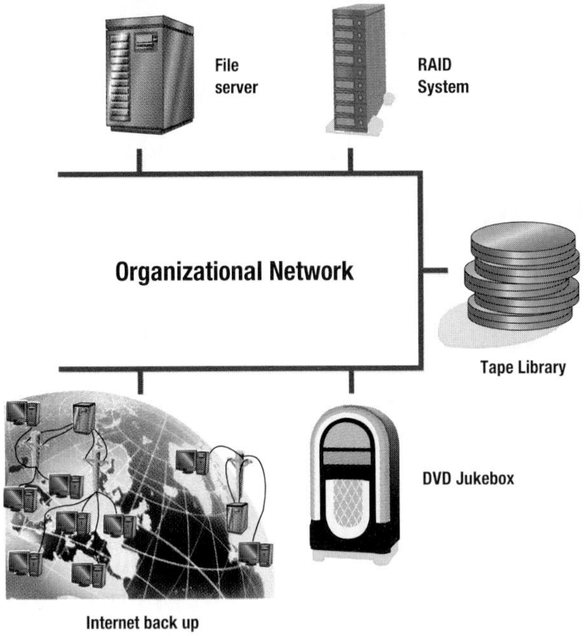

Mass storage refers to the tremendous amount of secondary storage required by large organizations. **Mass storage devices** are specialized high capacity secondary storage devices designed to meet organizational demands for data.

Most large organizations have established a strategy called an **enterprise storage system** to promote efficient and safe use of data across the networks within their organizations.

Mass storage devices that support this strategy are: file servers, RAID systems, tape libraries, DVD-ROM and CD-ROM jukeboxes, and organizational Internet storage.

- **File servers**—dedicated computers with very high storage with fast access.
- **RAID systems**—large RAID devices that enhance security by backing up files that move across network.
- **Tape library**—provides automatic access to large collection or library of magnetic tapes.
- **DVD-ROM** and **CD-ROM jukeboxes**—provide automatic access to large collection or library of optical disks.
- **Organizational Internet storage**—high speed Internet connection to dedicated remote organizational Internet drive site.

KEY TERMS

1.44 MB 3½-inch disk (324)
A drive (324)
allocation unit (324)
2HD (324)
access time (322)
access speed (322)
C drive (328)
capacity (322)
CD (compact disc) (333)
CD burner (335)
CD-R (CD-recordable) (333)
CD-ROM (compact disc-read only memory) (333)
CD-ROM jukebox (345)
CD-RW (compact disc rewritable) (335)
cluster (324)
computer output microfilm (COM) recorder (342)
cylinder (327)
DAT (digital audio tape) (342)
DataPlay (337)
density (324)
direct access (342)
disk caching (330)
diskette (323)
disk (323)
DLT (digital linear tape) (342)
DVD (digital versatile disc or digital video disc) (335)
DVD-RW (DVD rewritable) (337)
DVD+R (DVD-recordable) (335)
DVD-RAM (DVD-random-access memory) (337)
DVD player (335)
DVD-ROM (digital versatile disc-read only memory) (335)
DVD-ROM jukebox (345)
enhanced integrated drive electronics (EIDE) controller card (328)
enterprise storage system (344)
erasable optical disk (335)
file compression (331)
file decompression (331)
file server (345)
fixed disk (328)
flash memory card (340)
flexible disk (323)
floppies (323)
floppy disk (323)
floppy disk drive (FDD) (324)
floppy-disk cartridge (326)
formatting (324)
fragments (325)
hard disk (327)
hard-disk cartridge (328)
hard disk controller (HDC) card (328)
hard-disk pack (330)
head crash (327)
HiFD disk (326)
high capacity disk (326)
i-drive (341)
initializing (324)
internal hard disk (328)
Internet hard drive (341)
jewel box (333)
key chain hard drives (341)
key chain flash memory devices (341)
label (324)
land (333)
magnetic tape (342)
magnetic tape reel (342)
magnetic tape streamer (342)
mass storage (344)
mass storage device (344)
media (322)
medium (322)
microfiche (342)
microfilm (342)
multiread (335)
multisession (335)
nonvolatile storage (322)
online storage (341)
organizational Internet storage (345)
optical disk (333)
optical disk drive (333)
PC Card hard disk (330)
Photo CD (335)
Picture CD (335)
pits (333)
platters (327)
primary storage (322)
QIC (quarter-inch cartridge) (342)
RAID system (345)
reading (322)
read/write head (324)
redundant arrays of inexpensive disks (RAID) (330)
removable hard disk (328)
rotational speed (333)
secondary storage (322)
secondary storage device (322)
sector (324)
sequential access (342)
shutter (324)
single-session (335)
small computer system interface (SCSI) controller card (328)
solid-state storage (340)
storage devices (322)
SuperDisk (326)
tape cartridge (342)
tape library (345)
track (324)
volatile storage (322)
write-protection notch (324)
writing (322)
Zip disk (326)

To test your knowledge of these key terms with animated flash cards, select Flash Cards from Tim's Toolbox at http://www.mhhe.com/oleary/CT05.

CHAPTER REVIEW

CROSSWORD

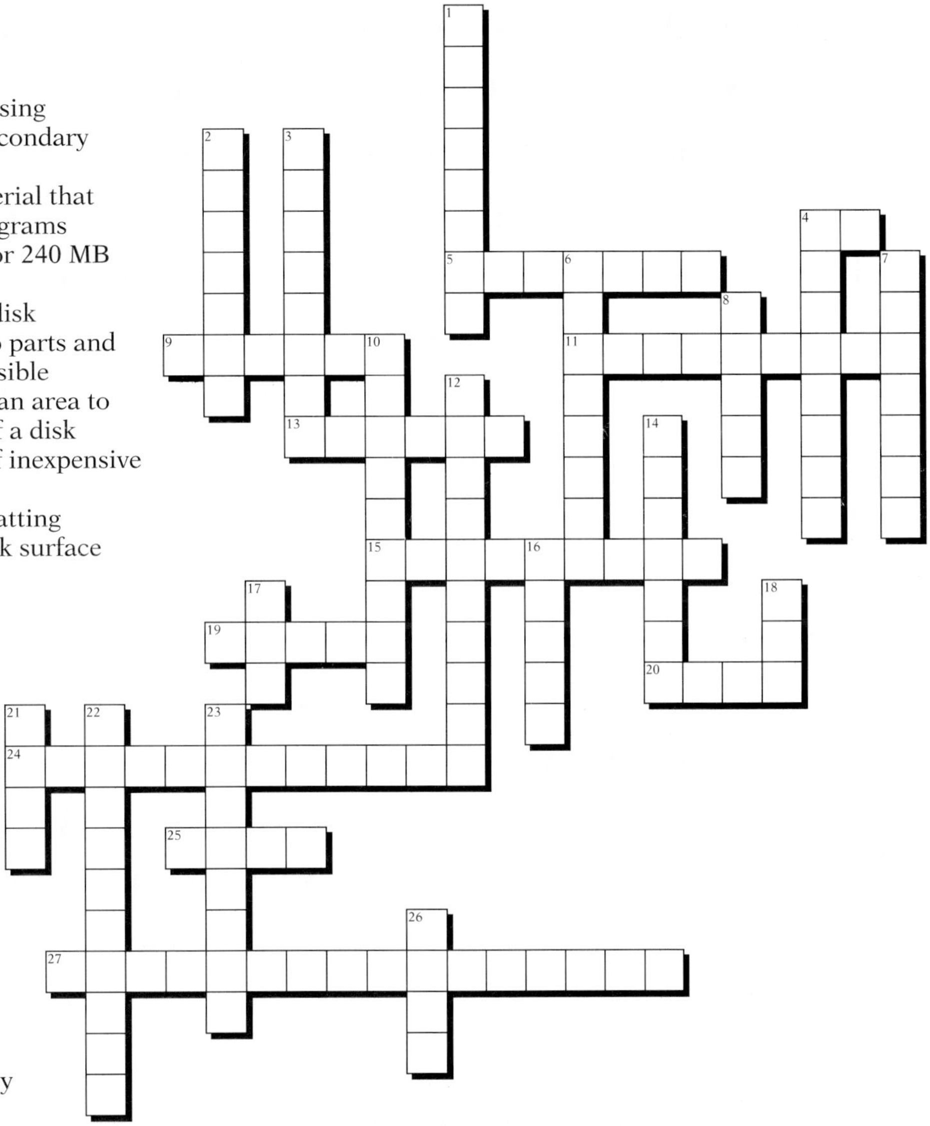

ACROSS

4 Compact disc
5 The process of accessing information from secondary storage devices
9 Actual physical material that retains data and programs
11 Disks with 120 MB or 240 MB capacity
13 Wedge shapes on a disk
15 A file broken up into parts and stored wherever possible
19 Provides users with an area to write the contents of a disk
20 Redundant arrays of inexpensive disks
24 Also known as formatting
25 Flat areas on the disk surface
27 DataPlay

DOWN

1 The actual storage surface within a hard disk
2 The smallest disk space that read/write heads can read from or write to a floppy disk
3 Also known as flexible disks
4 Runs through each track of a stack of platters
6 Also known as floppy disk
7 Provides automatic access to a library of optical disks
8 Concentric circles on a disk
10 Stores images on long rolls of film
12 Establishes tracks and sectors
14 Slides to expose a disk's recording surface
16 Actual physical material that retains data and programs
17 Digital audio tape
18 Two-sided, high-density
21 Bumpy areas on the disk surface
22 Stores microscopic images on cards
23 A measure of how much a particular storage medium can hold
26 Compact disc rewritable

For an interactive crossword puzzle select Crosswords from Tim's Toolbox at http://www.mhhe.com/oleary/CT05.

MULTIPLE CHOICE

Circle the letter or fill in the correct answer.

1. ________ is permanent storage used to preserve data and programs.
   a. Internal storage
   b. Volatile storage
   c. Nonvolatile storage
   d. File compression
   e. Read only memory
2. Another name for floppy disks is ________.
   a. diskettes
   b. disks
   c. flexible disks
   d. floppies
   e. all of the above
3. The internal hard disk is typically referred to as the ________ drive.
   a. A
   b. B
   c. C
   d. alternate
   e. main
4. Before a disk without tracks and sectors can be used for storage, it must be ________.
   a. opened
   b. compressed
   c. expanded
   d. initialized
   e. scanned
5. An internal hard disk is also known as a ________ because it is located inside the system unit.
   a. hard-disk pack
   b. PC Card hard disk
   c. fixed disk
   d. removable disk
   e. hard disk cartridge
6. ________ is a type of tape cartridge.
   a. Reel
   b. Streamer
   c. RAID
   d. DVD
   e. DAT
7. ________ is exclusively a sequential-access storage media.
   a. A floppy disk
   b. A hard disk
   c. Magnetic tape
   d. CD-ROM
   e. WORM
8. Files cannot be written onto a floppy disk when the write-protection notch is ________.
   a. zipped
   b. open
   c. closed
   d. sealed
   e. crossed
9. ________ is the process of accessing files from a disk.
   a. Reading
   b. Writing
   c. Printing
   d. Spanning
   e. Caching
10. ________ can provide over two hours of high quality video and sound comparable to that found in theaters.
   a. CD-RW
   b. CD
   c. CD-ROM
   d. DVD-R
   e. DVD-ROM

To test your knowledge of this chapter, select Self Test from Tim's Toolbox at http://www.mhhe.com/oleary/CT05.

MATCHING

Match each numbered item with the most closely related lettered item. Write your answers in the spaces provided.

- **a.** access speed
- **b.** CD burner
- **c.** cluster
- **d.** disk caching
- **e.** enterprise storage system
- **f.** file compression
- **g.** file server
- **h.** flash memory card
- **i.** floppy disk
- **j.** floppy-disk cartridge
- **k.** hard-disk pack
- **l.** head crash
- **m.** jewel box
- **n.** microfiche
- **o.** online storage
- **p.** Picture CD
- **q.** RAM
- **r.** solid-state storage
- **s.** track
- **t.** writing

1. Also known as a diskette. ____
2. Zip disks, SuperDisks, HiFD disks. ____
3. The process of saving a file to a secondary storage device. ____
4. Closed concentric ring on a disk on which data is recorded. ____
5. Special CD format for storing digital pictures. ____
6. Mass storage device that is a dedicated computer with large storage capacity. ____
7. Happens when the read/write heads contact the surface of a hard disk. ____
8. Several platters aligned one above the other, allowing greater storage capacity. ____
9. Time required to retrieve data and programs. ____
10. A combination of hardware and software that improves hard-disk performance by anticipating data needs. ____
11. Helps increase storage capacity by reducing the amount of space required to store data and programs. ____
12. Stores microscopic images on a card. ____
13. The smallest amount of disk space that can be read by floppy disk drive. ____
14. A type of storage that is volatile. ____
15. CD-R drive. ____
16. Used to protect optical disks. ____
17. Strategy employed by large organizations to ensure safe and efficient use of data. ____
18. Device that stores and retrieves data and information electronically and has no moving parts. ____
19. Free or low-cost storage available at special service Web sites. ____
20. Solid-state storage device used in portable computers. ____

OPEN-ENDED

On a separate sheet of paper, respond to each question or statement.

1. Discuss the three most likely successors to the 1.44 MB 3 ½-inch floppy.
2. What are the three types of hard disk? What is so disastrous about a head crash?
3. Describe three ways to improve hard disk performance.
4. What are the two most common optical disk formats? Describe the basic types for each format.
5. Explain the concept of Internet storage. What are the advantages and disadvantages of this type of storage?

USING TECHNOLOGY

1 Music from the Internet

Did you know that you could use the Internet to locate music, download it to your computer, and create your own compact discs? All it takes is the right software, hardware, and a connection to the Internet. To learn more about creating your own CDs, review Making IT Work for You: Music from the Internet on pages 338 and 339. Then visit our Web site at http://www.mhhe.com/oleary/CT05, select Using Technology from Tim's Toolbox, play the video, and answer the following questions: (a) What is the title of the song that was selected for download from the Internet? (b) Describe the procedure for adding music files to the playlist. (c) Describe the windows that popped up while creating the custom CD.

2 TiVo

TiVo is a device that, among other features, allows users to pause live television. Connect to our Web site at http://www.mhhe.com/oleary/CT05 and select Using Technology from Tim's Toolbox to connect to TiVo's Web site. Once connected, explore the TiVo product and then answer the following questions: (a) What are the basic functions of TiVo? (b) How could TiVo be an improvement on the traditional VCR? (c) What type of secondary storage does TiVo use? (d) How does TiVo receive updated television program information? (e) Would you use TiVo? Why or why not?

iPod 3

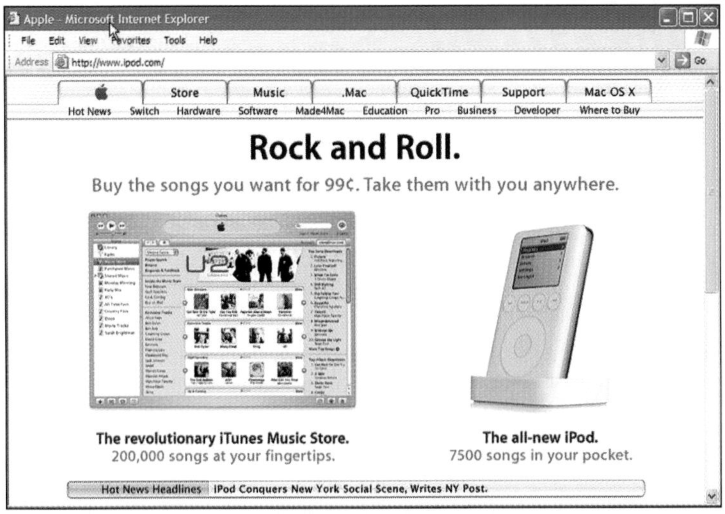

Apple's iPod is a personal portable music player that stores a large number of digital music files. Connect to our Web site at http://www.mhhe.com/oleary/CT05 and select Using Technology from Tim's Toolbox to link to the iPod Web site. Once connected, read about the features and capabilities of iPod, and then answer the following questions: (a) How are music files transferred to iPod? (b) What type of secondary storage does iPod use? (c) What is iPod's storage capacity?

Keychain Storage 4

Do you need to carry more data than will fit on a single floppy disk or CD? A keychain storage device might be for you. Keychain storage devices store large amounts of data in a package small enough to travel with your car keys. Connect to our Web site at http://www.mhhe.com/oleary/CT05 and select Using Technology from Tim's Toolbox to link to a site that features keychain storage devices. Explore the site, and then answer the following questions: (a) What type of secondary storage does the keychain storage device use? (b) How is data transferred to and from computer systems? (c) What system software is the keychain storage device compatible with? (d) What is the capacity of the keychain storage device?

EXPANDING YOUR KNOWLEDGE

1 Computing Today CD

One of the most popular activities on the Internet is to locate and download music files. Using a CD burner, the files are saved onto an optical disk. These disks can then be played in a variety of different types of devices. After reviewing Figure 9-22 and viewing the animation How Music is Downloaded from either your Computing Today CD or by selecting Expanding Your Knowledge from Tim's Toolbox at http://www.mhhe.com/oleary/CT05, consider the following questions: (a) Music is typically downloaded to the internal hard disk drive. Could music be downloaded directly onto a CD? Why or why not? (b) Locate and list five Web sites that provide access to compressed music. (c) Not all music sites provide access to music that can be downloaded legally. Identify the sites listed in (b) that provide legal access to music. (d) How did you determine the legality of these sites?

2 Disks

Several manufacturers are producing high capacity floppy disks including Iomega, Imation, and Sony Corporation. Conduct a Web search to learn more about high capacity floppy disks. Then answer the following: (a) What are the most widely used high capacity floppy disks? (b) Compare their capacities and costs. (c) Discuss their relative advantages and disadvantages. (d) If you were to use a high capacity floppy disk, which one would you select? Discuss and justify your choice.

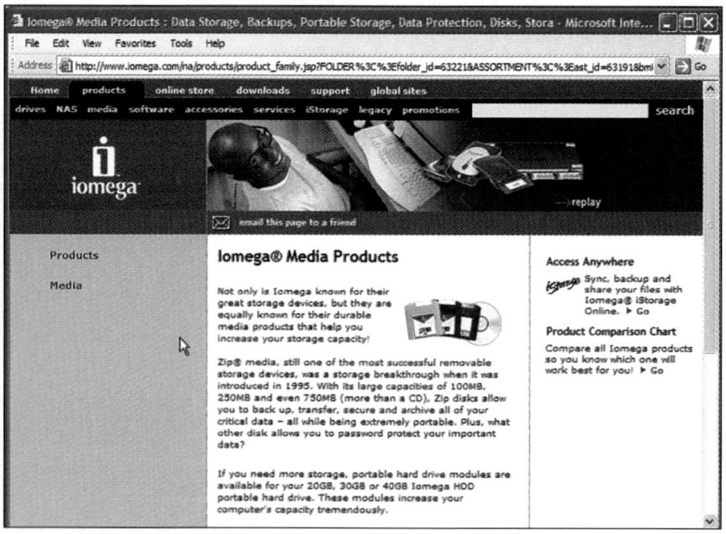

SimNet CD 3

Complete Chapter 9: Secondary Storage on the SimNet Computer Concepts CD and then answer the following questions:

a. Describe how to format a floppy disk.
b. Match the memory allocation to each type of disk shown below.

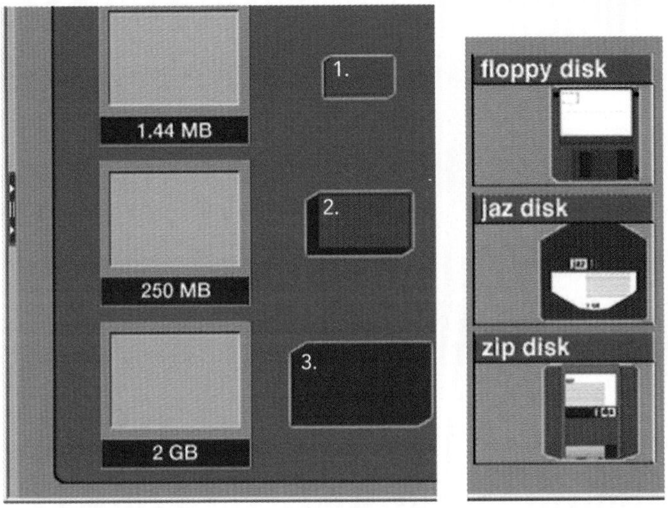

c. Describe the two types of storage.

Internet Hard Drives 4

Internet Hard Drives offer remote file storage or backup. Research an Internet Hard Drive service on the Web, and then answer the following questions: (a) What Internet Hard Drive did you research? (b) What is the cost for using the Internet Hard Drive, and what services do you get for that price? (c) How are files accessed from and uploaded to the Internet Hard Drive? (d) What assurances does the Internet Hard Drive service provider offer concerning availability of your data? What about security? (e) Would you use an Internet Hard Drive? Justify your answer.

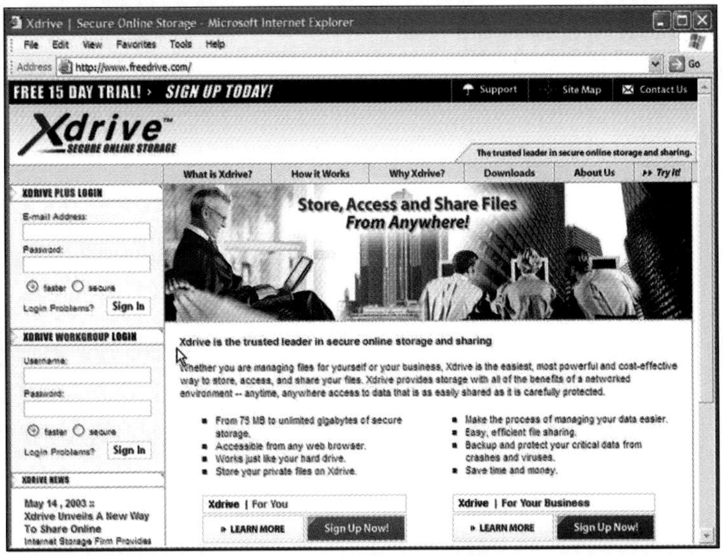

BUILDING YOUR PORTFOLIO

1 DVD

DVD is a newer optical format that is rapidly replacing CDs as the standard in optical disks. DVDs can store 17 gigabytes, more than 30 times the capacity of a CD. Many of today's microcomputers come with DVD drives. Write a one-page paper titled "DVD Technology" that answers the following questions: (a) Define DVD-ROM, DVD-R, and DVD-RW. (b) Compare DVD technology to other types of secondary storage in terms of speed, portability, and capacity. (c) Give examples of applications where DVD would be the best choice for storage. What are some applications where DVD would not be the best choice? Explain your answers.

2 RAID

Many organizations use RAID, or Redundant Arrays of Inexpensive Disks, to enhance performance and reliability. Research RAID on the Web, and write a one-page paper titled "An Overview of RAID" that addresses the following: (a) How does RAID enhance performance? (b) How does RAID enhance reliability? (c) List the three most commonly used RAID levels. Describe the purpose of each. (d) Describe the difference between software RAID and hardware RAID. (e) What type of error cannot be corrected by RAID? Why?

CD-R and Music Files 3

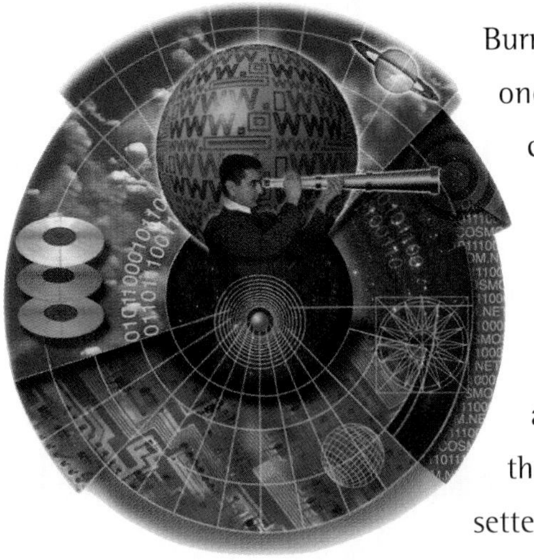

Burning a custom CD of your favorite music is a popular use of secondary storage. Many sites on the Web offer free music that you can download. However, not all music files that are available on the Internet are freely distributable. Consider the following questions and write a one-page paper addressing them: (a) Is it fair to make a copy of a CD you have purchased on your computer? (b) Would it be fair to give a burned copy of a CD to a friend? What if the friend would not have otherwise purchased that CD? (c) People have been making illegal copies of music cassette tapes for some time. How is using the Internet different?

Storage Trade-offs 4

As you have seen in this chapter, there are many different types of secondary storage. No one type is best for all situations or purposes, and any choice in selecting secondary storage involves certain trade-offs. Write a one-page paper titled "Secondary Storage Trade-offs" that addresses the following: (a) Summarize the following types of secondary storage: hard disks, optical disks, floppy disks, and solid state. Rank each type of storage based on the following considerations: capacity, access time, and cost. *Hint: You may wish to organize this in a table.* (b) Based on your summary, describe some situations for each type of secondary storage where that type is a good choice. (c) What relationships do you see between capacity and access time, cost and access time, and cost and capacity?

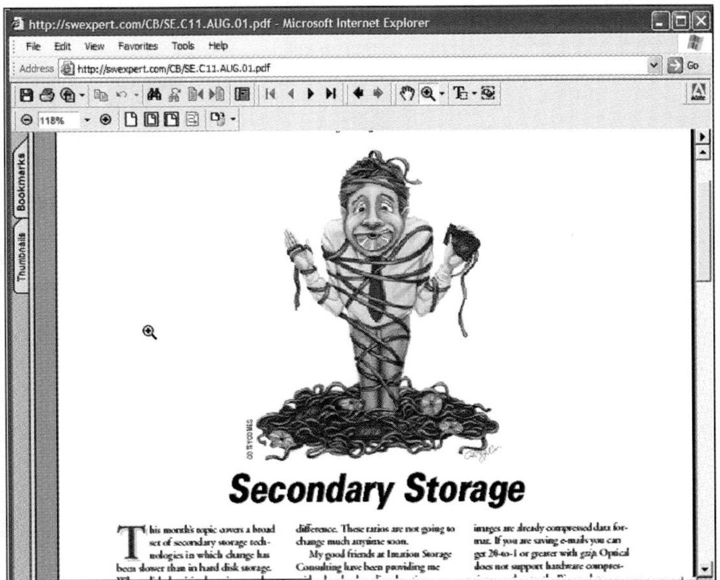

COMMUNICATIONS AND NETWORKS

OBJECTIVES

After you have read this chapter, you should be able to:

1. Discuss connectivity, the wireless revolution, and communication systems.
2. Describe physical and wireless communications channels.
3. Discuss connection devices including modems, T1, DSL, cable modem, and satellite connections.
4. Describe data transmission factors including bandwidths, data flow, data direction, and protocols.
5. Discuss networks and key network terminology.
6. Describe different types of networks including local area, metropolitan area, and wide area networks.
7. Describe network architectures including configurations and strategies.
8. Describe organizational uses of Internet technologies including intranets, extranets, and firewalls.

Communication
Electronic systems that transmit data over communication lines from one location to another

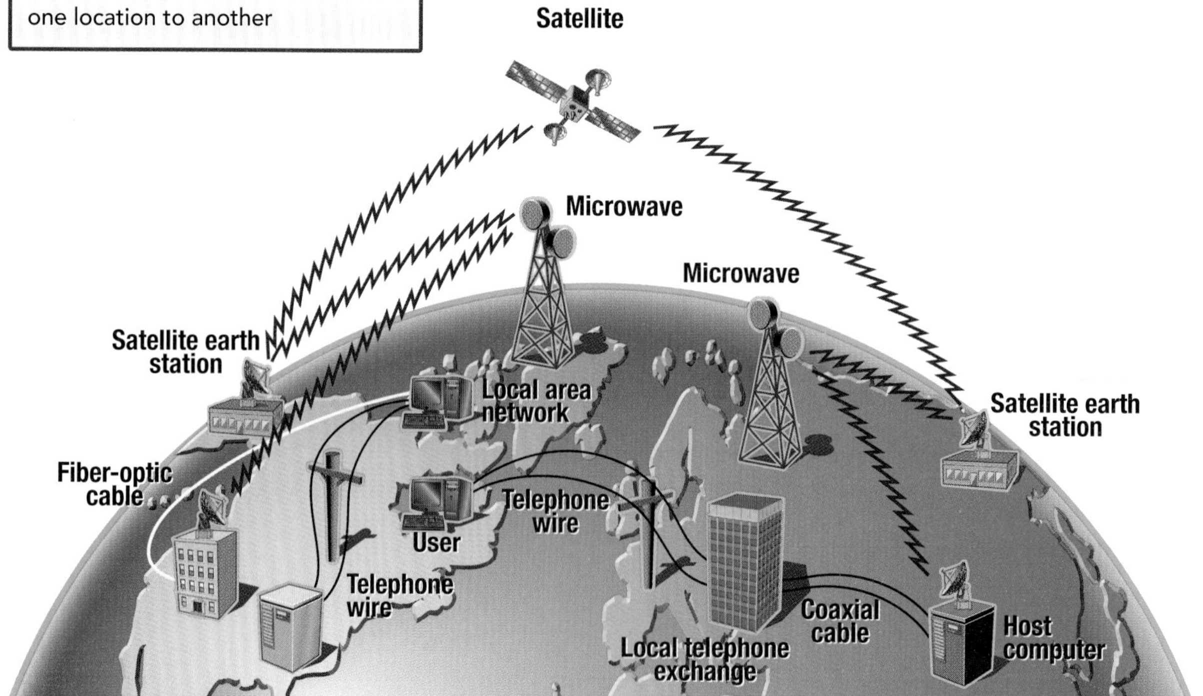

Communications has extended our uses for the microcomputer enormously. The mobile telephone and other wireless technologies are revolutionizing how we use computers today. You can connect your microcomputer to the other people's microcomputers, to the Internet, and to other, larger computers located throughout the world. As we've mentioned earlier, this connectivity puts incredible power on your desk. The result is increased productivity—for you as an individual and for the groups and organizations of which you are a member. Connectivity has become particularly important in business, where individuals now find themselves connected in networks to other individuals and departments.

Communication systems are the electronic systems that transmit data over communications lines from one location to another. You might use a wearable computer and a satellite communication system to access the Internet from almost anywhere. You might work for an organization whose computer system is spread throughout a building, or even throughout the country or world. Or you might use telecommunications lines—telephone lines—to tap into information located in an outside data bank. You could then transmit it to your microcomputer for your own reworking and analysis.

You can even set up a network in your home or apartment using existing telephone lines. Or, you can set up a wireless network. Then you can share files, use one Internet connection, and play interactive games with others in your home.

Competent and knowledgeable end users need to understand the concept of connectivity, the impact of the wireless revolution, and the elements of a communications system. Additionally, they need to understand the basics of communication channels, connection devices, data transmission, networks, network architectures, and network types.

Connectivity
Provides incredible power to you while at and away from your desk

Satellite

Microwave Dish

Wireless Revolution
Extends wireless voice communication to computer communication to free users from their desks

COMMUNICATIONS

Connectivity relates to linking people and resources by networks. The wireless revolution allows Web-enabled devices to connect to the Internet from almost anywhere in the world. Communication systems comprise sending and receiving devices, communication channel, connection devices, and transmission specifications.

Computer **communications** is the process of sharing data, programs, and information between two or more computers. We have discussed numerous applications that depend on communication systems including:

- **E-mail**—provides a fast, efficient alternative to traditional mail by sending and receiving electronic documents.
- **Instant messaging**—supports direct, "live" electronic communication between two or more friends or buddies.
- **Internet telephone**—provides a very low cost alternative to long-distance telephone calls using electronic voice delivery.
- **Electronic commerce**—buying and selling goods electronically.

In this chapter, we will focus on the communication systems that support these and many other applications. Most likely you have used some or all of the above applications. You may have a microcomputer connected to the Internet using a telephone. Perhaps you have a Web-enabled mobile telephone. Or you may have a microcomputer that is directly connected to other computers without using telephone lines. (See Figure 10-1.) Whatever the case, these situations allow you to connect to other people and resources, perhaps using wireless technologies that form a communication system. Connectivity, the wireless revolution, and communication systems are key concepts and technologies for the 21st century.

CONNECTIVITY

Connectivity is a concept related to using computer networks to link people and resources. For example, connectivity means that you can connect your microcomputer by telephone or other telecommunications links to other computers and information sources almost anywhere. With this connection, you are linked to the world of larger computers and the Internet. This includes minicomputers and mainframes and their extensive information resources. Thus, becoming computer competent and knowledgeable becomes a matter of knowing not only about connectivity through networks to microcomputers, but also about larger computer systems and their information resources.

THE WIRELESS REVOLUTION

The single most dramatic change in connectivity and communications in the past five years has been the widespread use of mobile or wireless telephones. Students, parents, teachers, business people, and others routinely talk and communicate with these devices. It is estimated that over 600 million mobile telephones are in use worldwide. This wireless technology allows individuals to stay connected with one another from almost anywhere at any time.

So what's the revolution? While this wireless technology was originally intended for voice communication, it is now becoming widely used to support all kinds of communication, especially computer communication. In addition, recently released wireless technology promises to allow a wide variety of nearby

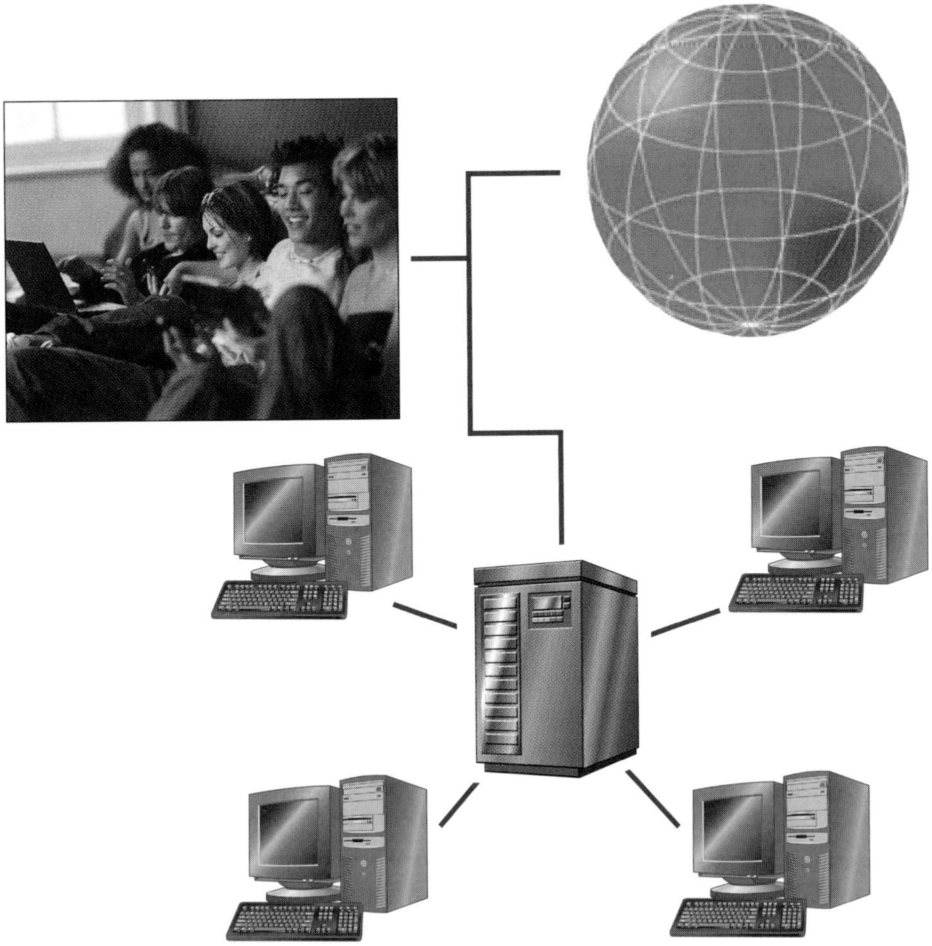

Figure 10-1 Communications

devices to communicate with one another without any physical connection. You can share a high-speed printer, share data files, and collaborate on working documents with a nearby coworker without having your computers connected by cables or telephone—wireless communication. Other wireless technology allows individuals to connect to the Internet and share information from almost anywhere in the world. (See Figure 10-2.) But is it a revolution? Most experts say yes and that the revolution is just beginning.

Figure 10-2 Connectivity options

COMMUNICATION SYSTEMS

Communication systems are electronic systems that transmit data from one location to another. Whether wired or wireless, every communication system has four basic elements. (See Figure 10-3.)

- **Sending** and **receiving devices.** These are often a computer or specialized communication device. They originate (send) as well as accept (receive) messages in the form of data, information, and/or instructions.
- **Communication channel.** This is the actual connecting or **transmission medium** that carries the message. This medium can be a physical wire or cable or it can be a wireless connection.

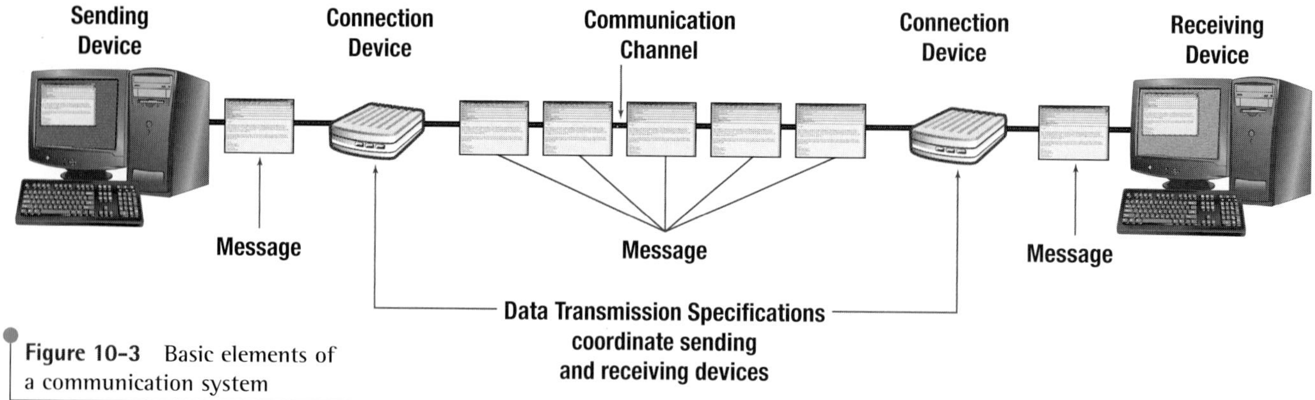

Figure 10-3 Basic elements of a communication system

- **Connection devices.** These devices, also known as **communication devices,** act as an interface between the sending and receiving devices and the communication channel. They convert outgoing messages into a form and format so that they can travel across the communication channel. They also reverse the process for incoming messages.
- **Data transmission specifications.** These are rules and procedures that coordinate the sending and receiving devices by precisely defining how the message will be sent across the communication channel.

For example, if you wanted to send an e-mail to a friend, you could create and send the message using your computer, the *sending device.* Your modem, a *connection device,* would modify and format the message so that it could travel efficiently across *communication channels* such as telephone lines. The specifics describing how the message is modified, reformatted, and sent would be described in the *data transmission specifications.* After your message traveled across the channel, the receiver's modem, a connection device, would reform it so that it could be displayed on your friend's computer, the *receiving device.* (Note: This example presents the basic communication system elements involved in sending e-mail. It does not and is not intended to demonstrate all the specific steps and equipment involved in an e-mail delivery system.)

Concept Check

- ✓ Define communications and connectivity.
- ✓ What is the wireless revolution?
- ✓ Describe the four elements of every communication system.

COMMUNICATION CHANNELS

Communication channels carry data. Telephone lines, coaxial cables, and fiber-optical cable are physical channels. Infrared, broadcast radio, microwave, and satellite are wireless channels.

Communication channels are an essential element of every communication system. These channels actually carry the data from one computer to another. There are two categories of communication channels. One category connects sending and receiving devices by providing a physical connection such as a wire or cable. The other category is wireless.

PHYSICAL CONNECTIONS

Physical connections use a solid medium to connect sending and receiving devices. These connections include telephone lines (twisted pair), coaxial cable, and fiber-optic cable.

- **Telephone lines** you see strung on poles consist of **twisted pair** cable, which is made up of hundreds of copper wires. A single twisted pair culminates in a wall jack into which you can plug your phone and computer. (See Figure 10-4.) Telephone lines have been the standard transmission medium for years for both voice and data. However, they are now being phased out by more technically advanced and reliable media.
- **Coaxial cable,** a high-frequency transmission cable, replaces the multiple wires of telephone lines with a single solid-copper core. (See Figure 10-5.) In terms of the number of telephone connections, a coaxial cable has over 80 times the transmission capacity of twisted pair. Coaxial cable is used to deliver television signals as well as to connect computers in a network.
- **Fiber-optic cable** transmits data as pulses of light through tiny tubes of glass. (See Figure 10-6.) In terms of the number of telephone connections, fiber-optic cable has over 26,000 times the transmission capacity of twisted pair. However, it is significantly smaller. Indeed, a fiber-optic tube can be half the diameter of a human hair. Although limited in the distance they can carry information, fiber-optic cables have several advantages. Such cables are immune to electronic interference, which makes them more secure. Compared to coaxial cable, they are lighter and more reliable at transmitting data. They transmit information using beams of light at light speeds instead of pulses of electricity, making them far faster than copper cable. Fiber-optic cable is rapidly replacing twisted pair telephone lines.

Figure 10-4 Twisted pair cable

Figure 10-5 Coaxial cable

Figure 10-6 Fiber-optic cable

WIRELESS CONNECTIONS

Wireless connections do not use a solid substance to connect sending and receiving devices. Rather, they use the air itself. Primary technologies used for wireless connections are infrared, broadcast radio, microwave, and satellite.

- **Infrared** use infrared light waves to communicate over short distances. It is sometimes referred to as **line of sight communication** because the light waves can only travel in a straight line. This requires that sending and receiving devices must be in clear view of one another without any obstructions blocking that view. As we discussed in Chapter 6, some desktops, notebooks, and handheld computers have **infrared (IrDA) ports.** Additionally some input devices like the infrared mouse and output devices like infrared printers eliminate the clutter of connecting cables and wires. These devices send and/or receive data and information using infrared light waves. One of the most common applications is to transfer data and information from a portable device such as a notebook computer or PDA to a desktop computer. (See Figure 10-7.)
- **Broadcast radio** communication uses special sending and receiving towers called **transceivers.** These transceivers send and receive radio signals from wireless devices. For example, cellular telephones and many Web-enabled devices use broadcast radio to place telephone calls and/or to connect to the Internet. Some end users connect their notebook or handheld computers to a cellular telephone to access the Web from remote locations. Most of these Web-enabled devices follow a standard known as **Wi-FI (wireless fidelity).** Also known as **802.11,** this wireless standard is widely used to connect computers to each other and to the Internet.
- **Microwave** communication uses high-frequency radio waves. Like infrared, microwave communication provides line of sight communication

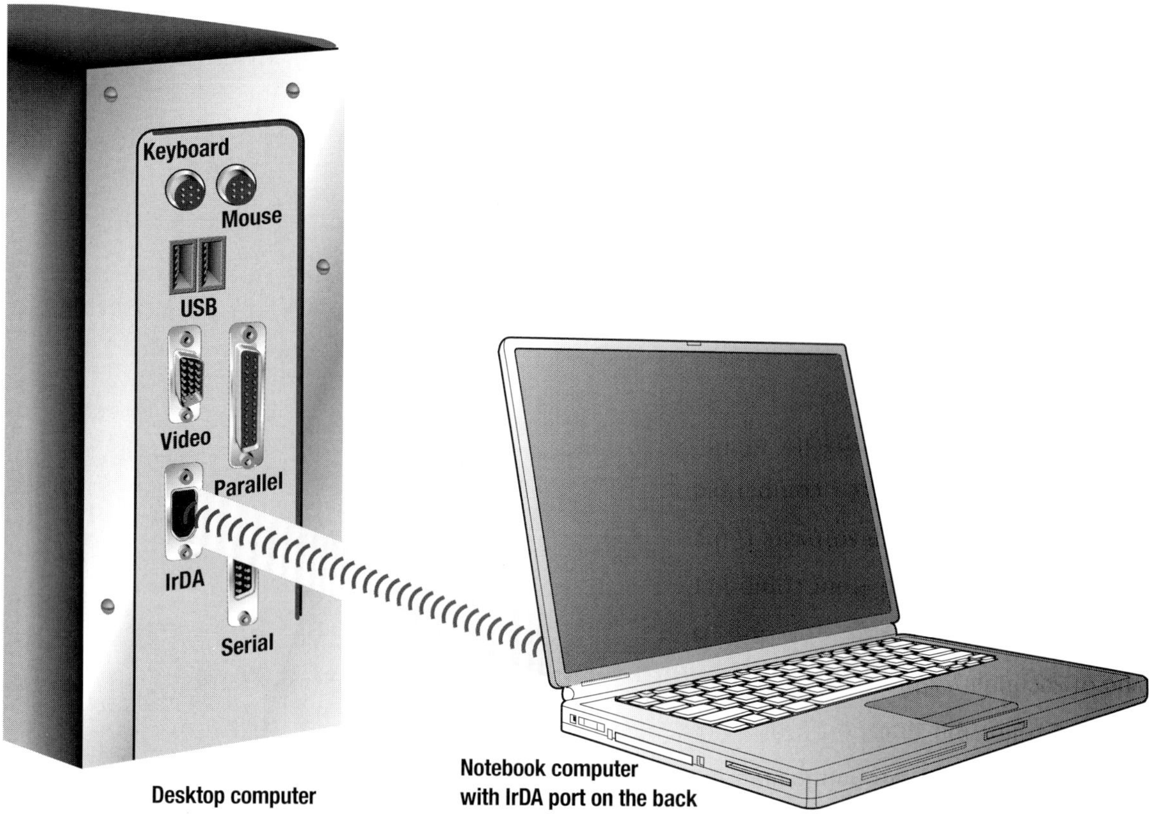

Figure 10-7 IrDA infrared wireless connection

Figure 10-8 Microwave dish

Figure 10-9 Satellite

because microwaves travel in a straight line. Because the waves cannot bend with the curvature of the earth, they can be transmitted only over relatively short distances. Thus, microwave is a good medium for sending data between buildings in a city or on a large college campus. For longer distances, the waves must be relayed by means of **microwave stations** with microwave **dishes** or antennas. (See Figure 10-8.) These stations can be installed on towers, high buildings, and mountaintops.

Bluetooth is a short range wireless communication standard that uses microwaves to transmit data over short distances of up to approximately 33 feet. Unlike traditional microwaves, Bluetooth does not require line of sight communication. Rather it uses radio waves that can pass through nearby walls and other nonmetal barriers. It is anticipated that within the next few years, this technology will be widely used to connect a variety of different communication devices. Currently, it is most widely used for special mice, keyboards, and printers. Using these Bluetooth devices, users are freed from cables. Additionally, unlike with infrared connections, these devices do not require a direct line of sight to communicate.

- **Satellite** communication uses satellites orbiting about 22,000 miles above the earth as microwave relay stations. (See Figure 10-9.) Many of these are offered by Intelsat, the International Telecommunications Satellite Consortium, which is owned by 114 governments and forms a worldwide communications system. Satellites rotate at a precise point and speed above the earth. They can amplify and relay microwave signals from one transmitter on the ground to another. Thus, satellites can be used to send and receive large volumes of data. **Uplink** is a term relating to sending data to a satellite. **Downlink** refers to receiving data from a satellite. The major drawback to satellite communication is that bad weather can sometimes interrupt the flow of data.

Figure 10-10 GPS Navigation

One of the most interesting applications of satellite communications is for **global positioning.** A network of 24 satellites owned and managed by the Defense Department continuously sends location information to earth. **Global positioning system (GPS)** devices use that information to uniquely determine the geographic location of the device. Available in some automobiles to provide navigational support, these systems are often mounted into the dash with a monitor to display maps and speakers to provide spoken directions. (See Figure 10-10.)

For a summary of communication channels, see Figure 10-11.

Channel	Description
Twisted pair	Copper wire, standard voice telephone line
Coaxial cable	Solid copper core, more than 80 times the capacity of twisted pair
Fiber-optic cable	Light carries data, more than 26,000 times the capacity of twisted pair
Infrared	Infrared light travels in straight line to IrDA ports
Broadcast radio	Radio waves used by cellular telephones and other wireless devices
Microwave	High-frequency radio waves, travels in straight line through the air
Satellite	Microwave relay station in the sky, used by GPS devices

Figure 10-11 Types of communication channels

Concept Check

- ✓ What are communication channels?
- ✓ Compare physical and wireless channels.
- ✓ What is Wi-FI? Bluetooth? GPS?

CONNECTION DEVICES

Conventional modems convert analog and digital signals. External, internal, PC Card, and wireless are types of modems. Leased high speed telephone lines, DSL, cable modems, and satellites provide other types of connections.

A great deal of computer communication takes place over telephone lines. However, because the telephone was originally designed for voice transmission, telephones typically send and receive **analog signals,** which are continuous electronic waves. Computers, in contrast, send and receive **digital signals.** (See Figure 10-12.) These represent the presence or absence of an electronic pulse—the on/off binary signals we mentioned in Chapter 6. To convert the digital signals to analog signals and vice versa, you need a modem.

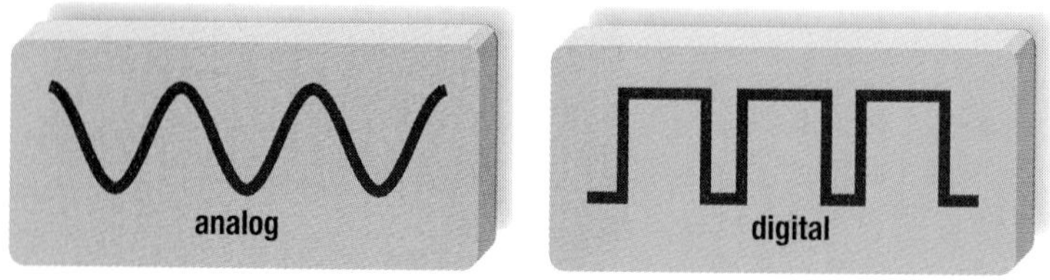

Figure 10-12 Analog versus digital signals

MODEMS

The word **modem** is short for *modulator-demodulator.* **Modulation** is the name of the process of converting from digital to analog. **Demodulation** is the process of converting from analog to digital. The modem enables digital microcomputers to communicate across analog telephone lines. This communication includes both voice and data communications.

The speed with which modems transmit data varies. This speed, called **transfer speed** or **transfer rate**, is typically measured in **bits per second (bps).** (See Figure 10-13.) The higher the speed, the faster you can send and receive information. For example, transferring an image like Figure 10-12, might take 75 seconds with a 33.6 kbps modem and only 45 seconds with a 56 kbps modem.

Unit	Speed
bps	bit per second
kbps	thousand bits per second
mbps	million bits per second
gbps	billion bits per second

Figure 10-13 Transfer speeds

There are four basic types of modems: external, internal, PC Card, and wireless. (See Figure 10-14.)

- The **external modem** stands apart from the computer and typically is connected by a cable to the computer's serial port. Another cable connects the modem to the telephone wall jack.
- The **internal modem** consists of a plug-in circuit board inside the system unit. A telephone cable connects the modem to the telephone wall jack.
- The **PC Card modem** is a credit card–size expansion board that is inserted into portable computers. A telephone cable connects the modem to the telephone wall jack.
- A **wireless modem** may be internal, external, or a PC Card. Unlike the other modems, it does not use cables. Instead, wireless modems send and receive through the air.

TYPES OF CONNECTIONS

Standard telephone lines and conventional modems provide what is called a **dial-up service.** Although still the most popular type of connection service, dial-up service is quite slow, and many users find it inadequate to meet their communication needs.

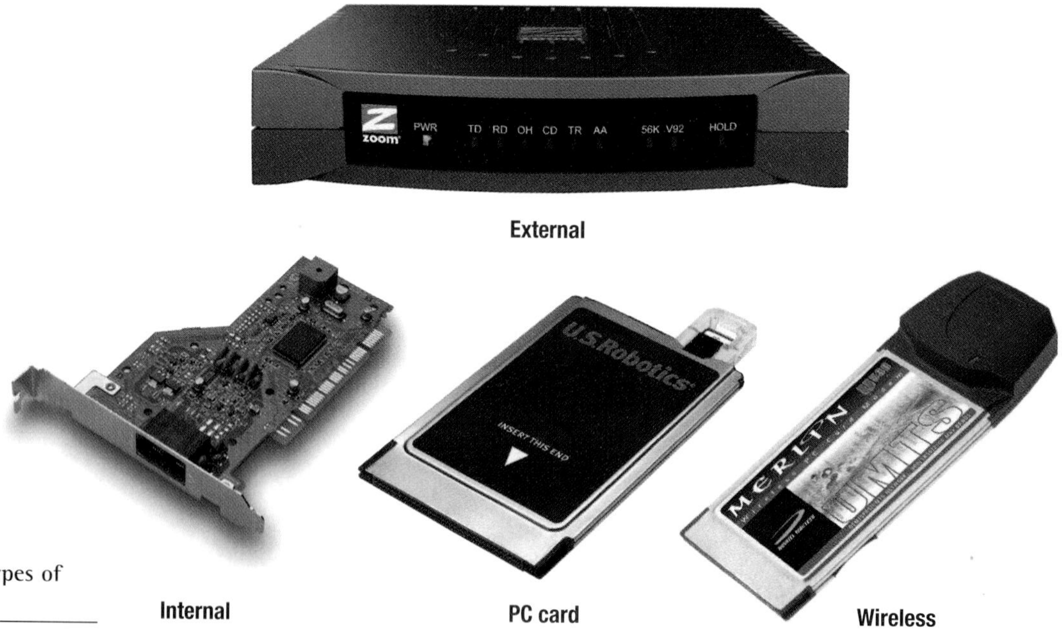

Figure 10-14 Basic types of modems

For years, large corporations have been leasing special high-speed lines from telephone companies. These lines—known as **T1, T2, T3,** and **T4 lines**—support all digital communications, do not require conventional modems, and provide very high capacity. Unfortunately, this type of connection is very expensive. For example, T1 lines provide a speed of 1.5 mbps (over 26 times as fast as a conventional modem) and cost several thousands of dollars.

While the special high-speed lines are too costly for most individuals, there are affordable connections that provide significantly higher capacity than standard dial-up service. These include DSL, cable modems, and satellite. For a comparison of typical user connection costs and speeds, see Figure 10-15.

Type	Monthly Fee	Speed	Seconds to Receive Image
Dial-up	$16	56 kbps	45.0 seconds
DSL	50	1.5 mbps	1.7 seconds
Cable modem	40	1.5 mbps	1.7 seconds
Satellite	70	900 kbps	2.8 seconds

Figure 10-15 Typical user connection costs and speeds

- **Digital subscriber line (DSL)** uses existing telephone lines to provide high-speed connections. **ADSL (asymmetric digital subscriber line)** is one of the most widely used types of DSL. This technology is widely available in most areas.
- **Cable modems** use existing television cables to provide high-speed connections as fast as a T1 or DSL connection, at a lower cost. Although cable connections reach 90 percent of the homes in America, all cable companies do not support cable modems. Industry observers, however, predict 100 percent availability within the next few years.
- **Satellite/air connection services** use satellites and the air to download (down link) or send data to users at a rate seven times faster than dial-up connections. While older satellite services could not upload (uplink) or send data to satellites and had to rely on slow dial-up connections, newer two-way satellite connections are now available. While slower than DSL and cable modems, satellite/air connections are available almost anywhere that a satellite-receiving disk can be aimed at the southern skies.

Concept Check

- ✓ What is the function of a modem?
- ✓ Compare the four types of modems.
- ✓ Describe the high-speed Internet connection options affordable to most users.

DATA TRANSMISSION

Bandwidth measures capacity of communication channel. Serial and parallel are two types of data flow. Simplex, half-duplex, and full-duplex are modes of data transmission. Protocols are rules for exchanging data.

Several factors affect how data is transmitted. These factors include bandwidth, data flow, data direction, and protocols.

BANDWIDTH

Bandwidth is a measurement of the width or capacity of the communication channel. Effectively, it means how much information can move across the communication channel in a given amount of time. For example, to transmit text documents, a slow bandwidth would be acceptable. However, to effectively transmit video and audio, a wider bandwidth is required. There are three categories of bandwidth.

- **Voiceband,** also known as **voice grade** and **low bandwidth,** is used for standard telephone communication. Microcomputers with standard modems and dial-up service use this bandwidth. While effective for transmitting text documents, it is too slow for many types of transmission including high-quality audio and video. Typical speeds are 56 to 96 kbps.
- **Medium band** is the bandwidth used in special leased lines to connect minicomputers and mainframes as well as to transmit data over long distances. Unlike voice band and broadband, medium band is not typically used by individuals.
- **Broadband** is the bandwidth used for high-capacity transmissions. Microcomputers with DSL, cable, and satellite connections as well as other more specialized high-speed devices use this bandwidth. It is capable of effectively meeting most of today's communication needs including transmitting high-quality audio and video. Speeds are typically 1.5 mbps, although much higher speeds are possible.

DATA FLOW

Data can flow or travel in one of two ways: serially and in parallel. (See Figure 10-16.)

- In **serial data transmission,** bits flow in a series or continuous stream, like cars crossing a one-lane bridge. Serial transmission is the way most data is sent over telephone lines. For this reason, external modems typically connect to a microcomputer through a serial port. More technical names for the serial port are **RS-232C connector** and **asynchronous communications port.**
- With **parallel data transmission,** bits flow through separate lines simultaneously. In other words, they resemble cars moving together at the same speed on a multilane highway. Parallel transmission is typically limited to communications over short distances and typically is not used over telephone lines. It is commonly used to send data from the system unit to a printer.

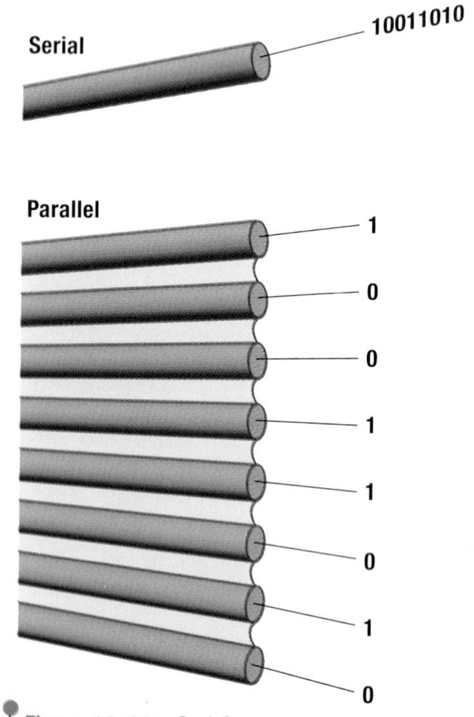

Serial
10011010
Parallel
1
0
0
1
1
0
1
0

Figure 10-16 Serial versus parallel transmission

DATA DIRECTION

There are three directions or modes for data transmission. (See Figure 10-17.)

- **Simplex communication** resembles the movement of cars on a one-way street. Data travels in one direction only. The simplex mode is not frequently used in data communications systems today. One instance in which it is used may be in point-of-sale (POS) terminals in which data is being entered only.
- In **half-duplex communication,** data flows in both directions, but not simultaneously. That is, data flows in only one direction at any one time. This resembles traffic on a one-lane bridge. Half-duplex is very common and frequently used for linking microcomputers by telephone lines to other microcomputers.
- In **full-duplex communication,** data is transmitted back and forth at the same time, like traffic on a two-way street. It is clearly the fastest and most efficient form of two-way communication. Full-duplex has been widely used for mainframe communications for years. Now, it is becoming the standard mode for microcomputers as well.

PROTOCOLS

For data transmission to be successful, sending and receiving devices must follow a set of communication rules for the exchange of information. These rules for exchanging data between computers are known as **protocols.**

The standard protocol for the Internet is **TCP/IP (transmission control protocol/ Internet protocol).** The essential features of this protocol involve (1) identifying sending and receiving devices and (2) reformatting information for transmission across the Internet.

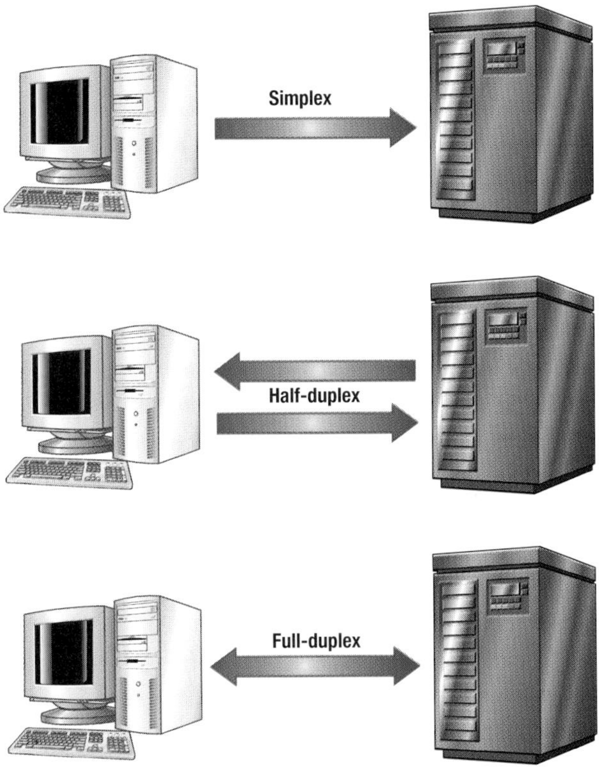

Figure 10-17 Simplex, half-duplex, and full-duplex communication

- **Identification:** Every computer on the Internet has a unique numeric address called an **IP address (Internet Protocol address).** Similar to the way a postal service uses addresses to deliver mail, the Internet uses IP addresses to deliver e-mail and to locate Web sites. Because these numeric addresses are difficult for people to remember and use, a system was developed to automatically convert text-based addresses to numeric IP addresses. This system uses a **domain name server (DNS)** that converts text-based addresses to IP addresses. For example, whenever you enter a URL, say www.McGraw-Hill.com, a DNS converts this to an IP address before a connection can be made. (See Figure 10-18.)
- **Reformatting:** Information sent or transmitted across the Internet usually travels through numerous interconnected networks. Before the message is sent, it is reformatted or broken down into small parts called **packets.** Each packet is then sent separately over the Internet, possibly traveling different routes to one common destination. At the receiving end, the packets are reassembled into the correct order.

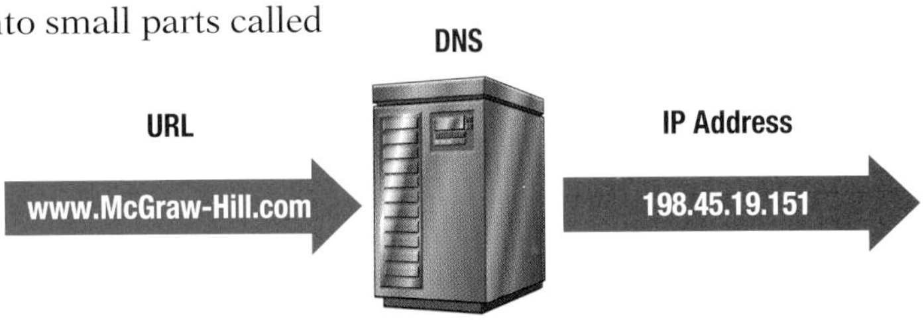

Figure 10-18 DNS converts text-based addresses to numeric IP addresses

There are numerous other widely used protocols, including HTTP, HTTPS, FTP, and WAP.

- **HTTP (hypertext transfer protocol)** is used to connect to Web sites and download Web pages.
- **HTTPS (hypertext transfer protocol secure)** supports secure (often encrypted) Web communication.
- **FTP (file transfer protocol)** supports the uploading and downloading of files from the Internet.
- **WAP (wireless application protocol)** supports wireless access to the Internet.

For a summary of data transmission, see Figure 10-19.

Concept Check

- ✓ What is bandwidth?
- ✓ Compare serial and parallel data transmission.
- ✓ Discuss the three directions or modes of data flow.
- ✓ What are protocols?

Factors	Description
Bandwidth	Measures capacity; voice, medium, and broadband
Data flow	Serial one lane; parallel multilane
Data direction	Simplex one-way only; half-duplex one-way at a time; full-duplex both ways simultaneously
Protocols	Rules for exchanging data; TCP/IP, HTTP, HTTPS, FTP, WAP

Figure 10-19 Data transmission

NETWORKS

Computer networks connect computers. A node may be a client, server, hub, or host computer. NICs connect computers to networks. NOS control and coordinate nodes. Shared processing at different locations is called distributed processing. Network managers manage networks.

A **computer network** is a communication system that connects two or more computers so that they can exchange information and share resources. Networks can be set up in different arrangements to suit users' needs. (See Figure 10-20.)

TERMS

There are a number of specialized terms that describe computer networks. There terms include:

- **Node**—any device that is connected to a network. It could be a computer, printer, or data storage device.
- **Client**—a node that requests and uses resources available from other nodes. Typically, a client is a user's microcomputer.
- **Server**—a node that shares resources with other nodes. **Dedicated servers** specialize in performing specific tasks. Depending on the specific task, they may be called an **application server, communication server, database server, file server, printer server,** or **Web server.**
- **Hub**—the center or central node for other nodes. This device can be a server or simply a connection point for cables from other nodes.
- **Network interface cards (NIC)**—as discussed in Chapter 6, these are expansion cards located within the system unit that connect the computer to a network. Sometimes referred to as a **LAN adapter.**
- **Network operating systems (NOS)**—controls and coordinates the activities of all computers and other devices on a network. These activities include electronic communication and the sharing of information and resources.
- **Distributed processing**—a system in which computing power is located and shared at different locations. This type of system is common in decentralized organizations where divisional offices have their own computer systems. The computer systems in the divisional offices are networked to the organization's main or centralized computer.
- **Host computer**—a large centralized computer, usually a minicomputer or a mainframe.
- **Network manager**—a computer specialist, also known as **network administrator,** responsible for efficient network operations and implementation of new networks.

Figure 10-20 Computer network

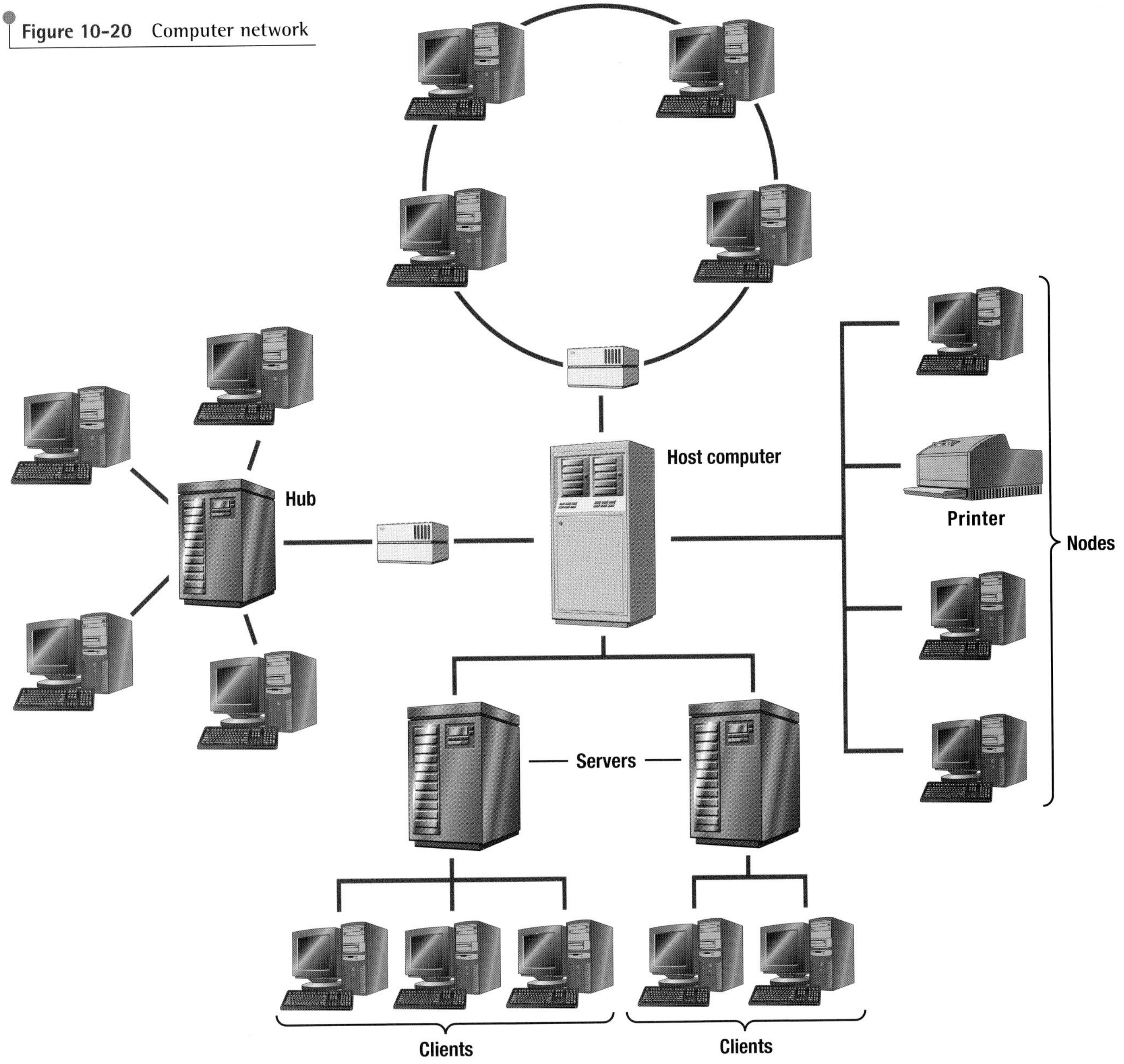

A network may consist only of microcomputers, or it may integrate microcomputers or other devices with larger computers. Networks can be controlled by all nodes working together equally or by specialized nodes coordinating and supplying all resources. Networks may be simple or complex, self-contained or dispersed over a large geographical area.

Concept Check

- ✓ What is a computer network? What are nodes, clients, servers, hubs, and host computers?
- ✓ What is the function of a network interface card and a network operating system?
- ✓ What is distributed processing and what is a network manager?

NETWORK TYPES

Communications networks differ in geographical size. LANs including home networks connect nearby devices. MANs connect buildings in a city. WANs are countrywide and worldwide networks.

Clearly, different types of channels—cable or air—allow different kinds of net works to be formed. Telephone lines, for instance, may connect communications equipment within the same building or within a home. Networks may also be citywide and even international, using both cable and air connections. Local area, metropolitan area, and wide area networks are distinguished by the geographic area they serve.

LOCAL AREA NETWORKS

Networks with nodes that are in close physical proximity—within the same building, for instance—are called **local area networks (LANs).** Typically, LANs span distances less than a mile and are owned and operated by individual organizations. LANs are widely used by colleges, universities, and other types of organizations to link microcomputers and to share printers and other resources. For a simple LAN, see Figure 10-21.

The LAN represented in Figure 10-21 is a typical arrangement and provides two benefits: economy and flexibility. People can share costly equipment. For instance, the four microcomputers share the laser printer and the file server, which are expensive pieces of hardware. Other equipment or nodes may also be added to the LAN—for instance, more microcomputers, mainframe computer, or optical-disk storage devices. Additionally, the **network gateway** is a device that allows one LAN to be linked to other LANs or to larger networks. For example, the LAN of one office group may be connected to the LAN of another office group.

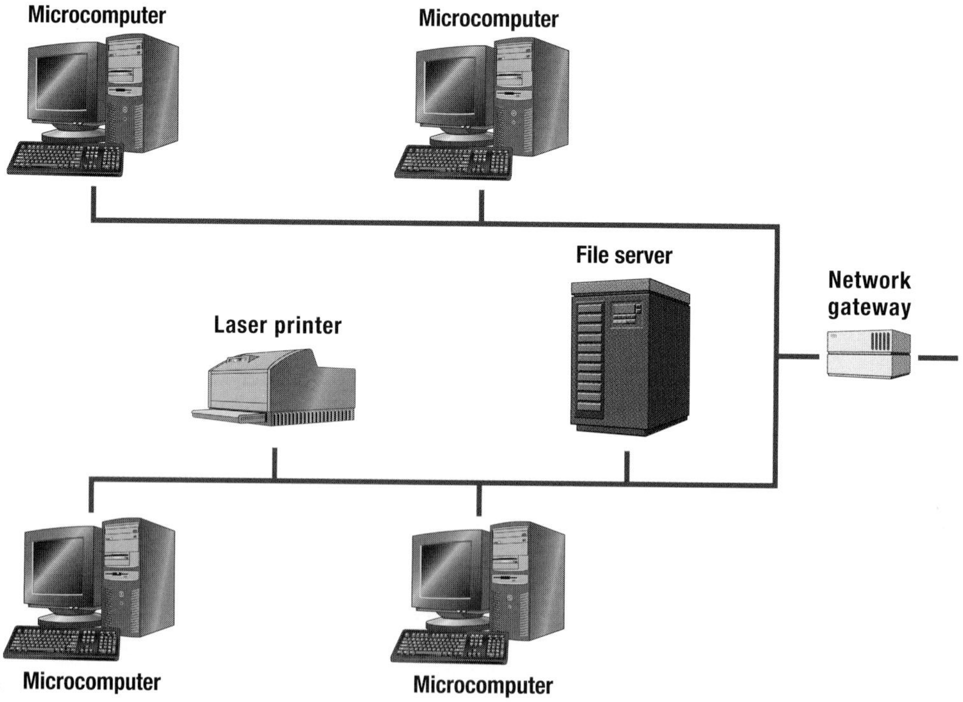
Microcomputer
Microcomputer
File server
Network gateway
Laser printer
Microcomputer
Microcomputer

Figure 10-21 Local area networks

There are a variety of different standards or ways in which nodes can be connected to one another and ways in which their communications are controlled in a LAN. The most common standard is known as **Ethernet.** LANs using this standard are sometimes referred to as **Ethernet LANs.**

HOME NETWORKS

While LANs have been widely used within organizations for years, they are now being commonly used by individuals in their homes and apartments. These LANs, called **home networks,** allow different computers to share resources including a common Internet connection. Computers can be connected in a variety of ways including electrical wiring, telephone wiring, and special cables. One of the simplest ways, however, is without cables or wireless.

A wireless local area network is typically referred to as a **wireless LAN (WLAN).** It uses radio frequencies to connect computers and other devices. All communications pass through the network's centrally located **wireless receiver** or **base station.** This receiver interprets incoming radio frequencies and routs communications to the appropriate devices. These devices may include separate microcomputers, a shared printer, and a modem to provide a gateway for access to the Internet. To see how home networks work, see Figure 10-22. Additionally, consult your Computing Today CD or visit us on the Web at http://www.mhhe.com/oleary/CT05 and select Animations from Tim's Toolbox.

To learn more about how to set up and use a wireless home network, see the nearby Making IT Work for You: Home Networking.

METROPOLITAN AREA NETWORKS

The next step up from the LAN is the **MAN**—the **metropolitan area network.** Also known as **regional networks,** MANs span distances up to 100 miles. These networks are frequently used as links between office buildings in a city. For example, they may be used to connect office buildings located at different locations within a city. (See Figure 10-23.)

Unlike a LAN, a MAN is typically not owned by a single organization. Rather, it is either owned by a group of organizations who jointly own and operate the network or by a single network service provider who provides network services for a fee. (See Figure 10-24.) **Cellular phone systems** expand the flexibility of MANs by allowing links to car phones and portable phones.

WIDE AREA NETWORKS

Wide area networks (WANs) are countrywide and worldwide networks. These networks provide access to regional service (MAN) providers and typically span distances greater than 100 miles. They use microwave relays and satellites to reach users over long distances—for example, from Los Angeles to Paris. Of course, the widest of all WANs is the Internet, which spans the entire globe. (See Figure 10-25.)

The primary difference between a LAN, MAN, and WAN is the geographical range. Each may have various combinations of hardware, such as microcomputers, minicomputers, mainframes, and various peripheral devices.

Concept Check

- What are the three types of networks? What is the primary difference between them?
- What is a network gateway? What is a wireless receiver?
- Who typically owns and operates WANs?

On the Web Explorations

Cirrus Logic is a leader in developing wireless home networks. To learn more about these companies, visit our Web site at http://www.mhhe.com/oleary/CT05 and select On the Web Explorations from Tim's Toolbox.

Computing Today CD

Figure 10-22 How wireless home networks work

How Wireless Home Networks Work

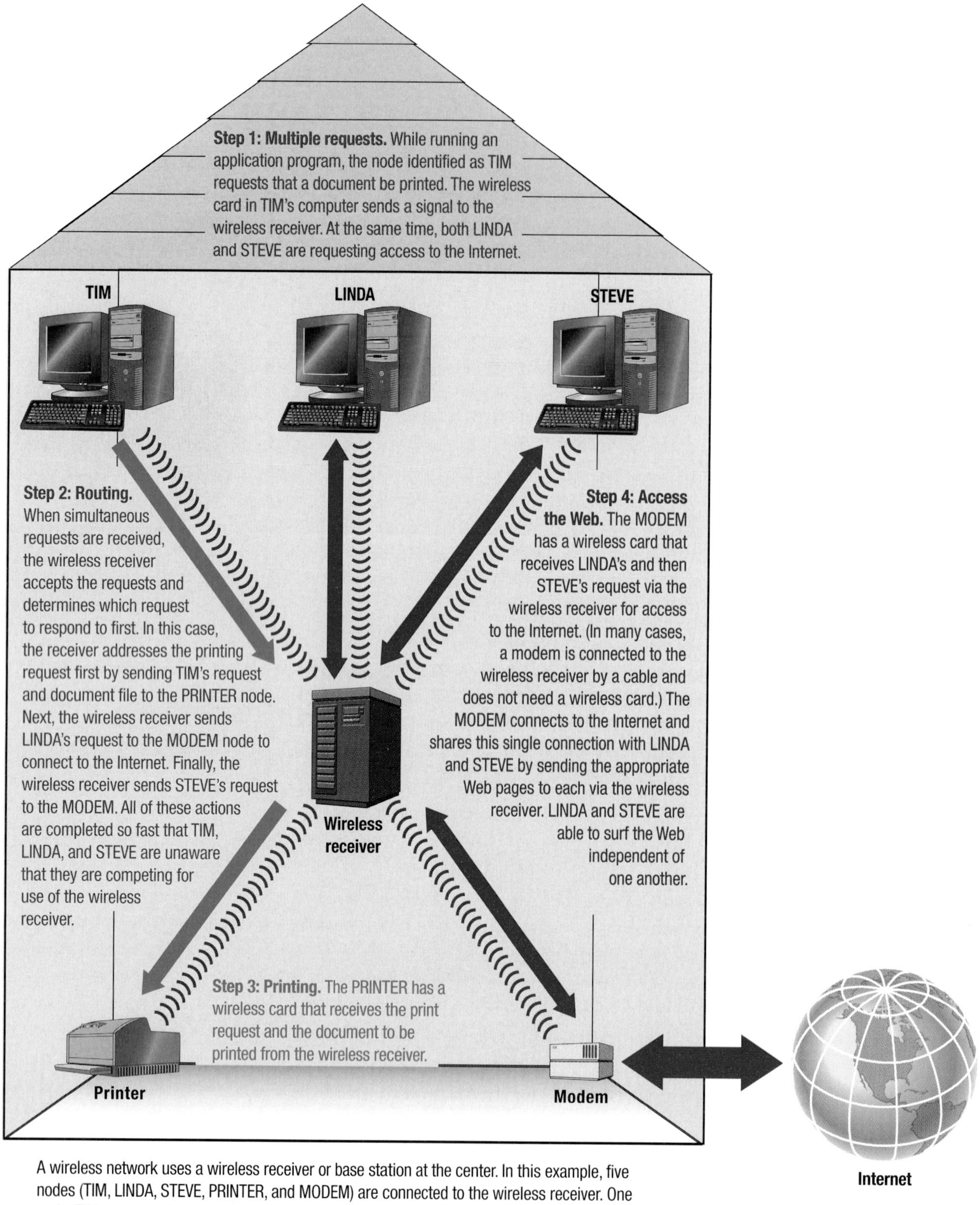

Step 1: Multiple requests. While running an application program, the node identified as TIM requests that a document be printed. The wireless card in TIM's computer sends a signal to the wireless receiver. At the same time, both LINDA and STEVE are requesting access to the Internet.
TIM
LINDA
STEVE
Step 2: Routing. When simultaneous requests are received, the wireless receiver accepts the requests and determines which request to respond to first. In this case, the receiver addresses the printing request first by sending TIM's request and document file to the PRINTER node. Next, the wireless receiver sends LINDA's request to the MODEM node to connect to the Internet. Finally, the wireless receiver sends STEVE's request to the MODEM. All of these actions are completed so fast that TIM, LINDA, and STEVE are unaware that they are competing for use of the wireless receiver.
Wireless receiver
Step 4: Access the Web. The MODEM has a wireless card that receives LINDA's and then STEVE's request via the wireless receiver for access to the Internet. (In many cases, a modem is connected to the wireless receiver by a cable and does not need a wireless card.) The MODEM connects to the Internet and shares this single connection with LINDA and STEVE by sending the appropriate Web pages to each via the wireless receiver. LINDA and STEVE are able to surf the Web independent of one another.
Step 3: Printing. The PRINTER has a wireless card that receives the print request and the document to be printed from the wireless receiver.
Printer
Modem
Internet

A wireless network uses a wireless receiver or base station at the center. In this example, five nodes (TIM, LINDA, STEVE, PRINTER, and MODEM) are connected to the wireless receiver. One node, TIM, is requesting a document to be printed. At the same time, two other nodes (LINDA and STEVE) are requesting access to the Internet.

Figure 10-23 Connecting people and organizations

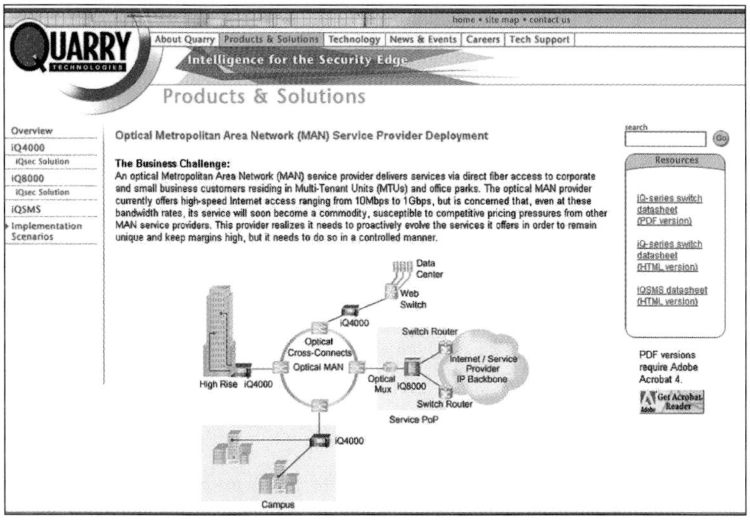

Figure 10-24 Metropolitan area service provider

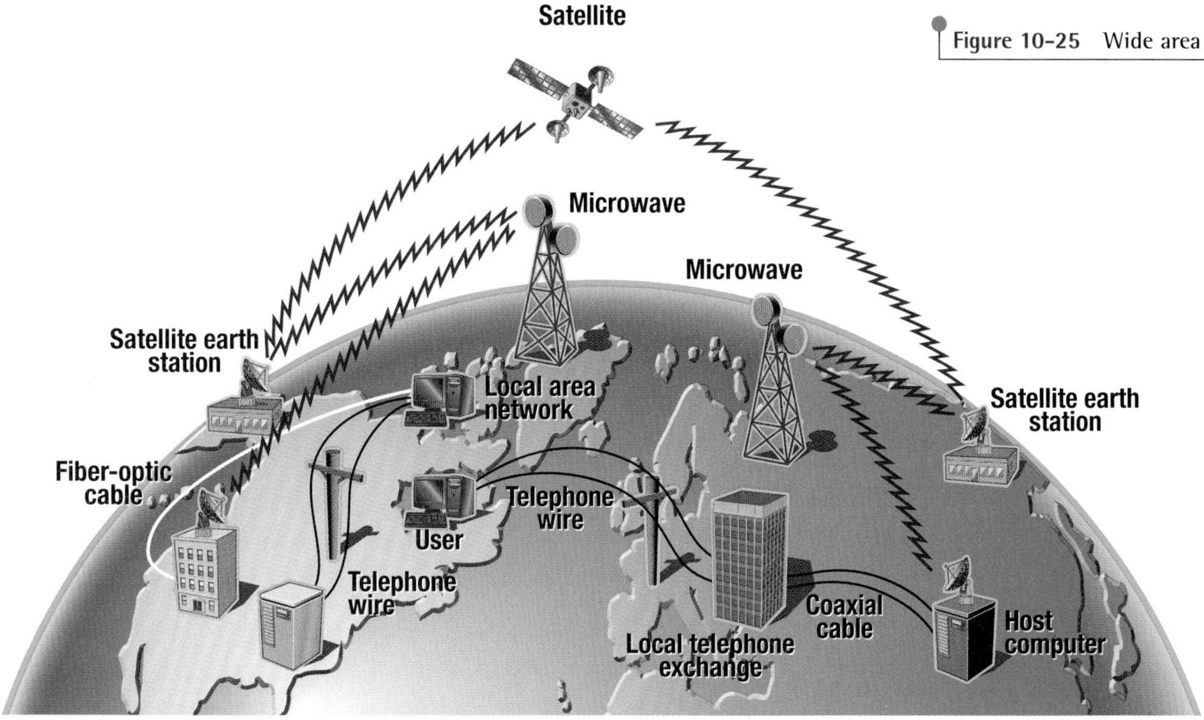

Figure 10-25 Wide area network

MAKING IT WORK FOR YOU

HOME NETWORKING

Computer networks are not just for corporations and schools anymore. If you have more than one computer, you can use a home network to share files and printers, to allow multiple users access to the Internet at the same time, and to play multiplayer computer games.

Installing the Network Each computer on a wireless network requires a wireless network card. Cards are often available in kits that also include a base station. Once the cards are installed in each computer, the base station must be configured for sharing the Internet. Then, each computer can be configured to share file and printers. For example, to set up a wireless network using Agere System's Residential Gateway and Windows XP:

1

- **Install a compatible wireless card in each computer. In most cases, simply plugging the card in is all that is required.**
- **Run the included software to set up the base station for accessing and sharing the Internet.**

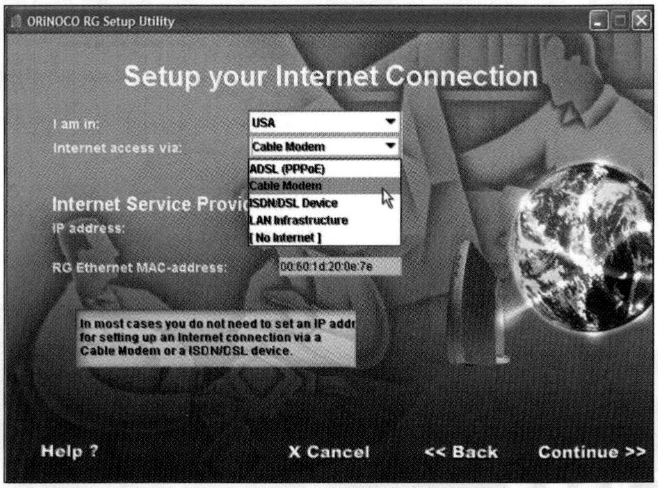

2

- **Click *Start/My Network Places* and click *Set up a home or small office network.***
- **Follow the instructions in the wizard to set up your computer for file and printer sharing, and to access the Internet through the residential gateway.**

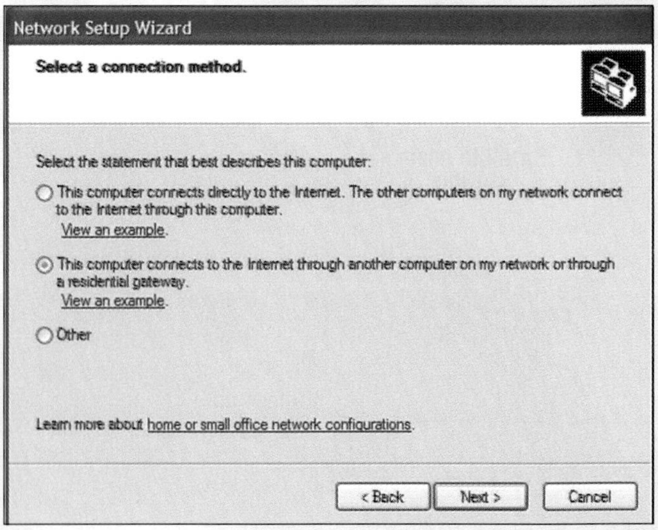

Using the Network Now your computers are ready to share their resources. The four most common uses of a home network are to share files, printers, and Internet access, and to run multiplayer computer games.

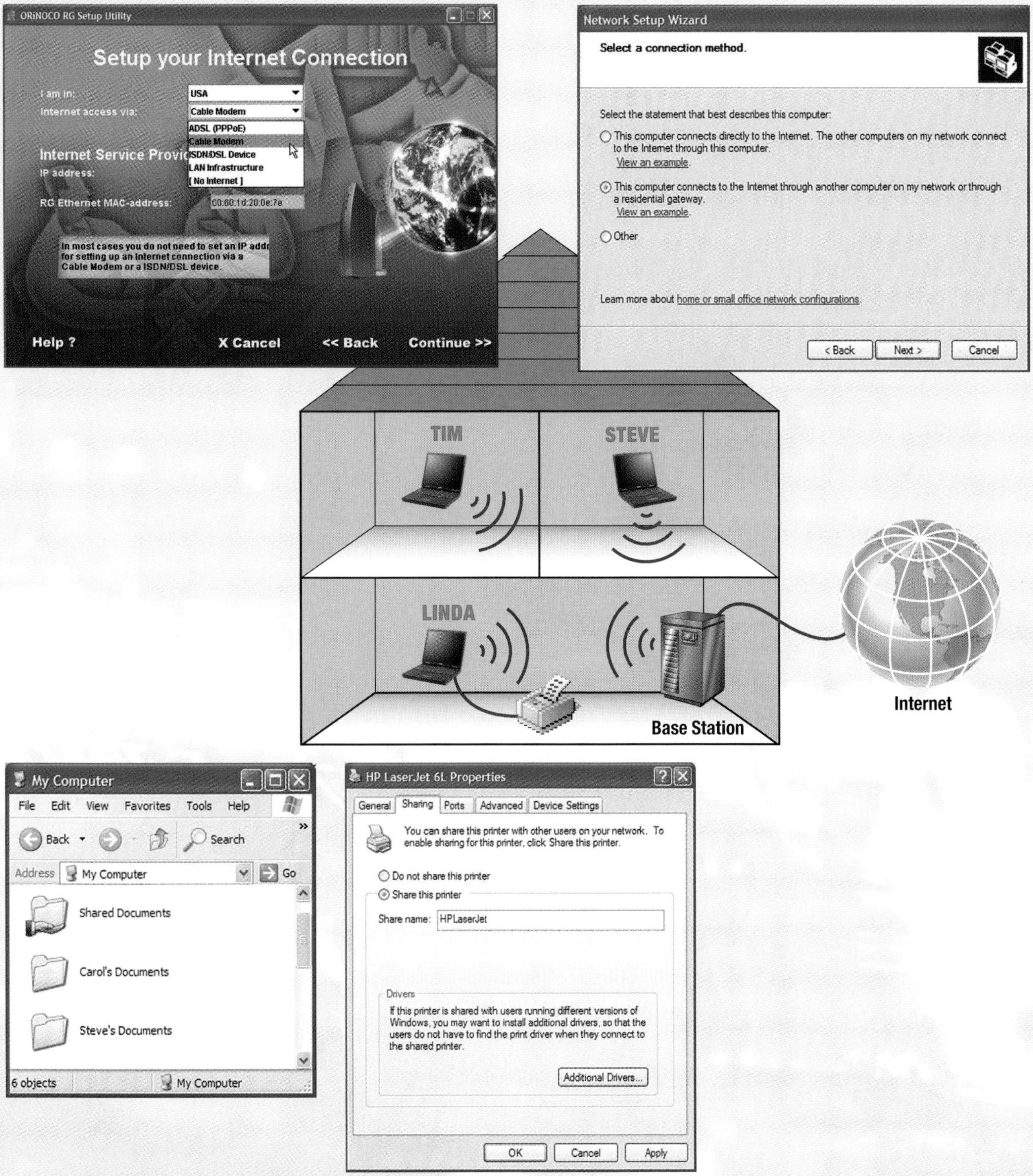

Home networks are continually changing and some of the specifics presented in this Making IT Work for You may have changed. To learn about other ways to make information technology work for you, visit our Web site at http://www.mhhe.com/oleary/CT05 and select Making IT Work for You from Tim's Toolbox.

NETWORK ARCHITECTURE

Network architecture describes how a computer network is configured and what strategies are employed. Configurations include star, bus, ring, and hierarchical. Strategies include terminal, client-server, and peer-to-peer.

Network architecture describes how a network is arranged and how resources are coordinated and shared. It encompasses a variety of different network specifics including network configurations and strategies. Network configurations describe the physical arrangement of the network. Network strategies define how information and resources are shared.

CONFIGURATIONS

A network can be arranged or configured in several different ways. This arrangement is called the network's **topology.** The four principal network topologies are star, bus, ring, and hierarchical.

In a **star network,** a number of small computers or peripheral devices are linked to a central unit. (See Figure 10-26.) The central unit is the **network hub** and is typically a host computer or file server.

All communications pass through this central unit. Control is maintained by **polling.** That is, each connecting device is asked ("polled") whether it has a message to send. Each device is then in turn allowed to send its message.

One particular advantage of the star topology is that it can be used to support a **time-sharing system.** That is, several users can share resources ("time") on a central computer. The star is a common topology for linking microcomputers to a mainframe that allows access to an organization's database.

In a **bus network** each device in the network handles its own communications control. There is no host computer. All communications travel along a common connecting cable called a **bus** or **backbone.** (See Figure 10-27.) As the information passes along the bus, it is examined by each device to see if the information is intended for it.

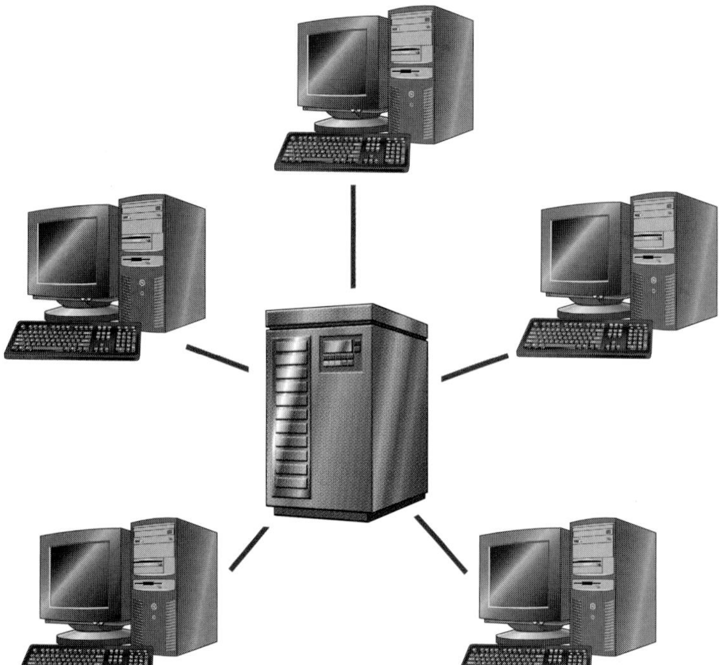

Figure 10-26 Star network

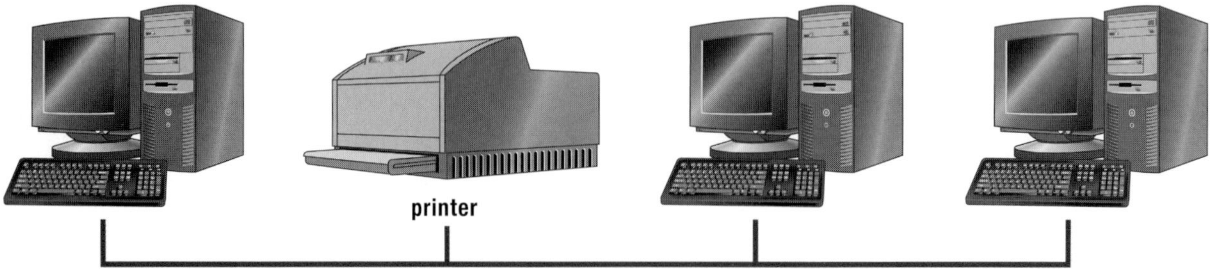

Figure 10-27 Bus network

The bus network is typically used when only a few microcomputers are to be linked together. This arrangement is common for sharing data stored on different microcomputers. Because a star network typically provides a more direct path to shared resources, it is more efficient than a bus network for sharing these resources. However, a bus network is easy to install and is less expensive.

In a **ring network,** each device is connected to two other devices, forming a ring. (See Figure 10-28.) There is no central file server or computer. Messages are passed around the ring until they reach the correct destination. With microcomputers, the ring arrangement is the least frequently used of the four networks. However, it often is used to link mainframes, especially over wide geographical areas. These mainframes tend to operate fairly autonomously. They perform most or all of their own processing and only occasionally share data and programs with other mainframes.

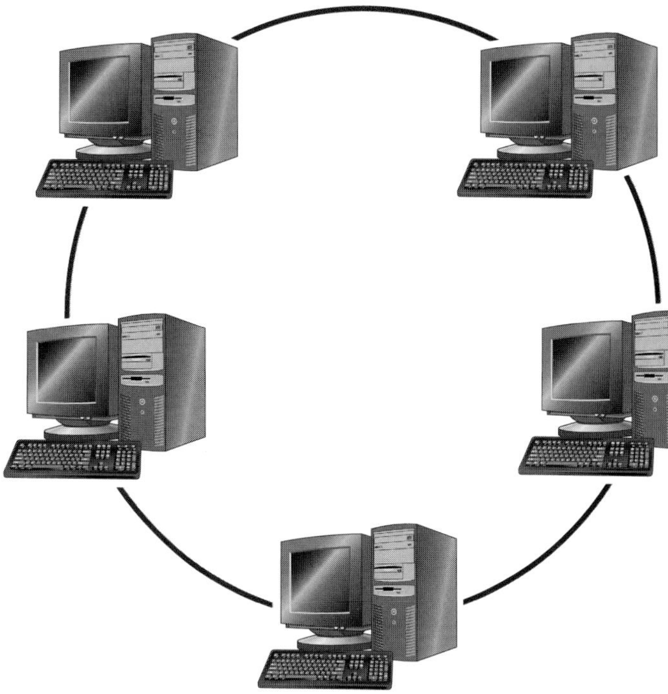

Figure 10-28 Ring network

A ring network is useful in a decentralized organization because it makes possible a **distributed data processing system.** That is, computers can perform processing tasks at their own dispersed locations. However, they can also share programs, data, and other resources with each other.

The **hierarchical network**—also called a **hybrid network**—consists of several computers linked to a central host computer, just like a star network. However, these other computers are also hosts to other, smaller computers or to peripheral devices. (See Figure 10-29.)

Thus, the host at the top of the hierarchy could be a mainframe. The computers below the mainframe could be minicomputers, and those below, microcomputers. The hierarchical network allows various computers to share databases, processing power, and different output devices.

A hierarchical network is useful in centralized organizations. For example, different departments within an organization may have individual microcomputers connected to departmental minicomputers. The minicomputers in turn may be connected to the corporation's mainframe, which contains data and programs accessible to all.

For a summary of the network configurations, see Figure 10-30.

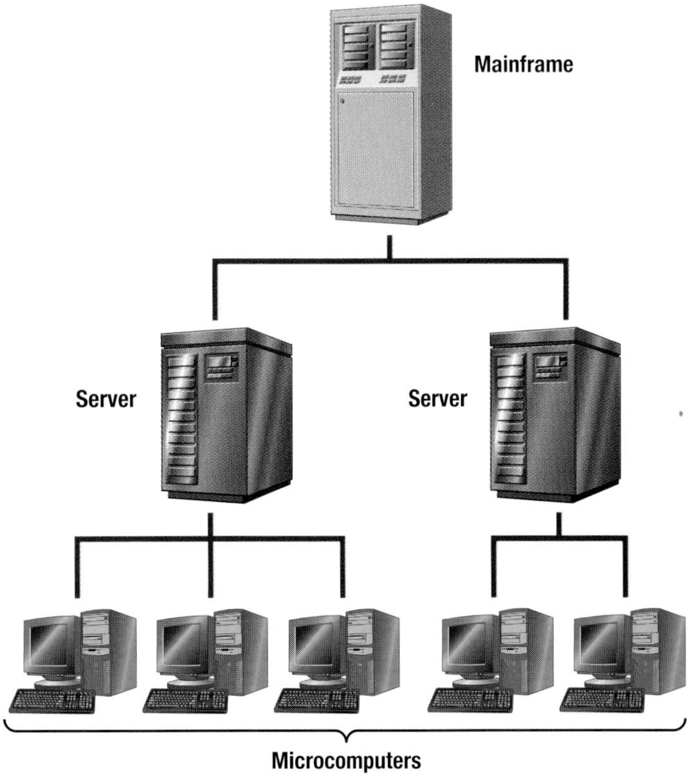

Figure 10-29 Hierarchical network

Topology	Description
Star	Several computers connected to a central server or host; all communications travel through central server; good for sharing common resources
Bus	Computers connected by a common line; communication travels along this common line; less expensive than star
Ring	Each computer connected to two others forming a ring; communications travel around ring; often used to link mainframe computers in decentralized organizations
Hierarchical	One top-level host computer connected to next-level computers, which are connected to third-level computers; often used in centralized organizations

Figure 10-30 Principal network configurations

Concept Check

- What is a network topology?
- What are the four principal network topologies?
- What is a distributed data processing system?
- What is time-sharing system?

STRATEGIES

Every network has a **strategy,** or way of coordinating the sharing of information and resources. The most common network strategies are terminal, client/server, and peer-to-peer systems.

In a **terminal network system,** processing power is centralized in one large computer, usually a mainframe. The nodes connected to this host computer are either terminals, with little or no processing capabilities, or microcomputers running special software that allows them to act as terminals. (See Figure 10-31.) The star and hierarchical networks are typical configurations with UNIX as the operating system.

Many airline reservation systems are terminal systems. A large central computer maintains all the airline schedules, rates, seat availability, and so on. Travel agents use terminals to connect to the central computer and use

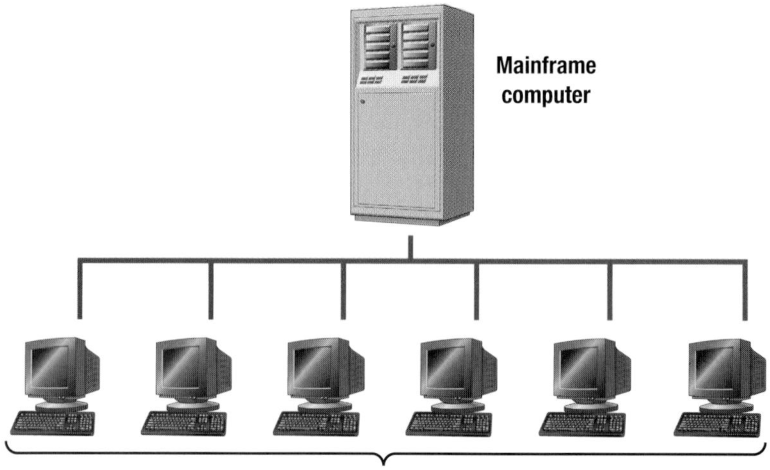

Figure 10-31 Terminal network system

it to schedule reservations. Although the tickets may be printed along with travel itineraries at the agent's desk, nearly all processing is done at the central computer.

One advantage of terminal network systems is the centralized location and control of technical personnel, software, and data. One disadvantage is the lack of control and flexibility for the end user. Another disadvantage is that terminal systems do not use the full processing power available with microcomputers. Though the terminal strategy was once very popular, most new systems do not use it.

Client/server network systems use one computer to coordinate and supply services to other nodes on the network. The server provides access to resources such as Web pages, databases, application software, and hardware. (See Figure 10-32.) This strategy is based on specialization. Server nodes coordinate and supply specialized services, and client nodes request the services. Commonly used network operating systems are Novell's NetWare, Microsoft's Windows NT, IBM's LAN Server, and Banyan Vines.

Client/server network systems are widely used on the Internet. For example, **Napster** (the once popular music service) employed a version of this strategy. Music enthusiasts used the Internet to connect to Napster servers. The Napster servers provided lists of music files (some of which were copyrighted) that were available to be copied from participating Napster users. The music enthusiasts were clients requesting services (information regarding the location of others willing to share music files) from Napster servers. (See Figure 10-33 and consult your Computing Today CD or visit us on the Web at http://www.mhhe.com/oleary/CT05 and select Animations from Tim's Toolbox.)

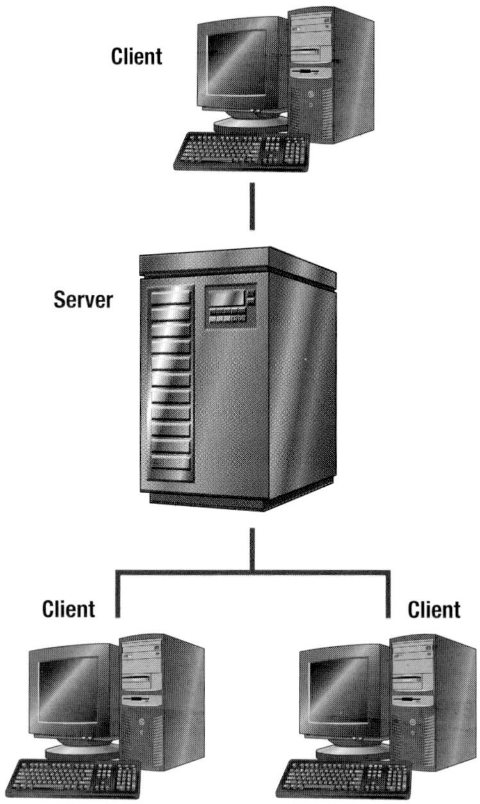

Figure 10-32 Client/server network system

It is important to note that Napster did not provide the music files that were to be copied. Rather, it provided information—the location of users who were willing to share specific music files. Once a requesting user had the location of the files, he/she would contact the provider directly and did not need to remain in the Napster network. Once disconnected from the Napster server, this direct connection formed a very simple peer-to-peer network which will be discussed next. When the music industry charged Napster for violating copyright laws, Napster responded that they did not provide the music files, noting that they only provided information. The courts ruled against Napster citing that Napster *facilitated* the illegal copying of copyright materials and the Napster sites were shut down. Once the servers were shut down, the Napster system fell apart.

One advantage of the client/server network strategy is the ability to handle very large networks efficiently. Another advantage is the availability of powerful network management software to monitor and control network activities. The major disadvantages are the cost of installation and maintenance.

In a **peer-to-peer network system,** nodes have equal authority and can act as both clients and servers. For example, one microcomputer can obtain files located on another microcomputer and can also provide files to other microcomputers. (See Figure 10-34.) A typical configuration for a peer-to-peer system is the bus network. Commonly used network operating systems are Novell's NetWare Lite, Microsoft's Windows NT, and Apple's Macintosh Peer-to-Peer LANs.

Many current popular music sharing services use this network strategy. In fact, the Napster approach discussed earlier was actually a hybrid network in which the Napster server worked in a client-server environment providing a service to clients. Once a Napster user had the location of requested music

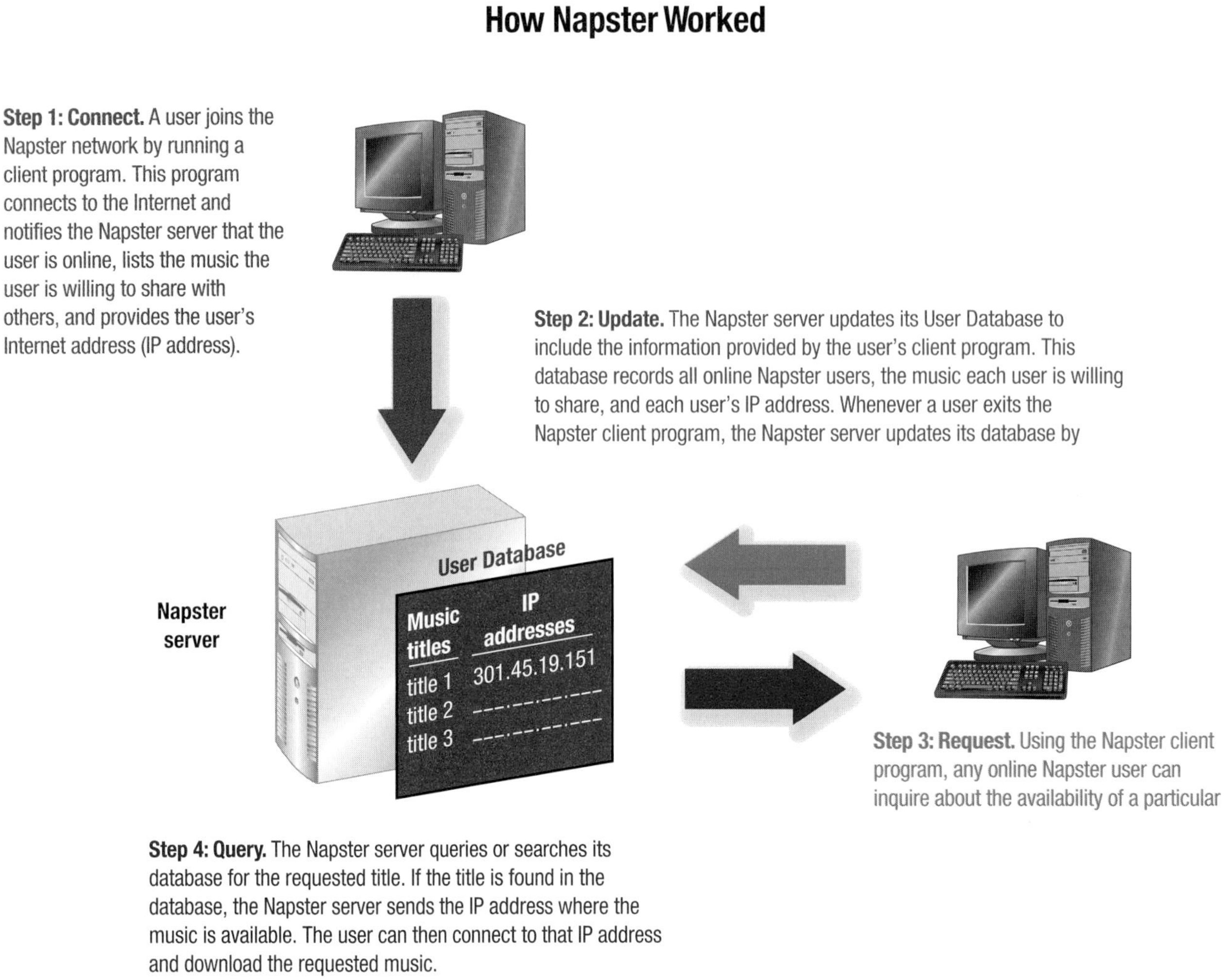
How Napster Worked
Step 1: Connect. A user joins the Napster network by running a client program. This program connects to the Internet and notifies the Napster server that the user is online, lists the music the user is willing to share with others, and provides the user's Internet address (IP address).
Step 2: Update. The Napster server updates its User Database to include the information provided by the user's client program. This database records all online Napster users, the music each user is willing to share, and each user's IP address. Whenever a user exits the Napster client program, the Napster server updates its database by
Napster server
User Database
Music titles
IP addresses
title 1
301.45.19.151
title 2
title 3
Step 3: Request. Using the Napster client program, any online Napster user can inquire about the availability of a particular
Step 4: Query. The Napster server queries or searches its database for the requested title. If the title is found in the database, the Napster server sends the IP address where the music is available. The user can then connect to that IP address and download the requested music.

Figure 10-33 How Napster worked

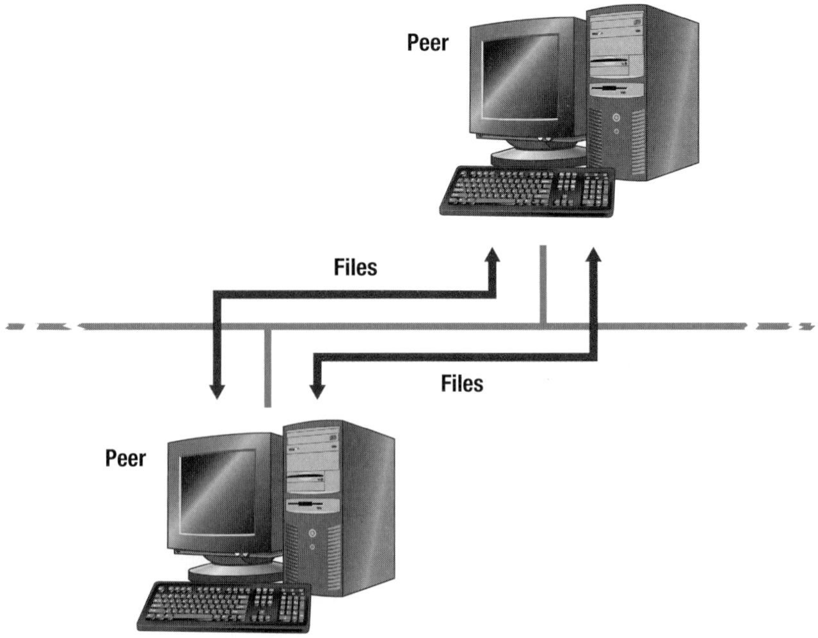
Peer
Files
Files
Peer

Figure 10-34 Peer-to-peer network system

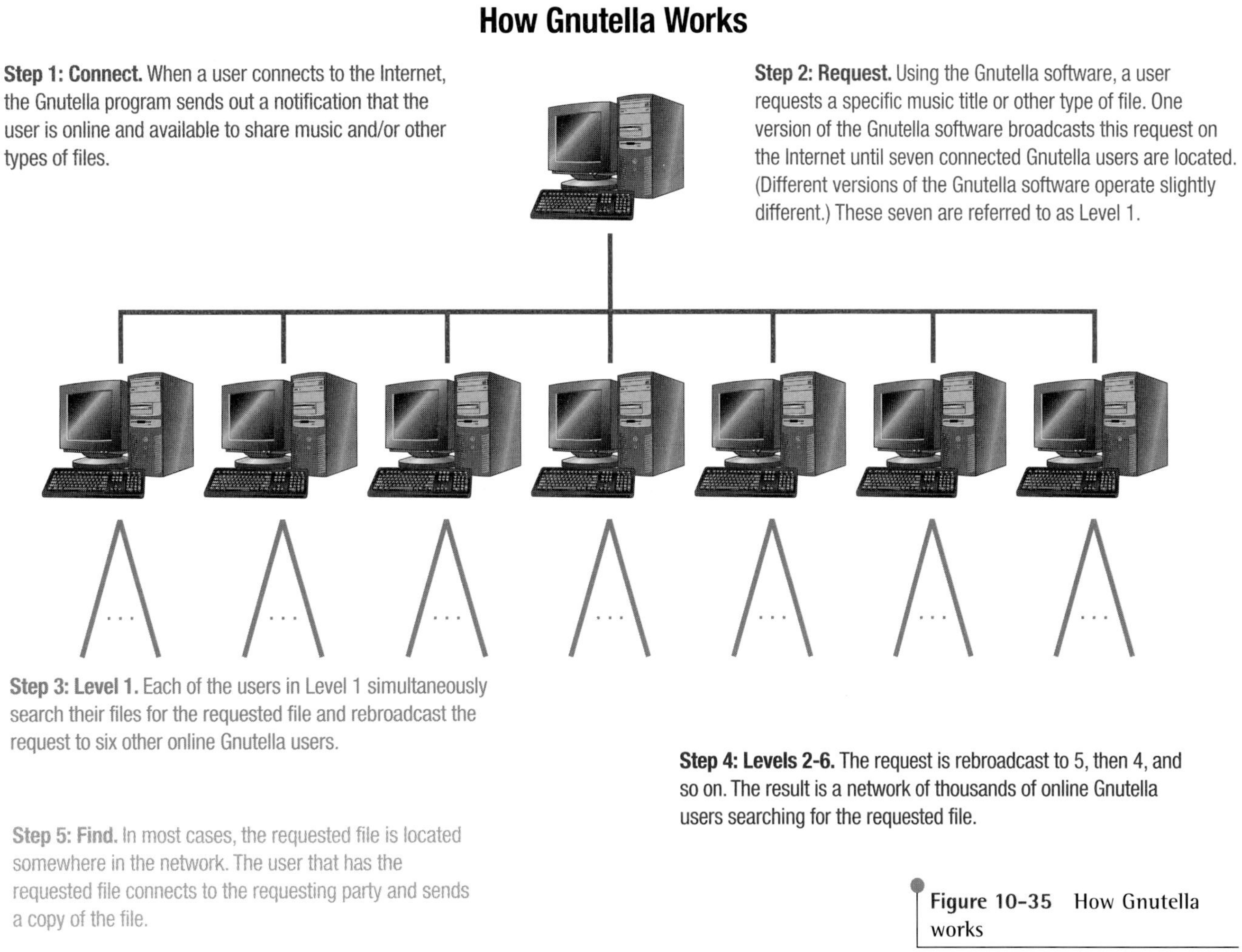
How Gnutella Works
Step 1: Connect. When a user connects to the Internet, the Gnutella program sends out a notification that the user is online and available to share music and/or other types of files.
Step 2: Request. Using the Gnutella software, a user requests a specific music title or other type of file. One version of the Gnutella software broadcasts this request on the Internet until seven connected Gnutella users are located. (Different versions of the Gnutella software operate slightly different.) These seven are referred to as Level 1.
Step 3: Level 1. Each of the users in Level 1 simultaneously search their files for the requested file and rebroadcast the request to six other online Gnutella users.
Step 4: Levels 2-6. The request is rebroadcast to 5, then 4, and so on. The result is a network of thousands of online Gnutella users searching for the requested file.
Step 5: Find. In most cases, the requested file is located somewhere in the network. The user that has the requested file connects to the requesting party and sends a copy of the file.

Figure 10-35 How Gnutella works

files, he or she could sign off the network and then connect directly to the source forming a very simple peer-to-peer network. Each node could act as a server by providing access to music files and a client by receiving copies of music files. Today, **Gnutella** is a widely used peer-to-peer network system for sharing all kinds of files including music files. Unlike the Napster approach, Gnutella networks directly connect users without a central server acting as the focal point for operations. There are various different versions of Gnutella. One of these is described in Figure 10-35. Also consult your Computing Today CD or visit us on the Web at http://www.mhhe.com/oleary/CT05 and select Animations from Tim's Toolbox.

Computing Today CD

Each online Gnutella user or node can act both as a client by requesting specific files and as a server by providing access to files to be copied. Unlike the Napster model which has centralized servers, the Gnutella model has thousands of independent servers. Even though Gnutella is often used to provide access to copyrighted music just as Napster did, it is not considered to be a likely target for legal action.

There are several advantages to the peer-to-peer network strategy. The networks are inexpensive and easy to install, and they usually work well for smaller systems with fewer than 10 nodes. Unlike the client-server network strategy, network operations are not dependent upon a single central node. As the number of nodes increases, however, the performance of the network declines. Another disadvantage is the lack of powerful management software to effectively monitor a large network's activities. For these reasons, peer-to-peer networks are typically used by smaller networks within organizations and for sharing files on the Internet.

For a summary of the network strategies, see Figure 10-36.

Strategy	Description
Terminal	One large computer provides all processing, strong central control, limited flexibility, and control for users
Client/server	Several clients or computers depend upon one server or computer to coordinate and supply services
Peer-to-peer	Computers act as both servers and clients, inexpensive and easy to install, works well in small networks and for sharing files on the Internet

Figure 10-36 Network strategies

Concept Check

- What is a network strategy?
- Discuss the three most common network strategies.
- Compare the network strategies employed by Napster and Gnutella.

ORGANIZATIONAL INTERNETS: INTRANETS AND EXTRANETS

Intranets are private networks within an organization. Extranets are private networks connecting organizations. Organizational firewalls typically use proxy servers to provide security.

Computer networks in organizations have evolved over time. Most large organizations have a complex and wide range of different network configurations, operating systems, and strategies. Integrating or connecting all of these networks has been a very challenging task. One way is to apply Internet technologies to support communication within and between organizations using intranets and extranets.

INTRANETS

An **intranet** is a *private* network within an organization that resembles the Internet. Like the *public* Internet, intranets use browsers, Web sites, and Web pages. Intranets typically provide e-mail, mailing lists, newsgroups, and FTP services accessible only to those within the organization.

Organizations use intranets to provide information to their employees. Typical applications include electronic telephone directories, e-mail addresses, employee benefit information, internal job openings, and much more. Employees find surfing their organizational intranets to be as easy and as intuitive as surfing the Internet.

EXTRANETS

An **extranet** is a *private* network that connects *more than one* organization. Many organizations use Internet technologies to allow suppliers and others

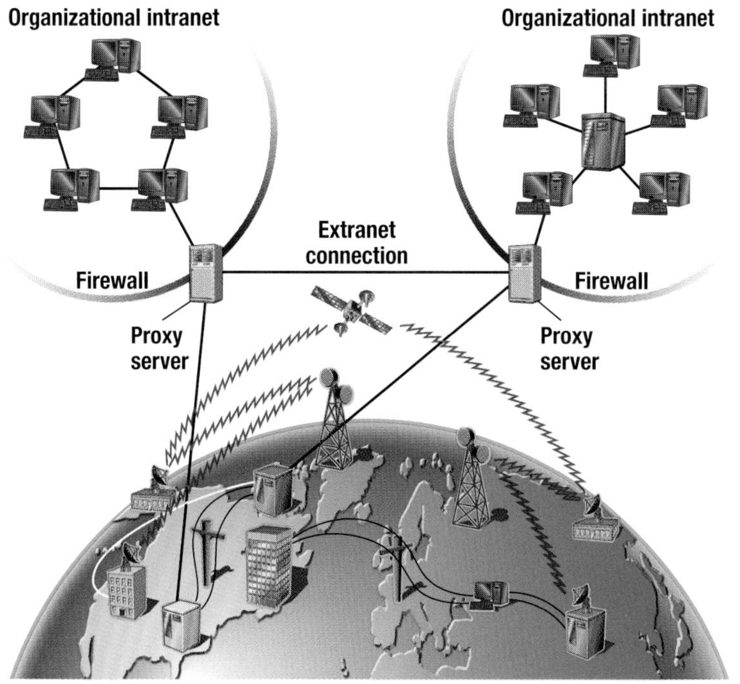
Organizational intranet
Organizational intranet
Extranet connection
Firewall
Firewall
Proxy server
Proxy server

Figure 10-37 Intranets, extranets, firewalls, and proxy servers

limited access to their networks. The purpose is to increase efficiency and reduce costs. For example, General Motors has thousands of suppliers for the parts that go into making an automobile. By having access to the production schedules, suppliers can schedule and deliver parts as they are needed at the General Motors assembly plants. In this way, General Motors can be assured of having adequate parts without maintaining large inventories.

FIREWALLS

Organizations have to be very careful to protect their information systems. A **firewall** is a security system designed to protect an organization's network against external threats. It consists of hardware and software that control access to a company's intranet or other internal networks.

Typically organizational firewalls include a special computer called a **proxy server.** This computer is a gatekeeper. All communications between the company's internal networks and the outside world must pass through it. By evaluating the source and the content of each communication, the proxy server decides whether it is safe to let a particular message or file pass into or out of the organization's network. (See Figure 10-37.)

Of course, end users have security issues as well. We are subject to many of the same types of security concerns that face organizations. Additionally, we need to be concerned about the privacy of our personal information. In the next chapter, we will discuss personal firewalls and other ways to protect personal privacy and security.

Concept Check

- ✔ What are intranets?
- ✔ What are extranets?
- ✔ What are firewalls? What is a proxy server?

Careers in IT

Network Administrator

Network administrators manage a company's LAN and WAN networks. They may be responsible for design, implementation, and maintenance of networks. Responsibilities usually include maintenance of both hardware and software related to a company's intranet and Internet networks. Network administrators are typically responsible for diagnosing and repairing problems with these networks. Some network administrators are responsible for planning and implementations of network security as well.

Employers typically look for candidates with a bachelor's degree in computer science and practical networking experience. Experience with network security and maintenance is preferred. Technical certification may also be helpful in obtaining this position. Because network administrators are involved directly with people in many departments, good communication skills are essential.

Network administrators can expect to earn an annual salary of $40,000 to $65,000. Opportunities for advancement typically include upper management positions. This position is expected to be among the fastest growing jobs in the near future. To learn about other careers in information technology, visit us at http://www.mhhe.com/oleary/CT05 and select Careers in IT from Tim's Toolbox.

A Look to the Future

Toyota and Sony Create Wireless Robotic Car

Have you ever found yourself driving around lost in an unfamiliar city, wishing you could connect to the Internet and download driving directions? Have you ever longed for access to your favorite Internet radio station while you drive around? What if you could send and receive e-mail while you wait in traffic? Wouldn't be convenient if your car would just send an e-mail whenever it needed maintenance? Toyota and Sony are collaborating on a car called "Pod" that does all this and more.

Pod stands for personalization on demand. Toyota hopes this new car will predict and respond to your moods, likes, and dislikes. It features lighting that may display red if you drive erratically or orange if you seem happy. It features voice recognition technology and responds to verbal commands. Pod is designed to learn and adapt to your driving habits and needs. Some say it is the car equivalent of the Sony AIBO robotic pet.

The Pod connects wirelessly to a portable terminal called the Mini Pod to share data and serve the user's needs. For example, Pod might use the information stored in the PDA-like Mini Pod to download songs from the Internet it thinks you might like. The Pod also uses GPS information and the Internet to make recommendations concerning local restaurants as you drive around.

Pod uses technology developed by Suzuki Motors to phone the owner if it is broken into or needs mechanical attention. Pod can communicate with other cars by using a horn messaging system. It also locates pedestrians and warns the driver to correct speed or course to avoid them. Pod can also phone ahead to your destination to advise those waiting if it detects you will be delayed. It may even alert you when you drive by restaurants that it thinks you may like.

Do these new features appeal to you? Do you think Americans will someday be driving cars that can connect to the Internet? Many new cars come equipped with wireless technology and GPS devices. Some car enthusiasts look forward to a car that senses your mood and downloads songs to match it. For now Pod is a concept vehicle, but many of the features it includes may soon be found in your new car. What do you think? Would you buy a car that communicates with other cars, the Internet, and you?

VISUAL SUMMARY

COMMUNICATIONS AND NETWORKS

COMMUNICATIONS

Communications is process of sharing data, programs, and information between two or more computers. Applications include **e-mail, instant messaging, Internet telephones,** and **electronic commerce.**

Connectivity

Connectivity is a concept related to using computer networks to link people and resources. You can link or connect to large computers and the Internet providing access to extensive information resources.

The Wireless Revolution

Mobile or wireless telephones have brought dramatic changes in connectivity and communications. These wireless devices are becoming widely used for computer communication.

Communication Systems

Communication systems transmit data from one location to another. Four basic elements:

- **Sending and receiving devices**
- **Communication channel (transmission medium)**
- **Connection (communication) devices**
- **Data transmission specifications**

COMMUNICATION CHANNELS

Communication channels carry data from one computer to another.

Physical Connections

Physical connections use a solid medium to connect sending and receiving devices. These connections include **telephone lines (twisted pair), coaxial cable,** and **fiber-optic cable.**

Wireless Connections

Wireless connections use air rather than solid substance to connect devices.

- **Infrared**—use light waves over short distance; **line of sight communication;** uses **IrDA ports.**
- **Broadcast radio**—use **transceivers** to collect radio waves. **Wi-FI (wireless fidelity, 802.11)** widely used standard.
- **Microwave**—uses high-frequency radio waves; line of sight communication; uses **microwave stations** and **disks; Bluetooth** widely used short range standards.
- **Satellite**—microwave relay station in the sky to **uplink** and **downlink** data; **GPS** provide **global positioning** to track geographic locations.

To be a competent and knowledgeable end user you need to understand the concepts of connectivity, the wireless revolution, and communication systems. Additionally, you need to know the essential parts of communications technology including channels, connection devices, data transmission, networks, network architectures, and network types.

CONNECTION DEVICES

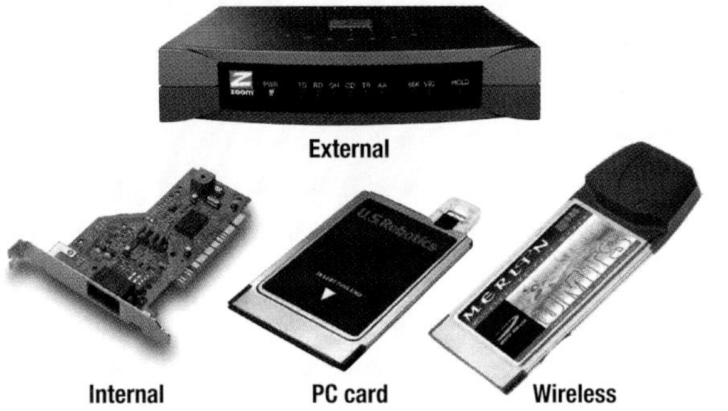

Many communication systems use standard telephone lines and **analog signals.** Computers use **digital signals.**

Modems

Modems modulate (convert digital signals to analog) and **demodulate. Transfer speed (rate)** measured in **bits per second.** Four types of conventional modems:

- **External**—outside the system cabinet.
- **Internal**—card that plugs into a slot on the system board.
- **PC Card modem**—a credit card–size expansion card for portable computers.
- **Wireless**—does not connect with a cable; receives data through the air.

Types of Connections

Dial-up services use standard telephone lines and conventional modems. **T1, T2, T3,** and **T4** support very high speed all-digital transmission. More affordable technologies include:

- **DSL (digital subscriber line)**—uses existing telephone lines; **ASDL** widely used.
- **Cable modems**—use existing cable lines.
- **Satellite/air**—uses **satellites** to download data.

DATA TRANSMISSION

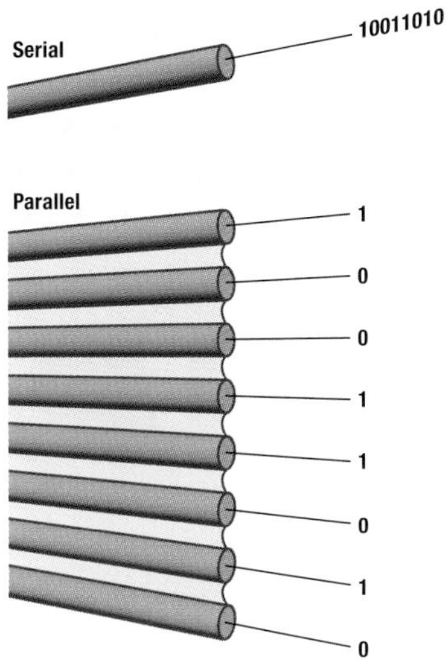

Several factors affect how data is actually transmitted from one point to another.

Bandwidth

Bandwidth is a measure of a communication channel's width or capacity. Three bandwidths: **voiceband (voice grade** or **low bandwidth), medium band** (uses special leased lines), **broadband** (high-capacity transmissions).

Data Direction

With **serial data transmission,** bits flow in a single lane. **RS-232C** and **asynchronous communications** are serial ports. With **parallel data transmission,** bits flow in multiple lanes.

Data Direction

There are three directions or modes: **simplex, half-duplex,** and **full-duplex** (data flows in both directions simultaneously).

Protocols

Protocols are rules for exchanging data. **TCP/IP** is standard Internet protocol. (**IP addresses** are unique numeric Internet address. **DNS** convert text based addresses to numeric IP address. **Packets** are small parts of messages.) Other protocols include: **HTTP, HTTPS, FTP,** and **WAP.**

NETWORKS

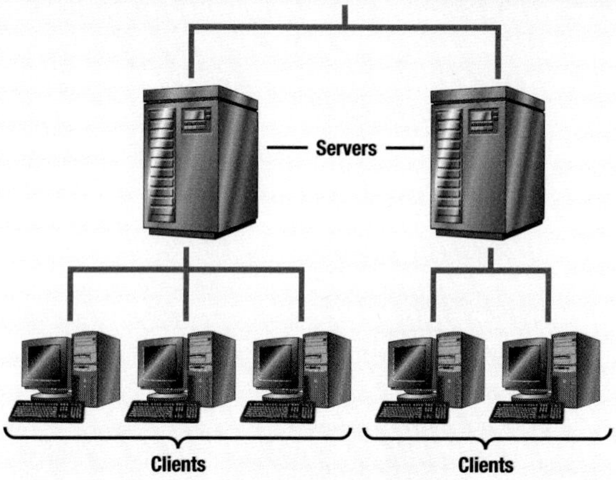
Servers
Clients
Clients

Computer networks connect two or more computers. Networks can be set up in different arrangements.

Some specialized network terms include:

- **Node**—any device connected to a network.
- **Client**—node requesting resources.
- **Server**—node providing resources; specialized servers such as **application, communication, database, file, print,** and **Web servers** are called **dedicated servers.**
- **Hub**—center or central node.
- **NIC (network interface cars)—LAN adapter** card for connecting to a network.
- **NOS (network operating system)**—controls and coordinates network operations.
- **Distributed processing**—system where processing located and shared at different locations.
- **Host computer**—large centralized computer.
- **Network manager (administrator)**—network specialist responsible for network operations.

NETWORK TYPES

Networks can be citywide or even international using both cable and air connections. Three network types are:

Local Area Networks

Local area networks (LAN) connect nearby devices. **Ethernet** is a LAN standard. These LANs are called **Ethernet LANs. Network gateways** connect networks to one another.

Home Networks

Home networks are LANs used in homes. **Wireless LANs (WLAN)** use **wireless receiver (base station)** as a hub.

Metropolitan Area Networks

Metropolitan area networks or **MANs** are used to link office buildings within a city. **Cellular phone systems** link car phones and portable phones.

Wide Area Networks

Wide Area Networks or **WANs** are the largest type. They span states and countries, or form worldwide networks. The Internet is the largest wide area network in the world.

NETWORK ARCHITECTURE

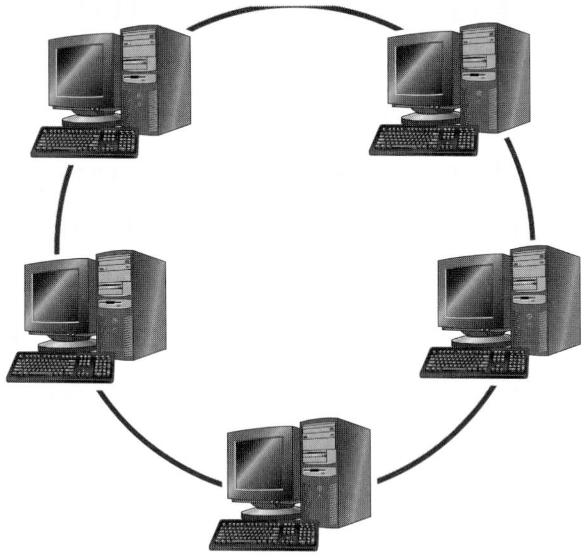

Network architecture describes how a computer network is configured and what strategies are employed.

Configurations

A network's configuration is called its **topology.** Principal topologies: **star network** (each device linked to **network hub;** control maintained by **polling;** often used for **time-sharing systems**), **bus network** (nodes connect by cable called a **bus** or **backbone**), **ring network, hierarchical network** (**hybrid network,** often used in **distributed data processing systems**).

Strategies

Every network has a **strategy,** or way of sharing information and resources. Common **strategies** include:

- **Terminal network system**—a centralized computer distributes power to several terminals.
- **Client/server network system**—client computers request resources from a server computer; **Napster** servers operated with client/server strategy.
- **Peer-to-peer network system**—each computer acts as both a server and a client. **Gnutella** supports peer-to-peer file sharing.

ORGANIZATIONAL INTRANETS

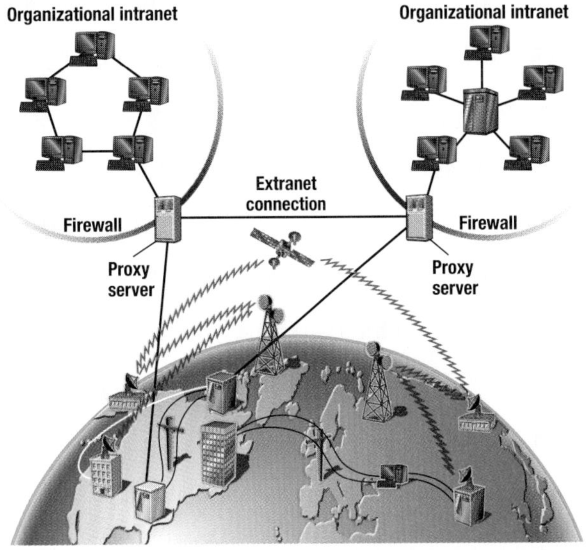

Many organizations use Internet technologies to support communication within and between organizations using intranets and extranets.

Intranets

Intranets are *private* networks within an organization that resemble the Internet. Like the Internet, they use browsers, Web sites, and Web pages. Unlike the Internet, intranets are available only to those within the organization.

Extranets

Extranets are similar to intranets, except that extranets connect more than one organization. Extranets are often used to connect suppliers and producers to increase efficiency.

Firewalls

A **firewall** is a security system to protect against external threats. It consists of both hardware and software. All communications into and out of an organization pass through a special security computer called a **proxy server.**

KEY TERMS

802.11 (367)
analog signal (369)
application server (374)
asymmetric digital subscriber line (ADSL) (371)
asynchronous communications port (372)
backbone (382)
bandwidth (371)
base station (377)
bits per second (370)
Bluetooth (368)
broadcast radio (367)
broadband (372)
bus (382)
bus network (382)
cable modem (371)
cellular phone system (377)
client (374)
client/server network system (385)
coaxial cable (367)
communications (364)
communication channel (365)
communication device (366)
communication server (374)
communication system (365)
computer network (374)
connection device (366)
connectivity (364)
database server (374)
data transmission specification (366)
dedicated server (374)
demodulation (370)
dial-up service (370)
digital signal (369)
digital subscriber line (DSL) (371)
dish (368)
distributed data processing system (383)
distributed processing (374)
domain name server (DNS) (373)
downlink (369)
electronic commerce (364)
e-mail (364)
Ethernet (377)
Ethernet LAN (377)
external modem (370)
extranet (388)
fiber-optic cable (367)
file server (374)
firewall (389)
FTP (file transfer protocol) (373)
full-duplex communication (372)
Gnutella (387)
global positioning (369)
global positioning system (GPS) (369)
half-duplex communication (372)
hierarchical network (383)
home network (377)
host computer (374)
hub (374)
HTTP (hypertext transfer protocol) (373)
HTTPS (hypertext transfer protocol secure) (373)
hybrid network (383)
infrared (367)
infrared (IrDA) port (367)
instant messaging (364)
Internet telephone (364)
internal modem (370)
intranet (388)
IP address (Internet Protocol address) (373)
line of sight communication (367)
local area network (LAN) (376)
low bandwidth (372)
medium band (372)
metropolitan area network (MAN) (377)
microwave (367)
microwave station (368)
modem (370)
modulation (370)
Napster (385)
network administrator (374)
network architecture (382)
network gateway (376)
network hub (382)
network interface card (NIC) (374)
network manager (374)
network operating system (NOS) (374)
node (374)
packet (373)
parallel data transmission (372)
PC card modem (370)
peer-to-peer network system (385)
polling (382)
printer server (374)
protocol (373)
proxy server (389)
receiving device (365)
regional network (377)
ring network (382)
RS-232C (372)
satellite (368)
satellite/air connection service (371)
sending device (365)
serial data transmission (372)
server (374)
simplex communication (372)
star network (382)
strategy (384)
TCP/IP (transmission control protocol/ Internet protocol) (373)
telephone line (367)
terminal network system (384)
time-sharing system (382)
T1, T2, T3, T4 lines (371)
topology (382)
transceiver (367)
transfer speed (370)
transfer rate (370)
transmission medium (365)
twisted pair (367)
uplink (369)
voiceband (372)
voice grade (372)
WAP (wireless application protocol) (373)
Web server (374)
wide area network (WAN) (377)
Wi-FI (wireless fidelity) (367)
wireless LAN (WLAN) (377)
wireless modem (370)
wireless receiver (377)

To test your knowledge of these key terms with animated flash cards, select Flash Cards from Tim's Toolbox at http://www.mhhe.com/oleary/CT05.

CHAPTER REVIEW

CROSSWORD

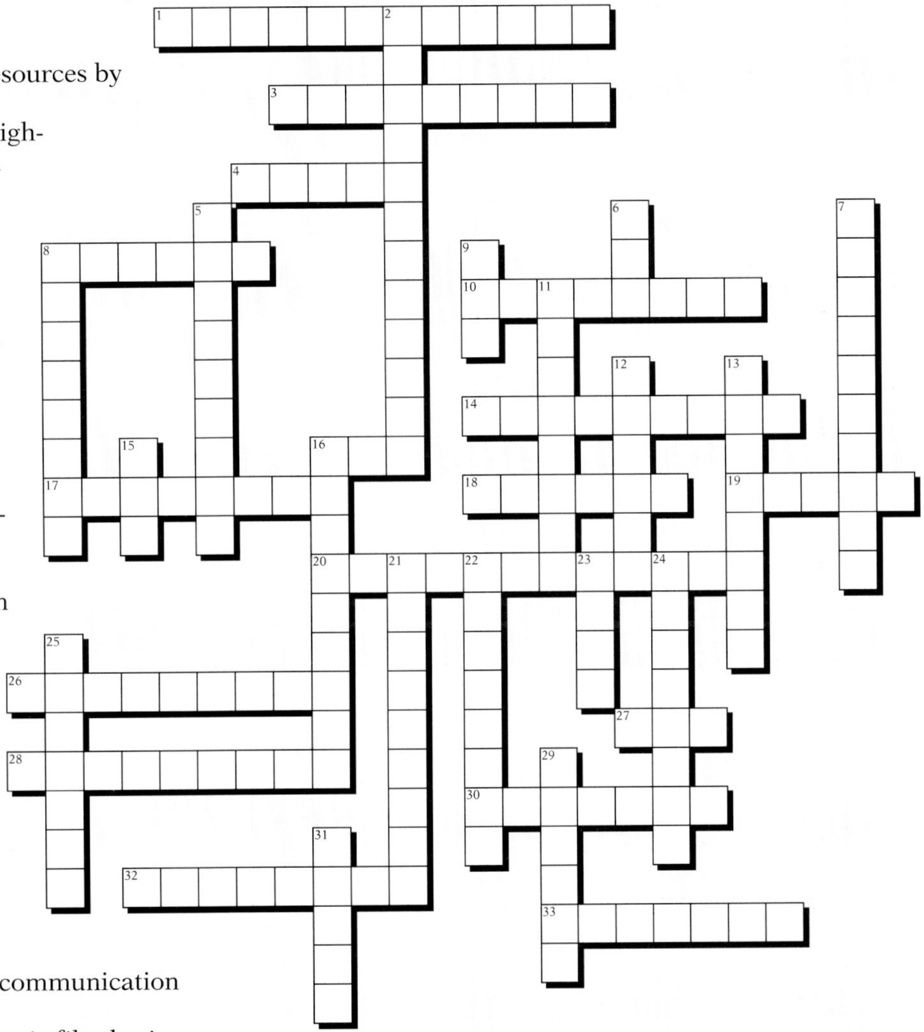

ACROSS

1 Linking people and resources by networks
3 Bandwidth used for high-capacity transmission
4 Supports secure Web communication
8 A node that shares resources with other nodes
10 The arrangement of a network
14 Microwave relay station in the sky
16 Common connecting cable
17 A widely used peer-to-peer network system
18 Small parts of a message broken down before being sent
19 A fast, efficient alternative to traditional mail
20 The process of converting from analog to digital
26 Bandwidth used for standard telephone
27 Supports wireless access to the internet
28 Short range wireless communication standard
30 Failed peer-to-peer music file sharing business
32 Also know as the bus
33 Connect computers

DOWN

2 Broadcast radio sending and receiving towers
5 A server that specializes in performing specific tasks
6 Uses existing telephone lines to provide high-speed connections
7 The process of converting from digital to analog
8 A network's way of coordinating the sharing of information and resources
9 Supports the uploading and downloading of files from the internet
11 Rules for exchanging data
12 Node requesting resources
13 The most common standard for connecting to a LAN
15 The center or central node for other nodes
16 Measures capacity of a communication channel
21 High frequency radio waves
22 Receiving data from a satellite
23 Asymmetric digital subscriber line
24 A light wave used to communicate over short distances
25 When each device is asked whether it has a message to send
29 Sending data to a satellite
31 Modulator-demodulator

For an interactive crossword puzzle select Crosswords from Tim's Toolbox at http://www.mhhe.com/oleary/CT05.

MULTIPLE CHOICE

Circle the letter or fill in the correct answer.

1. Modulation and demodulation are the processes of a(n) ________.
   a. connection device
   b. node
   c. modulator
   d. modem
   e. OSI
2. Standard telephone lines and conventional modems provide what is called ________.
   a. network architecture
   b. broadband
   c. dial-up service
   d. data transmission
   e. channels
3. ________ use wireless receivers as a hub.
   a. LANs
   b. Microwaves
   c. WLANs
   d. MANs
   e. Satellites
4. Gnutella uses a ________ network strategy.
   a. terminal
   b. peer-to-peer
   c. client-server
   d. wireless
   e. NIC
5. ________ is a measurement of the capacity of the communication channel.
   a. Protocol
   b. Packet
   c. Network architecture
   d. IP address
   e. Bandwidth
6. Every computer on the Internet has a unique numeric address called a(n) ________.
   a. packet
   b. protocol
   c. IP address
   d. bandwidth
   e. network bridge
7. ________ use satellites to determine geographic locations.
   a. TCP/IP
   b. OSI
   c. GPS
   d. DSL
   e. NOS
8. ________ describes how the network is arranged and how the resources are coordinated and shared.
   a. Topology
   b. Communication channel
   c. Sharing system
   d. Network architecture
   e. Domain name system
9. ________ controls and coordinates the activities of all computers and devices on a network.
   a. TCP/IP
   b. NOS
   c. DNS
   d. OSI
   e. none of the above
10. In a ________ network, each device in the network handles its own communications control.
    a. host
    b. client
    c. bus
    d. sharing
    e. polling

To test your knowledge of this chapter, select Self Test from Tim's Toolbox at http://www.mhhe.com/oleary/CT05.

MATCHING

Match each numbered item with the most closely related lettered item. Write your answers in the spaces provided.

a. ADSL
b. bandwidth
c. Bluetooth
d. coaxial cable
e. communication system
f. computer network
g. client
h. dedicated
i. distributed processing
j. FTP
k. host
l. hybrid network
m. infrared
n. packets
o. protocol
p. star
q. TCP/IP
r. topology
s. transfer speed
t. wide area network

1. Electronic system that transmits data over communication lines from one location to another. ____
2. Type of DSL. ____
3. High-frequency transmission cable with a single solid-copper core. ____
4. Uses microwaves to transmit data over short distances up to 33 feet. ____
5. The type of server that performs specific tasks. ____
6. Type of wireless connection that uses light waves over short distances. ____
7. Measured in bits per second. ____
8. Protocol for uploading and downloading files. ____
9. Measurement of a the width or capacity of a communication channel. ____
10. Rules for exchanging data between computers. ____
11. Standard protocol for the Internet. ____
12. Broken-down parts of a message that are sent over the Internet. ____
13. Communications system connecting two or more computers that work together to exchange information and share resources. ____
14. A node that requests and uses resources available from other nodes. ____
15. System in which computing power is located and shared at different locations. ____
16. The configuration of a network. ____
17. This type of network links computers and other devices to a central unit. ____
18. A large centralized computer. ____
19. Countrywide and worldwide networks. ____
20. Also known as hierarchical, this network consists of several computers linked to a central host that serve as hosts to smaller computers or devices. ____

OPEN-ENDED

On a separate sheet of paper, respond to each question or statement.

1. Define and discuss connectivity, the wireless revolution, and communications.
2. Identify and describe the various physical and wireless communication channels.
3. Identify the standard Internet protocol and discuss its essential features.
4. Define and discuss the four principal network topologies.
5. Define and discuss the three most common network strategies.

USING TECHNOLOGY

1 Home Networking

Computer networks are not just for corporations and schools anymore. If you have more than one computer, you can use a home network to share files and printers, to allow multiple users access to the Internet at the same time, and to play multiplayer computer games. To learn more about this technology, review Making IT Work for You: Home Networking on pages 380 and 381. Then answer the following questions: (a) Describe the window shown for the setup of the wireless base station. (b) What are the four most common uses of a home network? (c) What are the names of the folders displayed in the My Computer window?

2 Palm One

Palm One is the leader in Personal Digital Assistants, or PDAs. Recent advances in technology allow PDAs like the Palm One to communicate on the go. Visit our Web site at http://www.mhhe.com/oleary/CT05 and select Using Technology from Tim's Toolbox to link to Palm One's Web site. Once connected, review the latest PDA products and then answer the following questions: (a) What support for Internet connection is available? (b) What is required to connect their PDAs to the Internet? (c) What type of Internet information is accessible? Is there any type which is not accessible? (d) Would you use an Internet-connected PDA? Why or why not?

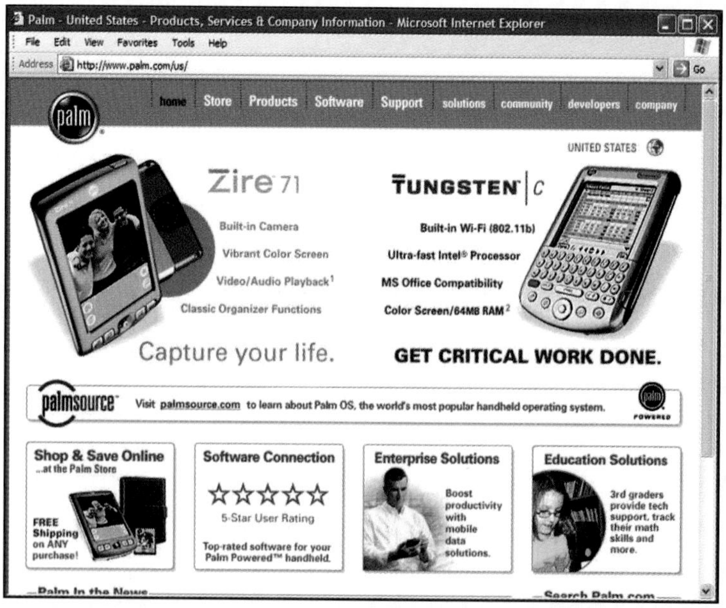

Ricochet Internet Access 3

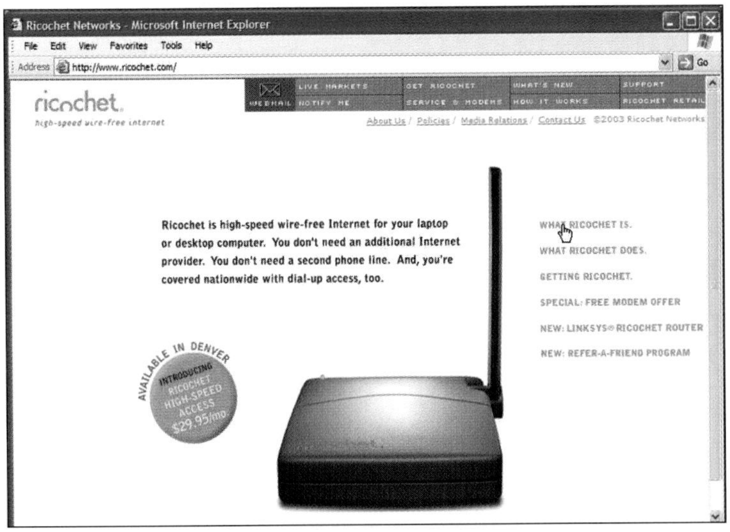

Ricochet is an innovative new technology that provides high-speed Internet access to mobile computer users. To learn more about this technology, visit our Web site at http://www.mhhe.com/oleary/CT05 and select Using Technology from Tim's Toolbox to connect to the Ricochet Web site. Once connected, explore the site, and then answer the following questions: (a) What equipment does a user require to connect to the Ricochet network? (b) How does the Ricochet network deliver the Internet to users? (c) What are the current limitations of this technology? (d) Would you use Ricochet over a more standard Internet connection? Why?

Distributed Computing 4

When networked computers are not in use, their processing power can be combined with other networked computers to perform a common task. In some cases, the problems that can be solved by many individual computers are far too large to be solved by any single computer. Connect to our site at http://www.mhhe.com/oleary/CT05 and select Using Technology from Tim's Toolbox to link to a site that features distributed computing. Explore the site, and answer the following questions: (a) What type of problem does this site solve with distributed computing? (b) How do users donate unused computer time to this project? (c) Would you donate your extra computer time to a distributed computing project? Why or why not?

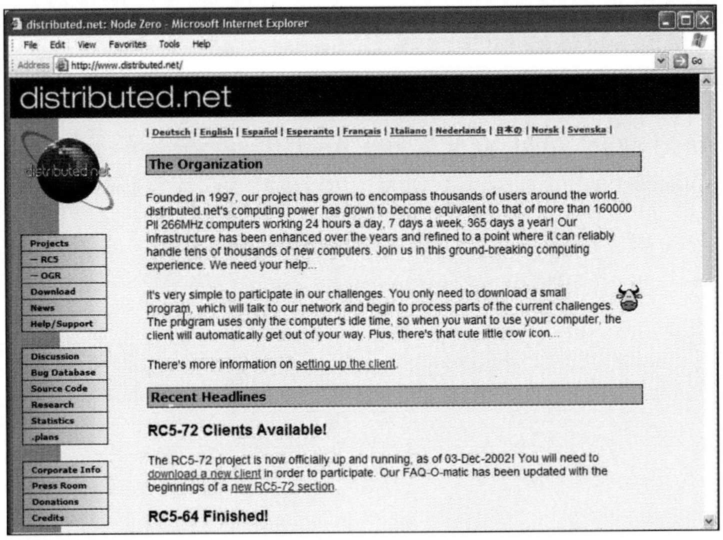

EXPANDING YOUR KNOWLEDGE

1 Computing Today CD

Wireless home networks are becoming very popular. These LANs are easy to set up and use. They allow different computers to share resources including a common Internet connection and printer. After reviewing Figure 10-22 and viewing the animation How Home Networks Work on your Computing Today CD, consider the following questions. (a) What is a node? Identify each node in Figure 10-22. (b) What is a base station and what is its function? (c) What is a wireless card and what is its function? (d) If one or more requests to print a document are made at exactly the same time, what node determines which document is printed first? (e) Can the Nodes TIM, LINDA, and STEVE access and use the Internet at the same time? If yes, how can this be done with a single Internet connection?

2 Virtual Private Networks

People who telecommute to work must often connect to a corporate LAN securely over the Internet. Virtual Private Networking, or VPN, is a solution for this. Conduct a Web search using the keyword "VPN" or "Virtual Private Networking" to learn more. Then answer the following questions: (a) Describe what VPN is and what it does. (b) How is using VPN different from accessing files from a company Web site? (c) What advantage does this offer individuals and organizations?

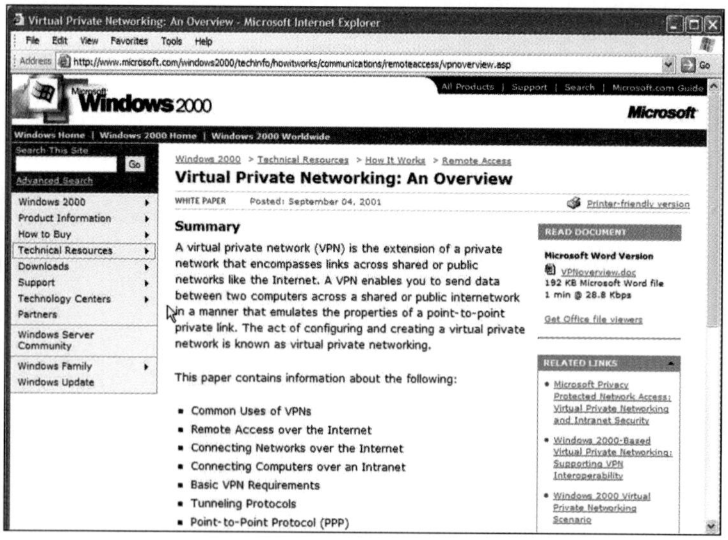

SimNet CD 3

Complete Chapter 10: Communications and Networks on the SimNet Computer Concepts CD and then answer the following questions: (a) Describe each of the physical connections. (b) Explain why and how Web sites are specially designed for handheld devices. (c) Explain how weather can be a factor of bandwidth. (d) Identify the topologies in the figure to the right. (e) Describe the benefits of peer-to-peer networking.

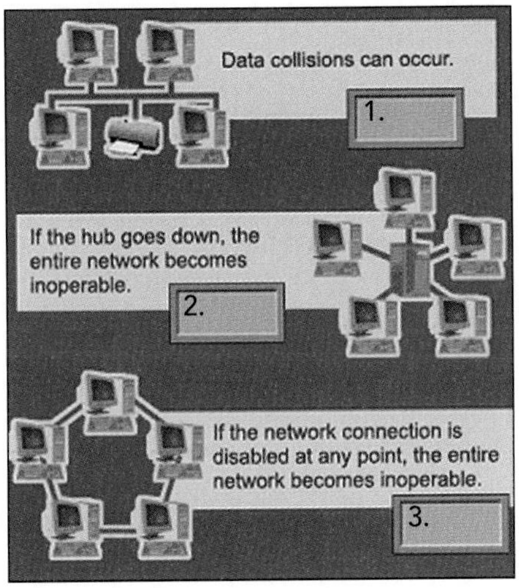

Hotspots 4

Hotspots are areas set up to provide public access to wireless Internet service. Find them in coffee shops, airports, or hotels. Connect to our Web site at http://www.mhhe/com/oleary/CT05 and select Expanding Your Knowledge from Tim's Toolbox. Link to a directory of hotspots to locate one near you. Where is the hotspot? What equipment is necessary to use the hotspot? What does it cost to use the hotspot?

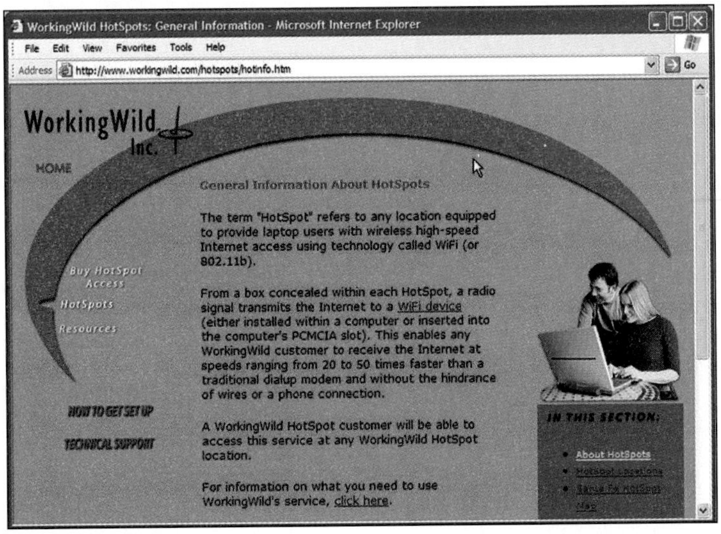

BUILDING YOUR PORTFOLIO

1 User Connection

One of the key determinants to enjoyable and effective use of the Internet is available bandwidth. As bandwidth increases, Internet content becomes richer and more varied. Write a one-page paper titled "Internet Connections" that addresses the following: (a) Define voiceband, medium band, and broadband. (b) Describe the four types of connections that are commonly available. (c) Discuss how faster Internet connections are shaping the way in which the Internet is used. (d) Research and discuss three specific examples.

2 Network-Attached Storage

Network-attached storage, or NAS, uses a special type of server for file sharing. Research NAS on the Web, and briefly answer the following questions in a one-page paper: (a) How does NAS differ from other types of servers? (b) What types of networks use NAS? (c) What are common alternatives to NAS? (d) What are the advantages and disadvantages to using NAS?

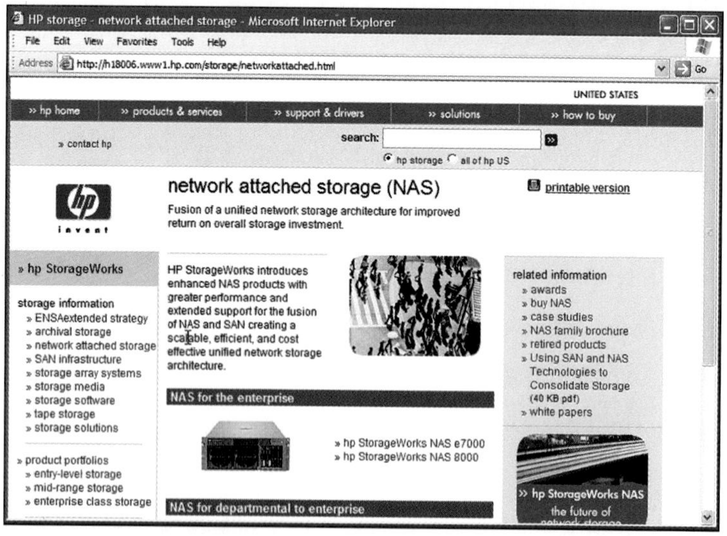

Electronic Monitoring 3

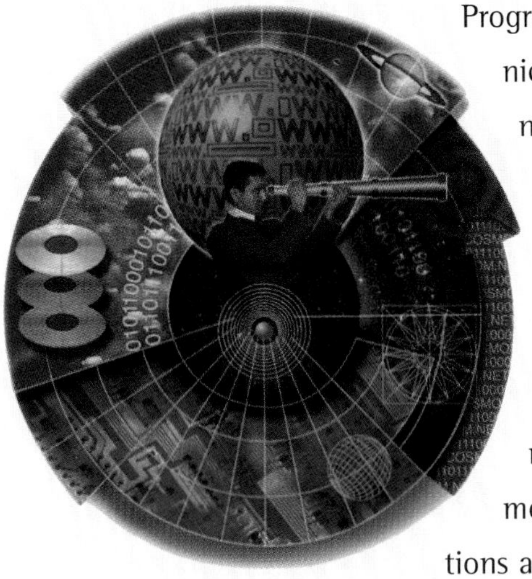

Programs known as "sniffers" are sometimes used to monitor communications on corporate networks. Recently, the FBI unveiled a technology known as Carnivore that can monitor an individual's Internet activity and eavesdrop on e-mail messages. Write a one-page paper that answers the following questions: (a) Is it a violation of an employee's privacy for an organization or corporation to use sniffer programs to monitor communications on their network? (b) Is it a violation of privacy for a government agency such as the FBI to use programs like Carnivore to monitor communications on the Internet? (c) Under what conditions are the types of monitoring discussed in parts (a) and (b) acceptable and ethical? (d) How can these conditions be enforced?

Digital Rights Management 4

In response to the sharing of copyrighted material over computer networks, as discussed in this chapter, many different forms of Digital Rights Management, or DRM, have been proposed. However, DRM is controversial, and hotly debated by industry groups and consumer advocates. Use the Web to research DRM, and then write a one-page paper titled "Digital Rights Management" that addresses the following topics: (a) Define "Digital Rights Management." (b) What systems have been proposed for DRM? (c) Why are some consumers opposed to these systems? (d) Do you think DRM is a fair solution to online piracy? Justify your answer.

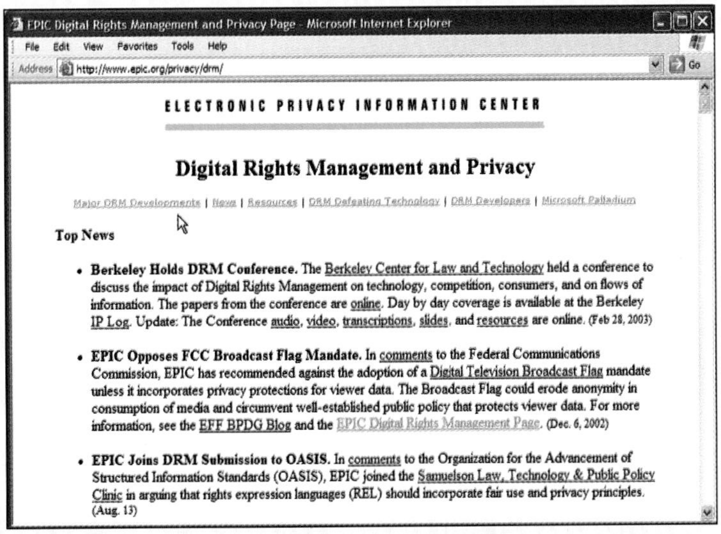

PRIVACY AND SECURITY

OBJECTIVES

After you have read this chapter, you should be able to:

1. Describe the most significant concerns associated with computer technology.
2. Discuss computer ethics and the guidelines that govern the morally acceptable use of computers in our society.
3. Discuss the privacy issues related to the presence of large databases, private networks, the Internet, and the Web.
4. Describe the major privacy laws and the Code of Fair Information Practice.
5. Describe the security threats posed by computer criminals, computer crime, and other hazards.
6. Discuss ways that individuals and organizations protect their security.
7. Describe the common types of physical and mental risks associated with computer use and ways to protect yourself against these risks.
8. Discuss what the computer industry is doing, and what you can do, to protect the environment.

Privacy
Concerns collection and use of data

Security
Keeping private information safe from criminals, natural hazards, and civil unrest.

The tools and products of the information age do not exist in a world by themselves. As we said in Chapter 1, a computer system consists not only of software, hardware, data, and procedures but also of people. Because of people, computer systems may be used for both good and bad purposes.

There are more than 300 million microcomputers in use today. What are the consequences of the widespread presence of this technology? Does technology make it easy for others to invade our personal privacy? When we apply for a loan or for a driver's license, or when we check out at the supermarket, is that information about us being distributed and used without our permission? When we use the Web, is information about us being collected and shared with others?

Does technology make it easy for others to invade the security of business organizations like our banks or our employers? What about health risks to people who use computers? What about the environment? Do computers pose a threat to our ecology?

This technology prompts lots of questions—very important questions. Perhaps these are some of the most important questions for the twenty-first century. Competent and knowledgeable end users need to be aware of the potential impact of technology on people and how to protect themselves on the Web. They need to be sensitive to and knowledgeable about personal privacy, organizational security, ergonomics, and the environmental impact of technology.

Ergonomics
Human factors related to the devices people use

Environment
Discovering ways to discourage waste in the microcomputer industry

PEOPLE

Information systems consist of people, procedures, software, hardware, and data. The most significant concerns for people are privacy, security, ergonomics, and the environment.

As we have discussed, information systems consist of people, procedures, software, hardware, and data. (See Figure 11-1.) This chapter focuses on people. While most everyone agrees that technology has had a very positive impact on people, it is important to recognize the negative or potentially negative impacts as well.

Effective implementation of computer technology involves maximizing its positive effects while minimizing its negative effects. The most significant concerns are:

- **Privacy:** What are the threats to personal privacy and how can we protect ourselves?
- **Security:** How can access to sensitive information be controlled and how can we secure hardware and software?
- **Ergonomics:** What are the physical and mental risks to technology and how can these risks be eliminated or controlled?
- **Environment:** What can individuals and organizations do to minimize the impact of technology on our environment?

Let us begin by examining privacy.

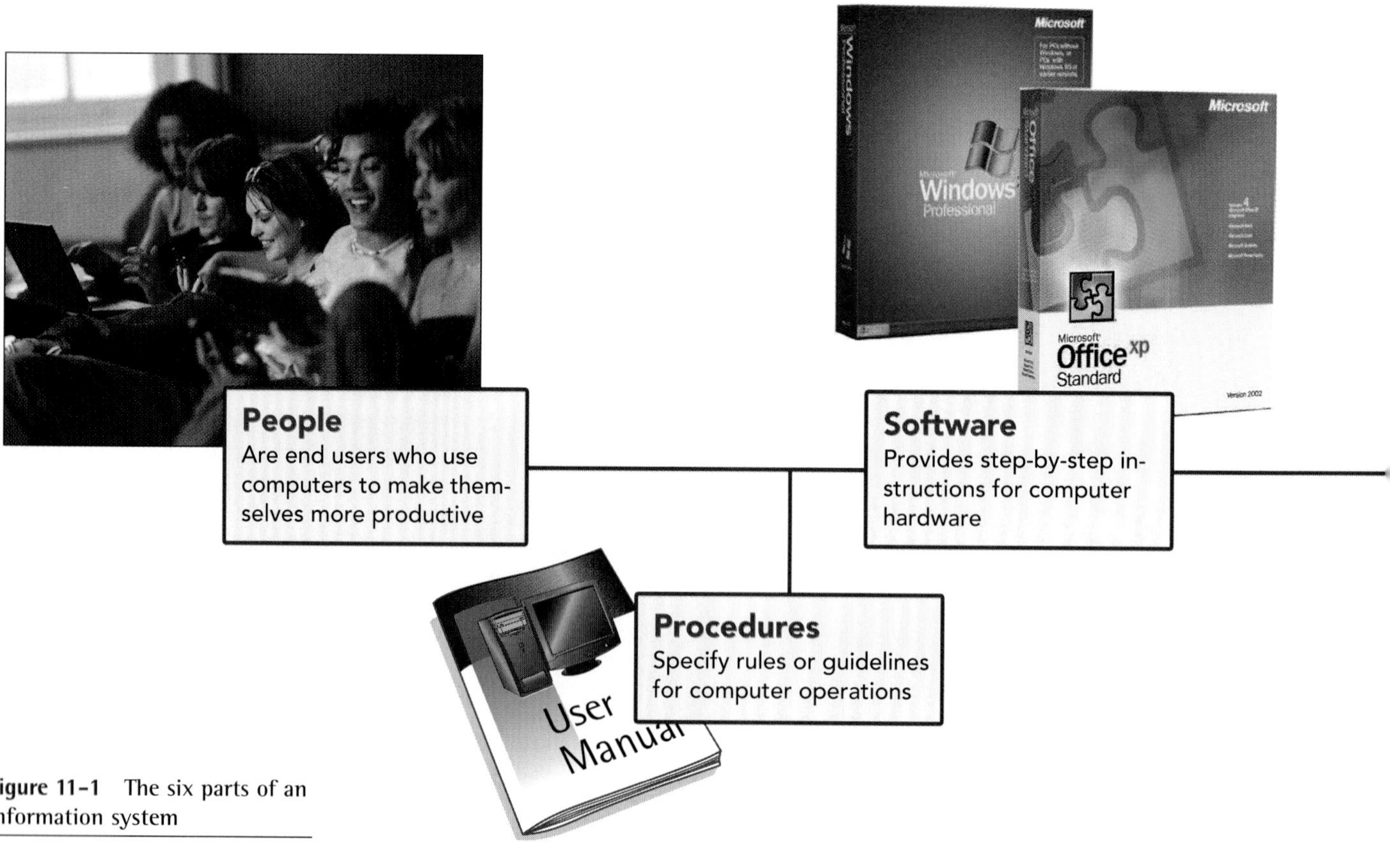
People
Are end users who use computers to make themselves more productive
Software
Provides step-by-step instructions for computer hardware
Procedures
Specify rules or guidelines for computer operations
User Manual
Microsoft
Windows
Professional
Microsoft
Office xp
Standard

Figure 11-1 The six parts of an information system

PRIVACY

Computer ethics provide guidelines for computer use. Privacy relates to the collection and use of personal information. Privacy concerns include large databases, private networks, the Internet, and the Web. While privacy laws exist, privacy remains primarily an ethical issue.

What do you suppose controls how computers can be used? You probably think first of laws. Of course that is right, but technology is moving so fast that it is very difficult for our legal system to keep up. The essential element that controls how computers are used today is *ethics.*

Ethics, as you may know, are standards of moral conduct. **Computer ethics** are guidelines for the morally acceptable use of computers in our society. There are four primary computer ethics issues:

- **Privacy** concerns the collection and use of data about individuals.
- **Accuracy** relates to the responsibility of those who collect data to ensure that the data is correct.
- **Property** relates to who owns data and rights to software.
- **Access** relates to the responsibility of those who have data to control and who is able to use that data.

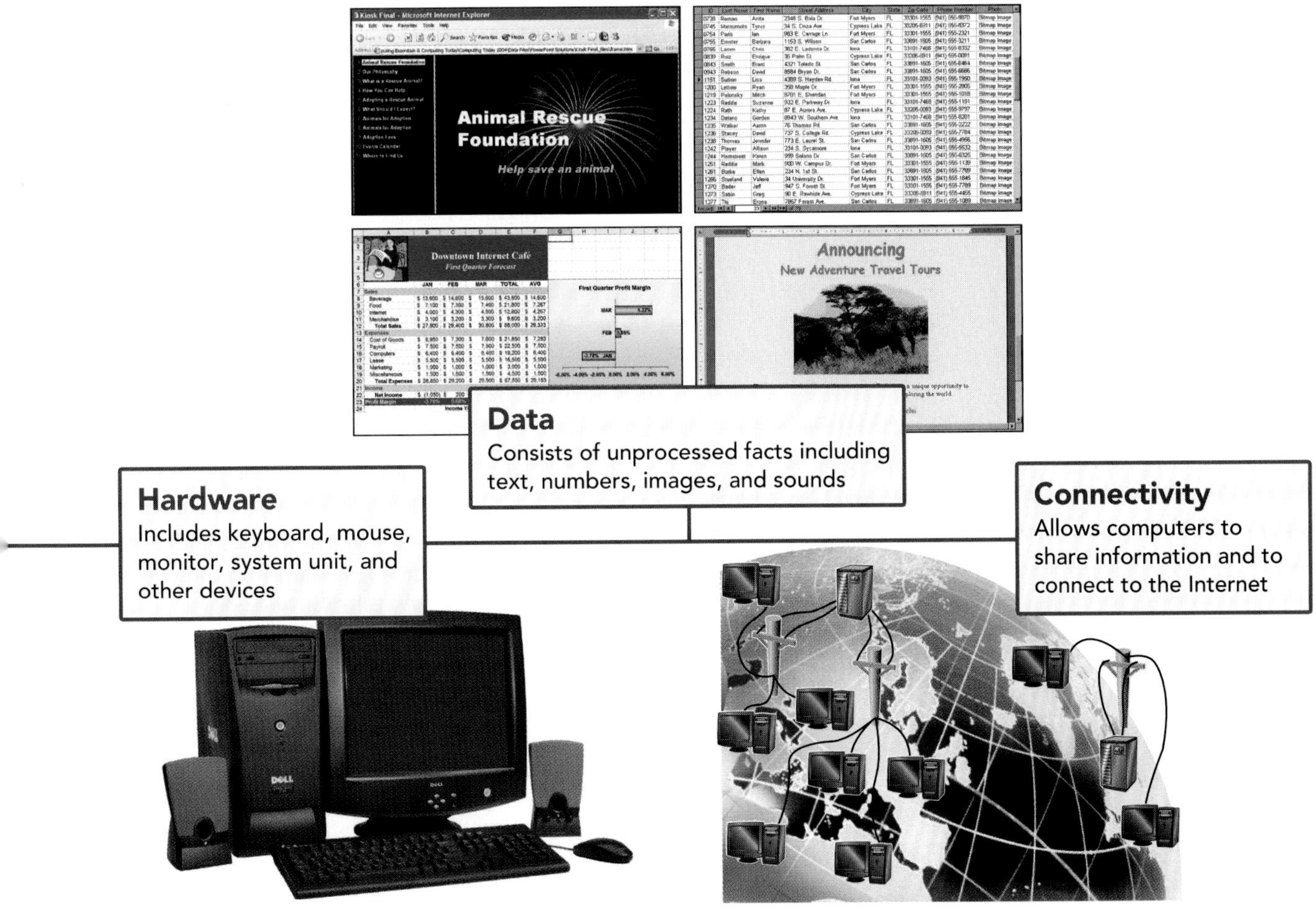

Animal Rescue Foundation
Help save an animal
Downtown Internet Café
First Quarter Forecast
Announcing
New Adventure Travel Tours
Data
Consists of unprocessed facts including text, numbers, images, and sounds
Hardware
Includes keyboard, mouse, monitor, system unit, and other devices
Connectivity
Allows computers to share information and to connect to the Internet

We are all entitled to ethical treatment. This includes the right to keep personal information, such as credit ratings and medical histories, from getting into unauthorized hands. Many people worry that this right is severely threatened. Let us see what some of the concerns are.

LARGE DATABASES

Large organizations are constantly compiling information about us. The federal government alone has over 2,000 databases. Our social security numbers have become a national identification number. This number has become a standard field in all kinds of databases including employment records, medical records, credit card records, and on and on. The vast majority of forms we fill out today require our Social Security number. Indeed, even children are now required to have Social Security numbers. Shouldn't we be concerned that cross-referenced information might be used for the wrong purposes?

Every day, data is gathered about us and stored in large databases. For example, for billing purposes, telephone companies compile lists of the calls we make, the numbers called, and so on. A special telephone directory (called a **reverse directory**) lists telephone numbers sequentially. Using it, government authorities and others can easily get the names, addresses, and other details about the persons we call. Numerous sites on the Web provide access to these reverse directories. (See Figure 11-2.) Additionally, some of the reverse directory Web sites will provide maps to the addresses associated with any telephone.

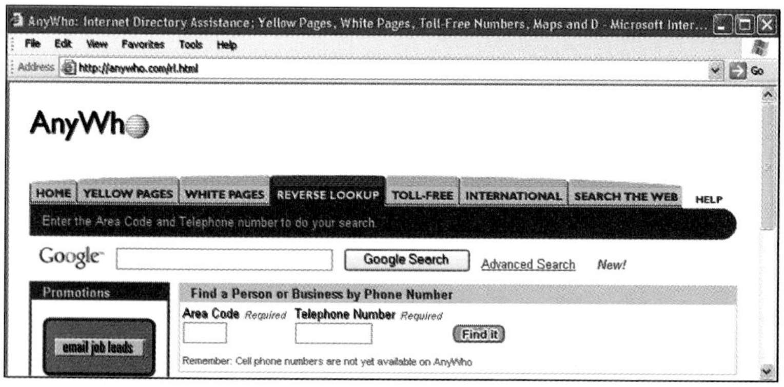

Figure 11-2 Reverse directory Web site

Credit card companies keep similar records. Supermarket scanners in grocery checkout counters record what we buy, when we buy it, how much we buy, and the price. (See Figure 11-3.) Financial institutions, including banks and credit unions, record how much money we have, what we use it for, and how much we owe. Publishers of magazines, newspapers, and mail-order catalogues have our names, addresses, phone numbers, and what we order.

Figure 11-3 Large organizations are constantly compiling information about us, such as the kinds of products we buy.

A vast industry of data gatherers known as **information resellers** or **information brokers** now exists that collects and sells such personal data. Using publicly available databases and in many cases nonpublic databases, information resellers create **electronic profiles** or highly detailed and personalized descriptions of individuals. Very likely, you have an electronic profile that includes your name, address, telephone number, Social Security number, driver's license number, bank account numbers, credit card numbers, telephone records, and shopping and purchasing patterns. Information resellers sell these electronic profiles to direct marketers, fund-raisers, and others. Many provide these services on the Web for free or for a nominal cost. (See Figure 11-4.)

Your personal information including preferences, habits, and financial data has become a marketable commodity. This raises many issues, including:

- **Spreading information without personal consent:** How would you feel if your name and your taste in movies were made available nationwide? For a while, Blockbuster, a large video rental company, considered doing just this.

What if a great deal of information about your shopping habits—collected about you without your consent—was made available to any microcomputer user who wanted it? Before dropping the project, Lotus Development Corporation and Equifax Inc. planned to market disks containing information on 120 million American consumers. (Lotus claimed it was providing small businesses with the same information currently available to larger organizations.)

How would you feel if an employer were using your medical records to make decisions about hiring, placement, promotion, and firing? A University of Illinois survey found that half the Fortune 500 companies were using medical records for just these purposes.

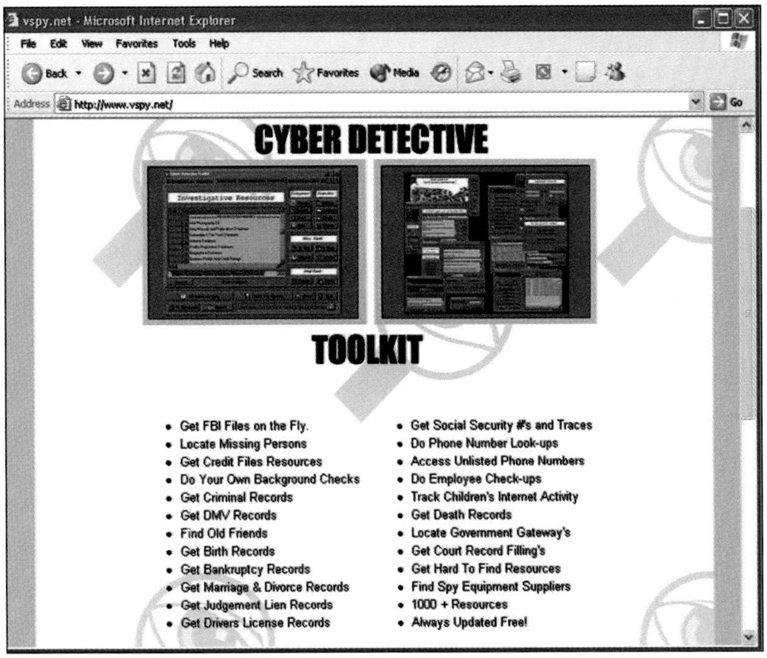

Figure 11-4 Information resellers Web site

How would you feel if someone obtained a driver's license and credit cards in your name? What if that person then assumed your identity to buy clothes, cars, and a house? It happens every day. Last year, over 1 million people were victimized in this way. It is called **identify theft.** Identity theft is the illegal assumption of someone's identity for the purposes of economic gain. It is one of the fastest growing crimes in the country. To learn more about identity theft and how to minimize your risk, consult your Computing Today CD or visit Tim's Toolbox at http://www.mhhe.com/oleary/CT05 and select Expansions.

Computing Today CD

- **Spreading inaccurate information:** How would you feel if inaccurate information about you were being used to make important decisions? Simple recording mistakes happen all the time and an error in one file can be quickly spread to other files. Unfortunately, even if an error is located and corrected in one file, it is often very difficult to locate and correct in all files.

How would you like to be turned down for a home loan because of an error in your credit history? This is much more common than you might expect. What if you could not find a job or were fired from a job because of an error giving you a serious criminal history? This can and has happened due to simple clerical errors. In one case, an arresting officer while completing an arrest warrant incorrectly recorded the social security number of a criminal. From that time forward, this arrest and subsequent conviction became part of another person's electronic profile. This is an example of **mistaken identity** in which the electronic profile of one person is switched with another.

It's important to know that you have some recourse. The law allows you to gain access to those records about you that are held by credit bureaus. Under the **Freedom of Information Act,** you are also entitled to look at

TIPS

Have you been a victim of identify theft? If you have or if you ever are, here are some suggestions on what you should do.

1. **Contact local and federal police authorities to report the crime.**
2. **Call the Federal Trade Commission (FTC) free Identity Theft Hotline at 1-877-IDTHEFT (438-4338) to obtain current advice relating to resolving credit-related problems.**
3. **Visit the ID Theft Web site at www.consumer.gov/idtheft for additional information and advice.**
4. **Obtain and file the ID Theft Affidavit available at the ID Theft Web site.**

your records held by government agencies. (Portions may be deleted for national security reasons.)

Computing Today CD

To learn more about mistaken identity, consult your Computing Today CD or visit us on the Web at http://www.mhhe.com/oleary/CT05 and select Expansions from Tim's Toolbox.

Concept Check

- What are four primary computer ethics issues?
- What is identity theft? What is mistaken identity? How are they different?
- What is the Freedom of Information Act?

PRIVATE NETWORKS

Suppose you use your company's electronic mail system to send a co-worker an unflattering message about your supervisor. Later you find the boss has been spying on your exchange. Or suppose you are a subscriber to an online discussion group. You discover that the company that supports the discussion group screens all your messages and rejects those it deems inappropriate. Both these situations have actually happened.

The first instance, of firms eavesdropping on employees, has inspired attempts at federal legislation. One survey revealed that nearly 75 percent of all businesses search employees' electronic mail and computer files using so-called **snoopware.** (See Figure 11-5.) These programs record virtually everything you do on your computer. Currently this is legal. One proposed law would not prohibit this type of electronic monitoring but would require employers to provide prior written notice. Employers would also have to alert employees during the monitoring with some sort of audible or visual signal.

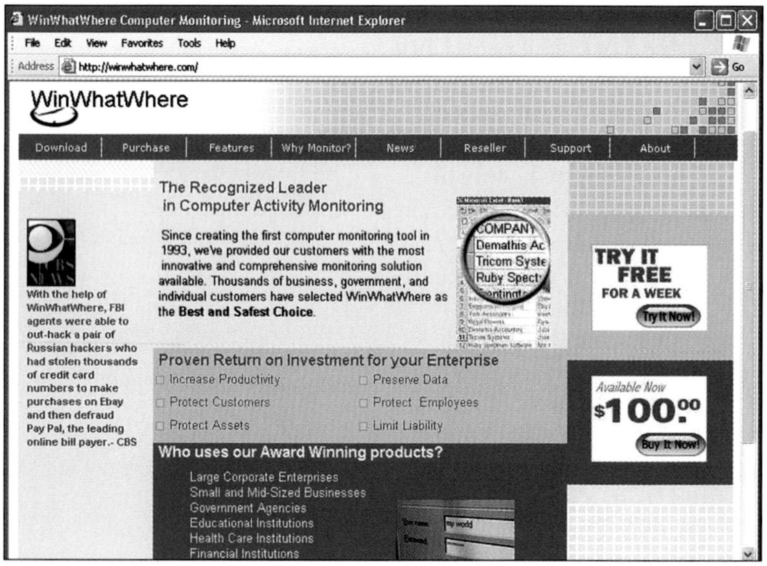

Figure 11-5 Snoopware

The second instance, in which online information services screen and reject messages, is a common activity with most commercial services. In one case, the Prodigy Information Service terminated the accounts of eight members who had been using the electronic mail system to protest Prodigy's rate hikes. Prodigy executives argued that the U.S. Constitution does not give members of someone's private network the right to express their views without restrictions. Opponents say that the United States is becoming a nation linked by electronic mail. Therefore, the government has to provide protection for users against other people reading or censoring their messages.

On the Web Explorations

The Center for Democracy and Technology monitors privacy issues and legislation. To learn more about this organization, visit our Web site at http://www.mhhe.com/oleary/CT05 and select On the Web Explorations from Tim's Toolbox.

THE INTERNET AND THE WEB

When you send e-mail on the Internet or browse the Web, do you have any concerns about privacy? Most people do not. They think as long as they are selective about disclosing their names or other personal information, then little can be done to invade their personal privacy. Experts call this the **illusion of anonymity** that the Internet brings.

As discussed earlier, many organizations monitor e-mail content of all messages sent within their private electronic networks. Likewise, for some unscrupulous individuals, it is also a common practice to eavesdrop or snoop into the content of e-mail sent across the Internet.

Furthermore, when you browse the Web, your activity is monitored. Whenever you visit a Web site, your browser stores critical information onto your hard disk, typically without your explicit permission or knowledge. For example, your browser creates a **history file** that includes the locations of sites visited by your computer system. This history file can be displayed by your browser. To view the history file using Internet Explorer version 6.0 follow the steps in Figure 11-6.

Another way your Web activity is monitored is by **cookies** or specialized programs that are deposited on your hard disk from Web sites you have visited. Typically, these programs are deposited without your explicit knowledge or consent. They record what sites you visit, what you do at the sites, and other information you provide such as passwords and credit card numbers. Most cookies can be displayed by your browser. To view the cookies on a hard drive using Internet Explorer version 6.0 follow the steps in Figure 11-7.

1 **Select *View* from the *menu bar***

Choose *Explorer bar*

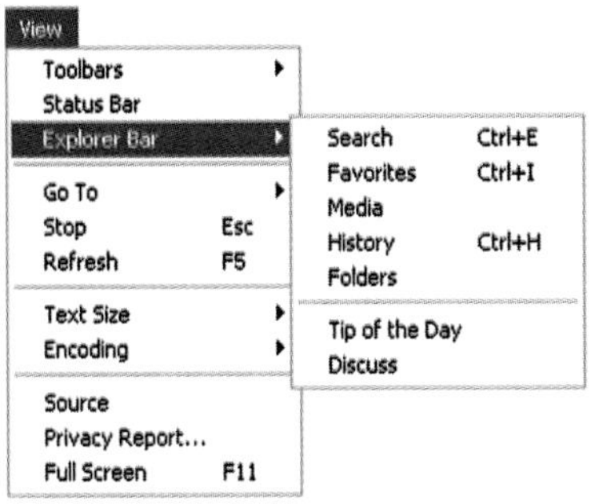

2 **Select *History***

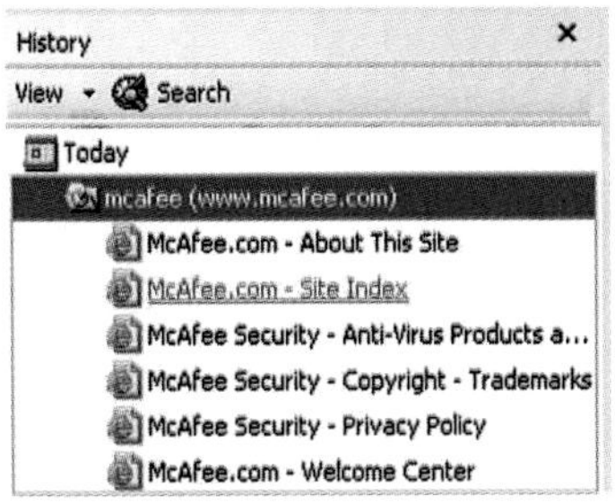

Figure 11-6 Viewing history files

1 **Select *Tools* from the *menu bar***

Choose *Internet Options*

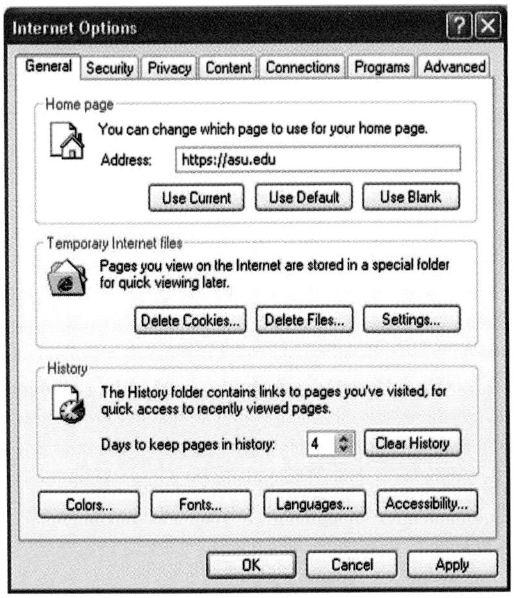

2 **Select *Settings* in the *General* tab**

Click *View files*

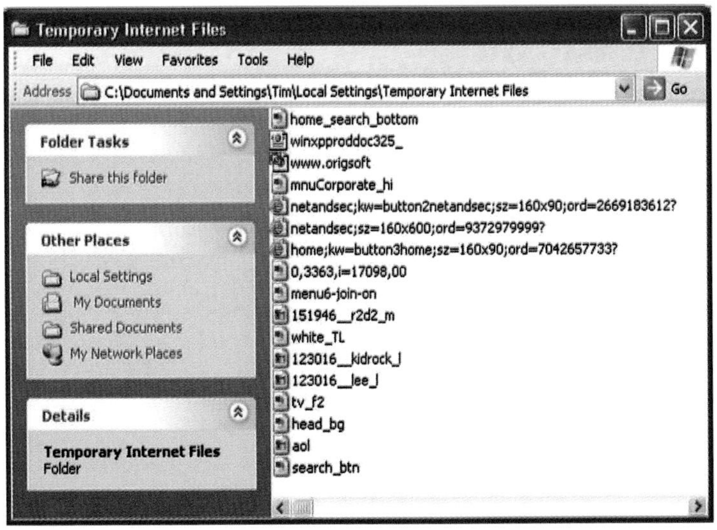

Figure 11-7 Viewing cookies

There are two basic types of cookies: traditional and ad network.

- **Traditional cookies** monitor your activities at a single site. When you first visit a site, a cookie is deposited and begins to monitor your activities. When you leave the site, the cookie becomes dormant. When you revisit, the cookie is reactivated and sends the previously collected information back to the site and then continues recording your activities. These cookies are intended to provide customized service. For example, when you revisit an electronic commerce site, you can be greeted by name, presented with customized advertising banners, and directed to Web pages promoting items you have previously purchased.
- **Ad network** or **adware cookies** monitor your activities across all sites you visit. Once deposited onto your hard drive, they are continually active collecting information on your Web activities. These cookies are secretly deposited on your hard disk by organizations that compile and market the information including individual personal profiles, mailing lists, and e-mail addresses. Two such organizations are DoubleClick and Avenue A.

Most browsers are able to control many types of cookies. For example, Internet Explorer version 6.0 provides settings to selectively block cookies from being deposited onto a system's hard disk. See Figure 11-8.

A more effective way to control unwanted cookies, however, is to use specialized programs. These programs, called **cookie-cutter programs,** allow users to selectively filter or block the most intrusive cookies while allowing selective traditional cookies to operate. (See Figure 11-9.) For a list of some of the most widely used cookie-cutter programs, see Figure 11-10.

1
- **Select *Tools* from the *menu bar***
- **Choose *Internet Options***

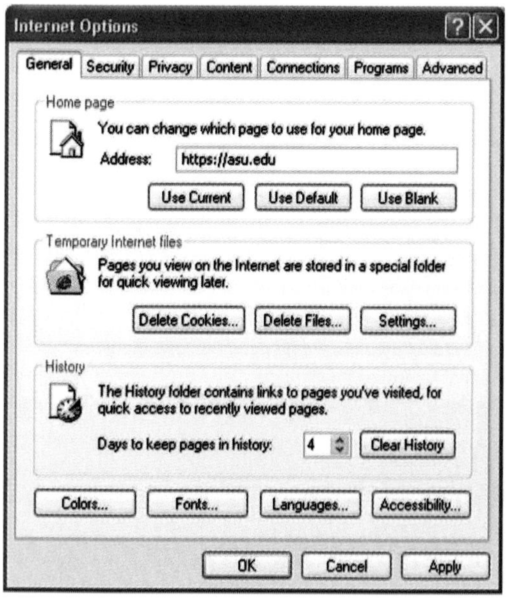

2
- **Select the *Privacy* tab**
- **Move the slide to desired level of protection**
- **Click *Apply;* Click *OK***

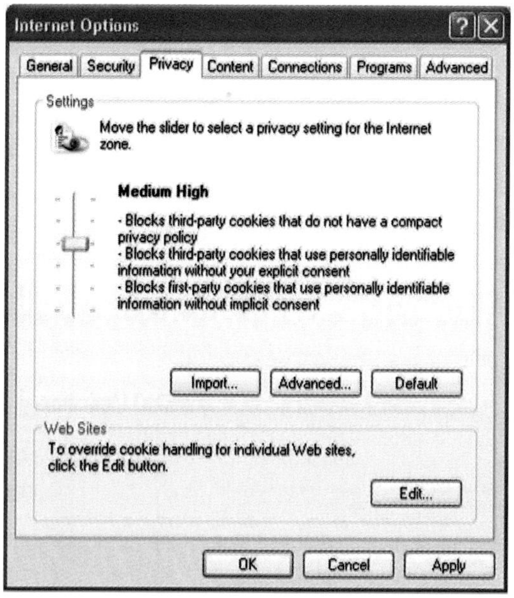

Figure 11-8 Blocking cookies

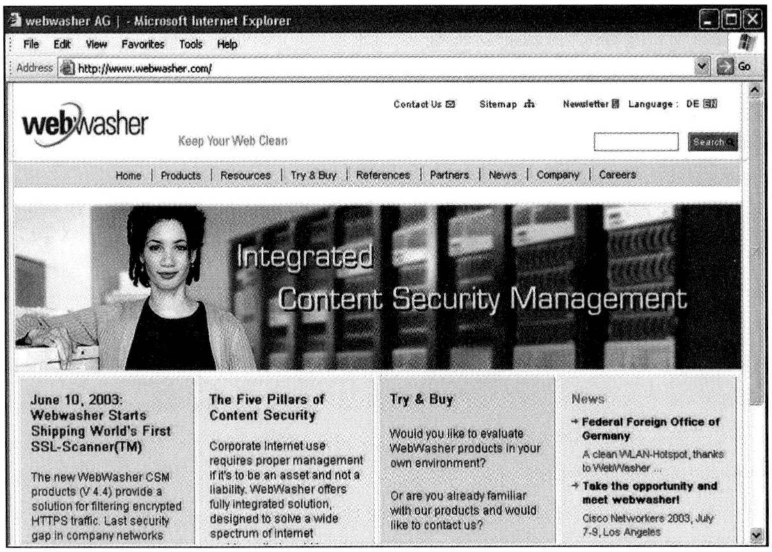

Figure 11-9 WebWasher

Program	Web Site
AdSubtract	adsubtract.com
Cookie Cleanup	softadd.com
Cookie Crusher	thelimitsoft.com
Cookie Pal	kburra.com
WebWasher	webwasher.com

Figure 11-10 Cookie-cutter programs

The term **spyware** is used to describe a wide range of programs that are designed to secretly record and report an individual's activities on the Internet. Ad network cookies are just one type of spyware. Two other types are Web bugs and computer monitoring software.

- **Web bugs** are small programs typically hidden within the HTML code for a Web page or email message as a graphical image. Web bugs migrate whenever an unsuspecting user visits a Web site containing a Web bug or opens an infected email message. Web bugs often work with cookies on the user's computer to collect and report information back to a predefined server on the Web. Web bugs can even be used to secretly read a user's email messages. To see how Web bugs can work, see Figure 11-11 and consult your Computing Today CD or visit Tim's Toolbox at http://www.mhhe.com/oleary/CT05 and select Animations.

Computing Today CD

- **Computer monitoring software** is the most invasive and dangerous type of spyware. These programs record every activity and keystroke made on your computer system including credit card numbers, bank account numbers, and e-mail messages. Also known as **sniffer programs** and **keystroke loggers,** computer monitoring software can be deposited onto your hard drive without your knowledge either from the Web or by someone installing the programs directly onto your computer. The previously mentioned snoopware is a type of computer monitoring software used by businesses to monitor their employees. Computer monitoring software has also been used by the FBI and the CIA to collect incriminating evidence on suspected terrorists and organized crime members. These programs are also widely used by private investigators, criminals, and spouses.

Unfortunately, it is more difficult to remove Web bugs and computer monitoring software than ad network cookies because they are more difficult to detect. A new category of programs known as **spy removal programs** has recently evolved designed to detect Web bugs and monitoring software. (See Figure 11-12.) For a list of some of these programs, see Figure 11-13.

To learn more about protecting yourself from Spyware, see Making IT Work for You: Spyware Removal on pages 418–419.

Figure 11-11 How Web Bugs Works

How Web Bugs Work

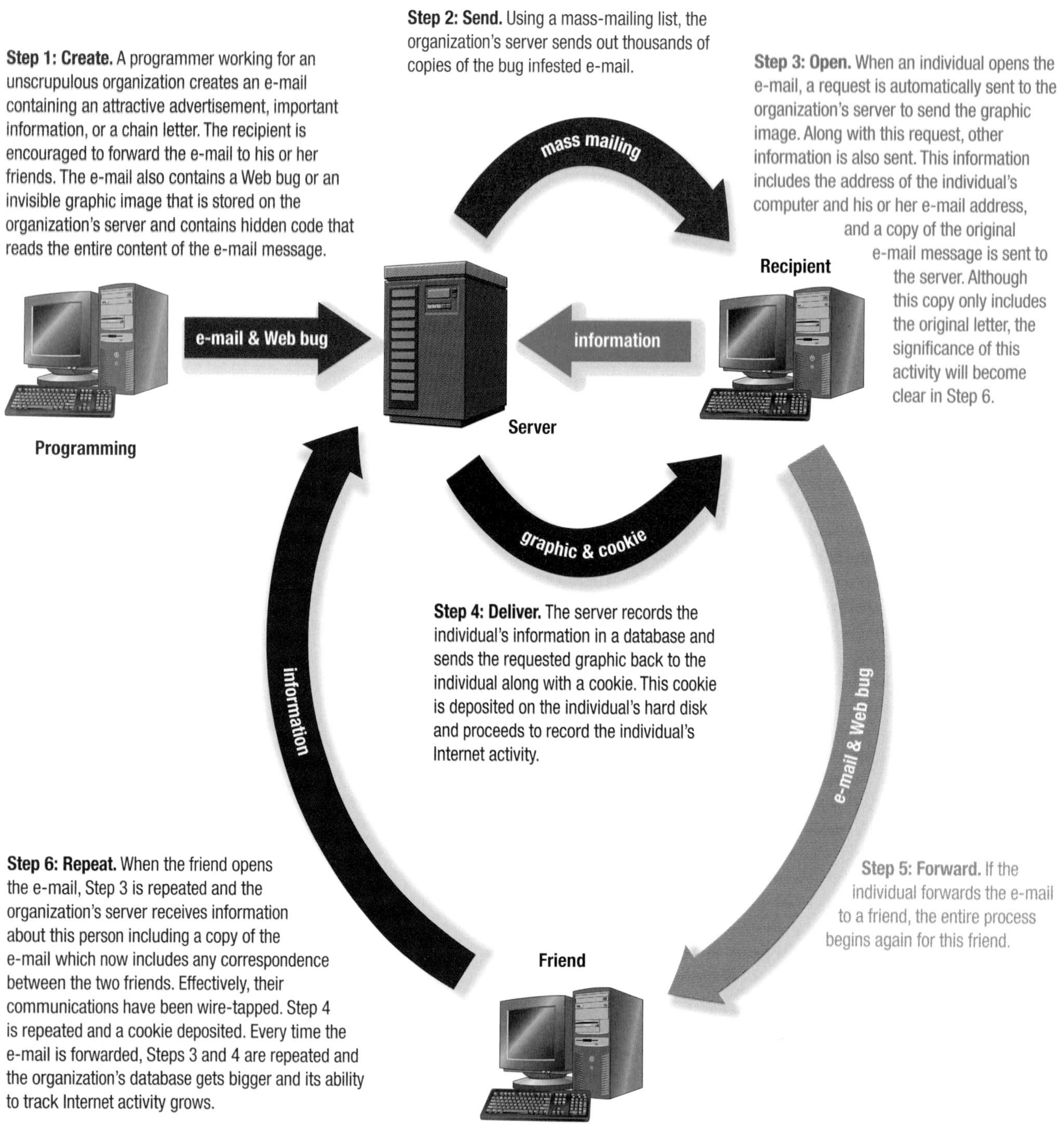
Step 1: Create. A programmer working for an unscrupulous organization creates an e-mail containing an attractive advertisement, important information, or a chain letter. The recipient is encouraged to forward the e-mail to his or her friends. The e-mail also contains a Web bug or an invisible graphic image that is stored on the organization's server and contains hidden code that reads the entire content of the e-mail message.
Step 2: Send. Using a mass-mailing list, the organization's server sends out thousands of copies of the bug infested e-mail.
Step 3: Open. When an individual opens the e-mail, a request is automatically sent to the organization's server to send the graphic image. Along with this request, other information is also sent. This information includes the address of the individual's computer and his or her e-mail address, and a copy of the original e-mail message is sent to the server. Although this copy only includes the original letter, the significance of this activity will become clear in Step 6.
mass mailing
Recipient
e-mail & Web bug
information
Server
Programming
graphic & cookie
Step 4: Deliver. The server records the individual's information in a database and sends the requested graphic back to the individual along with a cookie. This cookie is deposited on the individual's hard disk and proceeds to record the individual's Internet activity.
information
e-mail & Web bug
Step 5: Forward. If the individual forwards the e-mail to a friend, the entire process begins again for this friend.
Friend
Step 6: Repeat. When the friend opens the e-mail, Step 3 is repeated and the organization's server receives information about this person including a copy of the e-mail which now includes any correspondence between the two friends. Effectively, their communications have been wire-tapped. Step 4 is repeated and a cookie deposited. Every time the e-mail is forwarded, Steps 3 and 4 are repeated and the organization's database gets bigger and its ability to track Internet activity grows.

Figure 11-12 Protect your privacy

Program	Web Site
Ad-aware	lavasoftusa.com
PestPatrol	pestpatrol.com
Spybot-S&D	sypbot.com
Spy Sweeper	spysweeper.com

Figure 11-13 Spyware removal programs

MAJOR LAWS ON PRIVACY

Some federal laws governing privacy matters have been created (see Figure 11-14). However, most of the information collected by nongovernmental organizations is not covered by existing laws. As a result, privacy remains primarily an ethical issue. Increasingly, more and more individuals have become concerned about controlling who has the right to personal information and how that information is used.

To respond to these privacy concerns, a Code of Fair Information Practice has been established. (See Figure 11-15.) The code was recommended by a committee established by former Secretary of Health, Education, and Welfare Elliott Richardson. While this code has been adopted by many information-collecting businesses it is not a law. Privacy advocates strongly support legislation that makes this code an enforceable law.

TIPS

What can you do to protect your privacy while on the Web? Here are a few suggestions.

1. **Encrypt sensitive e-mail.** Encrypt or code sensitive e-mail using special encryption programs.
2. **Shield your identity.** Use an anonymous remailer or special Web site that forwards your e-mail without disclosing your identity.
3. **Block cookies.** Use your browser or a cookie-cutter programs to block unwanted cookies.
4. **Check for Web bugs and computer monitoring software.** Use spy removal programs to check for Web bugs and computer monitoring software.
5. **Notify providers.** Instruct your service provider or whomever you use to link to the Internet not to sell your name or any other personal information.
6. **Be careful.** Never disclose your telephone number, passwords, or other private information to strangers.

Concept Check

- What are history files? What are cookies?
- Identify and describe the two basic types of cookies.
- What are Web bugs? What is computer monitoring software? What is spyware?
- What does the PATRIOT act provide?
- Describe the Code of Fair Information Practice.

MAKING IT WORK FOR YOU

SPYWARE REMOVAL

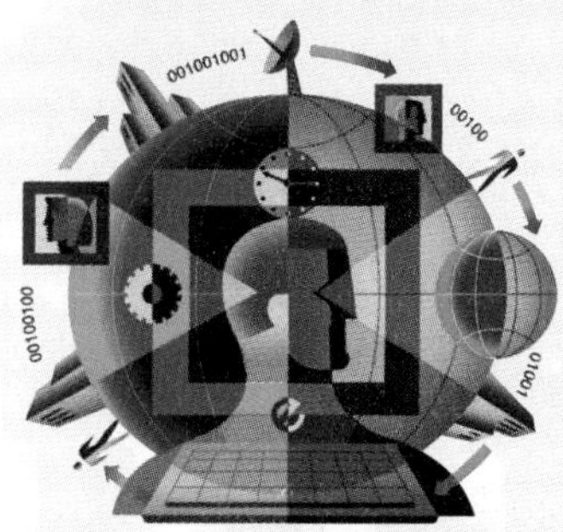

Have you installed any free software from the Internet? Did you know seemingly harmless software might actually be spying on you, even sending personal information to advertisers or worse? Fortunately, spyware removal software is available to keep your personal information private.

Getting Started The first step is to install spyware removal software on your system. Spyware removal software can be downloaded from the Internet easily and often for free. For instance, to install Lavasoft Ad-aware:

1. **Connect to *www.lavasoftusa.com.***
   - **Click the *Downloads* link.**
   - **Select a download site from the list and follow their instructions to download the *Ad-aware software.***
   - **Double-click the file you downloaded and follow the on-screen instructions to install it on your system.**

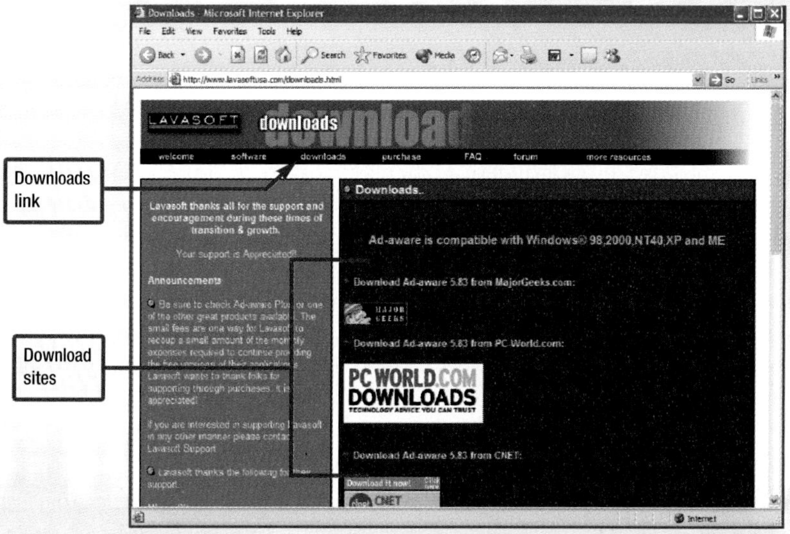

Finding and Removing Spyware Once spyware removal software is installed on your system, you can scan your system for known spyware and remove it. Follow the steps below to find and remove spyware using Ad-aware.

1. **Launch the *Ad-aware* application.**
   - **Click to place a check mark next to *My Computer* on the left.**
   - **Click the *Scan now* button.**
   - **Click *Continue* when the scan is complete.**

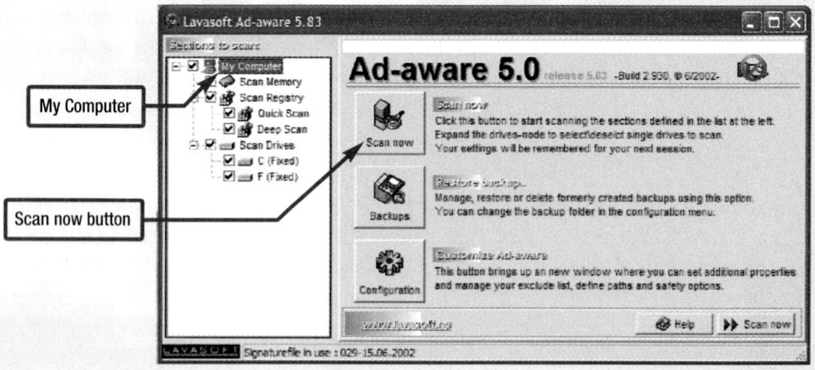

- Place a checkmark next to unwanted components by clicking them in the *Detected components . . .* list.
- Click *Continue.*

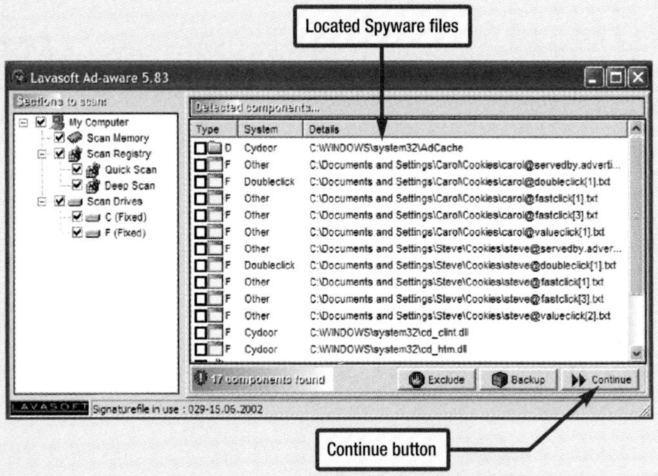

The detected spyware is removed from your system.

Staying Up To Date Now that your system is spyware-free, you'll want to keep it that way. Ad-aware uses a reference file to keep track of known spyware, similar to profiles kept by antivirus software for known viruses (see Making IT Work for You: Virus Protection on page 186). Follow the steps below to download and install a current spyware reference file.

1
- **Connect to *www.lavasoftusa.com.***
- **Click the *Downloads* link.**
- **Follow the instructions to download and install the *Refupdate* application.**

2
- **Launch the *Refupdate* application.**
- **Click the *Connect* button.**

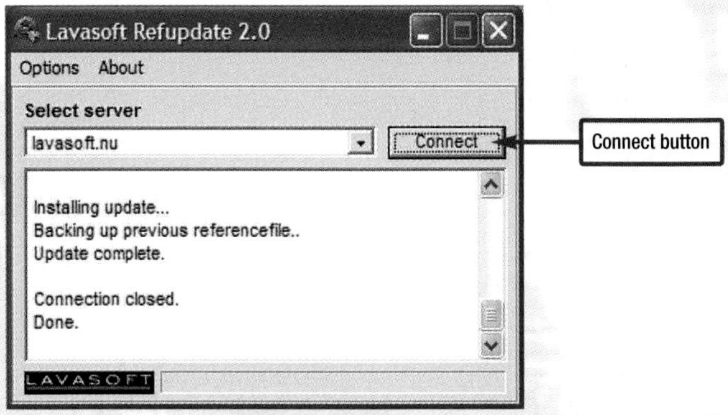

The newest Ad-aware reference file is installed automatically. You can now follow the steps in the "Finding and Removing Spyware" section to rid your system of the latest known spyware. The Web is continually changing and some of the specifics presented in the Making IT Work for You may have changed. To learn about other ways to make information technology work for you, visit our Web site at http://www.mhhe.com/oleary/CT05 and select Making IT Work for You from Tim's Toolbox.

Law	Year	Protection
Fair Credit Reporting Act	1970	Gives right to review and correct personal credit records; restricts sharing of personal credit histories.
Freedom of Information Act	1970	Gives right to see personal files collected by federal agencies.
Privacy Act	1974	Prohibits use of federal information for purposes other than original intent.
Right to Financial Privacy Act	1979	Limits federal authority to examine personal bank records.
Computer Fraud and Abuse Act	1986	Allows prosecution of unauthorized access to computers and databases.
Electronic Communications Privacy Act (ECPA)	1986	Protects privacy on public electronic-mail systems.
Video Privacy Protection Act	1988	Prevents sale of video-rental records.
Computer Matching and Privacy Protection Act	1988	Limits government's authority to match individual's data.
Computer Abuse Amendments Act	1994	Outlaws transmission of viruses.
National Information Infrastructure Protection Act	1996	Protects computer systems, networks, and information.
No Electronic Theft (NET) Act	1997	Prevents unauthorized distribution of copyrighted software on the Internet.
Child Online Protection Act (COPA)	1998	Prohibits commercial distribution of materials harmful to minors.
Digital Millennium Copyright Act (DMCA)	1998	Protects software manufacturers against sale of devices that illegally copy software. Prohibits tampering with antiprivacy schemes.
Provide Appropriate Tools Required to Intercept and Obstruct Terrorism (PATRIOT) Act	2001	Provides for legal monitoring of people's activities.

Figure 11-14 Summary of privacy laws

Principle	Description
No secret databases	There must be no record-keeping systems containing personal data whose very existence is kept secret.
Right of individual access	Individuals must be able to find out what information about them is in a record and how it is used.
Right of consent	Information about individuals obtained for one purpose cannot be used for other purposes without their consent.
Right to correct	Individuals must be able to correct or amend records of identifiable information about them.
Assurance of reliability and proper use	Organizations creating, maintaining, using, or disseminating records of identifiable personal data must make sure the data is reliable for its intended use. They must take precautions to prevent such data from being misused.

Figure 11-15 Principles of the Code of Fair Information Practice

SECURITY

Threats to computer security are criminals, computer crime, and hazards. Measures to protect security include encryption, restricting access, anticipating disasters, and making backup copies.

We are all concerned with having a safe and secure environment to live in. We are careful to lock our car doors and our homes. We are careful about where we walk at night and whom we talk to. This is personal security. What about computer security? What if someone gains unauthorized access to our computer or other computers that contain information about us? What if someone steals our computer or other computers that contain information about us? What are the major threats to computer security and how can we be protected?

THREATS TO COMPUTER SECURITY

Keeping information private depends on keeping computer systems safe from criminals, natural hazards, and other threats. (See Figure 11-16.)

COMPUTER CRIMINALS

A **computer crime** is an illegal action in which the perpetrator uses special knowledge of computer technology. Computer criminals are of five types:

- **Employees:** The largest category of computer criminals consists of those with the easiest access to computers—namely, employees. Sometimes the employee is simply trying to steal something from the employer—equipment, software, electronic funds, proprietary information, or computer time. Sometimes the employee may be acting out of resentment and is trying to get back at the company.
- **Outside users:** Not only employees but also some suppliers or clients may have access to a company's computer system. Examples are bank

Computer theft

Civil unrest

Natural hazards

Figure 11-16 There are numerous threats to computer security.

customers who use an automated teller machine. Like employees, these authorized users may be able to obtain confidential passwords or find other ways of committing computer crimes.

- **Hackers and crackers:** Some people think of these two groups as being the same, but they are not. **Hackers** are people who gain unauthorized access to a computer system for the fun and challenge of it. **Crackers** do the same thing but for malicious purposes. They may intend to steal technical information or to introduce what they call a bomb—a destructive computer program—into the system.
- **Organized crime:** Members of organized crime groups have discovered that they can use computers just as people in legitimate businesses do, but for illegal purposes. For example, computers are useful for keeping track of stolen goods or illegal gambling debts. In addition, counterfeiters and forgers use microcomputers and printers to produce sophisticated-looking documents such as checks and driver's licenses.
- **Terrorists:** Knowledgeable terrorist groups and hostile governments could potentially crash satellites and wage economic warfare by disrupting navigation and communication systems. The Department of Defense reports that its computer systems are probed approximately 250,000 times a year by unknown sources.

COMPUTER CRIME

The FBI estimates that businesses lost $1.5 trillion in the past year from computer crimes. The number of these crimes has tripled in the past two years. Computer crime can take various forms including the creation of malicious programs, denial of service attacks, Internet scams, theft, and data manipulation.

Malicious Programs

Hackers and crackers are notorious for creating and distributing malicious programs. These programs are called **malware,** which is short for **mal**icious soft**ware.** They are specifically designed to damage or disrupt a computer system. The three most common types of malware are viruses, worms, and Trojan horses.

- **Viruses** are programs that migrate through networks and operating systems and most attach themselves to different programs and databases. While most viruses are relatively harmless, some can be quite destructive. Once activated, these destructive viruses can alter and/or delete files. Some delete all files on the hard disk and can damage system components. Creating and knowingly spreading a virus is a very serious crime and a federal offense punishable under the **Computer Abuse Amendments Act of 1994.**

  See Figure 11-17 for a list of common viruses.

Name	Description
Apology-B	Follows every outgoing e-mail with a second e-mail containing virus
KuKworm	Automatically attaches to outgoing e-mail
Love Bug	Recreates itself through Microsoft Outlook; renames files
Stages-A	Copies itself on all available network drives
Thus	Deletes data on December 13th

Figure 11-17 Commonly encountered viruses

Name	Description
Bugbear	Most deposit viruses; some are e-mail viruses, others deposit computer monitoring software
Fizzer	Most deposit an e-mail virus; others locate and disable the infected computer system's virus protection programs
Klez	Duplicates itself through mass-mailing of e-mail; however, most do not deposit traditional viruses
Yaha	Most activated when an infected e-mail is opened; unsuspecting recipients are enticed to open the e-mail by displaying subject lines such as free screen saver and one way to love

Figure 11-18 Commonly encountered worms

- **Worms** are a special type of virus that does not attach itself to programs and databases. Rather it fills a computer system with self-replicating information, clogging the system so that its operations are slowed or stopped. A recent worm traveled across the world within hours stopping tens of thousands of computers along its way. Internet worms can also be carriers of more traditional viruses. Once the traditional virus has been deposited by a worm onto an unsuspecting computer system, the virus will either activate immediately or lie dormant until some future time.

  See Figure 11-18 for a list of common worms, each with different variations.

Viruses and worms typically find their way into microcomputers through e-mail attachments, copied floppy disks, or programs downloaded from the Internet. Because viruses can be so serious—certain "disk-killer" viruses can destroy all the information on one's system—computer users are advised to exercise care in accepting new programs and data from other sources.

As we discussed in Chapter 5, detection programs called **virus checkers** are available to alert users when certain kinds of viruses and worms enter their system. Four of the most widely used virus checkers are Dr. Solomon's Anti-Virus, McAfee VirusScan, eSafe, and Norton AntiVirus. Unfortunately, new viruses are being developed all the time, and not all viruses can be detected. (See Making IT Work for You: Virus Protection on pages 186–187 presented in Chapter 5.)

To learn more about viruses and how you could get one, study Figure 11-19.

- **Trojan horses** are programs that come into a computer system disguised as something else. Trojan horses are not viruses. Like worms, however, they are carriers of viruses. Two of the most common types of Trojan horses appear as free computer games and free screen saver programs that can be downloaded from the Internet. Once the Trojan horse is downloaded onto a computer system, the viruses are deposited and ready to activate. One of the most dangerous types of Trojan horse claims to provide free antivirus programs. These programs begin by locating and disabling any existing virus protection programs and then deposit the virus.

TIPS

Are you concerned about catching a virus? Here are a few suggestions that might help:

1. **Use an antivirus program.** Install antivirus programs on all computer systems you use and run them frequently.
2. **Check disks.** Before using any floppy or CD, check for viruses.
3. **Enable write protection.** Protect data and programs on floppy disks by enabling write protection.
4. **Check all downloads.** Check all files downloaded from the Internet.
5. **Update your antivirus program.** New viruses are being developed daily, and the virus programs are continually being revised. Update your antivirus program frequently.

Denial of Service

Like a worm, a **denial of service (DoS) attack** attempts to slow down or stop a computer system or network. Unlike a worm that

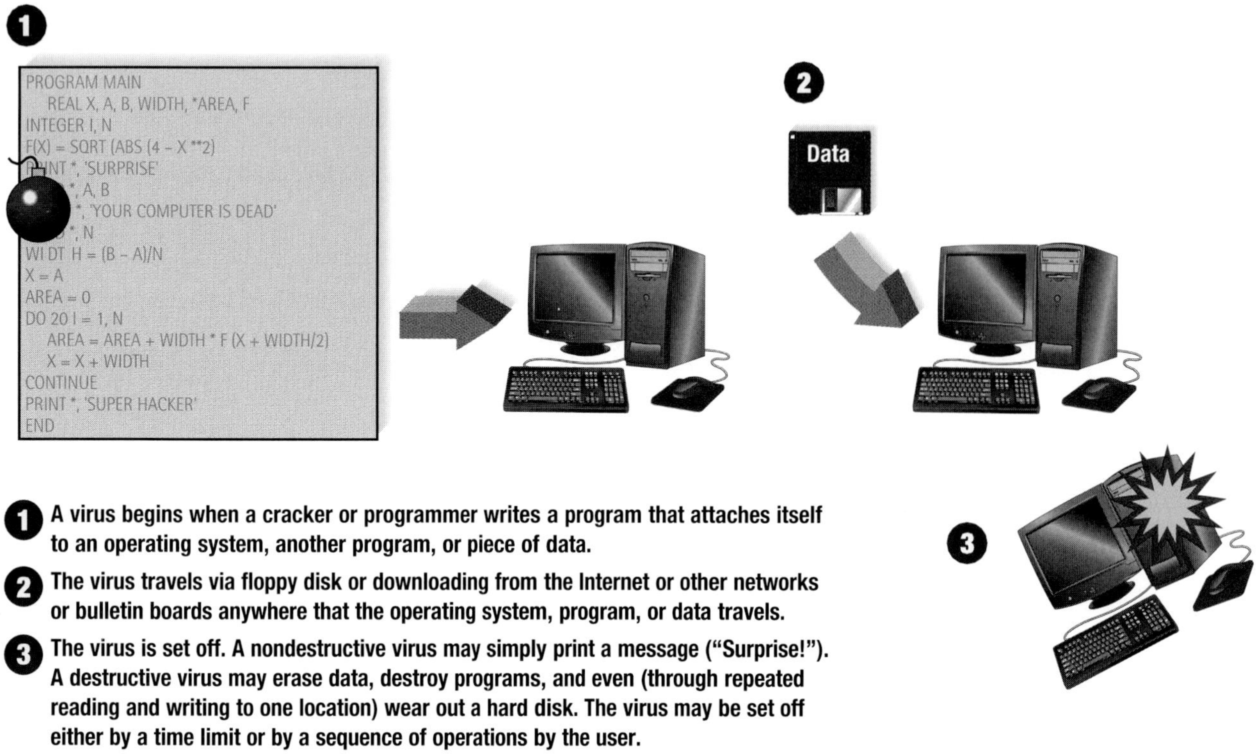
PROGRAM MAIN
REAL X, A, B, WIDTH, *AREA, F
INTEGER I, N
F(X) = SQRT (ABS (4 - X **2)
*, 'SURPRISE'
*, A, B
*, 'YOUR COMPUTER IS DEAD'
*, N
WI DT H = (B - A)/N
X = A
AREA = 0
DO 20 I = 1, N
AREA = AREA + WIDTH * F (X + WIDTH/2)
X = X + WIDTH
CONTINUE
PRINT *, 'SUPER HACKER'
END
Data
1 A virus begins when a cracker or programmer writes a program that attaches itself to an operating system, another program, or piece of data.
2 The virus travels via floppy disk or downloading from the Internet or other networks or bulletin boards anywhere that the operating system, program, or data travels.
3 The virus is set off. A nondestructive virus may simply print a message ("Surprise!"). A destructive virus may erase data, destroy programs, and even (through repeated reading and writing to one location) wear out a hard disk. The virus may be set off either by a time limit or by a sequence of operations by the user.

Figure 11-19 How a computer virus can spread

self-replicates, a DoS attack floods a computer or network with requests for information and data. The targets of these attacks are usually Internet service providers (ISP) and specific Web sites. Once under attack, the servers at the ISP or the Web site become overwhelmed with these requests for service and are unable to respond to legitimate users. As a result, the ISP or Web site is effectively shut down.

Internet Scams

A **scam** is a fraudulent or deceptive act or operation designed to trick individuals into spending their time and money for little or no return. An **Internet scam** is simply a scam using the Internet. Internet scams are becoming a serious problem and have created financial and legal problems for thousands of people. Almost all of the scams are initiated by a mass mailing to unsuspecting individuals.

See Figure 11-20 for a list of some of the most common types of Internet scams.

Theft

Theft can take many forms—of hardware, of software, of data, of computer time. Thieves steal equipment and programs, of course, but there are also white-collar crimes. These crimes include the theft of data in the form of confidential information such as preferred-client lists. Another common crime is the use (theft) of a company's computer time by an employee to run another business.

Unauthorized copying of programs for personal gain is a form of theft called **software piracy.** According to the **Software Copyright Act of 1980,** it is legal for a program owner to make only his or her own backup copies of that program. *It's important to note that none of these copies may be legally resold or given away. This may come as a surprise to those who copy software from a friend, but that's the law.*

Type	Description
Identity theft	Individual(s) pose as ISPs, bank representatives, or government agencies requesting personal information. Once obtained, criminal(s) assume identity for a variety of financial transactions.
Chain letter	Classic chain letter instructing recipient to send a nominal amount of money to each of five people on a list. The recipient removes the first name on the list, adds their name at the bottom and mails the chain letter to five friends. Almost all chain letters are fraudulent and illegal.
Auction fraud	Merchandise is selected and payment sent. Merchandise is never delivered.
Vacation prize	"Free" vacation has been awarded. Upon arrival at vacation destination, the accommodations are dreadful but can be "upgraded" for a fee.
Advance fee loans	Guaranteed low rate loans available to almost anyone. After applicant provides personal loan related information, the loan is granted subject to payment of an "insurance fee."

Figure 11-20 Common Internet scams

Pirated software accounts for over 40 percent of software used in the United States. The incidence of pirated software is even higher overseas in such countries as Italy (82 percent) and Thailand (92 percent). Penalties for violating this law are up to $250,000 in fines and five years in prison.

Data Manipulation

Finding entry into someone's computer network and leaving a prankster's message may seem like fun, which is why hackers do it. It is still against the law. Moreover, even if the manipulation seems harmless, it may cause a great deal of anxiety and wasted time among network users.

The Computer Fraud and Abuse Act of 1986 makes it a crime for unauthorized persons even to view—let alone copy or damage—data using any computer across state lines. It also prohibits unauthorized use of any government computer or computer used by any federally insured financial institution. Offenders can be sentenced to up to 20 years in prison and fined up to $100,000.

For a summary of computer crimes, see Figure 11-21.

Computer Crime	Description
Malicious programs	Include viruses, worms, and Trojan horses
DoS	Cause computer systems to slow down or stop
Internet scams	Are scams over Internet initiated by e-mail
Theft	Including hardware, software, and computer time
Data manipulation	Involves changing data or leaving prankster messages

Figure 11-21 Computer crimes

OTHER HAZARDS

There are plenty of other hazards to computer systems and data besides criminals. They include the following:

- **Natural hazards:** Natural forces include fires, floods, wind, hurricanes, tornadoes, and earthquakes. Even home computer users should store backup disks of programs and data in safe locations in case of fire or storm damage.
- **Civil strife and terrorism:** Wars, riots, and terrorist activities are real risks in all parts of the world. Even people in developed countries must be mindful of these acts.
- **Technological failures:** Hardware and software don't always do what they are supposed to do. For instance, too little electricity, caused by a

Figure 11-22 Crashes can result in lost data

brownout or blackout, may cause the loss of data in primary storage. Too much electricity, as when lightning or some other electrical disturbance affects a power line, may cause a **voltage surge,** or **spike.** This excess of electricity may destroy chips or other electronic components of a computer.

Microcomputer users should use a **surge protector,** a device that separates the computer from the power source of the wall outlet. When a voltage surge occurs, it activates a circuit breaker in the surge protector, protecting the computer system.

Another technological catastrophe occurs when a hard-disk drive suddenly crashes, or fails (as discussed in Chapter 9), perhaps because it has been bumped inadvertently. If the user has forgotten to make backup copies of data on the hard disk, data may be lost. (See Figure 11-22.)

- **Human errors:** Human mistakes are inevitable. Data-entry errors are probably the most commonplace and, as we have discussed, can lead to mistaken identity. Programmer errors also occur frequently. Some mistakes may result from faulty design, as when a software manufacturer makes a deletion command closely resembling another command. Some errors may be the result of sloppy procedures. One such example occurs when office workers save important documents under file names that are not descriptive and not recognizable by others.

MEASURES TO PROTECT COMPUTER SECURITY

Figure 11-23 Disasters—both natural and manmade—can play havoc with computers

Security is concerned with protecting information, hardware, and software, which must be protected from unauthorized use as well as from damage from intrusions, sabotage, and natural disasters. (See Figure 11-23.) Considering the numerous ways in which computer systems and data can be compromised, we can see why security is a growing field. Some of the principal measures to protect computer security are encryption, restricting access, anticipating disasters, and backing up data.

Concept Check

- ✔ Describe malware including viruses, worms, and Trojan horses.
- ✔ Compare a worm to a denial of service attack. How are they similar? How are they different?
- ✔ Describe the five most common types of Internet scams.

ENCRYPTING MESSAGES

Whenever information is sent over a network, the possibility of unauthorized access exists. The longer the distance the message has to travel, the higher the security risk is. For example, an e-mail message on a LAN meets a limited number of users operating in controlled environments such as offices. An e-mail message travelling across the country on the Internet affords greater opportunities for the message to be intercepted.

Businesses have been **encrypting,** or coding, messages for years. They have become so good at it that some law enforcement agencies are unable to wiretap messages from suspected criminals. Some federal agencies have suggested that a standard encryption procedure be used so that law enforcement agencies can monitor suspected criminal communications. Individuals are also using encryption programs to safeguard their private communications. One of the most widely used personal encryption programs is Pretty Good Privacy. (See Figure 11-24.)

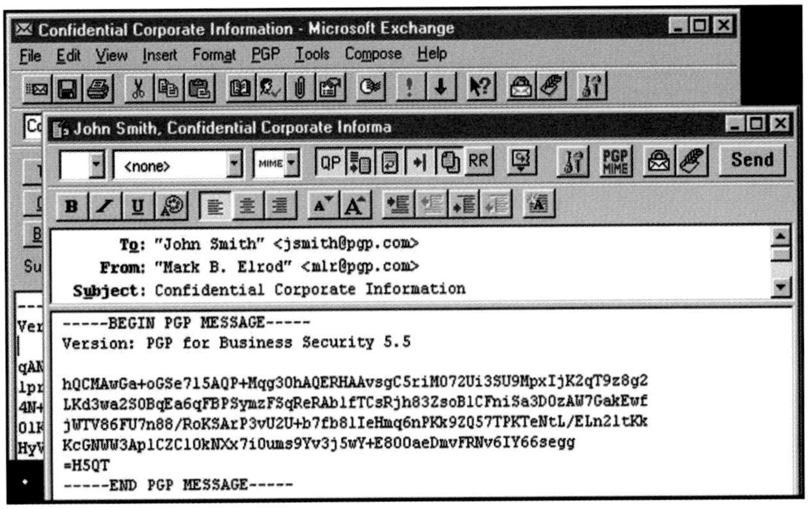

Figure 11-24 Encrypted e-mail

RESTRICTING ACCESS

Security experts are constantly devising ways to protect computer systems from access by unauthorized persons. Sometimes security is a matter of putting guards on company computer rooms and checking the identification of everyone admitted. Other times it is using **biometric scanning** devices such as fingerprint and retinal (eye) scanners. (See Figure 11-25.)

Oftentimes it is a matter of being careful about assigning passwords to people and of changing the passwords when people leave a company. **Passwords** are secret words or numbers that must be keyed into a computer system to gain access. In some dial-back computer systems, the user telephones the computer, punches in the correct password, and then hangs up. If the password is verified by the computer system, it then calls the user back at a certain preauthorized telephone number. For many applications on the Web, users assign their own passwords.

As mentioned in previous chapters, most major corporations today use special hardware and software called firewalls to control access to their internal computer networks. **Firewalls** act as a security buffer between the corporation's private network and all external networks, including the Internet. All electronic communications coming into and leaving the corporation must be evaluated by the firewall. Security is maintained by denying access to unauthorized communications. To learn how to use Windows XP's built-in firewall, consult your Computing Today CD or visit us on the Web at http://www.mhhe.com/oleary/CT05 and select Expansions from Tim's Toolbox.

On the Web Explorations

Pretty Good Privacy (PGP) is one of the leaders in the development of encryption programs. To learn more about the company, visit our Web site at

http://www.mhhe.com/oleary/CT05

and select On the Web Explorations from Tim's Toolbox.

Computing Today CD

Figure 11-25 Biometric scanning devices

ANTICIPATING DISASTERS

Companies (and even individuals) that do not make preparations for disasters are not acting wisely. **Physical security** is concerned with protecting hardware from possible human and natural disasters. **Data security** is concerned with protecting software and data from unauthorized tampering or damage. Most large organizations have a **disaster recovery plan** describing ways to continue operating until normal computer operations can be restored.

Hardware can be kept behind locked doors, but often employees find this restriction a hindrance to their work. As a result, security is often lax. Fire and water (including the water from ceiling sprinkler systems) can do great damage to equipment. Many companies therefore will form a cooperative arrangement to share equipment with other companies in the event of a catastrophe. Special emergency facilities called **hot sites** may be created that are fully equipped backup computer centers. They are called **cold sites** if they are empty shells in which hardware must be installed.

BACKING UP DATA

Equipment can always be replaced. A company's *data,* however, may be irreplaceable. Most companies have ways of trying to keep software and data from being tampered with in the first place. They include careful screening of job applicants, guarding of passwords, and auditing of data and programs from time to time. An essential procedure, however, is to make frequent backups of data and to store them in safe remote locations.

See Figure 11-26 for a summary of the different measures to protect computer security.

TIPS

What can you do to protect the security of your microcomputer system? Here are a few suggestions.

1. **Avoid extreme conditions:** Don't expose the computer to extreme conditions. Clean your equipment regularly. Use a surge protector to protect against voltage surges.
2. **Avoid viruses:** Install, use, and periodically update virus protection programs. All incoming files should be checked for viruses before they are executed or saved.
3. **Avoid attachments:** Never run an e-mail attachment with an .exe extension unless you are sure of its source.
4. **Install firewall:** Either use Windows XP firewall and/or obtain a commercially available product.
5. **Update software:** Occasionally programs (especially operating systems) have security weaknesses. Software manufacturers often provide corrective code to eliminate the security holes. This code is often referred to as a patch.
6. **Guard the computer:** If you are concerned that your computer may be stolen, put a cable lock on it. If you subscribe or belong to an online information service, do not leave passwords nearby in a place accessible to others. Etch your driver's license number into your equipment. That way it can be identified in the event it is recovered after theft.
7. **Guard programs and data:** Store disks properly, preferably in a locked container. Frequently and periodically make backup copies of all your important data files and programs. Store copies of your files in a different—and safe—location from the site of your computer.

Concept Check

- ✔ What is encryption? What is Pretty Good Privacy?
- ✔ Discuss ways to restrict access including biometric scanning, passwords, and firewalls.
- ✔ Discuss ways to anticipate disasters including physical and data security, disaster recovery plans, hot sites, and cold sites.

Measure	Description
Encrypting	Code all messages sent over a network
Restricting	Limit access to authorized persons using such measures as passwords, dial-back systems, and firewalls
Anticipating	Prepare for disasters by ensuring physical security and data security through a disaster recovery plan
Backing up	Routinely copy data and store it at a remote location

Figure 11-26 Measures to protect computer security

ERGONOMICS

Ergonomics is the study of human factors related to things people use. Physical risks include eyestrain, backache, neck pain, and RSI. Mental risks include noise and electronic monitoring.

Computers have become a common business tool because they increase productivity. Unfortunately, there are certain ways in which computers may actually make people less productive. Many of those affected are in positions that involve intensive data entry, such as clerks and word processor operators. However, anyone whose job involves heavy use of the computer may be affected. As a result, there has been great interest in a field known as *ergonomics.*

Ergonomics (pronounced "er-guh-nom-ix") is defined as the study of human factors related to things people use. It is concerned with fitting the job to the worker rather than forcing the worker to contort to fit the job. As computer use has increased, so has interest in ergonomics. People are devising ways that computers can be designed and used to increase productivity and avoid health risks.

On the Web Explorations

Workplace Designs is one of the leading distributors of ergonomic equipment. To learn more about the company, visit our Web site at http://www.mhhe.com/oleary/CT05 and select On the Web Explorations from Tim's Toolbox.

PHYSICAL HEALTH

Sitting in front of a screen in awkward positions for long periods may lead to physical problems such as eyestrain, headaches, and back pain. Computer users can alleviate these problems by taking frequent rest breaks and by using well-designed computer furniture. Some recommendations by ergonomics experts for the ideal microcomputer setup are illustrated in Figure 11-27.

The physical health matters related to computers that have received the most attention recently are the following:

- **Eyestrain and headache:** Our eyes were made for most efficient seeing at a distance. However, monitors require using the eyes at closer range for a long time, which can create eyestrain, headaches, and double vision.

  To make the computer easier on the eyes, take a 15-minute break every hour or two. Avoid computer screens that flicker. Keep computer screens away from windows and other sources of bright light to minimize reflected glare on the screen. Special antiglare screen coatings and glare shields are also available. Make sure the screen is three to four times brighter than room light. Keep everything you're focusing on at about the same distance. For example, the computer screen, keyboard, and a document holder containing your work might be positioned about 20 inches away. Clean the screen of dust from time to time.
- **Back and neck pain:** Many people work at monitors and keyboards that are in improper positions. The result can be pains in the back and neck. (See Figure 11-28.)

On the Web Explorations

The Mayo Clinic and the American Optometric Association provide free electronic newsletters that describe computer-related eyestrain. To learn more about these organizations, visit our Web site at http://www.mhhe.com/oleary/CT05 and select On the Web Explorations from Tim's Toolbox.

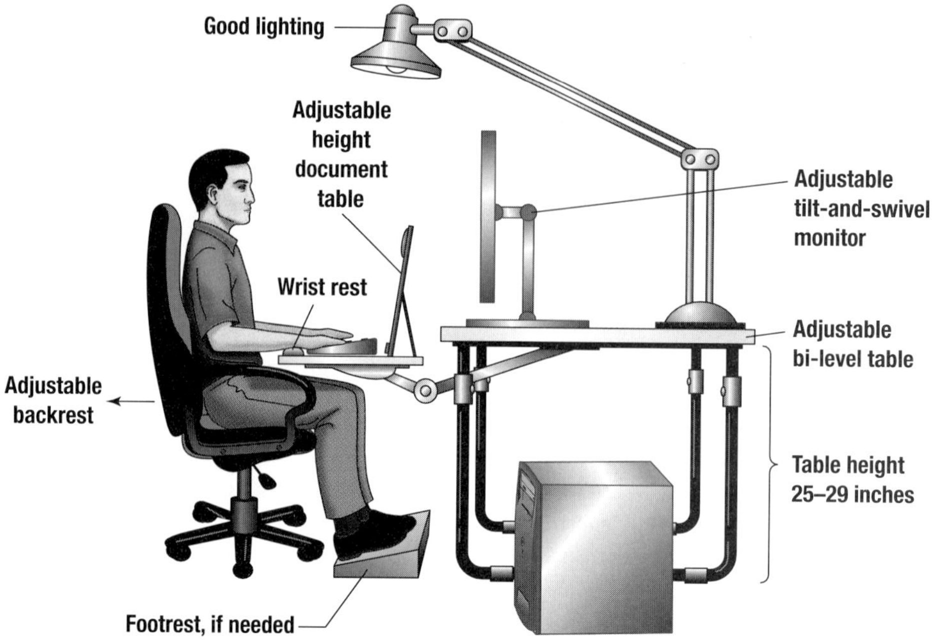
Good lighting
Adjustable height document table
Adjustable tilt-and-swivel monitor
Wrist rest
Adjustable bi-level table
Adjustable backrest
Table height 25–29 inches
Footrest, if needed

Figure 11-27 Recommendations for the ideal microcomputer work environment

Figure 11-28 Back and neck pain

To avoid such problems, make sure equipment is adjustable. You should be able to adjust your chair for height and angle, and the chair should have good back support. The table on which the monitor stands should also be adjustable, and the monitor itself should be of the tilt-and-swivel kind. The monitor should be at eye level or slightly below eye level. Keyboards should be detachable. Document holders should be adjustable. Use footrest, if necessary, to reduce leg fatigue.

- **Repetitive strain injury:** Data-entry operators may make as many as 23,000 keystrokes a day. Some of these workers and other heavy keyboard users have fallen victim to a disorder known as repetitive strain injury.

Repetitive strain injury (RSI)—also called **repetitive motion injury** and **cumulative trauma disorder**—is the name given to a number of injuries. These result from fast, repetitive work that can cause neck, wrist, hand, and arm pain. RSI is by far the greatest cause of workplace illnesses in private industry. It accounts for billions of dollars in compensation claims and lost productivity every year. Some RSI sufferers are slaughterhouse, textile, and automobile workers, who have long been susceptible to the disorder. One particular type of RSI, **carpal tunnel syndrome,** found among heavy computer users, consists of damage to nerves and tendons in the hands. (See Figure 11-29.) Some victims report the pain is so intense that they cannot open doors or shake hands and that they require corrective surgery.

Figure 11-29 Carpal tunnel syndrome

Figure 11-30 Ergonomic keyboard

Ergonomically correct keyboards have recently been developed to help prevent injury from heavy computer use. (See Figure 11-30.) In addition to using ergonomic keyboards, you should take frequent short rest breaks and gently massage your hands. Experts also advise getting plenty of sleep and exercise, watching your weight, sitting up straight and learning stress-management techniques.

MENTAL HEALTH

Computer technology offers many ways of improving productivity, but it also creates some irritants that may be counterproductive.

- **Noise:** Computing can be quite noisy. Voice input and output can be distracting for co-workers. Working next to some types of printers can leave one with ringing ears. Also, users may develop headaches and tension from continual exposure to the high-frequency, barely audible squeal produced by cooling fans and vibrating parts inside the system unit. This is particularly true for women, who according to recent studies hear high-frequency sounds better than men do.
  Head-mounted microphones and earphones greatly reduce the effect of voice input and output. Acoustical tile and sound-muffling covers are available for reducing the noise from co-workers and impact printers. Tightening loose system unit components will reduce high-frequency noise.
- **Electronic monitoring:** Research shows that workers whose performance is monitored electronically suffer more health problems than do those watched by human supervisors. For instance, a computer may monitor the number of keystrokes a data-entry clerk completes in a day. It might tally the time a customer-service person takes to handle a call. The company might then decide to shorten the time allowed and to continue monitoring to ensure compliance. By so doing, it may force a pace leading to physical problems, such as RSI, and mental health difficulties. One study found that electronically monitored employees reported more tension, extreme anxiety, depression, anger, and severe fatigue than those who were not electronically monitored.
  Recently it has been shown that electronic monitoring actually is not necessary. For instance, both Federal Express and Bell Canada replaced electronic monitoring with occasional monitoring by human managers. They found that employee productivity stayed up and even increased.

A new word—*technostress*—has been proposed to describe the stress associated with computer use that is harmful to people. **Technostress** is the tension that arises when we have to unnaturally adapt to computers rather than having computers adapt to us.

DESIGN

Electronic products from microcomputers to microwave ovens to VCRs offer the promise of more efficiency and speed. Often, however, the products are so overloaded with features that users cannot figure them out. Because a microprocessor chip handles not just one operation but several, some manufacturers feel obliged to pile on the bells and whistles. Thus, many home and office products, while being fancy technology platforms, are difficult for humans to use.

A recent trend among manufacturers is to deliberately strip down the features offered, rather than to constantly do all that is possible. In appliances, this restraint is shown among certain types of high-end audio equipment, which comes with fewer buttons and lights. In computers, there are similar trends. Surveys show that consumers want plug-and-play equipment—machines that they can simply turn on and with which they can quickly start working. Thus, computers are being made easier to use, with more menus, windows, icons, and pictures.

For a summary of ergonomic concerns, see Figure 11-31.

Problem	Remedy
Eyestrain and headache	Take frequent breaks, avoid screen glare, place object at fixed focal distance
Back and neck pain	Use adjustable equipment
Repetitive strain injury	Use ergonomically correct keyboards, take frequent breaks
Noise	Use head-mounted microphones and earphones, install acoustical tile and sound-muffling covers, tighten system unit components
Stress from excessive monitoring	Remove electronic monitoring

Figure 11-31 Summary of ergonomic concerns

Concept Check

- What is ergonomics and why is it important?
- Discuss some of the most significant physical concerns and how they can be avoided.
- Discuss some of the most significant mental concerns and how they can be avoided.

THE ENVIRONMENT

The computer industry has responded to the Energy Star program with the Green PC. You can help by conserving, recycling, and educating.

What do you suppose uses the greatest amount of electricity in the work place? Microcomputers do. They account for 5 percent of the electricity used. Increased power production translates to increased air pollution, depletion of nonrenewable resources, and other environmental hazards.

The Environmental Protection Agency (EPA) has created the **Energy Star** program to discourage waste in the microcomputer industry. Along with over 50 manufacturers, the EPA has established a goal of reducing power requirements for system units, monitors, and printers. The industry has responded with the concept of the **Green PC.** (See Figure 11-32.)

THE GREEN PC

The basic elements of the Green PC are:

- **System Unit:** Using existing technology from portable computers, the system unit (1) uses an energy-saving microprocessor that requires a minimal amount of power, (2) employs microprocessor and hard-disk drives that shift to an energy-saving or sleep mode when not in operation, (3) replaces the conventional supply unit with an adapter that requires less electricity, and (4) eliminates the cooling fan.
- **Display:** Displays have been made more energy efficient by using (1) flat panels that require less energy than the traditional monitors, (2) special power-down monitors that automatically reduce power consumption when not in use, and (3) screen-saver software that clears the display whenever it is not in use.

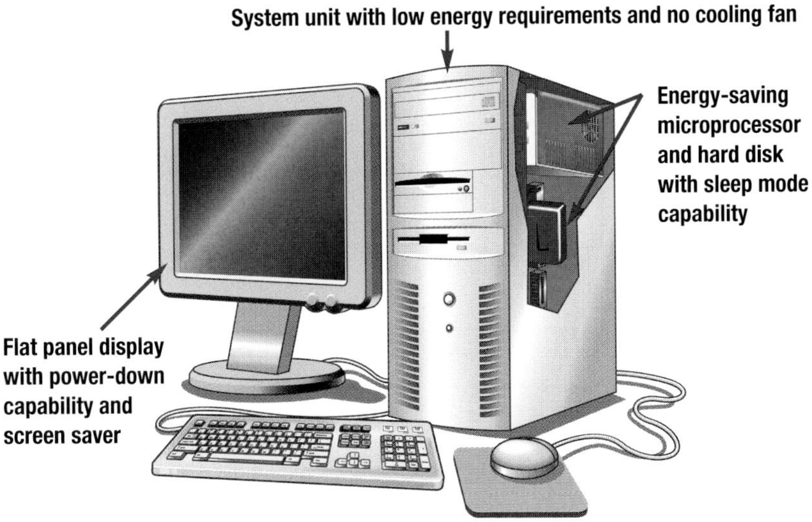
System unit with low energy requirements and no cooling fan
Energy-saving microprocessor and hard disk with sleep mode capability
Flat panel display with power-down capability and screen saver

Figure 11-32 The Green PC

- **Manufacturing:** Computer manufacturers such as Intel, Apple, Compaq, and others are using fewer harmful chemicals in production. Particular attention is given to **chlorofluorocarbons (CFCs)** in solvents and cleaning agents. (CFCs can travel into the atmosphere and are suspected by some in the scientific community to deplete the earth's ozone layer.) Toxic nickel and other heavy metals are being eliminated or reduced in the manufacturing processes.

Of course, not all of these technologies and manufacturing processes are used for all microcomputers. But more and more of them are.

PERSONAL RESPONSIBILITY

Some of the things that you, as a computer user, can do to help protect the environment are the following:

- **Conserve:** The EPA estimates that 30 to 40 percent of computer users leave their machines running days, nights, and weekends. When finished working for the day, turn off all computers and other energy-consuming devices. The EPA also estimates that 80 percent of the time a monitor is on, no one is looking at it. Use screen-saver programs that blank the computer screen after three to five minutes of inactivity.
- **Recycle:** U.S. businesses use an enormous amount of paper each year—a pile 48,900 miles high. Much of that, as well as the paper we throw out at home, can be recycled. Other recyclable items include computer boxes, packaging material, printer cartridges, and floppy disks. Last year over 24 million computers were thrown away. (See Figure 11-33.) Only 14 percent were recycled. Recycle discarded computers by contacting any one of the groups listed in Figure 11-34.
- **Educate:** Be aware of and learn more about ecological dangers of all types. Make your concerns known to manufacturers and retail agencies. Support ecologically sound products.

Figure 11-33 Discarded computer components

Figure 11-34 Computer recycling groups

Organization	Web Site
Computers for Schools Association	www.detwiler.org
Computers for Youth	www.cfy.org
National Cristina Foundation	www.cristinak.org
Share Technology	www.sharetechnology.org

Concept Check

- ✔ What is a Green PC?
- ✔ What are the basic elements of the Green PC?
- ✔ What other actions can you take to help protect the environment?

Careers in IT

Cryptographer

Cryptography is the science of disguising and revealing encrypted information. In terms of Information Technology, cryptography usually refers to keeping any intercepted information private. For example, such information may be financial data, like banking and credit card information used in online shopping, or private e-mail and correspondence. Cryptographers design systems, break systems, and do research on encryption. Responsibilities typically do not include building and maintaining the computer networks that use cryptography; these are the duties of security engineers and network administrators. In general, cryptographers are mathematicians who specialize in making and breaking codes.

Many cryptographers work as consultants or professors of cryptography, yet there are full-time positions available at some large corporations or for the government. A PhD in cryptography is usually an essential prerequisite for a position as a cryptographer. However, all cryptographers must have broad experience in both mathematics and computer science.

Cryptographers can expect to earn an annual salary of $60,000 to $85,000. Opportunities for advancement typically depend on experience; the most competitive field will be research positions at universities. Those with experience in computer science and information technology should be among the most employable mathematicians and increasingly in demand. To learn more about becoming a cryptographer visit us at http://www.mhhe.com/oleary/CT05 and select Careers in IT from Tim's Toolbox.

A Look to the Future

Presence Technology Makes Finding People Easy

How would you like the devices you use to alert others when you are using them? What if you sat down to watch television and a message popped up alerting you that a friend wants to chat? What if you could instantly know what is the best way to get in touch with someone you know? Presence technology is designed to meet all of these needs, and many more.

Many people are currently exposed to presence technology through their instant messaging software. When a user signs on to a system, friends are alerted to his or her presence. Many manufacturers of personal computing devices and cellular phones are currently developing presence technology. Analysts expect presence technology to become a feature of everything from your computer to your car. Some even anticipate that your friends will be able to tell where you are and which device (PDA, television, telephone) is the best way to contact you. While there are many advantages to such a system, the potential loss of privacy is of concern to many. They argue the potential abuse by advertisers and others makes presence technology a threat to privacy. Supporters of this technology suggest the user would have control over when and where they are "seen."

What do you think? Would you like to know that you are always available to those who need to get in touch with you? What are the potential advantages of this type of technology? Experts suggest presence technology will become a standard feature of new cars, phones, and appliances. What do you think? Would you buy a television that lets everyone know you are watching TV instead of working on homework?

VISUAL SUMMARY

PRIVACY AND SECURITY

PRIVACY

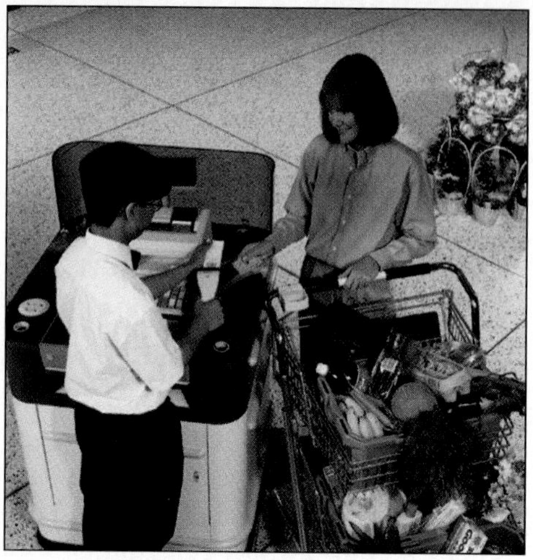

Computer ethics are guidelines for moral computer use. Four computer ethics issues:

- **Privacy** concerns collection and use of data about individuals.
- **Accuracy** relates to the responsibility of those who collect data to ensure correctness.
- **Property** relates to who owns the data.
- **Access** relates to the responsibility of those who have data to control who is able to use it.

Large Databases

Large organizations are constantly compiling information about us. **Reverse directories** are special telephone directories that list telephone numbers followed by subscriber names. **Information resellers (information brokers)** collect and sell personal data. **Electronic profiles** are compiled from databases to provide highly detailed and personalized descriptions of individuals.

Two key personal privacy issues are:

- Spreading information without personal consent. **Identity theft** is the illegal assumption of someone's identity for the purposes of economic gain.
- Spreading inaccurate information. **Mistaken identity** occurs when an electronic profile of one person is switched with another. The **Freedom of Information Act** entitles individuals access to governmental records.

PRIVACY

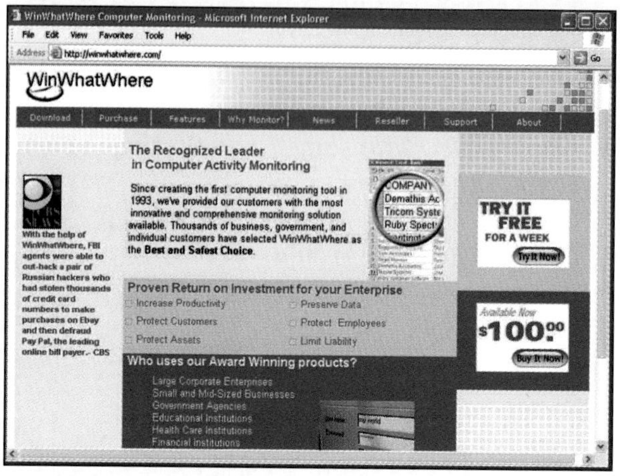

Private Networks

Many organizations monitor employee e-mail and computer files using special software called **snoopware.** Most online information services restrict libelous, obscene, or other offensive material.

Internet and the Web

Many people believe that while using the Web as long as they are selective about disclosing their name and other personal information, little can be done to invade their privacy. This is called the **illusion of anonymity.**

Created by browsers, **history files** record locations of sites visited by a computer system. **Cookies** are specialized programs deposited onto your computer system that record sites visited, activity at sites, and other information.

Two basic types of cookies:

- **Traditional cookies**—monitor activities at a single site.
- **Ad network cookies**—also known as **adware cookies,** monitor activities across all sites visited.

Special programs called **cookie-cutter programs** allow users to selectively filter or block the most intrusive cookies while allowing selective traditional cookies to operate.

To be a competent and knowledgeable end user you need to be aware of the potential impact of technology on people. You need to be sensitive to and knowledgeable about personal privacy, organizational security, ergonomics, and the environmental impact of technology.

PRIVACY

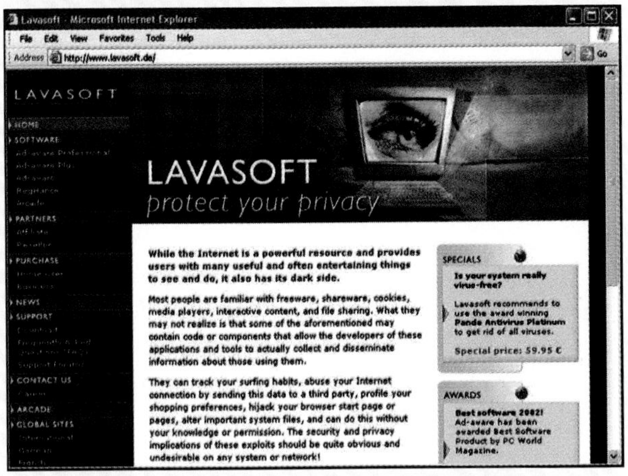

The term **spyware** is used to describe a wide range of programs that are designed to secretly record and report an individual's activities on the Internet. Ad network cookies are just one type of spyware. Two other types are:

- **Web bugs**—programs typically hidden within the HTML code as a graphic image. They migrate whenever an unsuspecting user visits a Web site containing a Web bug or opens an infected e-mail message. Often work with cookies to collect and report information back to a predefined server on the Web.
- **Computer monitoring—**record every activity and keystroke made on your computer system. Also known as **sniffer programs** and **keystroke loggers,** these programs are used by businesses, CIA, FBI, private investigators, and others.

A new category of programs known as **spy removal programs** has recently evolved designed to detect Web bugs and monitoring software.

Major Privacy Laws

There are numerous federal laws governing privacy matters. Nonetheless, privacy remains primarily an ethical issue. To respond to privacy concerns, a Code of Fair Information Practice has been established.

SECURITY

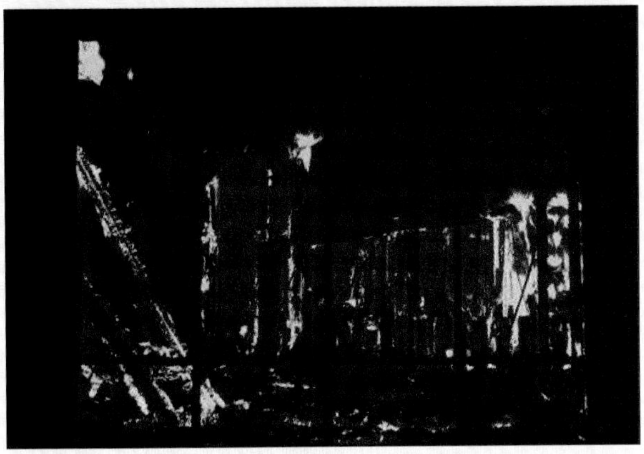

Threats to Computer Security

Keeping information private depends on keeping computers safe from computer criminals, natural hazards, and other threats.

Computer Criminals

There are a variety of different types of computer criminals including:

- Employees—the largest category of computer criminals.
- Outside users—often suppliers or clients that may have access to computer systems.
- Hackers and crackers—**hackers** gain access for the fun and challenge while **crackers** do it for malicious purposes.
- Organized crime—including counterfeiting and forgery.
- Terrorists—potentially crash satellites and wage economic warfare.

Computer Crime

Computer crime is an illegal action in which a criminal uses special knowledge of computer technology. These crimes can take a variety of different forms including:

SECURITY

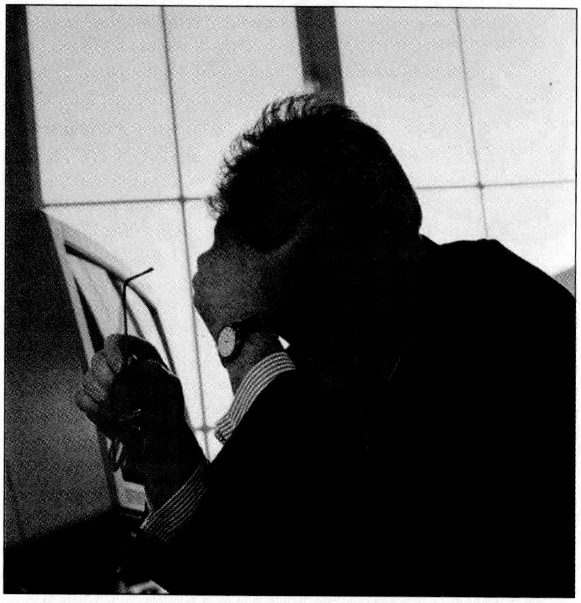

- **Malicious programs,** also known as **malware** (**mal**icious soft**ware**), include viruses, worms, and Trojan horses. **Viruses** migrate through networks and operating systems and most attach to programs and databases. **Computer Abuse Amendments Act of 1994** makes spreading a virus a federal offence. **Worms** are special viruses that self-replicate to slow or stop a computer's operations. **Trojan horses** are programs that come into a computer system disguised as something else. While not a virus, Trojan horses deposit viruses onto unsuspecting computer systems.
- **Denial of service (DoS)** attacks attempt to shut down or stop a computer system or network. Unlike a worm that self-replicates, a DoS attack floods a computer or network with request for information and data. Typical targets include Internet service providers and specific Web sites.
- **Internet scams** are fraudulent or deceptive acts or operations designed to trick individuals into spending their time and money with little or no return. Common scams include identity theft, chain letters, auction fraud, vacation prizes, and advance fee loans. Almost all Internet scams initiated by mass e-mails.

SECURITY

- **Theft** takes many forms including stealing hardware, software, data, and computer time. Unauthorized copying of programs is called software **piracy** and protected against by the **Software Copyright Act of 1980.**
- **Data manipulation** involves changing data or leaving prank messages. The **Computer Fraud and Abuse Act of 1986** makes it a federal crime for unauthorized viewing or copying data across state lines and prohibits unauthorized use of computers owned by the government or any federally insured financial institution.
- Other hazards include natural disasters, civil strife, terrorism, technological failures, and human error. **Surge protectors** protect against **voltage surges** or **spikes.**

Measures to Protect Computer Security

Security involves keeping hardware, software, data, and programs safe. Some measures are **encrypting** messages, restricting access by using **passwords** and **firewalls,** anticipating disasters (**hot sites** are emergency facilities; **cold sites** are empty shells), backing up data and storing the data in a safe remote location.

ERGONOMICS

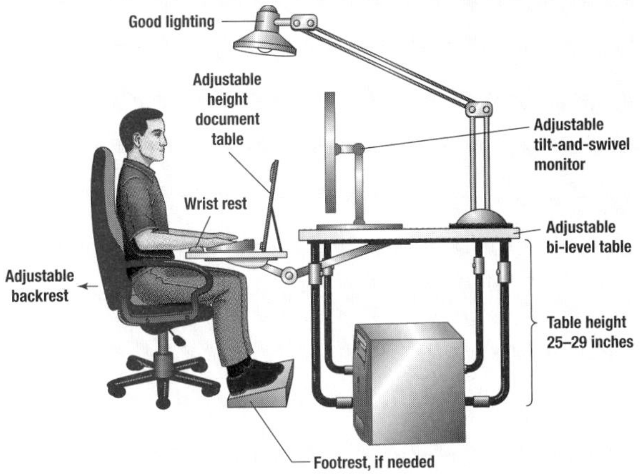
Good lighting
Adjustable height document table
Adjustable tilt-and-swivel monitor
Wrist rest
Adjustable bi-level table
Adjustable backrest
Table height 25–29 inches
Footrest, if needed

Ergonomics is the study of human factors related to things people use, including computers.

Physical Health

Physical health problems and their solutions include:

- Eyestrain and headache—take frequent breaks; avoid glare on the monitor.
- Back and neck pains—use adjustable chairs, tables, monitor stands, keyboards, footrests.
- **Repetitive strain injury (RSI),** also known as **repetitive motion industry,** includes **carpal tunnel syndrome**—take frequent breaks; use good posture; adopt healthy lifestyle; use ergonomic keyboards.

Mental Health

Counterproductive mental irritations include:

- Noise from clattering printers and high-frequency squeal from computers.
- Stress from electronic monitoring. Unnatural adaptation to computers can cause **technostress.**

Design

Computers are being designed for easier and healthier use. There is a trend toward simplifying features offered on new models.

THE ENVIRONMENT

Organization	Web Site
Computers for Schools Association	www.detwiler.org
Computers for Youth	www.cfy.org
National Cristina Foundation	www.cristinak.org
Share Technology	www.sharetechnology.org

Microcomputers are the greatest users of electricity in the workplace. The EPA has established the **Energy Star program** to promote energy-efficient computer use. The computer industry has responded with the concept of the **Green PC.**

The Green PC

The basic elements of the Green PC include:

- System units with energy-saving processors, sleep-mode capability, efficient adapters, and no cooling fans.
- Display units that replace CRT displays with flat panels, use special power-down monitors, and use screen-saver software.
- Manufacturing that eliminates or reduces the use of harmful chemicals such as **chlorofluorocarbons (CFCs),** nickel, and other heavy metals.

Personal Responsibility

As a responsible computer user, you can help protect the environment by:

- Conserving energy by turning off computer systems at night and using screen-savers.
- Recycling paper, computer boxes, packaging materials, printer cartridges, and floppy disks.
- Educating yourself and others about ecological dangers and using ecologically sound products.

KEY TERMS

access (409)
accuracy (409)
ad network cookie (414)
adware cookie (414)
biometric scanning (427)
carpal tunnel syndrome (430)
chlorofluorocarbons (CFCs) (433)
cold site (428)
Computer Abuse Amendments Act of 1994 (422)
computer crime (421)
computer ethics (409)
Computer Fraud and Abuse Act of 1986 (425)
computer monitoring software (415)
cookie (413)
cookie-cutter program (414)
cracker (422)
cumulative trauma disorder (430)
data security (428)
denial of service attack (DoS) (423)
disaster recovery plan (428)
electronic monitoring (431)
electronic profile (410)
encrypting (427)
Energy Star (432)
ergonomics (429)
ethics (409)
firewall (427)
Freedom of Information Act (411)
Green PC (432)
hacker (422)
history file (413)
hot site (428)
identity theft (411)
illusion of anonymity (412)
information brokers (410)
information resellers (410)
Internet scam (424)
keystroke logger (419)
malware (422)
mistaken identity (411)
password (427)
physical security (428)
privacy (409)
property (409)
repetitive motion injury (430)
repetitive strain injury (RSI) (430)
reverse directory (410)
scam (424)
security (426)
snoopware (412)
Software Copyright Act of 1980 (424)
software piracy (424)
sniffer program (419)
spike (426)
spy removal program (419)
spyware (415)
surge protector (426)
technostress (431)
traditional cookies (414)
Trojan horse (423)
virus (422)
virus checker (423)
voltage surge (426)
Web bug (419)
worm (423)

To test your knowledge of these key terms with animated flash cards, select Flash Cards from Tim's Toolbox at http://www.mhhe.com/oleary/CT05.

CHAPTER REVIEW

CROSSWORD

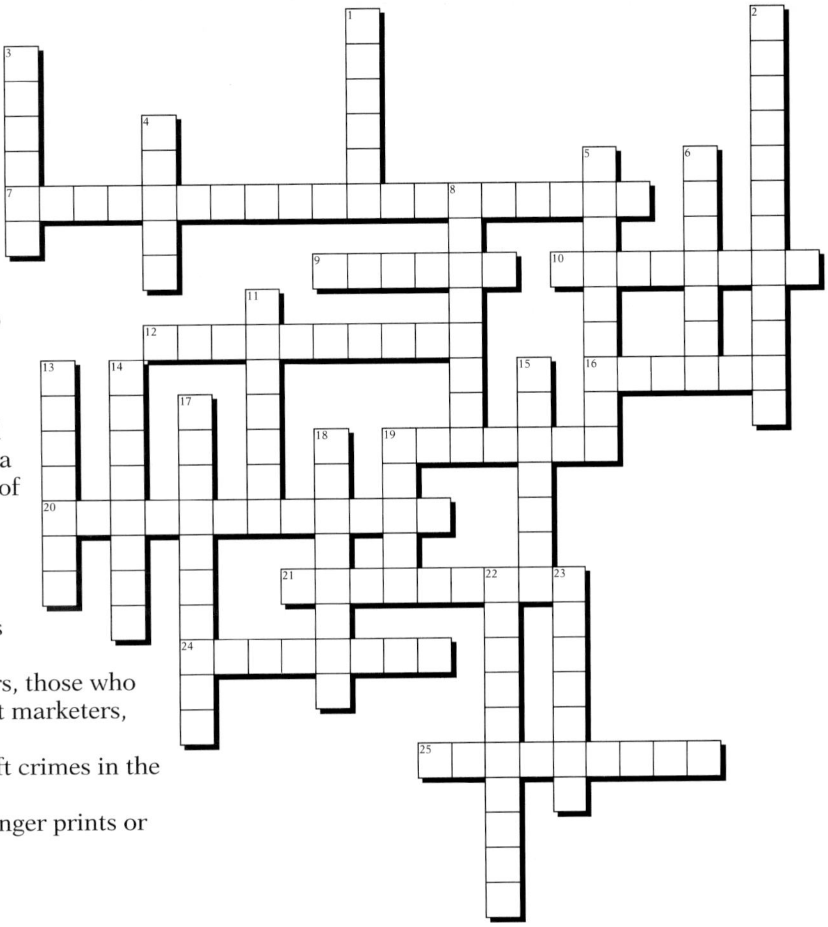

ACROSS

7 Can travel into the atmosphere and are suspected by some in the scientific community to deplete the earth's ozone layer
9 Unauthorized copying of software for personal gain
10 Empty shells in which hardware must be installed
12 Program created by the EPA to discourage waste in the microcomputer industry
16 Relates to the responsibility of those who have data to control and who is able to use that data
19 Used to describe a wide range of programs that are designed to secretly record and report an individual's activities on the Internet
20 Monitors your activities across all sites you visit
21 Also called information brokers, those who sell electronic profiles to direct marketers, fundraisers, and others
24 One of the fastest growing theft crimes in the country
25 Scanning device that checks finger prints or retinal scans

DOWN

1 Person who gains unauthorized access to a computer system for the fun and challenge of it
2 The tension that arises when we have to unnaturally adapt to computers rather than having computers adapt to us
3 Standards of moral conduct
4 Program that migrates through networks and operating systems and can attach itself to different programs and databases
5 A type of computer monitoring software used by businesses to monitor their employees
6 Special emergency facilities that are fully equipped backup computer centers
8 Relates to the responsibility of those who collect data to ensure that the data is correct
11 The computer industry has responded to the EPA Energy Star program with this concept
13 Relates to the collection and use of personal information and remains primarily an ethical issue
14 Acts as a security buffer between the corporation's private network and all external networks, including the Internet
15 Person who gains unauthorized access to a computer system for malicious purposes
17 Coding messages
18 Relates to who owns the data
19 This excess of electricity may destroy chips or other electronic components of a computer
22 The study of human factors related to things people use
23 Also called a keystroke logger, a program that records every activity and keystroke made on your computer system including credit card numbers, bank account numbers, and e-mail messages.

For an interactive crossword puzzle select Crosswords from Tim's Toolbox at http://www.mhhe.com/oleary/CT05.

MULTIPLE CHOICE

Circle the letter or fill in the correct answer.

1. The ethical issue that relates to the responsibility of those who collect data to ensure that the data is correct is ________.
   a. privacy
   b. accuracy
   c. property
   d. access
   e. ethics
2. The ethical issue that concerns the collection and use of data about individuals is ________.
   a. privacy
   b. accuracy
   c. property
   d. access
   e. ethics
3. ________ is a term used to describe a wide range of programs that secretly record and report an individual's activities on the Internet.
   a. Worm
   b. Utility
   c. Virus
   d. Spyware
   e. Suite
4. The largest category of computer criminals is ________.
   a. crackers
   b. hackers
   c. agents
   d. organized criminals
   e. employees
5. ________ is/are concerned with protecting information, hardware, and software.
   a. Users
   b. FBI agents
   c. Security
   d. The Department of Defense
   e. Protection programs
6. ________ is concerned with protecting hardware from possible human and natural disasters.
   a. Physical security
   b. Data security
   c. The FBI
   d. Encryption
   e. Energy Star
7. ________ is concerned with fitting the job to the worker rather than forcing the worker to contort to fit a job.
   a. Human Resources
   b. Ergonomics
   c. Energy Star
   d. RSI
   e. An HMO
8. ________ is also called repetitive motion injury and cumulative trauma disorder.
   a. RSI
   b. ARD
   c. TVT
   d. EMI
   e. BRM
9. ________ describes the stress that is associated with computers.
   a. RSI
   b. EMI
   c. Technostress
   d. Computer Use Distress
   e. Cumulative TechStress
10. Environmentally friendly system units, display, and manufacturing are the basic elements of the ________.
    a. Energy Star
    b. Green PC
    c. Standard System
    d. Millennium Plan
    e. EarthTech Program

To test your knowledge of this chapter, select Self Test from Tim's Toolbox at http://www.mhhe.com/oleary/CT05.

MATCHING

Match each numbered item with the most closely related lettered item. Write your answers in the spaces provided.

a. ad network cookies
b. cold site
c. computer crime
d. cookie
e. cookie-cutter program
f. cracker
g. denial of service attack
h. disaster recovery plan
i. encrypting
j. ethics
k. firewall
l. hacker
m. illusion of anonymity
n. property
o. reverse directory
p. snoopware
q. spike
r. virus checkers
s. viruses
t. worm

1. Standards of moral conduct. ____
2. Relates to who owns data and rights to software. ____
3. Directory that lists subscriber names followed by telephone numbers. ____
4. Programs that record virtually every activity on a computer system. ____
5. Belief that there is little threat to personal privacy via the Internet. ____
6. Specialized programs that record information on Web site visitors. ____
7. Cookies that continually monitor Web activity and report information back to marketing organizations. ____
8. Program that blocks the most intrusive ad network cookies. ____
9. Illegal action involving special knowledge of computer technology. ____
10. Person who gains unauthorized access to a computer system for the fun and challenge of it. ____
11. Person who gains unauthorized access to a computer system for malicious purposes. ____
12. Hidden instructions that migrate through networks and operating systems and become embedded in different programs. ____
13. Fills a computer system with self-replicating information. ____
14. Type of virus that overwhelms Web sites with data making them inaccessible to users. ____
15. Programs that alert users when certain viruses enter a system. ____
16. Excess of electricity that may destroy chips or other electronic computer components. ____
17. Coding information so that only authorized users can read or use it. ____
18. Security hardware and software that controls access to internal computer networks. ____
19. Plan used by large corporations describing ways to continue operations following a disaster until normal computer operations can be restored. ____
20. Special emergency facility in which hardware must be installed but which is available to a company in the event of a disaster. ____

OPEN-ENDED

On a separate sheet of paper, respond to each question or statement.

1. Discuss the relationship between databases and privacy.
2. Discuss the Code of Fair Information Act. Why has this Act not been made into law?
3. Discuss the various kinds of computer criminals.
4. What are the principal measures used to protect computer security? What is encryption? How is it used by corporations and individuals?
5. What is ergonomics? How does computer use impact mental health? Physical health? What steps can be taken to alleviate technostress? What is ergonomic design?

USING TECHNOLOGY

1 Spyware

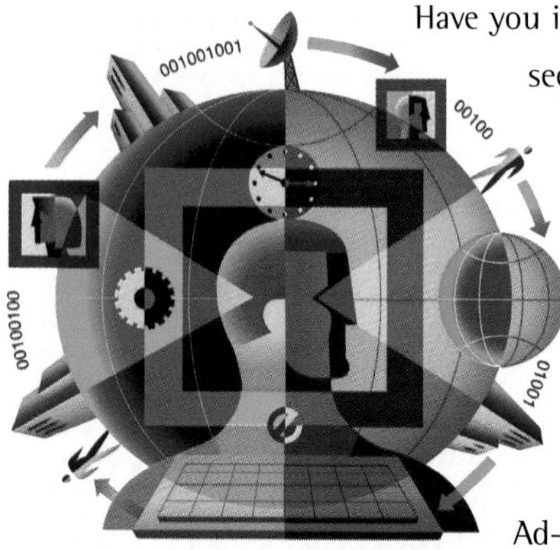

Have you installed any free software from the Internet? Did you know that seemingly harmless software might actually be spying on you, even sending personal information to advertisers or worse? Fortunately, spyware removal programs can help. After reviewing Making IT Work for You: Spyware Removal on pages 418 and 419 and visiting our Web site at http://www.mhhe.com/oleary/CT05 and selecting Using Technology from Tim's Toolbox, answer the following questions: (a) Define spyware and discuss how it works. (b) Describe the process for downloading and installing Lavasoft's Ad-Aware. (c) Describe the capabilities of Ad-Adware. (d) Do you think that spyware might be on your computer? If yes, how do suppose the spyware was deposited onto your system? If no, why are you so confident?

2 Anonymous Web Browsing

Are you concerned about others tracking your online activities? Did you know that it is possible to review all the Web sites you visited on a particular computer or network? The Anonymizer is one solution. Visit our site at http://www.mhhe.com/oleary/CT05 and select Using Technology from Tim's Toolbox to link to the Anonymizer Web site. Browse a couple of Web sites anonymously, and then answer the following questions: (a) How does Anonymizer ensure anonymity? (b) What are the drawbacks to using Anonymizer for all of your Web activities? (c) What type of monitoring cannot be averted by Anonymizer? (d) Would you use anonymous Web browsing? Why or why not?

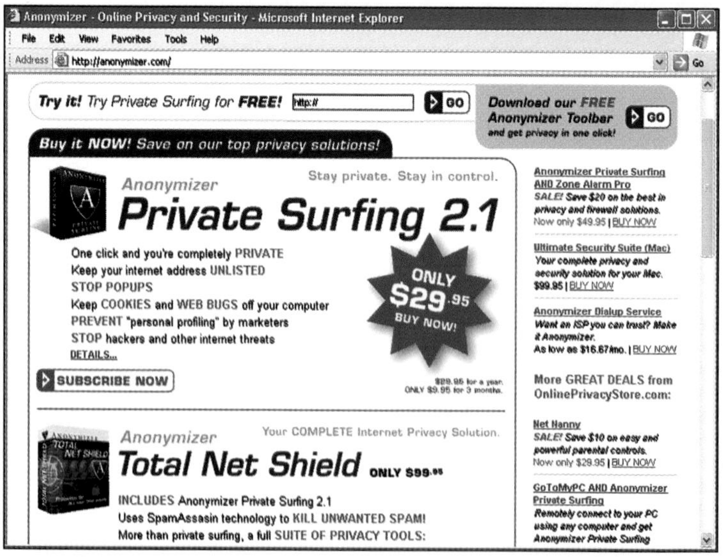

Personal Firewalls 3

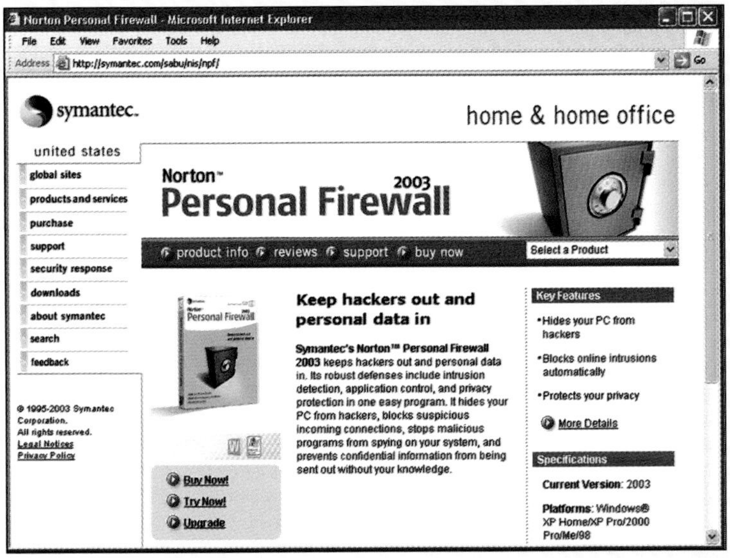

Firewalls used to just be for large servers. Today, firewalls are available for almost any device that connects to the Internet, and are essential to ensure security. Connect to our Web site at http://www.mhhe.com/oleary/CT05 and select Using Technology from Tim's Toolbox to link to a personal firewall product for home users. Once connected, read about the firewall, and then answer the following questions: (a) Is this firewall a hardware or software solution? (b) Describe the procedure for installing the firewall. (c) What types of security risks does this firewall protect against? (d) Are there any security risks the firewall does not cover? If so, how can those risks be reduced?

Ergonomic Workstations 4

As public awareness and understanding of repetitive motion workplace injuries have grown, more ergonomic products have become available. Visit our Web site at http://www.mhhe.com/oleary/CT05 and select Using Technology from Tim's Toolbox to link to a site that educates the public on correct ergonomics for safety and comfort. Once connected, explore the site, and briefly answer the following questions: (a) What office equipment or furniture is covered? (b) Summarize the recommendations for each component. (c) What additional resources are available from the site to assist in creating an ergonomic workplace?

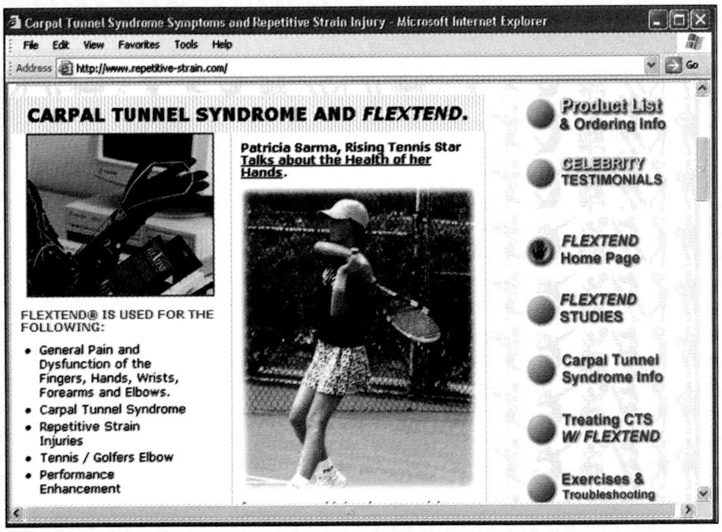

EXPANDING YOUR KNOWLEDGE

1 SimNet CD

Complete Chapter 11: Privacy and Security on the SimNet Computer Concepts CD and then answer the following questions:

a. Referencing the section "Ergonomics," when should a wrist rest not be used?

b. Referencing the section "Privacy Issues," describe how employers protect themselves from dishonest employees.

c. Referencing the section "Security Issues," describe the security issues that computer users should be aware of.

d. Referencing the section "Security Issues," describe the best steps in creating and maintaining a secure password.

2 Online Backup

One of the best ways to safeguard important personal or corporate data is to use an online backup service. Research three or four online backup services, and then answer the following questions: (a) What are the general features of online backup services? (b) What types of emergencies do online backups help with that other backup methods do not? (c) How are backups scheduled? (d) Is this service a replacement for making backups locally? Why or why not?

EXPANDING YOUR KNOWLEDGE

Privacy Avocation Online 3

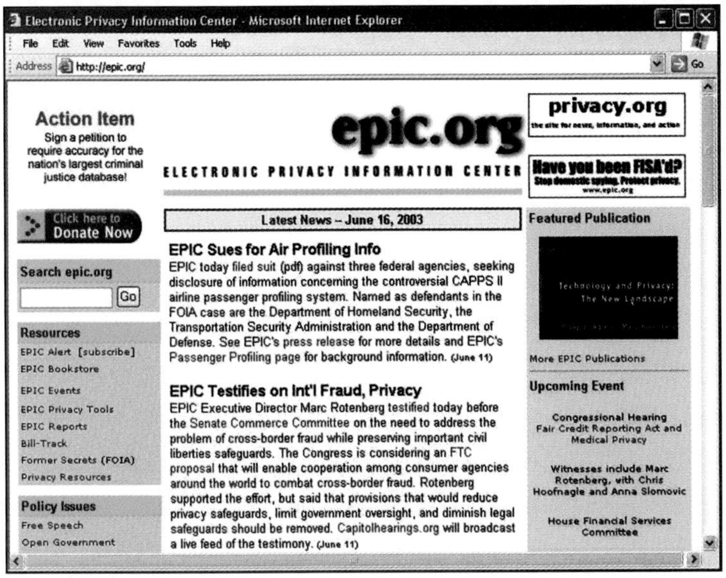

For those concerned with online privacy, there are many Web sites available that offer cutting-edge information on related software, hardware, and policy. Connect to our Web site at http://www.mhhe.com/oleary/CT05 and select Expanding Your Knowledge from Tim's Toolbox to link to a site that features online privacy information. Once connected, browse the site, and then answer to the following questions: (a) What topics does this site deal with? (b) Summarize the most useful or interesting information you found on the site. (c) Are concerns about online privacy justified or overly paranoid? Cite specific examples and justify your answer.

Air Travel Database 4

To curb possible terrorist threats, the government has implemented a controversial database, known as the Computer Assisted Passenger Pre-screening System (CAPPS), to perform background checks on travelers before allowing them on aircraft. This database determines a "possible threat score" for each individual to determine whether they can fly. This system relies on airlines to share information on passengers that once was considered confidential. Research CAPPS on the Internet, and then answer to the following questions: (a) How does CAPPS determine who is a security risk? (b) What personal information is gathered by CAPPS? (c) How might CAPPS infringe on personal privacy? (d) Would you prefer to travel with or without the CAPPS system in place? Justify your answer.

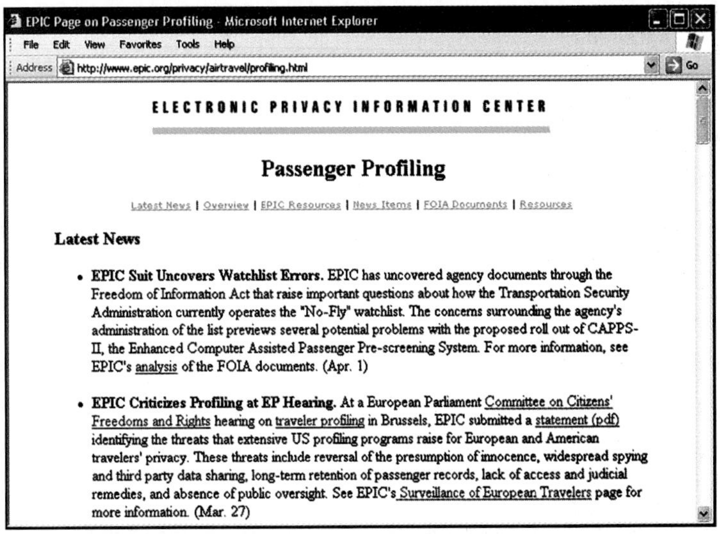

BUILDING YOUR PORTFOLIO

1 Firewalls

Firewalls are a necessary component of complete computer security. They consist of hardware and software that control access to internal networks. A firewall usually includes a proxy server as a gatekeeper. Research firewalls and computer crime and write a one-page paper titled "Firewall Security" that addresses the following: (a) Define the term firewall. (b) What types of computer crime do firewalls protect against? (c) What types of computer crime are firewalls unable to protect against? Why? (d) What type of firewall protection might a corporation use? (e) What firewall protection is available for home users?

2 Environmental Hazards

Many computer users are familiar with the frustration of a computer becoming obsolete after just a couple of years of service. PC technology advances at an incredible rate, and new computers must replace the old ones. But what happens to all that used computer equipment? Many PC components are toxic, and according to one recent report, more than 3.2 million tons will end up in landfills annually. Research computer component recycling on the Web, and then write a one-page paper titled "Environmental Hazards" that addresses the following topics: (a) What dangers do used PC components pose to safety and the environment? (b) What recycling options exist for used PCs? (c) In your opinion, what obligations do PC owners have regarding their used equipment? What about PC manufacturers? Explain your answers.

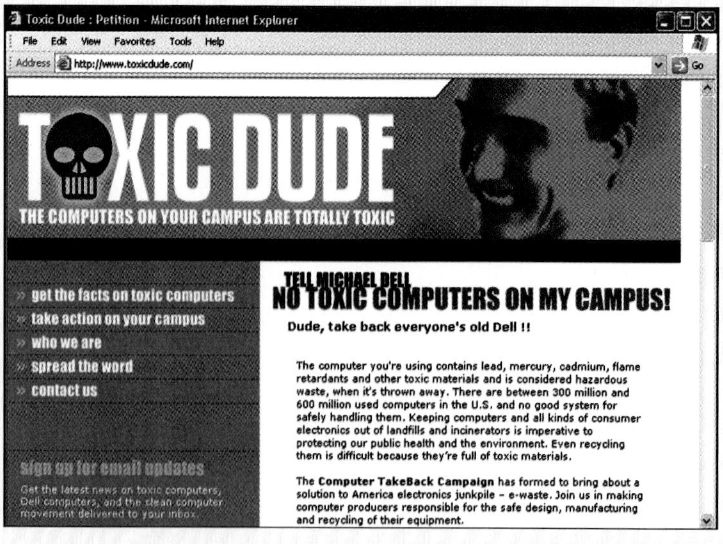

Plagiarism 3

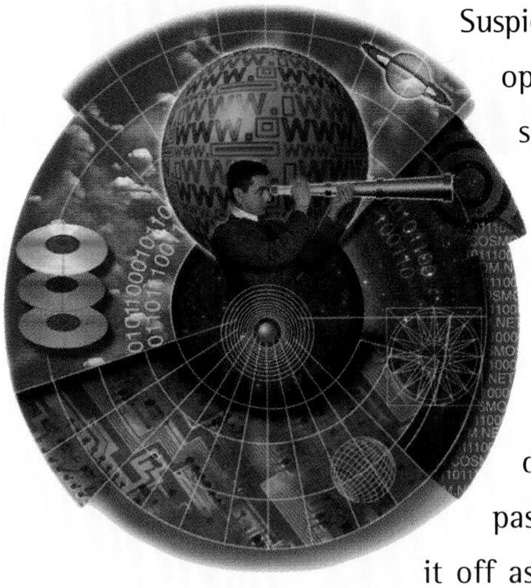

Suspicious of cheating, a professor at the University of Virginia developed a program to compare the term papers of his current and past students. Alarmingly, he found that 122 students' work suggested plagiarizing. Consider the implications of this case, and then write a one-page paper titled "Plagiarism" that addresses the following questions: (a) With more and more academic submissions being stored in an electronic format, how is the ease of copying another's work easier? (b) For the same reason, how is detecting an unoriginal work easier? (c) Have you ever copied and pasted text from a Web site or other electronic document and passed it off as your own? (d) How does "borrowing" work in this way affect other students? What about the original author? Explain.

Facial Recognition 4

As new technologies emerge which promise to enhance our security, our privacy may be at stake. A recent example is the introduction of facial recognition systems in public places for use by police officers. Such systems have recently caught the attention of privacy advocates, as well as the ACLU. Research facial recognition systems on the Web, and then write a one-page paper titled "Facial Recognition" that addresses the following topics: (a) Describe how facial recognition technology works. (b) How can facial recognition technology enhance security? (c) In what ways might facial recognition technology compromise privacy? (Hint: Consider security cameras in department or grocery stores.) (d) Do you approve of facial recognition technology? Explain your answer.

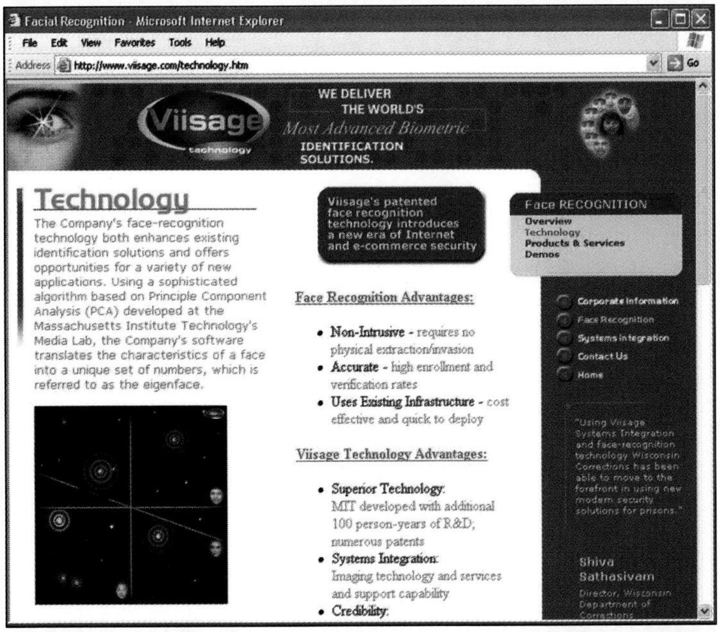

INFORMATION SYSTEMS

OBJECTIVES

After you have read this chapter, you should be able to:

1. **Explain how organizations can be structured according to five functions and three management levels.**
2. **Describe how information flows in an organization.**
3. **Distinguish among a transaction processing system, a management information system, a decision support system, and an executive support system.**
4. **Distinguish between office automation systems and knowledge work systems.**
5. **Explain the difference between data workers and knowledge workers.**

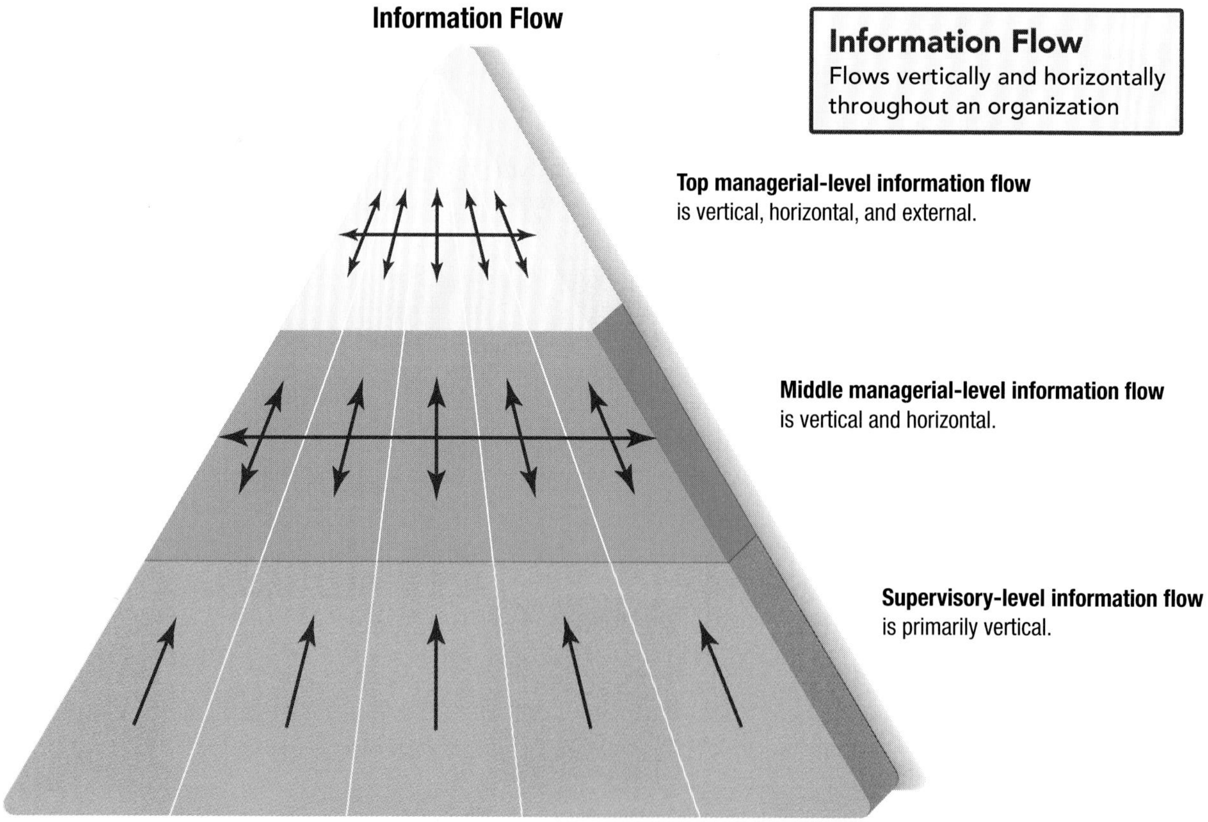
Information Flow
Information Flow
Flows vertically and horizontally throughout an organization
Top managerial-level information flow
is vertical, horizontal, and external.
Middle managerial-level information flow
is vertical and horizontal.
Supervisory-level information flow
is primarily vertical.

An information system is a collection of people, procedures, software, hardware, and data (as we discussed in Chapter 1). They all work together to provide information essential to running an organization. This is information that will successfully produce a product or service and, for profit-oriented enterprises, derive a profit.

Why are computers used in organizations? No doubt you can easily state one reason: to keep records of events. However, another reason might be less obvious: to help make decisions. For example, point-of-sale terminals record sales as well as which salesperson made each sale. This information can be used for decision making. For instance, it can help the sales manager decide which salespeople will get year-end bonuses for doing exceptional work.

The Internet, communication links, and databases connect you with information resources as well as information systems far beyond the surface of your desk. The microcomputer offers you access to a greater quantity of information than was possible a few years ago. In addition, you also have access to a better quality of information. As we show in this chapter, when you tap into a computer-based information system, you not only get information—you also get help in making decisions.

Competent and knowledgeable end users need to understand how the information flows in an organization as it moves through the organization's different functional areas and management levels. They need to be aware of the different types of computer-based information systems, including transaction processing systems, management information systems, decision support systems, and executive support systems. They also need to understand the role and importance of databases to support each level or type of information system.

Information Systems

Information Systems
Support the natural flow of information within an organization

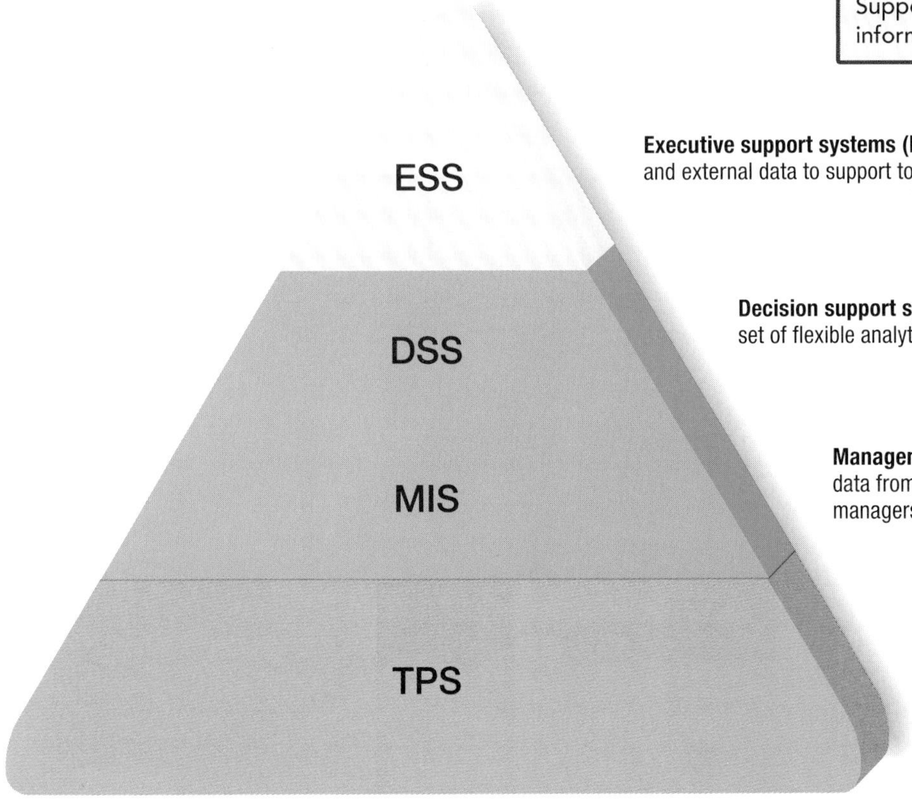

Executive support systems (ESS) use internal data from MIS and TPS and external data to support top-level managers.

Decision support systems (DSS) use data from TPS and a set of flexible analytical tools to support middle managers.

Management information systems (MIS) use data from the TPS to support middle-level managers.

Transaction processing systems (TPS) record day-to-day transactions to support middle managers.

ORGANIZATIONAL INFORMATION FLOW

Organizations can be viewed from a functional perspective. Management has three levels. Information flows up, down, and across among managers and departments.

In large and medium-sized organizations, computerized information systems don't just keep track of transactions and day-to-day business operations. They also support the flow of information within the organization. This information flows both vertically and horizontally. In order to understand this, we need to understand how an organization is structured. One way to examine an organization's structure is to view it from a functional perspective. That is, you can study the different basic functional areas in organizations and the different types of people within these functional areas.

As we describe these, you might consider how they apply to any organization you are familiar with. Or consider how they apply to a hypothetical manufacturer of sporting goods, the HealthWise Group. (See Figure 12-1.) Think of this as a large company that manufactures equipment for sports and physical activities, including those that interest you. These goods range from every type of ball imaginable (from golf to tennis to soccer) to hockey pads, leotards, and exercise bicycles.

Like many organizations, HealthWise Group can be viewed from a functional perspective with various management levels. Effective operations require an efficient and coordinated flow of information throughout the organization.

FUNCTIONS

Depending on the services or products they provide, most organizations have departments that specialize in one of five basic functions. These are accounting, marketing, human resources, production, and research. (See Figure 12-2.)

- **Accounting** records all financial activity from billing customers to paying employees. For example, at HealthWise, the accounting department tracks

Figure 12-1 At HealthWise manufacturing organizational flow makes managing operations flow smoothly

Figure 12-2 The five functions of an organization

Functional Perspective

Human resources finds and hires people and handles matters such as sick leave and retirement benefits. In addition, it is concerned with evaluation, compensation, and professional development.

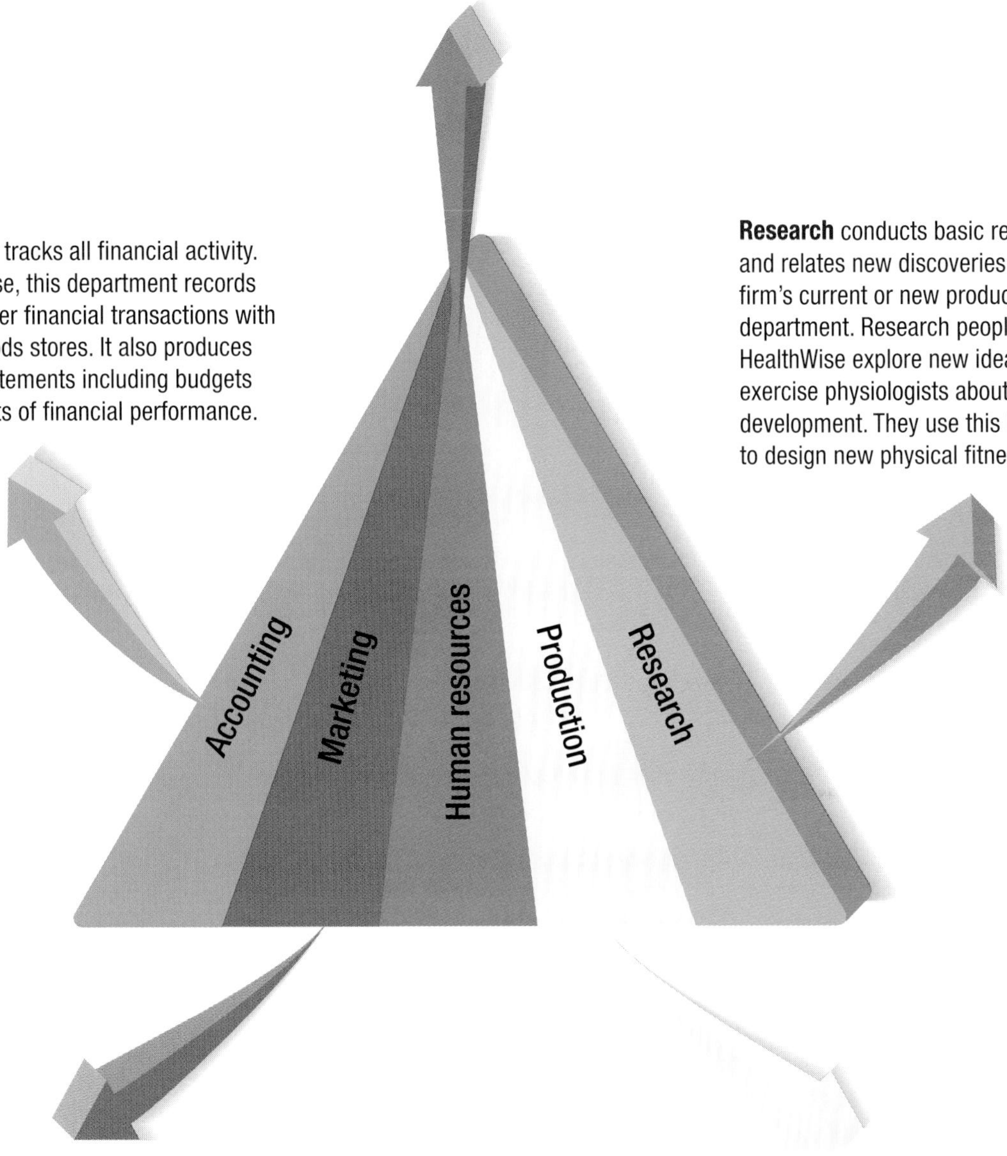

Accounting tracks all financial activity. At HealthWise, this department records bills and other financial transactions with sporting goods stores. It also produces financial statements including budgets and forecasts of financial performance.

Research conducts basic research and relates new discoveries to the firm's current or new products department. Research people at HealthWise explore new ideas from exercise physiologists about muscle development. They use this knowledge to design new physical fitness machines.

Marketing handles planning, pricing, promoting, selling, and distributing goods and services to customers. At HealthWise, they even get involved with creating a customer newsletter that is distributed via the corporate Web page.

Production takes in raw materials and people work to turn out finished goods (or services). It may be a manufacturing activity or—in the case of a retail store—an operations activity. At HealthWise, this department purchases steel and aluminum to be used in weight-lifting and exercise machines.

all sales, payments, and transfers of funds. It also produces reports detailing the financial condition of the company.

- **Marketing** plans, prices, promotes, sells, and distributes the organization's goods and services. At HealthWise, goods include a wide range related to sports and other types of physical activity.
- **Human resources** focuses on people—hiring, training, promoting, and any number of human-centered activities within the organization. This function relates to people in each of the functional areas including accountants, sales representatives, human resource specialists, production workers, and research scientists.
- **Production** actually creates finished goods and services using raw materials and personnel. At HealthWise, this includes manufacturing a variety of sports equipment and apparel.
- **Research** identifies, investigates, and develops new products and services. For example, at Healthwise, scientists are investigating a new light, inexpensive alloy for a new line of weight training equipment.

Although the titles may vary, nearly every large and small organization has departments that perform these basic functions. Whatever your job in an organization, it is likely to be in one of these functional areas.

MANAGEMENT LEVELS

Most people who work in an organization are not managers, of course. At the base of the organizational pyramid are the assemblers, painters, welders, drivers, and so on. These people produce goods and services. Above them are various levels of managers—people with titles such as supervisor, director, regional manager, and vice president. These are the people who do the planning, leading, organizing, and controlling necessary to see that the work gets done. At HealthWise, for example, the northwest district sales manager directs and coordinates all the salespeople in her area. Other job titles might be vice president of marketing, director of human resources, or production manager. In smaller organizations, these titles are often combined.

Management in many organizations is divided into three levels: supervisors, middle-level, and top-level. (See Figure 12-3.)

- **Supervisors:** Supervisors manage and monitor the employees or workers, those who actually produce the goods and services. Thus, these managers have responsibility relating to *operational matters.* They monitor day-to-day events and immediately take corrective action, if necessary. (See Figure 12-4.)
- **Middle management:** Middle-level managers deal with *control, planning* (also called *tactical planning*), and *decision making.* They implement the long-term goals of the organization.
- **Top management:** Top-level managers are concerned with *long-range planning* (also called *strategic planning*). They need information that will help them to plan the future growth and direction of the organization.

INFORMATION FLOW

Each level of management has different information needs. Top-level managers need information that is summarized in capsule form to reveal the overall condition of the business. They also need information from outside the organization, because top-level managers need to forecast and plan for long-range events. Middle-level managers need summarized information—weekly or monthly reports. They need to develop budget projections as well as to eval-

Managerial Levels

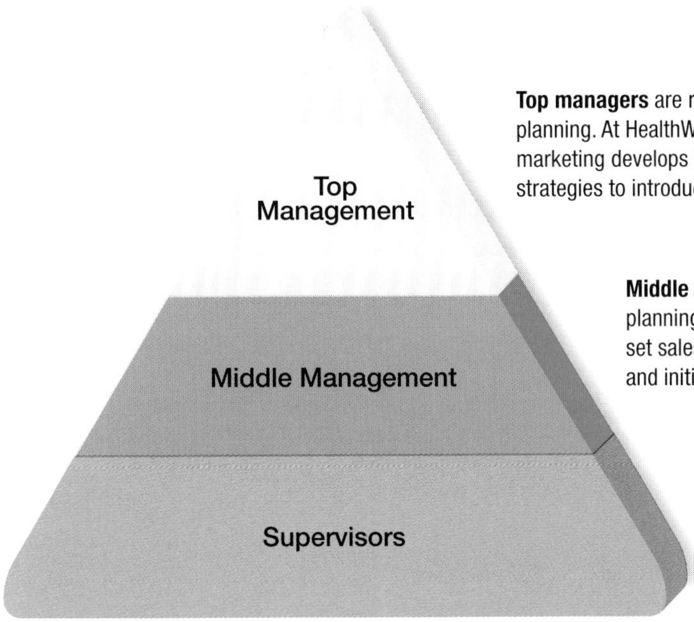

Top managers are responsible for long-range planning. At HealthWise, the vice president of marketing develops long-term marketing strategies to introduce newly developed products.

Middle managers are responsible for tactical planning. At HealthWise, regional sales managers set sales goals, monitor progress to meet goals, and initiate corrective action as needed.

Supervisors are responsible for operational matters. At HealthWise, a production supervisor monitors the inventory for parts and reorders when low.

Figure 12-3 Three levels of management

uate the performance of supervisors. Supervisors need detailed, very current, day-to-day information on their units so that they can keep operations running smoothly.

Figure 12-4 Supervisors monitor day-to-day events

To support these different needs, information *flows* in different directions. (See Figure 12-5.) For top-level managers, the flow of information from within the organization is both vertical and horizontal. The top-level managers, such as the chief executive officer (CEO), need information from below and from all departments. (See Figure 12-6.) They also need information from outside the organization. For example, at HealthWise, they are deciding whether to introduce a line of hockey equipment in the southwestern United States. The vice president of marketing must look at relevant data. Such data might include availability of ice rinks and census data about the number of young people. It might also include sales histories on related cold-weather sports equipment.

For middle-level managers, the information flow is both vertical and horizontal across functional lines within the organization. For example, the regional sales managers at HealthWise set their sales goals by coordinating with middle managers in the production department. They are able to tell sales managers what products will be produced, how many, and when. An example of a product might be an exercise bicycle. The regional sales managers also must coordinate with the strategic goals set by the top managers. They must set and monitor the sales goals for the supervisors beneath them.

For supervisory managers, information flow is primarily vertical. That is, supervisors communicate mainly with their middle managers and with the workers beneath them. For instance, at HealthWise, production supervisors rarely communicate with people in the accounting department. However, they are constantly communicating with production-line workers and with their own managers.

Information Flow

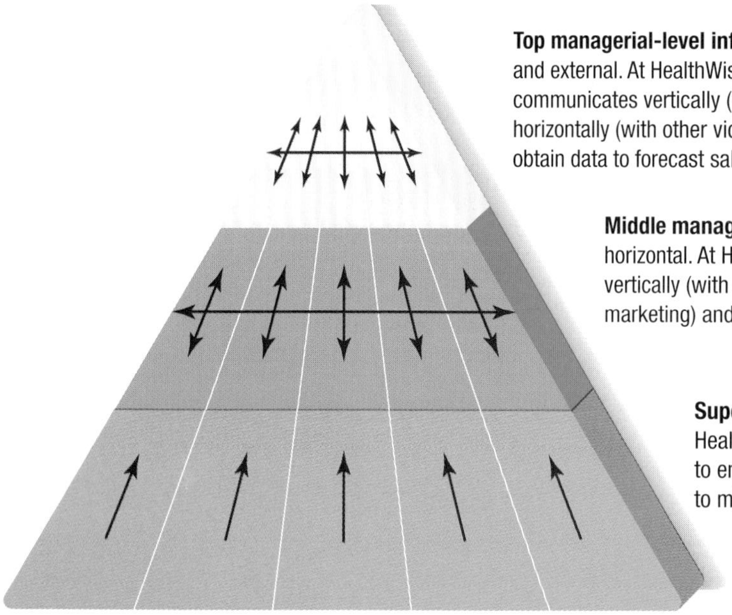

Top managerial-level information flow is vertical, horizontal, and external. At HealthWise, the vice president of marketing communicates vertically (with regional sales managers), horizontally (with other vice presidents), and externally to obtain data to forecast sales.

Middle managerial-level information flow is vertical and horizontal. At HealthWise, regional sales managers communicate vertically (with district sales managers and the vice president of marketing) and horizontally with other middle-level managers.

Supervisory-level information flow is primarily vertical. At HealthWise, production supervisors monitor worker activities to ensure smooth production. They provide daily status reports to middle-level production managers.

Figure 12-5 Information flow within an organization

Now we know how a large organization is usually structured and how information flows within the organization. But how is a computer-based information system likely to be set up to support its needs? And what do you, as a microcomputer user, need to know to use it?

Figure 12-6 Top-level managers handle both vertical and horizontal information flow

Concept Check

- ✔ What are the five basic functions within an organization?
- ✔ What are the three levels of management? Discuss each level.
- ✔ Describe the flow of information within an organization.

COMPUTER-BASED INFORMATION SYSTEMS

There are four kinds of computer-based information systems: transaction processing system, management information system, decision support system, and executive support system.

Almost all organizations have computer-based **information systems.** Large organizations typically have formal names for the systems designed to collect and use the data. Although different organizations may use different names, the most common names are transaction processing, management information, decision support, and executive support systems. (See Figure 12-7.)

Information Systems

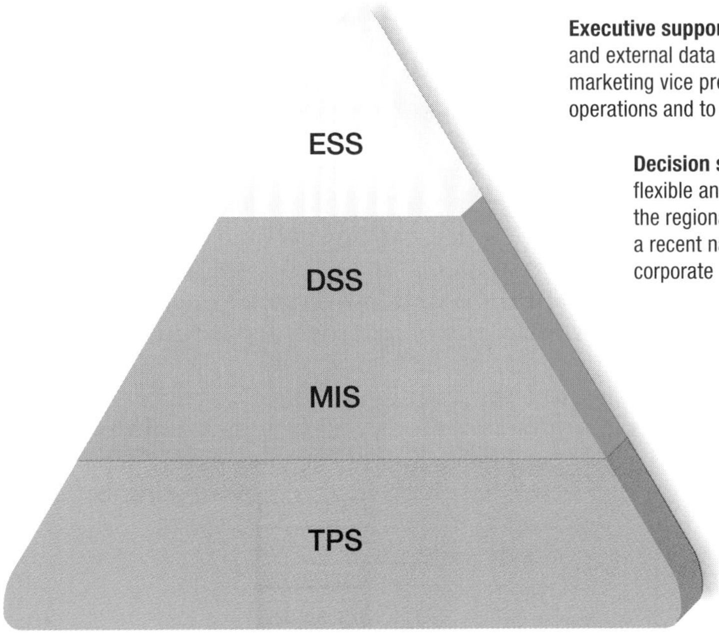
ESS
DSS
MIS
TPS
Executive support systems (ESS) use internal data from MIS and TPS and external data to support top-level managers. At HealthWise, the marketing vice president uses his ESS to view current marketing operations and to develop long-term marketing strategies.
Decision support systems (DSS) use data from TPS and a set of flexible analytical tools to support middle managers. At HealthWise, the regional sales managers use the DSS to evaluate the impact of a recent national promotion campaign on regional sales and corporate profit.
Management information systems (MIS) use data from the TPS to support middle-level managers. At HealthWise, regional sales managers use their MIS reports to monitor weekly divisional sales and to compare actual sales to established sales goals.
Transaction processing systems (TPS) record day-to-day transactions to support middle managers. At HealthWise, production supervisors use their TPS to record and to monitor current inventory levels and production line output.

Figure 12-7 Four kinds of computer-based information systems

- **Transaction processing system:** The transaction processing system (TPS) records day-to-day transactions such as customer orders, bills, inventory levels, and production output. The TPS helps supervisors by generating databases that act as the foundation for the other information systems.
- **Management information system:** The **management information system (MIS)** summarizes the detailed data of the transaction processing system in standard reports for middle-level managers. Such reports might include weekly sales and production schedules.
- **Decision support system:** The **decision support system (DSS)** provides a flexible tool for analysis. The DSS helps middle-level managers and others in the organization analyze a wide range of problems, such as the effect of events and trends outside the organization. Like the MIS, the DSS draws on the detailed data of the transaction processing system.
- **Executive support system:** The **executive support system (ESS),** also known as the **executive information system (EIS),** is an easy-to-use system that presents information in a very highly summarized form. It helps top-level managers oversee the company's operations and develop strategic plans. The ESS combines the internal data from TPS and MIS with external data.

Concept Check

- ✔ What are the four most common computer-based information systems? Describe each.
- ✔ Compare and contrast management information systems with decision support systems.

TRANSACTION PROCESSING SYSTEMS

A transaction processing system tracks operations and creates databases. Accounting TPS have six activities involving sales order processing, accounts receivables, inventory, accounts payable, payroll, and general ledger.

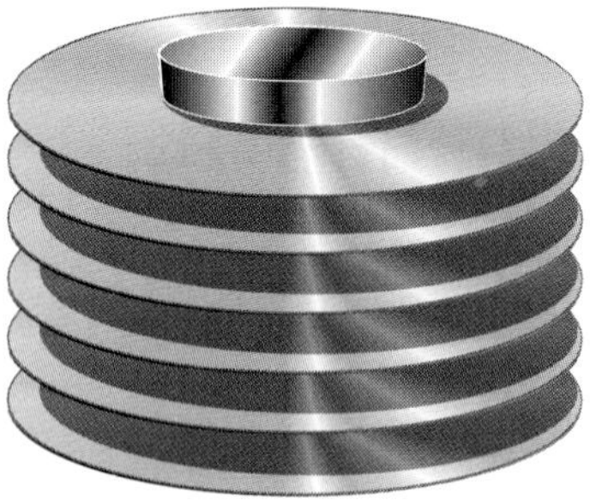

Figure 12-8 Transaction processing system database

A *transaction processing system (TPS)* helps an organization keep track of routine operations and records these events in a database. (See Figure 12-8.) For this reason, some firms call this the **data processing system (DPS).** The data from operations—for example, customer orders for HealthWise's products—makes up a database that records the transactions of the company. This database of transactions is used to support an MIS, DSS, and ESS.

One of the most essential transaction processing systems for any organization is in the accounting area. (See Figure 12-9.) Every accounting department handles six basic activities. Five of these are sales order processing, accounts receivable, inventory and purchasing, accounts payable, and payroll. All of these are recorded in the general ledger, the sixth activity.

Let us take a look at these six activities. They will make up the basis of the accounting system for almost any office you might work in.

- The **sales order processing** activity records the customer requests for the company's products or services. When an order comes in—a request for a set of barbells, for example—the warehouse is alerted to ship a product. (See Figure 12-10.)
- The **accounts receivable** activity records money received from or owed by customers. HealthWise keeps track of bills paid by sporting goods stores and by gyms and health clubs to which it sells directly.
- The parts and finished goods that the company has in stock are called **inventory**—all exercise machines in the warehouse, for example. (See Figure 12-11.) An **inventory control system** keeps records of the number of each kind of part or finished good in the warehouse. **Purchasing** is the buying of materials and services. Often a **purchase order** is used. This is a form that shows the name of the company supplying the material or service and what is being purchased.
- **Accounts payable** refers to money the company owes its suppliers for materials and services it has received—steel and aluminum, for example.
- The **payroll** activity is concerned with calculating employee paychecks. Amounts are generally determined by the kind of job, hours worked, and

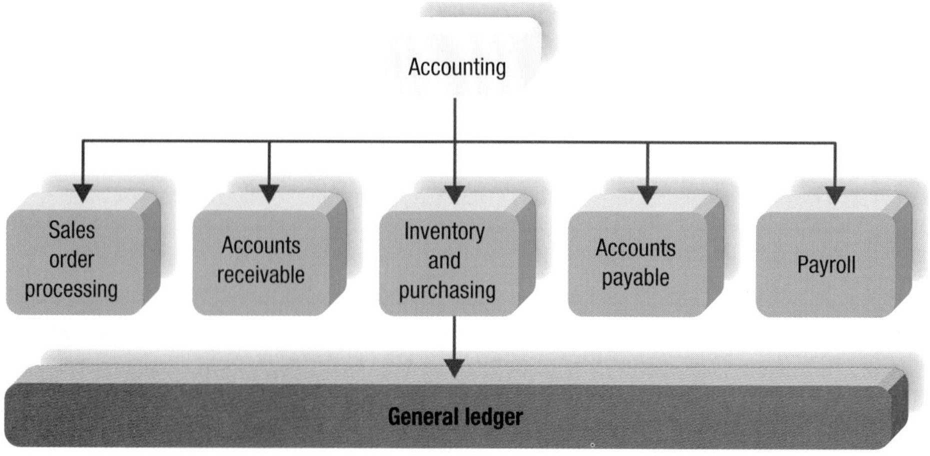

Figure 12-9 Transaction processing system for accounting

Figure 12-10 Customer orders are sent to the warehouse via sales order processing

Figure 12-11 Inventory control systems manage the merchandise in the warehouse

kinds of deductions (such as taxes, social security, medical insurance). Paychecks may be calculated from employee time cards or, in some cases, supervisors' time sheets.

- The **general ledger** keeps track of all summaries of all the foregoing transactions. A typical general ledger system can produce income statements and balance sheets. **Income statements** show a company's financial performance—income, expenses, and the difference between them for a specific time period. **Balance sheets** list the overall financial condition of an organization. They include assets (for example, buildings and property owned), liabilities (debts), and how much of the organization (the equity) is owned by the owners.

There are many other transaction systems that you come into contact with every day. These include automatic teller machines, which record cash withdrawals, online registration systems, which track student enrolments, and supermarket discount cards, which track customer purchases.

Concept Check

- ✓ What is the purpose of a transaction processing system?
- ✓ Describe the six activities of a TPS for accounting.

MANAGEMENT INFORMATION SYSTEMS

A management information system produces summarized, structured reports. Periodic, exception, and demand are three types of reports.

A *management information system (MIS)* is a computer-based information system that produces standardized reports in summarized structured form. (See Figure 12-12.) It is used to support middle managers. An MIS differs from a transaction processing system in a significant way. Whereas a transaction processing system *creates* databases, an MIS *uses* databases. Indeed, an MIS can draw from the databases of several departments. Thus, an MIS requires a *database management system* that integrates the databases of the different

The Sports Company
Regional Sales Report

Region	Actual Sales	Target	Difference
Central	$166,430	$175,000	($8,570)
Northern	137,228	130,000	7,228
Southern	137,772	135,000	2,772
Eastern	152,289	155,000	(2,711)
Western	167,017	160,000	7,017

Figure 12-12 Management information system report

departments. Middle managers need summary data often drawn from across different functional areas.

An MIS produces reports that are *predetermined*. That is, they follow a predetermined format and always show the same kinds of content. Although reports may differ from one industry to another, there are three common categories of reports: periodic, exception, and demand.

- **Periodic reports** are produced at regular intervals—weekly, monthly, or quarterly, for instance. Examples are HealthWise's monthly sales and production reports. The sales reports from district sales managers are combined into a monthly report for the regional sales managers. For comparison purposes, a regional manager is also able to see the sales reports of other regional managers. (See Figure 12-13.)
- **Exception reports** call attention to unusual events. An example is a sales report that shows that certain items are selling significantly above or below marketing department forecasts. For instance, if fewer exercise bicycles are selling than were predicted for the northwest sales region, the regional manager will receive an exception report. That report may be used to alert the district managers and salespeople to give this product more attention.
- The opposite of a periodic report, a **demand report,** is produced on request. An example is a report on the numbers and types of jobs held by women and minorities. Such a report is not needed periodically, but it may be required when requested by the U.S. government. At HealthWise, many government contracts require this information. It is used to certify that HealthWise is within certain government equal-opportunity guidelines.

Figure 12-13 Reports can be shared by regional managers with a management information system

Concept Check

- ✓ What is the purpose of a management information system?
- ✓ Describe the three common categories of MIS reports.

DECISION SUPPORT SYSTEMS

A DSS helps decision makers analyze unanticipated situations. Four parts of a DSS are user, system software, data, and decision models. GDSS supports collective work.

Managers often must deal with unanticipated questions. For example, the HealthWise manager in charge of manufacturing might ask how a strike would affect production schedules. A *decision support system (DSS)* enables managers to get answers to such unexpected and generally nonrecurring kinds of problems. Frequently, a team is formed to address large problems. A **group decision support system (GDSS)** is then used to support this collective work.

A DSS, then, is quite different from a transaction processing system, which simply records data. It is also different from a management information system, which summarizes data in predetermined reports. A DSS is used to analyze data. Moreover, it produces reports that do not have a fixed format. This makes the DSS a flexible tool for analysis.

At one time, most DSSs were designed for large computer systems. Now, microcomputers, with their increased power and sophisticated software, such as spreadsheet and database programs, are widely used for DSS. Users of a DSS are managers, not computer programmers. Thus, a DSS must be easy to use—or most likely it will not be used at all. A HealthWise marketing manager might want to know which territories are not meeting their monthly sales quotas. To find out, the executive could query the database for all "SALES < QUOTA." (See Figure 12-14.)

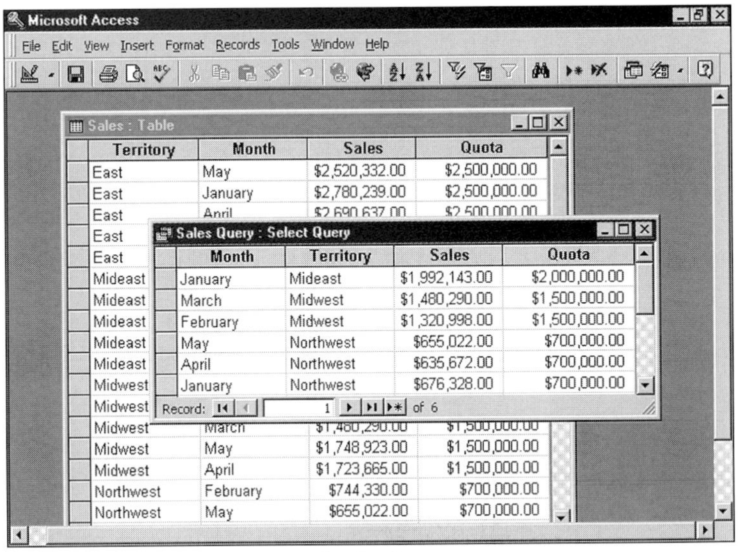

Figure 12-14 Decision support system query results for SALES < QUOTA

How does a decision support system work? Essentially, it consists of four parts: the user, system software, data, and decision models.

- The **user** could be you. In general, the user is someone who has to make decisions—a manager, often a middle-level manager.
- **System software** is essentially the operating system—programs designed to work behind the scenes to handle detailed operating procedures. In order to give the user a good, comfortable interface, the software typically is menu- or icon-driven. That is, the screen presents easily understood lists of commands or icons, giving the user several options.
- **Data** in a DSS is typically stored in a database and consists of two kinds. **Internal data**—data from within the organization—consists principally of transactions from the transaction processing system. **External data** is data gathered from outside the organization. Examples are data provided by marketing research firms, trade associations, and the U.S. government (such as customer profiles, census data, and economic forecasts).
- **Decision models** give the DSS its analytical capabilities. There are three basic types of models: strategic, tactical, and operational. **Strategic models** assist top-level managers in long-range planning, such as stating company objectives or planning plant locations. **Tactical models** help middle-level managers control the work of the organization, such as financial planning and sales promotion planning. **Operational models** help lower-level managers accomplish the organization's day-to-day activities, such as evaluating and maintaining quality control.

Concept Check

- What is the purpose of a decision support system?
- Describe the parts of a DSS.

EXECUTIVE SUPPORT SYSTEMS

Executive support systems include sophisticated software, are specifically designed for easy use, require little training, and use graphics extensively.

Using a DSS requires some training. Many top managers have other people in their offices running DSSs and reporting their findings. Top-level executives also want something more concise than an MIS—something that produces very focused reports.

Figure 12-15 ESS is designed for the executive

Executive support systems (ESSs) consist of sophisticated software that, like an MIS or a DSS, can present, summarize, and analyze data from an organization's databases. However, an ESS is specifically designed to be easy to use. This is so that a top executive with little spare time, for example, can obtain essential information without extensive training. Thus, information is often displayed in very condensed form with informative graphics. (See Figure 12-15.)

Consider an executive support system used by the president of Health-Wise. It is available on his microcomputer. The first thing each morning, the president calls up the ESS on his display screen, as shown in Figure 12-16. Note that the screen gives a condensed account of activities in the five different areas of the company. (These are Accounting, Marketing, Production, Human Resources, and Research.) On this particular morning, the ESS shows business in four areas proceeding smoothly. However, in the first area, Accounting, the percentage of late-paying customers—past due accounts—has increased by 3 percent. Three percent may not seem like much, but HealthWise has had a history of problems with late payers, which has left the company at times strapped for cash. The president decides to find out the details. To do so, she selects 1. Accounting.

Within moments, the display screen displays a graph of the past due accounts. (See Figure 12-17.) The status of today's late payers is shown in red. The status of late payers at this time a year ago is shown in yellow. The differences between today and a year ago are significant and clearly presented. For example, approximately $70,000 was late 1 to 10 days last year. This year, over

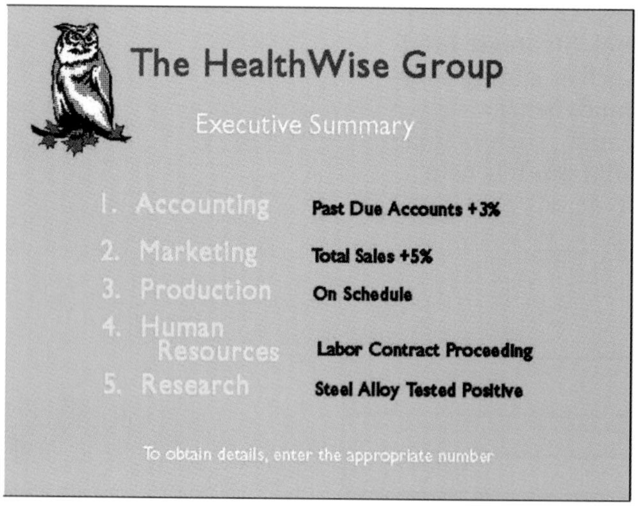

Information in condensed text form

Figure 12-16 Opening screen for an executive information system

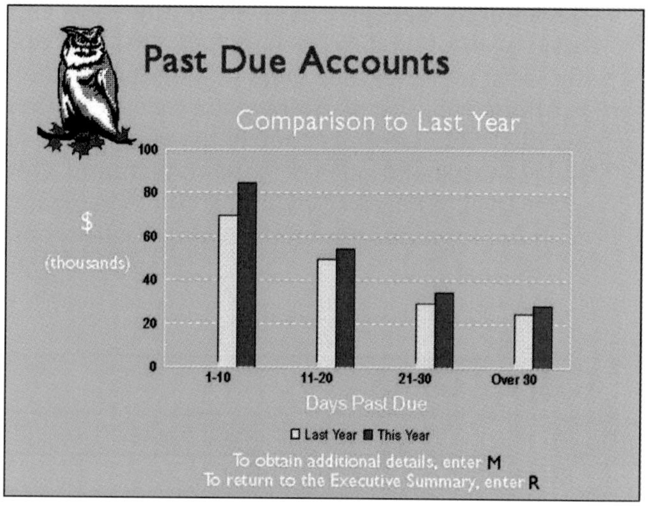

Details in graphic form

Figure 12-17 Graphic representation of Past Due Accounts

$80,000 was late. The president knows that she must take some action to speed up customer payments. (For example, she might call this to the attention of the vice president of accounting. The vice president might decide to implement a new policy that offers discounts to early payers or charge higher interest to late payers.)

ESSs permit a firm's top executives to gain direct access to information about the company's performance. Most provide direct electronic communication links to other executives. Some systems provide structured forms to help managers streamline their thoughts before sending electronic memos. In addition, an ESS may be organized to retrieve information from databases outside the company, such as business-news services. This enables a firm to watch for stories on competitors and stay current on relevant news events that could affect its business. For example, news of increased sports injuries caused by running and aerobic dancing, and the consequent lessened interest by people in these activities, might cause HealthWise to alter its sales and production goals for its line of fitness-related shoes.

For a summary of the different types of information systems, see Figure 12-18.

Type	Description
TPS	Tracks routine operations and records events in databases, also known as data processing systems
MIS	Produces standardized reports (periodic, exception, and demand) using databases created by TPS
DSS	Analyzes unanticipated situations using data (internal and external) and decision models (strategic, tactical, and operational)
ESS	Presents summary information in a flexible, easy-to-use, graphical format designed for top executives

Figure 12-18 Summary of information systems

Concept Check

- ✓ What is the purpose of an executive support system?
- ✓ How is an ESS similar to and different from an MIS or DSS?

OTHER INFORMATION SYSTEMS

Information workers include data workers and knowledge workers. Data workers distribute and communicate information and use office information systems. Knowledge workers create information and use knowledge work systems.

We have discussed only four information systems: TPS to support lower-level managers, MIS and DSS to support middle-level managers, and ESS to support top-level managers. There are many other information systems to support different individuals and functions. The fastest-growing are information systems designed to support information workers.

Information workers distribute, communicate, and create information. They are the organization's secretaries, clerks, engineers, and scientists, to name a few. Some are involved with distribution and communication of information (like the secretaries and clerks; see Figure 12-19). They are called **data workers.** Others are involved with the creation of information (like the engineers and scientists). They are called **knowledge workers.**

Figure 12-19 Secretaries and clerks are data workers

Figure 12-20 Videoconferencing: Individuals and groups can see and share information

Figure 12-21 CAD/CAM: Knowledge work systems used by design and manufacturing engineers

Two systems to support information workers are:

- **Office automation systems: Office automation systems (OASs)** are designed primarily to support data workers. These systems focus on managing documents, communicating, and scheduling. Documents are managed using word processing, Web authoring, desktop publishing, and other image technologies. **Project managers** are programs designed to schedule, plan, and control project resources. Microsoft Project is the most widely used project manager. **Videoconferencing systems** are computer systems that allow people located at various geographic locations to communicate and have in-person meetings. (See Figure 12-20.)
- **Knowledge work systems: Knowledge workers** use OAS systems. Additionally, they use specialized information systems called **knowledge work systems (KWSs)** to create information in their areas of expertise. For example, engineers involved in product design and manufacturing use **computer-aided design/computer-aided manufacturing (CAD/CAM) systems.** (See Figure 12-21.) These KWSs consist of powerful microcomputers running special programs that integrate the design and manufacturing activities. CAD/CAM is widely used in the manufacture of automobiles and other products.

Concept Check

- ✔ What is an information worker?
- ✔ Who are data workers? What type of information system is designed to support them?
- ✔ Who are knowledge workers? What type of information system is design to support them?

Careers in IT

Information Systems Manager

Information systems managers oversee the work of programmers, computer specialists, systems analysts and other computer professionals. They create and implement corporate computer policy and systems. These professionals consult with management, staff, and customers to achieve goals.

Most companies look for individuals with strong technical backgrounds, sometimes as consultants, with a master's degree in business. Employers seek individuals with strong leadership and excellent communication skills. Information systems managers must be able to communicate with people in technical and nontechnical terms. Information systems management positions are often filled with individuals who have been consultants or managers in previous positions. Those with experience in computer and network security will be in demand as businesses and society continue to struggle with important security issues.

Information systems managers can expect an annual salary of $60,000 to $100,000. Advancement opportunities typically include leadership in the field. To learn more about other careers in information systems visit us at http://www.mhhe.com/oleary/CT05 and select Careers in IT from Tim's Toolbox.

A Look to the Future

Information Overload

Have you ever questioned the value of technology? Has it really helped us and made us more productive? Is it possible that the various devices intended to increase our productivity have actually had the opposite effect?

E-mail, cell phones, notebook computers, and the Web are great. They allow us to communicate, work almost anywhere, and have access to vast amounts of data. However, unless we are careful, they can create "information overload" and have a negative effect on our ability to get work done.

Several recent studies have found that e-mail is the major source of information overload. It was recently reported that a typical knowledge worker in a large corporation sends and receives over 100 e-mail messages a day. Furthermore, the study concluded that the majority of these messages are not necessary. Here are some tips to control e-mail overload:

- **Be selective.** Look first at the subject line in an e-mail—read only those of direct and immediate interest to you. Look next at the sender line—read only those from people important to you; postpone or ignore the others.
- **Remove.** After reading an e-mail, respond if necessary; then either file it in the appropriate folder or delete it.
- **Protect.** Limit your e-mail by giving your address only to those who need it.
- **Be brief.** When responding, be concise and direct.
- **Stop spam.** Spam is unwanted e-mail advertisements. Avoid mailing lists, complain to those who send spam, and ask to have your name removed from their mailing list.
- **Don't respond.** You do not have to respond to an e-mail. Be selective; respond only to those worthy of your time.

Is information overload part of your future? If you are like today's busy executives, it probably will be. Don't let it get you down!

INFORMATION SYSTEMS AT DVD DIRECT

INTRODUCTION

DVD Direct is an entirely Web-oriented movie rental business. Unlike traditional movie rental businesses like Blockbuster, DVD Direct conducts all business over the Web at its Web storefront. For a monthly fee, their customers are able to order up to three movies at a time from a listing posted at the company Web site. The movies the customers select are delivered to them on DVD disks by mail within three working days. After viewing, customers return one or more disks by mail. They are allowed to keep the disks as long as they wish but can never have more than three disks in their possession at one time.

Although in operation for only three years, DVD Direct has experienced rapid growth. To help manage and to accelerate this growth, the company has just hired Alice, a recent college graduate. Let's follow Alice on her first day at DVD Direct which begins with a meeting with Bob, the vice president of Marketing.

Figure C12-1 "She said she was concerned about how our members were connecting to our Web site."

ALICE'S FIRST ASSIGNMENT

Bob: Oh, hi Alice . . . come on in! I know that we were scheduled for an orientation meeting this morning. But I'm afraid that will have to wait. There is an important fire to put out today. Let me introduce you to one of your coworkers. This is Jamal.

Alice and Jamal exchange hellos and Bob motions Alice to take one of the chairs across from his desk as he speaks.

Bob: I just came back from a meeting with Carol, our CEO. While we were discussing the Monthly Membership Report, she said she was concerned about how our members were connecting to our Web site. [See Figure C12-1.] This really caught me off guard! Our membership growth has exceeded projections and I had assumed that our meeting was to discuss how to handle all the new members. She requested that her Morning Report be modified to include the percentage of our customers who use high bandwidth, and she wants us to analyze the changes in low bandwidth customers versus high bandwidth customers over the past year.

Bob: Jamal, here is the Monthly Membership Report. I'd like you to review it and then create two profiles. One profile will describe our members who use low bandwidth. The other profile will be for our members who use high bandwidth. I'm interested in any differences or unique characteristics you can uncover.

Bob removes the cover page, hands the rest of the report to Jamal, and hands the cover page to Alice.

Bob: Alice, I want you to focus on these three values. [See Figure C12-2.] Start by locating their source. Then obtain data for low and high bandwidth members for the past twelve months and prepare a graph comparing the two. Start by talking with Dennis. He is the southwest marketing manager and his team developed the Monthly Membership Report.

Bob: Jamal, before you start your profiles, please introduce Alice to Dennis. On the way to his office, give Alice a rundown on our corporate structure. Okay, guys, get to work! Before 4:00 today, I want you to present your findings to Carol!

Alice and Jamal head toward Dennis's office.

Jamal: This is a hectic way to start your first day, but it should give you an overall view of the company.

Membership Profile	
Low Bandwith	118,098
High Bandwith	31,051
Total Membership	149,149

Figure C12-2 "Focus on these values."

DEPARTMENTS

DVD Direct has five departments: Accounting, Marketing, Production, Human Resources, and Research.

Jamal: We are in Marketing, which focuses on promoting and selling DVD Direct products. Production is in another building. The responsibility of production at DVD Direct is to ship, receive, and warehouse the DVDs. You dealt with Human Resources when you went through the interview process and filled out the paperwork to work at DVD Direct. Research looks into new technologies. I've heard that they are exploring the feasibility of delivering movies over the Web using streaming video technology. Accounting handles billing customers and creating the yearly shareholders report, among other responsibilities.

Management Levels

Jamal: Each department has different management levels. Bob is one of DVD Direct's top managers. As Vice President of Marketing, he determines long-range plans and sets the direction for marketing. We're on our way to see Dennis, who is a middle marketing manager. He takes the long-range goals set by Bob and formulates shorter objectives such as monthly sales quotas for his southwest regional supervisors. The regional supervisors take care of day-to-day operational matters, like contacting new potential customers and ensuring that our current customers are happy.

Alice and Jamal arrive at an open door to Dennis's office and Jamal knocks on the door frame. Looking up, Dennis asks them to come in and have a seat.

Jamal: Actually, Dennis, I have to head back. I just wanted to introduce you to our new marketing analyst, Alice. It's her first day and she has some questions about the bandwidth data in the Monthly Membership Report.

Dennis: Welcome, Alice. I've heard about Carol's interest in these figures. I don't understand why Carol is so concerned. Membership is up and everything seems positive. If things keep going this well, we will be one of the few Internet companies to post a profit this year. I'm confident in the accuracy of the numbers. They were compiled by Elizabeth, one of my best supervisors, and her team's work is always first rate.

Alice: So you didn't compile these numbers yourself? [See Figure C12-3.]

Figure C12-3 "So you didn't compile these numbers yourself?"

Dennis: Oh no, I rarely take part in the actual gathering of data anymore. When I was promoted to middle management, my job became more about communication and I leave much of the detail work for my team supervisors.

When I was a supervisor, my communications were pretty much limited to my team and my boss. Now that I am a middle manager, I communicate with supervisors below me, middle managers from other departments, and with top management. Life has gotten more complicated since my old supervisory days when I only had to worry about my immediate manager.

While almost all of my information comes from within the organization, top managers, like Bob, also use external information. For example, last week he and Carol attended the European Video Perspectives (EVEP) conference to learn how video is being using worldwide

Alice: That's interesting! Well, I'll need some advice about the Monthly Membership Report. From what you say it sounds like I need to talk to Elizabeth because it's at the supervisor level where the data is actually collected. Does that sound right? Do you think Elizabeth can make time in her schedule to help me track down these numbers?

Dennis: Whenever the CEO wants something, we'll make the time. Elizabeth is just down the hall on the left. I'll give her a call and tell her that you're on your way.

MANAGEMENT INFORMATION SYSTEMS AT DVD DIRECT

Alice: Hi Elizabeth, I'm Alice.

Elizabeth: Hi Alice, nice to meet you. Dennis just called and said you had some questions about the bandwidth data in the Monthly Membership Report. I did it about three months ago. When I wrote it I had no idea it would cause such a stir. Even looking at the numbers now, nothing seems particularly out of the ordinary. I wonder why Carol is so concerned.

Alice: You wrote this report three months ago? But the information in the report includes data from this month and last month.

She hands Elizabeth the cover page of the report.

Elizabeth: Well I didn't actually write *this* report. I determined the format and the formulas that this report is based on. This particular report was created by a program that is part of our MIS or Management Information System. The program is run at the end of each month and applies my formulas to the new monthly data to produce the report. To locate the specific formulas you are interested in, all we have to do is look at the program that generated the report.

Elizabeth turns to her computer and retrieves the MIS program. After quickly reviewing the program code, she points to her screen.

Elizabeth: There they are. The formulas use data from the production TPS database.

TRANSACTION PROCESSING SYSTEMS AT DVD DIRECT

Alice: What's a TPS?

Elizabeth: A TPS is a Transaction Processing System. It is a collection of programs that keep track of routine operations and record those operations in a database. The production department's TPS records what movies have been ordered, when they are sent out, and when they are returned. For example, if you needed a report on what movies are available right now, the TPS could provide you with that information. It can also provide the bandwidth data for the past several months that you're interested in. Go see Frank, a supervisor in production. He will help you locate the data you need. His office is located in Building B. Tell him I sent you.

Alice walks down to Building B where all the DVDs for DVD Direct are received, warehoused, packaged, and shipped. Although she knows that DVD Direct ships several thousand DVDs a day, she is still surprised at the size of the operation. Workers scan incoming DVDs into the Transaction Processing System with handheld scanners, while others scan outgoing DVDs. After asking around, Alice finally locates Frank in his office on the second floor.

Alice: Excuse me, Frank? I'm new here. My name's Alice. Elizabeth said you'd help me find some data.

Frank: Hello there, Alice. Elizabeth? Sure thing!

Alice: I'm helping my boss Bob prepare something for Carol for this afternoon. She is looking for some historical data for low and high bandwidth customers for the past year. I'm tracking down the source of data used to calculate these figures here.

She hands Frank the cover page from the Monthly Membership Report and a printout of the formulas that Elizabeth identified.

Alice: As you can see, the formulas reference data in the production database captured by your department's TPS. I was hoping that you could use the TPS to analyze the bandwidths used by new customers over the past twelve months.

For a moment Frank looks at the cover page and the formulas and chews on his pencil.

Frank: So this is the report everyone is talking about. I'm afraid the TPS won't help with the analysis. The TPS stores data on day-to-day activity and current inventory, but it doesn't analyze trends.

Alice: So you don't think we can get the data for the last twelve months?

Frank: We can get the data. Our TPS collects that data automatically from our Web site whenever an order is placed. However, the TPS does not analyze data.

Alice: Can't I use the MIS to analyze the data?

Frank: Not really. Our MIS is designed to produce standardized reports. I suppose you could create an MIS program to analyze the bandwidth data, but that would require more time and money than is necessary. Besides, you only need to do this analysis once . . . not every month. The best way is to use a DSS.

DECISION SUPPORT SYSTEMS

Alice: What's a DSS?

Frank: A DSS or Decision Support System is a fancy name for a collection of tools designed to analyze data. Unlike an MIS which produces standardized reports, a DSS is a more flexible tool designed to handle unexpected and nonrecurring types of information needs.

Alice: That sounds pretty complicated.

Frank: Not complicated at all. Are you familiar with Excel? It's a DSS and contains all the DSS tools that you'll need for this project.

Alice: Great! I'm pretty good with Excel. But where do I get the data.

Frank: I can download the data you need from the TPS database and save it for you in an Excel file.

Frank turns to his computer, accesses the database, extracts the necessary data, and saves it onto a disk. Frank hands the disk to Alice.

Frank: Here it is. Good luck!

Alice thanks Frank, returns to her new office, and uses Excel to create a chart comparing the number of low and high bandwidth customers over the past year. [See Figure C12-4.]

EXECUTIVE SUPPORT SYSTEMS

Alice returns to Bob's office to report her findings.

Bob: Alice, glad to see you. How is the analysis going? [See Figure C12-5.]

Alice: Hi Bob! I think I have what you need, I hope. Here is the data for the last twelve months and a chart showing the trend of low versus high bandwidth customers. I've also calculated the current percentage of our members who are high bandwidth users.

Bob: Excellent work . . . now, go down to computing services and have them add this information to Carol's ESS and then go straight to Carol's office and give her a quick rundown on the additions to the ESS.

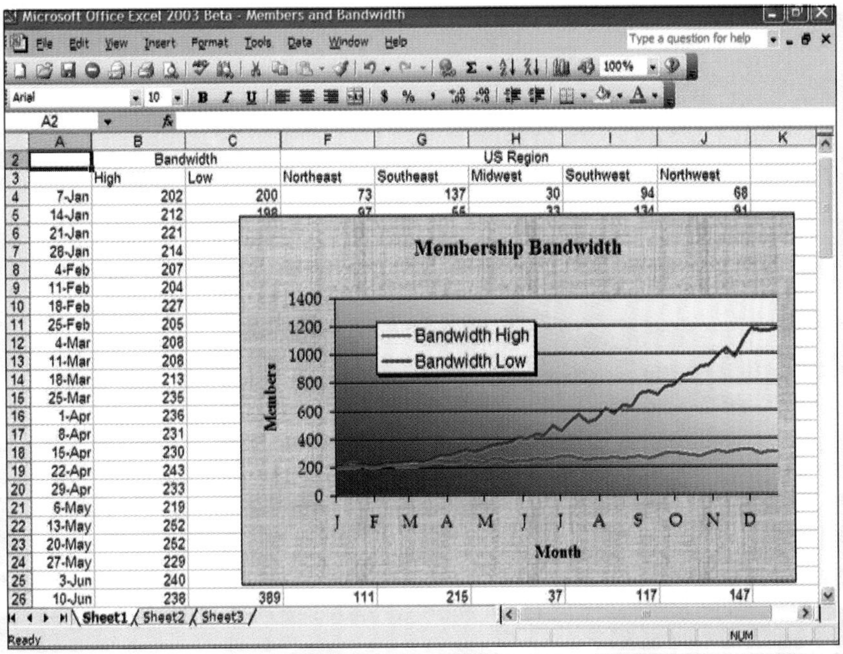

Figure C12-4 Alice's analysis

Alice: ESS?

Bob: Of course, I forgot you haven't been given the full tour. An ESS is an Executive Support System that generates a customized and very concise daily report for a particular top-level manager. If the manager wants additional detail, it is readily available. In this case, Carol's ESS will present the current percentage of high bandwidth customers along with other information. More detailed information will be available at a click of the mouse.

Alice: I'll go down to computing services right now and request these changes for Carol's ESS.

Figure C12-5 "How is the analysis going?"

ALICE MEETS WITH THE CEO

After visiting computing services, Alice goes to the CEO's office. Just as she arrives, the CEO's door opens and Jamal walks out, followed by Carol.

Carol: Jamal, thanks for these profiles. They'll give me a lot to think about. [Carol turns to Alice.] You must be our newest employee.

Alice: Yes, I'm Alice, your new marketing analyst.

Carol: Well come on in and show me what you've got.

At her desk Carol reviews Alice's data. Initially nervous talking to the CEO, Alice quickly warms to Carol and ventures to ask the question that everyone wants answered.

Alice: So what is it about the bandwidth data in the Monthly Membership Report that has caused you such concern? By everyone's estimate that I've talked to, membership is increasing and everything seems to be going better than anticipated. What do these numbers tell you that they don't tell them?

Carol: Right now everything does seem to be going well. But I'm concerned about our future, Alice, and I think I see evidence of upcoming problems. In this month's issue of *Video Trends in America,* an article discussed the rapid growth of high bandwidth users.

Carol hands Alice a graph that indicates that more and more Internet users are switching from low bandwidth to high bandwidth.

Carol: How would you expect this trend in higher bandwidth users to impact us?

Alice: I guess I would expect to see a similar increase in high bandwidth customers. However, my analysis shows that the number of our high bandwidth customers has remained fairly constant.

Carol: Exactly. It would seem that high bandwidth users don't take much interest in our services. Not only that. According to the results that Jamal compiled, 70 percent of our customers who switch from low bandwidth to high bandwidth connections cancel their membership with us! Why do you suppose that is happening?

Alice: There are several possibilities, but I am at a loss as to why a faster Internet connection would reduce a person's interest in renting our movies.

Carol: But that is exactly what is happening. As more people become high bandwidth users, we can expect to lose more and more members. Can you think of any reason why faster Internet connections would lead to fewer DVD rentals?

Alice: Well, perhaps high bandwidth users prefer to immediately download movies from the Internet rather than wait for them to be delivered by mail.

Carol: Exactly! We may be seeing the beginning of the end of our present way of doing business. [See Figure 12-6.] It may take two or three years, but I expect that the number of movies delivered via the Internet will greatly exceed those delivered by mail. And if we don't start providing movies over the Internet, we'll continue to lose our high bandwidth customers. In fact, recently I directed our Research people to start work on the feasibility of delivering movies via streaming video over the Web. I suspect that our competitors are already exploring the feasibility of Internet delivery. If we don't adapt and adapt fast, we just might go out of business. We are going to have to make a radical shift in the way we do business here. You've joined our company at an exciting time. There are some big changes on the horizon. Welcome to the new DVD Direct!

Figure 12-6 "We may be seeing the beginning of the end of our present way of doing business."

For more comprehensive discussion on DVD Direct's information systems, consult your Computing Today CD or visit us on the web at http://www.mhhe.com/oleary/CT05 and select DVD Direct from Tim's Toolbox.

NOTES

VISUAL SUMMARY

INFORMATION SYSTEMS

INFORMATION FLOW

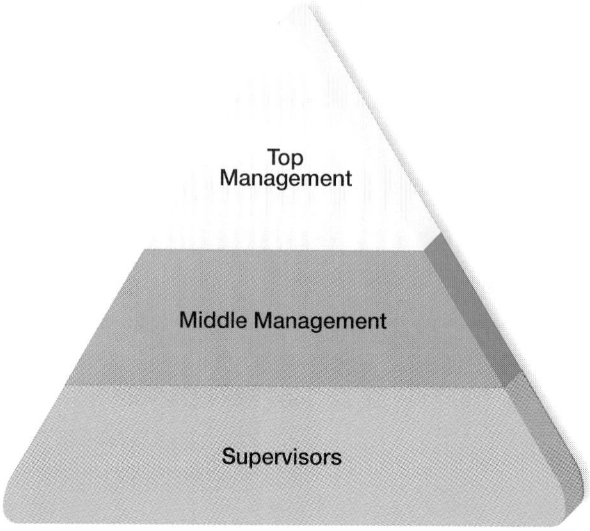

Information flows in an organization through functional areas and between management levels.

Functions

Most organizations have separate departments to perform five functions:

- **Accounting**—tracks all financial activities and generates periodic financial statements.
- **Marketing**—advertises, promotes, and sells the product (or service).
- **Production**—makes the product (or service) using raw materials and people to turn out finished goods.
- **Human resources**—finds and hires people, handles such matters as sick leave, retirement benefits, evaluation, compensation, and professional development.
- **Research**—conducts product research and development, monitors and troubleshoots new products.

Management Levels

The three basic management levels are:

- **Top-level**—long-range planning and forecasting.
- **Middle-level**—control, planning, and implementing long-term goals.
- **Supervisors**—control of operational matters, monitoring day-to-day events, and supervising workers.

Information Flow

Information flows within an organization in different directions.

- For **top-level managers** the informational flow is primarily up within the organization and into the organization from the outside.
- For **middle-level managers** the information flow is horizontally across and vertically within departments.
- For **supervisors** the information flow is primarily vertical.

To be a competent and knowledgeable end user you need to understand how information flows through functional areas and management levels. You need to be aware of the different types of computer-based information systems including transaction processing systems, management information systems, decision support systems, and executive support systems.

INFORMATION SYSTEMS

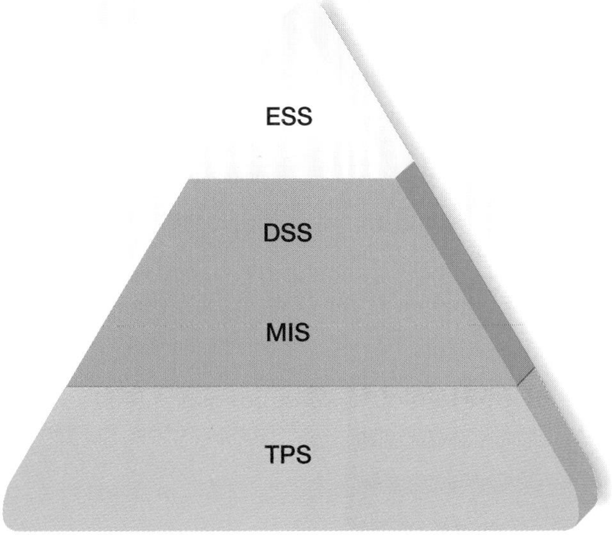

All organizations have computer-based **information systems,** including the following.

Transaction Processing Systems

Transaction processing systems (TPS), also known as **data processing systems (DPS),** record day-to-day transactions. An example is in accounting, which handles six activities: **sales order processing, accounts receivable, inventory (inventory control systems) and purchasing, accounts payable, payroll,** and **general ledger.** General ledger used to produce **income statements** and **balance sheets.**

Management Information Systems

Management information systems (MIS) produce predetermined **periodic, exception,** and **demand reports.** Management information systems use database management systems to integrate the databases of different departments.

Decision Support Systems

Decision support systems (DSS) enable managers to get answers for unanticipated questions. Teams formed to address large problems use **group decision support systems (GDSS).** A decision support system consists of the **user, system software, (data internal** and **external),** and **decision models.** Three types of decision models are **strategic, tactical,** and **operational.**

Executive Support Systems

Executive support systems (ESS) assist top-level executives. An executive support system is similar to MIS or DSS but easier to use. ESSs are designed specifically for top-level decision makers.

Other Systems

Many other systems are designed to support **information workers** who create, distribute, and communicate information. Two such systems are:

- **Office automation systems (OAS)** support **data workers** who are involved with distribution and communication of information. **Project managers** and **videoconferencing systems** are OAS.
- **Knowledge work systems (KWS)** support **knowledge workers,** who create information. Many engineers use **computer-aided design/computer-aided manufacturing system (CAD/CAM)** KWS.

KEY TERMS

accounting (452)
accounts payable (458)
accounts receivable (458)
balance sheet (459)
computer aided design/computer aided manufacturing (CAD/CAM) (464)
data (461)
data processing system (DPS) (458)
data worker (463)
decision model (461)
decision support system (DSS) (457, 460)
demand report (460)
exception report (460)
executive information system (EIS) (457)
executive support system (ESS) (457, 462)
external data (461)
general ledger (459)
group decision support system (GDSS) (460)
human resources (454)
income statement (459)
information system (456)
information worker (463)
internal data (461)
inventory (458)
inventory control system (458)
knowledge worker (463)
knowledge work system (KWS) (464)
management information system (MIS) (457, 459)
marketing (454)
middle management (454)
office automation system (OAS) (464)
operational model (461)
payroll (458)
periodic report (460)
production (454)
project manager (464)
purchase order (458)
purchasing (458)
research (454)
sales order processing (458)
strategic model (461)
supervisor (454)
system software (461)
tactical model (461)
top management (454)
transaction processing system (TPS) (457, 458)
user (461)
videoconferencing system (464)

To test your knowledge of these key terms with animated flash cards, select Flash Cards from Tim's Toolbox at http://www.mhhe.com/oleary/CT05.

CHAPTER REVIEW

CROSSWORD

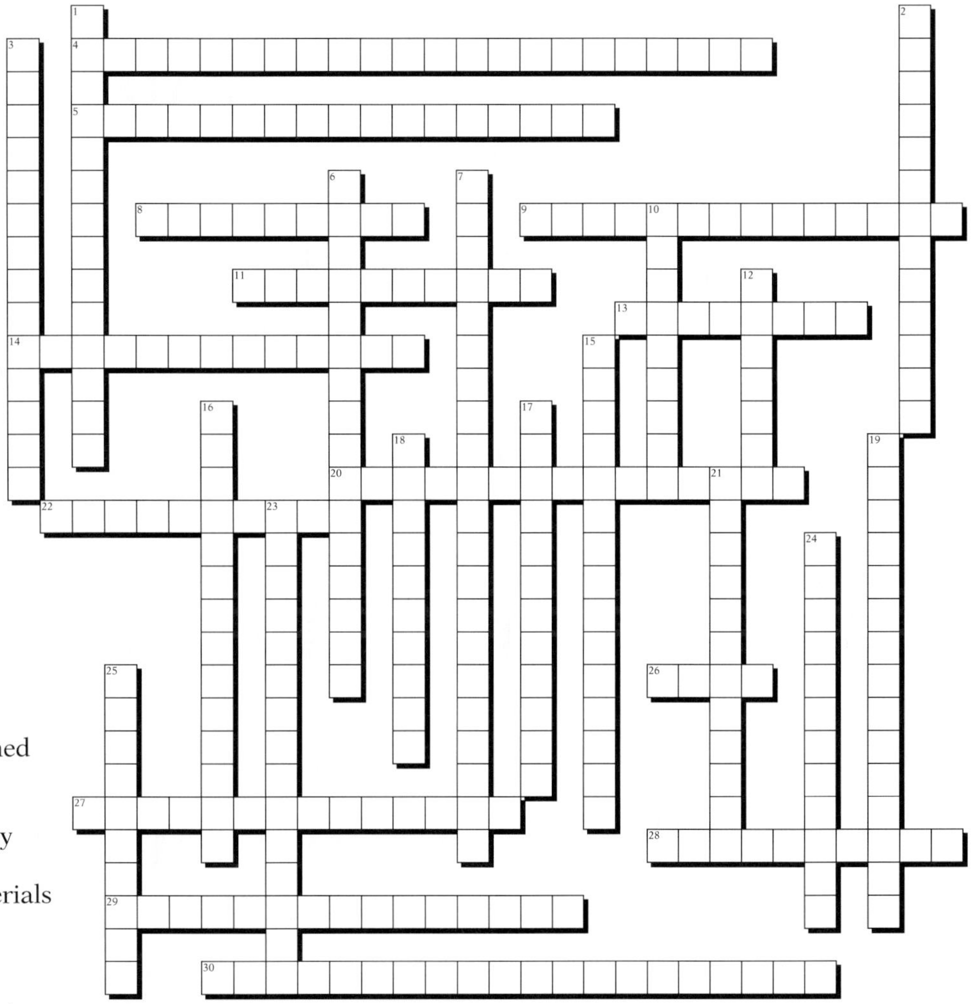

ACROSS

4 Designed for easy use, require little training, and use graphics extensively
5 People who distribute, communicate, and create information
8 Advertises, promotes, and sells the product or service
9 Help middle-level managers control the work of the organization
11 Uses raw materials and people to turn out finished goods
13 Conducts product research and development
14 Employees concerned with long-range planning
20 Money the company owes its suppliers
22 The buying of materials and services
26 Anyone who has to make decisions
27 Programs designed to schedule, plan, and control project resources
28 People involved with the distribution and communication of information
29 Assist top-level managers in the long-range planning
30 Records day-to-day transactions

DOWN

1 Produced at regular intervals
2 Keeps track of all summaries of all transactions
3 Programs that handle operating procedures
6 Employees who implement the long-term goals of the organization
7 Enables managers to get answers to problems
10 The parts and finished goods that a company has in stock
12 Activity concerned with calculating employee paychecks
15 Calls attention to unusual events
16 Focuses on people within the organization
17 Data gathered from outside the organization
18 Records all financial activity
19 People who create information
21 Lists the overall financial condition of an organization
23 Shows the company's income and expenses for a specific period of time
24 Produced on request
25 Manages and monitors the employees

For an interactive crossword puzzle select Crosswords from Tim's Toolbox at http://www.mhhe.com/oleary/CT05.

MULTIPLE CHOICE

Circle the letter or fill in the correct answer.

1. A(n) ________ is a collection of people, procedures, software, hardware, and data.
   - **a.** corporation
   - **b.** information system
   - **c.** knowledge work system
   - **d.** office automation system
   - **e.** data processing system
2. A general ledger usually includes both ________ and ________.
   - **a.** income statements, balance sheets
   - **b.** accounts receivable, purchasing
   - **c.** income statements, purchasing
   - **d.** payroll, purchasing
   - **e.** income statements, payroll
3. People involved in distribution and communication of information are called ________.
   - **a.** knowledge workers
   - **b.** users
   - **c.** data workers
   - **d.** managers
   - **e.** secretaries
4. Because it helps an organization keep track of routine operations and records these events in a database, some firms call a TPS a(n) ________.
   - **a.** decision support system
   - **b.** executive support system
   - **c.** executive information system
   - **d.** data processing system
   - **e.** management information system
5. Purchasing, accounts receivable, and inventory are examples of ________ activities.
   - **a.** executive
   - **b.** managerial
   - **c.** clerical
   - **d.** accounting
   - **e.** human resources
6. The ________ department focuses on hiring, training, and promoting.
   - **a.** marketing
   - **b.** production
   - **c.** research
   - **d.** accounting
   - **e.** human resources
7. ________ help lower-level managers accomplish the organization's day-to-day activities, such as evaluating and maintaining quality control.
   - **a.** Tactical models
   - **b.** Operational models
   - **c.** Strategic models
   - **d.** Exception reports
   - **e.** Periodic reports
8. ________ are designed primarily to support data workers.
   - **a.** Office automation systems
   - **b.** Knowledge work systems
   - **c.** CAD/CAM systems
   - **d.** Decision support systems
   - **e.** Management information systems
9. Information workers are also known as ________.
   - **a.** supervisors
   - **b.** managers
   - **c.** data workers
   - **d.** knowledge workers
   - **e.** executives
10. The level of manager whose information flow is primarily vertical is ________.
    - **a.** vice president
    - **b.** executive
    - **c.** top level manager
    - **d.** supervisor
    - **e.** data worker

To test your knowledge of this chapter, select Self Test from Tim's Toolbox at http://www.mhhe.com/oleary/CT05.

MATCHING

Match each numbered item with the most closely related lettered item. Write your answers in the spaces provided.

- **a.** computer-aided design (CAD)
- **b.** demand report
- **c.** DPS
- **d.** DSS
- **e.** EIS
- **f.** exception report
- **g.** GDSS
- **h.** general ledger
- **i.** internal data
- **j.** inventory
- **k.** knowledge workers
- **l.** MIS
- **m.** payroll
- **n.** periodic report
- **o.** purchasing
- **p.** research department
- **q.** strategic models
- **r.** supervisor
- **s.** tactical models
- **t.** transaction processing system

1. Manager responsible for administration and monitoring workers. ____
2. Department that identifies, investigates, and develops new products and services. ____
3. System that records day-to-day transactions. ____
4. Computer-based information system that produces standardized reports in summarized, structured form. ____
5. Sophisticated software that can draw together data from an organization's databases in meaningful patterns. ____
6. Transaction processing system that keeps track of routine operations and records these events in a database. ____
7. The parts and finished goods that a company has in stock. ____
8. Buying of raw materials and services. ____
9. Activity concerned with calculating employee paychecks. ____
10. Activity that produces income statements and balance sheets based on all transactions of a company. ____
11. Report generated at regular intervals. ____
12. Report that calls attention to unusual events. ____
13. The opposite of a scheduled report. ____
14. Flexible tool for analysis that helps managers make decisions about unstructured problems. ____
15. System used to support the collective work of a team addressing large problems. ____
16. Data gathered from within an organization. ____
17. Models that assist top-level managers in long range planning. ____
18. Models that help middle-managers control the work of the organization. ____
19. Individuals involved in the creation of information. ____
20. Type of program that integrates design and manufacturing activity. ____

OPEN-ENDED

On a separate sheet of paper, respond to each question or statement.

1. Name and discuss the five common departments explained in the chapter.
2. Discuss the roles of the three kinds of management in a corporation. What is information flow? How does this concept relate to the various managerial roles?
3. What are the four kinds of computer-based information systems? What kinds of employees is each designed to assist?
4. How are managerial reports utilized? Describe the different reports and their roles in managerial decision making.
5. What is the difference between an office automation system and a knowledge work system? Who is more likely to use each one? What is the difference between data workers and knowledge workers?

USING TECHNOLOGY

1 CAD

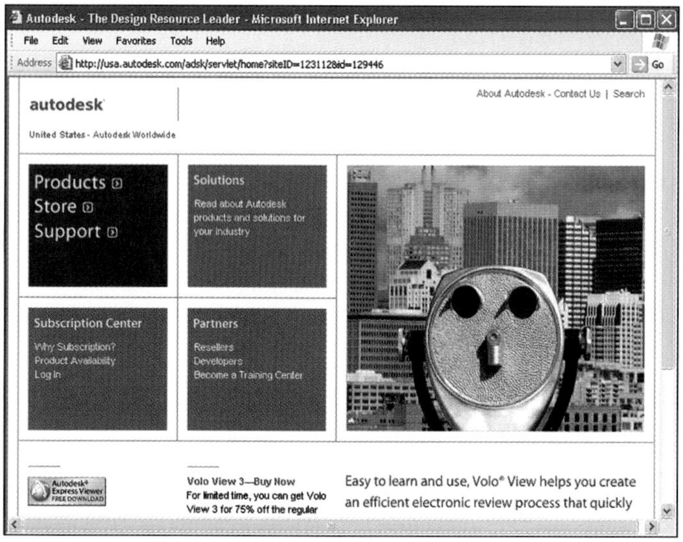

Many companies model plans or products using computer-aided design, or CAD. One of the most popular CAD applications is AutoCAD from Autodesk. To learn more about this product, visit our Web site at http://www.mhhe.com/oleary/CT05 to link to the AutoCAD site. Once connected, read about the features of the AutoCAD product, and then answer the following questions: (a) What type of modeling is AutoCAD used for? (b) What are the basic features of AutoCAD? (c) Cite some specific applications that AutoCAD is used for. (d) What special or advanced features does AutoCAD offer that set it apart from other CAD software?

2 Knowledge Work Systems

Companies always want to tailor their Web site to the needs of their customers to stay competitive; sites that are easier to navigate or provide the desired information quicker will be most in demand by consumers. One way to accomplish this is with Web site knowledge work software that monitors traffic on a Web server and provides reports for anomalous usage. Visit our Web site at http://www.mhhe.com/oleary/CT05 to link to a company that delivers such software. Once connected, review the company's products, and then answer the following questions: (a) What events can the software monitor for? Briefly describe each. (b) How are reports about Web site usage delivered? What information do they include? (c) How can a company apply this information to improve its Web site? Provide specific examples.

Online Personal Information Managers 3

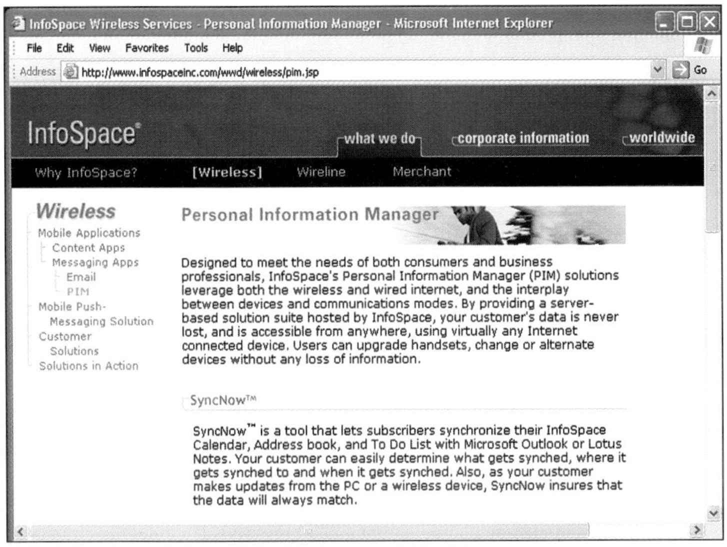

An important element for many personal information systems is a personal information manager or PIM. PIMs can either be stored onto your system's hard disk or accessed from the Web. Using the Web, locate and explore two or three online PIMs, and then answer the following questions in a one-page paper: (a) Describe the common features of online PIMs. (b) What is the advantage of using an online PIM versus one that is stored on your system's hard disk? (c) What are the disadvantages? (d) Of the PIMs you reviewed, which would you choose? Why?

Accounting Software 4

Accounting software packages are available to manage any organization's accounting needs, from small businesses to large corporations. Connect to our Web site at http://mhhe.comm/oleary/CT05 and select Using Technology from Tim's Toolbox to link to a leading accounting software package. Read about the product, and then answer the following questions in a one-page paper: (a) What type of organization is this product intended for? (b) List and describe the six basic accounting activities discussed in the chapter. (c) Describe how this product addresses each of the six activities.

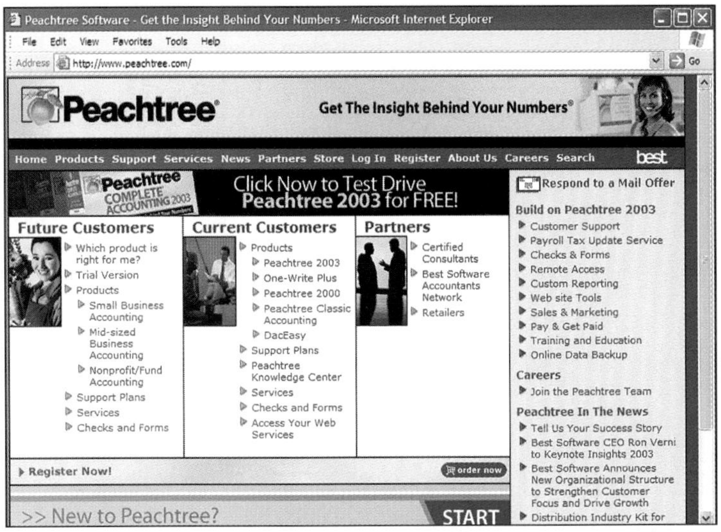

EXPANDING YOUR KNOWLEDGE

1 Computing Today CD

DVD Direct is similar to NETFLIX. Using the Web, locate and connect to the NETFLIX Web page. Once connected, explore the site and then answer the following: (a) How are DVD Direct and NETFLIX similar? (b) How are they different? (c) Does NETFLIX offer streaming video downloads? (d) If DVD Direct wanted to provide delivery via streaming video, what would you anticipate would be their greatest challenges?

2 Executive Support Systems

Research at least three different executive support systems using a Web search. Review each, and then answer the following questions: (a) Which ESSs did you review? (b) What are the common features of ESSs? (c) What specific types of decisions was each ESS designed to aid in? (d) What type of company is likely to use each? Provide some examples.

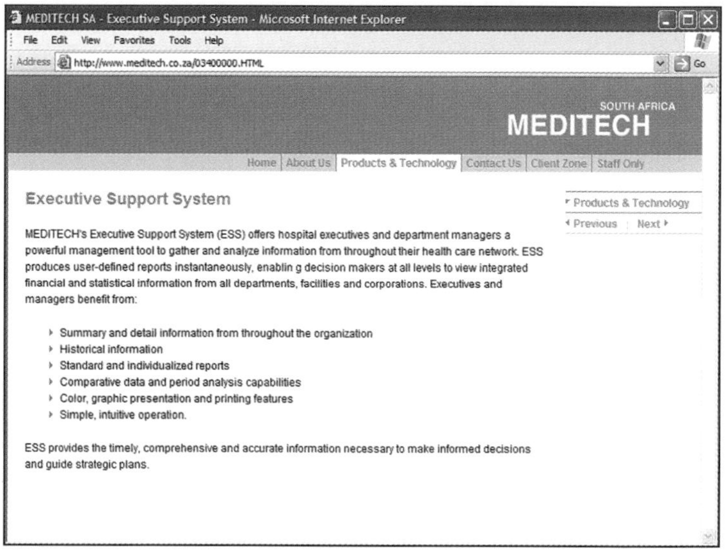

BUILDING YOUR PORTFOLIO

Office Automation Systems 1

Office Automation Systems are often used to minimize human error and enhance productivity in a variety of business disciplines. Used primarily to support data workers, these systems focus on managing documents, communicating, and scheduling. Write a one-page paper titled "Office Automation Systems" that addresses the following: (a) Define and describe an Office Automation System. (b) Describe the type of worker that an OAS supports. What is their role in a company? (c) Describe how OASs are used. Give specific examples.

Identity Theft 2

Identity theft occurs when someone acquires your personal information and uses it to hijack your finances. A common scenario is a thief's using your Social Security number to open a credit card account in your name. When they do not pay, it is your credit history that is blemished. Consider this scam thoroughly, and then answer the following questions in a one-page paper: (a) List three steps an individual should take to avoid identity theft. (b) List three steps a corporation that maintains your personal data in their information system should take to safeguard your data. (c) How can Internet activities contribute to the likelihood of identity theft? How can this be prevented?

DATABASES

OBJECTIVES

After you have read this chapter, you should be able to:

1. **Distinguish between the physical and logical view of data.**
2. **Describe how data is organized: characters, fields, records, files, and databases.**
3. **Describe databases, database issues, and database management systems (DBMS).**
4. **Describe five data models: hierarchical, network, relational, multidimensional, and object-oriented.**
5. **Distinguish among individual, company, distributed, proprietary, and Web databases.**
6. **Recognize strategic database uses and security concerns.**

Data Organization
Uses characters, fields, records, files, and databases

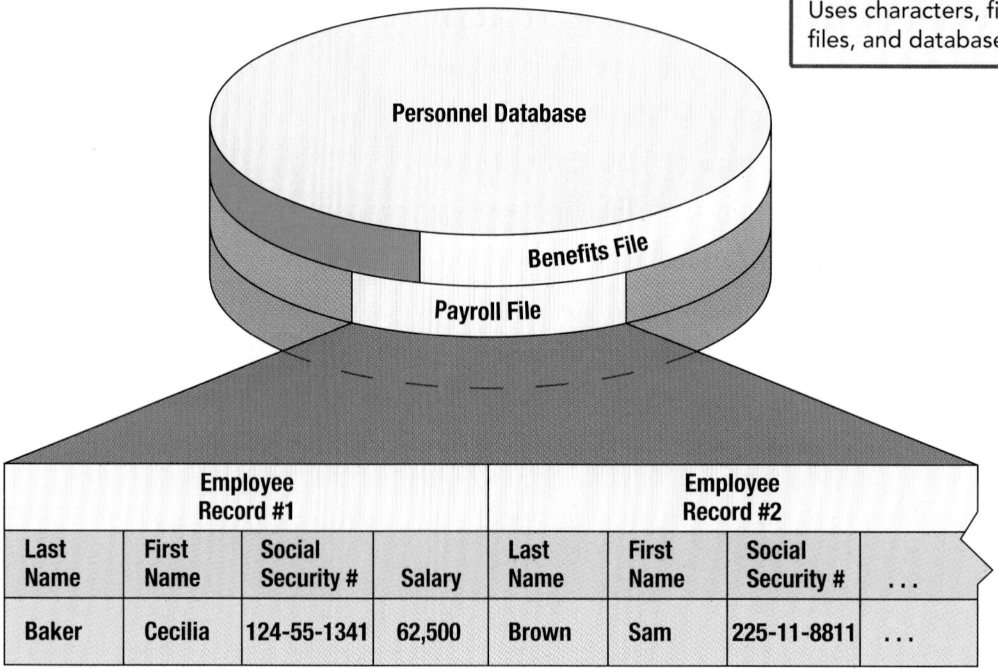
Personnel Database
Benefits File
Payroll File
Employee Record #1
Employee Record #2
Last Name
First Name
Social Security #
Salary
Last Name
First Name
Social Security #
...
Baker
Cecilia
124-55-1341
62,500
Brown
Sam
225-11-8811
...

Like a library, secondary storage is designed to store information. How is such stored information organized? What are files and databases and why do you need to know anything about them? Perhaps the answer is this: To be a competent and knowledgeable user of information in the Information Age, you have to know how to find information, and so you have to understand how it is stored.

At one time, it was not important for microcomputer users to know much about data files and databases. However, the recent arrival of very powerful microcomputers and their connectivity to communications networks and the Internet has changed that. Communications lines and the Internet extend the reach of your microcomputer well beyond the desktop.

Competent and knowledgeable end users need to understand data fields, records, files, and databases. They need to be aware of the different ways in which a database can be structured and the different types of databases. Also, they need to know the most important database uses and issues.

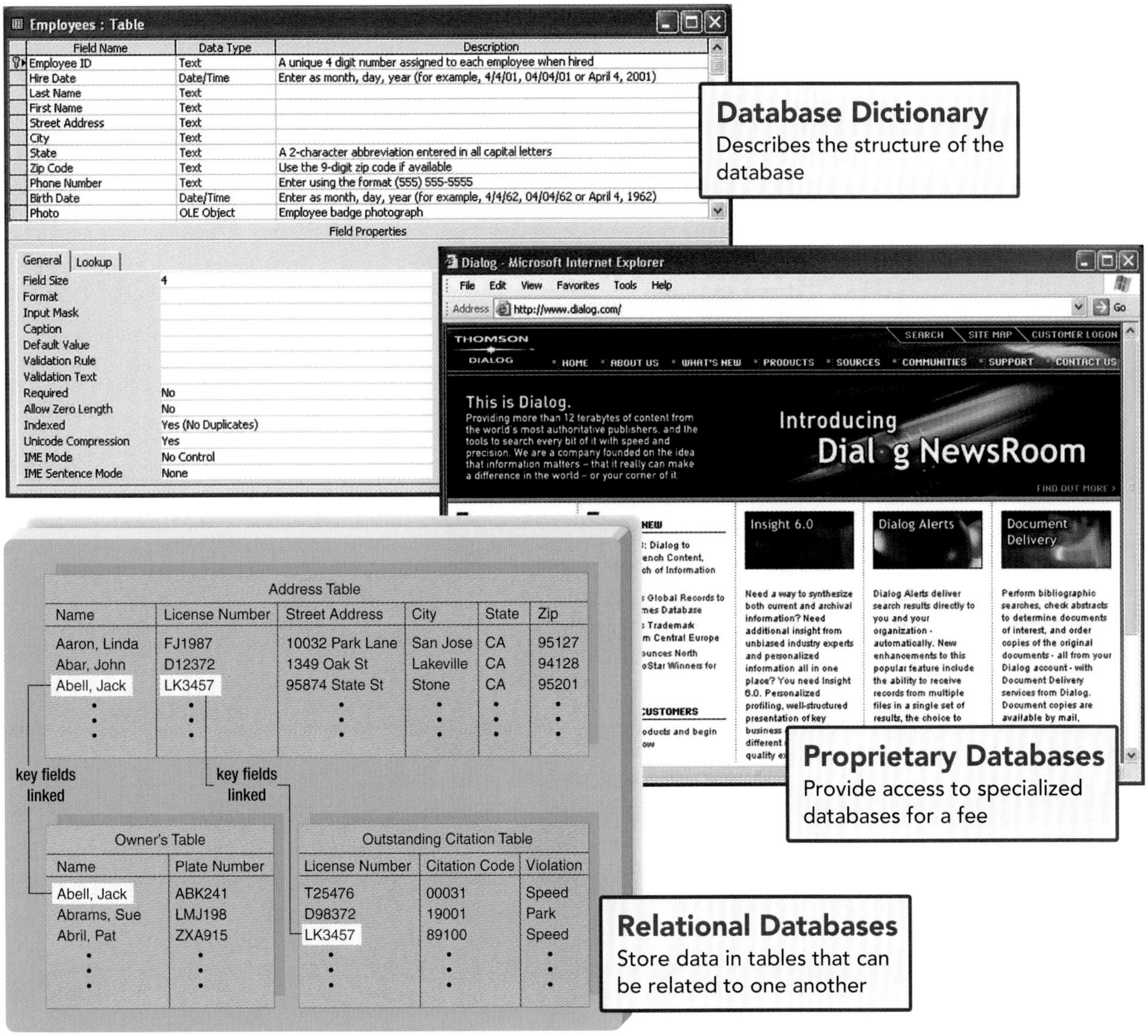
Database Dictionary
Describes the structure of the database
Proprietary Databases
Provide access to specialized databases for a fee
key fields linked
key fields linked
Relational Databases
Store data in tables that can be related to one another

DATA

Data is defined as facts or observations about people, places, things, and events. Physical view focuses on actual format and location of data. Logical view focuses on meaning and content of data.

As we have discussed throughout this book, information systems consist of people, procedures, software, hardware, and data. This chapter focuses on the last element, **data,** which can be defined as facts or observations about people, places, things, and events. More specifically, this chapter focuses on how databases are used to store, organize, and use data.

Not long ago, data was limited to numbers, letters, and symbols recorded by keyboards. Now, as depicted in Figure 13-1, data is much richer and includes:

- Audio captured, interpreted, and saved using microphones and voice recognition systems.
- Music captured from the Internet, from MIDI devices, and other sources.
- Photographs captured by digital cameras, edited by image editing software, and shared with others over the Internet.
- Video captured by digital video cameras, TV tuner cards, and WebCams.

There are two ways or perspectives to view data. These perspectives are the *physical view* and the *logical view.* The **physical view** focuses on the actual format and location of the data. As discussed in Chapter 6, data is recorded as digital bits that are typically grouped together into bytes that represent characters using a coding scheme such as ASCII. Typically, only very specialized computer professionals are concerned with the physical view. The other perspective, **logical view,** focuses on the meaning and content of the data. End users and most computer professionals are concerned with this view. They are involved with actually using the data with application programs. This chapter presents the logical view of data and how data is stored in databases.

Concept Check

- ✓ Describe some of the different types of data.
- ✓ What is the physical view of data?
- ✓ What is the logical view of data?

DATA ORGANIZATION

Character, field, record, file, and database are logical data groups. Key fields uniquely identify records. Batch processing processes data later. Real-time processing processes data now.

You want to know your final grades for the semester. You call your school's registrar after your last final exam to find out your grade point average. Perhaps you are told, "Sorry, that's not in the computer yet." Why can't they tell you? How is the school's computer system different from, say, your bank's, where deposits and withdrawals seem to be recorded right away?

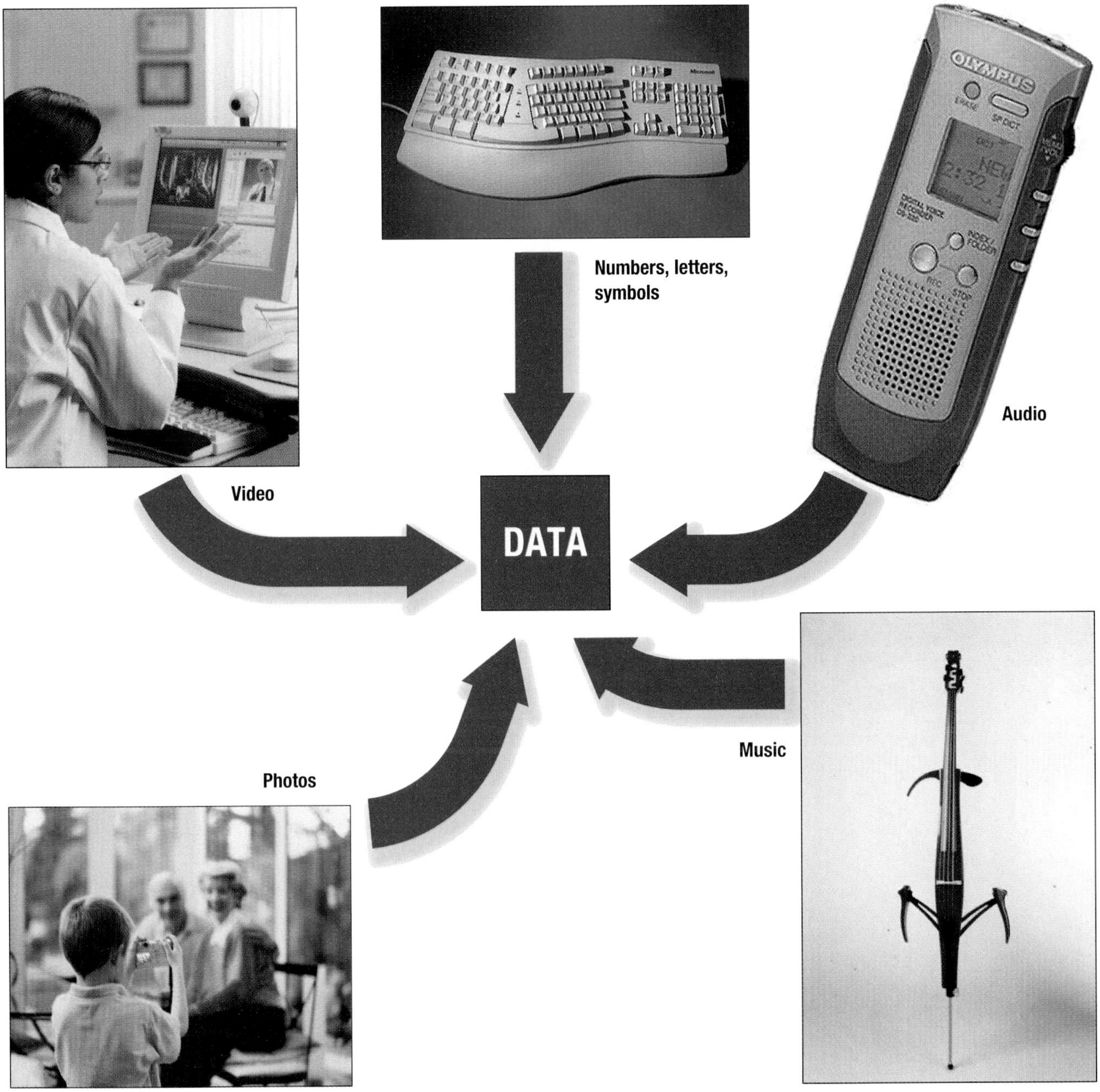

Figure 13-1 Different types of data

The answers to these questions lie in part in how the data is organized into logical groups or categories. Each group is more complex than the one before. (See Figure 13-2.)

- **Character:** A character is the most basic logical data element. It is a single letter, number, or special character such as a punctuation mark or a symbol such as $. For example, in Figure 13-2 the letter B is the first letter of an employee's name.
- **Field:** The next higher level is a field or group of related characters. In our example, Baker is the data field for the Last Name of an employee. It consists of the individual letters (characters) that make up the last name. A data field represents an **attribute** (description or characteristic) of some **entity** (person, place, thing, or object). For example, an employee is an entity with many attributes including their last name.

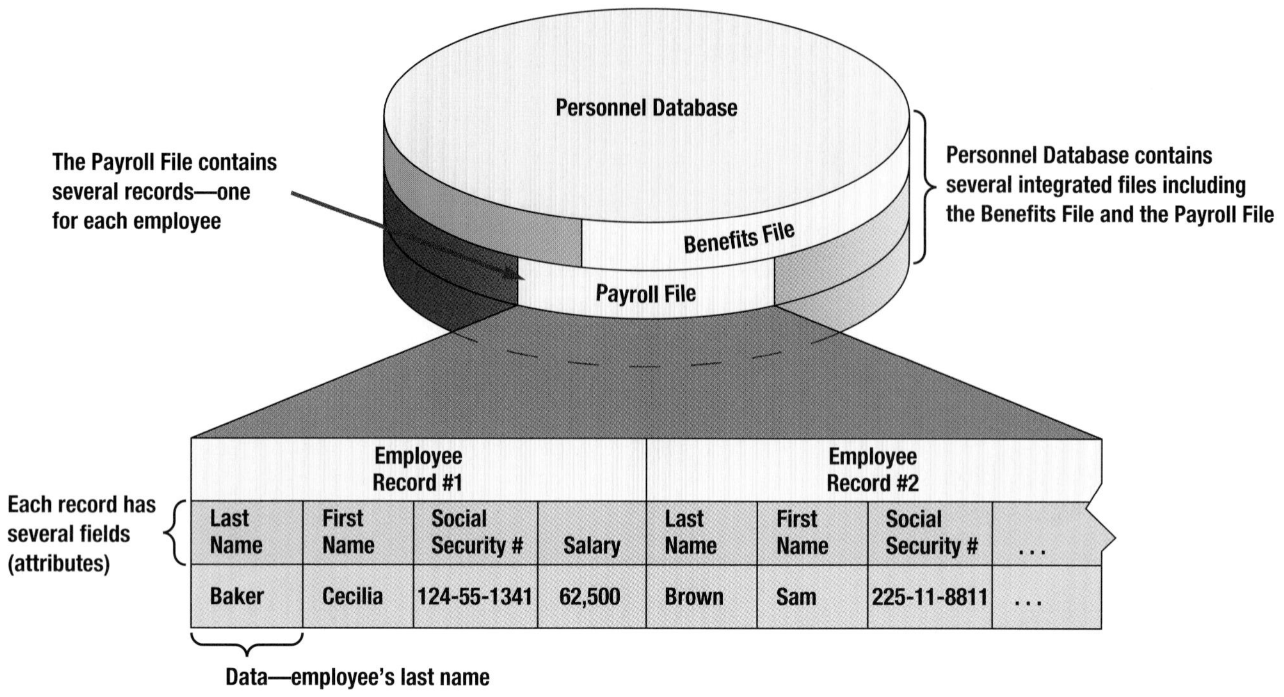
Personnel Database
The Payroll File contains several records—one for each employee
Personnel Database contains several integrated files including the Benefits File and the Payroll File
Benefits File
Payroll File
Employee Record #1
Employee Record #2
Each record has several fields (attributes)
Last Name
First Name
Social Security #
Salary
Last Name
First Name
Social Security #
. . .
Baker
Cecilia
124-55-1341
62,500
Brown
Sam
225-11-8811
. . .
Data—employee's last name

Figure 13-2 Logical data organization

- **Record:** A record is a collection of related fields. A record represents a collection of attributes that describe an entity. In our example, the payroll record for an employee consists of the data fields describing the attributes for one employee. These attributes are First Name, Last Name, Social Security Number, and Salary.
- **File:** A file is a collection of related records. For example, the payroll file would include payroll information (records) for all the employees (entities).
- **Database:** A database is an integrated collection of logically related records or objects. For example, the Personnel Database would include all related employee files including payroll file and benefits file.

KEY FIELD

Each record in a database has at least one distinctive field, called the **key field.** Also known as the **primary field,** this field uniquely identifies the record. For many employee and university databases, the key field is social security number. Key fields in different files can be used to integrate the data in a database. For example, in the Personnel Database, both the Payroll and the Benefits files include the field Social Security #. Data from the two files could be related by combining all records with the same key field (social security number). While social security number is the most commonly used key field, other widely used key fields are student identification numbers, employee identification numbers, part numbers, and inventory numbers.

BATCH VERSUS REAL-TIME PROCESSING

Traditionally data is processed in one of two ways. These are batch processing, what we might call "later," and real-time processing, what we might call "now." These two methods have been used to handle common record-keeping activities such as payroll and sales orders.

- **Batch processing:** In **batch processing,** data is collected over several hours, days, or even weeks. It is then processed all at once—as a "batch."

If you have a bank credit card, your bill probably reflects batch processing. That is, during the month, you buy things and charge them to your credit card. Each time you charge something, an electronic copy of the transaction is sent to the credit card company. At some point in the month, the company's data processing department puts all those transactions (and those of many other customers) together and processes them at one time. The company then sends you a single bill totaling the amount you owe. (See Figure 13-3.)

- **Real-time processing:** Totaling up the sales charged to your bank credit card is an example of batch processing. You might use another kind of card—your bank's automated teller machine (ATM) card—for the second kind of processing. **Real-time processing,** also known as **online processing,** occurs when data is processed at the same time the transaction occurs. As you use your ATM card to withdraw cash, the system automatically computes the balance remaining in your account. (See Figure 13-4.)

At one time, only magnetic tape storage, and therefore only sequential access storage (as we discussed in Chapter 9), was available. All processing then was batch processing and was done on mainframe computers. Even today, a great deal of mainframe time is dedicated to this kind of processing. Many smaller organizations, however, use microcomputers for this purpose.

Real-time processing is made possible by the availability of disk packs and direct access storage (as we described in Chapter 9). Direct access storage makes it possible to go quickly and directly to a particular record. (In sequential access storage, by contrast, the user must wait for the computer to scan several records one at a time. It continues scanning until the desired record is located.)

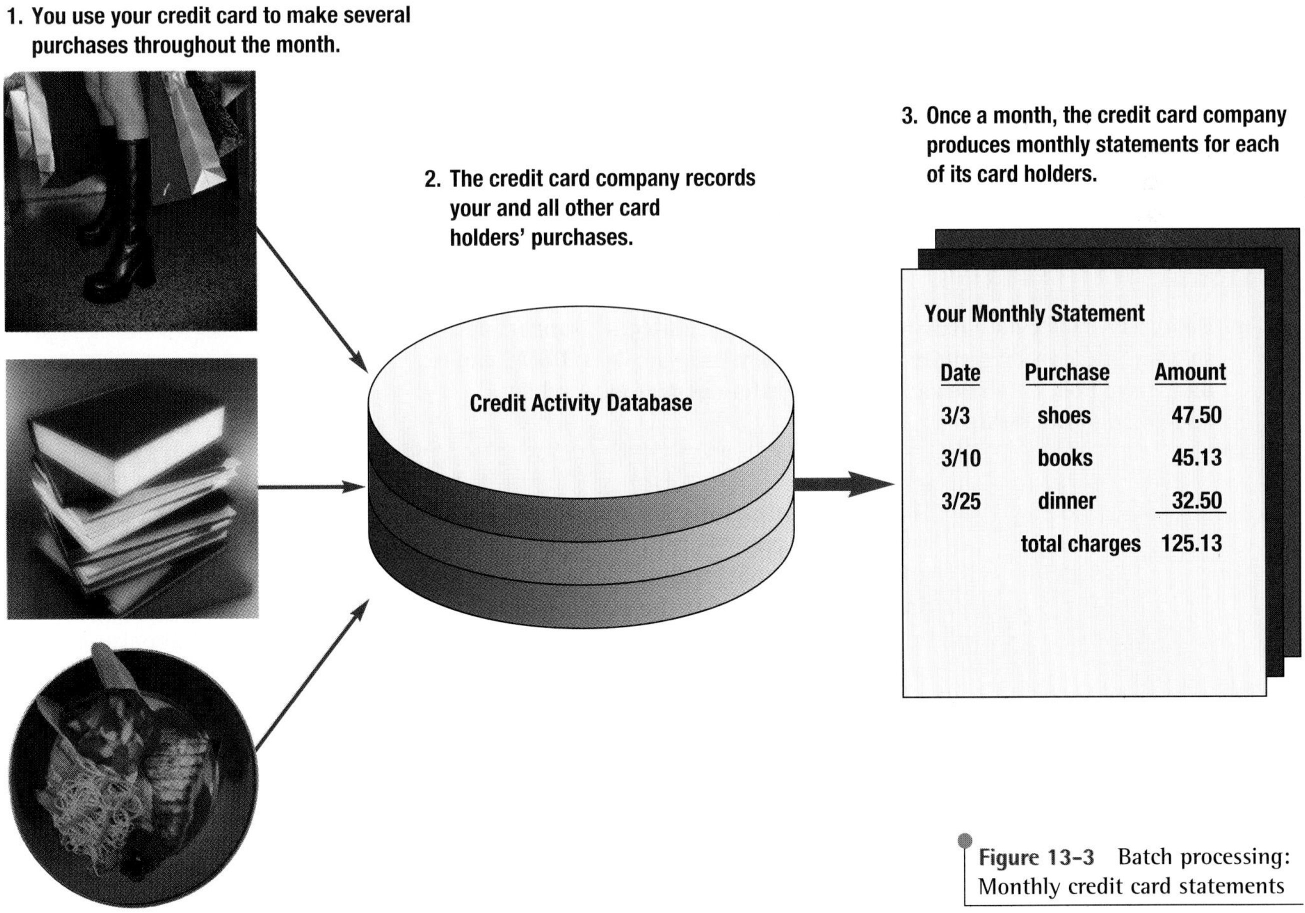
1. You use your credit card to make several purchases throughout the month.
2. The credit card company records your and all other card holders' purchases.
Credit Activity Database
3. Once a month, the credit card company produces monthly statements for each of its card holders.
Your Monthly Statement
Date Purchase Amount
3/3 shoes 47.50
3/10 books 45.13
3/25 dinner 32.50
total charges 125.13

Figure 13-3 Batch processing: Monthly credit card statements

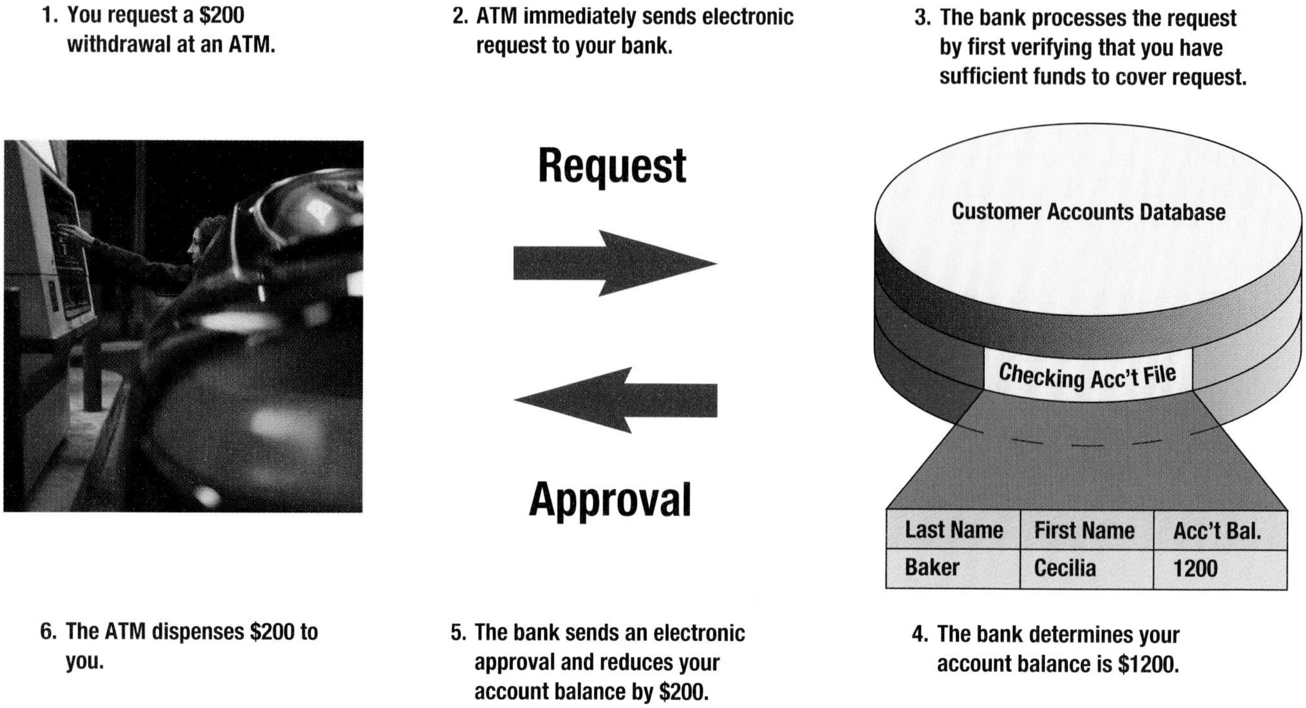
1. You request a $200 withdrawal at an ATM.
2. ATM immediately sends electronic request to your bank.
3. The bank processes the request by first verifying that you have sufficient funds to cover request.
Request
Customer Accounts Database
Checking Acc't File
Approval
Last Name
First Name
Acc't Bal.
Baker
Cecilia
1200
6. The ATM dispenses $200 to you.
5. The bank sends an electronic approval and reduces your account balance by $200.
4. The bank determines your account balance is $1200.

Figure 13-4 Real-time processing: ATM withdrawal

Concept Check

- ✔ Describe how data is organized.
- ✔ What are key fields and how are they used?
- ✔ Compare batch processing and real-time processing.

DATABASES

Databases reduce data redundancy, enhance data integrity, support data sharing, and provide security. DBMS software has five parts: DBMS engine, data definition, data manipulation, application generation, and data administration subsystems.

Many organizations have multiple files on the same subject or person. For example, records for the same customer may appear in different files in the sales department, billing department, and credit department. This is called **data redundancy.** If the customer moves, then the address in each file must be updated. If one or more files are overlooked, problems will likely result. For example, a product ordered might be sent to the new address, but the bill might be sent to the old address. This situation results from a lack of **data integrity.**

Moreover, data spread around in different files is not as useful. The marketing department, for instance, might want to offer special promotions to customers who order large quantities of merchandise. However, they may be unable to do so because the information they need is in the billing department. A database can make the needed information available.

NEED FOR DATABASES

For both individuals and organizations, there are many advantages to having databases:

- **Sharing:** In organizations, information from one department can be readily shared with others. Billing could let marketing know which customers ordered large quantities of merchandise.
- **Security:** Users are given passwords or access only to the kind of information they need. Thus, the payroll department may have access to employees' pay rates, but other departments would not.
- **Less data redundancy:** With several departments having access to one file, there are fewer files. Excess storage is reduced. Microcomputers linked by a network to a file server, for example, could replace the hard disks located in several individual microcomputers.
- **Data integrity:** Older filing systems many times did not have "integrity." That is, a change made in the file in one department might not be made in the file in another department. As you might expect, this can cause serious problems and conflicts when data is used for important decisions affecting both departments.

DATABASE MANAGEMENT

In order to create, modify, and gain access to a database, special software is required. This software is called a **database management system,** which is commonly abbreviated **DBMS.**

Some DBMSs, such as Access, are designed specifically for microcomputers. Other DBMSs are designed for mainframes and for specialized database or file servers. DBMS software is made up of five parts or subsystems: *DBMS engine, data definition, data manipulation, application generation,* and *data administration.*

- The **DBMS engine** provides a bridge between the logical view of the data and the physical view of the data. When users request data (logical perspective), the DBMS engine handles the details of actually locating the data (physical perspective).
- The **data definition subsystem** defines the logical structure of the database by using a **data dictionary.** This dictionary contains a description of the structure of data in the database. For a particular item of data, it defines the names used for a particular field. It defines the type of data for each field (text, numeric, time, graphic, audio, and video). An example of an Access data dictionary form is presented in Figure 13-5.
- The **data manipulation subsystem** provides tools for maintaining and analyzing data. Maintaining

Figure 13-5 Access data dictionary form

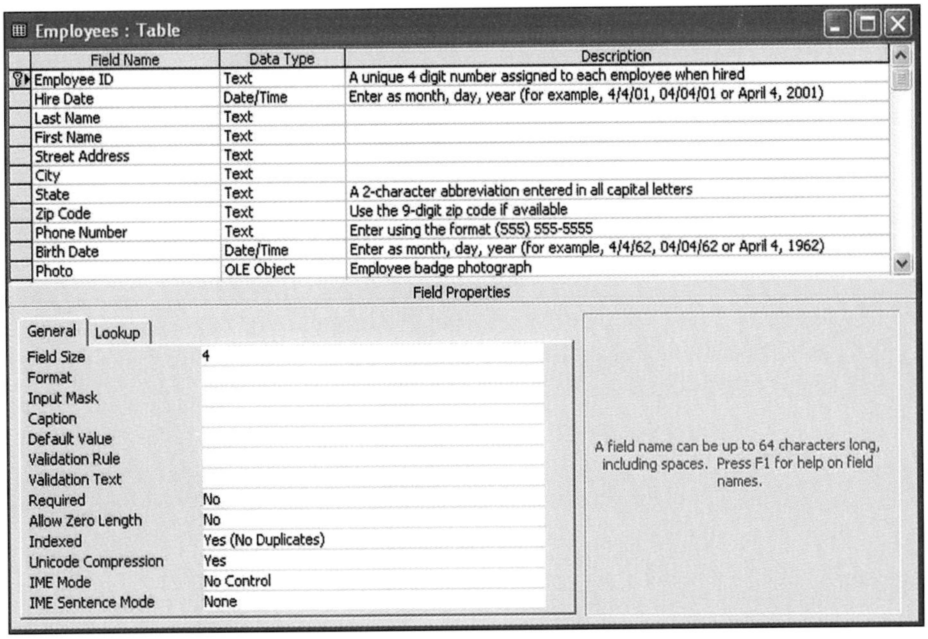

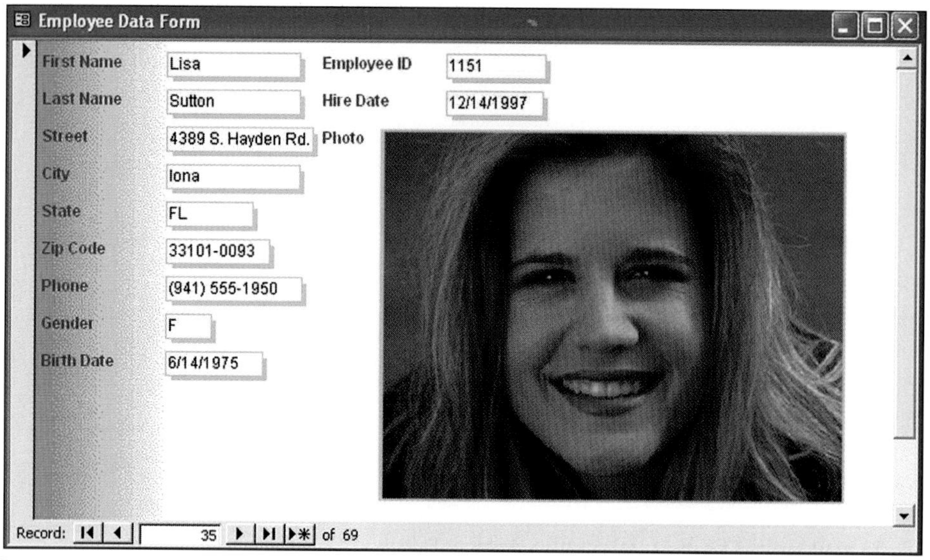
Employee Data Form
First Name
Lisa
Employee ID
1151
Last Name
Sutton
Hire Date
12/14/1997
Street
4389 S. Hayden Rd.
Photo
City
Iona
State
FL
Zip Code
33101-0093
Phone
(941) 555-1950
Gender
F
Birth Date
6/14/1975
Record:
35
of 69

Figure 13-6 Access data entry form

data is known as **data maintenance.** It involves adding new data, deleting old data, and editing existing data. Analysis tools support viewing all or selected parts of the data, querying the database, and generating reports. Specific tools include **query-by-example** and specialized programming languages called **structured query languages (SQL).** (Structured query languages and other types of programming languages will be discussed in Chapter 15.)

- The **application generation subsystem** provides tools to create data entry forms and specialized programming languages that interface or work with common and widely used programming languages such as COBOL. See Figure 13-6 for a data entry form created by the application generation subsystem in Access.
- The **data administration subsystem** helps to manage the overall database including maintaining security, providing disaster recovery support, and monitoring the overall performance of database operations. Larger organizations typically employ highly trained computer specialists, called **database administrators (DBAs),** to interact with the data administration subsystem. Additional duties of database administrators include determining **processing rights** or determining which people have access to what kinds of data in the database.

Concept Check

- ✓ What are some of the advantages to having databases?
- ✓ What is DBMS software?
- ✓ List the five basic subsystems and describe each.

DBMS STRUCTURE

Data models define rules and standards for data in a database. The five data models are hierarchical, network, relational, multidimensional, and object-oriented.

DBMS programs are designed to work with data that is logically structured or arranged in a particular way. This arrangement is known as the **data model.** These models define rules and standards for all the data in a database. For example, Access is designed to work with databases using the relational data model. There are five widely used data models: *hierarchical, network, relational, multidimensional,* and *object-oriented.*

HIERARCHICAL DATABASE

Figure 13-7 Airlines may use a hierarchical database for their reservations system

At one time, nearly every DBMS designed for mainframes used the hierarchical data model. In a **hierarchical database,** fields or records are structured in nodes. **Nodes** are points connected like the branches of an upside-down tree. Each entry has one **parent node,** although a parent may have several **child nodes.** This is sometimes described as a **one-to-many relationship.** To find a particular field you have to start at the top with a parent and trace down the tree to a child.

The nodes farther down the system are subordinate to the ones above, like the hierarchy of managers in a corporation. An example of a hierarchical database is a nationwide airline reservations system. (See Figure 13-7.) The parent node is the "departure" city, Los Angeles. This parent has four children, labeled "arrival." New York, one of the children, has three children of its own. They are labeled "flight number." Flight 110 has three children, labeled "passenger." (See Figure 13-8.)

The problem with a hierarchical database is that if one parent node is deleted, so are all the subordinate child nodes. Moreover, a child node cannot be added unless a parent node is added first. The most significant limitation is the rigid structure: one parent only per child, and no relationships or connections between the child nodes themselves.

NETWORK DATABASE

Responding to the limitations of the hierarchical data model, network models were developed. A **network database** also has a hierarchical arrangement of nodes. However, each child node may have more than one parent node. This is sometimes described as a **many-to-many relationship.** There are additional connections—called **pointers**—between parent nodes and child nodes. Thus, a node may be reached through more than one path. It may be traced down through different branches.

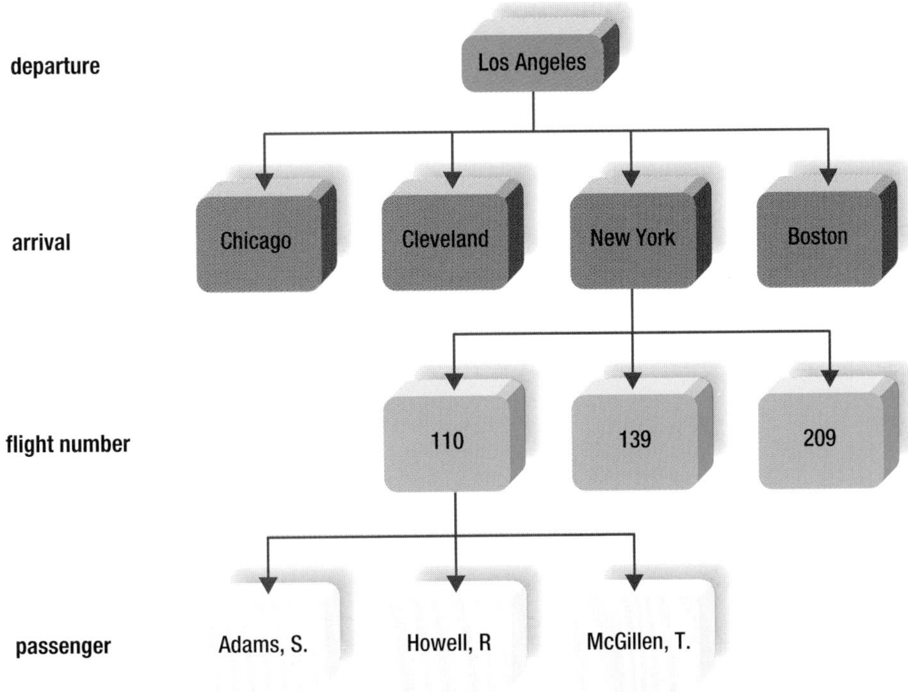

Figure 13-8 Hierarchical database

Figure 13-9 Universities may use a network database

For example a university could use this type of organization to record students taking classes. (See Figure 13-9.) If you trace through the logic of this organization, you can see that each student can have more than one teacher. (See Figure 13-10.) Each teacher can also teach more than one course. Students may take more than a single course. This demonstrates how the network arrangement is more flexible and in many cases more efficient than the hierarchical arrangement.

RELATIONAL DATABASE

A more flexible type of organization is the **relational database.** In this structure, there are no access paths down a hierarchy. Rather, the data elements are stored in different tables, each of which consists of rows and columns. A table is called a **relation.**

An example of a relational database is shown in Figure 13-11. The address table contains the names, driver's license numbers, and addresses for all registered drivers in a particular state. Within the table, a row resembles a record—

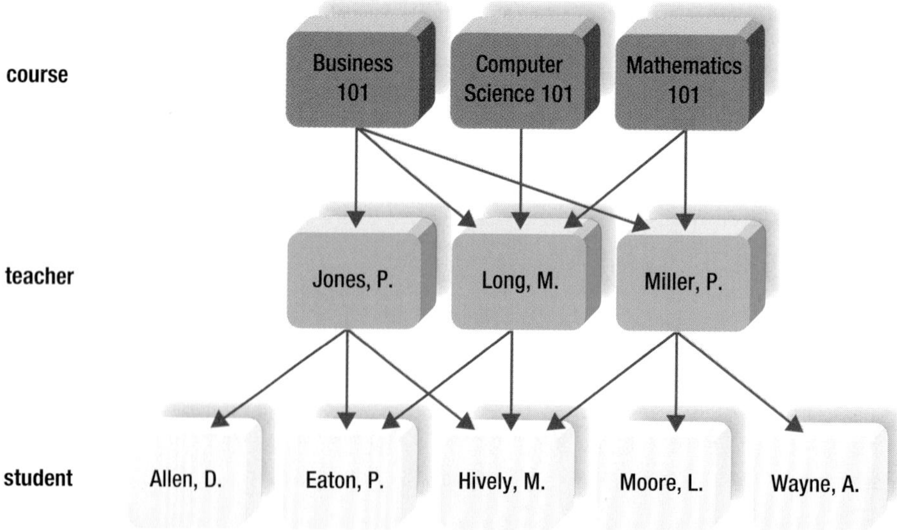
course
Business 101
Computer Science 101
Mathematics 101
teacher
Jones, P.
Long, M.
Miller, P.
student
Allen, D.
Eaton, P.
Hively, M.
Moore, L.
Wayne, A.

Figure 13-10 Network database

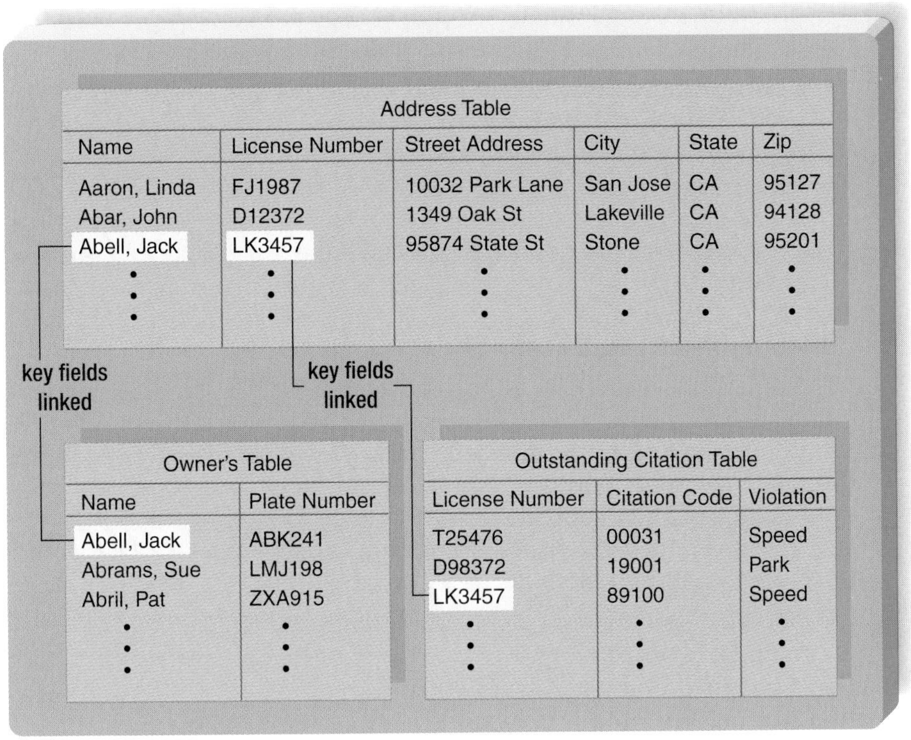
Address Table
Name
License Number
Street Address
City
State
Zip
Aaron, Linda
FJ1987
10032 Park Lane
San Jose
CA
95127
Abar, John
D12372
1349 Oak St
Lakeville
CA
94128
Abell, Jack
LK3457
95874 State St
Stone
CA
95201
key fields linked
key fields linked
Owner's Table
Name
Plate Number
Abell, Jack
ABK241
Abrams, Sue
LMJ198
Abril, Pat
ZXA915
Outstanding Citation Table
License Number
Citation Code
Violation
T25476
00031
Speed
D98372
19001
Park
LK3457
89100
Speed

Figure 13-11 Relational database

for example, information about one driver. A column entry resembles a field. The driver's name is one field; the driver's license number is another field. All related tables must have a **common data item** (key field). Thus, information stored on one table can be linked with information stored on another. One common field might be a person's social security number. Another might be a driver's license number.

Thus, police officers who stop a speeding car can radio the driver's license number and the car's license plate number to the Department of Motor Vehicles. They can use the driver's license number as the key field. With it they can find out about any unpaid traffic violations (such as parking tickets) or outstanding arrest warrants. Also using the license plate number they can obtain the car owner's name and address. If the owner's name and address do not match the driver who has been stopped, the police officer may check further for a stolen vehicle. (See Figure 13-12.)

The most valuable feature of relational databases is their simplicity. Entries can be easily added, deleted, and modified. The hierarchical and network databases are more rigid. The relational organization is common for microcomputer DBMSs, such as Access, Paradox, dBASE, and R: Base. Relational databases are also widely used for mainframe and minicomputer systems.

Figure 13-12 The Department of Motor Vehicles may use a relational database

MULTIDIMENSIONAL DATABASE

The multidimensional data model is a variation and an extension of the relational data model. While relational databases use tables consisting of rows and columns, **multidimensional databases** extend this two-dimensional data model to include additional or multiple dimensions sometimes called a **hyper cube.** Data can be viewed as a cube having three or more sides and consisting of cells. Each side of the cube is considered a dimension of the data. In this way, complex relationships between data can be represented and efficiently analyzed.

Figure 13-13 A fitness club may use an object-oriented database to organize employee and member data

Multidimensional databases provide several advantages over relational databases. Two of the most significant advantages are:

- **Conceptualization.** Multidimensional databases and hyper cubes provide users with an intuitive model in which complex data and relationships can be conceptualized.
- **Processing speed.** Analyzing and querying a large multidimensional database is much faster. For example, a query requiring just a few seconds on a multidimensional database could take minutes or hours to perform on a relational database.

OBJECT-ORIENTED DATABASE

The other data structures are primarily designed to handle structured data such as names, addresses, pay rates, and so on. **Object-oriented databases** are more flexible, store data as well as instructions to manipulate the data, and are able to handle unstructured data such as photographs, audio, and video.

Object-oriented databases organize data using objects, classes, entities, attributes, and methods.

- **Objects** are items that contain both data and instructions to manipulate the data.
- **Classes** are similar objects grouped together.
- **Entities** are a person, place, thing, or event that is to be described.
- **Attributes** are the description of entities. They are similar to fields.
- **Methods** are descriptions of how the data is to be manipulated.

For example, a health club might use an object-oriented employment database. (See Figure 13-13.)

The objects Trainers, Front Desk, and Managers describe the three types of employees at the health club. These objects are grouped together to form the class Employees. Time Cards are another class. Each object in a class has some common attributes. In the case of the Employee class, the common attributes are PHOTO, FIRST NAME, LAST NAME, and ADDRESS. YEARLY SALARY is a unique attribute assigned to the Managers object. The object-oriented database also contains methods for calculating weekly payroll checks for trainers, front desk, and manager employees. (See Figure 13-14.) While hierarchical

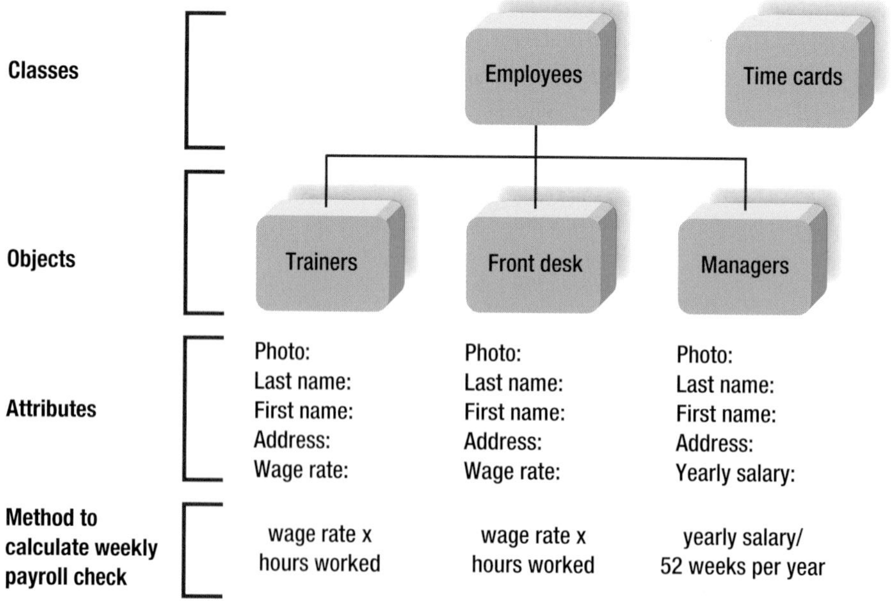

Figure 13-14 Object-oriented database

Organization	Description
Hierarchical	Data structured in nodes organized like an upside-down tree; each parent node can have several children; each child node can have only one parent
Network	Like hierarchical except that each child can have several parents
Relational	Data stored in tables consisting of rows and columns
Multidimensional	Data stored in hyper cubes with three or more dimensions
Object-oriented	Organizes data using objects, classes, entities, attributes, and methods

Figure 13-15 Summary of DBMS organization

and network databases are still widely used, the relational, multidimensional, and object-oriented data models are more popular today.

For a summary of DBMS organization, see Figure 13-15.

Concept Check

- What are data models?
- List the five principal DBMS formats and discuss each.
- What is the difference between a relational database and a multidimensional database?

TYPES OF DATABASES

There are five classifications of databases: individual, company, distributed, proprietary, and Web.

Databases may be small or large, limited in accessibility or widely accessible. Databases may be classified into five types: *individual, company (or shared), distributed, proprietary,* and *Web.*

INDIVIDUAL

The **individual database** is also called a **microcomputer database.** It is a collection of integrated files primarily used by just one person. Typically, the data and the DBMS are under the direct control of the user. They are stored either on the user's hard-disk drive or on a LAN file server.

There may be many times in your life when you will find this kind of database valuable. If you are in sales, for instance, a microcomputer database can be used to keep track of your customers. If you are a sales manager, you can keep track of your salespeople and their performance. If you are an advertising account executive, you can keep track of what work and how many hours to charge each client.

COMPANY OR SHARED

Companies, of course, create databases for their own use. The **company (shared) database** may be stored on a mainframe and managed by a database administrator. Users throughout the company have access to the database through their microcomputers linked to local area networks or wide area networks.

Company databases are of two types:

- The **common operational database** contains details about the operations of the company, such as inventory, production, and sales. It contains data describing the day-to-day operations of the organization.
- The **common user database** contains selected information both from the common operational database and from outside private (proprietary) databases. Managers can tap into this information on their microcomputers or terminals and use it for decision making.

As we discussed in Chapter 12, company databases are the foundation for management information systems. For instance, a department store can record all sales transactions in the database. A sales manager can use this information to see which salespeople are selling the most products. The manager can then determine year-end sales bonuses. Or the store's buyer can learn which products are selling well or not selling and make adjustments when reordering. A top executive might combine overall store sales trends with information from outside databases about consumer and population trends. This information could be used to change the whole merchandising strategy of the store.

DISTRIBUTED

Many times the data in a company is stored not in just one location but in several locations. It is made accessible through a variety of communications networks. The database, then, is a **distributed database.** That is, it is located in a place or places other than where users are located. Typically, database servers on a client/server network provide the link between users and the distant data.

For instance, some database information can be at regional offices. Some can be at company headquarters, some down the hall from you, and some even overseas. Sales figures for a chain of department stores, then, could be located at the various stores. But executives at district offices or at the chain's headquarters could have access to these figures.

PROPRIETARY

A **proprietary database** is generally an enormous database that an organization develops to cover particular subjects. It offers access to this database to the public or selected outside individuals for a fee. Sometimes proprietary databases are also called **information utilities** or **data banks.** An example is Dialog Information Services, which offers a variety of financial services. (See Figure 13-16.)

Some important proprietary databases are the following:

- **CSi:** Offers consumer and business services, including electronic mail.
- **Dialog Information Services:** Offers business information, as well as technical and scientific information.
- **Dow Jones Interactive Publishing:** Provides world news and information on business, investments, and stocks.
- **Prodigy:** Offers news and information on business and economics, as well as leisure services.

Most of the proprietary databases are designed for organizational as well as individual use. Organizations typically pay a membership fee plus hourly use fees. Often, individuals are able to search the database to obtain a summary of available information without charge. They pay only for those items selected for further investigation.

WEB DATABASE

While a **Web database** is similar to the other types of databases, its distinguishing feature is that it is available over the Web. Nearly every Web site you visit collects data about you and enters that data into a Web database. Specialized search sites use their Web databases to provide information to you.

As we discussed in Chapter 2, when you surf the Web, traditional and ad network cookies are collecting data about you. This data is sent back to a Web site that uses a Web database to store, organize, and use your data. One common use is by Web site developers who collect visitor information in order to better serve their customers and to improve the effectiveness of their Web sites. Another use is by information resellers who collect and market the data to others.

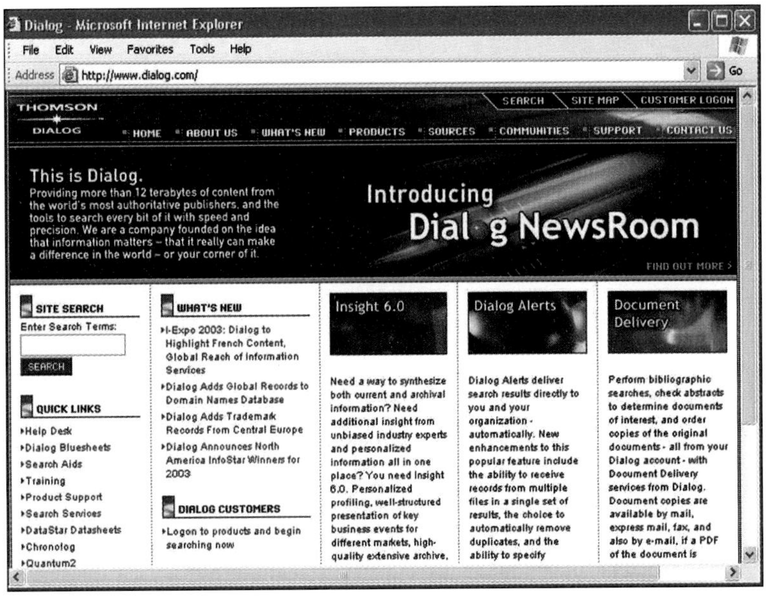

Figure 13-16 Proprietary database (Dialog Information Services)

As we discussed in Chapter 2, whenever you use a search engine on the Web, you are interacting with a database. For example, if you connect to the Yahoo! site and search using a keyword such as "travel," the site searches its Web database to locate all pages containing that keyword.

Whenever you complete a form or provide any information at a Web site, the data is recorded by that Web site's Web database. Typically, this is accomplished by special interface programs that create the input forms, accept your input, and send the data to the Web database. Typically, these programs consist of **CGI (Common Gateway Interface) scripts.**

See Figure 13-17 for a summary of the five types of databases.

Type	Description
Individual	Integrated files used by just one person
Company	Common operational or commonly used files shared in an organization
Distributed	Database spread geographically and accessed using database server
Proprietary	Information utilities or databanks available to users on a wide range of topics for a fee
Web	Used by Web sites collecting data and search sites providing data

Figure 13-17 Summary of the five types of databases

Concept Check

- ✔ What are the five types of databases?
- ✔ Give a brief example of each type of database.
- ✔ What distinguishes Web databases from the other types of databases?

DATABASE USES AND ISSUES

Data warehouse is a type of database. Data mining is a technique to locate related information and patterns. Firewalls are hardware and software to control access.

Databases offer great opportunities for productivity. In fact, in corporate libraries, electronic databases are now considered more valuable than books and journals. However, maintaining databases means users must make constant efforts to keep them from being tampered with or misused.

STRATEGIC USES

Databases help users to keep up to date and to plan for the future. To support the needs of managers and other business professionals, many organizations collect data from a variety of internal and external databases. This data is then stored in a special type of database called a **data warehouse.** A technique called **data mining** is often used to search these databases to look for related information and patterns.

There are hundreds of databases available to help users with both general and specific business purposes, including:

- *Business directories* providing addresses, financial and marketing information, products, and trade and brand names.
- *Demographic data,* such as county and city statistics, current estimates on population and income, employment statistics, census data, and so on.
- *Business statistical information,* such as financial information on publicly traded companies, market potential of certain retail stores, and other business data and information.
- *Text databases* providing articles from business publications, press releases, reviews on companies and products, and so on.
- *Web databases* covering a wide range of topics including all of the above. As mentioned earlier, Web search sites like Yahoo! maintain extensive databases of available Web sites.

SECURITY

Precisely because databases are so valuable, their security has become a vital issue. As we discussed in Chapter 11, there are several database security concerns. One concern is that personal and private information about people stored in databases may be used for the wrong purposes. For instance, a person's credit history or medical records might be used to make hiring or promotion decisions. Another concern is unauthorized users gaining access to a database. For example, there have been numerous instances in which a computer virus has been launched into a database or network.

Security may require putting guards in company computer rooms and checking the identification of everyone admitted. Some security systems electronically check fingerprints. (See Figure 13-18.) Security is particularly

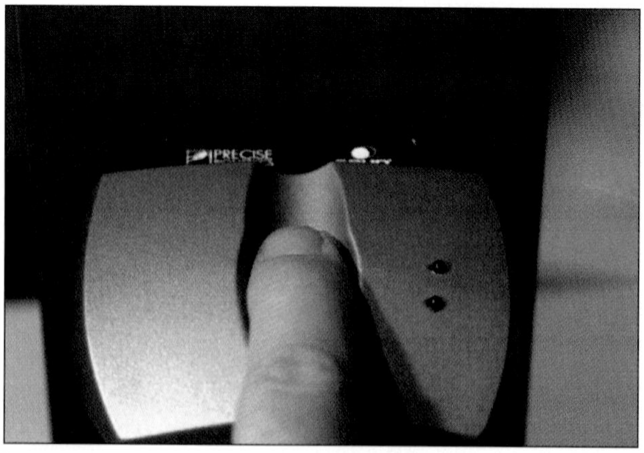

Figure 13-18 Security: Electronic fingerprint pads

important to organizations using WANs. Violations can occur without actually entering secured areas. As mentioned in previous chapters, most major corporations today use special hardware and software called **firewalls** to control access to their internal networks.

Concept Check

- ✔ What is a data warehouse? What is data mining?
- ✔ What are some database security concerns?
- ✔ What is a firewall?

Careers in IT

Database Administrator

Database administrators use database management software to determine the most efficient ways to organize and access a company's data. Additionally, database administrators are typically responsible for maintaining database security and backing up the system. Database administration is a fast growing industry and substantial job growth is expected.

Database administrator positions normally require a bachelor's degree in computer science and technical experience. Internships and prior experience with the latest technology are a considerable advantage for those seeking jobs in this industry. It is possible to transfer skills learned in one industry, such as finance, to a new career in database administration. In order to accomplish this objective, many people seek additional training in computer science.

Database administrators can expect to earn an annual salary of $35,000 to $75,000. Opportunities for advancement include positions as a chief technology officer or other managerial opportunities. To learn more about other careers in information technology visit us at http://www.mhhe.com/oleary/CT05 and select Careers in IT from Tim's Toolbox.

A Look to the Future

Xperanto Makes Database Searches Easier

Have you ever been frustrated by the results of a Web search? Have you ever wished you could search all the Word files on your computer for a specific word or phrase? Businesses with multiple databases and many types of data are even more frustrated with limited searches and unreachable data. IBM has recently announced technology they hope will help businesses access many kinds of data from many locations from one database interface.

Xperanto is designed to make both structured (relational databases) and unstructured data (word processing or spreadsheet files, for example) searchable in a database. For example, an organization might use a database that accesses all employee Word files. Xperanto might also be used to examine audio transcripts of phone calls. Using this technology an organization has access to all of its files, on all computers, and in all locations through a database.

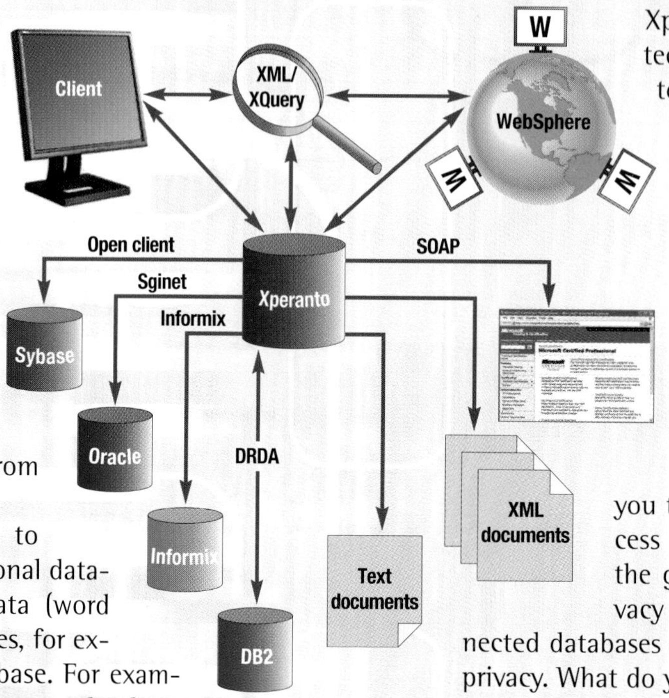

Xperanto combines various technological breakthroughs to make this possible, but the project relies heavily on XML. XML allows information in Web pages to be accessed by a database. XML uses special notation in the code to identify parts of the page, including names and dates.

What do you think of this development? Do you think this kind of easy access to data has benefits for the general public? Some privacy advocates worry connected databases are a danger to individual privacy. What do you think?

DATABASES AT DVD DIRECT

INTRODUCTION

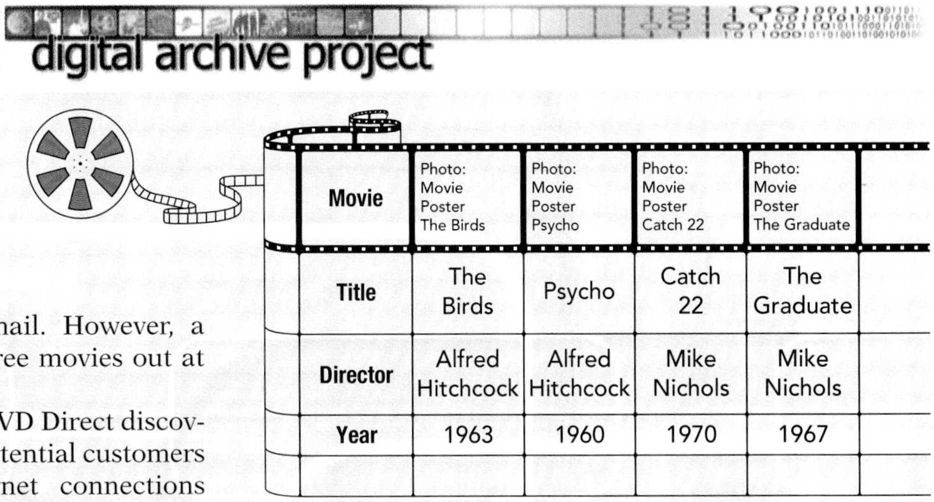
digital archive project
Movie
Photo: Movie Poster The Birds
Photo: Movie Poster Psycho
Photo: Movie Poster Catch 22
Photo: Movie Poster The Graduate
Title
The Birds
Psycho
Catch 22
The Graduate
Director
Alfred Hitchcock
Alfred Hitchcock
Mike Nichols
Mike Nichols
Year
1963
1960
1970
1967

Figure C13-1

DVD Direct is an entirely Web-oriented movie rental business. (See Figure C13-1.) Their members order movies from DVD Direct's Web site and the movies are delivered on DVD disks by mail. Members can keep the movies as long as they wish before returning them by mail. However, a member can have at most three movies out at one time.

A recent internal study at DVD Direct discovered that many current and potential customers with high bandwidth Internet connections would prefer to have movies delivered over the Internet. Further, the study indicated that current customers who recently switched to high bandwidth connections were very likely to drop their DVD Direct membership. Top management has become concerned that if DVD Direct does not address these findings they will continue to lose high bandwidth members and they may no longer be able to compete in the online movie rental business. This has led Carol, DVD Direct's CEO, to consider some dramatic changes to their business model—the way they do business.

So far, this issue has been formally discussed only in high-level meetings. However, the rumor mill has been working and almost everyone in the company knows that some type of change is in the works. Alice, a recently hired market analyst, has joined the company at this critical moment for DVD Direct and is about to learn more about the proposed changes. Let's follow Alice as she meets with Bob, the vice president of marketing. (See Figure C13-2.)

Figure C13-2 "I want you to focus on some critical database issues."

ALICE'S ASSIGNMENT

Bob: By now you're as aware as any of us, Alice, of the issue of DVD Direct's changing customer base and the necessity to adjust to these changes. Carol has asked us to investigate the implications of using streaming video to deliver movies directly to our customers over the Internet. In fact, Research has been working on this for some time from a technical angle.

Currently, as you know, members use our Web site only to select movies. In the future, our customers may use our Web site to select *and* to download movies. After selecting a movie, the movie would be immediately downloaded using streaming video technology to the member's hard disk. The movie would automatically erase from the member's hard disk after one week or after the movie was played, whichever occurs first.

A change like this has dramatic implications for how we conduct business. It affects almost everything from pricing to inventorying. Before the company can proceed with any of these changes a lot of questions need to be answered.

Alice, I want you to focus on some critical database issues. Find out how we currently store movie data and what, if anything, would need to be changed to support online delivery of movies. Go to Computing Services and talk with Harvey. He is their lead database administrator and very knowledgeable. I'll give him a call and tell him to expect you in fifteen minutes.

DATA FILES

While walking over to Harvey's office, Alice mentally reviews what she knows about databases. "Databases are large collections of data stored in a manner to allow efficient storage and retrieval. I don't see how a change to streaming video would require any changes to DVD Direct's databases. The movies are the same. The only thing that changes are how they are delivered to our customers," she thinks. Alice rounds the corner and knocks on the door to Harvey's office.

Alice: Hi, my name is Alice. Have you heard from Bob regarding my visit?

Harvey: Hi Alice. Yes, Bob just called. We all know the streaming video idea is in the wind. I understand that you're here to learn about our current databases.

Alice: Yes, and to discuss any changes that might be required to support streaming video delivery of movies to our customers.

Harvey: Well you came to the right place to learn about DVD Direct's databases. While I didn't create all the databases, I've revamped just about every one of them at one time or another. We have four main databases: PERSONNEL, CUSTOMER, INVENTORY, and MOVIE. The PERSONNEL database contains all information relevant to our employees. The CUSTOMER database keeps the information about our members. The INVENTORY database keeps track of the movie DVDs. The MOVIE database keeps information about our movies and is available to our customers at our Web site. So where would you like to begin?

Alice: Let's start with the MOVIE database. Could you walk me through the process of entering a new movie into the database? That should give me a good feel for how the database is set up.

Harvey: Perfect! I was just about to enter Alfred Hitchcock's classic, *Psycho,* into our Access database. To begin, we use a form to create a new record and enter the fields. [See Figure C13-3.]

Alice: What do you mean by a record and fields?

Harvey: That has to do with the way in which the data is stored in a database. For example, the title of our movie is *Psycho.* Each letter in the title *Psycho* will be stored as a character in the database. The string of characters *P, s, y, c, h,* and *o* will be stored in a field labeled TITLE. This way whenever someone wants to search for a particular movie title, the database knows to check the TITLE field. Other fields include the DIRECTOR, YEAR, and MOVIE ID.

Harvey enters the movie title, *Psycho,* the director, Hitchcock, Alfred, and year released, 1960.

Harvey: The MOVIE ID is automatically entered for us. To enter this record, all we need to do is to press the ENTER key.

Figure C13-3 "I was just about to enter Alfred Hitchcock's classic, Psycho."

Key Field

Alice: That was easy. But why do we need a MOVIE ID field?

Harvey: The MOVIE ID is a reference number assigned to this particular movie that uniquely identifies this particular record. Fields such as these are called key fields.

Alice: Okay, but why do I need a key field? If we wanted to locate this record, couldn't I just use the movie's title?

Harvey: You would think so, but not always. More than one movie can have the same title. For example, there are two versions of *Psycho,* one filmed in 1960 and another in 1998. Or some films such as the classic *Blade Runner* released in 1982 have two versions—the standard version that appeared in movie theaters and a director's cut version that includes the standard version plus additional scenes that were cut from the original. Even though these films have the same TITLE, each has a unique MOVIE ID.

Alice: I didn't think of that. So, all the Classic movies are stored in a file. I assume there are separate files for each type of movie such as Comedies, Westerns, and so on. Combined, all of these files comprise the MOVIE database. [See Figure C13-4.]

Harvey: You've got it.

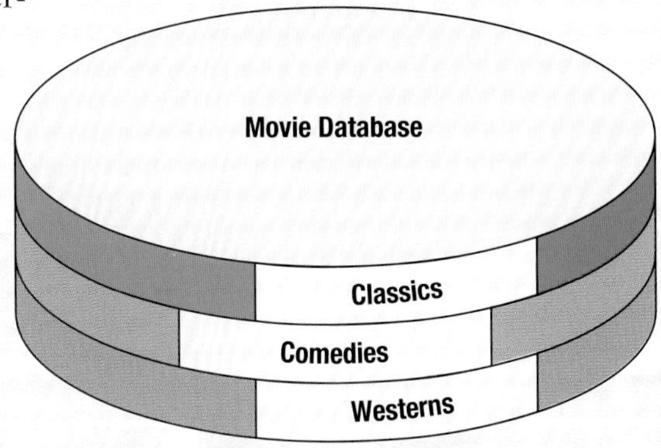

Figure C13-4 MOVIE database.

Batch versus Real-Time Processing

Alice: So now that we have entered the movie into the Classics file, we should be able to go to the Web site and view *Psycho* as one of the available movies to rent, right?

Harvey: Well not exactly. Although we've entered the movie into a file, the database has not been updated yet. During the day, we will be adding several other new movies. Rather than updating the database each time a movie is added or becomes available during the day, the changes are collected throughout the day or batched in special files called transaction files. The files in the database are called master files. At the end of the day, the transaction files are used to update the master files. This is called batch processing. Once the database is updated, the Web site will reflect all the new titles.

Alice: We may want to provide very time-sensitive videos to our customers, for example, a video of a championship boxing match recorded hours earlier in the day or video of recent breaking news events. In these cases, we would want the videos posted immediately to the Web site, wouldn't we? Can batch processing do the job?

Harvey: No. That would require real-time processing. With real-time processing, as soon as a record is added or changed, the database is updated. To support this type of processing we would need some hardware improvements. But it can definitely be done.

DBMS ORGANIZATION

Alice: Currently, we send out movies on DVD disk by mail. If we deliver them over the Web, where would the actual videos be located?

Harvey: I don't know a lot about streaming video over the Internet, but I am guessing that we will need to pre-process the movies into a special streaming video format, and the resulting file that we send to the customer will need to be an automated process that can occur fairly quickly. This means we will need the database to include the movie files.

Alice: But I thought that a database was a collection of files; files are a collection of records; records are a collection of fields; and fields are a collection of characters. Now it sounds like you are telling me that a database can also be a collection of movies. How can that be?

Harvey: Excellent question. Right now our database can't handle unstructured data, like movies. You see, our database is organized as a relational database. In a relational database, information is stored in tables and the tables' key fields create relationships between those tables that allow the database to quickly and simply return specified information.

But to be able to handle more complex data, like movies, we'll need to use an object-oriented data structure. An object-oriented database can store any type of data, from television video in TV format and movies in DVD format, to photos of movie posters and motion picture personalities, to special audio effects in a variety of different formats. [See Figure C13-5.]

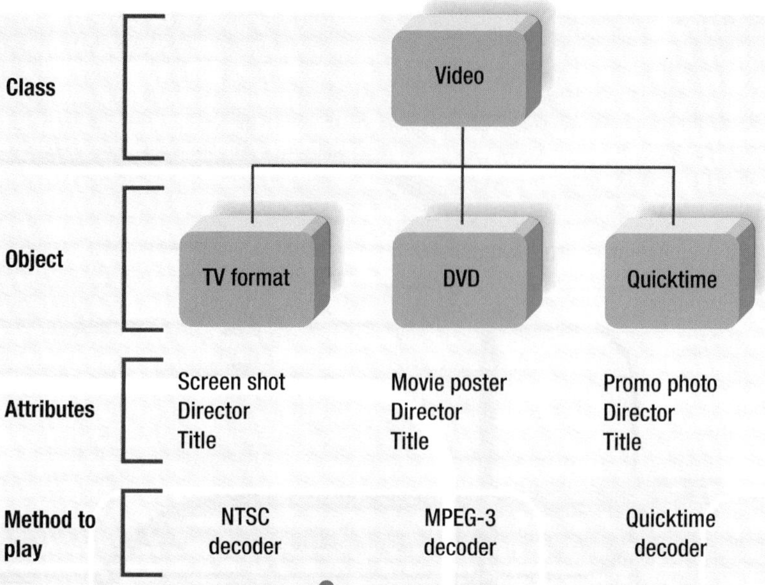

Figure C13-5 Object-oriented structure.

DATABASE SECURITY

Alice: I didn't expect that this proposed change to streaming video would affect our databases this much. Let me see if I have the major points. We will have to change our processing from batch to real-time, and we will have to overhaul the entire DBMS organization from relational to object-oriented to handle storage of movie formats in the database.

Harvey: Well, there's at least one more concern—security. Using our current system, when customers order movies online they provide their membership numbers and mailing addresses. The DVD is mailed out the next business day. Before mailing the DVD, we have plenty of time to consult the MEMBERSHIP database to verify the member's identity, mailing address, and payment history. This reduces the chance that a DVD is sent out to an unauthorized individual or an individual who is unlikely to pay for the rental.

Actually, the worst case is that we incorrectly send out a copy of the movie on a DVD disk. Or that someone is able to gain unauthorized access to the MOVIE database. In either case, the loss is minimal.

But with the proposed system, a customer orders and downloads a movie at the same time. There would be less time to verify membership or payment history. A greater concern, however, is that someone is able to gain unauthorized access to the MOVIE database. They could obtain a copy of the streaming video version of the movie. It is possible that they could then send, or broadcast, the movie to an unlimited number of people on the Internet! So, developing security controls is at least as important as the other two issues you mentioned, Alice.

Alice: That's a lot to think about. [See Figure C13-6.] Thanks for your time, Harvey. I need to get back to Bob so I can report my findings.

Figure C13-6 "That's a lot to think about."

Computing Today CD

For more comprehensive discussion on DVD Direct's database organization, consult your Computing Today CD or visit us on the web at http://www.mhhe.com/oleary/CT05 and select DVD Direct from Tim's Toolbox.

NOTES

VISUAL SUMMARY

DATABASES

DATA

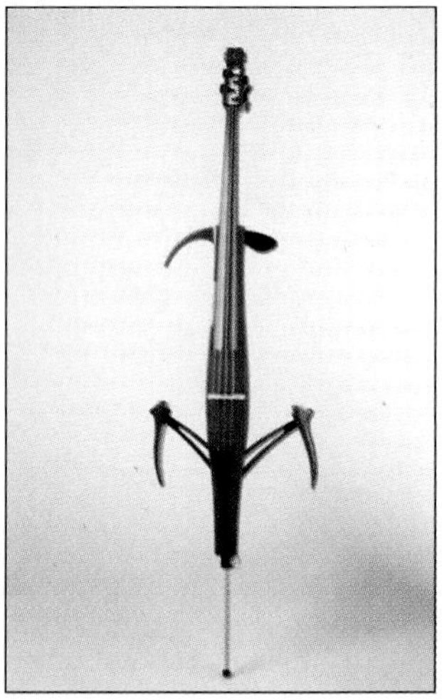

Data consist of facts or observations about people, places, things, and events.

Data Types

Not long ago, data was limited to numbers, letters, and symbols. Now data includes:

- Audio—captured, interpreted, and saved using microphones and voice recognition systems.
- Music—captured from the Internet and other sources, rearranged, and used to create customized CDs.
- Photographs—captured by digital cameras, edited by image editing software, and shared with others over the Internet
- Video—captured by digital video cameras and TV tuner cards, saved, and used in presentations.

Data Views

There are two ways or perspectives to view data: *physical view* and the *logical view.*

- **Physical view** focuses on actual format and location of data; very specialized computer professionals concerned with this view.
- **Logical view** focuses on meaning and content of data; end users and most computer professionals are concerned with this view.

DATA ORGANIZATION

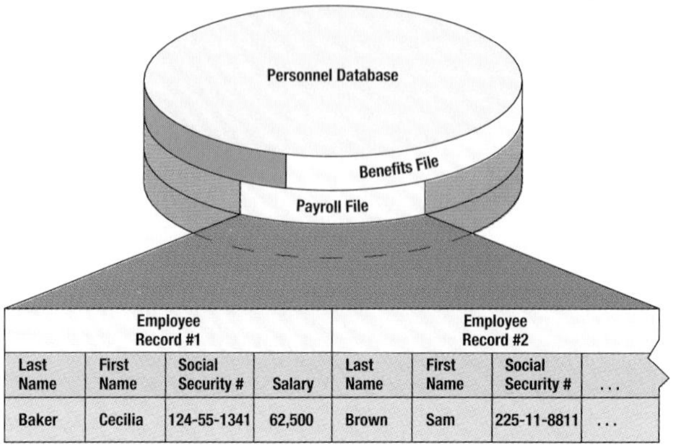

Data is organized by the following groups:

- **Character**—the most basic logical element, for example, characters can consist of individual letters.
- **Field**—next level consisting of a set of related characters, for example, a person's last name.
- **Record**—a collection of related fields, for example, a payroll record consist of fields of data relating to one employee.
- **File**—a collection of related records, for example, a payroll file consists of all the employee records.
- **Database**—an integrated collection of related files, for example, personnel database includes all related employee files including payroll file.

Key Field

A **key field (primary field)** is the field in a record that uniquely identifies each record. Common key fields are social security numbers and driver's license numbers.

To be a competent and knowledgeable end user you need to understand data fields, records, files, and databases. You need to be aware of the different ways in which a database can be structured and the different types of databases. Also, you need to know the most important database uses and issues.

DATA ORGANIZATION

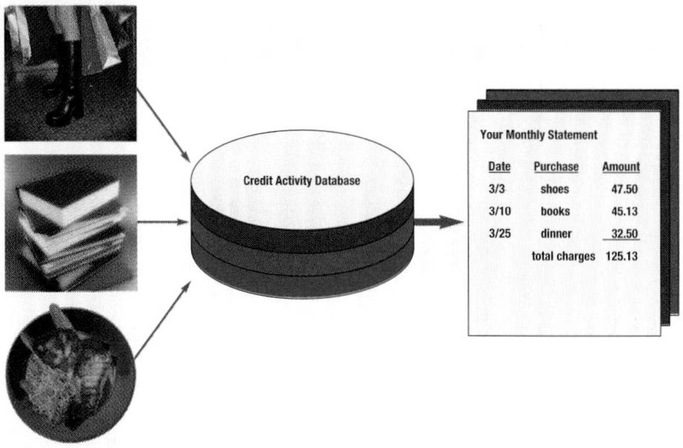

Batch versus Real-Time Processing

Traditionally, data processed in two ways:

- **Batch processing**—data collected over time and then processed later all at one time (batched).
- **Real-time processing** (**online processing**)—data is processed at the same time the transaction occurs; direct access storage devices make real-time processing possible.

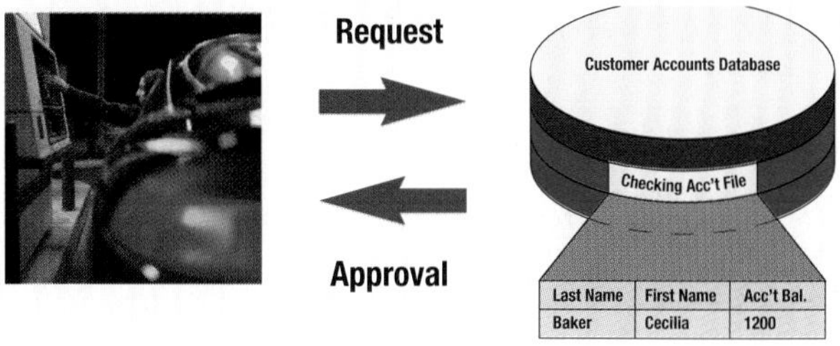

DATABASES

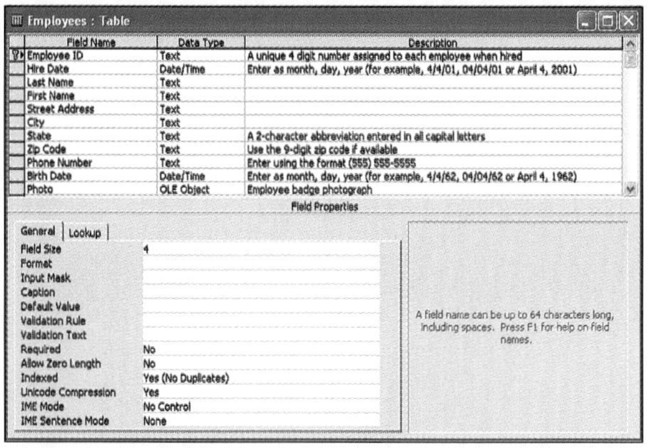

A **database** is a collection of integrated data—logically related files and records.

Need for Databases

Advantages of databases are sharing data, improved security, reduced **data redundancy**, and higher **data integrity**.

Database Management

A **database management system (DBMS)** is the software for creating, modifying, and gaining access to the database. A DBMS consists of five subsystems:

- **DBMS engine** bridges between logical and physical data views.
- **Data definition** defines logical structure using **data dictionary.**
- **Data manipulation** provides tools for **data maintenance** and data analysis; tools include **query-by-example** and **structure query languages (SQL).**
- **Application generation** provides tools for data entry forms and specialized programming languages.
- **Data administration** manages database; **database administrators (DBAs)** are computer professionals who help define **processing rights.**

DBMS STRUCTURE

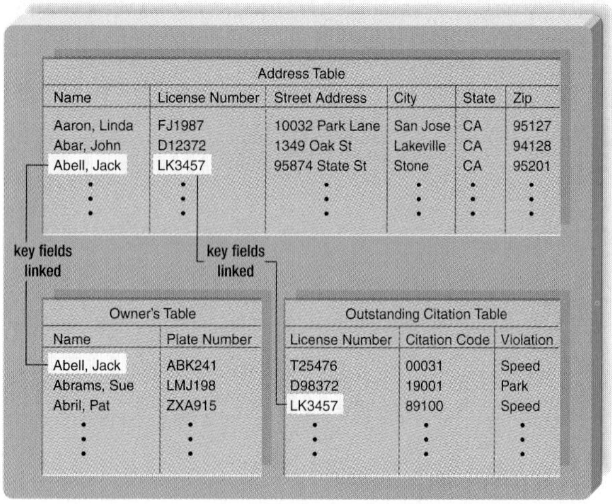

DBMS programs are designed to work with specific data structures or **data models.** These models define rules and standards for all the data in the database. Five principal data models are *hierarchical, network, relational, multidimensional,* and *object-oriented.*

Hierarchical Database

Hierarchical database uses **nodes** to link and structure fields and records; entries may have one **parent node** with several **child nodes** in a **one-to-many relationship.**

Network Database

Network database is like hierarchical except child node may have more than one parent in **many-to-many relationship;** additional connections called **pointers.**

Relational Database

Relational database data is stored in tables (**relations**); related tables have **common data item** (key field).

DBMS STRUCTURE

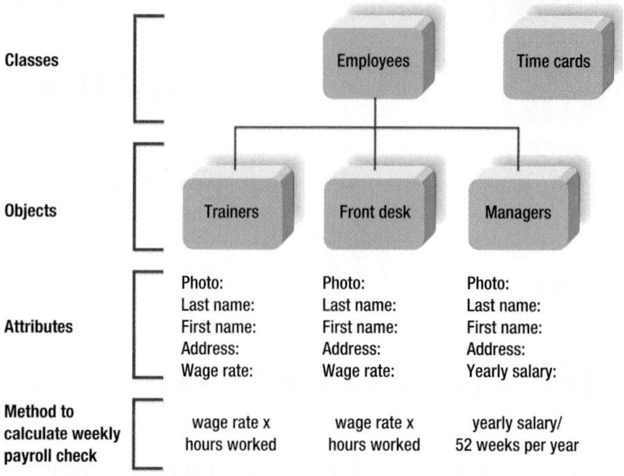

Multidimensional Database

Multidimensional databases extend two-dimensional relational tables to three or more dimensions sometimes called a **hyper cube.** Advantages include:

- Conceptualization—database provides an intuitive model for complex data and relationships.
- Processing speed—analyzing and querying is faster.

Object-Oriented Database

Object-oriented databases store data, instructions and unstructured data. Data organized using *objects, classes, entities, attributes,* and *methods.*

- **Objects** contain both data and instructions to manipulate data.
- **Classes** are similar to objects grouped together.
- **Entities** are a person, place, thing, or event.
- **Attributes,** similar to fields, are descriptions of entities.
- **Methods** describe how data is to be manipulated.

TYPES OF DATABASES

There are five types of databases:

Individual

Individual database or **microcomputer database** used by one person.

Company or Shared

Two types of **company (shared) databases** are **common operational database** (contains data on company operations) and **common user database** (contains selected data from common operational and outside private databases).

Distributed

Distributed database spread out geographically; accessible by communications links.

Proprietary

Proprietary database available by subscription, also known as **information utilities** and **data banks.**

Web

Web databases used by Web sites to record data collected from users and by Web search engines; **CGI (Common Gateway Interface)** scripts used in interface programs.

DATABASE USES AND ISSUES

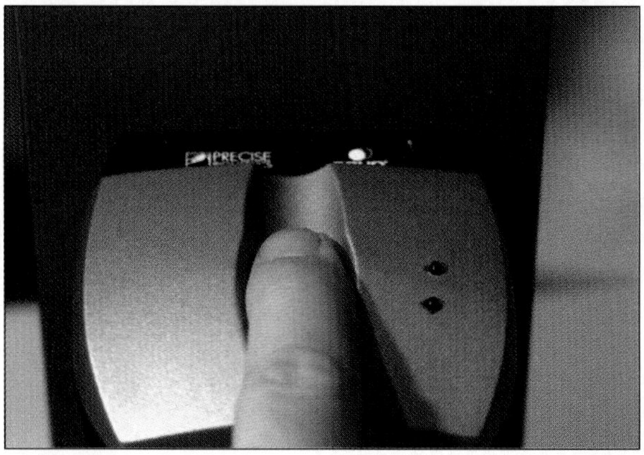

Databases offer a great opportunity for increased productivity; however, security is always a concern.

Strategic Uses

Data warehouses are a new type of database that supports data mining. **Data mining** is a technique for searching and exploring for related information and patterns in data.

Databases available for general and specific business purposes include:

- Business directories
- Demographic data
- Business statistical information
- Text databases
- Web databases

Security

Two important security concerns are illegal use of data and unauthorized access. Most organizations use **firewalls** to protect their internal networks.

KEY TERMS

application generation subsystem (492)
attribute (487)
batch processing (488)
CGI (Common Gateway Interface) (499)
character (487)
child node (493)
class (496)
common data item (495)
common operational database (498)
common user database (498)
company database (497)
data (486)
data administration subsystem (492)
data bank (498)
data definition subsystem (491)
data dictionary (491)
data integrity (490)
data maintenance (492)
data manipulation subsystem (491)
data mining (500)
data model (492)
data redundancy (490)
data warehouse (500)
database (488)
database administrator (DBA) (492, 501)
database management system (DBMS) (491)
DBMS engine (491)
distributed database (498)
entity (487)
field (487)
file (488)
firewall (501)
hierarchical database (493)
hyper cube (495)
individual database (497)
information utility (498)
key field (488)
logical view (486)
many-to-many relationship (493)
method (496)
microcomputer database (497)
multidimensional database (495)
network database (493)
node (493)
object (496)
object-oriented database (496)
one-to-many relationship (493)
online processing (489)
parent node (493)
physical view (486)
pointer (493)
primary field (488)
processing rights (492)
proprietary database (498)
query-by-example (492)
real-time processing (489)
record (488)
relation (494)
relational database (494)
shared database (497)
structured query language (SQL) (492)
Web database (499)

To test your knowledge of these key terms with animated flash cards, select Flash Cards from Tim's Toolbox at http://www.mhhe.com/oleary/CT05.

CHAPTER REVIEW

CROSSWORD

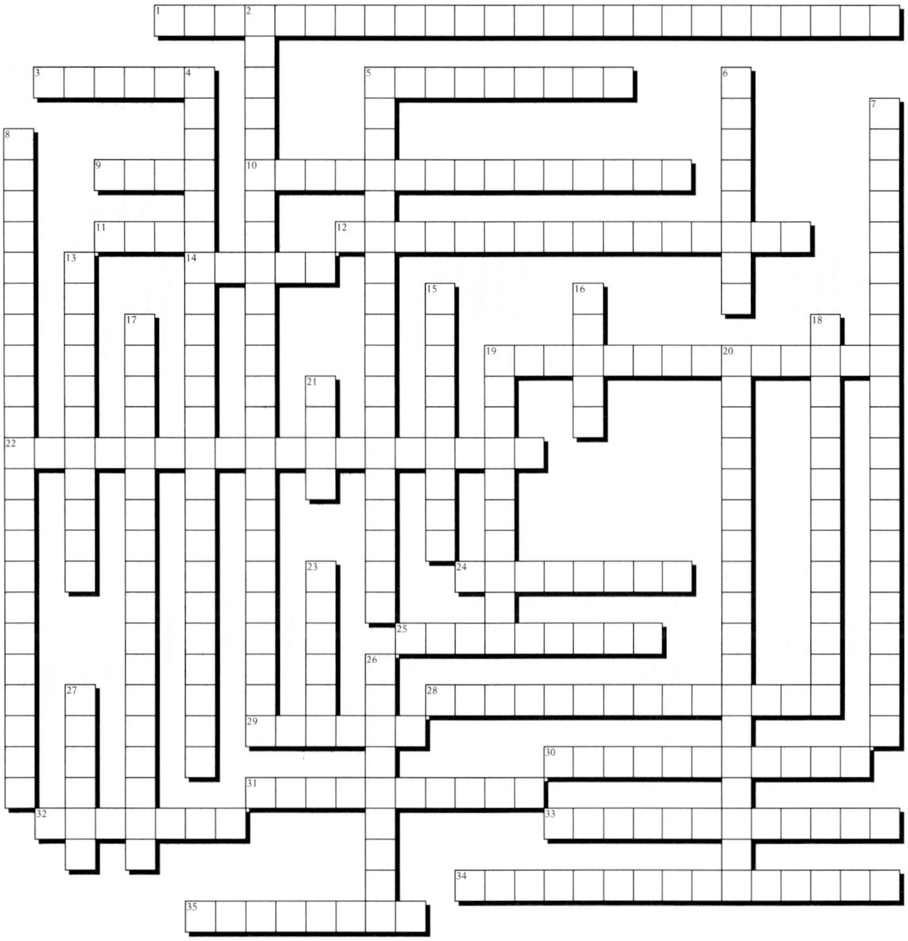

ACROSS

1 Contains details about the operations of the company
3 A collection of related fields
5 The most basic logical data element
9 Facts or observations about people, places, things, and events
10 Adding new data, deleting old data, and editing existing data
11 A collection of related records
12 When data is processed at the same time the transaction occurs
14 A group of related characters
19 Contains a description of the structure of data in the database
22 A database in which elements are stored in different tables, each consisting of rows and columns
24 Hardware and software that controls access
25 Relational tables with three or more dimensions
28 When records for the same customer appear in different files
29 Person, place, thing, or object
30 A database available over the Web
31 A technique to locate related information and patterns
32 Additional connections between parent and child nodes
33 Focuses on the actual format and location of data
34 Data collected over time and then processed later all at one time
35 Uniquely identify records

DOWN

2 A relational database extended to include additional dimensions
4 Defines the logical structure of the database by using a data dictionary
5 Contains selected information both from the common operational database and from outside private databases
6 Another term for table
7 When a parent node has several child nodes
8 When each child node has more than one parent node
13 Focuses on meaning and content of data
15 Description of entities
16 Similar objects grouped together
17 Processes data now
18 Changes in one file are made in other files as well
19 Bridges between logical and physical data views
20 A database used by one person
21 Points connected like the branches of an upside-down tree
23 A logically related file
26 Defines rules and standards for all the data in the database
27 Description of how the data is to be manipulated

For an interactive crossword puzzle select Crosswords from Tim's Toolbox at http://www.mhhe.com/oleary/CT05.

MULTIPLE CHOICE

Circle the letter or fill in the correct answer.

1. A ________ is a collection of related fields.
   - **a.** field
   - **b.** class
   - **c.** file
   - **d.** record
   - **e.** character
2. In ________ processing data is collected over time and then processed later all at one time.
   - **a.** real-time
   - **b.** relational
   - **c.** batch
   - **d.** database
   - **e.** direct
3. ________ are special hardware and software designed to control access to internal networks.
   - **a.** Firewalls
   - **b.** Data models
   - **c.** DBMS
   - **d.** Relations
   - **e.** Pointers
4. A database characteristic relating to the consistency and accuracy of data is ________.
   - **a.** data redundancy
   - **b.** security
   - **c.** data integrity
   - **d.** sharing
   - **e.** data dictionary
5. The arrangement used in a network database is an example of a ________.
   - **a.** one-to-one relationship
   - **b.** one-to-many relationship
   - **c.** many-to-many relationship
   - **d.** many-to-one relationship
   - **e.** none of the above
6. A common data item is also known as a ________.
   - **a.** field
   - **b.** transaction file
   - **c.** pointer
   - **d.** node
   - **e.** key field
7. ________ are persons, places, things, or events that are to be described in an object-oriented database.
   - **a.** Methods
   - **b.** Fields
   - **c.** Classes
   - **d.** Entities
   - **e.** Attributes
8. A collection of integrated records useful mainly to one person is a(n) ________.
   - **a.** common user database
   - **b.** individual database
   - **c.** company database
   - **d.** common operational database
   - **e.** distributed database
9. An enormous database an organization develops to cover certain objects is called a ________.
   - **a.** proprietary database
   - **b.** company database
   - **c.** common operational database
   - **d.** distributed database
   - **e.** data warehouse
10. The person responsible for structuring, coordinating, linking, and maintaining databases is commonly referred to as the ________.
   - **a.** database manager
   - **b.** database administrator
   - **c.** database operator
   - **d.** pointer
   - **e.** hasher

To test your knowledge of this chapter, select Self Test from Tim's Toolbox at http://www.mhhe.com/oleary/CT05.

MATCHING

Match each numbered item with the most closely related lettered item. Write your answers in the spaces provided.

a. batch processing
b. character
c. child node
d. class
e. data dictionary
f. data mining
g. data redundancy
h. DBMS
i. DBMS engine
j. distributed database
k. file
l. hierarchical database
m. key field
n. logical
o. multi-dimensional
p. network database
q. pointer
r. SQL
s. real-time processing
t. relational database

1. A single letter or number. ____
2. A collection of records. ____
3. The common field by which tables in a database are related to each other. ____
4. Processing performed all at once on data that has been collected over several days. ____
5. Processing that occurs when data is processed at the same time that the transaction occurs. ____
6. DBMS subsystem that bridges logical and physical data views. ____
7. DBMS structure that extends the two-dimensional relational data model. ____
8. End users and most computer professionals use this data view. ____
9. Database problem in which data is duplicated and stored in different files. ____
10. Software required to create, modify, and gain access to a database. ____
11. Dictionary with a description of the structure of the data in a database. ____
12. Database in which fields or records are structured in nodes. ____
13. Most widely used query language. ____
14. A node one level below the node being considered in a hierarchical database. ____
15. Database with hierarchical arrangement of nodes in which each child node may have more than one parent node. ____
16. Connection between parent node and a child node in a hierarchical database. ____
17. Database structure, in which data is organized into related tables. ____
18. Similar objects grouped together. ____
19. Database that can be made accessible through a variety of communications networks, allowing portions of the database to be located in different places. ____
20. Technique of searching data warehouses for related information and patterns. ____

OPEN-ENDED

On a separate sheet of paper, respond to each question or statement.

1. Describe the five logical data groups or categories.
2. What is the difference between batch processing and real-time processing? Give an example of each.
3. Identify and define the five parts of DBMS programs.
4. What are the five types of databases? Why does more than one kind of database exist?
5. What are some of the benefits and limitations of databases? Why is security a concern?

USING TECHNOLOGY

1 Free Database Software

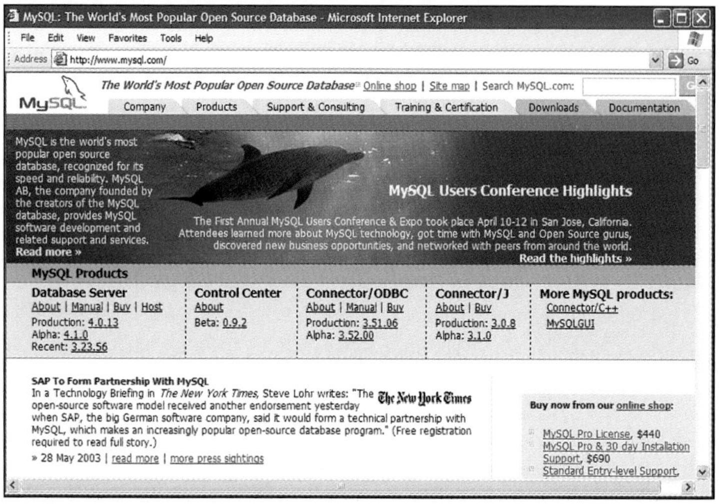

Software to manage relational databases is a key component in many corporate IS departments. Database software like Microsoft Access and Oracle can be money well spent when fast, reliable information retrieval is a must. But did you know that advanced database management software can be obtained for free? Visit our Web site at http://www.mhhe.com/oleary/CT05 and select Using Technology from Tim's Toolbox to connect to a site that features free database software. Read about this software, and then answer the following questions: (a) What is MySQL? What is its basic functionality? (b) How does MySQL compare to commercial software like Microsoft Access in terms of performance? (c) What support is available to users of MySQL? How is it provided? (d) Would you recommend MySQL as an IT solution? Why or why not?

2 Online Databases

As an Internet user, you have access to many interesting and informative databases via the Web. Locate at least five online databases that contain information that is interesting to you by conducting a Web search using the keywords "online database." Conduct a query of each database, and then answer the following questions: (a) Give the URL and a brief description of each online database you reviewed. (b) What features are common to online databases? (c) Which provided the most relevant or interesting information? Will you use this site again? Why or why not?

Reports 3

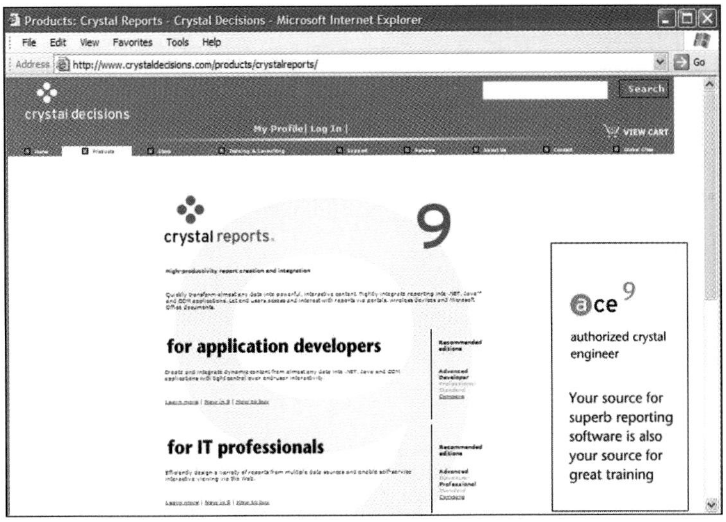

Many reports are often generated based on database query results. Specialized software is available to generate reports using the results from a database query. Connect to our Web site at http://mhhe.com/oleary/CT05 and select Using Technology from Tim's Toolbox to link to a product that generates reports from database queries. Once connected, read about the product, and then briefly answer the following questions: (a) What types of data can this product use to generate reports? (b) How does this product connect to a database to create a report? (c) Describe the process for creating a new report with this product.

Internet Movie Database 4

One popular Web database is the Internet Movie Database, or IMDB. Connect to our site at http://mhhe.com/oleary/CT05 and select Using Technology from Tim's Toolbox to link to the IMDB site. Once connected, try making a couple of queries and then answer the following questions: (a) What types of information does the IMDB contain? (b) What queries did you try? What were the results? (c) Based on your knowledge of databases, would you expect the IMDB to be relational or object-oriented? Justify your answer.

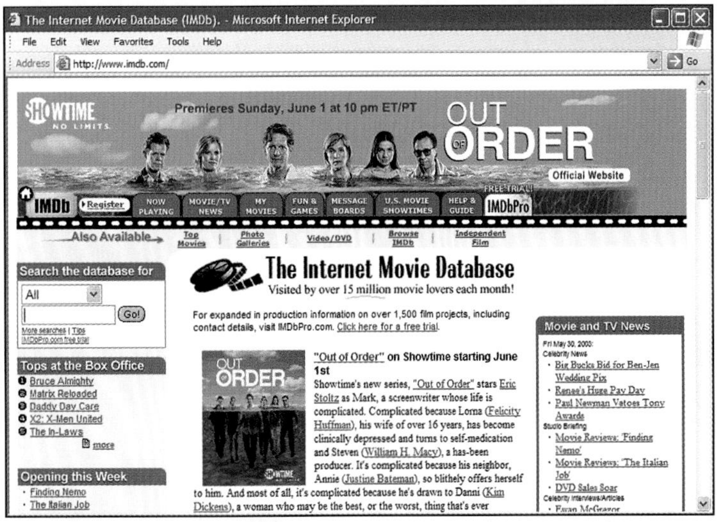

EXPANDING YOUR KNOWLEDGE

1 Computing Today CD

DVD Direct's MOVIE database is similar to the Internet Movie Database (IMDB). Using the Web, locate and connect to the IMDB database. Once connected, explore the site and then answer the following: (a) Compare the fields in the IMDB database to those in the DVD Direct MOVIE database. (b) Which fields are similar? (c) Are any unique? (d) Based on your knowledge of databases, would you expect the IMDB to be relational or object-oriented? Justify your answer.

2 ODBC

Open Data Base Connectivity is a technology standard for database administrators and application developers. To learn about ODBC, conduct a Web search with the keyword "ODBC." Research this topic, and then answer the following questions: (a) What is ODBC, and what does it do? (b) Who developed ODBC? (c) What is required of databases and applications in order to use ODBC? (d) How could ODBC benefit a database administrator? (e) How could ODBC benefit an application developer?

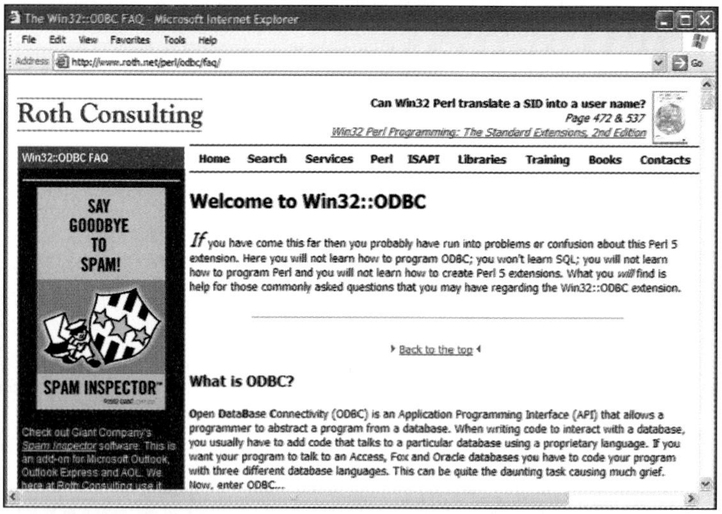

EXPANDING YOUR KNOWLEDGE

SimNet CD 3

Complete Chapter 13: Databases on the SimNet CD and then answer the following questions:

a. Describe the different ways of managing data.

b. Describe the process of using a DBMS.

c. Label the database organizations shown on the right.

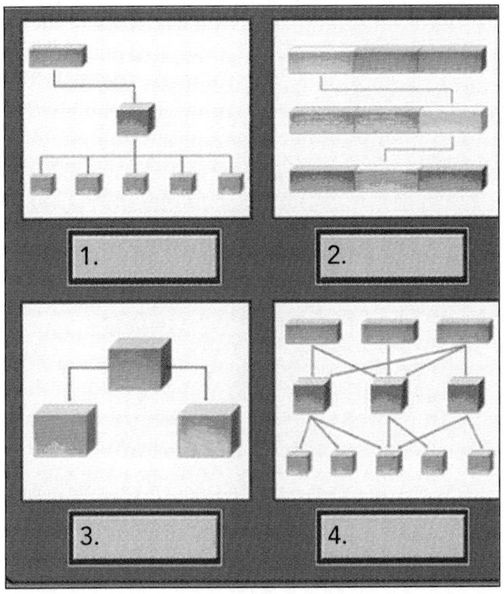

d. Describe the three basic types of data mining tools.

SQL 4

Structured Query Language (SQL) is the most widely-used language for database interaction today. Connect to our Web site at http://www.mhhe.com/oleary/CT05 and select Expanding Your Knowledge from Tim's Toolbox to link to a site that gives an overview of SQL. Explore the site, and answer the following questions: (a) What type of database is SQL designed for? (b) What database tasks can SQL be used for? (c) List some popular databases that use SQL. (d) In the DVD Direct case in the chapter, Alice is considering changes to the current database system. How might SQL be used to help accomplish that task? Be specific.

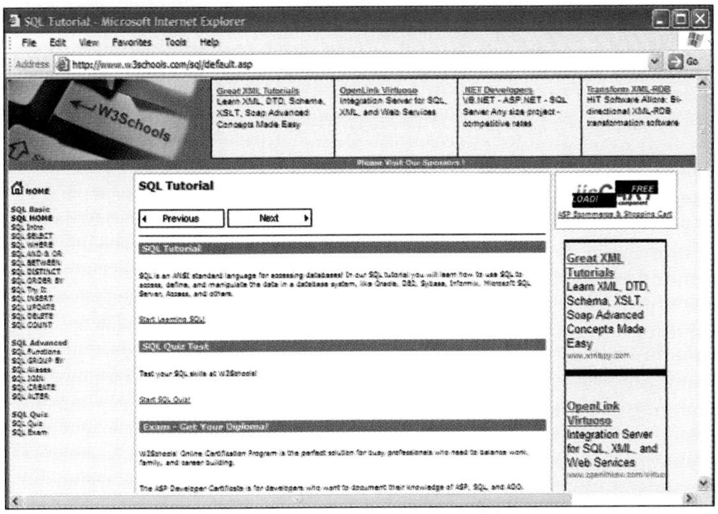

BUILDING YOUR PORTFOLIO

1 Web Databases

Web databases are a convenient way to deliver information access to a large audience. Write a one-page paper titled "Web Databases" that addresses the following: (a) What type of data is well suited for Web delivery? (b) What type of data would not be a good candidate for Web delivery? Why? (c) What are the benefits for a company to allow its users online access to information instead of through a DBMS application? (d) What are the benefits to the user?

2 Database Management Systems

A Database Management System, or DBMS, is a necessary part of any database. Review DBMS in the chapter, and then write a one-page paper that covers the following topics: (a) What is a DBMS? (b) How is a DBMS related to a database? (c) List and describe the five ways of organizing a DBMS. (d) Cite some popular DBMS available today. What are the strengths of each?

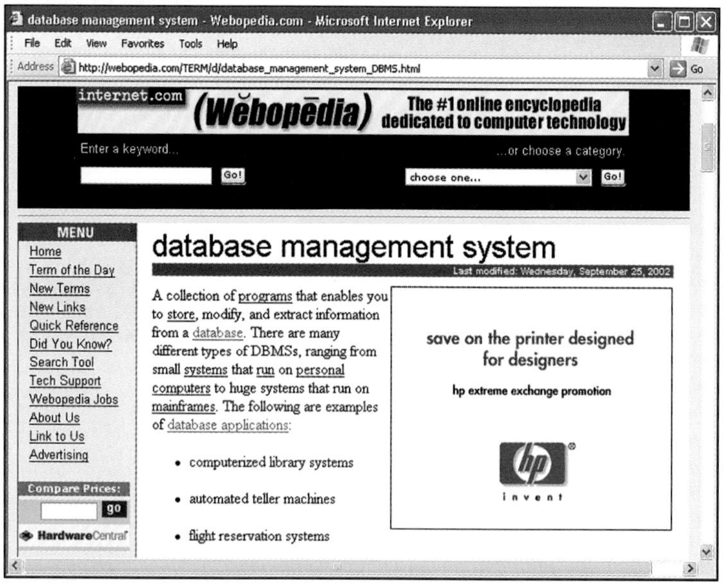

3 Personal Information 3

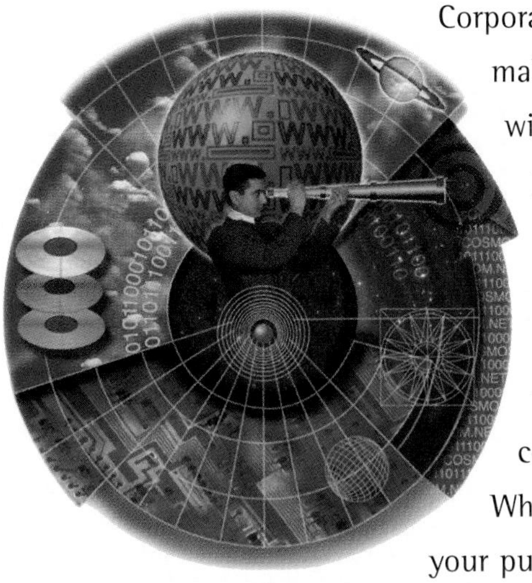

Corporations currently collect information about the purchases you make and your personal spending habits. Sometimes corporations will share information to build a more informative profile about you. There have been proposals for legislation to regulate or halt this type of exchange. Consider how you feel about this exchange of information, and then answer the following questions in a one-page paper: (a) What ethics and privacy concerns are related to corporations sharing personal data? (b) How might the consumer benefit from this? (c) Could this harm the consumer? What could happen if your grocery store shared information about your purchases with your life insurance carrier? (d) What rights do you feel consumers should have with regard to privacy of information collected about them? How should these rights be enforced? Defend your answer.

4 Database Security 4

Securing the data in a database is typically as important a concern as its design. Research database security on the Web, and then write a one-page paper that addresses the following topics: (a) Describe a few security risks that databases must be protected against. (b) Describe some steps that can be taken to ensure that a database is secured. (c) In the DVD Direct case in the chapter, Harvey cited some security concerns for the new database design. Summarize those concerns, and add any others you think would be important. (d) What obligations does DVD Direct have to the copyright owners of the streaming videos to keep its data secure? What obligations does it have to its customers?

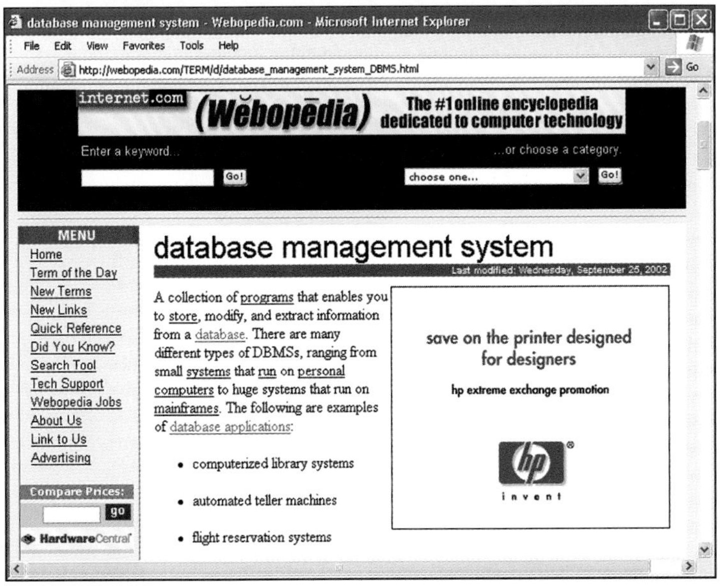

SYSTEMS ANALYSIS AND DESIGN

OBJECTIVES

After you have read this chapter, you should be able to:

1. Describe the six phases of the systems life cycle.
2. Identify information needs and formulate possible solutions.
3. Analyze existing information systems and evaluate the feasibility of alternative systems.
4. Identify, acquire, and test new system software and hardware.
5. Switch from an existing information system to a new one with minimal risk.
6. Perform system audits and periodic evaluations.

Systems Life Cycle
Consists of six phases to examine and improve information systems

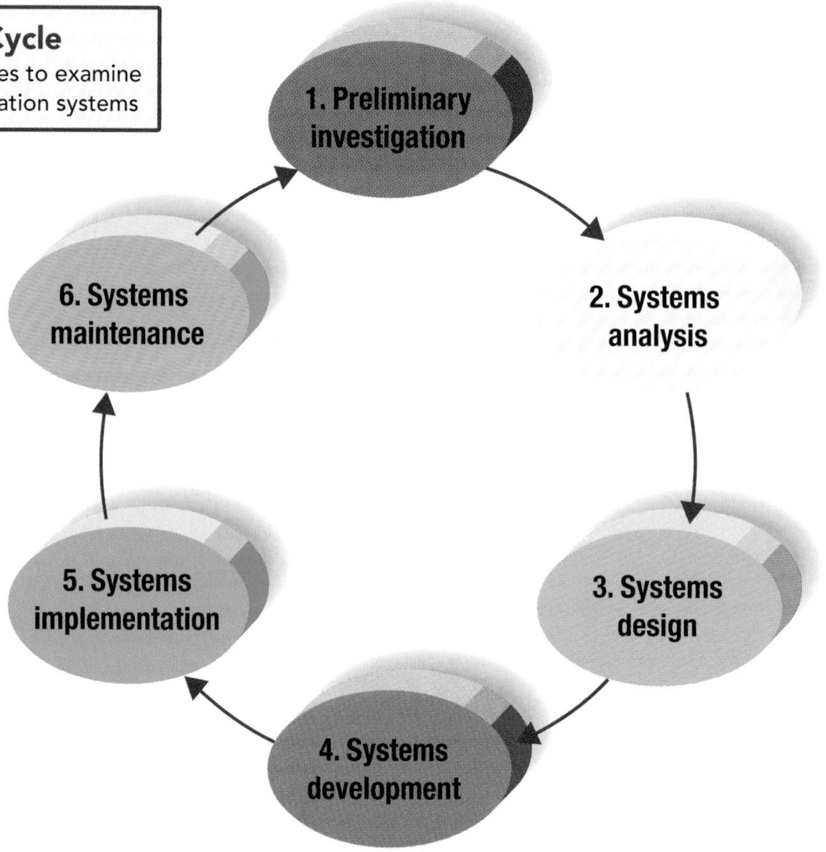
1. Preliminary investigation
2. Systems analysis
3. Systems design
4. Systems development
5. Systems implementation
6. Systems maintenance

Most people in an organization are involved with an information system of some kind, as we saw in the previous chapter. For an organization to create a system and for users to make it truly useful requires considerable thought and effort. Fortunately, there is a six-step problem-solving process for accomplishing this. It is known as systems analysis and design.

Big organizations can make big mistakes. For example, General Motors spent $40 billion putting in factory robots and other high technology in its auto making plants. It then removed much of this equipment and reinstalled that basic part of the assembly line, the conveyor belt. Why did the high-tech production systems fail? The probable reason was that GM didn't devote enough energy to training its workforce in using the new systems.

The government also can make big mistakes. In one year, the Internal Revenue Service computer system was so overwhelmed it could not deliver tax refunds on time. How did this happen? Despite extensive testing of much of the system, not all testing was completed. Thus, when the new system was phased in, the IRS found it could not process tax returns as quickly as it had hoped.

Both of these examples show the necessity for thorough planning—especially when an organization is trying to implement a new kind of system. Systems analysis and design reduces the chances for such spectacular failures.

Competent and knowledgeable end users need to understand the importance of systems analysis and design. They need to be aware of the relationship of an organization's chart to its managerial structure. Additionally, they need to know the six phases of the systems development life cycle: preliminary investigation, systems analysis, systems design, systems development, systems implementation, and systems maintenance.

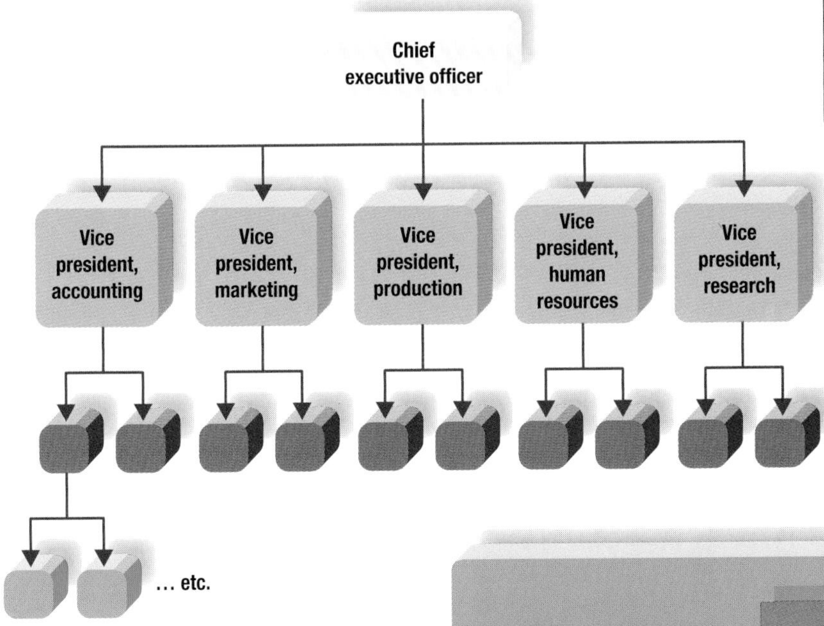
Chief executive officer
Vice president, accounting
Vice president, marketing
Vice president, production
Vice president, human resources
Vice president, research
... etc.

Organization Chart
Shows levels of management and formal lines of authority

Conditions	Decision rules 1	2	3	4
1. Project less than $10,000	Y	Y	N	N
2. Good credit history	Y	N	Y	N
Actions	**1**	**2**	**3**	**4**
1. Accept project	✓	✓	✓	
2. Require deposit		✓	✓	
3. Reject project				✓

Decision Table
Shows the decision rules that apply when certain conditions occur

SYSTEMS ANALYSIS AND DESIGN

Systems analysis and design is a six-phase problem-solving procedure for examining and improving an information system.

We described different types of information systems in the last chapter. Now let us consider: What, exactly, is a **system?** We can define it as a collection of activities and elements organized to accomplish a goal. As we saw in Chapter 12, an *information system* is a collection of hardware, software, people, procedures, and data. These work together to provide information essential to running an organization. This information helps to produce a product or service and, for profit-oriented businesses, derive a profit.

Information about orders received, products shipped, money owed, and so on, flows into an organization from the outside. Information about what supplies have been received, which customers have paid their bills, and so on, also flows within the organization. In order to avoid confusion, the flow of information must follow a route that is defined by a set of rules and procedures. However, from time to time, organizations need to change their information systems. Reasons include organizational growth, mergers and acquisitions, new marketing opportunities, revisions in governmental regulations, and availability of new technology.

Systems analysis and design is a six-phase problem-solving procedure for examining and improving an information system.

The six phases make up the **systems life cycle.** (See Figure 14-1.) The phases are as follows:

1. *Preliminary investigation:* The information problems or needs are identified.
2. *Systems analysis:* The present system is studied in depth. New requirements are specified.
3. *Systems design:* A new or alternative information system is designed.
4. *Systems development:* New hardware and software are acquired, developed, and tested.
5. *Systems implementation:* The new information system is installed and adapted to the new system, and people are trained to use it.
6. *Systems maintenance:* In this ongoing phase, the system is periodically evaluated and updated as needed.

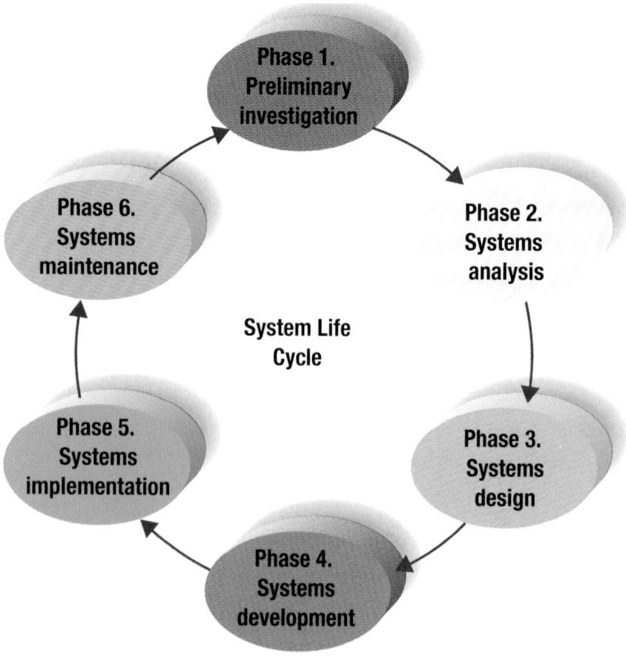

Figure 14-1 The six-phase systems life cycle

In organizations, this six-phase systems life cycle is used by computer professionals known as **systems analysts.** These people study an organization's systems to determine what actions to take and how to use computer technology to assist them. A recent survey by *Money* magazine compared salary, prestige, and security of 100 widely held jobs. The top job classification was computer engineer, followed by computer systems analyst.

As an end user, working alone or with a systems analyst, it is important that you understand how the systems life cycle works. In fact, you may *have* to use the procedure. More and more end users are developing their own information systems. This is because in many organizations there is a three-year backlog of work for systems analysts. For instance, suppose you recognize that there is a need for certain information within your organization. Obtaining this information will require the introduction of new hardware and software. You go to seek expert help from systems analysts in studying these information needs. At that point you discover that the systems analysts are so overworked it will take them three years to get to your request! You can see, then, why many managers are learning to do these activities themselves. In any case, learning the six steps described in this chapter will raise your computer competency. It will also give you skills to solve a wide range of problems. These skills can make you more valuable to an organization.

Concept Check

- ✓ What is a system?
- ✓ Name the six phases of the systems life cycle.
- ✓ What do systems analysts do?

PHASE 1: PRELIMINARY INVESTIGATION

In the preliminary investigation phase, the problems are briefly identified and a few solutions are suggested.

The first phase of the systems life cycle is a **preliminary investigation** of a proposed project to determine the need for a new information system. This usually is requested by an end user or a manager who wants something done that is not presently being done. For example, suppose you work for Advantage Advertising, a fast-growing advertising agency. Advantage Advertising produces a variety of different ads for a wide range of different clients. The agency employs both regular staff workers and on-call freelancers. One of your responsibilities is keeping track of the work performed for each client and the employees who performed the work. In addition, you are responsible for tabulating the final bill for each project. (See Figure 14-2.)

Figure 14-2 Preliminary investigation

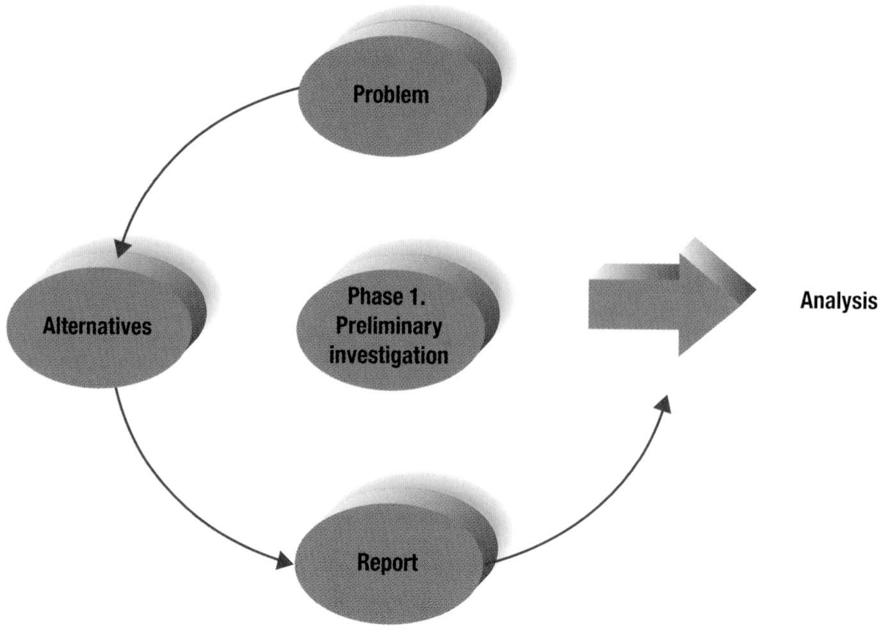

Figure 14-3 Phase 1: Preliminary investigation

How do you figure out how to charge which clients for which work done by which employees? This kind of problem is common to many service organizations (such as lawyers' and contractors' offices). Indeed, it is a problem in any organization where people charge for their "time" and clients need proof of hours worked.

In Phase 1, the systems analyst—or the end user—is concerned with three tasks. These are (1) briefly defining the problem, (2) suggesting alternative solutions, and (3) preparing a short report. (See Figure 14-3.) This report will help management decide whether to pursue the project further. (If you are an end user employing this procedure for yourself, you may not produce a written report. Rather, you would report your findings directly to your supervisor.)

DEFINING THE PROBLEM

Defining the problem means examining whatever current information system is in use. Determining what information is needed, by whom, when, and why is accomplished by interviewing and making observations. If the information system is large, this survey is done by a systems analyst. If the system is small, the survey can be done by the end user.

For example, suppose Advantage Advertising account executives, copywriters, and graphic artists currently just record the time spent on different jobs on their desk calendars. (Examples might be "Client A, telephone conference, 15 minutes"; "Client B, design layout, 2 hours.") After interviewing several account executives and listening to their frustrations, it becomes clear that the approach is somewhat helter-skelter. (See Figure 14-4.) Written calendar entries are too unprofessional to be shown to clients. Moreover, a large job often has many people working on it. It is difficult to pull together all their notations to make up a bill for the client. Some freelancers work at home, and their time slips are not readily available. These matters constitute a statement of the problem: The company has a manual time-and-billing system that is slow and difficult to implement.

As an end user, you might experience difficulties with this system yourself. You're in someone else's office, and a telephone call comes in for you from a client. Your desk calendar is back in your own office. You have two choices. You can always carry your calendar with you. As an alternative, you can re-

Figure 14-4 One step in defining problems with the current system is to interview executives

member to note the time you spent on various tasks when you return to your office. The secretary to the account executive is continually after you (and everyone else at Advantage) to provide photocopies of your calendar. This is so that various clients can be billed for the work done on various jobs. Surely, you think, there must be a better way to handle time and billing.

SUGGESTING ALTERNATIVE SYSTEMS

This step is simply to suggest some possible plans as alternatives to the present arrangement. For instance, Advantage could hire more secretaries to collect the information from everyone's calendars (including telephoning those working at home). Or it could use the existing system of network-linked microcomputers that staffers and freelancers presently use. Perhaps, you think, there is already some off-the-shelf packaged software available that could be used for a time-and-billing system. At least there might be one that would make your own job easier.

PREPARING A SHORT REPORT

For large projects, the systems analyst writes a report summarizing the results of the preliminary investigation and suggesting alternative systems. (See Figure 14-5.) The report may also include schedules for further development of the project. This document is presented to higher management, along with a recommendation to continue or discontinue the project. Management then decides whether to finance the second phase, the systems analysis.

For Advantage Advertising, your report might point out that billing is frequently delayed. It could say that some tasks may even "slip through the cracks" and not get charged at all. Thus, as the analyst has noted, you suggest the project might pay for itself merely by eliminating lost or forgotten charges.

Figure 14-5 Management meets to evaluate the preliminary investigation report

Concept Check

- What is the purpose of the preliminary investigation phase?
- What are the three tasks the systems analyst is concerned with during this phase?

PHASE 2: ANALYSIS

In the systems analysis phase, the present system is studied in depth, and new requirements are specified.

In Phase 2, **systems analysis,** data is collected about the present system. This data is then analyzed, and new requirements are determined. We are not concerned with a new design here, only with determining the *requirements* for a new system. Systems analysis is concerned with gathering and analyzing the data. It usually is completed by documenting the analysis in a report. (See Figure 14-6.)

GATHERING DATA

When gathering data, the systems analyst—or the end user doing systems analysis—expands on the data gathered during Phase 1. He or she adds details about how the current system works. Data is obtained from observation and interviews. In addition, data may be obtained from questionnaires given to people using the system. Data is also obtained from studying documents that describe the formal lines of authority and standard operating procedures. One document is the **organization chart,** which shows levels of management and formal lines of authority. (See Figure 14-7.) You might note that an organization chart resembles the hierarchy of three levels of management we described in Chapter 12. The levels are top managers, middle managers, and supervisors.

Note in our illustration in Figure 14-7 that we have preserved the department labeled "Production." However, the name in an advertising agency might

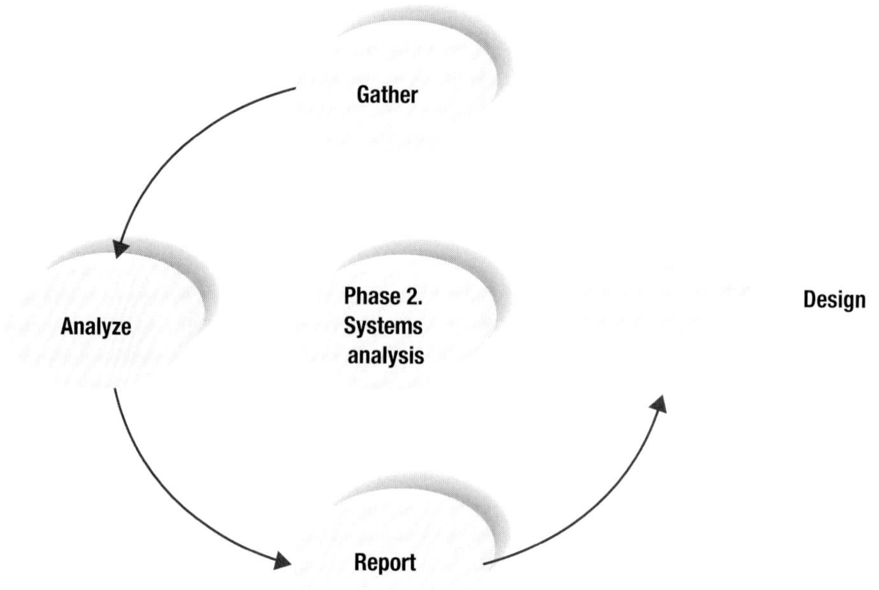

Figure 14-6 Phase 2: Systems Analysis

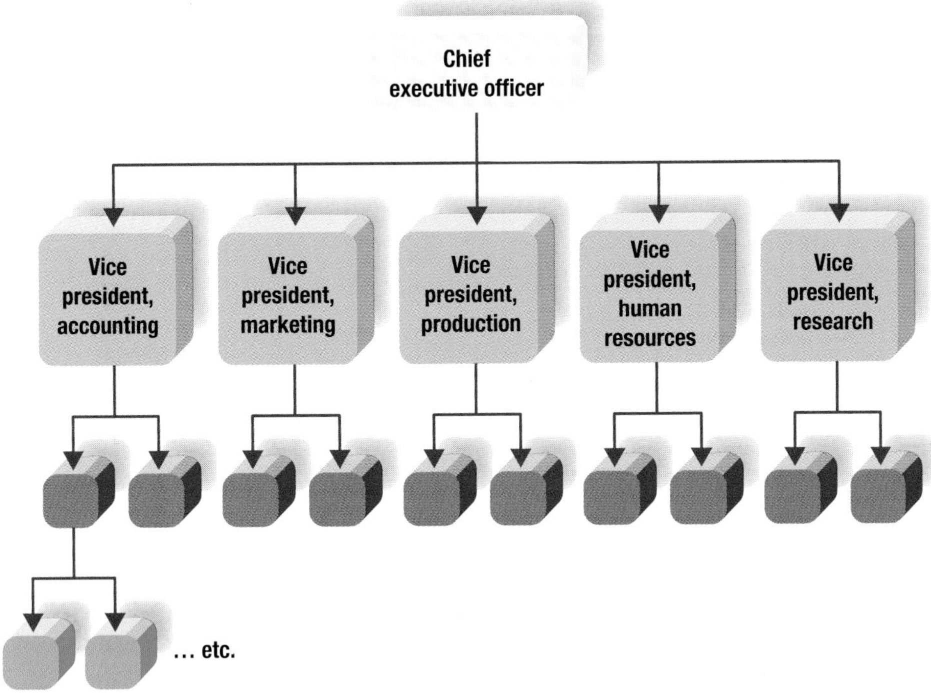

Figure 14-7 Example of an organization chart

be something like "Creative Services." Obviously, the products an advertising agency produces are ads: radio and television commercials, magazine and newspaper ads, billboard ads, and so on. In any case, if the agency is working on a major advertising campaign, people from several departments might be involved. There might also be people from different management levels within the departments. Their time charges will vary, depending on how much they are paid.

ANALYZING THE DATA

In the step of analyzing the data, the idea is to learn how information currently flows and to pinpoint why it isn't flowing appropriately. The whole point of this step is to apply logic to the existing arrangement to see how workable it is. Many times the current system is not operating correctly because prescribed procedures are not being followed. That is, the system may not really need to be redesigned. Rather, the people in it may need to be shown how to follow correct procedures.

Many different tools are available to assist systems analysts and end users in the analysis phase. Some of the principal ones are as follows:

- **Checklists:** Numerous checklists are available to assist in this stage. A checklist is a list of questions. It is helpful in guiding the systems analyst and end user through key issues for the present system.

  For example, one question might be "Can reports be easily prepared from the files and documents currently in use?" Another might be "How easily can the present time-and-billing system adapt to change and growth?"
- **Top-down analysis method:** The top-down analysis method is used to identify the top-level components of a complex system. Each component is then broken down into smaller and smaller components. This approach makes each component easier to analyze and deal with.

  For instance, the systems analyst might look at the present kind of bill submitted to a client for a complex advertising campaign. The analyst

Forms (input)	Reports (output): Client billing	Personnel expense	Support cost
Time sheet	✓	✓	
Telephone log	✓		✓
Travel log	✓		✓

Figure 14-8 Example of a grid chart

Conditions	Decision rules: 1	2	3	4
1. Project less than $10,000	Y	Y	N	N
2. Good credit history	Y	N	Y	N
Actions	**1**	**2**	**3**	**4**
1. Accept project	✓	✓	✓	
2. Require deposit		✓	✓	
3. Reject project				✓

Figure 14-9 Example of a decision table

might note the categories of costs—employee salaries, telephone and mailing charges, travel, supplies, and so on.

- **Grid charts:** A grid chart shows the relationship between input and output documents. An example is shown in Figure 14-8 that indicates the relationship between the data input and the outputs.

  For instance, a time sheet is one of many inputs that produces a particular report, such as a client's bill. Other inputs might be forms having to do with telephone conferences and travel expenses. On a grid sheet, rows represent inputs, such as time sheet forms. Columns represent output documents, such as different clients' bills. A checkmark at the intersection of a row and column means that the input document is used to create the output document.
- **Decision tables:** A decision table shows the decision rules that apply when certain conditions occur. Figure 14-9 shows a decision table to evaluate whether to accept a client's proposed advertising project. The first decision rule applies if both conditions are met. If the project is less than $10,000 and if the client has a good credit history, the firm will accept the project without requiring a deposit.
- **System flowcharts:** System flowcharts show the flow of input data to processing and finally to output, or distribution of information. An example of a system flowchart keeping track of time for advertising "creative people"

is shown in Figure 14-10. The explanation of the symbols used appears in Figure 14-11. Note that this describes the present manual, or noncomputerized, system. (A system flowchart is not the same as a program flowchart, which is very detailed. Program flowcharts are discussed in Chapter 15.)

- **Data flow diagrams:** Data flow diagrams show the data or information flow within an information system. The data is traced from its origin through processing, storage, and output. An example of a data flow diagram is shown in Figure 14-12. The explanation of the symbols used appears in Figure 14-13.
- **Automated design tools:** Automated design tools are software packages that evaluate hardware and software alternatives according to requirements given by the systems analyst. They are also called **computer-aided software engineering (CASE) tools.** These tools are not limited to system analysis. They are used in system design and development as well. CASE tools relieve the system analysts of many repetitive tasks, develop clear documentation, and, for larger projects, coordinate team member activities.

For a summary of the analysis tools, see Figure 14-14.

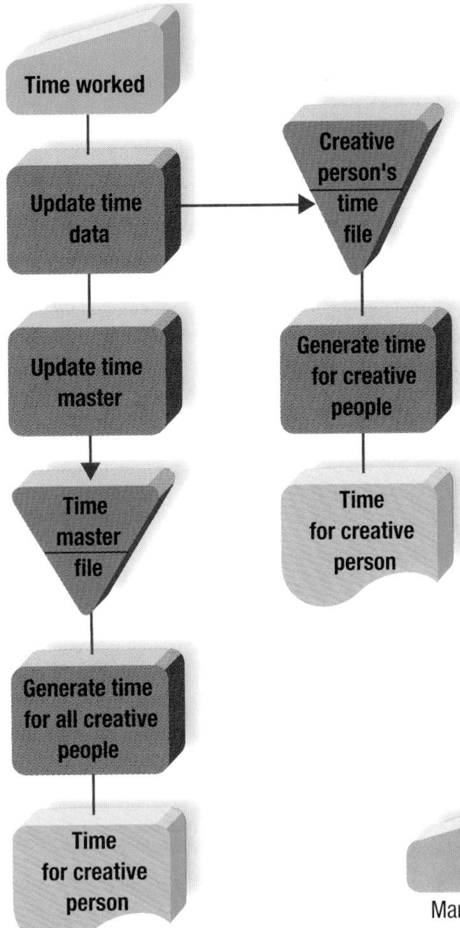

Figure 14-10 Example of a system flowchart

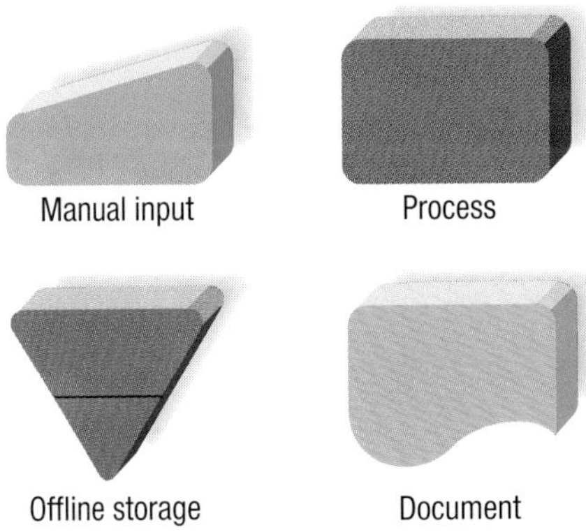

Figure 14-11 System flowchart symbols

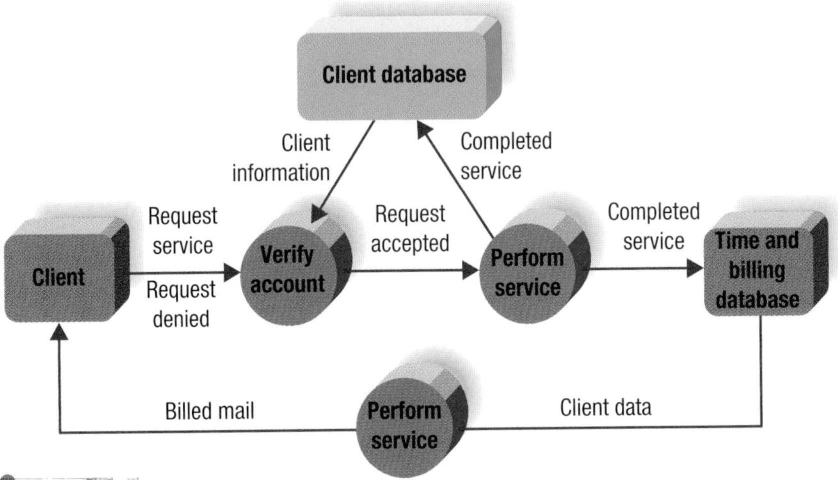

Figure 14-12 Example of a data flow diagram

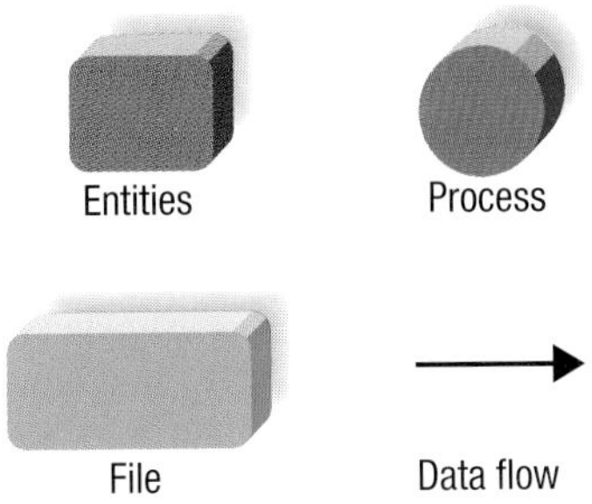

Figure 14-13 Data flow diagram symbols

Tool	Description
Checklist	Provides a list of questions about key issues
Top-down analysis	Divides a complex system into components, beginning at the top
Grid chart	Shows relationships between inputs and outputs
Decision table	Specifies decision rules and circumstances when specific rules are to be applied
System flowchart	Shows movement of input data, processing, and output or distribution of information
Data flow diagram	Shows data flow within an organization or application
Automated design tools	Automates the analysis, design, and development of information systems

Figure 14-14 Summary of analysis tools

Figure 14-15 Systems analysis documentation

DOCUMENTING SYSTEMS ANALYSIS

In larger organizations, the systems analysis stage is typically documented in a report for higher management. The **systems analysis report** describes the current information system, the requirements for a new system, and a possible development schedule. For example, at Advantage Advertising, the system flowcharts show the present flow of information in a manual time-and-billing system. Some boxes in the system flowchart might be replaced with symbols showing where a computerized information system could work better.

Management studies the report and decides whether to continue with the project. Let us assume your boss and higher management have decided to continue. You now move on to Phase 3, systems design. (See Figure 14-15.)

Concept Check

- ✔ What is the purpose of the analysis phase?
- ✔ List and describe the common analysis tools.
- ✔ What is a systems analysis report?

PHASE 3: DESIGN

In the systems design phase, a new or alternative information system is designed.

Phase 3 is **systems design.** It consists of three tasks: (1) designing alternative systems, (2) selecting the best system, and (3) writing a systems design report. (See Figure 14-16.)

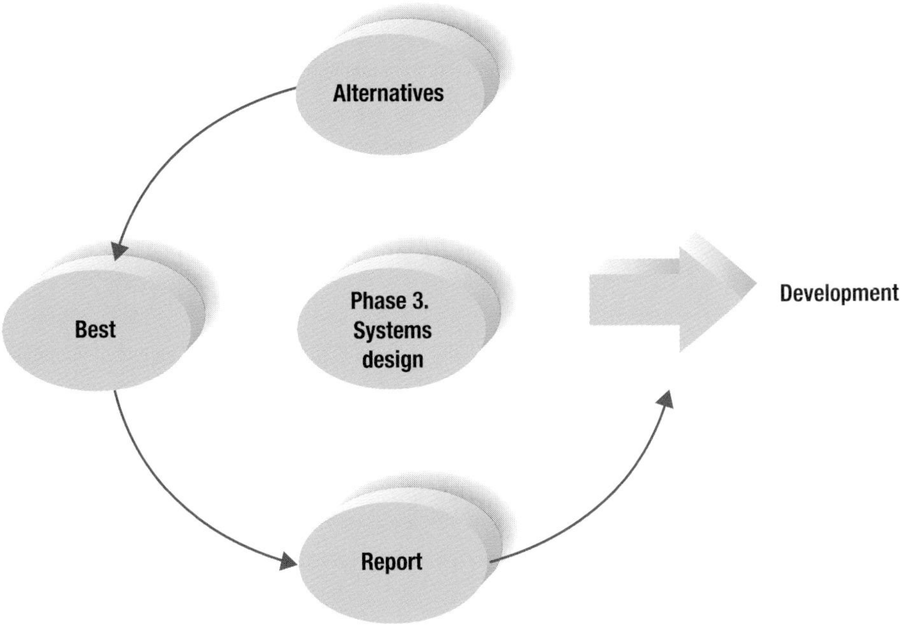

Figure 14-16 Phase 3: Systems Design

DESIGNING ALTERNATIVE SYSTEMS

In almost all instances, more than one design can be developed to meet the information needs. Systems designers evaluate each alternative system for feasibility. By feasibility we mean three things:

- **Economic feasibility:** Will the costs of the new system be justified by the benefits it promises? How long will it take for the new system to pay for itself?
- **Technical feasibility:** Are reliable hardware, software, and training available to make the system work? If not, can they be obtained?
- **Operational feasibility:** Can the system actually be made to operate in the organization, or will people—employees, managers, clients—resist it?

SELECTING THE BEST SYSTEM

When choosing the best design, managers must consider these four questions. (1) Will the system fit in with the organization's overall information system? (2) Will the system be flexible enough so it can be modified in the future? (3) Can it be made secure against unauthorized use? (4) Are the benefits worth the costs?

For example, one aspect you have to consider at Advantage Advertising is security. Should freelancers and outside vendors enter data directly into a computerized time-and-billing system, or should they keep submitting time slips manually? In allowing these outside people to directly input information, are you also allowing them access to files they should not see? Do these files contain confidential information, perhaps information of value to rival advertising agencies?

WRITING THE SYSTEMS DESIGN REPORT

The **systems design report** is prepared for higher management and describes the alternative designs. It presents the costs versus the benefits and outlines the effect of alternative designs on the organization. It usually concludes by recommending one of the alternatives.

Concept Check

- What is the purpose of the design phase?
- Distinguish between economic, technical, and operational feasibility.
- Identify the factors that need to be considered when choosing the best systems design.

PHASE 4: DEVELOPMENT

In the systems development phase, software and hardware are acquired and tested.

Phase 4 is **systems development.** It has three steps: (1) acquiring software, (2) acquiring hardware, and (3) testing the new system. (See Figure 14-17.)

ACQUIRING SOFTWARE

Application software for the new information system can be obtained in two ways. It can be purchased as off-the-shelf packaged software and possibly modified, or it can be custom designed. If any of the software is being specially created, the steps we will outline on programming (in Chapter 15) should be followed.

With the systems analyst's help, you have looked at time-and-billing packaged software designed for service organizations. Unfortunately, you find that none of the packaged software will do. Most of the packages seem to work well for one person (you). However, none seem to be designed for many people working together. It appears, then, that software will have to be custom designed. (We discuss the process of developing software in Chapter 15, on programming.)

ACQUIRING HARDWARE

Some new systems may not require new computer equipment, but others will. The kinds needed and the places they are to be installed must be determined.

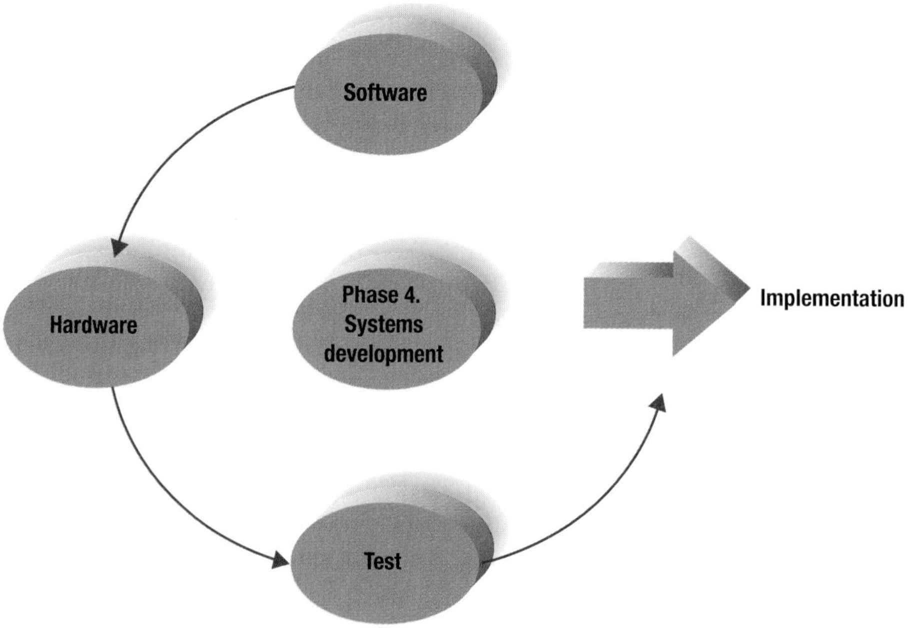

Figure 14-17 Phase 4: Systems Development

This is a very critical area. Switching or upgrading equipment can be a tremendously expensive proposition. Will a microcomputer system be sufficient as a company grows? Are networks expandable? Will people have to undergo costly training?

The systems analyst tells you that there are several different makes and models of microcomputers currently in use at Advantage Advertising. Fortunately, all are connected by a local area network to a file server that can hold the time-and-billing data. To maintain security, the systems analyst suggests that an electronic mailbox can be installed for freelancers and others outside the company. They can use this electronic mailbox to post their time charges. Thus, it appears that existing hardware will work just fine.

TESTING THE NEW SYSTEM

After the software and equipment have been installed, the system should be tested. Sample data is fed into the system. The processed information is then evaluated to see whether results are correct. Testing may take several months if the new system is complex.

For this step, you ask some people in Creative Services to test the system. (See Figure 14-18.) You observe that some of the people have problems knowing where to enter their times. To solve the problem, the software is modified to display an improved user entry screen. After the system has been thoroughly tested and revised as necessary, you are ready to put it into use.

Figure 14-18 To test a system, sample data is entered and problems are resolved

Concept Check
✓ What is the purpose of the development phase?
✓ What are the ways by which application software can be obtained?

PHASE 5: IMPLEMENTATION

In the systems implementation phase, the new information system is installed, and people are trained to use it.

Another name for Phase 5, **systems implementation,** is **conversion.** It is the process of changing—converting—from the old system to the new and training people to use the new system. (See Figure 14-19.)

TYPES OF CONVERSION

There are four approaches to conversion: *direct, parallel, pilot,* and *phased.*

- In the **direct approach,** the conversion is done simply by abandoning the old and starting up the new. This can be risky. If anything is still wrong with the new system, the old system is no longer available to fall back on.

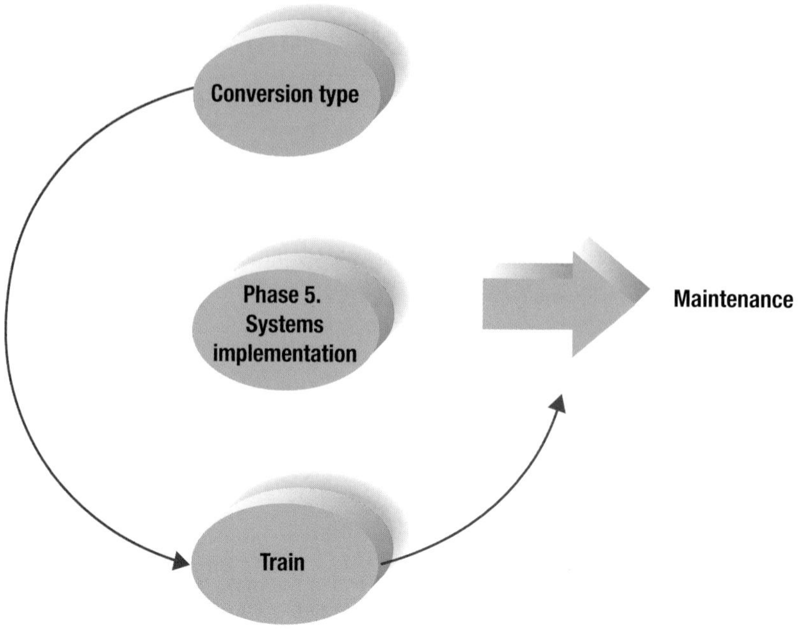

Figure 14-19 Phase 5: Systems Implementation

The direct approach is not recommended precisely because it is so risky. Problems, big or small, invariably crop up in a new system. In a large system, a problem might just mean catastrophe.

- In the **parallel approach,** old and new systems are operated side by side until the new one has proved to be reliable.

  This approach is low-risk. If the new system fails, the organization can just switch to the old system to keep going. However, keeping enough equipment and people active to manage two systems at the same time can be very expensive. Thus, the parallel approach is used only in cases in which the cost of failure or of interrupted operation is great.
- In the **pilot approach,** the new system is tried out in only one part of the organization. Once the system is working smoothly in that part, it is implemented throughout the rest of the organization.

  The pilot approach is certainly less expensive than the parallel approach. It also is somewhat riskier. However, the risks can be controlled because problems will be confined to only certain areas of the organization. Difficulties will not affect the entire organization.
- In the **phased approach,** the new system is implemented gradually over a period of time.

  The entire implementation process is broken down into parts or phases. Implementation begins with the first phase and once it is successfully implemented, the second phase begins. This process continues until all phases are operating smoothly. This is an expensive proposition, because the implementation is done slowly. However, it is certainly one of the least risky approaches.

In general, the pilot and phased approaches are the most favored methods. Pilot is preferred when there are many people in an organization performing similar operations—for instance, all sales clerks in a department store. Phased is more appropriate for organizations in which people are performing different operations. For a summary of the different types of conversions, see Figure 14-20.

You and the systems analyst, with top management support, have decided on a pilot implementation. This approach was selected in part based on cost and the availability of a representative group of users. The Creative Services

Type	Description	Discussion
Direct	Abandon the old	Very risky; not recommended
Parallel	Run old and new side by side	Very low risk; however, very expensive; not generally recommended
Pilot	Convert part of organization first	Less expensive but riskier than parallel conversion; recommended for situations with many people performing similar operations
Phased	Implement gradually	Less risky but more expensive than parallel conversion; recommended for situations with many people performing different operations

Figure 14-20 Types of conversion

department previously tested the system and has expressed enthusiastic support for it. A group from this department will pilot the implementation of the time-and-billing system. (See Figure 14-21.)

Figure 14-21 A pilot group from Creative Services tests the new system

TRAINING

Training people is important, of course. Unfortunately, it is one of the most commonly overlooked activities. Some people may begin training early, even before the equipment is delivered, so that they can adjust more easily. In some cases, a professional software trainer may be brought in to show people how to operate the system. However, at Advantage Advertising the time-and-billing software is simple enough that the systems analyst can act as the trainer.

Concept Check

- What is the goal of the implementation phase?
- Briefly describe the four approaches to conversion.

PHASE 6: MAINTENANCE

Systems maintenance is first a systems audit and then an ongoing evaluation to see whether a system is performing productively.

After implementation comes **systems maintenance,** the last step in the systems life cycle. This phase is a very important, ongoing activity. Most organizations spend more time and money on this phase than any of the others. Maintenance has two parts—a *systems audit* and a *periodic evaluation.* (See Figure 14-22.)

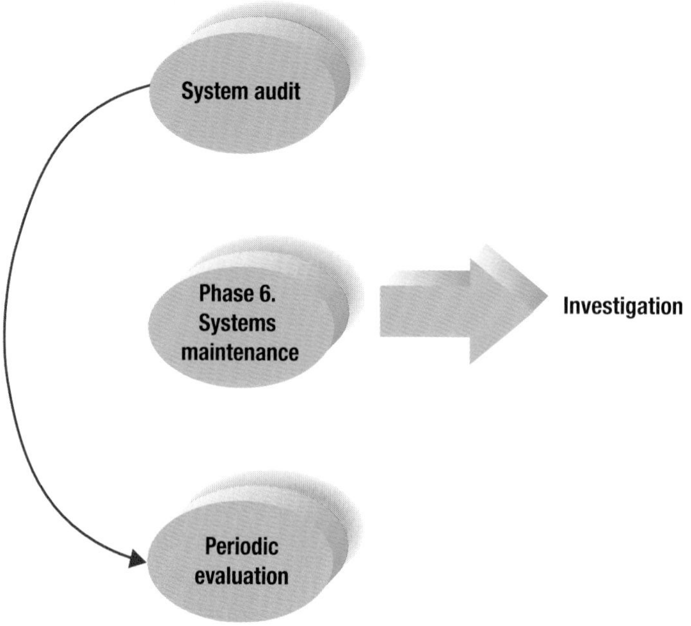

Figure 14-22 Phase 6: Systems Maintenance

Phase	Activity
1 Preliminary investigation	Define problem, suggest alternatives, prepare short report
2 Systems analysis	Gather data, analyze data, document
3 Systems design	Design alternatives, select best alternative, write report
4 Systems development	Develop software, acquire hardware, test system
5 Systems implementation	Convert, train
6 Systems maintenance	Perform system audit, evaluate periodically

Figure 14-23 Summary of systems life cycle

In the **systems audit,** the system's performance is compared to the original design specifications. This is to determine whether the new procedures are actually furthering productivity. If they are not, some redesign may be necessary.

After the systems audit, the new information system is further modified, if necessary. All systems should be evaluated from time to time to determine whether they are meeting the goals and providing the service they are supposed to.

The six-step systems life cycle is summarized in Figure 14-23.

Concept Check

- What is the purpose of the maintenance phase?
- Name the two parts of the maintenance phase.

PROTOTYPING AND RAPID APPLICATIONS DEVELOPMENT

Prototyping and RAD are two alternatives to the systems life cycle approach.

Is it necessary to follow every phase of the systems life cycle? It may be desirable, but often there is no time to do so. For instance, hardware may change so fast that there is no opportunity for evaluation, design, and testing as just described. Two alternative approaches that require much less time are *prototyping* and *rapid applications development*.

Figure 14-24 SimuSys from IBM

PROTOTYPING

Prototyping means to build a *model* or *prototype* that can be modified before the actual system is installed. For instance, the systems analyst for Advantage Advertising might develop a proposed or prototype menu as a possible screen display for the time-and-billing system. Users would try it out and provide feedback to the systems analyst. The systems analyst would revise the prototype until the users felt it was ready to put into place. Typically, the development time for prototyping is shorter; however, it is sometimes more difficult to manage the project and to control costs. (See Figure 14-24.)

RAPID APPLICATIONS DEVELOPMENT

Rapid applications development (RAD) involves the use of powerful development software; small specialized teams; and highly trained personnel. For example, the systems analyst for Advantage Advertising would use specialized development software like CASE, form small teams consisting of select users and managers, and obtain assistance from other highly qualified analysts. Although the resulting time-and-billing system would likely cost more, the time for development would be shorter and the quality of the completed system would be better.

Concept Check

- ✓ What is meant by prototyping?
- ✓ What is involved in RAD?

Careers in IT

Systems Analyst

A systems analyst follows the steps described in the systems life cycle. Analysts plan and design new systems or reorganize a company's computer resources to best utilize them. Analysts follow the systems life cycle through all steps of the systems life cycle: preliminary investigation, analysis, design, development, implementation, and maintenance.

Systems analyst positions normally require a bachelor's degree in computer science and technical experience. Internships and prior experience with the latest technology are a considerable advantage for those seeking jobs in this industry. Systems analysts can expect to earn an annual salary of $35,000 to $70,000. Opportunities for advancement include positions as a chief technology officer or other managerial opportunities.

To learn about other careers in information technology visit us at http://www.mhhe.com/oleary/CT05 and select Careers in IT from Tim's Toolbox.

A Look to the Future

Rapid Change

Most observers firmly believe that the pace of business is now faster than ever before. The time to develop a product and bring it to market in many cases is now months rather than years. Internet technologies, in particular, have provided tools to support the rapid introduction of new products and services.

To stay competitive, corporations must integrate these new technologies into their existing way of doing business. Existing systems are being modified, and entirely new systems are being developed. In most cases, the traditional systems life cycle approach takes too long—sometimes years—to develop a system. Many organizations are responding by aggressively implementing prototyping and RAD. Others are enlisting the services of outside consulting groups that specialize in system development.

One such company is Drapkin Technology. Drapkin provides technical expertise and managerial experience to the systems analysis and design process. Working with corporations such as Gateway and Sony, the company provides project assessment, analysis, design, development, implementation, and administration. Drapkin can also step in and quickly reorganize projects when the systems life cycle fails—a crucial service in and of itself.

As the pace of business continues to increase, more and more organizations are expected to move to prototyping and RAD approaches as well as enlisting the services of outside consulting groups.

SYSTEMS ANALYSIS AND DESIGN AT DVD DIRECT

INTRODUCTION

DVD Direct is an entirely Web oriented movie rental business. Their customers order movies from DVD Direct's Web site and the movies are delivered on DVD disks by mail. While business has been good, some recent indications have pointed to possible trouble ahead. Specifically, an internal study discovered that many current and potential customers with high bandwidth Internet connections prefer to have movies delivered over the Internet rather than by mail. Further, the study reported that current customers who recently switched to high bandwidth connections were very likely to drop their DVD Direct membership.

In response, top management has committed to expanding DVD Direct's business model to include online delivery of movies using streaming video technology. Once an order is placed, the Internet-delivered movies would be immediately downloaded onto the member's hard disk. The movie would remain there for a week, or until the movie was played, whichever occurs first.

Alice, a recently hired marketing analyst, has proposed the creation of a Frequent Renters Club that gives members points for each streaming movie they order. As a member's points accumulate, the points can be redeemed for gifts and for free rentals. Let's follow Alice as she meets with Bob, the vice president of marketing, to discuss the proposed Frequent Renters Club.

ALICE'S ASSIGNMENT

Bob: Good morning, Alice. Yesterday, I presented your Frequent Renters Club proposal to the Oversight Committee. This committee evaluates all new projects at DVD Direct. They liked your proposal and have given it tentative approval.

This is a big project and an important one for the company. You've made a contribution. I want this project to be yours and I'm confident that you'll be able to successfully implement it. The key is to develop an information system that accurately and consistently records reward points. [See Figure C14-1.]

To assist you, I have arranged for a systems analyst to provide you ongoing support. Her name is Mia. I called her just before—oh, here she is now. Mia, I'd like you to meet Alice. Mia has been a systems analyst at DVD Direct for the past three years and has developed several large systems over that time. She knows the ropes better than anyone.

Mia: Hello, Alice! Bob has discussed the Frequent Renters Club with me. Your proposal looks like a great idea. I'm looking forward to working with you to develop an information system to support it.

Bob: I wish we could have Mia's undivided attention on this project; however, she is working on several other projects right now. She'll provide overall guidance on the project and provide you technical support. Alice, why don't you take Mia to your office and get started immediately?

Eager to get to work, Mia and Alice leave Bob's office.

Figure C14-1 "The key is to develop an information system that accurately and consistently records reward points."

Alice: Wow! I didn't expect this! I've been with the company for less than a month and now I have this big project. I've never done anything like this before. I have to admit I'm a little nervous. I've heard that these big projects can sometimes blow up.

Mia: Projects like this always seem overwhelming at first, and it's true that many projects are not successful for one reason or another. But we're going to do fine. To maximize the chances of success, we are going to follow a carefully developed procedure that includes periodic updates to the Oversight Committee. It is called systems analysis and design.

Alice: Systems analysis and design—tell me more.

Mia: Well, it's a problem-solving approach that has six sequential phases: preliminary investigation, analysis, design, development, implementation, and maintenance. These phases make up a system life cycle for a project. As we proceed on the project, I'll walk you through the phases and help out as much as I can.

Alice: Great, how do we get started?

PRELIMINARY INVESTIGATION

Mia: Preliminary investigation is one of the most important phases and the one that often is overlooked. A common mistake is to rush into a project without a clear understanding of the problem to be addressed and clear support from management.

Alice: But I've already discussed the project with Bob and the project has been tentatively approved by the Oversight Committee.

Mia: Right, and that's a good beginning. But before proceeding we need to make sure that you, Bob, and the Oversight Committee are on the same page. If not, we could invest a lot of time only to learn later that Bob or the Oversight Committee were expecting something else. Taking a little time now can save us a great deal of time and money later.

Alice: I hear what you're saying. What do I do for this preliminary phase?

Mia: Start by writing a clear concise statement that describes the problem. In a way that's the hard part—being very brief and clear. It shouldn't be longer than four sentences. Then, identify some alternative systems or ways to address the problem. Again, be concise. You might run these by some of your coworkers to get their input. Let's meet Tuesday afternoon to review what you have by then.

Alice: Sounds good. I'll get on this right away!

On Tuesday, Alice and Mia meet again to discuss Alice's progress. Alice has put a good deal of time into exploring and describing the problem of installing the reward system.

Alice: Defining the problem was more challenging that I thought it would be. But some of my coworkers had some good suggestions. Here's the problem definition. [See Figure C14-2.]

Mia: That's excellent. It is clear, concise, and provides enough detail. Now let's hear your solutions.

Alice: I have identified three possible alternative solutions. The first one uses stamps. When a member orders a movie online, a stamp is sent to them by mail. When they have enough stamps, members return the stamps for rewards.

Frequent Renters Club

Problem definition:

Create a system to record the accumulation and the redemption of reward points for members participating in the Frequent Renters Club. Whenever a member rents a streaming video, he or she will receive points. The number of points will depend on such factors as the popularity and availability of the video, the date and the time of day the video is requested, and any special promotions offered at that time. Points can be redeemed for free videos, movie paraphernalia, and priority for video downloading at peak times.

Figure C14-2 Mia's problem definition

The second alternative uses the monthly billing statement. The current billing statement is sent monthly listing the member's account balance and the movies rented for the month. The program that generates the statements could be revised to also calculate and report reward points. Members redeem their reward points by mail or over the Web.

The third alternative uses a Web page to immediately record, report, and redeem award points. Whenever a member downloads a movie, reward points are awarded and reported. Members redeem their reward points over the Web.

Mia: I think you've got it. Now, we need to prepare a two- or three-page report presenting the problem definition and outlining each of your alternative solutions. If you could prepare a draft, we could revise it on Thursday, and I'll present it to the Oversight Committee on Friday.

Alice: I'll have the draft ready by Thursday morning.

ANALYSIS

Alice and Mia complete the report as scheduled and Mia presents it to the Oversight Committee on Friday. Late that day Mia enters Alice's office with a big smile on her face.

Mia: Alice—good news! The Oversight Committee has given us the go-ahead to continue the project.

Alice: Great! I'm so relieved. Let's get started programming the new system!

Mia: Not so fast. Before building something new, we need to know what we currently have. And we still have three alternative solutions. Before we can select one, we need to understand how the current information systems at DVD Direct work and how they might be affected by the Frequent Renters Club.

Alice: Of course you're right. Where should I start?

Mia: Start by talking with people in areas that might be affected by the new system. Learn about their operations and procedures. What areas do you think would be most affected by the Frequent Renters Club?

Alice: That would be Accounting and Production. Accounting produces the monthly billing statements and Production will be responsible for delivering the videos.

Mia: Start with Accounting. Learn more about their accounting software. Be particularly mindful of any documents that are created including managerial reports. Determine how a member's credit history is maintained and used. Consider any modifications that may be necessary for the expanded model.

Alice: Right. I'll do some interviewing and keep my eyes open for any documentation on current processes.

Mia: Next, visit Production and follow the same procedure. See if you can locate any documents that describe how current orders are processed and how DVDs are shipped out. Then consider how these documents might be altered to fit the expanded model.

Alice: This should be pretty interesting, but I think it will take some time.

Mia: I agree. It's important that we don't rush through this process. The success of this project is dependent on a thorough understanding of exactly what is needed. Let's meet again in three weeks, okay?

During the following three weeks, Alice interviews a number of people in Accounting and Production and collects numerous documents. She learns a great deal about how DVD Direct currently records and processes orders from their members. At the same time she identifies numerous changes or modifications that may be required for the expanded business model.

In her next meeting with Mia at the end of the three weeks, Alice discusses her findings and presents the documents she has collected related to DVD Direct's accounting and production systems. The documents include the decision table shown in Figure C14-3 and the data flow diagram shown in Figure C14-4. Mia and Alice discuss the requirements for the new system and formulate a tentative schedule to design, build, and implement the necessary systems to support the Frequent Renters Club. Over the next several days they prepare the systems analysis report that Mia will present to the Oversight Committee.

DESIGN

After her meeting with the Oversight Committee, Mia goes to Alice's office to report the committee's recommendation.

Mia: Alice, the committee is very interested in our project and has given approval for the design phase. The first design step is to evaluate the economic, technical, and operational feasibility of each alternative we identified in the first phase.

Alice: Sounds good! I'm so pleased. But I don't know much about computer technology.

Mia: No problem, that's my area. I'll take care of that and you focus on the economic and operational feasibility. I suggest that you consult with the people in Accounting and Production that you met with during the analysis phase.

Alice: Several of them seemed very interested in the project and asked me to keep them up-to-date. I'm confident that they will have some opinions regarding the feasibility of the different alternatives. This looks like a big job.

Mia: Yes it is and an extremely important one. Based on our findings, we'll select one system to recommend to the Oversight Committee. We need to take our time, be thorough, and not rush through this step. My guess is that it will take three to four weeks.

	Decision rules			
Conditions	**1**	**2**	**3**	**4**
1. Are they a member of the frequent renters club?	Y	Y	N	N
2. Have they requested a streaming video?	Y	N	Y	N
Actions	**1**	**2**	**3**	**4**
1. Add points to account	✓			
2. Create a new account			✓	
3. Nothing		✓		✓

Figure C14-3 Decision table

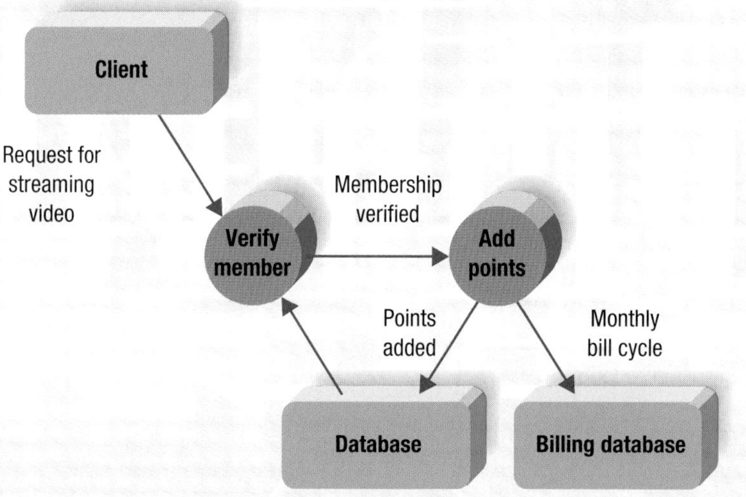

Figure C14-4 Data flow diagram

As they thought, the feasibility investigation does take nearly a month, during which Alice consults with people in Accounting and Production and Mia evaluates technical requirements. Let's follow them as they meet once again to discuss their findings.

Mia: Let's start with the first option involving stamps that are mailed. From a technical standpoint this is pretty low tech and would not be a problem.

Alice: From an operational standpoint it is very straightforward too. However, economically it may not be feasible. In addition to postal costs, we would need to hire additional staff to send out the stamps and record redemptions. Another issue, perhaps more significant, is counterfeiting. We would need to develop a system to ensure that redeemed stamps are actually authentic.

Mia: Good point. Also, while technically this approach is obviously feasible, this low tech approach is inconsistent with the high tech streaming video delivery system.

Alice: I agree. Our high bandwidth members would not be too impressed with a manual system. So let's forget that one. This leaves us with the other two alternatives, using the billing statement and using a Web page.

Alice and Mia conclude that both remaining alternative systems are economically, technically, and operationally feasible. Each system is similar, except that the Web site alternative supports immediate updates of reward points, while the monthly billing cycle alternative performs this operation just once a month. There may be more than meets the eye at first, however.

Mia: Some of the accounting programs would have to be modified for the monthly billing cycle approach. Even more changes, however, would be required for the new Web page approach.

Alice: Good point. The billing cycle approach would essentially be an extension to our existing information system.

Mia: Another factor to consider is the ability of the selected system to be modified or changed over time. For example, what if we ran a special promotion that allocated more reward points for certain movies?

Alice: Seems to me both would be equally capable of being modified. What about security? Does one alternative offer better security?

Mia: Our current billing system has built-in security measures, and we have never experienced any security problems. As an extension of this system, the monthly billing alternative would be just as secure. While the Web page alternative would present more security concerns, current Web technology is available that provides good security. But it would require more time and money to implement.

Alice: Both approaches have unique benefits and costs. The Web site provides the faster and better customer support. Monthly billing is a good fit with our current information systems. Both can provide security. However, the Web site approach will require more time and money.

Mia: While the immediate tabulation of club points by the Web site approach seems to offer more benefits, it would be more expensive. I think, from this perspective, we should go with modifying the monthly billing statement to include calculation and report of reward points.

Alice: I agree. Let's write our systems design report to include the costs and benefits of all the alternatives and recommend proceeding with the Monthly Billing approach.

DEVELOPMENT

The Oversight Committee reviewed the systems design report presented by Mia and approved the funding and support for final phases of the project. (See Figure C14-5.) Alice and Mia have been working on the development of the Monthly Billing option for the past six weeks. Let's check on them as they discuss their progress on the development phase.

Mia: Alice, because our Frequent Renters Club rewards are similar to airlines's frequent flyers rewards, I decided to talk with some of my contacts in the airline industry. They purchased their software from a company that specializes in sales and support of these types of programs.

Alice: Great. If we don't have to create our own programs, that would save a lot of development time. Have you contacted the software company?

Mia: Yes. I've met with them several times to discuss modifying their standard programs to meet our needs. Purchasing the modified programs will cost less than developing them on our own.

Alice: How about hardware? Will we have to purchase and install any new equipment?

Figure C14-5 The Oversight Committee

Mia: Originally I thought we would need to buy a new Web server. However, I located a company in Canada that provides Web server support and extensive data storage. Leasing the services from this firm is more cost effective than purchasing the equipment ourselves.

Alice: So did you manage to outsource all hardware and software?

Mia: Almost. I had to write some code for a login screen to integrate the new Web site for users to redeem their club points. But for the most part, I worked on integrating pre-existing software. We are ready to test the hardware and software.

Using the modified software and the Web services from the Canadian firm, Mia and Alice, along with a team from the Accounting department, tested the hardware and software. Numerous issues surfaced, including changes in the Web login screen and some minor errors in the procedures to calculate reward points. But after three weeks, the system was ready to go.

Let's look in on Alice and Mia as they discuss the completed design and prepare for the next phase, implementation.

IMPLEMENTATION

Mia: So, we have a working, tested system. Now we need to implement it. Any ideas on how we should do it?

Alice: I assumed we were going to promote the system to our members and make it available as soon as possible. If any problems arise, we'll fix them as they occur.

Mia: We could do that. But I think we should expect the unexpected. Even though we have carefully tested the system, it is very likely that problems will surface when our members use it.

Alice: That could be a challenge! I estimate that several hundred members will initially use the Frequent Renters Club. If the system blows up the first time our members use it, we're going to have some frustrated users on our hands. Some may never use the system again. Do you have any ideas how we can minimize this risk?

Mia: There are alternative ways. Instead of implementing the new system to everyone at one time, let's initially offer it in the southwest region. It is the smallest region. As problems arise we can quickly fix them. Then, after the system is working smoothly, we can expand the system throughout the country. This approach will cost a little more, and it does not eliminate all problems. But it does minimize the impact of the problems while we are working out the kinks in the system.

Alice: Sounds good to me.

For the next two months, the members in the southwest region used the Frequent Renters awards program. In the first two weeks, several minor problems surfaced and were quickly addressed. Since that time, the system has been working smoothly and has been implemented countrywide.

Again we find Alice and Mia in discussion, this time reviewing how the system has been performing and what needs to be done next.

MAINTENANCE

Alice: Our new system is working great and our high bandwidth members have reported that they like using it. Thanks for all your help on this project, and I hope that we'll work together again sometime in the future.

Mia: We're not done yet. We have one final phase to complete—maintenance. [See Figure C14-6.]

Alice: I thought that you and information services would be responsible for ensuring that the hardware and software continued to operate correctly.

Figure C14-6 "We're not done yet. We have one final phase to complete–maintenance."

Mia: That's true. We will address hardware and software problems as they occur. And we will periodically review the entire system to ensure that it is operating efficiently. But first you and I need to conduct a systems audit.

Alice: Audit, as in accounting?

Mia: The kind of audit I'm referring to evaluates how well the actual system performs relative to the requirements we originally specified. Maintenance may not be exciting, but it is a highly valuable effort. It starts with confirming that we have truly solved our initial problem!

Alice and Mia spend the next week evaluating the system's performance and comparing it to their original design specifications. They are very pleased to see that the system meets their expectations, the expectations of their managers, and the expectations of the Frequent Renters Club members.

For more comprehensive discussion on DVD Direct's systems analysis and design, consult your Computing Today CD or visit us on the web at http://www.mhhe.com/oleary/CT05 and select DVD Direct from Tim's Toolbox.

SYSTEM ANALYSIS AND DESIGN

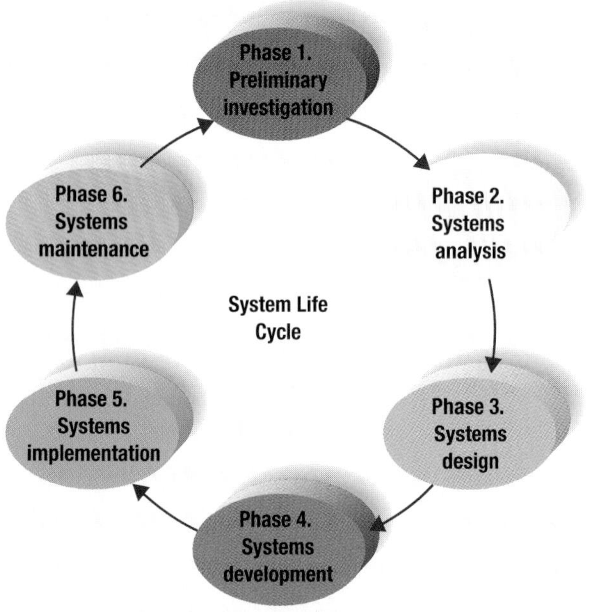

A **system** is a collection of activities and elements organized to accomplish a goal. **System analysis and design** is a six-phase problem solving procedure that makes up the **system life cycle.**

The phases are:

- *Preliminary investigation*—identifies problems or needs.
- *Systems analysis*—studies present system and specifies new requirements.
- *Systems design*—design new or alternative system to meet new requirements.
- *Systems development*—acquiring, developing, and testing needed hardware and software.
- *Systems implementation*—installing new system and training people.
- *Systems maintenance*—periodically evaluating and updating system as needed.

Systems analysts are computer professionals that typically conduct system analysis and design.

PHASE 1: PRELIMINARY INVESTIGATION

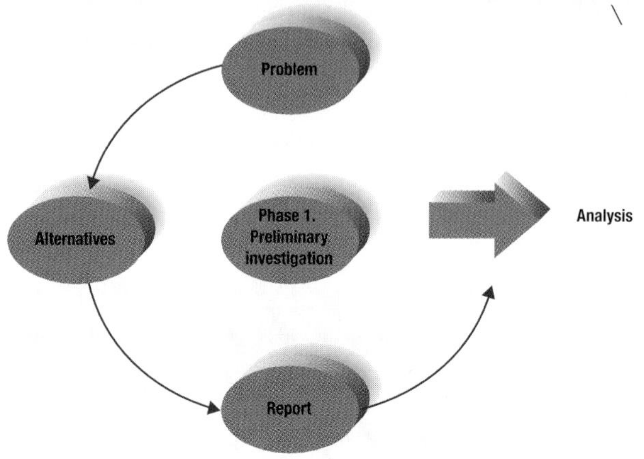

The **preliminary investigation** determines the need for a new information system. It is typically requested by an end user or a manager. Three tasks of this phase are defining the problem, suggesting alternative systems, and preparing a report

Defining the Problem

The current information system is examined to determine who needs what information, when the information is needed, and why.

If the existing information system is large, then a **systems analyst** conducts the survey. Otherwise, the end user conducts the survey.

Suggesting Alternative Systems

Some possible alternative systems are suggested. Based on interviews and observations made in defining the problem, alternative information systems are identified.

Preparing a Short Report

To document and to communicate the findings of Phase 1, preliminary investigation, a short report is prepared and presented to management.

To be a competent and knowledgeable end user you need to understand the importance of systems analysis and design. You need to know the six phases of the systems development life cycle: preliminary investigation, analysis, design, development, implementation, and maintenance. Additionally, you need to understand prototyping and RAD.

PHASE 2: ANALYSIS

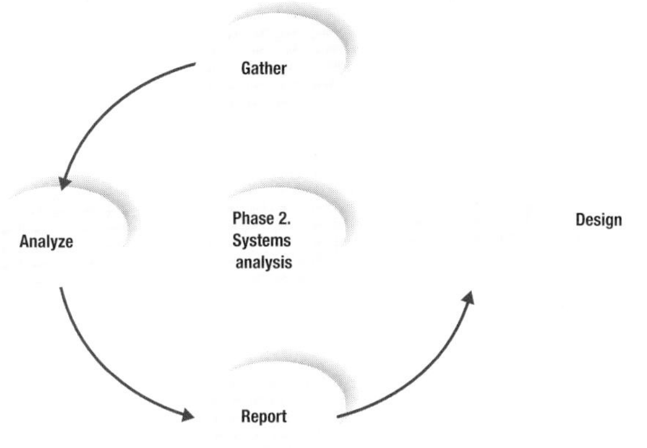

In **systems analysis** data is collected about the present system. The focus is on determining the requirements for a new system. Three tasks of this phase are gathering data, analyzing the data, and documenting the analysis.

Gathering Data

Data is gathered by observation, interviews, questionnaires, and looking at documents. One helpful document is the **organization chart,** which shows a company's functions and levels of management.

Analyzing the Data

There are several tools for the analysis of data, including **checklists, top-down analysis, grid charts, decision tables,** and **system flowcharts.**

Documenting Systems Analysis

To document and to communicate the findings of Phase 2, a **systems analysis report** is prepared for higher management.

PHASE 3: DESIGN

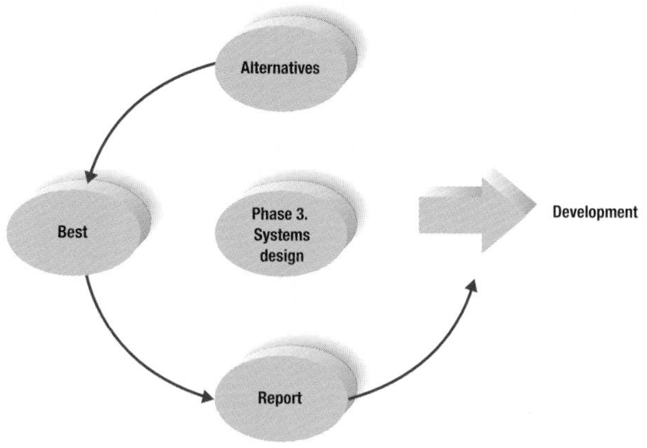

In the **systems design** phase, a new or alternative information system is designed. This phase consists of three tasks:

Designing Alternative Systems

Alternative information systems are designed. Each alternative is evaluated for:

- **Economic feasibility**—cost versus benefits; time for the system to pay for itself.
- **Technical feasibility**—hardware and software reliability; available training.
- **Operational feasibility**—system work within organization.

Selecting the Best System

Four questions considered when selecting the best system:

- Will the system fit into an overall information system?
- Will the system be flexible enough to be modified as needed in the future?
- Will it be secure against unauthorized use?
- Will the system's benefits exceed its costs?

Writing the System Design Report

To document and to communicate the findings of Phase 3, a **systems design report** is prepared for higher management.

PHASE 4: DEVELOPMENT

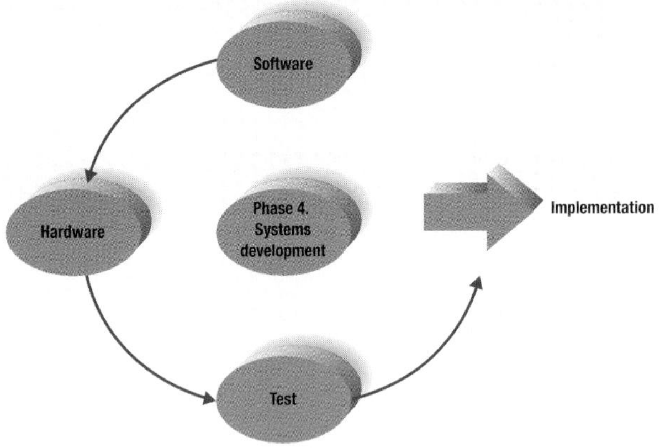

In the **systems development** phase, software and hardware are acquired and tested.

Acquiring Software

Two ways to acquire software are:

- Purchase—buying off-the-shelf packaged software to be modified if necessary.
- Custom designed—create programs following programming steps presented in Chapter 15.

Acquiring Hardware

Acquiring hardware is very critical and involves consideration for future company growth, existing networks, communication capabilities, and training.

Testing the New System

Using sample data, the new system is tested. This step can take several months for a complex system.

PHASE 5: IMPLEMENTATION

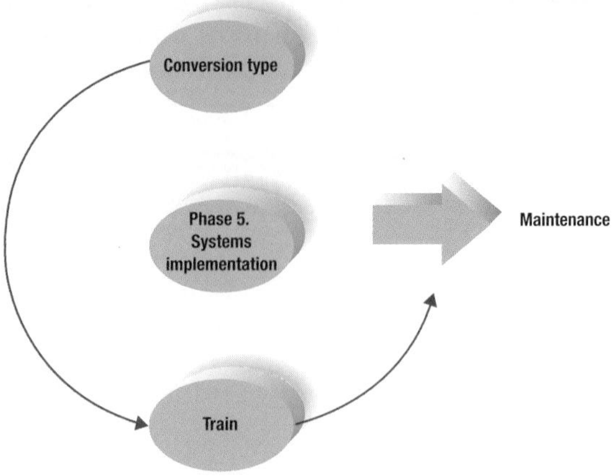

Systems implementation (conversion) is the process of changing to the new system and training people.

Types of Conversion

Four ways to convert are:

- **Direct approach**—abandoning the old and starting up the new; can be very risky and not recommended.
- **Parallel approach**—operating the old and new side by side until the new one proves its worth; low risk but expensive.
- **Pilot approach**—trying out the new system in only one part of an organization. Compared to parallel, pilot is riskier and less expensive.
- **Phased approach**—implementing the new system gradually; low risk but expensive.

Training

A software trainer may be used to train end users in the new system.

PHASE 6: MAINTENANCE

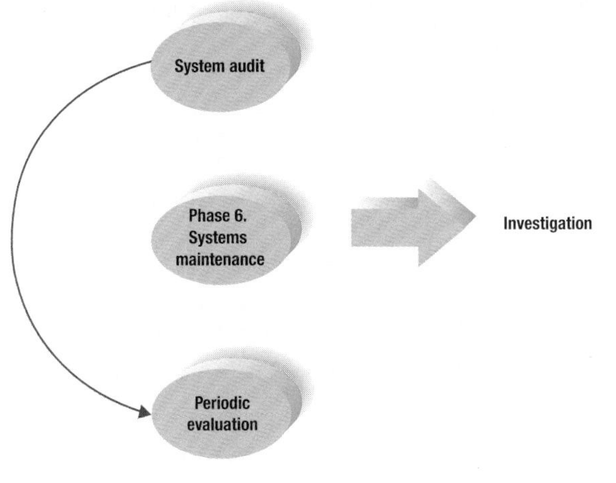

Systems maintenance is the final phase. It consists of a system audit followed by periodic evaluation.

System Audit

Once the system is operational, the systems analyst performs a **system audit** by comparing the new system to its original design specifications. If the system does not meet these specifications, some further redesign of the system may be required.

Periodic Evaluation

The new system is periodically evaluated to ensure that it is operating efficiently. If it is not, some redesign may be required.

Phase	Activity
1 Preliminary investigation	Define problem, suggest alternatives, prepare short report
2 Systems analysis	Gather data, analyze data, document
3 Systems design	Design alternatives, select best alternative, write report
4 Systems development	Develop software, acquire hardware, test system
5 Systems implementation	Convert, train
6 Systems maintenance	Perform system audit, evaluate periodically

PROTOTYPING AND RAD

Due to time pressures, it is not always feasible to follow every phase of the system life cycle. Two alternatives that require less time are *prototyping* and *RAD.*

Prototyping

Prototyping means to build a model or prototype that can be modified before the actual system is installed. Typically, the development time for prototyping is shorter; however, it can be more difficult to manage the project and to control costs.

Rapid Application Development

Rapid application development (RAD) uses powerful development software, small specialized teams, and highly trained personnel. Typically, the development costs more. However, the time is much less and the quality is often better.

KEY TERMS

automated design tools (531)
checklist (529)
computer-aided software engineering (CASE) tools (531)
conversion (535)
data flow diagram (531)
decision table (530)
direct approach (535)
economic feasibility (533)
grid chart (530)
operational feasibility (533)
organization chart (528)
parallel approach (536)
phased approach (536)
pilot approach (536)
preliminary investigation (525)
prototyping (539)
rapid applications development (RAD) (539)
system (524)
system flowchart (530)
systems analysis (528)
systems analysis report (532)
systems analyst (524)
systems audit (538)
systems design (532)
systems design report (533)
systems development (534)
systems implementation (535)
systems life cycle (524)
systems maintenance (537)
technical feasibility (533)
top-down analysis method (529)

To test your knowledge of these key terms with animated flash cards, select Flash Cards from Tim's Toolbox at http://www.mhhe.com/oleary/CT05.

CHAPTER REVIEW

CROSSWORD

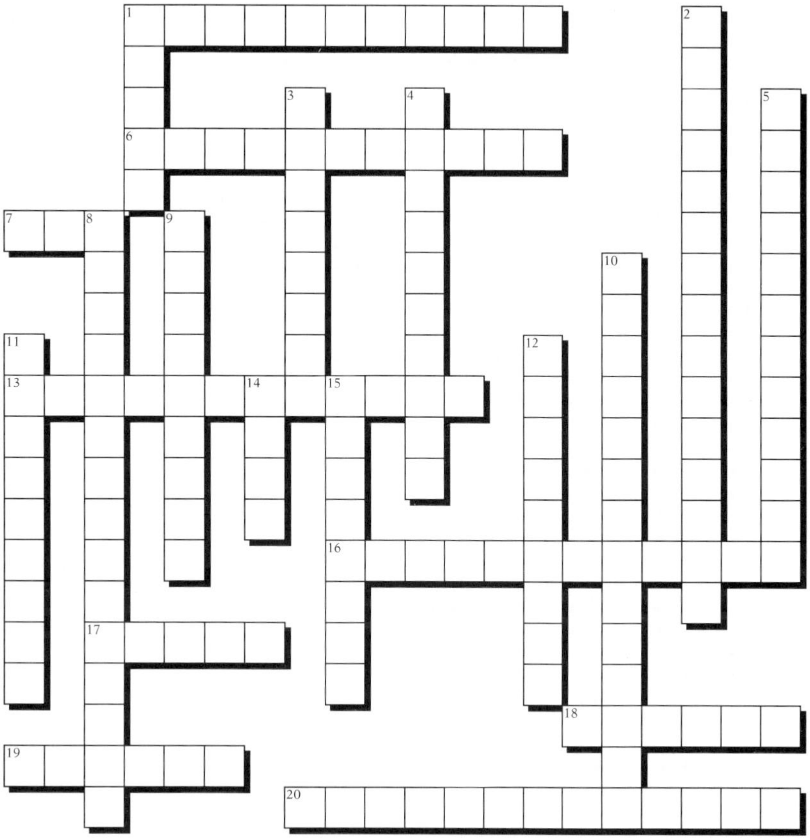

ACROSS

1 To build a model that can be modified before the actual system is installed
6 Feasibility being measured when the systems designer asks: can the system actually be made to operate in the organization, or will people resist it?
7 Rapid applications development
13 Sequential phases of a system: preliminary investigation, analysis, design, development, implementation, and maintenance
16 This type of chart shows levels of management and formal lines of authority
17 The system's performance is compared to the original design specifications
18 Defined as a collection of activities and elements organized to accomplish a goal
19 Approach to conversion where the new system is gradually implemented over a period of time
20 Shows the decision rules that apply when certain conditions occur

DOWN

1 Approach to conversion where the new system is tried out in only one part of the organization
2 Data is collected about the present system, then analyzed, and new requirements are determined
3 Approach to conversion where old and new systems are operated side by side until the new one has proved to be reliable
4 The process of changing from the old system to the new and training people to use the new system
5 Design new or alternative system to meet new requirements
8 Data is traced from its origination through processing, storage, and output
9 Shows relationships between inputs and outputs
10 People who study an organization's systems to determine what actions to take and how to use computer technology to assist them
11 Shows the flow of input data to processing and finally to output, or distribution of information
12 Feasibility being measured when the systems designer asks: are reliable hardware, software, and training available to make the system work and if not, can they be obtained?
14 Tools that relieve systems analysts of many repetitive tasks, develop clear documentation, and, for larger projects, coordinate team-member activities
15 Feasibility being measured when the systems designer asks: will the costs of the new system be justified by the benefits it promises and how long will it take for the new system to pay for itself?

For an interactive crossword puzzle select Crosswords from Tim's Toolbox at http://www.mhhe.com/oleary/CT05.

MULTIPLE CHOICE

Circle the letter or fill in the correct answer.

1. Preliminary investigation, systems analysis, systems design, systems development, systems implementation, and systems maintenance are elements of the ________.
   a. systems checklist
   b. systems life cycle
   c. technical feasibility chart
   d. parallel approach
   e. pilot approach
2. A ________ studies an organization's systems to determine what actions to take and how to use technology to assist them.
   a. RAD
   b. data worker
   c. CASE
   d. systems analyst
   e. data flow diagram
3. A(n) ________ is usually requested by an end user or manager who wants something done.
   a. prototype
   b. systems audit
   c. top-down analysis
   d. organization chart
   e. preliminary investigation
4. Defining the problem, suggesting alternative systems, and preparing a report are part of the ________ phase.
   a. preliminary investigation
   b. analysis
   c. design
   d. development
   e. implementation
5. Checklists, grid charts, decision tables, and system flowcharts are part of the ________ phase.
   a. preliminary investigation
   b. analysis
   c. design
   d. development
   e. implementation
6. Automated design tools are also called ________.
   a. data flow diagrams
   b. decision tables
   c. grid charts
   d. CASE tools
   e. system flowcharts
7. The ________ describes the current information system, the requirements for a new system, and a possible development schedule.
   a. systems analysis report
   b. systems design report
   c. system flowchart
   d. systems implementation report
   e. operational feasibility report
8. A(n) ________ shows the formal lines of authority.
   a. systems audit
   b. organization chart
   c. grid chart
   d. decision table
   e. RAD
9. ________ determines whether or not reliable hardware, software, and training are available to make a new system work.
   a. Economic feasibility
   b. Operational feasibility
   c. Technical feasibility
   d. Systems audit
   e. Top-down analysis
10. In the ________, conversion to a new system is done simply by abandoning the old and starting up the new.
    a. parallel approach
    b. direct approach
    c. pilot approach
    d. phased approach
    e. pilot and direct approaches

To test your knowledge of this chapter, select Self Test from Tim's Toolbox at http://www.mhhe.com/oleary/CT05.

MATCHING

Match each numbered item with the most closely related lettered item. Write your answers in the spaces provided.

- **a.** automated design tools
- **b.** checklist
- **c.** data flow diagram
- **d.** decision table
- **e.** direct approach
- **f.** economic feasibility
- **g.** grid chart
- **h.** operational feasibility
- **i.** organization chart
- **j.** phased approach
- **k.** preliminary investigation
- **l.** prototyping
- **m.** RAD
- **n.** system
- **o.** systems analysis and design
- **p.** systems analysis
- **q.** systems analyst
- **r.** systems audit
- **s.** systems design report
- **t.** systems development

1. Collection of activities and elements designed to accomplish a goal. ____
2. A six-phase problem-solving procedure for examining and improving an information system. ____
3. Computer professional who studies an organization's systems to determine what actions to take and how to use computer technology to assist them. ____
4. The first phase of the systems life cycle. ____
5. Data is collected about the present system. ____
6. Chart showing management levels and formal lines of authority. ____
7. A helpful record of questions that guides the systems analyst and end user through key issues for the present system. ____
8. Shows the relationship between input and output documents. ____
9. Table showing the decision rules that apply when certain conditions occur. ____
10. Shows the data or information flow within an information system. ____
11. Software package that evaluates hardware and software alternatives according to requirements given by the systems analyst. ____
12. Condition in which costs of designing a new system will be justified by the benefits it will provide. ____
13. Condition in which the design of a new system will be able to function within the existing framework of an organization. ____
14. Report prepared for higher management that describes the alternative designs suggested in the design phase. ____
15. Phase consisting of developing software, acquiring hardware, and testing the new system. ____
16. Approach for systems implementation whereby the old system is abandoned for the new. ____
17. Systems implementation in which the new system is implemented gradually over a period of time. ____
18. Compares the performance of a new system to the original design specifications to determine if new procedures are improving productivity. ____
19. Building a modifiable model before the actual system is installed. ____
20. Involves the use of powerful development software and specialized teams as an alternative to the systems development life cycle approach. ____

OPEN-ENDED

On a separate sheet of paper, respond to each question or statement.

1. What is a system? What are the six phases of the systems life cycle? Why do corporations undergo this process?
2. What are the tools used in the analysis phase? What is top-down analysis? How is it used?
3. Describe each type of system conversion. Which is the most commonly used?
4. What is system maintenance? When does it occur?
5. Explain prototyping and RAD. When might they be used by corporations?

USING TECHNOLOGY

1 Visio

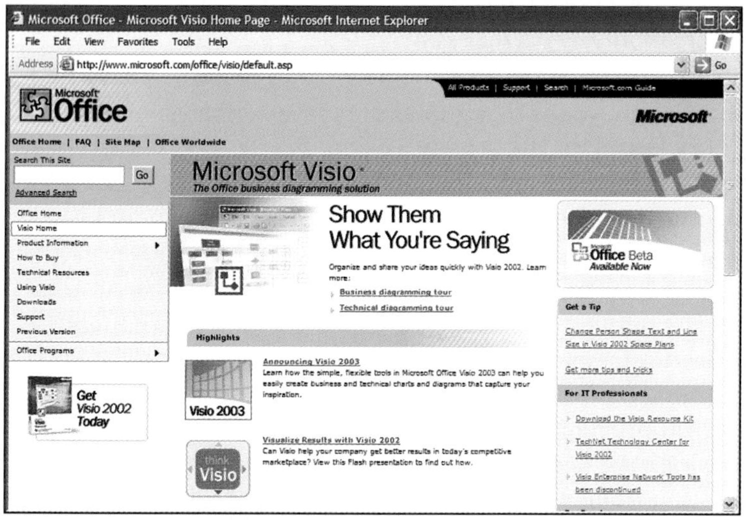

Software tools are often used to enhance understanding of the different phases of system design. One popular application is Visio. To learn more about this product, visit our Web site at http://www.mhhe.com/oleary/CT05 and select Using Technology from Tim's Toolbox to link to the Visio site. Once connected, read about Visio's features, and then answer the following questions: (a) What is Visio, and what does it do? (b) What types of projects could use Visio? (c) What types of professionals could use Visio? Provide specific examples.

2 RAD

Several software packages are available to assist developers with RAD, or Rapid Application Development. One such tool is EntireX from Software AG. To learn more about EntireX, connect to our Web site at http://www.mhhe.com/oleary/CT05 and select Using Technology from Tim's Toolbox to link to their site. Once there, read about this tool, and then answer the following questions: (a) What type of RAD applications is this tool designed for? (b) What types of companies use this tool? (c) What are the benefits of using this tool versus designing applications from scratch? (d) Are there any disadvantages? Explain.

Preliminary Investigation 3

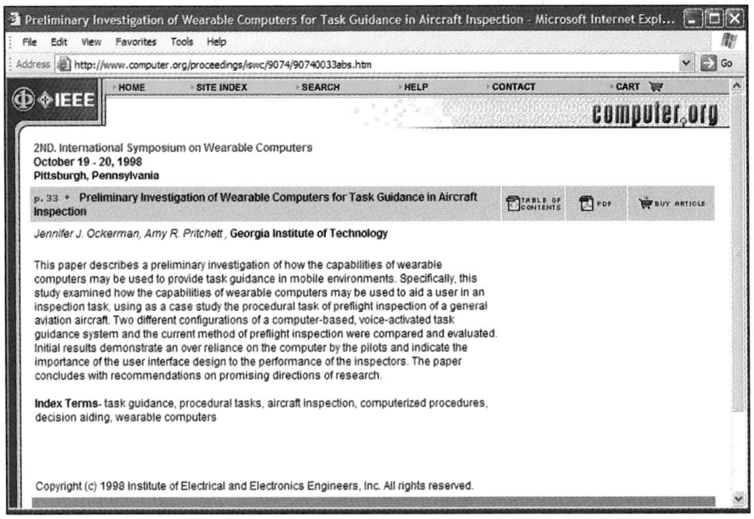

The systems analysis and design process can be applied to simple systems as well as complex ones. As discussed in the chapter, the first phase of the systems analysis and design process is a preliminary investigation. Perform the preliminary investigation step for either a new computer system you'd like to purchase, or an upgrade to your current system (Hint: see the Buyer's Guide and Upgrader's Guide at the end of this book). Include and document each step of preliminary investigation in a one-page paper: (a) Define the problem. (b) Suggest at least three alternatives. (c) Write a preliminary investigation summary of your findings, with a recommended course of action.

Rational Software 4

Rational is a leader in systems analysis support software. Connect to our Web site at http://www.mhhe.com/oleary/CT05 and select Using Technology from Tim's Toolbox to link to the Rational Software site. Explore the products that Rational offers, and then answer the following questions: (a) Describe the products Rational Software offers to enhance systems analysis. (b) For each product you described, list the phase or phases of the systems life cycle it applies to. (c) Review the DVD Direct case in the chapter. Pick a Rational Software product that could assist Alice and Mia, and describe how. Be specific.

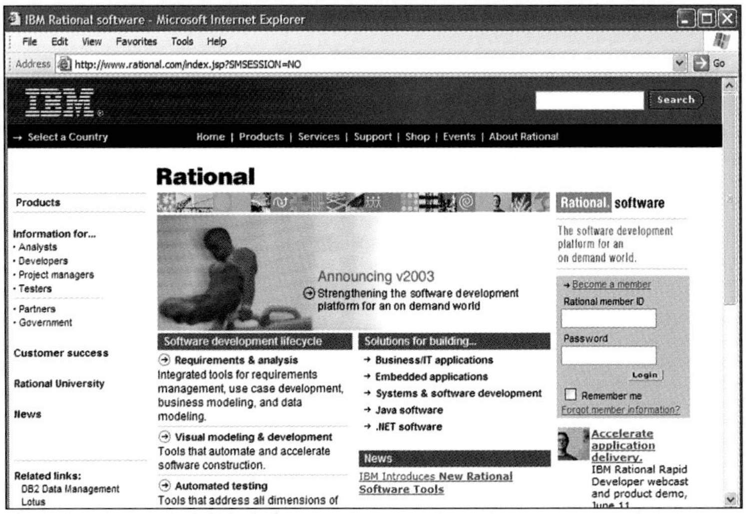

EXPANDING YOUR KNOWLEDGE

1 Computing Today CD

Review the DVD Direct case in the chapter, and briefly answer the following questions: (a) Define the term *conversion*, and briefly describe each conversion type. (b) Which phase of the systems life cycle does conversion occur in? (c) What type of conversion do Alice and Mia use for implementing the new DVD Direct system? (d) Do you agree that this was the best choice for DVD Direct? Why or why not?

2 UML

Uniform Modeling Language, or UML, is being used more extensively in industry to assist in system analysis. Research UML on the Internet, and then answer the following questions: (a) What is UML? (b) What details of a project does UML focus on? (c) How is defining a project with UML different than in plain English? What are the advantages and disadvantages to each? (d) UML could be an improvement for both the individuals who must understand a project and the software they use as well. How might CASE tools use UML? Explain.

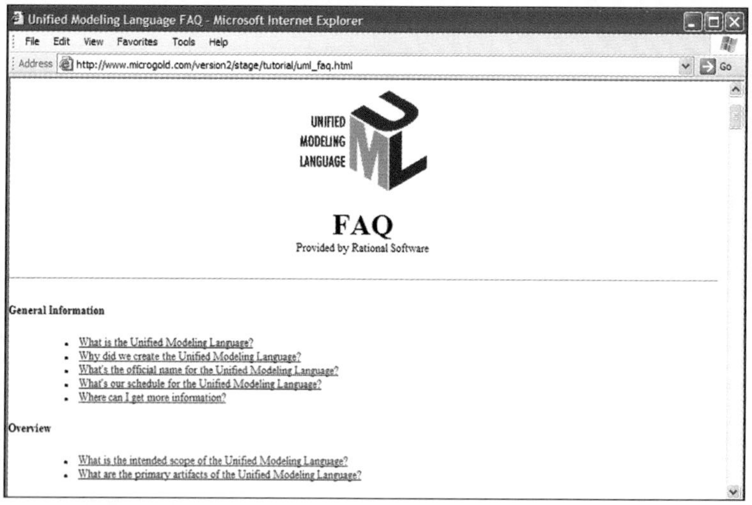

EXPANDING YOUR KNOWLEDGE

SimNet CD 3

Complete Chapter 14: Systems Analysis and Design on the SimNet Computer Concepts CD and then answer the following questions: (a) Referencing the section "Systems Development Overview," discuss the five phases in the Systems Development Life Cycle. (b) Referencing the section "Systems Development Overview," discuss the alternative 6th step to the Systems Development Life Cycle.

Automated System Testing 4

During the systems development phase, it can be difficult to ensure that a system has been tested adequately before implementation. Fortunately, many software applications exist to help meet this requirement. Research automated system testing software on the Web, and then answer the following questions: (a) What software package did you research? (b) What types of systems is the software intended to test? (c) What types of tests does the software perform? (d) Would this software be enough to reduce all risk of system errors? Justify your answer.

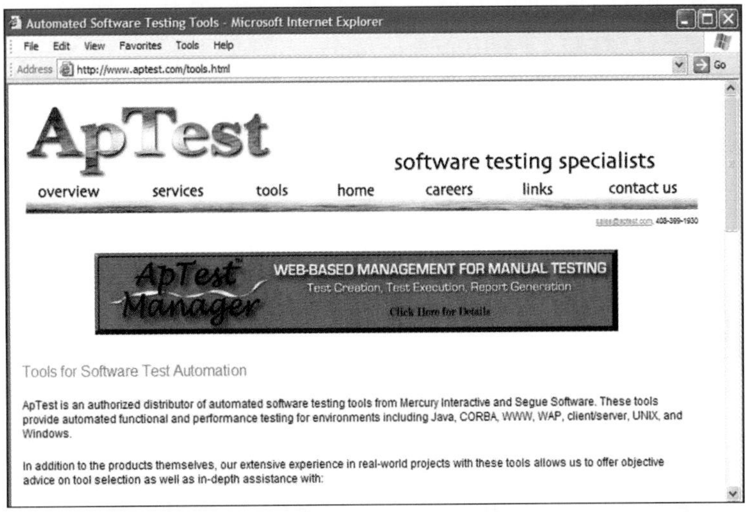

BUILDING YOUR PORTFOLIO

1 CASE Tools

Sometimes described as a CAD system for systems analysts, CASE tools are primarily used to automate and manage the elements of the analysis phase. In a one-page paper entitled "CASE tools," address the following: (a) Define CASE. (b) Give specific examples of how CASE tools can be used in each of the following instances: system analysis, system development, and system design.

2 Web Services

Many system components that relied on customized and costly methods of communication may soon be able to leverage the existing technology of the Web. Web Services is the latest technology for interconnecting system components. Research Web Services on the Web, and answer the following questions in a one-page paper: (a) Define the term *Web Services*, and briefly describe how Web Services technology works. (b) In what ways can Web Services reduce IT costs for an organization? (c) How are Web Services acquired or developed? (d) Analyze the DVD Direct case in the chapter. How might Web Services technology affect the alternative systems considered by Alice and Mia?

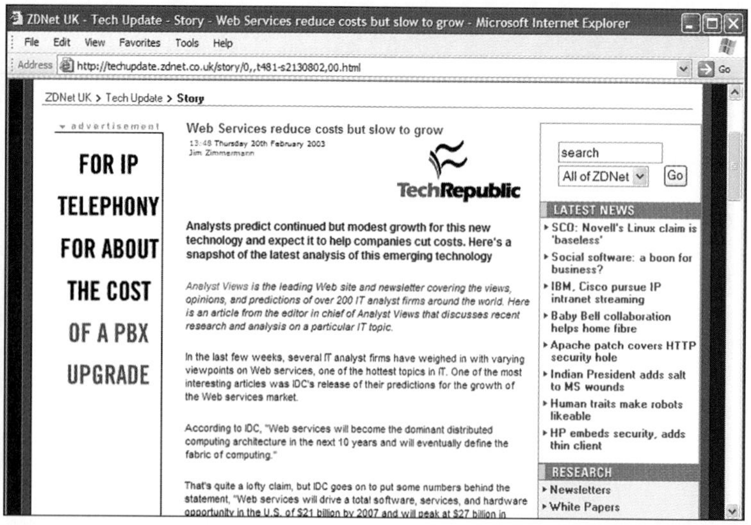

Managing Choices 3

Consider the following scenario, and then answer the questions that follow in a one-page paper: You're a manager who comes up with a new system that will make your company more efficient. However, implementing this system would make several tasks obsolete and cost many of your coworkers their jobs. (a) What is your ethical obligation to your company in this situation? (b) What is your ethical obligation to your coworkers? (c) What would you do in this situation? Defend your answer.

Legacy Systems 4

The term "legacy systems" refers to systems in which an organization has already invested significant time and money. Often, when a system audit reveals that a system change is necessary, it is cheaper to patch the existing system rather than create a new one. Over time, this can lead to systems which are expensive to maintain and difficult to modify. Research issues related to legacy systems and write a one-page paper that addresses the following: (a) Define the term "legacy system." (b) What problems can legacy systems present? (c) What problems can system upgrades present? (d) How can an analyst determine whether it is more cost-effective to maintain or upgrade a legacy system? (e) Identify any security and privacy concerns that might be associated with legacy systems.

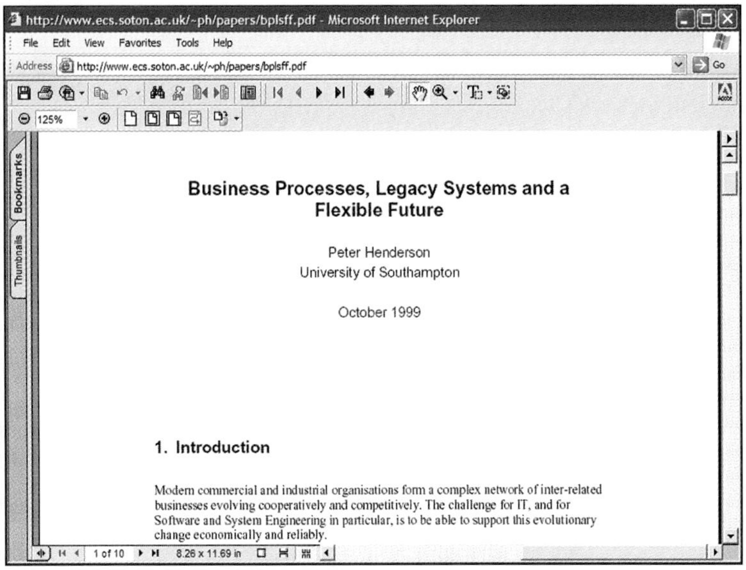

PROGRAMMING AND LANGUAGES

OBJECTIVES

After you have read this chapter, you should be able to:

1. Describe the six steps of programming.
2. Discuss design tools including top-down design, pseudocode, flowcharts, and logic structures.
3. Describe program testing and the tools for finding and removing errors.
4. Describe CASE tools and object-oriented software development.
5. Explain the five generations of programming languages.

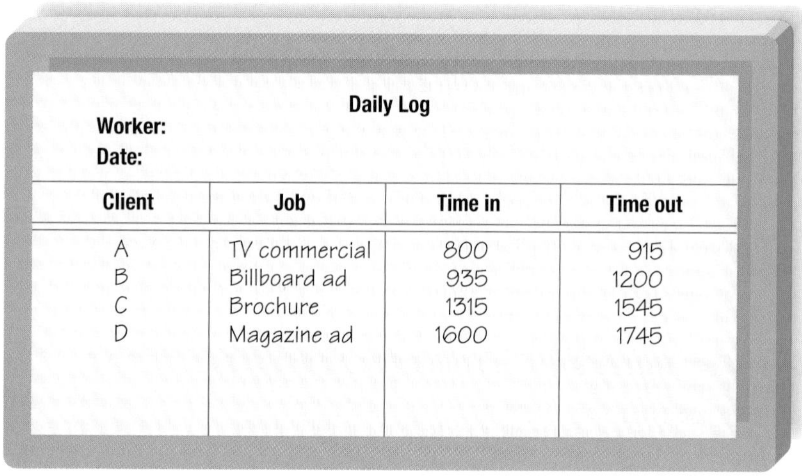

Daily Log

Worker:

Date:

Client	Job	Time in	Time out
A	TV commercial	800	915
B	Billboard ad	935	1200
C	Brochure	1315	1545
D	Magazine ad	1600	1745

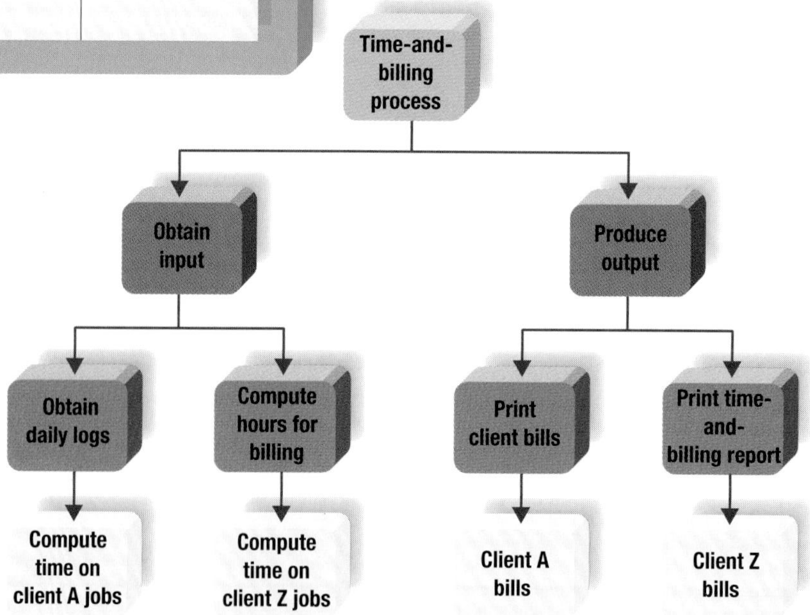

Programming
Consists of six steps to create and maintain good programs

How do you go about getting a job? You might look through newspaper classified ads, check with employment services, and write to prospective employers, and so on. In other words, you do some general problem solving to come up with a broad plan. This is similar to what you do in systems analysis and design. Once you have determined a particular job you would like to have, you then do some specific problem solving. That is what you do in programming. In this chapter, we describe programming in two parts: (1) the steps in the programming process and (2) some of the programming languages available.

Why should you need to know anything about programming? The answer is simple. You might need to deal with programmers in the course of your work. You may also be required to do some programming yourself in the future. A new field has emerged known as end user application development. In this field, users like you create their own business application programs, without the assistance of a programmer. Thus, organizations avoid paying high software development costs. You and other end users avoid waiting months for programmers to get around to projects important to you.

In Chapter 14, we described the six phases of the systems life cycle. Programming is part of phase 4, systems development. Competent and knowledgeable end users need to understand the relationship between the systems life cycle's phase 4, systems development, and programming. Additionally, they need to know the six steps of programming including program specification, program design, program code, program test, program documentation, and program maintenance.

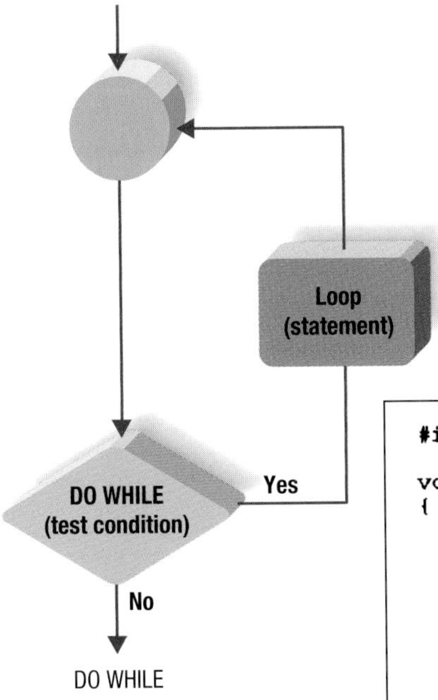

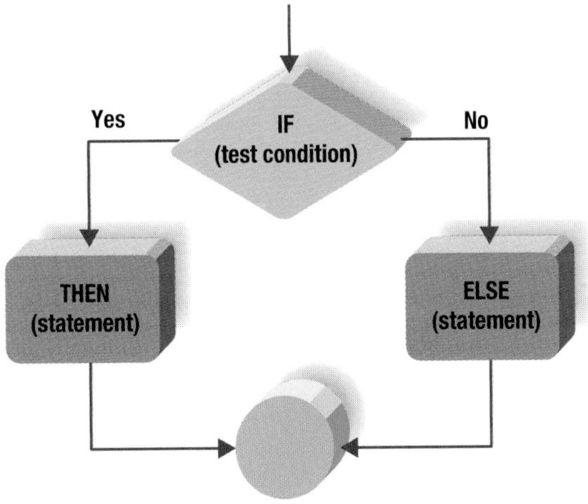


```
#include <fstream.h>

void main (void)
{
    ifstream input_file;

    float total_regular, total_overtime, regular, overtime;
    int hour_in, minute_in, hour_out, minute_out;
    input_file.open("time.txt",ios::in);

    total_regular = 0;
    total_overtime = 0;

    while (input_file != NULL)
    {
        input_file >> hour_in >> minute_in >> hour_out >> minute_out;

        if (hour_out > 17)
            overtime = (hour_out-17) +(minute_out/(float)60);
        else
            overtime = 0;
            regular = ((hour_out - hour_in) +(minute_out
                    - minute_in)/(float)60)    - overtime;
        total_regular += regular;
        total_overtime += overtime;
    }

    cout <<"Regular: " << total_regular <<endl;
    cout <<"Overtime " << total_overtime <<endl;
}
```

Languages
Range from low to high and have five generations

PROGRAMS AND PROGRAMMING

A program is a list of instructions. Programming is a six-step procedure for creating programs. Programmers use this six-step procedure.

What exactly is programming? Many people think of it as simply typing words into a computer. That may be part of it—but certainly not all of it. Programming, as we've hinted before, is actually a *problem-solving procedure.*

WHAT IS A PROGRAM?

To see how programming works, think about what a program is. A **program** is a list of instructions for the computer to follow to accomplish the task of processing data into information. The instructions are made up of statements used in a programming language, such as BASIC, C, or Java.

You are already familiar with some types of programs. As we discussed in Chapters 1 and 3, application programs are widely used to accomplish a variety of different types of tasks. For example, we use word processors to create documents and spreadsheets to analyze data. System programs, on the other hand, focus on tasks necessary to keep the computer running smoothly. These can be purchased and are referred to as prewritten or packaged programs. Programs can also be created or custom-made. In Chapter 14, we saw that the systems analyst looked into the availability of time-and-billing software for Advantage Advertising. Will off-the-shelf software do the job, or should it be custom-written? This is one of the first things that needs to be decided in programming.

WHAT IS PROGRAMMING?

A program is a list of instructions for the computer to follow to process data. **Programming,** also known as **software development,** is a six-step procedure for creating that list of instructions. Only one of those steps consists of typing (keying) statements into a computer. (See Figure 15-1.)

The six steps are as follows:

1. *Program specification:* The program's objectives, outputs, inputs, and processing requirements are determined.
2. *Program design:* A solution is created using programming techniques such as top-down program design, pseudocode, flowcharts, and logic structures.
3. *Program code:* The program is written or coded using a programming language.
4. *Program test:* The program is tested or debugged by looking for syntax and logic errors.
5. *Program documentation:* Documentation is an ongoing process throughout the programming process. This phase focuses on formalizing the written description and processes used in the program.
6. *Program maintenance:* Completed programs are periodically reviewed to evaluate their accuracy, efficiency, standardization, and ease of use. Changes are made to the program's code as needed.

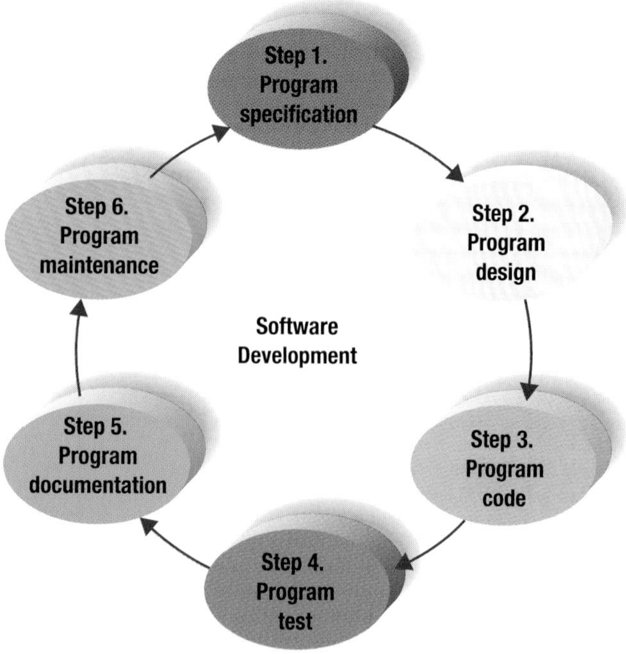

Figure 15-1 Software development

In organizations, computer professionals known as **software engineers** or **programmers** use this six-step procedure. Working closely with systems analysts in phase 4, systems development, of the systems life cycle, programmers create software required for information systems. In a recent survey by *Money* magazine, software engineers were ranked at the top of over 100 widely held jobs based on salary, prestige, and security.

You may well find yourself working directly with a programmer or indirectly through a systems analyst. Or you may actually do the programming for a system that you develop. Whatever the case, it's important that you understand the six-step programming procedure.

Concept Check

- What is a program?
- What are the six programming steps?

STEP 1: PROGRAM SPECIFICATION

In the program specification step, the objectives, outputs, inputs, and processing requirements are determined. This step concludes with documentation.

Program specification is also called **program definition** or **program analysis.** It requires that the programmer—or you, the end user, if you are following this procedure—specify five tasks: (1) the program's objectives, (2) the desired output, (3) the input data required, (4) the processing requirements, and (5) the documentation. (See Figure 15-2)

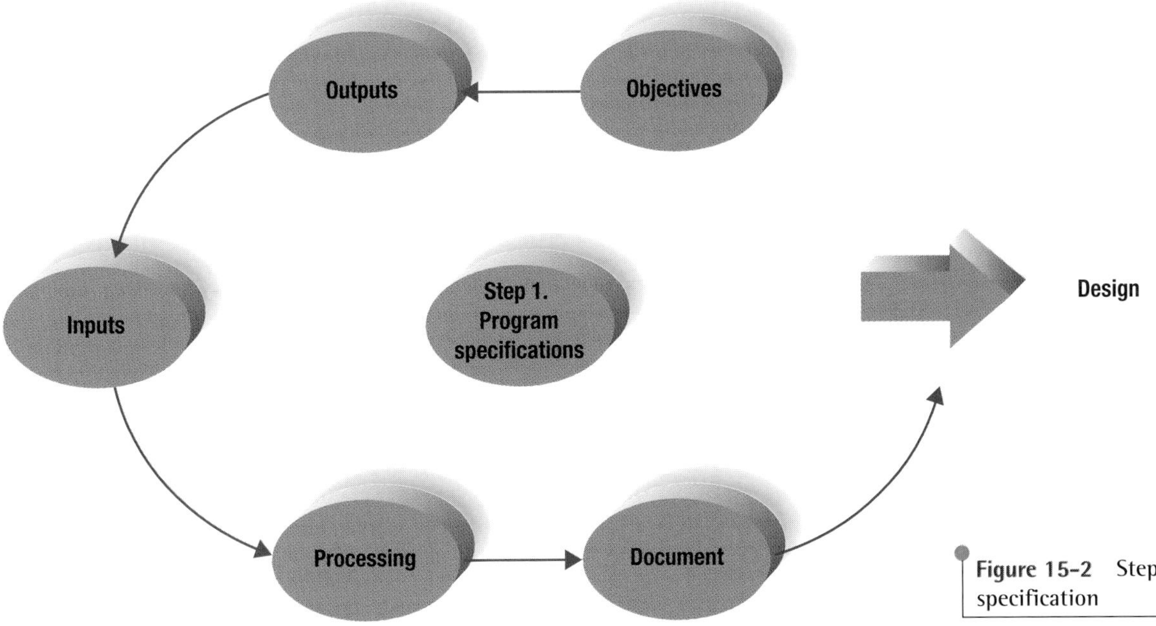

Figure 15-2 Step 1: Program specification

Figure 15-3 Problem definition: Make a clear statement of the problem

PROGRAM OBJECTIVES

You solve all kinds of problems every day. A problem might be deciding how to commute to school or work or which homework or report to do first. Thus, every day you determine your **objectives**—the problems you are trying to solve. Programming is the same. You need to make a clear statement of the problem you are trying to solve. (See Figure 15-3.) An example would be "I want a time-and-billing system to record the time I spend on different jobs for different clients of Advantage Advertising."

DESIRED OUTPUT

It is best always to specify outputs before inputs. That is, you need to list what you want to *get out* of the computer system. Then you should determine what will *go into it.* The best way to do this is to draw a picture. You—the end user, not the programmer—should sketch or write how you want the output to look when it's done. It might be printed out or displayed on the monitor.

For example, if you want a time-and-billing report, you might write or draw something like Figure 15-4. Another form of output from the program might be bills to clients.

INPUT DATA

Once you know the output you want, you can determine the input data and the source of this data. For example, for a time-and-billing report, you can specify

Client name: Allen Realty Month and year: Jan'00

Date	Worker	Regular Hours & Rate	Overtime Hours & Rate	Bill
1/2	M. Jones	5 @ $10	1 @ $15	$65.00
	K. Williams	4 @ $30	2 @ $45	$210.00

Figure 15-4 End user's sketch of desired output

Daily Log

Worker:
Date:

Client	Job	Time in	Time out
A	TV commercial	800	915
B	Billboard ad	935	1200
C	Brochure	1315	1545
D	Magazine ad	1600	1745

Figure 15-5 Example of statement of hours worked—manual system; hours are expressed in military time

that one source of data to be processed should be time cards. These are usually logs or statements of hours worked submitted on paper forms. The log shown in Figure 15-5 is an example of the kind of input data used in Advantage Advertising's manual system. Note that military time is used. For example, instead of writing "5:45 P.M.," people would write "1745."

PROCESSING REQUIREMENTS

Here you define the processing tasks that must happen for input data to be processed into output. For Advantage, one of the tasks for the program will be to add the hours worked for different jobs for different clients.

DOCUMENT PROGRAM SPECIFICATIONS

As in the systems life cycle, ongoing documentation is essential. You should record program objectives, desired outputs, needed inputs, and required processing. This leads to the next step, program design.

Concept Check

- ✔ What is program specification?
- ✔ What are the five tasks of the program specification phase?

STEP 2: PROGRAM DESIGN

In the program-design step, a solution is created using programming techniques such as top-down program design, pseudocode, flowcharts, and logic structures.

After program specification, you begin **program design**. (See Figure 15-6.) Here you plan a solution, preferably using **structured programming techniques.** These techniques consist of the following: (1) top-down program design, (2) pseudocode, (3) flowcharts, and (4) logic structures. (See Figure 15-7.)

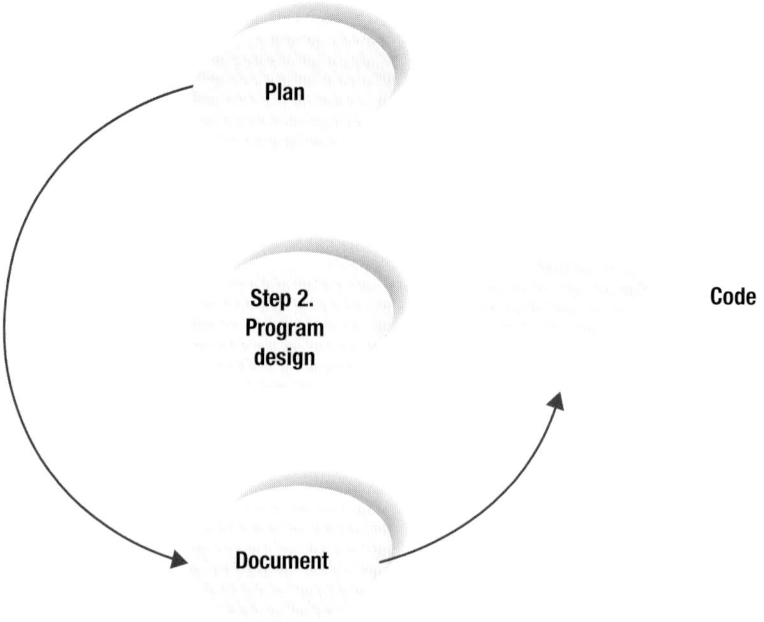

Figure 15-6 Step 2: Program design

Figure 15-7 Program design: Plan the solution

TOP-DOWN PROGRAM DESIGN

First you determine the outputs and inputs of the computer program you will create. Then you can use **top-down program design** to identify the program's processing steps. Such steps are called **program modules** (or just **modules**). Each module is made up of logically related program statements.

An example of a top-down program design for a time-and-billing report is shown in Figure 15-8. Each of the boxes shown is a module. Under the rules of top-down design, each module should have a single function. The program must pass in sequence from one module to the next until all modules have been processed by the computer. Three of the boxes—"obtain input," "compute hours for billing," and "produce output"—correspond to the three principal computer system operations: *input, process,* and *output.*

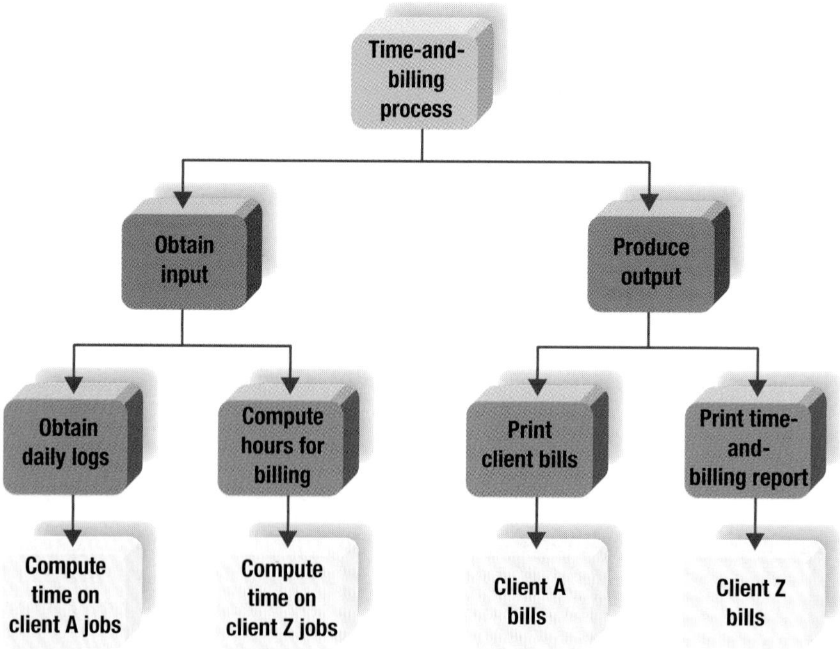

Figure 15-8 Example of top-down program design

PSEUDOCODE

Pseudocode (pronounced "soo-doh-code") is an outline of the logic of the program you will write. It is like doing a summary of the program before it is written. Figure 15-9 shows the pseudocode you might write for one module in the time-and-billing program. This shows the reasoning behind determining hours—including overtime hours—worked for different jobs for one client, Client A. Again, note this expresses the *logic* of what you want the program to do.

Compute time for Client A

Set total regular hours and total overtime hours to zero.
Get time in and time out for a job.
If worked past 1700 hours, then compute overtime hours.
Compute regular hours.
Add regular hours to total regular hours.
Add overtime hours to total overtime hours.
If there are more jobs for that client, go back and compute for that job as well.

Figure 15-9 Example of pseudocode

FLOWCHARTS

We mentioned system flowcharts in the previous chapter. Here we are concerned with **program flowcharts.** These graphically present the detailed sequence of steps needed to solve a programming problem. Figure 15-10 presents the standard flowcharting symbols. An example of a program flowchart is presented in Figure 15-11. This flowchart expresses all the logic for just one module—"Compute time on Client A jobs"—in the top-down program design.

Perhaps you can see from this flowchart why a computer is a computer, and not just a fancy adding machine. A computer does more than arithmetic. It also *makes comparisons*—whether something is greater than or less than, equal to or not equal to.

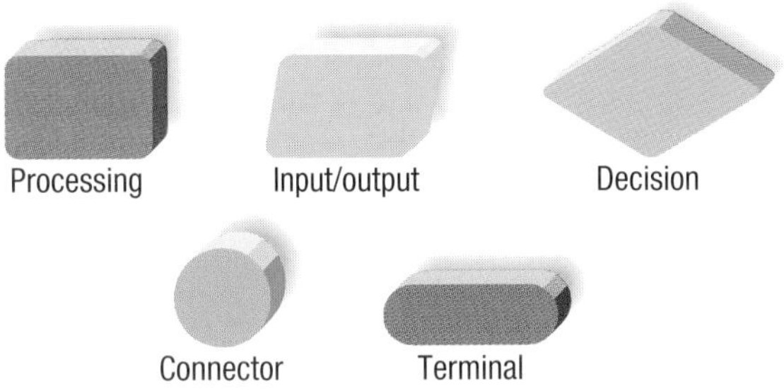
Processing
Input/output
Decision
Connector
Terminal

Figure 15-10 Flowchart symbols

But have we skipped something? How do we know which kind of twists and turns to put in a flowchart so that it will logically work? The answer is based on the use of logic structures, as we will explain.

LOGIC STRUCTURES

How do you link the various parts of the flowchart? The best way is a combination of three **logic structures** called *sequence, selection,* and *loop.* Using these arrangements enables you to write so-called structured programs, which take much of the guesswork out of programming. Let us look at the logic structures.

- In the **sequence structure,** one program statement follows another. (See Figure 15-12.) Consider, for example, the "compute time" flowchart. (Refer back to Figure 15-11.) The two "add" boxes are "Add regular hours to total regular hours" and "Add overtime hours to total overtime hours." They logically follow each other. There is no question of "yes" or "no," of a decision suggesting other consequences.
- The **selection structure** occurs when a decision must be made. The outcome of the decision determines which of two paths to follow. (See Figure 15-13.) This structure is also known as an **IF-THEN-ELSE structure,** because that is how you can formulate the decision. Consider, for example, the selection structure in the "compute time" flowchart, which is concerned about computing overtime hours. (Refer back to Figure 15-11.) It might be expressed in detail as follows:

  IF hour finished for this job is later than 1700 hours (5:00 P.M.),
  THEN overtime hours equal the number of hours past 1700 hours,
  ELSE overtime hours equal zero.

- The **loop structure** describes a process that may be repeated as long as a certain condition remains true. The structure is called a "loop" or "iteration" because the program loops around (iterates or repeats) again and

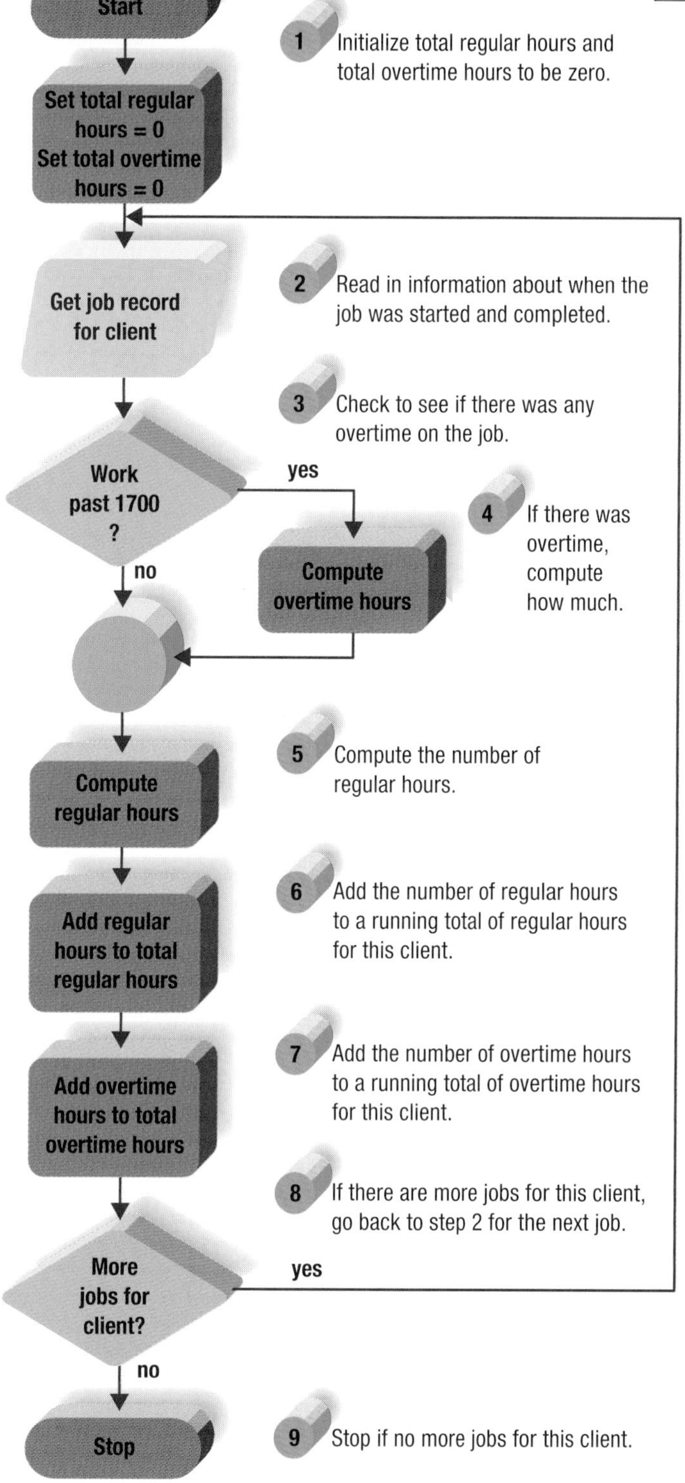

Start
Set total regular hours = 0
Set total overtime hours = 0
1 Initialize total regular hours and total overtime hours to be zero.
Get job record for client
2 Read in information about when the job was started and completed.
3 Check to see if there was any overtime on the job.
Work past 1700 ?
yes
no
Compute overtime hours
4 If there was overtime, compute how much.
Compute regular hours
5 Compute the number of regular hours.
Add regular hours to total regular hours
6 Add the number of regular hours to a running total of regular hours for this client.
Add overtime hours to total overtime hours
7 Add the number of overtime hours to a running total of overtime hours for this client.
8 If there are more jobs for this client, go back to step 2 for the next job.
More jobs for client?
yes
no
Stop
9 Stop if no more jobs for this client.

Figure 15-11 Flowchart example

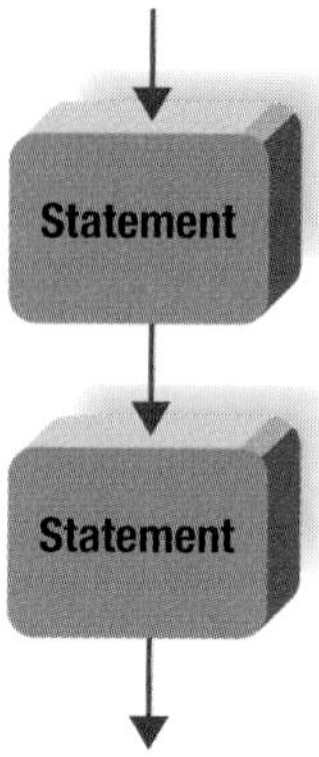

Statement
Statement

Figure 15-12 Sequence logic structure

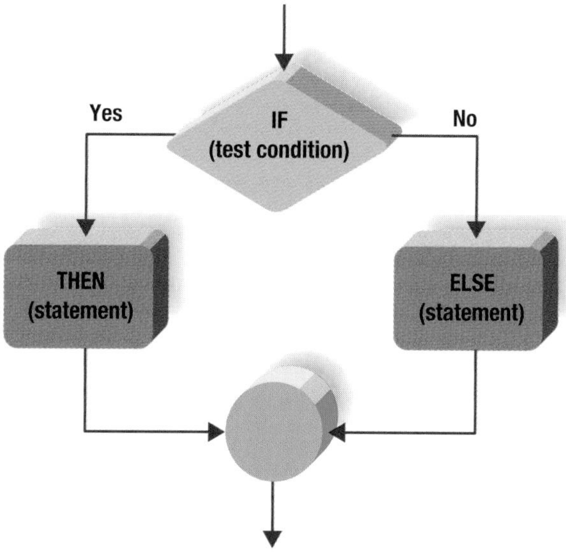

Yes
IF (test condition)
No
THEN (statement)
ELSE (statement)

Figure 15-13 Selection (IF-THEN-ELSE) logic structure

again. The loop structure has two variations: *DO UNTIL* and *DO WHILE.* (See Figure 15-14.) An example of the **DO UNTIL structure** follows.

DO read in job information UNTIL there are no more jobs.

An example of the **DO WHILE structure** is:

DO read in job information WHILE (that is, as long as) there are more jobs.

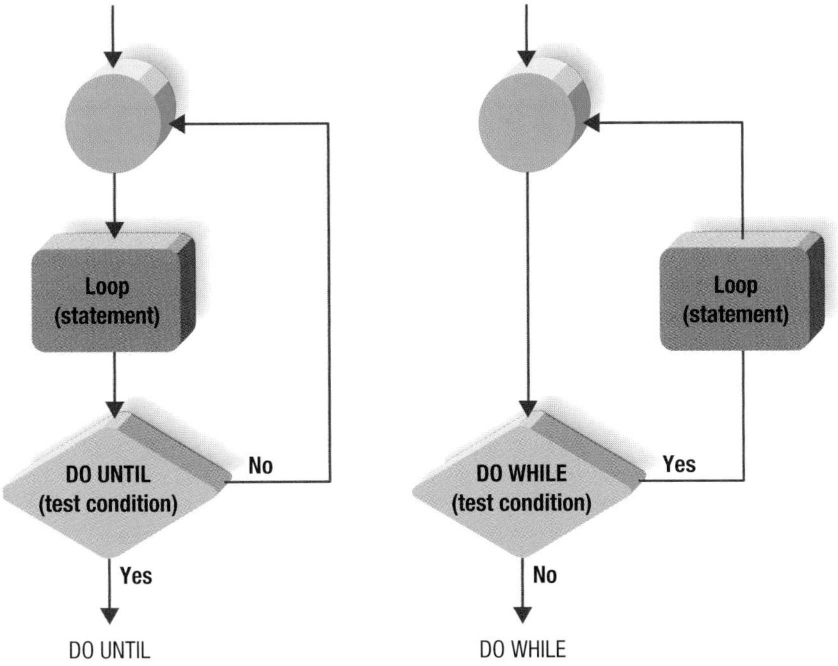

Figure 15-14 Loop logic structures: DO UNTIL and DO WHILE

There is a difference between the two loop structures. You may have several statements that need to be repeated. If so, the decision when to *stop* repeating them can appear at the *beginning* of the loop (DO WHILE). Or it can appear at the *end* of the loop (DO UNTIL). The DO UNTIL loop means that the loop statements will be executed at least once. This is because the loop statements are executed before you are asked whether to stop.

A summary of the structured programming techniques is presented in Figure 15-15.

The last thing to do before leaving the program design step is to document the logic of the design. This report typically includes pseudocode, flowcharts, and logic structures. Now you are ready for the next step, program code.

Technique	Description
Top-down design	Major processing steps, called program modules, are identified
Pseudocode	A narrative expression of the logic of the program is written
Program flowcharts	Graphic representation of the steps needed to solve the programming problem is drawn
Logic structures	Three arrangements are used in program flowcharts to write structured programs

Figure 15-15 Summary of structured programming techniques

Concept Check

- Define the goal of the program design step.
- Discuss top-down program design, pseudocode, flowcharts, and logic structures.
- Describe three logic structures.

STEP 3: PROGRAM CODE

Coding is the actual writing of a program. Good programs are structured programs. Formatting languages control the display of information. Programming languages specify the processing of data for specific operations.

Writing the program is called **coding.** Here you use the logic you developed in the program design step to actually write the program. (See Figure 15-16.) That is, you write out—using pencil and paper or typing on a computer keyboard—the letters, numbers, and symbols that make up the program. This is the "program code" that instructs the computer what to do. Coding is what many people think of when they think of programming. As we've pointed out, however, it is only one of the six steps in the programming process. (See Figure 15-17.)

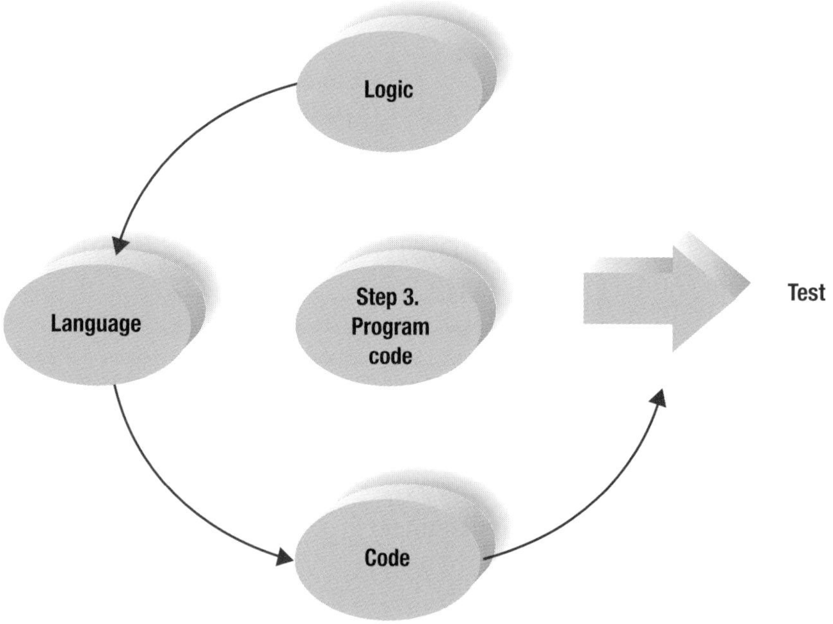
Logic
Language
Step 3.
Program
code
Test
Code
Figure 15-16 Step 3: Program code

THE GOOD PROGRAM

What are the qualities of a good program? Above all, it should be reliable—that is, it should work under most conditions. It should catch obvious and common input errors. It should also be well documented and understandable by programmers other than the person who wrote it. After all, someone may need to make changes in the program in the future. The best way to code effective programs is to write so-called **structured programs,** using the logic structures described in Step 2.

CODING

After the program logic has been formulated, the next step is to **code** or write the program using the appropriate computer language. There are hundreds of formatting and programming languages. A **formatting,** or **presentation language** uses symbols, words, and phrases that instruct a computer as to how to display information to the user. For example, HTML is a widely used formatting language to display Web pages. See Figure 15-18 for a partial listing of the HTML code used to display The Adventure Traveler's Explore the Nile Web page. Some of the most popular formatting languages are presented in Figure 15-19.

Figure 15-17 Program code: Write the program

A **programming language** uses a collection of symbols, words, and phrases that instruct a computer to perform specific operations. While formatting languages focus on displaying information primarily for Web pages, programming languages focus on processing data and information for a wide variety of different types of applications. Figure 15-20 presents the programming code using C++, a widely used programming

```
<html>

<head>
<meta http-equiv="Content-Type" content="text/html; charset=windows-1252">
<meta http-equiv="Content-Language" content="en-us">

<title>Explore the Nile</title>
<meta name="GENERATOR" content="Microsoft FrontPage 4.0">
<meta name="ProgId" content="FrontPage.Editor.Document">

<!--mstheme--><link rel="stylesheet" type="text/css"
href="_themes/artsy/arts1111.css"><meta name="Microsoft Theme" content="artsy 1111,
default">
<meta name="Microsoft Border" content="tb">
</head>
<body><!--msnavigation--><table border="0" cellpadding="0" cellspacing="0"
width="100%"><tr><td>



<p>
        </p>
<p>
<img border="0" src="images/logo_newletter.jpg" width="271" height="188"
align="left"></p>


<p>
 </p>


<p>
<img src="_derived/africa03.htm_cmp_artsy110_bnr.gif" width="600" height="60"
border="0" alt="Explore the Nile"></p>
```

Figure 15-18 Portion of HTML code to display Explore the Nile Web page

Language	Description
HTML	Stands for HyperText Markup Language and is the most common formatting language to present Web pages.
DHTML	Stands for Dynamic HTML, and improves HTML by including animations, interaction, and dynamic updating.
XHTML	Stands for eXtended HTML, combines HTML and XML to add structure and flexibility to HTML.
XML	Stands for eXtensible Markup Language, provides a standard way to present and use data on Web pages.
WML	Stands for Wireless Markup Language, provides a standard for describing data in wireless applications.

Figure 15-19 Widely used formatting languages

```
#include <fstream.h>

void main (void)
{
     ifstream input_file;

     float total_regular, total_overtime, regular, overtime;
     int hour_in, minute_in, hour_out, minute_out;
     input_file.open("time.txt",ios::in);

     total_regular = 0;
     total_overtime = 0;

     while (input_file != NULL)
     {
          input_file >> hour_in >> minute_in >> hour_out >> minute_out;

          if (hour_out > 17)
               overtime = (hour_out-17) +(minute_out/(float)60);
          else
               overtime = 0;
               regular = ((hour_out - hour_in) +(minute_out
                              - minute_in)/(float)60)    - overtime;
          total_regular += regular;
          total_overtime += overtime;
     }

     cout <<"Regular: " << total_regular <<endl;
     cout <<"Overtime " << total_overtime <<endl;
}
```

Figure 15-20 C++ code for compute time module

Language	Description
C	Widely used programming language, often associated with the UNIX operating system.
C++	Extends C to use objects or program modules that can be reused and interchanged between programs.
C#	Extends C++ to include XML functionality and support for a new Microsoft initiative called .Net.
Java	Primarily used for Internet applications, similar to C++, runs with a variety of operating systems.
JavaScript	Embedded into Web pages to provide dynamic and interactive content.
Visual Basic	Uses a very graphical interface making it easy to learn and to rapidly develop Windows and other applications.

Figure 15-21 Widely used programming languages

language, to calculate the compute time module. For a description of C++ and some other widely used programming languages, see Figure 15-21.

Once the program has been coded, the next step is testing, or debugging, the program.

Concept Check

- ✔ What is coding?
- ✔ What makes a good program?
- ✔ What is the difference between a formatting and a programming language?

STEP 4: PROGRAM TEST

Debugging is testing a program and eliminating errors. Syntax errors are violations of a programming language's rules. Logic errors are created by incorrect or missing specifications. The testing process is designed to identify and remove syntax and logic errors.

Debugging is a programmer's word for testing and then eliminating errors ("getting the bugs out"). (See Figure 15-22.) It means running the program on a computer and then fixing the parts that do not work. (See Figure 15-23.) Programming errors are of two types: *syntax errors* and *logic errors*.

SYNTAX ERRORS

A **syntax error** is a violation of the rules of the programming language. For example, in C++, each statement must end with a semicolon (;). If the semicolon is omitted, the program will not run due to a syntax error. For example, Figure 15-24 shows testing of the compute time module in which a syntax error was identified.

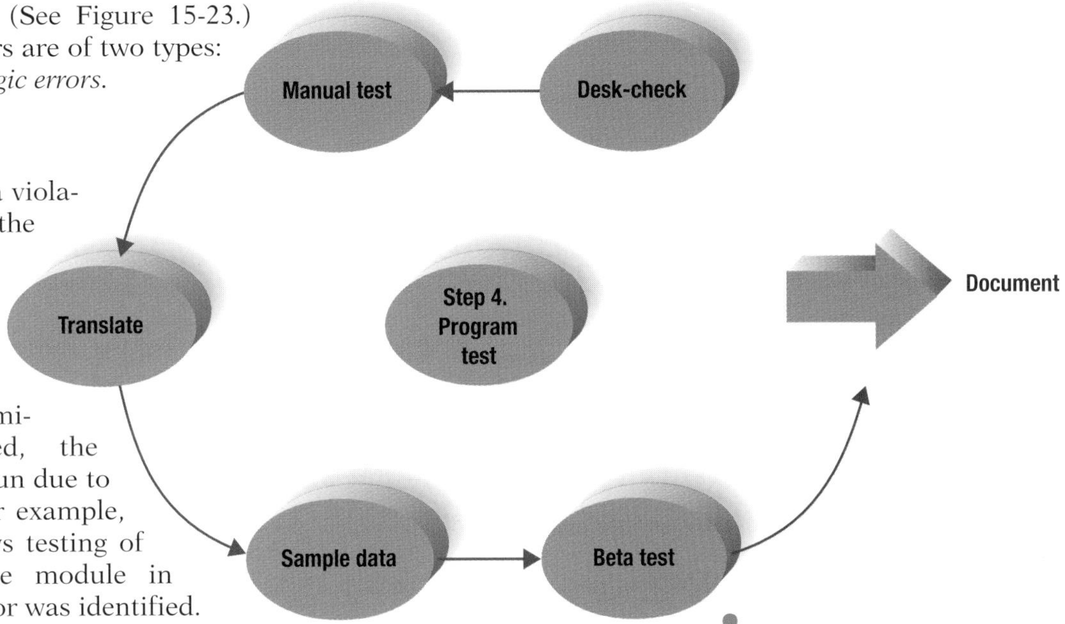
Manual test
Desk-check
Translate
Step 4. Program test
Document
Sample data
Beta test

Figure 15-22 Step 4: Program test

LOGIC ERRORS

A **logic error** occurs when the programmer uses an incorrect calculation or leaves out a programming procedure. For example, a payroll program that did not compute overtime hours would have a logic error.

TESTING PROCESS

Several methods have been devised for finding and removing both types of errors:

- **Desk checking:** In desk checking, a programmer sitting at a desk checks (proofreads) a printout of the program. The programmer goes through the listing line by line looking for syntax and logic errors.
- **Manually testing with sample data:** Using a calculator and sample data, a programmer follows each program statement and performs every calculation. Looking for programming logic errors, the programmer compares the manually calculated values to the correct values.
- **Attempt at translation:** The program is run through a computer, using a translator program. The translator attempts to translate the written program from the programming language (such as C++) into the machine language. Before the program will run, it must be free of syntax errors. Such errors will be identified by the translating program. (See Figure 15-24.)

Figure 15-23 Program test: locate errors

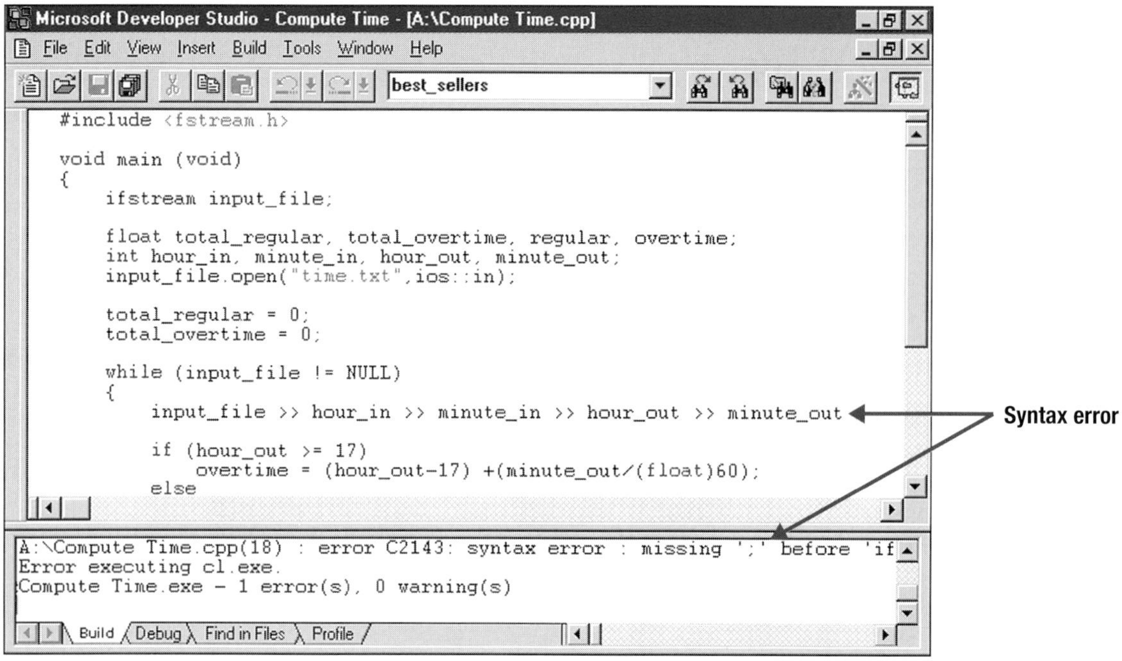
Microsoft Developer Studio - Compute Time - [A:\Compute Time.cpp]
File Edit View Insert Build Tools Window Help
best_sellers
#include <fstream.h>
void main (void)
{
ifstream input_file;
float total_regular, total_overtime, regular, overtime;
int hour_in, minute_in, hour_out, minute_out;
input_file.open("time.txt",ios::in);
total_regular = 0;
total_overtime = 0;
while (input_file != NULL)
{
input_file >> hour_in >> minute_in >> hour_out >> minute_out
if (hour_out >= 17)
overtime = (hour_out-17) +(minute_out/(float)60);
else
A:\Compute Time.cpp(18) : error C2143: syntax error : missing ';' before 'if
Error executing cl.exe.
Compute Time.exe - 1 error(s), 0 warning(s)
Build Debug Find in Files Profile
Syntax error

Figure 15-24 Syntax error identified

Task	Description
1	Desk-check for syntax and logic errors
2	Manually test with sample data
3	Translate program to identify syntax errors
4	Run program with sample data
5	Beta test with potential users

Figure 15-25 Step 4: Testing process

- **Testing sample data on the computer:** After all syntax errors have been corrected, the program is tested for logic errors. Sample data is used to test the correct execution of each program statement.
- **Testing by a select group of potential users:** This is sometimes called **beta testing.** It is usually the final step in testing a program. Potential users try out the program and provide feedback.

For a summary of Step 4: Program test, see Figure 15-25.

Concept Check

- ✓ What is debugging?
- ✓ What is the difference between syntax errors and logic errors?
- ✓ Briefly describe the testing process.

STEP 5: PROGRAM DOCUMENTATION

Documentation consists of written descriptions and procedures. Program documentation occurs throughout the programming process.

Documentation consists of written descriptions and procedures about a program and how to use it. (See Figure 15-26.) It is not something done just at the end of the programming process. **Program documentation** is carried on throughout all the programming steps. This documentation is typically within the program itself and in printed documents. In this step, all the prior docu-

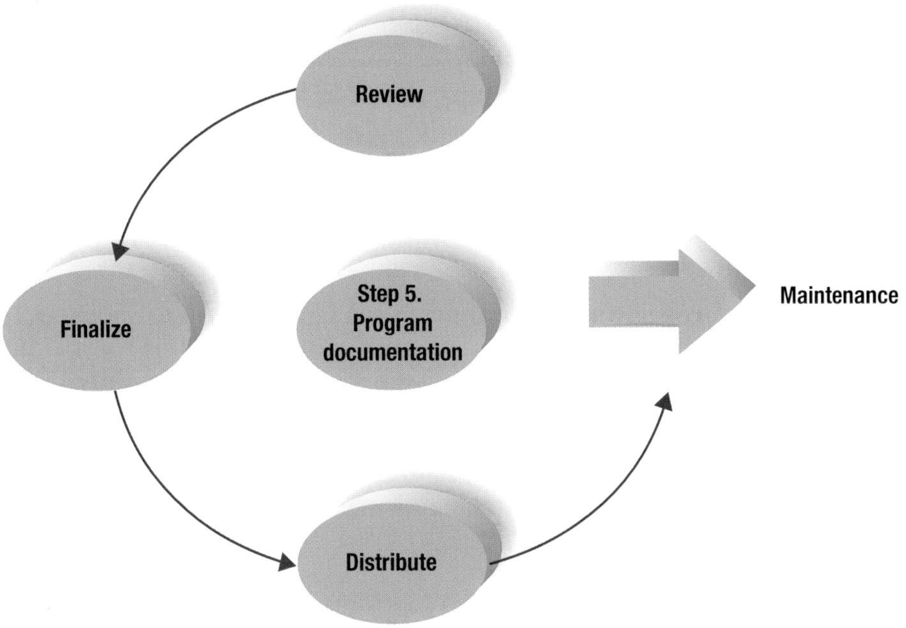

Figure 15-26 Step 5: Program documentation

mentation is reviewed, finalized, and distributed. Documentation is important for people who may be involved with the program in the future. (See Figure 15-27.) These people may include the following:

- **Users:** Users need to know how to use the software. Some organizations may offer training courses to guide users through the program. However, other organizations may expect users to be able to learn a package just from the written documentation. Two examples of this sort of documentation are the manuals that accompany the software and the help option within most microcomputer applications.
- **Operators:** Documentation must be provided for computer operators. If the program sends them error messages, for instance, they need to know what to do about them.
- **Programmers:** As time passes, even the creator of the original program may not remember much about it. Other programmers wishing to update and modify it—that is, perform program maintenance—may find themselves frustrated without adequate documentation. This kind of documentation should include text and program flowcharts, program listings, and sample output. It might also include system flowcharts to show how the particular program relates to other programs within an information system.

Figure 15-27 Program documentation: An ongoing process

Concept Check

- ✓ What is documentation?
- ✓ When does program documentation occur?
- ✓ Who is affected by documentation?

STEP 6: PROGRAM MAINTENANCE

Maintenance programmers are specialists in program maintenance. Operations activities focus on locating and correcting errors and standardizing software. Maintenance is also needed to adapt to the changing needs of an organization.

The final step is **program maintenance.** (See Figure 15-28.) As much as 75 percent of the total lifetime cost for an application program is for maintenance. This activity is so commonplace that a special job title, **maintenance programmer,** exists. (See Figure 15-29.)

The purpose of program maintenance is to ensure that current programs are operating error free, efficiently, and effectively. Activities in this area fall into two categories: operations and changing needs.

OPERATIONS

Operations activities concern locating and correcting operational errors, making programs easier to use, and standardizing software using structured programming techniques. For properly designed programs these activities should be minimal.

CHANGING NEEDS

The category of changing needs is unavoidable. All organizations change over time, and their programs must change with them. Programs need to be adjusted for a variety of reasons, including new tax laws, new information needs, and new company policies. Significant revisions may require that the entire programming process begin again with program specification.

Figure 15-30 summarizes the six steps of the programming process.

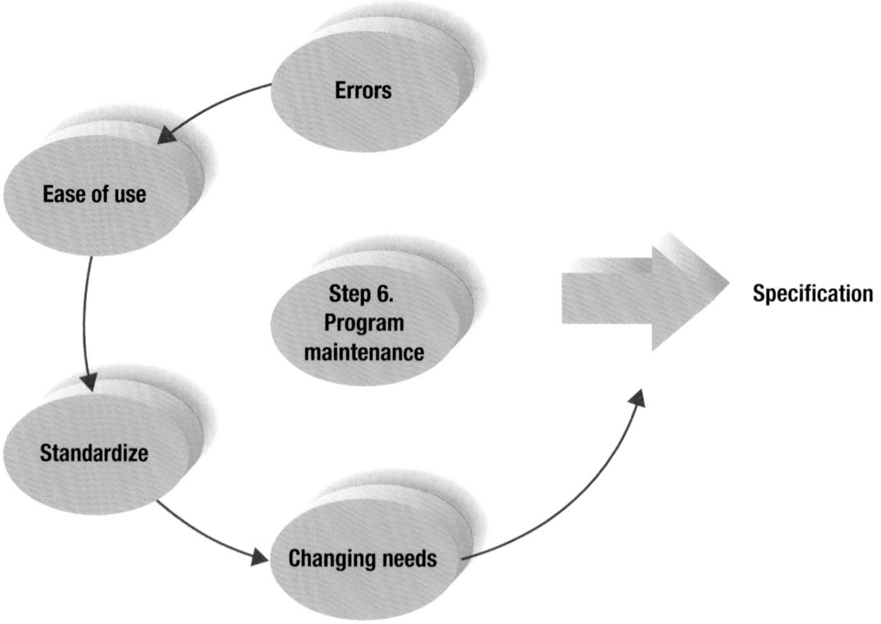

Figure 15-28 Step 6: Program maintenance

Figure 15-29 Program maintenance: Ensure program operating correctly

Step	Primary Activity
1. Program specification	Determine program objectives, desired output, required input, and processing requirements
2. Program design	Use structured programming techniques
3. Program code	Select programming language; write the program
4. Program test	Perform desk check and manual checks; attempt translation; test using sample data; beta test with potential users
5. Program documentation	Write procedure for users, operators, and programmers
6. Program maintenance	Adjust for errors, inefficient or ineffective operations, nonstandard code, and changes over time

Figure 15-30 Summary of six steps in programming

Concept Check

- ✔ What is the purpose of program maintenance?
- ✔ Discuss operational activities.
- ✔ What are changing needs and how do they affect programs?

CASE AND OOP

CASE tools automate the development process. Object-oriented software development focuses on relationships between procedures and objects. Object-oriented programming organizes a program into objects.

You hear about efficiency and productivity everywhere. They are particularly important for software development. Two resources that promise to help are *CASE tools* and *object-oriented software development.*

CASE TOOLS

Professional programmers are constantly looking for ways to make their work easier, faster, and more reliable. One tool we mentioned in Chapter 14, CASE, is meeting this need. **Computer-aided software engineering (CASE) tools** provide some automation and assistance in program design, coding, and testing. (See Figure 15-31.)

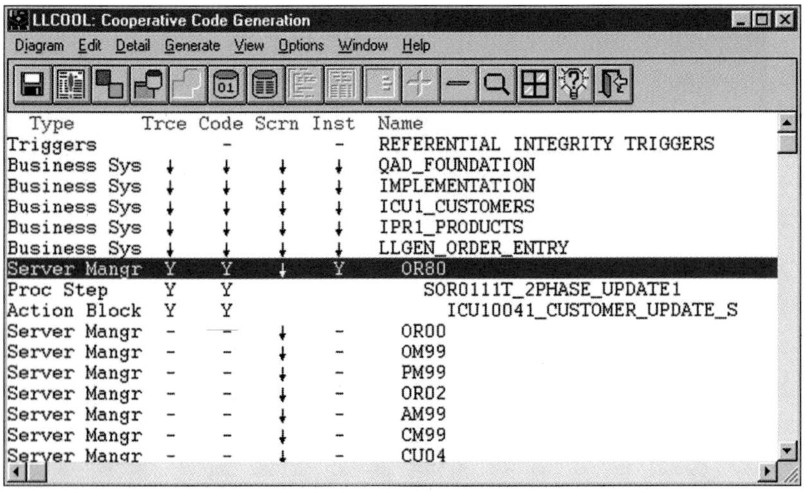

Figure 15-31 CASE tool: Providing code-generation assistance

OBJECT-ORIENTED SOFTWARE DEVELOPMENT

Traditional systems development is a careful, step-by-step approach focusing on the procedures needed to complete a certain objective. **Object-oriented software development** focuses less on the procedures and more on defining the relationships between previously defined procedures or "objects." **Object-oriented programming (OOP)** is a process by which a program is organized into objects. Each **object** contains both the data and processing operations necessary to perform a task. Let's explain what this means.

In the past, programs were developed as giant entities, from the first line of code to the last. This has been compared to building a car from scratch. Object-oriented programming is like building a car from prefabricated parts—carburetor, alternator, fenders, and so on. Object-oriented programs use **modules** called objects. Objects are reusable, self-contained components. Programs built with these objects assume that certain functions are the same. For example, many programs, from spreadsheets to database managers, have an instruction that will sort lists of names in alphabetical order. A programmer might use this module or object for alphabetizing in many other programs. There is no need to invent this activity anew every time. C++ is one of the most widely used object-oriented programming languages.

Concept Check

- What are CASE tools?
- What is object-oriented software development?
- What is object-oriented programming?

GENERATIONS OF PROGRAMMING LANGUAGES

Low-level languages are closer to computer languages consisting of 0s and 1s. High-level languages are closer to human language. Programming language generations include: machine, assembly, high level, problem-oriented, and natural and visual programming.

Computer professionals talk about **levels** or **generations** of programming languages, ranging from "low" to "high." Programming languages are called **lower level** when they are closer to the language the computer itself uses. The computer understands the 0s and 1s that make up bits and bytes. Programming languages are called **higher level** when they are closer to the language humans use—that is, for English speakers, more like English.

There are five generations of programming languages. These are (1) machine languages, (2) assembly languages, (3) procedural languages, (4) problem-oriented languages, and (5) natural languages.

MACHINE LANGUAGES: THE FIRST GENERATION

We mentioned in Chapter 6 that a byte is made up of bits, consisting of 1s and 0s. These 1s and 0s may correspond to electricity's being on or off in the computer. They may also correspond to a magnetic charge's being present or absent on storage media such as disk or tape. From this two-state system coding schemes have been developed that allow us to construct letters, numbers, punctuation marks, and other special characters. Examples of these coding schemes, as we saw, are ASCII and EBCDIC.

Data represented in 1s and 0s is said to be written in **machine language.** To see how hard this is to understand, imagine if you had to code this:

11110010011100111101001000010000011100000101011

Machine languages also vary according to make of computer—another characteristic that makes them hard to work with.

ASSEMBLY LANGUAGES: THE SECOND GENERATION

Before a computer can process or run any program, the program must be converted or translated into machine language. **Assembly languages** use abbreviations or mnemonics such as ADD that are automatically converted to the appropriate sequence of 1s and 0s. Compared to machine languages, assembly languages are much easier for humans to understand and to use. The machine language code we gave above could be expressed in assembly language as

ADD 210(8,13),02B(4,7)

This is still pretty obscure, of course, and so assembly language is also considered low level.

Assembly languages also vary from computer to computer. With the third generation, we advance to high-level languages, many of which are considered **portable languages.** That is, they can be run on more than one kind of computer—they are "portable" from one machine to another.

HIGH-LEVEL PROCEDURAL LANGUAGES: THE THIRD GENERATION

People are able to understand languages that are more like their own (e.g., English) than machine languages or assembly languages. These more English-like programming languages are called "high-level" languages. However, most people still require some training in order to use higher-level languages. This is particularly true of procedural languages.

Procedural languages, also known as **3GLs (third generation languages),** are designed to express the logic—the procedures—that can solve general problems. Procedural languages, then, are intended to solve general problems. C++ is a procedural language widely used by today's programmers. For example, C++ was used in Advantage's time-and-billing report. (See again Figure 15-20 for the "compute time" module of this program.)

Consider the following C++ statement from a program that assigns letter grades based on the score of an exam.

if (score > = 90) grade = 'A' ;

This statement tests whether the score is greater than or equal to 90. If it is, then the letter grade of A is assigned.

Like assembly languages, procedural languages must be translated into machine language so that the computer processes it. Depending on the language, this translation is performed by either a *compiler* or an *interpreter.*

- A **compiler** converts the programmer's procedural language program, called the **source code,** into a machine language code, called the **object**

code. This object code can then be saved and run later. Examples of procedural languages using compilers are the standard versions of Pascal, COBOL, and FORTRAN.

- An **interpreter** converts the procedural language one statement at a time into machine code just before it is to be executed. No object code is saved. An example of a procedural language using an interpreter is the standard version of BASIC.

What is the difference between using a compiler and using an interpreter? When a program is run, the compiler requires two steps. The first step is to convert the entire program's source code to object code. The second step is to run the object code. The interpreter, in contrast, converts and runs the program one line at a time. The advantage of a compiler language is that once the object code has been obtained, the program executes faster. The advantage of an interpreter language is that programs are easier to develop.

PROBLEM-ORIENTED LANGUAGES: THE FOURTH GENERATION

Third generation languages are valuable, but they require training in programming. Problem-oriented languages, also known as **4GLs** and **very high level languages,** require little special training on the part of the user.

Unlike general-purpose languages, **problem-oriented languages** are designed to solve specific problems. While 3GLs focus on procedures and *how* a program will accomplish a specific task, 4GLs are nonprocedural and focus on specifying *what* the program is to accomplish. 4GLs are more English-like, easier to program, and widely used by nonprogrammers. Some of these fourth generation languages are used for very specific applications. For example, **IFPS (interactive financial planning system)** is used to develop financial models. Many 4GLs are part of a database management system. 4GLs includes query languages and application generators:

- **Query languages: Query languages** enable nonprogrammers to use certain easily understood commands to search and generate reports from a database. One of the most widely used query languages is SQL (structured query language). For example, let's say that Advantage Advertising has a database containing all customer calls for service and that their management would like a listing of all clients who incurred overtime charges. The SQL command to create this list is:

  SELECT client FROM dailyLog WHERE serviceEnd > 17

  This SQL statement selects or identifies all clients (a field name from the dailyLog table) that required service after 17 (military time for 5:00 P.M.). Microsoft Access can generate SQL commands like this one by using its Query wizard.

- **Application generators:** An **application generator** or a **program coder** is a program that provides modules of prewritten code. When using an application generator, a programmer can quickly create a program by referencing the appropriate module(s). This greatly reduces the time to create an application. For example, Access has a report generation application and a Report wizard for creating a variety of different types of reports using database information.

NATURAL LANGUAGES AND VISUAL PROGRAMMING LANGUAGES: THE FIFTH GENERATION

As they have evolved through the generations, computer languages have become more human-like. Clearly the fourth generation query languages using commands that include words like SELECT, FROM, and WHERE are much more human-like than the 0s and 1s of machine language. However, 4GLs are still a long way from the natural languages such as English and Spanish that people use.

The standard definition of a **fifth generation language (5GL)** is a computer language that incorporates the concepts of artificial intelligence to allow direct human communication. Additionally, these languages would enable a computer to *learn* and to *apply* new information as people do. Rather than coding by keying in specific commands, we would communicate more directly to a computer using **natural languages** or human languages such as English or Spanish.

Consider the following natural language statement that might appear in a 5GL program for recommending medical treatment.

If patient is dizzy, then check temperature and blood pressure.

Recently, the definition of 5GL has been expanded to include **visual programming languages** that provide a natural visual interface for program development. This interface provides intuitive icons, menus, and drawing tools for creating program code. Under this definition, programs such as Microsoft's Visual Basic are fifth generation programming languages.

See Figure 15-32 for a summary of the generations of programming languages.

Generation	Sample Statement
First: Machine	111100100111001111010010000100000111000000101011
Second: Assembly	ADD 210(8, 13),02B(4, 7)
Third: Procedural	if (score > = 90) grade = 'A';
Fourth: Problem	SELECT client FROM dailyLog WHERE serviceEnd > 17
Fifth: Natural and Visual	If patient is dizzy, then check temperature and blood pressure.

Figure 15-32 Summary of five programming generations

Concept Check

- ✓ What distinguishes a lower-level language from a higher-level language?
- ✓ Outline the five generations of programming languages.
- ✓ Distinguish between natural and visual programming languages.

Careers in IT

Programmer

Computer programmers create, test, and troubleshoot programs used by computers. Programmers may also update and repair existing programs. Most computer programmers are employed by companies that create and sell software, but programmers may also be employed in various other businesses. Many computer programmers work on a project basis as consultants, meaning they are hired by a company only to complete a specific program. As technology has developed, the need for programmers to work on the most basic computer functions has decreased. However, demand for computer programmers with specializations in advanced programs continues.

Jobs in programming typically require a bachelor's degree. However, there are positions available in the field for those with a two-year degree. Employers looking for programmers typically put an emphasis on previous experience. Programmers who have patience, think logically, and pay attention to detail are continually in demand. Additionally, programmers who can communicate technical information to nontechnical people are preferred.

Computer programmers can expect to earn an annual salary in the range of $45,000 to $75,000. Advancement opportunities for talented programmers include a lead programmer position or supervisory positions. Programmers with specializations and experience may also have an opportunity to consult. To learn about careers in information technology visit us at http://www.mhhe.com/oleary/CT05 and select Careers in IT from Tim's Toolbox.

A Look to the Future

MI-tech Takes the Pain Out of Programming

What if you could instruct a computer to code a program with a simple wish list written in English? What if syntax errors didn't happen? What if the computer asked you to clarify your meaning rather than just reporting an error? What if you could create a program that would run on a Windows PC, an Apple Mac, or even a Linux computer? At Synapse Solutions they believe they have created a system that meets these needs.

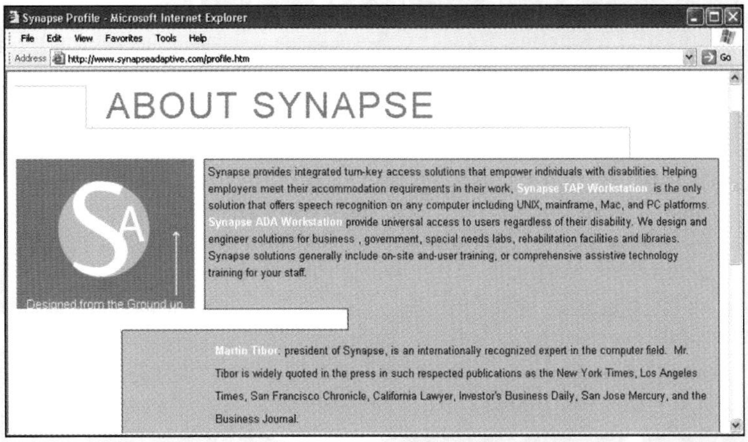

Traditional programming relies on a compiler and a translator to communicate the desires of the programmer to the computer. There are also precise rules that must be followed in order to correctly communicate with the computer. Natural language programming (using a human language to talk to the computer) has been the dream of programmers for a long time. Human languages can be confusing to a machine because it is possible to have double meanings and uncertainty.

Synapse Solutions has created a system called MI-tech that has an understanding of word order and meaning in English. In order to program using the system, you enter a "wish list" and the computer translates these sentences into machine language. If the system does not understand a "wish," it makes a request for clarification. It also uses a dictionary to look up words it doesn't recognize.

Would you like to create your own applications? What if you could create a Web page using a list of what you would like to appear on the page? Synapse Solutions believes it will soon be possible to use their system to do just that. What other programs do you think could utilize this system? Do you think someday all computer users will be programmers?

PROGRAMMING AT DVD DIRECT

INTRODUCTION

DVD Direct is an entirely Web oriented movie rental business in which customers select movies to rent from the company's Web site and choose the delivery method. One way is to receive selected movies on DVD disks by mail. This is how the business originally started out. The other way is to immediately download the movies onto the member's hard disk. Online delivery is a recent innovation. To encourage the choice of online delivery (which is more cost effective for DVD Direct), a Frequent Renters Club has been established. Whenever a member selects online delivery, they receive reward points which can be redeemed for a variety of items.

To support the record keeping of the Frequent Renters Club, an information system was developed by Alice, a marketing analyst, and Mia, a systems analyst. The hardware needed to support the system was leased and most of the software was purchased from an outside vendor. Mia created one program that integrated a login screen to the Frequent Renters Club Web site. After some initial modifications, the Frequent Renters Club has been successfully operating for the past two months.

One morning Mia receives a telephone call from Bob, the vice president of marketing, asking her to come to the meeting room to discuss the login program she wrote for the Frequent Renters Club Web site and to bring all her documentation from the project. This is a bit of a surprise and Mia wonders what it could be about. The system has been up and running for two months without problems. The login program is quite simple. Could that in itself somehow be the problem? Why aren't they meeting in Bob's office?

THE MEETING

When Mia opens the meeting room door her last question is answered when she is greeted not only by Bob but by four new faces.

Bob: Hi Mia. Good morning! I'd like you meet Laurence, Nicole, and Oscar. [See Figure C15-1.] They are from the Web development team. They have a few questions about the program you wrote.

Mia greets each person in turn, hoping her smile hides her nervousness, and waits apprehensively for the first question.

Laurence: Mia, would you walk us through the process you followed to develop your login application?

Mia: Sure! I closely followed the systems life cycle approach throughout the project. In the systems development phase, it became apparent that we would need some customized software to integrate the current login code with a new login screen. It was a fairly simple job to create a Java program.

Figure C15-1 "Hi Mia. Good morning! I'd like you meet Nicole, Oscar, and Laurence."

At this, Mia notices a series of glances between the Web developers. Do they question her abilities as a programmer? Are they unhappy with her choice of programming languages? Trying to clear these questions from her head, she hesitates.

Bob: Go on, Mia . . .

Mia: I followed the six steps in the software development life cycle: specification, design, code, test, documentation, and maintenance. I started with program specification and worked through all the steps in order.

Nicole: Mia, could you please walk us through each step?

PROGRAM SPECIFICATION

Mia: In the first step, I focused on identifying objectives, outputs, inputs, processing requirements, and documentation. Our program's objective is to accept user input, to verify valid membership, and to connect members to the appropriate Web site. The program's outputs are directions for the member's Web browser to connect to the appropriate Web site. The inputs are a member's name, password (in encrypted form), and a preference for mail-delivered DVDs or online delivery.

Nicole: What form is used to record their preferences? Did they type a phrase, pull down a menu...?

Mia: Users select their preference from a pull-down menu. That preference is associated with an integer sent to the server, so the input is an integer. The processing requirements are minimal. The user name and password are verified from the MEMBER database and the delivery preference is a simple comparison. Here's the documentation for this step.

Mia provides the team a copy of her program specifications document, of which she is quite proud, having meticulously researched the program specifications and documented the objectives, outputs, inputs, and processing requirements. Glancing around as they pass the document around, she is pleased to note that they seem impressed with her thoroughness.

PROGRAM DESIGN

Laurence: So how did you go about step two, program design?

Mia hands him a copy of her program design document.

Mia: Well, as you well know, the program design step is where you plan the solution to the problem identified in the specification step, and originally, I started with a top-down program design.

Oscar: How did you use that?

Mia: I divided the login process into its input and output components and defined the individual process of each step as indicated in the diagram you see on the document.

Laurence: What then?

Mia: Next, I developed pseudocode for each of the processes in the top-down program diagram. Here is one I did on verifying the user name and password. [See Figure C15-2.]

Oscar: And what are these diagrams here?

Mia: That chart is the final step in the program design. It is a flowchart and logic structure describing the process the computer uses to log in a user. [See Figure C15-3.]

Everyone looks at Mia's documentation with great interest, especially Oscar. Something in Oscar's tone makes Mia briefly worry that Oscar may find fault with her design decisions. The process she followed was clear and well documented. If he wants to make an issue of her work, she's prepared to defend her choices.

PROGRAM CODE

Oscar: So far you've done a lot of planning, but I haven't seen any actual code yet.

Mia: That's true, Oscar, but as you know only one of the six steps of the software development lifecycle is actually writing code. The first two phases, specification and design, in my opinion require as much of a programmer's talent as does the program code. Although writing code is an important part of my job as a programmer, to me it is only a small part of my overall responsibilities.

Nicole: Mia, I think you're right! But how did you decide on Java as a programming language?

Mia: I considered several possibilities. I wanted a language that was easy to use in Web applications, so

```
Get user name, password, and video type.
If user name/password invalid try again.
After 3 invalid entries, go to user login FAQ.
If valid, are they streaming.
If streaming, are they a frequent renter club member,
if no, go to new member page
if yes, go to their account page.
```

Figure C15-2 Pseudocode

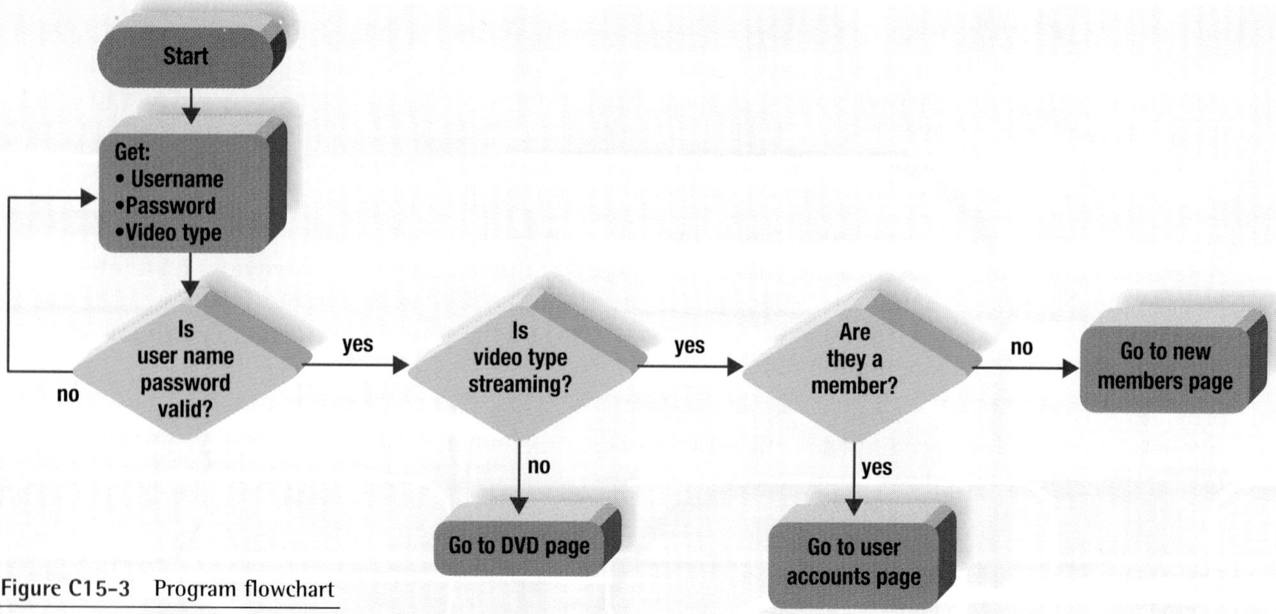

Figure C15-3 Program flowchart

I considered HTML, C++, and Java. I rejected HTML because it is a formatting language and not well suited to handle the required programming loops and if statements. While C++ could certainly handle the programming requirements, it does not integrate with the Web as well as Java. So I chose Java. It meets all of the program's needs. Here is the final Java code. [See Figure C15-4.]

As Mia speaks, she feels the interest of her audience rise. They are eager to see the code. It is certainly something about her decision to use Java.

TESTING

Laurence: Certainly you didn't write this code bug free your first time?

Mia: No, I don't know any programmers who write error-free code in the first draft, and I'd be a little suspicious of any programmer who claimed they did.

This gets a chuckle from the group and Nicole even blushes slightly. Mia can't help wondering if perhaps she has recently made such a claim.

Mia: Initially I had several syntax errors and typos. Once those were dealt with, I discovered a minor logic error.

Nicole: What testing methods did you use?

Mia: For syntax errors, I just did desk checking, going through the program line by line looking for errors. For logic errors, I manually tested with sample data. I assumed the role of a user going through the process of logging in to verify that the functions worked. Once it worked to my satisfaction, it was further tested by a select group of potential users.

DOCUMENTATION

Mia: There were just two steps left. First, I wrote up the documentation for the program. I wrote a FAQ for the users on how to log in to their new system, and I compiled my documentation of the previous four steps for programmers who might work on this code in the future—which I have been handing out to you.

```
/**
* This Applet accepts a username and password for logging in to a Web site.
*/
public class LoginApplet extends JApplet {
	private static final String USERNAME = "Alec";
	private static final String PASSWORD = "Guiness";
	private static final String LOGIN_SUCCESS_URL = "VideoPage.html";
	private static final String HELP_PAGE = "LoginHelp.html";
	private static final int MAX_LOGIN_ATTEMPTS = 3;
	private static final String[ ] VIDEO_TYPES= { "DVD", "Streaming" };
	private JTextField usernameField;
	private JPasswordField passwordField;
	private JComboBox videoTypeComboBox;
	private int counter = 0;

	/**
	 * Initialize this <code>LoginApplet</code>.
	 */
	public void init( ) {
		try {
```

Figure C15-4 Java code

MAINTENANCE

Mia: Lastly—maintenance. We have just completed a review of the streaming video system after two months of service. We checked for operational errors and none were identified. And with only two months of use, we feel that it is too soon to be checking for changes in the program based on the changing needs of our customers.

Coming to her conclusion, Mia realizes she has lost all her apprehension and is at ease about her work. Perhaps it's been the group that was nervous! Oscar smiles.

Oscar: Thank you Mia, you've been very helpful. We're looking into upgrading our code to an object oriented language like Java. The languages we currently use are all procedure oriented rather than object oriented. We really appreciate all you've told us.

Laurence: We've been investigating whether we will need to modify our established life cycle model. Your experiences are invaluable to us, Mia. Thanks for your presentation! You've done an excellent job on this project. [See Figure C15-5.]

Figure C15-5 "You've done an excellent job on this project."

Computing Today CD

For more comprehensive discussion of DVD Direct's programming, consult your Computing Today CD or visit us on the web at http://www.mhhe.com/oleary/CT05 and select DVD Direct from Tim's Toolbox.

VISUAL SUMMARY

PROGRAMMING AND LANGUAGES

PROGRAMS AND PROGRAMMING

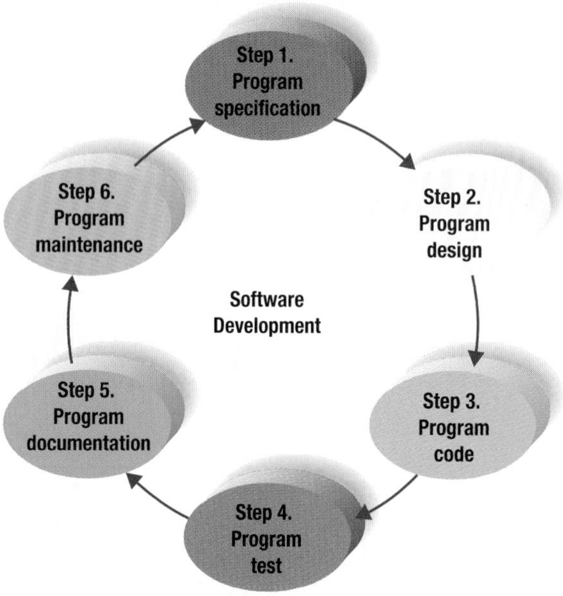

A **program** is a list of instructions for a computer to follow. **Programming (software development)** is a six-step procedure for creating programs.

The steps are:

- Program specification—defining objectives, inputs, outputs, and processing requirements.
- Program design—creating a solution using structured programming techniques.
- Program code—writing or coding the program.
- Program test—testing or debugging program.
- Program documentation—ongoing process throughout programming process.
- Program maintenance—evaluating and modifying program code as needed.

STEP 1: PROGRAM SPECIFICATION

Program specification, also called **program definition** or **program analysis,** consists of specifying five tasks related to objectives, outputs, inputs, requirements, and documentation.

Program Objectives

The first task is to clearly define the problem to solve in the form of program **objectives.**

Desired Output

Next, focus on the desired output before considering the required inputs.

Input Data

Once outputs are defined, determine the necessary input data and the source of the data.

Processing Requirements

Next, determine the steps necessary (processing requirements) to use input to produce output.

Program Specifications Document

The final task is to create a specifications document to record this step's program objectives, outputs, inputs, and processing requirements.

To be a competent and knowledgeable end user, you need to understand the six steps of programming: program specification, program design, program coding, program test, program documentation, and program maintenance. Additionally, you need to be aware of CASE, OOP, and the generations of programming languages.

STEP 2: PROGRAM DESIGN

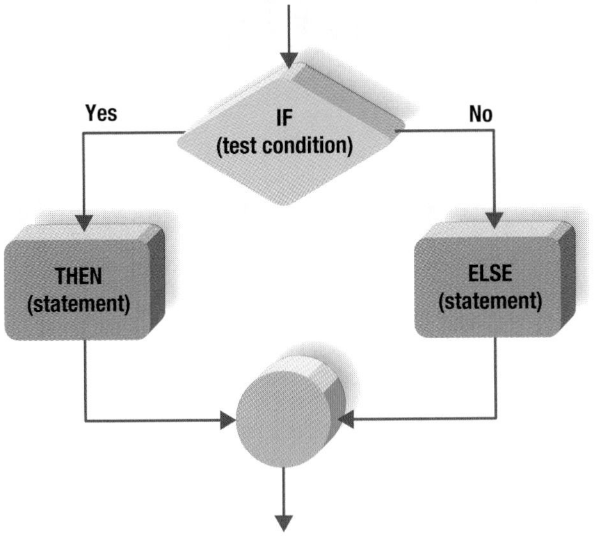

In **program design,** a solution is designed using, preferably, **structured programming techniques,** including the following.

Top-Down Design

In **top-down design,** major processing steps, called **program modules,** are identified.

Pseudocode

Pseudocode is an outline of the logic of the program you will write.

Flowcharts

Program flowcharts are graphic representations of the steps necessary to solve a programming problem.

Logic Structures

Logic structures are arrangements of programming statements. Three types are:

- **Sequence**—one program statement followed by another.
- **Selection (IF-THEN-ELSE)**—when a decision must be made.
- **Loop (DO UNTIL and DO WHILE)**—when process is repeated until condition is true.

STEP 3: PROGRAM CODE

```
<html>

<head>
<meta http-equiv="Content-Type" content="text/html; charset=windows-1252">
<meta http-equiv="Content-Language" content="en-us">

<title>Explore the Nile</title>
<meta name="GENERATOR" content="Microsoft FrontPage 4.0">
<meta name="ProgId" content="FrontPage.Editor.Document">

<!--mstheme--><link rel="stylesheet" type="text/css"
href="_themes/artsy/arts1111.css"><meta name="Microsoft Theme" content="artsy 1111,
default">
<meta name="Microsoft Border" content="tb">
</head>
<body><!--msnavigation--><table border="0" cellpadding="0" cellspacing="0"
width="100%"><tr><td>



<p>
        </p>
<p>
<img border="0" src="images/logo_newletter.jpg" width="271" height="188"
align="left"></p>


<p>
 </p>


<p>
<img src="_derived/africa03.htm_cmp_artsy110_bnr.gif" width="600" height="60"
border="0" alt="Explore the Nile"></p>
```

Coding is writing a program. There are several important aspects of writing a program. Two are writing good programs and actually writing or coding:

Good Programs

Good programs are reliable, detect obvious and common errors, and are well documented. Best way to create good programs is to write **structured programs** using the three basic logic structures presented in step 2.

Coding

There are hundreds of different programming languages. Two types are:

- **Formatting languages** that instruct a computer how to display information for the user. Widely used formatting languages include HTML, one of the most widely used formatting languages.
- **Programming languages** that instruct a computer to perform specific operations. C++ is a widely used programming language.

STEP 4: PROGRAM TEST

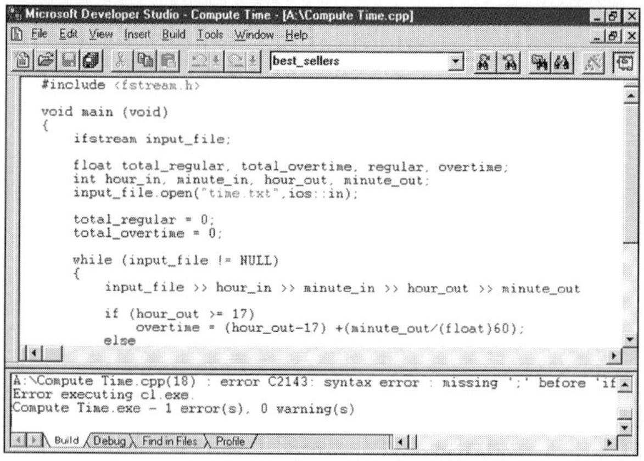

Debugging is a process of testing and eliminating errors in a program. Syntax and logic are two types of programming errors.

Syntax Errors

Syntax errors are violations in the rules of a programming language. For example, omitting a semicolon at the end of a C++ statement is a syntex error.

Logic Errors

Logic errors are incorrect calculations or procedures. For example, failure to include calculation of overtime hours in a payroll program is a logic error.

Testing Process

Five methods for testing for syntax and logic errors are:

- **Desk checking**—careful reading of a printout of the program.
- **Manual testing**—using a calculator and sample data to test for correct programming logic.
- **Attempt at translation**—running program using a translator program to identify syntax errors.
- **Testing sample data**—running the program and testing the program for logic errors using sample data.
- **Testing by users (beta testing)**—final step in which potential users try the program and provide feedback.

STEP 5: PROGRAM DOCUMENTATION

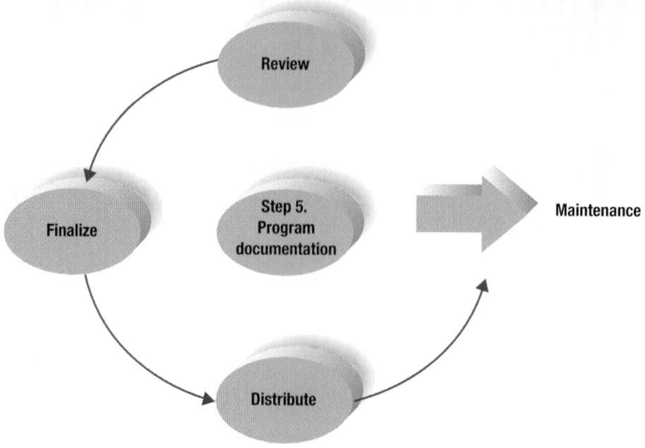

Program documentation consists of a written description of the program and the procedures for running it. People who use documentation include:

- **Users,** who need to know how to use the program.
- **Operators,** who need to know how to execute the program and how to recognize and correct errors.
- **Programmers,** who may need to update and maintain the program in the future.

STEP 6: PROGRAM MAINTENANCE

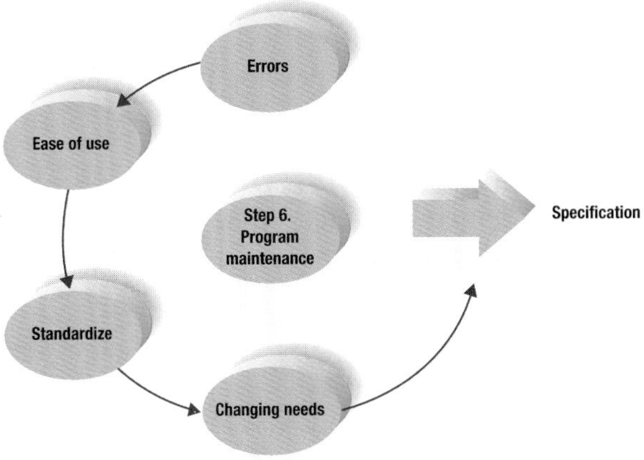

Program maintenance is designed to ensure that the program operates correctly, efficiently, and effectively. Two categories of maintenance activities are the following.

Operations

Operations activities include locating and correcting errors, improving usability, and standardizing software.

Changing Needs

Organizations change over time and their programs must change with them.

CASE AND OOP

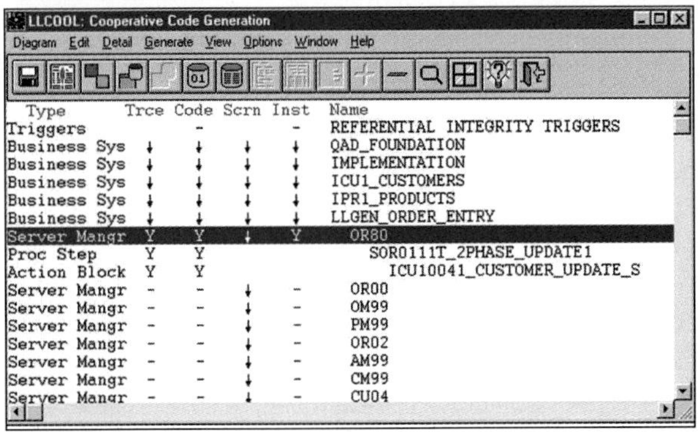

CASE

Computer-aided software engineering (CASE) tools provide automation and assistance in program design, coding, and testing.

OOP

Traditional systems development focuses on procedure to complete a specific objective.

Object-oriented software development focuses less on procedures and more on defining relationships between previously defined procedures or objects. **Object-oriented programming (OOP)** is a process by which a program is divided into **modules** called objects. Each object contains both data and processing operations necessary to perform a task.

These modules are reusable and self-contained components. C++ is one of the most widely used object-oriented programming languages.

PROGRAMMING GENERATIONS

Programming languages have **levels** or **generations** ranging from "low" to "high." **Lower-level** languages are closer to the 0s and 1s language of computers. **Higher-level** languages are closer to the languages of humans.

Generation	Sample Statement
First: Machine	111100100111001110
Second: Assembly	ADD 210(8, 13),02B(4, 7)
Third: Procedural	if (score > = 90) . . .
Fourth: Problem	SELECT client FROM . . .
Fifth: Natural and Visual	If patient is dizzy, then . . .

KEY TERMS

application generator (582)
assembly language (581)
beta testing (576)
code (572)
coding (572)
compiler (581)
computer-aided software engineering (CASE) tools (579)
debugging (575)
desk checking (575)
documentation (576)
DO UNTIL structure (570)
DO WHILE structure (570)
fifth generation language (5GL) (583)
formatting language (572)
fourth generation language (4GL) (582)
generations (580)
higher level (580)
IFPS (interactive financial planning system) (582)
IF-THEN-ELSE structure (569)
interpreter (582)
levels (580)
logic error (575)
logic structure (569)
loop structure (569)
lower level (580)
machine language (581)
maintenance programmer (578)
modules (580)
natural language (583)
object (580)
object code (581)
objectives (566)
object-oriented programming (OOP) (580)
object-oriented software development (580)
operators (577)
portable language (581)
presentation language (572)
problem-oriented language (582)
procedural language (581)
program (564)
program analysis (565)
program coder (582)
program definition (565)
program design (567)
program documentation (576)
program flowcharts (569)
program maintenance (578)
programmer (565)
programming (564)
programming language (572)
program modules (568)
program specification (565)
pseudocode (569)
query language (582)
selection structure (569)
sequence structure (569)
software development (564)
software engineer (565)
source code (581)
structured programs (572)
structured programming techniques (567)
syntax error (575)
third generation language (3GL) (581)
top-down program design (568)
users (577)
very high level language (582)
visual programming language (583)

To test your knowledge of these key terms with animated flash cards, select Flash Cards from Tim's Toolbox at http://www.mhhe.com/oleary/CT05.

CHAPTER REVIEW

CROSSWORD

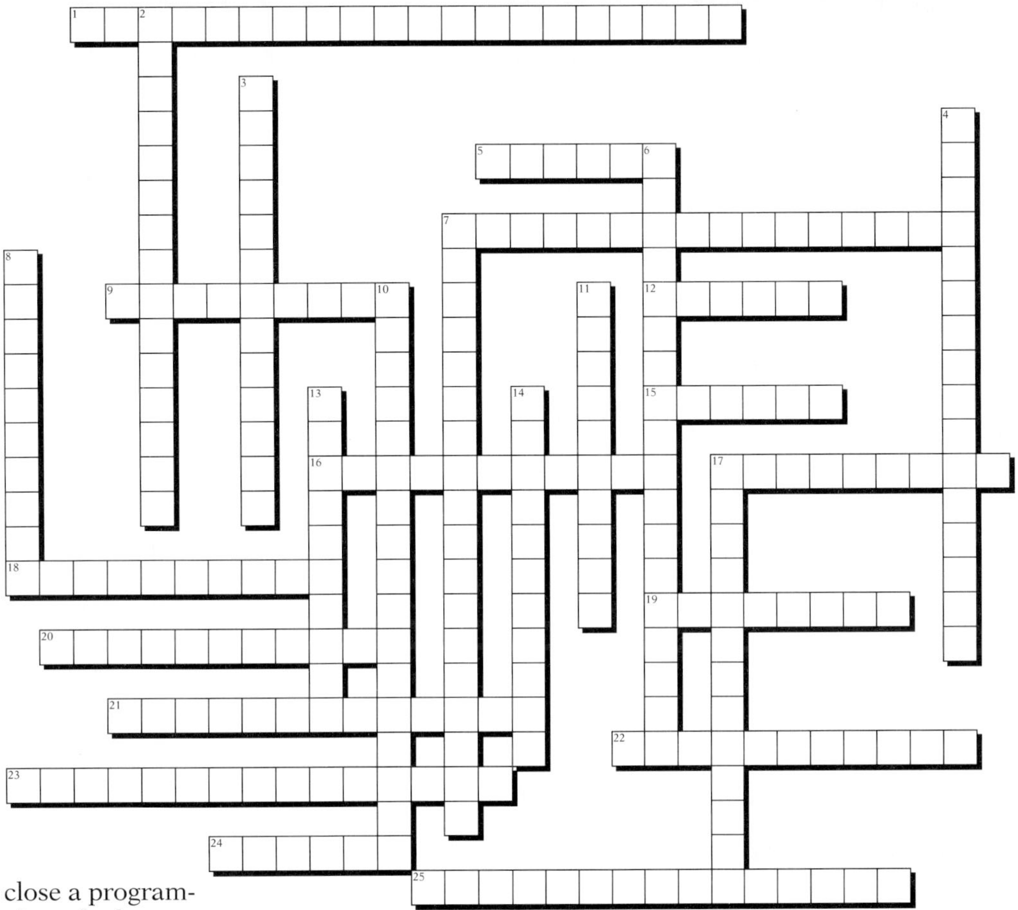

ACROSS

1 A program that provides modules of prewritten code
5 Describe how close a programming language is to the language of the computer itself
7 High-level procedural language
9 Need to know how to execute the program and how to recognize and correct errors
12 The actual writing of a program
15 Previously defined procedures
16 There are five __________ of programming languages
17 The process of testing and eliminating errors in a program
18 The programmer's procedural language program
19 Converts the programmer's procedural language program into machine language code
20 Violations of a programming language's rules
21 A process that may be repeated as long as a certain condition remains
22 Testing by a select group of potential users
23 Data represented in 1s and 0s
24 A program's processing steps
25 Human language

DOWN

2 Prewritten program
3 Allows nonprogrammers to search and generate reports from a database
4 Use abbreviations or mnemonics
6 Also known as the IF-THEN-ELSE structure
7 Designed to express the logic that can solve general problems
8 Graphically present the sequence of steps needed to solve a programming problem
10 One program statement follows another
11 An outline of logic of the program you will write
13 Created by incorrect or missing specifications
14 Converts the procedural language one statement at a time into machine code
17 The written description of the program and the procedures for running it

For an interactive crossword puzzle select Crosswords from Tim's Toolbox at http://www.mhhe.com/oleary/CT05.

MULTIPLE CHOICE

Circle the letter or fill in the correct answer.

1. Only the ________ step of software development involves keying statements into a computer.
   - **a.** program specification
   - **b.** program design
   - **c.** program code
   - **d.** program test
   - **e.** program documentation
2. In the ________ step a solution is created using programming techniques such as top-down program design, pseudocode, flowcharts, and logic structures.
   - **a.** program specification
   - **b.** program design
   - **c.** program code
   - **d.** program test
   - **e.** program documentation
3. Program specification is also called ________ and ________.
   - **a.** program definition, program analysis
   - **b.** program charting, program requirements
   - **c.** program design, program analysis
   - **d.** program charting, program design
   - **e.** program modeling, program definition
4. Under the rules of top-down design each module should have ________ function(s).
   - **a.** multiple
   - **b.** two
   - **c.** one
   - **d.** three
   - **e.** ten
5. The two variations of loop structure are ________ and ________.
   - **a.** DO NOW, DO LATER
   - **b.** DO WHILE, DO PARALLEL
   - **c.** DO WHILE, DO UNTIL
   - **d.** DO NOW, DO DURING
   - **e.** DO LATER, DO UNTIL
6. The best way to code effective programs is to write ________.
   - **a.** top-down programs
   - **b.** structured programs
   - **c.** coded programs
   - **d.** loop structured programs
   - **e.** selection structured programs
7. The omission of a semicolon at the end of a statement in C++ is an example of a ________ error.
   - **a.** loop
   - **b.** direct
   - **c.** calculation
   - **d.** design
   - **e.** syntax
8. ________ is carried on throughout all the programming steps.
   - **a.** Coding
   - **b.** Design
   - **c.** Beta testing
   - **d.** Documentation
   - **e.** Desk checking
9. Languages that can run on more than one kind of computer are called ________.
   - **a.** machine languages
   - **b.** portable languages
   - **c.** assembly languages
   - **d.** problem-oriented languages
   - **e.** query languages
10. A(n) ________ contains a number of modules that have been preprogrammed to accomplish various tasks.
    - **a.** application generator
    - **b.** natural language program
    - **c.** translator
    - **d.** interpreter
    - **e.** compiler

To test your knowledge of this chapter, select Self Test from Tim's Toolbox at http://www.mhhe.com/oleary/CT05.

MATCHING

Match each numbered item with the most closely related lettered item. Write your answers in the spaces provided.

a. assembly
b. beta testing
c. coding
d. debugging
e. desk checking
f. higher-level languages
g. logic error
h. logic structure
i. loop structure
j. maintenance
k. modules
l. objectives
m. OOP
n. procedural language
o. program specification
p. programmer
q. program
r. program flowchart
s. pseudocode
t. software development

1. A list of instructions for the computer to follow to process data. ____
2. A six-step procedure used to create a program. ____
3. Off-the-shelf programs. Designed to express the logic that can solve general problems. ____
4. Computer professional who creates new software or revises existing software. ____
5. Programming step in which objectives, outputs, inputs, and processing requirements are determined. ____
6. The problems you are trying to solve. ____
7. Logically related program statements. ____
8. An outline of the logic of the program to be written. ____
9. Graphically presents the detailed sequence of steps needed to solve a programming problem. ____
10. Structure that controls the logical sequence in which computer program instruction are executed. ____
11. Logic structure in which a process may be repeated as long as a certain condition remains true. ____
12. Actual writing of a program. ____
13. Testing and eliminating errors from a program. ____
14. Error that occurs when an incorrect calculation or incorrect procedure is used in a program. ____
15. Studying a computer program line by line looking for syntax and logic errors. ____
16. Potential users are given the opportunity to try out a program and provide feedback. ____
17. Computer specialist whose job is to ensure current programs run error free, efficiently, and effectively. ____
18. Process by which a program is organized into objects. ____
19. Programming languages closer to human languages. ____
20. Languages that use abbreviations or mnemonics. ____

OPEN-ENDED

On a separate sheet of paper, respond to each question or statement.

1. What are the six steps of programming? What part does coding play in program development?
2. Describe CASE tools and OOP. How does CASE assist programmers?
3. What is meant by "generation" in reference to programming languages? What is the difference between low-level and high-level languages?
4. What is the difference between a compiler and an interpreter? What role would these tools have in programming with natural languages?
5. What are logic structures? Describe the differences between the three types discussed in the chapter.

USING TECHNOLOGY

1 CVS

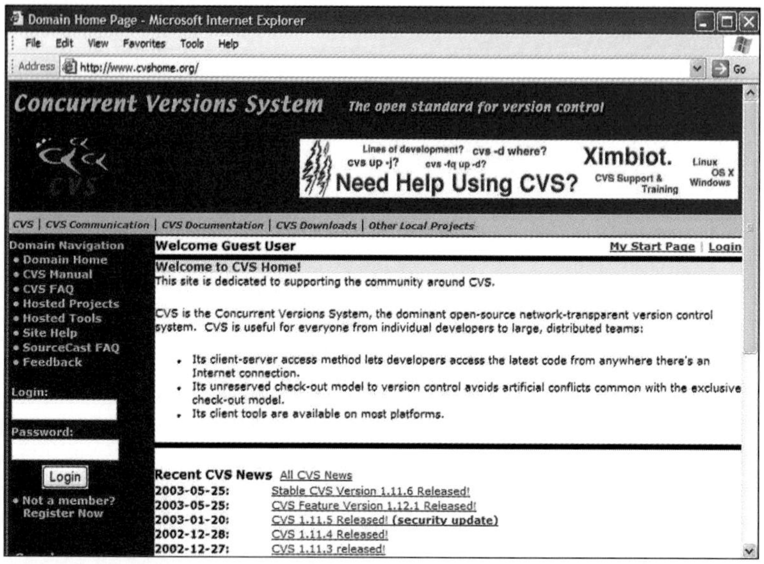

The Concurrent Versions System, or CVS, is an invaluable tool for large programming projects. Learn more about CVS by visiting our Web site at http://www.mhhe.com/oleary/CT05 and select Using Technology from Tim's Toolbox and linking to the CVS Web site. Once connected, read about CVS, and then answer the following questions: (a) What is CVS? Who uses it? (b) Describe what CVS does. Be specific. (c) What is CVS useful for? (d) When is CVS not a useful choice? Why?

2 JAVA

Java has become a very high profile language in recent years. Find out why by visiting our Web site at http://www.mhhe.com/oleary/CT05 and select Using Technology from Tim's Toolbox to connect to the official Java Web site. Explore the articles and information there, and then answer the following questions: (a) How is Java being used by companies today? (b) How is Java technology expected to be used by companies in the future? (c) Are these predictions realistic? Justify your answer. (d) How is Java licensed—is there a fee to use Java in a new product?

.NET Framework 3

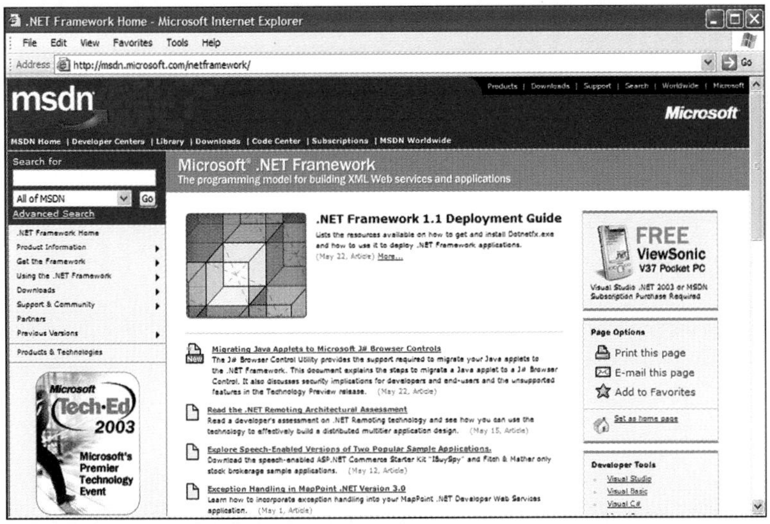

Microsoft's .NET Framework is a platform for developing applications that run on computers, small devices like mobile phones and PDAs, and even across the Internet. Visit our Web site at http://www.mhhe.com/oleary/CT05 and select Using Technology from Tim's Toolbox to link to the .NET site. Read about the .NET Framework, and then answer the following questions: (a) What are the basic components of the .NET Framework? (b) What programming languages does the .NET Framework include? (c) What are the benefits of using the .NET Framework for software developers?

Integrated Development Environments 4

As discussed in the chapter, source code is written in a programming language and then compiled or interpreted. Although source code can be written in most any word processor and compiled with a separate program, most programmers use an integrated development environment (IDE). Research IDEs on the Web, and then answer the following questions: (a) What is an IDE? What purpose does it serve? (b) What features are common to most IDEs? (c) In the DVD Direct case study, Mia programmed the login application herself. Locate and describe an IDE that would be appropriate for her chosen programming language.

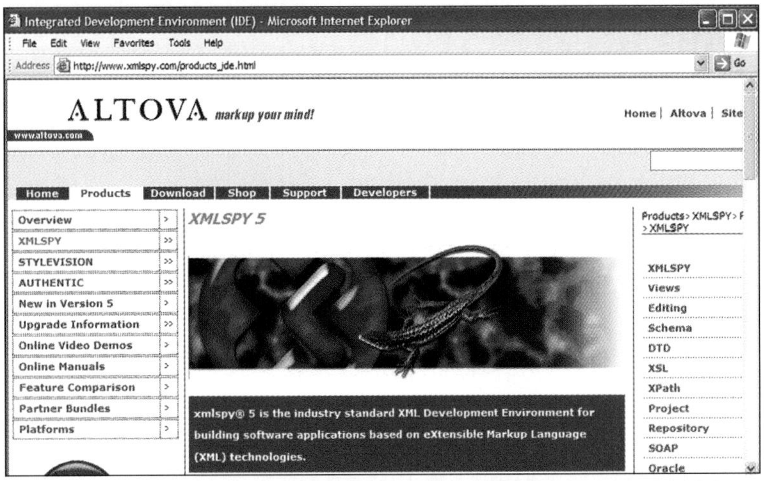

EXPANDING YOUR KNOWLEDGE

1 Computing Today CD

In the DVD Direct case study, Mia defended her choice of programming language. Review the case study, and then answer the following questions: (a) Which language did Mia choose? (b) What other languages did Mia consider? How did she make her choice? (c) Was the chosen language procedural, or object-oriented? (d) In this example, there were many languages available for Mia to choose from. Why doesn't everyone simply use the same language? Explore this topic thoroughly, and justify your answer.

2 Source Code Generators

Generally, the human resources that are devoted to a successful software project are its greatest single expense. Programming and testing applications is a time-consuming task. Recently, source code generators have become popular for handling some of the more routine programming tasks. Research source code generators on the Web, and answer the following questions: (a) What are source code generators? (b) How do source code generators work? (c) What programming tasks are source code generators best for? Why? (d) What programming tasks are beyond what source code generators can accomplish? Why?

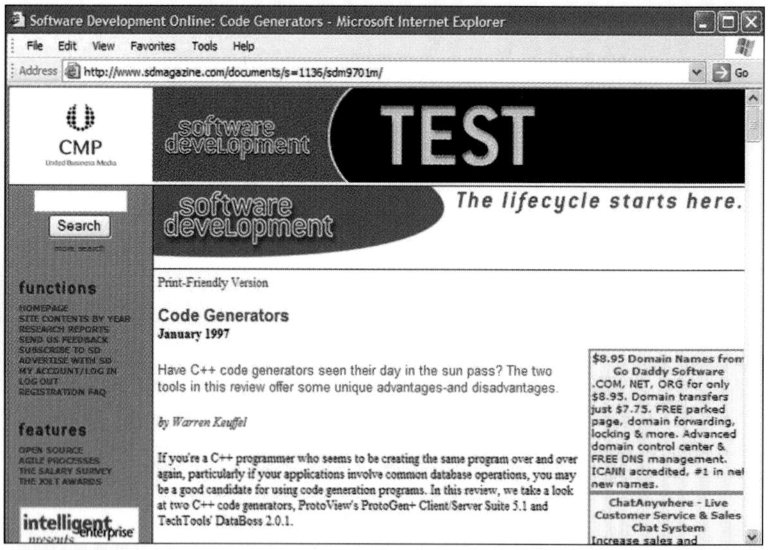

EXPANDING YOUR KNOWLEDGE

SimNet CD 3

Complete Chapter 15: Programming And Languages on the SimNet Computer Concepts CD and then answer the following questions: (a) Referencing the section "Object Oriented and Visual Programming," describe the differences between Object Oriented programming and Visual programming. (b) Referencing the section "Programming Languages," describe the programming used to code Internet programs.

Capability Maturity Model 4

Continuous improvement of the software development process is critical for an organization. A solid process lets an organization estimate needed resources for a new project more accurately, allows retaining knowledge gain from prior projects, and eliminates dependence on any particular person for success. The Capability Maturity Model, or CMM, is a way to address this need. Visit our Web site at http://mhhe.com/oleary/CT05 to connect to the CMM site. Read about CMM, and then answer the following questions: (a) What is CMM? Who created it? (b) List the five CMM levels, and describe the characteristics of each. (c) What CMM level was DVD Direct working at? Justify your answer. (d) Based on the CMM, what steps can DVD Direct take to use Mia's experience to improve their next software project? Be specific.

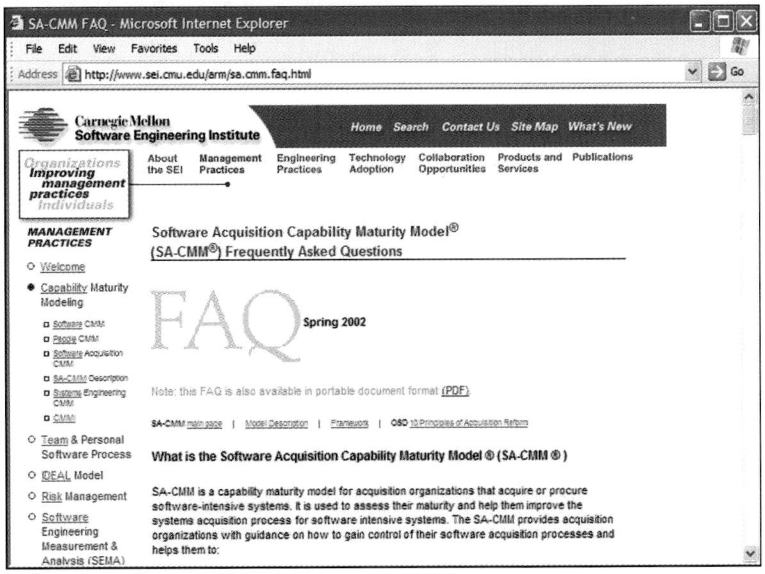

BUILDING YOUR PORTFOLIO

1 Java

Its ease of learning and its current momentum make Java an important and valuable programming language. In a one-page paper entitled "Java," address the following: (a) What generation of programming language is Java? (b) How is Java different from other programming languages? (c) What types of applications is Java best suited for? Why? (d) What types of applications is Java a poor choice for? Why?

2 Extreme Programming

Extreme Programming, also known as XP, is a newer model for the software development process. XP emphasizes simplified and accelerated development. Research Extreme Programming on the Web, and then answer the following questions in a one-page paper: (a) What are the 12 principles of XP? (b) How does XP differ from other models of software development? (c) For what kinds of software projects is XP most effective? When would a different model be a better choice? Explain your answers.

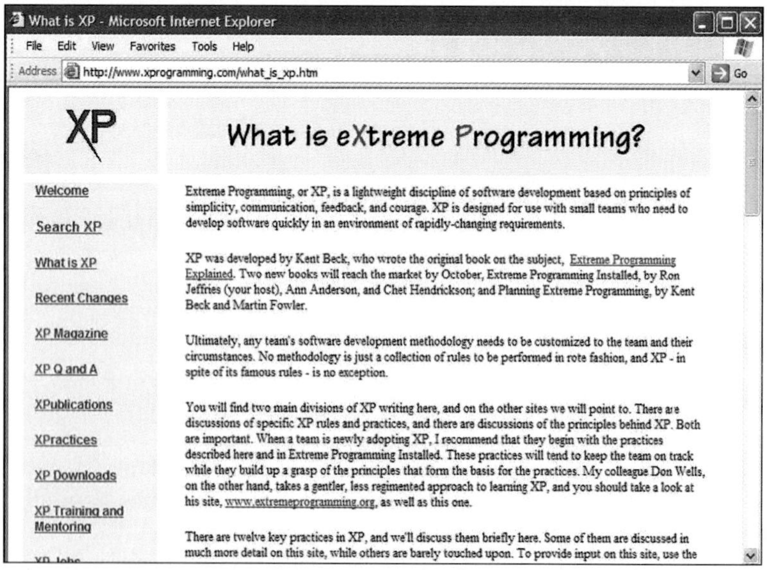

Bugs 3

In 1986, two people died and a third was maimed after receiving excessive radiation from a medical machine. It was only after the second incident that the problem was located—a bug in the software that controlled the machine. Consider the possible consequences of software failure in situations where life is at stake, and then answer the following questions in a one-page paper: (a) Are there situations when software bugs are unethical? Explain your answer. (b) No program of any significant complexity can reasonably be fully tested. When is it ethical to say that software is "tested enough"? (c) What responsibility does a programmer have in situations when a program fails in the field? What about the software company he or she works for? Does the consumer share any responsibility? Justify your answers.

Security and Privacy 4

Security and privacy are important concerns in the of development of any information system. Answer the following questions in a one-page paper: (a) In the development process, who would you expect to have the responsibility of identifying security and privacy concerns? (b) In what phase of the system life cycle, would security and privacy concerns be identified? (c) In the DVD Direct case, identify the most important security and privacy concerns. Be as specific as possible.

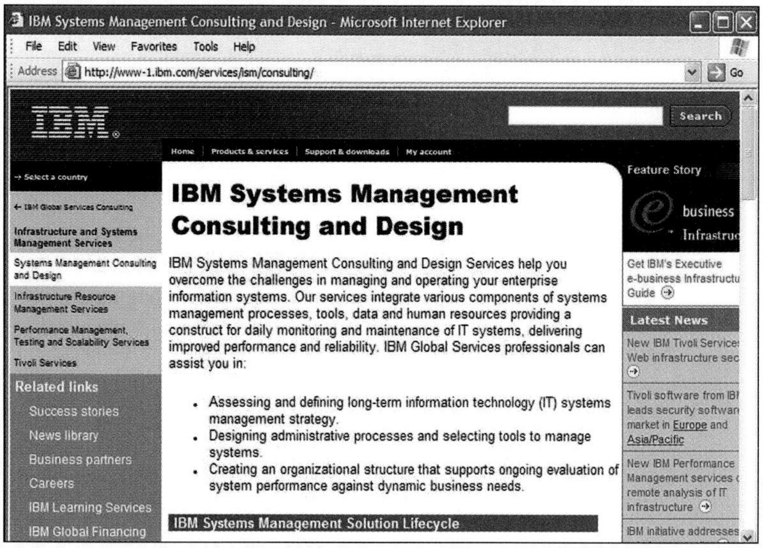

YOUR FUTURE AND INFORMATION TECHNOLOGY

OBJECTIVES

After you have read this chapter, you should be able to:

1. **Explain why it's important to have an individual strategy in order to be a "winner" in the information age.**
2. **Describe how technology is changing the nature of competition.**
3. **Discuss four ways people may react to new technology.**
4. **Describe how you can stay current with your career.**
5. **Describe different careers in information technology.**

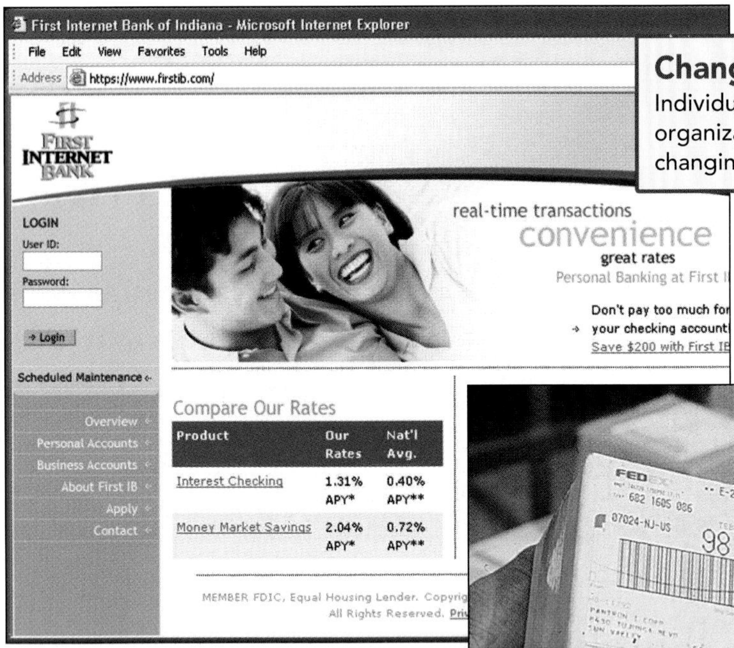

Changing Times
Individuals, businesses, and organizations must adapt to changing technology

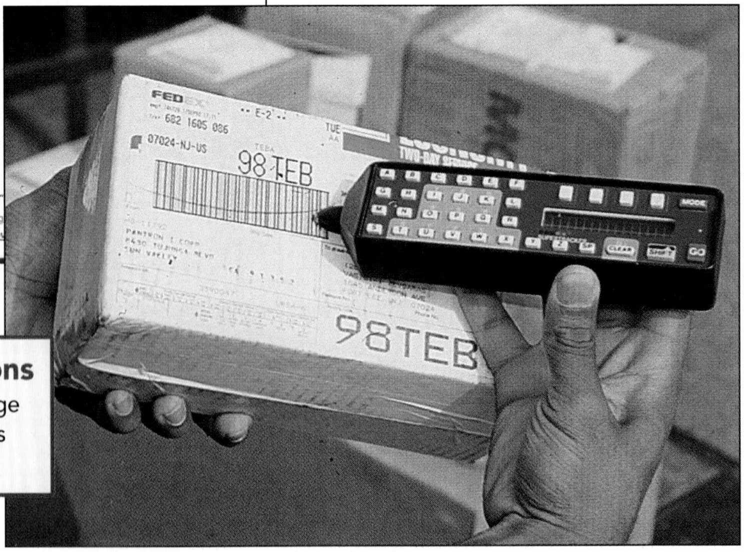

Technology and Organizations
Technology forces organizational change by introducing new ways for businesses to compete

CHAPTER 16

Throughout this book, we have emphasized practical subjects that are useful to you now or will be very soon. Accordingly, this final chapter is not about the far future, say, 10 years from now. Rather, it is about today and the near future—about developments whose outlines we can already see. It is about how organizations adapt to technological change. It is also about what you as an individual can do to keep your computer competency up to date.

Are the times changing any faster now than they ever have? It's hard to say. People who were alive when radios, cars, and airplanes were being introduced certainly lived through some dramatic changes. Has technology made our own times even more dynamic? Whatever the answer, it is clear we live in a fast-paced age. The challenge for you as an individual is to devise ways to stay current and to use technology to your advantage. For example, you can use the Web to locate job opportunities.

To stay competent and knowledgeable, end users need to recognize the impact of technological change on organizations and people. They need to know how to use change to their advantage and to be winners. Although end users do not need to be specialists in information technology, they should be aware of career opportunities in the area.

Be a Winner
By staying current, developing specialties, and being alert to organizational changes and opportunities for innovation

Technology and People
Some people react negatively to technological change by being cynical, naive, or frustrated but the most positive reaction to technological change is to be proactive

CHANGING TIMES

To be a winner in the information revolution, you need an individual strategy.

Almost all businesses have become aware that they must adapt to changing technology or be left behind. Most organizations are now making formal plans to keep track of technology and implement it in their competitive strategies. For example, banks have found that automated teller machines (ATMs) are vital to retail banking. (See Figure 16-1.) Not only do they require fewer human tellers, but they can also be made available 24 hours a day. More and more banks are also trying to go electronic, doing away with paper transactions wherever possible. ATM cards are used to buy almost anything from gas to groceries.

Figure 16-1 Automated teller machines are examples of technology used in business strategy

What's next for the banking industry? Almost all banks are also trying to popularize home banking so that customers can use microcomputers for certain financial tasks. Some banks, known as Internet banks, have even done away with physical bank buildings and conduct all business over the Web. (See Figure 16-2.) In addition, banks are exploring the use of some very sophisticated application programs. These programs will accept cursive writing (the handwriting on checks) directly as input, verify check signatures, and process the check without human intervention.

Clearly, such changes do away with some jobs—those of many bank tellers and cashiers, for example. However, they create opportunities for other people. New technology requires people who are truly capable of working with it. These are not the people who think every piece of equipment is so simple they can just turn it on and use it. Nor are they those who think each new machine is a potential disaster. In other words, new technology needs people who are not afraid to learn about it and are able to manage it. The real issue, then, is not how to make technology better. Rather, it is how to integrate the technology with people.

You are in a very favorable position compared with many other people in industry today. After reading the previous chapters, you have learned more than just the basics of hardware, software, connectivity, and the Internet. You have learned about the most current technology. You are therefore able to use these tools to your advantage—to be a winner.

How do you become and stay a winner? In brief, the answer is: You must form your own individual strategy for dealing with change. First let us look at how businesses are handling technological change. Then let's look at how people are reacting to these changes. Finally, we will offer a few suggestions that will enable you to keep up with—and profit from—the information revolution.

Concept Check

- ✓ Cite examples of ways computers are changing the business world.
- ✓ What are the human requirements of new technology?

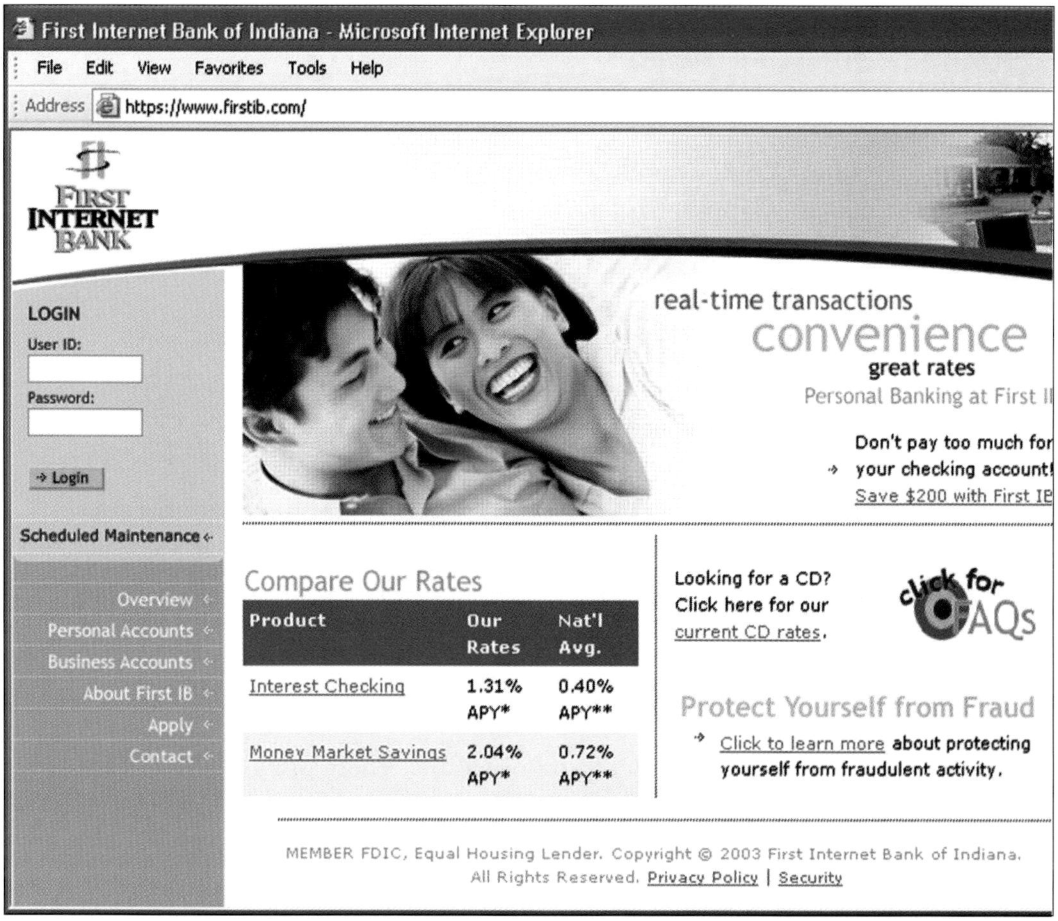

Figure 16-2 Internet banks conduct business over the Web

TECHNOLOGY AND ORGANIZATIONS

Technology changes the nature of competition by introducing new products, new enterprises, and new relationships among customers and suppliers.

Technology can introduce new ways for businesses to compete with each other. Some of the principal changes are as follows.

NEW PRODUCTS

Technology creates products that operate faster, are priced cheaper, are often of better quality, or are wholly new. Indeed, new products can be individually tailored to a particular customer's needs. For example, financial services companies such as Merrill Lynch have taken advantage of technology to launch cash management accounts. (See Figure 16-3.) These accounts combine information on a person's checking, savings, credit card, and securities accounts into a single monthly statement. It automatically sets aside "idle" funds into interest-bearing money market funds. Customers can access their accounts on the Web and get a complete picture of their financial condition at any time. However, even if they don't pay much attention to their statements, their surplus funds are invested automatically.

Figure 16-3 Merrill Lynch's cash management account

NEW ENTERPRISES

Information technology can build entirely new businesses. Two examples are Internet service providers and Web site development companies.

- Just a few years ago, the only computer connectivity options available to individuals were through online service providers like America Online and through colleges and universities. Now, hundreds of national service providers and thousands of local service providers are available.
- Thousands of small companies specializing in Web site development have sprung up in the past three years. These companies help small- to medium-sized organizations by providing assistance in evaluating, creating, and maintaining Web sites.

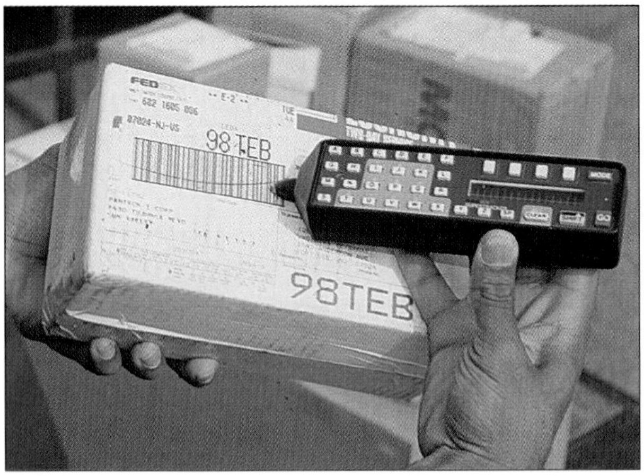

Figure 16-4 New technology helps Federal Express maintain customer loyalty

NEW CUSTOMER AND SUPPLIER RELATIONSHIPS

Businesses that make their information systems easily available may make their customers less likely to take their business elsewhere. For instance, Federal Express, the overnight package delivery service, does everything possible to make its customers dependent on it. Upon request, customers receive airbills with their name, address, and account number preprinted on them, making shipping and billing easier. Package numbers are scanned into the company's information system so that they can be tracked from pickup point to destination. (See Figure 16-4.) Thus, apprehensive customers can be informed very quickly of the exact location of their package as it travels toward its destination.

Concept Check

- What is the role of technology in creating new products?
- Describe two new enterprises built by information technology.
- Discuss how technology can create new customers and affect supplier relationships.

TECHNOLOGY AND PEOPLE

People may be cynical, naive, frustrated, or proactive in response to technology.

Clearly, recent technological changes, and those sure to come in the near future, will produce significant changes and opportunities in the years ahead. How should we be prepared for them?

People have different coping styles when it comes to technology. It has been suggested, for instance, that people react to changing technology in one of four ways. These ways are cynicism, naivete, frustration, and proactivity.

CYNICISM

The **cynic** feels that, for a manager at least, the idea of using a microcomputer is overrated. (See Figure 16-5.) Learning and using it take too much time, time that could be delegated to someone else. Doing spreadsheets and word processing, according to the cynic, are tasks that managers should understand. However, the cynic feels that such tasks take time away from a manager's real job of developing plans and setting goals for the people being supervised.

Cynics may express their doubts openly, especially if they are top managers. Or, they may only pretend to be interested in microcomputers, when actually they are not interested at all.

Figure 16-5 The cynic: "These gadgets are overrated."

NAIVETE

Many **naive** people are unfamiliar with computers. They may think computers are magic boxes capable of solving all kinds of problems that computers really can't handle. On the other hand, some naive persons are actually quite familiar with computers, but underestimate the difficulty of changing computer systems or of generating certain information.

FRUSTRATION

The **frustrated** person may already be quite busy and may hate having to take time to learn about microcomputers. Such a person feels it is an imposition to have to learn something new or is too impatient to try to understand the manuals explaining what hardware and software are supposed to do. The result is continual frustration. (See Figure 16-6.) Some people are frustrated because they try to do too much. Or they're frustrated because they find manuals difficult to understand. In some cases poorly written manuals are at fault.

Figure 16-6 The frustrated: "This stuff doesn't make sense half the time."

Figure 16-7 The proactive: "How can I use this new tool?"

PROACTIVITY

Webster's Collegiate Dictionary defines **proactive,** in part, as "acting in anticipation of future problems, needs, or changes." A proactive person looks at technology in a positive realistic way. (See Figure 16-7.) They are not cynics, underestimating the likely impact of technology on their lives. They are not naive, overestimating the ability of technology to solve the world's or their problems. They do not easily become frustrated and give up using technology. Proactive people are positive in their outlook and look at new technology as providing new tools that when correctly applied can positively impact their lives.

Most of us fall into one of the four categories. Cynicism, naivete, frustration, and proactivity are common human responses to change. Do you see yourself or others around you responding to technology in any of these ways? For those who respond negatively, just being aware of their reaction can help them become more positive and proactive to tomorrow's exciting new changes in technology.

Concept Check

- ✔ Describe three negative ways people cope with technological changes in the workplace.
- ✔ Describe one positive way people cope with technological change in the workplace.
- ✔ Define proactive.

HOW YOU CAN BE A WINNER

Individuals need to stay current, develop specialties, and be alert to organizational changes and opportunities for innovation.

So far we have described how progressive organizations are using technology in the information age. Now let's concentrate on you as an individual. (See Making IT Work for You: Locating Job Opportunities Online on pages 612–613.) How can you stay ahead? Here are some ideas.

STAY CURRENT

Whatever their particular line of work, successful professionals keep up both with their own fields and with the times. We don't mean you should try to become a computer expert and read a lot of technical magazines. Rather, you should concentrate on your profession and learn how computer technology is being used within it.

Every field has trade journals, whether the field is interior design, personnel management, advertising, or whatever. Most such journals regularly present articles about the uses of computers. It's important that you also belong to a trade or industry association and go to its meetings. Many associations sponsor seminars and conferences that describe the latest information and techniques.

Another way to stay current is by participating electronically with special-interest newsgroups on the Internet.

MAINTAIN YOUR COMPUTER COMPETENCY

Actually, you should try to stay ahead of the technology. Books, journals, and trade associations are the best sources of information about new technology that applies to your field. The general business press—*Business Week, Fortune, Inc., The Wall Street Journal,* and the business section of your local newspaper—also carries computer-related articles.

However, if you wish, you can subscribe to a magazine that covers microcomputers and information more specifically. Examples are *InfoWorld, PC World,* and *MacWorld.* You may also find it useful to look at newspapers and magazines that cover the computer industry as a whole. An example of such a periodical is *ComputerWorld.* Most of these magazines also have an online version available on the Web. (See Figure 16-8.)

Figure 16-8 PC World on the Web

MAKING IT WORK FOR YOU

LOCATING JOB OPPORTUNITIES ONLINE

Did you know that you can use the Internet to find a job? You can locate and browse through job listings. You can even electronically post your resume for prospective employers to review.

How It Works There are several Web sites designed to bring together prospective employers and employees. These sites maintain a database of available jobs and a database of résumés. Individuals are able to post resumes and to search through available jobs. Organizations are able to post job opportunities and to search through individual resumes.

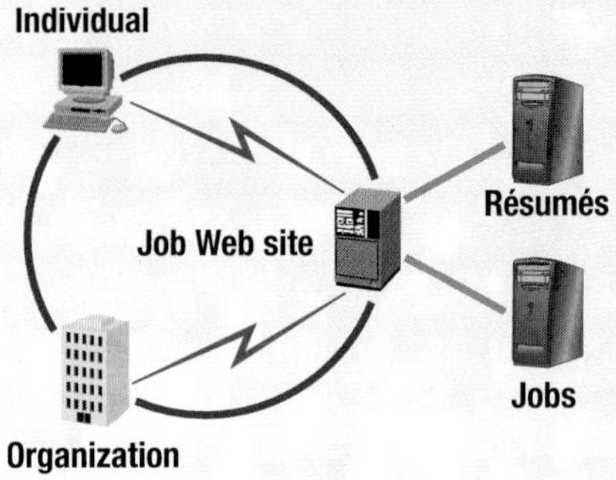

Browsing Job Listings Three well-known job search sites on the Web are hotjobs.com, Yahoo!jobs, and monster.com. You can connect to these sites and browse through job opportunities. For example, after connecting to monster.com, you can search for a job by following steps similar to those shown below.

1. - Connect to *www.monster.com.*
   - Click the *Search Jobs* link.

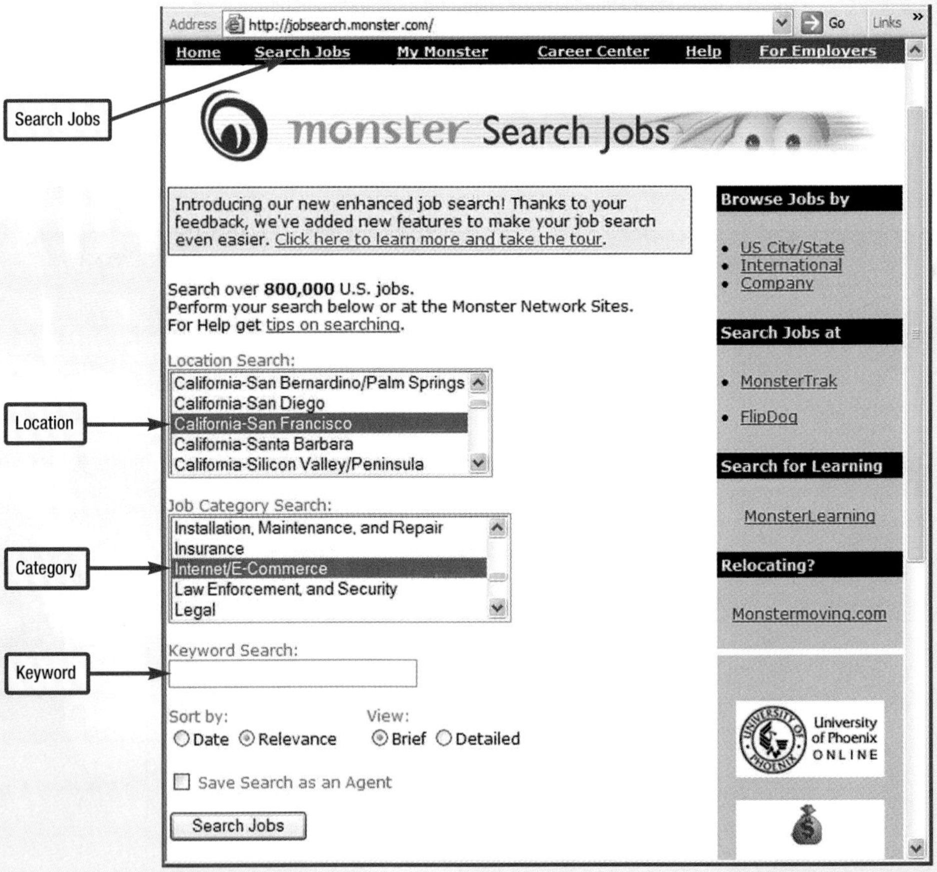

2 Select a location to search.

- Select a category to search.
- Optionally, enter any keywords to search.
- Click *Search Jobs.*

Jobs 1 to 40 of 40
Show Jobs Posted: Last 60 days
Sort: Date | Relevance
View: Brief | Detailed
Date
Location
Job Title
Company
Jul 10 US-CA-San Francisco WIN32 Developer TRS
Jul 10 US-CA-San Francisco Senior Software Sales Executive Management Recruiters Intntl
Jul 9 US-CA-San Francisco Software Developers Wanted! CFH Enterprises, Inc.
Jul 9 US-CA-San Francisco ASSOCIATE WEB EDITOR CFH Enterprises, Inc.
Jul 8 US-CA-San Francisco Director of Public Relations Management Recruiters Intntl
Jul 8 US-CA-San Francisco QUALITY ASSURANCE ANALYST 3 Wells Fargo

3 Select a job title to learn more about a job posting.

A detailed job posting, including description, company information, and contact information, is displayed.

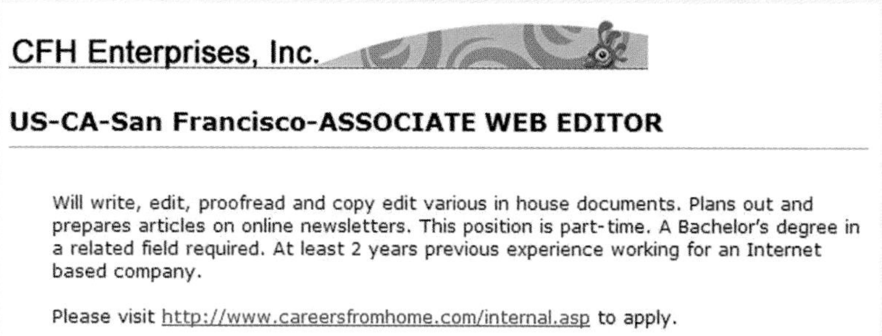
CFH Enterprises, Inc.
US-CA-San Francisco-ASSOCIATE WEB EDITOR
Will write, edit, proofread and copy edit various in house documents. Plans out and prepares articles on online newsletters. This position is part-time. A Bachelor's degree in a related field required. At least 2 years previous experience working for an Internet based company.
Please visit http://www.careersfromhome.com/internal.asp to apply.

Posting Your Resume To make your qualifications known to prospective employers, you can post your resume at the job search site.

1 Select *My Monster.*

- Select the *Create your new My Monster account* link.
- Follow the on-screen instructions to create an account.

My Monster
New Account Link
Home
Search Jobs
My Monster
Career Center
Help
For Employers
MY
monster
Career Operating System
My Monster: Build your resume and manage your career
Create your new My Monster account today so you can:
• Create up to five online resumes and cover letters to use to apply online to jobs
• Activate your resume so employers can view it or store it privately for your own use
• Track your online job applications
• Create automatic Job Search Agents that email you when a
Existing Members
Enter Username:
Enter Password:
Log In

2 Log onto your new account.

- Select the *Create a New Resume* link.
- Complete the on-screen resume form.
- Click *Submit Resume.*

Create a New Resume Link
MY
monster
Career Operating System
My Monster Home
Account Profile
Agents
Applications
Resumes
Letters
Career Talk
Welcome to My Monster. Your personal home on Monster.
Use all the links in this area to access your account profile, job search and career management tools and resources.
JUMPSTART your job search for less than $7 per month!
CLICK HERE
My Resumes
Create a New Resume
Profile Information
Student Name
If you're not Student Name, click here

Your agent will search new job listings and alert you to new opportunities by e-mail.

The Web is continually changing and some of the specifics presented in this Making IT Work for You may have changed. To learn about other ways to make information technology work for you, see our Web site at http://www.mhhe.com/oleary/CT05 and select Making IT Work for You from Tim's Toolbox.

DEVELOP PROFESSIONAL CONTACTS

Figure 16-9 Professional organizations and contacts help you keep up in your field

Besides being members of professional associations, successful people make it a point to maintain contact with others in their field. They stay in touch by telephone, e-mail, and newsgroups and go to lunch with others in their line of work. Doing this lets them learn what other people are doing in their jobs. It tells them what other firms are doing and what tasks are being automated. Developing professional contacts can keep you abreast not only of new information but also of new job possibilities. (See Figure 16-9.) It also offers social benefits. An example of a professional organization found in many areas is the local association of realtors.

DEVELOP SPECIALTIES

Develop specific as well as general skills. You want to be well-rounded *within* your field, but certainly not a "jack of all trades, master of none." Master a trade or two within your profession. At the same time, don't become identified with a specific technological skill that might very well become obsolete.

Figure 16-10 Desktop publishing: A good specialty to develop for certain careers

The best advice is to specialize to some extent. However, don't make your specialty so tied to technology that you'll be in trouble if the technology shifts. For example, if your career is in marketing or graphics design, it makes sense to learn about desktop publishing and Web page design. (See Figure 16-10.) In this way you can learn to make high-quality, inexpensive graphics layouts. It would not make as much sense for you to become an expert on, say, the various types of monitors used to display the graphics layouts, because such monitors are continually changing.

Expect to take classes during your working life to keep up with developments in your field. Some professions require more keeping up than others—a computer specialist, for example, compared to a human resources manager. Whatever the training required, always look for ways to adapt and improve your skills to become more productive and marketable. There may be times when you are tempted to start all over again and learn completely new skills. However, a better course of action may be to use emerging technology to improve your present base of skills. This way you can build on your current strong points and then branch out to other fields from a position of strength.

BE ALERT FOR ORGANIZATIONAL CHANGE

Every organization has formal lines of communication—for example, supervisor to middle manager to top manager. However, there is also the *grapevine*—informal lines of communication. (See Figure 16-11.) Some service departments will serve many layers of management and be abreast of the news on all levels. For instance, the art director for advertising may be aware of several aspects of a companywide marketing campaign. Secretaries and administrative assistants know what is going on in more than one area.

Figure 16-11 Informal communication can alert you to important organizational changes

Being part of the office grapevine can alert you to important changes—for instance, new job openings—that can benefit you. However, you always have to assess the validity of what you hear on the grapevine. Moreover, it's not advisable to be a contributor to office gossip. Behind-the-back criticisms of other people have a way of getting back to the person criticized.

Be especially alert for new trends within the organization—about future hiring, layoffs, automation, mergers with other companies, and the like. Notice which areas are receiving the greatest attention from top management. One tip-off is to see what kind of outside consultants are being brought in. Independent consultants are usually invited in because a company believes it needs advice in an area with which it has insufficient experience.

LOOK FOR INNOVATIVE OPPORTUNITIES

You may understand your job better than anyone—even if you've only been there a few months. Look for ways to make it more efficient. How can present procedures be automated? How can new technology make your tasks easier? Discuss your ideas with your supervisor, the training director, or the head of the information systems department. Or discuss them with someone else who can see that you get the recognition you deserve. (Co-workers may or may not be receptive and may or may not try to take credit themselves.)

A good approach is to present your ideas in terms of saving money rather than "improving information." Managers are generally more impressed with ideas that can save dollars than with ideas that seem like potential breakthroughs in the quality of decisions.

In general, it's best to concentrate on the business and organizational problems that need solving. Then look for a technological way of solving them. That is, avoid becoming too enthusiastic about a particular technology and then trying to make it fit the work situation.

Concept Check

- ✓ Outline the strategies you can use to stay ahead and be successful in your career.
- ✓ Discuss the advantages and disadvantages of specialization.
- ✓ Describe how you would stay alert for organizational changes.

Careers in IT

Being a winner does not necessarily mean having a career in information systems. There are, however, several jobs within information systems that you might like to consider. We have discussed several of these careers in the preceding chapters. (See Figure 16-12.)

To learn more about these careers, see your Computing Today CD or visit us at http://www.mhhe.com/oleary/CT05 and select careers in IT from TIm's Toolbox..

Career	Responsibilities
Computer support specialist	Provides technical support to customers and other users
Computer technician	Repairs and installs computer components and systems
Computer trainer	Instructs users on the latest software or hardware
Cryptographer	Designs, tests, and researches encryption procedures
Database administrator	Uses database management software to determine the most efficient ways to organize and access data
Data entry worker	Inputs customer information, lists, and other types of data
Desktop publisher	Creates and formats publication-ready material
Information systems manager	Oversees the work of programmers, computer specialists, systems analysts, and other computer professionals
Network administrator	Creates and maintains networks
Programmer	Creates, tests, and troubleshoots computer programs
Software engineer	Analyzes users' needs and creates application software
Systems analyst	Plans and designs information systems
Technical writer	Prepares instruction manuals, technical reports, and other scientific or technical documents
Webmaster	Develops and maintains Web sites and Web resources

Figure 16-12 Careers in Information Systems

A Look to the Future

Maintaining Computer Competency and Becoming Proactive

This is not the end, it is the beginning. Being a skilled computer end user and having computer competency is not a matter of thinking "Someday I'll have to learn all about that." It is a matter of living in the present and keeping an eye on the future. Computer competency also demands the discipline to keep up with emerging technology. Yet, it is important not to focus on the "what ifs" of technology. Computer competency demands concentration on your goals and dedication to learning how the computer can aid you in obtaining these goals. Being an end user, in short, is not about trying to avoid failure. Rather, it is about always moving toward success—about taking control of the exciting new tools available to you.

NOTES

VISUAL SUMMARY

YOUR FUTURE AND INFORMATION TECHNOLOGY

CHANGING TIMES

Individuals, businesses, and organizations must adapt to changing technology or be left behind.

Banking Industry

The banking industry uses automated teller machines (ATMs) to provide 24-hour service without incurring additional employee costs. Internet banks conduct all business over the Web.

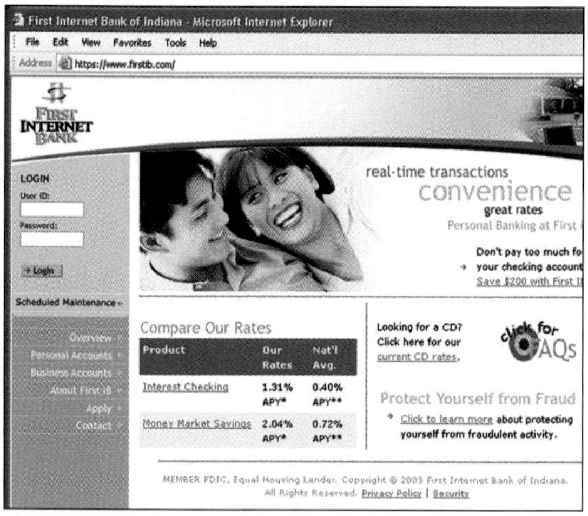

Many changes do away with jobs. Technology, however, creates opportunities. New technology requires people who are truly capable of working with it.

To become and stay a winner, you must form your own individual strategy for dealing with changes.

TECHNOLOGY AND ORGANIZATIONS

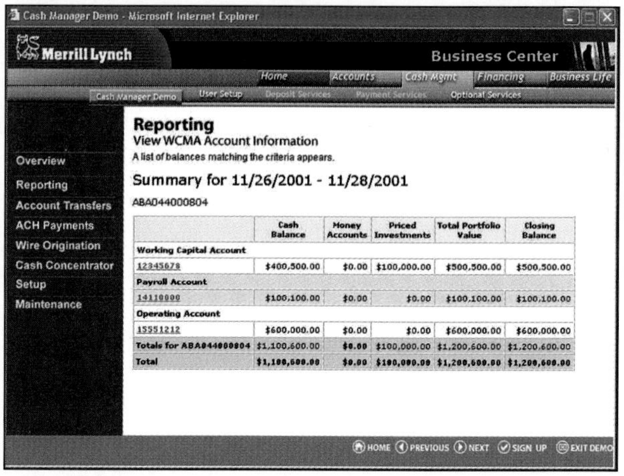

Technology can introduce new ways for businesses to compete with each other. They can compete by creating *new products, establishing new enterprises,* and *developing new customer and supplier relationships.*

New Products

Technology creates products that operate faster, are priced more cheaply, are often better quality, or are wholly new. New products can be individually tailored to a particular customer's needs.

New Enterprises

Technology can build entirely new businesses. Two examples:

- Internet service providers—just a few years ago, only a few Internet service providers were available. Now, thousands of national and local providers are available.
- Web site development companies—thousands of small companies specializing in developing Web sites have sprung up in just the past three years.

New Customer and Supplier Relationships

Businesses that make their information systems easily available may make their customers less likely to take their business elsewhere (e.g., overnight delivery services closely track packages and bills).

To stay competent and knowledgeable, you need to recognize the impact of technological change on organizations and people. You need to know how to use change to your advantage and to become a winner. Although you do not need to be a specialist in information technology, you should be aware of career opportunities in the area.

TECHNOLOGY AND PEOPLE

People have different coping styles when it comes to technology. Four common reactions to new technology are cynicism, naivete, frustration, and proactivity.

Cynicism

The **cynics** feel that new technology is overrated and too troublesome to learn. Some cynics openly express their doubts. Others pretend to be interested.

Naivete

Naive people may be unfamiliar or quite familiar with computers. Unfamiliar ones tend to think of computers as magic boxes. Even those familiar with technology often underestimate the time and difficulty of using technology to generate information.

Frustration

Frustrated users are impatient and irritated about taking time to learn new technology. Often these people have too much to do, find manuals difficult to understand, and/or feel stupid.

Proactivity

A **proactive** person looks at technology in a positive and realistic way. He or she is not cynical, naive, or frustrated regarding new technology. Proactive people are positive and look at new technology as providing new tools that can positively impact their lives.

HOW YOU CAN BE A WINNER

Six ongoing activities that can help you be successful are:

Stay Current

Read trade journals and the general business press, join professional associations, and participate in interest groups on the Internet.

Maintain Your Computer Competency

Stay current by reading computer-related articles in the general press and trade journals.

Develop Professional Contacts

Stay active in your profession and meet people in your field. This provides information about other people, firms, job opportunities, and social contacts.

Develop Specialties

Develop specific as well as general skills. Expect to take classes periodically to stay current with your field and technology.

Be Alert for Organizational Change

Use formal and informal lines of communication. Be alert for new trends within the organization.

Look for Innovative Opportunities

Look for ways to increase efficiency. Present ideas in terms of saving money rather than "improving information."

CAREERS IN IT

Computer Support Specialist
Computer support specialists provide technical support to customers and other users.

Computer Technician
Computer technicians repair and install computer components and systems.

Computer Trainer
Computer trainers instruct users on the latest software or hardware.

Cryptographer
Cryptographers design, test, and research encryption procedures.

Database Administrator
Database administrators use database management software to determine the most efficient ways to organize and access data.

Data Entry Worker
Data entry workers input customer information, lists, and other types of data.

CAREERS IN IT

Network Administrator
Network administrators create and maintain networks.

Programmer
Programmers create, test, and troubleshoot computer programs.

Software Engineer
Software engineers analyze users' needs and create application software.

Systems Analyst
Systems analysts plan and design information systems.

Technical Writer
Technical writers prepare instruction manuals, technical reports, and other scientific or technical documents.

Webmaster
Webmasters develop and maintain Web sites and Web resources.

Desktop Publisher
Desktop publishers create and format publication-ready material.

Information Systems Manager
Information system managers oversee the work of programmers, computer specialists, systems analysts, and other computer professionals.

KEY TERMS

computer support specialist (616)
computer technician (616)
computer trainer (616)
cryptographer (616)
cynic (609)
database administrator (616)
data entry worker (616)
desktop publisher (616)
frustrated (609)
information systems manager (616)
naive (609)
network administrator (616)
proactive (610)
programmer (616)
software engineer (616)
systems analyst (616)
technical writer (616)
webmaster (616)

To test your knowledge of these key terms with animated flash cards, select Flash Cards from Tim's Toolbox at http://www.mhhe.com/oleary/CT05.

CHAPTER REVIEW

CROSSWORD

ACROSS

2 Oversees the work of programmers, computer specialists, systems analysts and other computer professionals
3 Uses database management software to determine the most efficient
6 Repairs and installs computer components and systems
7 Acting in anticipation of future problems
10 Develops and maintains Web sites and Web resources
12 Creates, tests, and troubleshoots computer programs
13 Provides technical support to customers and other users

DOWN

1 Instructs users on the latest software or hardware
4 Inputs customer information, lists, and other types of data
5 Creates and maintains networks
8 Analyzes users' needs and creates application software
9 Prepares instruction manuals, technical reports, and other scientific or technical documents
11 Plans and designs information systems

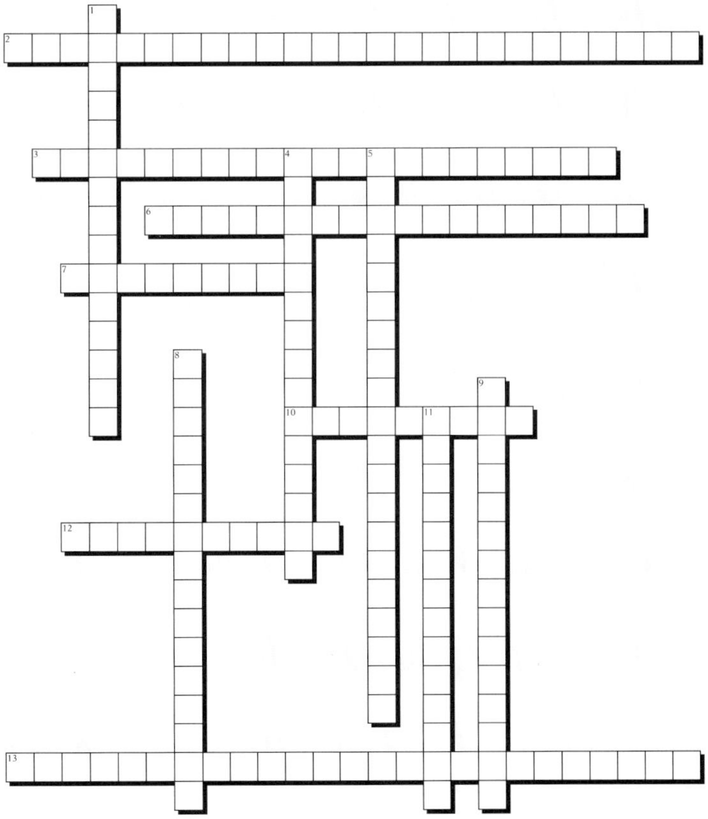

For an interactive crossword puzzle select Crosswords from Tim's Toolbox at http://www.mhhe.com/oleary/CT05.

MULTIPLE CHOICE

Circle the letter or fill in the correct answer.

1. The real issue with technology is _________.
   - **a.** finding qualified individuals
   - **b.** making it better
   - **c.** integrating it with people
   - **d.** teaching it to students
   - **e.** summarizing it for the general society
2. The principal changes technology brings to business are _________, new enterprises, and new customer and supplier relationships.
   - **a.** new computers
   - **b.** new problems
   - **c.** new agencies
   - **d.** new laws
   - **e.** new products
3. The _________ user believes that learning and using computers take time away from their real jobs.
   - **a.** cynical
   - **b.** proactive
   - **c.** frustrated
   - **d.** confused
   - **e.** naive
4. The _________ user believes all problems can be solved by computers.
   - **a.** proactive
   - **b.** optimistic
   - **c.** frustrated
   - **d.** naive
   - **e.** cynical
5. The _________ user does not easily become frustrated and give up using technology.
   - **a.** proactive
   - **b.** cynical
   - **c.** naive
   - **d.** inexperienced
   - **e.** advanced
6. The best advice in regard to specializing is _________.
   - **a.** don't do it
   - **b.** it is a necessity in today's business world
   - **c.** learn one program and learn it well
   - **d.** learn a little about every program
   - **e.** do so to some extent
7. _________ instruct users on the latest software or hardware.
   - **a.** Computer support specialists
   - **b.** Computer technicians
   - **c.** Computer trainers
   - **d.** Database administrators
   - **e.** Data entry workers
8. _________ oversee work of programmers, computer specialists, systems analysts and other computer professionals.
   - **a.** Data entry workers
   - **b.** Desktop publishers
   - **c.** Information systems managers
   - **d.** Network administrators
   - **e.** Programmers
9. _________ prepare instruction manuals, technical reports, and other scientific or technical documents.
   - **a.** Programmers
   - **b.** Software engineers
   - **c.** Systems analysts
   - **d.** Technical writers
   - **e.** Webmasters
10. _________ input customer information, lists, and other types of data.
    - **a.** Data entry workers
    - **b.** Desktop publisher
    - **c.** Information systems managers
    - **d.** Network administrators
    - **e.** Programmers create

MATCHING

Match each numbered item with the most closely related lettered item. Write your answers in the spaces provided.

a. database administrator
b. computer technician
c. computer trainer
d. cynic
e. software engineer
f. frustrated
g. technical writer
h. network administrator
i. proactive
j. programmer
k. systems analyst
l. data entry worker
m. Webmaster

1. A computer specialist employed to evaluate, create, and maintain Web sites. ____
2. Computer user who feels the idea of using microcomputers is overrated. ____
3. Computer user who feels it is an imposition to have to take the time to understand technology. ____
4. Computer user who looks at technology in a positive and realistic way.____
5. Computer professional who creates, tests, and troubleshoots computer programs. ____
6. Computer specialist that inputs customer information, lists, and other types of data. ____
7. Computer specialist who uses database management software to determine the most efficient ways to organize and access data. ____
8. Computer professional who analyzes users' needs and creates application software. ____
9. Computer professional who plans and designs information systems. ____
10. Computer professional who repairs and installs computer components and systems. ____
11. Computer professional who creates and maintains networks. ____
12. Computer professional who instructs users on the latest software or hardware. ____
13. Computer professional who prepares instruction manuals, technical reports, and other scientific or technical documents. ____

OPEN-ENDED

On a separate sheet of paper, respond to each question or statement.

1. Why is strategy important to individual success in the information age? What is your strategy?
2. Describe how technology changes the nature of competition.
3. How can your computer competencies and knowledge help you get ahead in today's market?
4. What does proactive mean? What is a proactive computer user? What advantages does this type of user have over the other types?
5. Discuss several different careers in information technology. Which one(s) are of interest to you?

To test your knowledge of this chapter, select Self Test from Tim's Toolbox at http://www.mhhe.com/oleary/CT05.

USING TECHNOLOGY

1 Jobs Online

Did you know that you can use the Internet to find a job? You can browse through job listings, post resumes for prospective employers, and even use special agents to continually search for that job that's just right for you. To learn more about online job searches, review Making IT Work for You: Locating Job Opportunities Online on pages 612 and 613. Then visit our Web site at http://www.mhhe.com/oleary/CT05 and select Using Technology from Tim's Toolbox. Once at that site, play the video and answer the following questions: (a) What locations and categories were selected for the job search? (b) Describe the process for posting a resume. (c) What search criteria were used to set up the job search agent?

2 Maintain Computer Competence

There are several sources of information to help keep you up to date on current computing trends. Visit our Web site at http://www.mhhe.com/oleary/CT05 and select Using Technology from Tim's Toolbox to link to a few computing sites. Connect to each and explore, and then answer the following: (a) List the sites you visited and describe the focus of each. (b) Which of these sites was most useful? Why? (c) Which of these sites was least useful? Why? (d) What are other ways you can stay in step with current computing issues?

EXPANDING YOUR KNOWLEDGE

Your Career 1

Have you thought about what your career might be? Perhaps it is in marketing, education, or information technology. If you have a career in mind, conduct a Web search to learn more about your chosen career. If you don't have a career in mind, select one of the information systems careers presented in this chapter and conduct a Web search to learn more about that career. After reviewing at least five sites, complete the following: (a) Describe your career of choice. (b) Why did you choose that career? (c) How is information technology used in this career? (d) How will changing technology impact your chosen career?

Resume Advice 2

There are several excellent resources available online to help you write a winning resume. Conduct a Web search using the keywords "resume help" to learn more. Review at least five sites, and then compose a sample resume for yourself applying the information from the sites.

BUILDING YOUR PORTFOLIO

1 Technology Portfolio

As discussed in Chapter 1, a portfolio typically consists of printed material that documents an individual's competence and knowledge. Personal information technology portfolios are often submitted to prospective employers to demonstrate an individual's knowledge and understanding of information technology. Create your personal information technology portfolio by (a) compiling all your responses to the technology-oriented Building Your Portfolio questions that you have completed throughout this term (questions 1 and 2 from each chapter's Building Your Portfolio are technology oriented); (b) adding a coverage page and a table of contents to the front of the paper; (c) adding a summary at the end of the paper; and (d) editing the material so that the topics flow logically (you may need to add additional material) and printing your assembled personal technology portfolio.

2 Information Systems Careers

The U.S. government is anticipating a need for over 1 million information systems workers in the next five years. Write a one-page paper titled "Careers in Information Systems" that addresses the following: (a) List and describe the seven types of careers available in IS. (b) Of those seven, single out one that is of particular interest to you and research it further. What types of companies are seeking this type of employee? What are the job requirements?

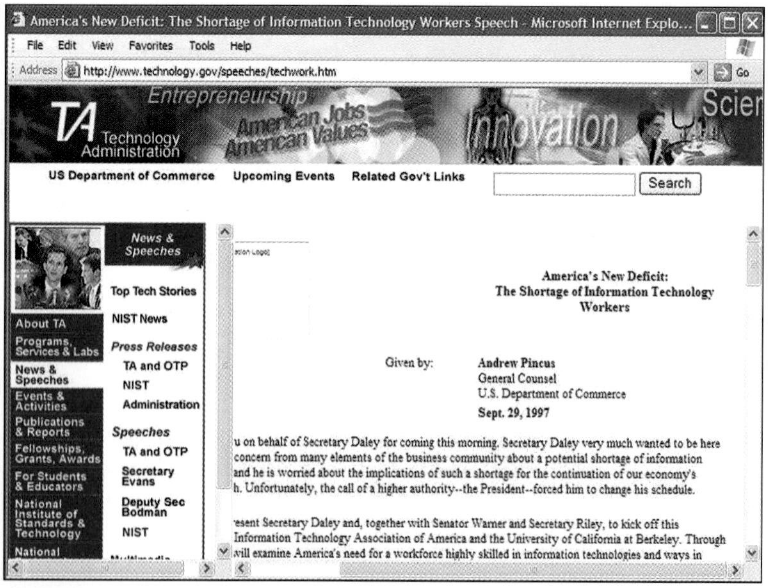

Ethics Portfolio 3

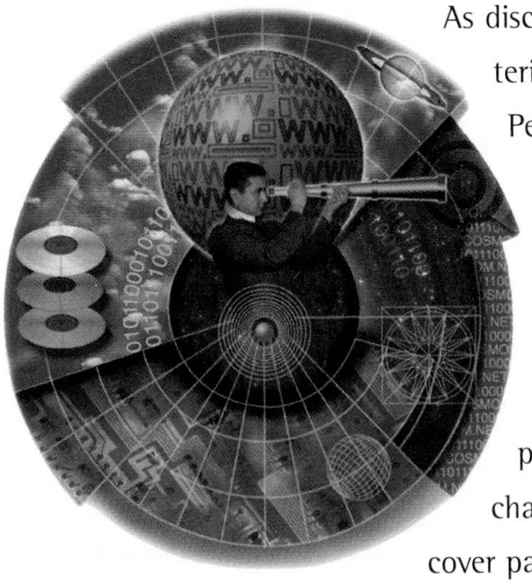

As discussed in Chapter 1, a portfolio typically consists of printed material that documents an individual's competence and knowledge. Personal ethics portfolios relating to information technology can be presented to prospective employers to demonstrate an individual's sensitivity, understanding, and commitment to secure, private, and ethical use of computers. Create your personal ethics portfolio by (a) compiling all your responses to the ethics-oriented Building Your Portfolio questions that you have completed throughout this term (questions 3 and 4 from each chapter's Building Your Portfolio are ethics oriented); (b) adding a cover page and a table of contents to the front of the paper; (c) adding a summary at the end of the paper; and (d) editing the material so that the topics flow logically (you may need to add additional material) and printing your assembled personal ethics portfolio.

Job Offers 4

Consider this scenario, and then answer the questions that follow in a one-page paper: You are at a new job for about six months and have stopped actively seeking new employment when you receive an unsolicited offer for a job that seems a better opportunity. (a) What are your obligations to your present company? (b) What are your obligations to yourself? (c) What would you do in this situation? Defend your answer.

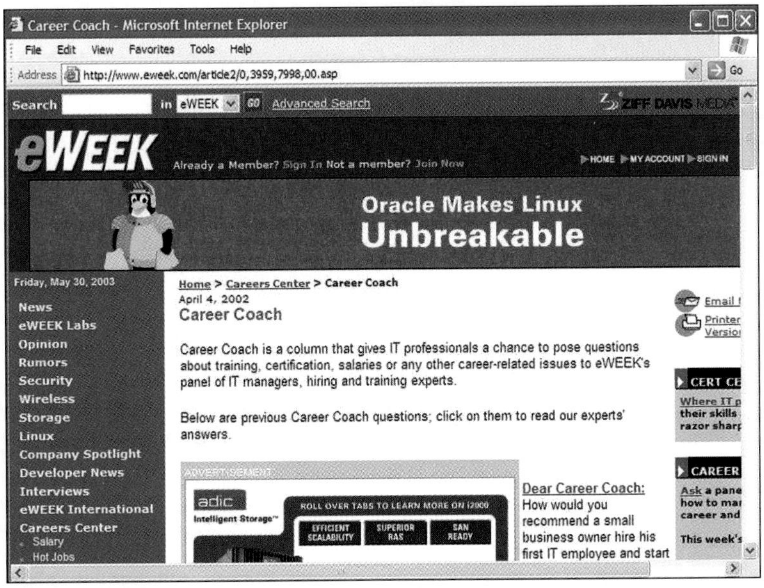

THE EVOLUTION OF THE COMPUTER AGE

Many of you probably can't remember a world without computers, but for some of us, computers were virtually unknown when we were born and have rapidly come of age during our lifetime.

Although there are many predecessors to what we think of as the modern computer—reaching as far back as the 18th century, when Joseph Marie Jacquard created a loom programmed to weave cloth and Charles Babbage created the first fully modern computer design (which he could never get to work)—the Computer Age did not really begin until the first computer was made available to the public in 1951.

The modern age of computers thus spans slightly more than 50 years (so far), which is typically broken down into five generations. Each generation has been marked by a significant advance in technology:

- **First Generation (1951–57):** During the first generation, computers were built with vacuum tubes—electronic tubes that were made of glass and were about the size of light bulbs.

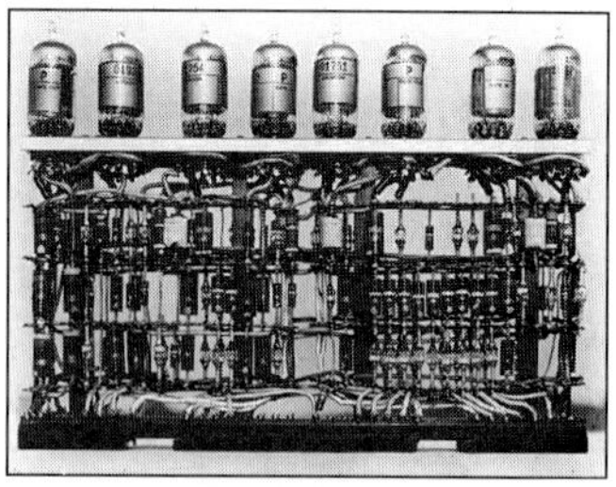

- **Second Generation (1958–63):** This generation began with the first computers built with transistors—small devices that transfer electronic signals across a resistor. Because transistors are much smaller, use less power, and create less heat than vacuum tubes, the new computers were faster, smaller, and more reliable than the first-generation machines.

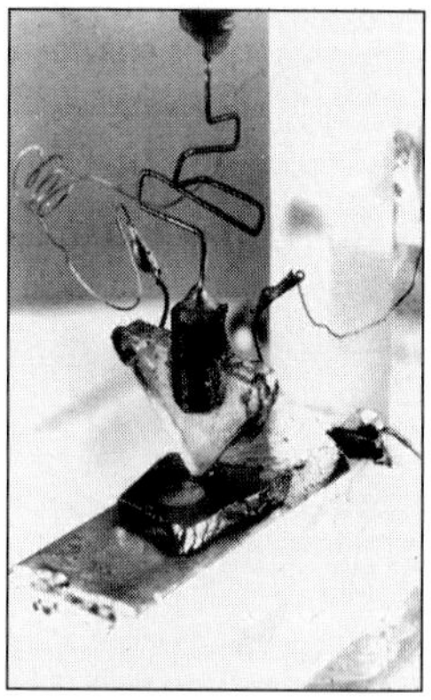

- **Third Generation (1964–69):** In 1964, computer manufacturers began replacing transistors with integrated circuits. An integrated circuit (IC) is a complete electronic circuit on a small chip made of silicon (one of the most abundant elements in the earth's crust). These computers were more reliable and compact than computers made with transistors, and they cost less to manufacture.
- **Fourth Generation (1970–90):** Many key advances were made during this generation, the most significant being the microprocessor—a specialized chip developed for computer memory and logic. Use of a single chip to create a smaller "personal" computer (as well as digital watches, pocket calculators, copy machines, and so on) revolutionized the computer industry.

- **Fifth Generation (1991–2005 and beyond):** Our current generation has been referred to as the "Connected Generation" because of the industry's massive effort to increase the connectivity of computers. The rapidly expanding Internet, World Wide Web, and intranets have created an information superhighway that has enabled both computer professionals and home computer users to communicate with others across the globe.

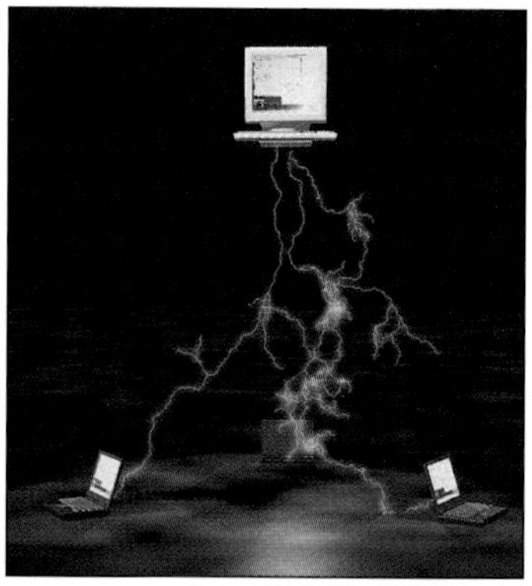

This appendix provides you with a timeline that describes in more detail some of the most significant events in each generation of the Computer Age.

First Generation

The Vacuum Tube Age

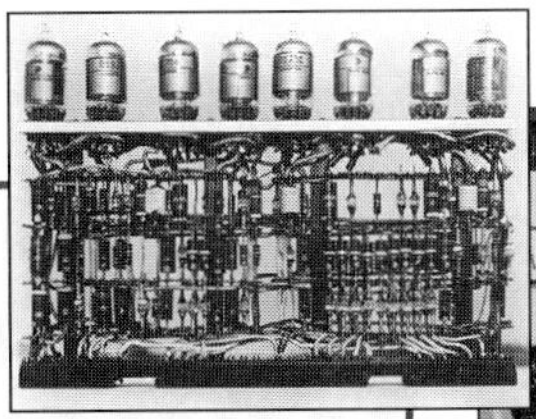

1951 Dr. John W. Mauchly and J. Presper Eckert Jr. introduce the first commercially available electronic digital computer—the UNIVAC—built with vacuum tubes.This computer was based on their earlier ENIAC (Electronic Numerical Integrator and Computer) design completed in 1946.

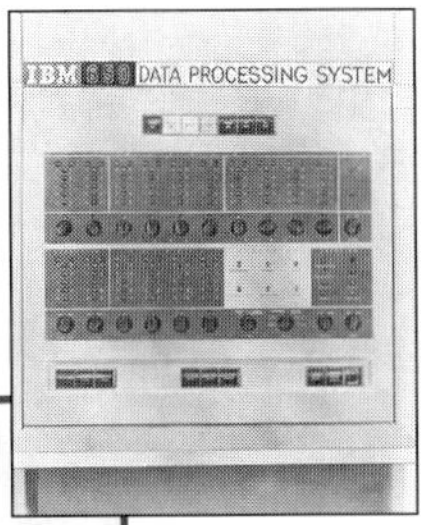

1951–53 IBM adds computers to its business equipment products and sells over 1,000 IBM 650 systems.

1951 1952 1953 1954 1955 1956 1957

1952 Development team led by Dr. Grace Hopper, former U.S. Navy programmer, introduces the A6 Compiler—the first example of software that converts high-level language symbols into instructions that a computer can execute.

1957 Introduction of first high-level programming language—FORTRAN (FORmula TRANslator).

Second Generation

The Transistor Age

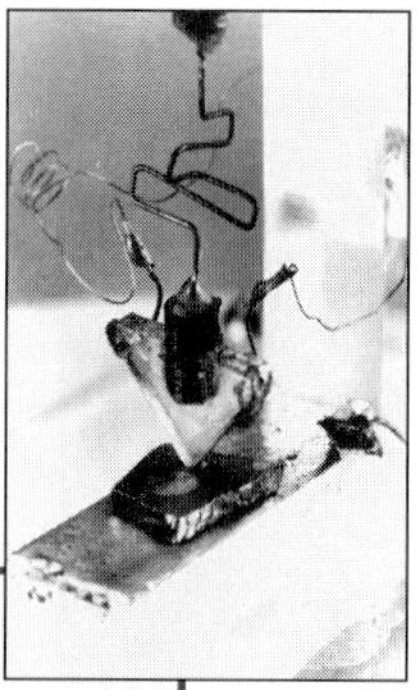

1958 Introduction of computers built with transistors—a 1947 Bell Laboratories invention.

1959 Introduction of the removable disk pack, providing users with fast access to stored data.

1960 Introduction of first business application programming language—COBOL (Common Business Oriented Language)—based on English-like phrases.

1958 1959 1960 1961 1962 1963

1963 Introduction of the first computer industry standard character set—ASCII (American Standard Code for Information Interchange) that enables computers to exchange information.

1959 General Electric Corporation introduces ERMA (Electronic Recording Machine Accounting)—the first technology that can read special characters, such as digitized information.

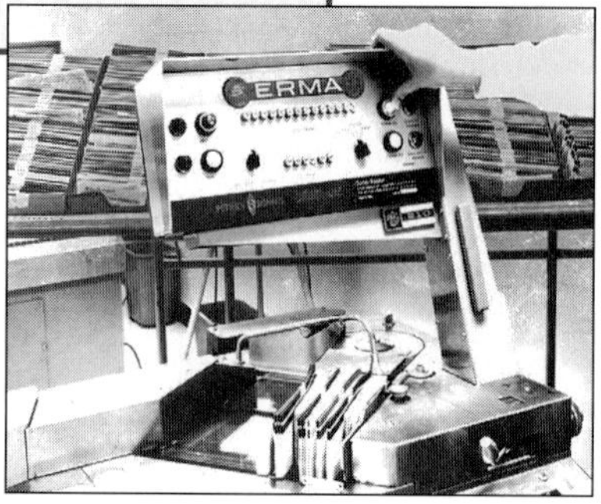

Third Generation

The Integrated Circuit Age

1964 Introduction of computers built with an integrated circuit (IC), which incorporates multiple transistors and electronic circuits on a single silicon chip.

1965 Digital Equipment Corporation (DEC) introduces the first minicomputer.

1969 Introduction of ARPANET and the beginning of the Internet.

1964 1965 1966 1967 1968 1969

1965 Introduction of the BASIC programming language.

1969 IBM announces its decision to offer unbundled software, priced and sold separately from the hardware.

1964 IBM introduces its System/360 line of compatible computers, which can all use the same programs and peripherals.

Fourth Generation

The Microprocessor Age

1970 Introduction of computers built with chips that used LSI (large-scale integration).

1971 Dr. Ted Hoff of Intel Corporation develops a microprogrammable computer chip—the Intel 4004 microprocessor.

1975 First local area network (LAN)—Ethernet—developed at Xerox PARC (Palo Alto Research Center).

1975 The MITS, Inc., Altair becomes the first commercially successful microcomputer, selling for less than $400 a kit.

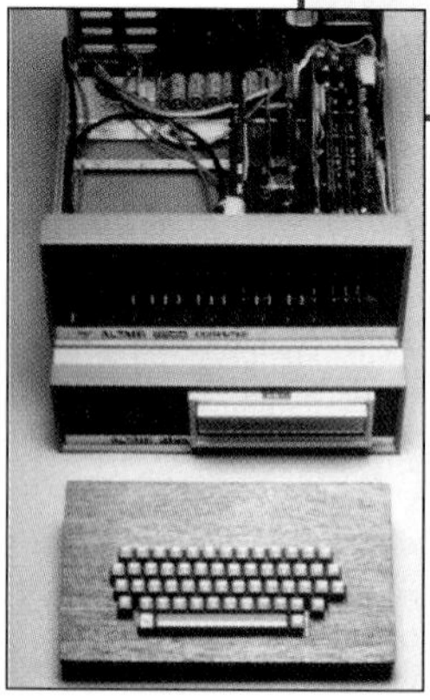

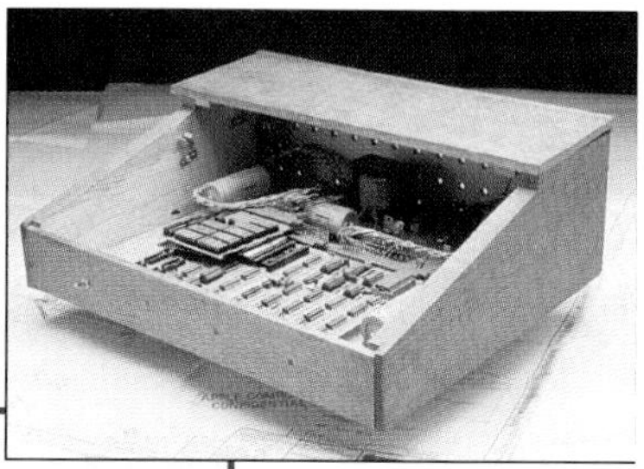

1977 Apple Computer, Inc., founded by Steve Wozniak and Steve Jobs, and Apple I introduced as an easy-to-use "hobbyist" computer.

1979 Introduction of the first public information services—Compuserve and the Source.

1970 1971 1972 1973 1974 1975 1976 1977 1978 1979

1980 IBM asks Microsoft founder, Bill Gates, to develop an operating system—MS-DOS—for the soon-to-be released IBM personal computer.

1981 Introduction of the IBM PC, which contains an Intel microprocessor chip and Microsoft's MS-DOS operating system.

1989 Introduction of Intel 486—the first 1,000,000 transistor microprocessor.

1980 1981 1982 1983 1984 1985 1986 1987 1988 1989 1990

1984 Apple introduces the Macintosh Computer, with a unique, easy-to-use graphical user interface.

1985 Microsoft introduces their Windows graphical user interface.

1990 Microsoft releases Windows 3.0, with an enhanced graphical user interface and the ability to run multiple applications.

Fifth Generation

The Age of Connectivity

1991 Release of World Wide Web standards that describe the framework of linking documents on different computers.

1992 Apple introduces the Newton MessagePad—a personal digital assistant (PDA) that incorporates a pen interface and wireless communications.

1993 Introduction of computer systems built with Intel's Pentium microprocessor.

1995 Intel begins shipping the Pentium Pro microprocessor.

1991 1992 1993 1994 1995

1991 Linus Torvalds, a graduate student at the University of Helsinki, develops a version of UNIX called the Linux operating system.

1993 Introduction of the Mosaic graphical Web browser, which led to the organization of Netscape Communications Corporation.

1995 Microsoft releases Windows 95, a major upgrade to its Windows operating system.

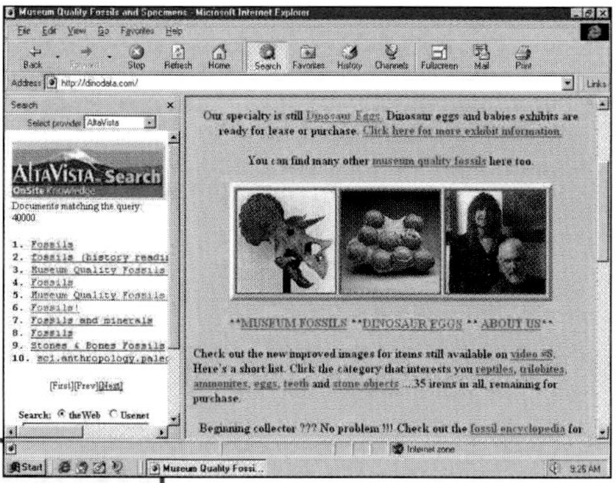

1998 Microsoft releases Office 98 integrated with Internet Explorer 4.0—antitrust legislation intensifies.

1997 Microsoft releases Office 97 with major Web enhancements integrated into its applications.

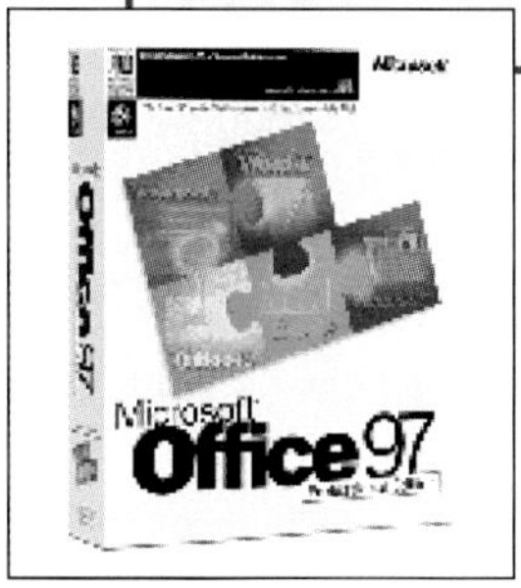

By 2004 A private Internet—Internet2—expected to be completed with higher speed, limited access, and tighter security is in the works. Expected to include advanced virtual reality interfaces called nanomanipulators.

1996 | 1997 | 1998 | 1999 | 2000+

1997 The number of Internet and World Wide Web users estimated at 50 million.

1999 Microsoft releases Office 2000 featuring extensive Web integration and document collaboration—soon followed by Windows 2000.

1996 More than 50 million PCs sold and more than 250 million PCs in use worldwide.

THE BUYER'S GUIDE
How to Buy Your Own Microcomputer System

Some people make snap judgments about some of the biggest purchases in their lives: cars, college educations, houses. People have been known to buy such things based solely on an ad, a brief conversation, or a one-time look. They may be making an impulsive decision about something costing thousands of dollars. Who is to blame, then, if they are disappointed later? They simply didn't take time to check it out.

The same concerns apply in buying a microcomputer system. You can make your choice on the basis of a friend's enthusiasm or a salesperson's promises. Or you can proceed more deliberately, as you would, say, in looking for a job.

FOUR STEPS IN BUYING A MICROCOMPUTER SYSTEM

The following is not intended to make buying a microcomputer an exhausting experience. Rather, it is to help you clarify your thinking about what you need and can afford.

The four steps in buying a microcomputer system are presented on the following pages. We divide each step into two parts on the assumption that your needs may change, but so may the money you have to spend on a microcomputer. For instance, later in your college career or after college graduation, you may want a far more powerful computer system than you need now. At that point you may have more money to spend. Or, if your employer provides you with a computer, you may not need to spend money at all.

STEP 1

What Needs Do I Want a Computer to Serve?
The trick is to distinguish between your needs and your wants. Sure, you *want* a cutting-edge system powerful enough to hold every conceivable program you'll ever need. And you want a system fast enough to process them all at the speed of light. But do you *need* this? Your main concern is to address the two-part question:

- What do I need a computer system to do for me today?
- What will I need it to do for me in another year or two?

The questionnaire at the end of this guide will help you determine the answers to both questions.

Suggestions

The first thing to establish is whether you need a computer at all. Some colleges offer computer facilities at the library or in some dormitories. Or perhaps you can borrow a roommate's. The problem, however, is that when you are up against a term-paper deadline, many others may be also. Then, the machine you want may not be available. To determine the availability of campus computers and network support, call the computer center or the dean of students' office.

Another matter on which you might want advice is what type of computer is popular on campus. Some schools favor Apple Macintoshes, others favor IBMs or IBM-compatibles. If you own a system that's incompatible with most others on campus, you may be stuck if your computer breaks down. Ask someone knowledgeable, who is a year or two ahead of you, if your school favors one system over another.

Finally, look ahead and determine whether your major requires a computer. Business and engineering students may find one a necessity, physical education and drama majors may not. Your major may also determine the kind of computer that's best. A journalism major may want an IBM or IBM-compatible notebook that can be set up anywhere. An architecture major may want a powerful desktop Macintosh with a laser printer that can produce elaborate drawings. Ask your academic advisor for some recommendations.

Example

Suppose you are a college student beginning your sophomore year, with no major declared. Looking at the courses you will likely take this year, you decide you will probably need a computer mainly for word processing. That is, you need a system that will help you write short (10- to 20-page) papers for a variety of courses.

By this time next year, however, you may be an accounting major. Having talked to some juniors and seniors, you find that courses in this major, such as financial accounting, will require you to use elaborate spreadsheets. Or maybe you will be a fine arts or architecture major. Then you may be required to submit projects for which drawing and painting desktop publishing software would be helpful. Or perhaps you will be out in the job market and will be writing application letters and resumes. In that case, you'll want them to have a professional appearance.

STEP 2

How Much Money Do I Have to Spend on a Computer System?

When you buy your first computer, you are not necessarily buying your last. Thus, you can think about spending just the bare-bones amount for a system that meets your needs while in college. Then you might plan to get another system later on. After all, most college students who own cars (quite often used cars) don't consider those the last cars they'll own.

You know what kind of money you have to spend. Your main concern is to answer this two-part question:

- How much am I prepared to spend on a computer system today?
- How much am I prepared to spend in another year or two?

The questionnaire at the end of this guide asks you this.

Suggestions

You can probably buy a good used computer of some sort for under $300 and a printer for under $50. On the other hand, you might spend $1,000 to $2,500 on a new state-of-the-art system. When upgraded, this computer could meet your needs for the next five years.

There is nothing wrong with getting a used system, if you have a way of checking it out. For a reasonable fee, a computer-repair shop can examine it prior to your purchase. Look at newspaper ads and notices on campus bulletin boards for good buys on used equipment. Also try the Internet. Often the sellers will include a great deal of software and other items (disks, reference materials) with the package. If you stay with recognized brands such as Apple, IBM, Compaq, or Dell, you probably won't have any difficulties. The exception may be with printers, which, since they are principally mechanical devices, may get a lot of wear and tear. This is even more reason to tell the seller you want a repair shop to examine the equipment before you buy.

If you're buying new equipment, be sure to look for student discounts. Most college bookstores, for instance, offer special prices to students. Mail-order houses also steeply discount their products. These firms run ads in such periodicals as *Computer Shopper* (sold on newsstands) and other magazines as well as on the Internet. However, using mail and telephone for repairs and support can be a nuisance. Often you can use the prices advertised by a mail-order house to get local retail computer stores to lower their prices.

Example

Perhaps you have access to a microcomputer at the campus student computing center, the library, or the dormitory. Or you can borrow a friend's. However, this computer isn't always available when it's convenient for you. Moreover, you're not only going to college but also working, so both time and money are tight. Having your own computer would enable you to write papers when it's convenient for you. Spending more than $350 might cause real hardship, so a new microcomputer system may be out of the question. You'll need to shop the newspaper classified ads or the campus bulletin boards to find a used but workable computer system.

Or, maybe you can afford to spend more now—say, between $1,000 and $2,000—but probably only $500 next year. By this time next year, however, you'll know your major and how your computer needs have changed. For example, if you're going to be a finance major, you need to have a lot more computer memory (primary storage). This will hold the massive amounts of data you'll be working with in your spreadsheets. Or maybe you'll be an architecture major—or maybe you'll be graduating and looking for a job. In these cases, you may need a laser printer to produce attractive-looking designs or application letters. Thus, whatever system you buy this year you'll want to upgrade next year.

STEP 3

What Kind of Software Will Best Serve My Needs?

Most computer experts urge that you determine what software you need before you buy the hardware. The reasoning here is that some hardware simply won't run the software that is important to you. This is certainly true once you get into *sophisticated* software. Examples include specialized programs available for certain professions (such as certain agricultural or retail-management programs). However, if all you are interested in today are the basic tools of software—word processing, spreadsheet, and communications programs—these are available for nearly all microcomputers. The main caution is that some more recent versions of application software won't run on older hardware. Still, if someone offers you a free computer, don't say no because you feel you have to decide what software you need first. You will no doubt find it sufficient for many general purposes, especially during your early years in college.

That said, you are better served if you follow step 3 after step 2—namely, finding the answers to the two-part question:

- What kind of software will best serve my needs today?
- What kind will best serve my needs in another year or two?

The questionnaire at the end of this guide will help you determine your answers.

Suggestions

No doubt some kinds of application software are more popular on your campus—and in certain departments on your campus—than others. Are freshman and sophomore students mainly writing their term papers in Word, WordPerfect, or Word Pro? Which spreadsheet is most often used by business students: Excel, Lotus 1-2-3, or Quattro Pro? Which desktop publishing program is most favored by graphic arts majors: PageMaker, Ventura Publisher, or Freehand? Do many students use their microcomputers to access the Internet, and, if so, which communications software is the favorite? Do engineering and architecture majors use their own machines for CAD/CAM applications? Start by asking other students and your academic advisor.

If you're looking to buy state-of-the-art software, you'll find plenty of advice in various computer magazines. Several of them rate the quality of newly issued programs. Such periodicals include *InfoWorld, PC World, PC/Computing,* and *MacWorld.*

Example

Suppose you determine that all you need is software to help you write short papers. In that case, nearly any kind of word processing program would do. You could even get by with some older versions or off-brand kinds of word processing software. This might happen if such software was included in the sale of a used microcomputer that you bought at a bargain price.

But will this software be sufficient a year or two from now? Looking ahead, you guess that you'll major in theater arts and minor in screenwriting, which you may pursue as a career. At that point a simple word processing program won't do. You learn from juniors and seniors in that department that screenplays are written using special screenwriting programs. This is software that's not available for some computers. Or, as an advertising and marketing major, you're expected to turn word-processed promotional pieces into brochures. For this, you need desktop publishing software. Or, as a physics major, you discover you will need to write reports on a word processor that can handle equations. In short, you need to look at your software needs not just for today but also for the near future. You especially want to consider what programs will be useful to you in building your career.

STEP 4

What Kind of Hardware Will Best Serve My Needs?

A bare-bones hardware system might include a three-year-old desktop or notebook computer with a 3½-inch floppy disk drive and a hard-disk drive. It should also include a monitor and a printer. With a newer system, the sky's the limit. On the one hand, as a student—unless you're involved in some very specialized activities—it's doubtful you'll really need such things as voice-input devices, touch screens, scanners, and the like. On the other hand, you will probably need speakers and a CD-ROM or DVD-ROM drive. The choices of equipment are vast.

As with the other steps, the main task is to find the answers to a two-part question:

- What kind of hardware will best serve my needs today?
- What kind will best serve my needs in another year or two?

There are several questions on the questionnaire at the end of this guide to help you determine answers to these concerns.

Suggestions

Clearly, you should let the software be your guide in determining your choice of hardware. Perhaps you've found that the most popular software in your department runs on a Macintosh rather than an IBM-compatible. If so, that would seem to determine your general brand of hardware.

Whether you buy IBM or Macintosh, a desktop or a notebook, we suggest you get a 3½-inch floppy disk drive, a hard-disk drive with at least 2 gigabytes of storage, a DVD-ROM drive, at least 128 megabytes of memory, and an ink-jet printer.

As with software, several computer magazines not only describe new hardware but also issue ratings. See *InfoWorld, PC World,* and *MacWorld,* for example.

Example

Right now, let's say, you're mainly interested in using a computer to write papers, so almost anything would do. But you need to look ahead.

Suppose you find that Word seems to be the software of choice around your campus. You find that Word 2000 will run well on a Pentium machine with 8 megabytes of memory and a 1-gigabyte hard disk.

Although this equipment is now outdated, you find from looking at classified ads that there are many such used machines around. Plus, they cost very little—well under $500 for a complete system.

If you're a history or philosophy major, maybe this is all the hardware and software you need. Indeed, this configuration may be just fine all the way through college. However, some majors, and the careers following them, may require more sophisticated equipment. Your choice then becomes: Should I buy an inexpensive system now that can't be upgraded, then sell it later and buy a better one? Or should I buy at least some of the components of a good system now and upgrade it over the next year or so?

As an advertising major, you see the value of learning desktop publishing. This will be a useful if not essential skill once you embark on a career. In exploring the software, you learn that Word includes some desktop publishing capabilities. However, the hardware you previously considered simply isn't sufficient. Moreover, you learn from reading about software and talking to people in your major that there are better desktop publishing programs. Specialized desktop publishing programs like Ventura Publisher are considered more versatile than Word. Probably the best software arrangement, in fact, is to have Word as a word processing program and Ventura Publisher for a desktop publishing program.

To be sure, the campus makes computers that will run this software available to students. If you can afford it, however, you're better off having your own. Now, however, we're talking about a major expense. A computer running a Pentium 4 microprocessor, with 512 megabytes of memory, a DVD-ROM disk drive, and a 10-gigabyte hard disk, plus a modem, color monitor, and laser printer, could cost in excess of $1,500.

Perhaps the best idea is to buy now, knowing how you would like your system to grow in the future. That is, you will buy a microcomputer with a Pentium 4 microprocessor. But at this point, you will buy only an ink-jet printer and not buy a DVD-ROM drive. Next year or the year following, you might sell off the less sophisticated peripheral devices and add a DVD-ROM drive and a laser printer.

DEVELOPING A PHILOSOPHY ABOUT COMPUTER PURCHASING

It's important not to develop a case of "computer envy." Even if you buy the latest, most expensive microcomputer system, in a matter of months something better will come along. Computer technology is still in a very dynamic state, with more powerful, versatile, and compact systems constantly hitting the marketplace. So what if your friends have the hottest new piece of software or hardware? The main question is: Do you need it to solve the tasks required of you or to keep up in your field? Or can you get along with something simpler but equally serviceable?

VISUAL SUMMARY

THE BUYER'S GUIDE: HOW TO BUY YOUR OWN MICROCOMPUTER SYSTEM

NEEDS

What do I need a computer system to do for me today? In another year or two?

I wish to use the computer for:

	Today	1–2 years
Word processing—writing papers, letters, memos, or reports	❑	❑
Business or financial applications—balance sheets, sales projections, expense budgets, or accounting problems	❑	❑
Record-keeping and sorting—research bibliographies, scientific data, or address files	❑	❑
Graphic presentations of business, scientific, or social science data	❑	❑
Online information retrieval to campus networks, service providers, or the Internet	❑	❑
Publications, design, or drawing for printed newsletters, architectural drawing, or graphic arts	❑	❑
Multimedia for video games, viewing, creating, presenting, or research	❑	❑
Other (specify): ________	❑	❑

BUDGET

How much am I prepared to spend on a system today? In another year or two?

I can spend:

	Today	1–2 years
Under $500	❑	❑
Up to $1,000	❑	❑
Up to $1,500	❑	❑
Up to $2,000	❑	❑
Up to $2,500	❑	❑
Over $3,000 (specify):__________	❑	❑

Buying a Microcomputer System

Step	Questions
1	*My needs:* What do I need a computer system to do for me today? In another year or two?
2	*My budget:* How much am I prepared to spend on a system today? In another year or two?
3	*My software:* What kind of software will best serve my needs today? In another year or two?
4	*My hardware:* What kind of hardware will best serve my needs today? In another year or two?

To help clarify your thinking about buying a microcomputer system, complete the questionnaire by checking the appropriate boxes.

SOFTWARE

What kinds of software will best serve my needs today? In another year or two?

The application software I need includes:

	Today	1–2 years
Word processing—Word, WordPerfect, Word Pro, or other (specify): ________	❑	❑
Spreadsheet—Excel, Lotus 1-2-3, Quattro Pro, or other (specify): ________	❑	❑
Database—Access, Paradox, Approach, or other (specify): ________	❑	❑
Presentation graphics—PowerPoint, Freelance, CorelPresentations, or other (specify): ________	❑	❑
Browsers—Netscape Navigator, Microsoft Internet Explorer, or other (specify): ________	❑	❑
Other—integrated packages, software suites, graphics, multimedia, Web authoring, CAD/CAM, other (specify): ________	❑	❑

The system software I need:

	Today	1–2 years
Windows 98	❑	❑
Windows 2000	❑	❑
Windows XP	❑	❑
Mac OS	❑	❑
UNIX	❑	❑
Other (specify):__________	❑	❑

HARDWARE

What kinds of hardware will best serve my needs today? In another year or two?

The hardware I need includes:

	Today	1–2 years
Microprocessor—Pentium 4, Pentium III, Apple G4, other (specify): ________	❑	❑
Memory—(specify amount): ________	❑	❑
Monitor—size (specify): ________	❑	❑
Floppy disk drives—3½" and/or Zip (specify): ________	❑	❑
Optical disk drive—CD-ROM, DVD-ROM (specify type, speed, and capacity): ________	❑	❑
Hard-disk drive—(specify capacity): ________	❑	❑
Portable computer—laptop, notebook, subnotebook, personal digital assistant (specify): ________	❑	❑
Printer—ink-jet, laser, color (specify): ________	❑	❑
Other—modem, network card, speakers, fax, surge protector (specify): ________	❑	❑

THE UPGRADER'S GUIDE
How to Upgrade Your Microcomputer System

If you own a microcomputer, chances are that your machine is not the latest and greatest. Microcomputers are always getting better—more powerful and faster. While that is a good thing, it can be frustrating trying to keep up.

What can you do? If you have lots of money, you can simply buy a new one. Another alternative is to upgrade or add new components to increase the power and speed of your current microcomputer. You probably can increase your system's performance at a fraction of the cost of a new one.

THREE STEPS IN UPGRADING A MICROCOMPUTER SYSTEM

The following is not intended to detail specific hardware upgrades. Rather, it is intended to help you clarify your thinking about what you need and can afford.

The three steps in upgrading a microcomputer system are presented on the following pages. Each step begins by asking a key question and then provides some suggestions or factors to consider when responding to the question.

STEP 1

Is It Time to Upgrade?

Almost any upgrade you make will provide some benefit; the trick is determining if it is worth the monetary investment. It is rarely practical to rebuild an older computer system into a newer model piece by piece. The cost of a complete upgrade typically far exceeds the purchase price of a new system. But if your system is just a piece or two away from meeting your needs, an upgrade may be in order.

Clearly defining what you hope to gain with an upgrade of some of your system's hardware will enable you to make the most relevant and cost-effective selections. Before deciding what to buy, decide what goal you hope to accomplish. Do you want to speed up your computer's performance? Do you need more space to save your files? Is it a new component you'd like to add, such as a DVD-ROM drive?

Suggestions

A good place to start is the documentation on the packaging of any software you use or plan to use. Software manufacturers clearly label the minimum requirements to use their product. These requirements are usually broken down into categories that relate to specific pieces of hardware. For instance, how much RAM (random access memory) does a new program require? How much hard disk space is needed? Keep in mind these ratings are typically the bare minimum. If your system comes very close to the baseline in any particular category, you should still consider an upgrade.

Another thing to investigate is whether there is a software solution that will better serve your needs. For instance, if you are looking to enhance performance or make more room on your hard disk, there are diagnostic and disk optimization utility programs that may solve your problem. In Chapter 5, we discuss a variety of utility programs, such as Norton SystemWorks, that monitor, evaluate, and enhance system performance and storage capacity.

Typical objectives of an upgrade are to improve system performance, increase storage capacity, or add new technology.

STEP 2

What Should I Upgrade?

Once you have clearly defined your objectives, the focus shifts to identifying specific components to meet those objectives.

Suggestions

If your objective is to improve performance, three components to consider are RAM, the microprocessor, and expansion cards. If your objective is to increase storage capacity, two components to consider are hard-disk drive and Zip disk drive. If you are adding new technology, consider the capability of your current system to support new devices.

Performance

If you want to increase the speed of your computer, consider increasing the amount of RAM. In most cases, this upgrade is relatively inexpensive and will yield the highest performance result per dollar invested. How much your system's performance will increase depends on how much RAM you start with, the size of programs you run, and how often you run large programs.

Another way to increase speed is to replace your system's microprocessor. Processor speed is measured in gigahertz (GHz). This rating is not a direct measurement of how fast the processor works, but rather gives you a general idea of how it compares to other processors. (Computing magazines such as *PC World* often publish articles comparing the relative effectiveness of different processors.) The concept behind a microprocessor upgrade is simple: A faster processor will process faster. This is often an expensive upgrade and not as cost-effective as increasing RAM.

If you are looking at upgrading for a specific type of application, perhaps an expansion card is your answer. Expansion cards connect to slots on the system board, provide specialized support, and often free up resources and increase overall system performance. For example, if you run graphics-intensive programs, such as a drafting program or a video game, a video-card upgrade may be a good buy. An upgraded video card can be used to support higher resolution displays, handle all video data, and speed up overall system performance.

Storage Capacity

It's not hard to know when it's time to upgrade your storage capacity. If you frequently have to delete old files to make way for new ones, then it is probably time for more space. A larger or an additional hard drive is usually the solution. Two things to consider when comparing new hard drives are (1) size, which is usually rated in gigabytes (GB) of data the drive can hold, and (2) seek time, which is a rating of the average time it takes the drive to access any particular piece of data.

If you are storing a lot of data that you no longer use, such as old term papers, you might consider adding a Zip drive. This is usually cheaper and is a good way to archive and transport data. Access time is slower than from a hard drive, so this is an option best suited for infrequently used data or for backing up data.

New Technology

Perhaps you are not looking to modify existing hardware, but would like to add a new device. Examples include large high-resolution monitors, DVD-ROM drives, and high-speed printers.

The key consideration is whether the new device will work with your existing hardware. The requirements for these devices are typically printed on the outside packaging. If not, then refer to the product's operating manuals. Obviously, if your current system cannot support the new technology, you need to evaluate the cost of the new device plus the necessary additional hardware upgrades.

STEP 3

Who Should Do the Upgrade?

Once you've decided that the cost of the upgrade is justified and you know what you want to upgrade, the final decision is who is going to do it. Basically, there are two choices. You can either do it yourself or pay for professional installation.

Suggestions

The easiest way, and many times the best way, is to have a professional perform the upgrade. If you select this option, be sure to include the cost of installation in your analysis. If you have had some prior hardware experience or are a bit adventurous, you may want to save some money and do it yourself.

Visit a few computer stores that carry the upgrades you have selected. Most stores that provide the parts will install them as well. Talk with their technical people, describe your system (better yet, bring your system unit to the store), and determine the cost of professional installation. If you are thinking of doing it yourself, ask for their advice. Ask if they will provide assistance if you need it.

If you decide to have the components professionally installed, get the total price in writing and inquire about any guarantees that might exist. Before leaving your system be sure that it is carefully tagged with your name and address. After the service has been completed, pay by credit card and thoroughly test the upgrade. If it does not perform satisfactorily, contact the store and ask for assistance. If the store's service is not satisfactory, you may be able to have your credit card company help to mediate any disputes.

VISUAL SUMMARY

THE UPGRADER'S GUIDE: HOW TO UPGRADE YOUR MICROCOMPUTER SYSTEM

Upgrading a Microcomputer System	
Step	**Questions**
1	*Needs:* Is it time to upgrade? What do I need that my current system is unable to deliver?
2	*Analysis:* What should I upgrade? Will the upgrade meet my needs and will it be cost-effective?
3	*Action:* Who should do the upgrade? Should I pay a professional or do it myself?

NEEDS

Is it time to upgrade? What do I need that my current system is unable to deliver?

I am considering an upgrade to:

- ❑ **Improve performance because**
  - ❑ My programs run too slow
  - ❑ I cannot run some programs I need
- ❑ Increase storage capacity because
  - ❑ I don't have enough space to store all my files
  - ❑ I don't have enough space to install new programs
  - ❑ I need a secure place to back up important files
  - ❑ I'd like to download large files from the Internet
- ❑ **Add new technology**
  - ❑ Zip drive
  - ❑ DVD-ROM
  - ❑ High-performance monitor
  - ❑ Printer
  - ❑ TV tuner card
  - ❑ Enhanced video card
  - ❑ Enhanced sound card
  - ❑ Other________________

ANALYSIS

What should I upgrade? Will the upgrade meet my needs and will it be cost-effective?

I will improve:

- ❑ **Performance by**
  - ❑ Adding random-access memory (RAM)
    Current RAM (MB) _________
    Upgrade to _________
    Cost $_________
    Expected improvement _________
    Other factors _________
  - ❑ Replacing the current microprocessor
    Current processor _________
    Upgrade processor _________
    Cost $_________
    Expected improvement _________
    Other factors _________
  - ❑ Adding an expansion card
    Type _________
    Purpose _________
    Cost $_________
    Expected improvement _________
    Other factors _________
- ❑ **Storage capacity by**
  - ❑ Adding a hard disk drive
    Current size (GB) _________
    Upgrade size (GB) _________
    Cost $_________
    Expected improvement _________
    Other factors _________
  - ❑ Adding a Zip disk drive
    Upgrade size (GB) _________
    Cost $_________
    Type _________
    Expected improvement _________
    Other factors _________
- ❑ **Functionality by adding**
  New technology _________
  System requirements _________
  Cost $_________
  Expected improvement _________
  Other factors _________

To help clarify your thinking about upgrading a microcomputer system, complete the questionnaire by checking the appropriate boxes.

ACTION

Who should do the upgrade? Should I do it myself or should I pay a professional?

The two choices are:

❑ **Professional installation**

The easiest way, and many times the best way, is to have a professional perform the upgrade. If you select this option, be sure to include the cost of installation in your analysis. Pay with a credit card, and make sure your system is tagged with your name and address before you part with it.

❑ **Do-it-yourself installation**

If you have had some prior hardware experience or are a bit adventurous, you may want to save some money and do it yourself. Avoid touching sensitive electronic parts and be sure to ground yourself by touching an unpainted metal surface in your computer.

Glossary

1.44 MB 3½-inch disk: The amount of data a floppy disk holds; equal to 350 typewritten pages.

3GLs (third generation languages): High-level procedural language. *See* Procedural languages.

4GLs (fourth generation languages): Very high level or problem-oriented languages. *See* Problem-oriented languages.

5GLs (fifth generation languages): *See* Fifth generation language.

802.11: *See* WiFI (wireless fidelity).

A

A drive: Floppy disk drive is designated as the A drive.

AC adapters: Notebook computers use AC adapters that are typically outside the system unit. They plug into a standard wall outlet, convert AC to DC, provide power to drive the system components and can recharge batteries.

Accelerated Graphics Port (AGP): A type of bus line that is dedicated to the acceleration of graphics performance.

Access: Refers to the responsibility of those who have data and to control who is able to use that data.

Access speed: *See* Access time.

Accessibility hardware: *See* Assistive devices.

Access time: Measures the amount of time required by the storage device to retrieve data and programs.

Accounting: The organizational department that records all financial activity from billing customers to paying employees.

Accounts payable: The activity that shows the money a company owes to its suppliers for the materials and services it has received.

Accounts receivable: The activity that shows what money has been received or is owed by customers.

Accuracy: Relates to the responsibility of those who collect data to ensure that the data is correct.

Active-matrix: Type of flat-panel monitor in which each pixel is independently activated. More colors with better clarity can be displayed; also known as thin film transistor (TFT) monitors.

Ad network cookies: Cookies that monitor your activities across all sites you visit and are continually active in collecting information on your Web activities.

Adapter card: *See* Expansion card.

Address: Located in the header of an e-mail message, the e-mail address of the persons sending, receiving, and optionally, anyone else who is to receive copies.

Advanced Research Project Agency Network (ARPANET): A national computer network from which the Internet developed.

Advanced transfer cache: Built into the microprocessor providing faster responses than cache located on the system board.

Adware cookie: *See* Ad Network Cookies.

Agent: Programs called agents, spiders, and bots continually look for new information to update search engines and databases.

Alignment: Text is positioned or aligned between margins or indents in 4 ways: left, centered, right, and justified.

Allocation unit: *See* cluster.

Alternating current (AC): Current from standard wall outlets.

Alternative keyboards: Designed to allow those with limited mobility to enter data and text. See large print keyboards, one- handed keyboards, and Braille keyboards.

Alternative mouse: These devices accept foot and/or head movements to control the mouse pointer and to select commands.

ALU: *See* Arithmetic-logic unit.

Analog signal: Signals that represent a range of frequencies, such as the human voice. They are a continuous electronic wave signal as opposed to a digital signal that is either on or off. To convert the digital signals of your computer to analog and vice versa, you need a modem. Another cable connects the modem to the telephone wall jack.

Analytical graphs or charts: Form of graphics used to put numeric data into objects that are easier to analyze, such as bar charts, line graphs, and pie charts.

Animation: Feature involving special visual and sound effects like moving pictures, audio, and video clips that play automatically when selected.

Antivirus programs: Programs that guard a computer system from viruses or other damaging programs.

Applets: Web pages contain links to programs called applets, written in a programming language called Java. These programs are used to add interest to a Web site by presenting animation, displaying graphics, providing interactive games, etc.

Application generation subsystem: Provides tools to create data entry forms and specialized programming languages that interface or work with common languages, such as COBOL.

Application generator: Or otherwise called program coder that provides modules of pre-written code to accomplish various tasks, such as calculation of overtime pay.

Application server: A dedicated server providing resources using the applications necessary to run that particular business.

Application service provider (ASP): Provides access to a wide range of application programs on the Internet and generally charges for their service.

Application software: Software that can perform useful work, such as word processing, cost estimating, or accounting tasks. The user primarily interacts with application software.

Applications: Programs, such as word processing and spreadsheets.

Aqua: As part of the Mac OS X operating system, Aqua is an instinctual user interface providing photo-quality icons and easy-to-use menus.

Arithmetic operations: Fundamental math operations: addition, subtraction, multiplication, and division.

Arithmetic-logic unit (ALU): The part of the CPU that performs arithmetic and logical operations.

Artificial intelligence (AI): A field of computer science that attempts to develop computer systems that can mimic or simulate human thought processes and actions.

Artificial reality: *See* Virtual reality.

ASCII (American Standard Code for Information Interchange): Binary coding scheme widely used on all computers, including microcomputers. Eight bits form each byte and each byte represents one character.

Assembly language: A step up from machine language, using names instead of numbers. These languages use abbreviations or mnemonics, such as ADD, that are automatically converted to the appropriate sequence of 1s and 0s.

Assistive devices: Also known as accessibility hardware, which allows those with visual or other physical impairments to use computers and access the Internet.

Asymmetric digital subscriber line (ADSL): One of the most widely used types of telephone high-speed connections (DSL).

Asynchronous communications port: Or RS-232C connector used to receive serial transmission through a serial port. *See* serial data transmission.

Attachment: A file, such as a document or worksheet that is attached to an e-mail message.

Attributes: A data field represents an attribute (description or characteristic) of some entity (person, place, thing, or object). For example, an employee is an entity with many attributes including their last name, address, phone, etc.

Auction house sites: Web sites that operate like a traditional auction to sell merchandise to bidders.

Audio editing software: Allows you to create and edit audio clips like filtering out pops and scratches in an old recording.

Audio input: The human voice and music are examples of audio input. *See* audio input device.

Audio input device: Converts sound into a form that can be processed by the computer. A microphone is an example of an audio input device.

Audio output: Converted digital signals from the system into analog sounds audible to humans, such as music played from speakers or voice output.

Audio-output devices: Devices, such as speakers and headphones, that translate audio information from the computer into sounds that people can recognize and understand.

AutoComplete: As user begins to enter specified words or phrases, AutoComplete will finish the text and enter it into the document at the user's request.

AutoContent wizard: This Microsoft wizard steps you through the process of creating a PowerPoint presentation.

AutoCorrect: A feature that automatically makes corrections for you.

Automated design tool: Software package that evaluates hardware and software alternatives according to requirements given by the systems analyst. Also called computer-aided software engineering (CASE) tools.

AutoText: Previously specified words or phrases can be directly inserted into a document upon the user's request.

B

Backbone: *See* Bus.

Background: Programs you are not using are running in the background.

Backup: A utility program that helps protect you from the affects of a disk failure by making a copy of selected or all files that have been saved onto a disk.

Balance sheet: Lists the overall financial condition of an organization.

Bandwidth: Bandwidth determines how much information can be transmitted at one time. It is a measurement of capacity of the communication channel. There are three bandwidths: voiceband, medium band, and broadband.

Bar code: Code consisting of vertical zebra-striped marks printed on product containers, read with a bar-code reader.

Bar-code reader: Photoelectric scanner that reads bar codes for processing. *See* Scanning devices.

Base station: *See* Wireless receiver.

Basic applications: *See* General-purpose applications.

Batch processing: Processing performed all at once on data that have been collected over time.

Beta testing: Testing by a select group of potential users in the final stage of testing a program.

Binary coding schemes: The representation of characters as 0s and 1s, or "off" and "on" electrical states, in a computer. Two of the most popular Binary coding schemes use eight bits to form each byte as in the ASCII and EBCDIC codes.

Binary system: Numbering system in which all numbers consist of only two digits; 0 and 1.

Biometric scanning: Devices that check fingerprints or retinal scans.

Bit (binary digit): Each 1 or 0 is a bit, short for binary digit.

Bitmap images: Graphic file in which images are made up of thousands of dots (pixels). *See* Paint programs.

Bits per second (bps): Speed at which data is transferred.

Blog: An easily updated personal page used as a diary of events. Some blogs are used for business or advocacy capacities but the majority of blogs are personal sites that share feelings and experiences in a public forum.

Bluetooth: This is recent wireless technology that allows nearby devices to communicate without the connection of cables or telephone systems.

Booting: Starting or restarting your computer.

Bot: Short for Robot. *See* Agent.

Braille display: Output device that uses specialized software to "read" text on a computer screen and then display the text on a type of monitor with moving Braille symbols.

Braille keyboards: Use keys identified by raised dots.

Braille printer: Also known as Braille embossers that work like dot-matrix printers to output Braille on printed pages.

Bricks and mortar: Actual business locations with standard business hours when sellers are open, as opposed to e-commerce when buyers and sellers can purchase goods any time of the day or night on their computer.

Broadband: Bandwidth that includes microwave, satellite, coaxial cable, and fiber-optic channels. It is used for very high-speed computers.

Broadcast radio: Communication using transceivers to send and receive signals from wireless devices.

Browser: Special Internet software connecting you to remote computers, opens and transfers files, displays text and images, and provides an uncomplicated interface to the Internet and Web documents. Examples of Browsers are Internet Explorer and Netscape Navigator.

Brush: Used to fill an area or object with a color.

Buddy: *See* Friend.

Builds: Used to display each bullet point, text, paragraph or graphic independently of the other text or objects on the slide.

Bulleted list: The sequence of topics arranged on a page and organized by bullets.

Bus: All communication travels along a common connecting cable called a bus or a backbone. As information passes along the bus, it is examined by each device on the system board to see if the information is intended for that device. *See* Bus line and Ethernet.

Bus line: Electronic data roadway, connecting the parts of the CPU to each other and linking the CPU with other important hardware, along which bits travel. The common connecting cable in a bus network.

Bus network: Also known as Ethernet. Network in which all communications travel along a common connecting cable called a bus. Each device in the network handles its own communications control. There is no host computer or file server.

Bus width: The number of bits travelling simultaneously down a bus is the bus width.

Business suite: *See* Productivity suite.

Business-to-business (B2B): A type of electronic commerce that involves the sale of a product or service from one business to another. This is typically a manufacturer-supplier relationship.

Business-to-consumer (B2C): Type of electronic commerce that involves the sale of a product or service to the general public or end users.

Button: A special area you can click to make links that "navigate" through a presentation.

Byte: Unit consisting of eight bits. There are 256 possible bit combinations in a byte and each byte represents one character.

C

C drive: For most systems the internal hard drive is designated as the C drive. Used to store programs and large data files such as the operating system and application programs like Word and Excel.

Cable: Cords used to connect input and output devices to the system unit.

Cable modem: Allows all digital communication, which is a speed of 27 million bps.

Cache memory: Area of random-access memory (RAM) set aside to store the most frequently accessed information. Cache memory improves processing by acting as a temporary high-speed holding area between memory and CPU allowing the computer to detect which information in Ram is most frequently used.

Calendar: Electronic appointment book that keeps track of events, holidays, assignments, project schedules, and more.

Capacity: Capacity is how much data a particular storage medium can hold and another characteristic of secondary storage.

Carder: Criminal who steals credit cards over the Internet.

Carpal tunnel syndrome: Disorder found among frequent computer users, consisting of damage to nerves and tendons in the hands. *See also* Repetitive strain injury.

Carrier package: The material that chips are mounted on which then plug into sockets on the system board.

Cathode-ray tube (CRT): Desktop-type monitor built in the same way as a television set. The most common type of monitor for office and home use. These monitors are typically placed directly on the system unit or on the top of the desk.

CD: *See* Compact disc.

CD Burner: Also known as CD-R drive. They can write to a CD-recordable only once, and is used to record custom music.

CD-R: Stands for CD-recordable and this optical disk can be written to only once. After that it can be read many times without deterioration but cannot be written on or erased. Used to create custom music CD's and to archive data.

CD-R/DVD: DVD players identified as CD-R/DVD also read CD format.

CD-ROM (compact disc-read-only memory): Optical disk that allows data to be read but not recorded. Used to distribute large databases, references and software application packages.

CD-ROM jukeboxes: See DVD-ROM jukeboxes.

CD-RW (compact disc-rewriteable): A reusable, optical disk that is not permanently altered when data is recorded. Used to create and edit large multimedia presentations.

Cell: The space created by the intersections of a vertical column and a horizontal row within worksheets in a program like Microsoft Excel. A cell can contain text or numeric entries.

Cellular phone systems: Links car phones and portable phones.

Center aligning: Centering text on a page to create a balanced appearance. Click center in the toolbar and all text will be automatically centered. Align left, align right and justify are other commands to adjust text.

Center for European Nuclear Research (CENR): In Switzerland, where the Web was introduced in 1992.

Central processing unit (CPU): Part of the computer that holds data and program instructions for processing the data. The CPU consists of the control unit and the arithmetic-logic unit. In a microcomputer, the CPU is on a single electronic component called a microprocessor chip.

CGI (Common Gateway Interface): Whenever you complete a form or provide information at a web site, the data is recorded by the web site's database. Programs called CGI scripts create input forms that accept your input, and send the data to the Web database.

Chain printer: An expensive high-speed machine typically used within organizations to serve several computers connected by a network or a mainframe computer requiring large quantities of printed output.

Channel: Topic for discussion in a chat group. You can communicate live with others by typing words on your computer once you've selected a channel or topic and other members immediately see those words on their computer and can respond.

Character: A single letter, number, or special character, such as a punctuation mark or $.

Character and mark recognition device: Specialty devices that are able to recognize special characters and marks.

Character based interface: In older operating systems the user communicated with the operating system through written commands such as "Copy A: assign.doc to C:".

Character effect: Change appearance of font characters by using bold, italic, shadows, and colors.

Chart: Displaying numerical data in a work sheet as a pie chart or a bar chart, making it easier to understand.

Chart types: In creating charts in Word or Excel, select a chart type that might show each month's projected sales for example. Using Word to create a chart, go to Insert; Object; Create New and then click Microsoft Graph 2000 Chart.

Chassis: The metal casing that houses the computer components. *See* System Unit.

Chat group: An online discussion group that allows direct "live" communication.

Checklist: In analyzing data a list of questions helps guide the systems analyst and end user through key issues for the present system.

Child node: A node one level below the node being considered in a hierarchical database or network. *See* Parent node.

Chip: A tiny circuit board etched on a small square of sandlike material called silicon. A chip is also called a silicon chip, semiconductor, or integrated circuit.

Chlorofluorocarbons (CFCs): Toxic chemicals found in solvents and cleaning agents. Chlorofluorocarbons can travel into the atmosphere and deplete the earth's ozone layer.

CISC: *See* Complex instruction set computer chip.

Clarity: Indicated by the resolution, or amount of pixels, on a monitor. The greater the resolution, the better the clarity.

Classes: In an object-oriented database, classes are similar objects grouped together.

Client: A node that requests and uses resources available from other nodes. Typically, a client is a user's microcomputer.

Client operating system: A type of desktop operating system that works with a network's operating system (NOS) to share and coordinate resources.

Client/server network system: Network in which one powerful computer coordinates and supplies services to all other nodes on the network. Server nodes coordinate and supply specialized services, and client nodes request the services.

Clip art: Graphic illustrations representing a wide variety of topics.

Clock rate: *See* Clock Speed.

Clock speed: Also called clock rate. It is measured in gigahertz or billions of beats per second. The faster the clock speed, the faster the computer can process information and execute instructions.

Closed architecture: Computer manufactured in such a way that users cannot easily add new devices.

Cluster: Smallest amount of disk space that can be read from or written to a floppy disk is a cluster or allocation unit.

Coaxial cable: High-frequency transmission cable that replaces the multiple wires of telephone lines with a single solid-copper core. It is used to deliver television signals as well as to connect computers in a network.

Code: Writing a program using the appropriate computer language.

Coding: Actual writing of a computer program, using a programming language.

Cold boot: Starting the computer after it has been turned off.

Cold site: Special emergency facility in which hardware must be installed but is available to a company in the event of a disaster to its computer system. *Compare* Hot site.

Collaboration: A number of people helping to create a draft or document depending on their field of expertise.

Color capability: Ability to choose between printing in black and white or color.

Color scheme: Combination for complimentary colors to apply to a slide background, text, and other elements.

Column: Using Microsoft Excel for example, a vertical block of cells is one cell wide all the way down the worksheet.

Combination devices: Combines features of input devices such as scanners with features of output devices like printers. Also known as multifunctional devices such as fax machines, Internet telephony, and terminals.

Combination key: Keys such as the *Ctrl* key that perform an action when held down in combination with another key.

Commerce server: *See* Web storefront creation packages.

Common data item: In a relational database, all related tables must have a common data item or key field.

Common operational database: Contains details about the operations of the company, such as inventory, production and sales.

Common user database: Company database that contains selected information from both the common operational database and from outside (proprietary) databases.

Communication: Process of sharing data, programs and information between two or more computers.

Communication aids: A combination of strategies is used to allow disabled individuals to interact with a computer and with others. Such input devices incorporate pictures ands symbols and can be programmed with spoken words and phrases.

Communication channel: The actual connecting medium that carries the message between sending and receiving devices. This medium can be a physical wire, cable, or a wireless connection.

Communication device: Computer systems that communicate with other computer systems using modems. For example, it modifies computer output into a form that can be transmitted across standard telephone lines.

Communication server: Dedicated server performing specific tasks in relation to communications between computers.

Communication systems: Electronic systems that transmit data over communications lines from one location to another.

Compact disc (CD): Widely used optical disk format. It holds 650 MB (megabytes) to 1 GB (gigabyte) of data on one side of the CD.

Compact disc rewritable: *See* CD-RW.

Compact disc-read only memory: *See* CD-ROM.

Company database: Also called shared databases. Stored on a mainframe, users throughout the company have access to the database through their microcomputers linked by a network.

Compiler: Software that converts the programmer's procedural-language program (source code) into machine language (object code). This object code can then be saved and run later.

Complementary metal-oxide semiconductor (CMOS): A CMOS chip provides flexibility and expandability for a computer system. Unlike RAM, it does not lose its contents if power is turned off and unlike ROM, its contents can be changed.

Complex instruction set computer (CISC) chip: The most common type of microprocessor that has thousands of programs written specifically for it. Intel's Pentium and Itanium are CISC chips.

Computer Abuse Amendments Act of 1994: Outlaws transmission of viruses and other harmful computer code.

Computer-aided design (CAD): Type of program that manipulates images on a screen.

Computer-aided design/computer-aided manufacturing (CAD/CAM): Knowledge work systems that run programs to integrate the design and manufacture activities. CAD/CAM is widely used in manufacturing automobiles.

Computer-aided software engineering (CASE) tool: A type of software development tool that helps provide some automation and assistance in program design, coding and testing. *See* Automated design tool.

Computer competency: Becoming proficient in computer-related skills.

Computer crime: Illegal action in which a perpetrator uses special knowledge of computer technology. Criminals may be employees, outside users, hackers and crackers, and organized crime members.

Computer ethics: Guidelines for the morally acceptable use of computers in our society.

Computer Fraud and Abuse Act of 1986: Law allowing prosecution of unauthorized access to computers and databases.

Computer knowledge: Understanding how technology works.

Computer Matching and Privacy Protection Act of 1988: Law setting procedures for computer matching of federal data for verifying eligibility for federal benefits or for recovering delinquent debts.

Computer monitoring software: The most invasive and dangerous type of spyware. These programs record every activity made on your computer, including credit card numbers, bank account numbers, and e-mail messages.

Computer network: Communications system connecting two or more computers and their peripheral devices to exchange information and share resources.

Computer output microfilm (COM) recorder: Microscopic images of documents stored on microfilm and microfiche are produced by a COM recorder.

Computer support specialist: Specialists include technical writers, computer trainers, computer technicians, and help desk specialists who provide technical support to customers and other users.

Computer technician: Specialist who installs hardware and software as well as trouble-shoots problems for users.

Computer trainer: Computer professional who provides classes to instruct users.

Computer Virus: Destructive programs that can come in e-mail attachments and Spam.

Conceptualization: Multidimensional databases and hyper cubes provide users with an intuitive model where by complex data and relationships can be compartmentalized which is an advantage over relational databases.

Connecting lines: Called bus lines that provide pathways to support communication among the various electronic components that are either located on the system board or attached to the system board.

Connection device: A device that acts as an interface between sending and receiving devices and the communication channel.

Connectivity: Capability of the microcomputer to use information from the world beyond one's desk. Data and information can be sent over telephone or cable lines and through the air so that computers can talk to each other and share information.

Consumer-to-consumer (C2C): A type of electronic commerce that involves individuals selling to individuals.

Contact: *See* Friend.

Contacts: Electronic address book that is linked to other parts of a PIM to save you time and energy.

Continuous-speech recognition system: Voice-recognition system with the ability to distinguish between same-sounding words by evaluating the context within which individual words are used.

Control unit: Section of the CPU that tells the rest of the computer how to carry out program instructions.

Controller card: *See* Expansion card.

Conversion: Also known as Systems implementation, which has four approaches to conversion: direct, parallel, pilot and phased. *See* Systems implementation.

Convertible tablet pc: Notebook computer with a monitor that swivels and folds onto its keyboard.

Cookie-cutter programs: Specialized programs that allow users to selectively filter or block the most intrusive ad network cookies while allowing selective traditional cookies to operate.

Cookies: Programs that record information on Web site visitors.

Coprocessor: Specialized processing chips designed to improve specific computer operations such as the graphics coprocessor.

Cordless mouse: A battery-powered mouse that typically uses radio waves or infrared light waves to communicate with the system unit. Also known as wireless mouse.

Cracker: One who gains unauthorized access to a computer system for malicious purposes.

Criteria: Set of conditions used to sort data in database management systems.

Cryptographer: Designs, tests, and researches encryption procedures.

Cumulative trauma disorder: *See* Repetitive strain injury.

Cybercash: *See* Electronic cash.

Cybermall: A place to visit on the Internet that provides access to a variety of different stores where you can make purchases.

Cyberspace: The Internet moves your ideas and information from one place to another through cyberspace. The space of electronic movement of ideas and information.

Cylinder: Hard disks store and organize files using tracks, sectors and cylinders. A cylinder runs through each track of a stack of platters. Cylinders differentiate files stored on the same track and sector of different platters.

Cynic: Individual who feels that the idea of using a microcomputer is overrated and too troublesome to learn.

D

DAT (digital audio tape): Tape cartridge with a capacity of 40GB.

Data: Raw, unprocessed facts that are input to a computer system that will give compiled information when the computer processes those facts. Data are also defined as facts or observations about people, places, things, and events.

Data administration subsystem: Helps manage the overall database including maintaining security, providing disaster recovery support, and monitoring the overall performance of database operations.

Data banks: *See* Proprietary database.

Data definition subsystem: This system defines the logical structure of the database by using a data dictionary.

Data dictionary: Dictionary containing a description of the structure of data in a database.

Data entry worker: Inputs customer information, lists, and other types of data.

Data flow diagram: Diagram showing data or information flow within an information system.

Data integrity: Database characteristics relating to the consistency and accuracy of data.

Data labels: Draws viewer's attention to selected pieces of information in a chart.

Data maintenance: Maintaining data includes adding new data, deleting old data, and editing existing data.

Data manipulation: Entering someone's computer network, leaving a seemingly harmless message but it's against the law.

Data manipulation subsystem: Provides tools to maintain and analyze data.

Data mining: Technique of searching data warehouses for related information and patterns.

Data model: Defines rules and standards for all data in a database. There are five data models: hierarchical, network, relational, multidimensional, and object-oriented. For example, Access uses the relational data model.

Data organization: Data is organized in groups of characters, fields, record files, databases, logical groups or categories.

Data processing system (DPS): Transaction processing system that keeps track of routine operations and records these events in a database. Also called transaction processing system (TPS).

Data projector: Specialized devices, similar to slide projectors, that connect to microcomputers and project computer output.

Data redundancy: A common database problem in which data is duplicated and stored in different files.

Data security: Protection of software and data from unauthorized tampering or damage.

Data transmission specifications: The rules and procedures that coordinate sending and receiving devices by precisely defining how messages will be sent across communication channels.

Data warehouse: Data collected from a variety of internal and external databases and stored in a database called a data warehouse. Data mining is then used to search these databases.

Data workers: People involved with the distribution and communication of information, such as secretaries and clerks.

Database: A collection of related information, like employee names, addresses and phone numbers. It is organized in a way that a computer program can quickly select the desired pieces of information and display them for you.

Database administrator (DBA): Uses database management software to determine the most efficient way to organize and access data.

Database file: File containing highly structured and organized data created by database management programs.

Database management system (DBMS): To organize, manage and retrieve data. DBMS programs have five subsystems: DBMS engine, data definition, data manipulation, applications generation, and data administration. An example of a database management system is Microsoft Access. *See* Database manager.

Database manager: Software package used to set up, or structure, a database such as an inventory list of supplies. It also provides tools to edit, enter, and retrieve data from the database.

Database server: Dedicated server that shares resources with other computers regarding tracking and storing vast amounts of information in databases.

Database types: Databases are classified into five types: individual, company, distributed, proprietary, and Web.

DataPlay: An optical write-once format, similar to CD-R, designed for optical disks with a capacity of 500 MB or enough to hold 5 hours of CD-quality sound. It is a specialized format used for music and digital photography.

DBMS engine: Provides a bridge between the logical view of data and the physical view of data.

DBMS structures: Organizations defined by data models.

Debugging: Programmer's word for testing and then eliminating errors in a program. Programming errors are of two types: syntax and logic errors.

Decision model: The Decision Model gives the Decision Support System its analytical capabilities. There are three types of models included in the Decision model: Tactical, Operational, and Strategic model.

Decision support system (DSS): Flexible tool for analysis helping managers make decisions about unstructured problems, such as effects of events and trends outside the organization.

Decision table: Table showing decision rules that apply when certain conditions occur and what action should take place as a result.

Decoding: Translating instructions and data into a form that can be processed. *See* Instruction cycle.

Dedicated server: Specializes in performing specific tasks like application server, database server, print server, and more.

Demand report: A demand report is produced on request. An example is a report on the numbers and types of jobs held by women and minorities done at the request of the government.

Demodulation: Process performed by a modem in converting analog signals to digital signals.

Denial of service attack (DoS): A variant virus in which Web sites are overwhelmed with data, resulting in the inability for users to access the Web site. Unlike a worm that self-replicates, a DoS attack floods a computer or network with requests for information and data.

Density: Refers to how tightly the bits (electromagnetic charges) can be packed next to one another on a floppy disk.

Design templates: Provides professionally selected combinations of color schemes, slide layouts, and special effects.

Desk checking: Process of checking out a computer program by studying a printout of the program line-by-line, looking for syntax and logic errors.

Desktop: The screen that is displayed on the monitor when the computer starts up. All items and icons on the screen are considered to be on your desktop and are used to interact with the computer.

Desktop computer: Computer small enough to fit on top or along the side of a desk and yet too big to carry around.

Desktop manager: *See* Personal Information Managers.

Desktop operating systems: *See* Stand-alone operating systems.

Desktop publishing: Program that allows you to mix text and graphics to create publications of professional quality.

Desktop system unit: A system unit that typically contains the system's electronic components and selected secondary storage devices. Input and output devices, such as the mouse, keyboard, and monitor, are located outside the system unit.

Destination file: A document in which a linked object is inserted. The object is created in the source file and then inserted into the new file, called the destination file.

Device driver: Every device that is connected to the computer has a special program associated with it called a device driver, which allows communication between the operating system and the device.

DHTML (Dynamic HTML): Improves HTML by including animations, interaction, and dynamic updating, which would automatically refresh the content.

Diagnostic utility: *See* Troubleshooting utility.

Dialog box: Provides additional information and requests user input.

Dial-up service: Method of accessing the Internet using a high-speed modem and standard telephone lines.

Dictation mode: Allows users to dictate text directly into a word document.

Digital: Computers are digital machines because they can only understand one's and zero's. It is either on or off. For example, a digital watch states the exact time on the face, whereas an analog watch has the second hand moving in constant motion as it tells the time.

Digital camera: Similar to a traditional camera except that images are recorded digitally in the camera's memory rather than on film.

Digital cash: *See* Electronic cash.

Digital notebook: An input device that records and stores pen movements. For example, notes you might take in a class can later be processed, edited, and used with a word processing program.

Digital signal: Computers can only understand digital signals. Before processing can occur within the system unit, a conversion must occur from what we understand (analog) to what the system unit can electronically process (digital). *See* Analog signal.

Digital subscriber line (DSL): Provides high-speed connection using existing telephone lines.

Digital versatile disc: *See* DVD.

Digital versatile disc-read only memory: A type of DVD disk providing over two hours of high-quality video and sound comparing to a motion picture theatre.

Digital versatile disk (DVD): A type of optical disk similar to CD-ROMs except that more data can be packed into the same amount of space.

Digital video camera: Input device that records motion digitally.

Digital video disc: *See* DVD (digital versatile disc).

Digitizing Device: These devices convert a sketch or a figure into a form that can be processed by a computer. Examples are graphic tablets and digital notebooks.

Direct access: A fast approach to external storage, provided by disks, where information is not in a set sequence.

Direct approach: Approach for systems implementation whereby the old system is simply abandoned for the new.

Direct current (DC): All computer hardware requires direct current (DC) to power their electronic components. DC power is provided by converting alternating current (AC) from standard outlets using a power supply or directly from batteries.

Direct file organization: File organization that makes use of key fields to go directly to the record being sought rather than reading records one after another.

Direct Rambus DRAM (Direct RDRAM): Fastest and most expensive DRAM chip.

Directories: Provide access to content organized into categories such as the arts, business and computers.

Directory search: A search engine option that provides a directory or list of categories or topics to choose from, such as Arts & Humanities, Business & Economics, or Computers & Internet, that help you narrow your search until a list of Web sites appears.

Disaster recovery plan: Plan used by large organizations describing ways to continue operations following a disaster until normal computer operations can be restored.

Discrete-speech recognition system: Voice-recognition system that allows users to dictate directly into a computer using a microphone. These systems are not able to distinguish between same-sounding words.

Discussion Group: Using e-mail to communicate in groups with people you do not know, but with whom you would like to share ideas and interests.

Disk: *See* Floppy disk; Hard disk; Optical disk.

Disk caching: Method of improving hard-disk performance by anticipating data needs. Frequently used data is read from the hard disk into memory (cache). When needed, data is then accessed directly from memory, which has a much faster transfer rate than from the hard disk. Increases performance by as much as 30 percent.

Disk cleanup: A windows troubleshooting utility that eliminates nonessential files.

Disk defragmenter: Windows utility that optimizes disk performance by eliminating unnecessary fragments and by rearranging files.

Disk Drives: Secondary storage devices for saving data, programs, and information.

Diskette: *See* Floppy disk.

Display: Displaying on the computer screen the information asked for from a database.

Display screen: Or screens, present visual images of text and graphics.

Distributed data processing system: In a network, computers that perform processing tasks at their own dispersed locations while also sharing programs, data, and other resources with each other.

Distributed database: Database that can be made accessible through a variety of communications networks, which allows portions of the database to be located in different places.

Distributed processing: System in which computing power is located and shared at different locations.

DLT (digital linear tape): Most expensive tape cartridge with a capacity of 110 GB.

Dock: The Mac OS X operating system features the "Dock" which is a new way of visually organizing applications, documents, Web sites, and more.

Document: Any kind of text material.

Document file: File created by a word processor to save documents such as letters, research papers, and memos.

Documentation: Written descriptions and procedures about a program and how to use it. *See* Program Documentation.

Domain code: Last part of an Internet address, which identifies the geographical description or organizational identification. For example, using www.aol.com, the .com is the domain code and indicates it is a commercial site.

Domain name: The second part of the URL and is the name of the server where the resource is located. For example www.mtv.com.

Domain name system (DNS): Internet addressing method that assigns names and numbers to people and computers. Because the numeric IP addresses are difficult to remember, the DNS system was developed to automatically convert text-based addresses to numeric IP addresses.

DoS: *See* Denial of Services attacks.

Dot-matrix printer: A type of printer that forms characters and images using a series of small pins on a print head. Used where high-quality output is not required.

Dots-per-inch (dpi): Printer resolution is measured in dpi. The higher the dpi, the better the quality of images produced.

Dot pitch: Distance between each pixel. The lower the dot pitch, the shorter the distance between pixels, and the higher the clarity of images produced.

Double data rate SDRAM (DDR SDRAM): Also known as SDRAM II. Faster and more reliable than SDRAM. Able to transfer twice as much data in the same amount of time as SDRAM.

DO UNTIL structure: Loop structure in programming that appears at the end of a loop. The DO UNTIL loop means that the loop statements will be executed at least once. In other words, this program tells you to DO option one UNTIL it is no longer true.

DO WHILE structure: Loop structure in programming that appears at the beginning of a loop. The DO WHILE loop will keep executing as long as there is information to be processed. For example, DO option one WHILE (or as long as) option one remains true.

Downlink: Refers to receiving data from a satellite.

Downloading: Process of transferring information from a remote computer to the computer one is using.

Draw program: Program used to help create artwork for publications. *See also* Illustration program.

Driver: *See* Device driver.

Drop-down menu: *See* Pull-down menu.

Dual-scan monitor: *See* Passive-matrix monitor.

Dumb terminal: Terminal that can be used to input and receive data but cannot process data independently. It is used to gain access to information. An example is the type of terminals airline reservation clerks use.

DVD (digital versatile, or video disc): Similar to CD-ROMs except that more data can be packed into the same amount of space. DVD drives can store 4.7 GB to 17 GB on a single DVD disk or 17 times the capacity of CDs.

DVD player: Also known as DVD-ROM drives. *See* DVD.

DVD rewriteable (DVD+RW): A type of reusable DVD disk and is more flexible than the DVD-RAM. DVD+RW is able to create and read CD disks along with creating and editing large-scale multimedia presentations.

DVD-R: *See* DVD recordable and Write once DVD-R.

DVD+R: See Write once DVD-R.

DVD+RW: *See* DVD-rewriteable.

DVD-RW: Another format to record and erase repeatedly. Able to create and read CD disks. Also known as DVD-rewritable.

DVD-random-access memory (DVD-RAM): A high capacity, maximum performance disk that allows the user to read the information, write over it and erase the data if necessary. Use like a floppy disk by copying, deleting files, and running programs. It has up to 8 times the storage capacity of a CD and can also be used to read CD and DVD formats.

DVD-recordable (DVD-R): A recordable DVD disk for large amounts of data.

DVD-ROM: Digital versatile disc-read-only memory. Used to distribute full-length feature films with theatre-quality video and sound.

DVD-ROM jukeboxe: Device that provides automatic access to a collection or library of optical disks.

Dynamic RAM: See Dynamic Random Access Memory (DRAM).

Dynamic Random Access Memory (DRAM): A Ram chip that requires a constant supply of power to refresh and retain its contents.

E

E-banking: *See* Online banking.

EBCDIC (Extended Binary Coded Decimal Interchange Code): Binary coding schemes that are a standard for minicomputers and mainframe computers.

E-book: Handheld, book-sized devices that display text and graphics. Using content downloaded from the web or special cartridges, these devices are used to read newspapers, magazines and books.

E-book reader: *See* E-book.

E-cash: *See* Electronic cash.

E-Commerce: Buying and selling goods over the Internet.

Economic feasibility: Justifying the costs of a new system to the benefits it promises.

Editing: Features that modify a document such as using a Thesaurus, find and replace, or spell check.

E-Learning: A web application allowing anyone to take classes on any subject and at all levels on the Internet.

Electronic book: *See* E-book.

Electronic cash (e-cash): Currency for Internet purchases. Buyers purchase e-cash from a third party (a bank that specializes in electronic currency) by transferring funds from their banks.

Electronic commerce (e-commerce): Buying and selling of goods over the Internet.

Electronic Communications Privacy Act of 1986: Law protecting the privacy of users on public electronic-mail systems.

Electronic Mail: Transmission of electronic messages over the Internet. Also known as E-mail.

Electronic monitoring: Workers whose performance is monitored electronically rather than by human supervisors.

Electronic profiles: Using publicly and privately available databases, information resellers create electronic profiles, which are highly detailed and personalized descriptions of individuals.

E-mail: Communicate with anyone in the world who has an Internet address or e-mail account with a system connected to the Internet. You can include a text message, graphics, photos, and file attachments.

Embedded object: Information inserted into a destination file of another application that becomes part of that file. Double clicking the object in the destination file causes the object to run.

Embedded operating system: An operating system that is completely stored within the ROM (read only memory) memory of the device that it is in; used for hand-held computers and smaller devices like PDAs.

Encrypting: Coding information so that only the user can read or otherwise use it.

End user: Person who uses microcomputers or has access to larger computers.

End user's sketch: Document the desired format and content for a program's output.

Energy Star: Program created by the Environmental Protection Agency to discourage waste in the microcomputer industry.

Enhanced integrated drive electronics (EIDE) controller card: A type of hard disk controller that can support as many as four separate hard disk drives. *See* hard disk controller card.

Enterprise storage system: Using mass storage devices, a strategy is designed for organizations to promote efficient and safe use of data across the networks within their organizations.

Entity: In an object-oriented database, a person, place, thing, or event that is to be described.

Environment: The computer industry has responded to the Energy Star program designed by the Environmental Protection Agency to discourage waste in the microcomputer industry. The Green PC has been the result.

Erasable optical disk: Optical disk on which the disk drive can write information and also erase and rewrite information. Also known as CD-RW or compact disc rewritable.

E-retailing: *See* Online shopping.

Ergonomic keyboards: Keyboard arrangement not rectangular with a palm rest, which is designed to alleviate wrist strain.

Ergonomics: Study of human factors related to things people use. It is concerned with fitting the job to the worker rather than forcing the worker to contort to fit the job.

E-tailing: *See* online shopping.

Ethernet: Otherwise known as Ethernet Bus or Ethernet LAN. The Ethernet bus is the pathway or arterial to which all nodes (PC's, file servers, print servers, web servers, etc.) are connected. All of this is connected to a Local Area Network (LAN) or a Wide Area Network (WAN). *See* Bus Network.

Ethernet LAN: *See* Ethernet.

Ethics: Standards of moral conduct.

E-time: *See* Execution time.

E-trading: *See* online stock trading.

Exception report: Report that calls attention to unusual events.

Executing: Carrying out the commands. *See* Instruction cycle.

Execution time: Also known as E-time, it is the time required to decode and execute the instruction. *See* Instruction cycle.

Executive information system (EIS): Sophisticated software that can draw together data from an organization's databases in meaningful patterns and highly summarized forms.

Executive support system (ESS): *See* Executive information system.

Expansion bus: Connects the CPU to slots on the system board. There are different types of expansion buses such as Industry standard architecture (ISA), Peripheral component interconnect (PCI), Accelerated graphics port (AGP), Universal bus (USB) and FireWire buses. *See* system bus.

Expansion card: Optional device that plugs into a slot inside the system unit to expand the computers' abilities. Ports on the system board allow cables to be connected from the expansion board to devices outside the system unit.

Expansion slot: Provides connections for expansion cards to the system board. *See* Expansion card.

Expert system: Computer program that provides advice to decision makers who would otherwise rely on human experts. It's a type of artificial intelligence that uses a database to provide assistance to users.

Extended graphics array: *See* XGA.

External cache: Slower than Level 1(L1) cache but has a greater capacity.

External data: Data gathered from outside an organization. Examples are data provided by marketing research firms.

External modem: Modem that stands apart from the computer and is connected by a cable to the computer's serial port.

Extranet: Private network that connects more than one organization.

F

Facsimile Transmission Machine: *See* Fax Machine.

FAQ (frequently asked questions): Many web sites have a FAQ page that provides answers to commonly asked questions.

Fast infrared (FIR): *See* Infrared data association (IrDA).

Fax machine: Device that scans an image and sends it electronically over telephone lines to a receiving fax machine, which converts the electronic signals back to an image and recreates it on paper.

Fetching: Retrieving a program instruction or data element from memory. *See* Instruction cycle.

Fiber-optic cable: Special transmission cable made of glass tubes that are immune to electronic interference. Data is transmitted through fiber-optic cables in the form of pulses of light.

Field: Each column of information within a record is called a field. A field contains related information on a specific item like employee names within a company department.

Fifth generation language (5GL): Computer language that incorporates the concept of artificial intelligence to allow direct human communication. *See* Visual programming languages.

File: A collection of related records that can store data and programs. Such as, the payroll file would include payroll information (records) for all of the employees (entities).

File compression: Process of reducing the storage requirements for a file.

File compression programs: Programs that reduce the size of files so as to require less storage on the computer and can be sent more efficiently over the Internet. Examples of such programs are Win Zip and Wizard.

File decompression: Process of expanding a compressed file.

File server: Dedicated computer with large storage capacity providing users access to shared folders or fast storage and retrieval of information used in that business.

File transfer protocol (FTP): Internet service for uploading and downloading files.

Filter: A filter will locate or display records from a table that fit a set of conditions or criteria when using programs like Excel.

Filter: Program to block selected Web sites, set time limits, monitor use, and generates reports on use. Such as programs parents will use to block children from selected sites.

Filter: When using programs like Paint and Photoshop, a filter creates special effects and textures to your pictures.

Find and replace: An editing tool that finds a selected word or phrase and replaces it with another. Click edit, find.

Firewall: Security hardware and software. All communications into and out of an organization pass through a special security computer called a proxy server in order to protect all systems against external threats.

FireWire Bus: They operate much like USB buses on the system board but at higher speeds.

FireWire port: Used to connect high-speed printers and even videocameras to system unit.

Firmware: *See* ROM.

Fixed disk: *See* Internal hard disk.

Flaming: A discussion group term meaning insulting, putting down, or attacking.

Flash: An interactive animation program from Macromedia that is usually full screen and highly dynamic, displaying moving text or complicated interactive features.

Flash memory card: A solid-state storage device widely used in notebook computers. Flash memory is also used in a variety of specialized input devices to capture and transfer data to desktop computers.

Flash RAM: RAM chips that retain data even when power is disrupted. Flash RAM is an example of solid-state storage and is typically used to store digitized images and record MP3 files.

Flat Panel Monitor: Or Liquid Crystal Display (LCD) monitor. These monitors are much thinner than CRT's and can be used for desktop systems as well.

Flatbed scanner: An input device similar to a copying machine.

Flexible disk: *See* Floppy disk.

Flexible keyboards: Fold or rollup for easy packing or storage designed for mobile users who want a full size keyboard.

Floppies: *See* Floppy disk.

Floppy disk: Flat, circular piece of magnetically treated mylar plastic that rotates within a jacket. A floppy disk is 3½ inches and holds 1.44 MB of information. It is a portable or removable secondary storage device.

Floppy-disk cartridge: They all require special disk drives. They include Zip disks, SuperDisks, and HiFD disks, all competing to become the next higher capacity floppy disk standard.

Floppy Disk Drive (FDD): Stores data programs by altering the electromagnetic charges on the disk's surface to represent one's and zero's. The Floppy Drive retrieves the data by reading these charges from the magnetic disk.

Folder: A named area on a disk that is used to store related subfolders and files.

Font: Also known as typeface, is a set of characters with a specific design.

Font size: The height of a character measured in points with each point being 1/72 inch.

Footer: Page numbers and other document related information located at the bottom of the page.

Footnote: A reference note automatically numbered and formatted at the bottom of the page the reference occurs.

Foreground: Programs you are currently working in are running in the foreground.

Form: Electronic forms reflecting the contents of one record or table. Primarily used to enter new records or make changes to existing records.

Format: Features that change the appearance of a document like font, font sizes, character effects, alignment, and bulleted and numbered lists.

Formatting: The process of adapting a floppy disk to the type of microcomputer and disk drive that you are using.

Formatting language: Also known as presentation language that use symbols, words, and phrases that instruct a computer on how to display information to the user. For example, HTML is a formatting language used to display web pages.

Formatting toolbar: A collection of buttons used as shortcuts to commands that enhance the appearance of a document. Generally located on the second row under the menu bar, you can format text to be bold or underlined, or change the font, etc.

Formula: Instructions for calculations in a spreadsheet. It is an equation that performs calculations on the data contained within the cells in a worksheet or spreadsheet.

Fragmented: Storage technique that breaks up large files and stores the parts wherever space is available in adjacent sectors and clusters.

Frame: A separate scrollable window on a web page that would provide a table of contents for the site with links to various areas within the site as if viewing information from two or more pages simultaneously.

Freedom of Information Act of 1970: Law giving citizens the right to examine data about them in federal government files, except for that restricted for national security reasons.

Friend: To use instant messaging, you specify a list of friends (also known as buddies or contacts) and register with an instant messaging server.

Frustrated: Person who feels it is an imposition to have to learn something new like computer technology.

Full-duplex communication: Data is transmitted back and forth at the same time, making it the fastest and most efficient form of two-way communication.

Function: A built-in formula in a spreadsheet that performs calculations automatically.

Fuzzy logic: Used by expert systems to allow users to respond by using qualitative terms, such as *great* and *OK*.

G

Gas discharge display: *See* gas plasma monitors.

Gas plasma monitors: Contain millions of pixels illuminated by charged neon gas. They are flat screens with no distortion, plasma displays and commonly used in home theatres and HDTV's. Also known as plasma display and gas discharge display.

General ledger: Activity that produces income statements and balance sheets based on all transactions of a company.

General-purpose applications: Applications used for doing common tasks, such as browsers and word processors, spreadsheets, databases, management systems and presentation graphics. Also known as basic applications and productivity applications.

Generations of programming languages: The five generations are machine languages, assembly languages, procedural languages, problem-oriented languages, and natural languages. *See* Levels.

Gigahertz: Billions of beats per second.

Global positioning: Satellite communication network of 24 satellites owned by the Defense Department that continuously sends location information to earth.

Global positioning system (GPS): Devices use location information to determine the geographic location of your car for example.

GNOME: A Linux interface providing a free, user-friendly suite of applications and easy-to-use desktop. It is also web developer friendly with large amounts of developer documentation.

Gnutella: Widely used peer-to-peer network system for sharing all kinds of files including music files.

Goal seek: Allows you to set a goal and then will analyze other parts of the workbook that would need to be adjusted to meet that goal.

Graffiti: A handwriting recognition system included in the Palm OS.

Grammar checker: In word processing, a tool that identifies poorly worded sentences and incorrect grammar.

Graphic Card: *See* Video Card.

Graphic tablet: Records sketches and tracings using a special graphics surface or tablet and a special stylus.

Graphical map: Diagram of a Web site's overall design.

Graphical user interface (GUI): Special screen that allows software commands to be issued through the use of graphic symbols (icons) or pull-down menus.

Graphics: Tool for creating and importing graphic elements.

Graphics coprocessor: Designed to handle requirements related to displaying and manipulating 2-D and 3-D graphic images.

Graphics suite: Group of graphics programs offered at lower cost than if purchased separately like CorelDraw.

Green PC: Microcomputer industry concept of an environmentally friendly, low-power-consuming machine.

Grid chart: Chart that shows the relationship between input and output documents.

Group decision support system (GDSS): System used to support the collective work of a team addressing large problems.

H

Hacker: Person who gains unauthorized access to a computer system for the fun and challenge of it.

Half-duplex communication: Data flows in both directions but not simultaneously. In other words, data flows in only one direction at any one time.

Handheld computer: *See* Personal digital assistant (PDA) and Palm computers.

Handwriting recognition software: Translates handwritten notes into a form that the system unit can process.

Hard copy: Images output on paper by a printer or plotter.

Hard disk: Enclosed disk drive containing one or more metallic disks. Hard disks use magnetic charges to record data, have large storage capacity and fast retrieval times.

Hard-disk cartridge: Hard disk that is easily removed. Used primarily to complement an internal hard disk.

Hard disk controller (HDC) card: The internal hard disk is connected with a cable to the HDC card which is attached to the system board allowing communication with the massive amount of data stored in the internal hard disk drive.

Hard-disk pack: Several platters aligned one above the other, thereby offering much greater storage capacity. They are removable storage devices with a massive amount of storage available. Used in big business companies.

Hardware: Equipment that includes a keyboard, monitor, printer, the computer itself, and other devices that are controlled by software programming.

Head crash: When a read-write head makes contact with the hard disk's surface or particles on its surface, the disk surface becomes scratched and some or all data is destroyed.

Header: In a typical e-mail, the header has 3 elements: header, message, and signature. The header appears first and includes addresses, subject, and attachments.

Headphone: Audio-output devices connected to a sound card in the system unit. The sound card is used to capture as well as play back recorded sound.

Head tracking: A motion capture method that records head movements and uses these movements to enter data and to issue commands.

Help: A feature in most application software providing options that typically include an index, a glossary, and a search feature to locate reference information about specific commands.

Hierarchical database: Database in which fields or records are structured in nodes. Organized in the shape of a pyramid and each node is linked directly to the nodes beneath them. Also called one-to-many relationship.

Hierarchical network: Also called a hybrid network consisting of several computers linked to a central host computer. The computers linked to the host are themselves hosts to other computers or devices.

HiFD disk: High-capacity floppy disk manufactured by Sony. They have a capacity of 200 MB and like the SuperDisk drives; HiFD, disk drives are able to read the 1.44 MB floppy disk.

High capacity disk: Also a 3½" floppy-disk cartridge. It is thicker than a floppy disk and requires a special drive. Examples are Zip Disks, HiFD and SuperDisks.

High performance serial bus (HPSB): *See* FireWire Bus.

High Performance Serial Bus (HPSB) Port: Also known as FireWire Ports and are faster than USB ports. They provide connections to specialized HPSB devices, such as camcorders.

High-definition television (HDTV): All-digital television that delivers a much clearer and more detailed wide-screen picture.

Higher level: Programming languages that are closer to the language humans use.

History file: Created by browser to store information on Web sites visited by your computer system.

Hits: The sites that a search engine returns after running a keyword search, ordered from most likely to least likely to contain the information requested.

Home network: LAN network for homes allowing different computers to share resources including a common Internet connection.

Home page: Top-level, or opening page of Web site, which displays information about the site and serves as a table of contents.

Home software: *See* Integrated package.

Home suite: *See* Personal suite.

Horizontal portal: Also known as consumer portals designed to appeal to mass audiences offering free e-mail, personal homepages, sports scores, instant messengers, and general-interest services.

Host computer: Also called a server or provider and is a large centralized computer. *See* Provider.

Hot site: Special emergency facility consisting of a fully equipped computer center available to a company in the event of disaster to its computer system. *Compare* Cold site.

HotSync: Communication support to share files and back up data with desktop and notebook computers.

HTML: *See* HyperText Markup language.

HTML editor: *See* Web authoring program.

HTTP (hypertext transfer protocol): Used to connect to Web sites and download Web pages.

HTTPS (hypertext transfer secure): Supports secure (often encrypted) Web communication.

Hub: The center or central node for other nodes. This device can be a server or a connection point for cables from other nodes.

Human resources: The organizational department that focuses on the hiring, training, and promoting of people, as well as any number of human center activities within the organization.

Hybrid network: *See* Hierarchical network.

Hypercube: An extension of relational databases and able to analyze more sides of the information. Also called multidimensional databases.

Hyperlink: Connection or link to other documents or Web Pages that contain related information.

Hypermedia: *See* Multimedia.

Hypertext links: Colored and underlined text that provides further details about a subject on another page.

Hypertext Markup Language (HTML): Programming language that creates document files used to display Web pages.

I

Icon: Graphic objects on the desktop used to represent programs and other files.

Identification: The unique numeric address, or IP address (Internet Protocol address) for every computer on the Internet.

Identity theft: The illegal assumption of someone's identity for the purpose of economic gain.

I-drive: *See* Internet hard drive.

IFPS (interactive financial planning system): A 4GL language used for developing financial models.

IF-THEN-ELSE structure: Logical selection structure whereby one of two paths is followed according to IF, THEN, and ELSE statements in a program. *See* Selection structure.

Illusion of anonymity: The misconception that being selective about disclosing personal information on the Internet can prevent an invasion of personal privacy.

Illustration program: Also known as drawing programs and are used to create digital illustrations, modify vector images and thus create line art, 3-D models, and virtual reality.

Image capturing device: A device, such as a digital camera or a digital video camera, that creates or captures original images.

Image editor: Used to create and modify bitmap files. Advanced paint programs are called image editors and they are designed to modify and improve scanned images.

Image gallery: Libraries of electronic images.

Immersive experience: Allows the user to walk into a virtual reality room or view simulations on a virtual reality wall.

Income statement: A statement that shows a company's financial performance, income, expenses, and the difference between them for a specific time period.

Index search: *See* Directory search.

Individual database: Collection of integrated records used mainly by just one person. Also called microcomputer database.

Industrial robots: Robots used in factories to perform a variety of tasks. For example, machines used in automobile plants to do painting and polishing.

Industry Standard Architecture (ISA): Bus-line standard developed for the IBM Personal Computer. It first consisted of an 8-bit-wide data path, then a 16-bit-wide data path. *See* Peripheral Component Interconnect (PCI).

Information: Data that has been processed by a computer system.

Information brokers: *See* Information Resellers.

Information flow: In large and medium organizations, computerized information flows both vertically and horizontally as it moves through the different functional areas and management levels.

Information resellers: Also known as Information Brokers. They gather personal data on people and sell it to direct markets, fund raisers, and others, usually for a fee.

Information system: Collection of hardware, software, people, data, and procedures that work together to provide information essential to running an organization.

Information systems manager: Oversees the work of programmers, computer specialists, systems analysts and other computer professionals.

Information technology (IT): Computer and communication technologies, such as communication links to the Internet that provide help and understanding to the end user.

Information utilities: *See* Proprietary database and databanks.

Information worker: Employee who creates, distributes, and communicates information.

Infrared: Uses infrared light waves to communicate over short distances. Sometimes referred to as line of sight communication because light waves can only travel in a straight line.

Infrared data association (IrDA): Ports that provide a wireless mechanism for transferring data between devices. Instead of cables, infrared light waves are used to transmit data from a notebook computer to a desktop computer as an example. Also known as Fast infrared (FIR).

Initializing: *See* Formatting.

Ink-jet printer: Printer that sprays small droplets of ink at high speed onto the surface of the paper producing letter quality images and can print in color.

Input: Any data or instructions used by a computer.

Input device: Piece of equipment that translates data into a form a computer can process. The most common input devices are the keyboard and the mouse.

Instant messaging: A program allowing communication and collaboration for direct, "live," connections over the Internet between two or more people.

Instruction cycle: The control unit coordinates the process of following a series of steps called the instruction cycle or machine cycle each time an instruction is executed. These basic operations are Fetching, Decoding, Executing, and Storing.

Instruction time: Also known as I-time, it is the time required to fetch the instruction. *See* Instruction cycle and Fetching.

Integrated circuit: *See* Silicon chip.

Integrated package: A single program providing functionality of a collection of programs but is not as extensive as a specialized program like Microsoft Word. Popular with home users who are willing to sacrifice some advanced features for lower cost and simplicity.

Intel-compatible: Chips referred to as Intel-compatible processors, are able to process programs originally written for Intel chips. Examples are Athlon and Hammer.

Intelligent smart card: Contains a microprocessor combined with input, output and storage capabilities.

Intelligent terminal: Terminal that includes a processing unit, memory, secondary storage, communications software, and a telephone hook-up or other communication links.

Interactivity: User participation in a multimedia presentation.

Interface card: *See* Expansion card.

Internal cache: *See* Primary cache.

Internal data: Data from within an organization consisting principally of transactions from the transaction processing system.

Internal hard disk: Storage device consisting of one or more metallic platters sealed inside a container. Internal hard disks are installed inside the system cabinet of a microcomputer. It stores the operating system and major applications like Word.

Internal modem: The internal modem consists of a plug-in circuit board inside the system unit. A telephone cable connects the modem to the telephone wall jack. *See* Modem card.

Internet: A huge computer network available to everyone with a microcomputer and a means to connect to it. It is the actual physical network made up of wires, cables and satellites as opposed to the Web, which is the multimedia interface to resources available on the Internet.

Internet Explorer: A web browser from Microsoft that connects to home pages and supports Web searching and surfing.

Internet hard drive: A special service site on the Web providing users with free or low cost storage, allowing access to information from any computer that is connected to the Internet.

Internet Radio: Listening to the radio on the Internet through your computer with Windows Media Player for example.

Internet relay chat (IRC): Leading type of chat group service.

Internet scam: Using the Internet, a fraudulent act or operation designed to trick individuals into spending their time and money for little or no return.

Internet service provider (ISP): Provides access to the Internet.

Internet telephone: Low cost alternative to long distance telephone calls using electronic voice delivery.

Internet telephony: *See* Telephony.

Internet terminal: Provides access to the Internet and displays Web pages on a standard television set. Also called Web terminal.

Interpreter: Software that converts a procedural language one statement at a time into machine language just before the statement is executed. No object code is saved.

Intranet: Like the Internet it typically provides e-mail, mailing lists, newsgroups, and FTP services but accessible only to those within the organization. Organizations use intranets to provide information to their employees.

Inventory: Material or products that a company has in stock.

Inventory control system: A system that keeps records of the number of each kind of part or finished goods in the warehouse.

IP address (Internet Protocol address): The unique numeric address of a computer on the Internet that facilitates the delivery of e-mail.

I-time: *See* Instruction time.

J

Java: Programming language for creating special programs like applets. *See* Applets.

Jewel boxes: Optical disks are stored in these clear, protective boxes.

Joined: Tables can be linked or joined by their common fields. *See* Field.

Joystick: Popular input device for computer games. You control game actions by varying the pressure, speed, and direction of the joystick.

K

KDE: Graphical user interface from Linux for Unix workstations.

Kernel: The foundation of the system; performs basic operations such as assigning computer resources, starting application programs, task scheduling, and error handling during the cold boot up phase of your computer.

Key chain hard drive: Also known as key chain flash memory devices. The size of a key chain, these hard drives connect to a computer's USB port enabling a transfer of files and has a capacity of 1GB.

Key chain memory devices: *See* Key chain hard drive.

Key field: The common field by which tables in a database are related to each other. This field uniquely identifies the record. For example in university databases, a key field is the social security number. Also known as Primary field or Primary key.

Keyboard: Input device that looks like a typewriter keyboard but has additional keys.

Keyboard shortcuts: Allow you to use the keyboard to issue commands rather than selecting items from a menu. For example, CTRL+P is a shortcut to print a document.

Keystroker loggers: Also known as computer monitoring software and sniffer programs. They can be loaded onto your computer without your knowledge.

Keyword search: A type of search option that causes the search engine to compare your entry against its database and return with a list of sites, or hits, that contain the keyword you entered.

Knowledge base: A system that uses a database containing specific facts, rules to relate these facts, and user input to formulate recommendations and decisions.

Knowledge work system (KWS): Specialized information system used to create information in a specific area of expertise.

Knowledge workers: People involved in the creation of information, such as engineers and scientists.

Knowledge-based systems: Programs duplicating human knowledge. It's like capturing the knowledge of a human expert and making it accessible through a computer program.

L

Label: Provides structure to a worksheet by describing the contents of the rows and columns. *See* Text entry.

Labels: Provide users with an area to document the contents of the disk.

LAN adapter: Expansion cards located within the system that connect the computer to a network. Also known as Network interface cards (NIC).

Lands: *See* Lands and pits.

Lands and pits: Flat and bumpy areas, respectively, that represent 1s and 0s on the optical disk surface to be read by a laser.

Language bar: Microsoft word 2003 supports voice recognition. Using Word 2003's language bar, you can switch between voice command mode and dictation mode.

Language translator: Converts programming instructions into a machine language that can be processed by a computer.

Laptop computer: *See* Notebook computer and Notebook system unit.

Large print keyboards: For those with limited eyesight.

Laser printer: Printer that creates dotlike images on a drum, using a laser beam light source.

Layout files: Most presentation graphics programs provide layout files that include sample text for many of the different types of presentations, from delivering a report to selling a product.

Layout view: One of the views of a PowerPoint slide presentation in which a miniature of each slide is displayed.

Legend: Defines a chart's different columns or depicts more than one set of data.

Level 1 (L1): *See* Primary cache.

Level 2 (L2): *See* External cache.

Level 3 (L3): Works with L2 caches. L3 caches are not built into the microprocessor but use SD RAM chips located on the system board.

Levels: Generations or levels of programming languages ranging from "low" to "high". *See* Generations of programming languages.

Light pen: A light sensitive pen-like device. Placing the pen against the monitor closes a photoelectric circuit and identifies the spot for entering or modifying data.

Line of sight communication: Microwave communication using high-frequency radio waves that travel in a straight line.

Link: A connection to related information.

Linked object: Information created in a source file from one application and inserted into a destination file of another application while maintaining a link between files.

Linux: Type of Unix operating system initially developed by Linus Torvalds designed to run on minicomputers in network environments. Now powerful microcomputers and servers on the Web use it.

Liquid crystal display (LCD): Display monitor consisting of liquid crystal molecules whose optical properties can be altered by an applied electric field.

List address: In Discussion groups, members of a mailing list communicate by sending messages to the list address. Each message is then copied and sent via e-mail to every member of the mailing list.

Local area network (LAN): Network consisting of computers and other devices that are physically near each other, such as within the same building.

Location: For Browsers to connect to resources, location or addresses must be specified. Also known as uniform resource locators or URL's.

Log on: Windows provides support for multiple users of one computer through log on procedures. For example, each person in a family can use separate log on names to access personal documents and files.

Log on names: *See* Log on.

Logic error: Error that occurs when a programmer has used an incorrect calculation or left out a programming procedure.

Logic structure: Programming statements or structures called sequence, selection, or loop that control the logical sequence in which computer program instructions are executed.

Logical operations: Comparing two pieces of data to see whether one is equal to (=), less than (<), or greater than (>) the other.

Logical view: Focuses on the meaning and content of the data. End users and computer professionals are concerned with this view as opposed to the physical view in which only specialized computer professionals are concerned.

Loop structure: Logic structure in which a process may be repeated as long as a certain condition remains true. This structure is called a "loop" because the program loops around or repeats again and again. There are two variations: DO UNTIL and DO WHILE.

Low bandwidth: *See* Voiceband.

Lower level: Programming language closer to the language the computer itself uses. The computer understands the 0s and 1s, which make up bits and bytes.

Luna: Windows XP new user interface emphasizes functions over programs. For example, the new Start menu displays categories like E-Mail and Internet, rather than individual programs such as Outlook and Internet Explorer.

Lurking: Before you submit a contribution to a discussion group, it is recommended that you observe or read the communications from others. This observing process is called lurking.

M

Mac OS: Operating system designed for Macintosh computers.

Mac OS X: Macintosh operating system featuring a user interface called Aqua.

Machine cycle: *See* Instruction cycle.

Machine language: Language in which data is represented in 1s and 0s. Most languages have to be translated into machine language in order for the computer to process the data. Either a compiler or an interpreter performs this translation.

Magnetic tape: In order to find specific information, you will have to go through the tape sequentially until that data comes up. On the other hand, using an audio compact disk, select the song and the disk moves directly to that song. Tape may be slow, but it is effective and a commonly used tool for backing up data.

Magnetic tape reels: Typically ½-inch wide and ½-mile long, this type of magnetic tape is used by mainframe computers due to its massive storage capacity.

Magnetic tape streamer: Device that allows duplication (backup) of the data stored on a microcomputer hard disk.

Magnetic-ink character recognition (MICR): Direct-entry scanning devices used in banks. This technology is used to automatically read the numbers on the bottom of checks.

Magnification/zoom: Tool to provide closeup and distance views of the document.

Mailing list: In discussion groups members of a mailing list can communicate by sending messages to a list address.

Main board: *See* System board.

Mainframe computer: This computer can process several million program instructions per second. Sizeable organizations rely on these room-size systems to handle large programs and a great deal of data.

Maintenance programmer: Programmers who maintain software by updating programs protecting them from errors, improve usability, standardize, and adjust to organizational changes.

Malicious programs: Hackers and crackers create and distribute malicious programs called malware.

Malware: Short for Malicious software.

MAN: *See* Metropolitan area network.

Management information system (MIS): Computer-based information system that produces standardized reports in a summarized and structured form. Generally used to support middle managers.

Many-to-many relationship: In a network database, each child node may have more than one parent node and vice versa.

Mark recognition device: Scanners that are able to recognize special characters and marks.

Mark sensing: *See* Optical-mark recognition (OMR).

Marketing: The organizational department that plans, prices, promotes, sells, and distributes an organization's goods and services.

Mass storage: Refers to the tremendous amount of secondary storage required by large organizations.

Mass storage devices: Devices such as file servers, RAID systems, tape libraries, optical jukeboxes, and more.

Master slide: A special slide that does not appear in a presentation but controls all the formats and placement of all slides in a presentation. The design template can be changed for an entire presentation using a master slide.

Mechanical mouse: Traditional and most widely used type of mouse. It has a ball on the bottom and is attached with a cord to the system unit.

Media: Media is the actual physical material that holds the data, such as a floppy disk, which is one of the important characteristics of secondary storage. Also known as medium.

Media Player: Listening to audio or playing video files requires a media player. These programs support multimedia activities such as playing audio and video files,

CD's, DVD's, listening to the radio, and locating digital media files on the Internet.

Medium: *See* Media.

Medium band: Bandwidth of special leased lines, used mainly with minicomputers and mainframe computers.

Memory: Memory is contained on chips connected to the system board and is a holding area for data instructions and information (processed data waiting to be output to secondary storage). RAM, ROM, and CMOS are three types of memory chips.

Memory: Printer memory used to store printing instructions and documents waiting to be printed.

Memory addresses: Also known as RAM addresses that are specific or unique locations where data is stored in RAM, which is the data the CPU is presently processing.

Memory card: A smart card that has only storage capabilities.

Memory resident: Programs that run in the background of other programs like the Kernel and they remain in memory as long as the computer is on.

Menu: List of commands.

Menu bar: Menus are displayed in a menu bar at the top of the screen.

Message: The content portion of e-mail correspondence.

Metasearch engine: Program that automatically submits your search request to several indices and search engines, and then creates an index from received information. One of the best known is MetaCrawler.

Methods: In an object-oriented database, descriptions of how the data are to be manipulated.

Metropolitan area network (MAN): These networks are used as links between office buildings in a city.

Microcomputer: Small, low-cost computer designed for individual users. These include desktop, notebook, and personal digital assistant computers.

Microcomputer database: *See* Individual database.

Microfiche: Stores small microscopic images of documents on four- by six-inch cards for large organizations and libraries.

Microfilm: Stores very small microscopic images of documents on long rolls of film for libraries and large organizations.

Microprocessor: The central processing unit (CPU) of a microcomputer controls and manipulates data to produce information. The microprocessor is contained on a single integrated circuit chip and is the brains of the system.

Microsecond: One-millionth of a second. Computers process data and instructions in microseconds.

Microwave: Communication using high-frequency radio waves that travel in straight lines through the air.

Microwave stations: For long line of sight distances, waves must be relayed by means of microwave stations with microwave dishes or antennas.

Middle management: Middle-level managers deal with control and planning. They implement the long-term goals of the organization.

MIDI: *See* musical instrument interface and musical interface digital interface.

MIDI devices: Specialized musical instruments that provide input in the form of encoded digital signals representing musical sounds like an electronic keyboard.

Midrange computer: Also known as Minicomputer.

Minicomputer: Refrigerator-sized machines falling in-between microcomputers and mainframes in processing speed and data-storing capacity. Medium-sized companies or departments of large companies use minicomputers.

Mistaken identity: When the electronic profile of one person is switched with another.

Mobile robots: Robots that act as transports. For example, the police use them to locate and disarm explosive devices.

Modem: Short for modulator-demodulator. It is a communications device that translates the electronic signals from a computer into electronic signals that can travel over telephone lines.

Modem card: Also known as an internal modem, a card that allows distant computers to communicate with one another by converting electronic signals from within the system unit into electronic signals that can travel over telephone lines and other types of connections.

Modulation: Process of converting digital signals to analog signals.

Module: *See* Program module.

Monitor: Output device like a television screen that displays data processed by the computer.

Morphing: Special effect in which one image seems to melt into another.

Motherboard: Otherwise called a System board; the communications medium for the entire system.

Motion capture devices: Designed to follow the movements of a disabled individual and translate those movements into commands the computer can process like head tracking.

Mouse: Device that typically rolls on the desktop and directs the cursor on the display screen.

Mouse pad: Provides a smooth surface to roll the mouse.

Mouse pointer: Typically in the shape of an arrow. *See* Pointing devices.

Multidimensional database: Data can be viewed as a cube having three or more sides consisting of cells. Each side of the cube is considered a dimension of the data, thus complex relationships between data can be represented and efficiently analyzed. Sometimes called hypercube and designed for analyzing large groups of records.

Multifunctional devices (MFD): Devices that typically combine the capabilities of a scanner, printer, fax, and copying machine.

Multimedia: Technology that can link all sorts of media into one form of presentation, such as video, music, voice, graphics and text.

Multimedia authoring programs: Programs used to create multimedia presentations bringing together video, audio, graphics and text elements into an interactive framework. Macromedia Director, Authorware, and Toolbook are examples of multimedia authoring programs.

Multiread: Newer CD-ROM drives are multiread or able to read both CD-R and CD-RW drives.

Multi-session: Photo CDs are multi-session meaning that new images can be added to the CD at any time. *See* Single-session.

Multitasking: Operating system that allows a single user to run several application programs at the same time.

Musical instrument interface (MIDI) port: Port for connecting musical instruments like an electronic keyboard to a sound card.

Musical interface digital interface (MIDI): A standard that allows musical instruments to connect to the system using MIDI ports.

N

Naive: People who underestimate the difficulty of changing computer systems or generating information.

Nanoseconds: Billionths of a second.

Napster: Napster was a client/server network system whereby client computers request resources from a server computer.

National service provider: Internet service providers, such as America Online (AOL), that provide access through standard telephone connections and allow users to access the Internet from almost anywhere within the country for a standard fee.

Natural language: Language designed to give people a more human connection with computers.

Net: Launched in 1969 and is a large network that connects smaller networks all over the world. Also known as the Internet.

Net PC: *See* Net Personal Computer.

Net personal computer (Net PC): Low-cost type of intelligent terminal that typically has only one type of secondary storage and no expansion slots.

Network: The arrangement in which various communications channels are connected through two or more computers. The largest network in the world is the Internet.

Network adapter card: Connects the system unit to a cable that connects to other devices on the network.

Network administrator: Also known as network manager, creates and maintains networks.

Network architecture: Describes how networks are configured and how the resources are shared.

Network bridge: Connects networks of the same configuration.

Network computer: *See* Network terminal.

Network database: Database with a hierarchical arrangement of nodes, except that each child node may have more than one parent node. Also called many-to-many relationship.

Network gateway: Connection by which a local area network may be linked to other local area networks or to larger networks.

Network hub: The central unit in a star network where all computers and peripheral devices are linked. Typically a host computer or file server.

Network interface cards (NIC): Also known as Network Adapter Cards. They are used to connect a computer to one or more computers forming a communication network whereby users can share data, programs, and hardware.

Network manager: Computer professional who ensures that existing information and communication systems are operating effectively and that new ones are implemented as needed. Also responsible for meeting security and privacy requirements.

Network operating system (NOS): Interactive software between applications and computers coordinating and directing activities between computers on a network. This operating system is located on one of the connected computer's hard disk, making that system the Network Server.

Network server: *See* Network operating system. This computer coordinates all communication between the other computers. Popular network operating systems include, NetWare, Windows NT Server, and more.

Network terminal: Low-cost alternative to intelligent terminal; relies on host computer or server for software. Also called network computer or thin client.

Newsgroup: Newsgroups are organized by major topic areas and use the UseNet network.

Newsletter-style column: Formatting text into two columns using this feature provides a magazine-like feel to the newsletter.

Node: Any device connected to a network. For example, a node is a computer, printer or data storage device and each device has its own address on the network. Also, within hierarchical databases, fields or records are structured in nodes.

Non-proprietary operating system: Free operating systems as opposed to being owned by a corporation and are called open source programs. For example Linux is an open source program.

Non-volatile storage: Permanent storage, such as data stored on a disk, is used to preserve data and programs. Also called secondary storage because it does not lose its memory contents when the power goes off.

Normal view: One of the views in a PowerPoint slide presentation, which creates individual slides.

Norton AntiVirus: Collection of antivirus programs from Symantec.

Norton CleanSweep: Collection of programs to safely remove files and programs you no longer need. It will also archive, move, make backup of programs, and clean up your hard disk.

Norton CrashGuard: Collection of programs that protect against system crashes, from Symantec.

Norton Utilities: Collection of 17 troubleshooting utilities from Symantec. These programs are used to find and fix problems, improve system performance, and prevent problems from occurring.

Norton Web Service: Service from Symantec that monitors a computer system for out-of-date software and notifies you of available updates.

Notebook computer: Portable computer, also known as laptop computer, weighing between 4 and 10 pounds.

Notebook system unit: A small, portable system unit that contains electronic components, selected secondary storage devices and input devices.

Numbered list: Sequence of steps or topics on a page organized by numbers.

Numeric entry: In a worksheet or spreadsheet, typically used to identify numbers or formulas.

Numeric keyboard: Enters numbers and arithmetic symbols and is included on all computer keyboards.

O

O'Leary Expansion CD: Contains animations of key concepts, videos relating to select Making IT Work for You applications, and in-depth coverage of select topics.

Object: An element, such as a text box, that can be added to a workbook, which can be selected, sized, and moved. For example, if a chart (object) in an Excel workbook file (source file) is linked to a word document (destination file), the chart appears in the word document. In this manner, the object contains both data and instructions to manipulate the data.

Object code: Machine language code converted by a compiler from source code. Object code can be saved and run later.

Object embedding: The object from the source file, like a chart, is embedded and added to the destination document. It then becomes part of the destination document.

Object linking: A copy of the object from the source file that is inserted into another document or file.

Object linking and embedding (OLE): Powerful feature of many application programs that allows sharing of information.

Objectives: In programming, it is necessary to make clear the problems you are trying to solve in order to create a functional program.

Object-oriented database: A more flexible type of database that stores data as well as instructions to manipulate data and is able to handle unstructured data, such as photographs, audio and video. Object-oriented databases organize data using objects, classes, entities, attributes, and methods.

Object-oriented programming (OOP): Methodology in which a program is organized into self-contained, reusable modules called objects. Each object contains both the data and processing operations necessary to perform a task.

Object-oriented software development: Software development approach that focuses less on the tasks and more on defining the relationships between previously defined procedures or objects.

Office automation system (OAS): System designed primarily to support data workers. It focuses on managing documents, communicating, and scheduling.

One Button Checkup: This program integrates several of the separate troubleshooting utilities from Norton Utilities.

One-handed keyboards: Features a contoured arrangement of keys for use with a single hand.

One-to-many relationship: In a hierarchical database, each entry has one parent node, and a parent may have several child nodes.

Online: Being connected to the Internet is described as being online.

Online banking: Also known as e-banking, when customers go online with a standard browser to perform banking operations such as accessing account information, balance checkbook, pay bills, transfer funds, and apply for loans.

Online processing: *See* Real-time processing.

Online shopping: Also known as e-retailing or e-tailing, which includes buying and selling a wide range of consumer goods over the Internet.

Online stock trading: Also known as e-trading when investors research, buy and sell stocks over the Internet.

Online storage: *See* Internet hard drive.

Open architecture: Microcomputer architecture allowing users to expand their systems by inserting optional devices known as expansion cards.

Open source: *See* Non-proprietary operating system.

Operating system: Software that interacts between application software and the computer, handling such details as running programs, storing and processing data, coordinating all computer resources including attached peripheral devices. It is the most important program on the computer. Windows XP and Mac OS X are examples of operating systems.

Operational feasibility: Making sure the design of a new system will be able to function within the existing framework of an organization.

Operational model: A decision model that helps lower-level managers accomplish the organization's day-to-day activities, such as evaluating and maintaining quality control.

Operators: Operators handle correcting operational errors in any programs. In order to do that, they need documentation, which gives them the understanding of the program, thus enabling them to fix any errors.

Optical disk: Storage device that can hold over 17 gigabytes of data which is an equivalent of several million typewritten pages. Lasers are used to record and read data on the disk. The two basic types of optical disks are compact disks (CD's) and digital versatile or video disks (DVD's).

Optical disk drive: A disk is read by an optical disk drive using a laser that projects a tiny beam of light. The amount of reflected light determines whether the area represents a 1 or a 0.

Optical mouse: A type of mouse that emits and senses light to detect mouse movement.

Optical scanner: *See* Scanner.

Optical-character recognition (OCR): Scanning device that uses special pre-printed characters, such as those printed on utility bills, that can be read by a light source and changed into machine-readable code.

Optical-mark recognition (OMR): Device that senses the presence or absence of a mark, such as a pencil mark. As an example, an OMR device is used to score multiple-choice tests.

Organization chart: Chart showing the levels of management and formal lines of authority in an organization.

Organizational Internet storage: High speed Internet connection to a dedicated remote organizational Internet drive site.

Output: Processed data or information from a computer.

Output device: Equipment that translates processed information from the central processing unit into a form that can be understood by humans. The most common output devices are monitors or video display screens and printers.

P

Packaged program: Application program also referred to as a prewritten program. *See* Prewritten program.

Packet: Before a message is sent on the Internet, it is broken down into small parts called packets. Each packet is then sent separately over the Internet. At the receiving end, the packets are reassembled into the correct order. *See* reformatting.

Paint program: Allows you to use tools that simulate painting on a digital image. Paint programs produce bitmaps, or images made of thousands of dots or pixels.

Palm computer: Also known as handheld computers. These systems combine pen input, writing recognition, personal organizational tools and communications capabilities. They contain an entire computer system including the electronic components, secondary storage, input and output devices.

Palm OS: An operating system designed to run on PDA devices.

Parallel approach: Systems implementation in which old and new systems are operated side by side until the new one has shown it is reliable.

Parallel data transmission: Bits flow through separate lines simultaneously. Used for communications over short distances and not over telephone lines.

Parallel port: Used to connect external devices that send or receive data over a short distance. Mostly used to connect printers to the system unit.

Parallel processing: Used by supercomputers to run large and complex programs. *See* Parallel processor.

Parallel processor: Works with one or more other parallel processor chips to run or process a large program by using software that takes a large program, breaks it down into parts and assigns the parts to separate processors. The processors then work simultaneously and share results. *See* Parallel processing.

Parent node: Node one level above the node being considered in a hierarchical database or network. Each entry has one parent node, although a parent may have several child nodes. Also called one-to-many relationship.

Passive-matrix monitor: Monitor that creates images by scanning the entire screen. This type requires little energy but clarity of images is not sharp. Also known as dual-scan monitors.

Password: Special sequence of numbers or letters that limits access to information, such as electronic mail.

Payroll: Activity concerned with calculating employee paychecks.

PC card hard disk: A hard disk cartridge for a notebook computer that typically holds a capacity of 10 gigabytes.

P PC card: *See* Personal Computer Memory Card International Association (PCMCIA) card.

C card modem: A credit card-sized expansion board that is inserted into portable computers. A telephone cable connects the modem to the telephone wall jack.

PC/TV: Or high-definition television (HDTV) and is a recent development in the merger of microcomputers and television.

PDA keyboards: Miniature keyboards for PDA's and used to send e-mail, create documents and more.

Peer-to-peer network system: Network in which nodes can act as both servers and clients. For example, one microcomputer can obtain files located on another microcomputer and can also provide files to other microcomputers.

People: End users who use computers to make themselves more productive.

Perception systems: Robots that imitate some of the human senses.

Periodic report: Reports for a specific time period as to the health of the company or a particular department of the company.

Peripheral Component Interconnect (PCI): Bus architecture that combines the capabilities of MCA and EISA with the ability to send video instructions at speeds to match the microprocessor. PCI is a 32-bit or 64-bit speed bus that is over 20 times faster than ISA bus.

Personal Computer Memory Card International Association (PCMCIA) card: Credit card-sized expansion cards developed for portable computers.

Personal digital assistant (PDA): A device that typically combines pen input, writing recognition, personal organizational tools, and communication capabilities in a very small package. Also called Handheld PC and palmtop computer.

Personal finance management: Programs like Microsoft's Money help users organize and manage their money.

Personal information managers (PIMs): Also known as desktop managers. Applications that provide an electronic alternative to the appointment calendar, address book and notepad. Microsoft Outlook and Palm Desktop are examples.

Personal laser printer: Inexpensive laser printer widely used by single users to produce black-and-white documents.

Personal software: *See* Integrated packages.

Personal suite: Also known as home suites containing personal software applications or programs intended for home use like Microsoft Works Suite.

Personal video recorder card: Also called TV Tuner cards and Television boards. *See* Television board.

Person-to-person auction site: A type of Web auction site where the owner provides a forum for numerous buyers and sellers to gather.

Phased approach: System implementation whereby a new system is implemented gradually over a period of time.

Photo CD: Multisession format to store digital images on a CD.

Photo printer: A special-purpose ink jet printer designed to print photo-quality images from digital cameras.

Physical security: Activity concerned with protecting hardware from possible human and natural disasters.

Physical view: This focuses on the actual format and location of the data. *See* Logical view.

Picoseconds: Trillionth of a second.

Picture CD: Single session format developed by Eastman Kodak to store digital images on a CD, which are delivered by the Internet or Picture CD.

Pilot approach: Systems implementation in which a new system is tried out in only one part of the organization. Later it is implemented throughout the rest of the organization.

Pits: *See* Lands and pits.

Pixel (picture elements): Smallest unit on the screen that can be turned on and off or made different shades. Pixels are individual dots that form images on a monitor. The greater the resolution, the more pixels creating better clarity.

Plasma display: *See* gas plasma monitors.

Platform scanner: Handheld direct-entry device used to read special characters on price tags. Also known as Wand Readers.

Platters: On a hard disk, platters where the data is stored are rigid, metallic and stacked on top of each other.

Plotter: Special-purpose output device for producing bar charts, maps, architectural drawings, and three-dimensional illustrations.

Plug and Play: Set of hardware and software standards developed to create operating systems, processing units, expansion cards, as well as other devices that are able to configure themselves. When the computer starts up, it will search for the plug and play device and automatically configure it to the system.

Plug-in: Program that is automatically loaded and operates as part of a browser.

Plug-in board: *See* Expansion card.

Pocket PC: *See* Windows CE.

Pointer: For a monitor, a pointer is typically displayed as an arrow and controlled by a mouse. For a database, a pointer is a connection between parent node and child node in a hierarchical database.

Pointers: Within a network database, pointers are additional connections between parent nodes and child nodes. Thus a node may be reached through more than one path and can be traced down through different branches.

Pointing: The ability to move the pointer on the monitor and select an item.

Pointing devices: Accepts pointing gestures and converts them into machine-readable input. These devices include mice, joystick, touch screen, light pens and styluses.

Pointing stick: Device used to control the pointer by directing the stick with your finger.

Points: The font size of each printed character. Each point measures approximately 1/72 of an inch.

Polling: Process whereby a host computer or file server asks each connecting device whether it has a message to send and then allows each message, in turn, to be sent.

Port: Connecting socket on the outside of the system unit. Used to connect input and output devices to the system unit.

Portable language: Language that can be run on more than one type of computer.

Portable printer: Small and lightweight printers designed to work with notebook computers.

Portable scanner: Handheld input device that slides across the image for scanning images and text.

Portal: Startup pages, home pages or directories that are designed to ease navigation and organize resources. There are many different kinds of portals like web, corporate, enterprise and vertical portals depending on the type of information you are looking for.

POST (power-on self test): In a cold boot, the computer system runs a series of programs that include a self-testing process called POST and this verifies that certain hardware components are operational.

Power Supply unit: Desktop computers have a power supply unit located within the system unit which plugs into a standard wall outlet, converting AC to DC which becomes the power to drive all of the system unit components.

Preliminary investigation: First phase of the systems life cycle. It involves defining the problem, suggesting alternative systems, and preparing a short report.

Presentation file: A file created by presentation graphics programs to save presentation materials. For example, a file might contain audience handouts, speaker notes and electronic slides.

Presentation graphics: Graphics used to combine a variety of visual objects to create attractive and interesting presentations.

Presentation language: *See* Formatting language.

Presentation style: PowerPoint slides are presented in various styles including onscreen, Web, overhead slides, and 35 mm presentations.

Prewritten program: Application program also referred to as a packaged program, such as word processors, spreadsheets and database managers.

Primary Cache: Also known as level 1(L1) or Internal cache and is built into the microprocessor.

Primary field: Also known as primary key.

Primary key: Every record has at least one primary key or primary field that uniquely identifies the record like a social security number or a student ID number.

Primary storage: Holds data and program instructions for processing data. It also holds processed information before it is output. *See* Memory.

Print server: Dedicated server performing specific tasks in regards to all of the printers within that organization.

Printer: Device that produces printed-paper output.

Privacy: Computer ethics issue concerning the collection and use of data about individuals.

Proactive: Person who looks at technology in a positive, realistic way.

Problem-oriented language: Programming language that is non-procedural and focuses on specifying what the program is to accomplish. Also known as 4GLs or very high-level languages.

Procedural language: Programming language designed to focus on procedures and how a program will accomplish a specific task. Also known as 3GLs or third generation languages.

Procedures: Rules or guidelines to follow when using hardware, software, and data.

Processing speed: Analyzing and querying large multi-dimensional databases is much faster than relational databases.

Processing rights: Refers to which people have access to what kind of data.

Processor: *See* Central processing unit.

Production: The organizational department that actually creates finished goods and services using raw materials and personnel.

Productivity Applications: *See* General-purpose applications.

Productivity suites: Also known as Business suites that contain professional grade application programs including word processing, spreadsheet and more. A good example is Microsoft Office.

Program: Instructions for the computer to follow in order to process data. *See also* Software.

Program analysis: *See* Program specification.

Program coder: *See* Application generator.

Program definition: *See* Program specification.

Program design: Creating a solution using programming techniques, such as top-down program design, pseudocode, flowcharts, logic structures, object-oriented programming, and CASE tools.

Program documentation: Written description of the purpose and process of a program. Documentation is written within the program itself and in printed documents. Programmers will find themselves frustrated without adequate documentation, especially when it comes time to update or modify the program.

Program flowchart: Flowchart graphically presents a detailed sequence of steps needed to solve a programming problem.

Program maintenance: Activity of updating software to correct errors, improve usability, standardize, and adjust to organizational changes.

Program module: Each module is made up of logically related program statements. The program must pass in sequence from one module to the next until the computer has processed all modules.

Program specification: Programming step in which objectives, output, input, and processing requirements are determined.

Programmable keys: Can connect you to your favorite web site or perform tasks on your computer.

Programmer: Computer professional who creates new software or revises existing software.

Programming: A program is a list of instructions a computer will follow to process data. Programming, also known as software development, is a six-step procedure for creating that list of instructions. The six steps are program specification, program design, program code (or coding), program test, program documentation, and program maintenance.

Project manager: Software that enables users to plan, schedule, and control the people, resources, and costs needed to complete a project on time.

Property: Computer ethics issue relating to who owns data and rights to software.

Proprietary database: Enormous database an organization develops to cover certain particular objects. Access to this type of database is usually offered for a fee or subscription. Also known as databanks and informational utilities.

Proprietary operating system: A network operating system that is owned and licensed by a company.

Protocol: Rules for exchanging data between computers. The protocol http:// is the most common.

Prototyping: Building a model or prototype that can be modified before the actual system is installed.

Provider: A host computer that is already connected to the Internet providing a path or connection for individuals to access the Internet.

Proxy server: Computer that acts as a gateway or checkpoint in an organization's firewall. *See* Firewall.

Pseudocode: An outline of the logic of the program to be written. It is the steps or the summary of the program before you actually write the program for the computer. Consequently, you can see beforehand what the program is to accomplish.

Publish: By saving a presentation as web pages, HTML commands are automatically created to display each page and thus it is published making it available to the public.

Pull-down menu: List of options or commands associated with the selected menu. Also known as drop-down menu.

Purchase order: A form that shows the name of the company supplying the material or service and what is being purchased.

Purchasing: Buying of raw materials and services.

Q

QIC (quarter-inch cartridge): Tape cartridge with a capacity up to 25GB.

Query: A question or request for specific data contained in a database. Used to analyze data.

Query language: Easy-to-use language and understandable to most users. It is used to search and generate reports from a database. An example is the language used on an airline reservation system.

Query-by-example: A specific tool in database management that shows a blank record and lets you specify the information needed, like the fields and values of the topic you are looking to obtain.

R

RAID systems: A larger version of mass storage that enhances organizational security by constantly making backup copies of files moving across the organizations' networks. *See* Redundant arrays of inexpensive disks.

RAM: *See* Random-access memory.

RAM cache: *See* Cache memory.

Random-access memory: Volatile, temporary storage that holds the program and data the CPU is presently processing. It is called temporary storage because its contents will be lost if electrical power to the computer is disrupted or the computer is turned off.

Range: A series of continuous cells in a worksheet.

Rapid applications development (RAD): Involves the use of powerful development software and specialized teams as an alternative to the systems development life cycle approach. Time for development is shorter and quality of the completed system development time is better, although cost is greater.

Raster images: *See* Bitmap images.

Reader/sorter: A magnetic-ink character recognition device that reads the numbers at the bottom of checks and deposit slips. This provides input allowing banks to maintain customer accounts and balances.

Reading: Process of accessing information from secondary storage.

Reading machine: *See* Speech reader.

Read-only: Formatting that prevents the user from writing any new data onto a disc or from erasing any data imprinted by the publisher.

ReadonlyCD-Rom: Also known as compact disk-read only memory. Similar to a commercial music CD whereby the user has access only to the data imprinted by the publisher and the user cannot change it.

ReadonlyDVD-ROM: *See* DVD-ROM.

Read-only memory: Refers to chips that have programs built into them at the factory. The user cannot change the contents of such chips. The CPU can read or retrieve the programs on the chip but cannot write or change information. ROM stores programs that boot the computer, for example. *See also* Firmware.

Read/write head: When a floppy disk is inserted into the drive, the disk's shutter opens and the drive's read/write head moves across the disk's surface to either retrieve (read) information or save (write) information.

Real-time processing: Or online processing, resulting when data is processed at the same time a transaction occurs.

Recalculation: If you change one or more numbers in your spreadsheet, all related formulas will automatically recalculate and charts will be recreated.

Receiving device: A computer accepting or receiving data from another location.

Record: Each row of information in a database is a record. Each record contains fields of data about some specific item, like employee name, address and phone, etc. A record represents a collection of attributes describing an entity.

Reduced instruction set computer (RISC) chip: Powerful microprocessor chip found in workstations.

Redundant arrays of inexpensive disks (RAIDs): Groups of inexpensive hard-disk drives related or grouped together using networks and special software. They improve performance by expanding external storage.

Reformatting: Before any information can be sent over the Internet, it is reformatted or broken down into packets and each packet is sent separately for faster travel time. At the receiving end, the packets are reassembled into the correct order.

Refresh rate: How often a displayed image is updated or redrawn on the monitor.

Regional service provider: An Internet service provider provides access through standard telephone connections in a specific area, typically several states, for a standard fee. If users access the Internet from outside the regional area, they incur long-distance connection charges.

Relation: A table in a relational database in which data elements are stored in rows and columns.

Relational database: A widely used database structure, in which data is organized into related tables. Each table is made up of rows called records and columns called fields. Each record contains fields of data about a specific item.

Removable hard disks: Also known as hard disk cartridges.

Repetitive motion injury: *See* Repetitive strain injury.

Repetitive strain injury (RSI): Category of injuries resulting from fast, repetitive work that causes neck, wrist, hand, and arm pain.

Reports: Can be lists of fields in a table or selected fields based on a query. Typical database reports include sales summaries, phone lists, and mailing labels.

Research: The organizational department that identifies, investigates, and develops new products and services.

Resolution: A measurement in pixels of a monitor's clarity. For a given monitor, the greater the resolution, the more pixels and better clarity of the image.

Resources: These programs coordinate all system resources that include the keyboard, mouse, printer, monitor, storage devices, and memory. They also monitor system performance, schedule jobs, provide security, and start the computer.

Reverse directory: A special telephone directory listing telephone numbers sequentially, followed by subscriber names.

Rewriteable: There are several rewritable formats and few DVD players read all standards. Three most widely used formats are DVD-RW, DVD+RW, and DVD-RAM.

Rewriteable-CD-RW: *See* CD-RW.

RFD (request for discussion): Discussion group term meaning request for discussion.

Ring network: Network in which each device is connected to two other devices, forming a ring. There is no host computer, and messages are passed around the ring until they reach the correct destination.

RISC: *See* Reduced instruction set computer chips.

Robot: Robots are computer-controlled machines that mimic the motor activities of living things, and some robots can solve unstructured problems using artificial intelligence.

Robotics: Field of study concerned with developing and using robots.

Roller ball: *See* Trackball.

ROM: *See* Read-only memory.

Rotational speed: Important characteristic of CD drives because it determines how fast data can be transferred from the CD.

Row: A horizontal block of cells one cell high all the way across the worksheet.

RS-232C connector: Also called asynchronous communications port used to connect external modems to the computer.

S

Saint: Someone who aids new users by answering questions in a discussion group.

Sales order processing: Activity that records the demands of customers for a company's products or services.

Satellite: This type of communication uses satellites orbiting about 22,000 miles above the earth as microwave relay stations.

Satellite/air connection services: Connection services that use satellites and the air to download or send data to users at a rate seven times faster than dial-up connections.

Scanner: Device that identifies images or text on a page and automatically converts them to electronic signals that can be stored in a computer to copy or reproduce.

Scanning devices: Converts scanned text and images into a form the system can process. Optical scanners, bar code readers, and character and mark recognition devices are examples of scanning devices.

Scenario: Set of estimated values.

Scenario manager: An Excel tool that helps create, edit and evaluate alternative scenarios.

Scenario summary: An Excel tool that reports the effects of different scenarios created by the Scenario Manager.

Screen: *See* Display screen.

Screen reader: *See* Speech reader.

SDRAM II: *See* Double data rate SDRAM.

Search: Quickly locates or finds characters, words or phrases. *See* Find.

Search engine: Specialized programs assisting in locating information on the Web and the Internet.

Search provider: *See* Search services.

Search services: Organizations that maintain databases relating to information provided on the Internet that also provide search engines to locate information.

Secondary storage: Permanent storage used to preserve programs and data that can be retained after the computer is turned off. These devices include floppy disks, hard disks, and magnetic tape, CDs and DVDs, and more.

Secondary storage devices: These devices are used to save, backup and transport files from one location or computer to another. *See* Secondary storage.

Sector: Section shaped like a pie wedge that divides the tracks on a disk.

Security: The protection of information, hardware, and software.

Selection: Tool to select, move and resize images and text.

Selection structure: Logic structure that determines which of two paths will be followed when a program must make a decision. Also called IF-THEN-ELSE structures. If something is true, then do option one, else do option two.

Semiconductor: Silicon chip through which electricity flows with some resistance.

Sending and receiving devices: Often a computer or specialized communication device sends as well as accepts messages in the form of data, information, and/or instructions.

Sequence structure: Logic structure in which one program statement follows another.

Sequential access: An approach to external storage, provided by magnetic tape, where information is stored in sequence. *See* Magnetic tape.

Serial data transmission: Bits flow in a continuous stream the way most data are sent over telephone lines so modems need to connect through a serial port. *See* RS-232C and serial port.

Serial port: Used to connect external devices that send or receive data one bit at a time over a long distance. Used for mouse, keyboard, modem, and many other devices.

Server: A host computer with a connection to the Internet that stores document files used to display web pages. Depending on the resources shared, it may be called a file server, printer server, communication server, Web server, or database server.

Service program: Another word for Utilities. They perform specific tasks related to managing computer resources.

Shared database: *See* Company database.

Shared laser printer: More expensive laser printer used by a group of users to produce black-and-white documents. These printers can produce over 30 pages a minute.

Sharing: One advantage of databases is to share information. Other benefits are security, less data redundancy and maintaining data integrity.

Sheet name: Each worksheet has a unique and descriptive sheet name that makes the workbook easier to navigate.

Sherlock: In the Mac OS X operating system, Sherlock locates information on the web as well as the user's computer system.

Shutter: The shutter on a disk slides to the side exposing the recording surface.

Signature line: Provides additional information about a sender of an e-mail message, such as name, address, and telephone number.

Single-session: Picture CD disks are single-session meaning that all images must be transferred at one time to the CD.

Silicon chip: Tiny circuit board etched on a small square of sandlike material called silicon. Chips are mounted on carrier packages, which then plug into sockets on the system board.

SimNet Concepts: Interactive tutorials on a variety of IT subjects.

Simplex communication: Data travels in one direction only. Not used frequently in data communications systems today but can be used in POS (point-of-sale) terminals when data is being entered only.

Site Index: A page listing the major categories of that particular web site showing each web page listed within that branch of the site.

Site Map: A diagram and name of each page within that particular web site. There are different types of structures depending on the material, how it needs to be displayed and the number of pages within that site giving an overview of the entire site.

Size: Also known as viewable size of a monitor, indicated by the diagonal length of the viewing area.

Slate tablet PC: Similar to a notebook computer except that its monitor is attached to the system unit and does not have a keyboard integrated into the system unit.

Slide: A PowerPoint presentation is made up of many slides shown in different views and presentation styles.

Slide layout: How items are arranged on a slide and each slide can have a different layout arrangement.

Slide show view: This view in a PowerPoint slide presentation is used to present all of the slides.

Slot: Area on a system board that accepts expansion cards to expand a computer system's capabilities.

Small computer system interface (SCSI) controller card: This high-speed connection is the fastest and most versatile way for a PC to communicate with many peripheral devices such as hard drives, CD-Rom drives, scanners, printers, and more through a single slot on the system board.

Smart card: Card about the size of a credit card containing a tiny built-in microprocessor. It can be used to hold such information as personal identification, medical and financial knowledge, and credit card numbers. Information on this card is protected by a password, which offers security and privacy.

Sniffer programs: *See* Computer monitoring software and Keystroker loggers.

Snoopware: Programs that record virtually every activity on a computer system.

Sockets: Sockets provide connection points on the system board for holding electronic parts.

Soft copy: Images or characters output on a monitor screen.

Software: Computer program consisting of step-by-step instructions, directing the computer on each task it will perform.

Software Copyright Act of 1980: Law allowing owners of programs to make copies for backup purposes, and to modify them to make them useful provided they are not resold or given away.

Software development: *See* Programming.

Software engineer: Programming professionals or programmers who analyze users' needs and create application software.

Software environment: Operating system also known as software platform consisting of a collection of programs to handle technical details depending on the type of operating system. For example, software designed to run on an apple computer is compatible with Mac OS environment.

Software piracy: Unauthorized copying of programs for personal gain.

Software platform: *See* Software environment.

Software suite: Individual application programs that are sold together as a group.

Solid-state storage: A secondary storage device that has no moving parts. Data is stored and retrieved electronically directly from these devices, much as they would be from conventional computer memory.

Sort: Tool that rearranges a table's records numerically or alphabetically according to a selected field.

Sound card: These cards are connected to speakers. They accept audio input from a microphone and convert it into a form that can be processed by the computer.

Source code: When a programmer originally writes the code for a program in a particular language. This is called source code until it is translated by a compiler in order for the computer to execute the program. It then becomes object code.

Source file: The document that stores the data for the linked object.

Spam: Unwelcome and unsolicited e-mail that can carry attached viruses.

Speakers: Audio-output devices connected to a sound card in the system unit. The sound card is used to capture as well as play back recorded sound.

Special effects: Animation, transitions, and builds add interest and motion to a presentation.

Special purpose application: Programs that are narrowly focused on specific disciplines and occupations. Some of the best known are multimedia, Web Authoring, graphics, virtual reality and artificial intelligence. *See* Advanced applications.

Specialized applications: *See* Special purpose applications.

Specialized search engine: Search engines that focus on subject-specific Web sites.

Specialized suite: Programs that focus on specialized applications such as graphics suites or financial planning suites.

Speech reader: Also called screen readers or reading machines, these devices use a scanner to process printed text, a program to read the text and your speakers to output the text as voice output.

Speed: Speed is measured in the number of pages printed per minute.

Spelling checker: Program used with a word processor to check the spelling of typed text against an electronic dictionary.

Spider: *See* Agent.

Spike: *See* Voltage surge.

Spreadsheet: Computer-produced spreadsheet based on the traditional accounting "worksheet" that has rows and columns used to present and analyze data.

Spy removal programs: Programs designed to detect web bugs and monitor software such as Spybot and Spysweeper.

Spyware: Wide ranges of programs designed to secretly record and report an individual's activities on the Internet.

Stand-alone operating system: Also called desktop operating systems, a type of operating system that controls a single desktop or notebook computer.

Standard toolbar: A collection of buttons used as shortcuts to the most frequently used menu commands, like save and print.

Star network: Network of computers or peripheral devices linked to a central computer through which all communications pass. Control is maintained by polling. The configuration of the computers looks like a star surrounding and connected to the central computer in the middle.

Start menu: A Windows menu listing commands used to gain access to information, change hardware settings, find information, get online help, run programs, log off a network, and shut down the computer system.

Static Ram (SRAM): Typically used for specialized applications and requires a constant supply of power although not as much power. It is also faster and more reliable than DRAM.

Stock photographs: Photographs on a variety of subject material from professional models to natural landscapes.

Storage Pyramid: Shows the relationship of access speed and cost for various types of storage. Floppy disks are the slowest and least expensive. RAM is the fastest and most expensive.

Storing: Saving the results in memory. *See* Instruction cycle.

Story boards: Design tool for planning the overall logic, flow and structuring of a multimedia presentation.

Strategic models: A decision model that assists top-managers in long-range planning, such as stating company objectives or planning plant locations.

Strategy: A way of coordinating the sharing of information and resources. The most common network strategies are terminal, peer-to-peer, and client/server systems.

Streaming audio: The delivery of sound files in which the multimedia files are first compressed before they are requested and then converted and played while they are being received.

Streaming Media: Also known as streaming audio and streaming video. A technique for delivering audio and video files over a network without downloading the entire file first, thus allowing the end user to view the contents almost as soon as he brings up a media player.

Streaming video: The delivery of video files in which the multimedia files are first compressed before they are requested and then converted and played while they are being received.

Structured problem: A problem which can be broken down into a series of well-defined steps.

Structured program: Program that uses logic structures according to the program design and the language in which you have chosen to write the program. Each language follows techniques like pseudocode, flowcharts, and logic structures.

Structured programming techniques: Techniques consisting of top-down program design, pseudocode, flowcharts, and logic structures.

Structured query language (SQL): A Program control language used to create sophisticated database applications for requesting information from a database.

Stylus: Penlike device used with tablet PCs and PDAs using pressure to draw images on a screen. A stylus interacts with the computer through handwriting recognition software.

Subject: Located in the head of an e-mail message, a one-line description used to present the topic of the message.

Subscription address: Mailing list address. To participate in a mailing list, you must first subscribe by sending an e-mail request to the mailing list subscription address.

Super extended graphics array: *See* SXGA.

Super video graphics array: *See* SVGA.

Supercomputer: Fastest calculating device ever invented, processing billions of program instructions per second. Used by very large organizations like NASA.

SuperDisk: High-capacity floppy disk manufactured by Imation. They have a capacity of 120 MB or 250 MB. SuperDisk drives are also able to read and store data on the standard 1.44 MB floppy disk.

Superscaler: Microprocessors that are able to process more than one operation per beat of the system clock. Clock speed is measured in gigahertz or billions of beats per second.

Supervisor: Manager responsible for managing and monitoring workers. Supervisors have responsibility for operational matters.

Surfing: Moving from one Web site to another.

Surge protector: Device separating the computer from the power source of the wall outlet. When a voltage surge occurs, a circuit breaker is activated, protecting the computer system.

SVGA: Stands for Super Video Graphics Array and refers to a resolution standard that displays 800 by 600 pixels.

SXGA: Stands for Super Extended Graphics Array and refers to a resolution standard of 1,280 by 1,024 pixels. It is popular with 19- and 21-inch monitors.

Synchronous DRAM (SDRAM): Faster than conventional RAM chips. SDRAM chips streamline operations by coordinating the movement of data and instructions between the chip and other components in the system unit.

Syntax error: Violation of the rules of a language in which the computer program is written. For example, leaving out a semicolon would stop the entire program from working, because it is not the exact form the computer expects for that language.

Synthesizer: Using a MIDI port, a sound card converts music into a series of instructions. A synthesizer located on a chip on the system board or an external device converts these instructions to music.

System: Collection of activities and elements designed to accomplish a goal.

System board: Flat board that usually contains the CPU and memory chips connecting all systems components to one another.

System bus: There are two categories of buses. One is the system bus that connects the CPU on the system board. The other is the expansion bus that connects the CPU to slots on the system board.

System cabinet: Also known as the Chassis, which is a container that houses most of the electronic components that make up a computer system. *See* System unit.

System clock: Clock that controls how fast all the operations within a computer take place.

System flowchart: A flowchart that shows the flow of input data to processing and finally to output, or distribution of information.

System Restore: A utility that can undo unexpected events. Windows saves system settings and you can go back to prior settings with the System Restore utility.

System software: "Background" software that enables the application software to interact with the computer. System software consists of the operating system, utilities, device drivers and language translators. It works with application software to handle the majority of technical details.

System unit: Part of a microcomputer that contains the CPU. Also known as the system cabinet or chassis and is the container that houses most of the electronic components that make up the computer system.

Systems analysis: This second phase of the systems life cycle determines the requirements for a new system. Data is collected about the present system, analyzed, and new requirements are determined.

Systems analysis and design: Six phases of problem-solving procedures for examining information systems and improving them.

Systems analysis report: Report prepared for higher management describing the current information system, the requirements for a new system, and a possible development schedule.

Systems analyst: Plans and designs information systems.

Systems audit: A systems audit compares the performance of a new system to the original design specifications to determine if the new procedures are actually improving productivity.

Systems design: Phase three of the systems life cycle, consisting of designing alternative systems, selecting the best system, and writing a systems design report.

Systems design report: Report prepared for higher management describing alternative designs, presenting cost versus benefits, and outlining the effects of alternative designs on the organization.

Systems development: Phase four of the systems life cycle, consisting of developing software, acquiring hardware, and testing the new system.

Systems implementation: Phase five of the systems life cycle is converting the old system to the new one and training people to use the new system. Also known as conversion.

Systems life cycle: The six phases of the systems analysis and design are called systems life cycle. The phases are: preliminary investigation, systems analysis, systems design, systems development, systems implementation, and systems maintenance.

Systems maintenance: Phase six of the systems life cycle consisting of a system audit and periodic evaluation.

T

T1, T2, T3, T4 lines: High-speed lines that support all digital communications, provide very high capacity, and are very expensive.

Table (in database): The list of records in a database. Tables make up the basic structure of a database. Their columns display field data and their rows display records. *See* Fields and records.

Tablet PC: A type of notebook computer that accepts handwritten data using a stylus or pen, which is converted to standard text and can be processed by a word processor program.

Tactical models: A decision model that assists middle-level managers to control the work of the organization, such as financial planning and sales promotion planning.

Tape cartridges: *See* Magnetic tape streamers.

Tape library: Device that provides automatic access to data archived on a large collection or library of tapes.

Tasks: An electronic to-do list that organizes, records, displays, and reminds you of tasks you need to complete for yourself individually and for a group.

TCP/IP: *See* Transmission control protocol/Internet protocol.

Technical feasibility: Making sure hardware, software, and training will be available to facilitate the design of a new system.

Technical writer: Prepares instruction manuals, technical reports, and other scientific or technical documents.

Technostress: Tension that arises when humans must unnaturally adapt to computers.

Telephone lines: A transmission medium for both voice and data.

Telephony: Communication that uses the Internet rather than traditional communication lines to connect two or more people via telephone.

Television board: Contains a TV tuner and video converter changing the TV signal into one that can be displayed on your monitor. Also known as TV tuner cards, Video recorder cards, and Video capture cards.

Telnet: Internet service that helps you to connect to another computer (host) on the Internet and log on to that computer as if you were on a terminal in the next room.

Template: A sample form or presentation that can be used as a pattern to help guide you in designing your own layout. Templates might include text and layout features to show what can be accomplished.

Temporary storage: Memory is sometimes referred to as temporary storage because its contents will be lost if electrical power to the computer is disrupted. RAM is this kind of memory.

Terminal: An input and output device connecting to a mainframe or other type of computer called a host computer or server.

Terminal network system: Network system in which processing power is centralized in one large computer, usually a mainframe. The nodes connected to this host computer are terminals, with little or no processing capabilities, or they are microcomputers running special software allowing them to act as terminals.

Text: Letters, words, sentences, and paragraphs. Tools to draw text frames, insert text, and control wrapping of text.

Text entry: In a worksheet or spreadsheet, a text entry is typically used to identify or label information entered into a cell as opposed to numbers and formulas. Also known as labels.

Textbox: A container that you can change color, add text, pictures or clipart. Go to insert on the menu bar, choose textbox, and then make the changes you want.

Theme: Provides a basic layout and color scheme for Web pages.

Thermal printer: Printer that uses heat elements to produce images on heat-sensitive paper.

Thesaurus: An editing tool that provides synonyms, antonyms, and related words for a selected word or phrase.

Thin client: *See* Network terminal.

Thin film transistor (TFT) monitor: Type of flat-panel monitor activating each pixel independently.

Thread: A sequence of ongoing messages on the same subject in a discussion group.

Time-sharing system: System allowing several users to share resources in the host computer.

Titling: Descriptive information that automatically aligns to an x-axis or y-axis in a chart, making it easier to understand.

Toggle key: These keys turn a feature on or off like the cap lock key.

Toolbar: Bar located typically below the menu bar containing icons or graphical representations for commonly used commands.

Top management: Top-level managers are concerned with long-range (strategic) planning. They supervise middle management.

Top-down analysis method: Method used to identify top-level components of a system, then break these components down into smaller parts for analysis.

Top-down program design: Used to identify the program's processing steps called program modules. The program must pass in sequence from one module to the next until the computer has processed all modules.

Topology: The configuration of a network. The four principal network topologies are *star, bus, ring,* and *hierarchical.*

Touch pad: Also known as touch surface. Used to control pointer by moving and tapping your finger on the surface of a pad.

Touch screen: Monitor screen allowing actions or commands to be entered by the touch of a finger.

Touch surface: Typically part of a portable computer, similar to a mouse.

Tower model: Vertical system units are called Tower Models.

Track: Closed, concentric ring on a disk on which data is recorded. Each track is divided into sections called sectors.

Trackball: Device used to control the pointer by rotating a ball with your thumb. Also called a Rollerball.

Tracking changes: A collaboration feature in which changes to the original document are identified. Rightclick on any toolbar and click "reviewing" to help with these abilities.

Traditional cookies: Intended to provide customized service. A program recording information on Web site visitors within a specific site. When you leave the site, the cookie becomes dormant, and is reactivated when you revisit the site.

Traditional keyboards: Fullsized, rigid, rectangular keyboards that include function, navigational, and numeric keys.

Transaction processing system (TPS): System that records day-to-day transactions, such as customer orders, bills, inventory levels, and production output. The TPS tracks operations and creates databases.

Transceivers: Sending and receiving communication towers that send and receive radio signals from wireless devices.

Transfer rate: Or transfer speed is the speed that modems transmit data typically measured in bits per second (bps).

Transfer speed: *See* Transfer rate.

Transition: Controls how one slide moves off the screen and the next one appears.

Transmission control protocol/Internet protocol (TCP/IP): TCP/IP is the standard protocol for the Internet. The essential features of this protocol involve (1) identifying sending and receiving devices, and (2) reformatting information for transmission across the Internet.

Transmission medium: The actual connection or communication channel carrying the message. It can be a physical wire, cable, or wireless connection.

Trojan horses: Programs that are not viruses but carriers of viruses. The most common Trojan horses appear as free computer games, screen savers, or antivirus programs. Once downloaded they locate and disable existing virus protection and then deposit the virus.

Troubleshooting utility: A utility program that recognizes and corrects computer-related problems before they become serious. Also called diagnostic programs.

TV tuner card: *See* Television board. Also known as Video recorder cards and Video capture cards.

Twisted pair: Copper-wire telephone line.

2HD: Two-sided, double-density disk. Also known as a floppy disk and holds 1.44 MB of data.

Two-state system: Many forms of technology use a two-state system creating on/off, yes/no, or a present/absent arrangement. A magnetized spot on a tape or disk may have a positive or negative charge. This is the reason two-state or binary system represents computer instructions.

Type I cards: The thinnest PC card and used primarily to expand the notebook or handheld computer memory. These memory cards are also known as flash memory cards.

Type II cards: Thicker in size and used for communication. They include modem cards and network interface cards.

Type III cards: Thickest of the PC cards, used to expand external storage and include hard disk cards.

U

Ultra extended graphics array: *See* UXGA.

Unicode: A 16-bit code designed to support international languages, like Chinese and Japanese.

Uniform resource locator (URL): For browsers to connect you to resources on the Web, the location or address of the resources must be specified. These addresses are called URLs.

Uninstall program: Programs that safely and completely remove unwanted programs and related files.

Universal Instant Messenger: An instant messaging service that communicates with any other messaging service programs.

Universal Product Code (UPC): A barcode system that identifies the product to the computer, which has a description and latest price for the product.

Universal serial bus (USB): Combines with a PCI bus on the system board to support several external devices without inserting cards for each device. USB buses are used to support high-speed scanners, printers, and video-capturing devices.

Universal serial bus (USB) port: Expected to replace serial and parallel ports. They are faster, and one USB port can be used to connect several devices to the system unit.

Unix: An operating system originally developed for minicomputers. It is now important because it can run on many of the more powerful microcomputers.

Unstructured problem: A problem that requires the use of intuition, reasoning, and memory.

Uplink: Refers to sending data to a satellite.

Uploading: Process of transferring information from the computer the user is operating to a remote computer.

UseNet: Special network of computers that supports newsgroups.

User: Any individual who uses a computer. *See* End user.

User interface: Means by which users interact with application programs and hardware. A window is displayed with information for the user to enter or choose, and that is how you as a user communicate with the program.

Utility: Performs specific tasks related to managing computer resources or files. Norton Utility for virus control and system maintenance is a good example of a utility. Also known as service programs.

Utility suite: A program that combines several utilities in one package to improve system performance. McAfee Office and Norton System Works are examples.

UXGA: Ultra Extended Graphics Array refers to a resolution standard of 1,600 by 1,200 pixels. Popular in 21-inch monitors.

V

Vector file: Composed of a collection of objects, such as lines, rectangles, and ovals. A vector file contains all the shapes and colors, along with starting and ending points necessary to recreate the image.

Vector image: Graphics file made up of a collection of objects such as lines, rectangles, and ovals. Vector images are more flexible than bitmaps because they can be stretched and resized. Illustration programs create and manipulate vector graphics. Also known as vector illustrations.

Vertical portal: Web portal designed to appeal to special interest groups and typically must be a member.

Very high-level languages: Problem-orientated languages that require little special training on the part of the user.

Video: Moving images displayed on a monitor.

Video capture card: *See* Television boards.

Video card: Also known as graphic cards. They connect the system board to the computer monitor. The cards convert the internal electronic signals to video signals so they can be displayed on the monitor.

Video display screen: *See* Monitor.

Video editing software: Allows you to reorganize, add effects, and more to your video footage.

Video Privacy Protection Act of 1988: Law preventing retailers from selling or disclosing video-rental records without the customer's consent or a court order.

Videoconferencing systems: Computer systems that allow people located at various geographic locations to have in-person meetings.

Visual programming languages: A 5GL that provides a natural visual interface for program development like intuitive icons, menus, and drawing tools for creating program code. Visual Basic is a visual programming language.

Virtual environment: *See* Virtual reality.

Virtual Library: Visit libraries on the Internet, read selected items, and check out books.

Virtual memory: Feature of an operating system that increases the amount of memory available to run programs. With large programs, parts are stored on a secondary device like your hard disk. Then each part is read in RAM only when needed.

Virtual reality: Interactive sensory equipment (headgear and gloves) allowing users to experience alternative realities generated in 3-D by a computer, thus imitating the physical world.

Virtual reality modeling language (VRML): Used to create real-time animated 3-D scenes.

Virtual reality wall: An immersive experience whereby you are viewing simulations on a virtual reality wall in stereoscopic vision.

Virus: Hidden instructions that migrate through networks and operating systems and become embedded in different programs. They may be designed to destroy data or simply to display messages.

Virus checker: Detection programs alerting users when certain kinds of viruses enter the system.

Voice command mode: Allows users to select menu items, toolbars and dialog box options using voice or a mouse.

Voice grade: *See* Voiceband.

Voice input: Entering data and issuing commands using your voice.

Voice output: Converting digital data into speechlike sounds. For example, voice output on telephone messages, voice synthesizers that read aloud words on the screen, and mapping software for vehicle navigation devices.

Voice recognition system: Using a microphone, sound card and speciality software, the user can operate a computer and create documents using voice commands.

Voiceband: Bandwidth of a standard telephone line. Also known as low bandwidth.

Volatile storage: Temporary storage that destroys the current data when power is lost or new data is read like RAM storage.

Voltage surge (spike): Excess of electricity, which may destroy chips or other electronic computer components.

VR: *See* Virtual reality.

W

WAN: *See* Wide area networks.

Wand reader: Special-purpose handheld device used to read OCR characters.

WAP (wireless application protocol): Supports wireless access to the Internet.

Warm boot: Restarting your computer while the computer is already on and the power is not turned off.

Web: A service providing a multimedia interface to resources on the Internet. *See also* World Wide Web.

Web appliance: *See* Internet terminal.

Web auction: Similar to traditional auctions except that buyers and sellers meet only on the Web. Ebay is one example.

Web authoring: Creating a Web site.

Web authoring program: Word processing program for generating Web pages. Also called HTML editor or Web page editor. Widely used Web authoring programs include Macromedia Dreamweaver and Microsoft FrontPage.

Web bugs: Programs hidden in the HTML code for a Web page or e-mail message as a graphical image. Web bugs can migrate whenever a user visits a Web site containing a Web bug or opens infected e-mail. They collect information on the users and report back to a predefined server.

Web cam: Specialized digital video camera for capturing images and broadcasting to the Internet.

Web database: Used by Web sites to record data collected from users and by Web search engines; CGI scripts used in interface programs that collect user information.

Web log: *See* Blog.

Web Page: Browsers interpret HTML documents to display Web pages.

Web page editor: *See* Web authoring programs.

Web portal: Site offering a variety of services, such as e-mail, news, and sports updates. These sites are designed to encourage you to visit each time you are on the Web, to act as your home base, and to use as a gateway to their resources.

Web server: Dedicated server that houses internal and external web page information.

Web site: A location on a server.

Web storefront creation packages: Programs for creating Web sites for virtual stores.

Web storefronts: Virtual stores where shoppers can go to inspect goods and make purchases.

Web terminal: *See* Internet terminal.

Web utilities: Specialized utility programs making the Internet and the Web easier and safer. Some examples are plug-ins that operate as part of a browser, filters that block access and monitor use of selected Web sites, and many more.

Web-based applications: By using the Web to connect with an Application Service Provider (ASP), you can copy an application program to your computer system's memory and then run the application.

Webcasting: The process of broadcasting audio or video over the Internet.

Webmaster: Develops and maintains Web sites and Web resources.

What-if analysis: Spreadsheet feature in which changing one or more numbers results in the automatic recalculation of all related formulas.

Wheel button: Some mice have a wheel button that can be rotated to scroll through information displayed on the monitor.

Wide area network (WAN): Countrywide and worldwide networks that use microwave relays and satellites to reach users over long distances.

WiFI (wireless fidelity): Wireless standard also known as 802.11, used to connect computers to each other and to the Internet.

Window: A rectangular area containing a document or message.

Windows: An operating environment extending the capability of DOS.

Windows CE (Pocket PC): Handheld operating system from Microsoft similar to Windows XP with support for special versions of Word, Excel, and Internet Explorer.

Windows Explorer: File management system. Go to Start; choose Programs; Then Windows explorer. The left side is showing the organization of your hard drive. The right is the contents of what is highlighted on the left.

Windows Media Player: Plays digital media including music, video, CDs, DVDs, and Internet radio.

Windows Messenger: Keeps track of and communicates with online friends.

Windows XP: The most recent Windows operating system featuring a user interface called Luna.

Wireless keyboards: Transmit input to the system through the air providing greater flexibility and convenience.

Wireless LAN(WLAN): Uses radio frequencies to connect computers and other devices. All communications pass through the network's centrally located wireless receiver or base station and is routed to the appropriate devices.

Wireless modem: Modem connecting to the serial port but does not connect to telephone lines. It receives through the air.

Wireless mouse: *See* Cordless mouse.

Wireless receiver: Or Base station. The receiver interprets incoming radio frequencies from a wireless LAN and routs communications to the appropriate devices which could be separate computers, a shared printer, or a modem.

Wireless revolution: A revolution that is expected to dramatically affect the way we communicate and use computer technology.

Wireless service provider: Provides Internet connections for computers with wireless modems and a wide array of wireless devices. They do not use telephone lines.

Wizard: Someone who has comprehensive knowledge about a subject in a discussion group.

WML (Wireless Markup Language): Provides a standard for describing data in wireless applications.

Word: Chip capacities are expressed in word sizes. A word is the number of bits (such as 16, 32, or 64) that can be accessed at one time by the CPU.

Word processing: The act of creating a word document on a computer using a program like Microsoft Word for example.

Word processor: The computer and the program allow you to create, edit, save, and print documents composed of text.

Word wrap: Feature of word processing that automatically moves the cursor from the end of one line to the beginning of the next.

WordArt: Stylizing a document by changing the shape, alignment; and giving a 3-D appearance to the text.

Workbook file: Contains one or more related worksheets or spreadsheets. *See* Spreadsheet.

Worksheet: Also known as spreadsheet, or sheet and is a rectangular grid of rows and columns used in programs like Excel.

Workstation: Usually a powerful, high-end microcomputer, but any PC can be a workstation if set up correctly. Workstations have high quality graphics capabilities that can create animations for television by using engineering applications like CAD/CAM for example. Workstations are typically connected to a network but can also be a standalone computer.

World Wide Web (WWW, the Web): Introduced in 1992 and prior to the Web, the Internet was all text. The Web made it possible to provide a multimedia interface, which included graphics, animations, sound, or video.

Worm: Virus that doesn't attach itself to programs and databases but fills a computer system with self-replicating information, clogging the system so that its operations are slowed or stopped.

Write once-CD-R: Stands for CD-recordable. *See* CD-R.

Write once-DVD-R: DVD-Rand DVD+R are competing write once formats; however, most DVD players use either format and both stand for DVD recordable.

Write protection notch: When you slide the tile on a floppy disk so you can see through the hole, none of the information on that disk can be modified or deleted and the disk is write protected. If the hole is covered, you can save or change any material on the disk.

Writing: Process of saving information to the secondary storage device.

WWW: *See* World Wide Web.

X

XGA (extended graphics array): It has a resolution of up to 1,024 X 768 pixels and is popular with 17–19inch monitors.

XHTML (Extended HTML): Combines HTML and XML to add structure and flexibility to HTML.

XML (Extensible Markup Language): Provides a standard way to present data used on Web pages.

Z

Zip disk: High capacity floppy disk manufactured by Sony and requires a special disk drive to run this type of storage unit. They typically have 100 MB or 250 MB capacity, over 170 times as much as the standard floppy disk.

Photo Credits

p. 2 left: Courtesy Wacom Technology Corporation
p. 2 right: Lester Lefkowitz/Taxi/Getty Images
p. 3: C/B Productions/Corbis
Fig. 1-1a: Antonio Mo/Taxi/Getty Images
Fig. 1-1b & c: Courtesy Microsoft Corporation
p.5: Courtesy Dell Computer
Fig. 1-2a: Walter Hodges/Corbis
Fig. 1-2b: C/B Productons/Corbis
Fig. 1-2c: Lester Lefkowitz/Taxi/Getty Images
Fig. 1-2d: Stewart Cohen/Index Stock
p. 7: Antonio Mo/Taxi/Getty Images
Fig. 1-10: Corbis
Fig. 1-11a: Susan Ragan/AP Wide World
Fig. 1-11b: Courtesy Sony Corporation
Fig. 1-11c: Courtesy Wacom
Fig. 1-11d: Photo courtesy of Handspring, Inc.
Fig. 1-15: Courtesy IBM
Fig. 1-16: Eyewire/Getty Images
Fig. 1-17: Victor Paris/Taxi/Getty Images
Fig. 1-19a: Courtesy Blackberry
Fig. 1-19b: Courtesy Casio, Inc.
Fig. 1-19c & d: Copyright © Nokia 2002
p. 18: Eyewire/Getty Images
p. 20 top left: Antonio Mo/Taxi/Getty Images
p. 20 top right: C/B Productions/Corbis
p. 20 bottom right: Lester Lefkowitz/Taxi/Getty Images
p. 21: Courtesy Microsoft
p. 21 right: Courtesy Dell Computer
p. 22: Courtesy Nokia
p. 27: Antonio Mo/Taxi/Getty Images
p. 30: Courtesy Dell Computer
Fig. 2-1: © TeleGeography, Inc. 2001
www.telegeography.com
Fig. 2-2: Digital Vision/Getty Images
Fig. 2-47: Dave J. Anthony/Getty Images
p. 61: Digital Vision/Getty Images
p. 62: Jose Luis Pelaez/Corbis
p. 64 left: © TeleGeography, Inc. 2001
www.telegeography.com
Fig. 3-28: Courtesy Apple Computer
Fig. 3-30: Courtesy Microsoft Corporation
p. 110: Fisher-Thatcher/Stone/Getty Images
p. 111: V. C. L./Taxi/Getty Images
p. 114: Courtesy Apple Computer
p. 115: Courtesy Microsoft
p. 127: Roger Ressmeyer/Corbis
Fig. 4-1a: Courtesy Adobe
Fig. 4-1b: Courtesy Apple Computer
Fig. 4-1c: Courtesy Macromedia
Fig. 4-1d: Courtesy Microsoft
Fig. 4-8: Courtesy Corel
Fig. 4-16: Courtesy Macromedia
Fig. 4-20: Courtesy Microsoft
Fig. 4-22: Photo courtesy of Handspring, Inc.
Fig. 4-24: Courtesy Microsoft
Fig. 4-26: Courtesy H&R Block
Fig. 4-27: Roger Ressmeyer/Corbis
Fig. 4-28: Rodney White/AP Wide World
Fig. 4-30: Courtesy Sony
Fig. 4-31: Digital Vision/Getty Images
p. 147: Lonnie Duka/Stone/Getty Images
p. 148: Itsuo Inouye/AP Wide World
p. 153 left: Roger Ressmeyer/Corbis
p. 153 right: Courtesy Sony
Fig. 5-1a: Antonio Mo/Taxi/Getty
Fig. 5-1b & c: Courtesy Microsoft
Fig. 5-2 & Fig. 5-8: Photo courtesy of Handspring, Inc.
Fig. 5-11: Courtesy Dell Computer
Fig. 5-15: Courtesy Apple Computer
Fig. 5-18: Courtesy IBM
Fig. 5-19: Courtesy Toshiba
p. 191: Digital Vision/Getty Images
p. 194 left: Courtesy Microsoft
p. 194 right & p. 195: Photo courtesy of Handspring, Inc.
p. 196: Courtesy Toshiba
Fig. 6-1a: Courtesy Sony
Fig. 6-1b: Dex Images/Corbis
Fig. 6-1c & d: Courtesy Acer America
Fig. 6-2a: Courtesy Acer America
Fig. 6-2b: Sam Yeh/AFP/Corbis
Fig. 6-3: Denis Scott/Corbis
Fig. 6-8: Roger DuBuisson/Corbis
Fig. 6-9: Lawrence Manning/Corbis
Fig. 6-10: Royalty Free/Corbis
Fig. 6-11a: Courtesy Intel Corporation
Fig. 6-16: Julia Malakie/AP Wide World

Fig. 6-17: Courtesy Kingston Technology Company, Inc.
Fig. 6-25: Courtesy Creative Labs, Inc.
Fig. 6-26: Courtesy Zoom
Fig. 6-28: Courtesy Datakey
Fig. 6-29: Photodisc
Fig. 6-35: Courtesy PC Power & Cooling Silencer 400 ATX power supply.
Fig. 6-36: Courtesy Toshiba PC
p. 234: Bill Miles/Corbis
p. 235: Courtesy Xybernaut Corporation
p. 236 left: Courtesy Acer America
p. 236 bottom: Lawrence Manning/Corbis
p. 237 left: Courtesy Intel Corporation
p. 237 right: Courtesy Kingston Technology Company, Inc.
p. 238 top left: Courtesy Creative Labs Inc.
p. 238 top right: Photodisc
p. 238 bottom: Courtesy Datakey
p. 239 top right: Courtesy PC Power & Cooling Silencer 400 ATX power supply.
p. 239 bottom: Courtesy Toshiba PC
p. 252: left: Palm, Inc./Getty Images
p. 252 center: Courtesy Sony Electronics, Inc.
p. 252 right: Digital Vison/Getty Images
p. 253 left: Courtesy Yamaha
p. 253 center: Courtesy Logitech
p. 253 right: Photo courtesy of Prentke Romich Company www.prentrom.com
Fig. 7-1a: Justin Sullivan/Getty Images
Fig. 7-1b: David Young Wolff/Photoedit
Fig. 7-2: Courtesy Man & Machine
Fig. 7-3: Amy Etra/Photoedit
Fig. 7-4: Palm, Inc./Getty Images
Fig. 7-8: Courtesy Microsoft
Fig. 7-9a: Lucidio Studio, Inc./Superstock
Fig. 7-9b: Bruce Avery/Superstock
Fig. 7-9c: Photodisc Blue/Getty Images
Fig. 7-10: Courtesy Logitech
Fig. 7-11: Spencer Grant/Photoedit
Fig. 7-12: Courtesy Sony Electronics, Inc.
Fig. 7-13: Photo courtesy of Handspring, Inc.
Fig. 7-14a: David Young Wolff/Photoedit
Fig. 7-14b: Christina Charisius/Reuters NewMedia/Corbis
Fig. 7-15: Charles O'Rear/Corbis
Fig. 7-16: David Young Wolff/Photoedit
Fig. 7-17: Digital Vison/Getty Images
Fig. 7-19: Ed Bock/Corbis
Fig. 7-20: Courtesy Wacom
Fig. 7-21: Courtesy IBM
Fig. 7-22: Courtesy Plantronics, Inc.
Fig. 7-23: Courtesy Olympus America
Fig. 7-25: Courtesy Yamaha
Fig. 7-26: Owen Franken/Corbis
Fig. 7-27: Courtesy Freedom Science
Fig. 7-28: Photo courtesy of Prentke Romich Company www.prentrom.com
p. 270: Peter M. Fisher/Corbis
p. 272 left: Amy Etra/Photoedit
p. 272 right: Courtesy Microsoft
p. 273 left: Courtesy Logitech
p. 273 right: David Young Wolff/Photoedit
p. 273 bottom: Palm, Inc./Getty Images
p. 274 top left: Digital Vision/Getty
p. 274 top right: Charles O'Rear/Corbis
p. 274 bottom left: Ed Bock/Corbis
p. 274 bottom right: Courtesy IBM
p. 275 left: Courtesy Plantronics, Inc.
p. 275 right: Owen Franken/Corbis
p. 286 left: Courtesy Acer America
p. 286 center: Courtesy Viewsonic
p. 286 right: Mark Duncan/AP Wide World
p. 287: left: Courtesy ENCAD, Inc.
p. 287 center: Royalty Free/Corbis
p. 287 right: Courtesy Communitech
Fig. 8-2a: Courtesy IBM
Fig. 8-2b: Royalty Free/Corbis
Fig. 8-2c: Courtesy Apple Computer
Fig. 8-2d: Courtesy Humanware
Fig. 8-5: Courtesy IBM
Fig. 8-6: Courtesy Acer America
Fig. 8-7: Mark Duncan/AP Wide World
Fig. 8-8: Courtesy Epson America
Fig. 8-9: Courtesy Viewsonic
Fig. 8-12: Royalty Free/Corbis
Fig. 8-13: © Teri Stratford
Fig. 8-14: Courtesy Lexmark International, Inc.
Fig. 8-16: Courtesy ENCAD, Inc.
Fig. 8-17: Picture of Canon CP-100 dye-sublimation printer, courtesy of Canon USA. Used with permission.
Fig. 8-18a: Courtesy Apple Computer
Fig. 8-18b: David Young Wolff/Photoedit
Fig. 8-19: Courtesy Communitech
Fig. 8-21: Klaus Lahnstein/Stone/Getty Images
Fig. 8-22: Courtesy Humanware
Fig. 8-23: Courtesy Index Braille
Fig. 8-24: Courtesy Freedom Science
p. 303: Photodisc
p. 304: Courtesy AT&T Labs
p. 307 left: Courtesy Viewsonic
p. 307 right: Royalty Free/Corbis
p. 308 left: Courtesy ENCAD, Inc.
p. 308 right: David Young Wolff/Photoedit
p. 309 to right: Courtesy Humanware
p. 309 left: Klaus Lahnstein/Stone/Getty Images

p. 309 top right: Courtesy Humanware
p. 309 bottom: Courtesy Index Braille
p. 320 left: Photo courtesy Iomega Corporation
p. 320 center: Photo courtesy Seagate Technology
p. 320 right: Photodisc
p. 321: Courtesy SCM Microsystems, Inc.
Fig. 9-1: Photodisc Blue/Getty Images
Fig. 9-4: Photodisc
Fig. 9-6: Photodisc Blue/Getty Images
Fig. 9-7: Photo courtesy Iomega Corporation
Fig. 9-11: Photo courtesy Seagate Technology
Fig. 9-12: Photo courtesy Iomega Corporation
Fig. 9-13: Courtesy Toshiba – Toshiba's 5GB 1.8-inch PC Card hard disk drive
Fig. 9-14: Courtesy IBM Archives
Fig. 9-17: JetStor III RAID photo provided by Advanced Computer & Network Corporation (AC&NC) www.raid.com
Fig. 9-20: Photodisc
Fig. 9-22 bottom right: Photodisc
Fig. 9-22 bottom center: Courtesy of Creative Labs
Fig. 9-23: Courtesy Dataplay (DPHI)
Fig. 9-25a: Courtesy Lexar Media
Fig. 9-25b: Courtesy Sandisk
Fig. 9-26: Courtesy Cyberkey
Fig. 9-29: R. Mainsonneuve/Publiphoto/Photo Researchers
Fig. 9-30a: Courtesy Sony
Fig. 9-30b: Courtesy Verbatim
Fig. 9-32a: Photodisc
Fig. 9-32b: Courtesy Toshiba –Toshiba's 5GB 1.8-inch PC Card hard disk drive
Fig. 9-32c: Courtesy SCM Microsystems
Fig. 9-32d: Photodisc
Fig. 9-32e: Courtesy Iomega Corporation
p. 339: Courtesy Creative Labs
p. 346: Royalty Free/Corbis
p. 347: Courtesy Sony
p. 348 top: Photodisc
p. 348 bottom: Courtesy Iomega Corporation
p. 349 left: Photo courtesy Seagate Technology
p. 349 right: Courtesy IBM Archives
p. 349 bottom: Courtesy Toshiba – Toshiba's 5GB 1.8-inch PC Card hard disk drive
p. 350: Photodisc
p. 351: Courtesy SCM Microsystems, Inc.
p. 363 left: Photodisc
p. 363 Center: Stocktrek/Corbis
p. 363 right: Lester Lefkowitz/Corbis
Fig. 10-1: Antonio Mo/Taxi/Corbis
Fig. 10-2: Dex Images/Corbis
Fig. 10-4, 10-5 & 10-6: Photodisc
Fig. 10-8: Lester Lefkowitz/Corbis
Fig. 10-9: Stocktrek/Corbis
Fig. 10-10: Courtesy Toyota
Fig. 10-14a: Courtesy Zoom
Fig. 10-14b & c: Courtesy U.S. Robotics
Fig. 10-15d: Courtesy Novatel
Fig. 10-23: Ron Chapple/Taxi/Getty Images
p. 390: Randy Faris/Corbis
p. 391: Charles Bennett/AP Wide World
p. 392 left: Dex Images/Corbis
p. 392 right: Stocktrek/Corbis
p. 393a: Courtesy Zoom
p. 293b & c: Courtesy U.S. Robotics
p. 393d: Coutesy Novatel
p. 394: Ron Chapple/Taxi/Getty Images
p. 406 left: Neal Wilson/Taxi/Getty
p. 406 right: Mark L. Stephenson/Corbis
p. 407 left: Eric Pearle/Taxi/Getty
p. 407 right: Gabe Palmer/Corbis
Fig. 11-1a: Antonio Mo/Taxi/Getty
Fig. 11-1b & c: Courtesy Microsoft
p. 409: Courtesy Dell Computer
Fig. 11-3: Neal Wilson/Taxi/Getty
Fig. 11-16a: Miquel S. Salmeron/Taxi/Getty
Fig. 11-16b: Mark L. Stephenson/Corbis
Fig. 11-16c: Photodisc Green/Getty
Fig. 11-22: Christopher Bissell/Stone/Getty
Fig. 11-23: AP/Wide World
Fig. 11-25a: Courtesy Security First
Fig. 11-25b: Courtesy Iridian Technologies, Inc.
Fig. 11-28: Jean Pierre Lescourret/Corbis
Fig. 11-29: Michael Keller/Corbis
Fig. 11-30: Eric Pearle/Taxi.Getty
Fig. 11-33: Gabe Palmer/Corbis
p. 434: Tim Pannell/Corbis
p. 435: Ed Kashi/Corbis
p. 436: Neal Wilson/Taxi/Getty
p. 437: Mark L. Stephenson/Corbis
p. 438 left: Christopher Bissell/Stone/Getty
p. 438 right: Courtesy Iridian Technologies, Inc.
Fig. 12-1: David Young Wolff/Photoedit
Fig. 12-4: Walter Hodges/Stone/Getty
Fig. 12-6: Bill Varie/Corbis
Fig. 12-10: Jiang Jin/Superstock
Fig. 12-11: Keith Wood/Corbis
Fig. 12-13: LWA-JDC/Corbis
Fig. 12-15: Picture Press/Corbis
Fgi. 12-19: Paul Barton/Corbis
Fig. 12-20: R.W. Jones/Corbis
Fig. 12-21: Roger Ball/Corbis
Fig. C12-1: Superstock

Fig. C12-3: Superstock
Fig. C12-5: Superstock
p. 465: Photodisc
p. 466: Bill Varie/Corbis
p. 472: Royalty Free/Corbis
Fig. 13-1a: Ed Bock/Corbis
Fig. 13-1b: Amy Etra/Photoedit
Fig. 13-1c: Courtesy Olympus
Fig. 13-1d: Courtesy Yamaha
Fig. 13-1e: Digital Vision/Getty
Fig. 13-3a, b, c: Photodisc
Fig. 13-4: Photodisc
Fig. 13-7: Superstock
Fig. 13-9: Gary Connor/Photoedit
Fig. 13-12: Michael Newman/Photoedit
Fig. 13-13: Eyewire/Getty
Fig. 13-18: Alex Farnsworth/The Image Works
Fig. C13-2, 3, 6: Superstock
p. 501: Jose Luis Pelaez/Corbis
p. 508: Courtesy Yamaha
p. 509 all: Photodisc
p. 511: Alex Farnsworth/The Image Works
Fig. 14-2: Tom & Dee Ann McCarthy/Corbis
Fig. 14-4: Photodisc
Fig. 14-5: Jon Feingersh/Corbis
Fig. 14-15: Photodisc
Fig. 14-18: Photodisc
Fig. 14-21: Photodisc
Fig. C14-1: Superstock
Fig. C14-5: Rob Lewine/Corbis
Fig. C14-6: Superstock
p. 540 top: Superstock
p. 540 bottom: Shizuo Kambayashi/AP Wide World
p. 550 both: Photodisc
Fig. 15-3, 15-7, 15-17, 15-23, 15-27, 15-29: Photodisc
p. 584: Spencer Grant/Photoedit
p. 590, 592, 593: Photodisc
Fig. C15-1, C15-5: Digital Vision/Getty Images
p. 604: Jeff Greenberg/Photoedit
p. 605 left: Lonnie Duka/Stone/Getty Images
p. 605 right: Louise Gubb/Corbis
Fig. 16-1: Ariel Skelley/Corbis
Fig. 16-4: Jeff Greenberg/Photoedit
Fig. 16-5, Fig.16-6: Ed Taylor Studio/Taxi/Getty Images
Fig. 16-7: Louise Gubb/Corbis
Fig. 16-9: Bebetow Matthews/AP Wide World
Fig. 16-10: Lonnie Duka/Stone/Getty Images
Fig. 16-11: Rob Lewine/Corbis
p. 616: LWA-Dann Tardif/Corbis
p. 618: Ariel Skelley/Corbis
p. 619 left: Ed Taylor Studio/Taxi/Getty Images
p. 619 right: Lonnie Duka/Stone/Getty Images
p. 620 left: Fisher-Thatcher/Stone/Getty Images
p. 620 right: Superstock
p. 628 top left: IBM Archives
p. 628 bottom left: Computer Museum History Center
p. 628 top right: IBM Archives
p. 628 bottom right: Masami Sano/Corbis
p. 629 top left: IBM Archives
p. 629 top right: Bettmann/Corbis
p. 629 center: IBM Archives
p. 629 bottom: Computer Museum History Center
p. 630 top left: Computer Museum History Center
p. 630 top right: IBM Archives
p. 630 bottom: Computer Museum History Center
p. 631 top: IBM Archives
p. 631 center: Computer Museum History Center
p. 631 bottom: IBM Archives
p. 632 top: Computer Museum History Center
p. 632 center: Courtesy Apple Computer
p. 632 bottom: Computer Museum History Center
p. 633 top: Courtesy Microsoft Corporation
p. 633 center left & right: Computer Museum History Center
p. 633 bottom, p. 634 top: Courtesy Apple Computer
p. 634 top right & center: Courtesy Intel
p. 634 bottom left: Paul Sakuma/AP Wide World
p. 634 bottom right, p. 635: Courtesy Microsoft Corporation

Index

DPS, 458
Dr. Solomon's AntiVirus, 423
Dragon Systems Inc., 267
DRAM, 220–221
Drapkin Technology, 540
Drawing programs, 131
Drive, 324
Driver, 189
DRM, 405
Drop-down menu, 81
DSL, 371
DSS, 460
Dual-scan monitors, 290
Dumb terminal, 299
DVD, 335, 337, 360
DVD jukebox, 345
DVD players, 335
DVD-R (DVD recordable), 335, 337
DVD-RAM (DVD random-access memory), 337
DVD-ROM (digital versatile disc-read only memory), 335, 337
DVD-RW (DVD rewritable), 337
DVD+R (DVD recordable), 335, 337
DVD+RW (DVD rewritable), 337
Dynamic RAM (DRAM), 220–221

E

E-banking, 56
E-book readers, 291, 316
E-books, 291, 292
E-cash, 58
E-commerce, 55–58
  B2B, 56
  B2C, 56–57
  C2C, 57
  growth, 55
  security, 58
E-learning sites, 42
E-mail, 44–46, 364
E-mail addresses, 45
E-mail attachment, 45, 428
E-retailing, 56
E-tailing, 56
E-time, 217
E-trading, 56
eBay, 58
EBCDIC, 212–214
ECash, 58
Eckert, J. Presper, Jr., 629
Economic feasibility, 533
ECPA, 420
Editing, 86
EIDE, 328
802.11, 367
Electronic cash, 58
Electronic cash providers, 58
Electronic commerce, 364. *See also* E-commerce
Electronic Communications Privacy Act (ECPA), 420
Electronic data and instruction, 212–214
Electronic fingerprint pads, 500
Electronic mail (e-mail), 44–46
Electronic monitoring, 405, 431
Electronic profiles, 410
Electronic security, 285
eLiza, 192
Embedded object, 109
Embedded operating systems, 172
Emerging applications, 144–147
  AI, 144
  expert systems, 145–146
  robotics, 146–147
  VR, 144–145
EmoneyMail, 58
Emotional robot, 148
Encrypting, 427
Energy Star, 432
Enhanced integrated drive electronics (EIDE), 328
ENIAC, 629
Enterprise storage system, 344–345
Entertainment site, 37
EntireX, 556
Entity, 487, 496
Environmental issues, 432–434, 448
Erasable optical disks, 335
Ergonomic concerns, 429–431, 432
Ergonomic keyboards, 255, 430
Ergonomic workstations, 430, 445
Ergonomics, 284, 429–432
ERMA, 630
eSafe, 187, 423
eSafe Desktop, 184
Escape key, 256
ESS, 457, 462–463, 482
Ethernet, 377
Ethernet LAN, 377
Ethics, 409
Ethics portfolio, 627
Evolution of computer age, 628–635
  age of connectivity, 628, 634–635
  integrated circuit age, 628, 631
  microprocessor age, 628, 632–633
  transistor age, 628, 630
  vacuum tube age, 628, 629
Exception reports, 460
Exchange of personal information, 521
Excite, 52
Execution time (E-time), 217
Executive support system (ESS), 457, 462–463, 482
Expansion bus, 227, 230
Expansion card, 224, 225, 248
Expansion slot, 224
Expert systems, 145–146, 163
External cache, 221
External data, 461
External modem, 370
Extranet, 388–389
Extreme Programming (XP), 602
Eyestrain, 429

F

Facial recognition, 449
Facsimile transmission machine, 296–297
Fair Credit Reporting Act, 420
FAO Schwarz, 140
FAQ (Frequently Asked Questions), 40, 41
Fashion specialized search engine, 53
Fast infrared (FIR), 232
Fax machine, 296–297
FDD, 323–325
Federal Express, 431, 608
Fiber-optic cable, 367, 369
Field size, 98
Fields, 98, 100, 487
Fifth generation computers, 628, 634–635
Fifth generation language (5GL), 583
File, 170, 171, 488
File compression, 331, 332
File compression programs, 179
File decompression, 331, 332
File servers, 345, 374
File transfer protocol (FTP), 59, 373
Filter, 60, 98, 130
Find, 86
Fingerprint scanner, 427
FIR, 232
Firewall, 389, 427, 445
FireWire bus, 230
FireWire ports, 231
Firmware, 222
First generation computers, 628, 629
Firstborn Multimedia, 136
Fixed disk, 328
Fizzer, 423
Flaming, 51
Flash, 140
Flash memory cards, 227, 340
Flash RAM (memory), 221
Flat-panel monitors, 290–291, 292
Flatbed scanner, 260
Flexible disks, 323
Flexible keyboards, 255
Floppies, 323
Floppy-disk capacities, 326
Floppy-disk cartridges, 326
Floppy disk drive (FDD), 323–325
Floppy disks, 323–326
Flowchart, 569, 570
Flyer, 88
Folder, 170, 171
Font, 86, 88
Font size, 86, 88
Footer, 89
Footnote, 89
Foreground, 168
Form, 99, 100
Format, 86
Formatting, 324
Formatting languages, 572, 573
Formula, 92, 94
Fourth generation computers, 628, 632–633
4GLs (fourth generation languages), 582
Fragment, 325
Fragmented, 182
Fragmented files, 328
Frame, 40
Free database software, 516
Free Internet, 38
Free speech online, 77
Freedom of Information Act, 411, 420
Freedom Scientific, 268
Freedrive, 341
Frequently Asked Questions (FAQ), 40, 41
Friends, 46
Frustrated person, 609
FTP, 59, 373
Full-duplex communication, 372, 373
Function keys, 256
Functions, 92–94
Future developments
  Blu-Ray, 347
  brain-machine interface, 271
  emotional robots, 148
  information overload, 466
  Internet2, 62
  MI-tech, 585
  presence technology, 435
  rapid change, 540
  self-maintaining server, 192
  voice portals, 304
  wearable computers, 235
  Web-based ASPs, 111
  wireless robotic car, 391
  Xperanto, 502
Fuzzy logic, 145

G

Gates, Bill, 633
Gas discharge display, 291
Gas plasma monitors, 291, 292
Gathering data, 528–529
GB, 222
gbps, 370
GDSS, 457, 460–461
General ledger, 459
General Motors, 389
General-purpose applications, 80
Gif files, 130
GifArt, 132
Gigabyte (GB), 222
Gigahertz, 223
Global internet map, 36
Global positioning, 369
Global positioning system (GPS), 369
GNOME, 177, 178
Gnutella, 387
Goal seek, 93, 96
Google, 52
Google Groups, 50
GPS, 369
Graffiti, 178
Grammar checker, 86, 88
Grapevine, 614, 615
Graphical map, 137, 140, 141
Graphical user interface (GUI), 80, 167
Graphics cards, 224
Graphics coprocessor, 219
Graphics Maps, 132
Graphics Pack, 132
Graphics programs, 129–132
  desktop publishing, 129–130
  graphics suites, 132
  illustration programs, 130–131
  image editors, 130
  image galleries, 131
Graphics suites, 132
Graphics tablet, 263
Graphics tool, 129, 130
Green PC, 432–433
Grid chart, 530
Group decision support (GDSS), 460–461
GUI, 80, 167

H

Hackers, 422
Half-duplex communication, 372, 373
Hammer, 219
Handheld computer, 343
Handheld computer system, 211
Handheld computers, 178
Handwriting recognition, 82, 282
Handwriting recognition software, 259
Hard copy, 292
Hard disk, 327–332
Hard-disk cartridges, 328, 330
Hard disk controller (HDC), 328
Hard-disk packs, 330, 331
Hard Rock Hotel, 140
Hardware acquisition, 534–535
HDC, 328
HDTV, 291, 292, 317
Head crash, 327, 426
Head tracking, 269
Headache, 429
Header, 45, 89
Headphones, 296
Help, 81
Hewlett-Packard, 297
Hierarchical database, 493
Hierarchical network, 383
HiFD disks, 326
High capacity disks, 326, 358
High-definition television (HDTV), 291, 292, 317
High-level procedural languages, 581–582
High performance serial bus (HPSB), 230
High performance serial bus (HPSB) ports, 231
Higher-level languages, 580
Hints/suggestions. *See* Tips
Historical overview. *See* Evolution of computer age
History file, 413
Hits, 52
Hoff, Ted, 632
Home automation, 315
Home network, 377, 378, 380–381, 400, 402
Home page, 40
Home software, 105, 141. *See also* Personal applications
Home suites, 107
Hopper, Grace, 629
Horizontal portals, 40, 41
Host computer, 37, 299, 374
Hot site, 428
Hotspots, 403
HotSync, 178

I

J

K

L

M

T